NINTH EDITION

Our Sexuality

Robert Crooks
Karla Baur

THOMSON

WADSWORTH

Australia • Canada • Mexico • Singapore • Spain
United Kingdom • United States

THOMSON

✦ ™

WADSWORTH

_____

Executive Editor: Vicki Knight
Psychology Editor: Marianne Taflinger
Development Editor: Kate Barnes
Assistant Editor: Jennifer Keever
Editorial Assistant: Monica Sarmiento
Technology Project Manager: Darin Derstine
Marketing Manager: Chris Caldeira
Marketing Assistant: Laurel Anderson
Advertising Project Manager: Brian Chaffee
Project Manager, Editorial Production: Kirk Bomont
Art Director: Vernon Boes

Print/Media Buyer: Becky Cross
Permissions Editor: Stephanie Lee
Production Service: Heckman & Pinette
Text Designers: John Walker, Linda Beaupre, and Joyce Weston
Photo Researcher: Laurie Frankenthaler
Copy Editor: Mimi Braverman
Illustrator: Rolin Graphics
Cover Designer: Irene Morris
Cover Image: © Corbis
Compositor: Parkwood Composition Service, Inc.
Printer: Courier/Kendallville
Cover Printer: Coral Graphics

Thomson Wadsworth
10 Davis Drive
Belmont, CA 94002-3098
USA

Asia
Thomson Learning
5 Shenton Way #01-01
UIC Building
Singapore 068808

Australia/New Zealand
Thomson Learning
102 Dodds Street
Southbank, Victoria 3006
Australia

Canada
Nelson
1120 Birchmount Road
Toronto, Ontario M1K 5G4
Canada

Europe/Middle East/Africa
Thomson Learning
High Holborn House
50/51 Bedford Row
London WC1R 4LR
United Kingdom

Latin America
Thomson Learning
Seneca, 53
Colonia Polanco
11560 Mexico D.F.
Mexico

Spain/Portugal
Paraninfo
Calle Magallanes, 25
28015 Madrid, Spain

For more information about our products, contact us at:
Thomson Learning Academic Resource Center
1-800-423-0563

For permission to use material from this text or product, submit a request online at
http://www.thomsonrights.com.
Any additional questions about permissions can be submitted by email to **thomsonrights@thomson.com.**

Library of Congress Control Number: 2003114976

Student Edition Casebound: ISBN 0-534-63375-7
Student Edition Paperback: ISBN 0-534-65176-3
Advantage Edition: ISBN 0-534-63381-1
Instructor's Edition: ISBN 0-534-63382-X

For our loving spouses, Sami Tucker and Jim Hicks,
and the dedicated staff of Act Now—a community-based organization
implementing an HIV/AIDS intervention program
for southeastern Kenya.

About the Authors

The integration of psychological, social, and biological components of human sexuality in this text is facilitated by the blending of the authors' academic and professional backgrounds. Robert Crooks has a Ph.D. in psychology. His graduate training stressed clinical and physiological psychology. In addition, he has considerable background in sociology, which served as his minor throughout his graduate training. His involvement with teaching human sexuality classes at the university, college, and medical school levels spans over two decades. Recently Bob has been involved in the establishment and implementation of an HIV/AIDS education and intervention program in Kenya. His work with this project includes designing a research strategy for assessing behavior change and a peer educator–based educational strategy as well as conducting training sessions for Kenyan peer educator staff. He spent several months in Africa during 2003 and 2004. His involvement will continue in future years as the program expands dramatically due, in large part, to a substantial grant recently provided by the European Union.

Karla Baur has a master's degree in social work; her advanced academic work stressed clinical training. She is a licensed clinical social worker in private practice, specializing in couples and sex therapy with adults. Karla is certified as a sex educator, therapist, and sex therapy supervisor by the American Association of Sex Educators, Counselors, and Therapists. She has instructed sexuality classes at several colleges and universities and provides training for other mental health professionals. Karla has also found a way to combine her clinical skills with her love of horses by providing performance enhancement training for equestrians. Further, Karla has become involved in the HIV/AIDS program in Kenya, and she spent several weeks in 2004 teaming up with Bob training peer educators.

The authors have a combined total of over 60 years of teaching, counseling, and research in the field of human sexuality. Together they taught sexuality courses at Portland Community College for a number of years. They present workshops and guest lectures to a wide variety of professional and community groups, and they counsel individuals, couples, and families on sexual concerns. Their combined teaching, clinical, and research experiences, together with their graduate training, have provided them with an appreciation and sensitive understanding of the highly complex and personal nature of human sexuality.

It is the authors' belief that a truly sensitive understanding of our sexuality must be grounded in both the female and the male perspectives and experiences. In this sense, their courses, their students, and this text have benefited from a well-balanced perception and a deep appreciation of human sexual behavior.

Brief Contents

Contents

▶ PART TWO: BIOLOGICAL BASIS

4 Female Sexual Anatomy and Physiology 81

5 Male Sexual Anatomy and Physiology 121

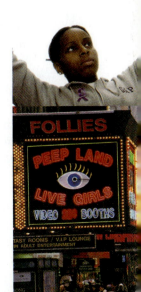

Preface

Our Sexuality, now in its ninth edition, provides students with an engaging, personally relevant, and academically sound introduction to human sexuality. The text's comprehensive integration of biological, psychological, behavioral, and cultural aspects of sexuality has been consistently well received in each previous edition.

New in This Edition

- More that **1,000 new citations,** reflecting the most recent research, have been added, many from studies reported in the last two years.
- A new, free *Our Sexuality* **CD-ROM** comes automatically bundled with every new copy of the text. The CD-ROM provides animations of difficult concepts, as well as video clips of people discussing various sexual issues. Topics include coming out in the workplace, a postsurgery transsexual, and a man with erectile dysfunction. The CD also has chapter quizzing and critical thinking questions, and students can easily print or e-mail their results. There is also a "Virtual Safer Sex Kit" that introduces major kinds of contraception.
- New **Spotlight on Research** boxes cover recent important research studies. Content topics include Media Reports on Hormone Therapy Research (Chapter 4), Monitoring Sexual Arousal in Women with Magnetic Resonance Imaging (Chapter 5), Sex Differences in Desire for Sexual Variety (Chapter 7), and the Impact of Prenatal Influences on the Brain (Chapter 10) as determinants of sexual orientation.
- **Sexuality and Diversity** discussions have been integrated directly into the flow of text, rather than separated out as boxes, emphasizing continuity of coverage.
- Several new **Sexuality and Diversity** discussions have been added throughout the text, dealing with topics such as American ethnic diversity in age of menarche and the HIV epidemic in Russia. Many other Sexuality and Diversity discussions have been revised, expanded, and updated for the ninth edition.
- New **At A Glance** tables are designed to present important information in summary form. Some examples of this new feature include tables that out-

line Factors Involved in Typical Prenatal Differentiation; Factors to Consider when Choosing a Birth Control Method; Common STDs: Transmission, Symptoms, and Treatment; and The Impact of Attachment Styles on Intimate Relationships.
- A wealth of **new and significantly updated information** in every chapter, highlights of which are described below.

Chapter 1: Perspectives on Sexuality

- Findings from the "Global Study of Sexual Attitudes and Behaviors" that describe how people around the world answer the question "How important is sex to you?"
- Significantly expanded coverage of diversity around the world, with emphasis on Islam and sexuality.
- New and expanded coverage of current trends in the media and its impact on our sexuality.
- Expanded discussion of sexuality from the perspective of the personal as political.

Chapter 2: Sex Research: Methods and Problems

- New *Spotlight on Research* box describing techniques used to assess the impact of an HIV/AIDS program in Kenya.
- Coverage of the *Youth Risk Behavior Survey.*
- Sex research in cyberspace: expanded and updated coverage.

Chapter 3: Gender Issues

- New *At a Glance* table outlining biological factors involved in typical prenatal differentiation.
- Expanded discussion of sex differences in cognitive functioning.
- Revised and updated coverage of atypical prenatal differentiation.
- Expanded and updated discussion of agents of gender-role socialization.
- New coverage of an evolutionary perspective on the origin of sex-typed toy preferences.

Chapter 4: Female Sexual Anatomy and Physiology

- Expanded coverage of female genital cutting with emphasis on clitoridectomy.
- New information about the health risks associated with douching.
- Expanded coverage of attitudes pertaining to sexuality and menstruation.
- New discussion and analysis of media reports pertaining to research on hormone therapy.
- Discussion of difficulties associated with hormone therapy research.
- Coverage of alternatives to hormone therapy.
- New *At a Glance* table listing benefits and problems associated with hormone therapy.
- Discussion of the use of magnetic resonance imaging to detect breast implant rupture.
- Coverage of the new recommendations/outlines for monthly breast exams provided by the American Cancer Society.

Chapter 5: Male Sexual Anatomy and Physiology

- New *Sexuality and Diversity* discussion of koro (genital retraction syndrome).
- New *On the Edge* box on the topic of penile augmentation.
- Updated coverage of circumcision.
- Description of the use of saw palmetto in the prevention of benign prostatic hyperplasia.
- Significantly updated coverage of prostrate cancer and treatment options.
- New *Spotlight on Research* box discussing the pros and cons of the PSA test as a diagnostic tool for prostate cancer.

Chapter 6: Sexual Arousal and Response

- Updated and significantly revised discussion of the role of hormones in sexual behavior.
- New coverage of the role of oxytocin in male and female sexual behavior.
- Expanded discussion of the brain and its relationship to sexual arousal, including specific regions in the hypothalamus and the neurotransmitters dopamine and serotonin.
- Discussion of the impact of selective serotonin reuptake inhibitors (SSRIs) on sexual arousal and response.
- Updated information about pheromones as sexual attractants.
- New *Spotlight on Research* box that describes the use of magnetic resonance imaging to monitor sexual arousal in women.

Chapter 7: Love, Attraction, Attachment, and Intimate Relationships

- New section dealing with attachment styles and love with a detailed discussion of how attachment styles are formed and how they influence adult intimate relationships.
- New *At a Glance* table that outlines the impact of attachment styles on intimate relationships.
- Expanded coverage of the relationship between love and sex.
- New *Spotlight on Research* box that describes a major cross-cultural study of sex differences in desire for sexual variety.

Chapter 8: Communication in Sexual Behavior

- Significantly revised discussion of "Expressing and Receiving Complaints" with substitution of the term "complaint" for the term "criticism."
- New section on "Communication Patterns in Successful and Unsuccessful Relationships" with particular attention to John Gottman's research on constructive and destructive communication tactics.

Chapter 9: Sexual Behaviors

- Expanded and revised section on celibacy with new discussion of celibacy as freedom from limitations of women's roles.
- Expanded coverage of fantasies about coerced sexual encounters.
- Discussion of factors associated with the taste of ejaculate.
- Coverage of new data indicting increased rates of anal intercourse.

Chapter 10: Sexual Orientations

- Discussion of new developments in the media portrayals of gays and lesbians.
- New research on sexual orientation conversion treatment.
- Inclusion of current examples of attitudes of acceptance and condemnation of homosexuality.
- Description of the first public high school for gay and lesbian students.
- Discussion of the characteristics of same-sex couples as compared to heterosexual couples.
- Percentages of gays and lesbians involved in ongoing relationships.
- Expanded coverage of gay and lesbian parents.
- Discussion of trends toward decriminalization of private sexual behavior between adults.
- Discussion of the effects of discrimination based on sexual orientation that occurs in the U.S. military.

Chapter 11: Contraception

- New information about contraception issues within American Catholicism.
- Updated coverage of the practice of using birth control at first intercourse.
- Revised and updated table: "Choosing a Birth Control Method."
- Discussion of the widespread occurrence of incorrect use of oral contraceptives.
- Coverage of new contraceptive methods, including: 1) the vaginal ring (NuvaRing); 2) Seasonale birth control pill; 3) the skin patch (Ortho Evra); 4) FemCap cervical barrier; 5) Lea's Shield cervical barrier; 6) Mirena intrauterine device; and 7) the Standard Days Method of fertility awareness.
- Discussion of advances in condom design and errors in condom use.
- Updated information about emergency contraception.
- Discussion of transcervical sterilization.
- Updated information about future contraceptive options for men and women.

Chapter 12: Conceiving Children: Process and Choice

- New information about sperm damage due to chemicals and environmental pollution.
- Birth rates from artificial reproductive technologies are updated and discussed.
- A discussion of caffeine's contribution to miscarriage.
- The political controversy raging over late-term abortion is discussed.
- Coverage of Islamic law as it relates to abortion.
- Coverage of the various states' child welfare policies and abortion restrictions.
- U.S. maternal and infant mortality rates.
- Maternal and infant mortality rates in developing countries are described.
- Information is presented about the increasing incidence of birth rates among older women in the United States.
- Discussion of characteristics of women who breast feed.

Chapter 13: Sexuality During Childhood and Adolescence

- New *Sexuality and Diversity* coverage of American ethnic diversity in age of menarche.
- Updated and revised discussion of the sexual double standard.
- Retitled "Petting" section to "Noncoital Sexual Expression" and revised content.
- Revised and updated discussion of adolescent coitus.
- New information on pregnant teenagers' risk for contracting sexually transmitted diseases.

Chapter 14: Sexuality and the Adult Years

- New information pertaining to cohabitation among older couples.
- New data on cohabitation.
- Discussion of the marriage ideal in collectivist and individualist cultures.
- New information about the status and controversy pertaining to legal marriage for same-sex couples.
- Coverage of the increased incidence of interracial marriage.
- Comparison of married men and women in their respective degree of sexual satisfaction.
- New information about DINS couples (Dual Income, No Sex).
- Discussion of the Internet's role in infidelity.
- An examination of the negative impact on relationships of secrecy about infidelity.
- Latest divorce rates data and updated and revised discussion of the various causes of divorce.
- A discussion of global beliefs about the relationship between sexual activity and aging.
- Information about the increasing phenomenon of older women dating younger men.
- A discussion of safer sex for senior citizens.

Chapter 15: The Nature and Origin of Sexual Difficulties

- Discussion of the use of a subjective definition of sexual problems.
- Consideration of men's concern about penis size and how this concern effects sexual functioning.
- Coverage of subjective reports of the degree of experienced sexual pleasure reported by people in countries around the world.

Chapter 16: Sex Therapy and Enhancement

- Discussion of the expanding use of erection-enhancing drugs.
- Coverage of the use of herbal treatment to enhance arousal.
- Discussion of the impact and implications of the limited knowledge about female physiological arousal processes.
- Coverage of the ongoing search for medical treatments for female sexual dysfunctions.
- Discussion of research inconsistencies in female sexual research.

Chapter 17: Sexually Transmitted Diseases

- Major updating of content throughout chapter with latest research findings on incidence data and treatment guidelines for all included STDs.
- Revised *At a Glance* table on mode of transmission, symptoms, and treatment of STDs.

- Revised and updated *Sexuality and Diversity* discussion of STDs in China.
- The latest data pertaining to the CDC's plan to eliminate syphilis by 2005.
- Expanded coverage of the use of antiviral drugs to manage herpes with a new discussion of *suppressive therapy* versus *episodic treatment*.
- Expanded and revised discussion of viral hepatitis.
- The latest incidence figures on HIV/AIDS with attention to the recent escalation in newly diagnosed HIV infections.
- New *Sexuality and Diversity* discussion of the HIV epidemic in Russia.
- Significantly revised and updated *Sexuality and Diversity* discussion of AIDS in Africa, including discussion of author involvement in a HIV/AIDS intervention program in Kenya.
- The latest developments in HIV testing.
- Heavily revised and updated discussion of treatment for HIV/AIDS.
- New *At a Glance* table listing potential benefits and risks of early or delayed treatment of HIV infection.
- New information on drug strategies for preventing mother-to-child transmission of HIV.
- Updated information on efforts to develop a vaccine(s) effective against HIV.
- Discussion of new research assessing the effectiveness of persuasive communication in HIV prevention.
- Expanded and revised coverage of the role of condoms in preventing STDs.
- Discussion of research findings demonstrating ineffectiveness (and potential adverse effects) of using spermicides containing nonoxynol-9.
- Updated and expanded *On the Edge* box describing efforts to develop vaginal microbicides.
- New information on the benefits of partner notification in reducing the spread of STDs.

Chapter 18: Atypical Sexual Behavior

- Updated *On the Edge* Box about video voyeurism with new information about unauthorized and authorized occurrences of video displays on the Internet that appeal to voyeuristic inclinations.
- New information about the use of selective serotonin reuptake inhibitors (SSRIs) in the treatment of coercive paraphilias.
- New *On the Edge* boxed discussion of cybersex addiction/compulsivity.

Chapter 19: Sexual Coercion

- New discussion of the research evidence linking the personality trait of *narcissism* to the inclination to be sexually coercive.
- Expanded coverage of date rape drugs and of ways to avoid being victimized by perpetrators who use these drugs as aids to their coercive behaviors.

- New section on the "Sexual Assault of Males."
- New *On the Edge* boxed discussion of declining trends in child sexual abuse.
- Discussion of the recent Supreme Court decision pertaining to the legality of Internet images of children engaged in sexual activity.
- Expanded coverage of what happens when a child tells about sexual abuse including recent research findings about why sexually abused children often delay disclosure or do not tell at all.

Chapter 20: Sex for Sale

- Discussion of trends in X-rated video rental rates.
- Description and discussion of how mainstream corporations profit from pornography.
- Evaluation of pornography's role in sex education.
- A discussion of the implications of men's preference for depictions of female enjoyment in pornography.
- Discussion of the advantages and disadvantages of legalization of prostitution for sex workers.
- Coverage of the various legal approaches to prostitution that occur in nations other than the United States.
- Discussion of teen involvement in prostitution.

Continuing Features

- A **personal approach.** Users of the text have responded favorably to our attempts to make the subject human and personal, and in this ninth edition we have retained and strengthened the elements that contribute to this approach.
- **Authors' files.** One of the most popular features of *Our Sexuality* has been the incorporation of voices of real people woven into the text through the use of Authors' Files. These quotations are taken from the experiences and observations of students, clients, and colleagues and appear interwoven in the text but highlighted by a color screen. The Authors' Files have been given fresh infusion for this edition thanks to feedback from students enrolled in college courses in human sexuality. Each chapter opens with an Authors' Files quote, illustrating an important concept pertinent to that chapter.
- **Nonjudgmental perspective.** Consistent with our personal focus, we have avoided a prescriptive stance on most issues introduced in the text. We have attempted to provide information in a sensitive, non-sexist, inclusive, nonjudgmental manner that assumes the reader is best qualified to determine what is most valid and applicable in her or his life.
- **Psychosocial orientation.** We focus on the roles of psychological and social factors in human sexual expression, reflecting our belief that human sexuality is governed more by psychosocial factors than by biological factors. At the same time, we provide the reader with a solid basis in the anatomy and physiology of human sexuality and explore new research

pertaining to the interplay of biology, psychology, and social learning.

■ **Critical Thinking Questions,** some of which are new to this edition, appear in the margin. These questions are designed to help students to apply their knowledge and experience while developing their own outlook. Each question encourages students to stop and think about what they are reading in an attempt to facilitate higher-order processing of information and learning.

■ **How About You?** questions, some new to this edition, also appear in the margin. These questions ask readers to consider their own experiences and attitudes on relevant sexual issues.

■ **InfoTrac search terms** are suggested several times in each chapter—called out by a margin icon. The Info-Trac® College Edition online searchable library (http://infotrac.thomsonlearning.com/) includes a multitude of journals, many which are specific to human sexuality. These journals include *Archives of Sexual Behavior, Archives of Sexual Health Behavior, Canadian Journal of Human Sexuality, Hispanic Journal of the Behavioral Sciences, Journal of Cross-Cultural Psychology, Journal of Physical Education, Journal of Sex Research,* and *Sex Roles.* A four-month subscription to InfoTrac College Edition is available free to purchasers of the ninth edition.

■ **Pedagogy.** Individuals learn in different ways. We therefore provide a variety of pedagogical aids to be used as the student chooses. Each chapter opens with an **outline** of major topic headings, complete with **chapter opening questions** that focus attention on important topics. **Key words** are boldfaced within the text, and a pronunciation guide follows selected key words. A **running glossary** in the text margin provides a helpful learning tool. Each chapter concludes with a **Summary** in outline form for student reference, annotated **Suggested Readings,** and annotated **Web Resources.** A complete **Glossary,** as well as a complete **Bibliography,** is provided at the end of the book.

Organization

The organization of this book has been designed to reflect a logical progression of topics. We begin, in **Part One—Introduction,** with the social and cultural legacy of sexuality in our society. We then describe how sex research is conducted and discuss the difficulties of gathering information in this sensitive area of human behavior. We conclude the opening unit with a detailed exploration of a variety of gender issues.

The three chapters of **Part Two—Biological Basis** present the biological foundations of sexuality, with separate chapters on male and female sexual anatomy, followed by coverage of sexual arousal and sexual response patterns integrated into one chapter.

In **Part Three—Sexual Behavior,** a variety of relationship issues and sexual behaviors are discussed.

In **Part Four—Sexuality and the Life Cycle,** we discuss contraception, pregnancy, and issues pertaining to sexuality throughout the life cycle.

Sexual problems and their treatment and a detailed chapter on sexually transmitted diseases constitute the three chapters of **Part Five—Sexual Problems.**

The final section, **Part Six—Social Issues,** includes discussions of atypical sexuality, sexual coercion, pornography, and prostitution.

Integrated Teaching and Learning Aids

Our Sexuality is accompanied by a wide array of supplements prepared for both the instructor and student. Many are available free to professors or students. Others can be packaged with this text at a discount. For more information on any of the listed resources, please call the Thomson Learning™ Academic Resource Center at 800-423-0563.

For the Instructor

Instructor's Resource Manual (ISBN 0-534-63394-3) by Caroline Clements of the University of North Carolina at Wilmington. The Introduction includes sections on "Making the First Week Count," "Involving Students in Important Decisions," "The Science and Art of Teaching," "Teaching Techniques from A to Z," and a new section, "How to Secure and Manage your Guest Speakers and Panels." For each chapter of the text, the manual includes teaching ideas, handouts, discussion topics, guest speaker suggestions, suggested Web sites, video suggestions and questions, Opposing Viewpoints questions and activities, InfoTrac College Edition search terms, and suggested questions for the free student CD-ROM. The manual also includes a detailed Resource Integration Guide that details, chapter by chapter, how all of the supplements Wadsworth offers for this course tie together.

Multimedia Manager Instructor's Resource CD-ROM (ISBN 0-534-63384-6) by Caroline Clements of the University of North Carolina at Wilmington. The CD-ROM includes PowerPoint slides, as well as electronic (Word) files of the *Instructor's Resource Manual* and *Test Bank.* A PowerPoint presentation contains lecture outlines for every chapter, including art from the text that has been integrated into the slides. Many of the chapters include embedded video clips from our CNN library.

Test Bank (ISBN 0-534-63437-0) by Rod Fowers of Highline Community College. This useful test resource contains at least 125 multiple choice, 25 true/false, and 15 short essay questions (with page references) per chapter with denotation as to whether each is a "knowledge" or "application" question.

ExamView (ISBN 0-534-63378-1). This supplement allows instructors to create, deliver, and customize tests and study guides (both print and online) in minutes. *ExamView* offers both a Quick Test Wizard and an Online Test Wizard that guides the instructor step-by-step through the process of creating tests, while its "what you see is what you get" interface allows instructors to see the test they are creating on the screen exactly as it will print or display online. Instructors can build tests of up to 250 questions using up to 12 question types. Using *ExamView*'s complete word processing capabilities, instructors can enter an unlimited number of new questions or edit existing questions.

CNN Today: Human Sexuality Volume I (ISBN 0-534-57985-X). This video, free to our adopters, offers clips ranging from one to three minutes in length to stimulate interest in relevant topics related to sexuality. Topics include: China sex shops, sex in America survey, transsexual teacher, female and male circumcision, prostate cancer, arranged marriage, sodomy law, same-sex marriage, morning-after pill, birth defects, covenant marriages, sexual dysfunction, the chlamydia test, herpes increase, date rape drugs, and the crime of rape.

CNN Today: Human Sexuality Volume II (ISBN 0-534-51598-3). This video, free to our adopters, offers clips ranging from one to three minutes in length to stimulate interest in relevant topics related to sexuality. Some topics include breast cancer, menopause, early puberty, New York sex shops, polygamy, Japanese bathhouses, premature ejaculation, sex laws, and more.

CNN Today: Human Sexuality Volume III (ISBN 0-534-51604-1). This video, free to our adopters, offers clips ranging from one to three minutes in length to stimulate interest in relevant topics related to sexuality. Some topics include: family planning in China, multiracial people and identity, pros and cons of abstinence sex education, parents and organized child porn, pornography and peer-to-peer file sharing, and more.

WebTutor Advantage (Web CT ISBN 0-534-63013-8; Blackboard ISBN 0-534-43012-X). An online, text-specific teaching and learning resource rich with course content and tools for study/mastery, course management, and communication. *WebTutor Advantage*'s course management tool gives you the ability to provide virtual office hours, post syllabi, set up threaded discussions, track student progress, and much more.

Transparency Acetates (ISBN 0-534-63377-3) (Figures chosen by Sue Frantz of Highline Community College). This is a collection of 125 acetates of four-color figures from the text and several additional figures not featured in the text.

Safer Sex Kit (ISBN 0-534-63376-5). This kit is intended for classroom demonstrations of various forms of con-traceptives. It includes the new O-ring, the patch, the diaphragm, contraceptive jelly, birth control pills, and more.

For the Student

Our Sexuality CD-ROM. This interactive CD-ROM comes automatically bundled with every new copy of the text. The CD-ROM provides animations of difficult concepts as well as video clips of people discussing various sexual issues. Topics include coming out in the workplace, a postsurgery transsexual, and a man with erectile dysfunction. The CD also has chapter quizzing and critical thinking questions, and students can easily print or e-mail their results. There is also a "Virtual Safer Sex Kit" that introduces major kinds of contraception. The CD also serves as a portal link to the *Our Sexuality* companion Web site.

Study Guide (ISBN 0-534-63385-4) by Rod Fowers of Highline Community College. Each chapter includes practice tests (which include multiple choice, essay, and true/false questions), learning objectives, concept maps, key terms, concept checks with page references to the text, crossword puzzles, and anatomical art figures that allow students to fill in the correct labels.

InfoTrac Workbook (ISBN 0-534-63383-8) by Paz Galupo of Towson University. This free guide contains student homework assignments that make good use of Info-Trac College Edition, our free online database of over 4,000 journals. Journals include *AIDS Weekly, Archives of Sexual Behavior, Sexuality & Culture, Gender Issues, Archives of Sexual Health Behavior, Canadian Journal of Human Sexuality, Hispanic Journal of the Behavioral Sciences, Journal of Cross-Cultural Psychology, Journal of Physical Education, Journal of Sex Research,* and *Sex Roles.* Assignments include class debates that teachers can assign. Includes a "quick start" to *InfoTrac College Edition* that explains how to get started using the database.

Web site (http://psychology.wadsworth.com/crooksbaur9e/). This companion Web site, free for students and not pin-coded, contains learning objectives, practice quizzes, InfoTrac College Edition activities, an online glossary in flashcard format for self-testing, Web links, and chapter summaries and outlines.

Acknowledgments

The quality and longevity of *Our Sexuality* are due to talents and insights that extend beyond those of the authors. We are especially indebted to the staff of Wadsworth, the reviewers, and our students, who have added immeasurably to the merit of our book. We also wish to acknowledge the contribution of William Zangwill, who revised Chapter 19 in the previous edition.

We owe special gratitude to reviewers and contributors to the ninth edition. Professors who lent their expertise at various stages of the revision process of this and previous editions are listed on the following pages.

Of all the members of the highly professional, competent, and supportive staff of Wadsworth who contributed to this and previous editions, we are especially indebted to developmental editor Kate Barnes, who worked tirelessly to ensure that the ninth edition of *Our Sexuality* would be the best yet. Kate had the unenviable task of succeeding Jim Strandberg, who worked his special magic as development editor for the seventh and eighth editions. Kate was more than up to the task as she brought fresh insights and new perspectives to the ninth edition. Among her many accomplishments were insightful suggestions for new topical content, valued recommendations for ways to reorganize and streamline content, and an educated and sharp eye for detail. Our sponsoring editor, Marianne Taflinger, again demonstrated the benefits of knowledgeable oversight in a project of this magnitude. We especially appreciate her role in securing excellent reviewers for the ninth edition. Marianne's ability to successfully and creatively resolve issues proved invaluable as she guided the birth of this, our ninth baby, from beginning to end. Editorial assistants Justin Courts, Lucy Faridany, and Nicole Root competently took care of a myriad of details. Kirk Bomont, senior production editor, again demonstrated his consummate professionalism as he managed the often complicated and hectic production schedule. Vernon Boes, John Walker, Linda Beaupre, and Joyce Weston managed in exemplary fashion the demanding job of designing and implementing the new design elements of this edition. Jennifer Keever adeptly supervised the development of the excellent supplements package, and Darin Derstine oversaw the creation of the exciting new *Our Sexuality* CD-ROM and technology resources.

Several freelance professionals added their talents at various stages of this edition. Research assistant Sami Tucker again demonstrated how invaluable her services are to the authors and to the academic strength of this book. The extremely current nature of the ninth edition is due in large part to Sami's exhaustive search of the recent journal literature in a wide range of academic disciplines, including—but not limited to—sexology, psychology, sociology, anthropology, biology, health, and medicine. Margaret Pinette again provided editorial and production services in an accomplished and professional manner. We are also indebted to Mimi Braverman, who performed superlatively as copy editor on this edition. Her contributions ranged far beyond our expectations. Photo researcher Laurie Frankenthaler was very instrumental in providing the ninth edition with a much-improved visual appeal. Laura Donahue performed the task of transcribing manuscript into electronic files in an exemplary fashion.

In addition, various field specialists added their expertise to the different aspects of this edition. Josephine Wilson at Wittenberg University provided her expertise on all aspects of biological psychology. Al Kielwasser and Michelle Wolf at San Francisco State helped us keep abreast of the latest media aspects related to human sexuality. Benjamin G. Rader at University of Nebraska, Lincoln, reviewed the historic aspects of the text, concentrating especially on Chapter 1. Jennifer Siciliani at the University of Missouri–St. Louis provided insights on the biological psychology of sexual arousal and response in Chapter 6.

An outstanding marketing team at Wadsworth was hard at work on promoting this revision long before the last words of the book were written. We offer special thanks to our marketing manager, Chris Caldeira, and Laurel Anderson, marketing assistant.

We would also like to extend our thanks to the many reviewers who provided guidance, support, and insight for the current edition:

Malinde Althaus
University of Minnesota

Ann Auleb
San Francisco State University

Janice Baldwin
University of California–Santa
Barbara

Tommy Begay
University of Arizona

Jim Belcher
Valencia Community College

M. Betsy Bergen
Kansas State University

Anthony Cantrell
University of Colorado

Nick Chittester
Washington State University

Richard Dienstbier
University of Nebraska–Lincoln

Mary Doyle
Arizona State University

April Few
Virginia Poly and State University

Rodney Fowers
Highline Community College

Bob Hensley
Iowa State University

Graham Higgs
Columbia College

Barbara Ilardi
University of Rochester

Al Kielwasser
San Francisco State

Kris Koehne
University of Tennessee

Luciana Lagana
California State
University–Northridge

Rhonda Martin
University of Tulsa

Shirley Ogletree
Texas State University–San Marcos

Valerie Pinhas
Nassau Community College

Benjamin G. Rader
University of Nebraska, Lincoln

Jennifer Siciliani
University of Missouri-St. Louis

Lee Spencer
Arizona State University

Veronica Tonay
University of California–Santa Cruz

David Ward
Arkansas Tech

Josephine Wilson
Wittenberg University

Michelle Wolf
San Francisco State

We also extend our continued thanks to reviewers of the previous eight editions.

Daniel Adame
Emory University

Sylvester Allred
Northern Arizona University

Linda Anderson
University of North Carolina

Veanne Anderson
Indiana State University

Wayne Anderson
University of Missouri, Columbia

Betty Sue Benison
Texas Christian University

M. Betsy Bergen
Kansas State University

Thomas E. Billimek
San Antonio College

Linda Bilsborough
California State University–Chico

Jane Blackwell
Washington State University

John Blakemore
Monterey Peninsula College

Marvin J. Branstrom
Cañada College

Tom Britton, M.D.
Planned Parenthood, Portland,
Oregon

Elizabeth Calamidas
Richard Stockton College

Charles Carroll
Ball State University

Joan Cirone
California Polytechnic State
University

Bruce Clear
The First Unitarian Church, Portland

David R. Cleveland
Honolulu Community College

Gretchen Clum
University of Missouri, St. Louis

Rosemary Cogan
Texas Tech University

Ellen Cole
Alaska Pacific University

Jeff Cornelius
New Mexico State University

Laurel Cox
Ventura College

John Creech
Collin Community College, Preston
Ridge Campus

Susan Dalterio
University of Texas, San Antonio

Joseph Darden
Kean College

Deborah Davis
University of Nevada, Reno

Brenda M. DeVellis
University of North Carolina

Lewis Diana
Virginia Commonwealth University

Beverly Drinnin
Des Moines Area Community
College

Judy Drolet
Southern Illinois University,
Carbondale

Andrea Parrot Eggleston
Cornell University

John P. Elia
San Francisco State University

Carol Ellison
Clinical Psychologist

Karen Eso
Bakersfield College

Peter Fabian
Edgewood College

Catherine Fitchen
Dawson College

Rod Flowers
Highline Community College

Karen Lee Fontaine
Purdue University, Calumet

Lin S. Fox
Kean College of New Jersey

Gene Fulton
University of Toledo

David W. Gallagher
Pima Community College

Carol Galletly
Ohio State University

Kenneth George
University of Pennsylvania

David A. Gershaw
Arizona Western College

Glen G. Gilbert
Portland State University

Brian A. Gladue
University of Cincinnati

Mike Godsey
College of Marin

Gordon Hammerle
Adrian College

Debra Hansen
College of the Sequoias

Stephen Harmon
University of Utah

Claudette Hastie-Beahrs
Clinical Social Worker

Pearl A. Hawe
New Mexico State University

Timothy Hulsey
Southwest Texas State University

Rosemary Iconis
York College

Barbara Iliardi
University of Rochester

Thomas Johns
American River College

David Johnson
Portland State University

James A. Johnson
Sam Houston State University

Kathleen Kendall-Tackett
University of New Hampshire

Sally Klein
Dutchess Community College

Peggy Kleinplatz
University of Ottawa

Patricia B. Koch
Pennsylvania State University

Robin Kowalski
Western Carolina University

Virginia Kreisworth
San Diego State University

Eric Krenz
California State University–Fresno

Vickie Krenz
California State University–Fresno

Lauren Kuhn
Portland Community College

Miriam LeGare
California State University–Sacramento

Sandra Leiblum
University of Medicine and Dentistry/Robert Wood Johnson

Sanford Lopater
Christopher Newport University

Joseph LoPiccolo
University of Missouri

Laura Madson
New Mexico State University

Peter Maneno
Normandale College

Milton Mankoff
Queens College

Christel J.Manning
Hollins College

Jerald J.Marshall
University of Central Florida

Donald Matlosz
California State University–Fresno

Leslie McBride
Portland State University

Deborah McDonald
New Mexico State University

Sue McKenzie
Dawson College

Brian McNaught
Gloucester, Massachusetts

Gilbert Meyer
Illinois Valley Community College

Deborah Miller
College of Charleston

John Money
Johns Hopkins University

Denis Moore
Honolulu Metropolitan Community Church

Charlene Muehlenhard
University of Kansas

Louis Munch
Ithaca College

Ronald Murdoff
San Joaquin Delta College

Kay Murphy
Oklahoma State University

James Nash
California Polytechnic State University

Jean L. Nash
Family Nurse Practitioner, Portland, Oregon

Teri Nicoll-Johnson
Modesto Junior College

William O'Donohue
University of Nevada, Reno

Roberta Ogletree
Southern Illinois University, Carbondale

Al Ono, M.D.
Obstetrician/Gynecologist

D. Kim Openshaw
Utah State University

Bruce Palmer
Washington State University

Monroe Pasternak
Diablo Valley College

Calvin D. Payne
University of Arizona

J. Mark Perrin
University of Wisconsin, River Falls

John W. Petras
Central Michigan University

Valerie Pinhas
Nassau Community College

Ollie Pocs
Illinois State University

Robert Pollack
University of Georgia

Patty Reagan
University of Utah

Deborah Richardson
University of Georgia

Barbara Rienzo
University of Florida

Barbara Safriet
Lewis and Clark Law School

Nancy Salisbury, M.D.
Portland, Oregon

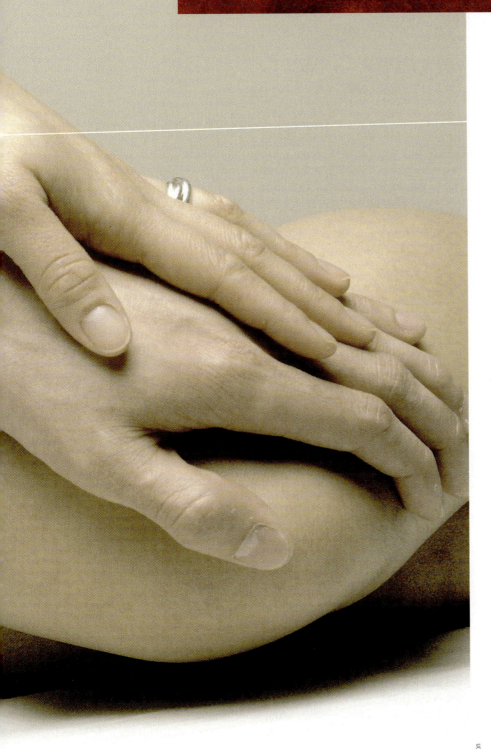

CHAPTER **1**

◆ Perspectives on Sexuality

▶ **Controversy and Diversity in Human Sexuality**

Why do the authors attempt to bring an inclusive approach to Our Sexuality?

▶ **Diversity Within the United States**

What factors contribute to diversity and similarity of sexual attitudes and behaviors within the United States?

▶ **A Psychosocial Orientation**

Why do the authors emphasize a psychosocial perspective in Our Sexuality?

▶ **Our Cultural Legacy: Sex for Procreation and Rigid Gender Roles**

What importance do the historical themes of sex for procreation and male/female gender roles have today?

▶ **Cross-Cultural Perspective of the Sex-for-Procreation and Gender-Role Themes**

How are sex for procreation and gender roles manifested in the Middle East and China?

▶ **Sexuality in the Western World: A Historical Perspective**

How did the legacies of sex for procreation and rigid gender roles develop through Western history?

What major scientific development has helped separate sexual pleasure from reproduction?

▶ **The Media and Sexuality**

How has mass media reflected and influenced sexual norms?

What are the unique elements to sexuality and the Internet compared to other mass media?

▶ **Sexuality: Where the Personal Is Political**

How can something as personal as sexuality be "political"?

© Joel Gordon

Most students take this course, at least in part, to enhance their personal understanding and development. We hope this book and your human sexuality class will help you do just that. We offer this book as a tool for exploring your perspectives on human sexuality. We present a wide array of information about attitudes, ideas, and behaviors. However, the final expert on your sexuality is *you,* and we encourage you to evaluate all the information we present within the framework of your own convictions and experience. We welcome you to this book and your human sexuality class.

▶ Controversy and Diversity in Human Sexuality

It is safe to assume that any controversial topic will elicit a wide range of responses. Few topics generate as much attention and evoke so much pleasure and distress as the many possibilities of the expression and control of human sexuality. In any beginning sexuality class—or in almost any other group, for that matter—attitudes toward sexuality are likely to range from very liberal to extremely conservative. Students in sexuality classes represent a diversity of ages, ethnic and religious backgrounds, and sexual and life experiences. Some have had sexual encounters with one or many partners; some have had long-term partnerships and marriages; others have not been sexually involved with another person. Many people relate sexually only with members of the other sex*; some seek sexual contact with members of the same sex; still others have sexual relationships with either sex. There are virtually no universals in sexual attitudes, experiences, or preferences. With this in mind, we have attempted to bring an inclusive philosophy to our book. We hope that something in the following pages will speak to the diversity of *all* our readers. We begin this chapter with an overview of the diversity within the United States.

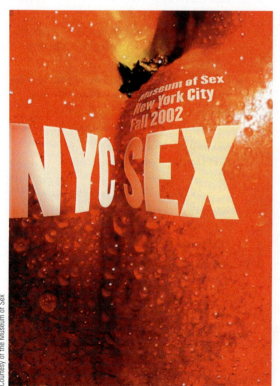

Courtesy of the Museum of Sex

The Museum of Sex opened its doors in New York in September 2002 with an exhibit about the history of sex in New York City. The museum's mission is to preserve and present the history and cultural significance of human sexuality.

▶ Diversity Within the United States

Our Sexuality explores the sexual attitudes and behaviors of many places around the globe, including the United States. Individuals of many ethnic and religious groups have made their homes in the United States, resulting in a wide range of sexual values and behaviors (South-Paul, 2003). Throughout this text, we will encounter many examples of the diversity that exists among different subcultures in our society. In studying these examples, we must note that within the same ethnic group, socioeconomic status and education are crucial in influencing sexual attitudes and behaviors. Low-income and middle-income people often differ; the same is often true of people at different educational levels. For instance, people with more education masturbate more often than less-educated people do (Kinsey et al., 1948; Michael et al., 1994). Another group-related difference is in oral–genital sex, which tends to be most common among young, college-educated whites and least common among African Americans and individuals with less education (Michael et al., 1994).

It should be stressed that differences between groups are generalities, not universal truths—even within groups, great diversity exists (Agbayani-Siewert, 2004). For example,

---

*We use the term *other sex* instead of *opposite sex* to emphasize that men and women are similar or alike in more ways than they are opposite.

A Child/Parent Sex Talk

To expand your understanding of your attitudes and experiences related to sexuality, you might consider interviewing your parents about their experiences and beliefs.

"WHAT!!! Talk to *my* parents about sex?!?"

The following ideas and suggestions may make this a less daunting endeavor.

"BUT, my mom and dad would *never* answer any questions about sex."

You might be quite surprised how open your parents are to your interest. The tell-the-children-when-they-ask parenting approach is common. Plus, you can test the waters first: Start with a low-key question, and if they respond with a direct or an indirect "I don't want to talk about it," stop the interview and change the subject.

The first step is to pick your interviewee.* It may be that you feel most comfortable to begin with a grandparent or another relative instead of a parent. Find a time when you will not be rushed and a place that will be private. (Alternatively, you can use e-mail, a phone call, or a letter; you might also find that several shorter conversations work best for you.) A possible way to begin is, "I'm taking a human sexuality class this term, and it made me wonder if you had any sex education in school."

Now you have broken the ice, and if you have had a good reception, you can ask specifics about your interviewee's sexual education: "What did you learn about sexuality from teachers? Friends? The church or synagogue? Your parents? Books? Is there any information you wish you had received? Wish you hadn't received?"

The next direction in the interview can be to ask about the information and ideas about sexuality that were the norm when your interviewee was a child and young adult. For example: "What were your parents' attitudes about sex? Your friends'? The media's? Did

*Do not choose someone to interview unless there is a lot of goodwill in the relationship.

 Universal/The Kobal Collection

The father–son "sex talk" scenes in the film American Pie *depict the awkwardness that parents and children often experience when they discuss sexuality.*

you think most people were virgins when they got married? What are the different standards for women and men? When did you first learn about homosexuality? What attitudes did people you knew have about homosexuality? What did people use for birth control? What was easier or more difficult about sexuality for your generation than for mine?"

If things are rolling along, you might take a more personal bent: "How did you feel about your body changing from a child to a teenager? How quickly did you mature compared to your classmates? Did you know about menstruation/ejaculation before you experienced it? When did you have your first crush on someone? What happened? What was your first kiss like? What do you wish you knew as a child or young adult that you know now?"

If your interview has come this far, you probably have a greater understanding and appreciation of important aspects of your interviewee's life and, hopefully, of your own. So, who's next?

Asian Americans include the descendants of Chinese laborers brought to the United States in the 19th century to build railroads. They also include refugees from the Vietnam and Korean wars and individuals who came from Hong Kong, Japan, the Pacific islands, and many other Asian countries to study, start businesses, or stay for other reasons. The Hispanic population comes from 22 different countries of origin, and some groups consider themselves culturally distinct from other Latino groups (Acosta-Belen & Bose, 2003; Larmer, 1999b). However, when research looks at patterns in groups, some differences emerge. For example, Asian Americans—*on the whole*—are less likely to engage in premarital intercourse than are Hispanic Americans, African Americans, or Americans of European descent (Cochran et al., 1991). Again, Hispanic culture—*on the whole*—often endorses sexual exploration for males but places a high value on chastity before marriage for women (Comas-Diaz & Greene, 1994).

The degree of *acculturation*—that is, replacing traditional beliefs and behavior patterns with those of the dominant subculture—also creates differences within subcultures. More recent immigrants are closer to the values of their countries of origin, but most individuals

Stand-up comic and second-generation Korean Margaret Cho shatters stereotypes of the submissive, reticent Asian female in her act. She takes provocative topics—such as bisexuality, what it would be like if men menstruated, and needing foreplay to have an orgasm—over the top.

Psychosocial Refers to a combination of psychological and social factors.

whose families have lived in North America for several generations are well assimilated (Barkley & Mosher, 1995). Films such as *My Big Fat Greek Wedding, American Desi,* and *Monsoon Wedding* depict the conflicts that can arise in families when the younger generation becomes more Americanized.

In contrast, some long-established groups, such as Hawaiians, African Americans, and Native Americans, are undergoing a process of ethnic revival. They are attempting to recapture aspects of their cultures to pass on to new generations (Williams & Ellison, 1996; Yim, 2000a). Many young Hispanics embrace Latin culture within the U.S. mainstream. They are building a strong bicultural identity, and a new wave of Latin-based popular music reflects their bicultural lives (Leland & Chambers, 1999).

A factor that blurs differences between ethnic groups is the fact that a significant—and ever-increasing—proportion of the U.S. population is *multiracial;* that is, some people have predecessors from two or more racial groups (Cose, 2000). Race and ethnicity are rarely simplistic, nonoverlapping classifications (Smith, 1995). "People all over the world have engaged in various degrees of mixing, particularly in the United States. . . . There is no way to look at every person and determine their exact racial background" (Wyatt, 1997, p. xv). The merging of ethnicity will likely increase over time in the United States because of the level of mixed-ethnic dating in young people. Almost 25% of teens have partners from different ethnic groups (Ford et al., 2002).

Sexual attitudes and behaviors often vary widely even within the same religious group. For example, although Pope John Paul II adheres to the traditional Roman Catholic view condemning all sexual activity that does not potentially lead to procreation, the views of American Catholics run the gamut on issues such as contraception, abortion, and homosexuality. Similarly, Orthodox Jews have much more conservative views regarding sexuality and gender roles than do Reform Jews. For example, Orthodox Jewish belief forbids sexual intercourse during menstruation, whereas Reform Jews follow individual preferences. Furthermore, fundamentalist Christians who interpret the Bible literally differ greatly in views about sexuality from Christians who do not (Ostling, 2000). For example, fundamentalist Christian belief typically holds that sexual intercourse before marriage is sinful, whereas a more liberal Christian might emphasize the importance of the quality and caring in the relationship.

These similarities and differences in sexual beliefs, values, and behaviors are part of the *psychosocial* orientation of this textbook.

▶ A Psychosocial Orientation

This book has a **psychosocial** orientation, reflecting our view that psychological factors (emotions, attitudes, motivations) and social conditioning (the process by which we learn our social groups' expectations and norms) have a crucial impact on sexual attitudes, values, and behavior. It is also clear that the biology of sex plays a significant role in human sexuality, and throughout this text we will be looking in some detail at the biological foundations of sexual behavior. Some examples include the role of hormones and the nervous system, theories about the role of genetic selection through thousands of years of human evolution, and the impact of specific genetic variables on an individual.

We may not always be aware of it, but our sexual attitudes and behaviors are strongly shaped by our society in general and by the particular social groups to which we belong (Laumann et al., 1994). The subtle ways in which we learn society's expectations regarding sexuality often lead us to assume that our behaviors or feelings are biologically innate, or natural. However, an examination of sexuality in other historical periods and in other societies (or even in different ethnic, socioeconomic, and age groups within our own society) reveals a broad range of acceptable behavior. What we regard as natural is clearly relative. The diversity of sexual expression throughout the world tends to mask a fundamental generalization that can be applied without exception to all social orders: All societies have rules regulating the conduct of sexual behavior. "Every society shapes, structures, and constrains the development and expression of sexuality in all of its members" (Beach, 1978, p. 116). Knowledge about the impact of culture and individual experience can make it easier to understand and make decisions about our own sexuality. Therefore the major emphasis in *Our Sexuality* will be on the psychosocial aspects of human sexuality.

► Our Cultural Legacy: Sex for Procreation and Rigid Gender Roles

The psychosocial impact on sexuality is highlighted by two themes pertaining to sexuality: the idea that procreation is the only legitimate reason for sexual activity and the belief in rigid distinctions between male and female roles. These themes make up significant parts of the foundation of patterns and conflicts related to sexuality and are long-standing in many cultures. In these initial sections we will review these elements in Western culture and then explore these themes in the Islamic Middle East and China.

Sex for Procreation

Prevalent in North America is the idea that procreation is the only legitimate reason for sexual activity. Therefore in this society "sex" and "intercourse" are often seen as synonymous, and anything other than a penis in a vagina is not "sex." In the Clinton–Lewinsky scandal that began in 1998, Clinton's initial declaration that he did not have "sex with that woman" was true if one considers the definition of "sex" to be only intercourse to the exclusion of kissing, oral sex, and genital petting. This line of thinking is rather common; in fact, a study of college students found that 60% did not consider engaging in oral sex as "having sex" (Sanders & Reinisch, 1999).

? Critical Thinking Question

If you overheard someone say, "I had sex last night," what *specific behaviors* would you think happened?

Certainly penile–vaginal intercourse can be a fulfilling part of heterosexual sexual expression, but excessive emphasis on intercourse can have negative consequences. For one, it perpetuates the notion that sexual response and orgasm are supposed to occur during penetration. Such a narrow focus places tremendous performance pressures on both women and men and can create unrealistic expectations of coitus itself. The sex-for-procreation view also might result in devaluing other forms of sexual behavior. Some activities—for instance, kissing, body caresses, and manual or oral stimulation of the genitals—are often relegated to the secondary status of *foreplay* (usually considered any activity before intercourse), implying that they are to be followed by the "real sex" of coitus. Furthermore, sexual activity between members of the same sex does not fit the model of sex for procreation. These and other non-coital sexual behaviors—such as masturbation, sexual fantasy, and anal intercourse—have been defined at various times in our own culture and in other cultures as immoral, sinful, perverted, or illegal, because they provide pleasure without procreation. However, we present them in this textbook as viable sexual options for those who choose them.

Male and Female Gender Roles in Sexuality

The second theme we question is a rigid distinction between male and female roles. This legacy is based on far more than the physiological differences between the sexes. Although research has found physiological differences between males and females that create gender characteristics and inclinations in each sex, socialization shapes and exaggerates our biological tendencies. Rigid gender-role conditioning can limit each person's full range of human potential and can produce a negative impact on sexuality. For example, teaching "appropriate" behavior for men and women might contribute to the notion that the man must always initiate sexual activity while the woman must either set limits or comply; this behavior places tremendous responsibility on the male and severely limits the woman's likelihood of discovering her own needs (Berman & Berman, 2001). Across most cultures women face more restrictions on and experience greater sanctions against their sexuality than men (Murphy, 2003). In the United States, for example, the word *slut* remains predominantly an indictment of females. A recent survey found this idea to be prevalent among today's teens: 90% of boys and 92% of girls stated that girls get bad reputations for having sex. In contrast, only 40% of boys and 43% of girls said that boys get bad reputations for the same behavior (Kaiser Family Foundation, 2003).

We hope that our discussions about gender roles and sexuality will help you to better navigate the challenges they present.

▶ Cross-Cultural Perspective of the Sex-for-Procreation and Gender-Role Themes

Before exploring sex for procreation and gender roles in sexuality more thoroughly in Western culture, let us consider how these beliefs are manifested in two other cultures: the Middle East and Asia. First, as we can see in Figure 1.1, most people around the world say that sex is important in their overall lives.

The Islamic Middle East

Islam is the world's fastest growing religion, and its followers are called Muslims. Islam predominates in the Middle East, yet it is present in many other parts of the world: one-fifth of the world's population is Muslim. Its followers adhere to the teachings of the Prophet Muhammad (c. A.D. 570–632), which are recorded in the Qur'an. Muhammad opposed intercourse before marriage but valued intercourse within marriage as the highest good in

▶ **Figure 1.1** Pfizer Global Study of Sexual Attitudes and Behaviors: How important is sex in your overall life? The study surveyed more than 26,000 people in 28 countries.

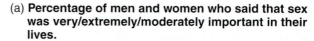

(a) **Percentage of men and women who said that sex was very/extremely/moderately important in their lives.**

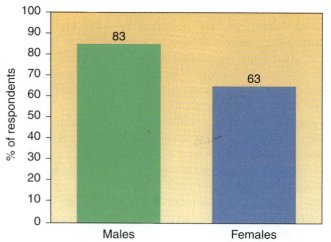

(b) **Percentage of people in each country who said that sex was very/extremely/moderately important to them.**

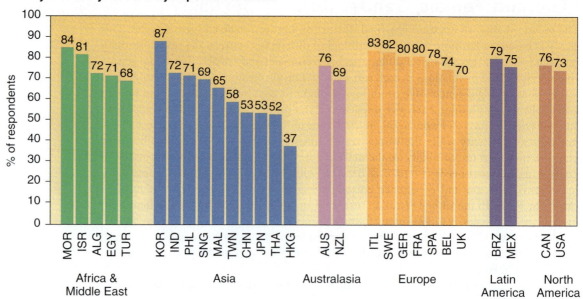

human life to be enjoyed by men and women alike, encouraging husbands to be "slow and delaying" (Abbott, 2000). Women are considered inherently sexual: Muhammad's son-in-law proclaimed, "Almighty God created sexual desire in ten parts: then he gave nine parts to women and one to men." The Qur'an requires modesty in public for both men and women by wearing loose-fitting, body-covering clothing. A woman in Islamic dress is said to be like "a pearl in a shell" (Jehl, 1998).

Before Islam's development, *polygamy* (*one* man having multiple wives at the same time) was a common practice. When war led to a disproportionate number of women compared to men, polygamy provided husbands for widows and orphans. The Qur'an did not subsequently prohibit polygamy. It allows men to have up to four wives, provided that the husband is fair to each of them.

Many of the extreme sexually related restrictions and punishments in Islamic countries do not stem from teachings in the Qur'an but from cultural traditions or the emergence of religious sects (Hays, 2004). Similarly, actions of some Christian extremists in the United States do not represent Christian tenets, as exemplified by Paul Hill, who, before his execution in 2003 for murdering a physician who performed abortions, stated, "I expect a great reward in heaven" (Dickey & Power, 2003, p. 50). Some Muslims believe that girls must be circumcised, but the Qur'an does not require it. In addition, in some areas local tradition sanctions "honor killings"; a wife who has dishonored her husband by having sex outside their marriage can be stoned or burned to death (Chigbo, 2003). Punishment for not wearing a veil in public, which occurred when the Taliban ruled Afghanistan, is also not a teaching in the Qur'an (Power, 1998a).

A Muslim man and woman in traditional conservative robes.

China

China has a rich history of erotic literature and art. Indeed, the earliest known sex manuals, produced in China sometime around 2500 B.C., portrayed sexual techniques and a great variety of intercourse positions. In ancient China, Taoism (dating from around the 2nd century B.C.) actively promoted sexual activity—oral sex, sensual touching, and intercourse—not only for procreation but also to achieve spiritual growth and harmony. The sexual connection of man and woman during intercourse was believed to join the opposing energies of yin (female) and yang (male), thereby balancing the essences of the two in each individual. Men were encouraged to ejaculate infrequently to conserve yang energy; orgasm for women helped create more yin energy and was sought after.

These liberal Taoist attitudes were replaced by a much stricter sexual propriety that emerged during a renaissance of Confucianism around A.D. 1000. Chinese sexual expression remains quite conservative today. After the Communist victory in 1949, the government attempted to eliminate "decadent" Western sexual behaviors by outlawing pornography and shutting down brothels (Ruan, 1998). Sex outside marriage was considered a bourgeois transgression, and sex more than once a week was deemed a counterproductive diversion of energy. As a result of these measures and attitudes, China all but eradicated sexually transmitted diseases (Wehrfritz, 1996).

Communist China's insulation from the Western world can be seen by its late involvement in the sexual sciences. China's first national conference on sexology was held in 1992. Only in the last few years has sex education been provided in Chinese schools (Contemporary Sexuality, 2004a).

Detail of a 19th-century Chinese illustration, part of a rich cultural history of erotic art.

Only 50% of rural and 35% of urban teenage girls have accurate knowledge about menstruation. Physicians maintain that inadequate sexual knowledge is the main cause of sexual disorders, which are most commonly seen in wives. Many men do not know that a woman has a clitoris. Most married women see procreation as the reason for sex, and once they have children, they are no longer interested. Most women see marital sex as a service to their husbands rather than as something pleasurable for themselves (Livingston, 1997). Furthermore, although 8% of university students report being gay, homosexuals are closeted (Contemporary Sexuality, 2001b; Livingston, 1997).

Changes in sexual attitudes and behavior in China have appeared in recent years. More sexual content is found in film, television, and advertising. The overall divorce rate rose from less than 5% in 1981 to 12% in 1996, with divorce rates in urban areas increasing to 25% of marriages (Pappas, 1998). Rates of premarital and extramarital sex are greater than before (Cowley et al., 1996). One study found that 68% of university students think that sex before marriage is "morally OK" (Pappas, 1998). However, adolescents and young adults are less sexually active than in the United States. Among Chinese college students 23% of men and 12% of women report having experienced intercourse. The statistics for young people in the United States are much higher; by age 19, 60% of women and 61% of men in the United States have experienced sexual intercourse (Centers for Disease Control, 2002g). Of those Chinese college students who do have intercourse, only half use birth control (Livingston, 1997). Unfortunately, some of these changes in behavior have led to an increase in sexually transmitted diseases, including AIDS. This increase is especially problematic because few doctors have been trained to treat these diseases (X. Chen et al., 2000) and because social stigma for having AIDS is extreme (Liu & Meyer, 2000).

? Critical Thinking Question

What would be the benefits to your sexuality if you lived in a more restrictive culture, such as China or the Islamic Middle East?

To better understand the influence of contemporary social beliefs on sexuality in the Western world, we must examine their historical roots, particularly those that pertain to the legacies of sex for procreation and rigid gender roles. Where did these ideas come from, and how relevant are they to us today?

▶ Sexuality in the Western World: A Historical Perspective

Judaic and Christian Traditions

By the time Hebraic culture was established, gender roles were highly specialized. The book of Proverbs lists the duties of a good wife: She must instruct servants, care for her family, keep household accounts, and obey her husband. Bearing children (especially sons) was essential; the Hebrews' history of subjugation by persecution and slavery made them determined to preserve their people—to "be fruitful, and multiply, and replenish the earth" (Genesis 1:28).

? How About You?

How do your religious views influence your decision making with regard to sexuality?

Yet sex within marriage was believed to be more than a reproductive necessity. To "know" a partner sexually, within marriage, was recognized in the Bible and by tradition as a profound physical and emotional experience (Carswell, 1969; Haffner, 2004). The Song of Songs in the Bible (or the Song of Solomon, depending on which Bible you use) contains sensuous love poetry. From a small excerpt, the bridegroom speaks:

> *How fair is thy love, . . . my bride!*
> *How much better is thy love than wine!*
> *And the smell of thine ointments than all manner of spices!*
> *Thy lips, oh my bride, drop honey—honey and milk are under thy tongue.*
> (Song of Songs 4:10–11).

And the bride:

> *I am my beloved's and his desire is toward me.*
> *Come, my beloved, let us go forth into the field; Let us lodge in the villages . . .*
> *There will I give thee my love.*
> (Song of Songs 7:11–13)

The joyful appreciation of sexuality displayed in these lines is part of the Judaic tradition. This view was overshadowed, however, by teachings of Christianity. To understand why this happened, we have to remember that Christianity developed during the later years of the Roman Empire. This was a period of social instability when many exotic cults were imported from Greece, Persia, and other parts of the empire to provide sexual entertainment and amusement. Early Christians separated themselves from these practices by associating sex with sin.

We know little about Jesus' specific views on sexuality, but the principles of love and tolerance were the foundation of his teachings. However, Paul of Tarsus, a follower of Christianity, had a crucial influence on the early church (he died in A.D. 66, and many of his writings were incorporated into the New Testament). Paul emphasized the importance of overcoming "desires of the flesh"—including anger, selfishness, hatred, and nonmarital sex—in order to inherit the Kingdom of God. He associated spirituality with sexual abstinence and saw **celibacy** (SEH-luh-buh-see), the state of being unmarried and therefore abstaining from sexual intercourse, as superior to marriage. Hence, sex, which is essential for reproduction, was a necessary but religiously denigrated act.

The teachings of Jesus Christ emphasized love, compassion, and forgiveness. Stoning was the prescribed punishment for a woman who committed adultery, but Jesus admonished the men who had brought her to him for judgment, "He that is without sin among you, let him first cast a stone at her" (John 4:7). After all the men left without throwing any stones, Jesus told the woman, "Neither do I condemn thee: go, and sin no more" (John 8:11).

© Erich Lessing/Art Resource, NY

Celibacy Historically defined as the state of being unmarried; currently defined as not engaging in sexual behavior.

Sex as Sinful

Later church fathers expanded on the theme of sex as sin. The bishop Augustine (354–430) declared that lust was the original sin of Adam and Eve; his writings formalized the notion that intercourse could take place only within marriage for the purpose of procreation (Bullough, 2001). Augustine also believed that female subordination was intrinsic to God's creation, which led to the idea that any intercourse position other than the one with the man on top was "unnatural" (Wiesner-Hanks, 2000).

Although attitudes varied from era to era across the thousand-year time span and from place to place within Europe, the belief that sex is sinful persisted throughout the Middle Ages (the period from the fall of the Western Roman Empire in A.D. 476 to the beginning of the Renaissance, about 1400). Theologian Thomas Aquinas (1224–1274) further refined this idea in a small section of his *Summa Theologica*. Aquinas maintained that human sexual organs were designed for procreation and that any other use—as in homosexual acts, oral–genital sex, anal intercourse, or sex with animals—was against God's will, heretical, and a "crime against nature." Local priests relied on handbooks called Penitentials, catalogs of sins with corresponding penances, to guide them in responding to confessions. Using withdrawal to avoid pregnancy was the most serious sin and could require a penance of fasting on bread and water for years. "Unnatural acts" of oral or anal sex were also viewed as gravely sinful and drew more severe penances than murder (Fox, 1995). Of course, homosexual relations precluded the possibility of reproduction and consisted of many "unnatural acts." From Aquinas's time on, homosexuals were to find neither refuge nor tolerance anywhere in the Western world (Boswell, 1980).

© Burstein Collection/CORBIS

Interpretations of Adam and Eve's transgressions in the Garden of Eden have influenced values about sexuality.

Eve versus Mary

The emphasis on sex for procreation during the Middle Ages supported two contradictory images of women, and each image had its own impact on women's place in society. The first image is the Virgin Mary; the second image is Eve as an evil temptress.

Initially, Mary was a figure of secondary importance in the Western church. Her status was elevated and she became more prominent when the Crusaders returned from Constantinople, bringing to the West a view of Mary as a gracious, compassionate protector and an exalted focus of religious devotion.

© SuperStock

Antagonism toward women reached a climax during the witch hunts of the 15th century.

The practice of *courtly love*, which evolved at about this time, reflected a compatible image of woman as pure and above reproach. Ideally, a young knight would fall in love with a married woman of higher rank. After a lengthy pursuit, he would find favor, but his love would remain unconsummated because her marriage vows ultimately proved inviolable. This paradigm caught the medieval imagination, and troubadours performed ballads of courtly love throughout the courts of Europe.

The other medieval image provides a counterpoint to the unattainable, compassionate Virgin Mary: Eve as the temptress in the Garden of Eden. This image, promoted by the Church, reflected an increasing emphasis on Eve's sin and ultimately resulted in heightened antagonism toward women. This antagonism reached its climax in the witch hunts that began in the late 15th century—after the Renaissance was well under way—and lasted for close to 200 years (Hitchcock, 1995). Witchcraft was blamed on carnal lust, and most "witches" were accused of engaging in sexual orgies with the devil (Wiesner-Hanks, 2000). Ironically, while Queen Elizabeth I (1533–1603) brought England to new heights, an estimated 50,000 women were executed as witches in Europe during and after her reign (Barstow, 1994).

A Sex-Positive Shift

The prevailing view of nonreproductive sex as sinful was modified by Protestant reformers of the 16th century. Both Martin Luther (1483–1546) and John Calvin (1509–1564) recognized the value of sex in marriage (Berman & Berman, 2001). According to Calvin, marital sex was permissible if it stemmed "from a desire for children, or to avoid fornication, or to lighten and ease the cares and sadnesses of household affairs, or to endear each other" (Taylor, 1971, p. 62). The Puritans, often maligned for having rigid views about sex, also shared an appreciation of sexual expression within marriage (D'Emilio & Freedman, 1988; Wiesner-Hanks, 2000). In fact, one man was expelled from Boston when, among other offenses, "he denied ... conjugal ... fellowship unto his wife for the space of 2 years" (Morgan, 1978, p. 364).

The 18th-century Enlightenment was partly an outgrowth of the new scientific rationalism: Ideas reflected facts that could be objectively observed, rather than subjective beliefs and superstition. Women were to enjoy increased respect, at least for a short time. Some women, such as Mary Wollstonecraft of England, were acknowledged for their intelligence, wit, and vivacity. Wollstonecraft's book, *The Vindication of the Rights of Women* (1792), attacked the prevailing practice of giving young girls dolls rather than schoolbooks. Wollstonecraft also asserted that sexual satisfaction was as important to women as to men and that premarital and extramarital sex were not sinful.

The Victorian Era

Unfortunately, these progressive views did not prevail. The Victorian era, which took its name from the queen who ascended the British throne in 1837 and ruled for over 60 years, brought a sharp turnaround. The sexes had highly defined roles. Women's sexuality was polarized between the images of Madonna and whore. Upper- and middle-class Victorian women in Europe and the United States were valued for their delicacy and ladylike manners—and consequently constrained by such restrictive devices as corsets, hoops, and bustles. Popular opinion of female sexuality was reflected by the widely quoted physician William Acton, who wrote, "The majority of women are not very much troubled with sexual feelings of any kind" (Degler, 1980, p. 250). Women's duties centered on fulfilling their families' spiritual needs and

? How About You?

How does the Madonna/whore dichotomy affect your sexuality today?

providing a comfortable home for their husbands to retreat to after working all day. Their presumed delicacy and limited roles resulted in marginalization through idealization (Glick & Fiske, 2001; Real, 2002). The world of women was clearly separated from that of men. Consequently, intensely passionate friendships sometimes developed between women, providing the support and comfort that were often absent in marriage.

In general, Victorians encouraged self-restraint in all aspects of their lives, and Victorian men were expected to conform to the strict propriety of the age (Rader, 2003). However, Victorian men often set morality aside in the pursuit of sexual companionship, because the societal separation between the worlds of husbands and wives created an emotional (and physical) distance in many Victorian marriages. Ironically, prostitution flourished at this time, as men sought the sexual companionship that they could not enjoy with their wives. Victorian men could smoke, drink, and joke with the women who had turned to prostitution out of economic necessity, whereas their wives were caught in the constraints of propriety and sexual repression.

Despite the prevailing notions of the asexual Victorian woman, Celia Mosher, a physician born in 1863, decided to ask women themselves about their sexuality. She conducted the only known research about the sexuality of women of that era. Over a span of 30 years, 47 married women completed her questionnaire. The information gathered from the research revealed a different picture of female sexuality from the one commonly described (perhaps even prescribed) by "experts" of the time. Mosher found that most of the women experienced sexual desire, enjoyed intercourse, and experienced orgasm (Ellison, 2000).

Nineteenth-century U.S. culture was full of sexual contradictions. Women's sexuality was polarized between the opposing images of Madonna and whore, and men were trapped between the ideal of purity and the frank pleasures of sexual expression. Gender-role beliefs about sexuality were taken to even greater extremes about African American men and women under slavery. Furthermore, the oppressive myths about African American men and women were used to justify slavery, as examined in the following "Sexuality and Diversity" discussion. Unfortunately, shades of these myths have persisted and play a role in contemporary racial tensions.

In the Victorian era the marriageable woman possessed morals that were as tightly laced as her corset. Ironically, prostitution flourished at this time.

 ## Sexuality and Diversity

Slavery's Assault on Sexuality and Gender Roles

An extreme manifestation of gender roles and sexuality was imposed on black slaves in the United States; stereotypes of black sexuality provided a justification for the institution of slavery and white power.* Europeans' ethnocentric reactions in their first encounters with Africans set the stage for the denigration of black sexuality during slavery. Europeans reacted to African customs with disgust and fear, comparing the sexual habits of the Africans to those of apes. Dehumanizing blacks as animalistic, oversexed "heathens" gave many white slave owners a rationale for their exploitation and domination (Moran, 2001).

The Madonna/whore dichotomy was drastically exaggerated for female slaves. The dominant image of black womanhood was the Jezebel—a treacherous seductress with an insatiable sexual appetite. To slave owners the image justified the life situation black women were forced to endure. Enslaved women lacked clothing to cover their bodies

*Adapted from Douglas (1999) and Wyatt (1997).

Slaves had no rights to physical privacy, protection from bodily harm, or reproductive autonomy.

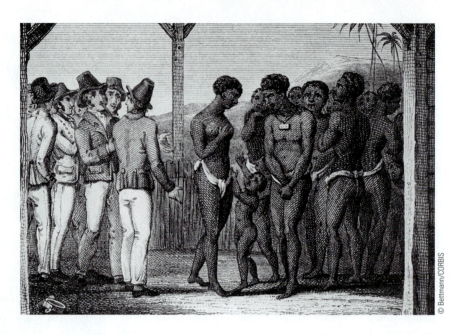

© Bettmann/CORBIS

"properly," and their field- and housework often required them to raise their dresses above their knees—nothing a "decent" woman would do. Slaves had no rights to their own bodies. During slave sales they were stripped naked so that prospective buyers could closely examine their bodies, including their genitals, as if they were cattle. The irrational logic that no self-respecting woman would allow herself to be put on such display was used by whites to confirm black women's wanton nature. Slave owners publicly discussed female slaves' reproductive capacity and managed their "breeding," forcing on them an imposed promiscuity that reinforced the Jezebel stereotype. White men (including some Union soldiers who raped slave women as they plundered towns and plantations) could then justify and avoid all responsibility for their sexual abuse and exploitation of black women and could rationalize having sexual outlets beyond the confines of their wives' sexually restrictive morality (Guy-Sheftall, 2003).

The stereotype of "Mammy" provided slave owners with a counterbalance to the Jezebel and represented the slave owner's successful civilizing of black women's sexuality. Mammy was supposed to be loyal, obedient, and asexual. She cooked, cleaned, and cared for white children, often even nursing infants. Her labors enabled many white women to maintain their delicate, ladylike images.

The male complement to the Jezebel was the stereotyped highly sexual, potentially violent "buck." Whites considered him a powerful animal and exploited his ability to work and to produce offspring with his mythical, larger-than-white-sized penis. On one hand, slave owners depended economically on black men's physical strength and sexual virility. On the other hand, they feared those same qualities. The fabricated threat of sexual seduction of white women and racist logic sanctioned the tools necessary to control black men and to assuage the slave owners' insecurities that their own stereotypes created. During slavery, black men were beaten, whipped, castrated, and lynched with impunity. With emancipation, freed slaves had greater opportunities to shape their own lives, but the lynching of black men and raping of black women continued as a means of maintaining social control over those who challenged the norms of white supremacy (Douglas, 1999; Wyatt, 1997).

The historical events and the controversies around them discussed in the previous sections show that the sex-for-procreation and gender-role issues are legacies of the Hebrew and Christian Bibles, of Augustine and Thomas Aquinas, of the Victorian era, and of slavery. These legacies are with us still, found in the complex conflicts among the values of personal pleasure, practicality, and tradition in 20th-century Western life (Jakobsen & Pellegrini, 2003).

The 20th Century*

Sigmund Freud (1856–1939) led the changes in perspectives about sexuality in the 20th century with the first of several books, *The Interpretation of Dreams* (1900). Freud's belief that sexuality was innate in women as well as in men helped expand Victorian concepts about sexuality. The physician Havelock Ellis (1859–1939), in his book *On Life and Sex* (1920), emphasized "the love-rights of women," and his seven-volume *Studies in the Psychology of Sex* regarded any sexual practice—including masturbation and homosexuality, previously considered "perversions"—as healthy so long as no one was harmed. Theodore Van de Velde (1873–1937) stressed the importance of sexual pleasure in his popular marriage manuals.

While ideas about the "proper" role of female sexuality were changing, the women's suffrage movement began in the late 19th century. Its goal of giving women the right to vote grew out of several related developments, such as the temperance movement to eliminate liquor consumption, the abolition of slavery, and the demand that women be permitted to attend universities and hold property. The passage in 1920 of the Nineteenth Amendment to the U.S. Constitution guaranteed women the right to vote but did not usher in a new era of equality.

However, subsequent historical events and technology brought new sexual perspectives and possibilities. U.S. involvement in World War I created an environment for increased equality and flexibility of gender roles, as thousands of women left the traditional homemaker role and took paying jobs for the first time. American men were introduced to the more open sexuality of Europe. When soldiers returned from WWI, Henry Ford's mass-produced automobiles of the 1920s provided increased independence and privacy for young people's sexual explorations. The advent of movies brought romance and sex symbols for public entertainment. The "flapper"—young, urban, single, middle-class women—rejected the ideals of Victorian restraint for short slinky dresses and exuberant, close-contact Roaring Twenties dancing. The changes in sexual mores mainly consisted of the prevalence of kissing and "petting" (sex play short of intercourse) among young unmarried people that went beyond acceptable Victorian standards, but women usually avoided premarital intercourse to prevent jeopardizing their reputations (Radar, 2001).

A return to more restrained behavior came with the Great Depression in the 1930s. Conversely, the hardships of the time also led to new laws mandating the right of women to have legal access to contraceptive information and devices. Before the development of penicillin in the 1940s, there was no effective treatment for life-threatening sexually transmitted diseases. Once penicillin became available, another feared consequence of sex became less harmful. During World War II, housewives once again filled the gaps in the workplace left by men fighting overseas and encountering European sexual morality.

*Our primary sources for this material are Czuczka (2000) and Glennon (1999).

© CORBIS

Many women in the 1920s broke out of traditional "at home" roles and enjoyed the independence the automobile provided. The clothing styles of the "flapper" expressed women's rejection of Victorian moral standards.

© Hulton-Deutsch Collection/CORBIS

During World Wars I and II, U.S. soldiers who socialized with European women were influenced by the more cosmopolitan sexual mores.

After World War II

After World War II, living in the suburbs became the ideal and goal of middle-class families, financed by the father as breadwinner. Women returned the workplace to men and devoted themselves to their homes, children, and husbands. Popular psychology of the era claimed that women who worked outside the home were neurotic and suffered from "penis envy." The fashion industry's ideal "refeminized" women with clothing that emphasized the bustline, small waist, and full skirts (Radar, 2001). During the postwar retreat into traditional gender roles, Alfred Kinsey and associates' *Sexual Behavior in the Human Male* (1948) and *Sexual Behavior in the Human Female* (1953) were best sellers in spite of (or possibly because of) medical professionals, clergy, politicians, and the press denouncing his work (Brown & Fee, 2003). Kinsey's data pertaining to the prevalence of women's sexual interest and response was particularly shocking to both professionals and the public. The surprising statistics on same-sex behavior, masturbation, and novel acts in the bedroom contributed to the growing acceptance of a variety of sexual behaviors.

In the 1950s, television, which emphasized suburban social conformity and whose sitcoms portrayed married couples in separate beds, entered American homes at the same time as the first issue of *Playboy*, which emphasized sex as recreation. Together, these media represent a dichotomy that played out through the 1950s.

The Times Are A-Changin'

It was not until the 1960s—after the flurry of post–World War II marriages, the baby boom, and widespread disappointment in the resulting domesticity of women—that a new movement for gender-role equality began. Starting in the 1960s and throughout the 1970s, feminism and the "sexual revolution" confronted the norms of previous decades. The oral contraceptive pill, introduced in the 1960s, and later the intrauterine device (IUD), morning after pills, and spermicides gave women newfound security in pursuing sexual pleasure with greatly reduced fear of pregnancy (Ofman, 2000). By 1965 contraceptive use was legal in all states by married couples, and by 1972 contraceptive use was legal in all states for single people. The widespread acceptance of these contraceptives and the subsequent availability of legal abortion in 1973 permitted sexuality to be separated from procreation as never before in Western cultures. The world had changed, too, so that many people were concerned with the ecological and economic costs of bearing children—costs that were not as relevant in the preindustrial world.

Masters and Johnson's *Human Sexual Response* (1966) and *Human Sexual Inadequacy* (1970) illuminated women's capacity for orgasm and propelled sex therapy into a legitimate endeavor. Sexual self-help books appeared, such as *Our Bodies, Ourselves* (Boston Women's Health Collective, 1971), and *For Yourself: The Fulfillment of Female Sexuality* (Barbach, 1975). These books emphasized women's sexual self-awareness, whereas *The Joy of Sex* (Comfort, 1972) highlighted varied, experimental sexual behavior for couples.

In the increasingly tolerant atmosphere of the late 1960s and 1970s, attitudes began to change about a long-standing taboo, homosexuality. Gays and lesbians began to openly declare their sexual orientation and to argue that such a personal matter should not affect their rights and responsibilities as citizens. In 1973, the American Psychiatric Association removed homosexuality from its diagnostic categories of mental disorders. Then, the early 1980s brought the first AIDS diagnosis. The so-called "gay plague" dramatically increased the visibility of homosexual individuals and amplified both negative and positive public sentiments toward homosexuality.

Each square of the enormous AIDS Quilt was made by the partner, friends, or family of a person who died from AIDS.

Increased violence against gays highlighted the extreme beliefs of some. For others, homosexuality remained a scapegoat for society's ills, as exemplified by the Reverend Jerry Falwell's comments about the cause of the September 11 attacks: "The pagans and the abortionists and the feminists and the gays and the lesbians . . . all of them who have tried to secularize America, I point the finger in their face and say, 'You helped this happen'" (Falwell, 2001, p. 61).

In contrast, the media, most notably television, reflected positive changing attitudes about homosexuality. Mainly as a result of gay activism, by the mid-1990s television began to incorporate gays and lesbians into programming (Hensley, 2001; Kielwasser, 1991). Gay and lesbian characters appeared on shows such as *ER, Sex and the City, Roseanne, Melrose Place, Friends,* and *NYPD Blue.* Ellen DeGeneres's coming-out show on *Ellen* was an event of the 1997 season (Marin & Miller, 1997). In the footsteps of *Ellen*'s trailblazing lesbian lead character, other series, such as *Will and Grace,* have included gay and lesbian story lines and main characters who are likable and well-rounded (Elber, 2000). Lesbian eroticism was first used in a Dior advertisement in 2000 and quickly became fairly common (Reichert, 2003). The hit cable series *Queer as Folk* is noted for its portrayal of explicit sexual content (Rowe, 2003b). Another first occurred in the fall 2003 television season: One of the characters in *It's All Relative* has two gay men as parents.

Changes in the media's portrayal of homosexuality illustrate how the media simultaneously reflect and influence sexual information, attitudes, and behaviors (Gross, 2001). What do the media say to us about sexuality? The following sections explore that very question.

In the 1990s advertising introduced "lesbian chic" ads in which two or more women are posed together, suggesting a sexual relationship.

▶ The Media and Sexuality

The phenomenon that we call mass media has existed for only a short time in human history. Printed books, magazines and newspapers, and radio and movies existed before the first black-and-white televisions of the late 1940s. The continued explosion of media technology since then—color and big-screen TVs, VCRs and DVDs, cable and satellite networks, and, of course, computer technology and the Internet—flood us with opportunities for media exposure. Greater sexualization of the media has accompanied the huge technological advances (American Academy of Pediatrics, 2001b). For example, 50 years ago a Hollywood movie would not be released to the public unless husband and wife were shown in separate beds (Lapham, 1997).

Television

Television likely has had the most significant effect on sexual attitudes, given the amount of time people spend watching it. By the time we are 18 years old, we have watched TV for an average of 20,000 hours, certainly enough time to have had some degree of influence on our perspectives about sexuality (Folb, 2000). At times, the way sexual issues are presented on television can have beneficial effects in promoting greater knowledge, tolerance, and positive social change, such as the media's portrayal of homosexuality (Keller & Brown, 2002; Silver, 2002).

Television news reporting broke new ground on several sexual issues in the 1990s. Anita Hill's televised testimony that Supreme Court nominee Clarence Thomas had sexually harassed her brought this issue to the public's attention. Consequently, workplace policies about sexual harassment were implemented across the country. In a different example, the Clinton–Lewinsky scandal raised numerous controversies, including the definition of *sex,* what a wife's response should be to infidelity, and whether words such as *penis* and *oral sex* should be on the evening news.

Television advice and educational programs can offer constructive guidance. For example, *Loveline* hosts Drew Pinsky and Adam Corolla discussed and gave teens advice on relationship and sexual concerns. *Berman and Berman,* a show hosted by psychologist and physician sisters, provides sex education for women. In addition, network and cable programs on child abuse, rape, and transgender concerns have helped to reduce the stigma associated with such topics (American Academy of Pediatrics, 2001b). Although many daytime talk shows take a sensationalist approach to sex, with topics such as "Pregnant Exotic Dancers," "Cousins in Love," or "Immortalized on Video in Compromising Positions," other talk shows have helped to break down cultural taboos and have revealed the enormous diversity of human sexual expression. *The Phil Donahue Show* (which began in the late 1960s and ended in 1996) and *Oprah* (which began airing in 1986) have provided a forum for people to learn about and discuss many aspects of human sexuality (Gross, 2001).

Information about the potential negative health and emotional consequences of sex has increased in programming. For example, in 2002 among television shows with depictions or talk about intercourse, 26% made reference to the risks and responsibilities of sex, twice the rate in 1998. Shows popular with teens had an even greater increase in safe-sex content (Elber, 2003; Kaiser Family Foundation, 2003b). One organization, called The Media Project, works with the television industry to incorporate realistic information about sexuality and responsibility into their programming. Some of the Project's accomplishments include episodes on *Felicity* about date rape, safe sex, and condom use, including a scene showing the correct way to use a condom. The Media Project also sponsors the annual SHINE Awards (Sexual Health in Entertainment) to recognize television programs that constructively portray sexual health issues (Folb, 2000).

On the other hand, some critics decry the degree and nature of sexual material on network and cable TV. Daytime soaps and talk shows were the first type of programs to emphasize more explicit sexual content (Greenberg & Woods, 1999). About 30 million adults in the United States admit to watching soap operas, in which 6 to 10 sex acts per hour occur, usually involving sexual intrigue based on infidelity, revenge, and exploitation (Greenberg & Busselle, 1996). Standard network programming is also rife with sexual innuendo and explicit sexual references, such as a female judge on *The Practice* who claimed to give "the

▶ **Figure 1.2** The evolution of broken taboos on TV.

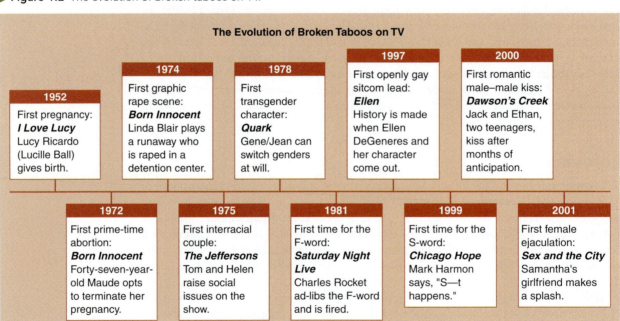

SOURCE: Modified from *TV Guide,* August 2, 2003.

best fellatio known to man" (Lipton, 2000). About 64% of prime-time shows contain sexual content. Eighty-five percent of television shows aimed at the teen audience include some sexual reference (Kaiser Family Foundation, 2003b; Warner, 2003b). Most sexual bantering occurred between single people; only 14% of all the sexual comments made on prime-time shows were between people married to each other (Poniewozik, 1999). Cable TV offers programs containing far more sexual explicitness than network television, as seen in *Sex in the City,* in which four New York women deal with men and talk with each other about faking orgasm, disappointment with penis size and rapid ejaculation, "funky spunk" (bad-tasting ejaculate), and an uncircumcised penis. Reality TV—*Real World, Temptation Island, The Bachelor,* and the like—are fueled by sexual themes. Videos and DVDs offer films of varying degrees of sexual explicitness for consumers to watch in the privacy of their own homes.

Music videos bridge television and the music industry. They are primarily designed as advertisements to sell CDs (Pardun & McKee, 2002). They arrived on the entertainment scene in 1981, and currently up to 50% of music videos (depending on type of music) have sexual content, sometimes mixed with portrayals of sexual coercion (Brown, 2002). In many music videos any initial sexual refusal by a women is only a front. She really means yes, and her false resistance is easily overcome by instant arousal (Samuels et al., 2000). Some music videos show love, tenderness, and respect in male–female interactions, but more express lust, power, impulsivity, and aggression, which raises questions about how these messages interfere with young people learning about healthy relationships (Wyatt, 1997).

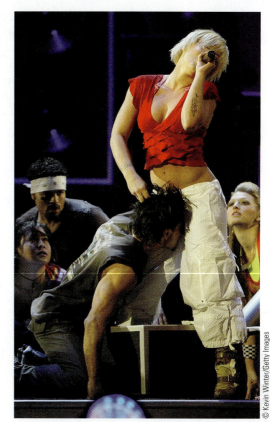

Sexual suggestion and expression in musical performances and music videos have become more explicit, as we see in a performance by Pink during the 2003 Billboard Music Awards.

Advertising

Advertising is present in most forms of media or stands alone, as with the ubiquitous billboards. Sexual images, often blatant but sometimes subtle, are designed to help attract attention to and sell products. Advertising relies on the false promises that love or sex or both will come with the acquisition of a certain beauty product, brand of liquor, clothing, sound system, or car. Most advertising trivializes sex and reinforces the idea that only young, hard bodies merit attraction, with the exception of advertising aimed at the large consumer group of maturing baby boomers. Occasionally, advertising helps to break down taboos. For example, presidential candidate Bob Dole's advertisements for Viagra helped bring erectile dysfunction into public discourse.

Using sex to sell usually does work: Jeans sales doubled following the 1980s ad with a young Brooke Shields promising that nothing came between her and her Calvin Klein jeans (Kuriansky, 1996). Sex in advertising seems to be most effective when the product is intrinsically linked to sex, as with perfume, lingerie

? How About You?

Can you think of an advertisement that helps reshape sexual stereotypes?

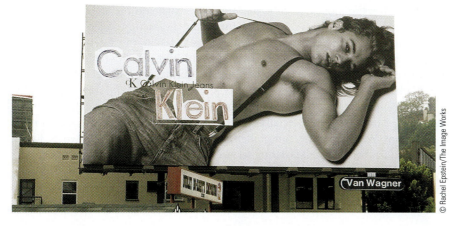

Calvin Klein's marketing technique of utilizing highly sexualized images in its advertising has proven to be lucrative.

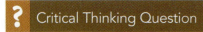
and underwear, liquor, and cars. When sexual imagery in an ad is not related to the nature of the product (e.g., a lawnmower), sex may get more notice than the product (Severn et al., 1990). Research has revealed that strong sexual content in TV programs distracts viewers from the products advertised in the programs' commercials. Randomly assigned viewers who watched neutral television shows had better memory of the products advertised on the shows than did viewers who watched shows with sexual content. The researchers believe that their data may dissuade advertisers from sponsoring sexually oriented programming (American Psychological Association, 2002; Bushman & Bonacci, 2002).

Magazines

Today, magazines such as *Playboy* have nude photos that take bikini wax to new extremes. Men's magazines such as *Details, Maxim,* and *Men's Health* offer how-to articles such as "Be Better Than Her Last Lover," "Can I Have Multiple Orgasms?" or a horror story about penis enlargement, "An Inch Too Far" (Dobosz, 1997). Women's magazines contain articles about sex, such as "The Secret, Sexual You. Turn Her Loose" and "His Sexual Fantasies—Your Worst Nightmare." Teen magazines, such as *Seventeen* and *YM,* teach their nearly 4 million combined subscribers how to make themselves prettier, skinnier, and sexier with "Boy Magnet Beauty" and "Mega Makeovers: Go from So-So to Supersexy" (Higgenbotham, 1996). Romance novels with studly, bare-chested men on their covers and euphemistic sexual scenes are common (Aronson, 1998). At the checkout stand the front pages of the tabloids titillate us with topics such as "Cops Probe Daddy's Secret Porn Life." News media—TV, radio, and newspapers—often give precedence to the sexual misadventures of politicians and media figures over critical local, national, and international issues and events (Dowd, 1997). In contrast, health-oriented or self-help magazines often have accurate, useful information about sexual and relationship concerns.

likes to be driven hard.

and put away wet.

THE 2004 SUBARU OUTBACK®

SUBARU

DRIVEN BY WHAT'S INSIDE™

subaru.com

© 2003, Subaru of America, Inc.

Even makers of automobiles known for durability and reliability instead of sex appeal utilize sexual innuendo in their advertising.

The Internet

The best research study about sexuality to date in the United States, the National Health and Social Life Survey (NHSLS), concluded that our attitudes and behaviors are dramatically influenced by the people in our social groups (Laumann et al., 1994). This research was conducted before the 1990s explosion in cyberspace communication. Now people in disparate social groups—different ages, races, religions, ethnic groups, economic groups—are able to discuss whatever they choose, in the privacy of the World Wide Web. By 2005 there will likely be 1.2 billion Internet users worldwide (Cooper, 2002). The impact of this communication revolution on sexual attitudes and behaviors is potentially epic.

Sexuality in myriad forms has made its presence known on the Internet. In fact, many of the Internet's technological innovations and business successes were advanced by the sex industry (Carnes, 2000). The Internet is an interactive sexual supermarket: Many users hunt for Web sites that offer the most explicit sexual images. Sexual commerce is plentiful with "cyberstrippers" and interactive sexual talk, pictures, and live-action video conferencing. Some use chat rooms to talk about their wildest fantasies in the safety of complete anonymity, but a few use the Internet to make contact with and sexually exploit young people. Some married people are using the Internet to have online extramarital affairs.

On the other hand, the Internet offers a dynamic source of self-help information, ranging from Web sites for breast cancer to up-to-the-minute findings in AIDS research to message boards posting wig-care tips for transsexuals. "Dear Abby" type sex columnists answer online questions and many Web sites offer comprehensive sexuality education (Brown & Keller, 2000). The Internet has become a huge dating service, an interactive personal ad opportunity where people can have online conversations to see if they want to meet face to face.

The constructive and destructive possibilities of cyberspace on sexuality appear as unlimited as those potentials in human nature. One research study that collected data online

from participants who chose to answer a questionnaire found some strong indications of problematic patterns of Internet use. About 75% of all study participants kept the time they spent online for sexual purposes secret from others. Almost 9% of the study's participants spent *at least* 11 hours a week online, resulting in problems in their lives. Otherwise, the researcher concluded that most people use sex Web sites as a benign recreational activity (Cooper et al., 1999).

▶ Sexuality: Where the Personal Is Political

The personal and political (laws, policies, and norms) are truly merged when it comes to sexuality. The historical, cross-cultural, and intracultural perspectives that we have examined in this chapter clearly show the impact of social norms on sexuality and may help us to appreciate the unique position in which we currently find ourselves. We can define our own sexuality on the basis of personal choices to a far greater degree than was possible for the ancient Hebrews, the early Christians, the Europeans of the Middle Ages, the Victorian Europeans and North Americans of the 19th century, and to a far greater degree than is possible for many contemporary non-Western societies. With the increased understanding and acceptance of diversity in human sexuality that developed during the 20th century, we have greater freedoms and responsibilities today. Although some would argue that increased tolerance of diversity creates more problems than it solves, in general we agree with the idea that "the sexual health of an individual or society is enriched with the understanding, tolerance, and compassion for the diversity of sexual identities and sexual expressions that are a part of the human condition" (Coleman, 2000, p. 4).

And yet, the exponential changes in the last century have left us with many unresolved questions. Consequently, in the 21st century we face controversies about social policies, laws, and ethics in almost every area related to human sexuality, many of which are heard and decided by the U.S. Supreme Court. As we have seen throughout this chapter, social norms, sometimes codified into law, can support or interfere with the individual's right to privacy and personal choice (Kaiser, 2004; Wildman, 2001). A few examples of controversies pertaining to sexuality that will continue in the 21st century include:

- Should same-sex couples be able to legally marry?
- Should health-care insurance be required to cover expenses for contraception?

- Should women past menopause be permitted to utilize fertility technology to get pregnant and have babies?
- Should access to abortion be limited in any way?
  - Should teens be able to obtain contraceptive services without parental consent?
  - Should a person's HIV status be part of the public record?
  - Should prostitution be legal?

? Critical Thinking Question

How do these current controversies relate to our sex-for-procreation and rigid gender-role legacies?

We hope that your experience grappling with today's challenges related to sexuality contributes to your intellectual development and your personal ability to navigate all the different topics that make up our sexuality.

▶ Summary

Controversy and Diversity in Human Sexuality
- Few topics generate as much attention and controversy as issues surrounding sexuality. (p. 2)

Diversity Within the United States
- Variations in acculturation, religious orthodoxy, and socioeconomic status create sexual diversity within ethnic groups of the United States. (pp. 2–4)

A Psychosocial Orientation
- This book stresses the role of psychological factors and social conditioning in shaping human sexuality. (p. 4)

Our Cultural Legacy: Sex for Procreation and Rigid Gender Roles
- The book critically explores the effects of two pervasive themes related to sexuality: sex limited to reproduction (procreation) and inflexible gender roles. (p. 5)

Cross-Cultural Perspective of the Sex-for-Procreation and Gender-Role Themes
- To better appreciate the importance of social conditioning, we can compare sexual attitudes and behaviors in other cultures. (p. 6)
- Followers of Islam, Muslims, believe enjoyment of sex in marriage is important for men and women. Female sexuality is seen as powerful, and in some parts of the Islamic Middle East, veils, female circumcision, and segregation of the sexes until marriage are considered necessary to contain women's sexuality. (pp. 6–7)
- In ancient China sexual activity was a means to spiritual growth. (p. 7)
- Communist China's government has attempted to isolate its people from Western sexual attitudes and practices, and its sexual norms have been conservative. (pp. 7–8)

Sexuality in the Western World: A Historical Perspective
- The ancient Hebrews stressed the importance of childbearing and also had an appreciation of sexuality within marriage. (p. 8)
- Gender-role differences between men and women were well established in ancient Hebraic culture. Women's most important roles were to manage the household and bear children, especially sons. (p. 8)

- Christian writers such as Paul of Tarsus, Augustine, and Thomas Aquinas contributed to the view of sex as sinful, justifiable only in marriage for the purpose of procreation. (p. 9)
- Two contradictory images of women developed in the Middle Ages: the pure and unattainable woman on a pedestal, manifest in the cult of the Virgin Mary and in courtly love; and the evil temptress represented by Eve and by the women persecuted as witches. (p. 10)
- Leaders of the Reformation of the 16th century challenged the requirement that clergy remain celibate and recognized sexual expression as an important aspect of marriage. (p. 10)
- Women were viewed as asexual in the Victorian era, and the lives of "proper" Victorian men and women were largely separate. Men often visited prostitutes for companionship as well as sexual relations. (pp. 10–11)
- The theories of Freud, research findings, and feminism changed the Victorian notion of women being asexual. (p. 13)
- U.S. involvement in World Wars I and II exposed soldiers to the more open sexuality of Europe and placed women, temporarily, in the workforce. (pp. 13–14)
- Technical advances in contraception in the 20th century have permitted people to separate sexuality from procreation to a degree not previously possible. (p. 14)
- Dramatic changes in understanding and acceptance of homosexuality began in the 1960s. (p. 14)

The Media and Sexuality
- Mass media as we know it has existed a short time relative to the greater human experience. (p. 15)
- The explosion of mass media—radio, movies, television, VCRs and DVDs, and the Internet—presents a vast array of sexual information and misinformation that, at the least, highlights the diversity in human sexuality. (p. 15)
- The amount and degree of sexual explicitness in all popular media continues to increase. (pp. 15–19)
- The impact of the Internet on sexual attitudes, knowledge, and behavior has both constructive and problematic possibilities. (pp. 18–19)

Sexuality: Where the Personal Is Political
- The scientific, psychological, and social changes in the 20th century have led to the contemporary individual's increased ability to make personal decisions regarding sexuality. (p. 19)

- Laws, social policies, and norms related to sexuality merge this personal subject with "politics." (pp. 19–20)

▶ Suggested Readings

Allyn, David (2000). *Make Love, Not War: The Sexual Revolution, an Unfettered History.* Boston: Little, Brown. A comprehensive journey beginning in the 1960s of social changes evolving into the "sexual revolution."

Barstow, Anne (1994). *Witchcraze.* San Francisco: Pandora. A compelling, comprehensive legacy of the witch hunts and gender-based violence.

D'Emilio, John, and Estelle Freedman (1988). *Intimate Matters.* New York: Harper & Row. A full-length examination of the history of sexuality and how the meaning and place of sexuality in the United States have changed.

Fox, Thomas (1995). *Sexuality and Catholicism.* New York: George Braziller. A thorough analysis of controversial issues concerning sexuality and Catholicism, including contraception, abortion, celibacy, and homosexuality.

Gamson, Joshua (1998). *Freaks Talk Back: Tabloid Talk Shows and Sexual Noncomformity.* Chicago: University of Chicago Press. An analysis of the social impact of sensationalist subjects on talk shows.

Kilbourne, Jean (2000). *Can't Buy My Love: How Advertising Changes the Way We Think and Feel.* New York: Simon & Schuster. An illuminating look at the messages about sex, power, and relationships in advertising.

Reichert, Tom (2003). *The Erotic History of Advertising.* New York: Prometheus Books. A detailed history of the use of the erotic in advertising.

Sweet, Matthew (2001). *Inventing the Victorians.* New York: St. Martin's Press. A presentation of the progressive side of the Victorians that has been overlooked and misinterpreted by history.

▶ Web Resources

Your *Our Sexuality* Web site **http://psychology.wadsworth.com/ crooksbaur9e/** has direct links to the Web sites described below. These links are checked often for changes, dead links, and new additions.

Human Sexuality Web

Designed, maintained, and updated by graduate students at the University of Missouri, Kansas City, this site contains information concerning sex education, sexual counseling, sexual health issues, and related topics on sexuality.

SIECUS

SIECUS, the Sexuality Information and Education Council of the United States, is a well-respected nonprofit organization specializing in sex education and sexuality. Its Web site provides current and reliable information.

Ask NOAH About Sexuality

NOAH (New York Online Access to Health) offers detailed and relevant resources on sexual issues in both English and Spanish on its Web site.

Variations in Sex Laws

This Web site provides an interesting collection of direct links to laws pertaining to sexuality in Australia, Canada, various U.S. states, and traditional Islamic nations.

Our Sexuality Web Site

For online resources directly related to this book, go to **http://psychology.wadsworth.com/ crooksbaur9e/**. You will find interactive exercises, study questions, chapter outlines, an online version of this text's glossary, and Web links and activities that complement your CD-ROM.

InfoTrac® College Edition Online Library

http://infotrac.thomsonlearning.com/
InfoTrac College Edition is an online searchable library that includes a multitude of journals, many of which are specific to human sexuality. These journals include *Archives of Sexual Behavior, Archives of Sexual Health Behavior, Canadian Journal of Human Sexuality, Hispanic Journal of the Behavioral Sciences, Journal of Cross-Cultural Psychology, Journal of Physical Education, Recreation, and Dance, Journal of Sex Research,* and *Sex Roles.*

Our Sexuality CD-ROM

Use your CD-ROM for further study of the concepts in this chapter. Your CD-ROM provides animations of difficult concepts, video clips of real people discussing sexuality, critical thinking questions, chapter quizzing, and more.

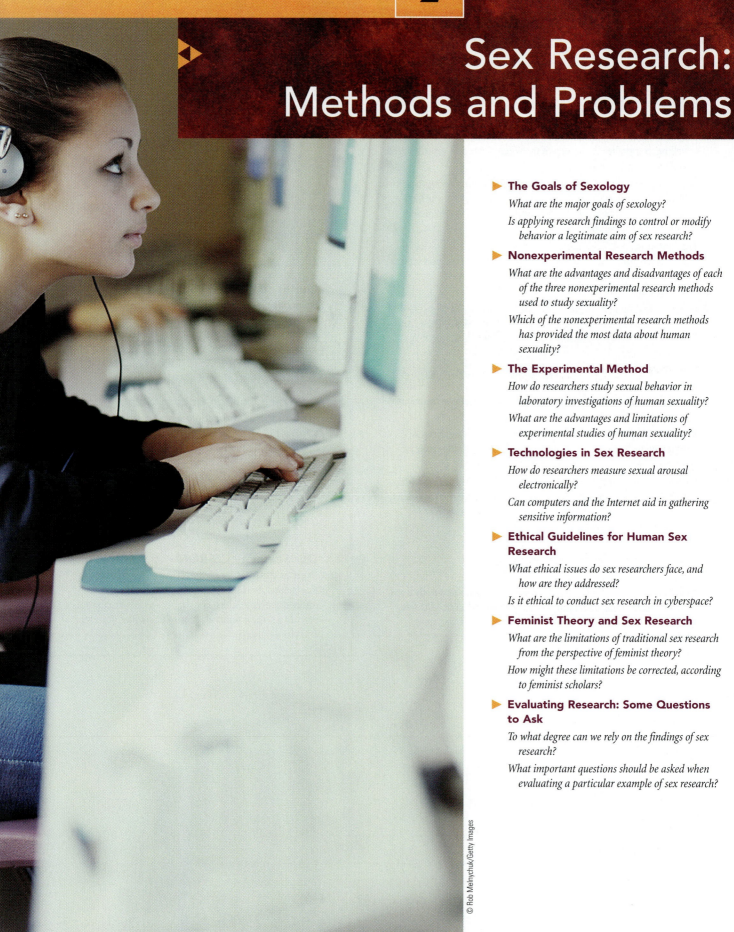

CHAPTER

2

Sex Research: Methods and Problems

▶ **The Goals of Sexology**

What are the major goals of sexology?

Is applying research findings to control or modify behavior a legitimate aim of sex research?

▶ **Nonexperimental Research Methods**

What are the advantages and disadvantages of each of the three nonexperimental research methods used to study sexuality?

Which of the nonexperimental research methods has provided the most data about human sexuality?

▶ **The Experimental Method**

How do researchers study sexual behavior in laboratory investigations of human sexuality?

What are the advantages and limitations of experimental studies of human sexuality?

▶ **Technologies in Sex Research**

How do researchers measure sexual arousal electronically?

Can computers and the Internet aid in gathering sensitive information?

▶ **Ethical Guidelines for Human Sex Research**

What ethical issues do sex researchers face, and how are they addressed?

Is it ethical to conduct sex research in cyberspace?

▶ **Feminist Theory and Sex Research**

What are the limitations of traditional sex research from the perspective of feminist theory?

How might these limitations be corrected, according to feminist scholars?

▶ **Evaluating Research: Some Questions to Ask**

To what degree can we rely on the findings of sex research?

What important questions should be asked when evaluating a particular example of sex research?

© Rob Melnychuk/Getty Images

I am always skeptical of sex studies reported in newspapers, magazines, and books. How can you accurately study something so private? (Authors' files)

- A number of social observers have suggested that men who are active consumers of sexually violent films, magazines, and other pornography are likely to adopt abusive attitudes toward women. As a result, they show an increased tendency to commit rape and other abusive acts toward women.
- Many people believe that a few drinks make sex more enjoyable. After imbibing a little alcohol, they say that their inhibitions relax; they feel more sensual and also more friendly toward the person they are with.
- Early in this century, Sigmund Freud asserted that women's orgasms resulting from vaginal penetration are more "mature" than those resulting from clitoral stimulation alone. A common assumption today is that "vaginal" orgasms are superior to clitoral orgasms.

You have probably heard each of these three assertions before, and you may agree with one or even all of them. But if you were called on to prove that they were true or untrue, how would you go about compiling evidence or, as the author of the quote at the top of this page asks, How do you study sex?

The role of **sexology,** the study of sexuality, is to test such assumptions in a scientific way, to find out whether they are true or false and to document what underlying relationships, if any, they reveal. This task is not easy. Although intrinsically interesting to most of us, human sexual behavior is also inherently difficult to study because it occupies an intensely private area in our lives that few of us are comfortable discussing with others. People often feel embarrassed or even threatened when asked to disclose details about their sexual attitudes or behavior to another, especially to a sex researcher who is a stranger to them (Turner, 1999). In addition, the subject matter of sexology abounds with myth, exaggeration, secrecy, and value judgments.

Sexology The study of sexuality.

Despite these problems, sex researchers are accumulating a growing body of knowledge about human sexual behaviors and attitudes—including the three assumptions with which we began this chapter: Does violent pornography lead to abusive behaviors such as rape? Does alcohol increase sexual pleasure? What are the differences between vaginal and clitoral orgasms? We will revisit these and other questions in this chapter as we discuss the methods used to study sexuality, the kinds of questions appropriate to each method, and also the problems inherent in each method. In the process we will also learn something about evaluating published research.

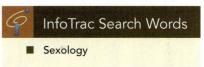

InfoTrac Search Words
- Sexology

We hope that in the following pages you will begin to appreciate what we know and what we do not know and how confident we can be about the available knowledge. You may also begin to sense the steps we can take to further expand our scientific knowledge of sexual behavior. Perhaps in the future you will contribute to our understanding of this important area of human experience. We invite you to do so.

▶ The Goals of Sexology

People who study human sexuality share certain goals with scientists in other disciplines. These include the goals of *understanding, predicting,* and *controlling* or influencing the events that are the subject matter of their respective fields.

The first two scientific goals—understanding and predicting behavior—are not difficult to comprehend. For example, a pharmacologist who knows how blood pressure medications interfere with sexual functioning can use this knowledge to predict what dosage of a drug could be tolerated by a patient with a particular health condition without experiencing impaired sexual functioning. Similarly, a psychologist who knows something about the way certain behavior patterns influence the quality of couples' interactions can help a couple predict whether they will have a happy marriage.

The third goal, using scientifically acquired knowledge to control behavior, is a more difficult concept to comprehend. Understandably, many people express concern about the legitimacy of applying scientific knowledge to control people's behavior. A certain amount of skepticism in this area is probably healthy, and it would be inaccurate to suggest that all knowledge acquired through research leads directly to behavior control. Nevertheless, sexologists have been able to influence, to some degree, a large body of phenomena. For example, understanding how adolescents make decisions about contraceptive use has resulted in the development of school-based sex-education programs, many of which are linked to family planning clinic services. These innovative programs have often resulted in positive behavioral changes, such as increased contraceptive use among sexually active teenagers. Similarly, knowledge about the psychobiological causes of certain sexual problems, such as premature ejaculation and lack of vaginal lubrication, has enabled specialists to develop therapies aimed at controlling such disruptive symptoms, as we will see in Chapter 16.

Most of us would not object to the goal of controlling or influencing events in the examples just described. However, sexologists, like other scientists, also must contend with situations in which the application of this goal raises important questions. For instance, is it appropriate for fertility specialists to use their knowledge to help a couple conceive a child of a desired biological sex? Is it appropriate for a sex therapist to subject imprisoned sex offenders to aversive stimuli (e.g., putrid odors) in an effort to control deviant sexual urges? Clearly, the goal of controlling or influencing human behavior should be carefully evaluated within a framework of ethical consideration.

Compared with many other disciplines, sexology is an infant science, having originated largely in the 20th century. The pioneering work of Alfred Kinsey, the first researcher to conduct an extensive general survey of American sexual behaviors, took place only in the late 1940s and early 1950s. Many questions remain unanswered, although a considerable body of knowledge is accumulating. In the remainder of this chapter we examine some of the research methods that have been used to explore human sexuality.

▶ Nonexperimental Research Methods

We began this chapter with three common notions about human sexual behavior: that exposure to violent pornography can increase a man's tolerance of and willingness to commit sexually violent acts such as rape, that alcohol can enhance sexual responsiveness, and that vaginal orgasms are superior to clitoral orgasms. How do researchers go about investigating hypotheses such as these? In this section we look at three nonexperimental methods: (1) the case study, (2) the survey, and (3) direct observation. Later in the chapter we will learn about a fourth method, experimental research. Table 2.1 summarizes these four major methods of studying sexual behavior. As we will see, not every research method is appropriate to every type of research question.

Case Studies

Case study A nonexperimental research method that examines either a single subject or a small group of subjects individually and in depth.

A **case study** examines either a single subject or a small group of subjects, each of whom is studied individually and in depth. Data are gathered using a variety of means, including direct observation, questionnaires, testing, and even experimentation.

People often become subjects for case studies because they behave in an atypical way or have a physical or emotional disorder. Thus a large portion of our information about sexual response difficulties (e.g., erectile disorder in men and lack of orgasmic response in women) comes from case studies of individuals seeking treatment for these problems. Also, much of what we know about sex offenders, transsexuals, incest victims, and the like has been learned from case studies.

Not surprisingly, a number of case studies have investigated the relationship between sexually violent media and rape. In many of these studies rapists report high levels of exposure to sexually violent films, magazines, and books (Marshall, 1988). For example, Kenneth Bianchi, the infamous Los Angeles "Hillside Strangler" who raped and killed several women, was shown to have "collected magazines and films that featured violent pornography" (Norris, 1988, p. 197).

It is unclear whether violent attitudes toward women and behaviors such as rape result directly from exposure to sexually violent media. The mere fact that rapists seem more

TABLE 2.1 A Summary of Research Methods

Method	Brief Description	Advantages	Disadvantages
Case study	Examines a single subject or a small group of subjects, each of whom is studied individually and in depth.	Flexibility in data-gathering procedures. In-depth explorations of behaviors, thoughts, and feelings.	Limited generalizability of findings. Accuracy of data limited by fallibility of human memory. Not suitable for many kinds of research questions.

Survey	Data pertaining to sexual attitudes and behaviors derived from relatively large groups of people by means of questionnaires or interviews.	Relatively cheap and quick method for obtaining large amounts of data.
		
		Can obtain data from more people than is practical to study in the laboratory or through case studies.
			Problems of:
			
			  Nonresponse
			
			  Demographic bias
			
			  Inaccurate information

Direct observation	Researchers observe and record responses of participating subjects.	Virtually eliminates the possibility of data falsification. Behavioral record can be kept indefinitely on videotapes or films.	Subjects' behavior can be influenced by presence of observer(s) or the artificial nature of the environment where observations are made.
Experimental method	Subjects presented with certain events (stimuli) under managed conditions that allow for reliable measurement of their reactions.	Provides a controlled environment for managing relevant variables. Suited to discovering causal relationships between variables.	Artificiality of laboratory settings can adversely influence or bias subjects' responses.

inclined than nonrapists to consume pornography does not necessarily imply a cause-and-effect relationship. Perhaps there are other plausible explanations. For example, the types of environments that tend to socialize men to be violent toward women might also be characterized by easy access to violent pornography. Thus, although the case-study method shows that this media exposure is often associated with rape, it cannot tell us the exact nature of the relationship.

The case-study method has also been used to investigate the common assertion that alcohol enhances sexual responsiveness and pleasure. In fact, evidence from some case studies suggests just the reverse, at least among chronic alcoholics. Case studies of alcoholic subjects have shown decreased arousability and lowered sexual interest, although it is possible that this effect is due to the general physical deterioration that accompanies heavy, long-term alcohol use.

The case-study approach offers some advantages to researchers. One advantage is the flexibility of data-gathering procedures. Although the open-ended format of the case study offers little opportunity for investigative control, it often provides opportunities to acquire insight into specific behaviors. The highly personal, subjective information about what individuals actually think and feel about their behavior is an important step beyond simply recording activities. This case-study method sacrifices some control, but it offers opportunities to explore specific behaviors, thoughts, and feelings in depth and can add considerable dimension to our information.

The case-study method does have some limitations, however. Because case studies typically focus on individuals or small samples of especially interesting or atypical cases, it is often difficult to generalize findings accurately to broader populations. A second limitation of case studies is that a person's past history,

? Critical Thinking Question

Many studies have reported an association between abnormally low levels of testosterone and decreased sexual desire in both sexes. Can case-study research clarify whether or not this association reflects a cause-and-effect relationship? If so, how? If not, why not?

especially the person's childhood and adolescence, usually does not become a target of research until the individual manifests some unusual behavior later in life, as an adult. Human memory is fallible: Is it possible for a researcher to accurately reconstruct a subject's earlier life from accounts provided by the subject? Even if family members and friends are also questioned, there are no guarantees, because people often have trouble accurately remembering events from years ago. Furthermore, memory is also subject to intentional efforts to distort or repress facts.

A third limitation of the case study is that it is not suitable for many kinds of research questions. For instance, a case study might not be the best method for testing the third assumption on this chapter's opening page—that vaginal orgasms are superior to clitoral orgasms. And because personal accounts can be influenced by factors such as emotions, values, and the vagaries of memory, the reliability of the case-study method can also be in doubt. As we will see shortly, this type of research problem is better suited to the direct-observation method.

All these cautions about limitations of the case-study method can be applied to the cases we cite in our Authors' Files selections throughout this book. Nevertheless, we believe that each of these cases presents relevant personal reflections of experiences, thoughts, and feelings, and we include them so that you can draw perspective, not conclusions, from them.

Surveys

Survey A research method in which a sample of people are questioned about their behaviors and/or attitudes.

Most of our information about human sexuality has been obtained from a second important research method, the **survey,** in which people are asked about their sexual experiences or attitudes. The survey method enables researchers to collect data from a large number of people, usually more than can be studied in a clinical setting or in the laboratory. Surveys can be conducted orally, through face-to-face or telephone interviews, or through paper-and-pencil questionnaires. Recently, computerized interviews have been used to gather information about sexual behaviors and other sensitive topics. We discuss this technological aid to sex research later in this chapter.

Although the methods of conducting written and oral surveys are somewhat different, their intent is the same. Each tries to use a relatively small group, called the *survey sample,* to draw inferences or conclusions about a much larger group with a particular characteristic (called a *target population*). Examples of target populations are married adults or high school adolescents.

Most information about human sexual behavior has been obtained through questionnaire or interview surveys.

Choosing the Sample

The questions asked by sexologists often apply to populations that are too large to study in their entirety. For example, if you wanted to obtain information about the sexual practices of American married couples in their later years, your population would include all married couples in the United States over a given age, say 65. Clearly, it would be impossible to question everyone in this group. Sex researchers resolve this problem by obtaining data from a relatively small sample of the target population. The confidence with which conclusions about the larger population can be drawn depends on the technique used to select this sample.

Typically, researchers strive to select a **representative sample** (sometimes called a *probability sample*)—that is, a sample in which various subgroups are represented proportionately to their incidence in the target population. Target populations can be subdivided into smaller subgroups by such criteria as age, economic status, geographic locale, and religious affiliation. In a representative sample every individual in the larger target population has a chance of being included.

What procedures would you use to select a representative sample that could be surveyed to assess the sexual practices of older American married couples? How would you ensure the representativeness of your selected sample? A good beginning would be to obtain U.S. Census Bureau statistics on the number of married couples whose partners are age 65 and older who reside in major geographic regions of the United States (East, South, etc.). Next, you would select subgroups of your sample according to the actual distribution of the larger population. Thus, if 25% of older married couples live in the East, 25% of your sample would be drawn from this region. Similarly, if 15% of older married couples in the East fall in an upper socioeconomic status category, 15% of those subjects selected from the East would be drawn from this group.

Once you had systematically compiled your lists of potential subjects, your final step would be to select your actual subjects from these lists. To ensure that all members of each subgroup had an equal chance of being included, you might use a table of random numbers to generate random selections from your lists. If these procedures were correctly applied and if your final sample was large enough, you could be reasonably confident that your findings could be generalized to all married American couples, age 65 or older.

Another kind of sample, the **random sample,** is selected from a larger population using randomization procedures. A random sample may or may not be the same as a representative sample. For example, assume that you are a social scientist on the faculty of a large urban university whose faculty, graduate students, and undergraduate students are inclined to hold liberal political and social views. You wish to conduct a survey that will provide an update on "swinging" (a form of consensual extramarital sex practiced by married couples). It is convenient to draw your subjects from married couples affiliated with your university. You obtain a roster of all married students and faculty at your university (which number several thousand), and you randomly select your survey sample from this group.

You design an excellent, anonymously administered questionnaire, with clear, concise questions, and are gratified that a substantial majority of your sample responds to your survey. Can you now be relatively confident that your results reflect the general attitude of married couples toward swinging, if not in the greater U.S. population, at least in your geographic region? Unfortunately, you cannot, because you have selected subjects from a sample that is not necessarily representative of the broader community. Your university population is characterized by liberal political and social views, traits that probably render them atypical of the broader population of married couples. (Indeed, surveys have shown that most swingers tend to be middle- to upper-middle-class whites with relatively conservative to moderate political and social views [Gilmartin, 1977; Karlen, 1988].)

Thus, even though randomization is often a valid selection tool, a study sample cannot be truly representative unless it reflects all the important subgroups in the target population. All things considered, representative samples generally allow for more accurate generalizations to the entire target population than do random samples. However, random samples are often quite adequate and thus are used widely.

Representative sample A type of limited research sample that provides an accurate representation of a larger target population of interest.

Random sample A randomly chosen subset of a population.

InfoTrac Search Words

- Survey sexual
- Random sample sexual

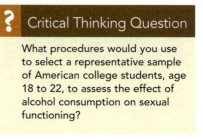
Critical Thinking Question

What procedures would you use to select a representative sample of American college students, age 18 to 22, to assess the effect of alcohol consumption on sexual functioning?

Questionnaires and Interviews

Once selected, subjects in a sample can be surveyed by either a written questionnaire or an interview. Both procedures involve asking the participants a set of questions, which might range from a few to over 1,000. These questions can be multiple-choice, true–false, or discussion questions; subjects can respond alone, in the privacy of their homes, or in the presence of a researcher.

Each survey method has advantages and disadvantages. Questionnaires tend to be quicker and cheaper to administer than interview surveys. In addition, because filling out a form affords greater anonymity than facing an interviewer, subjects might be considerably more likely to answer questions honestly, with minimal distortion. Sexual behavior is highly personal, and in interviews subjects might be tempted to describe their behaviors or attitudes in a more favorable light. Finally, because most written questionnaires can be evaluated objectively, their data are less subject to researcher bias than are interviews.

On the other hand, interviews have some advantages that questionnaires do not share. First, the format of an interview is more flexible. If a particular question is confusing to the subject, the interviewer can clarify it. In addition, interviewers have the option of varying the sequence of questions if it seems appropriate for a particular respondent. And finally, skillful interviewers can establish excellent rapport with subjects, and the resulting sense of trust may produce more revealing responses than is possible with paper-and-pencil questionnaires. Some sex researchers have found that combining face-to-face interviews, to establish rapport, with written questionnaires, to tap sensitive information, is an especially effective survey method (Laumann et al., 1994; Siegel et al., 1994).

The use of skilled interviewers can be especially advantageous when cultural, ethnic, and/or language barriers may create confusion among respondents to a sex survey. One of us, Bob Crooks, has found this to be especially true in the context of a study he is currently conducting in conjunction with an HIV/AIDS education project in Kenya. This research is described in the boxed discussion "Measuring the Impact of a Grassroots HIV/AIDS Education Project in Kenya."

? How About You?

Assume that you are a subject in a study of sexual attitudes and behavior. Would you prefer to answer questions presented by an anonymous questionnaire or in a face-to-face interview? Why? Do you think the survey method might influence your inclination to falsify your answers? If so, why?

Problems of Sex Survey Research: Nonresponse, Demographic Bias, and Inaccuracy

Regardless of the survey strategy used, sex researchers find that it is difficult to secure a representative sample. This is because many people do not want to participate in studies of this nature. For instance, assuming that you used proper sampling procedures to choose your sample of older married couples in the example discussed earlier, what proportion of your representative sample would actually be willing to answer your questions? **Nonresponse,** the refusal to participate in a research study, is a common problem that consistently plagues sex survey research (Turner, 1999).

No one has ever conducted a major sex survey in which 100% of the selected subjects voluntarily participated. In fact, some studies include results obtained from samples in which only a small minority responded. This raises an important question: Are people who agree to take part in sex surveys any different from those who refuse?

Perhaps volunteer subjects in sex research are a representative cross section of the population, but we have no theoretical or statistical basis for that conclusion. As a matter of fact, the opposite might well be true. People who volunteer to participate may be the ones who are the most eager to share their experiences, who have explored a wide range of activities, or who feel most comfortable with their sexuality. (Or it may be that the most experienced people are those who are least willing to respond because they feel that their behaviors are atypical or extreme.) A preponderance of experienced, inexperienced, liberal, or conservative individuals can bias any sample.

Research suggests that **self-selection,** or volunteer bias, is an important concern for sex researchers (Plaud et al., 1999; Wiederman, 1999). Studies strongly suggest that volunteers for sex research are more sexually experienced and hold more positive attitudes toward sexuality and sex research than do nonvolunteers (Boynton, 2003; Plaud et al., 1999; Trivedi & Sabini, 1998; Wiederman, 1999). In addition, research indicates that women are less likely than men to volunteer for sex research (Boynton, 2003; Plaud et al., 1999; Wiederman et al.,

Nonresponse The refusal to participate in a research study.

Self-selection The bias introduced into a research study results because of participants' willingness to respond.

Measuring the Impact of a Grassroots HIV/AIDS Education Project in Kenya

Bob Crooks is currently involved in the implementation of an HIV/AIDS education project in the Makindu region of southeastern Kenya. Crooks and James Curtis, program director of a community-based organization called Act Now, began developing a program in January 2003 that involves the use of *peer educators* drawn from the local population. These peer educators are presently conducting a comprehensive grassroots HIV/AIDS education and prevention outreach program that will ultimately reach a large percentage of the teenagers and adults who live in Makindu. This project, which is described in more detail in a boxed discussion in Chapter 17, illustrates the use of survey research to assess the impact of this program on the attitudes and behavior of the people of Makindu.

Peer educators meet with small groups of 14 to 18 people twice weekly in various locations throughout the greater Makindu region. The entire outreach education program, designed by Crooks, is completed in 6 to 8 weeks. Crooks developed a survey containing 13 yes/no questions to help determine whether this project promotes safer sexual behavior and an increased sense of *self-efficacy*—an individual's belief that she or he can

effectively deal with the HIV/AIDS pandemic and remain disease free. The assessment design involves administering the questionnaire twice to participants in the outreach program: before the educational sessions begin and again at some point after the participant has completed the program.

Respondents are provided with answer sheets to record their responses to each question after it is orally recited by the group leader/peer educator. All communication is conducted in the preferred language of the group participants. The people of Makindu are an educationally diverse population, and, because two African dialects and English are commonly spoken, language is an important consideration in both the construction and the administration of the questionnaire. (All peer educators are fluent in these three languages.) In addition, some of the terms for sexual concepts commonly used in American sex surveys might prove confusing in this cultural context. Consequently, the peer educators have been trained to clarify any aspects of the questionnaire not understood by the participants. Respondents circle either yes or no on the answer sheet for each of the 13 questions. If an item is not applicable,

the respondent is instructed to leave it blank. No names are listed on the questionnaire answer sheets, and the only demographic data collected are sex and age. Respondent anonymity, a feature not typically associated with an interview survey, is ensured by having each participant fold his or her completed answer sheet, which is then inserted in a sealed slotted box that contains many other completed answer forms.

At the time of this writing, Crooks and Curtis are in the early stages of the project. Thirty-six peer-educator-led groups and more than 500 Makindu residents are involved in this initial phase, with both sexes represented in approximately equal numbers. Some of the noteworthy findings from the initial administration of the questionnaire are the following:

- 22% of the male respondents and only 11% of the females reported using a condom every time they engage in sexual intercourse. (Distribution of free condoms and training on the proper use of condoms and condom negotiation skills are all integral parts of the outreach program.)
- About half the men and one-third of the women circled no in response to the question, "Is it possible to be sexually active and avoid being infected with HIV?"
- Only 15% of women and 28% of men have been tested for HIV. (Free voluntary and confidential counseling and testing for the presence of the HIV virus is provided at two separate centers operated by Act Now.)
- Almost half of both sexes indicated having experienced sexual intercourse with someone whose HIV status was unknown to them.
- Four of 10 male respondents and one-fourth of females reported having sexual intercourse with someone other than their primary partner in the last year.

Program director James Curtis (left) and Bob Crooks (second from the right) stand with the staff of Act Now outside the Voluntary Counseling and Testing (VCT) Center at the central headquarters compound in Makindu, Kenya.

How About You?

Would you volunteer to be a subject in a study dealing with sex? Why or why not?

1994), a finding that suggests female sex research samples are more highly selected than male samples.

Another kind of problem inherent in sex survey research has to do with the accuracy of subjects' responses. Most data about human sexual behavior are obtained from respondents' own reports of their experiences. How closely does actual behavior correspond to these subjective, after-the-fact reports?

As we saw in the discussion of case studies, people's actual behavior can be quite different from what they report (Catania, 1999b; Ochs & Binik, 1999). In the survey method human memory is also a potential problem (Catania et al., 1990). How many people accurately remember when they first masturbated and with what frequency or at what age they first experienced orgasm? Some people may also distort or falsify their self-disclosures to maintain or even enhance their social image (Catania, 1999b). This tendency to provide *socially desirable* responses can involve people who consciously or unconsciously conceal certain facts about their sexual histories because they view them as abnormal, foolish, or painful to remember. People can also feel pressure to deny or minimize their experiences regarding behaviors for which strong taboos exist, such as incest, homosexuality, and masturbation. In other cases, people can purposely inflate their experience, perhaps out of a desire to appear more liberal, experienced, or proficient.

A third type of problem that affects sex surveys is **demographic bias.** Most of the data available from sex research in the United States have come from samples weighted heavily toward white middle-class volunteers. Typically, college students and educated white-collar workers are overrepresented. White ethnic minorities and less educated individuals are underrepresented.

Demographic bias A kind of sampling bias in which certain segments of society (such as white, middle-class, white-collar workers) are disproportionately represented in a study population.

How much effect do nonresponse and demographic bias have on sex research findings? We cannot say for sure. But so long as elements of society, including the less educated and ethnic and racial minorities, are underrepresented, we must be cautious in generalizing findings to the population at large. The informational deficit pertaining to sexual behaviors of American racial and ethnic minorities is lessening with the recent emergence of several studies that included members of various ethnic minority groups in the United States. These studies demonstrate that ethnicity often exerts considerable influence on sexual attitudes and behaviors (Laumann et al., 1994; Meston et al., 1996; Weiderman et al., 1996). Throughout this textbook we describe results from several studies as we discuss ethnicity in relation to a variety of topics.

InfoTrac Search Words

- Demographic bias
- Volunteer bias

The Kinsey Reports

The studies of Alfred Kinsey are perhaps the best known and most widely cited example of survey research. With his associates Kinsey published two large volumes in the decade following World War II: One, on male sexuality, was published in 1948; the follow-up report on female sexuality was published in 1953. These volumes contain the results of extensive survey interviews, the aim of which was to determine patterns of sexual behavior in American males and females.

Alfred Kinsey, a pioneer sex researcher, conducted one of the most comprehensive surveys on human sexuality.

© Wallace Kirkland/Time Life Pictures/Getty Images

The Kinsey sample consisted of 5,300 white males and 5,940 white females. Respondents came from both rural and urban areas in each state and represented a range of ages, marital status, occupations, educational levels, and religions. However, the sample had a disproportionately greater number of better-educated city-dwelling Protestants, whereas older people, rural dwellers, and those with less education were underrepresented. African Americans and other racial minorities were completely omitted from the sample. And, finally, all subjects were volunteers. Thus in no way can Kinsey's study population be viewed as a representative sample of the American population.

Although published over 50 years ago, many of Kinsey's data are relevant today (Reinisch & Beasley, 1990). The passage of time has not altered the validity of certain findings—for example, that sexual behavior is influenced by educational level or that heterosexuality or homosexuality is often not an all-or-none proposition. However, certain other areas—such as coital rates among unmarried people—are more influenced by changing societal norms. Therefore we might expect the Kinsey data to be less predictive of contemporary practices in these areas. Nevertheless, even here the data are still relevant; they provide one possible basis for estimating the degree of behavioral change over the years.

The National Health and Social Life Survey

The outbreak of the devastating AIDS epidemic in the 1980s occurred at a time when the U.S. public health community was ill-informed about the contemporary sexual practices of the citizenry. To fill this informational void with data that could be used to predict and prevent the spread of AIDS, in 1987 an agency within the U.S. Department of Health and Human Services called for proposals to study the sexual attitudes and practices of American adults. A team of distinguished researchers at the University of Chicago answered this call with a plan for a national survey to assess the prevalence of a broad array of sexual practices and attitudes and to place them in their social contexts within the U.S. population. The research team—Edward Laumann and his colleagues John Gagnon, Robert Michael, and Stuart Michaels—was initially heartened by the acceptance of their proposal in 1988 and by the provision of government funds adequate to support a survey of 20,000 people.

A sample size this large would have allowed the investigators to draw reliable conclusions about various subpopulations in America, such as diverse ethnic minorities and homosexuals. However, after more than 2 years of extensive planning, the research team's efforts were dealt a crushing blow when federal funding for their study was withdrawn. In 1991 conservative members of Congress, offended by the prospect of government funding of sex research, introduced legislation that effectively eliminated federal funding for such studies.

? Critical Thinking Question

Should the federal government fund sex research? Are there potential benefits for the American people that justify such expenditures?

Undaunted by this setback, Laumann and his colleagues secured funding from several private foundations that enabled them to proceed with their project, with a much smaller sample size. The research team, working with the National Opinion Research Center at the University of Chicago, used sophisticated sampling techniques to select a representative sample of 4,369 Americans, age 18 to 59. An amazing 79% of the sample subjects agreed to participate, yielding a final study group of 3,432 respondents. This high response rate dramatically demonstrates that a broad array of people will participate in a highly personal sex survey when they are assured that the societal benefits for the research are important and that the confidentiality of their responses is guaranteed. Furthermore, this unusually high participation rate, together with the fact that the study population closely approximated many known demographic characteristics of the general U.S. population, yielded data that most social scientists believe reliably indicate the sexual practices of most 18- to 59-year-old American adults.

Forced to limit their sample size, Laumann and his associates had to forgo sampling a broad range of subpopulations and instead oversampled African Americans and Hispanic Americans to secure valid information about these two largest ethnic minorities in America. Thus, although the study population was representative of white Americans, African Americans, and Hispanic Americans, too few members of other racial and ethnic minorities

The NHSLS research team (left to right): Robert Michael, John Gagnon, Stuart Michaels, and Edward Laumann.

© Bruce Powell

(such as Jews, Asian Americans, and Native Americans) were included to provide useful information about these groups.

Laumann and his colleagues trained 220 professionals, with prior interview experience, to interview all 3,432 respondents face to face. They designed the questionnaire to be easily understood and to flow naturally across various topics. Using trained and experienced interviewers ensured that respondents understood all the questions posed. In addition, the questionnaire contained internal checks to measure the consistency of answers, to validate the overall responses.

This study, titled the National Health and Social Life Survey (NHSLS), provided the most comprehensive information about adult sexual behavior in America since Kinsey's research. In fact, because Laumann and his associates used far better sampling techniques than did the Kinsey group, the NHSLS study stands alone as the most representative U.S. sex survey and as one that reliably reflects the sexual practices of the general U.S. adult population in the 1990s. An analysis of the NHSLS findings was published in two books. The first book is a detailed and scholarly text titled *The Social Organization of Sexuality: Sexual Practices in the United States* (Laumann et al., 1994). Michael, Gagnon, Laumann, and Gina Kolata—a respected *New York Times* science author—wrote a less technical companion volume for the general public titled *Sex in America: A Definitive Study*. This book, also published in 1994, emerged as a popular trade book.

Like all sex research, the NHSLS has its share of critics. However, most sexologists, including us, are impressed with the excellent research design and scope of the study and generally accept the findings as representing the most accurate data currently available. Not surprisingly, publication of the two descriptive books created a storm of media attention. This was especially true because the NHSLS findings contradicted conventional wisdom—promulgated by magazine surveys and mass media images—that envisioned a "sex crazy" American populace madly pursuing excessive indulgence in all kinds of conventional and unconventional sexual practices. In reality, the results of the NHSLS reflect an American people who are more content with their erotic lives, less sexually active, and more sexually conservative than was widely believed. These findings are especially ironic in view of the judgmental opposition by conservative legislators to the Laumann study, who feared it would provide a mandate for excessive sexual expression.

As previously mentioned, our understanding of the impact of ethnic diversity on sexual behavior has been improving as a result of several research studies. The NHSLS is a good example of this expanding knowledge base. In the following "Sexuality and Diversity" discussion we describe a few pertinent findings from this landmark study that add to our awareness of the association between ethnicity and sexuality.

Sexuality and Diversity

Pertinent Findings from the NHSLS

Of the 3,432 American adult respondents to the NHSLS, approximately 75% were white Americans, 12% were African Americans, 8% were Hispanic Americans, and the balance was drawn from other ethnic and racial groups, notably Asian Americans and Native Americans (Laumann et al., 1994.) This ethnic distribution in the research population reflects U.S. demographics; African Americans are the largest ethnic minority in the United States, followed in frequency by Hispanic Americans. The following information provides a brief overview of some important ethnicity findings of this study.

The NHSLS revealed the effect of ethnicity on several sexual behaviors, including the number of sexual partners, the likelihood of choosing sex partners from the same ethnic group, oral sex, anal sex, masturbation, and experience with coercive sex. A larger percentage of African Americans (27.1%) reported having more than one sex partner in the past year than both Hispanic Americans (19.9%) and white Americans (15.1%). However, ethnic differences in the number of sex partners are less pronounced when assessed over a longer time frame. The relevant statistics for a 5-year span are 48.0% for African Americans, 36.6% for Hispanic Americans, and 37.2% for white Americans.

One finding of interest was that the percentage of noncohabitational sexual partnerships from the same ethnic group was very high, more than 90%, for both African Amer-

| TABLE 2.2 | Ethnicity and Sexual Practices |

Sexual Practice	White Americans		African Americans		Hispanic Americans	
	Men	Women	Men	Women	Men	Women
Experience with giving oral sex (%)	81.4	75.3	50.5	34.4	70.7	59.7
Experience with receiving oral sex (%)	81.4	78.9	66.3	48.9	73.2	63.7
Experience with anal sex (%)	25.8	23.2	23.4	9.6	34.2	17.0
Did not masturbate at all in last year (%)	33.4	55.7	60.3	67.8	33.3	65.5
Masturbated at least once per week in last year (%)	28.3	7.3	16.9	10.7	24.4	4.7
Women ever sexually forced by a man (%)		23.0		19.0		14.0

Source: Laumann et al. (1994).

icans and white Americans. In marked contrast, Hispanic American respondents reported that only about 50% of their noncohabitational sexual partnerships were with members of their ethnic group. Table 2.2 outlines several other notable ethnic variations in sexuality. Two of the most pronounced differences are in the area of oral sex and masturbation. African Americans report markedly lower rates of involvement in both these sexual practices than either white Americans or Hispanic Americans.

The Youth Risk Behavior Survey: United States, 2001

The Youth Risk Behavior Survey (YRBS) is a biennial report provided by the Centers for Disease Control and Prevention (CDC). The YRBS summarizes and analyzes data from a variety of surveys that assess the prevalence of six categories of health-risk behaviors among American youth. One of the six categories, sexual behaviors that contribute to unintended pregnancies and sexually transmitted diseases, is of particular interest to sexologists. The 2001 report covers data gathered during February–December 2001 from a representative national sample and 52 state and local surveys conducted among students in grades 9–12 (Centers for Disease Control, 2002h). Information gleaned from the YRBS has proved beneficial to the planning of programs designed to alter behaviors that increase youths' vulnerability to unintended pregnancies and sexually transmitted diseases. We list a few of the key findings of the 2001 YRBS:

- Nationwide, 45.6% of students (48.5% of males and 42.9% of females) reported having experienced sexual intercourse during their lifetime.
- Overall, 6.6% of student respondents reported experiencing sexual intercourse before age 13 (9.3% of males and 4% of females).
- Nationwide, 14.2% of students reported having had sexual intercourse with four or more partners during their lifetime (17.2% of males and 11.4% of females).
- One-third of students nationwide (33.4% for both sexes) reported being currently sexually active (defined as having experienced sexual intercourse during the previous 3 months).
- Among the currently sexually active students, 57.9% reported that either they or their partner had used a condom during their last sexual intercourse. Overall, male students (65.1%) were significantly more likely than female students (51.3%) to report condom use.
- Nationwide, 4.7% of students reported that they had ever been pregnant or had ever gotten someone pregnant.

Survey Findings Regarding Two Issues: Violent Pornography and Alcohol Use

How might the survey method be used to clarify the three assertions with which we began this chapter? The first assertion, concerning violent media and men's likelihood to develop abusive attitudes and behaviors toward women, has been the subject of a number of surveys in the last decade or so.

One of the more notable studies involved 222 male nonoffender college students who were administered a questionnaire regarding their use of pornography and their self-reported likelihood of committing rape or using sexual force. Of these men, 81% had used nonviolent pornography during the previous year, whereas 35% had used sexually violent pornography. Of the subjects who used sexually violent pornography, many more indicated a likelihood of raping or using sexual force against a woman than did subjects who used only nonviolent pornography (Démare et al., 1988). Other surveys of different populations of men (including some imprisoned rapists) have provided further indications that exposure to sexually violent media can lead to increased tolerance for sexually aggressive behavior, greater acceptance of the myth that women want to be raped, reduced sensitivity to rape victims, desensitization to violence against women, and, in some cases, an increased probability of committing a rape (Donnerstein & Linz, 1984; Rosen & Beck, 1988).

The second assertion, concerning the effect of alcohol on sexual responsiveness, has also been the subject of survey research. One study conducted in 1970 asked 20,000 middle- and upper-middle-class Americans whether drinking enhanced their sexual pleasure (Athanasiou et al., 1970). Most respondents answered yes—60% stated that alcohol helped put them "in the mood" for sex, with a significantly higher proportion of women providing this response. This finding should be interpreted with some caution, however, because people's memories of events can differ considerably from their actual behaviors. For the third assertion, regarding the superiority of vaginal orgasms, any survey results would also need to be interpreted with caution, for the same reasons. A more appropriate method for studying this question is direct observation, to which we turn next.

Direct Observations

Direct observation A method of research in which subjects are observed as they go about their activities.

A third method for studying human sexual behavior is **direct observation.** Here, researchers observe and record responses of participating subjects. Although observational research is quite common in the social sciences, such as anthropology, sociology, and psychology, little research of this nature occurs in sexology because of the highly personal and private nature of human sexual expression.

The most famous example of direct observational research is the widely acclaimed work of William Masters and Virginia Johnson. Along with the Kinsey research Masters and Johnson's study of human sexual response is probably the most often mentioned sex research, and it is cited frequently in this textbook. Masters and Johnson used direct observation in a laboratory setting to learn about physiological changes during sexual arousal. The result, *Human Sexual Response* (1966), was based on laboratory observations of 10,000 completed sexual response cycles. Results of these observations are presented in Chapter 6. The Masters and Johnson research sample consisted of sexually responsive volunteers (382 women and 312 men), drawn largely from an academic community, of above-average intelligence and socioeconomic background—obviously not a representative sample of the entire U.S. population. However, the physical signs of sexual arousal, the subject of their study, appear to be rather stable across a wide range of people with diverse backgrounds.

Masters and Johnson used a number of techniques to record physiological sexual responses. These included the use of photographic equipment and instruments to measure and record muscular and vascular changes throughout the body. They also used direct observation as well as ingenious measurement devices to record changes in sex organs. (Electronic devices for measuring sexual arousal are described later in this chapter.) Masters and Johnson recorded responses to a variety of stimulus situations in their laboratory: masturbation, coitus with a partner, artificial coition, and stimulation of the breasts alone. As a follow-up to all recorded observations, each participant was extensively interviewed.

Masters and Johnson's observational approach provided a wealth of information about the manner in which women and men respond physiologically to sexual stimulation. Among other findings, they observed no biological difference between women's orgasms resulting from clitoral and vaginal stimulation. This observation will be discussed at greater length in Chapter 6.

Direct observation has clear advantages as a research method. For studying sexual response patterns, seeing and measuring sexual behavior firsthand is clearly superior to relying on subjective reports of past experiences. Direct observation virtually eliminates the possibility of data falsification through memory deficits, boastful inflation, or guilt-induced repression. Furthermore, records of such behaviors can be kept indefinitely on videotapes or films. But this approach also has disadvantages. A major problem lies in the often unanswerable question of just how much a subject's behavior is influenced by the presence of even the most discreet observer. This question has been asked often since the publication of Masters and Johnson's research. Researchers using direct observation attempt to minimize this potential complication by being as unobtrusive as possible, remaining in a fringe location, observing through one-way glass, or perhaps using remotely activated video cameras. But the subject is still aware that he or she is being observed.

Although there is merit to criticisms of the direct observation method, Masters and Johnson's research has demonstrated that it can withstand the test of time. Their findings are still applied in many areas—including infertility counseling, conception control, sex therapy, and sex education—with beneficial results.

William Masters and Virginia Johnson used direct observation to study the physiological sexual responses of women and men.

▶ The Experimental Method

A fourth method, **experimental research,** is being used with increasing frequency to investigate human sexual behavior. This method involves presenting subjects with certain events (stimuli) under managed conditions that allow for reliable measurement of their reactions.

Experimental research, as typically conducted in a laboratory environment, has a major advantage over other methods because it provides a controlled environment in which all possible influences on subjects' responses, other than the factors that are being investigated, can be ruled out. A researcher using the experimental method manipulates a particular set of conditions, or variables, and observes the effect of this manipulation on subjects' behavior. The experimental method is particularly suited to discovering causal relationships between variables.

There are two types of *variables* (behaviors or conditions that can have varied values) in any experimental research design: independent and dependent. An **independent variable** is a condition or component of the experiment that is under the control of the researcher, who manipulates or determines its value. Conversely, a **dependent variable** is an outcome or resulting behavior that the experimenter observes and records but does not control.

With this brief summary of the experimental method in mind, let us consider how this technique might clarify the relationship between sexually violent media and rape attitudes and behavior. A number of research studies have provided compelling evidence that sexually violent media can cause attitudes to shift toward greater tolerance of sexually aggressive behavior and can actually contribute to some rapists' assaultive behaviors. We consider three experiments, the first involving college men and the other two using convicted rapists as subjects.

The first study was conducted with 271 college men who were divided into two groups. Subjects in the first group were exposed to movies with nonviolent sexual themes, whereas subjects in the second group saw R-rated films in which men were shown committing sexual violence against women (who eventually experienced a transformation from victim to willing partner). A few days after viewing the movies, all subjects completed an attitude questionnaire. The results demonstrated that the men who viewed the violent films were generally much more accepting of

Experimental research
Research conducted in precisely controlled laboratory conditions so that subjects' reactions can be reliably measured.

Independent variable In an experimental research design, a condition or component that is under the control of the researcher, who manipulates or determines its value.

Dependent variable In an experimental research design, an outcome or resulting behavior that the experimenter observes and records but does not control.

? Critical Thinking Question

What were the independent and dependent variables in this study? (See p. 44 for the answer.)

sexual violence toward women than those subjects who were exposed to movies with consensual, nonviolent erotic themes (Malamuth & Check, 1981).

Two other research studies, with comparable research designs, compared the erectile responses (dependent variable) of matched groups of rapists and nonrapists to two different taped descriptions of sexual activity (the independent variable), one involving rape and the other mutually consenting sexual activity (Abel et al., 1977; Barbaree et al., 1979). While subjects listened to tapes, penile tumescence (engorgement) was measured with a penile strain gauge, which is described in the next section of this chapter. In both experiments rapists experienced erections while listening to violent descriptions of rape, whereas their nonrapist counterparts did not. Descriptions of consenting sexual activity produced similar levels of arousal in both groups of men. These findings suggest that repetitive exposure to sexually violent media not only encourages attitudes of violence toward women but also influences at least some men who rape to "sexualize" violence.

The experimental method has also been used to study the relationship between alcohol use and sexual responsiveness (although it has not been used to study vaginal orgasms). In one study of 48 male college students a penile strain gauge was used to measure engorgement as subjects watched a sexually explicit film, first while not under the influence of alcohol and then several days later after the subjects had consumed controlled amounts of alcohol. Findings showed that sexual arousal was reduced by drinking alcohol and that the more alcohol consumed, the greater the reduction (Briddell & Wilson, 1976). A similar experiment tested the relationship between arousal and alcohol intake in women, with consistent results (Wilson & Lawson, 1976).

❓ Critical Thinking Question

Of the four research techniques discussed (case study, survey, direct observation, and experimental study), which method do you think would be most helpful for investigating the effect of chronic pain on sexual functioning? Why?

These studies illustrate one of the primary advantages of the experimental method. Because researchers can control variables precisely, they are able to draw conclusions about causal relationships to a degree not possible with other research methods. However, this method also has disadvantages. One of the most important limitations has to do with the artificiality of laboratory settings, which can adversely influence or bias subjects' responses. As in direct-observation research, the fact that people know they are in an experiment can alter their responses from those that might occur outside the laboratory.

Before concluding this chapter, we turn our attention to several additional areas of concern regarding how we acquire information about sexual practices. First, we examine three technologies used in sex research. Next we discuss ethical guidelines for conducting human sex research. Then we examine feminist theory and scholarship as applied to contemporary sex research. Finally, we end this chapter by describing a process for evaluating research.

▶ Technologies in Sex Research

Sex researchers have benefited from the development of three distinct technologies for collecting data. The first technology we discuss, electronic devices for measuring sexual arousal, has been around for several decades. The other technologies—computerized assessment of sexual behavior and sex research in cyberspace—are both relatively new.

Electronic Devices for Measuring Sexual Arousal

Experimental research and direct-observation studies of human sexual responses often use measures of sexual arousal. In the early years of sex research, investigators had to rely largely on subjective reports of these responses. However, advances in technology over the last few decades have produced several devices for electronically measuring arousal (see Figure 2.1).

The penile strain gauge is a flexible loop that looks something like a rubber band with a wire attached. It is actually a thin rubber tube filled with a fine strand of mercury. A tiny electrical current from the attached wire flows through the mercury continuously. The gauge is placed around the base of the penis. As an erection occurs, the rubber tube stretches, and the strand of mercury becomes thinner, changing the flow of the current. These changes are registered by a recording device. The penile strain gauge can measure even the slightest changes in penis size and is so sensitive that it can even record every pulse of blood into the penis. In the interests of privacy a subject can attach the gauge to his own penis. Researchers can also measure male sexual arousal with a penile plethysmograph or a metal-band gauge, devices that also fit around the penis and reflect small changes in its circumference.

When a woman is sexually aroused, her vaginal walls fill with blood in a manner comparable to the engorgement of a man's penis. The vaginal photoplethysmograph is a device designed to measure this increased vaginal blood volume. It consists of an acrylic cylinder, about the size and shape of a tampon, that is inserted into the vagina. The cylinder contains a light that is reflected off the vaginal walls and a photocell that is sensitive to the reflected light. When the vaginal walls fill with blood during sexual arousal, less light is reflected to the photocell. These changes in light intensity, continuously recorded by an electronic device, provide a measure of sexual arousal comparable to that provided by the penile strain gauge. Like the male device, the vaginal photoplethysmograph can be inserted in privacy by the research subject. In addition to the vaginal photoplethysmograph, two other devices are currently being used to measure sexual response; the vaginal myograph and the rectal myograph are implements inserted into the vagina or rectum that measure muscular activity in the pelvic area.

Computerized Assessment of Sexual Behavior

When an interviewer-administered questionnaire (IAQ) is used in sex research, the human element involved in a face-to-face encounter can influence the respondent to underreport certain sensitive behaviors and to overreport more normative or socially acceptable behaviors (Gribble et al., 1999). A written or self-administered questionnaire (SAQ) provides an alternative survey method that can overcome some of the difficulties of an IAQ by providing a more private and less threatening means of reporting sensitive behavior. However, SAQs can also be limited by the reading ability or literacy of respondents (Couper & Stinson, 1999). Failure to understand written survey questions can be a significant limiting factor when people with relatively low literacy are surveyed.

The recent advent of computer-assisted self-interview (CASI) technology for surveying children, adolescents, and adults has provided an excellent tool for overcoming these barriers to successful sex research. With CASI technologies literacy problems and the potential negative effect of a human interviewer are minimized. Furthermore, researchers can be confident that key elements of questions' presentation and measurement are standardized for all respondents.

▶ **Figure 2.1** Devices for electronically measuring sexual arousal.

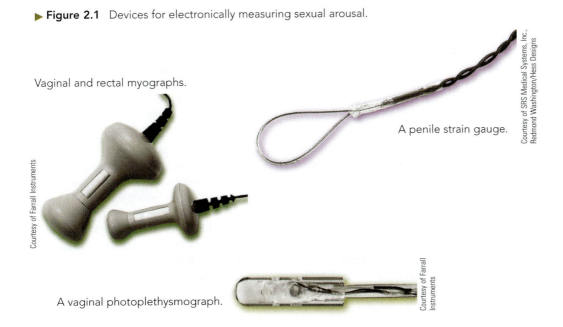

Vaginal and rectal myographs.

Courtesy of Farrall Instruments

Courtesy of SRS Medical Systems, Inc.,
Redmond Washington/Hess Designs

A penile strain gauge.

A vaginal photoplethysmograph.

Courtesy of Farrall Instruments

Two varieties of CASI technology are currently used. In video CASI technology, respondents view questions on a computer screen and enter their answers by pressing labeled keys on the computer keyboard. Audio CASI offers a somewhat more advanced technology in which respondents listen to questions through headphones (which may also be simultaneously displayed by on-screen print) and enter their answers by keystrokes. The audio component has voice-quality sound. Unlike video CASI and more traditional survey methods, audio CASI does not require that respondents be literate. Furthermore, because questions are prerecorded, this technology allows multilingual administration without requiring that researchers be multilingual.

The application of CASI technology is becoming more widespread, and numerous studies have demonstrated that this method is an effective tool for collecting sensitive information on a variety of topics (Couper & Stinson, 1999; Gribble et al., 1999; Johnson et al., 2001; Turner et al., 1998). An interesting example of combining video and audio CASI is provided by the work of David Paperny (1997), who recently reported on a decade of research using an interactive multimedia computer program titled Youth Health Provider. This program is used to obtain a comprehensive social and behavioral history from adolescent respondents.

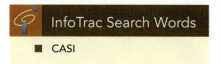

InfoTrac Search Words

■ CASI

Questions are presented both orally and on-screen and are answered by pressing a key or touching the computer screen. Assessment of data from over 5,000 computer interviews with adolescents revealed that this new technology provides valid response data on sensitive issues in a manner that teenagers clearly preferred over written questionnaires or face-to-face interviews.

Sex Research in Cyberspace

With the Internet rapidly evolving into a common household technology, opportunities are emerging to conduct sex research using this technology (Cooper et al., 2000; Rhodes et al., 2003). Traditionally, the Internet has been used by scientists to distribute research information rather than to collect data. Today, the Internet provides access to a diverse and growing population of potential research participants and is becoming an important medium for conducting research. In this section we describe the advantages and disadvantages of sex research in cyberspace and examine some of the ethical issues posed by this technology.

Almost any kind of survey questionnaire can be posted on the Internet, and these survey instruments can be visually and functionally similar or identical to conventional questionnaires (Rhodes et al., 2003). So what are the advantages of Internet-based surveys over more conventional instruments? Cyberspace questionnaires are considerably cheaper than traditional paper-and-pencil questionnaires because they eliminate printing costs, decrease the need for data collection staff, and do not require distribution and collection costs such as postage and envelopes. Online surveys can save 20–80% of the total costs associated with traditional questionnaires (Rhodes et al., 2003). In comparison with mailed, self-administered questionnaires, time can also be saved with Internet-based surveys (Pealer & Weiler, 2000). Research also indicates that people responding to electronic surveys are less influenced by social desirability and more inclined to share information that they might not disclose through traditional written questionnaires or interviews. Perhaps this is because they believe that their responses are more anonymous and secure (Buchanan, 2000; McKenna & Bargh, 2000; Rhodes et al., 2003).

The collection and management of data are also typically more efficient with Internet-based surveys. For example, survey data can be automatically inserted, by means of e-mail, into a corresponding database. Furthermore, researchers can make adjustments to Internet-based surveys as unforeseen problems related to item comprehension are discovered (Rhodes et al., 2003). In addition to the ease of revising items, new follow-up queries, based on preliminary data analysis, can be added as desired.

With tens of millions of people worldwide accessing the Internet daily, the World Wide Web provides "nearly limitless numbers of potential study respondents across geographical and cultural boundaries" (Rhodes et al., 2003, p. 68). For example, a recent Internet-based investigation of factors associated with gay men being tested for hepatitis C infection reported data obtained from men located throughout North America, Europe, Asia, Australia, and Africa (Rhodes et al., 2001b). Researchers conducting sex research in cyberspace can also recruit hidden populations of geographically isolated participants or those who might otherwise be difficult to find locally.

A final advantage of this approach to sex research is that online data collection can yield information that is more usable or accurate than data obtained through other methods (Rhodes et al., 2003). This is accomplished by reducing errors in two ways. First, errors are minimized by including prompts, menus, and clearly stated explanations designed to guide a respondent to accurately complete the entire survey. Problems commonly encountered with paper-and-pencil questionnaires include unanswered questions or multiple responses to questions asking for a single answer. Internet surveys can make completion of all items a requirement for questionnaire submission and acceptance, and multiple responses can be eliminated by appropriate prompts. Second, errors associated with incorrect data entry or problems that stem from variations in how traditional surveys are administered or in how interviewers interpret responses are eliminated by Internet surveys that standardize respondents' interactions with the survey document (Rhodes et al., 2003).

The effectiveness of the Youth Health Provider program, developed by David Paperny, suggests that teenagers are more willing to share sensitive information on sexual behavior when they are working with a computer.

A significant disadvantage of Internet-based sex surveys is that considerable sample-selection bias exists. At present, a digital divide exists, meaning that Internet users are still not representative of the general U.S. population. Internet users tend to be younger, better educated, more affluent, and more likely to be male than nonusers (Rhodes et al., 2003). Because of this demographic bias, findings from Internet surveys must be cautiously interpreted. However, as the popularity of the Internet attracts an increasingly diverse population of users, we can expect that Internet-user demographics will become more comparable to the general population. Internet-user demographics are rapidly evolving. By the early 2000s, over 50% of U.S. adults had computers at home and more than 80% of these individuals routinely logged on to the Internet. These figures represent a significant increase from 1996, when only 30% of U.S. adults owned computers and 27% logged on to the Internet (Rhodes et al., 2003; U.S. Government Working Group on Electronic Commerce, 2000).

Other challenges and disadvantages of this approach to sex research include low response rates for Internet-based surveys and multiple survey submissions (Pealer & Weiler, 2000; Rhodes et al., 2003). Response rates are presently incalculable because Web counters that allow researchers to document the number of visits to a Web site are unable to differentiate between respondents and nonrespondents. Thus the problem of nonresponse or volunteer bias that plagues all sex survey research is a concern for online investigators. Although multiple submissions have yet to surface as a major problem in cyberspace research (Rhodes et al., 2003), the potentially damaging effect of multiple submissions remains a concern. Several methods for limiting this problem are being used by Internet researchers and include the use of identifying information (zip code, date of birth, etc.) to detect multiple or duplicate responses and embedding a question within the survey asking if the respondent has previously completed the same survey (Rhodes et al., 2001a, 2001b).

We have seen that the Internet offers a "virtual world" for conducting innovative sex research. However, this new world also poses new ethical issues in the areas of subject recruitment and privacy. A major ethical issue is associated with the use of unsolicited e-mail to recruit research participants. People rightfully may be upset when charged by their Internet service provider for the time spent downloading unsolicited e-mail. In addition, people who read e-mail at work might be justifiably concerned that their employer could misinterpret their being targeted for a sex study. (Employers are legally entitled to monitor employees' e-mail.) Furthermore, people who read e-mail at home often share their computer with family members or friends, who may misinterpret an e-mail requesting participation in sex research.

Privacy issues are especially acute when doing sex research in cyberspace. Unfortunately, "promises of anonymity on the Internet can rarely, if ever, be given with 100% certainty, since a persistent hacker or an official with a court order may be able to discover the identity of research participants" (Binik et al., 1999, p. 86). Risks of exposure are small, but a few incidents have been reported. To minimize participants' risks, Internet researchers are increasingly utilizing special techniques to provide anonymity.

Two recent articles dealing with ethical issues in Internet sex research outlined several suggestions for researchers who use this technology (Binik et al., 1999; Rhodes et al., 2003). Some of these suggestions are:

1. Researchers must not send unsolicited e-mail for sex research.
2. Internet researchers must endeavor to obtain informed consent and to ascertain that respondents truly understand the nature of the research they are participating in.
3. When investigating emotionally sensitive issues, researchers should make provisions for referral services in the event that participants require help as a direct result of their participating in the research.
4. Researchers should use appropriate strategies, such as encryption and anonymous remailers, to provide anonymity to respondents.
5. Researchers should not store raw data received over the Internet in vulnerable electronic files for long periods but rather should transfer these files as quickly as possible to separate and more secure databases.

► Ethical Guidelines for Human Sex Research

Researchers in a range of investigative fields, including sexology, share a common commitment to maintain the welfare, dignity, rights, well-being, and safety of their human subjects. Detailed lists of ethical guidelines have been prepared by a number of professional organizations, including the American Psychological Association (APA), the American Medical Association (AMA), and the Society for the Scientific Study of Sex (SSSS).

The ethical guidelines require, among other things, that no pressure or coercion be applied to ensure the participation of volunteers in research and that researchers avoid procedures that might cause physical or psychological harm to human subjects. Researchers need to obtain informed consent from participants before conducting an experiment. Informed consent involves explaining the general purpose of the study and each participant's rights as a subject, including the voluntary nature of participation and the potential costs and benefits of participation (Seal et al., 2000). Researchers must also respect a subject's right to refuse to participate at any time during the course of a study. In addition, special steps must be taken to protect the confidentiality of the data and to maintain participants' anonymity unless they agree to be identified (Margolis, 2000).

The issue of deception in research remains controversial. Some studies would lose their effectiveness if participating subjects knew in advance exactly what the experimenter was studying. The ethical guideline generally applied to this issue is that if deception must be used, a postexperiment debriefing must thoroughly explain to participants why it was necessary. At such time, subjects must be allowed to request that their data be removed from the study and destroyed.

Sometimes it is hard for researchers to weigh objectively the potential benefits of a study against the possibility of harming subjects. Recognizing this difficulty, virtually every institution conducting research in the United States has established an ethics committee that reviews all proposed studies. If committee members perceive that the subjects' welfare is insufficiently safeguarded, the proposal must be modified or the research cannot be conducted. In addition, federal funding for research is denied to any institution that fails to conduct an adequate ethics committee review before data collection begins.

InfoTrac Search Words
■ Sex research ethical

► Feminist Theory and Sex Research

Feminism is perhaps best defined as "a movement that involves women and men working together for equality" (McCormick, 1996, p. 99). Feminism, as both a field of study and a social movement, seeks to give voice to as many different individuals and groups as possible.

A feminist theory of research emerged as an important influence on research in sexology and other areas of the social sciences in the 1970s and 1980s. Feminist sexologists who espouse this theoretical position are more focused on giving voice to the people who are studied, especially women, than are sexologists who are not feminists (McCormick, 1996). Because feminism is a perspective on the people studied rather than a particular methodology, there is no single feminist position on research. However, several common threads are worth noting in reference to sex research.

One viewpoint, widely held among feminist sexologists, is that research in sexology has been largely dominated by white middle-class men who develop research strategies based on a model of male sexuality that also promotes heterosexuality as the norm (Irvine, 1990; Jackson, 1984). Feminist scholars believe that this emphasis on male sexuality consistently promotes a narrow view of sexual activity as centered on a penis in a vagina (see our discussion "Sex for Procreation" in Chapter 1). Such a limiting perspective often results in sex researchers de-emphasizing and devaluing the female experience of sex (MacKinnon, 1986; McCormick, 1996; Pollis, 1988). This inevitably creates a dearth of scientific knowledge about important aspects of female sexuality, such as the female orgasm and the importance to women of nonintercourse activities, such as shared touching and kissing.

This lack of attention to women has been especially evident in studies of homosexuals, where until recently almost all scientific research focused on gay men, essentially ignoring lesbian women. Women have also been largely forgotten and marginalized in much of the research conducted in the medical and health care systems of the United States, according to a book by Sue Rosser titled *Women's Health—Missing from U.S. Medicine* (1994). Rosser presents a persuasive case that this minimization of women has influenced health policies in many adverse ways. She powerfully documents the fact that resources and attention are often devoted to women's health issues only when those problems are related to men's interest in controlling reproduction. Another wrenching example described by Rosser is the limited research on AIDS in women. Even though the AIDS epidemic has increasingly involved women as patients, most of the drug trials have included only men—a potentially serious oversight because women might respond differently to drug therapy. Although there have been some improvements on both of these fronts in the last few years, Rosser's book remains a compelling indictment of contemporary research practices.

Feminist scholars also believe that the scope of sex research, with its primary emphasis on quantitative data collection, should be expanded to include more detailed exploration of the subjective and qualitative experience and meaning of sexuality for both women and men (Hyde, 2001; Peplau & Conrad, 1989; *Psychology of Women Quarterly*, 1999, v. 23 [special issue, "Innovative Methods in Feminist Research"]). Examples of this type of research include the studies by Francine Klagsbrun (1985) and Ruthellen Josselson (1992), both of whom conducted in-depth interviews with married couples in which they explored the meaning, impact, and relationship value of a range of intimate experiences.

More recent examples of feminist research methodology include two investigations of men's experiences after surgery to treat prostate disease (Jakobsson et al., 2000; Pateman & Johnson, 2000). Researchers in both of these studies sought to give voice to their male subjects by encouraging them to talk freely, in a relaxed environment, about their preoperative and postoperative life experiences. Open-ended questions allowed participants to discuss topics such as urinary problems and sexual life consequences of surgery. (We discuss prostate disease in detail in Chapter 5.)

Psychologist Janet Hyde (2001) recently expressed the view that the most progress in sex research in future years will be made by researchers who integrate quantitative and qualitative information collection. A good example of this integrative approach is provided by the work of Deborah Tolman and Laura Szalacha (1999), who used a combination of quantitative and qualitative methods to discover how adolescent females think about sexual desire.

Feminist scholars do not seek to replace traditional empirical sex research. Rather, they are committed to correcting some of the limitations that stem from this perspective while adding a rich body of data, particularly qualitative information, to enhance our understanding of how women and men experience their sexuality. We can expect the future impact of a feminist perspective on research to increase in accordance with the growing number of women who make contributions to the research literature in sexology and other disciplines.

▶ Evaluating Research: Some Questions to Ask

We hope that the material presented here and elsewhere in our book will help differentiate legitimate scientific sex research from the many frivolous nonscientific polls and opinion surveys that are widespread in the contemporary media. Even when you are exposed to the results of serious investigations, it is wise to maintain a critical eye and to avoid the understandable tendency to accept something as factual just because it is presented as being "scientific." The following list of questions may prove useful as you evaluate the legitimacy of any research, sex or otherwise, that you are exposed to.

1. What are the researchers' credentials? Are the investigators professionally trained? Are they affiliated with reputable institutions (research centers, academic institutions, etc.)? Are they associated with any special-interest groups that may favor a particular research finding or conclusion?

2. In what type of media were the results published: reputable scientific journals, scholarly textbooks, popular magazines, newspapers, the Internet?

3. What approach or type of research method was used, and were proper scientific procedures adhered to?

4. Were a sufficient number of subjects used, and is there any reason to suspect bias in the selection method?

5. Is it reasonable to apply the research findings to a larger population beyond the sample group? To what extent can legitimate generalizations be made?

6. Is there any reason to believe that the research methods could have biased the findings? (Did the presence of an interviewer encourage false responses? Did the cameras place limitations on the response potentials?)

7. Are there any other published research findings that support or refute the study in question?

▶ Summary

The Goals of Sexology
- The goals of sexology include understanding, predicting, and controlling behavior. (p. 23)
- Pursuit of the goal of controlling behavior is often modified or tempered by ethical issues. (p. 24)

Nonexperimental Research Methods
- Nonexperimental methods for studying sexuality include case studies, surveys, and direct observation. (p. 24)
- Case studies typically produce a great deal of information about one or a few individuals. They have two advantages: flexibility and the opportunity to explore specific behaviors and feelings in depth. Disadvantages include lack of investigative control, possible subjective bias on the researcher's part, and poor sampling techniques that often limit the possibility of making generalizations to broad populations. (pp. 24–26)
- Most information about human sexual behavior has been obtained through questionnaire or interview surveys of relatively large populations of respondents. Questionnaires have the advantage of being anonymous, inexpensive, and quickly administered. Interviews are more flexible and allow for more rapport between researcher and subject. (p. 28)

- Sex researchers who use surveys share certain problems. These include the following:
- The virtual impossibility of getting 100% participation of randomly selected subjects, making it difficult to obtain a representative sample. Self-selection of samples, or volunteer bias, is a common problem. (p. 28)
- Biases created by nonresponse: Do volunteer participants have significantly different attitudes and behaviors from nonparticipants? (p. 28)
- The problem of accuracy: Respondents' self-reports may be less than accurate because of limitations of memory, boastfulness, guilt, or simple misunderstandings. (p. 30)
- Demographic biases: Most samples are heavily weighted toward white, middle-class, better-educated participants. (p. 30)
- Research has demonstrated that ethnicity often exerts considerable influence on sexual attitudes and behaviors. (p. 30)
- The Kinsey surveys were broad-scale studies of human sexual behavior that were somewhat limited by sampling techniques that overrepresented young, educated, city-dwelling people. (p. 30)

- The National Health and Social Life Survey (NHSLS) stands alone as the single most representative sex survey ever conducted in the United States. It has provided a reliable view of the sexual practices of the general U.S. adult population in the 1990s. (pp. 31–32)
- The Youth Risk Behavior Survey (YRBS) is a biennial report that summarizes data on several categories of youth health-risk behaviors, including sexual behavior that contributes to unintended pregnancies and sexually transmitted diseases. (p. 33)
- There is little direct-observation sex research because of the highly personal nature of sexual expression. When direct observation can be used, the possibility of data falsification is significantly reduced. However, subjects' behavior might be altered by the presence of an observer. Furthermore, the reliability of recorded observations can sometimes be compromised by preexisting researcher biases. (pp. 34–35)

The Experimental Method
- In experimental research, subjects are presented with events (stimuli) under managed conditions that allow for reliable measurement of their reactions. (p. 35)
- The purpose of the experimental method is to discover causal relationships between independent and dependent variables. (p. 35)
- An independent variable is a condition or component of the experiment that is controlled or manipulated by the experimenter. A dependent variable is an outcome or resulting behavior that the experimenter observes and records but does not control. (p. 35)
- Experimental research offers two advantages: control over the relevant variables and direct analysis of possible causal factors. However, the artificial nature of the experimental laboratory setting can alter subject responses from those that might occur in a natural setting. (p. 36)

Technologies in Sex Research
- The penile strain gauge, vaginal photoplethysmograph, vaginal myograph, and rectal myograph are devices used for electrically measuring human sexual response. (pp. 36–37)
- Video CASI and audio CASI are two versions of computer-assisted self-interview technology that are increasingly being effectively used to collect sensitive information from children, adolescents, and adults. (pp. 37–38)
- The Internet has become an important medium for conducting sex research. The collection and management of data are more efficient with Internet-based surveys and are also cheaper, faster, and more error free than traditional survey methods. Disadvantages of Internet-based sex surveys include sample-selection bias, low response rates, and multiple survey submissions. (pp. 39–40)

Ethical Guidelines for Human Sex Research
- Sexologists and other researchers operate under ethical guidelines that seek to ensure the welfare, dignity, rights, well-being, and safety of their human subjects. (p. 40)
- These ethical guidelines require that researchers obtain informed consent from participants, avoid procedures that might cause physical or psychological harm to subjects, and maintain confidentiality of both data and participants. (p. 40)

Feminist Theory and Sex Research
- Feminist scholars believe that sex researchers place too great an emphasis on males, a perspective that often results in the de-emphasis and devaluing of the female experience of sex. Feminist scholars also believe that the scope of sex research, with its primary emphasis on quantitative data, should be expanded to include more detailed exploration of the subjective and qualitative experience and meaning of sexuality for both sexes. (pp. 40–41)

Evaluating Research: Some Questions to Ask
- In evaluating any study of sexual behavior, it is helpful to consider who conducted the research, examine the methods and sampling techniques, and compare the results with those of other reputable studies. (p. 42)

▶Suggested Readings

Abramson, Paul (1990). "Sexual Science: Emerging Discipline or Oxymoron?" *Journal of Sex Research, 27,* 147–165. An excellent article that discusses some of the methodological problems that sex researchers encounter while making a strong case for the importance of scientific rigor in this area of research.

Bancroft, John (Ed.) (2000). *The Role of Theory in Sex Research.* Bloomington, IN: Indiana University Press. A scholarly book that presents the proceedings from a workshop, hosted at the Kinsey Institute, that focused on the role of theory in sex research.

Brannigan, Gary, Elizabeth Allgeier, and Albert Allgeier (1998). *The Sex Researchers.* New York: Longman. An interesting and illuminating discussion of a diverse group of contemporary sex researchers and some of the issues and concerns that have influenced their research.

Bullough, Vern (1994). *Science in the Bedroom: A History of Sex Research.* New York: Basic Books. A scholarly, highly readable, and enlightening discussion of the history of sex research from the early 19th century to the present.

Davis, Clive, William Yarber, Robert Bauserman, Sandra Davis, and George Schreer (Eds.). (1998). *Handbook of Sexuality: Related Measures.* Thousand Oaks, CA: Sage. An informative collection of articles that provides in-depth discussions of investigation methods used by contemporary sex researchers.

Journal of Sex Research, February 1999, v. 36. A special issue of this journal devoted entirely to issues related to methods used in sex research.

Laumann, Edward, John Gagnon, Robert Michael, and Stuart Michaels (1994). *The Social Organization of Sexuality.* Chicago: University of Chicago Press. An informative report on the most comprehensive and representative survey to date of sexual practices and attitudes in the American population.

Pomeroy, Wardell (1972). *Dr. Kinsey and the Institute for Sex Research.* New York: Harper & Row. An informed and entertaining look at Kinsey and his research, as seen through the "insider" eyes of one of his original research colleagues.

Psychology of Women Quarterly, 1999, v. 23. A special issue of this journal devoted entirely to articles describing innovative methods in feminist research.

Wiederman, Michael (2001). *Understanding Sexuality Research.* Belmont, CA: Wadsworth. A helpful new guide to thinking critically about research in human sexuality.

Web Resources

Your *Our Sexuality* Web site **http://psychology.wadsworth.com/ crooksbaur9e/** has direct links to the Web sites described below. These links are checked often for changes, dead links, and new additions.

Kinsey Institute for Research in Sex, Gender, and Reproduction

The Kinsey Institute, founded by the pioneer sexologist Alfred Kinsey, sponsors a Web site dedicated to supporting interdisciplinary research in the study of human sexuality. The Research and Publications section describes the center's most recent studies.

The Society for the Scientific Study of Sexuality (SSSS)

Meetings and research sponsored by the SSSS, a respected organization of scholars and professionals dedicated to the advancement of knowledge about sexuality, are announced on its Web site.

Society for the Psychological Study of Lesbian, Gay, and Bisexual Issues

One of more than 50 divisions of the American Psychological Association, Division 44 focuses on sexual orientation issues, and its Web site provides information on recent research in this field.

Centers for Disease Control and Prevention

Many of the issues addressed by the Centers for Disease Control and Prevention (CDC) deal with aspects of human sexuality, including such topics as adolescent sexuality, contraception and pregnancy, and sexually transmitted diseases. The Web site contains a wealth of recent research information about sexual behavior and related health issues.

The U.S. Census Bureau

Census data as they relate to human sexuality are cited frequently in our textbook. This Web site can be accessed to obtain accurate research data pertaining to a range of issues involving sexuality, such as recent trends in marriages and divorces, family composition, single living, and cohabitation.

The National Health and Social Life Survey

This Web site provides an overview and summary of this important survey research study.

ANSWER TO QUESTION ON P. 35

The independent variable in this experiment was the degree of violence in the movies observed by the participants. The dependent variable was the subjects' responses to the questionnaire.

Our Sexuality Web Site

For online resources directly related to this book, go to **http://psychology.wadsworth.com/ crooksbaur9e/**. You will find interactive exercises, study questions, chapter outlines, an online version of this text's glossary, and Web links and activities that complement your CD-ROM.

InfoTrac® College Edition Online Library

http://infotrac.thomsonlearning.com/
InfoTrac College Edition is an online searchable library that includes a multitude of journals, many of which are specific to human sexuality. These journals include *Archives of Sexual Behavior, Archives of Sexual Health Behavior, Canadian Journal of Human Sexuality, Hispanic Journal of the Behavioral Sciences, Journal of Cross-Cultural Psychology, Journal of Physical Education, Recreation, and Dance, Journal of Sex Research,* and *Sex Roles.*

Our Sexuality CD-ROM

Use your CD-ROM for further study of the concepts in this chapter. Your CD-ROM provides animations of difficult concepts, video clips of real people discussing sexuality, critical thinking questions, chapter quizzing, and more.

Gender Issues

Examine the following sentence and fill in the blanks: In this particular society, "the _____ is the dominant, impersonal, managing partner, while the _____ is the less responsible, emotionally dependent person."

If you assumed that the word *man* belongs in the first space and *woman* belongs in the second, you are mistaken. In the society in question, the Tchambuli of New Guinea, traditional masculine and feminine behavior patterns are complete opposites of stereotypical American patterns (Mead, 1963). (The opening anecdotal account illustrates common American gender-role stereotypes.) The sharp difference between Tchambuli expectations for men and women and those that predominate in American culture raises certain fundamental questions: What constitutes maleness and femaleness? How can the expectations and assumptions for each sex differ so greatly from one society to another? If some gender-related behaviors are learned, do any of the behavioral differences between men and women have a biological basis? How do gender-role expectations affect sexual interactions? These are questions that we address in this chapter.

▶ Male and Female, Masculine and Feminine

Through the ages people have held to the belief that we are born males or females and just naturally grow up doing what men or women do. The only explanation required has been a simple allusion to "nature taking its course." This viewpoint has a simplicity that helps make the world seem like an orderly place. However, closer examination reveals a much greater complexity in the process by which our maleness or femaleness is determined and in the way our behavior, sexual and otherwise, is influenced by this aspect of our identity. This fascinating complexity is our focus in the pages that follow. But first it will be helpful to clarify a few important terms.

Sex and Gender

Sex Biological maleness and femaleness.

Gender The psychological and sociocultural characteristics associated with our sex.

Many writers use the terms *sex* and *gender* interchangeably. However, each word has a specific meaning. **Sex** refers to our biological femaleness or maleness. There are two aspects of biological sex: *genetic sex,* which is determined by our sex chromosomes, and *anatomical sex,* the obvious physical differences between males and females. **Gender** is a concept that encompasses the special psychosocial meanings added to biological maleness or femaleness. Thus, although our sex is linked to various physical attributes (chromosomes, penis, vulva, and so forth), our gender refers to the psychological and sociocultural characteristics associated with our sex—in other words, our femininity or masculinity. In this chapter we use the terms *masculine* and *feminine* to characterize the behaviors that are typically attributed to males and females. One undesirable aspect of these labels is that they can limit the range of behaviors that people are comfortable expressing. For example, a man might hesitate to be nurturing lest he be labeled feminine, and a woman might be reticent to act assertively for fear of being considered masculine. It is not our intention to perpetuate the stereotypes often associated with these labels. However, we find it necessary to use these terms when discussing gender issues.

Gender assumptions Assumptions about how people are likely to behave based on their maleness or femaleness.

When we meet people for the first time, most of us quickly note their sex and make assumptions about how they are likely to behave based on their maleness or femaleness. These are **gender assumptions.** For most people gender assumptions are an important part of routine social interaction. We identify people as being either the same sex as ourselves or the other sex. (We have avoided using the term *opposite sex* because we believe it overstates the differences between males and females.) In fact, many of us find it hard to interact with a person whose gender is ambiguous. When we are unsure of our identification of someone's gender, we may become confused and uncomfortable.

Gender Identity and Gender Role

Gender identity refers to each individual's subjective sense of being male or female. Most of us realize in the first few years of life that we are either male or female. However, there is no guarantee that a person's gender identity will be consistent with his or her biological sex, and some people experience considerable confusion in their efforts to identify their own maleness or femaleness. We look into this area in more detail later in this chapter.

Gender role (sometimes called *sex role*) refers to a collection of attitudes and behaviors that are considered normal and appropriate in a specific culture for people of a particular sex. Gender roles establish sex-related behavioral expectations that people are expected to fulfill. Behavior thought to be socially appropriate for a male is called masculine; for a female, feminine. When we use the terms *masculine* and *feminine* in subsequent discussions, we are referring to these socialized notions.

Gender-role expectations are culturally defined and vary from society to society. For example, Tchambuli society considers emotionally expressive behavior appropriate for males. American society takes a somewhat different view. A kiss on the cheek is considered a feminine act and therefore inappropriate between men in American society. In contrast, such behavior is consistent with masculine role expectations in many European and Middle Eastern societies.

Besides being culturally based, our notions of masculinity and femininity also depend on the era in which they occur. For instance, if an American father in the 1950s had stayed home to care for his preschool children while his wife traveled on business, his behavior would probably have raised eyebrows, if not engendered ridicule. Today, young couples are more likely to divide household labor according to practical needs rather than preconceived notions of how men and women "should" behave. More than any other time in our history, the present era is marked by redefinition of male and female roles. Many of us who have grown up subjected to strong gender-role conditioning are now exploring how these roles have shaped our lives and are seeking to break away from their limiting influences. Being part of this change can be both exciting and confusing. We consider the impact of traditional and changing gender roles later in this chapter (and also throughout this textbook). But first, let us turn our attention to the processes by which we acquire our gender identity.

Gender identity How one psychologically perceives oneself as either male or female.

Gender role A collection of attitudes and behaviors that are considered normal and appropriate in a specific culture for people of a particular sex.

InfoTrac Search Words

- Gender identity
- Gender role

▶ Gender-Identity Formation

Like the knowledge that we have a particular color hair or eyes, gender is an aspect of our identity that most people take for granted. Certainly, gender identity usually—but not always—comes with the territory of having certain biological parts. But there is more to it than simply looking like a female or a male. As we will see in the following paragraphs, the question of how we come to think of ourselves as either male or female has two answers. The first explanation centers on biological processes that begin shortly after conception and are completed before birth. But a second important explanation has to do with social-learning theory, which looks to cultural influences during early childhood to explain both the nuances of gender identity and the personal significance of being either male or female. We explore first the biological processes involved in gender-identity formation, summarized in Table 3.1.

Gender Identity as a Biological Process: Typical Prenatal Differentiation

From the moment of conception many biological factors contribute to the differentiation of male or female sex. In the following paragraphs we explore how biological sex differentiation occurs during prenatal development. Our discussion follows a chronological sequence. We begin at conception, looking at chromosomal differences between male and female, and then continue with the development of gonads, the production of hormones, the development of internal and external reproductive structures, and, finally, sex differentiation of the brain.

TABLE 3.1	Gender Identity as a Biological Process—Typical Prenatal Differentiation	
Characteristic	**Female**	**Male**
Chromosomal sex	XX	XY
Gonadal sex	Ovaries	Testes
Hormonal sex	Estrogens	Androgens
	Progestational compounds	
Internal reproductive structures	Fallopian tubes	Vas deferens
	Uterus	Seminal vesicles
	Inner portions of vagina	Ejaculatory ducts
External genitals	Clitoris	Penis
	Inner vaginal lips	Scrotum
	Outer vaginal lips	
Sex differentiation of the brain	Hypothalamus becomes estrogen sensitive, influencing cyclic release of hormones.	Estrogen-insensitive male hypothalamus directs steady production of hormones.
	Two hypothalamic areas are smaller in the female brain.	Two hypothalamic areas are larger in the male brain.
	Cerebral cortex of right hemisphere is thinner in the female brain.	Cerebral cortex of right hemisphere is thicker in the male brain.
	Corpus callosum is thicker in the female brain.	Corpus callosum is thinner in the male brain.
	Less lateralization of function in the female brain compared to the male brain.	More lateralization of function in the male brain compared to the female brain.

Chromosomal Sex

Sperm The male reproductive cell.

Ovum The female reproductive cell.

Autosomes The 22 pairs of human chromosomes that do not significantly influence sex differentiation.

Sex chromosomes A single set of chromosomes that influences biological sex determination.

Our biological sex is determined at conception by the chromosomal makeup of the **sperm** (male reproductive cell) that fertilizes an **ovum,** or egg (female reproductive cell). Except for the reproductive cells, human body cells contain 46 chromosomes, arranged in 23 pairs (see Figure 3.1). Twenty-two of these pairs are matched; that is, the two chromosomes of each pair look almost identical. These matched sets, called **autosomes** (AW-tuh-sohmes), are the same in males and females and do not significantly influence sex differentiation. One chromosome pair, however—the **sex chromosomes**—differs in females and males. Females have two similar chromosomes, labeled XX, whereas males have dissimilar chromosomes, labeled XY.

As noted, the reproductive cells are an exception to the 23-pair rule. As a result of a biological process known as *meiosis,* mature reproductive cells contain only half the usual complement of chromosomes—one member of each pair. (This process is necessary to avoid doubling the chromosome total when sex cells merge at conception.) A normal female

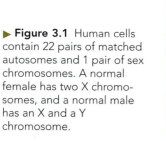

▶ **Figure 3.1** Human cells contain 22 pairs of matched autosomes and 1 pair of sex chromosomes. A normal female has two X chromosomes, and a normal male has an X and a Y chromosome.

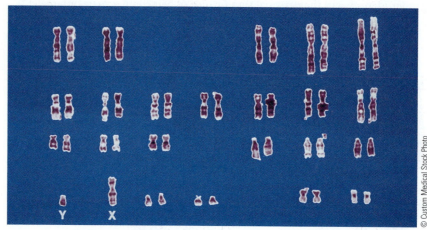

ovum (or egg) contains 22 autosomes plus an X chromosome. A normal male sperm cell contains 22 autosomes plus either an X or a Y chromosome. If the ovum is fertilized by a sperm carrying a Y chromosome, the resulting XY combination will produce a male child. In contrast, if an X-chromosome-bearing sperm fertilizes the ovum, the result will be an XX combination and a female child. Two X chromosomes are necessary for internal and external female structures to develop completely. But if one Y chromosome is present, male sexual and reproductive organs will develop (Harley et al., 1992; Page et al., 1987).

Researchers have recently located a single gene on the short arm of the human Y chromosome that seems to play a crucial role in initiating the sequence of events that leads to the development of the male gonads, or **testes.** This maleness-determining gene is called *SRY* (Bancroft, 2002; Jegalian & Lahn, 2001b).

> **Testes** Male gonads inside the scrotum that produce sperm and sex hormones.

Findings from a study conducted by scientists from Italy and the United States suggest that a gene or genes for femaleness also exist. These researchers studied four cases of chromosomal males with feminized external genitals. All these individuals were found to have XY chromosomes and a working *SRY* (maleness) gene. Three of the four individuals exhibited clearly identifiable female external genitals; the fourth had ambiguous genitals. If the maleness gene was the dominant determinant of biological sex, the external genitals of these individuals would have developed in a typical male pattern. What, then, triggered this variation from the expected developmental sequence? Examination of these individuals' DNA revealed that a tiny bit of genetic material on the short arm of the X chromosome had been duplicated. As a result, each of the subjects had a double dose of a gene designated as *DSS*. This condition resulted in feminization of an otherwise chromosomally normal male fetus (Bardoni et al., 1994).

These findings suggest that a gene (or genes) on the X chromosome helps to push the undifferentiated gonads in a female direction just as the *SRY* gene helps to start construction of male sex structures. Such observations contradict the long-held belief that the human fetus is inherently female and that, unlike male prenatal differentiation, no gene triggers are necessary for female differentiation.

Gonadal Sex

In the first weeks after conception the structures that will become the reproductive organs, or **gonads,** are the same in males and females (see Figure 3.2a). Differentiation begins about 6 weeks after conception. Genetic signals determine whether the mass of undifferentiated sexual tissue develops into male or female gonads (Bancroft, 2002; Hiort and Holterhus, 2000). At this time an *SRY* gene product (or products) in a male fetus triggers the transformation of embryonic gonads into testes. In the absence of *SRY* and perhaps under the influence of the *DSS* or other femaleness gene, the undifferentiated gonadal tissue develops into **ovaries** (see Figure 3.2b).

> **Gonads** The male and female sex glands—ovaries and testes.

> **Ovaries** Female gonads that produce ova and sex hormones.

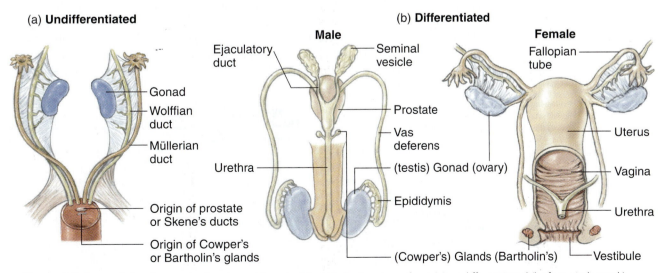

(a) **Undifferentiated**

(b) **Differentiated**

Male

Ejaculatory duct

Seminal vesicle

Gonad

Wolffian duct

Müllerian duct

Urethra

Origin of prostate or Skene's ducts

Origin of Cowper's or Bartholin's glands

Prostate

Vas deferens

(testis) Gonad (ovary)

Epididymis

(Cowper's) Glands (Bartholin's)

Female

Fallopian tube

Uterus

Vagina

Urethra

Vestibule

▶ **Figure 3.2** Prenatal development of male and female internal duct systems from (a) undifferentiated (before sixth week) to (b) differentiated.

Once the testes or ovaries develop, these gonads begin releasing their own sex hormones. As we will see next, these hormones become the critical factor in further sex differentiation, and genetic influence ceases.

Hormonal Sex

The gonads produce hormones and secrete them directly into the bloodstream. Ovaries produce two classes of hormones: **estrogens** (ES-troh-jens) and **progestational compounds.** Estrogens, the most important of which is *estradiol,* influence the development of female physical sex characteristics and help regulate the menstrual cycle. Of the progestational compounds only *progesterone* is known to be physiologically important. It helps to regulate the menstrual cycle and to stimulate development of the uterine lining in preparation for pregnancy. The primary hormone products of the testes are **androgens** (AN-droh-jens). The most important androgen is *testosterone,* which influences both the development of male physical sex characteristics and sexual motivation. In both sexes the adrenal glands also secrete sex hormones, including small amounts of estrogen and greater quantities of androgen.

Sex of the Internal Reproductive Structures

By about 8 weeks after conception the sex hormones begin to play an important role in sex differentiation. The two duct systems shown in Figure 3.2a—the *Wolffian ducts* and the *Müllerian ducts*—begin to differentiate into those internal structures shown in Figure 3.2b. In a male fetus androgens secreted by the testes stimulate the Wolffian ducts to develop into the vas deferens, seminal vesicles, and ejaculatory ducts. Another substance released by the testes is known as *Müllerian-inhibiting substance* (MIS). MIS causes the Müllerian duct system to shrink and disappear in males (Bancroft, 2002; Lee et al., 1997). In the absence of androgens the fetus develops female structures (Clarnette et al., 1997). The Müllerian ducts develop into the fallopian tubes, uterus, and the inner third of the vagina, and the Wolffian duct system degenerates.

Sex of the External Genitals

The external genitals develop according to a similar pattern. Until the gonads begin releasing hormones during the sixth week, the external genital tissues of male and female fetuses are undifferentiated (Figure 3.3). These tissues will develop into either male or female external genitals, depending on the presence or absence of a testosterone product known as *dihydrotestosterone* (DHT). DHT stimulates the *labioscrotal swelling* to become the scrotum and the *genital tubercle* and *genital folds* to differentiate into the glans and shaft of the penis, respectively. The genital folds fuse around the urethra to form the shaft of the penis, and the two sides of the labioscrotal swelling fuse to form the scrotum; these fusions do not occur in females. In the absence of testosterone (and possibly under the influence of a substance(s) triggered by the *DSS* or femaleness gene), the genital tubercle becomes the clitoris, the genital folds become the inner vaginal lips (labia minora), and the two sides of the labioscrotal swelling differentiate into the outer vaginal lips (labia majora). By the twelfth week the differentiation process is complete: The penis and scrotum are recognizable in males; the clitoris and labia can be identified in females.

Because the external genitals, gonads, and some internal structures of males and females originate from the same embryonic tissues, it is not surprising that they have corresponding, or homologous, parts. Table 3.2 summarizes these female and male counterparts. We will look at the form and function of human sex organs in more detail in Chapters 4 and 5.

TABLE 3.2	Homologous Sex Organs
Female	**Male**
Clitoris	Glans of penis
Hood of clitoris	Foreskin of penis
Labia minora	Shaft of penis
Labia majora	Scrotal sac
Ovaries	Testes
Skene's ducts	Prostate gland
Bartholin's glands	Cowper's glands

Undifferentiated before sixth week

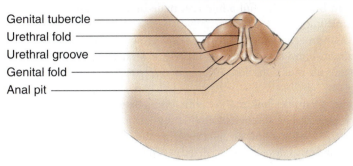

Genital tubercle
Urethral fold
Urethral groove
Genital fold
Anal pit

Seventh to eighth week

Male

Female

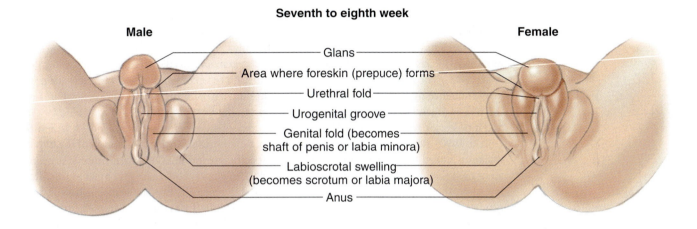

Glans
Area where foreskin (prepuce) forms
Urethral fold
Urogenital groove
Genital fold (becomes shaft of penis or labia minora)
Labioscrotal swelling (becomes scrotum or labia majora)
Anus

Fully developed by twelfth week

Male

Female

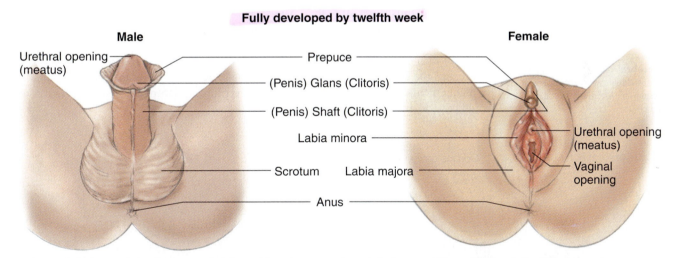

Urethral opening (meatus)
Prepuce
(Penis) Glans (Clitoris)
(Penis) Shaft (Clitoris)
Labia minora
Urethral opening (meatus)
Scrotum   Labia majora
Vaginal opening
Anus

▶ **Figure 3.3** Prenatal development of male and female external genitals from undifferentiated to fully differentiated.

Sex Differentiation of the Brain

Important structural and functional differences in the brains of human females and males are in part a result of prenatal sex-differentiation processes (Coe et al., 2002; Leibenluft, 1996; Reiner, 1997a, 1997b; Wilson, 2003). Many areas of the developing prenatal brain are significantly affected by circulating hormones (both testosterone and estrogen), which contribute to the development of these sex differences (Sanders et al., 2002; Segovia, 1999; Wilson, 2003).

InfoTrac Search Words

■ Sex differentiation

At the broadest level there is a significant sex difference in overall brain size. By age 6, when human brains reach full adult size, male brains are approximately 15% larger than female brains (Gibbons, 1991). Researchers believe that this size difference results from the influence of androgens, which stimulate faster growth in boys' brains (Wilson, 2003). Other specific human brain sex differences involve at least three major areas: the *hypothalamus* (hy-poh-THAL-uh-mus), the left and right *cerebral hemispheres,* and the *corpus callosum* (Figure 3.4).

A number of studies link marked differences between the male and female **hypothalamus** to the presence or absence of circulating testosterone during prenatal differentiation (Reiner, 1997a, 1997b; Zhou et al., 1995). In the absence of circulating testosterone the female hypothalamus develops specialized receptor cells that are sensitive to estrogen in the bloodstream. In fetal males the presence of testosterone prevents these cells from developing sensitivity to estrogen. This prenatal differentiation is critical for events that take place later. During puberty the estrogen-sensitive female hypothalamus directs the pituitary gland to release hormones in cyclic fashion, initiating the menstrual cycle. In males the estrogen-insensitive hypothalamus directs a relatively steady production of sex hormones.

Research has uncovered several intriguing findings pertaining to sex differences in one tiny hypothalamic region called the *bed nucleus of the stria teminalis* (BST) (Chung et al., 2002; Gu et al., 2003). The BST contains androgen and estrogen receptors and appears to exert a significant influence on human sex differences and human sexual functioning. One central area of the BST is much larger in heterosexual men than in heterosexual women (Zhou et al., 1995), and a posterior region of the BST is more than twice as large in men as in women (Allen & Gorski, 1990). Researchers have also reported sex differences in an anterior region of the hypothalamus, called the *preoptic area* (POA). One specific site in the POA is significantly larger in adult men than in adult women (Allen et al., 1989). Evidence from these and other studies has led some theorists to hypothesize that both sex differences in human sexual behavior and gender-biased behavior in children and adults result, in part, from a generalized sex-hormone-induced masculinization or feminization of the brain during prenatal development (Bancroft, 2002; Diamond & Sigmundson, 1997; Lerman et al., 2000).

Other key brain sex differences have been demonstrated in the function and structure of the cerebral hemispheres and the corpus callosum. The **cerebrum,** consisting of two **cerebral hemispheres** and the interconnection between them, is the largest part of the human brain. The two hemispheres, although not precisely identical, are almost mirror images of each other (see Figure 3.4b). Both cerebral hemispheres are covered by an outer layer, called the **cerebral cortex,** which is a major structure of the brain that is responsible for higher mental processes, such as memory, perception, and thinking. Without a cortex we would cease to exist as unique, functioning individuals.

Hypothalamus A small structure located in the central core of the brain that controls the pituitary gland and regulates motivated behavior and emotional expression.

Cerebrum The largest part of the brain, consisting of two cerebral hemispheres.

Cerebral hemispheres The two sides (right and left) of the cerebrum.

Cerebral cortex Outer layer of the cerebral hemispheres that is responsible for higher mental processes.

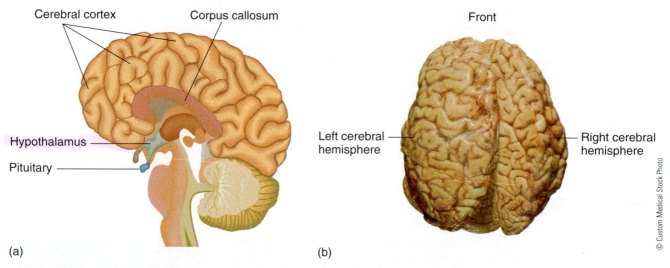

(a)

(b)

© Custom Medical Stock Photo

▶ **Figure 3.4** Parts of the brain: (a) cross section of the human brain showing the cerebral cortex, corpus callosum, hypothalamus, and pituitary gland; (b) top view showing the left and right cerebral hemispheres. Only the cerebral cortex covering of the two hemispheres is visible.

As Figure 3.4b illustrates, the two hemispheres are approximately symmetric, with areas on the left side roughly matched by areas on the right side. A variety of functions, such as speech, hearing, vision, and body movement, are localized in various regions of the cortical hemispheres. Furthermore, each hemisphere tends to be specialized for certain functions. For example, in most people verbal abilities, such as the expression and understanding of speech, are governed more by the left than by the right hemisphere. In contrast, the right hemisphere seems to be more specialized for spatial orientation, including the ability to recognize objects and shapes and to perceive relationships between them.

The term *lateralization of function* is used to describe the degree to which a particular function is controlled by one rather than both hemispheres. If, for example, a person's ability to deal with spatial tasks is controlled exclusively by the right hemisphere, we could say that this ability in this person is highly lateralized. In contrast, if both hemispheres contribute equally to this function, the person would be considered bilateral for spatial ability.

Even though each cerebral hemisphere tends to be specialized to handle different functions, the hemispheres are not entirely separate systems. Rather, our brain functions mostly as an integrated whole. The two hemispheres constantly communicate with each other through a broad band of millions of connecting nerve fibers, called the **corpus callosum** (Wilson, 2003) (see Figure 3.4a). In most people a complex function such as language is controlled primarily by regions in the left hemisphere, but interaction and communication with the right hemisphere also play a role. Furthermore, if a hemisphere that is primarily responsible for a particular function is damaged, the remaining intact hemisphere might take over the function (Ogden, 1989).

Corpus callosum The broad band of nerve fibers that connects the left and right cerebral hemispheres.

Keeping in mind this general overview of brain lateralization, we note that research has revealed some important sex differences in the structure of the cerebrum. First, studies of the fetal brains of both humans and rats have found that the cerebral cortex in the right hemisphere tends to be thicker in male brains than in female brains (de Lacoste et al., 1990; Diamond, 1991b). Perhaps of even greater significance is the finding that there are sex differences in the overall size of the corpus callosum in a number of animals, including humans (Coe et al., 2002; Holloway et al., 1993). Several studies have demonstrated that this structure is significantly thicker in women's brains than in men's brains (Allen et al., 1991; de Lacoste et al., 1990). This greater thickness of the corpus callosum allows for more intercommunication between the two hemispheres, which could account for why female brains are less lateralized for function and male brains have larger asymmetries in function (Kimura, 1992; Wilson, 2003).

Research has clearly demonstrated sex differences in the degree of hemispheric specialization for verbal and spatial cognitive skills. Women tend to use both brain hemispheres when performing verbal and spatial tasks, whereas men are more inclined to use only one hemisphere for each of these functions (Hiscock et al., 1999; Lambe, 1999; Leibenluft, 1996). The stronger communication network between the two halves of a female's brain might explain why women typically exhibit less impairment of brain function than men do after comparable neurological damage to one hemisphere (Majewska, 1996).

Currently, researchers and theorists are debating whether these structural differences in the cerebrums of men and women can explain sex differences in cognitive functioning. Females often score somewhat higher than males on tests of verbal skills, whereas the reverse is often true for spatial tests (Beller & Gafni, 2000; Gron et al., 2000; Halpern, 1997; Halpern & LaMay, 2000). Some researchers suggest that differences in hemispheric and corpus callosum structure indicate a possible biological basis for such sex differences in cognition (Geer & Manguno-Mire, 1997; Gur et al., 1995; Leibenluft, 1996). However, many theorists argue that reported sex differences in cognitive skills are largely due to psychosocial factors (Fausto-Sterling, 2000; Green et al., 1999). They cite substantial evidence that such differences have declined sharply in recent years (Carter, 2000; Fausto-Sterling, 2000; Hyde, 1996).

Two studies conducted by the American Association of University of Women (AAUW) provide striking indications of movement toward cognitive parity of the sexes. This organization reported in 1992 that girls start school demonstrating abilities in math and science equal to those shown by boys, but by the time they complete high school, girls have fallen considerably behind boys in these two cognitive areas (AAUW, 1992). A follow-up AAUW study conducted in 1998 found that the achievement gap between the sexes in science and math performance had largely disappeared, except at the highest levels of high school math, such as calculus (Carter, 2000). Of related interest are two studies which found that, when female subjects are provided with a few hours of training in spatial skills, they learn to perform as well as males on tests of these skills (Azar, 1997; Lawton & Morrin, 1999).

Some writers argue that biological explanations for sex differences in cognitive (and behavioral) traits, far from being based on solid scientific evidence, are merely unsubstantiated justification for supporting traditional gender roles. (See, for example, *Sexing the Body: Gender Politics and the Construction of Sexuality*, a book written by developmental geneticist Anne Fausto-Sterling [2000].)

In the past many feminists have been reluctant to acknowledge differences between the sexes, instead arguing that all but the most visibly obvious sex differences "are the products of culture, not genes, and could be erased by the appropriate legislation and child-rearing practices" (Ehrenreich, 1999, p. 58). However, a number of influential women writers are now both acknowledging and celebrating differences between the sexes, even those that may be biological in nature (Angier, 1999; Fisher, 1999; Hales, 1999). As data continue to roll in, we may soon be able to draw reliable conclusions about whether or not there is a biological basis for alleged sex differences in cognitive skills and behavioral traits.

Atypical Prenatal Differentiation

Thus far we have considered only typical prenatal differentiation. However, much of what is known about the impact of biological sex differentiation on the development of gender identities comes from studies of atypical differentiation.

We have seen that the differentiation of internal and external sex structures occurs under the influence of biological cues. When these signals deviate from normal patterns, the result can be ambiguous biological sex. A person with ambiguous or contradictory sex characteristics is sometimes called a *hermaphrodite* (her-MAF-roh-dite), a term derived from the mythical Greek deity Hermaphroditus, who was thought to possess biological attributes of both sexes. Today it is becoming more common to refer to these people as **intersexed** rather than hermaphroditic (Morris, 2003).

When discussing the condition of being intersexed, it is important to distinguish between **true hermaphrodites** and **pseudohermaphrodites.** True hermaphrodites, who have both ovarian and testicular tissue in their bodies, are exceedingly rare (Blackless et al., 2000; Parker, 1998). Their external genitals are often a mixture of female and male structures. Pseudohermaphrodites are much more common, occurring with an approximate frequency of 1 in every 2,000 births (Colapinto, 2000). These individuals also possess ambiguous internal and external reproductive anatomy, but unlike true hermaphrodites, pseudohermaphrodites are born with gonads that match their chromosomal sex. Studies of pseudohermaphrodites have helped to clarify the relative roles of biology and social learning in the formation of gender identity. This intersex condition can occur because of an atypical combination of sex chromosomes or as a result of prenatal hormonal irregularities. In this section we consider evidence from five varieties of pseudohermaphrodites, summarized in Table 3.3.

Sex-Chromosome Disorders

Errors occasionally occur at the first level of biological sex determination, and individuals are born with one or more extra sex chromosomes or missing one sex chromosome. More than 70 atypical conditions of the sex chromosomes have been identified (Nielson & Wohlert, 1991). These irregularities are associated with various physical, health, and behavioral effects. We consider two of the most widely researched of these conditions: Turner's syndrome and Klinefelter's syndrome.

Turner's Syndrome Turner's syndrome is a relatively rare condition characterized by the presence of only one sex chromosome, an X. This condition is estimated to occur in about 1 in every 2,000 live female births (Blackless et al., 2000; Gravholt et al., 1998). The number of chromosomes in the fertilized egg is 45 rather than the typical 46; the sex-chromosome combination is designated XO. People with this combination develop normal external

Intersexed A term applied to people who possess biological attributes of both sexes.

True hermaphrodites Exceedingly rare individuals who have both ovarian and testicular tissue in their bodies; their external genitals are often a mixture of male and female structures.

Pseudohermaphrodites Individuals whose gonads match their chromosomal sex but whose internal and external reproductive anatomy has a mixture of male and female structures or structures that are incompletely male or female.

InfoTrac Search Words
- Intersex(ed)
- Hermaphrodite

Turner's syndrome A relatively rare condition, characterized by the presence of one unmatched X chromosome (XO), in which affected individuals have normal female external genitals but their internal reproductive structures do not develop fully.

TABLE 3.3 Summary of Some Examples of Atypical Prenatal Sex Differentiation

Syndrome	Chromosomal Sex	Gonadal Sex	Reproductive Internal Structures	External Genitals	Fertility	Secondary Sex Characteristics	Gender Identity
Turner's syndrome	45, XO	Fibrous streaks of ovarian tissue	Uterus and fallopian tubes	Normal female	Sterile	Undeveloped; no breasts	Female
Klinefelter's syndrome	47, XXY	Small testes	Normal male	Undersized penis and testes	Sterile	Some feminization of secondary sex characteristics; may have breast development and rounded body contours.	Usually male, although higher than usual incidence of gender identity confusion.
Androgen insensitivity syndrome	46, XY	Undescended testes	Lacks a normal set of either male or female internal structures	Normal female genitals and a shallow vagina	Sterile	At puberty, breast development and other signs of normal female sexual maturation appear, but menstruation does not occur.	Female
Fetally androgenized females	46, XX	Ovaries	Normal female	Ambiguous (typically more male than female)	Fertile	Normal female (individuals with adrenal malfunction must be treated with cortisone to avoid masculinization).	Female, but significant level of dissatisfaction with female gender identity; oriented toward traditional male activities.
DHT-deficient males	46, XY	Undescended testes at birth; testes descend at puberty	Vas deferens, seminal vesicles, and ejaculatory ducts but no prostate; partially formed vagina	Ambiguous at birth (more female than male); at puberty, genitals are masculinized.	Sterile	Female before puberty; become masculinized at puberty.	Prepuberty gender identity difficult to ascertain (lack of data); approximately 90% have assumed traditional male gender role at puberty.

female genitals and consequently are classified as females. However, their internal reproductive structures do not develop fully—ovaries are absent or represented only by fibrous streaks of tissue. Females with Turner's syndrome do not develop breasts at puberty (unless given hormone treatment), do not menstruate, and are sterile. As adults, women with this condition tend to be unusually short (Gravholt et al., 1998).

Because the gonads are absent or poorly developed and because the hormones are consequently deficient, Turner's syndrome permits gender identity to be formed in the absence of gonadal and hormonal influences (the second and third levels of biological sex determination). Individuals with Turner's syndrome identify themselves as female, and as a group they are not distinguishable from biologically normal females in their interests and behavior (Kagan-Krieger, 1998). This characteristic strongly suggests that a feminine gender identity can be established in the absence of ovaries and their products.

Klinefelter's Syndrome A much more common sex-chromosome error in humans is **Klinefelter's syndrome.** This condition, estimated to occur once in about every 500 live male births (Kruse et al., 1998), results when an atypical ovum containing 22 autosomes and 2 X chromosomes is fertilized by a Y-chromosome-bearing sperm, creating an XXY individual. Despite the presence of both the XY combination characteristic of normal males and the XX pattern of normal females, individuals with Klinefelter's syndrome are anatomically male. This condition supports the view that the presence of a Y chromosome triggers the formation of male structures. However, the presence of an extra female sex chromosome impedes the continued development of these structures, and males with Klinefelter's syndrome typically are sterile and have undersized penises and testes. Furthermore, these individuals often have little or no interest in sexual activity (Money, 1968; Rabock et al., 1979). Presumably, this low sex drive is related, at least in part, to deficient production of hormones from the testes.

Males with Klinefelter's syndrome tend to be tall and are often somewhat feminized in their physical characteristics; they might exhibit breast development and rounded body contours. Testosterone treatments during adolescence and adulthood can enhance the development of male secondary sexual characteristics and can increase sexual interest (Kolodny et al., 1979). These individuals usually identify themselves as male; however, they not uncommonly manifest some degree of gender-identity confusion (Mandoki et al., 1991).

Disorders Affecting Prenatal Hormonal Processes

The ambiguous sex characteristics associated with pseudohermaphroditism can also result from genetically induced biological errors that produce variations in prenatal hormonal processes. We consider three examples of disorders caused by hormonal errors: androgen insensitivity syndrome, fetally androgenized females, and DHT-deficient males.

Androgen Insensitivity Syndrome A rare genetic defect causes a condition known as **androgen insensitivity syndrome (AIS),** also called *testicular feminization syndrome*. In AIS the body cells of a chromosomally normal male fetus are insensitive to androgens (Blackless et al., 2000; Hines et al., 2003). The result is feminization of prenatal development, so that the baby is born with normal-looking female genitals and a shallow vagina. Not surprisingly, babies with AIS are identified as female and reared accordingly. The anomaly is often discovered only in late adolescence, when a physician is consulted to find out why menstruation has not started. A study of 10 individuals with AIS revealed that all but one—a child reared in a dysfunctional environment—had acquired a clear female gender identity and behaved accordingly (Money & Masica, 1968).

A more recent investigation confirmed that individuals with AIS typically identify themselves as female and engage in traditional feminine behavior. In this study investigators compared psychological outcomes and gender development in a group of 22 women with AIS to a control group of 22 women without AIS. The women in the two groups were matched with respect to sex of rearing, age, and race. No significant differences were found between the women with AIS and the matched control subjects for any psychological outcome measures, including gender identity, sexual orientation, gender-role behaviors, and overall quality of life (Hines et al., 2003).

At first glance these observations seem to support the importance of social learning in shaping gender-identity formation. However, a case can also be made that these findings indicate the strong impact of biological factors in gender-identity formation. The lack of receptivity to androgen in individuals with AIS might prevent the masculinization of their brains necessary to develop a male identity, just as it results in failure to develop male genitals.

Fetally Androgenized Females In a second type of rare atypical sex differentiation, chromosomally normal females are prenatally masculinized by exposure to excessive androgens, either from a genetically induced malfunctioning of their own adrenal glands (*adrenogenital* *syndrome*) or from androgenlike substances ingested by their mothers during pregnancy (Blackless et al., 2000; Clarnette et al., 1997). (In the 1950s some pregnant women were given androgenlike drugs to reduce the risk of miscarriage.) As a result, such babies are born with masculine-looking external genitals: An enlarged clitoris can look like a penis, and fused labia can resemble a scrotum (Figure 3.5). These babies are usually identified as female by medical tests, treated with minor surgery or hormone therapy to eliminate their genital ambiguity, and reared as girls. Nevertheless, one noteworthy study reported that 20 out of 25 **fetally androgenized females** identified themselves as tomboys, engaged in traditionally male activities, and rejected behaviors and attitudes commonly associated with a female gender identity (Money & Ehrhardt, 1972).

Another investigation compared fetally androgenized women with their cousins or sisters who were unaffected by this syndrome. Researchers found that the fetally androgenized women had expressed more cross-gender role behavior and experienced less comfort with a feminine gender identity than did their nonandrogenized counterparts (Zucker et al., 1996). Furthermore, although most professionals have maintained that fetally androgenized females should be "assigned" a female gender identity, many of these individuals have problems with gender identity and gender roles. In fact, some eventually assume a male gender identity with commensurate male gender-role behavior (Meyer-Bahlburg et al., 1996; Slijper et al., 1998). These various studies of fetally androgenized females appear to reflect the significant impact of biological factors in gender-identity formation.

DHT-Deficient Males A third variety of atypical prenatal differentiation is caused by a genetic defect that prevents conversion of testosterone into the hormone dihydrotestosterone (DHT), which is essential for normal development of external genitals in a male fetus. In males with this disorder the testes do not descend before birth, the penis and scrotum remain undeveloped so that they resemble a clitoris and labia, and a shallow vagina is partially formed. Because their genitals look more female than male, **DHT-deficient males** are typically identified as female and reared as girls. However, because their testes are still functional, an amazing change occurs at puberty as accelerated testosterone production reverses the DHT deficiency. This causes the testes to descend and the clitorislike organs to enlarge into penises. In short, these DHT-deficient males undergo rapid transformation, from apparently female to male! How do they respond?

In one study a team of Cornell University researchers investigated 18 DHT-deficient males who had been reared as females in rural communities in the Dominican Republic (Imperato-McGinley et al., 1979).When their bodies changed at puberty, 16 of the subjects responded to this transformation by embracing traditional male gender roles mandated by their culture. These findings challenge the widely held belief that once gender identity is formed in the first few years of life, it cannot be changed without severe emotional trauma.

Some important questions have been raised about this study, however. First, the culture of this Caribbean nation is male oriented, which may have influenced these youths to switch gender identity more readily. Indeed, some of the subjects were exposed to extreme social pressure in the form of ridicule; locals called them *quevedoces*, which means "penis at 12," or *machihembra* ("first woman, then man"). Second, the research was conducted retrospectively, after the subjects were adults. Because people's recollections are not always reliable, it cannot be determined with certainty whether all these youths had experienced unambiguous female gender socialization as children.

These three examples of atypical sex differentiation appear to provide contradictory evidence. In the first example of males with AIS, chromosomal males insensitive to their own androgens acquired a female gender identity consistent with the way they were reared. In the second example, prenatally

Fetally androgenized female A chromosomally normal (XX) female who, as a result of excessive exposure to androgens during prenatal sex differentiation, develops external genitalia resembling those of a male.

DHT-deficient male A chromosomally normal (XY) male who develops external genitalia resembling those of a female as a result of a genetic defect that prevents the prenatal conversion of testosterone into dihydrotestosterone (DHT).

▶ **Figure 3.5** Masculinized external genitals of a fetally androgenized female baby.

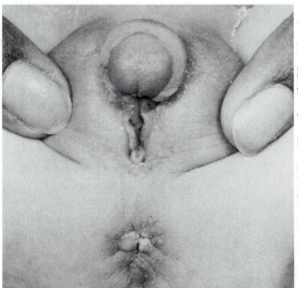

From Money, John, and Anke A. Ehrhardt. Man and Woman, Boy and Girl: Differentiation and Dimorphism of Gender Identity from Conception to Maturity, p. 115 (fig 6.2). © 1973. Reprinted with permission of the Johns Hopkins University Press.

masculinized chromosomal females behaved in a typically masculine manner even though they were reared female. Finally, in the third example chromosomal males whose biological maleness was not apparent until puberty were able to successfully switch their gender identity to male, despite early socialization as girls. Are these results at odds with one another, or is there a plausible explanation for their seeming inconsistencies?

? Critical Thinking Question

What research design would allow investigators to determine whether DHT-deficient males experience a gender-identity change in adolescence that is genuine rather than an artifact of cultural contamination? Would an investigation of this design be ethically responsible?

As described earlier, some data suggest that prenatal androgens influence sex differentiation of the brain just as they trigger masculinization of the sex structures. The same gene defect that prevents masculinization of the genitals of males with AIS might also block masculinization of their brains, thus influencing the development of a female gender identity. Similarly, the masculinizing influence of prenatal androgens on the brain might also account for the tomboyish behaviors of fetally androgenized females. But what about DHT-deficient males who appear to make a relatively smooth transition from a female to a male gender identity? Perhaps these boys' brains were prenatally programmed along male lines. Presumably, they had normal levels of androgens and, with the exception of genital development, were able to respond appropriately to these hormones at critical stages of prenatal development. We cannot state with certainty that prenatal androgens masculinize the brain. However, this interpretation offers a plausible explanation for how DHT-deficient individuals, already hormonally predisposed toward a male gender identity despite being identified as female, are able to change to a male identity at adolescence in response to changes in their bodies.

These fascinating studies underscore the complexity of biological sex determination. We have seen that many steps, each susceptible to errors, are involved in sex differentiation before birth. These investigations also raise a fundamental question: Just what makes us female or male? To further amplify this question, we now turn to the role of social-learning factors in influencing gender-identity formation *after* birth.

Social-Learning Influences on Gender Identity

Thus far we have considered only the biological factors involved in the determination of gender identity. Our sense of femaleness or maleness is not based exclusively on biological conditions, however. Social-learning theory suggests that our identification with either masculine or feminine roles or a combination thereof (androgyny) results primarily from the social and cultural models and influences that we are exposed to during our early development (Lips, 1997; Lorber, 1995).

Even before their baby is born, parents (and other adults involved in child rearing) have preconceived notions about how boys and girls differ. And through a multitude of subtle and not-so-subtle means, they communicate these ideas to their children (Witt, 1997). Gender-role expectations influence the environments in which children are raised, from the choice of room color to the selection of toys. They also influence the way parents think of their children. For example, in one study parents were asked to describe their newborn infants. Parents of boys described them as "strong," "active," and "robust," whereas parents of girls used words such as "soft" and "delicate"—even though all their babies were of similar size and muscle tone (Rubin et al., 1974). Not surprisingly, gender-role expectations also influence the way parents respond to their children: A boy might be encouraged to suppress his tears if he scrapes a knee and to show other "manly" qualities, such as independence and aggressiveness, whereas girls might be encouraged to be nurturing and cooperative (Hyde, 1996; Mosher & Tomkins, 1988).

By age 3 most children have developed a firm gender identity (DeLamater & Friedrich, 2002). From this point gender-identity reinforcement typically becomes somewhat self-perpetuating, as most children actively seek to behave in ways that they are taught are appropriate to their own sex (Bussey & Bandura, 1999; DeLamater & Friedrich, 2002). It is not unusual for little girls to go through a period of insisting that they wear fancy dresses or practice baking in the kitchen—sometimes to the dismay of their own mothers, who have themselves adopted more practical wardrobes and have abandoned the kitchen for a career! Likewise, young boys may develop a fascination for superheroes, policemen, and other cultural role models and try to adopt behaviors appropriate to these roles.

cathy®   by Cathy Guisewite

Anthropological studies of other cultures also lend support to the social-learning interpretation of gender-identity formation. In several societies the differences between males and females that we often assume to be innate are simply not evident. In fact, Margaret Mead's classic book *Sex and Temperament in Three Primitive Societies* (1963) reveals that other societies may have different views about what is considered feminine or masculine. In this widely quoted report of her fieldwork in New Guinea, Mead discusses two societies that minimize differences between the sexes. She notes that among the Mundugumor both sexes exhibit aggressive, insensitive, uncooperative, and nonnurturing behaviors that would be considered masculine by our society's norms. In contrast, among the Arapesh both males and females exhibit gentleness, sensitivity, cooperation, nurturing, and nonaggressive behaviors that would be judged feminine in our society. And, as we saw in this chapter's opening paragraphs, among the Tchambuli masculine and feminine gender roles

Although parents are becoming more sensitive to the kinds of toys children play with, many still choose different toys and play activities for boys and girls.

are actually reversed from what Americans view as typical. Because there is no evidence that people in these societies are biologically different from Americans, their often diametrically different interpretations of what is masculine and what is feminine seem to result from different processes of social learning.

Finally, proponents of the social-learning interpretation of gender-identity formation refer to various studies of intersexed children born with ambiguous external genitals who are assigned a particular sex and reared accordingly. Much of the early work in this area was performed at Johns Hopkins University Hospital by a team headed by John Money. When these treatment approaches were being implemented, Money and his colleagues believed that a person is psychosexually neutral or undifferentiated at birth and that social-learning experiences are the essential determinants of gender identity and gender-role behavior (Money, 1961, 1963; Money & Ehrhardt, 1972). Therefore little attention was paid to matching external genitals with sex chromosomes. Rather, because the guiding principle was how natural the genitals could be made to look, many of these intersexed infants were assigned to the female sex, because surgical reconstruction of ambiguous genitalia to those of a female form is mechanically easier and aesthetically and functionally superior to constructing a penis (Diamond & Sigmundson, 1997; Nussbaum, 2000).

Money and his colleagues followed these surgically altered children over a period of years and reported that in most cases children whose assigned sex did not match their chromosomal sex developed a gender identity consistent with the manner in which they were reared (Money, 1965; Money & Ehrhardt, 1972). Additional evidence supporting these earlier findings was recently published. Researchers surveyed 39 adult participants who had undergone surgical alteration as infants at Johns Hopkins. All of these individuals are genetic males who were born with a micropenis with a urethral opening located on its underside. Some of the individuals were altered to be anatomical females and others to be anatomical males, with gender assigned accordingly. Most of these respondents (78% of women and 76% of men) reported being satisfied with the gender chosen for them and with their body image, sexual functioning, and sexual orientation. However, 2 of the 39 switched gender as adults (Migeon et al., 2002).

In recent years research has revealed that at least some intersexed children may not be as psychosexually neutral at birth as originally believed. Long-term follow-ups of several intersexed children treated under the Johns Hopkins protocol revealed that some of these individuals have had serious problems adjusting to the gender assigned to them (Diamond, 1997; Diamond & Sigmundson, 1997). One especially compelling account involved two identical twin boys, one of whom experienced a circumcision accident that destroyed most of his penile tissue. Because no amount of plastic surgery could adequately reconstruct the severely damaged penis, it was recommended that the child be raised as a female and receive appropriate sex-change surgery. A few months later the parents decided to begin raising him as a girl. Shortly thereafter, castration and initial genital surgery were performed to facilitate feminization. Further surgery to fashion a full vagina was to wait until the child was older. Follow-up analyses of these twins during their early childhood years revealed that, despite possessing identical genetic materials, they responded to their separate social-learning experiences by developing opposite gender identities. Furthermore, the child reassigned to the female gender was described as developing into a normally functioning girl child.

If the story of these twins ended here, we would have strong evidence of the dominant role of social learning in gender-identity formation. However, in 1979 the psychiatrist following the twins revealed that the assigned female member of the pair was experiencing considerable difficulty in making her adjustment as a female (Williams & Smith, 1979). A more recent follow-up (Diamond & Sigmundson, 1997) found that, beginning at age 14, still unaware of the XY chromosome status and against the recommendations of family and treating clinicians, this person decided to no longer live as a female. This adamant rejection of living as a female, together with a much improved emotional state when living as a male, convinced therapists of the appropriateness of sexual reassignment. His postsurgical adjustment was excellent and, aided by testosterone treatments, he "emerged" as an attractive young man. At the age of 25 he married a woman, adopted her children, and comfortably assumed his role as father and husband. This remarkable story is told in a book written by John Colapinto (2000), titled *As Nature Made Him: The Boy Who Was Raised as a Girl.*

This case study illustrates the critical importance of long-term longitudinal studies of children who have been sex reassigned. The early childhood phase of the follow-up of this child was widely reported in the press and the academic and medical community as providing clear evidence that gender identity is psychologically neutral at birth, as yet unwritten upon by social-learning experiences. Now, after many years during which this viewpoint remained predominant, we find out how wrong this interpretation may be. Even John Money, formerly a major proponent of this perspective, no longer holds such an extreme view (see Money, 1994b).

Another recent study raised questions about the common practice of surgically assigning a sex to a child with ambiguous external genitals. This investigation reported on the development of 27 children born without penises (a condition known as *cloacal exstrophy*) but who were otherwise males with normal testes, chromosomes, and hormones. Twenty-five of the 27 were sex reassigned shortly after birth, by means of castration, and their parents raised them as females. All 25 exhibited play activities typical of males, and 14 eventually declared themselves boys. The two boys who were not reassigned and thus were raised as boys seemed to be better adjusted than their reassigned counterparts. These results led William Reiner, lead researcher on this investigation, to conclude that "with time and age, children may well know what their gender is, regardless of any and all information and child rearing to the contrary" (Reiner, 2000, p. 1).

Several prominent researchers now argue that prevailing assumptions about gender neutrality at birth and the efficacy of sex reassignment of children may be wrong. In fact, evidence is increasing that, despite great care in rearing chromosomal males sex reassigned as females, some—perhaps many—of them manifest strong male tendencies in their developmental years and may even change their assigned sex after they reach puberty (Colapinto, 2000; Diamond & Sigmundson, 1997; Reiner, 1997, 2000). Concerns about the benefits and ethics of standard treatment practices used with intersexed individuals have instigated a lively debate among intersexed individuals, researchers, and practitioners, described in the boxed discussion "Treatment Strategies for Intersexed People: Debate and Controversy."

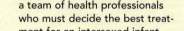

? Critical Thinking Question

Assume that you are the leader of a team of health professionals who must decide the best treatment for an intersexed infant. Would you assign a gender identity and perform the surgical and/or hormonal treatments consistent with the assigned gender? If so, what gender would you select? Why? If you would elect not to assign a gender, what kind of follow-up or management strategy would you suggest during the child's developmental years?

The Interactional Model

Scientists have argued for decades about the relative importance of nature (biological determinants) versus nurture (social learning and the environment) in shaping human development. Today it seems clear that gender identity is a product of both biological factors and social learning. The evidence is simply too overwhelming to conclude that normal infants are psychosexually neutral at birth. We have seen that human infants possess a complex and yet to be fully understood biological substrate that predisposes them to interact with their social environment in either a masculine or a feminine mode. However, few contemporary researchers believe that human gender identity has an exclusively biological basis. There is simply too much evidence supporting the important role of life experiences in shaping the way we think about ourselves—not only as masculine or feminine but in all aspects of how we relate to those around us. Consequently, most theorists and researchers support an *interactional model,* which acknowledges both biology and experience in the development of gender identity (Golombok & Fivush, 1995). Hopefully, as we acquire more data from further research, especially from long-term longitudinal analyses, we will gain a clearer understanding of the relative impact of these two powerful forces on gender-identity formation and gender-role behavior.

? How About You?

Do you think that your gender identity was biologically wired at birth or socialized by your early childhood experiences?

▶ Transsexualism and Transgenderism

We have learned that gender-identity formation is a complex process influenced by many factors, with congruity between biological sex and gender identity by no means guaranteed. In recent years we have become increasingly aware of the rich diversity in gender identities and roles. Many people fall somewhere within a range of variant gender identities. The community of gender-variant people, composed of *transsexual* and *transgendered*

People born with ambiguous external genitals are often viewed as biological accidents that need to be fixed. John Money and his colleagues at Johns Hopkins Medical School were the primary architects of a treatment protocol for intersexed individuals that became standard practice by the early 1960s and persists to the present. According to this protocol, a team of professionals, in consultation with the parents, choose which gender to assign an intersexed child. To reduce the possibility of future adjustment problems or gender confusion, the physicians usually provide surgical and/or hormonal treatments. Money and his associates reported that most intersexed individuals treated according to this protocol develop into relatively well-adjusted people with gender identities consistent with the manner in which they were reared (Money, 1965; Money and Ehrhardt, 1972).

In recent years serious questions have emerged about both the long-term benefits and the ethical appropriateness of this standard treatment protocol (Dreger, 1998, 2003; Fausto-Sterling, 2000; Kessler, 1998). Milton Diamond, an outspoken critic of John Money's treatment strategies, has conducted long-term follow-ups of a number of intersexed individuals treated under this standard protocol. His research has revealed that some of these individuals experience significant adjustment problems that they attribute to the biosocial "management" of their intersexed conditions (Diamond, 1997, 1998; Diamond & Sigmundson, 1997).

The research of Diamond and others, and the testimony of people who have been harmed by treatment they have received via the standard protocol, has triggered an intense debate among intersexed people, researchers, and health care professionals about what constitutes proper treatment of intersexed infants. Many specialists still support Money's protocol and argue that intersexed infants should be unambiguously assigned a gender at the earliest possible age, certainly before the emergence of gender identity in the second year of life. This position endorses surgical and/or hormonal intervention to minimize gender confusion. An alternative viewpoint, championed by Diamond and others, suggests a threefold approach to treating intersexed peo-

Michael Geissinger Photography

Cheryl Chase and a number of her intersexed colleagues have attempted to halt the traditional practice of performing surgery on intersexed infants unable to provide informed consent.

individuals, has acquired considerable voice in both the professional literature and the popular media.

A **transsexual** is a person whose gender identity is opposite to his or her biological sex (Cole et al., 1997). Such people feel trapped in a body of the "wrong" sex, a condition known as **gender dysphoria.** Thus an anatomically male transsexual feels that *she* is a woman who, by some quirk of fate, has been provided with male genitals but who wishes to be socially identified as female. Many transsexuals undergo sex-reassignment procedures involving extensive screening, hormone therapy, and genital-altering surgery. However, not all gender-dysphoric people want complete sex reassignment. Instead, they may want only the physical body, gender role, or sexuality of the other sex. Although many gender-dysphoric individuals want to accomplish all three of these aims, as is the case with most transsexuals, some are content to take on only one or two aspects of the other sex (Carroll, 1999). Furthermore, some transgendered people who manifest variant gender-role behaviors experience little or no gender dysphoria.

Transsexual A person whose gender identity is opposite to his or her biological sex.

Gender dysphoria Unhappiness with one's biological sex or gender role.

ple. First, health care professionals should make an informed best guess about the intersexed infant's eventual gender identity and then counsel parents to rear the child in this identity. Second, genital-altering surgeries (which later might need to be reversed) should be avoided during the early years of development. And third, quality counseling and accurate information should be provided to both the child and his or her parents during the developmental years to ensure that the child is eventually able to make an informed decision about any additional treatment steps, such as surgery and/or hormone treatments.

Both Diamond's treatment strategy and the standard protocol raise important questions. Does genital-altering surgery performed on mere babies violate their rights as humans to give informed consent? Would intersexed children left with ambiguous genitals have problems functioning in schools or other settings where their condition might become known to others? Might society eventually evolve beyond the two-sex model and embrace the legitimacy of a third intersexed condition located somewhere on the spectrum between male and female?

A number of case studies have reported instances of people who comfortably adjusted to their untreated intersexed condition (Fausto-Sterling, 1993, 2000; Laurent, 1995). Furthermore, in recent years a number of intersexed people treated under the standard protocol have expressed strong resentment over being subjected to medical intervention as infants (Angier, 1996; Goodrum, 2000; Morris, 2003). In fact, "many intersexed people, now adults, are advocating for an end to the way intersexed children are seen as 'damaged goods' needing to be fixed" (Goodrum, 2000, p. 2). It is not uncommon for intersexed adults to report feeling violated by the practice of "medical display," in which, as presurgical children, they were repeatedly stripped naked and put on display for physicians, nurses, students, and others who prodded, probed, and perhaps laughed as well. "Children who experience this get the distinct sense that there is something terribly wrong with who they are and are deeply traumatized" (Koyama, quoted in Morris, 2003, p. 22).

Intersex activists, who have established many advocacy organizations, such as Bodies Like Ourselves and the Intersex Society of North America (ISNA), argue that intersexed people are cases of genital variability, not genital abnormality. The ISNA advocates a noninterventionist, child-centered approach in which an intersexed child is not subjected to genital-altering surgery; he or she may choose such procedures later in life (Melby, 2002a; Nussbaum, 2000). Furthermore, intersex activists and many medical ethicists believe that violations of medical ethics occur (1) when genital-altering surgery is performed on babies unable to provide informed consent, (2) when intersexed people are denied the right to remain intersexed people with their own identity, and (3) when parents are encouraged to withhold information from their children about their intersex condition.

Intersex activists have also strongly denounced one aspect of intersex treatment that previously was largely ignored. Genital-altering surgery can impair an individual's capacity for sexual pleasure (Chase, 2003; Creighton & Liao, 2004; Kessler, 1998; Morris, 2003). For example, surgical reduction of an enlarged clitoris in a fetally androgenized female can result in reduced erotic sensation and thus can interfere with genital pleasure and orgasmic capacity (Morris, 2003). One recent study of 28 intersexed adults living as females found that 18 women who had undergone clitoral surgery had higher rates of sexual difficulties (such as inability to achieve orgasm) than the 10 women in the study who had not had clitoral surgery (Minto et al., 2003).

There are currently more questions than answers about the most appropriate treatment strategy for intersexed infants. This uncertainty is due in large part to a scarcity of long-term outcome studies on intersexed individuals (Lerman et al., 2000). We hope that time and research will eventually resolve this dilemma.

The term **transgendered** is generally applied to individuals whose appearance and behaviors do not conform to the gender roles ascribed by society for people of a particular sex. In other words, transgendered people "to varying degrees, 'transgress' cultural norms as to what a man or woman 'should be'" (Goodrum, 2000, p. 1). These "transgressions" often involve cross-dressing either occasionally or full-time. Until recently, nontranssexual cross-dressers were labeled *transvestites*. This term is now generally applied only to people who cross-dress to achieve sexual arousal (see the discussion of *transvestic fetishism* in Chapter 18). Transgendered people who cross-dress typically do so to obtain psychosocial rather than sexual gratification.

Some intersexed people, who were born exhibiting a mixture of male and female external genitals, also consider themselves members of the transgendered community. This group can include intersexed individuals who have undergone surgical and/or hormonal treatments to establish congruence between their anatomical sex structures and their gender identity (Goodrum, 2000).

Transgendered A term applied to people whose appearance and/or behaviors do not conform to traditional gender roles.

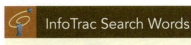

InfoTrac Search Words

■ Transsexual
■ Transgender

Clearly, not everyone who refrains from wholehearted embodiment of culturally defined gender roles is included in the transgendered community. Today, many people are embracing more *androgynous* lifestyles, blending aspects of masculinity and femininity into their personalities and behaviors. Some writers place androgynous males or females in a continuum of transgenderism. However, others, including ourselves, are less inclined to equate androgyny with transgenderism. (We discuss androgyny at the end of this chapter.)

The primary difference between a transsexual and a transgenderist is that the transgenderist does not want to change his or her physical body to create a better fit with personal and/or societal role expectations. Transsexuals often undergo major surgeries to make their physical bodies congruent with their gender identity. In contrast, most transgendered people have no wish to undergo anatomical alterations but do occasionally or frequently dress like and take on the mannerisms of the other sex. Some transgenderists live full-time manifesting gender-role behaviors opposite to those ascribed by society to someone of their biological sex (Bolin, 1997).

Variant Gender Identity and Sexual Orientation

Many people are confused about the difference between gender identity (especially variant gender identity) and sexual orientation. Simply stated, gender identity is who we are—our own subjective sense of being male, female, or some combination of the two. Sexual orientation refers to which of the sexes we are emotionally and sexually attracted to (see Chapter 10).

Most transsexuals, before sex reassignment, are attracted to people who match them anatomically but not in gender identity. Thus a transsexual with a female gender identity, feeling trapped in a man's body (and probably identified as a male by society), is likely to be attracted to men. In other words, she has a heterosexual orientation based on her own self-identification as female. If she acts on her sexual desires before undergoing sex reassignment, she may be falsely labeled as homosexual. In terms of postsurgical sexual orientation almost all female-to-male transsexuals desire female sexual partners, whereas male-to-female transsexuals can be sexually oriented to either sex, with most preferring male sex partners (Zhou et al., 1995).

Although transsexuals are predominantly heterosexual, the transgendered community has a more eclectic composition of gay men, lesbians, bisexuals, and heterosexuals (Goodrum, 2000).

Are Transsexualism and Transgenderism Gender-Identity Disorders?

The fourth edition of the *Diagnostic and Statistical Manual of Mental Disorders,* text revision version (DSM-IV-TR), contains the most widely used system for classifying psychological disorders (American Psychiatric Association, 2000). According to this classification scheme, a person must meet four distinct criteria to be diagnosed as having a **gender-identity disorder:** He or she must (1) have a strong and persistent cross-gender identification, (2) demonstrate persistent discomfort with his or her sex or a sense of inappropriateness in the gender role of that sex, (3) have a disturbance that is not concurrent with a physical intersex condition, and (4) manifest a disturbance that causes clinically significant distress or impairment in social, occupational, or other important areas of functioning. North American data indicate that boys are much more likely than girls to be referred for assessment and/or treatment of gender-identity disorders (Cohen-Kettenis et al., 2003). However, in one major study referred girls typically manifested more extreme cross-gender behavior than did referred boys, a finding that suggests a higher threshold for referral for girls than boys (Zucker et al., 1997).

Before the guidelines for diagnosing a gender-identity disorder were published, almost all transsexuals and many transgendered people were assumed to be afflicted with pathological gender-identity disorders. However, an emerging awareness of the dynamics of variant gender identities and roles has resulted in an increased tendency among professionals and laypersons to challenge the traditional male–female polarization of gender. Even

Gender-identity disorder A disorder characterized by a cross-gender identification that produces persistent discomfort with one's sex and impaired functioning.

Respecting a Transsexual or Transgendered Person Through Communication

Alexander John Goodrum (2000) recently wrote an informative article on transsexualism and transgenderism in which he discussed how people should communicate or interact with individuals with variant gender identities and/or behaviors. We summarize his suggestions as follows:

- It is important to refer to transsexual or transgendered individuals appropriately. If someone identifies himself as male, refer to him as *he;* if she identifies herself as female, refer to her as *she.* If you are not sure, it is all right to ask what this person prefers or expects. Once you know, try to be consistent. If you occasionally forget and use the wrong pronoun, make the correction. Most transsexual or transgendered people will understand slipups and appreciate your efforts.

- Never "out" someone by telling others without permission that he or she is transsexual or transgendered. Furthermore, do not assume that other people know about a person's variant gender identity. Many transgendered and transsexual individuals pass very well, and the only way others would know about their variant gender status would be by being told. Clearly, the decision whether or not to communicate gender status should be made only by the individual, and failure to honor this right would be highly disrespectful.

- Common sense and good taste mandate that we never ask transsexual or transgendered people what their genital anatomy looks like and/or how they relate sexually to others.

- Finally, make no assumptions about whether a person has a homosexual, bisexual, or heterosexual orientation. A person who believes that it is appropriate to reveal information about sexual orientation may elect to communicate this to you.

though most transsexual people and perhaps some transgendered individuals *do* meet the criteria for a gender-identity disorder, it is now becoming more acceptable to live in a permanent nonsurgically altered state without pressure to seek a "cure" (Denny, 1997). However, sex reassignment remains a viable option for many transsexuals. In the next section we examine transsexuals in more depth.

Transsexualism: Etiology, Sex-Reassignment Procedures, and Outcomes

In the 1960s and early 1970s, when medical procedures for altering sex were first being developed in the United States, approximately three out of every four people requesting a sex change were biological males who wished to be females (Green, 1974). Although most health professionals believe that males seeking sex reassignment still outnumber females, there is evidence that the ratio has narrowed appreciably in recent years (Landen et al., 1998).

A vast accumulation of clinical literature has focused on the characteristics, causes (etiology), and treatment of transsexualism. Certain factors are well established. We know that most transsexuals are biologically normal individuals with healthy sex organs, intact internal reproductive structures, and the proper complement of XX or XY chromosomes. Furthermore, transsexualism is usually an isolated condition and not part of any general psychopathology, such as schizophrenia or major depression (Cohen-Kettenis & Gooren, 1999). One study found that less than 10% of a sample of 137 transsexuals had symptoms associated with mental illness (Cole et al., 1997). What is less understood is why these individuals reject their anatomies.

Many transsexuals develop a sense of being at odds with their genital anatomy in early childhood; some recall identifying strongly with characteristics of the other sex as early as 5, 6, or 7 years of age. In some cases these children's discomfort is partially relieved by imagining themselves to be members of the other sex, but many of them eventually progress beyond mere imagining to actual cross-dressing. Less commonly, a strong identity with the other sex may not emerge until adolescence or adulthood.

At present, there is no clear understanding of the etiology of transsexualism. Considerable controversy also exists regarding the most appropriate clinical strategies for dealing with this condition. Keeping this continued debate in mind, we will summarize our current tenuous state of knowledge about this highly unusual variant gender identity.

Etiology

Many theories have tried to explain transsexualism, but current evidence is inconclusive (Cole et al., 2000; Money, 1994a). Some writers maintain that biological factors play a decisive role. One theory suggests that prenatal exposure to inappropriate amounts of hormones of the other sex causes improper brain differentiation (Dessens et al., 1999; Pauly, 1974; Zhou et al., 1995). There is also some evidence that in transsexuals sexual differentiation of the brain and the genitals occurs in a discordant fashion (Krujiver et al., 2000). It has also been suggested that transsexualism can be induced by abnormal levels of adult sex hormones. However, this explanation is contradicted by numerous indications that sex hormone levels are normal in adult transsexuals (Meyer et al., 1986; Zhou et al., 1995).

Another theory, which has some supporting evidence, holds that social-learning experiences contribute significantly to the development of transsexualism. A child may be exposed to a variety of conditioning experiences that support behaving in a manner traditionally attributed to the other sex (Bradley & Zucker, 1997; Cohen-Kettenis & Gooren, 1999). The child may develop a close identifying relationship with the parent of the other sex, and this identification may be strongly reinforced by the adult's reaction. The little boy may play at being a girl, and the girl may be "Daddy's little man." Such cross-gender behaviors may be so exclusively rewarded that it may be difficult or impossible for the individual to develop the appropriate gender identity.

Difficult as it is to determine the causes of transsexualism, it is perhaps even more challenging to resolve the problem of reversed gender identity. As discussed earlier, most transsexuals follow a heterosexual script and prefer to have sexual relations with a member of the other sex. The fact that the "other sex" happens to have the same genitals as they do makes it difficult to find a partner. Most transsexuals want to interact with heterosexuals: A male transsexual wants to be desired as a woman by a heterosexual man, and most transsexual women are not satisfied with a lesbian relationship. These romantic and sexual needs are often hard to meet. Heterosexuals and homosexuals can generally find willing sex partners who match their orientations, but transsexuals' most desired partners are likely to reject them for making such advances.

Options for Transsexuals

The mental health field has traditionally considered only two possible solutions for overcoming the gender dysphoria of transsexuals: changing gender identity to match the physical body or changing the body to match gender identity (Carroll, 1999). There are, however, other options, and recent clinical evidence has indicated that some preoperative transsexuals have discovered that it may be psychologically sufficient to express themselves through such activities as gender blending or cross-dressing (Carroll, 1999). Nevertheless, in most cases, psychotherapy, without accompanying biological alterations, has generally been inadequate to help transsexuals adjust to their bodies and gender identities. For such individuals the best course of action might be to change their bodies to match their minds, through surgical and hormonal alteration of genital anatomy and body physiology. However, the process of medical alteration is not a simple solution, because it is both time consuming and costly.

One leading authority on the treatment of transsexualism suggested that all possible alternatives, including psychotherapy, be explored before considering irreversible sex-change surgery (Pauly, 1990). Certainly, not every adult with a gender-identity disorder requires psychotherapy to proceed with sex-reassignment procedures. However, the Harry Benjamin International Gender Dysphoria Association (HBIGDA) recently published revised standards of care for gender-identity disorders that require psychotherapy in certain situations (S. Levine, 1999). Psychotherapy can provide education about and opportunities to discuss a range of options not previously considered by a transsexual person.

Sex-Reassignment Procedures

The initial step of a sex change involves extensive screening interviews, during which the person's motivations for undergoing the change are thoroughly evaluated. Individuals with real conflicts and confusion about their gender identity are not considered for surgical alteration. Individuals with an apparently genuine incongruence between their gender identity and biological sex are then instructed to adopt a lifestyle consistent with their gender identity (i.e., dress style and behavior patterns). If, after several months to a year or longer, it appears that the individual has successfully adjusted to that lifestyle, the next step is hormone therapy, a process designed to accentuate latent traits of the desired sex. Thus males wishing to be females are given drugs that inhibit testosterone production together with doses of estrogen that induce some breast growth, soften the skin, reduce facial and body hair, and help to feminize body contours. Muscle strength also diminishes, as does sexual interest, but there is no alteration of vocal pitch. Women who want to become men are treated with testosterone, which helps to increase growth of body and facial hair and produces a deepening of the voice and a slight reduction in breast size. Testosterone also suppresses menstruation. Most health professionals who provide sex-change procedures require that a candidate live for at least 1 year as a member of the other sex, while undergoing hormone therapy, before surgery. At any time during this phase the process can be successfully reversed, although few transsexuals choose this option.

The final step of a sex change is surgery (Figure 3.6). Surgical procedures are most effective for men wishing to be women. The scrotum and penis are removed, and a vagina is created through reconstruction of pelvic tissue (see Figure 3.6a). During this surgical procedure, great care is taken to maintain the sensory nerves that serve the skin of the penis, and this sensitive skin tissue is relocated to the inside of the newly fashioned vagina. Intercourse is possible, although use of a lubricant may be necessary, and many male-to-female transsexuals report postsurgical capacity to experience sexual arousal and orgasm (Lief & Hubschman, 1993; Schroder & Carroll, 1999). Hormone treatments can produce sufficient breast development, but some individuals also receive implants. Body and facial hair, which were reduced by hormone treatments, can be further removed by electrolysis. Finally, if desired, an additional surgical procedure can be performed to raise the pitch of the voice in male-to-female transsexuals (Brown et al., 2000).

A biological female who desires to be male generally has her breasts, uterus, and ovaries surgically removed and her vagina sealed off. The process of constructing a penis is much more difficult than that of fashioning a vagina. In general, the penis is fashioned from abdominal skin or from tissue from the labia and perineum (see Figure 3.6b). This constructed organ is not capable of natural erection in response to sexual arousal. However,

▶ **Figure 3.6** The genitals following sex-change surgery: (a) Male-to-female sex-change surgery is generally more effective than (b) female-to-male sex-change surgery.

(a)

Courtesy of Dr. Daniel Greenwald

(b)

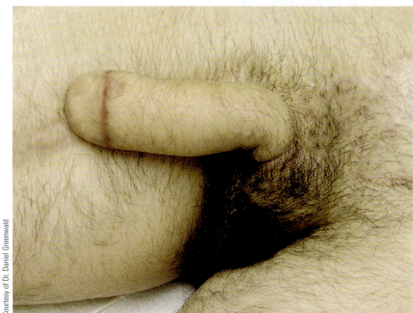

Courtesy of Dr. Daniel Greenwald

several artificial devices are available for providing a rigid penis for purposes of intercourse. One involves fashioning a small, hollow skin tube on the underside of the penile shaft into which a rigid silicone rod can be inserted. Another alternative is to use an implanted inflatable device, which will be described in Chapter 16. If erotically sensitive tissue from the clitoris is left embedded at the base of the surgically constructed penis, erotic feelings and orgasm are sometimes possible. In fact, one study of 25 surgically altered transsexuals found that, although 90% of the total group reported satisfaction with surgical results and with postoperative sexual activity, orgasmic capacity actually increased in the female-to-male group, whereas it declined somewhat in the male-to-female subjects (Lief & Hubschman, 1993).

Outcomes of Sex Reassignment

Numerous studies of the psychosocial outcome of gender reassignment provide a basis for optimism about the success of sex-reassignment procedures. The single most consistent finding of these investigations is that most people who have undergone these procedures experience significant improvement in their overall adjustment to life (Blanchard et al., 1985; Campo et al., 2003; Carroll, 1999; Pfafflin, 1992; Rakic et al., 1996).

▶ Gender Roles

We have seen that social learning is an important influence on the formation of gender identity early in life, so that even by the age of 2 or 3 years, most children have no doubt about whether they are boys or girls. This influence continues throughout our lives, because we are influenced by *gender roles* (or *sex roles*)—that is, behaviors that are considered appropriate and normal for men and women in a society.

The ascribing of gender roles leads naturally to certain assumptions about how people will behave. For example, men in North American society have traditionally been expected to be independent and aggressive, whereas women were supposed to be dependent and submissive. Once these expectations are widely accepted, they may begin to function as stereotypes. A **stereotype** is a generalized notion of what a person is like based only on that person's sex, race, religion, ethnic background, or similar category. Stereotypes do not take individuality into account.

Many common gender-based stereotypes are widely accepted in our society. Some of the prevailing notions about men maintain that they are aggressive (or at least assertive), logical, unemotional, independent, dominant, competitive, objective, athletic, active, and above all, competent. Conversely, women are frequently viewed as nonassertive, illogical, emotional, subordinate, warm, and nurturing.

Not all people hold these gender-role stereotypes, and in recent years we have seen a trend away from strict adherence to gender-typed behavior. This emerging digression from rigid gender-role stereotypes is perhaps most notable in a shift away from traditional markers of adolescent femininity. Passivity, acquiescence, and docility are increasingly less representative as primary standards for typical or normative girlhood, and many adolescent females are learning that independence, self-determination, and assertiveness are desirable traits of a young woman (Adams & Bettis, 2003). Research also suggests that women may be less entrenched than men in rigid gender-role stereotypes and are perhaps more inclined to embrace positions of equality with men (Larsen & Long, 1988). However, many men also feel constrained by traditional roles.

Despite the potentially limiting impact of stereotypical gender roles on our lives, they still pervade our society (Hyde, 1996; Rider, 2000). Indeed, many individuals are comfortable fulfilling a traditional masculine or feminine role, and we do not wish to demean or question the validity of their lifestyles. Rather, we are concerned with finding out why gender roles are so prevalent in society. We turn to this question next.

How Do We Learn Gender Roles?

You have probably heard the argument that behavioral differences between men and women are biologically determined, at least to some degree. Men cannot bear or nurse children. Likewise, biological differences in hormones, muscle mass, and brain structure and function

Stereotype A generalized notion of what a person is like based only on that person's sex, race, religion, ethnic background, or similar criterion.

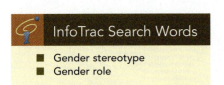

InfoTrac Search Words

- Gender stereotype
- Gender role

can influence some aspects of behavior. However, most theorists explain gender roles as largely a product of **socialization**—that is, the process by which individuals learn, and adopt, society's expectations for behavior. In the following "Sexuality and Diversity" discussion we see how cultural and ethnic groups within a society have varying expectations of men's and women's behavior.

Socialization The process by which our society conveys behavioral expectations to the individual.

Sexuality and Diversity

Ethnic Variations in Gender Roles

Throughout this textbook we have focused primarily on gender assumptions that are prevalent among the traditional mainstream—white Americans of European origin. Here we look briefly at gender roles among three different American ethnic groups: Hispanic Americans, African Americans, and Asian Americans.

Traditional Hispanic American gender roles are epitomized by the cultural stereotypes of *marianismo* and *machismo*. Marianismo derives from the Roman Catholic notion that women should be pure and self-giving—like the Virgin Mary. It ascribes to women the primary role of mothers who are faithful, virtuous, passive, and subordinate to their husbands and who act as the primary preserver of the family and tradition (Bryjak & Soroka, 1994; McNeill et al., 2001; Reid & Bing, 2000). Not surprisingly, this emphasis often places considerable stress on Hispanic American women. Although entering the workplace in increasing numbers, they are still expected to care for their children, perform household chores, and serve their husbands' needs.

The concept of machismo projects an image of the Hispanic American male as strong, virile, and dominant—the head of the household and major decision maker in the family (Bryjak & Soroka, 1994; McNeill et al., 2001; Torres, 1998). Machismo also embodies the notion that it is acceptable to be sexually aggressive and to seek conquests outside the marriage. Thus Hispanic culture is often expressive of a double standard in which wives are to remain faithful to one man and husbands can have outside affairs (McNeill et al., 2001). Machismo has another side, because it is also characterized by generosity, respect for others, the use of fair and just authority, courage, and responsibility for the safety and honor of one's family (McNeill et al., 2001; Torres, 1998).

Of course, marianismo and machismo are just stereotypes, and many Hispanic Americans do not embrace these gender-role assumptions (Vasquez, 1994). Furthermore, assimilation, urbanization, and upward mobility of Hispanic Americans are combining to diminish the impact of these cultural stereotypes as they reduce gender-role inequities (McNeill et al., 2001; Sanchez, 1997).

Among a second ethnic group, African Americans, women play a central role in families that tends to differ from the traditional nuclear family model of mother, father, and children (Bulcroft et al., 1996; Greene, 1994; Reid & Bing, 2000). African American women have traditionally been a bulwark of strength in their communities since the days of slavery. Because women were not economically dependent on men under the system of slavery, African American men did not typically assume the dominant role in the family. This accounts, in part, for why relationships between African American women and men have tended more toward egalitarianism and economic parity than has been true of other cultural groups, including the dominant white culture (Blee & Tickamyer, 1995; Bulcroft et al., 1996). The historical absence of economic dependence also helps explain why so many African Americans households are headed by women who define their own status.

Another factor is the high unemployment rate among African American males—almost three times that for whites (Bureau of Labor Statistics, 2003). The realities of unemployment and the American welfare system undoubtedly contribute to some African American men's avoidance of marriage and absenteeism from the home. Consequently, African American women often assume gender-role behaviors that reflect a reversal of the gender patterns traditional among white Americans.

Although African Americans may not adhere as strongly as other cultural groups to the concept of the nuclear family, certain characteristics contribute to stability and cohesion in both family and community. These include (1) intense kinship bonds among a variety of households; (2) strong work, achievement, and education ethics; and (3) unusually high levels of adaptability and flexibility in family and gender roles (Reid & Comas-Diaz, 1990; Schaefer, 1990).

A third minority group, Asian Americans, represents great diversity both in heritage and country of origin (China, the Philippines, Japan, India, Korea, Vietnam, Cambodia, Thailand, and others). Asian Americans tend to place more value on family, group solidarity, and interdependence than do white Americans (Bradshaw, 1994). Like her Hispanic counterparts, the Asian American woman expects her family obligations to take higher priority than her own individual aspirations (Pyke & Johnson, 2003). Thus, although more Asian American women work outside the home than do women in any other American ethnic group, many spend their lives supporting others and subordinating their needs to the family (Bradshaw, 1994; Cole, 1992). As a result, achievement-oriented Asian women are often caught in a double bind, torn between contemporary American values of individuality and independence and the traditional gender roles of Asian culture.

Although there is no typical pattern, the diverse Asian cultures still tend to allow greater sexual freedom for men than for women while perpetuating the gender-role assumption of male dominance (Ishii-Kuntz, 1997a, 1997b; Pyke & Johnson, 2003). In Chinese American families, for instance, even when husband and wife occupy equal breadwinning roles, the wife usually assumes the role of helper to her husband rather than equal partner (Wong, 1988). This gender hierarchy is also reflected in parenting practices. For example, in both Korean American and Vietnamese American families daughters are generally expected to be at home helping with household chores (when not in school) and sons are typically given more freedom (Pyke & Johnson, 2003).

As these accounts illustrate, social learning and cultural traditions influence gender-role behaviors within American society. How does society convey these expectations? In the following sections we look at five agents of socialization: parents, peers, schools, television, and religion.

Parents as Shapers of Gender Roles

Many social scientists view parents as influential agents of gender-role socialization (Hardesty et al., 1995; Leaper et al., 1998; Witt, 1997). A child's earliest exposure to what it means to be female or male is typically provided by parents (Witt, 1997). As we saw earlier in the discussion of gender-identity formation, parents often have different expectations for girls and boys, and they demonstrate these expectations in their interactions. Baby girls often

? How About You?

Take a few moments to think about parents, peers, school, television, and religion as agents of socialization in your own life. In what ways did each of these influences shape your gender-role expectations?

receive more attention than baby boys (Jacklin et al., 1984), and parents are more likely to treat baby girls as if they were fragile—for instance, hesitating to bounce them up and down (Doyle & Paludi, 1991). Likewise, a girl may be cuddled when she cries out of pain or frustration, whereas a boy may be admonished that "boys don't cry." In general, parents tend to be more protective and restrictive of girl babies and provide less intervention and more freedom for boys (Skolnick, 1992). Furthermore, research has found that sons are more likely than daughters to receive parental encouragement for self-assertion behaviors and for controlling or limiting their emotional expression, whereas girls receive more encouragement for expressing social engagement behavior (Block, 1983; Leaper et al., 1998).

Although an increasing number of parents are becoming sensitive to the gender-role implications of a child's playthings, many others encourage their children to play with toys that help prepare them for specific adult gender roles. Girls are often given dolls, tea sets, and miniature ovens. Boys frequently receive things like trucks, cars, balls, and toy weapons. Children who play with toys thought appropriate only for the other sex are often rebuked by their parents. Because children are sensitive to these expressions of displeasure, they usually develop toy preferences consistent with their parents' gender-role expectations.

That there are significant toy preferences throughout childhood, usually evident by age 2 or 3, is well established by evidence and not a subject of debate among social scientists (Berenbaum & Snyder, 1995; Rubble & Martin, 1998). However, the causes of these preferences are a source of varied opinions. Many writers, including us, believe that social learning significantly influences toy selection. Another perspective is offered by the developing field of *evolutionary psychology*. Evolutionary psychology maintains that many of our behaviors, even some that appear to be exclusively a product of social learning, have been molded by a long period of human evolution that has favored the selection of genes that predispose individuals to certain sex-specific behaviors and thus assist the survival and reproduction of the species (Bjorklund & Pellegrini, 2000).

Recently, Gerianne Alexander (2003) proposed an evolutionary perspective on the origin of sex-typed toy preferences. Briefly stated, Alexander argues that boys' preferences for "masculine" toys, such as trucks and balls, which can be used actively and observed moving in space, reflect the adaptive significance of acquiring spatial abilities that are useful in such species-survival tasks as hunting and killing wild game for food. Similarly, girls' preferences for "feminine" toys, such as dolls, might reflect the adaptive benefit of acquired gender-role behaviors that are useful for taking care of infants and for child rearing. From this evolutionary perspective the association between toy preferences and gender-role behaviors evolved from the social roles of early males and females and "preferences for objects such as toys may indicate a biological preparedness for a 'masculine' or 'feminine' gender role" (G. Alexander, 2003, p. 7).

Although more and more parents today try to avoid teaching their children gender stereotypes, many still encourage their children to engage in gender-typed play activities and household chores (Lytton & Romney, 1991; McHale et al., 1990). Even when parents do make a conscious effort not to teach gender roles, some behaviors may seem so natural that they occur unconsciously. Thus a boy's father may invite him to play catch, change the oil in the family car, or mow the lawn, whereas a girl may receive more frequent reminders to keep her room tidy or invitations to help prepare meals. This differential treatment has the effect of guiding children toward specific and different adult roles (Fisher-Thompson, 1990).

Parents, especially fathers, who have only female children demonstrate a stronger commitment to gender equity than do parents of sons (Warner & Steel, 1999). This suggests that in North American society, which often tends to favor males, wanting the best for their children might encourage parents of daughters to embrace principles of gender equity in their child-rearing practices.

The establishment of stereotypical masculine or feminine roles can be influenced by traditional child-rearing practices.

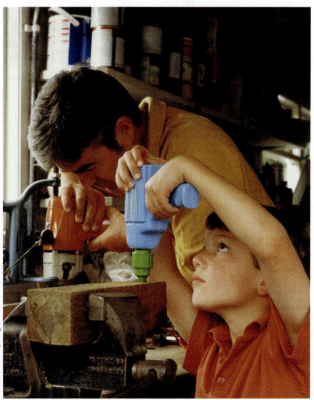

© Stephen Simpson/Getty Images

© Ian Shaw/Getty Images

The Peer Group

A second important influence in the socialization of gender roles is the peer group (Fagot, 1995). One element of peer-group influence that begins early in life is a voluntary segregation of the sexes (Maccoby, 1988, 1990, 1998; Powlishta et al., 1993). This begins during the preschool years, and by first grade children select members of their own sex as playmates about 95% of the time (Maccoby, 1998; Maccoby & Jacklin, 1987). Segregation of the sexes, which continues into the school years, contributes to sex typing in play activities that help prepare children for adult gender roles (Moller et al., 1992). Girls often play together with dolls and tea sets, and boys frequently engage in athletic competitions and play with toy guns. Such peer influences contribute to the socialization of women who are inclined to be nurturing and nonassertive and men who are comfortable being competitive and assertive.

One aspect of peer-group structure among American children that helps to perpetuate traditional gender roles is the tendency to select same-sex playmates most of the time.

By late childhood and adolescence the influence of peers becomes even more important (Doyle & Paludi, 1991; Hyde, 1996). Children of this age tend to view conformity as important, and adhering to traditional gender roles promotes social acceptance by their peers (Absi-Semaan et al., 1993; Moller et al., 1992). Most individuals who do not behave in ways appropriate to their own sex are subjected to pressure in the form of ostracism or ridicule. Evidence also indicates that contemporary children continue to respond to their peers in gender-stereotyped ways, despite important changes in our society in recent years (McAninch et al., 1996).

Schools, Textbooks, and Gender Roles

Research studies published in the 1970s, 1980s, and early 1990s generally concurred that girls and boys receive quite different treatment in the classroom (AAUW, 1992; Eccles & Midgley, 1990; Eccles et al., 1999; Kantrowitz, 1992; Sadker & Sadker, 1990, 1994; Serbin, 1980). Among other findings, these studies reported that

- Teachers call on and encourage boys more than girls.
- Boys who call out answers without being recognized are generally not penalized, whereas girls tend to be reprimanded for the same behavior.
- Boys are more likely to receive praise for the content of their work, whereas girls receive praise for its neatness.
- Teachers are more tolerant of bad behavior among elementary school boys than girls.
- Boys are more likely than girls to receive attention, remedial help, and praise from their teachers.
- Teachers pay more attention to girls who act dependently, but they are more likely to respond to boys who behave in independent or aggressive ways.
- Girls frequently suffer a loss of confidence in their math and science abilities in the middle school years.

As these findings illustrate, schools are another important influence in gender-role socialization. Teachers are often guided by their own gender-role stereotypes in their interaction with students. Thus instructors might expect boys to excel in subjects such as math and science while assuming that girls will do better in English and literature. As a result, boys and girls might receive differential encouragement. This can have a restrictive influence on students, who might not try as hard in fields in which they receive little encouragement.

Fortunately, schools in the United States are now acting to reduce classroom perpetuation of stereotypical gender roles. An influx of younger teachers who are products of a more gender-aware generation has aided in this gradual transformation of classroom environments. One of the most striking examples of this change has been a concerted effort by American schools to ensure equal educational opportunities for both sexes in math and science.

School textbooks have also perpetuated gender-role stereotypes. In the early 1970s two major studies of children's textbooks found that girls were typically portrayed as dependent, unambitious, and not very successful or clever, whereas boys were shown to have just the opposite characteristics (Saario et al., 1973; Women on Words and Images, 1972). In the early 1980s men played the dominant roles in about two out of every three stories in American reading texts—an improvement from four out of every five stories in the early 1970s (Britton & Lumpkin, 1984). Textbook publishers in the 1990s and early 2000s have continued to improve markedly in their efforts to avoid gender stereotypes. However, like the culture they represent, textbooks are still not completely free of stereotyped gender roles.

Television and Gender-Role Stereotypes

Another powerful agent of gender-role socialization is television. Depictions of men and women on the TV screen are often blatantly stereotypical (Huston et al., 1998; Larson, 1996; Ward & Rivadeneyra, 1999). Whereas men most often appear as active, intelligent, adventurous, and in charge, women are more likely to play passive, less competent characters who are better at domestic tasks than at thinking for themselves. In commercials and even on the television news, men often appear as the authoritative sources on most topics (Furnham & Mak, 1999). It is safe to assume that these depictions have some impact as agents of socialization, considering that most American children spend hours in front of the TV each day. By the time the typical teenager graduates from high school, he or she will probably have spent more time watching television than engaging in any other single activity besides sleep (Baran & Davis, 2003).

An analysis of popular television sitcoms from the 1950s through the 1990s found that, even though portrayals of gender equality have become more common over the years, gender stereotyping was still largely the norm in the 1990s (Olson & Douglas, 1997). One of the all-time most popular programs, the 1990s series *Home Improvement,* received the lowest ratings on gender-role equity. Another recent study conducted by the National Organization for Women (NOW) evaluated 82 television programs during the February 2000 sweeps period. Based on their observations, NOW concluded that prime-time television remains largely a male-dominated medium and that sexist stereotypes abound in prime time. Although the report gave high marks to a few TV dramas, such as *Family Law* and *ER* (programs that consistently featured multidimensional and competent women characters), most of the programs reviewed, especially comedies, were judged to either underrepresent women or present them stereotypically (Aucoin, 2000).

Children's programs are also not averse to portraying gender-role stereotypes (Barner, 1999). For example, even *Sesame Street*—public television's immensely popular and long-running children's show—is guilty of sexism in its programming. In 1992, 84% of the characters featured on the show were male, compared to 76% in 1987 (Media Report to Women, 1993b). However, in recent years child-oriented networks such as Nickelodeon and Disney have featured both cartoons and action/drama programs that are noteworthy for their positive, nonstereotypical portrayals of girls and women. These programs include *The Wild Thornberrys, Lizzie McGuire, So Weird, Dora the Explorer,* and *Kim Impossible* (an action/adventure cartoon that features a girl in the title role).

The television industry is in the process of gradually reducing gender biases in its adult-oriented programming, partly because of the influence of media advocacy groups who have worked tirelessly to reduce the portrayal of traditional stereotypes of male and female roles. Today, the lead roles played by women in prime-time television shows more often allow them to behave in assertive and competent ways. Examples of strong, independent women acting with authority and rejuvenating prime-time television include *The West Wing*'s press secretary C. J. Cregg (portrayed by Allison Janney), *Alias*'s superstar Sydney Bristow (played by Jennifer Garner), Judge Amy Gray (played by Amy Brenneman) in *Judging Amy,* and attorney Ellenor Frutt (Camryn Manheim) in *The Practice.*

However, even popular television series that feature strong women often have a disproportionate number of male characters in lead roles (e.g., *NYPD Blue, The West Wing,* and *Law and Order*). Furthermore, the increased presence of strong women on television may have more to do with product marketing than with deliberate efforts to erase longtime gender stereotypes. Women make up almost 60% of the prime-time television audience (Schulberg, 1999), and women are more likely than men to purchase products advertised in commercials (Waters & Huck, 1989).

In recent years there has been a dramatic increase in the number of women ordained as clergy.

Religion and Gender Roles

Organized religion plays an important role in the lives of many Americans. Despite differences in doctrines, most religions exhibit a common trend in their views about gender roles (Eitzen & Zinn, 2000). As one writer noted, any child who receives religious instruction is likely to be socialized to accept certain gender stereotypes (Basow, 1992). In Jewish, Christian, and Islamic traditions these stereotypes commonly embrace an emphasis on male supremacy, with God presented as male through language such as *Father, He,* or *King.* The biblical conceptualization of Eve as created from Adam's rib provides a clear endorsement of the gender assumption that females are meant to be secondary to males.

The composition of the leadership of most religious organizations in the United States provides additional evidence of male dominance and of the circumscription of female gender roles. Until 1970 no women were ordained as clergy in any American Protestant denomination. There were no female rabbis until 1972, and the Roman Catholic Church still does not allow female priests.

Currently, there are movements to change the traditional patriarchal nature of organized religion in America, as evidenced by several recent trends. Over the last two decades female enrollment in seminaries and divinity schools has increased dramatically, the number of ordained women in Protestant ministries has more than doubled, and the number of female rabbis has also increased significantly (Eitzen & Zinn, 1994; Renzetti & Curran, 1992; Ribadeneira, 1998).

Efforts are also under way to reduce sexist language in church proceedings and religious writings. In 1983 the National Council of Churches published guidelines for a more "inclusive language" designed to eliminate exclusively male metaphors for God and to replace other terms such as *God the Father, mankind,* and *fellowship* with more gender-neutral terms such as *Creator, humanity,* and *community.* More recently, the International Bible Society announced in February 2002 plans for a new Bible translation with gender-accurate wording. This updated version, called *Today's New International Version,* will drop gender-specific terms when it is clear that the original text did not intend exclusively male terms. For example, in this version *brothers* becomes *brothers and sisters* and *sons of God* becomes *children of God* (Gorski, 2002). Some religious groups, such as Reform Judaism, are vocal in their support of equal rights for and equal treatment of women. We can expect these new trends toward gender-role parity eventually to reduce or minimize organized religion's reinforcement of traditional gender-role stereotypes.

We see, then, that family, friends, schools and textbooks, television (and other media, such as movies, magazines, and popular music), and religion frequently help to develop and reinforce traditional gender-role assumptions and behaviors in our lives. We are all affected by gender-role conditioning to some degree, and we could discuss at great length how this process discourages development of each person's full range of potential. However, this textbook deals with our sexuality, so it is the impact of gender-role conditioning on this aspect of our lives that we examine in the next section.

Gender-Role Expectations: Their Impact on Our Sexuality

Gender-role expectations exert a profound impact on our sexuality. Our beliefs about males and females together with our assumptions about what constitutes appropriate behaviors for each can affect many aspects of sexual experience. Our assessment of ourselves as sexual beings, the expectations we have for intimate relationships, our perception of the quality of such experiences, and the responses of others to our sexuality are all significantly influenced by our identification as male or female.

In the following pages we examine some of our gender-role assumptions and their potential effects on relations between the sexes. We do not mean to imply that only heterosexual couples are limited by these assumptions. Gender-role stereotypes can influence people regardless of their sexual orientation, although homosexual couples might be affected somewhat differently by them.

? **How About You?**

What are some ways in which gender-role expectations and stereotypes have influenced your views of sexuality and the manner in which you relate intimately to others?

Women as Undersexed, Men as Oversexed

A long-standing assumption in many Western societies is the mistaken belief that women are inherently less sexually inclined than men. Such gender stereotypes can result in women being subjected to years of negative socialization during which they are taught to suppress or deny their natural sexual feelings. Legions of women have been told by parents, peers, and books that sex is something a woman engages in to please a man, preferably her husband. A related gender assumption is the view that "normal women" do not enjoy sex as much as men.

Although these stereotypes are beginning to fade as people strive to throw off some of the behavior constraints of generations of socialization, many women are still influenced by such views. How can a woman express interest in being sexual or actively seek her own pleasure if she believes that women are not supposed to have sexual needs? Some women, believing that it is not appropriate to be easily aroused sexually, direct their energies to blocking or hiding these normal responses. Some people who adhere to these stereotypes believe that any woman who openly expresses sexual interest or responds sexually is "easy," "sleazy," or a "slut." However, men who manifest similar behavior are characterized as "studs" or "playboys," terms that are often meant to be ego enhancing rather than demeaning.

Males can be harmed by being stereotyped as supersexual. A man who is not instantly aroused by a person he perceives as attractive and/or available can feel somehow inadequate. After all, are not all men supposed to be instantly eager when confronted with a sexual opportunity? We believe that such an assumption is demeaning and reduces men to insensitive machines that respond instantly when the correct button is pushed. Male students in our classes frequently express their frustration and ambivalence over this issue. The following account is typical of these observations:

When I take a woman out for the first time, I am often confused over how the sex issue should be handled. I feel pressured to make a move, even when I am not all that inclined to hop into the sack. Isn't this what women expect? If I don't even try, they may think there is something wrong with me. I almost feel like I would have to explain myself if I acted uninterested in having sex. Usually it's just easier to make the move and let them decide what they want to do with it. (Authors' files)

Clearly, this man believes that he is expected to pursue sex, even when he does not want to, as part of his masculine role. This stereotypical view of men as the initiators of sex in developing relationships can be distressing for both sexes, as we see in the next section.

Men as Initiators, Women as Recipients

In our society traditional gender roles establish the expectation that men will initiate intimate relationships (from the opening invitation for an evening out to the first overture toward sexual activity) and that women will respond with permission or denial (Rickert et al., 2002). As the following comments reveal, this can make men feel burdened and pressured:

Women should experience how anxiety-provoking it can be. I get tired of always being the one to make the suggestion, since there's always the potential of being turned down. (Authors' files)

During lovemaking, my wife usually expects me to make all the initial moves. Sometimes I wish I could just lie back and be taken over sexually instead of being the one who must orchestrate the whole thing. (Authors' files)

This last comment reflects a concern voiced by many of our male students and clients. Even in established relationships, men are frequently expected to initiate each sexual encounter. This can result in sex becoming more of a duty than a pleasure. Yet men who grow up being socialized to be active, assertive, and even aggressive are usually accustomed to being in control in most situations. It can be difficult to relinquish this role in the bedroom. Thus, even though a man might fantasize about being taken over sexually, actually having such an experience can be stressful.

A woman who feels compelled to accept a passive female role can have a difficult time initiating sex. It could be even harder for her to assume an active role during sexual activity.

Many women are frustrated, regretful, and understandably angry that such cultural expectations are so deeply ingrained in our society. The following comments, expressed by women talking together, reflect some of these thoughts:

I like to ask men out and have often done so. But it's frustrating when many of the men I ask out automatically assume that I want to jump in bed with them just because I take the initiative to make a date. (Authors' files)

It is hard for me to let my man know what I like during lovemaking. After all, he is supposed to know, isn't he? If I tell him, it's like I am usurping his role as the all-knowing one. (Authors' files)

The last comment relates to another common gender myth about sexual functioning—the notion that men are more knowledgeable and better able than women to direct a sexual encounter.

Men as "Sexperts"

Considering that gender-role socialization conditions males to be competent leaders and females to be passive followers, is it any wonder that men are expected to act as experts in sexual matters? Men are not the only ones who see themselves as "sexperts"; women, in fact, can coerce men into playing the expert role by subscribing to this mistaken notion. Some men enjoy being cast as teacher or mentor. However, others feel burdened by the need to play the expert and thus, by implication, to be responsible for the outcome of sexual sharing.

Fortunately, some of these destructive patterns are showing signs of eroding. Many of our male students speak with a sense of delight and relief about their sexual encounters with women who initiate sex, play an active role during lovemaking, and assume responsibility for their own pleasure. In recent years women too have seemed more inclined to view men as sexual equals rather than as all-knowing experts.

Women as Controllers, Men as Movers

Many women grow up believing that men always have sex on their minds. For such a woman it may be a logical next step to become the controller of what takes place during sexual interaction. By this we do not mean actively initiating certain activities, which she sees as the prerogative of men, the movers. Rather, a woman may see her role as controlling her male partner's rampant lust by making certain he does not coerce her into unacceptable activities. Thus, instead of enjoying how good it feels to have her breasts caressed, she may concentrate her attention on how to keep his hand off her genitals. This concern with control can be particularly pronounced during the adolescent dating years. It is not surprising that a woman who spends a great deal of time and energy regulating sexual intimacy might have difficulty experiencing sexual feelings when she finally allows herself to relinquish her controlling role.

Conversely, men are often conditioned to see women as sexual challenges and to go as far as they can during sexual encounters. They too may have difficulty appreciating the good feelings of being close to and touching someone when all they are thinking about is what they will do next. Men who routinely experience this pattern can have a hard time relinquishing the mover role and being receptive rather than active during sexual interaction. They might be confused or even threatened by a woman who switches roles from controller to active initiator.

Men as Unemotional and Strong, Women as Nurturing and Supportive

Perhaps one of the most undesirable of all gender-role stereotypes is the notion that being emotionally expressive, tender, and nurturing is appropriate only for women (Plant et al., 2000). We have already seen that men are often socialized to be unemotional. A man who is trying to appear strong might find it difficult to express vulnerability, deep feelings, and doubts. This conditioning can make it exceedingly difficult for a man to develop emotionally satisfying intimate relationships.

For example, a man who accepts the assumption of nonemotionality might approach sex as a purely physical act during which expressions of feelings have no place. This results in a limited kind of experience that can leave both parties feeling dissatisfied. Women often have a negative reaction when they encounter this characteristic in men because women tend to place great importance on openness and willingness to express feelings in a relationship. However, we need to remember that many men must struggle against a lifetime of "macho" conditioning when they try to express long-suppressed emotions. Women, on the other hand, can grow tired of their role as nurturers, particularly when their efforts are greeted with little or no reciprocity.

We have discussed how strict adherence to traditional gender roles can limit and restrict the ways we express our sexuality. These cultural legacies are often expressed more subtly today than in the past, but rigid gender-role expectations linger on, inhibiting our growth as multidimensional people and our capacity to be fully ourselves with others. Although many people are breaking away from stereotyped gender roles and are learning to accept and express themselves more fully, we cannot underestimate the extent of gender-role learning that still occurs in our society.

Many people are now striving to integrate both masculine and feminine behaviors into their lifestyles. This trend, often referred to as androgyny, is the focus of the final section of this chapter.

Transcending Gender Roles: Androgyny

The word **androgyny** (an-DRAW-ji-nee), meaning "having characteristics of both sexes," is derived from the Greek roots *andr*, meaning man, and *gynē*, meaning woman. The term is used to describe flexibility in gender role. Androgynous individuals are those who have integrated aspects of masculinity and femininity into their personalities and behavior. Androgyny offers the option of expressing whatever behavior seems appropriate in a given situation instead of limiting responses to those considered gender appropriate. Thus androgynous men and women might be assertive on the job but nurturing with friends, family members, and lovers. Many men and women possess characteristics that are consistent with traditional gender assumptions but also have interests and behavioral tendencies typically ascribed to the other sex. Actually, people can range from being very masculine or feminine to being *both* masculine and feminine—that is, androgynous.

Androgyny A blending of typical male and female behaviors in one individual.

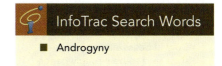
InfoTrac Search Words
■ Androgyny

A social psychologist, Sandra Bem (1974, 1993), developed a paper-and-pencil inventory for measuring the degree to which individuals are identified with masculine or feminine behaviors or a combination thereof. Other similar devices have been developed since Bem's pioneering work (Spence & Helmreich, 1978). Armed with these devices for measuring androgyny, a number of researchers have investigated how androgynous individuals compare with strongly gender-typed people.

A number of studies indicate that androgynous people are more flexible in their behaviors, are less limited by rigid gender-role assumptions, have higher levels of self-esteem, make better decisions in group settings, and exhibit more social competence and motivation to achieve than do people who are strongly gender-typed or those who score low in both areas (Katz & Ksansnak, 1994; Kirchmeyer, 1996; Rose & Montemayor, 1994; Shimonaka et al., 1997; Vonk & Ashmore, 1993). Research also demonstrates that masculine and androgynous people of both sexes are more independent and less likely to have their opinions swayed than are individuals who are strongly identified with the feminine role (Bem, 1975). In fact, both androgyny and high masculinity appear to be adaptive for both sexes at all ages (Sinnott, 1986). However, feminine and androgynous people of both sexes appear to be significantly more nurturing than those who adhere to the masculine role (Bem, 1993; Coleman & Ganong, 1985; Ray & Gold, 1996).

We need to be cautious about concluding that androgyny is an ideal state, free of potential problems (Sampson, 1985). One study found that masculine-typed males demonstrated better overall emotional adjustment than did androgynous males (Jones et al., 1978). Another study, of college professors in their early careers, found that androgynous individuals exhibited greater personal satisfaction but more job-related stress than those who were strongly gender typed (Rotheram & Weiner, 1983). In a large sample of college students masculine personality characteristics were also more closely associated with being versatile and adaptable than was the trait of androgyny (Lee & Scheurer, 1983). Other studies have also indicated that it may be masculinity, not femininity or androgyny, that is more closely associated with successful adjustment and positive self-esteem (Basoff & Glass, 1982; Unger & Crawford, 1992; Williams & D'Alessandro, 1994). This may be "because masculine attributes are viewed more positively and consequently lead to greater social rewards" (Burn et al., 1996, p. 420). Thus, although androgyny is often associated with emotional, social, and behavioral competence, more information is necessary for a complete picture of its effect on personal adjustment and satisfaction.

Androgynous individuals, both male and female, seem to have more positive attitudes toward sexuality and are more aware of and expressive of feelings of love than are those who are traditionally gender typed (Ganong & Coleman, 1987; Walfish & Myerson, 1980). Androgynous people also appear to be more tolerant and less likely to judge or criticize the sexual behaviors of others (Garcia, 1982). Studies have found that androgynous women are more orgasmic and experience more sexual satisfaction than do feminine-typed women (Kimlicka et al., 1983; Radlove, 1983). However, two separate investigations revealed that masculine males were significantly more comfortable with sex than were androgynous females, indicating that biological sex may still exert a stronger effect than gender typing (Allgeier, 1981; Walfish & Myerson, 1980).

Our own guess is that androgynous people tend to be flexible and comfortable in their sexuality. We would expect such people, whether men or women, to have great capacity to enjoy both the emotional and the physical aspects of sexual intimacy. Androgynous lovers are probably comfortable both initiating and responding to invitations for sexual sharing, and they are probably not significantly limited by preconceived notions of who must do what—and how—during their lovemaking. These observations are supported by research indicating that androgynous couples experience more emotional and sexual satisfaction and personal commitment in their relationships than do gender-typed couples (Rosenzweig & Daily, 1989; Stephen & Harrison, 1985).

Research on androgyny continues, and we certainly have good reasons to be cautious about an unequivocally enthusiastic endorsement of this behavioral style. Nevertheless, most of the evidence collected thus far suggests that people who are able to transcend traditional gender roles are able to function more comfortably and effectively in a wider range of situations. Androgynous individuals can select from a broad repertoire of feminine and masculine behaviors. They can choose to be independent, assertive, nurturing, or tender, based not on gender-role norms but rather on what provides them and others optimum personal satisfaction in a given situation.

? How About You?

Do you believe that you were socialized to be strongly gender typed, or were you raised in a manner supporting androgynous behavior?

► Summary

Male and Female, Masculine and Feminine

- The processes by which our maleness and femaleness are determined and the manner in which they influence our behavior, sexual and otherwise, are highly complex. (p. 46)

- Sex refers to our biological maleness or femaleness, as reflected in various physical attributes (chromosomes, reproductive organs, genitals, and so forth). (p. 46)

- Gender encompasses the special psychosocial meanings added to biological maleness or femaleness or, in other words, our masculinity or femininity. Our ideas of masculinity and femininity involve gender assumptions about behavior based on a person's sex. (p. 46)

- Gender identity refers to each individual's subjective sense of being male or female. (p. 46)

- Gender role refers to a collection of attitudes and behaviors considered normal and appropriate in a specific culture for people of a particular sex. (p. 47)

- Gender roles establish sex-related behavioral expectations, which are culturally defined and therefore vary from society to society and from era to era. (p. 47)

Gender-Identity Formation

- Research efforts to isolate the many biological factors that influence a person's gender identity have resulted in the identification of six biological categories, or levels: chromosomal sex, gonadal sex, hormonal sex, sex of the internal reproductive structures, sex of the external genitals, and sex differentiation of the brain. (pp. 47–54)

- Under normal conditions these six biological variables interact harmoniously to determine our biological sex. However, errors can occur at any of the six levels. The resulting irregularities in the development of a person's biological sex can seriously complicate acquisition of a gender identity. (pp. 54–58)

- The social-learning interpretation of gender-identity formation suggests that our identification with either masculine or feminine roles results primarily from the social and cultural models and influences to which we are exposed. (pp. 58–61)
- Most contemporary theorists embrace an interactional model in which gender identity is seen as a result of a complex interplay of biological and social-learning factors. (p. 61)

Transsexualism and Transgenderism

- A transsexual is a person whose gender identity is opposite to his or her biological sex. (p. 62)
- The term *transgendered* is generally applied to individuals whose appearance and behaviors do not conform to the gender roles ascribed by society for people of a particular sex. (p. 63)
- Most transsexuals are heterosexually oriented. The transgendered community has a more eclectic composition of gay men, lesbians, bisexuals, and heterosexuals. (p. 64)
- Most transsexual people and perhaps some transgendered individuals meet the DSM-IV-TR criteria for a gender-identity disorder. (pp. 64–65)
- The scientific community has not reached a consensus about the causes and best treatment for transsexualism. Some transsexuals have successfully undergone sex-reassignment procedures in which their physical bodies are altered to match their gender identities. (pp. 65–68)

Gender Roles

- Widely accepted gender-role assumptions can begin to function as stereotypes, which are notions about what people are like based not on their individuality but on their inclusion in a general category, such as age or sex. (p. 68)
- Many common gender-based stereotypes in our society encourage us to prejudge others and restrict our opportunities. (p. 68)
- Socialization is the process by which society conveys its behavioral expectations to us. (p. 69)
- Ethnic variations in gender roles are observed among Hispanic Americans, African Americans, and Asian Americans. (pp. 69–70)
- Parents, peers, schools, textbooks, television, and religion all act as agents in the socialization of gender roles. (pp. 70–74)
- Gender-role expectations can have a profound effect on our sexuality. Our assessment of ourselves as sexual beings, the expectations we have for intimate relationships, our perception of the quality of such experiences, and the responses of others to our sexuality are all significantly influenced by our own perceptions of our gender roles. (p. 74)
- Androgynous individuals are people who have moved beyond traditional gender roles by integrating aspects associated with both masculinity and femininity into their lifestyles. (pp. 77–78)

▶ Suggested Readings

Dreger, Alice (1998). *Hermaphrodites and the Medical Invention of Sex.* Cambridge, MA: Harvard University Press. A fascinating discussion of how and why medical and social scientists have historically construed the sex, gender, and sexuality of intersexed people. An epilogue contains informative narratives of several intersexed individuals treated according to the still standard protocol developed in the 1950s.

Fausto-Sterling, Anne (2000). *Sexing the Body: Gender Politics and the Construction of Sexuality.* New York: Basic Books. This book provides information about how the scientific community has historically politicized the human body. Three chapters describe how intersexed people have traditionally been dealt with as "damaged goods" and why such individuals should not be coerced into compromising their differences to fit a flawed societal definition of normality.

Levant, Ronald, and William Pollack (Eds.). (1995). *A New Psychology of Men.* New York: Basic Books. An excellent collection of articles that provides an informative overview of an emerging field. Topics include men's changing roles, male development and psychological functioning, and men's health and gender-role stress.

Lips, Hilary (2001). *Sex and Gender* (4th ed.). Mountain View, CA: Mayfield. An informative text that provides a thorough review of the professional literature pertaining to sex differences in social behavior and experiences. Lips presents information suggesting that gender differences are relatively small and, when present, stem largely from the socialization of gender-role expectations.

Maccoby, Eleanor (1998). *The Two Sexes: Growing Up Apart, Coming Together.* Cambridge, MA: Harvard University Press. A highly informative book that presents the findings of an influential researcher who has spent much of her career investigating the origins of gender differences.

Mead, Margaret (1963). *Sex and Temperament in Three Primitive Societies.* New York: Morrow. An eminent anthropologist's analysis of three societies in which male and female gender roles differ from those of North American society.

Preves, Sharon (2002). *Intersex and Identity.* Piscataway, NJ: Rutgers University Press. An illuminating and informative book that gives voice to people with intersex conditions. Preves, a sociologist, provides insights into intersexuality through her analyses of life-history interviews with 37 adults who were treated for this condition as children.

▶ Web Resources

Your *Our Sexuality* Web site **http://psychology.wadsworth.com/ crooksbaur9e/** has direct links to the Web sites described below. These links are checked often for changes, dead links, and new additions.

Gender Talk

Detailed explanations and challenges to conventional attitudes about gender issues, gender identity, and transgenderism in particular are explored on this Web site.

Intersex Society of North America

The ISNA is an advocacy organization devoted to educating the public about issues related to intersexed individuals.

Ingersoll Gender Center

The Ingersoll Center is a nonprofit agency for the transsexual, transvestite, and transgender community. Among the highlights of its Web site are a catalog of publications, opinion pieces, and a host of links to related organizations.

Bodies Like Ours

Valuable Web resource that provides information about the condition of intersex and support for intersexed people.

International Foundation for Gender Education

A good source of information about gender issues, including transgenderism and transsexualism.

Gender Inn

This Web site lists many valuable resources for further information about the topic of gender, including lists of books, articles, and other Web sites that deal with gender.

Our Sexuality Web Site

For online resources directly related to this book, go to **http://psychology.wadsworth.com/ crooksbaur9e/**. You will find interactive exercises, study questions, chapter outlines, an online version of this text's glossary, and Web links and activities that complement your CD-ROM.

InfoTrac® College Edition Online Library

http://infotrac.thomsonlearning.com/
InfoTrac College Edition is an online searchable library that includes a multitude of journals, many of which are specific to human sexuality. These journals include *Archives of Sexual Behavior, Archives of Sexual Health Behavior, Canadian Journal of Human Sexuality, Hispanic Journal of the Behavioral Sciences, Journal of Cross-Cultural Psychology, Journal of Physical Education, Recreation, and Dance, Journal of Sex Research,* and *Sex Roles.* You may search topics suggested in the margins of this chapter or terms of your own.

Our Sexuality CD-ROM

Use your CD-ROM for further study of the concepts in this chapter. Your CD-ROM provides animations of difficult concepts, video clips of real people discussing sexuality, critical thinking questions, chapter quizzing, and more.

Female Sexual Anatomy and Physiology

▶ **Genital Self-Exam**

What are two reasons to do a genital self-exam?

▶ **The Vulva**

Does the clitoris serve any purpose other than sexual pleasure?

What are some myths about the hymen?

▶ **Underlying Structures**

What is the function of the bulbs and glands that underlie the vulval tissue?

What are Kegel exercises, and how can they affect a woman's sexual responsiveness?

▶ **Internal Structures**

How (and why) does vaginal lubrication occur?

Which internal structure produces the most hormones?

▶ **Menstruation**

Are there physiological signs that a woman is ovulating and therefore at the most fertile point in her menstrual cycle?

What are the symptoms of premenstrual syndrome and dysmenorrhea?

What can a woman do to minimize these symptoms?

▶ **Menopause**

What are some positive effects of menopause?

What are the potential benefits and risks of hormone replacement therapy?

▶ **Gynecological Health Concerns**

Why do vaginal infections and urinary tract problems occur?

How effective is the Pap smear in detecting cervical cancer?

▶ **The Breasts**

What are the steps for a breast exam?

What percentage of breast cancers are attributed to a genetic flaw?

I had three children and was 45 years old before I ever really looked at my genitals. I was amazed at the delicate shapes and subtle colors. I'm sorry it took me so long to do this because I now feel more sure of myself sexually after becoming more acquainted with me. (Authors' files)

Many women are as unacquainted with their genitals as this woman was. However, gaining a knowledge and understanding of her body can be an important aspect of a woman's sexual well-being. In this chapter we present a detailed description of all female genital structures, external and internal. The discussion is intended to be easy to use for reference, and we encourage women readers to do a self-exam as part of reading it (see "Your Sexual Health" on page 84). We begin with a discussion of the external structures, then discuss the underlying structures and the internal organs. The chapter continues with information about menstruation, menopause, and breasts and then closes with women's health information.

Vulva The external genitals of the female, including the pubic hair, mons veneris, labia majora, labia minora, clitoris, and urinary and vaginal openings.

▶ The Vulva

The **vulva** encompasses all female external genital structures—the hair, the folds of skin, and the urinary and vaginal openings. *Vulva* is the term we use most frequently in this textbook to refer to the external genitals of the female. For reference, see Figure 4.1.

▶ **Figure 4.1**
The structures and variations of the vulva: (a) external structures and (b–d) different colors and shapes. There are many common variations of external female genitals.

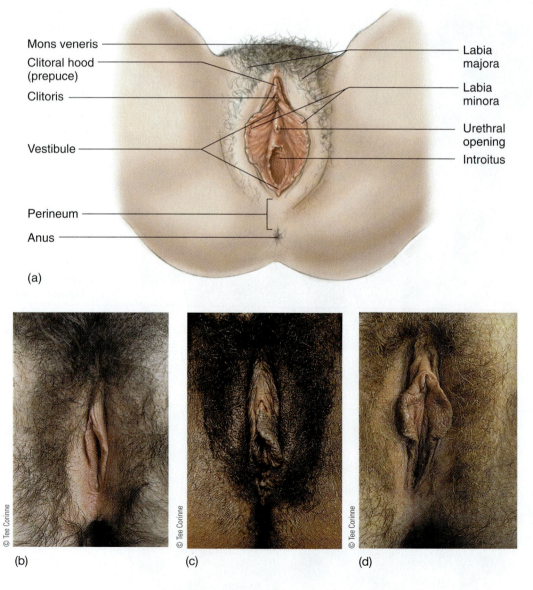

Mons veneris
Clitoral hood (prepuce)
Clitoris
Vestibule
Perineum
Anus

Labia majora
Labia minora
Urethral opening
Introitus

(a)

© Tee Corinne
© Tee Corinne
© Tee Corinne

(b)   (c)   (d)

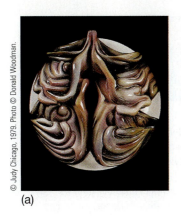
(a)

(b)

Vulva shapes in art and nature:
(a) one of the plates in Judy
Chicago's *The Dinner Party*, an
exhibit symbolizing women in
history that is on permanent
exhibit at the Brooklyn Museum
of Art; (b) the vulvalike beauty of
a flower.

The appearance of the vulva, which varies from person to person, has been likened to that of certain flowers, seashells, and other forms found in nature. Transformed vulvalike shapes have been used in artwork, including *The Dinner Party* by Judy Chicago. This work consists of 39 ceramic plates symbolizing significant women in history.

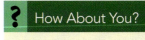

? How About You?

For women only: Have you ever looked closely at your genitals?

The Mons Veneris

Translated from Latin, **mons veneris** means "the mound of Venus." Venus was the Roman goddess of love and beauty. The mons veneris, or mons, is the area covering the pubic bone. It consists of pads of fatty tissue between the pubic bone and the skin. Touch and pressure on the mons can be sexually pleasurable because of the presence of numerous nerve endings.

At puberty the mons becomes covered with hair that varies in color, texture, and thickness from woman to woman. Sometimes women are concerned about these differences:

I always felt uncomfortable in college physical education classes because I had very thick, dark pubic hair, more so than most other women. One day my best friend and I were talking and she mentioned that she felt self-conscious in the showers after P.E. class because her pubic hair was light-colored and sparse. I told her my concerns. We laughed and both decided to stop worrying about it. (Authors' files)

During sexual arousal the scent that accompanies vaginal secretions is held by the pubic hair and can add to sensory erotic pleasure.

Mons veneris A triangular mound over the pubic bone above the vulva.

The Labia Majora

The **labia majora** (LAY-bee-uh muh-JOR-uh), or outer lips, extend downward from the mons on each side of the vulva. They begin next to the thigh and extend inward, surrounding the labia minora and the urethral and vaginal openings. Next to the thigh the outer lips are covered with pubic hair; their inner parts, next to the labia minora, are hairless. The skin of the labia majora is usually darker than the skin of the thighs. The nerve endings and underlying fatty tissue are similar to those in the mons.

Labia majora The outer lips of the vulva.

The Labia Minora

The **labia minora** (LAY-bee-uh muh-NOR-uh), or inner lips, are located within the outer lips and often protrude between them. The inner lips are hairless folds of skin that join at the **prepuce** (PREE-pyoos), or clitoral hood, and extend downward past the urinary and vaginal openings. They contain sweat and oil glands, extensive blood vessels, and nerve endings. They also vary considerably in size, shape, length, and color from woman to woman, as Figure 4.1 shows. (In the Hottentot culture of Africa pendulous labia are considered a sign of beauty, and women start pulling on them early in childhood in an effort to increase their size.) During pregnancy the inner lips become darker in color.

Labia minora The inner lips of the vulva, one on each side of the vaginal opening.

Prepuce The foreskin or fold of skin over the clitoris.

◆ Genital Self-Exam for Women

Women are born with curiosity about their bodies. In fact, physical self-awareness and exploration are important steps in a child's development. Unfortunately, many women receive negative conditioning about the sexual parts of their bodies from earliest childhood. They learn to think of their genitals as "privates" or "down there"—parts of their body not to be looked at, touched, or enjoyed. It is common for people to react with discomfort to the suggestion of a genital self-exam.

This self-exploration exercise can help women become more aware of their genitals. Like many other exercises and information throughout this textbook that are aimed to help students improve their own self-knowledge or sexual health, some female readers may choose to read about this exercise but not do it. Others may wish to try some or all of the steps. If you choose to do the exploration, you may experience a variety of feelings. Some women feel selfish for spending time on themselves. You may find it difficult to remain focused on the experience instead of thinking about daily concerns. The exercise may be enjoyable for some women but not for others. Primarily, it provides an opportunity to learn about yourself—your body and your feelings.

Routine self-examination is an aspect of preventive health care.

To begin the examination, use a hand mirror, perhaps in combination with a full-length mirror, to look at your genitals from different angles and postures—standing, sitting, lying down. As you are looking, try to become aware of whatever feelings you have about your genital anatomy. You may find it helpful to draw a picture of your genitals and label the parts (identified in Figure 4.1). All women have the same parts, but the shades of color, shapes, and textures vary from woman to woman.

Women have different kinds of reactions to looking at their genitals:

I don't find it to be an attractive part of my body. I wouldn't go as far as to call it ugly. I think it would be easier to accept if it was something you weren't taught to hide and think was dirty, but I've never been able to understand why men find the vulva so intriguing. (Authors' files)

I think it looks very sensuous; the tissues look soft and tender. I was told by a previous partner that my vulva was very beautiful. His comment made me feel good about my body. (Authors' files)

Besides examining yourself visually, use your fingers to explore the various surfaces of your genitals. Focus on the sensations produced by the different kinds of touching. Note which areas are most sensitive and how the nature of stimulation varies from place to place. The primary purpose of doing this exercise is to explore, not to become sexually aroused. However, if you do become sexually excited during this self-exploration, you may be able to notice changes in the sensitivity of different skin areas that occur with arousal.

The genital self-exam serves another purpose besides helping women feel more comfortable with their anatomy and sexuality. Monthly self-examinations of the genitals can augment routine medical care. Women who know what is normal for their own bodies can often detect small changes and seek medical attention promptly. Problems usually require less extensive treatment when they are detected early. If you discover any changes, consult a health practitioner immediately. **Gynecology** (guy-nuh-KOL-uh-jee) is the medical specialty for female sexual and reproductive anatomy.

Gynecology The medical practice specializing in women's health and in diseases of the female reproductive and sexual organs.

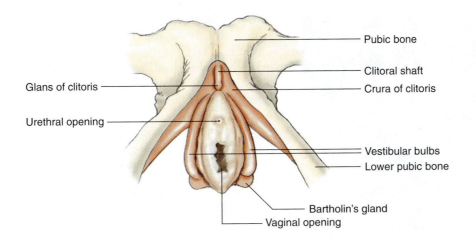

Pubic bone

Clitoral shaft

Crura of clitoris

Glans of clitoris

Urethral opening

Vestibular bulbs

Lower pubic bone

Bartholin's gland

Vaginal opening

The Clitoris

The **clitoris** (KLIT-uh-rus) comprises the external **shaft** and **glans** and the internal **crura** (KROO-ra), or roots, which project inward from each side of the clitoral shaft. The shaft and glans are located just below the mons area, where the inner lips converge. They are covered by the clitoral hood, or prepuce. Genital secretions, skin cells, and bacteria combine to form **smegma,** which can accumulate under the hood and occasionally form lumps and cause pain during sexual arousal or activity. Smegma can be prevented from collecting in this area by drawing back the hood when washing the vulva. If the smegma is already formed, a health care practitioner can remove it. ■

If you look at Figure 4.2, which shows the clitoris with the hood removed, you can see that the glans is supported by the shaft. The shaft itself cannot be seen, but it can be felt and its shape can be seen through the hood. The shaft contains two small spongy structures called the **cavernous bodies,** which engorge with blood during sexual arousal (Hamilton, 2002). These become the crura (internal leglike stalks) where they connect to the pubic bones in the pelvic cavity. The glans is often not visible under the clitoral hood, but it can be seen if a woman gently parts the labia minora and retracts the hood. The glans looks smooth, rounded, and slightly translucent. The size, shape, and position of the clitoris vary from woman to woman. These normal differences have no known relation to sexual arousal and functioning.

Initially, it may be easier for a woman to locate her clitoris by touch rather than sight because of its sensitive nerve endings. The external part of the clitoris, although tiny, has about the same number of nerve endings as the head of the penis. The clitoral glans in particular is highly sensitive, and women usually stimulate this area with the hood covering it to avoid direct stimulation, which may be too intense. Research into female masturbation patterns has produced findings in keeping with the physiological data about the location and concentrations of nerve endings. Clitoral stimulation, not vaginal insertion, is the most common way women achieve arousal and orgasm when masturbating.

Although all other sexual organs, male and female, have additional functions in reproduction or waste elimination, the only purpose of the clitoris is sexual pleasure and arousal. Sexual pleasure as the exclusive purpose of the clitoris confounds the notion of women as less sexual than men. In some parts of the world the sexual role of the clitoris is so troubling that it is removed during female genital cutting, as described in the following discussion.

Clitoris A highly sensitive structure of the female external genitals, the only function of which is sexual pleasure.

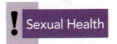

Shaft The length of the clitoris between the glans and the body.

Glans The head of the clitoris, which is richly endowed with nerve endings.

Crura The innermost tips of the cavernous bodies that connect to the pubic bones.

Smegma A cheesy substance of glandular secretions and skin cells that sometimes accumulates under the hood of the clitoris.

Cavernous bodies The structures in the shaft of the clitoris that engorge with blood during sexual arousal.

How should parents educate their daughters about their clitorises?

 # Sexuality and Diversity

Female Genital Cutting: Torture or Tradition?

Various forms of female genital cutting have been practiced at some time in almost all parts of the world, including in the United States from 1890 through the late 1930s to "cure" masturbation (Hamilton, 2002; Nour, 2000). Genital cutting still occurs today in

A baby girl is about to undergo female genital cutting in Ethiopia, where both Muslims and Christians still continue this practice despite a constitutional ban.

the United States when girls are born with a larger than normal clitoris—a topic of increasing controversy (Coventry, 2000). It also occurs in more than 40 countries in Africa, the Middle East, and Asia (Al-Krenawi & Wiesel-Lev, 1999). Females in these parts of the world undergo several types of genital cutting, usually as part of an initiation from childhood to womanhood. The village midwife performs the procedures, which are usually arranged by the girl's mother (Prince-Gibson, 2000). The simplest procedure, *circumcision,* consists of cutting off the clitoral hood. Another common practice is the removal of the clitoris itself, called *clitoridectomy.* In the most extreme practice, *genital infibulation,* the clitoris is entirely removed and the labia are cut off. Then both sides of the vulva are scraped raw and stitched up (sometimes with thorns) while the girl is held down. Razor blades or broken glass are used to cut the tissue, and the procedure is done without anesthetics, disinfectants, or sterile instruments (McCormack, 2001). The girl's legs are bound closed around the ankles and thighs for about a week (Nour, 2000). The tissue then grows together, leaving only a small opening for urine and menstrual flow to pass through (Woolard & Edwards, 1997). It is estimated that 80 million women and girls now living have undergone one of these forms of genital cutting (Hopkins, 1999).

The main objective of genital cutting is to ensure virginity before marriage. Young girls are considered unmarriageable if they do not have the prescribed excision. Because marriage is usually the only role for a woman in these cultures, her future and her family's pride depend on upholding this tradition. The social stigma for remaining uncircumcised is severe. For example, in Sudan one of the most vile invectives a man can be called is "the son of an uncircumcised mother" (Al-Krenawi & Wiesel-Lev, 1999).

The clitoris is seen as a small penis and therefore inherently male. Clitoridectomy is consequently performed to reassure men that they are not having sex with another man. As one African woman explained, "At the time of sexual relations, if the clitoris is uncut, it gets a big erect. So the woman is compared to a man because the penis is in erection and also the clitoris, so it's two men, you see" (Vissandjee et al., 2003, p. 118). In addition, the women themselves may not see themselves as completely female without this procedure.

Serious gynecological and obstetric complications often arise from genital infibulation. Complications following the procedure include bleeding and pain that lead to shock and death, prolonged bleeding that leads to anemia, infection that causes delayed healing, tetanus, and gangrene. Long-term consequences include urinary obstruction, blockage of menstrual flow, and serious difficulties during labor and delivery. Extensive vaginal scarring can make childbirth difficult, and fetal death sometimes results (Armstrong, 2003). In an attempt to minimize the health risks of female genital cutting, some believe that the procedures should be offered in medical clinics. Others maintain that doing so would legitimize a destructive practice (Shell-Duncan, 2001).

In recent years the outcry over female genital cutting pushed the United Nations to suspend its policy of nonintervention in the cultural practices of individual nations. In 1990 the Organization of African Unity condemned traditional practices that are harmful to children. The United Nations Fourth World Conference on Women in 1995 also condemned female genital cutting. Unfortunately, the strength of cultural tradition in many societies remains difficult to overcome (Gauch, 2001). Because of recent immigration patterns, U.S. obstetricians and gynecologists are encountering some of the estimated 168,000 girls and women now living in the United States who have undergone genital cutting (Hoban, 2003; Nour, 2003).

Complex legal and ethical questions are arising related to this issue (Vissandjee et al., 2003). Canada was the first nation to recognize female genital cutting as a basis for granting refugee status. In 1996 the highest U.S. immigration court granted asylum to a West African teenager for protection against female genital cutting (Superville, 1996).

A good deal of controversy has surrounded the role of the clitoris in sexual arousal and orgasm. Despite long-existing scientific knowledge about the highly concentrated nerve endings in the clitoris, the erroneous belief has persisted that vaginal rather than clitoral stimulation is—or should be—exclusively responsible for female sexual arousal and orgasm. However, the vagina has relatively fewer nerve endings than the clitoris, and the clitoris is more sensitive to touch than the vagina. Some nerve endings respond to light touch in the outer third of the vagina, but almost no nerve endings are present in the inner two-thirds. (This is why women do not feel tampons or diaphragms when they are correctly in place.) Nevertheless, many women experience erotic feelings in the vagina and find the internal pressure and stretching sensations during manual stimulation or intercourse highly pleasurable. Some experience more intense arousal from vaginal stimulation than from clitoral stimulation, especially when a woman is aroused and the vaginal tissues are fully engorged. As more and more scientific research is done, a wider range of individual variation becomes apparent (Ellison, 2000).

The Vestibule

The **vestibule** (VES-ti-byool) is the area of the vulva inside the labia minora. It is rich in blood vessels and nerve endings, and its tissues are sensitive to touch. (In architectural terminology the word *vestibule* refers to the entryway of a house.) Both the urinary and the vaginal openings are located within the vestibule.

Vestibule The area of the vulva inside the labia minora.

The Urethral Opening

Urine collected in the bladder passes out of a woman's body through the urethral opening. The **urethra** (yoo-REE-thruh) is the short tube connecting the bladder to the urinary opening, located between the clitoris and the vaginal opening.

Urethra The tube through which urine passes from the bladder to outside the body.

The Introitus and the Hymen

The opening of the vagina, called the **introitus** (in-TROH-i-tus), is located between the urinary opening and the anus. Partially covering the introitus is a fold of tissue called the **hymen** (HIGH-men), which is typically present at birth and usually remains intact until initial coitus. Occasionally, this tissue is too thick to break easily during intercourse; a medical practitioner might then be needed to make a minor incision. In rare cases an *imperforate hymen,* tissue that completely seals the vaginal opening, causes menstrual flow to collect inside the vagina. When this condition is discovered, a medical practitioner can open the hymen with an incision. Usually, however, the vaginal opening is partially open and flexible enough to insert tampons with the hymen intact (Pokorny, 1997). Although it is rare, it is possible for a woman to become pregnant even if her hymen is still intact and she has not experienced penile penetration. If semen is placed on the labia minora, the sperm can swim from outside to inside the vagina. Unless pregnancy is desired, sexual play involving rubbing the penis and vulva together should be avoided without contraception. ■

Introitus The opening to the vagina.

Hymen Tissue that partially covers the vaginal opening.

Although the hymen can protect the vaginal tissues early in life, it has no other known function. Nevertheless, many societies, including our own, have placed great significance on its presence or absence. Euphemisms such as *cherry* or *maidenhead* have been used to describe the hymen. In our society and many others people have long believed that a woman's virginity can be proved by the pain and bleeding that can occur with initial coitus, or "deflowering." At different times in various cultures bloodstained wedding night bedsheets were seen as proof that the groom had wed "intact goods" and that the marriage had been consummated. Even today, some women, particularly women from Japan and the Middle East, undergo *hymenalplasty,* surgical reconstruction of the hymen, to conceal the loss of their virginity (Ollivier, 2000).

Although pain or bleeding sometimes occurs, the hymen can be partial, flexible, or thin enough for there to be no discomfort or bleeding; it may even remain intact after intercourse.

If a woman manually stretches her hymen before initial intercourse, she may be able to minimize the discomfort that sometimes occurs. To do this, first insert a lubricated finger

(using saliva or a water-soluble sterile lubricant) into the vaginal opening and press downward toward the anus until you feel some stretching. After a few seconds, release the pressure and relax. Repeat this step several times. Next, insert two fingers into the vagina and stretch the sides of the vagina by *opening* the fingers. Repeat the downward stretching with two fingers as well. ■

The Perineum

Perineum The area between the vagina and anus of the female and the scrotum and anus of the male.

The **perineum** (per-uh-NEE-um) is the area of smooth skin between the vaginal opening and the anus (the sphincter through which bowel movements pass). The perineal tissue is endowed with nerve endings and is sensitive to touch.

During childbirth, an incision called an *episiotomy* is sometimes made in the perineum to prevent the ragged tearing of tissues that can occur when the newborn passes through the birth canal. We will discuss this in more detail in Chapter 12.

▶ Underlying Structures

If the hair, skin, and fatty pads were removed from the vulva, several underlying structures could be seen (see Figure 4.2). The shaft of the clitoris would be visible, no longer concealed by the hood, as would the crura. These bodies are part of the vast network of bulbs and vessels that engorge with blood during sexual arousal. The **vestibular** (veh-STIB-yoo-ler) **bulbs** alongside the vagina also fill with blood during sexual excitement, causing the vagina to increase in length and the vulvar area to become swollen. These bulbs are similar in structure and function to the spongy tissue in the penis that engorges during arousal and causes erection (Bartlik & Goldberg, 2000). Compression of these tissues by the penis during intercourse causes internal sensations that some women find pleasurable (Ellison, 2000).

Vestibular bulbs Two bulbs, one on each side of the vaginal opening, that engorge with blood during sexual arousal.

Bartholin's glands Two small glands slightly inside the vaginal opening that secrete a few drops of fluid during sexual arousal.

Bartholin's glands, one on each side of the vaginal opening, were once believed to be the source of vaginal lubrication during sexual arousal; however, they typically produce only a drop or two of fluid just before orgasm. The glands are usually not noticeable, but sometimes the duct from a Bartholin's gland becomes clogged, and the fluid that is normally secreted remains inside and causes enlargement. If this occurs and the swelling does not subside within a few days, it is best to see a health care practitioner. ■

Besides the glands and network of vessels, a complex musculature underlies the genital area (Figure 4.3). The *pelvic floor muscles* have a multidirectional design that allows the vaginal opening to expand greatly during childbirth and to contract afterward.

▶ Figure 4.3
The underlying muscles of the vulva. These muscles can be strengthened using the Kegel exercises described in the "Your Sexual Health" box.

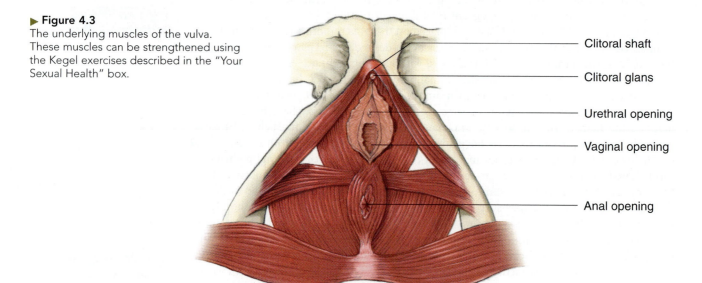

Clitoral shaft

Clitoral glans

Urethral opening

Vaginal opening

Anal opening

Kegel Exercises

The pelvic floor muscles squeeze involuntarily at orgasm; they also can be trained to contract voluntarily through a series of exercises known as **Kegel** (KAY-gul) **exercises.** These exercises were developed by Arnold Kegel in 1952 to help women regain urinary control after childbirth. (Not uncommonly, women who have recently given birth lose urine when they cough or sneeze as a result of excessive stretching and tearing of perineal muscles during childbirth.)

Kegel exercises have been shown to have other effects besides restoring muscle tone (Beji, 2003). After about 6 weeks of regular exercise many women report increased sensation during intercourse and a general increase in genital sensitivity. This seems to be associated with their increased awareness of their sex organs and their improved muscle tone.

The steps for the Kegel exercises are (Ono, 1994):

1. Locate the muscles surrounding the vagina. This can be done by stopping the flow of urine to feel which muscles contract. An even more effective way of contracting the pelvic floor muscles is to contract the anal sphincter as if to hold back gas.
2. Insert a finger into the opening of your vagina and contract the muscles you located in Step 1. Feel the muscles squeeze your finger.
3. Squeeze the same muscles for 10 seconds. Relax. Repeat 10 times.
4. Squeeze and release as rapidly as possible, 10 to 25 times. Repeat.
5. Imagine trying to suck something into your vagina. Hold for 3 seconds.
6. This exercise series should be done three times a day.

> **Kegel exercises** A series of exercises that strengthen the muscles underlying the external female or male genitals.

▶ Internal Structures

Internal female sexual anatomy consists of the vagina, cervix, uterus, and ovaries. These are discussed in the following sections. Refer to Figure 4.4 for cross-section and front views of the female pelvis.

The Vagina

The **vagina** is a canal that opens between the labia minora and extends into the body, angling upward toward the small of the back to the cervix and uterus. Women who are unfamiliar with their anatomy can have a difficult time when they first try inserting a tampon into the vagina:

No matter how hard I tried, I couldn't get a tampon in until I inserted a finger and realized that my vagina slanted backward. I had been pushing straight up onto the upper wall. (Authors' files)

The unaroused vagina is approximately 3 to 5 inches long. The walls form a flat tube. The analogy of a glove is often used to illustrate the vagina as a potential rather than an actual space, with its walls able to expand enough to serve as a birth passage. In addition, the vagina changes in size and shape during sexual arousal, as we will discuss in Chapter 6.

The vagina contains three layers of tissue: mucous, muscle, and fibrous tissue. All these layers are richly endowed with blood vessels. The **mucosa** (myoo-KOH-suh) is the layer of mucous membrane that a woman feels when she inserts a finger inside her vagina. The folded walls, or **rugae** (ROO-jee), feel soft, moist, and warm, resembling the inside of one's mouth. The walls normally produce secretions that help maintain the chemical balance of the vagina. During sexual arousal, a lubricating substance exudes through the mucosa.

Most of the second layer, composed of muscle tissue, is concentrated around the vaginal opening. Because of the concentration of musculature in the outer third and the expansive ability of the inner two-thirds of the vagina, a situation often develops that can be at best funny and at worst embarrassing. During headstands and certain yoga or coital positions with the pelvis elevated, gravity causes the inner two-thirds to expand and draw air into the vagina. The outer muscles tighten, and the trapped air is forced back out through the

> **Vagina** A stretchable canal in the female that opens at the vulva and extends about 4 inches into the pelvis.

> **Mucosa** Collective term for the mucous membranes; moist tissue that lines certain body areas such as the penile urethra, vagina, and mouth.

> **Rugae** The folds of tissue in the vagina.

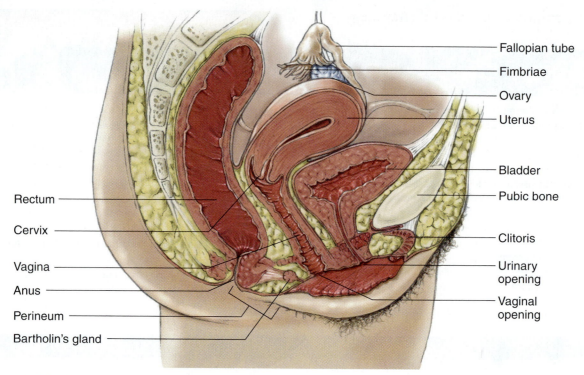

Fallopian tube

Fimbriae

Ovary

Uterus

Bladder

Pubic bone

Rectum

Cervix

Clitoris

Vagina

Urinary opening

Anus

Perineum

Vaginal opening

Bartholin's gland

(a) **Side view**

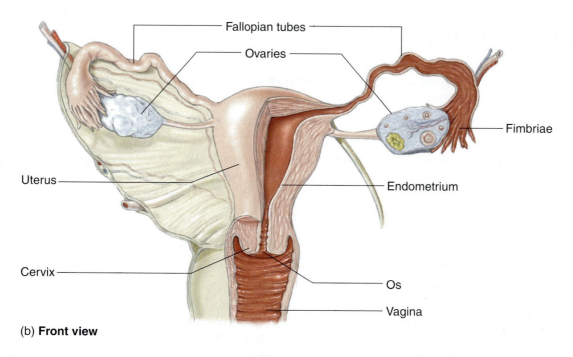

Fallopian tubes

Ovaries

Fimbriae

Uterus

Endometrium

Cervix

Os

Vagina

(b) **Front view**

▶ **Figure 4.4**
Internal female sexual anatomy: (a) cross-sectional side view of female internal structures; (b) front view of the internal organs. Parts of the ovaries, uterus, and vagina are shown cut away.

tightened muscles, creating a sound we usually associate with a different orifice. One student has suggested calling this phenomenon "varting," because the sound is similar to that of a fart (fortunately, there is no unpleasant smell).

Surrounding the muscular layer is the innermost vaginal layer, composed of fibrous tissue. This layer aids in vaginal contraction and expansion and acts as connective tissue to other structures in the pelvic cavity.

Arousal and Vaginal Lubrication

So far in this chapter, we have described the parts of the female sexual anatomy, but we have said relatively little about how these structures function. Because lubrication is a unique feature of the vagina, the process is explained here. Other physiological aspects of female arousal will be discussed in Chapter 6.

During sexual arousal, a clear, slippery fluid begins to appear on the vaginal mucosa within 10 to 30 seconds after effective physical or psychological stimulation begins. By inserting a clear phallus-shaped camera into the vagina, Masters and Johnson determined that this lubrication is a result of **vasocongestion,** the pooling of blood in the pelvic area. During vasocongestion the extensive network of blood vessels in the tissues surrounding the vagina engorges with blood. Clear fluid seeps from the congested tissues to the inside of the vaginal walls to form the characteristic slippery coating of the sexually aroused vagina.

Vaginal lubrication serves two functions. First, it enhances the possibility of conception by helping to alkalinize the normally acidic vaginal chemical balance. Vaginal pH level changes from 4.5 to 6.0–6.5 with sexual arousal (Meston, 2000).* Sperm travel faster and survive longer in an alkaline environment than in an acidic one. (The seminal fluid of the male also helps alkalinize the vagina.) Second, vaginal lubrication can increase sexual enjoyment. During manual genital stimulation, the slippery wetness can increase the sensuousness and pleasure of touching. During oral–genital sex, some women's partners enjoy the erotic scent and taste of the vaginal lubrication. During intercourse, vaginal lubrication makes the walls of the vagina slippery, which facilitates entry of the penis into the vagina. Lubrication also helps make the thrusting of intercourse pleasurable. Without adequate lubrication, entry of the penis and subsequent thrusting can be uncomfortable for the woman—and often for the man. Irritation and small tears of the vaginal tissue can result.

Insufficient vaginal lubrication can be remedied in several ways, depending on the source of the difficulty. Changing any anxiety-producing circumstances and engaging in effective stimulation are important. Saliva, lubricated condoms, or a nonirritating water-soluble jelly can be used to provide additional lubrication. Occasionally, hormone treatment is necessary. ■

Vasocongestion The engorgement of blood vessels in particular body parts in response to sexual arousal.

The Grafenberg Spot

The **Grafenberg spot** is an area located within the anterior (or front) wall of the vagina, about 1 centimeter from the skin's surface and one-third to one-half the way in from the vaginal opening. It consists of a system of glands (Skene's glands) and ducts that surround the urethra. This area is believed to be the female counterpart to the male prostate gland, developed from the same embryonic tissue (Heath, 1984).

The Grafenberg spot has generated considerable interest because of reports that some women experience sexual arousal, orgasm, and perhaps even an ejaculation of fluid when stimulated there (Darling et al., 1990), although many women do not have such an area of increased sensation. We will further discuss the role of the Grafenberg spot in female sexual response in Chapter 6.

Grafenberg spot Glands and ducts located in the anterior wall of the vagina. Some women experience sexual pleasure, arousal, orgasm, and an ejaculation of fluids from stimulation of the Grafenberg spot.

Vaginal Secretions and Chemical Balance of the Vagina

Both the vaginal walls and the cervix produce white or yellowish secretions. These secretions are normal and are a sign of vaginal health. They vary in appearance according to hormone-level changes during the menstrual cycle. (Keeping track of these variations is the basis for one method of birth control, discussed in Chapter 11.) The taste and scent of vaginal secretions can also vary with the time of a woman's cycle and her level of arousal.

The vagina's natural chemical and bacterial balance helps promote healthy mucosa. The chemical balance is normally rather acidic (pH 4.5—the same as is found in red wine [Angier, 1999]). A variety of factors can alter this balance, resulting in vaginal problems. Among these are **douching** (rinsing out the inside of the vagina) and using feminine-hygiene sprays. Douching is definitely *not* necessary for routine hygiene and can alter the

Douching Rinsing out the vagina with plain water or a variety of solutions. It is usually unnecessary for hygiene, and too frequent douching can result in vaginal irritation.

*pH is a measure of acidity or alkalinity. A neutral substance (neither acidic nor alkaline) has a pH of 7. A lower number means a substance is more acidic; a higher number means it is more alkaline.

natural chemical balance of the vagina. Douching can increase a woman's susceptibility to infections and other health risks, although most women mistakenly believe douching is healthy (Ness et al., 2003). Various studies have found that douching increases the risk of pelvic inflammatory disease, endometriosis, transmission of HIV, ectopic pregnancy, and decreased fertility. Furthermore, douching during pregnancy increases the likelihood of preterm births (Cottrell, 2003).

Feminine-hygiene sprays can cause irritation, allergic reactions, burns, infections, dermatitis of the thighs, and numerous other problems. In fact, genital deodorant sprays and body powders have been associated with an increased risk of ovarian cancer (Cook et al., 1997). Furthermore, deodorant tampons are unnecessary: Menstrual fluid has virtually no odor until it is outside the body. Regular bathing with a mild soap and washing between the folds of the vulva are all that are necessary for proper hygiene.

Advertising has played on our cultural negativity about female sexual organs, turning misguided attempts to eradicate normal secretions and scents into an extremely profitable business. Women grow up hearing slogans such as "Unfortunately, the trickiest deodorant problem a girl has isn't under her pretty little arms," and "Our product eliminates the moist, uncomfortable feeling most women normally have just because they're women."

Consequently, women in the United States spend about $500 million each year on over-the-counter douches. "Feminine hygiene products" are heavily advertised and take advantage of women's discomfort with their genitals. Ads act as a kind of education, which, in some cases, is inaccurate (Wolf & Kielwasser, 2003). Minorities and educationally and economically disadvantaged women appear more vulnerable to misinformation: Twice as many African American women douche than white women, and, regardless of race, the prevalence of douching is higher in women who have less education and income (Cottrell, 2003).

The Cervix

The **cervix** (SER-viks), located at the back of the vagina, is the small end of the pear-shaped uterus (see Figure 4.4). The cervix contains mucus-secreting glands. Sperm pass through the vagina into the uterus through the **os,** the opening in the center of the cervix.

A woman can see her own cervix if she learns to insert a **speculum** into her vagina. She can also ask for a mirror when she has her pelvic exam. A woman can feel her own cervix by

© George DeSota/Getty Images

Eve Ensler's one-woman play *The Vagina Monologues* answers the question "If your vagina could talk, what would it say?" Ensler's play has spurred a global grassroots movement, called V-Day, to stop violence against women and girls.

Cervix The small end of the uterus, located at the back of the vagina.

Os The opening in the cervix that leads to the interior of the uterus.

Speculum An instrument used to open the vaginal walls during a gynecological exam.

The speculum opens the walls of the vaginal canal.

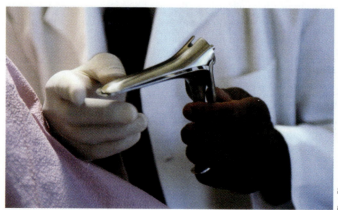

PhotoDisc

inserting one or two fingers into the vagina and reaching to the end of the canal. (Sometimes squatting and bearing down brings the cervix closer to the vaginal entrance.) The cervix feels somewhat like the end of a nose, firm and round in contrast to the soft vaginal walls.

The Uterus

The **uterus** (YOO-tuh-rus), or womb, is a hollow, thick, pear-shaped organ, approximately 3 inches long and 2 inches wide in a woman who has never had a child. (It is somewhat larger after pregnancy.) The uterus is suspended in the pelvic cavity by ligaments; in different women its position can vary from *anteflexed* (tipped forward toward the abdomen) to *retroflexed* (tipped back toward the spine). Women with retroflexed uteri are more likely to experience menstrual discomfort or have difficulty inserting a diaphragm. Although it was once thought that a retroflexed uterus interfered with conception, it does not impair fertility.

The walls of the uterus consist of three layers. The external layer is a thin membrane called the **perimetrium** (pear-ee-MEE-tree-um). The middle layer, or **myometrium** (my-oh-MEE-tree-um), is made of longitudinal and circular muscle fibers that interweave like the fibers of a basket; this enables the uterus to stretch during pregnancy and contract during labor and orgasm. At the top of the uterus, an area called the *fundus,* the uterine walls are especially thick. The inner lining of the uterus is called the **endometrium** (en-doh-MEE-tree-um). Rich in blood vessels, the endometrium nourishes the *zygote* (united sperm and egg), which travels down to the uterus from the fallopian tubes after fertilization. In preparation for this event, the endometrium thickens and sheds in response to hormone changes during the monthly menstrual cycle, discussed later in this chapter. The endometrium is also a source of hormone production.

Uterus A pear-shaped organ inside the female pelvis, within which the fetus develops.

Perimetrium The thin membrane covering the outside of the uterus.

Myometrium The smooth muscle layer of the uterine wall.

Endometrium The tissue that lines the inside of the uterine walls.

The Fallopian Tubes

Each of the two 4-inch **fallopian** (fuh-LOH-pee-un) **tubes** extends from the uterus toward an ovary, at the left or the right side of the pelvic cavity (see Figure 4.4). The outside end of each tube is shaped like a funnel, with fringelike projections called **fimbriae** (FIM-bree-eye) that hover over the ovary. When the egg leaves the ovary, it is drawn into the tube by the fimbriae.

Once the egg is inside the fallopian tube, the movements of tiny, hairlike *cilia* and the contractions of the tube walls move it along at a rate of approximately 1 inch every 24 hours. The egg remains viable for fertilization for about 24 to 48 hours. Therefore fertilization occurs while the egg is still close to the ovary. After fertilization the zygote begins developing as it continues traveling down the tube to the uterus.

An **ectopic pregnancy** occurs when a fertilized ovum implants outside the uterus, most commonly in the fallopian tube. This implantation can rupture the tube and cause uncontrolled bleeding, which is a serious medical emergency. The most common symptoms of ectopic pregnancy are abdominal pain and spotting that occur 6 to 8 weeks after the last menstrual period. Diagnostic tests can establish the presence of an ectopic pregnancy, and medical and surgical procedures are used to treat it (Morlock et al., 2000; Tenore, 2000).

Fallopian tubes Two tubes, extending from the sides of the uterus, in which the egg and sperm travel.

Fimbriae Fringelike ends of the fallopian tubes into which the released ovum enters.

Ectopic pregnancy A pregnancy that occurs when a fertilized ovum implants outside the uterus, most commonly in the fallopian tube.

The Ovaries

The two **ovaries,** which are about the size and shape of almonds, are located at the ends of the fallopian tubes, one on each side of the uterus. They are connected to the pelvic wall and the uterus by ligaments. The ovaries are endocrine glands that produce three classes of sex hormones. The estrogens, as mentioned in Chapter 3, influence development of female physical sex characteristics and help regulate the menstrual cycle. The progestational compounds also help regulate the menstrual cycle and promote maturity of the uterine lining in preparation for pregnancy. The ovaries also produce about half of a woman's testosterone (Lemonick, 2004). Around the onset of puberty the female sex hormones play a critical role in initiating maturation of the uterus, ovaries, and vagina and in developing the *secondary sex characteristics,* such as pubic hair and breasts.

The ovaries contain up to 472,000 immature ova at birth. During the years between puberty and menopause, one or the other ovary typically releases an egg during each cycle. Only 400 ova are destined for full maturation during a woman's reproductive years

Ovaries Female gonads that produce ova and sex hormones.

Ovulation The release of a mature ovum from the ovary.

(Macklon & Fauser, 2000). **Ovulation** (ahv-yoo-LAY-shun), or egg maturation and release, occurs as the result of the complex chain of events we know as the menstrual cycle, discussed in the next section.

▶ Menstruation

Menstruation The sloughing off of the built-up uterine lining that takes place if conception has not occurred.

Menstruation (men-stroo-Ā-shun), the sloughing off of uterine lining that takes place if conception has not occurred, is a sign of normal physical functioning. Negative attitudes about it, however, persist in contemporary American society.

Attitudes About Menstruation

American folklore reveals many interesting ideas about menstruation. In the 1920s women commonly believed that a permanent wave given during menstruation would not curl their hair. Other myths include the belief that it is harmful for a woman to be physically active during menstruation, that a corsage worn by a menstruating woman will wilt, and that a tooth filling done during menstruation will fall out (Milow, 1983).

Controversy exists about the meaning of menstrual rituals in some cultures. The meanings are often ambiguous, and little is actually known about the significance of menstrual taboos. In some societies a menstruating woman is isolated from the community and remains in a "menstrual hut." Researchers have rarely asked about the meaning of and experiences in the menstrual huts. Do women feel resentful and diminished or honored and pleased by the break from normal labor? Scattered reports suggest considerable variability, with positive meanings being fairly common. Menstrual customs can provide women with a means of solidarity, influence, and autonomy. For example, in some Native American traditions women were believed to be at their most powerful during menstruation. They would retreat to a "moon lodge" to be free of mundane daily chores. Blood flow was believed to purify women and to enable them to gather spiritual wisdom to benefit the entire tribe. Most Native American tribes also had celebrations for a girl's first menstruation (Angier, 1999; Owen, 1993). In South America, Inca Indians celebrated a girl's first menstruation by giving her adult clothing and her adult name. Shedding blood symbolized the transformation into adulthood; boys bled when elders pierced the boys' ears and inserted large ear spools as part of their coming-of-age ceremony (Wiesner-Hanks, 2000).

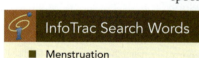

InfoTrac Search Words

■ Menstruation

Native American women retreated to special huts during menstruation.

© Bettmann/CORBIS

In a few cultures menstruation is described in lyrical words and positive images. The Japanese expression for a girl's first menstruation is "the year of the cleavage of the melon," and one East Indian description of menstruation is the "flower growing in the house of the god of love" (Delaney et al., 1976).

Another possibility is that the taboos are meant to constrain women and reinforce their lower social status (Forbes et al., 2003). A Roman historian wrote that bees will leave their hive, boiling linen will turn black, and razors will become blunt if touched by a menstruating woman. In the Bible, Leviticus states, "And if a woman have an issue and her issue in her flesh be blood, she shall be apart seven days: and whosoever touchet her shall be unclean until the even" (Leviticus 15:19). Contemporary Orthodox Judaism follows this teaching: Women are not to engage in sexual activity until they have attended a ceremonial cleansing bath following menstruation (Rothbaum & Jackson, 1990). One intention of this abstinence during menstruation is to keep the couple's desire for each other as fresh as in early married life.

Despite any negative myths and societal attitudes toward menstruation, most women associate regular menstrual cycles with healthy functioning and femininity. Further, research finds that women who have positive attitudes and comfort with menstruation are more likely to be more comfortable with their personal sexual feelings and behaviors than are women who have more negative attitudes about menstruation. In addition, women who had been sexual with their partner during menses were particularly comfortable with menstruation and were more aroused by sexual activities (Rempel & Baumgartner, 2003). Some women and families are redefining menstruation from a more positive perspective. For example, some may have a celebration or give a gift to a young woman when she has her first menstrual period (Kissling, 2002). Some view menstruation as an "emblem of primal female power" (Ehrenreich, 1999). One aspect of the menstrual cycle that people often see as positive is its cyclic pattern, typical of many natural phenomena.

The poet May Sarton describes the analogy of the menstrual cycle and nature in this 1937 poem:

> *There were seeds*
> *within her*
> *that burst at intervals*
> *and for a little while*
> *she would come back*
> *to heaviness,*
> *and then before a surging miracle*
> *of blood,*
> *relax,*
> *and re-identify herself,*
> *each time more closely*
> *with the heart of life.*
> *'I am the beginning,*
> *the never-ending,*
> *the perfect tree.'*
> *And she would lean*
> *again as one*
> *on the great curve of the earth,*
> *part of its turning,*
> *as distinctly part*
> *of the universe as a star—*
> *as unresistant,*
> *as completely rhythmical.*

Menarche

The menstrual cycle usually begins in the early teens, between the ages of 11 and 15, although some girls begin earlier or later. The average age of first menstruation in the United States is 12.8 years of age for white girls and 12.2 years for African American girls (Lemonick, 2000; Monsen, 2001). The first menstrual bleeding is called **menarche** (MEH-nar-kee). The timing of menarche appears to be related to heredity, general health, and altitude (average menarche is earlier in lower altitudes) and occurs during a time of other changes in body size and development (Forbes, 1992). Menstrual cycles end at menopause, which in most women occurs between the ages of 45 and 55. Differences in the age of menarche are often a concern for young women, especially those who begin earlier or later than the norm.

Menarche The initial onset of menstrual periods in a young woman.

Many young women are not fully informed about the developments and changes that accompany the onset of menstruation. Without adequate information girls may feel confused or frightened about their first periods. Young men are often uninformed about menstruation.

Menstrual Physiology

During the menstrual cycle the uterine lining is prepared for the implantation of a fertilized ovum. If conception does not occur, the lining sloughs off and is discharged as menstrual flow. The length of the menstrual cycle is usually measured from the beginning of the first day of flow to the day before the next flow begins. The menstrual period itself typically lasts 2 to 6 days. It is normal for the volume of the menstrual flow (usually 6 to 8 ounces) to vary. The cycle length varies from woman to woman; it can be anywhere from 24 to 42 days

(Belsey & Pinol, 1997). These time differences occur in the phase before ovulation. The interval between ovulation and the onset of menstruation is 14 days, plus or minus 2 days, even when there is several weeks' difference in the total length of the cycle. Life changes and stress can affect cycle length. If a woman experiences a dramatic change in her usual pattern, she should seek medical attention.

Menstrual Synchrony

An interesting phenomenon known as **menstrual synchrony** sometimes occurs among women who live together and have considerable contact with one another: They develop similar menstrual cycles (Cutler, 1999). The function of the uniform cycles is unknown, but the trigger is believed to be related to the sense of smell.

To test this hypothesis, researchers had subjects with normal menstrual cycles swab their upper lips with either perspiration extract from another woman or with plain alcohol. Within three menstrual cycles 80% of the subjects who had received the perspiration extract were menstruating in sync with their perspiration donors. The control group showed no menstrual cycle changes (Cutler et al., 1986).

The Menstrual Cycle

The menstrual cycle is regulated by intricate relationships between the hypothalamus and various endocrine glands, including the pituitary gland (located in the brain), the adrenal glands, and the ovaries and uterus (see Figure 4.5). The hypothalamus monitors hormone levels in the bloodstream throughout the cycle, releasing chemicals that stimulate the pituitary to produce two hormones that affect the ovaries: **follicle-stimulating hormone (FSH)** and **luteinizing** (LOO-te-uh-ny-zing) **hormone (LH).** FSH stimulates the ovaries to produce estrogen and also causes ova to mature in follicles (small sacs) within the ovaries. LH causes the ovary to release a mature ovum. LH also stimulates the development of the **corpus luteum** (the portion of the follicle that remains after the matured egg has been released), which produces the hormone progesterone.

The menstrual cycle is a self-regulating and dynamic process. Each hormone is secreted until the organ it acts on is stimulated; at that point the organ releases a substance that circulates back through the system to reduce hormonal activity in the initiating gland. This *negative-feedback mechanism* provides an internal control that regulates hormone fluctuation during the three phases of the menstrual cycle: the menstrual phase, the proliferative phase, and the secretory phase. These phases, described in the following paragraphs, are illustrated in Figures 4.5 and 4.6.

Menstrual Phase

During the **menstrual phase** the uterus sheds the thickened inner layer of the endometrium, which is discharged through the cervix and vagina as menstrual flow. Menstrual flow typically consists of blood, mucus, and endometrial tissue.

The shedding of the endometrium is triggered by reduced progesterone and estrogen levels in the bloodstream. As these hormone levels fall, the hypothalamus stimulates the pituitary gland to release FSH. This action initiates the second, proliferative, phase of the menstrual cycle.

Proliferative Phase

During the **proliferative phase** the pituitary gland increases production of FSH, which stimulates the developing follicles to mature and to produce several types of estrogen. Estrogen in turn causes the endometrium to thicken. Although several follicles begin to mature, usually only one reaches maturity; the other follicles degenerate. When the level of ovarian estrogen circulating in the bloodstream reaches a peak, the pituitary gland depresses the release of FSH and stimulates LH production.

Regardless of cycle length, ovulation occurs 14 days prior to the onset of menstruation, as shown in Figure 4.7. In response to the spurt of LH secreted by the pituitary gland, the mature follicle ruptures and the ovum is released. Some women experience a twinge, cramp,

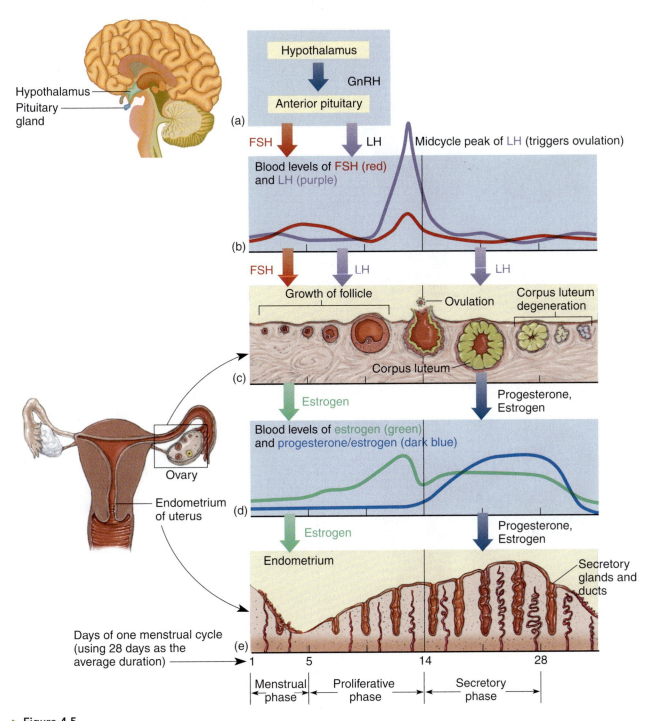

Hypothalamus
Pituitary gland

Hypothalamus

GnRH

Anterior pituitary

(a)

FSH   LH   Midcycle peak of LH (triggers ovulation)

Blood levels of FSH (red)
and LH (purple)

(b)

FSH   LH   LH

Growth of follicle   Ovulation   Corpus luteum degeneration

Corpus luteum

(c)

Estrogen   Progesterone, Estrogen

Blood levels of estrogen (green)
and progesterone/estrogen (dark blue)

Ovary

Endometrium
of uterus

(d)

Estrogen   Progesterone, Estrogen

Endometrium   Secretory glands and ducts

Days of one menstrual cycle
(using 28 days as the
average duration)

(e)

1   5   14   28

Menstrual phase | Proliferative phase | Secretory phase

▶ Figure 4.5

Changes during the menstrual cycle: (a) The hypothalamus in the brain measures levels of hormones and releases GnRH (gonadotropin-releasing hormone) to stimulate the pituitary to secrete FSH and LH into the bloodstream. (b) The levels of FSH (red line) and LH (purple line) vary during the complete cycle. (c) Ovarian changes during the phases of the cycle. (d) Fluctuations in blood levels of estrogen and progesterone produced by the ovaries. (e) Effects of estrogen and progesterone on the lining of the uterus. After ovulation, the glands and ducts inside the endometrium (drawn as vertical tubes and spirals) develop and secrete nutrients that, if the woman became pregnant, would support the embryo.

or pressure in the lower abdomen, called *Mittelschmerz* (German for *middle pain*), at ovulation. Mittelschmerz is caused by the swelling and bursting of the follicle or by a little fluid or blood from the ruptured follicle irritating the sensitive abdominal lining. The released ovum then travels to the fallopian tube. Occasionally, more than one ovum is released. If two ova are fertilized, nonidentical twins will develop. When one egg is fertilized and then divides into two separate zygotes, identical twins result.

(a) Proliferative phase

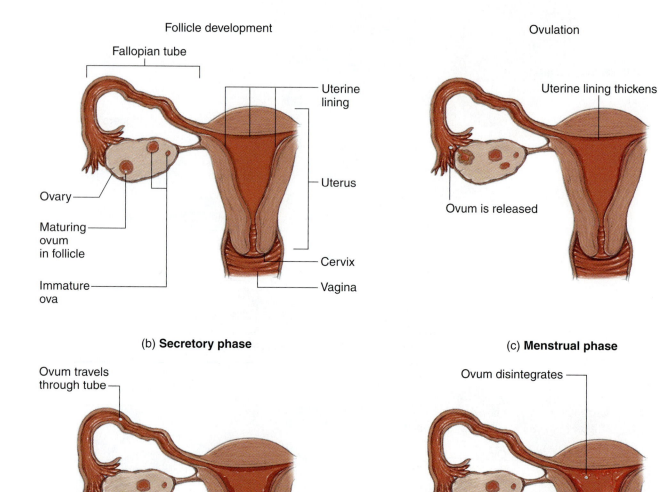

Follicle development

Ovulation

Fallopian tube

Uterine lining

Uterine lining thickens

Ovary

Maturing ovum in follicle

Immature ova

Uterus

Cervix

Vagina

Ovum is released

(b) Secretory phase

Ovum travels through tube

Remaining cells of follicle develop into corpus luteum

Lining continues to thicken

(c) Menstrual phase

Ovum disintegrates

Uterine lining sloughs off and passes out of the body through the cervix and vagina

▶ **Figure 4.6**
The changes to the ovaries and uterus during (a) the proliferative phase, including ovulation, (b) the secretory phase, and (c) the menstrual phase of the menstrual cycle.

Around the time of ovulation, secretions of cervical mucus increase because of increased levels of estrogen. The mucus also changes, becoming clear, slippery, and stretchy. The pH of this mucus is more alkaline; as noted earlier, a more alkaline vaginal environment contributes to sperm motility and longevity. This is the time in the cycle when a woman can most easily become pregnant.

Secretory Phase

Secretory phase The phase of the menstrual cycle in which the corpus luteum develops and secretes progesterone.

During the **secretory phase** continued pituitary secretions of LH cause the cells of the ruptured follicle to develop into a yellowish bump called the corpus luteum. The corpus luteum secretes progesterone, which inhibits the production of the cervical mucus during ovulation.

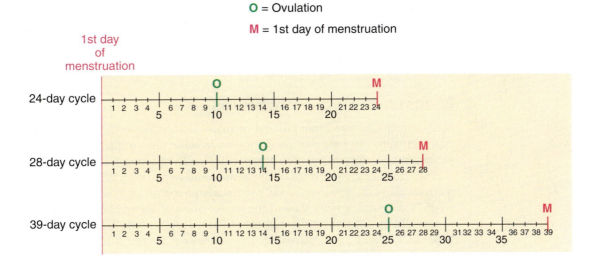

▶ **Figure 4.7**
Ovulation timing and cycle length. Regardless of the length of the cycle, ovulation occurs 14 days *before* menstruation.

Together with estrogen produced by the ovaries, progesterone causes the endometrium to thicken and engorge with blood in preparation for implantation of the **blastocyst.** Glands and ducts in the endometrium develop and secrete nutrients to ensure development of the blastocyst, the reason this phase is called the secretory phase. If implantation does not occur, the pituitary gland responds to high estrogen and progesterone levels in the bloodstream by shutting down production of LH and FSH. This causes the corpus luteum to degenerate, and estrogen and progesterone production decreases. This reduction of hormone levels triggers the sloughing off of the endometrium, initiating the menstrual phase once again.

Blastocyst Multicelled descendant of the united egg and sperm.

Sexual Activity and the Menstrual Cycle

A number of studies have tried to determine whether sexual behavior is affected by the menstrual cycle. The findings have been varied. Some studies show little variation in sexual arousal at different points in the menstrual cycle (Meuwissen & Over, 1991). Other studies suggest that sexual feelings and behavior increase during ovulation (Lemonick, 2004) and also during menstruation and the preceding few days (Friedman et al., 1980). In an attempt to control for external variables such as contraceptive use, fear of pregnancy, and male influence, one research group examined the relationship between cycle phase and sexual response and activity in a sample of lesbians. In this sample, partner- and self-initiated sexual activity increased in frequency at midcycle, as did orgasm, but sexual thoughts and fantasies peaked in the first 3 days after the onset of menstruation (Matteo & Rissman, 1984). Great individual variation exists; we encourage women readers and their partners to notice their own patterns and to talk about their feelings about sexual activity and menstruation.

Intercourse during menstruation is often avoided (Barnhart et al., 1995). One study found that both men and women initiated substantially fewer sexual activities during menstruation than at any other time during the cycle (Harvey, 1987). Although from a medical point of view there are no health reasons to avoid intercourse during menstruation (except in the case of excessive bleeding or other menstrual problems), many couples do so.

Reasons for avoiding sex during a woman's period vary. Uncomfortable physical symptoms of breast tenderness and menstruation can reduce sexual desire or pleasure, and the messiness can inhibit sexual playfulness. Religious beliefs can also be a factor. Some women and men avoid sexual activity because of culturally induced shame about menstruation.

If people do prefer to abstain from coitus during menstruation, the remaining repertoire of sexual activities is still available:

When I'm on my period, I leave my tampon inside and push the string in, too. My husband and I have manual and oral stimulation, and a great time! (Authors' files)

Some women use a diaphragm or cervical cap to hold back the menstrual flow during coitus. Orgasm by any means of stimulation can be beneficial to a menstruating woman. The uterine contractions and release of vasocongestion often reduce backache, feelings of pelvic fullness, and cramping.

Menstrual Cycle Problems

Most women undergo some physical or mood changes, or both, during their menstrual cycles. In many cases the changes are minor. In some cases women experience heightened pleasant moods during ovulation or menstruation (McFarlane et al., 1988).

Popular culture, as reflected by the media, tends to put forth negative and distorted perspectives about the menstrual cycle, particularly premenstrual syndrome (PMS). An analysis of 78 magazine articles showed the perpetuation of the stereotype of the maladjusted woman, listing 131 different symptoms of PMS. Titles include "The Taming of the Shrew Inside of You" and "Premenstrual Frenzy" (Chrisler & Levy, 1990). Most scientific research about menstruation has focused on negative effects. However, one study compared women's responses to the Menstrual Joy Questionnaire (MJQ) with those of a commonly used research tool, the Menstrual Distress Questionnaire. The MJQ's questions about such positive qualities as increased sexual desire, high spirits, feelings of affection, and self-confidence did result in subjects later reporting more positive attitudes and fewer negative symptoms about menstruation. The researchers concluded that the way menstruation is portrayed by research and popular culture affects how women think about their menstrual cycles (Chrisler et al., 1994).

Premenstrual Syndrome

Premenstrual syndrome (PMS) is a catchall term used to identify myriad physical and psychological symptoms that can occur before each menstrual period. As many as 200 premenstrual symptoms are listed in medical and research literature (O'Brien et al., 2000). Typical symptoms include bloating, breast swelling, and pain. (Fat layers in the waist and thighs become slightly thicker before menstruation—hence the period-related tight-jeans syndrome [Pearson, 2000].) Psychological symptoms include irritability, tension, depression, mood swings, and a feeling of a lack of emotional control. Some of these PMS symptoms can be disruptive to close relationships. Research finds that partners of women with PMS symptoms reported problems from increased conflict and withdrawal (Pearlstein et al., 2000).

Approximately 80–95% of women experience mild discomfort premenstrually, and only 5% have no PMS symptoms before menstruation. Five percent of women have symptoms severe enough for a diagnosis of **premenstrual dysphoric disorder (PMDD),** with symptoms significantly affecting their normal functioning (Grady-Weliky, 2003; O'Brien et al., 2000).

The causes of PMS and PMDD are unknown (Girman et al., 2003). Placebo-controlled studies have shown that medications used for depression, called SSRIs, alleviate physical and psychological symptoms and improve quality of life and interpersonal functioning (Dickerson et al., 2003). Oral contraceptives can also help some women (Grady-Weliky, 2003).

Dysmenorrhea

Painful menstruation is called **dysmenorrhea** (dis-meh-nuh-REE-uh). *Primary dysmenorrhea* occurs during menstruation and is usually caused by the overproduction of **prostaglandins,** chemicals that cause the muscles of the uterus to contract. Problems with primary dysmenorrhea usually appear with the onset of menstruation at adolescence. The symptoms are generally most noticeable during the first few days of a woman's period and include abdominal aching and/or cramping. Some women also experience nausea, vomiting, diarrhea, headache, dizziness, fatigue, irritability, or nervousness.

Secondary dysmenorrhea occurs before or during menstruation and is characterized by constant and often spasmodic lower abdominal pain that typically extends to the back and thighs. The symptoms are often similar to those of primary dysmenorrhea and are caused by factors other than prostaglandin production; possible causes include the presence of an intrauterine device (IUD), pelvic inflammatory disease (chronic infection of the reproductive

---

Premenstrual syndrome (PMS) Symptoms of physical discomfort and emotional irritability that occur 2 to 12 days before menstruation.

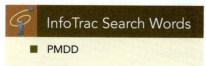
InfoTrac Search Words

■ PMDD

Premenstrual dysphoric disorder (PMDD) Premenstrual symptoms severe enough to significantly disrupt a woman's functioning.

Dysmenorrhea Pain or discomfort before or during menstruation.

Prostaglandins Hormones that induce uterine contractions.

organs), benign uterine tumors, obstruction of the cervical opening, and **endometriosis** (en-doh-mee-tree-OH-sis). Endometriosis, which affects up to 15% of premenopausal women (including adolescents), occurs when endometrial-like tissue implants in the abdominal cavity. The implanted tissue often adheres to other tissue in the pelvic cavity, reducing mobility of the internal structures and engorging with blood during the proliferative phase. The engorged tissues and adhesions can cause painful menstruation, lower backache, and pain from pressure and movement during intercourse. Once the cause of secondary dysmenorrhea has been diagnosed, appropriate treatment can begin (Propst & Laufer, 1999).

Endometriosis A condition in which uterine tissue grows on various parts of the abdominal cavity.

Amenorrhea

Besides discomfort or pain, another fairly common menstrual difficulty is **amenorrhea** (ay-meh-nuh-REE-uh), the absence of menstruation. There are two types of amenorrhea—primary and secondary. *Primary amenorrhea* is the failure to begin to menstruate at puberty. It can be caused by problems with the reproductive organs, hormonal imbalances, poor health, or an imperforate hymen. *Secondary amenorrhea* involves the disruption of an established menstrual cycle, with the absence of menstruation for 3 months or more. This is a normal condition during pregnancy and breast-feeding. It is also common in women who have just begun menstruating and in women approaching menopause. Women who discontinue birth control pills occasionally do not menstruate for several months, but this situation is usually temporary and resolves spontaneously.

Amenorrhea The absence of menstruation.

Amenorrhea is more common among athletes than among the general population. Research indicates that women who experience athletic amenorrhea also have decreased estrogen levels. This reduction in estrogen can place them at increased risk for developing serious health problems, such as decreased bone mineral density, with a resultant increased incidence of bone fractures, and atrophy of the genital tissues. Athletic amenorrhea can be reversed by improving diet, gaining weight, or in some cases, decreasing training intensity (Epp, 1997).

Medical or hormonal problems can produce amenorrhea (Hagan & Knott, 1998; Stener-Victorin et al., 2000). Women with *anorexia nervosa,* an eating disorder that often results in extreme weight loss, frequently stop menstruating because of hormonal changes that accompany emaciation (Ghizzani & Montomoli, 2000).

Planned amenorrhea can be desirable at times; most women would prefer not to be menstruating on their honeymoons, while camping, at a swim competition, or in many other situations. Since the standard oral contraceptive pill was introduced, many women have skipped the last seven dummy pills and begun a new pack to adjust the timing of their menses (Miller, 2001). An oral contraceptive pill called Seasonale, designed so that women have only four periods a year, became available in 2003 (Kalb, 2003a).

Self-Help for Menstrual Problems

Women may be able to alleviate some of the unpleasant symptoms before and during menstruation by their own actions. Moderate exercise throughout the month as well as proper diet can contribute to improvement of menstrual-related difficulties (Stearns, 2001). For example, an increase in fluids and fiber helps with the constipation that sometimes occurs before and during menstruation. Decreasing salt intake and avoiding foods high in salt (salad dressing, potato chips, bacon, pickles, to name a few) can help reduce swelling and bloating caused by water retention. Food supplements such as calcium, magnesium, and B vitamins can also help relieve PMS cramps and bloating (Bendich, 2000; Girman et al., 2003).

A woman who experiences menstrual-related pain may find it useful to keep a diary to track symptoms, stresses, and daily habits such as exercise, diet, and sleep. She may be able to note a relationship between symptoms and habits and modify her activities accordingly. The information can also be helpful for specific diagnosis if she consults a health care practitioner. ◼

Toxic Shock Syndrome

In May 1980 the Centers for Disease Control (CDC) published the first report of **toxic shock syndrome (TSS)** in menstruating women. Symptoms of TSS, which is caused by toxins produced by the bacterium *Staphylococcus aureus,* include fever, sore throat, nausea, vomiting,

Toxic shock syndrome (TSS) A disease that occurs most commonly in menstruating women and that can cause a person to go into shock.

diarrhea, red skin flush, dizziness, and low blood pressure (Hanrahan, 1994). Because TSS progresses rapidly and can cause death, a person with several of the symptoms of TSS should consult a physician immediately.

TSS is a rare disorder, and the number of reported TSS cases has fallen sharply since the peak in 1980, most likely as a result of the removal of highly absorbent tampons from the market (Petitti & Reingold, 1988). Some guidelines have been developed that can help to prevent toxic shock. One suggestion has been to use sanitary napkins instead of tampons. For women who want to continue using tampons, it is advisable to use regular instead of super-absorbent tampons, to change tampons three to four times during the day, and to use napkins for some time during each 24 hours of menstrual flow. A woman should consult her health care practitioner for further up-to-date suggestions pertaining to prevention and detection of TSS.

▶ Menopause

Climacteric Physiological changes that occur during the transition period from fertility to infertility in both sexes.

Perimenopause The time period before menopause when estrogen is decreasing.

InfoTrac Search Words
■ Menopause

Menopause Cessation of menstruation as a result of the aging process or surgical removal of the ovaries.

The term **climacteric** (kli-MAK-tuh-rik) refers to the physiological changes that occur during the transition period from fertility to infertility in both sexes. In women around 40 years of age the ovaries begin to slow the production of estrogen. This period before complete cessation of menstruation is called **perimenopause,** and it can last for up to 10 years. Menstruation continues but cycles can become irregular, with erratic and absent or heavy bleeding as menopause approaches (Bastian et al., 2003). Up to 90% of women experience a change in menstrual patterns and sexual response during perimenopause. Also, by age 40 a woman's level of circulating testosterone is half what it was when she was 20 years old, and supplementation might be appropriate (S. Davis, 2000; Mansfield et al., 1995). Some women experience increased fatigue, irritability, forgetfulness, and headaches during this transition (Harlow et al., 2003; Li et al., 2000). About 10% of women begin to experience hot flashes and night sweats while they continue to menstruate, and some may notice vaginal dryness during perimenopause (Torpy, 2003). Low-dose birth control pills are sometimes prescribed to alleviate the perimenopausal symptoms and to prevent bone loss (Seibert et al., 2003).

Menopause, one of the events of the female climacteric, is the permanent cessation of menstruation. Menopause occurs as a result of certain physiological changes and takes place at a mean age of 51 but can occur in the 30s or as late as the 60s (O'Neill, 2000b). Research indicates that women who experience earlier menopause smoke tobacco, began their periods by age 11, had shorter cycle lengths, had fewer pregnancies, and had less time of oral contraceptive use than women who experience menopause later. In essence, other than the variable of smoking, many women who have early menopause have a history of more ovulatory cycles (Cramer et al., 1995; Palmer et al., 2003).

The general public and the medical community have begun to focus more on menopause because of the great increase in the number of women who live many years after menopause. In 1900 the average life expectancy of a woman in the United States was 51 years. Today the average life expectancy for U.S. women is 82 years. Currently, almost 42 million women in the United States are over age 50 (Watt et al., 2003). By 2020 there will be 60 million postmenopausal women. In practical terms this means that millions of women will experience the second half of their adult life following menopause; menopause can be seen as the gateway to a second adulthood (Brewster et al., 1999). There are already signs that the "baby boom" generation will encourage the health care system to deal with menopause more thoroughly than before (Kingsberg, 2002).

During menopause, the pituitary gland continues to secrete FSH; however, the ovaries cease production of mature ova. Ovarian estrogen output also slows, although the adrenal glands, liver, and adipose (fat) tissue continue to produce some estrogen after menopause. After menopause the ovaries and the adrenal glands continue to produce androgens (Hughes et al., 1991).

The experience of menopause varies greatly from woman to woman. Some women experience few physical symptoms other than cessation of menstruation. For these women menopause is surprisingly uneventful:

In addition, most women feel relieved that they no longer need to be concerned about pregnancy, contraception, and menstruation. They may experience an increased sense of freedom in sexual intimacy as a result.

However, for many women, menopause brings a range of symptoms that can vary from mild to severe. These symptoms are caused by the decline in estrogen. The most acute menopausal symptoms occur in the 2 years before and the 2 years following the last menstrual period. Hot flashes and night sweats are also common difficulties. Hot flashes can range from a mild feeling of warmth to a feeling of intense heat and profuse perspiration, especially around the chest, neck, and face. A severe hot flash can soak clothing or sheets in perspiration. The flashes usually last for 3 to 6 minutes, although they may last up to an hour. Hot flashes occur because hormones influence the nerves that control the blood vessels. As hormone levels fluctuate, the diameter of the blood vessels changes. Rapid dilation of the vessels causes a woman to experience a momentary rush of heat. The sensation can be quite disconcerting. Hot flashes can occur several times a day and during sleep; they usually cease within 2 years. About 75% of women experience hot flashes (C. Shaw, 1997), and African American women experience more hot flashes and night sweats than other racial and ethnic groups (Avis et al., 2001). Women smokers also experience hot flashes more frequently than nonsmokers (Staropoli et al., 1997).

Other symptoms arising from the decrease in estrogen can significantly affect a woman's daily life. Sleep disturbance can increase during menopause. A typical example is a woman who can readily fall asleep but wakes one or more times during the night feeling agitated and has difficulty falling back to sleep. This pattern can easily result in fatigue and irritability during the day. Menopausal symptoms can also include dizziness, difficulty with balance, diminished pleasure from touch, itchy or burning skin, sensitivity to clothing or touch, and numbness or tingling in hands and feet. In addition, estrogen deficiency can cause severe headaches, short-term memory loss, difficulty concentrating, depression, and increased anxiety (Kurpius et al., 2001; Pearce et al., 1997; Yaffe et al., 1998). Thinning of the vaginal walls and less lubrication from the decline in estrogen can make intercourse uncomfortable or painful (Meston, 2000; Modelska & Cummings, 2003).

▶ Hormone Therapy

Hormone therapy (HT) for women involves using supplemental hormones—estrogen, progesterone, and/or testosterone—to alleviate problems that can arise from the decrease in natural hormone production that occurs during the female climacteric.* Also, younger women with hormone deficiencies following removal of their ovaries often use HT. Few current medical topics are in such a state of flux and as controversial as hormone therapy related to menopause (Lagro-Janssen et al., 2003). A great amount of research is being conducted and reported. However, the information that the media provide sometimes creates more confusion than clarification, as discussed in the Spotlight on Research box, "Media Reports on Hormone Therapy Research: Clarification or Confusion?" In this section we discuss current findings about the benefits and risks of HT.

Hormones used in HT come from three main sources. Estrogen and progesterone can be derived from plants or made from synthetic chemicals. Plant-based and synthetic hormones are bio-identical to human estrogen (i.e., they have the same chemical structure). Testosterone is made from synthetic chemicals. The third source of estrogen, and the one most

Hormone therapy (HT) The use of supplemental hormones during and after menopause or following surgical removal of the ovaries.

*Another abbreviation commonly seen for hormone therapy is HRT, or hormone replacement therapy. In the past, treatment with hormones was intended to replace the hormone levels after menopause to premenopause levels. Currently, the smallest dose of hormone therapies that alleviates symptoms associated with menopause is the usual treatment approach. Some other abbreviations used in association with general hormone therapy are ET (estrogen therapy; i.e., treatments that contain only estrogen), CEPT (combined estrogen and progesterone therapy; i.e., treatments that contain estrogen and progesterone), and CEE (conjugated equine estrogen). Sometimes these abbreviations also have an R (for replacement).

Media Reports on Hormone Therapy Research: Clarification or Confusion?

"The scientists found a 29% increase in heart attacks, a 41% increase in strokes, and a 26% increase in breast cancer" (Hendricks, 2002, p. 60). The media widely quoted these statistics from the Women's Health Initiative (WHI) research findings released in 2002. These results were particularly credible because the WHI study employed an excellent research methodology for investigating the effects of Prempro (a combined estrogen and progesterone therapy [CEPT]) in postmenopausal women. Although the often-cited percentages of increased problems sounded alarming, they also have been misleading to the general public because the following WHI study results are also accurate but much less sensationalistic: The scientists found a 0.07% increased risk of heart attack and a 0.08% increased risk for stroke and breast cancer.

For a woman evaluating the risks of hormone therapy, a 26% increase in breast cancer looks very different from a 0.08% increased risk. How can both of these research results be accurate?

Both sets of results are accurate (Table 4.1), but they were derived by two different methods of analyzing the data. The larger percentages represent the *hazard ratio*, which the media primarily used in its reporting. The hazard ratio is a statistical analysis that compares the difference between the numbers of women in each treatment condition who experienced the health problems or benefits. The hazard ratio also includes in its analysis the length of time between the start of the study and when the heart attack, stroke, or breast cancer occurred. The hazard ratio does *not* mean that 26% of women who used Prempro developed breast cancer.

The smaller set of risk percentages represent *absolute risk* and result from comparing the difference between the actual numbers of women in each treatment condition per 10,000 who experienced these health problems or benefits. For example, out of 10,000 women in a year's time, 30 taking the placebo and 38 taking Prempro developed breast cancer. Thus the absolute risk of developing breast cancer is calculated to be 0.3% for the placebo group and 0.38% for the Prempro group. The difference between 0.3% and 0.38% yields a 0.08% absolute increased risk of breast cancer attributable to 1 year of Prempro use. These figures reveal that the increased absolute risk of developing one of these health problems as a direct result of Prempro is dramatically smaller than the impression given by the well-publicized hazard ratio statistics. Even though both sets of statistics are accurate, the actual interpretation of one's risk is quite different depending on which statistics are used (Women's Health Initiative, 2002).

TABLE 4.1 Rate of Occurrence and Change in Risk/Benefit per 10,000 Women Using Hormone Therapy per Year

Health Risk or Benefit	Rate of Occurrence			Change in Risk/Benefit	
	Placebo	Prempro	Increase or Decrease in Number of Women	Hazard Ratio (%)	Absolute Risk (%)
Heart disease	30	37	+7	+29	+0.07
Breast cancer	30	38	+8	+26	+0.08
Stroke	21	29	+8	+41	+0.08
Blood clots	16	34	+18	+111	+0.18
Colorectal cancer	16	10	−6	−37	−0.06
Hip fracture	15	10	−5	−34	−0.05

widely used in the United States, is pregnant mares' urine, called conjugated equine estrogen (CEE). The CEE used in the HT products Premarin (estrogen only) and Prempro (estrogen and progesterone) is not bio-identical to human estrogen, and it contains impurities with unknown medical properties (Food and Drug Administration, 1997).

HT is available in many different delivery systems. It can be ingested in pills, put on the skin with patches or cream, inserted into the vagina by means of creams, tablets, or rings, or

TABLE 4.2	Benefits and Problems from Hormone Therapy	
Hormone	**Benefits**	**Problems**
Estrogen	Maintains thickness and vascularity of vaginal and urethral tissue for comfort and lubrication during sexual interaction (Bachmann & Nevadansky, 2000). Reduces hot flashes and sleep disturbance from night sweats (Hansen, 2003). Protects against osteoporosis (abnormal bone loss) and resultant fractures, particularly of the hip (Gelfand, 2000). Reduces risk of colon cancer (Humphries & Gill, 2003).	Increases the incidence of endometrial, ovarian, and breast cancer (Schairer et al., 2000). Increases risk of blood clots.
Progesterone	Eliminates the estrogen-caused increase in endometrial and ovarian cancer (Schairer et al., 2000).	Alters the type of fats in the bloodstream and increases the risk of cardiovascular disease. Increases the incidence of breast cancer (Million Women Study Collaborators, 2003).
Testosterone	Helps maintain or restore sexual interest (Lobo et al., 2003). Increases overall energy.	Side effects include increase in hair growth and acne.

placed under the skin in implants or by injection. In addition, a nasal spray is under development (Wattanakumtornkul et al., 2003).

Benefits and Risks of HT

Table 4.1 lists the main benefits and risks from a recent study of Prempro, a combination of conjugated equine estrogen and progesterone. Some of the general benefits and risks specific to estrogen, progesterone, and testosterone are given in Table 4.2.

Challenges in HT Research

Numerous variables involved in hormone therapy research make some of the findings difficult to generalize to all types of HT. First, most of the HT research in the United States used conjugated equine estrogen (CEE), including the WHI study of 16,000 women taking either Prempro or a placebo. Results from CEE research do not necessarily provide clear data for the risk/benefit profile for bio-identical plant-based and synthetic hormones (Northrup, 2002; Women's Health Initiative, 2002). Second, most studies focus on women who take pills rather than those who use other delivery systems. All the nonpill delivery systems allow hormones to enter the body without going through the digestive system, which can create some side effects. Unfortunately, research about nonpill delivery systems is, to date, rather limited (Hendricks, 2002; Northrup, 2002; Watt et al., 2003). However, a few studies do show differing effects according to the delivery system used. For example, women who received estrogen through their skin had a reduced incidence of blood clots compared to women who took estrogen orally in pill form (Scarabin et al., 2003). Women who used vaginal estrogen tablets experienced improvement in urogenital symptoms (such as painful urination, incontinence, and frequent urge to urinate) without the occurrence of endometrial growth or raised estrogen levels in their blood, both common side effects of pill delivery systems (Simunic et al., 2003). However, the first large study to compare effects of oral pills, implants, and skin cream and patches on breast cancer rates found similar incidence rates regardless of the delivery system women used (Million Women Study Collaborators, 2003).

The Estrogen and Breast Cancer Controversy

Two recent, large, well-designed studies validate that estrogen therapy and combined estrogen and progesterone therapy (CEPT) increase the incidence of breast cancer (Million Women Study Collaborators, 2003; Women's Health Initiative, 2002). These and other studies also reported that breast cancer risk increases with duration of HT use, but the risk is eliminated several years after HT is discontinued (Chlebowski et al., 2003; Cockey, 2003). However, unlike the consistent findings about breast cancer risk and CEPT, findings regarding exclusive estrogen use vary considerably (Stahlberg et al., 2003). One large study found that the incidence of breast cancer in women using CEPT was four times greater than the cancer rate in women using estrogen therapy (ET) (Million Women Study Collaborators, 2003). Other smaller studies found that ET did not increase users' risk of breast cancer, even after more than 25 years of taking it (C. Li et al., 2003; Stahlberg et al., 2003), and that even women who had previously had breast cancer and subsequently took ET for 3 years had no greater rate of recurrence of breast cancer than women in a matched control group (Decker et al., 2003).

The Prempro and Heart Disease Controversy

The increased risk of heart attack was an unanticipated finding from the 2002 WHI investigation. It has long been hypothesized that the low incidence of heart disease in women before menopause was due, in part, to the presence of estrogen. Conversely, the marked increase in incidence of heart disease in women 10 to 15 years after menopause was believed to be due to a decrease in estrogen (Grady, 2003; Hamelin et al., 2003). Furthermore, most previous research indicated that HT provided some protection against heart attack (Piantadosi, 2003; Whittemore & McGuire, 2003). These earlier studies were observational cohort studies in which researchers compared the health status of two groups of women who, on their own initiative, decided either to use HT or to forgo HT. In contrast, the WHI study used a double-blind placebo-controlled design in which subjects were randomly assigned to either the Prempro (CEPT) or placebo group; neither the investigators nor the subjects knew who was in which treatment group.

These different research designs resulted in variations in the study population, and the inconsistency of results could be due to differences in the characteristics of the women studied. For example, research has found that women who independently choose to take HT tend to have better general health, have better access to medical care, and are thinner than those who do not use HT (Hendricks, 2002). In addition, women in the observational cohort studies began taking HT at the onset of menopause in their late 40s or early 50s. They may have had more problematic menopause symptoms that led them to take HT, possibly indicating innate hormonal differences between women who seek treatment for menopause compared to those who do not. In contrast, in the WHI study, only some of the women had previously used HT. Furthermore, 66% of the WHI subjects were age 60 or older and 21% were age 70 or older when they began taking Prempro for the study (Michels, 2003). Therefore the differences in both the age when the woman began HT and the health characteristics of women who do or do not initiate HT at menopause could account, in part, for the inconsistent results and the subsequent difficulty in making direct comparisons between the WHI study and observational cohort studies.

Alternatives to Hormone Replacement

Alternatives to HT include lifestyle factors, health behaviors, vitamins and herbs, and non-hormonal medication. Research has found that changes in vaginal tissues and reduction in vaginal lubrication during arousal that result from aging are less pronounced in women who are sexually active through intercourse or masturbation compared to sexually inactive women (Bachmann & Nevadansky, 2000). Vaginal lubricants and moisturizers can also be used to improve vaginal lubrication. Calcium supplements and vitamin D, weight-bearing exercise, and various medications help to maintain bone density and prevent osteoporosis. Exercise, avoiding caffeine, tobacco, alcohol, and spicy foods, or using low doses of certain antidepressants can help reduce hot flashes (Dormire, 2003; Kligler, 2003; Stearns et al., 2003). Vitamin E and various herbs, such as dong quai or black cohosh, help relieve menopausal symptoms such as hot flashes for some women (Gingrich & Fogel, 2003; Kligler, 2003). Research has shown insignificant reduction in hot flashes from supplements or foods with isoflavones (compounds found in soy that are similar to estrogen) (Tice et al., 2003). However, one study found that isoflavone supplements improved cognitive functions

(Kritz-Silverstein et al., 2003). Evidence of the benefits and risks of foods and herbs is limited because few controlled studies have been done (Dormire, 2003; Spake, 2001).

Another alternative to HT became available in 1998 to address osteoporosis without increasing the risks of breast and uterine cancer. SERMs (selective estrogen receptor modulators) mimic estrogen's effects in some sites of the body and interfere with estrogen's effects in others. SERMs reduce bone fracture and breast cancer risk and do not increase the risk of uterine cancer. However, SERMs do exacerbate hot flashes and increase the risk of blood clots (Cowley & Springen, 2002). Research continues to develop therapies that will provide all the benefits and none of the liabilities of current treatments.

A Challenging Decision

A menopausal woman should weigh the potential benefits and risks of HT against the symptoms of hormone deficiency. For many women the benefits far outweigh the risks, and for other women the opposite is true (Hendricks, 2002; Utian, 2003). In general, taking the smallest effective dose for the shortest length of time is an approach to consider (Oliver et al., 2003; Underwood, 2003). New research results emerge continuously, and although they can be contradictory, it is this information that women and their health care providers have available to make the important decision of whether or not to use HT (Berlin, 2003; Michels, 2003). We recommend that women thoroughly discuss the available evidence and their individual health history and lifestyle with a health care practitioner specializing in menopause and HT.

▶ Gynecological Health Concerns

Gynecological health problems range from minor infections to cancer. In this section we provide information and self-help suggestions on several topics.

Urinary Tract Infections

Women often develop infections of the urinary tract, the organ system that includes the urethra, bladder, and kidneys. If the infection progresses all the way to the kidneys, severe illness can result (Pace, 2000). About 15% of women will have a urinary tract infection in their lifetimes; many have more than one (Delzell & Lefevre, 2000; Mayo Clinic Health Oasis, 1999). The symptoms of urinary tract infections include a frequent need to urinate, a burning sensation when urinating, blood or pus in the urine, and sometimes lower pelvic pain (D'Epiro, 1997). A conclusive diagnosis of a urinary tract infection requires laboratory analysis of a urine sample. Such an infection generally responds to short-term antibiotic treatment (Uehling et al., 1997).

Urinary tract infections are usually caused by bacteria that enter the urethral opening (Raz et al., 2000). Coitus is the most frequent means by which bacteria enter the urinary tract; the bacteria are massaged into the urethra by the thrusting motions of intercourse. Bladder infections often occur during periods of frequent intercourse. Poor hygiene or wiping the genitals from back to front after defecation can also introduce bacteria into the urethra. Using a diaphragm and spermicide also increases the risk of urinary tract infections (Hooton, 1996). Repeatedly stretching the bladder muscle beyond its normal capacity (which is reached with the first urge to urinate) weakens the muscle so that it cannot expel all the urine; thus some urine remains in the bladder, increasing the risk of infection. Changes in the tissue of postmenopausal women can also predispose women to urinary tract infections (Bachmann & Nevadansky, 2000).

Observing a few routine precautions can help prevent urinary tract infections. Careful wiping from front to back after both urination and bowel movements helps keep bacteria away from the urethra. Washing the genital and rectal areas thoroughly each day and urinating as soon as you feel the urge also reduce the likelihood of infection. For those who have frequent problems with such infections, it is important that both partners wash their hands and genitals before and after intercourse. Using intercourse positions that cause less friction against the urethra can also help. Women can also use sterile water-soluble

Sexual Health

lubricating jelly (not petroleum jelly) when vaginal lubrication is insufficient, because irritated tissue is more susceptible to infection. Urinating immediately after intercourse helps wash out bacteria (Leiner, 1997). Having your health care practitioner recheck the fit of your diaphragm is a good idea. It also can be helpful to drink plenty of liquids, especially cranberry juice (Kiel & Nashelsky, 2003), and to avoid substances such as coffee, tea, and alcohol, which have an irritating effect on the bladder. ■

Vaginal Infections

Vaginitis Inflammation of the vaginal walls caused by a variety of vaginal infections.

When the natural balance of the vagina is disturbed or when a nonnative organism is introduced, a vaginal infection, or **vaginitis** (va-juh-NYE-tus), can result. Usually the woman herself first notices symptoms of vaginitis: irritation or itching of the vagina and vulva, unusual discharge, and sometimes a disagreeable odor. (An unpleasant odor can also be due to a forgotten tampon or diaphragm.) Some of the different types of vaginal infections are yeast infections, bacterial infections, and trichomoniasis, discussed further in Chapter 17.

A number of factors increase a woman's susceptibility to vaginitis: diabetes, antibiotic use, emotional stress, a diet high in carbohydrates, hormonal changes caused by pregnancy or birth control pills, chemical irritants, coitus without adequate lubrication, and heat and

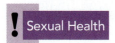

moisture retained by nylon underwear and panty hose. One study found that women who wore panty hose had three times more yeast infections than those who did not (Heidrich et al., 1984). Menstrual flow increases the alkalinity of the vagina, which promotes yeast growth in some women. Vaginal douching disturbs the normal balance of the vagina and increases the risk of vaginal infection (Cottrell, 2003).

It is important for vaginitis to be treated and cured. Chronic irritation resulting from long-term infections can play a part in predisposing a woman to cervical cell changes that can lead to cancer. Over-the-counter treatments for yeast infections are now available. Some health care practitioners provide suggestions for nondrug treatment of vaginitis. The following suggestions may help prevent vaginitis from occurring in the first place (Solimini, 1991):

1. Eat a well-balanced diet low in sugar and refined carbohydrates.
2. Maintain general good health with adequate sleep, exercise, and emotional release.
3. Use good hygiene, including (a) bathing regularly with mild soap; (b) wiping from front to back, vulva to anus, after urinating and having bowel movements; (c) wearing clean cotton underpants (nylon holds in heat and moisture that encourages bacterial growth); (d) avoiding the use of feminine hygiene sprays, colored toilet paper, bubble bath, and other people's washcloths or towels to wash or wipe your genitals; and (e) ensuring that your sexual partner's hands and genitals are clean before beginning sexual activity.
4. Be sure that you have adequate lubrication before coitus: natural lubrication or a sterile water-soluble lubricant. Do not use petroleum-based lubricants (such as Vaseline), because they are not water soluble and are likely to remain in the vagina and harbor bacteria. Petroleum-based lubricants can also weaken and will eventually degrade latex condoms or diaphragms.
5. Use condoms if you or your partner are nonmonogamous. ■

Self-Exams and Vaginal Health Care

A self-exam can sometimes help detect vaginal infection. The skin of the genital area turns red instead of its usual pink, and this, along with irritation, is a sign that treatment may be necessary. A woman can use a speculum, flashlight, and mirror at home to do vaginal self-exams. At the beginning of the women's health movement in the early 1970s, women began to do vaginal and cervical exams individually and in self-help groups—quite a radical practice when speculum exams were the sole province of physicians (Sandelowski, 2000). Now, many health care practitioners use a mirror to show a woman the inside of her vagina during her regular exam, and some will teach her how to use the speculum, the instrument that holds the vaginal walls open. ■

The Pap Smear

The **Pap smear,** a screening test for cervical cancer, is taken from the cervix. The vaginal walls are held open with a speculum, and a few cells are removed with a cervical brush or a small wooden spatula; these cells are put on a glass slide and sent to a laboratory to be examined. The cells for a Pap smear are taken from the *transition zone,* the part of the cervix where long, column-shaped cells called *columnar cells* meet flat-shaped cells called *squamous cells.* A Pap smear is not painful, because there are so few nerve endings on the cervix. A vaginal Pap smear is done when the woman's cervix has been removed, although the incidence of vaginal cancer is low (Stevermer, 2001; Volm, 1997). New technologies for detecting cervical cancer are being developed, and a vaccine to prevent some cervical cancer is under study (Mishra, 2002).

The Pap smear is an essential part of routine preventive health care for all women, including sexually active adolescents (Selvin & Brett, 2003) and postmenopausal women (Holmquist, 2000). Since the widespread use of Pap smears began in the 1950s, the death rate from cervical cancer has decreased dramatically (Wright et al., 2000). Nevertheless, each year 13,000 women in the United States are diagnosed with cervical cancer, and 4,100 die from the disease (Centers for Disease Control, 2002e). The worldwide ratio of death to diagnosis is worse: 200,000 women die out of the 400,000 diagnosed yearly worldwide (Grady, 2000).

Women should have their first Pap smear no more than 3 years after becoming sexually active, or by age 21. Based on a health care provider's recommendation, a woman may have this test once every 2 years, every year, twice a year, or even more frequently. Pap tests are not always accurate in detecting cervical cancer, and regular tests increase the likelihood of discovering cancer (Felix, 2003). ■

Some subgroups of women are less likely than others to have routine Pap smears. For example, lesbians get Pap smears less often than heterosexuals (Fields & Scout, 2001). This may be due to their lack of need for routine contraceptive visits to a gynecologist or to medical professionals' lack of knowledge or discomfort with homosexuality (Brogan, 2001; Saulnier, 2002). Socioeconomic level can also affect the rate of Pap test screening (Schorge et al., 2003). Unlike the general rate of decline in mortality from cervical cancer, the death rate has increased among low-income Native American women. The main cause seems to be the inefficient and unskilled health care system available to most Native Americans (Mahmoodian, 1997).

When the results of a Pap smear indicate abnormal cells, further tests are necessary before a conclusive diagnosis can be made (Wistuba et al., 2000). A *colposcopy* (an exam using a special microscope) and a tissue *biopsy* (surgical removal of a small piece of cervical tissue, which is then examined under a microscope) are two of the additional tests that can be done (Massad et al., 1997).

Abnormal cell changes occur up to 15 years before cancer develops (Higgins, 1997). Several simple, highly effective lifesaving treatments are used for cervical abnormalities. *Cryosurgery* (freezing of tissues) is one method of removing a small number of abnormal cells from the surface of the cervix. Elimination of tissue by means of a biopsy is also often effective (Soutter et al., 1997). In more severe cases a woman may need a complete hysterectomy. The most important factor leading to invasive cervical cancer is infrequent or no cervical cancer screening (Centers for Disease Control, 2002e).

An increased risk of developing cervical cancer has been linked to a number of factors. Having sexual intercourse early, having multiple sexual partners, smoking tobacco, inhaling secondary smoke, and having had a virus called human papillomavirus (HPV) increase the risk of developing cervical cancer (Canavan & Doshi, 2000; Centers for Disease Control, 2002e).

Surgical Removal of the Uterus and Ovaries

Sometimes a woman needs to have a **hysterectomy** (his-tuh-REK-tuh-mee), surgical removal of the uterus, or an **oophorectomy** (oh-uh-fuh-REK-tuh-mee), surgical removal of the ovaries, or both. These procedures are necessitated by various medical problems, including bleeding disorders, severe pelvic infections, and the presence of benign (noncancerous)

Pap smear A screening test for cancer of the cervix.

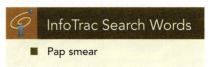

Hysterectomy Surgical removal of the uterus.

Oophorectomy Surgical removal of the ovaries.

tumors (Clark & Johnson, 2000; Faerstein et al., 2001; Kilbourne & Richards, 2001). Cancer of the cervix, uterus, or ovaries is also cause for hysterectomy or oophorectomy (Yuan et al., 1999). Ovarian cancer is by far the most deadly of these three (Tingulstad et al., 2003). Ovarian cancer victims have about a 40% survival rate for 5 years because the cancer is difficult to detect in early stages (Werness & Eltabbakh, 2001). About 75% of women with ovarian cancer have advanced disease at the time of diagnosis (Beard et al., 2000; Gnagy et al., 2000). Two major international trials have found that immediate treatment with chemotherapy after surgery improves survival rates (Mayor, 2003). In addition, new technology is being developed for earlier detection of ovarian cancer.

InfoTrac Search Words

■ Hysterectomy

An estimated 33% of women have a hysterectomy by age 65, making it the second most frequently performed major operation for women in the United States. Hysterectomy rates are higher among low-income women, women with less than a high-school education, and women who live in the South. Researchers suspect that a lack of preventive health care in these groups allows problems to advance to the point where other treatments are not viable (Palmer et al., 1999). In some situations the reasons for a hysterectomy are discretionary: A woman can often be treated successfully with other medical options, such as laser treatments or medications for bleeding disorders. Before consenting to undergo a hysterectomy or similar surgery, it is important for a woman to obtain a second opinion; to fully inform herself of the benefits, risks, and alternatives to surgery; and to arrange for thorough preoperative and postoperative information and counseling (Wade et al., 2000). Women will also want to consider newer, less expensive surgical procedures (Poirot, 2000).

The effects of hysterectomy on a woman's sexuality vary. First of all, hysterectomy does not affect the sensitivity of the clitoris. Some women find that the elimination of medical problems and painful intercourse, assured protection from unwanted pregnancy, and lack of menstruation enhance their quality of life in general and their sexual functioning and enjoyment (Kjerulff et al., 2000; Rannestad et al., 2001). However, other women experience an alteration or decrease in their sexual response after removal of the uterus. Sensations from uterine vasocongestion and elevation during arousal as well as uterine contractions during orgasm are absent and can change the physical experience of sexual response. Some changes result from damage to the nerves in the pelvis. The exact locations of nerves vital to female sexual function have not been identified, and no nerve-sparing procedures are done during pelvic surgeries in women (Berman & Berman, 2000; Lefkowitz & McCullough, 2000). Scar tissue or alterations to the vagina can also have an effect. When ovaries are removed, symptoms common to menopause will occur without hormone therapy.

An important variable in postsurgical sexual adjustment is the quality of the partner relationship and how the woman and her partner perceive the surgery (Helstrom et al., 1995).

▶ The Breasts

Secondary sex characteristics The physical characteristics other than genitals that indicate sexual maturity, such as body hair, breasts, and deepened voice.

Mammary glands Glands in the female breast that produce milk.

Breasts are not a part of the internal or external female genitalia. Instead, they are **secondary sex characteristics** (physical characteristics other than genitals that distinguish male from female). In a physically mature woman the breasts are composed internally of fatty tissue and **mammary** (MAM-uh-ree), or milk, **glands** (Figure 4.8). There is little variation from woman to woman in the amount of glandular tissue present in the breast, despite differences in size. This is why the amount of milk produced after childbirth does not correlate with the size of the breasts. Variation in breast size is due primarily to the amount of fatty tissue distributed around the glands. It is common for one breast to be slightly larger than the other. Breasts come in a multitude of sizes and shapes. One writer explained, "On real women, I've seen breasts as varied as faces: breasts shaped like tubes, breasts shaped like tears, breasts that flop down, breasts that point up, breasts that are dominated by thick, dark nipples and areolae, breasts with nipples so small and pale they look airbrushed" (Angier, 1999, p. 128).

Breast size is a source of considerable preoccupation for many women and men in our society:

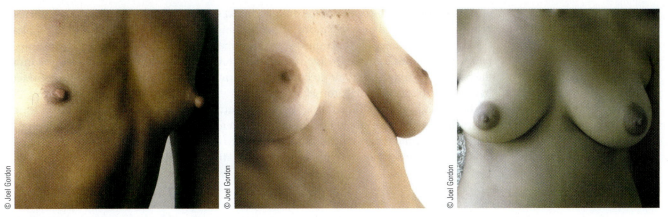

Breast size and shape vary from woman to woman.

In talking with my friends about how we feel about our breasts, I discovered that not one of us feels really comfortable about how she looks. I've always been envious of women with large breasts because mine are small. But my friends with large breasts talk about feeling self-conscious about their breasts too. (Authors' files)

Surgeries to enlarge or reduce breast size reflect the dissatisfaction many women feel because their breasts do not fit the cultural ideal. Breast augmentation practices may or may not be influenced by media images. However, in some plastic surgery clinics the average age of women requesting breast augmentation has dropped since the late 1980s (Farr, 2000).

The glandular tissue in the breast responds to sex hormones. During adolescence, both the fatty and the glandular tissue develop markedly. Breasts show some size variations at different phases of the menstrual cycle and when influenced by pregnancy, nursing, or birth control pills.

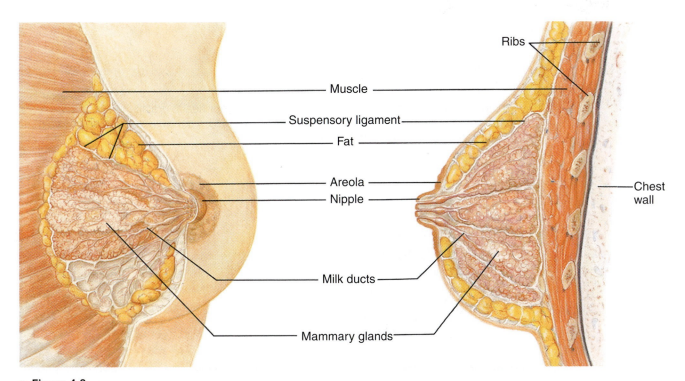

▶ **Figure 4.8**
Cross section front and side views of the female breast.

The **nipple** is in the center of the **areola** (ah-REE-oh-luh), the darker area of the external breast. The areola contains sebaceous (oil-producing) glands that help lubricate the nipples during breast-feeding. The openings of the mammary glands are in the nipples. Some nipples point outward from the breast, others are flush with the breast, and still others sink into the breast. The nipples become erect when small muscles at the base of the nipple contract in response to touch, sexual arousal, or cold.

Breast and nipple stimulation is an important source of pleasure and arousal during masturbation or sexual interaction for many women. Some find that breast and nipple stimulation helps build the sexual intensity that leads to orgasm; others enjoy it for its own sake. Other women find breast and nipple touching neutral or unpleasant.

Breast Self-Exam

A breast self-examination (BSE) is an important part of self–health care for women. This exam can help a woman know what is normal for her own breasts. She can do the breast exam herself and can also teach her partner to do it. As of 2003 the American Cancer Society stopped recommending monthly breast self-exams for early cancer detection because recent large, rigorous studies have shown that BSE does not decrease deaths from breast cancer. Women find most cancerous tumors accidentally by routine touching in the shower, while dressing, or by their partners noticing a lump. Therefore the American Cancer Society recommends that women use BSE occasionally for self-awareness in order to know how their breasts normally feel so that they can detect changes (Smith et al., 2003). The steps of a breast exam are illustrated in the box "How to Examine Your Breasts." It is helpful to fill out a chart, such as the one shown in Figure 4.9, to keep track of lumps in the breasts (Schifeling & Hamblin, 1991). Many breasts normally feel lumpy. Once a woman becomes familiar with her own breasts, she can notice any changes. If there is a change, she should consult a health care practitioner, who might recommend further diagnostic testing. Ninety percent of breast lumps, most of which are not malignant, are found by women themselves. ■

Fill out a chart, like the one shown here, when you examine your breasts. For any lump you find, mark

1. its location
2. its size (BB, pea, raisin, grape)
3. its shape (rounded or elongated)

Compare each record with the last one, and consult your health practitioner regarding any changes. A new or changing lump should be checked as soon as possible. Most such lumps will prove to be benign.

Today's date _____

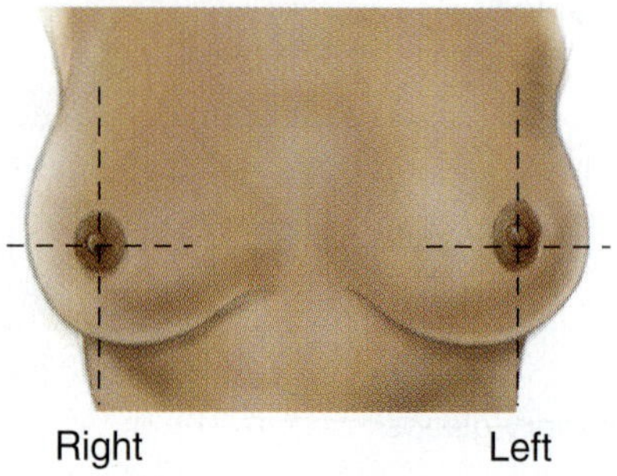

Right   Left

▶ **Figure 4.9**
It is helpful to use a chart similar to this one to keep track of lumps in the breasts.

How to Examine Your Breasts

1. **In the shower:** Examine your breasts during a bath or shower; hands glide more easily over wet skin. With fingers flat, move your hands gently over every part of each breast. Use your right hand to examine your left breast and your left hand to examine your right breast. Check for any lump, hard knot, or thickening.

2. **Before a mirror:** Inspect your breasts with your arms at your sides. Next, raise your arms high overhead. Look for any changes in the contour of each breast: a swelling, dimpling of the skin, or changes in the nipple. Then rest your palms on your hips and press down firmly to flex your chest muscles. Left and right breasts will not match exactly—few women's breasts do.

3. **Lying down:** To examine your right breast, put a pillow or folded towel under your right shoulder. Place your right hand behind your head—this distributes breast tissue more evenly

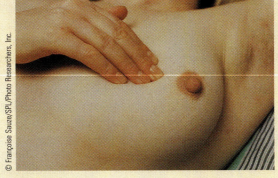

© Françoise Sauze/SPL/Photo Researchers, Inc.

on the chest. With your left hand, fingers flat, press gently in small circular motions around an imaginary clock face. Begin at the outermost top of your right breast for 12 o'clock, then move to 1 o'clock, and so on around the circle back to 12. A ridge of firm tissue in the lower curve of each breast is normal. Then move in an inch, toward the nipple, and keep circling to examine *every part of your breast,* including the nipple. This requires at least three more circles. Now slowly repeat this procedure on your left breast.

Finally, squeeze the nipple of each breast gently between thumb and index finger. Any discharge, clear or bloody, should be reported to your doctor immediately—as should the discovery of any unusual lump, swelling, or thickening anywhere in the breast.

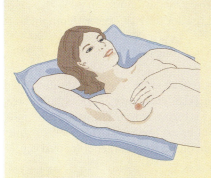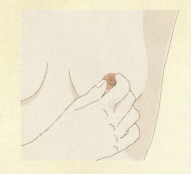

▶ **Figure 4.10**
Breast self-exam.

Breast Cancer Screening

Breast self-exam and routine breast exams by your health care provider are important screening tools. In addition, **mammography** (ma-MAWG-ruh-fee) is a highly sensitive X-ray screening test to help detect cancerous breast cells and lumps. Mammography uses low levels of radiation to create an image of the breast, called a *mammogram,* on film or paper. Mammography can often detect a breast lump up to several years before it can be felt manually; it can also sometimes find cancerous cell changes that occur even before a lump develops (Smith-Bindman et al., 2000). With earlier detection of breast cancer, a decrease in mortality (Table 4.3) and an increase in breast-conserving treatments are possible (Caplan et al., 2000; Hamilton et al., 2003). The mammogram also provides information about the type of tumor and the kinds of treatment needed (Tabár et al., 2000).

Mammography A highly sensitive X-ray test for the detection of breast cancer.

TABLE 4.3	Five-Year Survival Rate for U.S. Women by Stage of Cancer at Diagnosis	
Stage of Cancer	Percentage of Cancer Diagnosed at This Stage	Survival Rate at 5 Years (%)
Local (confined to breast)	60	98
Regional (spread to lymph nodes)	31	76
Distant (spread to other organs)	6	16

In North America one woman dies of breast cancer approximately *every 12 minutes.*

SOURCES: American Cancer Society (2003).

There has been considerable disagreement among medical professionals about the routine use of mammography in women age 40 to 49 years old. Mammography is less effective for detecting breast cancer in women less than 50 years of age than in those older than 50, mainly because of the greater density of the breast tissue, which makes it more difficult for the mammogram to illuminate potential problem areas (Mitka, 2003b). However, almost 6,000 women in their 40s die each year from breast cancer, and the American Medical Association, the American Cancer Society, and the National Cancer Institute recommend yearly mammograms for this age group (Pace, 2001).

Although mammography is an effective screening test, it can miss a significant number of tumors or result in a false-positive test (Cardenas & Frisch, 2003). Research is exploring better breast-screening technology (Flobbe et al., 2003). Currently, the best method for early detection of breast cancer is a combination of monthly manual self-exams, routine exams by a health care practitioner, and mammography as recommended (Caplan et al., 2000). ■

It is especially important for lesbians to be conscientious about scheduling regular exams and mammograms; they tend to be screened less often than heterosexual women because they do not have birth control medical appointments. Lesbians also tend to avoid health care services rather than confront the insensitivity and ignorance of some medical practitioners. Many lesbians report that past negative experiences have made them less likely to seek services when they have a problem (Saulnier, 2002).

In 5–10% of women breast cancer can develop from flaws in a gene that is now detectable (Burke et al., 1997). Women with this gene flaw have up to an 80% chance of developing breast cancer and may have an increased risk for ovarian cancer (Humphries & Gill, 2003). Women now have the opportunity to decide whether or not to use drugs for cancer prevention or to have a preventive mastectomy (Armstrong et al., 2000; Frost et al., 2000; Guthrie, 2000; Schrag et al., 2000).

Breakthrough research in 1998 found that tamoxifen, an antiestrogen medication used to treat breast cancer, can help prevent breast cancer (U.S. Preventive Services Task Force, 2003a). The study subjects were women at high risk for breast cancer. The group who took tamoxifen instead of a placebo had 45% fewer cases of breast cancer (Koglin, 1998). Significant side effects are possible, however, including fatal blood clots and endometrial cancer (Cuzick et al., 2003).

Breast Lumps

Three types of lumps can occur in the breasts. The two most common are *cysts,* which are fluid-filled sacs, and *fibroadenomas,* which are solid, rounded tumors. Both are benign (not cancerous or harmful) tumors, and together they account for approximately 80% of breast lumps. In some women the lumps create breast tenderness that ranges from mild to severe discomfort, which is called *fibrocystic disease* (Deckers & Ricci, 1992). The causes of fibrocystic disease are unknown but are believed to be hormonally related. Caffeine in coffee, tea, cola drinks, and chocolate might contribute to the development of benign breast lumps. Dietary changes that have helped some women reduce their symptoms include a diet high in fish, chicken, and grains and low in red meat, salt, and fats. Vitamin supplements of 600 units of vitamin E and vitamin-B complex in 110-mg daily doses have also helped some women (Sloane, 1985).

The third kind of breast lump is a *malignant tumor* (a tumor made up of cancer cells). Breast cancer affects approximately 1 in 9 North American women; 190,000 cases are diagnosed each year. Breast cancer kills about 40,000 U.S. women a year (Cardenas & Frisch, 2003) and 370,000 woman worldwide per year (Prentice, 2003). The risk of breast cancer rises with age; half of all breast cancer is diagnosed in women age 65 and older (Nattinger, 2000). On the other hand, although breast cancer is less common in women in their 20s and

30s, cancers that occur in younger women are often more aggressive and result in a higher mortality rate (Fraunfelder, 2000; Kroman et al., 2000). However, the good news is that overall mortality from breast cancer is at its lowest since 1950, most likely because of earlier detection (Higa, 2000). Unfortunately, the 5-year survival rate is lower for minority women than for white women (C. Li et al., 2003; Marbella & Layde, 2001). For example, only 50% of African American women diagnosed with breast cancer have early-stage, more treatable tumors, compared to 62% of white women (Disease-a-Month, 1999). Hispanic women, on average, also have larger tumors at diagnosis than white women (Hedeen & White, 2001). Socioeconomic characteristics leading to differences in preventive health care probably account for the differences (Russell et al., 2003). The fact that physicians are less likely to refer women of lower socioeconomic status for mammograms also contributes to the problem, because a recommendation from a health care provider is an important predictor of whether or not women obtain mammograms (Lukwago et al., 2003).

Certain risk factors that increase or decrease a woman's chances of developing breast cancer are outlined in Table 4.4. Women often worry most about genetic factors with breast cancer, but environmental factors account for twice as much risk of cancer as do genes (Begley, 2000a), even working at night instead of during the day increases breast cancer risk (Hansen, 2001). Environment's significance is validated by research that found that adopted children whose adoptive parents died of cancer had five times the risk of the average person of developing the same disease (D. Davis, 2000). Exposure to environmental pollution, pesticides, chemicals, and radiation is an underresearched cause of breast cancer. Growing evidence indicates that some synthetic chemicals found in plastics, detergents, and pharmaceutical drugs mimic estrogen's effects on the body and can cause cells to grow out of control and form tumors (Ginsburg, 1999; Hinrichsen & Robey, 2000). Some breast cancer activist groups are attempting to have a greater percentage of cancer research funds allocated to investigations into environmental causes of cancer to assist advances in prevention

TABLE 4.4	Risk Factors for Breast Cancer[a]
Higher Risk	**Lower Risk**
Higher lifetime cumulative estrogen exposure	Lower lifetime estrogen exposure
Menstruation onset before age 12	Menstruation onset after age 12
No pregnancies	One or more pregnancies
First child after age 30 and subsequent children later in life	First child before age 30 and subsequent children early in life
Never breast-fed a child	Breast-fed a child[b]
Menopause after age 54	Early menopause
Obesity	Slenderness
Intact ovaries	Both ovaries removed early in life
Family history of breast cancer	No family history of breast cancer
Two or more first-degree relatives with breast cancer	
One first-degree relative with bilateral premenopausal breast cancer	
Cancer in one breast	No cancer
Sedentary lifestyle	Regular exercise
More than 14 alcoholic drinks a week	Less than 1 alcoholic drink a week
High-fat diet	Low-fat diet
Normal dose of aspirin or ibuprofen (Advil) less than 3 times per week	Normal dose of aspirin or ibuprofen (Advil) 3 times per week

a. Eighty percent of women who develop breast cancer have *no* known risk factors (Heck & Pamuk, 1997; Pritchard, 1997).

b. An analysis of 50 worldwide epidemiologic studies suggests that the longer women breast-feed, the more they are protected against breast cancer (Collaborative Group on Hormonal Factors in Breast Cancer, 2002).

SOURCES: Bingham et al. (2003), Cain (2000), Cardenas & Frisch (2003), Higa (2000), Marchioni (2003), Verloop et al. (2000).

(McCormick, 2002). Some critics contend that the medical, pharmaceutical, and industrial establishment is not interested in prevention because current diagnostic and treatment methods and future innovations are their source of profits. Breast cancer prevention research and implementation are not likely to be profitable; corporations and taxpayers would need to finance the changes required to reduce environmental cancer risks (Fraser, 2002).

If a lump is found, further diagnostic testing is necessary. *Needle aspiration* involves inserting a fine needle into the lump to determine whether or not there is fluid inside. If there is, the lump is usually a cyst and can be drained. If there is no fluid, a surgical biopsy of the tissue of any lump can be analyzed for cancer cells (Meyer et al., 2000). Seventy-five percent of breast lump biopsies are negative for cancer (Muller, 1999).

Breast Cancer

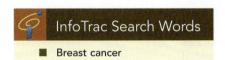

InfoTrac Search Words

■ Breast cancer

In 1974 Betty Ford and Happy Rockefeller were the first public figures to openly discuss their breast cancer and mastectomies. Before their courageous actions most women kept their breast cancer and its treatment as private as possible. In the ensuing years extensive resources have arisen to help women and their loved ones better manage a diagnosis of breast cancer. Political activism has also increased the previous disproportionately small percentage of research funding for breast cancer (Thorne & Murray, 2000).

Once breast cancer has been diagnosed, several forms of treatment can be used and others are being developed (E. Cohen, 2001; Fischman, 2001; Voelker, 2000). Radiation therapy, chemotherapy, hormone therapy, immunotherapy, *breast-conserving surgery* (BCS) (only the lump and small amounts of surrounding tissue are removed), **mastectomy** (surgical removal of all or part of the breast), or a combination of these procedures can be performed. In some cases chemotherapy is the first intervention used, in the hopes of reducing the tumor to allow more conservative surgery (Sapunar & Smith, 2000).With mastectomy the amount of the breast and surrounding tissue that is surgically removed varies from *radical mastectomy* (the entire breast, underlying muscle, and lymph nodes are removed) to *simple*

Mastectomy Surgical removal of the breast(s).

The Breast Cancer Fund's "Obsessed with Breasts" campaign used this attention-getting photo to promote breast cancer education.

mastectomy (breast tissue, the nipple and areola, and a sample of lymph nodes are removed) to BCS. If the cancer is small, localized, and in an early stage, BCS with chemotherapy or radiation can provide as good a chance of cure as a mastectomy (Julien et al., 2000; Love, 1997). Breast-conserving surgeries have become more common in the last 10 years (Morris et al., 2000).

The loss of one or both breasts is usually significant to women. Breasts symbolize many aspects of femininity and can be an important aspect of self-image (Potter & Ship, 2001). One writer who had a mastectomy described the many meanings her breasts have had during her life. "[I] remember the joy and power I felt as an adolescent when my breasts finally began to grow. How I had always enjoyed them, been proud of them, wanted them to be admired under my sweaters. How I liked them being fondled and appreciated by men. What pleasure I had nursing my three children, rocking and being suckled by their small mouths, while their small hands patted my breast" (Ostriker, 1999, p. 200).

Breast cancer and its treatments can adversely affect a woman's sexuality (Henson, 2002). Research indicates that approximately 50% of women who have had breast cancer experience sexual problems resulting from the physical effects of chemotherapy and radiation and hormone therapy (Fleming & Kleinbart, 2001). The stimulation of a woman's breasts during lovemaking, by massaging, licking, or sucking—and the stimulation her partner receives from doing these things and from simply looking at her breasts—is often an important component of sexual arousal for both the woman and her partner. Consequently, surgical removal of one or both breasts can create challenges in sexual adjustment for the couple (Polinsky, 1995).

A mastectomy presents unique problems for a woman who is not in a long-term relationship. She may have difficulty deciding when to tell someone she is dating about her surgery. Her own feelings of acceptance and her judgment about timing are important. Also, she needs to understand that her partner will require some time to adjust to the information about her mastectomy. Still, it may help her to keep in mind that a loving relationship is based on more than physical characteristics.

The American Cancer Society's Reach to Recovery program provides an important service to women with breast cancer. Volunteers in the program, who have all had one or both breasts removed, meet with women who have recently undergone a mastectomy and offer them emotional support and encouragement. They also provide positive models of women who have made a successful adjustment to the results of their surgery.

Breast Implants

Reconstructive breast surgery can enhance a woman's emotional and sexual adjustment following a mastectomy. In many cases a new breast can be made with a silicone pouch containing saline water that is placed under the woman's own skin and chest muscle. In 2002 about 70,000 women in the United States had implants following mastectomy (Healy, 2003). To improve the possibilities for breast reconstruction, a woman might find it helpful to have presurgical discussions with both the surgeon removing the tissue and the plastic surgeon doing the reconstruction. Issues regarding implants are discussed further in the On the Edge box, "Risks of Breast Implants?"

? Critical Thinking Question

Should adolescents be allowed to have breast enlargement surgery?

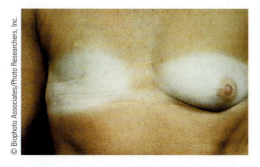 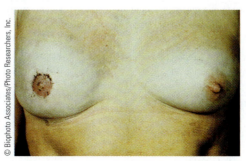

Reconstructive surgery following a mastectomy can enhance a woman's general and sexual adjustment.

Risks of Breast Implants?

The safety of breast implants for breast reconstruction and cosmetic augmentation has been widely debated since the early 1990s. The first implants came on the market in 1963 and were made from a silicone pouch filled with silicone gel. These implants and the saline-filled silicone pouch that followed did not require FDA approval because they were defined as medical products, not medications. Therefore implants were widely used before there was any requirement for premarket assessment of toxicity or postmarket surveillance of long-term complications (Bondurant, 2000). Almost 30 years later, in 1992, silicone implants were taken off the market after reports of implant-induced illnesses, mainly autoimmune symptoms. Saline-filled implants remain available and were approved in 2000 by the FDA. After reviewing the research and testimony, the FDA determined that neither saline nor silicone-gel implants cause serious illnesses (Allen, 2003).

Others disagree with this conclusion because the studies were financed by implant manufacturers, who have a vested interest in the results. The studies also did not select enough women who had had implants for at least 10 years; most autoimmune symptoms do not appear until 8–10 years have passed. Also, women who had symptoms that did not fit with known autoimmune diseases were excluded from the study; critics maintain that silicone-gel-induced symptoms are often atypical (Stott-Kendall, 1997; Washburne, 1996). A recent study supports the critics' views. This study used magnetic resonance imaging (MRI) to determine whether silicone implants had remained intact or had ruptured and whether the health status of the women was therefore different. The research further compared the health of women with ruptured capsules when the silicone gel stayed within the fibrous scar-tissue capsule that forms around the implant to the health of women who had gel leak outside the ruptured capsule. The research found no association with health problems when the implants rupture and the silicone gel remains within the capsule. However, the study found an increase in connective tissue disease when the silicone gel leaked outside the capsule (Brown, 2001). It will take many more years to establish the validity of these criticisms.

 Sexual Health

Although the FDA approved saline implants, it also recommended that women receive strong warnings about possible complications and poor results, such as loss of breast sensation, asymmetric breasts, and capsular contraction (scar tissue hardens around the implant and presses the soft capsule into a hard disk). One study found that 73% of women with saline implants experienced side effects, and 27% of women had their implants removed within 3 years because of infection, a broken or leaking implant, or painful scar tissue. Implants that break open or leak require women to undergo repeated surgeries; about 15% rupture by 10 years (Springen, 2003). Each year over 200,000 women in the United States receive cosmetic breast implants, and many will have complications (Farr, 2000; Springen, 2003). These complications can be painful and disfiguring, and women should inform themselves thoroughly when considering this surgery.

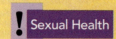
Summary

Genital Self-Exam
- Genital self-exploration is a good way for a woman to learn about her own body and to notice any changes that may require medical attention. (p. 84)

The Vulva
- The female external genitals, also called the vulva, are composed of the mons veneris, labia majora, labia minora, clitoris, and urethral and vaginal openings. Each woman's vulva is unique in shape, color, and texture. (pp. 82–83)
- The mons veneris and labia majora have underlying pads of fatty tissue and are covered by pubic hair beginning at adolescence. (pp. 82–83)
- The labia minora are folds of sensitive skin that begin at the hood over the clitoris and extend downward to below the vaginal opening, or introitus. The area between them is called the vestibule. (p. 83)
- The clitoris is composed of the external glans and shaft and the internal crura. The glans contains densely concentrated nerve endings. The only function of the clitoris is sexual pleasure. (p. 85)

- The urethral opening is located between the clitoris and the vaginal introitus. (p. 87)
- Many cultures have placed great importance on the hymen as proof of virginity. However, there are various sizes, shapes, and thicknesses of hymens, and many women can have initial intercourse without pain or bleeding. Also, women who have decided to have coitus can learn how to stretch their hymens to help make their first experience comfortable. (pp. 87–88)

Underlying Structures
- Below the surface of the vulva are the vestibular bulbs and the pelvic floor muscles. (p. 88)

Internal Structures
- The vagina, with its three layers of tissue, extends about 3 to 5 inches into the pelvic cavity. It is a potential rather than an actual space and increases in size during sexual arousal, coitus, and childbirth. The other internal reproductive structures are the cervix, uterus, fallopian tubes, and ovaries. (pp. 89–94)

- Kegel exercises are voluntary contractions of the vaginal muscles. (p. 89)
- Vaginal lubrication, the secretion of alkaline fluid through the vaginal walls during arousal, is important both in enhancing the longevity and motility of sperm cells and in increasing the pleasure and comfort of intercourse. (p. 91)
- The Grafenberg spot is located about 1 centimeter along the surface of the top wall of the vagina. Many women report erotic sensitivity to pressure in some area of their vaginas. (p. 91)
- The vaginal walls and cervix produce normal secretions. (pp. 91–92)

Menstruation

- The menstrual cycle results from a complex interplay of hormones. The cycle is divided into the proliferative, the secretory, and the menstrual phases. Although negative social attitudes have been historically attached to menstruation, some people are currently redefining it in a more positive fashion. (pp. 94–99)
- There are usually no medical reasons to abstain from intercourse during menstruation. However, many people do limit their sexual activity during this time. (pp. 99–100)
- Some women have difficulties with PMS (premenstrual syndrome), PMDD (premenstrual dysphoric disorder), or primary or secondary dysmenorrhea. Knowledge about the physiological factors that contribute to these problems is increasing, and some of the problems can be treated. (p. 100)
- Amenorrhea occurs normally during pregnancy, while breastfeeding, and after menopause. It can also be due to medical problems or poor health. A pill that prevents menstruation for three months has been developed. (p. 101)
- Toxic shock syndrome (TSS) is a rare condition that occurs most often in menstruating women. Its symptoms include fever, sore throat, nausea, red skin flush, dizziness, and low blood pressure. If untreated, it can be fatal. (pp. 101–102)

Menopause

- Menopause is the cessation of menstruation, and it signals the end of female fertility. The average age of menopause is 51. Because of increases in life expectancy, women can expect to live half their adult lives following menopause. (p. 102)
- Most women experience few uncomfortable symptoms during the aging process and maintain sexual interest and response. Others experience symptoms such as hot flashes, sleep disturbance, depression or anxiety, headaches, and sensitivity to touch as a result of declining estrogen levels. (p. 103)
- Hormone therapy (HT) is a medical treatment for menopausal symptoms and helps to protect against osteoporosis and heart disease. Potential side effects necessitate careful use of such therapy. (p. 103–107)

Gynecological Health Concerns

- About 15% of women will experience a urinary tract infection caused by bacteria that enter the urethra. (p. 107)
- Occasionally, a vaginal infection occurs that results in irritation, unusual discharge, or a disagreeable odor. (p. 108)
- The Pap smear has significantly reduced deaths from cervical cancer. A woman can use her own speculum to examine her cervix. (p. 109)
- There is considerable medical controversy about the appropriate use of hysterectomy. A hysterectomy or oophorectomy can have an effect—either positive or negative—on a woman's sexuality. (pp. 109–110)

The Breasts

- The breasts are composed of fatty tissue and milk-producing glands. Self-exam of the breasts is an important part of health care. (pp. 110–113)
- Three types of lumps can appear in the breasts: cysts, fibroadenomas, and malignant tumors. Careful diagnosis of a breast lump is important. Mammography and other tests can help detect and diagnose breast cancer. Less radical surgeries for breast cancer are often as effective as more severe procedures. (pp. 114–117)
- Saline-filled breast implants now have FDA approval with warnings that women inform themselves fully about possible complications. (pp. 117–118)

▶ Suggested Readings

Angier, Natalie (1999). *Woman: An Intimate Geography.* Boston: Houghton Mifflin. A fresh perspective on the female body by a Pulitzer Prize–winning author. Challenges evolutionary psychologists' theories about women's roles and sexuality.

Boston Women's Health Book Collective (1998). *Our Bodies, Ourselves for the New Century: A Book by and for Women.* New York: Simon & Schuster. An easy-to-use resource for all aspects of women's bodies, inclusive of heterosexual, bisexual, and lesbian orientations.

Boston Women's Health Book Collective. (2000). *Nuestros Cuerpos, Nuestros Vidas.* New York: Seven Stories Press. The classic *Our Bodies, Ourselves* reoriented for the Latina culture.

Bouris, Karen (1993). *The First Time.* Berkeley, CA: Conari Press. A collection of personal stories about "losing virginity" as a pivotal female experience.

Chalker, R. (2000). *The Clitoral Truth: The Secret World at Your Fingertips.* New York: Seven Stories Press. An in-depth exploration of understanding and appreciating the clitoris.

Ellison, Carol (2000). *Women's Sexualities.* Oakland, CA: New Harbinger Publications. Illuminating information and analysis, based on in-depth interviews with women, age 23 to 90, emphasizing the challenges and triumphs of sexual development.

Ensler, Eve (2002). *The Vagina Monologues: The V-Day Edition.* New York: Villard Books. (Also available on DVD and VHS.) A play about the delights and pathos of the vagina.

Foley, Sallie, Sally Kope, and Dennis Sugue (2002). *Sex Matters for Women: A Complete Guide to Taking Care of Your Sexual Self.* New York: Guilford Press. A comprehensive guide to female sexuality.

Girman, Andrea, Roberta Lee, and Benjamin Klinger (2003). An integrative medicine approach to premenstrual syndrome. *Am. J. Obstet. Gynecol., 188,* 556–563. A comprehensive review of complementary medicine and its benefits for premenstrual problems.

Link, John (2000). *The Breast Cancer Survival Manual: A Step-by-Step Guide for the Woman with Newly Diagnosed Breast Cancer.* New York: Owl Books. Practical and accessible advice from a leading expert on breast cancer who was recently honored by the American Cancer Society for his contributions to women with cancer.

Meshorer, Marc, and Judith Meshorer (1986). *Ultimate Pleasure: The Secrets of Easily Orgasmic Women.* New York: St. Martin's Press. A study based on in-depth interviews with easily orgasmic women; describes how women take an active role in creating, building, and experiencing arousal.

Murcia, Andy, and Bob Stewart (1989). *Man to Man: When the Woman You Love Has Breast Cancer.* New York: St. Martin's Press. Personal stories and practical information for men confronted with their partners' diagnosis of breast cancer.

Northrup, Christine (2003). *The Wisdom of Menopause.* New York: Bantam Doubleday Dell. Detailed information about medicine, including approaches of complementary medicine.

Raz, Hilda (1999). *Living on the Margins: Women Writers on Breast Cancer.* New York: Peresa Books. A collection of poems and essays in which writers describe the courage and resilience they experienced in their trials with breast cancer.

Stewart, Elizabeth, and Paula Spencer (2002). *The V Book: A Doctor's Guide to Complete Vulvovaginal Health.* New York: Bantam Books. This book draws on the latest medical research and clinical gynecological experience to provide extensive information about women's genital health.

Web Resources

Your *Our Sexuality* Web site **http://psychology.wadsworth.com/ crooksbaur9e/** has direct links to the Web sites described below. These links are checked often for changes, dead links, and new additions.

Gyn101
A visit to this Web site walks you through a first visit to a gynecologist. Among the resources available are how to choose a gynecologist, what to expect in a gynecological exam, and suggested questions to ask your health care provider.

OBGYN.net Women and Patients
This site includes valuable reference information on gynecological health, including links to recent research articles on a host of topics.

National Vaginitis Association
This site spells out the differences in symptoms and treatment of various vaginal infections.

National Women's Information Center
This Web site serves as a wide-ranging resource center on women's health issues and is sponsored by the Office on Women's Health of the U.S. Department of Health and Human Services.

North American Menopause Society
The resources available at this Web site include basic facts about menopause, a helpful FAQ, and information about educational materials available to both consumers and health care providers.

Our Sexuality Web Site
For online resources directly related to this book, go to **http://psychology.wadsworth.com/ crooksbaur9e/**. You will find interactive exercises, study questions, chapter outlines, an online version of this text's glossary, and Web links and activities that complement your CD-ROM.

InfoTrac® College Edition Online Library
http://infotrac.thomsonlearning.com/
InfoTrac College Edition is an online searchable library that includes a multitude of journals, many of which are specific to human sexuality. These journals include *Archives of Sexual Behavior, Archives of Sexual Health Behavior, Canadian Journal of Human Sexuality, Hispanic Journal of the Behavioral Sciences, Journal of Cross-Cultural Psychology, Journal of Physical Education, Recreation, and Dance, Journal of Sex Research,* and *Sex Roles.* You may search topics suggested in the margins of this chapter or terms of your own.

Our Sexuality CD-ROM
Use your CD-ROM for further study of the concepts in this chapter. Your CD-ROM provides animations of difficult concepts, video clips of real people discussing sexuality, critical thinking questions, chapter quizzing, and more.

CHAPTER 5

Male Sexual Anatomy and Physiology

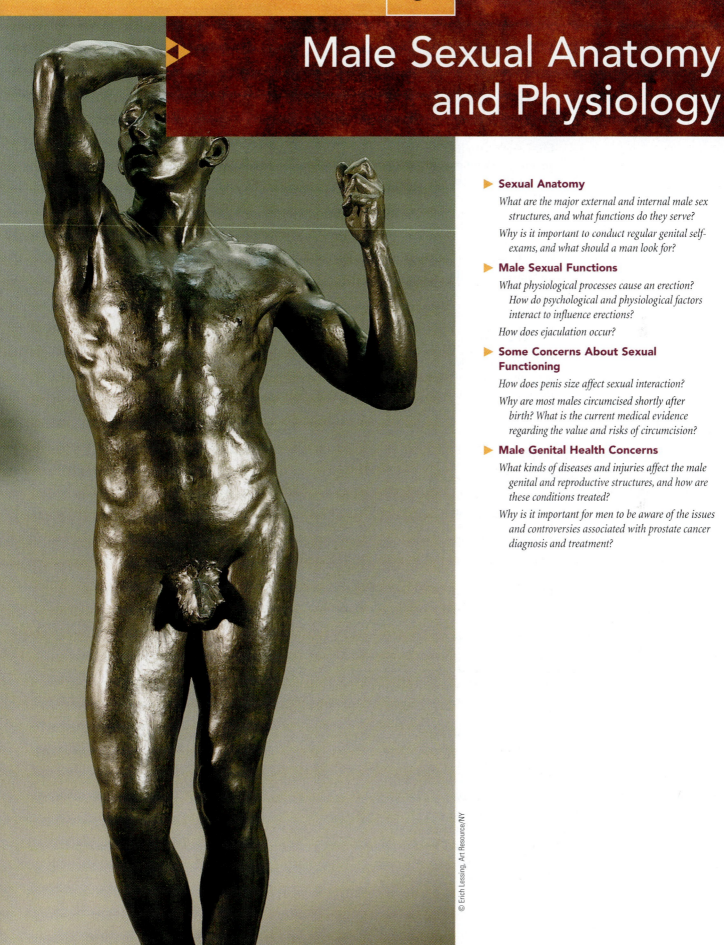

▶ **Sexual Anatomy**

What are the major external and internal male sex structures, and what functions do they serve?

Why is it important to conduct regular genital self-exams, and what should a man look for?

▶ **Male Sexual Functions**

What physiological processes cause an erection? How do psychological and physiological factors interact to influence erections?

How does ejaculation occur?

▶ **Some Concerns About Sexual Functioning**

How does penis size affect sexual interaction?

Why are most males circumcised shortly after birth? What is the current medical evidence regarding the value and risks of circumcision?

▶ **Male Genital Health Concerns**

What kinds of diseases and injuries affect the male genital and reproductive structures, and how are these conditions treated?

Why is it important for men to be aware of the issues and controversies associated with prostate cancer diagnosis and treatment?

Who needs a lecture on male anatomy? Certainly not the men in this class. It's hanging out there all our lives. We handle and look at it each time we pee or bathe. So what's the mystery? Now the female body—that's a different story. That's why I'm in the class. Let's learn something that isn't so obvious. (Authors' files)

This quote, from a student in a sexuality class, illustrates two common assumptions. The first is that male sexual anatomy is simple. All you need to know is "hanging out there." The second, perhaps more subtle implication is that female genital structures are considerably more complicated and mysterious than men's.

These assumptions call for some rethinking, for a few reasons. One is that there is more than meets the eye. The sexual anatomy of men and women is complex and varies widely from one individual to another. Another reason is that knowing about our own sexual anatomy and functioning, although it does not guarantee sexual satisfaction, at least provides a degree of comfort with our bodies and perhaps a greater ability to communicate with a partner. Equally important, an understanding of our own bodies provides an important basis for detecting potential health problems. In this chapter we provide information that every man should know regarding self-exams and health care. (For further information on this important topic, see the Suggested Readings at the end of this chapter.) As in Chapter 4, we encourage readers to use the pages that follow as a reference for their own self-knowledge and improved health.

▶ Sexual Anatomy

We begin with discussions of the various structures of the male sexual anatomy. Descriptive accounts are organized according to parts of the genital system for easy reference. Later in this chapter (and in Chapter 6) we will look more closely at the way the entire system functions during sexual arousal.

The Penis

Penis A male sexual organ consisting of the internal root and the external shaft and glans.

The **penis** consists of nerves, blood vessels, fibrous tissue, and three parallel cylinders of spongy tissue. It does not contain a bone or an abundance of muscular tissue, contrary to some people's beliefs. However, an extensive network of muscles are present at the base of the penis. These muscles help eject both semen and urine through the urethra.

Root The portion of the penis that extends internally into the pelvic cavity.

A portion of the penis extends internally into the pelvic cavity. This part, including its attachment to the pubic bones, is referred to as the **root.** When a man's penis is erect, he can feel this inward projection by pressing a finger up between his anus and scrotum. The external, pendulous portion of the penis, excluding the head, is known as the **shaft.** The smooth, acorn-shaped head is called the **glans.**

Shaft The length of the penis between the glans and the body.

Glans The head of the penis; it is richly endowed with nerve endings.

Running the entire length of the penis are the three cylinders referred to earlier. The two larger ones, the **cavernous bodies** (*corpora cavernosa*), lie side by side above the smaller third cylinder, the **spongy body** (*corpus spongiosum*). At the root of the penis the innermost tips of the cavernous bodies, or *crura*, are connected to the pubic bones. At the head of the penis the spongy body expands to form the glans. These structures are shown in Figure 5.1.

Cavernous bodies The structures in the shaft of the penis that engorge with blood during sexual arousal.

All these cylinders are similar in structure. As the terms *cavernous* and *spongy* imply, the cylinders are made of spongelike irregular spaces and cavities. Each cylinder is also richly supplied with blood vessels. When a male is sexually excited, the cylinders become engorged with blood, resulting in penile erection. During sexual arousal the spongy body may stand out as a distinct ridge along the underside of the penis.

Spongy body A cylinder that forms a bulb at the base of the penis, extends up into the penile shaft, and forms the penile glans.

The skin covering the penile shaft is usually hairless and quite loose, which allows for expansion when the penis becomes erect. Although the skin is connected to the shaft at the neck (the portion just behind the glans), some of it folds over and forms a cuff, or hood, over the glans. This loose covering is called the **foreskin,** or *prepuce*. In some males the foreskin covers the entire head, whereas in other males only a portion of the head is covered. Typically, the foreskin can be retracted (drawn back from the glans) quite easily. *Circumcision* involves the surgical removal of this sleeve of skin. Although familiar in our culture,

Foreskin A covering of skin over the penile glans.

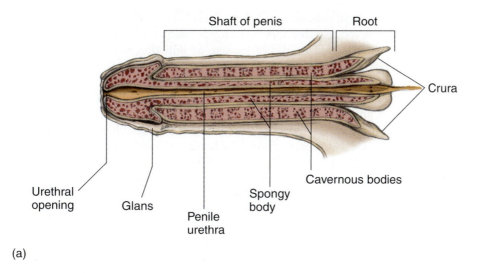

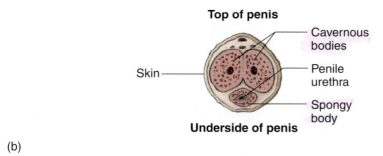

▶ **Figure 5.1** Interior structure of the penis: (a) view from above and (b) cross section of the penis.

circumcision is only one of many procedures for altering male genitalia that are practiced around the world, as described in the following "Sexuality and Diversity" discussion on male genital modification and mutilation.

 Sexuality and Diversity

Male Genital Modification:
Some Cultural Beliefs and Practices

Throughout the world people hold strong beliefs about the importance and implications of altering male genitals using a variety of procedures. These rituals and customs have been chronicled through the ages. (Female genital modification is also widespread, as discussed in Chapter 4.)

The most common genital alteration is *circumcision,* the surgical removal of the foreskin. Circumcision is practiced in many societies for religious, ritual, or hygienic reasons. Historically, circumcision is an old practice. Examinations of Egyptian mummies have revealed evidence of circumcision as far back as 6000 B.C., and Egyptian records at least 5,000 years old depict circumcised men. Australian aborigines, Muslims, and some African tribes have also used male circumcision to mark a rite of passage or to signify a covenant with God (Melby, 2002b).

For thousands of years Jews have practiced circumcision according to scripture (Genesis 17:9–27) as a religious rite. The ceremony, called a *bris,* takes place on the eighth day after birth. Similarly, the followers of Islam have a long-standing tradition of circumcision. Although circumcision is widespread among Middle Eastern and African societies, it is relatively uncommon in Europe today.

A variation of circumcision, called *superincision* (in which the foreskin, instead of being removed, is split lengthwise along its top portion), is practiced among certain South Pacific cultures as a kind of rite of passage or initiation ritual into sexual maturity (Gregersen, 1996). Mangaia and the Marquesas Islands are two societies that perform this procedure when a boy reaches adolescence (Marshall, 1971; Suggs, 1962).

Castration, removal of the testes, is a more extreme male genital mutilation that also has its roots in antiquity. This practice has been justified for a variety of reasons: to prevent sexual activity between harem guards (eunuchs) and their charges, to render war captives docile, to preserve the soprano voices of European choirboys during the Middle Ages, and as part of religious ceremonies (in ancient Egypt hundreds of young boys were castrated in a single ceremony). In the United States in the mid-19th century castration was sometimes performed as a purported cure for the evils of masturbation (Melby, 2002b). During this same time period American medical journals also reported that castration was often a successful treatment for "insanity."

In more modern times castrations have occasionally been performed for legal reasons, either as a method of eugenic selection (e.g., to prevent a mentally disabled person from having offspring) or as an alleged deterrent to sex offenders (see Chapter 6). The ethical basis of these operations is highly controversial. Finally, castration is sometimes performed as medical treatment for diseases, such as prostate cancer and genital tuberculosis (Parker & Dearnaley, 2003; Pickett et al., 2000).

The entire penis is sensitive to touch, but the greatest concentration of nerve endings is found in the glans. Although the entire glans area is extremely sensitive, many men find that two specific locations are particularly responsive to stimulation. One is the rim, or crown, which marks the area where the glans rises abruptly from the shaft. This distinct ridge is called the **corona** (kuh-ROH-nuh). The other is the **frenulum** (FREN-yoo-lum), a thin strip of skin connecting the glans to the shaft on the underside of the penis. The location of these two areas is shown in Figure 5.2.

Most men enjoy having the glans stimulated, particularly the two areas just mentioned, but individuals vary in their preferences. Some men occasionally or routinely prefer being stimulated in genital areas other than the glans of the penis. The mode of stimulation, either manual (by self or partner) or oral, can influence the choice of preferred sites. Some of these variations and individual preferences are noted in the following accounts:

Corona The rim of the penile glans.

Frenulum A highly sensitive thin strip of skin that connects the glans to the shaft on the underside of the penis.

▶ **Figure 5.2** The underside of the uncircumcised penis, showing the location of the corona and frenulum—two areas on the penis that harbor a high concentration of sensitive nerve endings.

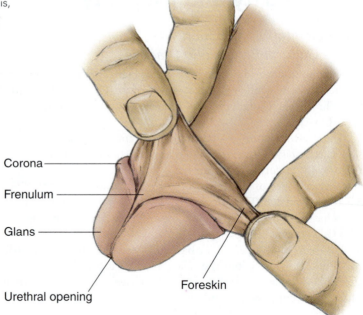

Corona

Frenulum

Glans

Urethral opening

Foreskin

When I masturbate I frequently avoid the head of my penis, concentrating instead on stroking the shaft. The stimulation is not so intense, which allows a longer time for buildup to orgasm. The result is that the climax is generally more intense than if I focus only on the glans. (Authors' files)

During oral sex with my girlfriend, I sometimes have to put my hand around my penis, leaving just the head sticking out, so she will get the idea what part feels best. Otherwise, she spends a lot of time running her tongue up and down the shaft, which just doesn't do it for me. (Authors' files)

Strengthening Musculature Around the Penis

As previously mentioned, the internal extension of the penis is surrounded by an elaborate network of muscles. This musculature is comparable to that in the female body, and strengthening these muscles by doing Kegel exercises can produce benefits for men similar to those experienced by women. In most men these muscles are quite weak because they are usually only contracted during ejaculation. The following description, adapted from *Male Sexuality* (Zilbergeld, 1978, p. 109), is a brief outline of how these muscles can be located and strengthened:

! **Sexual Health**

1. Locate the muscles by stopping the flow of urine several times while urinating. The muscles you squeeze to accomplish this are the ones on which you will concentrate. If you do a correct Kegel while not urinating, you will notice your penis move slightly. Kegels done when you have an erection will cause your penis to move up and down.
2. Begin the exercise program by squeezing and relaxing the muscles 15 times, twice daily. Do not hold the contraction at this stage. (These are called "short Kegels.")
3. Gradually increase the number of Kegels until you can comfortably do 60 at a time, twice daily.
4. Now practice "long Kegels" by holding each contraction for a count of 3.
5. Combine the short and long Kegels in each daily exercise routine, doing a set of 60 of each, once or twice a day.
6. Continue with the Kegel exercises for at least several weeks. You may not notice results until a month or more has passed. By this time the exercises will probably have become automatic, requiring no particular effort.

Some of the positive changes men have reported after doing the male Kegel exercises include stronger and more pleasurable orgasms, better ejaculatory control, and increased pelvic sensation during sexual arousal. ■

The Scrotum

The **scrotum** (SKROH-tum), or scrotal sac, is a loose pouch of skin that is an outpocket of the abdominal wall in the groin area directly underneath the penis (Figure 5.3). Normally, it hangs loosely from the body wall, although cold temperatures or sexual stimulation can cause it to move closer to the body.

The scrotal sac consists of two layers. The outermost layer is a covering of thin skin that is darker in color than other body skin. It typically becomes sparsely covered with hair at adolescence. The second layer, known as the *tunica dartos,* is composed of smooth muscle fibers and fibrous connective tissue.

Within the scrotal sac are two separate compartments, each of which houses a single **testis** (plural *testes*), or *testicle.* (For a diagram of the testes within the scrotal sac, see Figure 5.4.) Each testis is suspended in its compartment by the **spermatic** (spur-MAT-ik) **cord.** The spermatic cord contains the sperm-carrying tube, or *vas deferens,* and blood vessels, nerves, and *cremasteric muscle* fibers, which

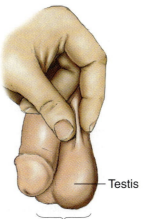

▶ **Figure 5.3** The scrotum and the testes. The spermatic cord can be located by palpating the scrotal sac above either testis with the thumb and forefinger.

Scrotum The pouch of skin of the external male genitals that encloses the testes.

Testis Male gonad inside the scrotum that produces sperm and sex hormones.

Spermatic cord A cord attached to the testis that contains the vas deferens, blood vessels, nerves, and cremasteric muscle fibers.

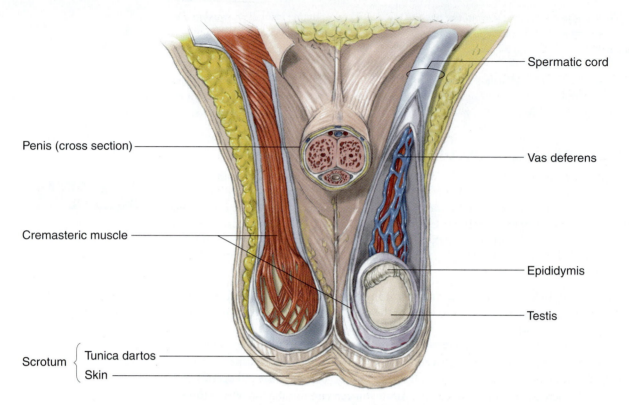

Penis (cross section)

Cremasteric muscle

Scrotum { Tunica dartos
Skin

Spermatic cord

Vas deferens

Epididymis

Testis

▶ **Figure 5.4** Underlying structures of the scrotum. This illustration shows portions of the scrotum cut away to reveal the cremasteric muscle, spermatic cord, vas deferens, and a testis within the scrotal sac.

influence the position of the testis in the scrotal sac. These muscles can be voluntarily contracted, causing the testes to move upward. Most males find that they can produce this effect with practice; this exercise is one way for a man to become more familiar with his body. As shown in Figure 5.3, the spermatic cord can be located by palpating the scrotal sac above either testis with the thumb and forefinger. The cord is a firm, rubbery tube that is generally quite pronounced.

The scrotum is sensitive to any temperature change, and numerous sensory receptors in its skin provide information that prevents the testes from becoming either too warm or too cold. When the scrotum is cooled, the tunica dartos contracts, wrinkling the outer skin layer and pulling the testes up closer to the warmth of the body. This process is involuntary, and the reaction sometimes has amusing ramifications:

When I took swimming classes in high school, the trip back to the locker room was always a bit traumatic. After peeling off my swimsuit, it seemed like I had to search around for my balls. The other guys seemed to have the same problem, since they were also frantically tugging and pulling to get everything back in place. (Authors' files)

Another kind of stimulation that causes the scrotum to draw closer to the body is sexual arousal. One of the clearest external indications of impending male orgasm is the drawing up of the testes to a position of maximum elevation. The major scrotal muscle involved in this response is the cremasteric muscle. Sudden fear can also cause strong contractions of this muscle, and it is also possible to initiate contractions by stroking the inner thighs. This response is known as the *cremasteric reflex*.

The movements of the testes and scrotal sac are influenced by factors other than temperature change, sexual arousal, and strong emotion. These structures have the rather amazing property of virtually constant movement, a result of the continuous contraction–relaxation cycles of the cremasteric musculature.

The Testes

The testes, or testicles, have two major functions: the secretion of sex hormones and the production of sperm. The testes form inside the abdominal cavity, and late in fetal development they migrate through the *inguinal canal* from the abdomen to the scrotum (Ferrer & McKenna, 2000).

At birth the testes are normally in the scrotum, but in some cases one or both fail to descend. This condition, known as **cryptorchidism** (krip-TOR-kuh-di-zum) (meaning "hidden testis"), affects 3–4% of male infants and up to 30% of premature male infants (Ferrer & McKenna, 2000). Undescended testes often move into place spontaneously sometime after birth. However, if they have not descended by age 1, the likelihood of spontaneous descent is small (Ferrer & McKenna, 2000).

Parents should watch out for cryptorchidism, especially when both testes are affected. Sperm production is affected by temperature. Average scrotal temperature is several degrees lower than body temperature, and sperm production appears to be optimal at this lower temperature. Undescended testes remain at internal body temperature, which is too high for normal sperm production, and infertility could result (Ferrer & McKenna, 2000). Cryptorchidism is also associated with an increased risk for developing a hernia or testicular cancer (Herrinton et al., 2003; Noh et al., 2000). Surgical or hormonal treatment is sometimes necessary to correct this condition (Vinardi et al., 2001). ■

In most men the testes are asymmetric. Note in Figure 5.3 that the left testis hangs lower than the right testis. This is usually the case because the left spermatic cord is generally longer than the right. Although this difference has often been attributed to excessive masturbation, there is no truth to this assertion. It is no more unusual than a woman having one breast that is larger than the other. Our bodies simply are not perfectly symmetric.

It is important for men to become familiar with their testes and to examine them regularly. The testes can be affected by a variety of diseases, including cancer, sexually transmitted diseases, and an assortment of infections. (Diseases of the male sex organs are discussed at the end of this chapter and in Chapter 17.) Most of these conditions have observable symptoms, and early detection allows for rapid treatment; early detection can also prevent far more serious complications. ■

Unfortunately, most men do not regularly examine their testes. Research suggests that among high-school-age males the percentage is extremely low, perhaps 2% at most. Even among male college students the rate is very small, probably less than 10% (Adelman & Joffe, 2000; Best & Davis, 1997). Furthermore, one study indicated that instruction about testicular self-examination in high school health classes is also relatively uncommon (Wohl & Kane, 1997). Yet this simple, painless, and potentially lifesaving process, which takes only a few minutes, is an excellent method for detecting early signs of disease. This procedure is described and illustrated in the boxed discussion, "Male Genital Self-Examination."

The Seminiferous Tubules

Within and adjacent to the testes are two separate areas involved in the production and storage of sperm. The first of these, the **seminiferous** (seh-muh-NI-fuh-rus) **tubules** (sperm-bearing tubules), are thin, highly coiled structures located in the approximately 250 cone-shaped lobes that make up the interior of each testis (Figure 5.5). Sperm production takes place in these tubules, usually beginning sometime after the onset of puberty. Men continue to produce viable sperm well into their old age, often until death, although the production rate diminishes with aging. The **interstitial** (in-ter-STI-shul) **cells,** or *Leydig's cells,* are located between the seminiferous tubules. These cells are the major source of androgen, and their proximity to blood vessels allows direct secretion of their hormone products into the bloodstream. (We will discuss the role of hormones in sexual behavior in Chapter 6.)

The Epididymis

The second important area for sperm processing is the **epididymis** (eh-puh-DID-uh-mus) (literally, "over the testes"). Sperm produced in the seminiferous tubules moves through a maze of tiny ducts into this C-shaped structure that adheres to the back and upper surface

---

Cryptorchidism A condition in which the testes fail to descend from the abdominal cavity to the scrotal sac.

InfoTrac Search Words

■ Cryptorchidism

Sexual Health

Sexual Health

Seminiferous tubules Thin, coiled structures in the testes in which sperm are produced.

Interstitial cells Cells located between the seminiferous tubules that are the major source of androgen in males.

Epididymis The structure along the back of each testis in which sperm maturation occurs.

YOUR SEXUAL HEALTH

Male Genital Self-Examination

Our male readers can conduct a self-examination of their genitals standing, reclining against a backrest, or in a sitting position (see photo). A good time is after a hot shower or bath, because heat causes the scrotal skin to relax and the testes to descend. This relaxed, accessible state of the testes can make detecting any unusual condition easier.

First, notice the cremasteric cycle of contraction and relaxation, and experiment with initiating the cremasteric reflex. Then explore the testes one at a time. Place the thumbs of both hands on top of a testis and the index and middle fingers on the underside. Then apply a small amount of pressure and roll the testis between your fingertips. The surface should be fairly smooth and firm in consistency. The contour and texture of male testes varies from individual to individual, and it is important to know your own anatomy so that you can note changes. Having two testes allows for direct comparison, which is helpful in spotting abnormalities (although it is common for the two testes to vary slightly in size). Areas that appear swollen or are painful to the touch can indicate the presence of an infection. The epididymis, which lies along the back of each testis, occasionally becomes infected, sometimes caus-

Self-examination can increase a man's familiarity with his genitals. Any irregularity, such as a lump or tender area in the scrotum, should be examined immediately by a physician.

© Joel Gordon

ing an irregular area to become tender to the touch. Also, be aware of any mass within the testis that feels hard or irregular to the fingertips but that can be painless to touch. This mass, which may be no larger than a BB shot or small pea, could be an indication of early-stage testicular cancer. This cancer, although relatively rare, can progress rapidly. Early detection and prompt treatment are essential to successful recovery. Testicular cancer is discussed further at the end of this chapter.

While examining your genitals, also be aware of any unusual changes in your penis. A sore or unusual growth anywhere on its surface can be a symptom of an infection, sexually transmitted disease, or in rare cases, penile cancer. Although cancer of the penis is among the rarest of cancers, it is also one of the most traumatic and, unless diagnosed and treated early, deadly (Gordon et al., 1997). Penile cancer usually begins as a small, painless sore on the glans or, in the case of uncircumcised men, the foreskin. The sore can remain the same for weeks, months, or even years until it changes into a cauliflower-like mass that is chronically inflamed and tender. Clearly, the time to first seek medical attention is immediately after first noticing the sore, when the prospect for a cure remains good.

of each testis (see Figure 5.5). Evidence suggests that the epididymis serves primarily as a storage chamber where sperm cells undergo additional maturing, or ripening, for a period of several weeks. During this time they are completely inactive. Researchers theorize that a selection process also occurs in the epididymis, in which abnormal sperm cells are eliminated by the body's waste removal system.

The Vas Deferens

Vas deferens A sperm-carrying tube that begins at the testis and ends at the urethra.

Vasectomy Male sterilization procedure that involves removing a section from each vas deferens.

Sperm held in the epididymis eventually drain into the **vas deferens** (vas DEH-fuh-renz), a long, thin duct that travels up through the scrotum inside the spermatic cord. The vas deferens is close to the surface of the scrotum along this route, which makes the common male sterilization procedure, **vasectomy** (vuh-SEK-tuh-mee), relatively simple. (Vasectomy is described in Chapter 11.)

The spermatic cord exits the scrotal sac through the inguinal canal, an opening that leads directly into the abdominal cavity. From this point the vas deferens continues its upward journey along the top of the bladder and loops around the ureter, as shown in Figure 5.6.

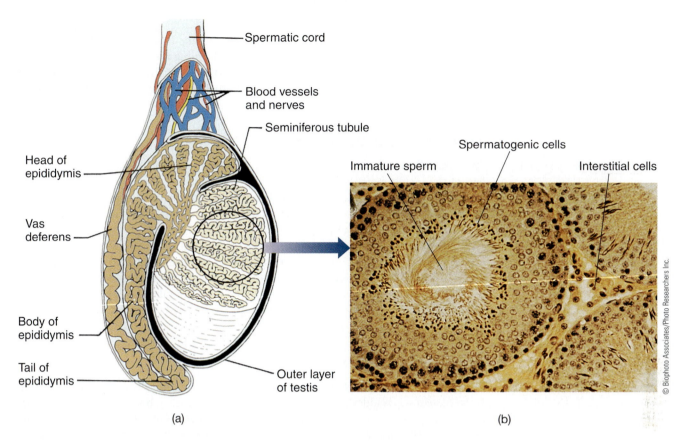

Head of
epididymis

Vas
deferens

Body of
epididymis

Tail of
epididymis

Spermatic cord

Blood vessels
and nerves

Seminiferous tubule

Outer layer
of testis

(a)

Spermatogenic cells

Immature sperm

Interstitial cells

© Biophoto Associates/Photo Researchers Inc.

(b)

▶ **Figure 5.5** (a) Internal structure of a testis. Sperm are produced in the seminiferous tubules and transported to the epididymis, which serves as a storage chamber. (b) The cross-section enlargement view of the seminiferous tubules shows spermatogenic (sperm-making) cells and the interstitial cells.

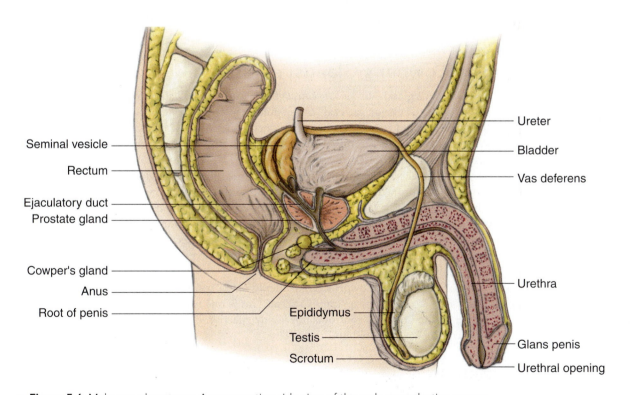

Seminal vesicle

Rectum

Ejaculatory duct
Prostate gland

Cowper's gland
Anus
Root of penis

Ureter

Bladder

Vas deferens

Urethra

Epididymus

Testis

Scrotum

Glans penis

Urethral opening

▶ **Figure 5.6** Male sexual anatomy: A cross-section side view of the male reproductive organs.

(This pathway is essentially the reverse of the route taken by the testis during its prenatal descent.) Turning downward, the vas deferens reaches the base of the bladder, where it is joined by the excretory duct of the *seminal vesicle,* forming the **ejaculatory duct.** The two ejaculatory ducts (one from each side) are very short, running their entire course within the prostate gland. At their ends they open into the prostatic portion of the **urethra** (yoo-REE-thruh), the tube through which urine passes from the bladder.

The Seminal Vesicles

70% of Seminal Fluid

The **seminal vesicles** (SEH-muh-nul VEH-si-kuls) are two small glands adjacent to the terminals of the vas deferens (see Figure 5.6). Their role in sexual physiology is not completely understood. It was once assumed that they functioned primarily as storage centers for sperm. However, we now know that they secrete an alkaline fluid that is rich in fructose. This secretion constitutes a major portion of the seminal fluid, perhaps as much as 70%, and its sugar component seems to contribute to sperm nutrition and motility (Spring-Mills & Hafez, 1980). Up to this point in its journey from the testis, a sperm cell is transmitted through the elaborate system of ducts by the continuous movement of *cilia,* tiny hairlike structures that line the inner walls of these tubes. Once stimulated by energy-giving secretions of the seminal vesicles, however, sperm propel themselves by the whiplike action of their own tails.

The Prostate Gland

The **prostate** (PROS-tayt) **gland** is a structure about the size and shape of a walnut, located at the base of the bladder (see Figure 5.6). As described earlier, both ejaculatory ducts and the urethra pass through this gland. The prostate is made up of smooth muscle fibers and glandular tissue, whose secretions account for about 30% of the seminal fluid released during ejaculation.

Although the prostate is continually active in a mature male, it accelerates its output during sexual arousal. Its secretions flow into the urethra through a system of sievelike ducts, and here the secretions combine with sperm and the seminal vesicle secretions to form the seminal fluid. The prostatic secretions are thin, milky, and alkaline. This alkalinity helps counteract the unfavorable acidity of the male urethra and the female vaginal tract, making a more hospitable environment for sperm. We will discuss some prostate gland health concerns at the end of this chapter.

The Cowper's Glands

The **Cowper's glands,** or *bulbourethral glands,* are two small structures, each about the size of a pea, located one on each side of the urethra just below where the urethra emerges from the prostate gland (see Figure 5.6). Tiny ducts connect both glands directly to the urethra. When a man is sexually aroused, these organs often secrete a slippery, mucuslike substance that appears as a droplet at the tip of the penis. Like the prostate's secretions, this fluid is alkaline and helps buffer the acidity of the urethra; it is also thought to lubricate the flow of seminal fluid through the urethra. Contrary to some reports, though, this droplet has virtually no function as a vaginal lubricant during coitus. In many men this secretion does not appear until well after the beginning of arousal, often just before orgasm. Other men report that the droplet appears immediately after they get an erection, and still others rarely or never produce these preejaculatory droplets. All these experiences are normal variations of male sexual functioning.

The fluid from the Cowper's glands should not be confused with semen; however, it does occasionally contain active, healthy sperm. This is one reason among many why the withdrawal method of birth control is not highly effective. (Withdrawal and other methods of birth control are discussed in Chapter 11.)

Semen

As we have seen, the **semen** or **seminal fluid** ejaculated through the opening of the penis comes from a variety of sources. Fluids are supplied by the seminal vesicles, the prostate gland, and Cowper's glands, with the seminal vesicles providing the greatest portion (Eliasson & Lindholmer, 1976; Spring-Mills & Hafez, 1980). The amount of seminal fluid that a man ejaculates—roughly 1 teaspoon on average—is influenced by a number of factors, including the length of time since the last ejaculation, the duration of arousal before ejaculation, and age (older men tend to produce less fluid). The semen of a single ejaculation typically contains between 200 and 500 million sperm, which account for only about 1% of the fluid's total volume. Chemical analysis shows that semen is also made up of ascorbic and citric acids, water, enzymes, fructose, bases (phosphate and bicarbonate buffers), and a variety of other substances. None of these materials is harmful if swallowed during oral sex. However, semen of an HIV-infected man can transmit the virus to the man's partner if the recipient has open sores or bleeding gums in his or her mouth (see Chapter 17).

Sperm, as seen under a microscope.

▶ Male Sexual Functions

Up to this point in the chapter we have looked at the various *parts* of the male sexual system, but we have not described their *functioning* in much detail. In the following pages we examine two of these functions: erection and ejaculation.

Erection

An **erection** is a process coordinated by the autonomic nervous system (Manecke & Mulhall, 1999). When a male becomes sexually excited, the nervous system sends out messages that cause expansion of the arteries leading to the three erectile cylinders in the penis. As a result, the rate of blood flow into these parallel cylinders increases rapidly. Because blood flowing out of the penis through veins cannot keep up with the inflow, it accumulates in the spongelike tissues of the three erectile cylinders, causing erection. The penis remains erect until the messages from the nervous system stop and the inflow of blood returns to normal.

Erection The process by which the penis or clitoris engorges with blood and increases in size.

The capacity for erection is present at birth. It is common and quite natural for infant boys to experience erections during sleep or diapering, from stimulation by clothing, and later by touching themselves. Nighttime erections occur during the rapid eye movement (REM), or dreaming, stage of sleep (Chung & Choi, 1990). Erotic dreams can play a role, but the primary mechanism seems to be physiological, and erections often occur even when the dream content is clearly not sexual. Often a man awakens in the morning just after completing a REM cycle. This explains the phenomenon of morning erections, which were once erroneously attributed to a full bladder.

Although an erection is basically a physiological response, it also involves psychological components. In fact, some writers distinguish between psychogenic (from the mind) and physiogenic (from the body) erections, although in most cases of sexual arousal there are simultaneous inputs from both thoughts and physical stimulation.

How great an influence does the mind have on erections? We know that it can inhibit the response: When a man becomes troubled by erection difficulties, the problem might be psychological, as we will discuss in Chapter 16. There is also extensive evidence that men are able to enhance their erection (as reflected in increased penile tumescence) by forming vivid mental images or fantasies of sexual activity (Dekker et al., 1985; Smith & Over, 1987).

Logically, one might expect erection to occur only in response to obvious sexual stimuli. That this is not always the case can be embarrassing, perplexing, amusing, or anxiety arousing. Nearly every man can recall scenes of unwanted erections during adolescent school days—the teacher saying, "Bob, come up here and do the math problem on the board," when math was the farthest thing from Bob's mind; the trips down school halls with a notebook held in a strategic location; the delayed exit from the swimming pool after playful frolicking.

Erections also happen in situations that seem entirely nonsexual, such as riding a bike, lifting heavy weights, or straining during defecation (particularly in little boys).

Ejaculation

The second basic male sexual function is **ejaculation**—the process by which semen is expelled through the penis to the outside of the body. Many people equate male orgasm with ejaculation. However, these two processes do not always take place simultaneously. Before

Ejaculation The process by which semen is expelled from the body through the penis.

puberty a boy might experience hundreds of "dry orgasms"—orgasms without any ejaculation of fluid. Occasionally, a man may have more than one orgasm in a given sexual encounter, with the second or third orgasm producing little or no expelled semen. Conversely, research reveals that some men experience a series of nonejaculatory orgasms culminating in a final orgasm accompanied by expulsion of semen (Dunn & Trost, 1989; Hartman & Fithian, 1984). Thus, although male orgasm is generally associated with ejaculation, these two processes are not one and the same and they do not necessarily occur together.

From a neurophysiological point of view, ejaculation—like erection—is basically a spinal reflex (Truitt & Coolen, 2002). Effective sexual stimulation of the penis (manual, oral, or coital) results in the buildup of neural excitation to a critical level. When a threshold is reached, several internal physical events are triggered.

Emission phase The first stage of male orgasm, in which the seminal fluid is gathered in the urethral bulb.

The actual ejaculation occurs in two stages (Figure 5.7). During the first stage, sometimes called the **emission phase,** the prostate, seminal vesicles, and *ampulla* (upper portions of the vas deferens) undergo contractions. These contractions force various secretions into the ejaculatory ducts and prostatic urethra. At the same time, both internal and external *urethral sphincters* (two muscles, one located where the urethra exits the bladder and the other below the prostate) close, trapping seminal fluid in the *urethral bulb* (the prostatic portion of the urethra, between these two muscles). The urethral bulb expands like a balloon. A man typically experiences this first stage as a subjective sense that orgasm is inevitable, the "point of no return" or "ejaculatory inevitability."

Expulsion phase The second stage of male orgasm, during which the semen is expelled from the penis by muscular contractions.

In the second stage, sometimes called the **expulsion phase,** the collected semen is expelled out of the penis by strong, rhythmic contractions of muscles that surround the urethral bulb and root of the penis. In addition, there are contractions along the entire urethral route. The external urethral sphincter relaxes, allowing fluid to pass through, while the inter-

▶ **Figure 5.7** Male sexual anatomy during ejaculation: (a) the emission phase and (b) the expulsion phase.

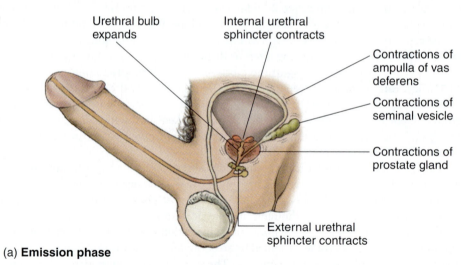

Urethral bulb expands

Internal urethral sphincter contracts

Contractions of ampulla of vas deferens

Contractions of seminal vesicle

Contractions of prostate gland

External urethral sphincter contracts

(a) **Emission phase**

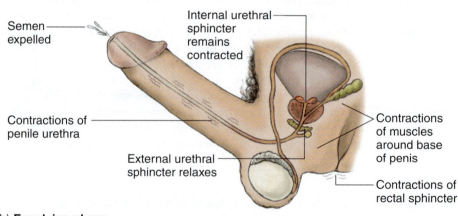

Semen expelled

Internal urethral sphincter remains contracted

Contractions of penile urethra

External urethral sphincter relaxes

Contractions of muscles around base of penis

Contractions of rectal sphincter

(b) **Expulsion phase**

nal sphincter remains contracted to prevent the escape of urine. The first two or three muscle contractions around the base of the penis are quite strong and occur at close intervals. Most of the seminal fluid is expelled in spurts corresponding to these contractions. Several more muscle responses typically occur, with a gradual diminishing of intensity and lengthening of time intervals between contractions. The entire expulsion stage usually occurs in 3 to 10 seconds.

Some men have an experience known as **retrograde ejaculation,** in which semen is expelled into the bladder rather than through the penis. This results from a reversed functioning of the two urethral sphincters (the internal sphincter relaxes while the external sphincter contracts). The condition sometimes occurs in men who have undergone prostate surgery (Kassabian, 2003). In addition, illness, congenital anomaly, and certain drugs, most notably tranquilizers, can induce this reaction. Retrograde ejaculation itself is not harmful (the seminal fluid is later eliminated with the urine). However, a man who consistently experiences this response would be wise to seek medical attention, not only because the effective result is sterility but also because retrograde ejaculation could be a sign of an underlying health problem. ▪

Sometimes a man experiences orgasm without direct genital stimulation. The most familiar of these occurrences are **nocturnal emissions,** which are commonly known as wet dreams. The exact mechanism that produces this response is not fully understood. (Women also experience orgasm during sleep.) The possibility of a man using fantasy alone to reach orgasm in a waking state is exceedingly remote, and we have never heard a firsthand account of this phenomenon. Kinsey and his associates (1948) stated that only 3 or 4 of the males in their sample of over 5,000 reported this experience. In contrast, significantly greater numbers of women in Kinsey's sample (roughly 2%) reported orgasms from fantasy alone (Kinsey et al., 1953). Another kind of nongenitally induced ejaculation that men sometimes report is reaching orgasm during sex play (activities such as mutual kissing or manual or oral stimulation of his partner) when there is no penile stimulation.

Retrograde ejaculation The process by which semen is expelled into the bladder instead of out of the penis.

Sexual Health

Nocturnal emission Involuntary ejaculation during sleep, also known as a wet dream.

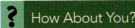
How About You?

If applicable, how did you respond to your initial experiences with nocturnal emissions or sleep orgasms?

▶ Some Concerns About Sexual Functioning

Men frequently voice a variety of concerns about sexual functioning. Several of these are addressed throughout this textbook. At this point we want to discuss two areas that receive considerable attention: the significance of penis size and the necessity and impact of circumcision. Claims are frequently made that one or both of these physical characteristics can influence the sexual pleasure of a man or his partner. In the following sections we examine the available evidence.

Penis Size

When I was a kid, my friends were unmerciful in their comments about my small size. They would say things like, "I have a penis, John has a penis, but you have a pee-pee." Needless to say, I grew up with a very poor self-image in this area. Later it was translated into anxiety-ridden sexual encounters where I would insist that the room be completely dark before I would undress. Even now, when I realize that size is irrelevant in giving sexual pleasure, I still worry that new partners will comment unfavorably about my natural endowment. (Authors' files)

All my life I have been distressed about the size of my penis. I have always avoided places such as community showers where I would be exposed to others. When my penis is hard it is about five inches long; but when it is flaccid, it is rarely longer than an inch or inch and a half, and thin as well. I don't like to be nude in front of the girls I sleep with, and that feeling of uneasiness is often reflected during sex. (Authors' files)

These men are not alone in their discomfort. Their feelings are echoed in more accounts than we can remember. Penis size has occupied the attention of most men and many women at one time or another. In general, it is more than idle curiosity that stimulates interest in

Penile Augmentation

Concern over penis size has contributed to a recent surge in cosmetic surgery to enlarge this body part. Penis enlargement ads have become a ubiquitous portion of e-mail spam, and in the United Kingdom penile augmentation has become the number one cosmetic surgery elected by British men (Reuters, 2003). Introduced in the United States over a decade ago, *phalloplasty*, or *penis augmentation*, involves lengthening the penis, increasing its girth, or a combination of both. To increase length, a surgeon makes an incision at the base of the penis and severs the ligaments that attach the penile root to the pelvic bone. This allows the portion of the penis normally inside the body cavity to drop down to the exterior, increasing its visible length by an inch or more. Additional thickness or girth can be added by tissue grafts or by injections of fat taken by liposuction from other body areas, usually the abdomen (Austoni & Guarneri, 1999; Taylor, 1995).

Although there have been no controlled clinical studies of penile augmentation to date, a number of anecdotal reports suggest that the results of these procedures are rarely impressive and can be disconcerting, disfiguring, and even dangerous (Fraser, 1999; Shuit, 1996). Ligament-cutting surgery can result in some loss of sensation, scarring, and a changed angle of erection (the erect penis may point down instead of up). Sometimes scar tissue reconnects the severed ligaments to the pelvic bone; this can result in more retraction of the penis into the body cavity than was the case before surgery. Portions of injected fat are often rejected by the body, and this can leave the penis with a lumpy, misshapen appearance. Many men who have undergone these procedures have reported being dissatisfied, embarrassed, and embittered by the results (Shuit, 1996; Wessells et al., 1996).

Men who elect to have penis augmentation often do not have undersized penises (Alexander, 1994). This fact, combined with the rising incidence of this cosmetic surgery, adds further evidence to how widespread men's concerns are about the acceptability of their penises. Anyone contemplating this potentially dangerous or disfiguring procedure should be extremely cautious. Currently, there is little good evidence about the procedure's efficacy. Furthermore, neither the American Urological Association nor the American Society of Plastic and Reconstructive Surgeons has endorsed penile augmentation.

Preoccupation with penis size is evident in a variety of cultures and art forms.

this topic. For many it is a matter of real concern, perhaps even cause for apprehension or anguish.

It does not take much imagination to understand why penis size often seems so important. As a society we tend to be overly impressed with size and quantity. Bigger cars are better than compacts, the bigger the house the better it is, and by implication, big penises provide more pleasure than smaller ones. Certainly, the various art forms, such as literature, painting, sculpture, and movies, do much to perpetuate this obsession with big penises.

The modern Western world is not alone in its preoccupation with penis size, as the photograph on this page illustrates. Even the fascinating Indian sex manuals, the *Ananga Ranga* and the *Kama Sutra*, classify men according to three categories: the hare-man (whose erect penis measures 6 finger widths in length), the bull-man (9 finger widths long), and the horse-man (12 or more finger widths). In ancient Greek mythology emphasis on penis size found a focal point in Priapus, son of the goddess Aphrodite and the god Dionysus. Priapus was usually portrayed as a lasciviously grinning little man with a greatly oversized penis. The concern some men feel over perceived size inadequacy has led them to seek a surgical solution, as described in the box titled "Penile Augmentation."

The result of all this attention to penis size is that men often come to view size in and of itself as an important attribute in defining their masculinity or their worth as lovers. Such a concept of virility can contribute to a poor self-image. Furthermore, if either a man or his partner views his penis as being smaller than it should be, this can decrease sexual satisfaction for one or both of them—not because of physical limitations but rather as a self-fulfilling prophecy.

As we learned in Chapter 4, the greatest sensitivity in the vaginal canal is concentrated in its outer portion. (We focus here on heterosexual penile–vaginal intercourse because concerns about penis size often relate to this kind of sexual activity.) Although some women do find pressure and stretching deep within the vagina to be pleasurable, this is not usually required for female sexual gratification. In fact, some women find deep penetration painful, particularly if it is quite vigorous:

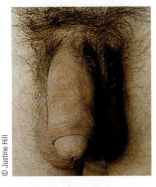

▶ **Figure 5.8** There are many variations in the shape and size of the male genitals. The penis in the right-hand photo is uncircumcised.

You asked if size was important to my pleasure. Yes, but not in the way you might imagine. If a man is quite large, I worry that he might hurt me. Actually, I prefer that he be average or even to the smaller side. (Authors' files)

There is a physiological explanation for the pain or discomfort some women feel during deep penetration. Because the female ovaries and male testes originate from the same embryonic tissue source, they share some of the same sensitivity. If the penis bangs into the cervix and causes the uterus to be slightly displaced, this action can in turn jar an ovary. The resulting sensation is somewhat like a male's experience of getting hit in the testes. Fast stretching of the uterine ligaments has also been implicated in deep-penetration pain. However, some women find slow stretching of these same ligaments pleasurable.

These observations indicate the importance of being gentle and considerate during intercourse. If one or both partners want deeper or more vigorous thrusting, they can experiment by gradually adding these components to their coital movements. It might also be helpful for the woman to be in an intercourse position other than underneath her partner (see Figure 9.8), so that she has more control over the depth and vigor of penetration.

Figure 5.8 shows several flaccid (nonerect) penises of different sizes, all well within the normal range. It is worth noting that penis size is not related to body shape, height, length of fingers, race, or anything else (Money et al., 1984). It should also be mentioned that small flaccid penises tend to increase more in size during erection than do penises that are larger in the flaccid state (Jamison & Gebhard, 1988; Masters & Johnson, 1966). It is also important to note that, even though physiological evidence indicates that large penises are not necessary for female sexual pleasure during coitus, some women do have subjective preferences regarding penis size and shape, just as some men have such preferences about breasts. Research indicates, however, that women are no more sexually aroused by depictions of large penises than by portrayals of medium or small penises (Fisher et al., 1983).

Finally, as we close this section, we take a look at another interesting cultural phenomenon that reflects a rather unusual, even bizarre, concern about penises that some men in other cultures experience in epidemic proportions: koro.

? Critical Thinking Question

Assume that you are assigned to debate whether or not a cause-and-effect relationship exists between penis size and sexual satisfaction of women during penile–vaginal intercourse. Which position would you argue? What evidence would you use to support your position?

? How About You?

What effect, if any, has the "bigger is better" view of penis size had on your own sexual functioning?

▸ Sexuality and Diversity

Koro: The Genital Retraction Syndrome

Genital retraction syndrome (GRS) is an unusual culture-bound phenomenon that has attracted considerable attention in many areas of the world community, especially Asia and Africa. GRS, known under a variety of local names or phrases that mean "shrinking penis," is most widely referred to as **koro.** A man afflicted with koro typically believes that he is the victim of a contagious disease that causes his penis to shrink and retract into his body, an alarming prospect made worse by local traditions or folklore that adds the warning that this condition is usually fatal (Bartholomew, 2001; Ritts, 2003; Vaughn, 2003). The belief in koro is thousands of years old, and numerous accounts of its existence have surfaced in Malaysia, Indonesia, China, India, and several countries in West Africa. The origin of the term *koro* is believed to derive from the Malaysian word for tortoise, the association being the capacity of the tortoise to retract its head and legs into its body (carapace). In Malaysia the word for tortoise is often used as a local slang word for penis (Vaughn, 2003).

Although koro is sometimes manifested as an isolated anomaly in a single individual (Ritts, 2003), it is most commonly expressed as a fast-spreading social belief that affects hundreds or even thousands of males, causing widespread panic and hysteria. One such instance took place in Singapore in 1967 (Vaughn, 2003). A rapidly spread rumor that contaminated pork was causing penis shrinkage resulted in Singapore hospitals being swamped with thousands of men who were convinced that their penises were shrinking and retracting. Many of these men had used mechanical means—clamps made from chopsticks, weights hung from their penises, and even relatives or friends grabbing firmly on to their "disappearing" anatomy—to keep their penises from slipping away. A coordinated public education program initiated by local physicians resulted in the eventual dissipation of this mass hysteria with no fatalities or lost penises, although many bruised private parts were undoubtedly left in its wake.

The mass-hysteria nature of GRS was also reflected in an epidemic of koro in northeast India in 1982 that was caused by a fast-moving rumor that the penises of boys were shrinking. Thousands of panicked parents brought their sons to hospitals, usually with their penises bound up or otherwise restrained to prevent further shrinkage. This epidemic was quelled by medical authorities, who toured the region with loudspeakers to reassure anxious citizens. The authorities also conducted large-scale public measuring of penises at regular intervals to demonstrate that no shrinking was taking place (Nixin, 2003).

In countries along the west coast of Africa, from Cameroon to Nigeria, koro is commonly associated with black magic and sorcerers and typically involves penis theft rather than retraction (Vaughn, 2003). Recent outbreaks of "penis thievery" have been reported in Nigeria, Cameroon, Ghana, and Ivory Coast. These episodes usually involve public accusations of penis theft, usually as the result of an unexpected or unwelcome touch from a stranger (Huyghe, 2003; Trull, 2003). Accused perpetrators of penis snatching are often physically assaulted and sometimes killed by angry victims and other concerned citizens. In January 2002 a dozen accused penis snatchers/sorcerers in Ghana were beaten to death by mobs of men who accused them of using witchcraft to make their penises vanish. Apparently, the accused sorcerers had taken advantage of vulnerable men by first inflicting them with the prospect of penis loss and then asking for money to either restore the penis or prevent its disappearance. When examined by police officials, the alleged victims were found to have intact genitals (Huyghe, 2003).

Epidemics of koro are best explained as anxiety-based delusions that are modeled and communicated among vulnerable men (Huyghe, 2003). GRS appears to have much in common with the Western phenomenon of panic attacks, with the added dimension of sexual overlay. In some Asian and African cultures where sexual anxiety is high and stories of genital retraction are common, it is not surprising that a man might panic in response to widespread rumors of genital retraction or thievery, especially when such rumors are reinforced by his own observations of the natural process of genital shrinking in response to cold or anxiety. Furthermore, when a man's guilt and/or anxiety arise out of real or imagined sexual excesses, he can be easily transformed into a prime candidate for irrational beliefs and receptivity to the seemingly bizarre syndrome of koro (Ritts, 2003).

Circumcision

A characteristic that many people associate with differences in male sensitivity—and also differences in hygiene—is the presence or absence of the foreskin.

Circumcision (ser-kum-SI-zhun) is the surgical removal of the foreskin (Figure 5.9). As previously described in the "Sexuality and Diversity" discussion on male genital modifica-

Circumcision Surgical removal of the foreskin of the penis.

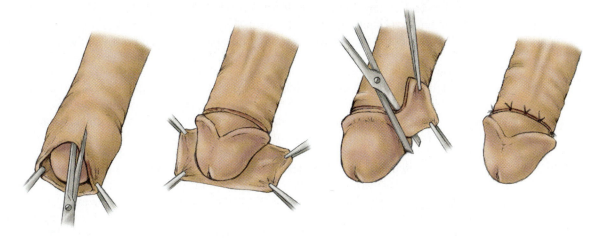

▶ **Figure 5.9** Circumcision, the surgical removal of the foreskin.

tion and mutilation, circumcision is widely practiced throughout the world for religious, ritual, or hygienic reasons. In the United States this operation is performed on most male infants (with parental consent), generally on the second day after birth. At least 1.2 million newborn boys (60%) are circumcised annually in the United States (Christakis et al., 2000; Melby 2002b).

Based on results from the National Health and Social Life Survey (NHSLS), both ethnicity and parental education level influence which males in America are likely to be circumcised. White males in this study were considerably more likely to be circumcised than African American or Hispanic American males (81% vs. 65% or 54%). Circumcision rates among the men in the NHSLS study were also significantly related to the level of education attained by their mothers. A strong majority (87%) of sons of mothers with a college degree were circumcised, compared to 62% of men whose mothers did not earn a high school degree (Laumann et al., 1997).

The routine practice of circumcision in the United States reflects the concern of the medical profession about hygiene. If not routinely cleaned, the area under the foreskin of an uncircumcised male can harbor a variety of infection-causing organisms. Indeed, many people assume that circumcision is important for hygiene. How do such assumptions affect a person's self-image and sexual relations? Consider the following account provided by a surgeon:

When I was serving as ship's surgeon on a large carrier during the Vietnam conflict, I had a very interesting experience. A young sailor came to me requesting circumcision. When I asked him why he wanted to undergo such an operation, he stated that his wife refused to engage in oral sex because she viewed him as unclean. After I performed the simple operation, an amazing thing happened. Many more men came with the same request. Apparently the word had circulated rapidly. Their reasons were essentially the same as the first seaman's. They either felt unclean themselves or were viewed in this way by partners. (Authors' files)

Accounts such as this one raise the question: Does medical evidence support the view that circumcision is necessary for good hygiene?

Numerous studies have looked into the question with mixed results. In support of circumcision, research has shown that uncircumcised males are more at risk for penile cancer, a rare malignancy, than are circumcised males (Gange, 1999; Schoen et al., 2000). In addition, organisms harbored under the foreskin can cause vaginal infections in women who have sexual relations with uncircumcised men. Some investigators have also suggested that the female partners of uncircumcised men are at increased risk for cervical cancer (Adami & Trichopoulos, 2002; Snyder, 1991; Wiswell, 1997). Several studies reported that uncircumcised men were more likely to have gonorrhea and syphilis than were circumcised men (Cook et al., 1994; Moses et al., 1998). Furthermore,

InfoTrac Search Words
■ Circumcision

uncircumcised men might be more likely to become infected with the AIDS virus (HIV) than their circumcised counterparts (Lipsky & Schaberg, 2000; Schoen et al., 2000).

There are several arguments against routine circumcision, and many of them have been raised with greater frequency in recent years. First, the foreskin could serve some important function yet to be determined. Second, some investigators have expressed concern that sexual function may be altered by excising the foreskin; we consider this question shortly. Finally, some health professionals think that performing this procedure on a newborn is unnecessarily traumatic and an invitation to possible surgical complications. Because it is inadvisable to use general anesthesia and narcotic analgesia on infants, circumcision is often performed without anesthesia (Herschel et al., 1998; Taddio et al., 1997a). However, infants undergoing circumcision without anesthesia feel and respond to pain (Howard et al., 1998; Wiswell, 1997). Furthermore, research indicates that the pain experienced by infants during circumcision can have long-lasting effects on future infant behavior. For example, in one study infants who were circumcised without anesthesia demonstrated a stronger pain response to subsequent routine vaccination than uncircumcised infants (Taddio et al., 1997b). In response to such findings, an increasing number of physicians who perform infant circumcision are either applying a topical analgesic or injecting a local anesthetic agent directly into the penis to reduce or eliminate pain associated with this operation (Task Force on Circumcision, 1999; Wiswell, 1997). Some of the health risks of circumcision include hemorrhage, infections, mutilation, shock, psychological trauma, and even death in extremely rare cases (Task Force on Circumcision, 1999; Wiswell, 1997).

Because circumcision is an issue with so many pros and cons, it is not surprising that the medical profession in the United States has historically gone back and forth on the matter. In the 1970s the assumed health benefits of circumcision underwent serious reconsideration. The 1975 policy statement of the American Academy of Pediatrics (AAP) concluded that there was no medical indication for circumcision and recommended against its routine practice. Many American hospitals followed this lead by establishing the policy of performing circumcision only at parents' request. However, most parents continued to ask for the procedure, in part because of social concerns, such as appearance and perceived future ridicule by peers. A number of studies conducted in the late 1980s reported higher rates of urinary tract infection among uncircumcised boys compared to circumcised boys, a finding that prompted the AAP to adopt a more neutral stance. Thus in March 1989 the AAP suggested that circumcision has both medical advantages and some risks (Schoen et al., 1989). In March 1999 the AAP again modified its position on circumcision by shifting from neutrality to a position of moderate opposition to this medical procedure (Task Force on Circumcision, 1999).

? Critical Thinking Question

Which of the research methods described in Chapter 2 might be effective to demonstrate whether or not being circumcised affects a man's sexual response and pleasure? What kind of research design would you use in such a study?

Clearly, the debate about the potential health benefits of infant circumcision will continue, and future editions of this textbook may present still other modifications of the AAP position on circumcision. However, to put this continuing debate and current medical evidence into proper perspective, we note that in most cases good personal genital hygiene practices allow uncircumcised boys to grow into adulthood without encountering significant health problems (Gange, 1999; Van Howe, 1998).

Beyond the issue of hygiene, another question has often been raised about circumcision: Do circumcised men enjoy any erotic or functional advantages over uncircumcised men (or vice versa)?

Some people assume that circumcised men respond more quickly during penile–vaginal intercourse because of the fully exposed glans. However, except when there is a condition known as **phimosis** (an extremely tight foreskin), there is no difference in contact during intercourse. The foreskin of an uncircumcised man is retracted during coitus, so the glans is fully exposed. It might be assumed, in fact, that the glans of a circumcised man is less sensitive, because of the toughening effect of constant exposure to chafing surfaces.

Masters and Johnson (1966) investigated both of these questions and found no evidence of differences in responsiveness. However, the Masters and Johnson data failed to include the all-important dimension of subjective assessment by men who have experienced both conditions after achieving sexual maturity. There are anecdotal reports in the medical literature that some men experience less sexual satisfaction after undergoing adult circumcision (Gange, 1999; Melby 2002b; Task Force on Circumcision, 1999). Occasionally, we have

Phimosis A condition characterized by an extremely tight penile foreskin.

encountered men in our classes who have been circumcised during their adult years. Some of these men have reported experiencing physiological differences in sexual arousal—such as a decrease in the sensitivity of the glans—following circumcision. But these reactions have not been consistent. Other men afforded this unique comparative opportunity have found no perceivable differences in sexual excitability. It would seem that there are still unanswered questions about the relationship between circumcision and male sexual arousal, and "little consensus exists regarding the role of the foreskin in sexual performance and satisfaction" (Laumann et al., 1997, p. 1052).

Data gathered from 1,410 men in the NHSLS study do, however, reveal a relationship between circumcision status and sexual activity. Circumcised respondents in this study reported engaging with greater frequency in a variety of sexual activities, including oral sex, anal sex, and masturbation. Sexual problems, such as erectile difficulties and low sex drive, were reported by a higher percentage of uncircumcised men (58%) compared to circumcised men (40%) (Laumann et al., 1997). The reasons for these behavior differences between circumcised and uncircumcised men, although unclear at present, might have a physical basis or might be rooted in psychosocial factors (such as feeling unclean or stigmatized by being a minority in America), or they might reflect a combination of these influences.

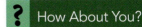

? How About You?

If you had a newborn son, would you have him circumcised? Why or why not?

▶ Male Genital Health Concerns

The male genital and internal reproductive structures can be adversely affected by a variety of injuries and diseases. We describe some of these health concerns in the following pages. Should any of our male readers become affected by one of these conditions, we urge immediate consultation with a physician. **Urology** (yoo-ROL-oh-jee) is the medical specialty that focuses on the male reproductive structures.

Urology The medical specialty dealing with reproductive health and genital diseases of the male and urinary tract diseases in both sexes.

The Penis: Health Care Issues

Caring for the penis is an important aspect of sexual self-health. Washing the penis regularly with soap and water, at least once a day, is an excellent self-health practice. (There is also evidence, discussed in Chapter 17, that washing the genitals before and after sex can reduce the chances of exchanging infectious organisms with one's partner.) Uncircumcised males should pay particular attention to drawing the foreskin back from the glans and washing all surfaces, especially the underside of the foreskin. A number of small glands located in the foreskin secrete an oily, lubricating substance. If these secretions are allowed to accumulate under the foreskin, they combine with sloughed-off dead skin cells to form a cheesy substance called **smegma.** When smegma builds up over time, it generally develops an unpleasant odor, becomes grainy and irritating, and can serve as a breeding ground for infection-causing organisms. Sometimes the glans or shaft of the penis can develop an eczema-like reaction—"weepy" and sore—that results from an allergic reaction to the vaginal secretions of the man's partner. Using a condom can help to alleviate this condition, but it is important that a physician is consulted to clarify the condition's origin and treatment.

! Sexual Health

Smegma A cheesy substance of glandular secretions and skin cells that sometimes accumulates under the foreskin of the penis or hood of the clitoris.

Men can protect their penises by using a condom during all sexual encounters with individuals whose health status is unknown to them. This affords improved protection against the transmission of sexually transmitted diseases for both partners. Other strategies for preventing disease transmission are described in Chapter 17.

Some sexual gadgets can also be hazardous to penile health. For example, a "cock ring" (a tight-fitting ring that encircles the base of the penis) that may be successful in accomplishing its intended purpose of sustaining erections can also destroy penile tissue by cutting off the blood supply. In the past, sexually oriented magazines published testimonials attesting to the pleasure of masturbating with a vacuum cleaner. This is not a good idea! Research suggests that severe penile injuries (including decapitation of the glans) resulting from masturbating with vacuum cleaners and electric brooms are much more common than reported (Benson, 1985; Grisell, 1988).

On rare occasions, the penis can be fractured (Adducci & Ross, 1991; Hargreaves & Plail, 1994). This injury involves a rupture of the cavernous bodies when the penis is erect. This injury most commonly occurs during coitus. A student reported his encounter with this painful injury:

I was having intercourse with my girlfriend in a sitting position. She was straddling my legs using the arms of the chair and her legs to move her body up and down on my penis. In the heat of passion, she raised up a little too far, and I slipped out. She sat back down hard, expecting me to repenetrate her. Unfortunately, I was off target and all of her weight came down on my penis. I heard a cracking sound and experienced excruciating pain. I bled quite a bit inside my penis, and I was real sore for quite a long time. (Authors' files)

This account suggests that it is wise to take some precautions during coitus. This injury usually happens in the heat of passion and often involves putting too much weight on the penis when attempting to gain or regain vaginal penetration. When the woman is on top, the risk increases. Communicating the need to go slow at these times can avert a painful injury. Treatment of penile fractures varies from splinting and ice packs to surgery. Most men injured in this fashion regain normal sexual function. ■

Penile Cancer

As stated earlier in this chapter, men can be afflicted with penile cancer, a rare malignancy that can be deadly if not diagnosed and treated in its earliest stages. Of the approximately 1,300 men in the United States who develop penile cancer in a given year, only half will be alive 5 years later. However, if the cancer is caught early and if it has not spread to lymph nodes, the 5-year survival rate is about 90% (Gordon et al., 1997). Such startling figures argue eloquently for the critical importance of seeking medical attention for any sore on the penis (see the boxed discussion "Male Genital Self-Examination" earlier in this chapter for a description of the early symptoms of penile cancer). Risk factors associated with penile cancer include being over age 50; a history of multiple sexual partners and sexually transmitted diseases, especially genital herpes; poor genital hygiene, which contributes to smegma-induced inflammation of the glans; being uncircumcised (see earlier discussion of circumcision); and a long history of tobacco use, which increases a man's lifetime chance of developing penile cancer from 1 in 100,000 to 1 in 600 (Fair et al., 1993; Gordon et al., 1997). Penile cancer, left untreated, will ultimately destroy the entire penis and spread to lymph nodes and beyond.

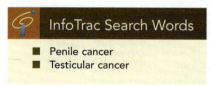

InfoTrac Search Words

■ Penile cancer
■ Testicular cancer

Testicular Cancer

Testicular cancer accounts for only about 1% of all cancers that occur in males; however, it is one of the most common of the malignancies that occur in young men age 15 to 34, with about half of all cases occurring in men younger than age 35 (Adelman & Joffe, 2000; Whiteford & Wordley, 2003). Furthermore, the incidence of testicular cancer seems to be on the increase in many Western countries (Srivastava & Krieger, 2000; Whiteford & Wordley, 2003). During the early stages of testicular cancer, there are usually no symptoms beyond a mass within the testis. The mass feels hard or irregular to the fingertips and is distinguishable from surrounding healthy tissue. It may be painless to touch, but some men do report tenderness in the area of the growth. Occasionally, other symptoms are reported; these include fever, a dull ache in the groin area, sensation of dragging or heaviness in a testis, tender breasts and nipples, and painful accumulation of fluid or swelling in the scrotum. Some types of testicular cancers tend to grow more rapidly than any other tumors that have been studied. Therefore, for successful treatment, it is important to detect the mass as soon as possible and to seek medical attention immediately. Improved therapeutic procedures have consistently yielded a survival rate better than 90% among men treated for early-detected testicular cancer (Whiteford & Wordley, 2003). Some men procrastinate in seeking medical treatment because they are afraid that such procedures will create erectile problems or reduce their capacity to enjoy sexual pleasure. In fact, this occurs in only a small minority of men treated for testicular cancer (Hartmann et al., 1999).

Diseases of the Prostate

As you will recall from our earlier discussion, the prostate gland is a walnut-sized structure at the base of the bladder that contributes secretions to the seminal fluid. The prostate is a focal point of some of the more common "male problems," which range from inflammation and enlargement to cancer.

Prostatitis

One of the most frequent disorders of the prostate gland, *prostatitis*, occurs when the prostate becomes enlarged and inflamed, often as a result of an infectious agent, such as the gonococcus bacterium (responsible for gonorrhea) or the protozoan *Trichomonas*. (These agents are discussed in Chapter 17.) Prostatitis can occur in a man of any age. Its symptoms include pain in the pelvic area or base of the penis, lower abdominal ache, backache, aching testes, the urgent need to urinate frequently, a burning sensation while urinating, a cloudy discharge from the penis, and difficulties with sexual functions, such as painful erections or ejaculations and reduced sexual interest. Prostatitis can be effectively treated with a variety of prescription drugs, most commonly antibiotics.

Benign Prostatic Hyperplasia

As men grow older, the prostate gland tends to increase in size, a condition known as *benign prostatic hyperplasia* (BPH) (Kassabian, 2003). About 50% of men between the ages of 50 and 70 and close to 90% of men over age 80 experience this problem (Gacci et al., 2003; Gaynor, 2003). The enlarged gland tends to put pressure on the urethra, thus decreasing urine flow. If this problem is severe, surgery or medications can help (Gacci et al., 2003; Kassabian, 2003). Recent evidence demonstrates that saw palmetto, an herbal product derived from the American dwarf palm tree, effectively reduces the symptom of restricted urine flow associated with BPH (Gordon & Shaughnessy, 2003). Saw palmetto appears to be as effective as prescription medications and is better tolerated and less expensive. Clinical studies of this herb have used a dosage of 160 mg twice a day or 320 mg once a day. However, as with most herbal medications, "the recommended dosage for saw palmetto may vary because of the lack of standardization of such products in the United States" (Gordon & Shaughnessy, 2003, p. 1282).

Prostate Cancer

Some men develop benign or malignant tumors of the prostate, and the potential for this increases with age. Each year almost 200,000 American men are diagnosed with prostate cancer, and about 30,000 deaths occur each year as a result of this disease (Hoffman, 2003; U.S. Preventive Services Task Force, 2003b). Among U.S. males cancer of the prostate is the most frequently diagnosed cancer (other than that of the skin) and is currently the second leading cause of cancer death after lung cancer (Jewett et al., 2003; U.S. Preventive Services Task Force, 2003b). Factors known to be associated with the development of prostate cancer include old age, family history of prostate cancer, being African American, a prior history of sexually transmitted disease(s), and a diet high in saturated fats (Bruner et al., 2000; DeMarzo et al., 2003; Eastham & Kattan, 2000; Gronberg, 2003). The incidence of prostate cancer is 60% higher among African American men than among white men, and black men have a poorer survival rate than white men for comparable stages of prostate cancer (U.S. Preventive Services Task Force, 2003b). The reasons for the increased risk and poorer survival rate among African American men are not known, but genetic, hormonal, and nutritional factors have been implicated (Eastham & Kattan, 2000). Compared with white Americans, mortality from prostate cancer

© Doug Pensinger/Getty Images

American cyclist Lance Armstrong won the 1999, 2000, 2001, 2002, and 2003 Tour de France cycling races after undergoing successful treatment for testicular cancer.

InfoTrac Search Words

■ Prostate cancer

SPOTLIGHT ON RESEARCH

PSA Test: Beneficial or Not?

There is persuasive research evidence that the PSA test can detect prostate cancer many years before symptoms occur and that radical prostatectomy can reduce mortality caused by prostate cancer in men whose cancer is detected clinically (Coldman et al., 2003; U.S. Preventive Services Task Force, 2003b). Why, then, is there a reluctance among some medical practitioners and researchers to recommend routine PSA testing, and why has the practice of using this test as a screening device remained controversial? The brief answer to this question is that the balance of potential benefits (reduced disease-related suffering and mortality) and harms (false-positive results, unnecessary biopsies, and treatment complications) remains uncertain at the present time (U.S. Preventive Services Task Force, 2003b). Therefore the benefits of PSA screening for early prostate cancer remain unknown (Hoffman, 2003; Sirovich et al., 2003). Let us examine some of the evidence.

Even though PSA screening might detect early-stage prostate cancer, it has not yet been shown to result in reduced death rates (Jewett et al.,

2003). Furthermore, a recent analysis of available research data reported mixed and inconclusive evidence that early detection improves health outcomes (U.S. Preventive Services Task Force, 2003b). These findings raise serious questions about the advisability of routine PSA screening. As mentioned earlier, such screening can yield various adverse outcomes, including false-positive results with commensurate and unnecessary anxiety and potential complications from treatment of some cancers that might never have affected a man's overall health (Frankel et al., 2003; Hoffman, 2003; U.S. Preventive Services Task Force, 2003b). If the overall mortality rate of men afflicted with prostate cancer is not influenced by whether or not they undergo PSA screening, one might wonder how advisable it is to subject them to the psychological discomfort associated with knowledge of above-normal PSA levels. Many practitioners now believe that because the complications associated with prostate cancer treatments can be significant, the detection and treatment of clinically unimportant disease may do more harm than good

(Coldman et al., 2003; Frankel et al., 2003; Hoffman, 2003).

Hopefully, future research will clarify whether or not PSA testing is beneficial. Two large studies, one in America and one in Europe, are currently under way. These studies should help to clarify the efficacy of screening for prostate cancer, but results are several years away (Hoffman, 2003). At present, the absence of compelling evidence supporting the use of PSA screening as a diagnostic tool has led to differing guidelines on PSA screening among medical practitioners: Some favor routine screening; some recommend providing information to patients so that they can make their own decision regarding testing; and some recommend against screening (Coldman et al., 2003). Given the current uncertain state of knowledge, perhaps the best advice is that physicians should not order a PSA test before first discussing with their patients the limits of current evidence and "the potential but uncertain benefits and the possible harms of prostate cancer screening" (U.S. Preventive Services Task Force, 2003b, p. 788).

is 40% lower among Asian American men and 35% lower in Hispanic American men (U.S. Preventive Services Task Force, 2003b).

Symptoms of prostate cancer include many of those previously listed for prostatitis, especially pain in the pelvis and lower back and urinary complications. However, prostate cancer often lacks easily detectable symptoms in its early stages. An early diagnosis can be obtained with a physical examination and a blood test. In the physical examination a physician inserts a finger into the rectum, a procedure called a digital rectal examination (DRE). Under normal conditions this exam is only mildly uncomfortable. The discovery of a marker for prostate cancer—*prostate-specific antigen* (PSA)—detectable by a blood test, has added another tool for physicians to use in diagnosing early prostate cancer. A normal PSA level is less than 4 nanograms PSA per milliliter of blood (U.S. Preventive Services Task Force, 2003b).

Efforts to detect prostate cancer using the DRE and PSA level as screening tools are far from precise (Hoffman, 2003). Many tumors are not detected by DRE. Both benign and malignant tumors can cause elevations in PSA levels (Woodrum et al., 1998). The U.S. government sponsors a task force of medical experts who regularly issue statements that address preventive health services for use in primary care clinical settings, including screening tests, counseling of patients, and treatment strategies. This task force, called the U.S.

Prostate Cancer Treatment Choices: The Patient's Dilemma

Most medical practitioners would agree that involving patients in decisions about treatment is generally desirable. However, this can be a daunting task when the patient must choose one treatment from several available alternatives when there is no clear evidence supporting one specific treatment. Medical writers have called this dilemma the medical "toss-up" and use the example of men with localized prostate cancer to illustrate the difficulties patients face when selecting a treatment (Patel et al., 2003).

At present, a man who is diagnosed with localized prostate cancer faces a bewildering array of treatment options (Jani & Hellman, 2003). Furthermore, because of insufficient data, there are currently no established evidence-based guidelines that clearly favor one treatment over another (Patel et al., 2003). Consequently, a newly diagnosed man is typically presented with a number of treatment options to be discussed with his physician and perhaps his family. In his effort to make an informed decision and resolve his "dilemma of choice," he may consult with several experienced clinicians and conduct his own research in medical journals, the popular media, and on the Internet. In the following paragraphs we summarize current knowledge about treatment options.

Medical experts differ widely as to whether treatment should be immediate or deferred after a diagnosis of prostate cancer. Arguments for immediate surgical, radiation, or antiandrogen treatments, especially for younger men, include longer survival time, significantly less pain, and prevention of metastatic disease (i.e., the spread of cancer to other areas, notably the spinal cord). Support for watchful waiting is provided by studies indicating that surgical, radiation, or hormonal treatments can result in a variety of complications, including incontinence, erection difficulties, and inability to experience orgasm (Jewett et al., 2003; Waxman & Mazhar, 2003). However, the urinary and erectile difficulties associated with radical prostatectomy can sometimes be averted by nerve-sparing surgical techniques that avoid cutting bundles of nerves and blood vessels supporting these functions (Jewett et al., 2003).

A complicating factor in this issue of treatment choice is that many men, especially those afflicted after age 70, die from unrelated causes before developing health-impairing symptoms of this often slow-to-progress disease (Hoffman, 2003; Waxman & Mazhar, 2003). The substantial possibility of dying without any serious complications from untreated prostate cancer should give some men thoughtful pause; they may not want to subject themselves to medical treatment that might erode the quality of their lives. It may be better to defer treatment of men over age 70 (or any man with a projected life span of less than 10 years) with asymptomatic prostate cancer that has not spread to other areas of the body (Kirby & Fitzpatrick, 2003). In contrast, many men diagnosed before age 70 develop indicators for treatment sometime after diagnosis, a finding that indicates the benefit of immediate treatment in younger men (Cunningham & Newton, 2003).

A recent Swedish study added new data about prostate cancer treatment while further complicating the dilemma of choice confronting newly diagnosed men. A total of 695 men, younger than age 75, with newly diagnosed prostate cancer were randomly assigned to two treatment conditions: watchful waiting (348 men) and radical prostatectomy (347 men). In a 10-year follow-up, death attributed to prostate cancer was halved by radical prostatectomy. In the watchful-waiting group there were twice as many men who developed distant metastases in other parts of their bodies. However—and this is the kicker from the patient dilemma perspective—the overall mortality rate did not differ significantly between these two groups of men (28.3% of men assigned to watchful waiting died and 22% in the prostatectomy group died) (Holmberg et al., 2002). The implications of this finding are perhaps best expressed in the recent words of a urologist: "Based on the results of this study, practitioners treating men with early prostate cancer can inform them that, over 10 years of follow-up, radical prostatectomy reduces the rate of local recurrence, progression to metastatic disease, and disease-specific mortality, but it offers no advantage over watchful waiting in overall mortality" (Siemens, 2003, p. 67).

Until well-controlled long-term studies of treatment outcomes provide clear evidence supporting a specific prostate cancer treatment, both clinicians and patients will continue to struggle with the dilemma of treatment choice. Hopefully, by the time our young male readers reach middle age, better treatment options and more powerful diagnostic tools for determining which prostate tumors are relatively insignificant and which warrant aggressive treatment will have been in place for some time.

Preventive Services Task Force (USPSTF), released its latest recommendations for prostate cancer screening in 2003. The report concluded that "the evidence is insufficient to recommend for or against routine screening for prostate cancer using prostate-specific antigen (PSA) testing or digital rectal examination (DRE)" (U.S. Preventive Services Task Force, 2003b, p. 787). This finding adds considerable fuel to a growing controversy among practitioners and researchers as to whether or not PSA screening is even advisable or beneficial in most cases. The evidence fueling this controversy is discussed in the box, "PSA Test: Beneficial or Not?"

Although the lifetime risk of being diagnosed with prostate cancer is 12.3% (about 1 in 8 men), the lifetime risk of dying from this disease is only 3.8% (about 1 in 26 men) (Jewett et al., 2003). In this respect, prostate cancer is clearly different from most other cancers, because it often progresses slowly in older men, who often have other life-threatening medical conditions, "and most men with prostate cancer will die from other causes" (Hoffman, 2003, p. 664). The natural history of prostate cancer, as reflected in the great disparity between diagnostic rates and mortality rates, makes treatment decisions difficult.

Once prostate cancer has been diagnosed, it can be treated in a number of ways, including just monitoring the cancer to determine whether its rate of progression poses a serious health threat. Medical practitioners often recommend medical intervention (usually surgery or radiation) for men with a life expectancy of at least 10 years (Cunningham & Newton, 2003). Among surgical options are radical prostatectomy (removal of the entire prostate gland), and cryoprostatectomy, in which the cancerous cells are destroyed by freezing. Two forms of radiation—external-beam radiotherapy and internal radiotherapy by means of implanted radioactive iodine or palladium seeds—are currently used. Because growth of prostatic cancer tumors is stimulated by androgen, another treatment option is either orchidectomy (surgical removal of the testes) or the use of androgen-blocking drugs or hormones (Parker & Dearnaley, 2003; Waxman & Mazhar, 2003). Finally, because the dangers or complications of surgery, radiation therapy, or hormone therapy can outweigh potential benefits, especially for older men, an approach called expectant management, which involves "watchful waiting" with deferred treatment, is sometimes most appropriate (Cunningham & Newton, 2003; Jani & Hellman, 2003).

At the time of this writing there is considerable controversy about what is the optimal approach to treating early-detected prostate cancer. Furthermore, a debate rages over whether or not the benefits outweigh the health risks of treatment. These timely issues are discussed in the box "Prostate Cancer Treatment Choices: The Patient's Dilemma."

Summary

Sexual Anatomy

- The penis consists of an internal root within the body cavity; an external, pendulous portion known as its body, or shaft; and the smooth, acorn-shaped head, called the glans. Running the length of the penis are three internal cylinders filled with spongelike tissue that becomes engorged with blood during sexual arousal. (p. 122)

- The scrotum is a loose outpocket of the lower abdominal wall, consisting of an outer skin layer and an inner muscle layer. Housed within the scrotum are the two testes, or testicles, each suspended within its respective compartment by the spermatic cord. (pp. 125–126)

- Human testes have two major functions: sperm production and secretion of sex hormones. (p. 127)

- Sperm development requires a scrotal temperature slightly lower than normal body temperature. (p. 127)

- The interior of each testis is divided into a large number of chambers that contain the thin, highly coiled seminiferous tubules, in which sperm production occurs. (p. 127)

- Adhering to the back and upper surface of each testis is a C-shaped structure, the epididymis, within which sperm cells mature. (pp. 127–128)

- Sperm travel from the epididymis of each testis through a long, thin tube, the vas deferens, which eventually terminates at the base of the bladder, where it is joined by the ejaculatory duct of the seminal vesicle. (pp. 128–130)

- The seminal vesicles are two small glands, each near the terminal of a vas deferens. They secrete an alkaline fluid that makes up about 70% of the semen and appears to nourish and stimulate sperm cells. (p. 130)

- The prostate gland, located at the base of the bladder and traversed by the urethra, provides about 30% of the seminal fluid released during ejaculation. (p. 130)

- Two pea-sized structures, the Cowper's glands, are connected by tiny ducts to the urethra just below the prostate gland. During sexual arousal, the Cowper's glands often produce a few drops of slippery alkaline fluid, which appear at the tip of the penis. (p. 130)

- Semen consists of sperm cells and secretions from the prostate, seminal vesicles, and Cowper's glands. The sperm component is only a tiny portion of the total fluid expelled during ejaculation. (pp. 130–131)

Male Sexual Functions

- Penile erection is an involuntary process that results from adequate sexual stimulation—physiological, psychological, or both. (p. 131)

- Ejaculation is the process by which semen is transported out through the penis. It occurs in two stages: the emission phase, when seminal fluid is collected in the urethral bulb, and the expulsion phase, when strong muscle contractions expel the semen. In retrograde ejaculation semen is expelled into the bladder. (pp. 131–133)

Some Concerns About Sexual Functioning

- Penis size does not significantly influence the ability to give or receive pleasure during penile–vaginal intercourse. Nor is it correlated with other physical variables, such as body shape or height. (pp. 133–135)

- Circumcision, the surgical removal of the foreskin, is widely practiced in the United States. The potential medical benefits of circumcision include reduced risks of penile cancer, HIV infection, and urinary tract infection. Data concerning the effect of circumcision on erotic function are limited and inconclusive. (pp. 136–139)

Male Genital Health Concerns

- The male genital and internal reproductive structures can be adversely affected by a variety of diseases and injuries. (p. 139)
- Injuries to the penis can be avoided by not using various sexual gadgets and by taking precautions during coitus. (pp. 139–140)
- Penile cancer is a rare malignancy that can be deadly if not diagnosed and treated in its earliest stage. Testicular cancer is more common than penile cancer, especially in young men. If detected in its early stages, testicular cancer is also highly curable. (p. 140)
- The prostate gland is a focal point of some of the more common male problems, including prostatitis, benign prostatic hyperplasia, and prostate cancer. A variety of drugs and surgical procedures are used to treat these conditions. Considerable controversy exists about what constitutes the best treatment strategy for prostate cancer. (pp. 141–144)

▷ Suggested Readings

Garnick, Marc (1996). *The Patient's Guide to Prostate Cancer: An Expert's Successful Treatment Strategies and Options.* New York: NAL-Dutton. An excellent, accessible book, written by one of the top physician experts on prostate cancer. Provides potentially life-saving information about all aspects of prostate cancer, including risk factors, diagnostic procedures, impact of the disease on sexual functioning, and treatment strategies.

Gilbaugh, James (1993). *Men's Private Parts.* New York: Crown Publishers. Practical advice from a urologist about male sexual anatomy and physiology in an easy-to-read and sometimes humorous format.

Kinsey, Alfred C., Wardell B. Pomeroy, and Clyde E. Martin (1948). *Sexual Behavior in the Human Male.* Philadelphia: Saunders. An abundance of details about male sexual anatomy, the manner in which males respond physiologically to sexual stimulation, and extensive data on male sexual behaviors.

Zilbergeld, Bernie (1999). *The New Male Sexuality: A Guide to Sexual Fulfillment.* New York: Bantam. An exceptionally well-written and informative treatment of male sexuality, including such topics as sexual functioning, self-awareness, and overcoming difficulties.

▷ Web Resources

Your *Our Sexuality* Web site **http://psychology.wadsworth.com/ crooksbaur9e/** has direct links to the Web sites described below. These links are checked often for changes, dead links, and new additions.

Male Health Center

An array of information is offered on this Web site, much of it related to male genital health, birth control from the male perspective, and sexual functioning.

Circumcision Information and Resource Pages

Although this Web site provides general information about the pros and cons of circumcision and articles written by those with various opinions on the subject, it takes the point of view that, other than for religious or cultural reasons, in most cases male circumcision is an unnecessary surgery.

The Journal of Urology

This Web site for a leading American medical journal provides content often related to genital health concerns of both men and women. Free access is provided to tables of contents and article abstracts.

Prostate Cancer

This Web site, sponsored by the Prostate Cancer Research and Education Foundation, is devoted to providing current information on prostate cancer and its treatment. The numerous resources available here include journal abstracts, discussion forums, and descriptions of various treatment strategies.

Testicular Cancer Resource Center

Testicular self-examinations, treatment options for testicular cancer, and issues involved in the posttreatment period—including an e-mail support group—are described and discussed on this Web site.

Lance Armstrong Foundation

This Web site is an excellent resource for information about testicular cancer, including topics such as prevention and awareness, treatment, caregiver resources, and survivor stories.

Our Sexuality Web Site

For online resources directly related to this book, go to **http://psychology.wadsworth.com/ crooksbaur9e/**. You will find interactive exercises, study questions, chapter outlines, an online version of this text's glossary, and Web links and activities that complement your CD-ROM.

InfoTrac® College Edition Online Library

http://infotrac.thomsonlearning.com/
InfoTrac College Edition is an online searchable library that includes a multitude of journals, many of which are specific to human sexuality. These journals include *Archives of Sexual Behavior, Archives of Sexual Health Behavior, Canadian Journal of Human Sexuality, Hispanic Journal of the Behavioral Sciences, Journal of Cross-Cultural Psychology, Journal of Physical Education, Recreation, and Dance, Journal of Sex Research,* and *Sex Roles.* You may search topics suggested in the margins of this chapter or terms of your own.

Our Sexuality CD-ROM

Use your CD-ROM for further study of the concepts in this chapter. Your CD-ROM provides animations of difficult concepts, video clips of real people discussing sexuality, critical thinking questions, chapter quizzing, and more.

CHAPTER

6

Sexual Arousal and Response

▶ **The Role of Hormones in Sexual Behavior**

What is the role of hormones in human sexual arousal?

▶ **The Brain and Sexual Arousal**

In what ways does the brain influence sexual arousal?

▶ **The Senses and Sexual Arousal**

How do the senses of touch, vision, smell, taste, and hearing contribute to erotic arousal?

▶ **Aphrodisiacs and Anaphrodisiacs in Sexual Arousal**

What substances have been shown to either heighten or reduce sexual arousal?

▶ **Sexual Response**

What common physiological changes accompany each stage of the sexual response cycles?

▶ **Aging and the Sexual Response Cycle**

What are some of the common variations that occur in the sexual response cycles of older women and men?

▶ **Some Differences Between the Sexes in Sexual Response**

What are some of the significant differences between the sexes in response patterns?

© Steve Prezant/CORBIS

There was never any heat or passion in my five-year relationship with Doug. He was a nice man, but I could never bridge the gap between us, which was due, in large part, to his unwillingness or inability to let go and express his feelings and vulnerability. Our lovemaking was like that too—kind of mechanical, as though he was there physically but not emotionally. I seldom felt any sexual desire for Doug, and sometimes my body barely responded during sex. How different it is with Matt, my current and, hopefully, lifetime partner. There was an almost instant closeness and intimacy at the beginning of our relationship. The first time we made love I felt like I was on fire. It was like we were melded together, both physically and emotionally. Sometimes just hearing his voice or the slightest touch arouses me intensely. (Authors' files)

Sexual arousal and sexual response in humans are influenced by many factors: hormones, our brain's capacity to create images and fantasies, our emotions, various sensory processes, the level of intimacy between two people, and a host of other influences. We begin this chapter by discussing some of the things that influence sexual arousal. We then turn our attention to the ways in which our bodies respond to sexual stimulation. We concentrate primarily on biological factors and events associated with human sexual arousal and response, but this focus on physiology is not meant to minimize the importance of psychological and cultural influences. In fact, psychosocial factors probably play a greater role than biological factors do in the extremely varied patterns of human sexual response, as we will discover in later chapters. However, it is always difficult, if not impossible, to differentiate between the complementary roles of psychological and biological factors as they influence our sexuality. In the final analysis, how do you separate the rich diversity of psychological influences from where they are collected, interpreted, and stored in the human nervous system? Clearly, the expression of our sexuality is determined by a complex interplay or interaction between social, emotional, and cognitive factors, hormones, brain neurons, and spinal reflexes.

► The Role of Hormones in Sexual Behavior

A number of hormones influence sexuality, sensuality, and interpersonal attraction in humans. Among the most widely discussed are androgens and estrogens, commonly referred to as sex hormones. These substances belong to the general class of **steroid hormones** that are secreted by the gonadal glands (testes and ovaries) and the adrenal glands.

No doubt you have heard the common descriptive expressions *male sex hormones* and *female sex hormones*. As we will see, linking specific hormones to one or the other sex is somewhat misleading—*both* sexes produce male and female sex hormones. As discussed in Chapter 3, the general term for male sex hormones is *androgens*. In males about 95% of total androgens are produced by the testes. Most of the remaining 5% are produced by the outer portions of the adrenal glands (called the adrenal cortex). A woman's ovaries and adrenal glands also produce androgens in approximately equal amounts (Davis, 1999; Rako, 1996). The dominant androgen in both males and females is testosterone. Men's bodies typically produce 20 to 40 times more testosterone than women's bodies (Crenshaw, 1996; Rako, 1999; Worthman, 1999). Female sex hormones, estrogens, are produced predominantly by the ovaries in females. Male testes also produce estrogens but in much smaller quantities than what occurs in female's bodies.

The arousal, attraction, and response components of human sexuality are also influenced by **neuropeptide hormones,** which are produced in the brain. One of the most important neuropeptide hormones, *oxytocin,* is sometimes referred to as a "love hormone"—it appears to influence our erotic and emotional attraction to one another. In the following sections we discuss research findings that link oxytocin to human sexual attraction, arousal, and behavior. But first we consider the evidence linking testosterone to sexual functioning in both sexes and examine the role of estrogens in female sexuality.

Steroid hormones The sex hormones and the hormones of the adrenal cortex.

Neuropeptide hormones Chemicals produced in the brain that influence sexuality and other behavioral functions.

Sex Hormones in Male Sexual Behavior

A number of research studies have linked testosterone with male sexuality (Dabbs, 2000; Freeman et al., 2001; McNicholas et al., 2003). This research indicates that testosterone generally has a greater effect on male sexual desire (libido) than on sexual functioning

(Crenshaw, 1996). Thus a man with a low testosterone level might have little interest in sexual activity but nevertheless be fully capable of erection and orgasms. However, testosterone does influence sensitivity of the genitals, and thus a testosterone deficiency can decrease sexual pleasure (Crenshaw, 1996; Rako, 1996). Furthermore, some men experience erectile difficulties that are associated with testosterone deficiency.

One source of information about testosterone's effect on male sexual function is studies of men who have undergone **castration.** This operation, called **orchidectomy** in medical language, involves removal of the testes, and it is sometimes performed as medical treatment for such diseases as genital tuberculosis and prostate cancer (Parker & Dearnaley, 2003; Pickett et al., 2000). Two European studies reported that surgically castrated men experience significantly reduced sexual interest and activity within the first year after undergoing this operation (Bremer, 1959; Heim, 1981). Other researchers have recorded incidences of continued sexual desire and functioning for as long as 30 years following castration, without supplementary testosterone treatment (Ford & Beach, 1951; Greenstein et al., 1995). However, even when sexual behavior persists following castration, the levels of sexual interest and activity generally diminish, often markedly (Bradford, 1998; Rosler & Witztum, 1998). The fact that this reduction occurs so frequently indicates that testosterone is an important biological instigator of sexual desire.

A second line of research investigating links between hormones and male sexual functioning involves androgen-blocking drugs. In recent years a class of drugs known as *antiandrogens* has been used in Europe and America to treat sex offenders as well as certain medical conditions, such as prostate cancer (Bradford, 1998; Waxman & Mazhar, 2003). Antiandrogens drastically reduce the amount of testosterone circulating in the bloodstream (Prior & Waxman, 2000; Waxman & Mazhar, 2003). One of these drugs, medroxyprogesterone acetate (MPA; also known by its trade name, Depo-Provera), has received a great deal of media attention in the United States in the last few years. A number of studies have found that MPA and other antiandrogens are often effective in reducing both sexual interest and sexual activity in human males (and females) (Crenshaw, 1996; Crenshaw & Goldberg, 1996). However, altering testosterone levels is not a completely effective treatment for sex offenders, especially in cases where sexual assaults stem from nonsexual motives, such as anger or the wish to exert power and control over another person.

A third source of evidence linking testosterone to sexual motivation in males is research on **hypogonadism,** a state of <u>testosterone deficiency</u> that results from certain diseases of the endocrine system. (Hypogonadism is also associated with the aging process in some older men.) If this condition occurs before puberty, maturation of the primary and secondary sex characteristics is retarded, and the individual may never develop an active sexual interest. The results are more variable if testosterone deficiency occurs in adulthood. Extensive studies of hypogonadal men provide strong evidence that testosterone plays an important role in male sexual desire (Freeman et al., 2001; McNicholas et al., 2003; Rabkin et al., 2000). For example, hypogonadal men who receive hormone treatments to replace testosterone often experience a return of normal sexual interest and activity (McNicholas et al., 2003). If the treatments are temporarily suspended, sexual desire and activity decline within 2 to 3 weeks (Cunningham et al., 1989; Findlay et al., 1989).

Sex Hormones in Female Sexual Behavior

Although it is known that estrogens contribute to a general sense of well-being, help maintain the thickness and elasticity of the vaginal lining, and contribute to vaginal lubrication (Bancroft, 2002; Kingsberg, 2002; Traish et al., 2002a), the role of estrogens in female sexual behavior is still unclear. Some researchers have reported that when postmenopausal women (menopause is associated with marked reduction in estrogen production) or women who have had their ovaries removed for medical reasons receive <u>estrogen therapy (ET)</u>, they experience not only heightened vaginal lubrication but also somewhat increased sexual desire, pleasure, and orgasmic capacity (Dennerstein et al., 1980; Dow et al., 1983; Kingsberg, 2002). The sexual benefits that often result from ET occur because estrogen provides "mood-mellowing" benefits and thus creates an emotional atmosphere receptive to sexual involvement (Crenshaw, 1996; Janowsky et al., 1996; Wilson, 2003). In addition, estrogen might play a somewhat subtle yet facilitating role in sexual arousal "in that the feminizing

Castration Surgical removal of the testes.

Orchidectomy The surgical procedure for removing the testes.

Hypogonadism Impaired hormone production in the testes that results in <u>testosterone</u> deficiency.

*EPT -estrogen replacement therapy

effects of estrogen on breasts, skin, and genitals may improve self-confidence and, indirectly, sexual desire" (Bartlik et al., 1999a, p. 51). See Chapter 4 for a more detailed discussion of ET, including the link between ET and breast cancer.

Other investigators have found that ET has no discernible impact on sexual desire, and, when estrogen is administered in relatively high doses, it can even decrease libido (Graham et al., 1995; Levin, 2002; Redmond, 1999). In view of these contradictory findings, the role of estrogens in female sexual motivation and functioning remains unclear.

There is far less ambiguity about the role of testosterone in female sexuality. In recent years an accumulation of evidence from many sources leaves little doubt that testosterone plays an important role as the major libido hormone in females (Apperloo et al., 2003; Bancroft, 2002; Kingsberg, 2002; Levin, 2002; Traish et al., 2002a; Traish et al. 2002b). Numerous experimental evaluations of the effects of testosterone on female sexuality provide evidence of a clear causal relationship between levels of circulating testosterone and sexual desire, genital sensitivity, and frequency of sexual activity. For instance, many studies have shown that testosterone replacement therapy enhances sexual desire and arousal in postmenopausal women (Apperloo et al., 2003; Davis, 1999; Gelfand, 2000). Of particular interest are several studies conducted at Canada's McGill University Menopause Clinic. These studies showed that postmenopausal women who received a combination estrogen—testosterone therapy reported restored feelings of sexuality, enhanced sexual desire, increased energy, and a heightened sense of well-being (Gelfand, 2000).

Other investigations have found that women who received testosterone or estrogen–testosterone therapy after natural menopause or surgical removal of their ovaries (ovariectomy) experience remarkably greater levels of sexual desire, sexual arousal, and sexual fantasies than women who received estrogen alone or no hormone therapy after surgery (Apperloo et al., 2003; Braunstein, 1999; Sarrel, 2000; Shifen et al., 2000).

Most of the evidence indicating the importance of testosterone in female sexual functioning has come from studies of women with low levels of this hormone as a result of ovariectomy, adrenalectomy, or natural menopause. One recent study of considerable interest sought to determine the effects of supplemental testosterone on the physiological and subjective sexual arousal in a group of sexually functional women with normal hormone levels. The investigators found that sublingually administered testosterone (under-the-tongue tablets) caused a significant increase in genital responsiveness within a few hours and that there was a strong and significant association between the increase in genital arousal and subjective reports of "genital sensation" and "sexual lust" (Tuiten et al., 2000).

InfoTrac Search Words

■ Estrogen therapy

Other studies have found that when testosterone is administered to women with a history of low sex drive and inhibited sexual arousal, the reported frequencies of sexual fantasies, masturbation, and sexual interaction with a partner typically increase (S. Davis, 2000; Shifen et al., 2000). Furthermore, when researchers compared testosterone levels in a group of healthy, sexually functional women with another group of women with a reported lifetime history of low sex drive, they found evidence linking low libido with reduced testosterone levels. Women in the low-libido group were found to have significantly lower levels of testosterone than those in the sexually functional group (Riley & Riley, 2000). Theresa Crenshaw, a renowned specialist in sexual medicine, believes that the results of studies such as these, considered in combination with her own extensive clinical and research experience, provides clear evidence "that testosterone plays a powerful role in female sexuality, and that when a women's testosterone dwindles, so does her sex life" (Crenshaw, 1996, p. 146).

How Much Testosterone Is Necessary for Normal Sexual Functioning?

Now that we have learned that testosterone plays a critical role in maintaining sexual desire in both sexes, we might ask, How much testosterone is necessary to ensure normal sexual arousability? The answer to this question is complex and is influenced by several factors.

Testosterone in the bodies of both sexes comes in two forms: attached (bound) and unattached (free). About 95% of the testosterone circulating in a man's blood is testosterone bound on a protein molecule (either albumin or globulin), where it is inactive or metabolically ineffective. The remaining 5% is the unattached version of testosterone, which is metabolically active and influences male libido (Crenshaw, 1996; Donnelly & White, 2000). Comparable figures for women are 97–99% bound testosterone and only 1–3% free testosterone to produce effects on bodily tissues (Rako, 1996). The sum of free and bound testosterone in both sexes is total testosterone. The normal range of total testosterone in the blood of a man is 300–1,200 ng/dl (nanograms per deciliter). In women the normal range of total testosterone is 20–50 ng/dl (Crenshaw, 1996; Rako, 1996; Winters, 1999). The essential amount, or critical mass, of testosterone necessary for adequate functioning varies from person to person in both sexes (Crenshaw, 1996; Rako, 1996). The fact that women normally have much smaller amounts of testosterone than men do does not mean that women have lower or weaker sex drives. Rather, it appears that women's body cells are more sensitive to testosterone than men's body cells are. Therefore for females a little testosterone is all that is necessary to stimulate libido (Bancroft, 2002; Crenshaw, 1996).

Too much testosterone can have adverse effects on both sexes (Redmond, 1999). Excess testosterone supplements in men can cause a variety of problems, including disruption of natural hormone cycles, salt retention, fluid retention, and hair loss. Furthermore, although there is no evidence that testosterone causes prostate cancer, excess testosterone can stimulate growth of preexisting prostate cancer (Bain, 2001; Pickett et al., 2000). In women excess testosterone can stimulate significant growth of facial and body hair, increase muscle mass, reduce breast size, and enlarge the clitoris (Kingsberg, 2002). However, in most instances only the use of irresponsibly high doses of testosterone over a sustained period of time results in the development of adverse side effects in either sex (Rako, 1999). Furthermore, as we have seen, supplementary testosterone can help restore sexual desire to men and women with deficient levels of this libido hormone.

Sexual Health

A normal level of total testosterone in either sex does not necessarily rule out a biological basis for a flagging sex drive, because the key hormonal component in libido—free testosterone—can be abnormally low even though the total testosterone level is within normal limits. Consequently, should you find yourself experiencing testosterone deficiency (see next section), it is important that, as an informed consumer of health care, you have your free testosterone levels assessed in addition to your total testosterone level. Until recently, most physicians ordered testing of only total testosterone. Even today, this improper and incomplete testing procedure is still followed by some medical practitioners. ■

Finally, the rate at which testosterone production diminishes with aging is markedly different in men and women. When a woman's ovaries begin to shut down at menopause, her total body testosterone levels often rapidly decrease, falling quickly in just a matter of months. For other women the onset of testosterone deficiency is more gradual, taking place over a period of several years (Davis, 1999; Gelfand, 2000; Kingsberg, 2002). (Women who have their ovaries surgically removed are more likely to experience an abrupt or precipitous loss of testosterone.) Even though a women's adrenal glands continue to produce testosterone, their output also diminishes when her ovaries are no longer producing normal levels of testosterone (Rako, 1999).

In contrast, in men the decline in testosterone with aging is usually much less rapid or precipitous. Although it is true that testosterone production in both the testes and the adrenal glands diminishes with aging, the changes are generally gradual rather than abrupt and typically take place over an extended number of years (McNicholas et al., 2003; Morales et al., 2000). This is probably due in large part to the continued functioning of the testes, which, unlike the ovaries, do not undergo a fairly rapid shutdown in the middle of life.

The general signs of testosterone deficiency are similar in both sexes, even though they have a more rapid onset in women than in men. The most obvious symptoms of testosterone deficiency are listed in Table 6.1.

TABLE 6.1	Common Signs of Testosterone Deficiency in Both Sexes

- Decrease in one's customary level of sexual desire.
- Reduced sensitivity of the genitals and the nipples to sexual stimulation.
- Overall reduction in general levels of sexual arousability, possibly accompanied by decreased orgasmic capacity and/or less intense orgasms.
- Diminished energy levels and possibly depressed mood.
- Increased fat mass.
- Decreased bone mineral density, which can result in osteoporosis in both sexes.
- Reduced body hair.
- Decreased muscle mass and strength.

SOURCES: Bain (2001), Gelfand (2000), Kingsberg (2002), McNicholas et al. (2003), Morales et al. (2000), and Rako (1999).

Testosterone Replacement Therapy

If you find yourself experiencing some of the symptoms listed in Table 6.1, you might want to seek medical advice regarding possible testosterone replacement therapy (TRT). At present, men generally find it much easier than women to secure medical advice about TRT. The use of testosterone supplements to treat male sexual difficulties is relatively common. In marked contrast, the medical community is reluctant to prescribe supplementary testosterone for women who manifest symptoms of deficiency. Too often, physicians adhere rigidly to the notion that "testosterone for women is unnatural" (Rako, 1996, p. 36). This misinformed position completely overlooks the obvious fact that testosterone is a sex hormone that occurs naturally in females as well as males (Gelfand, 2000). In recent years, however, there has been a gradual awakening to the benefits of testosterone supplement therapy. In fact, several leading authorities on gynecology and menopause stress the need for educating medical practitioners as well as health care consumers, especially postmenopausal women, about the use of supplementary testosterone (Gelfand, 2000; Utian & Schiff, 1994).

Because of the highly individualized manner in which both men and women respond to hormones, there is no clear-cut right or wrong approach to TRT. Furthermore, TRT is not necessary for every person whose testosterone levels are lower than normal. Ideally, a person will seek the counsel of an informed physician who will both determine the appropriateness of TRT and who will work with him or her to find the best dosage and method of administration to effectively alleviate the symptoms of testosterone deficiency.

Testosterone supplements can be administered to men or women orally (swallowing), sublingually (under-the-tongue tablets), by injection, by implantation of a pellet, or by direct application to the skin by means of either a testosterone gel formulation or a transdermal skin patch (McNicholas et al., 2003; Morales, 2003; Redmond, 1999). Testosterone can also be applied to women by means of vaginal creams and gels. Experts on TRT caution against taking too much testosterone. Taking a dose greater than necessary to eliminate deprivation symptoms is not likely to improve libido and general energy level and could result in adverse side effects.

Oxytocin in Male and Female Sexual Behavior

The neuropeptide hormone **oxytocin,** which is produced in the hypothalamus, exerts significant influence on sexual response, sensuality, and interpersonal erotic and emotional attraction (Blaicher et al., 1999; Love, 2001; McEwen, 1997; Wilson, 2003). A well-known biological function of oxytocin is to facilitate ejection of milk from the nipple during breast-feeding (Wilson, 2003). Some refer to oxytocin as the snuggle chemical because its release during breast-feeding facilitates mother–child bonding (Love, 2001). The release of oxytocin during sexual arousal and response possibly has a similar bonding effect on sexual partners.

Oxytocin A neuropeptide produced in the hypothalamus that influences sexual response and interpersonal attraction.

Oxytocin is secreted during cuddling and physical intimacy, and touch is an especially powerful triggering mechanism for its release. Increased levels of circulating oxytocin have been shown to stimulate sexual activity in a variety of animals, including humans (Anderson-Hunt & Dennerstein, 1994; Wilson, 2003). This hormone increases skin sensitivity to touch and thus encourages or facilitates affectionate behavior (Love, 2001; McEwen, 1997). In humans oxytocin levels increase as a person moves through a sexual response cycle from initial excitement to orgasm, and high levels of oxytocin are associated with orgasmic release in both sexes (Anderson-Hunt & Dennerstein, 1994; Carmichael et al., 1994; Wilson, 2003). Oxytocin also stimulates contractions of the uterine wall during orgasm (Wilson, 2003).

The significant escalation of oxytocin release at the point of orgasm, together with the fact that blood levels of this hormone remain elevated for a time afterward, could contribute to the emotional and erotic bonding of sexual partners and to a sense of shared attraction (Love, 2001; Pedersen, 1992). Research with human subjects indicates that oxytocin plays an important role in facilitating social attachment with others and in the development and fostering of feelings of being in love (Carter, 1998; Pedersen, 1992; Wilson, 2003). Autistic children, who commonly exhibit a reduced ability to form social attachments and express love, often have significantly reduced levels of oxytocin (Green et al., 2001). This finding provides further evidence of the association between oxytocin levels and the capacity to form attachments and loving interactions.

The Brain and Sexual Arousal

From our experience we know that the brain plays an important role in our sexuality. Our thoughts, emotions, and memories are all mediated through the brain's complex mechanisms. Sexual arousal can occur without any sensory stimulation; it can be produced by the process of *fantasy* (in this case, thinking of erotic images or sexual interludes), and some individuals can even reach orgasm during a fantasy experience without any physical stimulation (Kinsey et al., 1948, 1953; Whipple & Komisaruk, 1999; Whipple et al., 1992).

We know that specific events can cause us to become aroused. Less apparent is the role of individual experience and cultural influence, both of which are mediated by our brains. Clearly, we do not all respond similarly to the same stimuli. Some people can become highly aroused if their partners use explicit sexual language; others find such words threatening or a sexual turnoff. Cultural influences also play an important role. For example, the smell of genital secretions may be more arousing to many Europeans than to members of our own deodorant-conscious society. Before turning to a more detailed discussion of the brain and sexual arousal, we take a brief look at cultural influences on sexual arousal in the following "Sexuality and Diversity" discussion.

Sexuality and Diversity

Cultural Variations in Sexual Arousal

Although the biological mechanisms underlying human sexual arousal and response are essentially universal, the particular sexual stimuli and/or behaviors that people find arousing are greatly influenced by cultural conditioning. For example, in Western societies, in which the emphasis during sexual activity tends to be heavily weighted toward achieving orgasm, genitally focused activities are frequently defined as optimally arousing. In contrast, in some Asian societies sexual practices are interwoven with spiritual traditions of Hinduism, Buddhism, and Taoism, in which the *primary* goal of sexual interaction is not the mere achievement of orgasm but an extension of sexual arousal for long periods of time, often several hours (Stubbs, 1992). Devotees of Eastern Tantric traditions often achieve optimal pleasure by emphasizing the sensual and spiritual aspects of shared intimacy rather than orgasmic release (Devi, 1977).

In many non-Western societies, especially some African cultures, female orgasm is either rare or completely unknown (Ecker, 1993). Furthermore, in some of these societies, vaginal lubrication is negatively evaluated and male partners may complain about it (Ecker, 1993). This societal attitude provides an impetus for the practice of "dry sex," described in Chapter 17.

Even in American society ethnicity influences sexual response, and its effect is evident in female orgasm rates reported in the National Health and Social Life Survey (NHSLS). In this study 38% of African American women reported that they always have an orgasm during sexual interaction with their primary partner, compared to 26% of white American women and 34% of Hispanic women (Laumann et al., 1994). In the following paragraphs we provide brief examples of some other facets of cultural diversity in human sexual arousal.

Kissing on the mouth, a universal source of sexual arousal in Western society, is rare or absent in many other parts of the world. Certain North American Eskimo people and inhabitants of the Trobriand Islands would rather rub noses than lips, and among the Thonga of South Africa kissing is viewed as odious behavior. The Hindu people of India are also disinclined to kiss because they believe that such contact symbolically contaminates the act of sexual intercourse. In their survey of 190 societies, Clellan Ford and Frank Beach (1951) found that mouth kissing was acknowledged in only 21 societies and was practiced as a prelude or accompaniment to coitus in only 13.

Oral sex (both cunnilingus and fellatio) is a common source of sexual arousal among island societies of the South Pacific, in industrialized nations of Asia, and in much of the Western world. In contrast, in Africa (with the exception of northern regions), such practices are likely to be viewed as unnatural or disgusting.

Foreplay in general, whether it be oral sex, sensual touching, or passionate kissing, is subject to wide cultural variation. In some societies, most notably those with Eastern traditions, couples strive to prolong intense states of sexual arousal for several hours (Devi, 1977). Although varied patterns of foreplay are common in Western cultures, these activities often are of short duration as lovers move rapidly toward the "main event" of coitus. In still other societies foreplay is either sharply curtailed or absent altogether. For example, the Lepcha farmers of the southeastern Himalayas limit foreplay to men briefly caressing their partners' breasts, and among the Irish inhabitants of Inis Beag, precoital sexual activity is reported to be limited to mouth kissing and rough fondling of the woman's lower body by her partner (Messenger, 1971).

Another indicator of cultural diversity is the wide variety in standards of attractiveness. Although physical qualities exert a profound influence on human sexual arousal in virtually every culture, standards of attractiveness vary widely, as can be seen in the accompanying photos of women and men from around the world who are considered attractive in their own cultures. What may be attractive or a source of erotic arousal in one culture may seem strange or unattractive in others. For instance, although some island societies attach erotic significance to the shape and textures of female genitals, most Western societies do not. To cite a final example, in many societies bare female breasts are not generally viewed as erotic stimuli, as they are in the United States.

Our standards of physical attractiveness vary widely, as can be seen in these six photos of women and men from around the world who are considered attractive in their cultures.

The brain is the storehouse of our memories and cultural values, and consequently its influence over our sexual arousability is profound. Strictly mental events, such as fantasies, are the product of the **cerebral cortex,** the thinking center of the brain that controls such functions as reasoning, language, and imagination. The cerebral cortex represents only one level of functioning at which the brain influences human sexual arousal and response. At a subcortical level the **limbic system** seems to play an important part in determining sexual behavior, both in humans and in other animals.

Figure 6.1 shows some key structures in the limbic system. These include the *cingulate gyrus,* the *amygdala,* the *hippocampus,* and parts of the *hypothalamus,* which plays a regulating role. Research links various sites in the limbic system with sexual behavior. Some of the most striking findings come from the research of James Olds, who in the 1950s conducted a series of experiments involving limbic system stimulation of rats. Olds designed a system that enabled the rats to self-stimulate their brains; he implanted tiny electrodes in several regions of the limbic system and connected these electrodes to a special apparatus with a lever. The results? The rats responded by pressing the lever over and over again, to the point of exhaustion—as frequently as several thousand times per hour. This response, and the intense pleasure that the rats seemed to be experiencing, led Olds to call these limbic system regions "pleasure centers" (Olds, 1956). Olds's rats were unable to tell him whether the pleasure they were experiencing was sexual in nature. Subsequent research with humans is more enlightening.

For ethical reasons few experiments have studied the effects of brain stimulation on humans. However, some evidence indicates that electrical stimulation of the hypothalamus

Cerebral cortex The outer layer of the brain's cerebrum that controls higher mental processes.

Limbic system A subcortical brain system composed of several interrelated structures that influences the sexual behavior of humans and other animals.

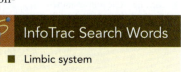

InfoTrac Search Words

■ Limbic system

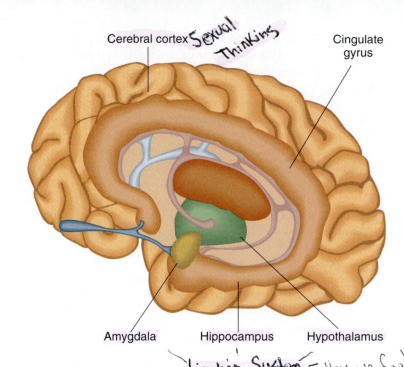

▶ **Figure 6.1** The limbic system, a region of the brain associated with emotion and motivation, is important in human sexual function. Key structures, shaded in color, include the cingulate gyrus, portions of the hypothalamus, the amygdala, and the hippocampus.

Cerebral cortex *Sexual Thinking*

Cingulate gyrus

Amygdala   Hippocampus   Hypothalamus

Limbic System – How we feel & act sexually

in human subjects produces sexual arousal, sometimes culminating in orgasm (Sem-Jacobsen, 1968). Furthermore, there are recorded cases in which electrical and chemical brain stimulation of humans, done for therapeutic purposes, has had similar impact.

Medical researcher Robert Heath (1972) experimented with limbic system stimulation in patients suffering from various disorders. He theorized that stimulation-induced pleasure would prove to have some therapeutic value. One patient, a man with an emotional disorder, was provided with a self-stimulation device that he used up to 1,500 times per hour to administer stimulation to an area in his limbic system. He described the stimulation as producing intense sexual pleasure, protesting each time the unit was taken away from him. Another patient, a woman with an epileptic disorder, reported intense sexual pleasure and experienced multiple orgasmic responses as a direct result of brain stimulation.

Several studies have implicated the hypothalamus in sexual functioning. For instance, researchers have reported increased sexual activity in rats, including erections and ejaculations, triggered by stimulation in both anterior and posterior regions of the hypothalamus (Paredes & Baum, 1997). When certain parts of the hypothalamus are surgically destroyed, the sexual behavior of both males and females of several species can be dramatically reduced (Hitt et al., 1970; Paredes & Baum, 1997). One region in the preoptic area of the hypothalamus, the *medial preoptic area* (MPOA), has been implicated in sexual arousal and sexual behavior. Electrical stimulation of the MPOA increases sexual behavior, and damage to this area reduces or eliminates sexual activity in males of a wide variety of species (Paredes & Baum, 1997; Wilson, 2003). Opiate drugs, such as heroin and morphine, have a suppressive effect on the MPOA and are known to inhibit sexual performance in both sexes (Argiolas, 1999).

Certain naturally occurring brain substances, called *neurotransmitters* (chemicals that transmit messages in the nervous system) are also known to influence sexual arousal and response by their effect on the MPOA. One of these transmitter substances, **dopamine,** has both an excitatory effect on the MPOA and a facilitatory effect on sexual arousal and response in males of many species (Hull et al., 1999; Wilson, 2003). Furthermore, testosterone is known to stimulate the release of dopamine in the MPOA in both males and females (Wilson, 2003). This finding indicates one possible mechanism by which testosterone stimulates libido in both sexes.

In contrast to the facilitatory impact of dopamine on sexual behavior, the neurotransmitter **serotonin** appears to inhibit sexual activity. Male ejaculation causes a release of serotonin in both the MPOA and the *lateral hypothalamus,* an area on the sides of the hypothalamus. This released serotonin temporarily reduces sex drive and behavior by inhibiting the release of dopamine (Hull et al., 1999). Serotonin also suppresses sexual

Dopamine A neurotransmitter that facilitates sexual arousal and activity.

Serotonin A neurotransmitter that inhibits sexual arousal and activity.

arousal by blocking the action of oxytocin (Wilson, 2003). Humans who suffer from depression are often provided antidepressant medications called *selective serotonin reuptake inhibitors* (SSRIs). These drugs, whose effect is to increase serotonin levels in the brain, often interfere with libido and sexual response. Research has shown that SSRIs diminish genital sensitivity and reduce orgasmic capacity in both sexes (Michelson et al., 2002; Wilson, 2003).

These various findings considered collectively provide strong evidence that dopamine facilitates sexual arousal and activity in women and men, whereas serotonin appears to provide an inhibitory effect on both sexes.

It is doubtful that researchers will ever find one specific "sex center" in the brain. However, it is clear that both the cerebral cortex and the limbic system play important roles in initiating, organizing, and controlling human sexual arousal and response. In addition, the brain interprets a variety of sensory inputs that often exert a profound influence on sexual arousal. We examine this topic in the next section.

© Deborah Egan

▶ The Senses and Sexual Arousal

It has been said that the brain is the most important sense organ for human sexual arousal. This observation implies that any sensory event, if so interpreted by the brain, can serve as an effective sexual stimulus. The resulting variety in the sources of erotic stimulation helps explain the tremendous sexual complexity of humans.

Of the major senses, touch tends to predominate during sexual intimacy. However, all the senses have the potential to become involved, and sights, smells, sounds, and tastes can all be important contributors to erotic arousal. There are no blueprints for the what and how of sensory stimulation. Each of us is unique; we have our own individual triggers of arousal.

Sensual touching is one of the most frequent sources of erotic stimulation.

? How About You?

Which of your senses are most influential in triggering your own sexual arousal?

✴Touch

Stimulation of the various skin surfaces is probably a more frequent source of human sexual arousal than any other type of sensory stimulus. The nerve endings that respond to touch are distributed unevenly throughout the body, which explains why certain areas are more sensitive than others. Those locations that are most responsive to tactile pleasuring are commonly referred to as the **erogenous zones.** A distinction is often made between primary erogenous zones (those areas that contain dense concentrations of nerve endings) and secondary erogenous zones (other areas of the body that have become endowed with erotic significance through sexual conditioning).

A list of **primary erogenous zones** generally includes the genitals, buttocks, anus, perineum, breasts (particularly the nipples), inner surfaces of the thighs, armpits, navel, neck, ears (especially the lobes), and the mouth (lips, tongue, and the entire oral cavity). It is important to remember, however, that just because a given area qualifies as a primary erogenous zone, there is no guarantee that stimulating it will produce arousal in a sexual partner. What is intensely arousing for one person may produce no reaction—or even irritation—in another.

The **secondary erogenous zones** include virtually all other regions of the body. For example, if your lover tenderly kissed and stroked your upper back during each sexual interlude, this area could be transformed into an erogenous zone. These secondary locations become eroticized because they are touched within the context of sexual intimacies. A man and a woman describe how touch enhances their sexual experiences:

I love being touched all over, particularly on my back. Each touch helps to develop trust and a sense of security. (Authors' files)

Soft touches, not necessarily genital, arouse me most. When he lightly traces my neck and back with his fingers, my nerves become highly sensitive, and my entire body starts tingling with arousal. (Authors' files)

InfoTrac Search Words

■ Erogenous zones

Erogenous zones Areas of the body that are particularly responsive to sexual stimulation.

Primary erogenous zones Areas of the body that contain dense concentrations of nerve endings.

Secondary erogenous zones Areas of the body that have become erotically sensitive through learning and experience.

? Critical Thinking Question

It has been said that women enjoy hugging and touching more than genital sex, whereas men have little interest in the "preliminaries," preferring to "get down to the real thing." Do you believe this statement reflects a genuine difference between the sexes? If so, is it learned or biologically determined?

*Vision

In our society visual stimuli appear to be of great importance. Prime evidence is the emphasis we often place on physical appearance, including such activities as personal grooming, wearing the right clothes, and the extensive use of cosmetics. Therefore it is not surprising that vision is second only to touch in the hierarchy of stimuli that most people view as sexually arousing.

The popularity of sexually explicit men's magazines in our society suggests that the human male is more aroused by visual stimuli than is the female. Early research seemed to support this conclusion. Kinsey found that more men than women reported being sexually excited by visual stimuli, such as pinup erotica and stag shows (Kinsey et al., 1948, 1953). However, this finding reflects several social influences, including the greater cultural inhibitions attached to such behavior in women at the time of his research and the simple fact that men had been provided with far more opportunities to develop an appetite for such stimuli. Furthermore, many women found the old-style porn films and videos, which were made to appeal exclusively to men, to be offensive and insensitive and thus not something they would acknowledge as a source of sexual arousal (Striar & Bartlik, 2000). This interpretation is supported by later research that used physiological recording devices (see Chapter 2) to measure sexual arousal under controlled laboratory conditions. These studies have demonstrated strong similarities in the physical responses of males and females to visual erotica (Murnen & Stockton, 1997; Rubinsky et al., 1987). Most women display physiologically measurable arousal while watching erotic films, even those who report no feelings of being aroused (Laan & Everaerd, 1996). Recent research findings suggest that when sexual arousal is measured by self-reports rather than by physiological devices, women are less inclined than men to report being sexually aroused by visual erotica (Koukounas & McCabe, 1997; Mosher & MacIan, 1994). This finding could reflect the persistence of cultural influences that make women reluctant to acknowledge being aroused by filmed erotica or it could indicate that females have greater difficulty than males identifying signs of sexual arousal in their bodies, or it could be a combination of these factors.

*Smell

A person's sexual history and cultural conditioning often influence what smells he or she finds arousing. We typically learn through experience to view certain odors as erotic and others as offensive. From this perspective there may be nothing intrinsic to the fragrance of genital secretions that causes them to be perceived as either arousing or distasteful. We might also argue the contrary—that the smell of genital secretions would be universally exciting to humans were it not that some people learn to view them as offensive. This latter interpretation is supported by the fact that some societies openly recognize the value of genital smells as a sexual stimulant. For example, in areas of Europe where the deodorant industry is less pervasive, some women use the natural bouquet of their genital secretions, strategically placed behind an ear or in the nape of the neck, to arouse their sexual partners.

Two people describe the impact of smell on their sexuality:

Sometimes my partner exudes a sex smell that makes me instantly aroused. (Authors' files)

There is really something stimulating about the scent of a woman, and I enjoy both the smell and taste of a woman's skin. (Authors' files)

The near obsession of many people in our society with masking natural body odors makes it difficult to study the effects of these smells. Any natural odors that might trigger arousal tend to be well disguised by frequent bathing, perfumes, deodorants, and antiperspirants. Nevertheless, each person's unique experiences allow certain smells to acquire erotic significance, as the following anecdote reveals:

I love the smells after making love. They trigger little flashes of erotic memories and often keep my arousal level in high gear, inducing me to go on to additional sexual activities. (Authors' files)

In a society that is often concerned about natural odors, it is nice to see that some people appreciate scents associated with sexual intimacy and their lovers' bodies.

Among many nonhuman animals smells are often more important than visual stimuli in eliciting sexual response. The females of many species secrete certain substances, called **pheromones** (FARE-oh-mones), during their fertile periods (Cutler, 1999; Roelofs, 1995; Small, 1999). If you have ever owned a female dog in heat and observed male dogs coming from miles around to scratch at your door, you will not doubt for a moment the importance of smell in sexual arousal. The relationship of sexual arousal to pheromones has been likened to that between salivation and the smell of food. Actually, these responses are quite different. The noses of dogs and other animals contain two channels of sensory input, "each with its own organ, nerves, and bumps in the brain" (Moran, quoted by Blakeslee, 1993, p. B11). One of these channels, the *olfactory system,* responds to conventional smells, such as the odor of fresh meat. A second system, called the *vomeronasal system,* is composed of two tiny pitlike organs (vomeronasal organs) whose exclusive task is detecting pheromones. This system appears to be distinct and separate from odor-sensing olfactory organs (Cutler, 1999; Weller, 1998).

Pheromones Certain odors produced by the body that relate to reproductive functions.

Most medical textbooks describe the vomeronasal organs as a minor structure in humans that appears in the fetus and then diminishes to a point of nonfunctionality later in development (Small, 1999; Smith & Bhatnagar, 2000). However, recent evidence indicates that this viewpoint may not be accurate. The findings of a number of recent studies support the contention that human females and males possess a vomeronasal system that can be activated by pheromones (Cutler, 1999; Kohl et al., 2001; Leinders-Zufall et al., 2000; McCoy & Pitino, 2001).

InfoTrac Search Words

■ Pheromones

Although mounting evidence suggests that humans do indeed secrete pheromones, there is insufficient evidence to determine whether or not these substances act as sexual attractants. Undaunted by the inconclusive nature of the available data, a number of American and international corporations have invested in the commercial development and marketing of perfumes and colognes allegedly containing substances that possess human pheromone properties (Cutler, 1999; Kohl, 2002; Small, 1999). However, the jury is still out on whether or not these products contain genuine sexual-attractant pheromones.

Contrary to what the marketers of commercial scents would like us to believe, Alan Hirsch, a researcher at the Smell and Taste Treatment and Research Foundation in Chicago, recently found that the odors reported to be most sexually arousing for either sex were not colognes or perfumes. In Hirsch's study, which used measures of penile tumescence and vaginal blood flow as physiological markers of arousal, women were most stimulated by the scents of licorice, cucumbers, and banana nut bread. Men reacted most strongly to the smells of lavender, pumpkin pie, and doughnuts. Although none of the tested odors inhibited the arousal of men, some smells did inhibit vaginal blood engorgement in women, including the odor of barbecued meat, cherries, and men's colognes (Adamson, 2003)!

We know that in nonhuman animals, whose sense of smell is paramount, pheromones play a major role as sexual attractants. Only time will tell if pheromones in perfumes and colognes prove to be genuine sexual attractants for humans. It is unlikely that such products, even if eventually proven to have a true pheromone effect, will ever produce irresistible sexual compulsions in humans comparable to those exhibited by animals influenced by sexual scents. Rather, it seems more likely that fragrances containing human pheromones will be shown to influence sensuality rather than sexuality, creating a sense of well-being and intimacy with another person rather than raw lust (Crenshaw, 1996).

Critical Thinking Question

In your opinion, which of the senses has the greatest impact on sexual arousal and sexual interaction? Why? Do men and women differ in reference to which senses predominate during sexual intimacy?

Taste

Taste, which has yet to be fully investigated, seems to play a relatively minor role in human sexual arousal. This is no doubt at least partly influenced by an industry that promotes breath mints and flavored vaginal douches. Besides making many individuals extremely self-conscious about how they taste or smell, such commercial products can mask any natural tastes that relate to sexual activity. Nevertheless, some people are still able to detect and appreciate certain tastes that they learn to associate with sexual intimacy, such as the taste of vaginal secretions or semen.

taste plays a minor role [handwritten]

Hearing

Whether or not people make sounds during sexual activity is highly variable, as is a partner's response. Some people find words, intimate or erotic conversation, moans, and orgasmic cries to be highly arousing; others prefer that their lovers keep silent during sex play. Some people, out of fear or embarrassment, make a conscious effort to suppress spontaneous noises during sexual interaction. Because of the silent, stoic image accepted by many males, it may be exceedingly difficult for men in particular to talk, cry out, or groan during arousal.

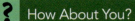
Yet in one research study many women reported that their male partners' silence hindered their own sexual arousal (DeMartino, 1970). Female reluctance to emit sounds during sex play might be influenced by the notion that "nice" women are not supposed to be so passionate that they make noises.

Besides being sexually arousing, talking to each other during a sexual interlude can be informative and helpful ("I like it when you touch me that way," "A little softer," and so on). If you happen to be a person who enjoys noisemaking and verbalizations during sex, your partner may respond this way if you discuss the matter beforehand. We will discuss talking about sexual preferences in Chapter 8.

Two people describe how sounds affect their lovemaking:

It is very important for me to hear that my partner is enjoying the experience. A woman who doesn't mind moaning is a pleasure to be with. It is good to be with someone who does not mind opening up and letting you know she is enjoying you. If my partner doesn't provide enough voice communication with sex, forget it. (Authors' files)

I like to hear our bodies slapping together as we make love and to hear him moan and groan for more. I also like to hear my name being called, and I like to say his. (Authors' files)

▶ Aphrodisiacs and Anaphrodisiacs in Sexual Arousal

Up to this point, we have considered the impact of hormones, brain processes, and sensory input on human sexual arousal. Several other factors also can affect a person's arousability in a particular situation. Some of these directly affect the physiology of arousal; others can have a strong impact on a person's sexuality through the power of belief. In the pages that follow we examine the effects of a number of products that people use to attempt to heighten or reduce sexual arousal.

Aphrodisiacs: Do They Work?

Aphrodisiac A substance that allegedly arouses sexual desire and increases the capacity for sexual activity.

An **aphrodisiac** (a-fruh-DEE-zee-ak) (named after Aphrodite, the Greek goddess of love and beauty) is a substance that supposedly arouses sexual desire or increases a person's capacity for sexual activities. Almost from the beginning of time people have searched for magic potions and other agents to revive flagging erotic interest or to produce Olympian sexual performances. That many have reported finding such sexual stimulants bears testimony, once again, to the powerful role of the mind in human sexual activity. We first consider a variety of foods that have been held to possess aphrodisiac qualities, and then we turn our attention to other alleged sexual stimulants, including alcohol and an assortment of chemical substances.

Almost any food that resembles the male external genitals has at one time or another been viewed as an aphrodisiac (Eskeland et al., 1997). Many of us have heard the jokes about oysters, although for some a belief in the special properties of this particular shellfish is no joking matter. One wonders to what extent the oyster industry profits from this pervasive myth. Other foods sometimes considered aphrodisiacs include bananas, asparagus, cucumbers, tomatoes, ginseng root, and potatoes (Castleman, 1997). Particularly in Asian countries there is a widespread belief that the ground-up horns of animals such as rhinoceros and reindeer are powerful sexual stimulants. (Have you ever used the term *horny* to describe a sexual state? Now you know its origin.) Unfortunately, the rhinoceros population in Africa

Strawberries

has dwindled to the point of near extinction, largely as a result of the erroneous belief that rhinoceros horn is an effective aphrodisiac (Tudge, 1991).

A number of drugs are also commonly thought to have aphrodisiac properties. Of these drugs, perhaps more has been written about the supposed stimulant properties of alcohol than about any other presumed aphrodisiac substance. In our culture the belief in the erotic enhancement properties of alcoholic beverages is widespread:

I am a great believer in the sexual benefits of drinking wine. After a couple glasses I become a real "hound in bed." I can always tell my partner is in the mood when she brings out a bottle of chilled rosé. (Authors' files)

Far from being a stimulant, alcohol has a depressing effect on higher brain centers and thus reduces cortical inhibitions such as fear and guilt that often block sexual expression (Cocores & Gold, 1989). Alcohol can also impair our ability to cognitively process information (e.g., values and expectations for behavioral consequences) that might otherwise put the brakes on sexual impulses (MacDonald et al., 2000). In addition, alcohol can facilitate sexual activity by providing a convenient rationalization for behavior that might normally conflict with one's values ("I just couldn't help myself with my mind fogged by booze").

Consumption of significant amounts of alcohol, however, can have serious negative effects on sexual functioning. Research has demonstrated that with increasing levels of intoxication both men and women experience reduced sexual arousal (as measured physiologically), decreased pleasurability and intensity of orgasm, and increased difficulty in attaining orgasm (Briddell & Wilson, 1976; Heaton & Varrin, 1991; Rosen & Ashton, 1993; Wilson & Lawson, 1976). Heavy alcohol use can also result in general physical deterioration, a process that commonly reduces a person's interest in and capacity for sexual activity.

Alcohol use can have even more serious potential consequences in conjunction with sexual activity. Research has demonstrated a strong association between alcohol use and an inclination to participate in sexual practices that have a high risk for contracting a life-threatening disease such as AIDS (Dittman, 2003; MacDonald et al., 2000; Sieving et al., 1997). (Other mind-altering drugs, such as marijuana and cocaine, have also been implicated in high-risk sexual behavior.) ■

In addition to alcohol, several other drugs have also been ascribed aphrodisiac qualities. Some of the substances included in this category are amphetamines, such as methylenedioxymethamphetamine (MDMA), commonly known as ecstasy; barbiturates; cantharides, also known as Spanish fly; cocaine; LSD and other psychedelic drugs; marijuana; amyl nitrite (a drug used to treat heart pain), also known as poppers; and L-dopa (a medication used in the treatment of Parkinson's disease). As you can see in the summary provided in Table 6.2, not one of these drugs possesses attributes that qualify it as a true sexual stimulant.

Researchers are currently studying one drug that may eventually be shown to have aphrodisiac qualities for at least some people. Since the 1920s there have been reports of the aphrodisiac properties of yohimbine hydrochloride, or yohimbine, a crystalline alkaloid derived from the sap of the tropical evergreen yohimbe tree, which grows in West Africa. Experiments conducted by Stanford University researchers with male rats have found that injections of yohimbine induce intense sexual arousal and performance in these animals (Clark et al., 1984). The data suggest that this drug is a true aphrodisiac, at least for rats. Several recent studies with male humans suggest that yohimbine treatment has the capacity to positively affect sexual desire or performance, at least in men with erectile disorders (Ernst & Pittler, 1998; Mann et al., 1996; Rowland et al., 1997). A recent study also demonstrated that yohimbine increases physiologically measured sexual arousal in postmenopausal women who report below-normal levels of sexual desire (Meston & Worcel, 2002).

How About You?

Have you ever experienced a sexual episode while under the influence of a substance that altered your typical patterns of sexual arousal and response? If so, what changes did you observe? Was the experience positive or negative?

In view of the widespread inclination of humans to seek out substances with aphrodisiac qualities and in light of escalating advances in the realm of sexual medicine, it seems likely that genuine aphrodisiacs will be introduced in the near future. At present, people continue to use various substances despite clear-cut evidence that they lack true aphrodisiac qualities. Why do so many people around the world swear by the effects of a little powdered rhino horn, that special meal of oysters and banana salad, or the marijuana cigarette before an

TABLE 6.2 Some Alleged Aphrodisiacs and Their Effects

Name (and Street Name)	Reputed Effect	Actual Effect
Alcohol	Enhances arousal; stimulates sexual activity.	Can reduce inhibitions to make sexual behaviors less stressful. Alcohol is actually a depressant and in quantity can impair erectile ability, arousal, and orgasm.
Amphetamines ("speed," "uppers")	Elevate mood; enhance sexual experience and abilities.	Central nervous system stimulants; amphetamines reduce inhibitions. High doses or long-term use can cause erectile disorder, delayed ejaculation, and inhibition of orgasm in both sexes and can reduce vaginal lubrication in women.
Amyl nitrite ("snappers," "poppers")	Intensifies orgasms and arousal.	Dilates arteries to brain and also to genital area; produces time distortion and warmth in pelvic area. Can decrease sexual arousal, delay orgasm, and inhibit or block erection.
Barbiturates ("barbs," "downers")	Enhance arousal; stimulate sexual activity.	Reduce inhibitions in similar fashion to alcohol and may decrease sexual desire, impair erection, and inhibit ejaculation.
Cantharides ("Spanish fly")	Stimulates genital area, causing person to desire coitus.	Not effective as a sexual stimulant. Cantharides acts as a powerful irritant that can cause inflammation to the lining of the bladder and urethra.
Cocaine ("coke")	Increases frequency and intensity of orgasm; heightens arousal.	Central nervous system stimulant; cocaine loosens inhibitions and enhances sense of well-being; may impair ability to enjoy sex, inhibit erection, or cause spontaneous or delayed ejaculation.
LSD and other psychedelic drugs (including mescaline, psilocybin)	Enhance sexual response.	No direct physiological enhancement of sexual response. Can produce altered perception of sexual activity; frequently associated with unsatisfactory erotic experiences.
L-dopa	Sexually rejuvenates older males.	No documented benefits to sexual ability. L-dopa occasionally produces a painful condition known as priapism (constant, unwanted erection).
Marijuana	Elevates mood and arousal; stimulates sexual activity.	Enhances mood and reduces inhibitions in a way similar to alcohol. Can inhibit sexual response and may distort the time sense, with the resulting illusion of prolonged arousal and orgasm.
Yohimbine	Induces sexual arousal and enhances sexual performance.	Appears to have genuine aphrodisiac effect on rats. Recent evidence suggests it may enhance sexual desire or performance in some humans.

SOURCES: Crenshaw (1996), Crenshaw & Goldberg (1996), Eisner et al. (1990), Finger et al. (1997), Rosen & Ashton (1993), Rowland et al. (1997), and Yates & Wolman (1991).

? Critical Thinking Question

Assume that research eventually reveals that yohimbine or some other substance has genuine aphrodisiac qualities. What possible benefits might be associated with its use? What possible abuses might arise? Would you consider using an aphrodisiac? If so, under what conditions?

evening's dalliance? The answer lies in faith and suggestion; these are the ingredients frequently present when aphrodisiac claims are made. If a person believes that something will improve his or her sex life, this faith is often translated into the subjective enhancement of sexual pleasure. From this perspective, literally anything has the potential of serving as a sexual stimulant. Consistent with this perspective is Theresa Crenshaw's (1996) cogent observation that "love, however you define it, seems to be the best aphrodisiac of all" (p. 89).

Anaphrodisiacs

Several drugs are known to inhibit sexual behavior. Substances that have this effect are called **anaphrodisiacs** (an-a-fruh-DEE-zee-aks). Common drugs with anaphrodisiac potential include previously discussed antiandrogens, opiates, tranquilizers, antihypertensives (blood pressure medicine), antidepressants, antipsychotics, nicotine, birth control pills, sedatives, ulcer drugs, appetite suppressants, steroids, anticonvulsants used for treating epilepsy, over-the-counter allergy medicines that cause drowsiness, and drugs for treating cancer, heart disease, fluid retention, and fungus infections (Crenshaw, 1996; Crenshaw & Goldberg, 1996; Finger et al., 1997).

A great deal of evidence indicates that regular use of opiates, such as heroin, morphine, and methadone, often produces a significant—and sometimes dramatic—decrease in sexual interest and activity in both sexes (Ackerman et al., 1994; Finger et al., 1997). Serious impairment of sexual functioning associated with opiate use can include erectile problems and inhibited ejaculation in males and reduced capacity to experience orgasm in females.

Tranquilizers, used widely in the treatment of a variety of emotional disorders, have been shown sometimes to reduce sexual motivation, impair erection, and delay or inhibit orgasm in both sexes (Crenshaw & Goldberg, 1996; Olivera, 1994).

Many antihypertensives, drugs used for treating high blood pressure, have been experimentally demonstrated to seriously inhibit erection and ejaculation, reduce the intensity of orgasm in male subjects, and reduce sexual interest in both sexes (Finger et al., 1997; Prisant et al., 1994).

Another class of commonly prescribed psychiatric medications, antidepressants, almost without exception cause adverse changes in sexual response. These changes include decreased desire in both sexes, erectile disorder in men, and delayed or absent orgasmic response in both sexes (Gregorian et al., 2002; Michelson et al., 2002; Wilson, 2003).

Antipsychotic drugs are also likely to disrupt sexual response. Potential adverse reactions include erectile disorder and delay of ejaculation in men and orgasm difficulties and reduced sexual desire in both sexes (Finger et al., 1997).

Many people are surprised to hear that birth control pills are also commonly associated with reduced sexual desire. A recent study of the effects of four different oral contraceptives on various sex hormones found that all four produced a marked reduction in the blood levels of free testosterone (Wiegratz et al., 2003). As we learned earlier, free testosterone influences both female and male libido. Most oral contraceptives contain the hormone progesterone or a synthetic version of progesterone. (*Progestin* is a term used to describe a large group of synthetic drugs that have a progesterone-like effect.) Progesterone is so potent in inhibiting desire that injections of the progesterone compound Depo-Provera (see earlier discussion) are sometimes used to "chemically castrate" sex offenders (Crenshaw & Goldberg, 1996).

Perhaps the most widely used and least recognized anaphrodisiac is nicotine. There is evidence that smoking can significantly retard sexual motivation and function by constricting the blood vessels (thereby retarding vasocongestive response of the body to sexual stimulation) and by reducing testosterone levels in the blood (Hirschkowitz et al., 1992; Mannino et al., 1994; Rosen, 1991).

Anaphrodisiac A substance that inhibits sexual desire and behavior.

▶ Sexual Response

Human sexual response is a highly individual physical, emotional, and mental process. Nevertheless, there are a number of common physiological changes that allow us to outline some general patterns of the sexual response cycle. Masters and Johnson (1966) and Helen Singer Kaplan (1979), a noted sex therapist and author, have described these patterns. We briefly outline Kaplan's ideas before turning to a detailed analysis of Masters and Johnson's work.

✳Kaplan's Three-Stage Model

Kaplan's model of sexual response, an outgrowth of her extensive experience as a sex therapist, contains three stages: *desire, excitement,* and *orgasm* (see Figure 6.2). Kaplan suggested that sexual difficulties tend to fall into one of these three categories and that it is possible for a person to have difficulty in one while continuing to function normally in the other two.

One of the most distinctive features of Kaplan's model is that it includes desire as a distinct stage of the sexual response cycle. Many other writers, including Masters and Johnson,

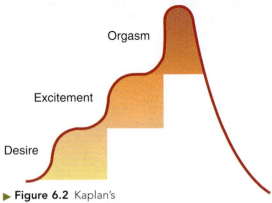

▶ **Figure 6.2** Kaplan's three-stage model of the sexual response cycle. This model is distinguished by its identification of desire as a prelude to sexual response.

SOURCE: Kaplan (1979).

do not discuss aspects of sexual response that are separate from genital changes. Kaplan's description of desire as a prelude to physical sexual response stands as a welcome addition to the literature. Kaplan's model was initially widely embraced as one that rectified a perceived deficiency in the Masters and Johnson model. However, it is now realized that simply adding a desire phase does not necessarily provide a complete model of human sexual arousal and response. One problem with assuming that desire belongs in such a model is that perhaps as much as 30% of sexually experienced, orgasmic women rarely or never experience spontaneous sexual desire (Levin, 2002). Fewer men appear to be included in this category. For example, in the NHSLS, 33% of women reported being uninterested in sex compared to 16.5% of men (Laumann et al., 1994).

It is clear, then, that not all sexual expression is preceded by desire. For example, a couple might agree to engage in sexual activity even though they are not feeling sexually inclined at the time. Frequently, they may find that their bodies begin to respond sexually to the ensuing activity, despite their lack of initial desire.

✴Masters and Johnson's Four-Phase Model

Masters and Johnson distinguish four phases in the sexual response patterns of both men and women: *excitement, plateau, orgasm,* and *resolution.* In addition, they include a *refractory period* (a recovery stage in which there is a temporary inability to reach orgasm) in the male resolution phase. Figures 6.3 and 6.4 illustrate these four phases of sexual response in women and men. These charts provide basic maps of common patterns, but a few cautions are in order.

First, the simplified nature of these diagrams can easily obscure the richness of individual variation that can and does occur. Masters and Johnson were charting only the physiological responses to sexual stimulation. Biological reactions might follow a relatively predictable course, but the variability in individual responses to sexual arousal is considerable. These variations are suggested in the several individual reports of arousal, orgasm, and resolution included later in this chapter.

The second caution has to do with a too literal interpretation of the so-called plateau stage of sexual response. In the behavioral sciences the term *plateau* is typically used to describe a leveling-off period during which no observable changes in behavior can be detected. For example, it might refer to a flat spot in a learning curve where no new behaviors occur for a certain period of time. The plateau stage has been diagrammed in just this manner in the male chart (Figure 6.4) and in pattern A of the female chart (Figure 6.3).

▶ **Figure 6.3** Female sexual response cycle. Masters and Johnson identified three basic patterns in female sexual response. Pattern A most closely resembles the male pattern, except that a woman can have one or more orgasms without dropping below the plateau level of sexual arousal. Variations of this response include an extended plateau with no orgasm (pattern B) and a rapid rise to orgasm with no definitive plateau and a quick resolution (pattern C).

SOURCE: Masters & Johnson (1966).

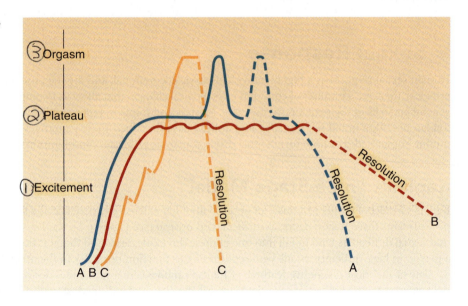

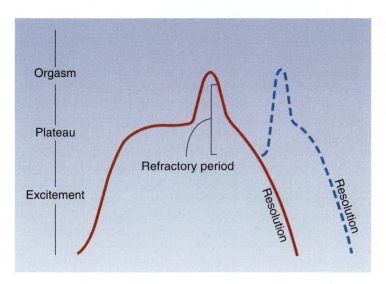

▶ **Figure 6.4** Male sexual response cycle. Only one male response pattern was identified by Masters and Johnson. However, men do report considerable variation in their response pattern. Note the refractory period; males do not have a second orgasm immediately after the first.

SOURCE: Masters & Johnson (1966).

Actually, the plateau level of sexual arousal involves a powerful surge of sexual tensions that are definitely measurable (e.g., as increased heart and breathing rates). Thus it is far from an unchanging state.

Our third caution is a warning against a tendency to use such charts as personal checklists. Although we encourage self-references throughout this book, this is one area where a too enthusiastic self-check can lead to potential problems in the form of "spectatoring." The following quote illustrates this point:

After learning about the four stages of sexual response in class, I found myself "standing back" and watching my own reactions, wondering if I had passed from excitement into plateau. Also, I began to monitor the responses of my partner, looking for the telltale signs that would tell me at what point he was. Suddenly I found myself doing clinical observations rather than allowing myself to fully experience the good feelings. It was a real put-off, and I had to force myself to stop being the observer and become more of a participant. (Authors' files)

The descriptions in the following pages should not be viewed as standards for analyzing or intellectualizing your feelings or for evaluating how "normal" your reactions are. We stress that these patterns have many natural variations. Consequently, the response profiles we outline are merely general patterns that do vary from person to person and within any person across situations. Perhaps familiarity with these generalized descriptions will help to illuminate some of the complexity of your own responses.

In much of the discussion that follows we will be looking at the physiological reactions and subjective reports of women and men. Before we become too involved in the several specific processes of sexual response, it is important to note that the basic responses of men and women are quite similar—a point Masters and Johnson stressed in their research:

Certainly there are reactions to sexual stimulation that are confined by normal anatomic variation to a single sex. There also are differences in established reactive patterns to sexual stimuli—for example, duration and intensity of response—that usually are sex-linked in character. However, parallels in reactive potential between the two sexes must be underlined. Similarities rather than differences of response have been emphasized by this investigation. (Masters & Johnson, 1966, p. 273)

Two fundamental physiological responses to effective sexual stimulation occur in both women and men. These are *vasocongestion* and *myotonia*. These two basic reactions are the primary underlying sources for almost all biological responses that take place during sexual arousal.

Vasocongestion is the engorgement with blood of body tissues that respond to sexual excitation. Usually the blood flow into organs and tissues through the arteries is balanced by an equal outflow through the veins. During sexual arousal, however, the arteries dilate, increasing the inflow beyond the capacity of the veins to carry blood away. This results in

Vasocongestion The engorgement of blood vessels in particular body parts in response to sexual arousal.

widespread vasocongestion in both superficial and deep tissues. The visible congested areas might feel warm and appear swollen and red as a result of increased blood content. The most obvious manifestations of this vasocongestive response are the erection of the penis in men and lubrication of the vagina in women. In addition, other body areas can become engorged—the labia, testes, clitoris, nipples, and even the earlobes.

As described in Chapter 2, Masters and Johnson and other researchers have used devices such as the vaginal photoplethysmograph and the penile strain gauge to electronically measure vasocongestion during sexual arousal. Recently, investigators have begun to explore the benefits of using magnetic resonance imaging (MRI) technology to study sexual response. This new approach to assessing the physiology of sexual arousal is described in the "Spotlight on Research" box.

The second basic physiological response is **myotonia** (my-uh-TOH-nee-uh), the increased muscle tension that occurs throughout the body during sexual arousal. Myotonia is evident in both voluntary flexing and involuntary contractions. Its most dramatic manifestations are facial grimaces, spasmodic contractions of the hands and feet, and the muscular spasms that occur during orgasm.

The phases of the response cycle follow the same general patterns regardless of the method of stimulation. Masturbation, manual stimulation by one's partner, oral pleasuring, penile–vaginal intercourse, dreaming, fantasy, and, in some women, breast stimulation can all result in completion of the response cycle. Often the intensity and rapidity of response vary according to the kind of stimulation.

In the next several pages we outline the major physiological reactions to sexual stimulation that occur during each of the four phases of the sexual response cycle. Subjective reports of several individuals are included. For each stage we list reactions common to both sexes and those unique to just one. Table 6.3 summarizes the major changes that occur in women and men during the four phases of the sexual response cycle. Note the strong similarities in the sexual response patterns of men and women. We discuss some important differences in greater detail at the conclusion of this chapter.

Excitement Phase

The first phase of the sexual response cycle, the **excitement phase,** is characterized by a number of responses common to men and women, including muscle tension and some increase in the heart rate and blood pressure. In both sexes several areas of the sexual anatomy become engorged. For example, the clitoris, labia minora, vagina, nipples, penis, and testes all increase in size, and most of them deepen in color. Some responses, such as the appearance of a **sex flush** (a pink or red rash on the chest or breasts), occur in both sexes but are more common in women. Still other responses, specific to just one sex, are illustrated in Figures 6.5–6.8, which show changes in the sexual anatomy of women and men throughout the phases of the cycle.

The excitement phase varies in duration from less than a minute to several hours. Both males and females show considerable variation in the degree of their arousal during this phase. For example, a man's penis might vary from flaccid to semierect to fully erect. Similarly, vaginal lubrication in women may vary from minimal to copious.

Although the physiological characteristics outlined in Figures 6.5–6.8 represent general patterns, different people experience these changes in differing ways. The following two reports give some indication of the subjective variations in how women describe their own feelings during sexual arousal:

Sexual arousal for me is something I look forward to when I realize my husband and I will have sex. His touching, kissing, and loving me in this way brings me to a height of excitement that is incredible. At first I felt selfish about him giving me so much satisfaction through stimulation, but he enjoys it so much, it's a wonderful time. Often we don't have intercourse because we are caught up in the "foreplay" of lovemaking. (Authors' files)

When I am aroused, I get warm all over, and I like a lot of holding and massaging of other areas of my body besides my genitals. After time passes with that particular stimulation, I prefer more direct manual stroking if I want orgasm. (Authors' files)

Myotonia Muscle tension.

Excitement phase Masters and Johnson's term for the first phase of the sexual response cycle, in which engorgement of the sexual organs and increases in muscle tension, heart rate, and blood pressure occur.

Sex flush A pink or red rash that can appear on the chest or breasts during sexual arousal.

Monitoring Sexual Arousal in Women with Magnetic Resonance Imaging

To date, most of the research on human sexual function and dysfunction has focused on men. Numerous scientific investigations have provided a wealth of knowledge about the physiology and pathophysiology of erectile function and dysfunction. This information has led to major advances in diagnostic tools and treatment strategies for male sexual dysfunction (Bechara et al., 2003), especially the use of pharmaceutical agents to treat sexual problems (Boynton, 2003). For example, expanded knowledge of male genital vascular responses to sexual arousal have resulted in the development of Viagra, Levitra, and Cialis, medications used to treat erectile problems (see Chapter 16). In sharp contrast to the abundant data on the physiology of male sexual response, evidence pertaining to the physiology and pathophysiology of female genital vascular responses to sexual stimulation is quite limited, despite the higher prevalence of female sexual dysfunction (Bechara et al., 2003).

This marked deficit in research findings on female sexual arousal is due in large part to the lack of a simple, objective, quantitative, and reproducible method for measuring the sexual arousal response in women (Maravilla et al., 2003). Until recently, studies measuring sexual arousal in women have been largely limited to the use of vaginal photoplethysmography, which, as described in Chapter 2, uses a device designed to measure increased vaginal blood volume during sexual arousal. Unfortunately, this technique is somewhat limited because of its invasive nature (i.e., insertion of the photoplethysmograph device into the vagina) and because it provides only an approximate measure of vaginal blood flow that is subject to error caused by subject movement. Furthermore, vaginal photoplethysmography provides no information about anatomical changes, such as increased size of the clitoral glans resulting from blood engorgement (Heiman, 1998; Laan & Everaerd, 1998).

The possibility of overcoming these limitations has recently emerged with the development of a new method for monitoring and measuring sexual arousal in women: dynamic magnetic resonance imaging of the female genitalia. The benefits of this exciting new technology have recently been demonstrated in a number of studies (Deliganis et al., 2000; Grist et al., 1997; Maravilla et al., 2000, 2003). **Magnetic resonance imaging (MRI)** is a research and diagnostic device that uses magnetic fields and radio-wave pulses to construct extremely detailed three-dimensional images of the brain and other areas of the body. In addition to providing images of the soft tissue of the brain and blood flow in various brain regions, MRI technology can also provide images of the soft tissue of the genitals. These images can be used to map and monitor changes in blood engorgement of the genital tissues that occur during sexual arousal. Because blood engorgement of the genitalia (vasocongestion) is a key component of arousal in both sexes, researchers reasoned that measuring genital vascular responses in women with noninvasive MRI technology would add immeasurably to the understanding of female sexual response.

An excellent recent example of dynamic MRI of the sexual arousal response in women is provided by research conducted by University of Washington researcher Kenneth Maravilla and his colleagues (2003). These investigators recruited a number of healthy, sexually functional women to participate in a series of three studies to determine the feasibility of using MRI technology to measure female sexual response. In each of the studies changes in the genital tissues of the participants were monitored using MRI while the women viewed video containing erotic content sandwiched in between beginning and ending segments of nonerotic, neutral images (documentary material). Study subjects also rated their subjective levels of sexual arousal by completing questionnaires related to overall feelings of

sexual arousal during the course of the study.

Each of the three investigations yielded similar results. All subjects exposed to the erotic video material reported sexual arousal on the subjective questionnaires that was closely associated with increased clitoral blood volume and size. Maravilla and his colleagues found that the magnetic resonance images recorded over a 45-minute period of video viewing provided excellent visualization of the genital anatomic structures of the participants, including major blood vessels involved in vasocongestion. In addition, the images allowed precise calculation of changes in clitoral size and in blood volume of the genital tissues during sexual arousal. Among the findings was an increase in both the degree of blood engorgement and overall size of the clitoris during the erotic video segment compared to the neutral segment. On average, clitoral size more than doubled from the unaroused to the aroused state for all subjects.

The results of these investigations and of similar studies demonstrate that dynamic MRI is an excellent noninvasive method for observing and quantitatively measuring the sexual arousal response in women. These findings strongly indicate that future applications of this simple, objective, and quantifiable technology will greatly benefit the process of evaluating and treating female sexual arousal disorders. In this vein, Maravilla and colleagues concluded that "this technique holds great promise for improving our understanding of the physiology of the female sexual response and may serve as a useful tool for testing new therapeutic methods in the future" (Maravilla et al., 2003, p. 76). It now seems likely that the development of new research techniques, such as dynamic MRI, together with the growing interest of pharmaceutical companies in female sexual functioning (Shah, 2003) will eventually yield drugs and other therapeutic methods to treat female sexual dysfunction.

	TABLE 6.3 Major Physiological Changes During Each of the Four Phases of the Sexual Response Cycle		
Phase	**Reactions Common to Both Sexes**	**Female Responses**	**Male Responses**
Excitement	• Increase in myotonia, heart rate, and blood pressure. • Sex flush and nipple erections occur (more common in females).	• Clitoris swells. • Labia majora separate away from vaginal opening. • Labia minora swell and darken in color. • Lubrication begins. • Uterus elevates. • Breasts enlarge.	• Penis becomes erect. • Testes elevate and engorge. • Scrotal skin thickens and tenses.
Plateau	• Myotonia becomes pronounced, and involuntary muscular contractions may occur in hands and feet. • Heart rate, blood pressure, and breathing increase.	• Orgasmic platform forms. • Clitoris withdraws under its hood. • Uterus becomes fully elevated. • Areola becomes more swollen.	• Engorgement and elevation of testes becomes more pronounced. • Cowper's gland secretions may occur.
Orgasm	• Involuntary muscle spasms throughout body. • Blood pressure, breathing, and heart rates at maximum levels. • Involuntary contractions of rectal sphincter.	• Orgasmic platform contracts rhythmically 3 to 15 times. • Uterine contractions occur. • Clitoris remains retracted under its hood. • No further changes in breasts or nipples.	• During emission phase, internal sex structures undergo contractions, causing pooling of seminal fluid in urethral bulb. • During expulsion phase, semen expelled by contractions of muscles around base of penis.
Resolution	• Myotonia subsides, and heart rate, blood pressure, and breathing rates return to normal immediately after orgasm. • Sex flush disappears rapidly. • Nipple erection subsides slowly.	• Clitoris descends and engorgement slowly subsides. • Labia return to unaroused size. • Uterus descends to normal position. • Lack of orgasm after period of high arousal may dramatically slow resolution.	• Erection is lost over a period of a few minutes. • Testes descend and return to their normal size. Scrotum resumes wrinkled appearance. • Resolution quite rapid in most men.

Two men provide their descriptions of sexual arousal in the following accounts:

When I am sexually aroused, my whole body feels energized. Sometimes my mouth gets dry, and I may feel a little light-headed. I want to have all of my body touched and stroked, not just my genitals. I particularly like the sensation of feeling that orgasm is just around the corner, waiting and tantalizing me to begin the final journey. Sometimes a quick rush to climax is nice, but usually I prefer making the arousal period last as long as I can stand it, until my penis feels like it is dying for the final strokes of ecstasy. (Authors' files)

When aroused, I feel very excited, and I fantasize a lot. Then all of a sudden, a warm feeling comes over me, and it feels like a thousand pleasure pins are being stuck into my loins all at the same time. (Authors' files)

Plateau Phase

Plateau phase Masters and Johnson's term for the second phase of the sexual response cycle, in which muscle tension, heart rate, blood pressure, and vasocongestion increase.

During the **plateau phase** sexual tension continues to mount until it reaches the peak that leads to orgasm. It is difficult to define clearly the point at which a sexually responding individual makes the transition to this phase. Unlike the excitement phase, the plateau phase has no clear external sign, such as lubrication or erection, to mark its onset. Instead, several of these signs become more pronounced as they accelerate toward the peaks reached in the next phase. Both heart rate and blood pressure continue to rise; breathing grows faster; sex flushes and coloration of the genitals become more noticeable. Muscle tension continues to build up, and the face, neck, hands, and feet may undergo involuntary contractions and spasms in both the plateau and orgasm phases. Among women the plateau phase is also distinguished by development of the *orgasmic platform,* a term used by Masters and Johnson to describe the markedly increased engorgement of the outer third of the vagina.

(a) Excitement phase

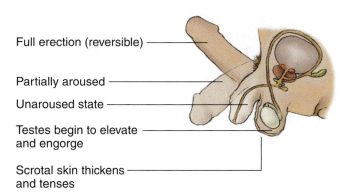

Full erection (reversible)

Partially aroused

Unaroused state

Testes begin to elevate and engorge

Scrotal skin thickens and tenses

(b) Plateau phase

Cowper's gland secretion

Corona may become further engorged

Cowper's gland becomes active

Testes become completely engorged and elevated

Scrotum maintains its thickened and tensed state

Loss of erection unlikely

(c) Emission phase of orgasm

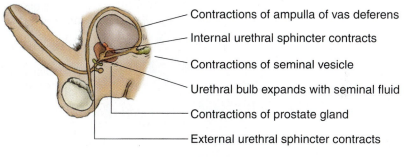

Contractions of ampulla of vas deferens

Internal urethral sphincter contracts

Contractions of seminal vesicle

Urethral bulb expands with seminal fluid

Contractions of prostate gland

External urethral sphincter contracts

(d) Expulsion phase of orgasm

Contractions of penile urethra

Internal urethral sphincter remains contracted

External urethral sphincter relaxes

Contractions of muscles around base of penis

Contractions of rectal sphincter

(e) Resolution phase

Erection loss begins

Unstimulated state (erection loss completed)

Testes descend and return to unstimulated size

Scrotum thins and resumes wrinkled appearance

▶ **Figure 6.5** Major changes in external and internal male sexual anatomy during the sexual response cycle.

The plateau phase is often brief, typically lasting a few seconds to several minutes. However, many people find that prolonging sexual tensions at this high level produces greater arousal and ultimately more intense orgasms. This is reported in the following subjective accounts:

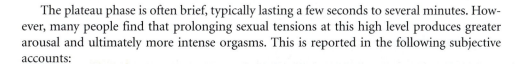

When I get up there, almost on the verge of coming, I try to hang in as long as possible. If my partner cooperates, stopping or slowing when necessary, I can stay right on the edge for several minutes, sometimes even longer. I know that all it would take is one more stroke and I'm over the top. Sometimes my whole body gets to shaking and quivering, and I can feel incredible sensations shooting through me like electric charges. The longer I can make this supercharged period last, the better the orgasm. (Authors' files)

When I masturbate, I like to take myself almost to the point of climaxing and then back off. I can tell when orgasm is about to happen because my vagina tightens up around the opening, and sometimes I can feel the muscles contract. I love the sensations of balancing myself on the brink, part of me wanting to come and the other part holding out for more. The longer I maintain this delicate balance, the more shattering the climax. Sometimes the pleasure is almost beyond bearing. (Authors' files)

(a) Unaroused state

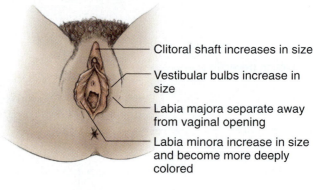

Clitoral hood
Clitoral glans
Urethral opening
Labia minora
Labia majora
Anus

(b) Excitement phase

Clitoral shaft increases in size

Vestibular bulbs increase in size

Labia majora separate away from vaginal opening

Labia minora increase in size and become more deeply colored

(c) Plateau

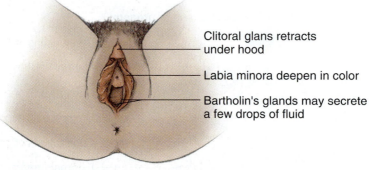

Clitoral glans retracts under hood

Labia minora deepen in color

Bartholin's glands may secrete a few drops of fluid

(d) Orgasm

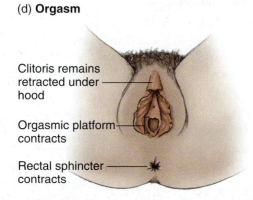

Clitoris remains retracted under hood

Orgasmic platform contracts

Rectal sphincter contracts

(e) Resolution phase

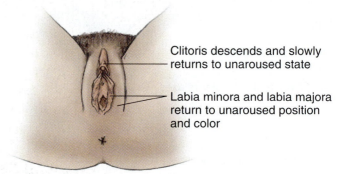

Clitoris descends and slowly returns to unaroused state

Labia minora and labia majora return to unaroused position and color

▶ **Figure 6.6** Major changes in the external female genitals during the sexual response cycle.

Orgasm A series of muscular contractions of the pelvic floor muscles occurring at the peak of sexual arousal.

? Critical Thinking Question

Do you believe that men and women differ in the importance they attach to experiencing orgasm during sexual sharing? Why or why not?

Orgasm Phase

As effective stimulation continues, many people move from plateau to **orgasm.** This is particularly true for men, who almost always experience orgasm after reaching the plateau level. (However, as described in Chapter 5, orgasm is not always accompanied by ejaculation.) When ejaculation occurs, it takes place in two phases. During the first or *emission phase,* the seminal fluid is gathered in the urethral bulb, a process accompanied by a subjective sense that orgasm is inevitable. In the second or *expulsion phase,* semen is expelled out of the penis by muscular contractions.

In contrast to men, women sometimes obtain plateau levels of arousal without the release of sexual climax. This is often the case during penile–vaginal intercourse when the man reaches orgasm first or when effective manual or oral stimulation is replaced with penetration as the female approaches orgasm.

Orgasm is the shortest phase of the sexual response cycle, typically lasting only a few seconds. Female orgasms often last slightly longer than male orgasms. Figures 6.5–6.8 summarize the primary physiological responses during orgasm.

(a) Unaroused state

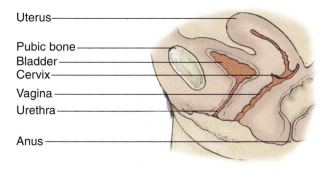

Uterus

Pubic bone
Bladder
Cervix
Vagina
Urethra

Anus

(b) Excitement phase

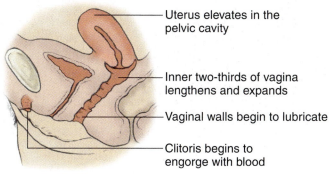

Uterus elevates in the pelvic cavity

Inner two-thirds of vagina lengthens and expands

Vaginal walls begin to lubricate

Clitoris begins to engorge with blood

(c) Plateau phase

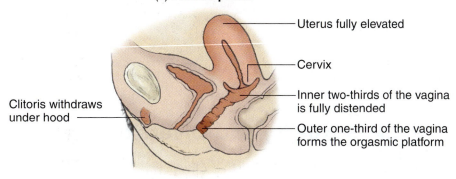

Uterus fully elevated

Cervix

Inner two-thirds of the vagina is fully distended

Outer one-third of the vagina forms the orgasmic platform

Clitoris withdraws under hood

(d) Orgasm

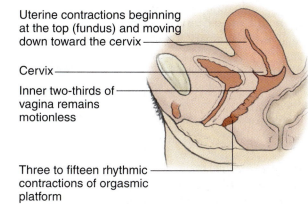

Uterine contractions beginning at the top (fundus) and moving down toward the cervix

Cervix

Inner two-thirds of vagina remains motionless

Three to fifteen rhythmic contractions of orgasmic platform

(e) Resolution phase

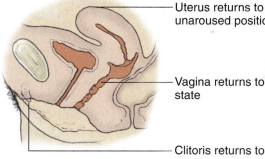

Uterus returns to unaroused position

Vagina returns to unaroused state

Clitoris returns to unaroused position

▶ **Figure 6.7** Major changes in the internal female genitals during the sexual response cycle.

For both sexes the experience of orgasm can be an intense mixture of highly pleasurable sensations, but whether that experience differs from male to female has been the subject of considerable debate. This question was evaluated in two separate experimental analyses of orgasm descriptions provided by college students (Wiest, 1977; Wiest et al., 1995). When compared using a standard psychological rating scale, women's and men's subjective descriptions of orgasm were indistinguishable in both investigations. Similar results were obtained in an earlier study, in which a group of 70 expert judges were unable to distinguish reliably between the written orgasm reports of men and women (Proctor et al., 1974).

Beyond the question of sex differences in orgasmic experiences, it is clear that there is great individual variation in how people, both men and women, describe orgasms. The following "Sexuality and Diversity" discussion provides some indication of the varied ways people experience and describe their orgasmic experiences.

(a) Excitement phase **(b) Plateau and orgasm phase** **(c) Resolution phase**

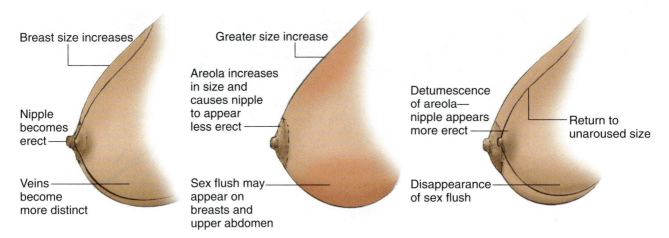

Breast size increases

Greater size increase

Nipple becomes erect

Areola increases in size and causes nipple to appear less erect

Detumescence of areola— nipple appears more erect

Return to unaroused size

Veins become more distinct

Sex flush may appear on breasts and upper abdomen

Disappearance of sex flush

▶ **Figure 6.8**
Changes in the breasts during the sexual response cycle.

▶▶ Sexuality and Diversity

Subjective Descriptions of Orgasm

The following accounts, selected from our files, illustrate the diversity of orgasmic descriptions. The first account is by a woman and the second by a man. The final three descriptions—labeled Reports A, B, and C—contain no specific references that identify the sex of the describer. Perhaps you would like to try to determine whether they were reported by a man or a woman. The answers follow the summary at the end of the chapter.

Female: *When I'm about to reach orgasm, my face feels very hot. I close my eyes and open my mouth. It centers in my clitoris, and it feels like electric wires igniting from there and radiating up my torso and down my legs to my feet. I sometimes feel like I need to urinate. My vagina contracts anywhere from 5 to 12 times. My vulva area feels heavy and swollen. There isn't another feeling like it—it's fantastic!*

Male: *Orgasm for me draws all my energy in toward a core in my body. Then, all of a sudden, there is a release of this energy out through my penis. My body becomes warm and numb before orgasm; after, it gradually relaxes and I feel extremely serene.*

Report A: *It's like an Almond Joy, "indescribably delicious." The feeling runs from the top of my head to the tips of my toes as I feel a powerful surge of pleasure. It raises me beyond my physical self into another level of consciousness, and yet the feeling seems purely physical. What a paradox! It strokes all over, inside and out. I love it simply because it's mine and mine alone.*

Report B: *An orgasm to me is like heaven. All my tensions and anxieties are released. You get to the point of no return, and it's like an uncontrollable desire that makes things start happening. I think that sex and orgasm are one of the greatest phenomena that we have today. It's a great sharing experience for me.*

Report C: *Having an orgasm is like the ultimate time I have for myself. I am not excluding my partner, but it's like I can't hear anything, and all I feel is a spectacular release accompanied with more pleasure than I've ever felt doing anything else. (Authors' files)*

Although the physiology of female orgasmic response can be clearly outlined, some past and present issues about its nature need to be discussed. Misinformation about female orgasm has been prevalent in our culture. Sigmund Freud (1905), writing in the early 1900s, developed a theory of the vaginal versus the clitoral orgasm that has had a great, if misguided, impact on people's thinking about female sexual response. Freud viewed the vaginal orgasm as more mature than the clitoral orgasm and thus preferable. The physiological basis for this theory was the assumption that the clitoris is a stunted penis. This led to the conclusion that erotic sensations, arousal, and orgasm resulting from direct stimulation of the clitoris were all expressions of "masculine" rather than "feminine" sexuality—and therefore undesirable (Sherfey, 1972). During adolescence a woman was supposed to transfer her erotic center from the clitoris to the vagina. If she was not able to make this transition, psychotherapy was sometimes used to attempt to help her attain vaginal orgasms. Unfortunately, this theory led many women to believe incorrectly that they were sexually maladjusted.

Our modern knowledge of embryology has established the falseness of the theory that the clitoris is a masculine organ, as we have seen in our discussion of the genital differentiation process in Chapter 3. In one researcher's words, "to reduce clitoral eroticism to the level of psychopathology because the clitoris is an innately masculine organ . . . must now be considered a travesty of the facts" (Sherfey, 1972, p. 47). Travesty of facts or not, during Freud's time, this sexual-center transfer theory was taken so seriously that surgical removal of the clitoris was recommended for little girls who masturbated, to help them later attain "vaginal" orgasms.

Surgical clitoridectomies are no longer performed in our culture. Yet social conditioning, which can be as effective as a scalpel, continues. Freud's operational definition of female sexual health is still with us in many respects. For example, a woman's reluctance to ask her partner to stimulate her clitoris manually during coitus (or to do it herself) typifies the learned belief that she "should" experience orgasm from vaginal stimulation alone. However, cultural conditioning can work two ways. With knowledge and support a woman can change her attitude about her sexual feelings and behaviors.

Contrary to Freud's theory, the research of Masters and Johnson suggests that there is one kind of orgasm in females, physiologically speaking, regardless of the method of stimulation. The intensity of orgasms, however, often varies with the type of stimulation. Most female orgasms result from direct or indirect stimulation of the clitoris. However, as we note elsewhere, females can experience orgasm from fantasy alone, during sleep (nocturnal orgasms), or by means of stimulation of other body areas, such as the nipples or the *Grafenberg spot*.

The Grafenberg Spot A number of studies have reported that some women are capable of experiencing orgasm, and perhaps ejaculation, when an area along the anterior wall of the vagina is vigorously stimulated (Levin, 2003; Whipple & Komisaruk, 1999; Zaviacic & Whipple, 1993). This area of erotic sensitivity, briefly mentioned in Chapter 4, has been named the Grafenberg spot (or *G spot*) in honor of Ernest Grafenberg (1950), a gynecologist who first noted the erotic significance of this location in the vagina over 50 years ago. However, the presence of glandular structures in this area was noted in the medical literature over 100 years ago (Skene, 1880). It has been suggested that the Grafenberg spot is not a point that can be touched by the tip of one finger but rather is a fairly large area composed of the lower anterior wall of the vagina and the underlying urethra and surrounding glands (Skene's glands) (Heath, 1984).

The Grafenberg spot can be located by "systematic palpation of the entire anterior wall of the vagina between the posterior side of the pubic bone and the cervix. Two fingers are usually used, and it is often necessary to press deeply into the tissue to reach the spot" (Perry & Whipple, 1981, p. 29). This exploration can be conducted by a woman's partner, as shown in Figure 6.9. Some women are able to locate their Grafenberg spots through self-exploration.

During initial searching for the sometimes elusive Grafenberg spot, a woman or her partner must rely on the sensations produced by manual stimulation. When the area is located, women report a variety of initial sensations, including a slight feeling of discomfort, a brief sensation of needing to urinate, or a pleasurable feeling. After a minute or more of stroking, the sensations usually become more pleasurable, and the area may begin to swell discernibly. Continued stimulation of the area can result in an orgasm that is often quite intense. The following account describes a 19-year-old college student's orgasm, experienced as a result of Grafenberg spot stimulation.

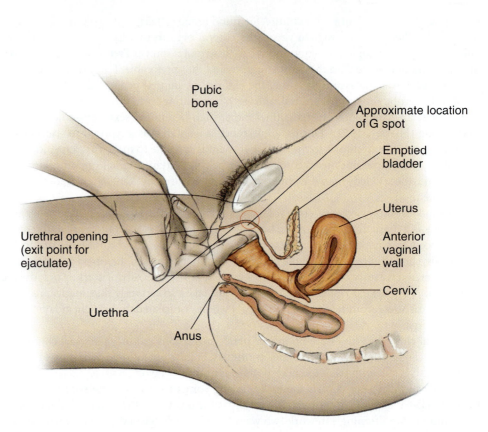

Figure 6.9 Locating the Grafenberg spot. Usually two fingers are used, and it is often necessary to press deeply into the anterior wall of the vagina to reach the spot.

After hearing about the G-spot in class I decided to try and locate it in my body. I could tell when I located it because the sensation was strange at first, like I urgently had to pee. After awhile it felt like a huge force was building inside me, and then an intense release. I was so surprised and excited. (Authors' files)

Perhaps the most amazing thing about Grafenberg spot orgasms is that they are sometimes accompanied by the ejaculation of fluid from the urethral opening (Schubach, 1996; Whipple, 2000). Research indicates that the source of this fluid may be the "female prostate," discussed in Chapter 4. The ducts from this system empty directly into the urethra. In some women Grafenberg spot orgasms result in fluid being forced through these ducts and out the urethra. In view of the homologous nature of Grafenberg spot tissue and the male prostate, we can speculate that the female ejaculate is similar to the prostatic component of male seminal fluid (Zaviacic & Whipple, 1993). This notion has been supported by research in which specimens of female ejaculate were chemically analyzed and found to contain high levels of an enzyme, prostatic acid phosphatase (PAP), characteristic of the prostatic component of semen (Addiego et al., 1981; Belzer et al., 1984). Some women report that the fluid has a mild semenlike scent. However, other research suggests that the ejaculated fluid is chemically more similar to urine than to male semen (Alzate, 1990; Goldberg et al., 1983; Schubach, 1996).

Although the existence of Grafenberg spot orgasms, sometimes accompanied by ejaculation, has been reported with some degree of reliability, our understanding of this phenomenon is far from complete. For example, how common are these responses? (A survey of 2,350 U.S. and Canadian professional women revealed that 40% of the respondents reported sometimes experiencing a fluid-release ejaculation at the moment of orgasm [Darling et al., 1990].) Is the female Grafenberg area a genuine homologue of the male prostate? Clearly, considerably more research is necessary before conclusive answers can be obtained for these and other questions. In the meantime, we encourage women and their partners who want to explore this intriguing information in relation to their own sexual response and activities to do so. However, it may be self-defeating to treat Grafenberg spot orgasm as a new sexual achievement to be relentlessly pursued. It would be unfortunate if the reexamination of some of our beliefs about female orgasm were to lead to a reemergence of attributing emotional or physiological superiority to any one orgasmic pattern.

Resolution Phase

During the final phase of the sexual response cycle, **resolution,** the sexual systems return to their nonexcited state. If no additional stimulation occurs, the resolution begins immediately after orgasm. Some of the changes back to a nonexcited state take place rapidly, whereas others occur more slowly. Figures 6.5–6.8 summarize the major physiological changes associated with resolution.

The self-reports that follow provide some indication of how people vary in their feelings after orgasm. The first two are by females, the third by a male.

After a satisfying experience with my husband, I want to be held, as if to finalize and complete our union. Sometimes I like to talk and sometimes I just like to be able to touch him and be touched by his whole body. (Authors' files)

After orgasm I feel very relaxed. My moods do vary—sometimes I'm ready to start all over; other times I can jump up and really get busy; and at other times I just want to sleep. (Authors' files)

After orgasm I feel relaxed and usually very content. Sometimes I feel like sleeping, and other times I feel like I want to touch my partner if she is willing. I like to hold her and just be there. (Authors' files)

These subjective reports sound similar. But there is one significant difference in the responses of women and men during this phase—their physiological readiness for further sexual stimulation. After orgasm the male typically enters a **refractory period**—a time when no amount of additional stimulation will result in orgasm. The length of this period ranges from minutes to days, depending on a variety of factors, such as age, frequency of previous sexual activity, and the degree of the man's emotional closeness to and sexual desire for his partner. In contrast to men, women generally experience no comparable refractory period. They are physiologically capable of returning to another orgasmic peak from anywhere in the resolution phase. However, a woman may or may not want to do so. In the last two sections of this chapter we discuss the effect of aging on sexual arousal and response and then consider some differences between men's and women's patterns of sexual response.

Resolution phase The fourth phase of the sexual response cycle, as outlined by Masters and Johnson, in which the sexual systems return to their nonexcited state.

Refractory period The period of time following orgasm in the male during which he cannot experience another orgasm.

▶ Aging and the Sexual Response Cycle

As people grow older, they will notice changes in sexual arousal and response patterns. In this section we briefly summarize some of the more common variations that occur in the sexual response cycles of women and men.

The Sexual Response Cycle of Older Women

In general, all phases of the response cycle continue to occur for older women but with somewhat decreased intensity (Masters & Johnson, 1966; Segraves & Segraves, 1995).

Excitement Phase

The first physiological response to sexual arousal, vaginal lubrication, typically begins more slowly in an older woman. Instead of 10 to 30 seconds, it may take several minutes or longer before vaginal lubrication is observed. In most cases the amount of lubrication is reduced (DeLamater & Friedrich, 2002; Kingsberg, 2002). Research using the vaginal photoplethysmograph found that postmenopausal women's vaginal blood-volume increase during sexual arousal is smaller than in premenopausal women. However, women in both groups reported similar levels of sexual activity and enjoyment, indicating that the somewhat lowered vasocongestion response is within the range necessary for normal function (Morrell et al., 1984). Another study found that older women who engage in sexual relations once or twice weekly lubricate more readily than women who experience infrequent sexual relations (Brackett et al., 1994).

The decrease in circulating estrogen also changes urethral and vaginal tissues. Urethral tissue can lose tone and become dry, often leading to urinary tract infections and urinary incontinence when sneezing, coughing, exercising, or engaging in sexual activity (Capewell et al., 1992). Vaginal mucosa become thinner and change to a lighter pinkish color. Both the length and the width of the vagina decrease, and these changes contribute to the diminished expansive ability of the inner vagina during sexual arousal.

When there is considerably diminished lubrication and vaginal expansion during sexual response, uncomfortable or painful intercourse can result (Mansfield et al., 1995). In addition, some women report decreased sexual desire and sensitivity of the clitoris, both of which interfere with sexual excitement. Hormone therapy, estrogen creams applied to the vagina, and vaginal lubricants can often help these symptoms (Kingsberg, 2002). ■

Plateau Phase

During the plateau phase, the vaginal orgasmic platform develops, and the uterus elevates. In a postmenopausal woman these changes occur to a somewhat lesser degree than before menopause (Masters & Johnson, 1966).

Orgasm Phase

Contractions of the orgasmic platform and the uterus continue to occur at orgasm, although the number of these contractions is typically reduced in older women. In some postmenopausal women uterine contractions that take place at orgasm can be painful. Several women in Masters and Johnson's study continued to experience multiple orgasmic response. However, one-third of the women in another study reported significantly reduced capacity or inability to experience orgasm (Sarrel, 1988).

Orgasm appears to be an important aspect of sexual activity to older women. One survey found that 69% of women, age 60 to 91, listed "orgasm" first in response to the question "What do you consider a good sexual experience?" (Starr & Weiner, 1981). Only 17% of the women answered "intercourse" to this same question. In addition, "orgasm" was the most frequent response to the question "What in the sex act is most important to you?" Sixty-five percent of the women reported that their frequency of orgasm was the same as when they were younger.

Resolution Phase

The resolution phase typically occurs more rapidly in postmenopausal women. Labia color change, vaginal expansion, orgasmic platform formation, and clitoral retraction all disappear soon after orgasm. This is most likely due to the overall reduced amount of pelvic vasocongestion during arousal.

In summary, the effects of aging on female sexuality vary considerably. Most women experience minor changes, and some others find their sexual interest, excitement, and orgasm seriously affected. An active sex life helps maintain vaginal health, and a functional and interested partner and good couple communication contribute to gratifying sexual relations for the older woman. Hormone therapy can also resolve many of the problems that interfere with enjoyable sexual response.

The Sexual Response Cycle of Older Men

Most changes in the sexual response cycle of older men involve alterations in the intensity and duration of response (Masters & Johnson, 1966; Segraves & Segraves, 1995).

Excitement Phase

During youth, many males can experience an erection in a few seconds. This ability is typically altered with the aging process. Instead of 8 to 10 seconds, a man might require several minutes of effective stimulation to develop an erect penis. Furthermore, an older man's erection may be less firm than was typical of his younger days. More direct physical stimulation, such as hand caressing or oral stimulation, may also be desirable or necessary. This slowed rate of erectile response can cause alarm, stimulating a fear of impotence in some men:

I guess it was the little things adding up that finally made me realize it was taking me longer to get a hard-on—the fact that I could go to bed with an extremely desirable woman and still be flaccid; that kissing and hugging often wasn't enough to get me started. At first I was shaken up at this discovery, thinking that maybe I would lose my potency. However, I received some good advice from my physician, who assured me that while things may slow down a bit, they continue to remain functional. (Authors' files)

Fortunately, this man received good advice. Most men retain their erectile capacities throughout their lifetimes. When a man and his partner understand that a slowed rate of obtaining an erection is normal, the altered pattern has little or no effect on their enjoyment of sexual expression.

However, some men who are fearful that they will ultimately lose their erectile function can develop such anxiety that their fears become reality. A preoccupation with erection leads some men to stop being sexually active (Friedan, 1994). Other real complications have to do with health problems; heart disease, high blood pressure, diabetes, and associated medications can also interfere with erection (Feldman et al., 1994).

Plateau Phase

Older men do not typically experience as much myotonia (muscle tension) during the plateau phase as when they were younger. The testes may not elevate as close to the perineum. Complete penile erection is frequently not obtained until late in the plateau phase, just before orgasm. One result of these changes is that an older man is often able to sustain the plateau phase much longer than he did when he was younger, which can significantly enhance his pleasure. Many men and their partners appreciate this prolonged opportunity to enjoy other sensations of sexual response besides ejaculation. When a man engages in intercourse, his partner also may appreciate his greater ejaculatory control.

Orgasm Phase

Most aging males continue to experience considerable pleasure from their orgasmic responses. In fact, 73% of older men in one study reported that orgasm was "very important" in their sexual experiences (Starr & Weiner, 1981). However, they may note a decline in intensity. Frequently absent are the sensations of ejaculatory inevitability that correspond with the emission phase of ejaculation. The number of muscular contractions occurring during the expulsion phase are typically reduced and so is the force of ejaculation. The seminal fluid is usually less copious and somewhat thinner in consistency.

Resolution Phase

Resolution typically occurs more rapidly in older men. Loss of erection is usually quite rapid, especially compared to younger men. The testes generally descend immediately after ejaculation. Although resolution becomes faster with aging, the refractory period between orgasm and the next excitement phase gradually lengthens (DeLamater & Friedrich, 2002). Men may begin to notice this as early as their 30s or 40s. Often, by age 60 the refractory period lasts for several hours, even days in some cases.

Table 6.4 summarizes the common changes in the sexual response cycles of older women and men.

► Some Differences Between the Sexes in Sexual Response

More and more, writers are emphasizing the basic similarities of sexual response in men and women. We see this as a positive trend away from the once-popular notion that great differences exist between the sexes—an opinion that undoubtedly helped create a big market for many "love manuals" designed to inform readers about the mysteries and complexities of the "opposite sex." Now we know that much can be learned about our partners by carefully observing our own sexual patterns. Nevertheless, there are some real and important primary differences. In the following pages we outline and discuss some of them.

Greater Variability in Female Response

One major difference between the sexes is the range of variations in the sexual response cycle. Although the graphs in Figures 6.3 and 6.4 do not reflect individual differences, they do demonstrate a wider range in the female response. One pattern is outlined for the male, and three patterns are drawn for the female.

In the female chart the sexual response pattern represented by line A is most similar to the male pattern (see Figure 6.3). It differs in an important way, however, in its potential for additional orgasms without dropping below the plateau level. Line B represents quite a different female pattern: a smooth advance through excitement to the level of plateau, where the responding woman may remain for some time without experiencing orgasm. The consequent resolution phase is more drawn out. Line C portrays a rapid rise in excitement, followed by one intense orgasm and a quick resolution.

Although it appears that women often have more variable sexual response patterns than men, this does not imply that all males experience the response cycle in exactly the same way. Men report considerable variation from the Masters and Johnson standard, including several mild orgasmic peaks followed by ejaculation, prolonged pelvic contractions after the expulsion of semen, and extended periods of intense excitement before ejaculation that feel like one long orgasm (Zilbergeld, 1978). In other words, there is no single pattern of sexual response, nor is there one "correct way." All patterns and variations—including one person's different reactions to sexual stimuli at different times or in different situations—are completely normal.

The Male Refractory Period

The presence of a refractory period in the male cycle is certainly one of the most significant differences in sexual responses between the sexes. Men typically find that a certain minimum time must elapse after an orgasm before they can experience another climax. Most women have no such physiologically imposed shutdown phase.

Speculation about why only men have a refractory period is considerable. It seems plausible that some kind of short-term neurological inhibitory mechanism is triggered by ejac-

AT A GLANCE

TABLE 6.4	Typical Age-Related Changes in the Sexual Response Cycles of Older Men and Women	
Phase	**Typical Changes in Women**	**Typical Changes in Men**
Excitement	• Vaginal lubrication is somewhat delayed and occurs with less volume. • Vaginal mucosa thins, and length and width of vagina decrease.	• Longer time required to obtain an erection. • Erection may be less firm.
Plateau	• Vaginal platform less pronounced. • Less elevation of uterus.	• Less overall muscle tension. • Less elevation of testes. • This phase often elongated in time.
Orgasm	• Fewer orgasmic contractions. • Occasionally uterine contractions may be painful.	• Number of muscular contractions decrease, and force of ejaculation is lessened. • Sensations of ejaculatory inevitability may be absent.
Resolution	• Typically occurs more rapidly as vaginal expansion, orgasmic platform, and clitoral retraction disappears soon after orgasm.	• Occurs more quickly with rapid loss of erection. • Refractory period between orgasm and the next excitement phase gradually lengthens.

ulation. This notion is supported by some fascinating research conducted by British scientists (Barfield et al., 1975). These researchers speculated that certain chemical pathways between the midbrain and the hypothalamus—pathways known to be involved in regulating sleep—might have something to do with postorgasm inhibition in males. To test their hypothesis, the researchers destroyed a specific site, the *ventral medial lemniscus,* along these pathways in rats. For comparative purposes they surgically eliminated three other areas in hypothalamic and midbrain locations in different rats. Later observations of sexual behavior revealed that the elimination of the ventral medial lemniscus had a dramatic effect on refractory periods, cutting their duration in half.

Other research with rats has provided further evidence implicating the brain in the male refractory period. In two studies large lesions made in an area below the hypothalamus resulted in greatly increased ejaculatory behavior (Heimer & Larsson, 1964; Lisk, 1966). Another investigation revealed that electrical stimulation of the posterior hypothalamus can produce dramatic declines in the intervals between a male rat's copulatory activities (Caggiula, 1970).

Some people believe that the answer to the riddle of refractory periods is somehow connected with the loss of seminal fluid during orgasm. Most researchers have been skeptical of this idea because there is no known substance in the expelled semen to account for an energy drain, marked hormone reduction, or any of the other implied biochemical explanations.

Still another explanation suggests that there is an evolutionary advantage in male refractory periods—that is, that the ultimate goal of survival of the species is served best if men experience a shutdown after orgasm and women do not. According to this theory, it is advantageous for women to be able to continue copulatory activity with more than one male because this practice increases the number of sperm in the reproductive tract, thus increasing the possibility of impregnation. The presence of additional sperm might also allow for increased natural selection of the fittest (the fastest swimmers, the longest living, etc.). The evidence for this theory is tenuous at best, but it is nevertheless a provocative thesis. Whatever the reason for it, the refractory period is common not just to human males but to males of virtually all other species for which data exist, including rats, dogs, and chimpanzees.

Multiple Orgasms

Differences between the sexes occur in still a third area of sexual response patterns: the ability to experience **multiple orgasms.** Technically speaking, the term *multiple orgasms* refers to having more than one orgasmic experience within a short time interval.

Multiple orgasms More than one orgasm experienced within a short time period.

Although researchers differ in their views of what constitutes a multiple orgasmic experience, for our own purposes we can say that if a man or woman has two or more sexual climaxes within a short period, that person has experienced multiple orgasms. There is, however, a distinction between males and females that is often obscured by such a definition. It is not uncommon for a woman to have several sequential orgasms, separated in time by the briefest of intervals (perhaps only seconds). In contrast, the spacing of male orgasms is typically more protracted.

How many women experience multiple orgasms? Kinsey and colleagues (1953) reported that about 14% of their female study subjects regularly had multiple orgasms. In 1970 a survey of *Psychology Today* readers revealed a 16% figure (Athanasiou et al., 1970). Surveys of our own student population over the years have produced a similar percentage of women who regularly experience more than one orgasm during a single sexual encounter.

On the surface it might seem that the capacity for multiple orgasms is limited to a minority of women. However, the research of Masters and Johnson showed that this assumption is false:

> If a female who is capable of having regular orgasms is properly stimulated within a short period after her first climax, she will in most instances be capable of having a second, third, fourth, and even a fifth and a sixth orgasm before she is fully satiated. As contrasted with the male's usual inability to have more than one orgasm in a short period, many females, especially when clitorally stimulated, can regularly have five or six full orgasms within a matter of minutes. (Masters and Johnson, 1961, p. 792)

Thus we find that most women have the capacity for multiple orgasms, but apparently only a small portion of the female population experiences them. Why is there a large gap between capacity and experience? The answer may lie in the source of stimulation. The Kinsey report, the *Psychology Today* survey, and our own student surveys are all based on orgasm rates during penile–vaginal intercourse. For a variety of reasons—not the least of which is the male's tendency to stop after his orgasm—women are not likely to continue coitus beyond their initial orgasm. In sharp contrast, several researchers have demonstrated that women who masturbate and those who relate sexually to other women are considerably more likely both to reach initial orgasm and to continue to additional orgasms (Athanasiou et al., 1970; Masters & Johnson, 1966).

We do not mean to imply by this discussion that all women should be experiencing multiple orgasms. On the contrary, many women prefer sexual experiences during which they have a single orgasm or perhaps no orgasm at all. The data on multiple orgasmic capacities of women are not meant to be interpreted as the way women "should" respond. This could lead to a new kind of arbitrary sexual standard. The following quotes illustrate the tendency to set such standards:

When I was growing up, people considered any young, unmarried woman who enjoyed and sought active sexual involvements to be disturbed or promiscuous. Now I am told that I must have several orgasms each time I make love in order to be considered "normal." What a switch in our definitions of normal or healthy—from the straightlaced, noninvolved person to this incredible creature who is supposed to get it off multiply at the drop of a hat. (Authors' files)

Sometimes men ask me why I don't come more than once. It is as though they want me to perform for them. The truth is, one orgasm is all I typically need to be satisfied. Sometimes it is nice not even to worry about having a climax. All this emphasis on producing multiple orgasms is a real put-off to me. (Authors' files)

As suggested earlier, multiple orgasms are considerably less common among males. They are most often reported by very young men, and their frequency declines with age. It is unusual to find men, even those of college age, who routinely experience more than one orgasm during a single sexual encounter. However, we agree with Alex Comfort (1972), who asserted that most men are probably more capable of multiple orgasms than they realize. Many have been conditioned by years of masturbation to get it over as quickly as possible to avoid detection. Such a mental set hardly encourages an adolescent to continue experimenting after the initial orgasm. Through later experimentation, though, many men make discoveries similar to the one described in the following personal reflection of a middle-aged man:

Somehow it never occurred to me that I might continue making love after experiencing orgasm. For 30 years of my life, this always signaled endpoint for me. I guess I responded this way for all the reasons you stated in class and a few more you didn't cover. My wife was with me the night you discussed refractory periods. We talked about it all the way home, and the next day gave it a try. Man, am I mad at myself now for missing out on something really nice all of these years. I discovered that I could have more than one orgasm in one session, and while it may take me a long time to come again, the getting there is a very nice part. My wife likes it, too! (Authors' files)

There is evidence to suggest that some men are actually capable of experiencing a series of orgasms in a short time period. In one study 13 men reported that they had the capacity to experience a series of preejaculatory orgasms culminating in a final orgasm with ejaculation. Most of these men related having 3 to 10 orgasms per sexual encounter. Unfortunately, only 1 of these 13 individuals was studied in the laboratory, where his claim was substantiated with physiological data. Apparently, the key to these multiple responses was the men's ability to withhold ejaculation, because the final orgasm in the series, accompanied by ejaculation, triggered a refractory period (Robbins & Jensen, 1978).

More recently, Marian Dunn and Jan Trost reported their findings from interviews with 21 men, age 25 to 69, all of whom stated that they were usually but not always multiply orgasmic. For the purpose of their investigation, Dunn and Trost defined male multiple orgasms as "two or more orgasms with or without ejaculation and without, or with only very limited, detumescence [loss of erection] during one and the same sexual encounter" (Dunn & Trost, 1989, p. 379). The men's patterns varied, with some men experiencing ejaculation with the first orgasm, followed by more "dry" orgasms. Other men reported having several orgasms without ejaculation followed by a final ejaculatory orgasm. Still others reported variations on these two themes.

These studies provide mounting evidence that some men do experience multiple orgasms. If these findings are ultimately verified and if more men become aware of the possibility of experiencing multiple orgasms, future surveys might reveal that the percentage of men experiencing more than one orgasm during one sex session is closer to that of their female counterparts than presently believed.

It is not necessary for lovemaking always to end with ejaculation. Many men find it pleasurable to continue sexual activity after a climax:

One of the best parts of sex for me is having intercourse again shortly after my first orgasm. I find it is relatively easy to get another erection, even though I seldom experience another climax during the same session. The second time round I can concentrate fully on my partner's reactions without being distracted by my own building excitement. The pace is generally mellow and relaxed, and it is a real high for me psychologically. (Authors' files)

Thus multiple orgasms can be seen not as an ultimate goal to be sought above all else but rather as a possible area to explore. A relaxed approach to this possibility can give interested women and men an opportunity to experience more of the full range of their sexual potentials.

◣ Summary

The Role of Hormones In Sexual Behavior

- Both sexes produce so-called male sex hormones and female sex hormones. In men the testes produce about 95% of total androgens and some estrogens. A woman's ovaries and adrenal glands produce androgens in roughly equal amounts, and estrogens are produced predominantly by her ovaries. (p. 147)

- The dominant androgen in both sexes is testosterone. Men's bodies typically produce 20 to 40 times as much testosterone as women's bodies, but women's body cells are more sensitive to testosterone than men's are. (p. 147)

- Although it is difficult to distinguish the effects of sex hormones and those of psychological processes on sexual arousal, research strongly indicates that testosterone plays a critical role in maintaining sexual desire in both sexes. (pp. 147–149)

- A major symptom of testosterone deficiency in both sexes—a decrease in one's customary level of sexual desire—can be eliminated by testosterone replacement therapy. However, raising the level of testosterone above a normal range can have adverse effects on both sexes. (p. 151)

- The neuropeptide hormone oxytocin, produced in the hypothalamus, exerts significant influence on sexual responses, sensuality, and interpersonal erotic and emotional attraction. (p. 151)

The Brain and Sexual Arousal

- The brain plays an important role in human sexual arousal by mediating our thoughts, emotions, memories, and fantasies. (pp. 152–155)

- There is evidence linking stimulation and surgical alteration of various brain sites with sexual arousal in humans and other animals. (pp. 154–155)

- The limbic system, particularly the hypothalamus, plays an important part in sexual function. (p. 153)

- Certain neurotransmitter substances in the brain are known to influence sexual arousal and response. Dopamine facilitates sexual arousal and activity in women and men, and serotonin provides an inhibitory effect on both sexes. (pp. 154–155)

The Senses and Sexual Arousal

- Touch tends to predominate among the senses that stimulate human sexual arousal. Locations on the body that are highly responsive to tactile pleasuring are called erogenous zones. Primary erogenous zones are areas with dense concentrations of nerve endings; secondary erogenous zones are other areas of the body that become endowed with erotic significance as the result of sexual conditioning. (p. 155)

- Vision is second only to touch in providing stimuli that most people find sexually arousing. Recent evidence suggests that women respond to visual erotica as much as men do. (p. 156)

- Research has yet to clearly demonstrate whether or not smell and taste play a biologically determined role in human sexual arousal, but our own unique individual experiences may allow certain smells and tastes to acquire erotic significance. However, our culture's obsession with personal hygiene tends to mask natural smells or tastes that relate to sexual activity. (pp. 156–157)

- Research on nonhuman animals has isolated a variety of pheromones (sexual odors) that are strongly associated with reproductive sexual activities. (p. 157)

- Recent studies have also provided tentative but not conclusive evidence that humans also produce pheromones that act as sexual attractants. (p. 157)

- Some individuals find sounds during lovemaking to be highly arousing, whereas others prefer that their lovers be silent during love play. Besides being sexually stimulating to some, communication during a sexual interlude can also be informative. (p. 158)

Aphrodisiacs and Anaphrodisiacs in Sexual Arousal
- At this point there is no clear evidence that any substance that we eat, drink, smoke, or inject has genuine aphrodisiac qualities. Faith and suggestion account for the apparent successes of a variety of alleged aphrodisiacs. (pp. 158–160)
- Certain substances are known to have an inhibitory effect on sexual behavior. These anaphrodisiacs include drugs such as opiates, tranquilizers, antihypertensives, antidepressants, antipsychotics, nicotine, birth control pills, and sedatives. (pp. 160–161)

Sexual Response
- Kaplan's model of sexual response contains three stages: desire, excitement, and orgasm. This model is distinguished by its inclusion of desire as a distinct stage of the sexual response cycle separate from genital changes. (pp. 161–162)
- Masters and Johnson describe four phases in the sexual response patterns of both women and men: excitement, plateau, orgasm, and resolution. (p. 162)
- During the excitement phase both sexes experience increased myotonia (muscle tension), heart rate, and blood pressure. Sex flush and nipple erection often occur, especially among women. Female responses include engorgement of the clitoris, the labia, and the vagina (with vaginal lubrication), elevation and enlargement of the uterus, and breast enlargement. Males experience penile erection, enlargement and elevation of the testes, and sometimes Cowper's gland secretions. (pp. 164–166)
- The plateau phase is marked by dramatic accelerations of myotonia, hyperventilation, heart rate, and blood pressure. In females the clitoris withdraws under its hood, the labia minora deepen in color, the orgasmic platform forms in the vagina, the uterus is fully elevated, and the areolas become swollen. In males the corona becomes fully engorged, the testes continue both elevation and enlargement, and Cowper's glands are active. (pp. 166–167)
- Orgasm is marked by involuntary muscle spasms throughout the body. Blood pressure, heart rate, and respiration rate peak. Orgasm is slightly longer in duration in females. Male orgasm typically occurs in two stages, emission and expulsion. It is difficult to distinguish subjective descriptions of female and male orgasms. (pp. 166–167)
- Masters and Johnson suggest that there is one kind of physiological orgasm in females, regardless of the method of stimulation. (p. 171)
- Some women are capable of experiencing orgasm and perhaps ejaculation when the Grafenberg spot, an area along the anterior wall of the vagina, is vigorously stimulated. (pp. 171–173)
- During the resolution phase sexual systems return to their nonexcited state, a process that can take several hours, depending on a number of factors. Erection loss occurs in two stages, the first rapid and the second more protracted. (p. 173)

Aging and the Sexual Response Cycle
- As women and men grow older, they notice changes in their sexual arousal and response patterns. For both sexes all phases of the response cycle generally continue to occur but with somewhat decreased intensity. (pp. 173–175)
- An older woman typically requires more time to achieve vaginal lubrication. The sexual response cycle of the older woman is also characterized by less vaginal expansion, diminished orgasmic intensity, and a more rapid resolution. (pp. 173–174)
- Less commonly, women can experience a decrease in sexual desire, clitoral sensitivity, and/or the capacity for orgasm. (p. 174)
- Older men typically require longer periods of time to achieve erection and reach orgasm. Greater ejaculatory control may be beneficial to sexual pleasure for both their partners and themselves. (pp. 174–175)
- The sexual response cycle of the aging male is also characterized by less myotonia, reduced orgasmic intensity, more rapid resolution, and longer refractory periods. (p. 175)

Some Differences Between the Sexes in Sexual Response
- Many writers now emphasize the fundamental similarities in the sexual responses of men and women. However, there are certain important primary differences between the sexes. (pp. 175–176)
- As a group, females demonstrate a wider variability in their sexual response patterns than do men. (p. 176)
- The presence of a refractory period in the male is one of the most significant differences in the response cycles of the two sexes. No cause for this period has been clearly demonstrated, but there is some evidence that neurological inhibitory mechanisms are activated by ejaculation. (pp. 176–177)
- Multiple orgasms occur more often in females than in males. Women are more likely to experience multiple orgasms while masturbating than during coitus. Recent evidence suggests that some men are also capable of experiencing a series of orgasms in a short time period. (pp. 177–179)

▶▶ ANSWER TO SEXUALITY AND DIVERSITY QUIZ ON P. 170

Report A = Male

Report B = Female

Report C = Female

▶▶ Suggested Readings

Brecher, Ruth, and Edward Brecher (1966). *An Analysis of Human Sexual Response.* New York: New American Library. A simplified, accurate reporting of the Masters and Johnson (1966) research findings.

Crenshaw, Theresa (1996). *The Alchemy of Love and Lust.* New York: Putnam. A superbly informative and entertaining book by one of America's leading authorities on sexual medicine. In addition to providing current data on the impact of testosterone and estrogens on our sexuality, Crenshaw also provides compelling information about such diverse topics as love, attraction, the senses, aging, and longevity.

Crenshaw, Theresa, and James Goldberg (1996). *Sexual Pharmacology: Drugs That Inhibit Sexual Function.* New York: Norton. A must-read for anyone wishing to expand his or her knowledge about a broad array of prescription medications that have adverse sexual side effects.

Jaffe, Maurice, and Elizabeth Fenwick (1995). *Sexual Happiness for Women: A Practical Approach* and *Sexual Happiness for Men: A Practical Approach.* Both books published by Holt (New York). Two companion books that provide valuable information and serve as helpful resource guides to enhanced sexual responsiveness and pleasure. Each book is recommended for both sexes.

Maines, Rachel (1999). *The Technology of Orgasm: Hysteria, the Vibrator, and Women's Sexual Satisfaction.* Baltimore: Johns Hopkins University Press. A fascinating, enlightening, and comprehensive discussion of many aspects of sexuality, with especially valuable information on many aspects of female sexual response, including an informative look at the history of the female orgasm.

Masters, William, and Virginia Johnson (1966). *Human Sexual Response.* Boston: Little, Brown. A highly technical book that outlines the authors' major contributions to the understanding of the physiology of human sexual response. It is a good source for those readers who would like more detailed information about physiological responses to sexual stimulation.

Rako, Susan (1996). *The Hormone of Desire.* New York: Harmony Books. A moving, often profound gem of a book that began as one woman physician's search for answers to her own personal and sexual discomfort associated with menopause-induced testosterone deficiency. Meticulously researched and packed with valuable facts, this book is an excellent source of information about testosterone-replacement therapy.

▶ Resource

North American Menopause Society, P.O. Box 94527, Cleveland, OH 44101. This organization will provide a referral list of member physicians, grouped by states, who can provide informed medical advice about testosterone replacement therapy.

▶ Web Resources

Your *Our Sexuality* Web site **http://psychology.wadsworth.com/ crooksbaur9e/** has direct links to the Web sites described below. These links are checked often for changes, dead links, and new additions.

The Facts About Aphrodisiacs
On this Web page from the U.S. Food and Drug Administration's Web site, claims of traditional aphrodisiacs are described and shot down.

Mysteries of Odor in Human Sexuality
This Web site serves as a comprehensive information resource for general and for scientific knowledge about human pheromones. Access to free abstracts of journal publications is provided.

Our Sexuality Web Site
For online resources directly related to this book, go to **http://psychology.wadsworth.com/ crooksbaur9e/**. You will find interactive exercises, study questions, chapter outlines, an online version of this text's glossary, and Web links and activities that complement your CD-ROM.

InfoTrac® College Edition Online Library
http://infotrac.thomsonlearning.com/
InfoTrac College Edition is an online searchable library that includes a multitude of journals, many of which are specific to human sexuality. These journals include *Archives of Sexual Behavior, Archives of Sexual Health Behavior, Canadian Journal of Human Sexuality, Hispanic Journal of the Behavioral Sciences, Journal of Cross-Cultural Psychology, Journal of Physical Education, Recreation, and Dance, Journal of Sex Research,* and *Sex Roles.* You may search topics suggested in the margins of this chapter or terms of your own.

Our Sexuality CD-ROM
Use your CD-ROM for further study of the concepts in this chapter. Your CD-ROM provides animations of difficult concepts, video clips of real people discussing sexuality, critical thinking questions, chapter quizzing, and more.

CHAPTER 7

Love, Attraction, Attachment, and Intimate Relationships

For me, the potential for falling in love begins with a physical attraction. But looks only count for so much. I need an intimate friendship and closeness in order to possibly fall in love. Trust is another important part of a relationship that can lead to love. A prospective partner would also need to share some of my interests, and I would need to share some of his. Finally, and perhaps most important, good communication in a relationship is essential for me to be truly in love. (Authors' files)

Love, attraction, attachment, and intimate relationships are important and complex aspects of people's lives. In this chapter we look at these interactions from various perspectives and examine some of the research dealing with them. We consider a number of questions: What is love? What kinds of love are there? What determines why we fall in love with one person and not another? How do various styles of attraction influence our relationships with others? How does sex fit into relationships? How does love relate to jealousy? And finally, what qualities or behaviors help to maintain relationship satisfaction over many years?

▶ What Is Love? An emotion

O Love is the crooked thing,
There is nobody wise enough
To find out all that is in it
For he would be thinking of love
Till the stars had run away
And the shadows eaten the moon.

(William Butler Yeats, "Brown Penny")

Love has intrigued people throughout history. Its joys and sorrows have inspired artists and poets, novelists, filmmakers, and other students of human interaction. Indeed, love is one of the most pervasive themes in the art and literature of many cultures. Each of our own lives has been influenced in significant ways by love, beginning with the love we received as infants and children. Our best and worst moments in life can be tied to a love relationship.

But what is love, and how do we define it?

Love is a special kind of attitude with strong emotional and behavioral components. It is also a phenomenon that eludes easy definition or explanation. As the following definitions suggest, love can mean different things to different people:

> Love is patient and kind; love is not jealous or boastful; it is not arrogant or rude. Love does not insist on its own way; it is not irritable or resentful; it does not rejoice at wrong, but rejoices in the right. Love bears all things, believes all things, hopes all things, endures all things. (I Corinthians 13:4–7)

> Love is a temporary insanity curable by marriage or by removal of the patient from the influences under which he incurred the disorder. (Bierce, 1943, p. 202)

> Love is that condition in which the happiness of another person is essential to your own. (Heinlein, 1961, p. 345)

As difficult as love is to define, can it be meaningfully measured? Some social scientists have attempted to do so, with varied results (Davis & Latty-Mann, 1987; Hatfield & Sprecher, 1986a; Pam et al., 1975; Rubin, 1970). Perhaps the most ambitious attempt to measure love was undertaken years ago by psychologist Zick Rubin (1970, 1973). Using responses to a questionnaire administered to several hundred dating couples at the University of Michigan, Rubin developed a 13-item measurement device that he called the Love Scale. On this scale people are asked to indicate whether a particular statement accurately reflects their feelings about another person, usually someone they are interested in romantically.

Love has been the inspiration for some of our greatest works of literature, art, and music.

© Culver Pictures

According to Rubin's Love Scale, love consists of three components: attachment, caring, and intimacy.

As measured by Rubin's scale, love has three components: attachment, caring, and intimacy. *Attachment* is a person's desire for the physical presence and emotional support of the other person. *Caring* is an individual's concern for the other's well-being. *Intimacy* is the desire for close, confidential communication with the other.

Some people would argue that it is simply not possible to measure an emotion such as love, particularly with a paper-and-pencil measurement device such as the Love Scale. Nevertheless, Rubin did obtain some evidence supporting the validity of his scale. For example, the scale was used to investigate the popular belief that lovers spend a great deal of time looking into one another's eyes (Rubin, 1970). Couples were observed through a one-way mirror while they waited to participate in a psychological experiment. The findings revealed that weak lovers (couples who scored below average on the Love Scale) made significantly less eye contact than did strong lovers (those with above-average scores).

Perhaps in the years ahead we will have access to a variety of new perspectives on the question of what love is, largely because of a marked increase in the number of scientists, especially social psychologists, who have begun to study love (Neto, 2001). What accounts for this rise in interest in love studies? An interview with a leading social scientist, psychologist Elaine Hatfield (author of *Love, Sex, and Intimacy* [1993]), provided one plausible explanation: The ranks of women scientists are swelling, and women may be more willing than men to consider love a legitimate topic for serious research (Gray, 1993).

▶ Types of Love

Love takes many forms. Love exists between parent and child and between family members. Love between friends, known to the ancient Greeks as *philia*, involves concern for the other's well-being. Lovers may experience two additional types of love: passionate love and companionate love. In this section we look more closely at these two widely discussed types of love and then present two contemporary models or theories of love.

Passionate Love

Passionate love State of extreme absorption in another person. Also known as romantic love.

Passionate love, also known as romantic love or infatuation, is a state of extreme absorption with and desire for another. It is characterized by intense feelings of tenderness, elation, anxiety, sexual desire, and ecstasy. Generalized physiological arousal, including increased heartbeat, perspiration, blushing, and stomach churning along with a feeling of great excitement, often accompanies this form of love.

Intense passionate love typically occurs early in a relationship. It sometimes seems as though the less one knows the other person, the more intense the passionate love. In passionate love people often overlook faults and avoid conflicts. Logic and reasoned consideration are swept away by the excitement. One perceives the object of one's passionate love as providing complete personal fulfillment.

Not surprisingly, passionate love is often short-lived, typically measured in months rather than years. Love that is based on ignorance of a person's full character is bound to change with increased familiarity. However, this temporary aspect of passionate love is often overlooked, especially by young people who lack experience with long-term love relationships. Many couples, convinced of the permanence of their passionate feelings, choose to make some kind of commitment to each other (becoming engaged, moving in together, getting married, etc.) while still fired by the fuel of passionate love—only to become disillusioned later. When ecstasy gives way to routine, and the annoyances and conflicts typical of ongoing relationships surface, lovers may begin to have some doubts about their partners.

The first weeks and months of my relationship with Bob were incredible. I felt like I had found the perfect partner, someone who filled all that was missing in my life. Then, suddenly, he started to get on my nerves, and we started fighting every time we saw each other. It took a while to realize that we were finally seeing each other as real people instead of dream companions. (Authors' files)

Some couples are able to work through this period to ultimately find a solid basis on which to build a lasting relationship of mutual love. Others discover, often to their dismay, that the only thing they ever really shared was passion. Unfortunately, many people who experience diminishing passion believe that this is the end of love rather than a possible transition into a different kind of love.

Companionate Love

Companionate love is a less intense emotion than passionate love. It is characterized by friendly affection and a deep attachment that is based on extensive familiarity with the loved one. It involves a thoughtful appreciation of one's partner. Companionate love often encompasses a tolerance for another's shortcomings along with a desire to overcome difficulties and conflicts in a relationship. This kind of love is committed to ongoing nurturing of a partnership. In short, companionate love is often enduring, whereas passionate love is almost always transitory.

Sex in a companionate relationship typically reflects feelings associated with familiarity, especially the security of knowing what pleases the other. This foundation of knowledge and sexual trust can encourage experimentation and subtle communication. Sexual pleasure strengthens the overall bond of a companionate relationship. Although sex is usually less exciting than in passionate love, it is often experienced as richer, more meaningful, and deeply satisfying, as the following statement reveals:

Between my first and second marriages, I really enjoyed the excitement of new sexual relationships, especially after so much sexual frustration in my first marriage. Even though I sometimes miss the excitement of those times, I would never trade it for the easy comfort, pleasure, and depth of sexual intimacy I now experience in my 17-year marriage. (Authors' files)

Although most relationships begin with a period of passionate love and only later evolve into companionate love, some have the opposite history. Companionate love can develop first when two people have known each other for an extended period as acquaintances, friends, or co-workers. Often an initial sexual attraction is not present or is de-emphasized because of circumstances. In these relationships passionate love is based on familiarity with the other person rather than on the excitement of the unknown. One woman describes her experience:

My boyfriend Victor and I started out as really close friends. I considered him to be my best friend. I do not know when everything changed, but somewhere during our friendship, we fell in love. It is the most wonderful relationship I have ever experienced. Not too long ago, we made love to each other for the first time. It was enormously incredible. I think it was exceptional because we communicate totally with each other. I can tell him what I like and dislike without being ashamed for talking about sex, and vice versa. I know the reason we are so in love is because we began our relationship as friends. (Authors' files)

Sternberg's Triangular Theory of Love

The distinction between passionate and companionate love has been further refined by psychologist Robert Sternberg (1986, 1988), who has proposed an interesting theoretical framework for conceptualizing what people experience when they report being in love. According to Sternberg, love has three faces: passion, intimacy, and commitment (Figure 7.1):

- **Passion** is the motivational component that fuels romantic feelings, physical attraction, and desire for sexual interaction. Passion instills a deep desire to be united with

Companionate love A type of love characterized by friendly affection and deep attachment based on extensive familiarity with the loved one.

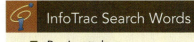

InfoTrac Search Words

- Passionate love
- Companionate love

Critical Thinking Question

What do you think are the key differences between passionate love and companionate love? How do these characteristics fit into a list of things that you believe are essential to a successful, lasting love relationship?

Passion The motivational component of Sternberg's triangular love theory.

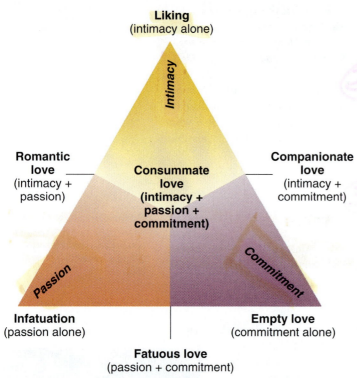

Figure 7.1 In Sternberg's love triangle, various combinations of the three components of love (passion, intimacy, and commitment) make up the different kinds of love. Note that nonlove is the absence of all three components.

Intimacy The emotional component of Sternberg's triangular love theory.

Commitment The thinking component of Sternberg's triangular love theory.

the loved one. In a sense, passion is like an addiction, because its capacity to provide intense stimulation and pleasure can exert a powerful craving in a person.

- **Intimacy** is the emotional component of love that encompasses the sense of being bonded with another person. It includes feelings of warmth, sharing, and emotional closeness. Intimacy also embraces a willingness to help the other and an openness to sharing private thoughts and feelings with the beloved.

- **Commitment** is the thinking or cognitive aspect of love. It refers to the conscious decision to love another and to maintain a relationship over time despite difficulties that may arise.

Sternberg maintains that passion tends to develop rapidly and intensely in the early stages of a love relationship and then declines as the relationship progresses. In contrast, intimacy and commitment continue to build gradually over time, although at different rates (Figure 7.2). Thus Sternberg's theory provides a conceptual basis for the transition from passionate to companionate love. Passionate love, consisting mainly of romantic feelings and physical attraction, peaks early and quickly subsides. However, as passion grows weaker, many couples experience a growth in both intimacy and commitment as their relationship evolves into one of companionate love (Sprecher & Regan, 1998). If intimacy does not flourish and if a couple does not make a mutual decision to commit to each other, their relationship will be on shaky ground when passion fades and conflicts surface. In contrast, commitment and a sense of bondedness and mutual concern can sustain a relationship during periods of dissatisfaction and conflict.

All three of Sternberg's love components are important dimensions of a loving relationship, but they typically exist in different patterns and to varying degrees in different relationships. Moreover, they often change over time within the same relationship. Sternberg suggests that such variations yield different kinds of love—or at least differences in how people experience love. For instance, the absence of all three components yields what Sternberg calls *nonlove* (what most of us feel for casual acquaintances). When only intimacy is present, the experience is one of *friendship* or *liking*. If only passion exists, without intimacy or commitment, one experiences *infatuation*. The presence of commitment without passion and intimacy yields *empty love* (such as might be experienced in a long-term, static relationship). If intimacy and commitment exist without passion, one experiences *companionate love* (often characteristic of happy couples who have shared many years together). When passion and commitment are present but without intimacy, the experience is *fatuous love*, a kind of foolish involvement characteristic of whirlwind courtships or situations in which one worships and longs for another person from afar. Love characterized by passion and intimacy but no commitment is described by Sternberg as *romantic love*. Finally, when all three components are present, the experience is *consummate*

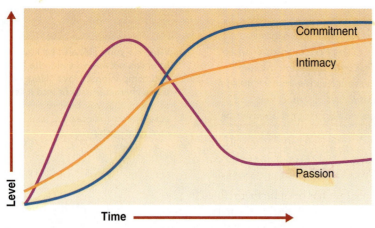

Figure 7.2 Sternberg theorizes that the passion component of love peaks early in a relationship and then declines, whereas the other two components, intimacy and commitment, continue to build gradually over time.

love, the fullest kind of love that people often strive for but find difficult to achieve and/or sustain.

Empirical research on love models, including Sternberg's, is generally limited to only a few studies. One study of dating couples reported that the presence of two of Sternberg's love components—intimacy and commitment—was predictive of relationship stability and longevity (Hendrick et al., 1988). Another investigation found that married people demonstrated higher levels of commitment to their relationships than unmarried people did, a finding consistent with Sternberg's model (Acker & Davis, 1992). This same study found that, although intimacy continued to rise in longer relationships, passion declined for both sexes, but more sharply for women than for men. A more recent investigation of Sternberg's triangular theory found that lovers' definition and communication of the three components of love remained relatively stable over time (Reeder, 1996).

Lee's Styles of Loving

Instead of attempting to describe different patterns or *types* of love, John Allan Lee (1974, 1988, 1998) proposed a theory that describes six different *styles of loving* that characterize intimate human relationships: romantic, game playing, possessive, companionate, altruistic, and pragmatic.

- People with a *romantic* love style *(eros)* tend to place their emphasis on physical beauty as they search for ideal mates. Romantic, erotic lovers delight in the visual beauty and tactile and sensual pleasures provided by their lovers' bodies, and they tend to be very affectionate and openly communicative with their partners.
- People with a *game-playing* love style *(ludus)* like to play the field and acquire many sexual "conquests" with little or no commitment. Love is for fun, the act of seduction is to be enjoyed, and relationships are to remain casual and transitory.
- People with a *possessive* love style *(mania)* are inclined to seek obsessive love relationships that are often characterized by turmoil and jealousy. These people live a roller-coaster style of love in which each display of affection from the lover brings ecstasy and the mildest slight produces painful agitation.
- People with a *companionate* love style *(storge)* (STOR-gay) are slow to develop affection and commitment but tend to experience relationships that endure. This style is love without fever or turmoil, a peaceful and quiet kind of relating that usually begins as friendship and develops over time into affection and love.
- People with an *altruistic* love style *(agape)* are characterized by selflessness and a caring, compassionate desire to give to another without expectation of reciprocity. Such love is patient and never demanding or jealous.
- People with a *pragmatic* love style *(pragma)* are inclined to select lovers based on rational, practical criteria (such as shared interests) that are likely to lead to mutual satisfaction. These individuals approach love in a businesslike fashion, trying to get the best "romantic deal" by seeking partners with social, educational, religious, and interest patterns that are compatible with their own.

What happens when two different people in a relationship are naturally inclined toward different styles of loving? For Lee this is a critical question. He suggests that loving relationships frequently fail to thrive over time because "too often people are speaking different languages when they speak of love" (Lee, 1974, p. 44). Even though both partners try to build a lasting involvement, their efforts can be undermined by a losing struggle to integrate incompatible loving styles. In contrast, satisfaction and success in loving relationships often depend on finding a mate who "shares the same approach to loving, the same definition of love" (Lee, 1974, p. 44).

An inventory called the Love Attitude Scale has been developed to measure Lee's six loving styles (Hendrick & Hendrick, 1986), and this research tool has generated some empirical studies of his theory. Studies that have used this scale provide some support for Lee's hypothesis that relationship success is influenced by compatibility in styles of loving (Davis & Latty-Mann, 1987; Hendrick et al., 1988). A recent investigation found that college students prefer to date people with love styles similar to their own (Hahn & Blass, 1997).

Another recent study used the Love Attitude Scale to investigate the relationship between styles of loving and relationship satisfaction at different stages of life (Montgomery & Sorell, 1997). The study sample included 250 adults in 4 groups: college-age single youths, young childless married adults, married adults with children living at home, and married adults whose grown-up children had left home. Two loving styles, *eros* and *agape*, were positively associated with relationship satisfaction for all life stages. Predictably, *ludus* was negatively associated with satisfaction for all three groups of married adults. *Storge* was significantly related to relationship satisfaction only for the married couples with children at home. *Mania* and, surprisingly, *pragma* were not significantly related to relationship satisfaction for any life-stage group. These findings are supported by other research demonstrating that *ludus* is a strong predictor of relationship dissatisfaction and that individuals who score high on the love styles of *eros, storge,* or *agape* experience greater relationship satisfaction than individuals with other love styles (Meeks et al., 1998).

? How About You?

Which of Lee's styles of love is most descriptive of your approach to romantic relationships?

▶ Falling in Love: Why and with Whom?

What determines why people fall in love and with whom they fall in love? These questions are exceedingly complex. Some writers believe that people fall in love to overcome a sense of aloneness and separateness. Psychoanalyst Erich Fromm (1965) suggested that union with another person is the deepest need of humans. Another psychoanalyst and writer, Rollo May, author of *Love and Will* (1969), also believed that as people experience their own solitariness, they long for the refuge of union with another through love. Some other observers see loneliness as a by-product of our individualistic and highly mobile society rather than as an inherent part of the human condition. This view emphasizes the connectedness that we all have with the people around us—through all our social relationships, language, and culture. According to this view, love relationships are one aspect of a person's social network rather than a cure for the "disease" of loneliness (Solomon, 1981).

We have seen that love is a complex human emotion that can be explained, at least in part, by various psychosocial interpretations of its origins. However, the answer to why we fall in love also encompasses, to some degree, complex neurochemical processes that occur in our brains when we are attracted to another person. We discuss some findings about the chemistry of love in the next section.

The Chemistry of Love

People caught up in the intense passion of blooming love often report feeling swept away or a kind of natural high. Such reactions might have a basis, at least in part, in brain chemistry, according to researchers Michael Liebowitz, author of *The Chemistry of Love* (1983), and Anthony Walsh, author of *The Science of Love* (1991). These investigators contend that the initial elation and the energizing "high" of excitement, giddiness, and euphoria characteristic of passionate love are a result of surging levels of three key brain chemicals: norepinephrine, dopamine, and especially phenylethylamine (PEA). These chemicals, called *neurotransmitters,* allow brain cells to communicate with each other and are chemically similar to amphetamine drugs; thus they produce amphetamine-like effects, such as euphoria, giddiness, and elation. As Walsh noted, "When we meet someone who is attractive to us, the whistle blows at the PEA factory" (quoted in Toufexis, 1993, p. 50). Furthermore, as we learned in Chapter 6, dopamine and oxytocin both contribute to sexual arousal, which adds further fire to passionate love. Oxytocin, which is secreted during cuddling and physical intimacy, also plays an important role in facilitating social attachment and in fostering feelings of being in love (Carter, 1998; Love, 2001; McEwen, 1997).

Unfortunately, particularly from the perspective of love junkies, the amphetamine-like highs and elevated sexual arousal associated with new love typically do not last—perhaps in part because the body eventually develops a tolerance to PEA and related neurotransmitters, just as it does for amphetamines. With time our brains simply become unable to keep up with the demand for more and more PEA to produce love's special kick. Thus the highs that we feel at the beginning of a relationship eventually diminish. This observation provides a plausible biological explanation for why passionate or romantic love is short-lived.

Liebowitz points out another parallel to amphetamine use. He notes that the anxiety, despair, and pain that follow the loss—or even potential loss—of a romantic love relationship are similar to what a person addicted to amphetamines experiences during drug withdrawal. In both cases the loss of mood-lifting chemicals results in a sometimes protracted period of emotional pain.

Are there other brain chemicals that help to explain why some relationships endure beyond the initial highs of passionate love? According to both Walsh and Liebowitz, the answer is yes. The continued progression from infatuation to the deep attachment characteristic of long-term loving relationships results, at least in part, from the brain gradually stepping up production of another set of neurotransmitters called *endorphins*. These morphinelike, pain-blunting chemicals are soothing substances that help produce a sense of euphoria, security, tranquility, and peace. Thus they can cause us to feel good when we are with a loved partner. This could be another reason abandoned lovers feel so terrible after their loss—they are deprived of their daily dose of feel-good chemicals.

Just as we know little about why people fall in love, we have no simple explanation for why they fall in love with one particular person instead of another. A number of factors are often important: proximity, similarity, reciprocity, and physical attractiveness.

? **How About You?**

If you are now (or have been) in a love relationship, what factors or personal traits were most influential in attracting you to the loved person?

Proximity

Although people often overlook **proximity,** or geographic nearness, in listing factors that attracted them to a particular person, proximity is one of the most important variables. We often develop close relationships with people whom we see frequently in our neighborhood, in school, at work, or at our place of worship.

Why is proximity such a powerful factor in interpersonal attraction? Social psychologists have offered a number of plausible explanations. One is simply that familiarity breeds liking or loving. Research has shown that when we are repeatedly exposed to novel stimuli—unfamiliar musical selections, works of art, human faces, and so on—our liking for such stimuli increases (Bornstein, 1989; Brooks & Watkins, 1989; Nuttin, 1987). This phenomenon, called the **mere exposure effect,** explains in part why we are attracted to people in close proximity to us.

Another reason why proximity influences who we are attracted to is that people often meet each other in locations where they are engaging in activities that reflect common interests. This observation is supported by the National Health and Social Life Survey (NHSLS) (see Chapter 2), which included questions about where people are most likely to meet their sex partners. Laumann and his associates (1994) sorted their data into high and low preselection locales. High preselection meant that people were together in locations where they shared common interests, such as physical health and fitness (working out at the local fitness center) or topics of study (taking the same classes at school). Low preselection locales included places that bring a diverse group of people together, such as bars and vacation sites. Predictably, Laumann and colleagues found that places with high levels of preselection were more likely to yield sex partner connections than locales with low preselection values.

Work and school were especially prevalent as places where people connect

Proximity The geographic nearness of one person to another, which is an important factor in interpersonal attraction.

Mere exposure effect The phenomenon by which repeated exposure to novel stimuli tends to increase an individual's liking for such stimuli.

People who fall in love often share common interests.

© Duomo/CORBIS

TABLE 7.1 — Percentage of Couples in Various Types of Relationships That Are Homophilous for Age, Educational Status, and Religion

Type of Homophily	Type of Relationship			
	Marriage (%)	Cohabitation (%)	Long-Term Partnership (%)	Short-Term Partnership (%)
Age (defined as difference of no more than 5 years in partners' ages)	78	75	76	83
Educational status (defined as difference of no more than one educational category[a])	82	87	83	87
Religion (defined as having same affiliation)	72	53	56	60

[a]Categories: Less than high school, high school graduate, vocational training, 4-year college degree, postgraduate degree.

SOURCE: Adapted from Laumann et al. (1994).

with future intimate partners. This finding reflects both the amount of time people spend in these locations and the possible effect of shared common interests. In addition, working with or taking classes with potential partners provides opportunities for repeated contacts. Many of us are reluctant to initiate a relationship the first time or two we meet or interact with another person. However, at work or in class, we come into contact with a desired person day after day. This allows us to get to know this person better, to become more comfortable interacting with him or her, and eventually to muster the motivation to ask for a first date.

Another likely reason that proximity influences who we fall in love with is that the more we see of others, the more familiar we become with their ways and thus the better able we are to predict their behavior. If we have a good idea of how someone is likely to behave in any given situation, we will probably be more comfortable with this person. It is also possible that when we know we will be seeing a lot of a person, we may be more motivated to see his or her good traits and to keep our interactions as positive as possible.

Similarity

Similarity The similarity of beliefs, interests, and values, which is a factor in attracting people to one another.

Similarity is also influential in determining whom we fall in love with. Contrary to the old adage that opposites attract, people who fall in love often share common beliefs, values, attitudes, interests, and intellectual abilities (Byrne, 1997; Douglass & Douglass, 1993; Hatfield & Rapson, 1993; Sherman & Jones, 1994). We also are inclined to pair romantically with people whose level of physical attractiveness is similar to our own (Feingold, 1988; Folkes, 1982). This tendency to match physical attractiveness with a partner might be related to our fear of being rejected if we approach someone whom we perceive to be much more attractive than ourselves (Bernstein et al., 1983).

We also tend to be attracted to people who are similar to us in the categories of age, educational status, and religious affiliation. Similarity in personal characteristics is referred to as *homophily,* or the tendency to form relationships with people of similar or equal status on various social and personal attributes. Data from the NHSLS reflecting homophily in age, educational status, and religion for various types of relationships are presented in Table 7.1.

The NHSLS also revealed that people are generally inclined to form partnerships with people of similar race and ethnicity. The following "Sexuality and Diversity" discussion describes this dimension of attraction.

 ## Sexuality and Diversity

Partner Choice and Race

The NHSLS provided data about the extent to which people form intimate relationships with members of the same race. As described in Chapter 2, a lack of funds forced Edward Laumann and his associates (1994) to include adequate numbers of only the two largest racial minorities in America. Consequently, Table 7.2 contains data pertaining only to white Americans, African Americans, and Hispanic Americans. Furthermore, these data summarize a sample of almost 2,000 nonmarital, noncohabitational heterosexual partnerships.

As you can see by examining the values in Table 7.2, the percentages of same-race noncohabitational partnerships are very high for both sexes among whites and African Americans. In contrast, the percentage of same-race noncohabitational partnerships is considerably lower among Hispanic respondents. Thus it would appear that "Hispanics as a group are less exclusive with respect to sexual partnering than are whites or blacks" (Laumann et al., 1994, p. 246).

A more recent study examined partner choice and race among 75,000 cohabiting couples and 480,000 married couples in the United States (Blackwell & Lichter, 2000). In contrast to the findings of the NHSLS, Blackwell & Lichter found that the inclination to select same-race partners was less pronounced among white Americans than among other racial groups. Specifically, the incidence of same-race partnerships among both cohabiting and married couples was highest among African Americans, followed in order by Asian Americans, Hispanic Americans, and whites.

TABLE 7.2	Noncohabitational Sexual Partnerships by Race and Sex	
	Percentage of Same-Race Partnerships	
Race	Men (%)	Women (%)
White	92	87
African American	82	97
Hispanic American	54	65

SOURCE: Laumann et al. (1994).

Why are we drawn to people who are like us? For one thing, people with similar attitudes and interests are often inclined to participate in the same kinds of leisure activities. Even more important, we are more likely to communicate well with people whose ideas and opinions are similar to ours, and communication is an important aspect of enduring relationships. It is also reassuring to be with similar people, because they confirm our view of the world, validate our own experiences, and support our opinions and beliefs (Byrne et al., 1986; Sanders, 1982).

In the final analysis, perceived similarity in others could be especially attractive to us because we have strong expectations of being accepted and appreciated by people who are like us (Sprecher & McKinney, 1993). That these expectations are often fulfilled is reflected in research findings which indicate that people who are similar in a variety of social and personal traits are more likely to stay together than couples who are more dissimilar (Weber, 1998).

Reciprocity

Still another factor drawing us to a particular individual is our perception that that person is interested in us. People tend to react positively to flattery, compliments, and other expressions of liking and affection. In the study of interpersonal attraction this concept is reflected in the principle of **reciprocity,** which holds that when we are the recipients of expressions of liking or loving, we tend to respond in kind (Byrne & Murnen, 1988). In turn, reciprocal responses can set in motion a further escalation of the relationship: By responding warmly to people who we believe feel positively toward us, we often induce them to like us even more (Curtis & Miller, 1988). Furthermore, our sense of self-esteem is affected by the extent to which we feel attached to and liked by others. Knowing that someone likes us increases our sense of belonging or being socially integrated in a relationship and hence bolsters our self-esteem (Baumeister & Leary, 1995).

Relationships that are mutually gratifying and enduring are likely to have a balance of positive exchanges or reciprocity within the partnership. Relationships characterized by a marked inequity of reciprocity, where only one member of the couple provides most of the compliments and other expressions of affection and love, are unlikely to endure. Most of us have a limited tolerance for one-way giving.

Reciprocity The principle which states that when we are recipients of expressions of liking or loving, we tend to respond in kind.

Physical Attractiveness

Physical attractiveness
Physical beauty, which is a powerful factor in attracting lovers to each other.

As you might expect, **physical attractiveness** often plays a dominant role in drawing lovers together. Despite the saying that beauty is only skin deep, it has been experimentally demonstrated that physically attractive people are more likely to be sought as friends and lovers and to be perceived as more likable, interesting, sensitive, poised, happy, sexy, competent, and socially skilled than people of average or unattractive appearance (Feingold, 1992; Hatfield & Rapson, 1993; Marcus & Miller, 2003; Speed & Gangestad, 1997).

Why is physical beauty such a powerful factor in attracting us to others? One answer has to do with aesthetics. We all enjoy looking at something or someone whom we consider beautiful. Another factor is that many people apparently believe that beautiful people have more to offer in terms of desirable personal qualities than those who are less attractive. We might also be attracted to beautiful people because they offer us the possibility of status by association. And perhaps beautiful people, by virtue of having been treated well by others over the course of their lives, are secure and comfortable with themselves, a fact that can translate into especially satisfying relationships with others. Finally, there is evidence that people consider physical beauty an indicator of health and that, other things being equal, we are attracted to healthy people (Gangestad & Buss, 1993; Kalick et al., 1998; Marcus & Miller, 2003).

Whatever the reason, good looks seem to attract people, even when we would normally discount beauty as a factor. Research by Judith Langlois and her colleagues strongly suggests that even infants exhibit a preference for beauty long before they are exposed to cultural standards of attractiveness and beauty. In one study infants from 2 to 8 months old demonstrated marked preferences for attractive faces. When they were shown pairs of color slides of the faces of adult women previously rated by other adults for attractiveness, the infants demonstrated a strong inclination to look longer at the more attractive face in the pair (Langlois et al., 1987). In another study 12-month-old infants demonstrated positive emotional and play responses when interacting with an adult stranger who wore a professionally constructed, lifelike, and attractive latex theater mask. In contrast, when the stranger wore a mask portraying an unattractive face, the infants demonstrated more negative emotions and less play involvement (Langlois et al., 1990). In still another experiment 1-year-old infants played significantly longer with attractive dolls than with unattractive dolls (Langlois et al., 1990).

Researchers have sought to determine whether both sexes are equally influenced by physical attractiveness in forming impressions of people they meet. Several studies have found that male college students place significantly greater emphasis on physical appearance in selecting a partner for a sexual or long-term relationship than do college women, who tend to place greater emphasis on such traits as ambition, status, interpersonal warmth, and personality characteristics (Nevid, 1984; Townsend & Wasserman, 1998). Other studies have found that American men place a greater emphasis on physical attractiveness than do American women (Bailey et al., 1994; Sprecher et al., 1994; Wiederman & Allgeier, 1992). Is this difference typical of men and women in other cultures as well?

A cross-cultural study of sex differences in heterosexual mate preferences provided strong evidence that men worldwide place greater value than do women on mates who are both young and physically attractive. In this study, conducted by psychologist David Buss (1994), subjects from 37 samples drawn from Africa, Asia, Europe, North and South America, Australia, and New Zealand were asked to rate the importance of a wide range of personal attributes in potential mates. These characteristics included dependability, good looks, age, good financial prospects, intelligence, sociability, and chastity.

Without exception, men in all the surveyed cultures placed greater emphasis on a potential mate's youth and attractiveness than women did (Buss, 1994). In contrast, women placed greater value on potential mates who were somewhat older, had good financial prospects, and were dependable and industrious. This is not to say that physical attractiveness was unimportant to women of these varied cultures. In fact, many women considered physical attractiveness important—although less so than financial responsibility and dependability.

What accounts for the apparent consistency across so many cultures in what appeals to men and to women in a potential mate? And what accounts for the differences between men and women? Buss provides a *sociobiological* explanation—that is, he explains a species' behavior in terms of its evolutionary needs. According to Buss (1994), evolution has biased mate preferences in humans, as it has in other animals. Males are attracted to younger, physically attractive females because these characteristics are good predictors of reproductive success. Simply put, a younger woman has more reproductive years remaining than does an older woman. Furthermore, smooth unblemished skin, good muscle tone, lustrous hair, and similar features of physical attractiveness are indicators of good health—and thus are strong cues to reproductive value. On the other hand, women tend to find older, established men more attractive because characteristics such as wealth, a desirable environment, or high rank are predictors of security for their offspring. Youth and physical attractiveness are less important to females, because male fertility is less related to age than it is for females.

Physical attractiveness seems to play the most important role in the early stages of a relationship. As researchers Elton McNeil and Zick Rubin concluded, "It seems likely that as the relationship progresses the impact of physical attractiveness tends to recede in importance. And we often perceive people whom we love as being beautiful, regardless of what anyone else might think" (1977, p. 581). Furthermore, both sexes consider the qualities exhibited by their mates, such as kindness, understanding, and intelligence, more important than physical attractiveness in long-term relationships (Buss, 1989; Buss and Barnes, 1986).

Studies have also revealed that American women typically consider traits such as ambition and being a good provider more important in mate selection than do their male counterparts (Buss & Schmitt, 1993). Sex differences in other aspects of mate selection among adults in the United States are described in the following "Sexuality and Diversity" discussion.

Sexuality and Diversity

Sex Differences in Mate Selection Preferences in the United States

Some years ago researchers Susan Sprecher, Quintin Sullivan, and Elaine Hatfield (1994) surveyed a national representative sample of more than 13,000 English- or Spanish-speaking people in the United States, age 19 or older. Figure 7.3 illustrates the average response rating of men and women to several items on a questionnaire used in the survey. One part of the

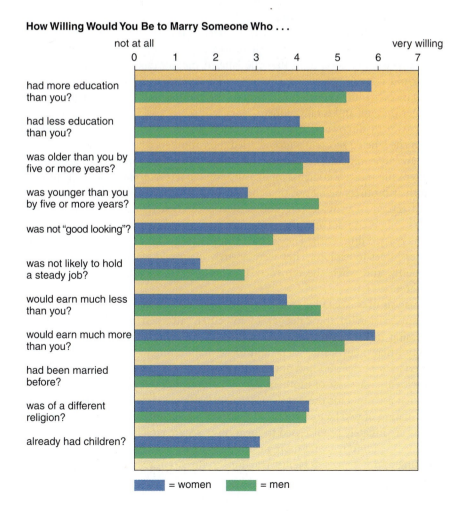

How Willing Would You Be to Marry Someone Who . . .

▶ **Figure 7.3** Sex differences in aspects of mate selection among adults in the United States.

questionnaire contained several items that asked respondents how willing they would be to marry someone who had more or less education, was older or younger, was not likely to hold a steady job, and so on. Subjects indicated their level of agreement with each item on a scale from 1 ("not at all") to 7 ("very willing").

The results indicate that women respondents were significantly more willing than men to marry someone who was better educated, older, would earn more, and was not good looking. Conversely, women were significantly less willing than men to marry someone who had less education, was younger, was not likely to hold a steady job, and would earn less. There were only minor sex differences on items related to prior marriages, religion, and already having children.

▶ Love and Styles of Attachment

Attachment Intense emotional tie between two individuals, such as an infant and a parent or adult lovers.

Attachment is the term applied to the intense emotional tie that develops between two individuals, such as the tie between an infant and a parent or between adult lovers. Attachment is a key ingredient in many definitions of love, and it is one of the three components of love measured by Rubin's Love Scale. It is possible to experience attachment without love, but it is unlikely that love of one person for another can exist in the absence of attachment. Although love itself is difficult to measure and study, researchers have had considerable success investigating various aspects of attachment, including how it forms, effects of attachment deprivation, and styles of attachment. The last of these dimensions, styles of attachment, is of particular interest to social scientists. In the following pages we examine some of the key research findings pertaining to attachment and human relationships.

Attachment Styles

The manner in which we form attachments, which has its roots in infancy, has a great impact on how we relate to loved partners. Much of our scientific knowledge about how attachment styles are established and how they later affect us is derived from the work of developmental psychologist Mary Ainsworth (Ainsworth 1979, 1989; Ainsworth et al., 1978). Ainsworth used a laboratory procedure that she labeled the "strange situation." In this procedure a 1-year-old infant's behavior in an unfamiliar environment is assessed under various circumstances—with mother present, with the mother and a stranger present, with only a stranger present, and totally alone.

Ainsworth discovered that infants react differently to these strange situations. Some, whom she labeled *securely attached,* used their mothers as a safe base for happily exploring the new environment and playing with the toys in the room. When separated from their mothers, the securely attached infants appeared to feel safe, expressed only moderate distress with their mothers being out of sight, and seemed confident in their expectations that she would return to provide care and protection. When reunited with their mothers, these infants sought contact and often resumed exploring their environments. *Insecurely attached* infants reacted differently. They showed more apprehension and less tendency to leave their mothers' sides to explore. They were severely distressed when their mothers left, often crying loudly, and when she returned, they often seemed angry, behaving with hostility or indifference.

Analysis of the data emerging from Ainsworth's strange situation research allowed further subdivision of the category of insecurely attached infants into those classified as expressing *anxious-ambivalent attachment* (these infants manifested extreme separation anxiety when their mothers left) and those manifesting *avoidant attachment* (these infants seemed to want close bodily contact with their mothers but were reticent to seek this because of apparent awareness of mothers' detachment or indifference).

What accounts for these differences in attachment styles? The answer probably lies in a combination of two factors: inborn differences among infants and parenting practices. Some infants are innately predisposed to form more secure attachments than others, just as some newborns seem to respond more positively to being held and cuddled. A second factor contributing to differences in babies' reactions to the strange situation was the way their mothers responded to them at home. Mothers of securely attached infants were inclined to be sensitive and responsive to their infants. For example, some mothers fed their babies when they were hungry rather than following a set schedule. They also tended to cuddle their babies at times other than during feeding or diapering. In contrast, mothers of infants classified in one of the two insecurely attached categories tended to be less sensitive and responsive and were inconsistent in their reactions to their babies. For example, they fed their infants when they felt like it and sometimes ignored their babies' cries of hunger at other times. These mothers also tended to avoid close physical contact with their offspring.

According to research on attachment, the quality of cuddling and snuggling behaviors that occur between babies and parents influences comparable interactions in adult lovers.

The establishment of a trusting, secure attachment between a child and a parent appears to have demonstrable effects on a child's later development. Several studies have shown that securely attached children, who learn that parents are a source of security and trust, are likely to demonstrate much greater social competence than individuals in either category of insecure attachment (Aspelmeier & Kerns, 2003; Sroufe, 1985; Sroufe et al., 1983). Anxious-ambivalent children, who have learned that parents respond inconsistently to their needs, are often plagued with uncertainty in new situations, and they frequently exhibit negative reactions to life situations, such as angry outbursts, an obsessive need to be near the parent, and an inconsistency in responses to others that reflects some degree of ambivalence about how to best respond. Avoidant children, whose parents often neglect them, develop negative views of others and are reticent to let others get close to them.

These varied attachment styles, developed during infancy, tend to continue throughout our lives and to exert considerable influence on both our capacity to form loving attachments and the manner in which we relate to significant others.

Adult Intimate Relationships as an Attachment Process

In recent years a number of social scientists have conceptualized adults' close or romantic relationships as an attachment process (e.g., Aspelmeier & Kerns, 2003; Bartholomew, 1990; Feeney & Noller, 1996). From this perspective individuals are seen to transfer attachment styles and patterns acquired from parent–child relationships to peers with whom they become emotionally and sexually involved. In this sense romantic partners come to serve as attachment figures (Aspelmeier & Kerns, 2003; Hazan & Zeifman, 1999).

These adult attachments between lovers or partners can be one of the three varieties previously described. Securely attached adults seem to be best equipped to establish stable, satisfying relationships. These individuals find it relatively easy to get close to others and are comfortable with others being close to them. They feel secure in relationships and do not fear being abandoned. In contrast, adults with an anxious-ambivalent attachment style often have a poor self-image and are insecure in relationships. These individuals might want to be close to a partner very much but have some ambivalence about getting too close because they fear that their partner does not want to be close to them. They may try to overcome their ambivalence in desperate attempts to get close to a partner, often relinquishing much of their independence in the process. The third attachment style, avoidant adults, are uncomfortable with any degree of closeness with a partner. These individuals often have issues with trusting or depending on a partner. They frequently view others negatively and thus have difficulties in letting others get close to them and in sharing intimacy. Avoidant adults desire a great deal of independence. Research reveals that slightly more than half of U.S. adults are securely attached, about one-fourth are avoidant, and one-fifth are anxious-ambivalent (Hazan &

Shaver, 1987). Table 7.3 outlines some of the common ways the three attachment styles influence interpersonal relationships.

Research indicates that paired couples often are similar in their styles of attachment—further evidence of how influential similarity is in determining whom we fall in love with (Latty-Mann & Davis, 1996). The most common pairing is between two people who both have secure attachment styles (Chappell & Davis, 1998). This is not surprising because secure people respond more positively to others and are comfortable with closeness, both attributes that result in these individuals being more preferred as love partners than any other attachment style. In one study of 354 couples, over half the pairs were a match of secure attachment styles. Predictably, there were no pairings in which both partners were anxious-ambivalent, nor were there any avoidant–avoidant couples, no doubt because people paired in such dyads would be quite incompatible. People with a secure attachment style reported the highest level of relationship satisfaction, especially if their partner also had a secure style of attachment (Kirkpatrick & Davis, 1994).

Still another study of 128 couples found that attachment style influences how partners in a relationship interact. Securely attached individuals reported dealing constructively and effectively with relationship conflicts and/or their partner's potentially damaging behavior. For example, when problems surfaced, their approach was to open lines of communication for discussing and resolving issues. In contrast, people with either of the two insecure attachment styles tended to respond to problems or conflicts with avoidance or withdrawal (Scharfe & Bartholomew, 1995).

These various findings, considered collectively, provide strong evidence of the impact of attachment styles on liking, loving, and relationship satisfaction.

▶ Issues in Loving Relationships

In many ways loving sexual relationships build on and amplify the positive features of friendly relationships, but they also pose more complications than friendships do. Sexual relationships tend to have less acceptance than nonsexual friendships; they are also characterized by more criticism, conflict, ambivalence, and discussions about the relationship and its problems.

Why is this so? In the following paragraphs we explore some of the dynamics that cause complications in intimate relationships, focusing on three questions in particular: What is the relationship between love and sex? How can we make the very personal decision about whether to become sexually involved in a relationship (and what is the best way of saying no to sexual involvement)? How does jealousy relate to love, and what can be done about jealousy in relationships? We turn next to these issues in loving relationships.

TABLE 7.3	Impact of Attachment Styles on Intimate Relationships	
Securely Attached Adults	**Anxious-Ambivalent Adults**	**Avoidant Adults**
Find it relatively easy to get close to others. Comfortable having others close to them.	Want to be close to others but believe that others may not want to be close to them.	Very uncomfortable with being close to others.
Feel secure in relationships and do not fear abandonment.	Worry that partners do not really love them and thus may leave them.	Believe that love is only transitory and that their partner will inevitably leave at some point in time.
Comfortable with both depending on partner and being depended upon.	May want to merge completely and be engulfed by partner.	Worry about becoming dependent on another and distrustful of someone depending on them.
Love relationships typically characterized by happiness, satisfaction, trust, and reciprocal emotional support.	Relationships characterized by roller-coaster emotional shifts and obsessive sexual attraction and jealousy.	Generally want less closeness than their partners seem to desire. Fear intimacy and experience emotional shifts from highs to lows.
Relationship duration averages 10 years.	Relationship duration averages about 5 years.	Relationship duration averages 6 years.

SOURCE: Adapted from Ainsworth (1989), Ainsworth et al. (1978), and Shaver et al. (1988).

What Is the Relationship Between Love and Sex?

Although we tend to associate sex with love, the connection is not always clear. It is certainly true that some couples, unmarried and married, engage in sexual relations without being in love. For example, in one study 53% of women and 79% of men agreed with the statement "I have been sexually attracted without feeling the slightest trace of love" (Tennov, 1979, p. 223). Love can also exist independently of any sexual attraction or expression. However, the ideal intimate relationship for most of us is one that is replete with both feelings of mutual love and sexual gratification for both partners.

Feelings of being both in love with and sexually attracted to another person are frequently intertwined, and these feelings are especially pronounced in the early stages of a developing relationship. Research with college students indicates that both women and men consider sexual desire and attraction an important ingredient of romantic love (Regan, 1998). The complex interplay between love and sex gives rise to many questions: Does sexual intimacy deepen a love relationship? Do men and women have different views of the relationship between sex and love? And is sex without love appropriate? Here, we attempt to shed some light on these and related questions.

Does Sexual Intimacy Deepen a Love Relationship?

I had known Chris for some time and thought I was ready to be sexual with him. So, after an evening out together, I asked him if I could stay at his place, and he said yes. I felt really aroused as we got in bed. I really enjoyed exploring the shapes and textures of his body. As we started to touch each other's genitals, though, I felt uncomfortable. If we proceeded in the direction we were headed, we would be going beyond the level of emotional intimacy I felt. It seemed that I would have to shut out the closeness I felt in order to go further. I had to choose between intimacy and genital contact. Our closeness was more important to me, and I told him that I wanted us to know each other more before going further sexually. (Authors' files)

The woman just quoted made the decision to postpone further sexual involvement until she became more comfortable in her relationship. Many individuals take a different course, moving quickly to sexual intimacy. In some cases this can deepen a relationship. However, this result is certainly not assured. In fact, when a relationship becomes sexual before a couple has established a more generalized bond of intimacy fostered by a growing awareness, understanding, and appreciation of each other, the individuals involved can actually experience a reduction in feelings of emotional closeness.

It is reasonable to suspect that some people have attempted to justify their sexual behavior by deciding they are in love. Indeed, it is likely that some couples enter into premature commitments (such as going steady, moving in together, becoming engaged, or even getting married) to convince themselves of the depth of their love and thus of the legitimacy of their sexual involvement.

Do Men and Women Have Different Views of Sex and Love?

In general, men and women tend to have somewhat different views about the relationship between sex and love (Hendrick & Hendrick, 1995; Quadagno & Sprague, 1991; Regan & Berscheid, 1995). For instance, men are more likely than women to define being in love and to assess the quality of the romantic involvement in terms of the degree of sexual satisfaction they experience in the relationship (Fischer & Heesacker, 1995; McCabe, 1999). Furthermore, in our own sexuality classes women have consistently associated love with sex to a greater extent than have men. In one survey of several hundred of our students, for instance, roughly 36% of women indicated that love is a necessary component of sexual relationships, compared to only 12% of men. Other studies have reported similar findings, indicating that it is easier for men than for women to have sexual intercourse for pleasure and physical release without an emotional commitment (Buss, 1999; Chara & Kuennen, 1994; Townsend, 1995). However, this difference between men and women in motivations for engaging in sexual relations diminishes somewhat with age; older women are more likely than younger women to list desire for physical pleasure as an important motivation for sex (Murstein & Tuerkheim, 1998).

Despite these apparent differences, both men and women value love and affection in sexual relationships. Furthermore, two nationwide surveys of large representative samples of American men and women, conducted for *Parade* magazine in 1984 and 1994, revealed a trend toward convergence of male and female attitudes about the relationship between love and sex. In the 1984 study 59% of men and 86% of women reported that it was difficult to have sex without love (Ubell, 1984). However, 10 years later, 71% of the men indicated it was difficult to relate sexually to someone without love, whereas the percentage of women expressing this viewpoint remained the same (86%) (Clements, 1994).

? How About You?

Do you believe that sex without love is appropriate? Why or why not?

Other studies have confirmed that, even though there are some sex differences in how men and women view the association between love and sex, both sexes are similar in what they consider important ingredients of successful and rewarding loving relationships (Regan, 1998; Sprecher et al., 1995). Among attributes ranked as very important by both men and women are good communication, commitment, and a high quality of emotional and physical intimacy (Byers & Demmons, 1999; Fischer & Heesacker, 1995; McCabe, 1999).

Do Heterosexuals, Gay Men, and Lesbians Have Different Views of Love and Sex?

I would not consider myself to be biased against homosexuals. However, I do feel some degree of disapproval of the gay lifestyle, which often seems to involve casual affairs based more on sex than genuine caring. Some gay men I know have had more partners in the last couple of years than I have had in a lifetime. (Authors' files)

This opinion reflects a belief widespread among heterosexuals that gay men and lesbians form sexual liaisons with same-sex lovers that are based primarily on sexual interaction and that are often devoid of genuine attachment, love, commitment, and overall satisfaction. A number of researchers have revealed the essential fallacy of this thinking by demonstrating that homosexuals, like heterosexuals, generally seek out loving, trusting, caring relationships that embrace many dimensions of sharing in addition to sexual intimacy (Adler et al., 1989; Kurdek, 1988, 1995b; Zak & McDonald, 1997). Lesbians and gay men differ in the degree to which they associate emotional closeness or love with sex, consistent with overall sex differences in views of sex and love. Whereas men in general are more likely than women to separate sex and love, as previously noted, gay men have shown a particularly strong inclination to make this separation. Some gay men engaged in frequent casual sexual encounters without love or caring attachment, especially before the AIDS epidemic (Bell & Weinberg, 1978; Gross, 2003a). Rather than indicating that gay men do not value love, this finding merely reveals that some gay men value sex as an end itself. In contrast, most lesbians postpone sexual involvement until they have developed emotional intimacy with a partner (Leigh, 1989; Zak & McDonald, 1997). A number of researchers have suggested that these differences between gay men and lesbians result from patterns of gender-role socialization that give more permission for casual sex for males than for females. Furthermore, they argue that heterosexual men would be as likely as gay men to occasionally engage in loveless, casual sex if women were equally interested and if it were not for the fact that most heterosexual couples assume that their relationship is exclusive (Foa et al., 1987; Leigh, 1989; Peplau, 1981).

Finally, love plays a prominent role in the lives of homosexual people as a nexus for establishing a self-imposed identity as either a lesbian or a gay man. Many heterosexually oriented people have had sexual contact with same-sex partners. This is especially true during the late childhood years and adolescence, when same-sex contact can be either experimental and transitory or an expression of a lifelong orientation (see Chapter 13). These same-sex sexual activities are not sufficient in and of themselves to establish an identity as a homosexually oriented person. Rather, it is falling in love with a same-sex person that often supplies the key element necessary to establish a gay or lesbian identity. Sexologist John Money (1980) maintains that loving someone of the same sex, rather than simply having sex with her or him, is the essential ingredient that distinguishes being homosexual from being heterosexual. It has also been suggested that loving a same-sex person unifies the emotional and physical aspects of a shared relationship, thereby solidifying commitment to being gay or lesbian (Troiden, 1988).

Sex and Relationships on Your Terms

Sexual expression can have many different meanings. It can be a validation of deep intimacy within a relationship. On the other hand, people can choose to be sexual as part of a friendship or as a way of getting to know someone. For some, reproduction is the primary purpose. For others, reducing sexual tension is the motivation. Sex can be used as a way of experiencing new feelings, excitement, and risk. It can even be a kind of recreational pastime. People can use sex to try to alleviate feelings of insecurity—to prove their manhood or womanhood, to please someone, or to persuade someone to care. People can also use sex to experience the power to attract others or to avenge earlier rejections by enticing partners and then turning them down.

Each of us has the task of deciding how to express sexuality—but this task is complicated by the fact that many of the old rules that have governed sexual relationships are changing. Consider the comments of a recently divorced woman:

> When I was dating 25 years ago in college, a kiss at the door on a first date was considered to mean I really liked the guy. And I was determined to be a virgin until I got married. These guidelines were held by most of my friends, and I felt a lot of security in them. Now I don't know how to behave. There really don't seem to be any standard rules. It's exciting and frightening to know I can make decisions because I want to. It is also confusing at times, and I sometimes wish I could still rely on the old standards. (Authors' files)

Some people base their decisions about sexuality on clear, preexisting rules expressed by their family, religion, or peer group. Many others do not have such specific guidelines, or they disagree with the values they have been taught. These people need to understand their own personal values and develop their own guidelines. In the following section we discuss some options for making decisions about sexual expression.

Know What You Want

The first step in integrating sex into your life in a meaningful way is to consider what you value in life and relationships before becoming sexually involved. This is a variation on the "Know thyself" theme. Consider the following:

> Often when I meet a man for the first time, I end up being swept off my feet and into bed. At the time it seems like the thing to do, but afterward I'm often left confused and a bit empty inside. It's not that I don't like sex. I'm just not sure about what role it should play in my life. (Authors' files)

This woman might be able to reduce the confusion and discomfort she experiences by evaluating her own expectations and needs. An important question for each of us to ask is, What role do I want relationships and sex to occupy in my life at this time? The answer to this question often changes over time as a person faces new life situations.

As a part of this self-inventory, it might be helpful to consider the following questions:

- How comfortable am I with some of the contemporary approaches to sex and relationships?
- Which of the more traditional norms do I value?
- What are my values regarding sexual relationships, and where do they come from (family, religious beliefs, friends, media)?
- What will I do to protect myself and a partner from sexually transmitted diseases or unwanted pregnancy?

You can further clarify your values in relation to a specific decision about sexual activity by asking another question: Will a decision to engage in a sexual relationship—with this person and at this time—enhance my positive feelings about myself and the other person? The answer to this question can help you act in a way that is consistent with your value system. It can also help prevent exploitative sexual encounters in which people do not consider each other's feelings. ■

What if the answer to the previous question is no? Then it may be appropriate to think about what kind of relationship, if any, might enhance positive feelings. Perhaps a sexual relationship is not right, but a nonsexual friendship would be. Or perhaps you do not feel ready for a sexual relationship yet but want to leave open that possibility. At this point, communication and negotiation are important.

One risk of understanding and acting on your own feelings, desires, and values is that someone else might not see things the same way. Many people take such differences to mean that either they are wrong or the other person is wrong. However, more often than not, differences simply indicate that two people do not want the same thing at the same time. Occasionally, a relationship cannot be established without compromising one person's situation or values. When this occurs, one option is to end the relationship, thereby allowing each individual to seek someone else with similar perspectives.

On other occasions, strategies such as clarification, negotiation, and compromise can establish a common foundation for a relationship. However, direct communication sounds easier than it is. The following sections illustrate some options for dealing with several specific relationship situations. In Chapter 8 we provide additional information on communication in sexual relationships.

Friendships Without Sex

Some people find it difficult to communicate a desire for a friendship without sex, especially when it appears that the other person wants a sexual relationship. Often they are concerned that the other person will feel bad or decide to end the relationship. However, most people would probably prefer to be told the truth directly rather than have to decipher vague, confusing responses. The following comment is fairly typical of our students:

I hate it when I find myself in a relationship, and all I get is the runaround. I eventually get the picture when someone else doesn't reciprocate my feelings, but what a waste of time and energy. Why can't they just come out and say what they are feeling? At least I would know where I stand and could act accordingly. (Authors' files)

This person's feeling of frustration is understandable. However, one can attempt to resolve some of the uncertainty by asking the other person about his or her feelings. The following illustrates how one student did this:

Jake and I had gone out several times, and at first he acted like he was attracted to me. But then he began to treat me more like a friend. He continued to ask me out but made no sexual gestures. I finally told him I was confused about how he felt about me. He seemed very concerned about my feelings as he told me that he wanted a friendship with me instead of a romantic relationship. I felt disappointed, and it was a little tough on my ego to not be desired sexually, but I decided that a friendship with him would be nice. And several years later, we are still friends. (Authors' files)

Nonsexual friendships can offer companionship and enjoyment.

Saying "Not Yet" to a Sexual Relationship

One of the benefits of less rigid rules about "proper" sexual behavior is that they can make it easier for people to set their own pace in sexual relationships. It is common for a person to feel sexual attraction and to want a sexual relationship with someone—but not yet. The ability to delay sexual involvement until both people feel ready can do much to enhance the initial experience. Waiting until familiarity and trust are established and making sure that personal values are consistent can enhance not only a relationship but also positive feelings about oneself. Also, as we will discuss in Chapter 17, the possibility of contracting AIDS or other serious sexually transmitted diseases can be reduced by taking some time to assess the risk status of a prospective partner before beginning sexual relations.

When sexual attraction exists within a relationship, sex is not necessarily an either/or situation. There are progressive stages of intimacy, from holding hands to genital contact, and some people move slowly through these stages to savor and grow comfortable with the increasingly intimate contact. Gratification can be greater when the progression toward intimacy is gradual rather than rushed:

I felt sexually attracted to Mike the first time I met him, but somehow, almost by mutual instinct, we moved very slowly sexually. We both agreed that was how we wanted it for this relationship. We spent several extremely enjoyable months kissing, touching, holding each other, and even sleeping together before we had intercourse. The entire experience has given new light to the expression "haste makes waste." (Authors' files)

Social expectations of "instant sex" can present a challenge to those who want to move gradually into a sexual relationship. What can you do to let another person know that you are not yet ready for sex or that you want the relationship to progress slowly? It is often helpful to begin by indicating that you find the person attractive. You can acknowledge your desire for greater sexual intimacy yet be definite about not being ready. Finally, you can let a partner know what kind of physical contact you want at a given point in the relationship; this can help avoid misunderstandings and reassure the other person.

Ending a Relationship

Over the years, our sexuality classes have included many lively discussions of the question, How do you prefer to be informed when someone does not wish to continue a relationship with you? Although students have many different opinions and experiences, most want to be told in a clear, unmistakable manner that their desire for a relationship is not reciprocated. A simple statement such as "I appreciate your interest in me, but I'm not attracted to you enough to want to develop a relationship with you" is the kind of ending that most of our students have indicated they would prefer.

Most of our students report that it is more difficult to break the news that they want to end a relationship than to receive the news. This finding has been supported by a survey of college students. Respondents who had decided to call off a relationship reported greater feelings of guilt, uncertainty, discomfort, and awkwardness than did those who had been rejected (Baumeister et al., 1993). It is rarely easy to

 How About You?

How would you want to be informed that a desired other person wishes to end a relationship with you?

end a relationship when one person is interested in maintaining it. This situation requires communication that is both effective and compassionate.

Managing Rejection

Unrequited love The experience of one person loving someone who does not return that love.

Most of us have experienced loving someone who does not reciprocate these feelings. Furthermore, we are probably familiar with both sides of this phenomenon of **unrequited love.** One study of college students found that most had experienced multiple episodes of unreciprocated attractions during the previous 5 years. More than 90% of this sample reported having had at least one painful experience of being rejected in an instance of unrequited love (Baumeister et al., 1993). Fear of rejection, perhaps stemming from previous episodes of unrequited love, can often inhibit people from initiating a relationship or expressing their desires within one. One man expressed his concern as follows:

I find it extremely stressful to ask a woman out for the first time. I just can't deal with the prospect of being turned down. I know it's irrational, but when someone says no, I feel lousy. (Authors' files)

To many people, a "no" affects their feelings of self-worth (Baumeister et al., 1993). A person who is rejected might feel unattractive, boring, unsexy, unintelligent, or inherently unlovable. But all of us experience rejection at some time, because our traits cannot match every person's preferences. The very characteristics that one person finds undesirable may well appeal to another, and the right to choose not to become involved with someone is certainly a right that most people want. Furthermore, in some instances people reject romantic advances because they are already involved in an intimate relationship with another or because they do not wish to experience a close relationship at that point in their lives.

Although rejection can be a painful experience, a few strategies are helpful in dealing with being turned down. It is important to remember that each of us has worth, regardless of whether all people approve of us. Also, defending yourself to someone who has said no is not likely to be helpful, because being turned down is usually not a criticism but simply an expression of individual preference. Finally, even though rejection can make us want to give up on continued attempts to form close relationships, we can avoid rejection completely only if we isolate ourselves from most kinds of social interaction.

It is not always easy to maintain such a positive attitude in response to rejection. Indeed, especially when individuals have become close to one another, feelings can become quite intense. We look next at one response to real or imagined rejection—jealousy—and explore how it affects relationships and what can be done, if anything, to keep feelings of jealousy under control.

Jealousy in Relationships

Jealousy has been defined as an aversive emotional reaction evoked by a real or imagined relationship involving one's partner and a third person (Bringle & Buunk, 1991). Many people think that jealousy is a measure of devotion and that the absence of jealous feelings implies a lack of love (Buss, 2000). It is not uncommon for people to have ambivalent attitudes about jealousy, "seeing it sometimes as a sign of insecurity, sometimes as a sign of love, and sometimes as both simultaneously" (Puente & Cohen, 2003, p. 458). Jealousy is related more to injured pride, or to people's fear of losing what they want to control or possess, than to love. For example, a person who finds that a spouse enjoys someone else's company might feel inadequate and therefore jealous. As previously described in our discussion of reciprocity, we often enter into and remain in relationships because they provide a sense of belongingness and bolster our self-esteem. We often rely on our partner to validate our positive sense of self. Consequently, we can feel threatened and sense a potential loss of both reciprocity and a positive self-image if we perceive that our partner is considering a replacement for us (Boekhout et al., 1999).

The intense emotions of jealousy are therefore often due to our imagining and fearing being abandoned by our partner for someone else (Sharpsteen & Kirkpatrick, 1997). Jealous feelings can be further heightened by envy of certain characteristics of the rival, because we are more likely to be jealous of individuals who have qualities that we desire. In general, traits for which women show the most

InfoTrac Search Words

■ Jealousy

envy are attractiveness and popularity, whereas men are more envious of wealth and fame (Barker, 1987; Salovey & Rodin, 1985).

Some people are more prone to feeling jealousy than others. Individuals who have a low opinion of themselves, reflected in feelings of insecurity and inadequacy, are more likely to feel jealousy in a relationship (Buss, 1994, 1999; Fisher, 1992). This relates back to a point we have already made—that a healthy self-esteem is the foundation for building intimate relationships. Second, people who see a large discrepancy between who they are and who they would like to be are also prone to jealousy. Not surprisingly, such individuals also are likely to have low self-esteem. And third, people who place a high value on traits such as wealth, fame, popularity, and physical attractiveness might be more likely to feel jealousy in a relationship (Salovey & Rodin, 1985).

Jealousy is frequently a factor in precipitating violence in marriages (Buss, 1999; Buunk et al., 1996; Puente & Cohen, 2003) and dating relationships (Himelein et al., 1994; Puente & Cohen, 2003). Research demonstrates that jealousy-precipitated violence is most commonly directed toward one's partner or lover rather than against a third-party rival (Mathes & Verstrate, 1993; Paul & Galloway, 1994).

Jealousy is an uncomfortable feeling that can stifle the development of a relationship and the pleasure associated with being together. For both men and women the emotions and thoughts associated with jealousy are negative and include feeling anxious, depressed, or angry and having a sense of being less valued by and attractive to one's partner (Bush et al., 1988). Jealousy also has a paradoxical effect, because although the jealous person desires to maintain both the relationship and his or her self-image, both of these desires are likely to be damaged when jealous feelings are expressed (Buunk & Bringle, 1987).

* self-acceptance

Although it is clear that jealousy has many negative effects, it is not always clear how jealous feelings should be handled when they occur in a relationship. The box "Coping with the Green-Eyed Monster" offers some suggestions to people who want to decrease feelings of jealousy, either in themselves or in their partners.

Sex Differences in Jealousy

Not everyone responds to jealousy in the same way, and a number of studies have found differences in the ways women and men react. In general, women are more likely to acknowledge jealous feelings and men are more likely to deny them (Barker, 1987; Clanton & Smith, 1977). Furthermore, a jealous woman is more inclined to focus on and become distressed by the emotional involvement of her partner with another person, whereas a jealous man is more likely to be upset about the sexual relationship his lover has with another (Buss et al., 1992, 1996; Buunk et al., 1996; Fisher, 1999). These sex differences in sexual jealousy appear to be consistent across other cultures, according to a study that reported finding them in Germany and the Netherlands in addition to the United States (Buunk et al., 1996).

David Buss and his colleagues have suggested that these sex differences in the instigators of jealousy emerged during the evolutionary history of humans (Buss, 1999, 2000; Buss et al., 1992, 1996). According to this viewpoint, which emphasizes the consequences of infidelity for the primary relationship, men are especially concerned about sexual infidelity because the biological parentage of offspring will be uncertain and they do not want to expend their resources on other men's children. Women, who need male investment in their offspring, have evolved to be more concerned about their partner's emotional infidelity or falling in love with others, which might result in abandoning the primary relationship.

> **? Critical Thinking Question**
>
> Research indicates that women are more likely to acknowledge jealous feelings and that men are more likely to deny them. What do you think accounts for this sex difference?

Another sex difference in jealousy patterns is that women often blame themselves when a conflict over jealousy arises, whereas men typically attribute their jealousy to a third party or to their partner's behavior (Barker, 1987; Clanton & Smith, 1977; Daly et al., 1982). Women have also been shown to be more inclined than men to deliberately provoke jealousy in their partners (Sheets et al., 1997; White & Helbick, 1988). This sex difference in jealousy patterns might stem from the fact that women experiencing jealousy often suffer simultaneously from feelings of inadequacy and worthlessness. Consequently, efforts to arouse jealousy in a partner can actually be an attempt to bolster self-worth by eliciting increased attention from a partner concerned about her actions. Men also often attach feelings of inadequacy to jealousy. However, the relationship is frequently reversed in men, with awareness of jealousy occurring first, followed by feeling inadequate (White & Helbick, 1988).

Coping with the Green-Eyed Monster

It is common for the green-eyed monster, jealousy, to raise its ugly head at least sometime during the course of a relationship. Dealing with jealousy can be difficult, because such feelings often stem from a deep sense of inadequacy that resides within the jealous individual rather than within the relationship. A person threatened by insecurity-induced feelings of jealousy often withdraws from his or her partner or goes on the attack with accusations and/or threats. These ineffective

Jealousy is an uncomfortable feeling that often harms a relationship and stifles the pleasure associated with being together.

coping behaviors often provoke a similar reaction in the nonjealous partner—withdrawal or counterattack. A more effective approach, from the perspective of the jealous person, is to acknowledge his or her own feelings of jealousy and to clarify their source. Thus a jealous person might initiate discussion by saying something like "Mary, I am afraid for us, and a little bit crazy over all the time you spend working late with your co-workers, especially with that guy Bill!" Such an open acknowledgment of feelings without threats or accusations might prompt Mary to respond with reassurances, and a positive dialogue might ensue.

In many situations the jealous person will not acknowledge the existence of a problem and will not express a desire to work on it. If this is the case, the essential first step toward successful coping is to instill the motivation to begin working to eliminate the painful jealousy feelings and the destructive behaviors that these feelings often induce. Robert Barker (1987), a marital therapist, provided valuable guidelines for how to accomplish this in his book *The Green-Eyed Marriage: Surviving Jealous Relationships.* Barker maintains that a jealous person is most likely to become motivated to work on the problem and to permit help from others when he or she:

- *is confident that there is no danger of losing the valued partner.* Direct reassurance that the relationship is not in danger is often ineffective and sometimes can even be counterproductive. A more effective strategy is to make references, at varied times, to being together in the future. Consequently, a nonjealous partner planning to initiate a discussion about jealousy at some future point might first pick a few opportune times to say such things as "It will be great when the children are all grown and we have more time just for us."
- *is assured that the problem comes from the relationship rather than from defects in his or her character.* A jealous person is much more likely to pursue a coping process when both partners acknowledge that jealousy is a shared problem. The nonjealous

partner can move thinking in this direction by stating, "This is a problem we share, and we both have to work equally to overcome it."

- *is confident about being genuinely loved and respected.* Because jealousy often stems from feelings of inadequacy and insecurity, the nonjealous partner can help minimize these negative emotions and bolster self-esteem and confidence by "regularly reaffirming affection for the jealous person verbally, emotionally, and physically" (Barker, 1987, p. 100).
- *is not provoked into feeling shame or guilt.* Understandably, many people who are undeservedly targets of jealousy become angry and inclined to strike back with sarcasm, ridicule, or put-downs in an effort to make their jealous partners feel so much guilt that they will be too ashamed to persist in their unfounded accusations. Unfortunately, these negative counterattacks are likely to have the opposite effect by promoting more anger and defensiveness. Worse yet, the jealous person might be even less willing to acknowledge a need for change.
- *is able to empathize with the person who has been hurt by the jealous behavior.* When jealous people are able to understand and empathize with the pain that their behavior has created in their partners, the incentive to change might be increased. The challenge for the nonjealous partner is to facilitate the development of empathy rather than guilt. This can be accomplished by verbalizing the hurt and pain but not attributing its cause to the jealous partner. Thus, Mary might say to her jealous partner, "I really love you, Mike, and I feel really bad when I have to work late and I know you are at home wishing we could be together. It is really painful to think that my work situation sometimes appears to be more important than our relationship."

Once the motivation for change is established and once a couple begins a dialogue aimed at coping with jealousy, several of the communication strategies outlined in Chapter 8 can facilitate this process. Some of the suggestions for self-disclosure, listening, feedback, and asking questions can help to clearly establish what each partner wants and expects of the relationship. For example, after disclosing his fears, Mike might communicate to Mary that it would reduce his concerns if she would spend less time working with Bill after hours or maybe just include others from the office at these times.

One interesting investigation assessed the relationship between perceived parenthood quality and jealousy. Women respondents in this study were more likely to become jealous over infidelity if their partner was perceived as potentially bad parent material, because an inadequate father who abandons a relationship would be less likely than a good father to continue support of his children. In sharp contrast, male respondents were more likely to become jealous if their mates were perceived as potentially good parents, because they might lose an ideal partner for producing and caring for their children (Sharpsteen, 1995).

▶ Maintaining Relationship Satisfaction

Human relationships present many challenges. To begin, there is the challenge of building positive feelings about ourselves. There is the added task of establishing satisfying and enjoyable relationships with family, peers, teachers, co-workers, employers, and other people in our social network. A third challenge involves developing special intimate relationships with friends and, when we want them, sexual relationships. Finally, many people confront the challenge of maintaining satisfaction and love within an ongoing committed relationship. Commitment in a relationship is often demonstrated by the decision to marry. However, many couples have long-term committed relationships, either heterosexual or homosexual, that do not involve marriage. In this section we present some of the factors that contribute to ongoing satisfaction in relationships. We also discuss the value of sexual variety within a relationship.

Ingredients in a Lasting Love Relationship

Ingredients often present in a lasting love relationship include self-acceptance, acceptance by one's partner, appreciation of one another, commitment, good communication, realistic expectations, shared interests, equality in decision making, and the ability to face conflict effectively. These characteristics are not static; they evolve and change and influence one another over time. Often they need to be deliberately cultivated. The efforts that partners make toward preservation are probably more important to relationship stability today than in the past, when marriage as an institution was sustained more strongly by culture, religion, law, and the extended family.

One review of the research on marital satisfaction reported that successful marriages that remain strong over the long haul often exhibit certain other characteristics (Karney & Bradbury, 1995):

- Parents of both spouses had successful, happy marriages.
- Spouses have similar attitudes, interests, and personality styles.
- Both spouses are satisfied with their sexual sharing.
- The couple has an adequate and steady income.
- The woman was not pregnant when the couple married.
- Spiritual Outcome

In another study researchers asked a sample of 560 women and men to judge the importance of a number of different relationship elements to the success of a marriage or a long-term committed relationship. Among the characteristics judged to be reflective of high-quality relationships are (Sprecher et al., 1995):

- Supportive communication: Open and honest communication and a willingness to talk about difficult issues and concerns.
- Companionship: Sharing mutual interests and enjoying many activities together.
- Sexual expression: Spontaneity and variety in sexual sharing and feeling sexually attractive to one's partner.

In still another study of 300 happily married couples, the most frequently named reason for an enduring and happy marriage was seeing one's partner as one's best friend. Qualities that individuals especially appreciated in a partner were caring, giving, having integrity, and having a sense of humor. These couples were aware of flaws in their mates, but they believed that the likable qualities were more important. Many said that their mates had become more interesting to them over time. They preferred shared rather than separate activities, which appeared to reflect the richness in the relationship. Another key was their belief in marriage as

An older couple's intimacy and affection develop from years of shared experiences.

a long-term commitment and a sacred institution. Most couples were generally satisfied with their sex lives, and for some the sexual passion had become more intense over time (Lauer & Lauer, 1985).

Maintaining frequent positive interactions is crucial to continued satisfaction in a relationship. The saying "It's the little things that count" is especially meaningful here. When one partner says to the other, "You do not love me anymore," that often means "You are not doing as many of the things you used to do that I interpret as meaning you love me." These behaviors are often so small that the partners may not really notice them. However, when couples do fewer things to make one another feel loved (or when they stop doing them entirely), the deficit is often experienced as a lack of love. Continuing affectionate and considerate interaction helps maintain a feeling of love. One person wrote:

The kinds of things that enhance my feeling that my partner still loves me may seem quite inconsequential, but to me they aren't. When he gets up to greet me when I come home, when he takes my arm crossing the street, when he asks, "Can I help you with that," when he tells me I look great, when he holds me in the middle of the night, when he thanks me for doing a routine chore—I feel loved by him. Those little things—all added up—make a tremendous difference to me. (Authors' files)

It is also useful to talk with our partners, to communicate what is especially enjoyable, or to suggest new ideas. The golden rule ("Do unto others as you would have them do unto you") is not always applicable in relationships, because people's preferences are often quite different. One partner may not know what the other partner wants unless that person expresses it.

Enjoyment with and appreciation of one another in nonsexual areas typically enhance sexual interest and interactions. Often couples report a lack of desire for sexual intimacy when they are not feeling emotionally intimate.

Sexual Variety: An Important Ingredient

There is a special little restaurant with great steaks and a cozy, intimate atmosphere that I love to visit once every few months. Good companionship, a favorite bottle of wine, a tasty dinner, and I am living. Let a friend invite me back the next day, and it is still good, but not quite so stimulating. Given an invitation for a third trip in as many days, and I might just as soon stop off for a McDonald's quarter-pounder. (Authors' files)

helps. w/ communication (intimate)

Many people have a strong desire to seek variety in life's experiences. They might acquire an assortment of friends, each of whom provides a unique enrichment to their lives. Likewise, they read different kinds of books, pursue a variety of recreational activities, eat a variety of foods, and take a mixture of classes. Yet many of these same people settle for routine in their sex lives.

Unfortunately, many people enter into a committed relationship thinking that intense sexual excitement will always follow naturally when two people are in love. But, as we have seen in this chapter, the initial excitement must eventually be replaced by realistic and committed efforts to maintain the vitality and rewards of a working relationship. Once a person is committed to a primary partner, the variety offered by a succession of relationships is no longer available. For some individuals it may be necessary to seek variety in other ways.

Not every couple feels the need for sexual variety. Many people are quite comfortable with established routines and have no desire to change them. However, if you prefer to develop more variety in your sexual relationship, the following paragraphs may be helpful.

Communication is critical. Talk to your partner about your needs and feelings. Share with him or her your desire to try something different. Perhaps some of the guidelines in Chapter 8 will facilitate making requests and exchanging information.

Even though time inevitably erodes the novelty associated with the newness of a relationship, the resulting decline of passion can be countered by introducing novelty into patterns of sexual sharing. This can be accomplished by avoiding routine times and places. Make love in places other than the bed (on the laundry room floor, in the shower, alongside a mountain trail) and at various times ("birdsong in the morning," a "nooner," or in the middle of the night when you wake up feeling sexually aroused).

Some of the most exciting sexual experiences are those that take place on the spur of the moment with little or no planning. It is easy to see how these encounters might occur frequently during courtship. It is also true that they can become distant memories after a couple settles into the demanding daily schedule of living together. Nevertheless, you may find that striving to maintain this spontaneity will stand you in good stead as your relationship is nurtured over months or years together.

On the other hand, planning for intimate time—sexual and nonsexual—can also help maintain closeness. Make dates with one another and consciously continue the romantic gestures that came naturally early in the relationship. Make a commitment to place your energy and time toward your sexual relationship.

Do not let questions of what is "normal" get in the way of an enriched and varied erotic life. Too often, people refrain from experiencing something new because they believe that different activities are "abnormal." In reality, only you can judge what is normal for you. Contemporary writers in the field of sexology concur that any sexual activity is normal, so long as it gives pleasure and does not cause emotional or physical discomfort or harm to either partner. Emotional comfort is an important variable because "discomfort and conflict rather than intimacy and satisfaction can result if behaviors are tried which are too divergent from personal values and attitudes" (Barbach, 1982, p. 282).

SPOTLIGHT ON RESEARCH

Sex Differences in the Desire for Sexual Variety

A number of evolutionary psychologists have hypothesized that the mating strategies of men and women have evolved differentially; a sex difference is especially pronounced in the motivations underlying the pursuit of short-term sexual relationships. According to this perspective, men seeking short-term mates are often motivated by a desire for sexual variety, which is reflected in their inclinations to pursue both numerous sex partners and to consent to sex relatively quickly. In contrast, women's underlying motivations for seeking short-term relationships seem to be more focused on selectively obtaining men of higher status and/or excellent genetic quality (Buss & Schmitt, 1993; Gangestad & Simpson, 2000; Gangestad & Thornhill, 1997; Schmitt, 2003; Schmitt et al., 2001).

Support for this interpretation was recently provided by a cross-cultural survey of 16,288 people selected from 10 major world regions, including North America, South America, Western Europe, Eastern Europe, Southern Europe, the Middle East, Africa, Oceania, South and Southeast Asia, and East Asia. This investigation, conducted by evolutionary psychologist David Schmitt (2003), used an anonymous nine-page survey questionnaire, translated into local languages, that was designed to assess three primary variables: (1) the number of sexual partners desired at differing time intervals ("Number of Partners" measure), (2) relationship duration before experiencing sexual intercourse ("Time Known" measure), and (3) the extent to which participants were actively seeking short-term mating partners ("Short-Term Seeking" measure).

The results of this comprehensive investigation provided strong evidence that men and women differ fundamentally in their short-term mating psychology, especially in the desire for sexual variety, and that these differences appear to be culturally universal throughout the sampled world regions. Schmitt's findings revealed that "men not only possess a greater desire than women do for a variety of sexual partners, men also require less time to elapse than women do before consenting to sexual intercourse, and men tend to more actively seek short-term mateships than women do" (Schmitt, 2003, p. 101). Schmitt concluded that his investigation provides strong support for the evolutionary psychology viewpoint that men's evolved short-term mating strategies are rooted in a desire for sexual variety. For example, even among women participants who responded that they were "strongly seeking" a short-term partner, less than 20% of these women desired more than one partner in the next month. In contrast, among men in the "strongly seeking" category, over 50% desired more than one partner in the next month. This percentage increased to 69% and 75% for the next 6 months and 1 year, respectively. For women respondents the percentage increases for the same time periods were minimal.

Related to concerns about what is normal are concerns about frequency. Forget the magazine article that said that couples in your age category are having sex 2.7 times per week. The only right standard for you is to have sex as often as you and your partner desire.

Finally, partners sometimes find that books dealing with sexual techniques benefit their erotic lives. We recommend that you read them together rather than separately. Discussing a particular written suggestion can often open up new possibilities of sexual sharing. Such books sometimes provide the necessary information and support for trying something new.

? How About You?

Of the various ingredients of lasting love relationships discussed in this section, which seem most important to you?

We do not mean to imply that all people must have active, varied sex lives to be truly happy; this is not the case. As we have already seen, some partners find comfort and contentment in repeating familiar patterns of sexual interaction. Others consider sex relatively unimportant compared with other aspects of their lives and choose not to exert special efforts in pursuing its pleasures. However, if your sexuality is an important source of pleasure in your life, perhaps these suggestions and others in this textbook will be valuable to you. ■

Do men and women differ in their desire for sexual variety? Recent cross-cultural research, described in the "Spotlight on Research" box on the previous page, provides strong evidence that the sexes do differ in the desire for sexual variety.

► Summary

What Is Love?

- Zick Rubin's Love Scale is a subjective rating scale that measures what Rubin defines as the three components of love: attachment, caring, and intimacy. (pp. 183–184)

Types of Love

- Passionate love is characterized by intense, vibrant feelings that tend to be relatively short-lived. (pp. 184–185)
- Companionate love is characterized by deep affection and attachment. (p. 185)
- Robert Sternberg's triangular theory maintains that love has three dimensions: passion and intimacy, which are the motivational and emotional components, respectively, and commitment, the cognitive component. Variations in the combinations in which these three components exist yield eight different kinds of love. (pp. 185–187)
- John Allan Lee proposed a theory that describes six different styles of loving: romantic, game playing, possessive, companionate, altruistic, and pragmatic. (pp. 187–188)

Falling in Love: Why and with Whom?

- Falling in love has been explained as resulting from the need to overcome a sense of aloneness or from the desire to justify sexual involvement or as a consequence of sexual attraction. (p. 188)
- The intense feelings of being passionately in love might have a basis in surging levels of the brain chemicals norepinephrine, dopamine, and especially phenylethylamine (PEA). The progression from passion to deep attraction might result from the gradual increase of endorphins in the brain. (pp. 188–189)
- Factors known to contribute strongly to interpersonal attraction and falling in love with another include proximity, similarity, reciprocity, and physical attractiveness. We often develop loving relationships with people whom we see frequently, who share similar beliefs, who seem to like us, and whom we perceive as physically attractive. (pp. 189–194)

Love and Styles of Attachment

- The manner in which we form attachments, which has its roots in infancy, has a great effect on how we relate to loved partners. (p. 194)

- Securely attached children, who learn that parents are a source of security and trust, demonstrate much greater social competence than insecurely attached children, who are classified as either anxious-ambivalent or avoidant. (p. 194)
- Attachment styles developed during infancy continue throughout life to exert considerable influence on a person's capacity to form loving attachments and the manner in which the person relates to significant others. (p. 195)
- Securely attached adults are best equipped to establish stable, satisfying relationships. They are comfortable being close to others, feel secure in relationships, and do not fear being abandoned. (p. 195)
- Anxious-ambivalent adults often have a poor self-image, are insecure in relationships, and struggle with ambivalence about achieving closeness with others. (p. 195)
- Avoidant adults are uncomfortable with any degree of closeness, have problems trusting or depending on a partner, and often view others negatively. (p. 195)
- Paired couples are often similar in their styles of attachment. The most common pairing is between partners who both have secure attachment styles. (p. 196)
- People with secure attachment styles report the highest levels of relationship satisfaction, especially if both partners also have a secure attachment style. (p. 196)

Issues in Loving Relationships

- There are various perspectives on the connections between love and sex. Most students in our surveys report that love enriches sexual relations but is not necessary for enjoyment of sex. (p. 197)
- Women consistently link love with sexual behavior more than men do, but research indicates that men and women are becoming more similar on this issue. (pp. 197–198)
- Gay men and lesbian women, like heterosexuals, generally seek out loving, trusting, caring relationships that embrace many dimensions of sharing in addition to sexual intimacy. (p. 198)
- Deciding one's own values in relation to sexual experiences is especially important today, in a time of changing expectations. To help you act in a way that is consistent with your value system, ask

yourself, Will a decision to engage in a sexual relationship—with this person at this time—enhance my positive feelings about myself and the other person? (p. 199)

- There are many types of intimate relationships, including friendships without sex and love relationships in which the sexual component progresses gradually. (pp. 200–201)
- You can develop strategies for minimizing the pain of rejection, particularly if you remember that rejection usually occurs because your traits do not match another's subjective preferences, not because you are unworthy. (pp. 201–202)
- Some people consider jealousy a sign of love, but it might actually reflect fear of losing possession or control of another. (p. 202)
- Jealousy is frequently a factor in precipitating violence in marriages and dating relationships. (p. 203)
- Research indicates that men and women react differently to jealousy. (pp. 203, 205)

Maintaining Relationship Satisfaction

- Ingredients often present in a lasting love relationship include self-acceptance, acceptance of one's partner, appreciation of one another, commitment, good communication, realistic expectations, shared interests, equality in decision making, and the ability to face conflict effectively. (pp. 205–206)
- Sexual variety is often an important ingredient of enjoyable sex in a long-term relationship. For some, however, the security of routine is most satisfying. (pp. 206–207)

 ## Suggested Readings

Ackerman, Diane (1994). *A Natural History of Love.* New York: Random House. A highly praised book that provides a readable, entertaining, and informative exploration of the historical, cultural, and biological roots of love.

Barker, Robert (1987). *The Green-Eyed Marriage: Surviving Jealous Relationships.* New York: Free Press. An excellent book by a marriage and family therapist that covers the causes and effects of jealousy and strategies for overcoming its negative effect on relationships.

Buss, David (2000). *The Dangerous Passion: Why Jealousy Is as Necessary as Love and Sex.* New York: Free Press. A book about the psychology of jealousy, relationships, and relationship violence. Buss argues the controversial viewpoint that jealousy is an evolutionary adaptation that is both an inherent component of romantic relationships and an index of love or commitment.

Fromm, Erich (1963). *The Art of Loving.* New York: Bantam Books. A classic on the topic of love. Fromm elucidates the power of love to develop human potential within oneself and within a relationship.

Hatfield, Elaine, and Richard Rapson (1993). *Love, Sex, and Intimacy: Their Psychology, Biology, and History.* New York: HarperCollins College. An excellent text that describes research and theories in the area of loving relationships.

Hendrick, Clyde, and Susan Hendrick (2000). *Close Relationships: A Sourcebook.* Thousand Oaks, CA: Sage. An informative overview of research on the related topics of attraction, love, intimacy, and the development and maintenance of relationships.

Hendrix, Harville (1990). *Getting the Love You Want: A Guide for Couples.* New York: Perennial Library. A best-selling book by an educator and couples therapist that provides a wealth of practical information for couples who wish to heal conflicts and develop a lasting and mature love relationship.

Pines, Ayala Malach (1998). *Romantic Jealousy: Causes, Symptoms, and Cures.* New York: Routledge. A valuable resource that provides practical advice for ways to effectively deal with jealousy in a relationship.

Schwartz, Pepper (2000). *Everything You Know About Love and Sex Is Wrong.* New York: Putnam. An informative and entertaining look at 25 myths pertaining to love and sexual relationships by a sociologist and frequent contributor to the literature on sexuality and relationships.

Weber, Ann, and John Harvey (Eds.) (1994). *Perspectives on Close Relationships.* Boston: Allyn & Bacon. A collection of scholarly articles that deal with a variety of relationship issues, including attraction, attachment, love, sexual intimacy, and jealousy.

 # Web Resources

Your *Our Sexuality* Web site **http://psychology.wadsworth.com/crooksbaur9e/** has direct links to the Web sites described below. These links are checked often for changes, dead links, and new additions.

Romance 101

Sponsored by womensforum.com, this Web site, directed primarily at girls and young women, provides a somewhat lighthearted look at romantic relationships.

Relationship Issues

Although aimed at teenagers, this short series of Web pages on the Planned Parenthood Web site addresses questions faced by many young adults with regard to relationships and sexual activity.

Our Sexuality Web Site

For online resources directly related to this book, go to **http://psychology.wadsworth.com/crooksbaur9e/**. You will find interactive exercises, study questions, chapter outlines, an online version of this text's glossary, and Web links and activities that complement your CD-ROM.

InfoTrac® College Edition Online Library

http://infotrac.thomsonlearning.com/
InfoTrac College Edition is an online searchable library that includes a multitude of journals, many of which are specific to human sexuality. These journals include *Archives of Sexual Behavior, Archives of Sexual Health Behavior, Canadian Journal of Human Sexuality, Hispanic Journal of the Behavioral Sciences, Journal of Cross-Cultural Psychology, Journal of Physical Education, Recreation, and Dance, Journal of Sex Research,* and *Sex Roles.* You may search topics suggested in the margins of this chapter or terms of your own.

Our Sexuality CD-ROM

Use your CD-ROM for further study of the concepts in this chapter. Your CD-ROM provides animations of difficult concepts, video clips of real people discussing sexuality, critical thinking questions, chapter quizzing, and more.

CHAPTER 8

Communication in Sexual Behavior

© Joyce Choo/CORBIS

I want to talk with my girlfriend about our sex life. So many times I have made up my mind to do this, but I can't seem to come up with how I should do this. How can I tell her about my body and its needs? What words do I use? Do I say, "I like it best when you caress along the entire length of my penis," or should I say, "It feels good when you touch all of my cock"? The first word sounds too clinical, but I am afraid the term cock might shock her and put her off. Just what words do lovers use? (Authors' files)

This is a chapter about sexual communication: the ways people express their feelings and convey their needs and desires to sexual partners. We consider the reasons that such attempts are sometimes unsuccessful; we also explore some ways to enhance this important aspect of our sexual lives.

▶ The Importance of Communication

Sexual communication can contribute greatly to the satisfaction of an intimate relationship. Good communication about sexual desires and concerns has frequently been identified as a valuable asset to the development and maintenance of a satisfying and enduring sexual relationship (Byers & Demmons, 1999; Ferroni & Jaffee, 1997). We do not mean that extensive verbal dialogue is essential to all sexual sharing; there are times when spoken communication is more disruptive than constructive. Nevertheless, partners who never talk about the sexual aspects of their relationship are denying themselves an opportunity to increase their closeness and pleasure through learning about each other's needs and desires.

Central to this chapter is our belief that the basis for effective sexual communication is **mutual empathy**—the underlying knowledge that each partner in a relationship cares for the other and knows that the care is reciprocated. With this perspective in mind we discuss various approaches to sexual communication that have proved helpful in the lives of many people. We do not claim to have the final word on the many nuances of human communication, nor do we suggest that the ideas offered here will work for everyone. Communication strategies often need to be individually modified; and sometimes the differences between two people are so profound that even the best communication cannot ensure a mutually satisfying relationship. We hope, though, that some of these shared experiences and suggestions can be helpful in your own life.

Mutual empathy The underlying knowledge that each partner in a relationship cares for the other and knows that the care is reciprocated.

Some Reasons That Sexual Communication Is Difficult

Some of the most important reasons that sexual communication is difficult lie in our socialization, the language available for talking about sex, and the fears many people have about self-expression.

Socialization and Sexual Communication

The way we were reared as children often contributes to later difficulties in talking about sexual needs. Learning to cover our genitals, to think that eliminative functions are "dirty," or to hide self-pleasuring for fear of adverse reactions can contribute to a sense of shame and discomfort with the sexual areas and functions of our bodies. We discuss the development of sexual attitudes during childhood and adolescence in Chapter 13.

The lack of communication about sexual matters in many American homes is detrimental in a number of ways. Not talking about sex at home deprives a young child of one valuable source of a vocabulary for talking about sex later in life. This lack of communication can also convey the implicit message that sex is not an acceptable topic for conversation. Furthermore, children acquire communication skills most effectively when they are provided with models of verbal interaction followed by the opportunity to express their own thoughts in an accepting atmosphere. None of these elements is typically available in a home where people simply do not talk about sex.

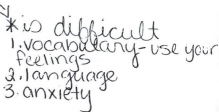

? How About You?

Are you able to talk candidly with a partner about sexual needs? If so, what do you attribute your comfort to? If not, what are the main stumbling blocks for you in this area?

Lack of positive models frequently extends beyond the home. Few people have access to classroom or textbook sources that portray how couples talk about sex. Neither peer groups nor the popular media fill the gap by providing realistic or positive information. Widely viewed movies rarely depict any meaningful verbal communication between on-screen lovers and, when dialogue does occur, it is typically ambiguous and insensitive (Striar & Bartlik, 2000).

Language and Sexual Communication

Another obstacle to effective communication is the lack of a suitable language of sex. By the time we are grown up and eager to communicate sexual needs and feelings, many of us do not know how to go about doing it. The very words we have learned to describe sex might have become associated with negative rather than positive emotions. Many of us have learned to snicker over taboo sex words or to use them in an angry, aggressive, or insulting manner. Consequently, it can be uncomfortable to use those same words to describe an activity with someone whom we really care for.

Thus, when we want to begin engaging in sexual communication, we find ourselves struggling to find the right language for this most intimate kind of dialogue. The range of words commonly used to describe genital anatomy gives some indication of our society's mixed messages about sexuality. Two extremes tend to predominate: street language at one end and clinical terminology at the other.

The anecdote at the beginning of this chapter revealed one man's consternation over trying to figure out what words to use for his own genitals. As this man discovered, our language lacks a comfortable sexual vocabulary. Many of us are not at ease with the words commonly available. We may find them to be too clinical, too harsh, or too juvenile to use in a caring way. Words such as *penis* and *vagina* often seem too technical or medical; but *cock, prick, cunt,* and *snatch* can sound too aggressive or insulting. And the terms available to describe sexual activity can produce similar problems. Invitations such as "Let's fuck" may be lovingly delivered and excitedly received by some but may seem too cold, graphic, or aggressive to others. But a more scientific description, such as "Let's have sexual intercourse," may seem clumsy and impersonal.

Indeed, as authors of this textbook we face the same limitations of language. What is the best word or phrase to describe how two people interact together in explicitly sexual ways? Some of the more common street terms tend to sound crude and can objectify the participants, diminishing their interaction to the purely physical level. More formal terms such as *coitus* and *sexual intercourse* tend to put too much emphasis on heterosexual genital contact. We do not want our language to exclude homosexual interactions, nor do we want it to exclude a whole range of nongenital interactions, including touching, talking, and communicating through facial expressions. When the context of our discussion focuses more on the physical aspects of sexual interactions, we use the terms *sexual activity* and *sexual play,* which we consider both broad and neutral. When the focus is more on the emotional and spiritual aspects of sexual interactions, we use the terms *sexual intimacy, sexual sharing,* and *love-making* to emphasize the larger emotional and intellectual relationship between the participants. We recognize, though, that even these terms have different connotations—both good and bad—for different people. What terms are you most comfortable with, and why?

Within the context of our culture it is natural—or at least common—to feel shy or embarrassed when talking about sexuality with friends and lovers. However, this awkwardness can often be avoided or overcome, and people certainly find ways of learning to live with the vocabulary. For example, the context and tone in which sexual terms are used can create totally different meanings and reactions, as this woman's comment shows:

I have very different feelings about words depending on how they are used. My lover saying "I love your sweet cunt" is very different from hearing "You stupid cunt." (Authors' files)

Also, some people give their own or their partners' genitals nicknames, such as Fuzzylove, Slurpy, Artesia, Pokey, Peter, or Moby, in an attempt to avoid negative associations with much of the existing terminology. When both partners in a couple choose personal names for their genitalia—ones that are easy to say and have positive connotations—it can "open up their communication by fostering playfulness" (Contemporary Sexuality,

1999d, p. 1). Couples who are experiencing sexual problems in their relationship have been shown to benefit from using playful names for their genitals (Godow, 1999). A key element in the success of using personal or playful names for sexual anatomy and sexual interaction is that both partners are comfortable with the terms used.

Many benefits and joys are associated with talking to our lovers while we touch their bodies. This is a wonderful time to develop intimacy while learning about each other's needs and preferences. It is a particularly good way to discover what words are mutually acceptable.

Ethnic variations in communication styles also significantly affect how people talk about sex. The following "Sexuality and Diversity" discussion examines ethnic variations in communication.

 ## Sexuality and Diversity

Ethnic Variations in Intimate Communication

Textbooks, lectures, and general media sources that portray how couples can effectively communicate about intimate matters, especially sex, are not overly plentiful. Thus it should come as no surprise that research data pertaining to ethnic variations in intimate communication are also limited. In this discussion we draw on a sparse database to offer a few generalizations about variations in styles of communicating about sexual intimacy that occur among white Americans, African Americans, Hispanic Americans, and Asian Americans.

The belief that good communication is the heart and soul of healthy intimate relationships is rather common among white Americans (especially white women) and, to a lesser extent, African Americans; however, among Hispanic Americans and Asian American couples, "working on" communication competence is generally much less emphasized (Bradshaw, 1994; Chang & Holt, 1991; Hecht et al., 1993; Ting-Toomey & Korzenny, 1991). Thus, although white Americans and African Americans may openly discuss sex with a partner, the general assumption among Hispanic American couples is that they will not discuss their sexual relationship (Guerrero-Pavich, 1986; Van Oss Marin & Gomez, 1994). Asian American couples are also less inclined to discuss sex, consistent with a general tendency to value nonverbal, indirect, and intuitive communication over explicit verbal interaction (Bradshaw, 1994; Del Carmen, 1990).

White Americans and, to a lesser extent, African Americans tend to be more self-oriented in intimate relationships than either Hispanic Americans or Asian Americans (Gudykunst et al., 1996; Hecht et al., 1990, 1993; Trafimow et al., 1991). This stress on *individualism*—an ideology that places greater emphasis on the individual than on the couple or group—is perhaps best reflected by the statement "I'm doing something with you, and I will get my needs met (and you might as well)" (Hecht et al., 1993, p. 155). In contrast, Hispanic Americans and Asian Americans are more likely to stress *collectivism*— an ideology that focuses on the couple or group rather than on the individual (Hecht et al., 1993; Parks & Vu, 1994). This perspective on intimate relationships is reflected by the statement "We are doing something together that we are both getting something out of" (Hecht et al., 1993, p. 155).

Perhaps because of the emphasis on individualism in white American relationships, overt conflict is considered natural and something to be dealt with and resolved. African American couples are less comfortable dealing with conflict, and Hispanic American couples tend to view conflicts as a negative indicator that a relationship is disharmonious or unbalanced (Collier, 1991; Ting-Toomey & Korzenny, 1991). Because harmonious relationships and the collective good of the group are valued over individualism and rewards for oneself, Asian Americans are also strongly inclined to avoid conflicts that involve direct confrontation with a primary partner (Del Carmen, 1990).

In light of these general differences among ethnic groups in the United States, it follows that, although Asian and Hispanic American couples may not necessarily encounter more relational sexual problems than white or African Americans, they are certainly less inclined to acknowledge or discuss such concerns. Furthermore, it is unlikely that members of either of these ethnic groups, Asian or Hispanic, would be inclined to seek professional help for relationship problems, especially those of a sexual nature.

Ethnic variations also exist in the area of nonverbal sexual communication. Hispanic Americans rely heavily on nonverbal communication to reveal sexual information, and they place particular emphasis on the use of touching to convey love, a desire for intimacy, or sexual intent (Hecht et al., 1990). Touching also plays a major role among African Americans, who touch more than white Americans; Asian Americans touch even less (Butts, 1981; Hecht et al., 1990; Parham et al., 1999).

Interpersonal distance—another important aspect of nonverbal sexual communication discussed later in this chapter—is much more contracted among Hispanic Americans than among white Americans, a fact that can lead to misunderstandings when members of these two ethnic groups interact. Thus a white American may misinterpret a close-standing Hispanic person as issuing an invitation for intimacy when, in actuality, the close proximity to another is typical of Hispanic culture (Bryjak & Soroka, 1994; Sluzki, 1982). African Americans also tend to establish smaller interpersonal distances than white Americans (Halberstadt, 1985).

Gender-Based Communication Styles

Still another factor that can hinder communication between heterosexual partners is the difference in women's and men's styles of relating to other people (Canary & Dindia, 1998; James & Cinelli, 2003; Tannen, 1994). According to Deborah Tannen (1990, 1994), a professor of linguistics at Georgetown University, men and women often have different communication goals. Men use language to convey information, to achieve status in a group, to challenge others, and to prevent being pushed around. Men often enter into conversations concerned about who is one-up and who is one-down. From this perspective, communication becomes something of a contest to avoid being put in a one-down position. A man operating within this framework might be overly sensitive about asking for advice or for suggestions about how to respond in a particular situation (sexual or otherwise), being told to do something, or engaging in any other behavior that even remotely resembles being in a one-down or pushed-around position.

In contrast, Tannen maintains that women use language to achieve and share intimacy, to promote closeness, and to prevent others from pushing them away. Women are not typically socialized to use language as a defensive weapon to avoid being dominated or controlled. Rather, their concern is often to use dialogue as a way to get close to another person—and to judge how close to or distant from a valued partner they are.

A woman's goal in talking about her concerns is often to foster a sense of sharing and rapport and to achieve the feeling that she is not alone. She wants a response that says, "I understand; I have been there too"—a reaction that puts both communicators on equal footing, allowing intimacy to be built around equality. A woman may only be looking for understanding or a willingness to talk openly about a concern, but her male partner is often likely to respond with advice or solutions. This response frames him "as more knowledgeable, more reasonable, more in control—in a word, one-up. And this contributes to the distancing effect" (Tannen, 1990, p. 53). Women can minimize this relationship-eroding influence by clearly telling their male partners that,

Communication between heterosexual partners can be hindered by the difference in women's and men's styles of relating to other people.

© Jose Luiz Pelaez, Inc./CORBIS

when dealing with intimacy or emotional troubles, they do not want to hear quickly offered solutions. Instead, they would prefer that their partner listen to their concerns and be willing to openly discuss and share viewpoints about problems on an equal footing.

Tannen stresses that the first step in improving communication is understanding and accepting that there are gender differences in communication styles; it is not a question of one style being more right or wrong than the other. As Tannen reports, many people have indicated that once they came to understand these differences in how the sexes use language, they were better able to put their problems of communication with the other sex in a manageable context—and often to arrive at solutions to difficult or seemingly unresolvable problems or predicaments.

Since the publication of Tannen's research, a considerable number of research investigations have been directed toward examining gender differences in communication styles. A recent review of a large number of these studies concluded that the differences in men's and women's styles of communicating with other people are, in general, relatively small (Canary & Dindia, 1998). Clearly, the gender differences described by Tannen and others do exist, as verified by this literature review. However, the differences are not so large as to suggest that the two sexes are from different cultures. Men and women can and do communicate effectively about a broad array of topics, including sexual intimacy. Being aware of and responsive to the gender differences outlined by Tannen can only improve communication between the sexes.

Anxieties About Sexual Communication

Beyond the handicaps imposed by socialization and language limitations, difficulties in sexual communication for some people can also be rooted in anxieties about exposing themselves. Any sexual communication involves a certain amount of risk: By talking, people place themselves in a position vulnerable to judgment, criticism, and even rejection. The willingness to take risks can be related to the amount of trust that exists within a relationship. Some couples lack this mutual trust, and for them the risks of openly expressing sexual needs are too great to overcome. Others have a high degree of reciprocal caring and trust; for them the first hesitant steps into sexual dialogue can be considerably easier.

Even when a climate of goodwill prevails, however, it still can be difficult to establish a satisfying pattern of sexual dialogue. In such circumstances a couple might be frustrated in their efforts to resolve their communication problems strictly on their own. Instead, they should probably seek professional counseling. (In Chapter 16 we provide some guidelines for seeking professional assistance.)

We have outlined some reasons many people find it difficult to engage in meaningful and effective sexual communication. Despite these difficulties, communication is an important part of sexual sharing, just as it is an important part of many other aspects of a relationship. The potential rewards are enhanced sexual experiences and enriched relationships.

▶ Talking: Getting Started

How does one begin communicating about sex? In this section we explore a few of the many ways of breaking the ice. These suggestions may be useful not just at the beginning of a relationship but throughout its course.

Talking About Talking

When people feel uneasy about a topic, often the best place to start is to talk about talking. Discussing *why* it is hard to talk about sex can be a good place to begin. All of us have individual reasons why this is difficult, and understanding those reasons can help set a relationship on a solid foundation. Perhaps you can share experiences about earlier efforts to discuss sex with parents, teachers, physicians, friends, or lovers. It might be helpful to move gradually into the arena of sexual communication by directing your initial discussions to non-threatening, less personal topics (such as new birth control methods, pornography laws, etc.). Later, as your mutual comfort increases, you may be able to talk about more personal feelings and concerns.

Reading and Discussing

Because many people find it easier to read about sex than to talk about it, articles and books dealing with the subject can provide the stimulus for personal conversations. Partners can read the material separately, then discuss it together; or a couple can read it jointly and discuss their individual reactions. Often it is easier to make the transition from a book or article to personal feelings than to begin by talking about highly personal concerns.

Sharing Sexual Histories

Another way to start talking is to share sexual histories. There may be many questions that you would feel comfortable discussing with your partner. For instance, how was sex education handled in your home or at school? How did your parents relate to each other—were you aware of any sexuality in their relationship? When did you first learn about sex, and what were your reactions? Many other items could be added to this brief list; the questions depend on the feelings and needs of each individual.

Javier Pierini/Getty Images

Reading together about sensitive matters facilitates discussion.

▶ Listening and Feedback

Communication, sexual or otherwise, is most successful when it is two-sided, involving both an effective communicator and an active listener. In this section we focus on the listening side of this process.

Have you ever wondered why certain people seem to draw others to themselves like iron to a magnet? With some thought you will probably conclude that, among other things, these individuals are often good listeners. What special skills do they possess that make us feel that they really care about what we have to say? The next time you are with such a person, observe closely. Make a study of his or her listening habits. Perhaps your list of good listening traits will include several of the following: being an active listener, maintaining eye contact, providing feedback, supporting one's partner's communication efforts, expressing unconditional positive regard, and using paraphrasing.

Be an Active Listener

Some people are *passive* listeners. They stare blankly into space as their companion talks, perhaps grunting uh-huh now and then. Such responses make us, the talker, think that the listener is indifferent, even when this is not the case, and we may soon grow tired of trying to share important thoughts with someone who does not seem to be receptive:

When I talk to my husband about anything really important, he just stares at me with a blank expression. It is like I am talking to a piece of stone. I think he hears the message, at least sometimes, but he rarely shows any response. Sometimes I feel like shaking him and screaming, "Are you still alive?" Needless to say, I don't try communicating with him very much anymore. (Authors' files)

Being an *active* listener means actively communicating that you are both listening to and genuinely interested in what your partner is saying (Cole & Cole, 1999; Gottman et al., 1998). You can communicate this through attentive body language, appropriate and sympathetic facial expressions, nodding your head, asking questions ("Could you give me an example?"), or making brief comments ("I see your point"). Sometimes it is helpful to reciprocate in the conversation. For example, as your partner relates a feeling or incident, you may be reminded of a similar point in your own life. Making these associations and candidly expressing them—provided that you do not sidetrack the conversation to your own needs—can encourage your partner to continue voicing important concerns.

Maintain Eye Contact

Maintaining eye contact is one of the most vital aspects of good face-to-face communication. Our eyes are wondrously expressive of feelings. When our partners maintain eye contact when we are sharing important thoughts or feelings with them, the message is clear: They care about what we have to say. When we fail to maintain eye contact, we deny our partners valuable feedback about how we are perceiving their messages.

Provide Feedback

The purpose of communication is to provide a message that has some effect on the listener. However, a message's impact is not always the same as its intent, because communications can be (and often are) misunderstood. This is particularly true with a topic such as sexuality, where language is often roundabout or awkward. Therefore, giving our partners some *feedback,* or reaction to their message, *in words* can be helpful. Besides clarifying how we have perceived our partners' comments, such verbal feedback reinforces that we are actively listening.

We can also benefit by asking our partners to provide some response to a message we think is important. A comment such as "What are your thoughts about what I have just said?" can encourage feedback that can help us determine the impact of our message on our partners.

Support Your Partner's Communication Efforts

Many of us can feel vulnerable when communicating important messages to our partners. Support for our efforts can help alleviate our fears and anxieties and can encourage us to continue building the communication skills so important for a viable relationship.

Think how good it can feel, after struggling to voice an important concern, to have a partner say, "I'm glad you told me how you really feel," or "Thanks for caring enough to tell me what was on your mind." Such supportive comments can help foster mutual empathy while ensuring that we will continue to communicate our thoughts and feelings candidly.

Express Unconditional Positive Regard

The concept of unconditional positive regard is borrowed from the immensely popular *Client-Centered Therapy,* by Carl Rogers (1951). In personal relationships unconditional positive regard means conveying to our partners the sense that we will continue to value and care for them regardless of what they do or say. Unconditional positive regard encourages a person to talk about even the most embarrassing or painful concerns. The following anecdote reveals one person's response to this valued attribute:

I know that my wife will continue to love me no matter what I say or reveal. In an earlier marriage, I could never express any serious concerns without my wife getting defensive or just plain mean. As a consequence, I quit talking about the things that really mattered. What a relief it is to be with someone who I can tell what is on my mind without worrying about the consequences. (Authors' files)

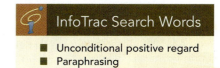

InfoTrac Search Words

- Unconditional positive regard
- Paraphrasing

Use Paraphrasing

One way to increase the probability that you and your partner will listen more effectively to each other is to use a technique called **paraphrasing.** This involves a listener summarizing, in his or her own words, the speaker's message.

Paraphrasing A listener's summarization of the speaker's message in his or her own words.

He: It would be nice if you could be a little gentler. Do you know what I mean?

She: I think so—you want me to be less aggressive.

He: That's not quite what I mean. I mean that when we make love, I would like you to touch me very lightly. I am so sensitive right before I come that anything more feels too rough.

She: Oh. I always thought you liked it when I'm sort of rough. I'm sorry I misunderstood. I'll try to be more gentle.

If the paraphrase is not satisfactory, the speaker can try to express the message again in different words. Then the listener can try to paraphrase again. Several attempts may be necessary to clear away discrepancies between the speaker's intent and the listener's interpretation. As time goes by, a couple typically finds that the need to use this approach diminishes as listening skills improve.

▶ Discovering Your Partner's Needs

Discovering what is pleasurable to your partner is an important part of sexual intimacy. Many couples want to know each other's preferences but are uncertain how to find out. In this section we look at some effective ways of learning about our partners' wants and needs.

Asking Questions

One of the best ways to discover your partner's needs is simply to ask. However, there are several ways of asking: Some can be helpful, whereas others may be ineffective or even counterproductive. We review a few of the most common ways of asking questions and the effect each is likely to have.

Yes/No Questions

Imagine being asked one or more of the following questions in the context of a sexual interlude with your partner:

1. Was it good for you?
2. Do you like oral sex?
3. Was I gentle enough?
4. Did you come?
5. Do you like it when I stimulate you this way?

At first glance these questions seem reasonably worded. However, they all share one characteristic that reduces their effectiveness: They are **yes/no questions.** Each asks for a one-word answer, even though people's thoughts and feelings are rarely so simple.

For example, consider Question 2, "Do you like oral sex?" Either answer—"Yes, I do," or "No, I don't"—gives the couple little opportunity to discuss the issue. Certainly, the potential for discussion exists. Nevertheless, in a world where sexual communication is often difficult under the best of circumstances, the asker may get no more than the specific information requested. In some situations, of course, a brief yes or no is all that is necessary. But the person responding might have mixed feelings about oral sex (for example), and the phrasing of the question leads to oversimplification. **Open-ended questions,** or questions that allow the respondent to state a preference, can make it easier for your partner to give accurate replies.

Open-Ended Questions

Some people find that asking open-ended questions is a particularly helpful way to discover their partners' desires. This approach places virtually no restrictions on possible answers; in a sense, it is like responding to a general essay question on an exam. ("What are some of the important aspects of human sexuality that you have learned thus far this term?") The following list gives some examples of open-ended questions:

1. What gives you the most pleasure when we make love?
2. What things about our sexual relationship would you most like us to change?
3. Where do you like to be touched?
4. What is the easiest or most enjoyable way for you to reach orgasm?
5. What are your feelings about oral sex?

Yes/no question A question that asks for a one-word answer (yes or no) and thus provides little opportunity for discussing an issue.

Open-ended question A question that allows a respondent to share any feelings or information she or he thinks is relevant.

A primary advantage of open-ended questions is that they allow your partner freedom to share any feelings or information she or he thinks is relevant. With no limitations or restrictions attached, you can learn much more than a simple yes/no answer could provide.

One possible drawback of the open-ended approach is that your partner may not know where to begin when asked such general questions. Consider being asked something like "What aspects of our lovemaking do you like best?" Some people might welcome the unstructured nature of this question, but others might find it difficult to respond to such a broad query, particularly if they are not accustomed to openly discussing sex. If this is the case, a more structured approach may have a better chance of encouraging talk. There are several ways of structuring your approach; one is the use of either/or questions.

Either/Or Questions

The following list gives some examples of **either/or questions:**

1. Would you like the light on when we make love, or should we turn it off?
2. Am I being gentle enough, or am I being too gentle?
3. Is this the way you want to be touched, or should we experiment with a different kind of caress?
4. Would you like to talk now, or would you prefer we wait for another time?

Either/or questions offer more structure than do open-ended questions, and they also encourage more participation than simple yes/no queries. People often appreciate the opportunity to consider a few alternatives. The either/or question also shows your concern about your partner's pleasure. Thus this kind of question can encourage a response at a time when a more open-ended question might be overwhelming. However, either/or questions can still be somewhat restrictive. There is always the possibility that your partner will not like either of the choices you offer. In this case he or she can state another alternative that is preferable.

Beside asking questions, we can discover the sexual needs of our partners in other ways. Here, we discuss three other communication techniques: self-disclosure, comparing notes, and giving permission.

Either/or question A question that allows statement of a preference.

© Bruce Ayres/Getty Images

Discovering what is pleasurable to your partner is an important part of sexual intimacy.

Self-Disclosure

Direct questions often put people on the spot. Whether you have been asked "Do you enjoy oral sex?" or "How do you feel about oral sex?" it may be difficult to respond candidly, simply because you do not know your partner's feelings on the subject. If the topic has strong emotional overtones, it may be difficult to reply—no matter how thoughtfully the question has been phrased. It is the content, not the communication technique, that causes the problem.

With potentially loaded topics, a way to broach the subject may be to start with a self-disclosure:

For the longest time, I avoided the topic of oral sex with my lover. We did just about everything else, but this was one thing we had not tried—and hadn't even talked about. I personally was both excited and repelled by the prospect of this kind of sex. I didn't have the slightest idea what she felt about it. I was afraid to bring it up for fear she would think I was some kind of pervert. Eventually I could no longer tolerate not knowing her feelings. I brought it up by first talking about my mixed emotions, like feeling that maybe it wasn't natural but at the same time really wanting to try it out. As it turned out, she had similar feelings but was afraid to bring them up. Afterward we laughed about how we had both been afraid to break the ice. Once we could talk freely, it was easy to add this form of stimulation to our sex life. (Authors' files)

Personal disclosures require some give and take. It is much easier to share feelings about strongly emotional topics when a partner is willing to make similar disclosures. Admittedly, such an approach has risks, and occasionally one can feel vulnerable sharing personal thoughts and feelings. In general, more men than women find it difficult to make disclosures of a personal nature, and many women express a preference for hearing more self-disclosures from their male partners, including those of a sexual nature (Byers & Demmons, 1999; Lips, 1997). It can be especially difficult for men to discuss their feelings, as described in the boxed discussion "Men Who Cannot Communicate About Their Emotions." Nevertheless, the increased possibility for open, honest dialogue may be worth the discomfort a person may feel about making the first disclosure. Research clearly reveals that self-disclosure of sexual desires and needs is positively associated with obtaining sexual satisfaction in intimate relationships (Byers & Demmons, 1999; Derlego et al., 1993; Purnine & Carey, 1997). Research also indicates that when one partner openly discusses his or her own feelings, the other partner is likely to do the same (Derlego et al., 1993; Hendrick & Hendrick, 1992).

A Canadian study examined the effect of dating individuals' self-disclosure about their sexual likes and dislikes to their partner (Byers & Demmons, 1999). Fifty-two college women and 47 college men, involved in dating relationships of 3 to 36 months' duration, completed a questionnaire designed to measure sexual and nonsexual self-disclosure with their partners, sexual communication satisfaction, sexual satisfaction, and relationship satisfaction. The study findings revealed that both sexual and nonsexual self-disclosure contributed positively to the participants' overall sexual communication satisfaction and to their relationship satisfaction. The researchers suggested that self-disclosure enhances sexual satisfaction through two routes: first, by increasing sexual rewards in the relationship; and second, by increasing overall relationship satisfaction (Byers & Demmons, 1999).

A form of self-disclosure that some people find exciting and informative involves telling their partners about personal fantasies, as revealed in the following anecdote:

I had this sexual fantasy that kept going through my mind. I would imagine coming home after a long, hard day of classes and being met by my partner, who would proceed to take me into the bedroom and remove all my clothes. Then he would pick me up and carry me into the bathroom, where the tub was full of hot water and bubbles. The fantasy would end with us making passionate love in the bathtub, with bubbles popping off around us. Finally, I shared my fantasy with him. Guess what happened when I came home after the next long day? It was even better than I had imagined! (Authors' files)

Understandably, many people might be concerned about the potentially negative effects of revealing such highly personal thoughts. Certain precautions can help reduce the possibility of an unpleasant outcome.

Sharing fantasies like this is usually most successful when it is mutual rather than one-way. If your partner is unwilling to engage in such a conversation, at least for the present, it would be wise to respect this wish. Sometimes starting out with mild fantasies can help desensitize fears and embarrassment and allow you to gauge the effect of such sharing on your partner and yourself. If you sense that your companion is feeling uncomfortable, it may be best not to press. It is probably advisable to avoid altogether any fantasies that you anticipate will be shocking to your companion; fantasies that involve other lovers can be particularly threatening.

Discussing Sexual Preferences

While planning an evening out, many couples consider it natural to discuss each other's preferences: "Would you like to go to a concert, or would you rather go to the movies?" "How close do you like to sit?" "Do you prefer vegetarian, Italian, or meat and potatoes?" Afterward they may candidly evaluate the evening's events: "The drummer was great." "I think we should sit farther from the speakers next time." "Boy, I wouldn't order the scampi again." Yet many of the same couples never think of sharing thoughts about mutual sexual enjoyment.

? Critical Thinking Question

Is it beneficial for partners to discuss their sexual likes and dislikes with each other, or should they be more selective in what they share? Would your opinion about the appropriate level of disclosure be influenced by the nature of the relationship (i.e., dating, cohabiting, or married)?

? How About You?

Have you ever shared sexual fantasies with an intimate partner? If so, was it helpful?

► Men Who Cannot Communicate About Their Emotions

The inability to put one's feelings or emotions into words, or even to be aware of them—a condition labeled *alexithymia* in the psychological literature—was first described in people suffering from severe psychological dysfunctions, such as post-traumatic stress disorder (Krystal, 1982). In the late 1990s a new perspective on alexithymia emerged with the work of Ronald Levant (1997), a respected author, Harvard Medical School professor, and founder of a counseling center that specializes in treating men. Levant's extensive clinical experiences led him to conclude that mild to moderate alexithymia is so widespread among men that it can be properly labeled *normative male alexithymia*.

This pervasive condition has its origins in male gender-role socialization processes in the home and peer group. In Chapter 3 we learned that many parents communicate to their male children, by words and actions, the messages that "boys do not cry" and that "real men" are strong, unemotional, and silent. Many men were raised (and continue to be raised) to believe that they should be emotionally stoic. Evidence indicates that both parents contribute to the suppression of emotions in their male children.

Mothers express less emotion to their sons than to their daughters (Dunn et al., 1987; Malatesta et al., 1989). Fathers' communication with their sons is more likely to be expressed as verbal bantering, joking, and kidding around, whereas their conversations with their daughters tend to focus more on emotions (Levant, 1997). The expression of vulnerable emotions (such as sadness, fear, and hurt) as well as of caring and connection emotions (such as fondness or affection) is actively encouraged in girls and discouraged in boys (Dunn et al., 1987; Siegal, 1987). In contrast, the expression of anger, although discouraged in girls, is the one emotion that is commonly allowed or encouraged in boys (Levant, 1997).

This decidedly negative aspect of male socialization is further ingrained by the peer group. Boys engage in play activities that often focus on dominance and aggression, where toughness and emotional stoicism are the proper operating style. These male patterns of recreation are typically devoid of the elements of play for girls that promote emotional self-awareness and empathy, such as expressing and responding to each others' emotions, resolving conflicts, and maintaining harmony (Levant, 1997; Maccoby, 1990).

According to Levant, this "normative" aspect of conventional masculinity, so strongly ingrained in many men by early socialization, "has such broad and negative consequences that, at least in the context of modern life, it must be considered dysfunctional" (1997, p. 10). Men who are conditioned to live detached from their emotions and the emotions of their significant others have great difficulty

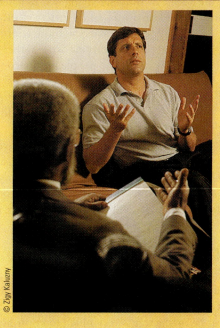

© Zigy Kaluzny

in both communicating their intimate feelings and experiencing true intimacy. When men are unable to discuss or express tender, caring, and vulnerable emotions, they are left with aggression and sexuality as the primary channels for emotional release. Because anger is one of the few emotions allowed under traditional male rearing, boys and then men often learn to channel vulnerable feelings such as sadness, fear, and shame into anger-induced aggression. In similar fashion, caring emotions are frequently channeled into sexuality. For many men sexual sharing is the only acceptable context in which to display and express affection and love.

Levant created a treatment strategy to help his male clients develop "emotional intelligence." The major emphasis is on "psychoeducation," in which various exercises are used to awaken a man's ability to empathize with others and to connect his emotional experience to thoughts about it. The first step in treatment is to expand a client's working vocabulary for emotions. An impoverished emotional vocabulary is typical of men with normative male alexithymia. The next step involves helping the client to become more aware of the emotions of others and to be able to identify them. Levant has found that it is often less threatening to start with the feelings of others rather than with one's own feelings. In the third phase of treatment the client begins to keep an "emotional log" in which he describes the context in which an emotion occurs (social situation, event, etc.) and identifies the emotion he is experiencing. The final phase involves continued practice in fostering the development of these new emotional skills. In group therapy sessions men might engage in role playing followed by feedback. Videotaping is also sometimes used; it allows men to observe and discuss the manner in which they express emotions. In individual therapy sessions clients are encouraged to continue practicing by raising such questions as "How did you feel?" or "How do you think your partner felt?"

Levant has found that his clients' lives provide the most effective feedback and reinforcement for these new emotional skills. Men are energized and gratified by the often profound changes that are taking place in their lives. One of Levant's clients said that "he felt like he had been living in a black-and-white television that had suddenly turned into a color set" (Levant, 1997, p. 23). Such changes become highly motivational as men discover that their emerging emotional empathy and increased ability to communicate intimate feelings reduce personal pain and conflicts, increase harmony in their relationships, and allow them to better integrate love and affection with sexuality.

Admittedly, discussing sexual preferences and evaluating specific sexual encounters are a big step up from discussing an evening out. Nevertheless, people do engage in this type of sexual dialogue. Some people feel comfortable discussing sexual preferences with a new lover before progressing to lovemaking. They might talk about what areas of their bodies are most responsive, how they like to be touched, what intercourse positions are particularly desirable, the easiest or most satisfying way to reach orgasm, time and location preferences, special turn-ons and turn-offs, and a variety of other likes and dislikes.

? How About You?

If you are comfortable sharing thoughts with your partner about mutual sexual enjoyment, do you prefer to engage in this communication before, during, or after lovemaking?

The appeal of this open, frank approach is that it allows a couple to focus on particularly pleasurable activities rather than discovering them by slow trial and error. However, some people feel that such dialogues are far too clinical, perhaps even robbing the sexual experience of the excitement of experimentation and mutual discovery. Furthermore, what a person finds desirable might be different with different partners, so it may be difficult to assess one's own preferences in advance.

Couples might also find it helpful to discuss their feelings after having sex. They can offer reactions about what was good and what could be better. They can use this time to reinforce the things they found particularly satisfying in their partner's lovemaking ("I loved the way you touched me on the insides of my thighs"). A mutual feedback session can be extremely informative; it can also contribute to a deeper intimacy between two people.

Giving Permission

Giving permission Providing reassurance to one's partner that it is okay to talk about specific feelings or needs.

Discovering your partner's needs can be made immeasurably easier by the practice we call **giving permission.** Basically, giving permission means providing encouragement and reassurance. One partner tells the other that it is okay to talk about specific feelings or needs—in fact, that he or she wants very much to know how the other feels about the subject.

He: I'm not sure how you like me to touch you when we make love.
She: Any way you want to is good.
He: Well, I want to know what you like best, and you can help me by saying what feels good while I touch you.

Many of us have had experiences in which we felt rebuffed in our efforts to communicate our needs to others. It is no wonder that people often remain silent even when they want to share personal feelings. Giving and receiving permission to express needs freely can contribute to the exchange of valuable information.

▶ Learning to Make Requests

People are not mind readers. Nevertheless, many lovers seem to assume that their partners know (perhaps by intuition?) just what they need. People who approach sex with this attitude are not taking full responsibility for their own pleasure. If sexual encounters are not satisfactory, it is often more convenient to blame a partner—"You don't care about my needs"—than to admit that one's own reluctance to express needs may be the problem. Expecting partners to somehow know what is wanted without telling them places a heavy burden on them. Many people think that they shouldn't have to ask. But in fact, asking a partner to do something can be an affirmative, responsible action that is helpful to both people.

Taking Responsibility for Our Own Pleasure

When two people are really in harmony with each other, you don't have to talk about your sexual wants. You each sense and respond to the other's desires. Talking just tends to spoil these magical moments. (Authors' files)

The situation this person describes seems to exist more in the fantasyland of idealized sex than in the real world. As we just noted, people are not mind readers, and intuition leaves much to be desired as a substitute for genuine communication. A person who expects another to know his or her needs by intuition is saying, "It's not my business to let you know my needs, but it is yours to know what they are," and by inference, "If my needs are not fulfilled, it is your fault, not mine." Needless to say, this is a potentially destructive approach that can lead to blaming, misunderstandings, and unsatisfying sex.

In a similar vein, some people take too much responsibility for their partners' sexual pleasure. Such a person says, in effect, "It is my job to satisfy you sexually. I will make all the decisions and assume responsibility for your pleasure." A person so intent on figuring out and fulfilling a partner's needs might find that his or her own needs are largely overlooked. Furthermore, such a take-charge attitude undermines a partner's inclination to assume responsibility for her or his own satisfaction.

In summary, the best way to get our needs met is to speak up. Two individuals willing to communicate their desires and take responsibility for their own pleasure create an excellent framework for effective, fulfilling sexual intimacy.

One woman stated her experience with assuming responsibility for her own pleasure:

For much of my life, sex has been a hit-or-miss proposition, with the miss part predominating. Only recently have I discovered how to change this pattern. I know what I need sexually to be satisfied. I am very good at giving myself pleasure. Finally it occurred to me how futile it was to hope that my partners would somehow automatically know what I want, when it took me years to discover this for myself. I decided that the better I could express myself about my sexual needs, the greater the likelihood they would be fulfilled. Assuming this responsibility for my own pleasure was a big step, and I took it with a great deal of hesitancy and anxiety. But I have been pleasantly surprised. Most of my subsequent lovers have been relieved to have the guesswork taken out of our sexual experiences. One man praised me for being so open, and confided that I had relieved him of one of his greatest concerns, namely, not knowing what his partner desired from him during sex. (Authors' files)

Deciding to assume responsibility for our own satisfaction is an important step. Just as important are the methods we select for expressing our needs. The way a request is made has a decided effect on the reaction it draws. Some suggestions are listed in the next two sections.

Making Requests Specific

The more specific a request is, the more likely it is to be understood and heeded. Although this principle is frequently noted by social psychologists and communication specialists, many of us neglect to apply it to our sexual dialogues. Lovers often ask for changes in the sexual aspects of their relationships in the vaguest language. It can be uncomfortable, even anxiety provoking, to be on the receiving end of an ill-defined request. Just how does one respond? Probably by doing little, if anything.

The key to preventing unnecessary stress for both partners lies in delivering requests in as clear and concise a manner as possible. Thus an alternative to the vague request "I'd like you to try touching me differently" might be something like "I would like you to touch me gently around my clitoris but not directly on it." Other examples of specific requests include the following:

1. I would like you to spend more time touching and caressing me all over before we have intercourse.
2. I want to be on top this time. It feels really good to me, and I love being able to watch you respond.
3. I like it when you lick the underside of the head of my penis. Not too hard, though— I'll tell you if I want it harder or softer.
4. I really enjoy it when you keep on kissing and caressing me after you're inside me.
5. I would like you to stroke my penis with your hand.

Using "I" Language

Many counselors encourage their clients to use "I" language when stating their needs to others (Worden & Worden, 1998). This forthright approach brings the desired response more often than does a general statement. For example, saying "I would like to be on top" is considerably more likely to produce that result than "What would you think about changing positions?"

Many people find it difficult to ask for what they want in such clear, unequivocal language. Saying "I want . . ." may seem selfish, as the following two anecdotes illustrate:

I have trouble expressing my needs to my partner. Sometimes I think that all the energy I put out to please him distracts me from focusing on what feels good to my body. But it would be selfish for me to say so, so I don't. (Authors' files)

My main problem in talking about sex is asking for gratification for myself. I am always trying to please my partner, and often I do not receive sexual fulfillment. I find it difficult to ask her for certain forms of sexual expression. It is just not my nature to ask for anything. (Authors' files)

There is, however, a difference between being self-centered and recognizing that "I am as important as others in my life, and my needs are worthy of being met." Individuals whose own needs have been satisfied are often able to give much of themselves to others. Conversely, the philosophy of never putting oneself first can ultimately produce so much frustration and resentment that a person is left with few positive feelings to share.

Expressing requests directly may not always be effective. Some people want to make all the decisions, and they may not take kindly to requests from their partners during lovemaking. A partner's assertiveness might be offensive to them. You might want to determine whether this is your partner's attitude before a sexual encounter, because doing so can help you avoid an awkward situation. One way to do this is to ask the open-ended question "How do you feel about asking for things during lovemaking?" Or you might choose to wait and find out during sex play. At any rate, if a person appears closed to direct requests, you may wish to reevaluate your strategy. Perhaps making your needs known at some time other than during sexual interaction will give your partner a more relaxed opportunity to consider your desires. Nevertheless, we strongly encourage you to use "I" language in whatever context you make your requests. It may help you to avoid the type of awkward scenario illustrated in the "without 'I' language" dialogue that follows (compare the results to the "with 'I' language" dialogue):

WITHOUT "I" LANGUAGE

She: What do you think about oral sex?

He: Oh, I'm not sure. What do you think?

She: Well, I'm wondering if it is something we might enjoy.

He I'm not sure. I guess it's something that we could consider.

This conversation might continue for some time without resolving anything, because both partners seem hesitant to do anything more than talk around the topic.

WITH "I" LANGUAGE

She: I have been thinking about oral sex, and I would very much like to try it when we make love.

He: Well, I was thinking about it too, but I was nervous about bringing it up.

She: I think I would enjoy it. Would you be comfortable experimenting a little?

He: Sure. I'm glad you suggested it.

▶ Expressing and Receiving Complaints

Contrary to the popular romantic image, no two people can fill all of each other's needs all the time. It seems inevitable in an intimate relationship that people will sometimes need to register complaints and request changes. This is not an easy process for caring individuals whose involvement is characterized by mutual empathy. The most effective way to voice a concern is to complain rather than to criticize (Gottman, 1994). Complaining involves the constructive expression of relationship concerns and is different from criticism (and is by no means synonymous with whining). Occasional and constructive complaining is actually beneficial for a relationship because it helps to identify problems or issues that need to be discussed and resolved. Complaining involves several of the strategies outlined in the following sections, such as being sensitive about when to express a complaint, using "I" language, tempering complaints with praise, and so forth. Complaints are voiced in the expectation that constructive change beneficial to both partners will occur. In contrast, criticisms are often leveled to hurt, downgrade, express contempt, get even, or gain dominant status over a partner. Criticism often involves "attacking someone's personality or character—rather than a specific behavior—usually with blame" (Gottman, 1994, p. 73). Couple-communication patterns that are tainted by expressions of denigration, criticism, and contempt can be extremely harmful to a relationship. We discuss the effect of these negative communication tactics in more detail in a later section of this chapter. When complaints pertain to the emotionally intense area of sexual intimacy, it can be doubly difficult. Partners will want to think carefully about appropriate strategies and potential obstacles to accomplishing this delicate task.

Constructive Strategies for Expressing Complaints

Perhaps the best way to begin, before verbalizing a complaint to your partner, is to examine the motivations underlying your need to express a complaint.

Be Aware of Your Motivation

The way a complaint is expressed depends largely on the complainer's motive. Consider the following two anecdotes:

My husband is a lousy lover. He doesn't know the first thing about how to turn me on, and when I tell him I don't get any pleasure out of our sex life he just clams up. I don't know what's the matter with him, but it sure burns me up. (Authors' files)

A couple of years ago I found out that my wife was involved in an affair with a man she works with. She claimed he was kind and gentle and that she couldn't help being attracted to him. Faced with my ultimatum, she changed jobs and stopped seeing him (I think). Since that time our sex life has been a real bust. She seems to lack enthusiasm, and we engage in sex much less frequently. Sometimes I think her having sex with the other guy has ruined our sex life. Maybe she thinks he was better than me. When I confront her about my dissatisfaction with her lack of enthusiasm she gets upset, and we usually end up having a fight. (Authors' files)

"If something is bothering you about our relationship, Lorraine, why don't you just spell it out."

It seems clear that these people's motivations for complaining are not based on a caring desire to make their relationships better. If the aim is to hurt, humiliate, blame, ridicule, or get even, it is likely that criticizing a partner will prove to be far more destructive than constructive. Being aware of your motives for expressing a complaint can help avoid this pitfall.

It is not always easy to effectively express a complaint while maintaining mutual empathy and a sense of togetherness. However, certain strategies can help maintain empathy in a confrontational situation. One important consideration is picking the right time and place.

Choose the Right Time and Place

Whenever my lover brings up something that is bothering her about our sex life, it inevitably is just after we have made love. Here I am, relaxed, holding her in my arms, thinking good thoughts, and she destroys the mood with some criticism. It's not that I don't want her to express her concerns, but her timing is terrible. The last thing I want to hear after lovemaking is that it could have been better. (Authors' files)

This man's dismay is obvious. His partner's decision to voice her concerns during the afterglow of lovemaking works against her purpose. He may feel vulnerable, and he clearly resents having his good mood following sex broken by the prospect of a potentially difficult conversation. Of course, other couples find this to be a time when they are exceedingly close to each other and thus a good time to air their concerns.

Many people, like the woman in the example, do not choose the best time to confront their lovers. Rather, the time chooses them: They jump right in when the problem is uppermost in their minds. Although there are some benefits to dealing with an issue immediately, it is not always the best strategy. When we are feeling disappointed, resentful, or angry, these negative emotions, when running full tide, can easily get in the way of constructive interaction. We should avoid expressing complaints when anger is at its peak. Although we may have every intention of making our complaint constructive, anger has a way of disrupting a search for solutions. Sometimes, however, it is necessary to express anger; at the end of this section we consider how to do so appropriately.

Choosing the right time and place to express sexual concerns can facilitate communication.

In most cases it is unwise to tackle a problem when either you or your partner has limited time or is tired, stressed, preoccupied, or under the influence of drugs or alcohol. Rather, try to select an interval when you have plenty of time and when you both are relaxed and feeling close to each other.

A pragmatic approach to timing is to simply ask your lover, "I really value our sexual relationship, but there are some concerns I would like to talk over with you. Is this a good time, or would you rather we talk later?" Be prepared for some anxiety-induced stalling. If your partner is hesitant to talk now, support his or her right to pick another time or place. However, it is important to agree on a time, particularly if you sense that your partner might prefer to let the matter go.

Choosing the right place for expressing sexual concerns can be as important as timing. Some people find that sitting around the kitchen table while sharing a pot of coffee is a more comfortable setting than the place where they make love; others might prefer the familiarity of their bed. A walk through a park or a quiet drive in the country, far removed from the potential interferences of a busy lifestyle, may prove best for you. Try to sense your partner's needs. When and where is she or he most likely to be receptive to your requests for change?

Picking the right time and place to deliver a complaint does not ensure a harmonious outcome, but it certainly improves the prospects of your partner responding favorably to your message. Using some other constructive strategies can also increase the likelihood of beneficial interaction. One of these is to combine a complaint with praise.

Temper Complaints with Praise

The strategy of tempering complaints with praise is based largely on common sense. All of us tend to respond well to compliments, whereas a harsh complaint or criticism alone is difficult to accept. The gentler approach of combining the two is a good way to reduce the negative impact of a complaint. It also gives your partner a broader perspective from which to evaluate the complaint, reducing the likelihood that he or she will respond in a defensive or angry manner. Consider how you might react differently to the following complaints depending on whether or not they are accompanied by praise:

COMPLAINT ALONE	COMPLAINT WITH PRAISE
1. When we make love, I feel that you are inhibited.	1. I like it when you respond to me while we make love. I think it could be even better if you would take the initiative sometimes. Does this seem like a reasonable request?
2. I am really getting tired of your turning off the lights every time we make love.	2. I enjoy hearing and feeling you react when we make love. I also want to watch you respond. How would you feel about leaving the lights on sometimes?
3. I think our lovemaking is much too infrequent. It almost seems like sex is not as important to you as it is to me.	3. I love having sex with you, and it has been bothering me that we don't seem to have as much time for it recently. What do you think about this?

Sadly, just about all of us have been on the receiving end of complaints, such as those in the left-hand column. Common reactions are anger, humiliation, anxiety, and resentment. Although some people respond to such harsh complaints with a resolve to make things better, it is more likely that this will not occur. On the other hand, affirmative complaints, such as the examples in right-hand column, are more likely to encourage efforts to change.

There is a good deal of wisdom in the saying "People are usually more motivated to make a good thing better than to make a bad thing good." This applies as much to sexual activity as to any other area of human interaction. One of us was once approached by a woman who complained that her husband was often too rough with her during love play. She was reluctant to discuss her concern with him, however, for fear that he would feel put down or angered. She also had mixed feelings about her husband's roughness—it was part of the unbridled enthusiasm with which he related to her sexually, a zestfulness she very much enjoyed. On those rare occasions when he did take the time to be gentle with her, she was very pleased. Now, the problem: How could she tell him she did not like his roughness while at the same time assuring that he would maintain his enthusiasm and not feel angry or inept?

What she finally told him was essentially what she had expressed in seeking advice. Sometimes it was terrific when he was gentle. She loved being pursued with enthusiasm and vigor. It could be even better if he would include more gentleness in their lovemaking. Although he was somewhat surprised and dismayed that he had not been able to detect her needs without being told, her husband's response was quite positive. What do you suppose his reaction might have been had she coldly complained, "Do you have to be so rough when we make love?"

It is also a good idea to ask for feedback when delivering complaints. Regardless of how much warmth and goodwill we put into this difficult process, there is always the possibility that our partners will become silent or change the subject. Asking them how they feel about our requests for change helps to reduce these prospects. (Note that in the preceding list, all "Complaint with Praise" examples end with requests for feedback.)

? Critical Thinking Question

Some people think that combining praise with a complaint is a manipulative technique, designed to coerce behavior changes by tempering requests with insincere praise. Do you agree with this point of view? Why or why not?

Nurture Small Steps Toward Change

Complete behavioral changes rarely occur immediately following expression of a complaint—no matter how positively the complaint is stated. Rather, they must be patiently nurtured, with each small step along the way properly acknowledged with words of appreciation. In the example of the woman wanting more gentleness from her husband, it would have been unreasonable for her to assume that once she expressed her complaint, her partner would completely change his ways. In fact, what occurred was a noticeable but minimal effort to be less vigorous in the next sexual encounter. Soon the old patterns ingrained over many years took over again.

Backsliding is natural and predictable, and, as with other unwanted behaviors, responding to it requires tact. Have you ever heard the words "I see you didn't pay a bit of attention to what I said"? Such a negative reaction could easily cool your desire to follow through with change. It is far more encouraging and reassuring to be on the receiving end of a message such as the one delivered by the wife to her "trying to be more gentle" husband: "I really appreciate the time you took to be gentle when we made love. It means a great deal that you care about my needs." With such a caring and supportive reaction, few people are likely to stick to old, undesirable behaviors.

Avoid "Why" Questions

People frequently use "why" questions as thinly veiled efforts to criticize or attack their partners while avoiding full responsibility for what is said. Have you ever asked or been asked any of the following questions:

1. Why don't you make love to me more frequently?
2. Why don't you show more interest in me?
3. Why don't you get turned on by me anymore?
4. Why can't you be more loving toward me?
5. Why are you so lazy?

Such queries have no place in a loving relationship: They are hurtful and destructive. Rather than representing simple requests for information, they are typically used to convey hidden messages of anger that people are unwilling to communicate honestly. These are hit-and-run tactics that cause defensiveness and seldom induce positive changes.

Express Negative Emotions Appropriately

Earlier in this chapter, we noted that it is wise to avoid confronting our partners when resentment or anger is riding high. However, there probably will be times when we feel compelled to express negative feelings. If so, certain guiding principles can help to defuse a potentially explosive situation.

Avoid focusing your anger on the character of your partner ("You are an insensitive person"). Instead, try directing your dissatisfaction toward his or her behaviors ("When you don't listen to my concerns, I think they are unimportant to you and I feel sad"). At the same time, express appreciation for your partner as a person ("You are very important to me, and I don't like feeling this way"). This acknowledges that we can be distressed by our partners' behaviors yet still feel loving toward them—an often overlooked but important truth.

Negative feelings are probably best expressed with clear, honest "I" statements rather than with accusatory and potentially inflammatory "you" statements. Consider the following:

"YOU" STATEMENTS	"I" STATEMENTS
1. You don't give a damn about me.	1. Sometimes I feel ignored, and this makes me afraid for us.
2. You always blame me for our problems.	2. I don't like being blamed.
3. You make me upset.	3. I am upset.
4. You make me sad.	4. I feel sad.
5. You don't love me.	5. I feel unloved.

"I" statements are self-revelations that express how we feel without placing blame or attacking our partner's character. In contrast, "you" statements frequently are interpreted as attacks on the other person's character or attempts to fix blame. When we express a concern with a statement that begins with *I* instead of *you*, our partners are less likely to feel criticized and thus to become defensive. Furthermore, using "I" statements to express emotions such as sadness, hurt, or fear conveys a sense of our vulnerability to our partners, who may find it easier to respond to these "softer" emotional expressions than to blaming emotions associated with resentment, such as anger or disgust.

Limit Complaints to One per Discussion

Many of us are inclined to avoid confrontations with our partners. This understandable reluctance to deal with negative issues can result in an accumulation of unspoken complaints. Consequently, when we finally reach the point where we need to say something, it may be difficult to avoid unleashing a barrage of complaints that includes everything on our current list of grievances. Such a response, although understandable, only serves to magnify rather than resolve conflicts between lovers, as reflected in the following account:

My wife lets things eat on her without letting me know when I do something that she disapproves of. She remembers every imagined shortcoming and blows it way out of proportion. But I never learn about it until she has accumulated a long list of complaints. Then she hits me with all of them at once, dredging them up like weapons in her arsenal, all designed to make me feel like an insensitive creep. I sometimes hear about things that happened years ago. She wonders why I don't have anything to say when she is done haranguing me. But what do you say when somebody has just given you 10 or 20 reasons why your relationship with her is lousy? Which one do you respond to? And how can you avoid being angry when somebody rubs your face in all your shortcomings, real or imagined? (Authors' files)

You can reduce the likelihood of creating such a counterproductive situation in your own relationships by limiting your complaints to one per discussion. Even if you have a half-dozen complaints you want to talk about, it will probably serve your relationship better to pick one and relegate the remaining concerns to later conversations.

Most of us find it hard to listen to a complaint that goes on and on, even when it is about just one thing. Consequently, when delivering a singular complaint, it is more effective to be concise. Just briefly describe the concern, limit examples to one or two, and then stop.

Receiving Complaints

Delivering complaints to a partner is difficult; likewise, receiving complaints from someone you love can also be an emotionally rending experience. However, as we have already said, people involved in an intimate, loving relationship inevitably experience the need to register complaints on occasion. How you respond to a complaint can have a significant effect not only on your partner's inclination to openly share concerns in the future but also on the probability that the complaint will be resolved in a manner that strengthens rather than erodes the relationship.

When your partner delivers a complaint, take a few moments to gather your thoughts. A few deep breaths is probably a much better initial response than blurting out, "Yeah, well what about the time that you . . .!" Ask yourself, Is this person trying to give me some information that may be helpful? In a loving relationship where mutual empathy prevails, perhaps you will be able to see some potential for positive consequences, even though you have just received a painful message. There are several ways you can respond to such a communication. We hope one or more of the following suggestions provides helpful guidelines in these circumstances.

Empathize with Your Partner and Paraphrase the Complaint

Many of us have had the experience of expressing concerns to people we care about, only to have them come back with a complaint of their own. Such a response will likely result in increased defensiveness, which may precipitate withdrawal or antagonistic confrontation. Furthermore, when people match a complaint with a countercomplaint, it appears that they are not trying to understand and empathize with the concern. In contrast, paraphrasing your partner's complaint suggests that you are making an effort to understand and appreciate what he or she is experiencing. For example, saying to your partner, "It sounds like you have been frustrated with our lovemaking," will probably have a much more beneficial effect than a comment such as "Well, you're not such a hot lover either!"

Paraphrasing a partner's complaint does not mean that you agree with it. Rather, you are simply saying, "This is what I am hearing. Do I understand correctly?" We can empathize with our lovers' concerns even if we have different thoughts and feelings about them. This type of positive response increases the likelihood that your partner will voice important concerns in the future.

Responding appropriately to a complaint can help strengthen a relationship.

© Nancy Richmond/The Image Works

Acknowledge a Complaint and Find Something to Agree With

Perhaps if you allow yourself to be open to a complaint, you will see that there is some basis for it. For example, suppose that your partner feels angry about your busy schedule and complains that you are not devoting enough time to the relationship. Maybe you think he or she is overreacting or forgetting all the time you have spent together. However, you also know that there is some basis for this concern. It can be helpful to acknowledge this by saying something like "I can understand how you might feel neglected because I have been so preoccupied with my new job." Such constructive acknowledgment can occur even if you think the criticism is largely unjustified. By reacting in an accepting and supportive manner, you are conveying the message that you hear, understand, and appreciate the basis for your partner's concern.

Ask Clarifying Questions

In some cases your partner may deliver a complaint in such a vague manner that further clarification is needed. If this happens, ask questions. For example, suppose that your partner complains that you do not take enough time in your lovemaking. You might respond by asking, "Do you mean that we should spend more time touching before we have intercourse, or that I should wait longer before coming, or that you want me to hold you for a longer time after we have sex?"

Express Your Feelings

It can be helpful to talk about your feelings with regard to the complaint rather than letting these emotions dictate your response. For instance, your partner's complaint may cause you to feel angry, hurt, or dejected. It is probably better to verbalize these emotional reactions by expressing feeling statements rather than by acting them out. Responses such as yelling, stomping out of the room, crying, or retreating into a shell of despair are unlikely to lead to productive dialogue. Instead, it may help to tell your partner, "That was really hard to hear, and I am hurt," or "Right now I feel angry, so I need to stop and take a few breaths and figure out what I am thinking and feeling."

Focus on Future Changes You Can Make

An excellent closure to receiving a complaint is to focus on what the two of you can do to make things better. Perhaps this is the time to say, "My new job is really important to me, but our relationship is much more important. Maybe we can set aside some specific times each week where we both agree not to let outside concerns intrude on our time together."

Sometimes people agree to make things better but neglect to discuss concrete changes that will resolve the issue that triggered the complaint. Taking the time to identify and agree on specific future changes is a crucial step in resolving the basis for the complaint.

▶ Saying No

Many of us have difficulty saying no to others. Our discomfort in communicating this direct message is perhaps most pronounced when it applies to intimate areas of relationships. This is reflected in the following anecdotes:

Sometimes my partner wants to be sexual when I only want to be close. The trouble is, I can't say no. I am afraid she would be hurt or angry. Unfortunately, I am the one who ends up angry at myself for not being able to express my true feelings. Under these circumstances, sex isn't very good. (Authors' files)

It is so hard to say no to a man who suggests having sex at the end of a date. This is especially true if we have had a good time together. You never know if they are going to get that hangdog hurt look or become belligerent and angry. (Authors' files)

These accounts reveal some of the common concerns that inhibit us from saying no. We might believe that a rejection will hurt the other person or perhaps cause him or her to become angry or even combative. Laboring under such fears, we might decide that it is less stressful to simply comply. Unfortunately, this reluctant acquiescence can create such negative feelings that the resulting shared activity may be less than pleasurable for both ourselves and our partners.

Many of us have not learned that it is okay to say no. Perhaps more important, we may not have learned strategies for doing so. In the following section we consider some potentially useful ways to say no.

A Three-Step Approach to Saying No

Many people have found it helpful to have a definite plan or strategy in mind for saying no to invitations for intimate involvements. This can help to prevent being caught off guard and not knowing how to handle a potentially unpleasant interaction with tact. One approach that you may find helpful involves three distinct steps, or phases:

1. Express appreciation for the invitation ("Thanks for thinking of me," "It's nice to know that you like me enough to invite me," etc.). Perhaps you may also wish to validate the other person ("You are a good person").
2. Say no in a clear, unequivocal fashion ("I would prefer not to make love, go dancing, get involved in a dating relationship," etc.).
3. Offer an alternative, if applicable ("However, I would like to have lunch sometime, give you a back rub," etc.).

The positive aspects of this approach are readily apparent. We first indicate our appreciation for the expressed interest in us. At the same time, we clearly state our wish not to comply with the request. Finally, we end the exchange on a positive note by offering an alternative. Of course, this last step will not always be an option (e.g., when turning down a request from someone with whom we wish to have no further social contact). Between lovers, however, there is often a mutually acceptable alternative.

Avoid Sending Mixed Messages

Saying no in clear, unmistakable language is essential to the success of the strategy just outlined. Nevertheless, many of us are probably guilty, at least sometimes, of sending mixed messages about our sexual and other intimate needs. Consider, for example, someone who responds positively to a partner's request for sexual intimacy but then spends an inordinate amount of time soaking in the bathtub while a patiently waiting partner falls asleep, or the person who expresses a desire to have sex but instead becomes engrossed in a late-night talk show. Both of these people are sending mixed messages that can reflect some of their own ambivalence about engaging in sexual relations.

As described in the next section, many of the messages we send about our sexual desires are conveyed nonverbally. When our nonverbal messages seem to contradict our verbal statements, it can be difficult for our partners to decipher the true nature of our intent. For example, we might say we are not interested in being sexual but then touch our partner in an intimate manner, or we might express willingness to engage in intercourse but then not be very responsive. In these circumstances, where our verbal and nonverbal messages are seemingly discordant, our partners are likely to have difficulty determining what we are actually communicating.

The effect of such mixed messages is usually less than desirable. The recipient is often confused about the other person's intent. He or she may feel uncertain or even inadequate ("Why can't I figure out what you really want?"), and these feelings may evolve into anger ("Why do I have to guess?") or withdrawal. These reactions are understandable under such circumstances. Faced with contradictory messages, most of us are unsure what to do—act on the first message or on the second one? Consider the following:

It really bothers me when my partner says we will make love when I get home from night school and then she is too busy studying to take a break. Even though it was her suggestion, sometimes I wonder if she had any intention to make love. (Authors' files)

All of us can benefit from taking stock from time to time to see if we send mixed messages. Try looking for inconsistencies between your verbal messages and your subsequent actions. Does your partner seem confused or uncertain when interacting with you? If you do spot yourself sending a double message, decide which one you really mean, then state it in unmistakable language. It can also be helpful to consider why you sent contradictory messages.

If you are on the receiving end of such contradictory messages, it may help to discuss your confusion and ask your partner which one of the two messages you should act on. Perhaps your partner will recognize your dilemma and act to resolve it. If she or he seems unwilling to acknowledge the inconsistency, it may help to express your feelings of discomfort and confusion as the recipient of the two conflicting messages.

▶ Nonverbal Sexual Communication

Sexual communication is not confined exclusively to words. Sometimes a touch or a smile can convey a great deal of information. Tone of voice, gestures, facial expression, and changes in breathing are also important elements of the communication process:

I can usually tell when my sweetheart is in the mood for some loving. There is a certain softness about her face and a huskiness that comes into her voice. She touches me more with her hands, and it almost seems like she presents her body as more open and vulnerable. There is some truth to all this stuff about body language. She rarely needs to verbalize her desire for sex because I usually get the message. (Authors' files)

Sometimes when I want my lover to touch me in a certain place, I move that portion of my body closer to his hands or just shift my position to make the area more accessible. Occasionally, I will guide his hand with mine to show him just what kind of stimulation I want. (Authors' files)

These examples reveal some of the varieties of nonverbal communication that have particular significance for our sexuality. In this section we direct our attention to four important components of nonverbal sexual communication: facial expression, interpersonal distance, touching, and sounds.

Facial Expression

Facial expressions often communicate the feelings a person is experiencing. Although people's expressions certainly vary, most of us have learned to accurately identify particular emotions from facial expressions. The rapport and intimacy between lovers can further increase the reliability of this yardstick.

Looking at our lovers' faces during sexual activity often gives us a quick reading of their level of pleasure. If we see a look of complete rapture, we are likely to continue providing the same type of stimulation. However, if the look conveys something less than ecstasy, we may decide to try something different or perhaps encourage our partners to provide some verbal direction.

Facial expressions can also provide helpful cues when talking over sexual concerns with a partner. If a lover's face reflects anger, anxiety, or some other disruptive emotion, it might be wise to deal with this emotion immediately ("I can tell you are angry. Can we talk about it?"). Conversely, a face that shows interest, enthusiasm, or appreciation can encourage us to continue expressing a particular feeling or concern. It is also a good idea to be aware of the nonverbal messages you are giving when your partner is sharing thoughts or feelings with you. Sometimes we inadvertently shut down potentially helpful dialogue by tightening our jaws or frowning at an inappropriate time.

Facial expressions of emotion are often a powerful component of nonverbal communication.

Interpersonal Distance

Social psychologists and communication specialists have much to say about *personal space*. In essence, this idea suggests that we tend to maintain differing degrees of interpersonal distance between ourselves and the people we have contact with, depending on the nature of our relationships (actual or desired). The intimate space to which we admit close friends and lovers restricts contact much less than the distance we maintain between ourselves and people we do not know or like.

It is instructive to watch what takes place between people meeting each other at such places as singles bars and parties. Consider the following:

When I meet people I am attracted to, I pay close attention to body language. If they seem uneasy or retreat when I move closer, it is a pretty good indication that my interest is not reciprocated. (Authors' files)

When someone attempts to decrease interpersonal distance, it is generally interpreted as a nonverbal sign that she or he is attracted to the other person or would like more intimate contact. Conversely, if someone withdraws when another person moves close, this action can usually be interpreted as a lack of interest or a gentle kind of rejection.

Lovers, whose interpersonal distance is generally at a minimum, can use these cues to signal desire for intimacy. When your lover moves in close, making his or her body available for your touches or caresses, the message of wanting physical intimacy (not necessarily sex) is apparent. Similarly, when he or she curls up on the other side of the bed, it may be a way of saying, "Please don't come too close tonight."

Decreased interpersonal space often indicates attraction and perhaps a desire for more intimate contact.

Touching

Touch is a powerful vehicle for nonverbal sexual communication between lovers. Hands can convey special messages. For example, increasing or decreasing the tempo with which you rub your lover's

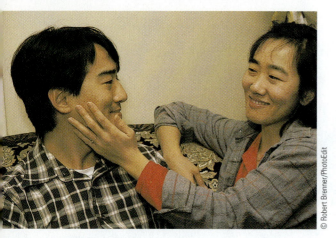
Touch is a powerful vehicle for nonverbal sexual communication.

back can signal a desire for more or less intense reciprocated stimulation. Reaching out and drawing your partner closer can indicate your readiness for more intimate contact. In the early stages of a developing relationship, touch can also be used to express a desire to become closer.

When I meet a man and find myself attracted to him, I use touch to convey my feelings. Touching him on the arm to emphasize a point or letting my fingers lightly graze across his hand on the table generally lets my feelings be known. (Authors' files)

Touch can also defuse anger and heal rifts between temporarily alienated lovers. As one man stated:

I have found that a gentle touch, lovingly administered to my partner, does wonders in bringing us back together after we have exchanged angry words. Touching her is my way of reestablishing connection. (Authors' files)

Sounds

Many people, although by no means all, like making and hearing sounds during sexual activity. Some individuals find increased breathing, moans, groans, and orgasmic cries extremely arousing. Also, such sounds can be helpful indicators of how a partner is responding to lovemaking. Some people find the absence of sounds to be frustrating:

My man rarely makes any sounds when we make love. I find this to be very disturbing. In fact, it is a real turn-off. Sometimes I can't even tell if he has come or not. If he wasn't moving, I'd think I was making love to a corpse. (Authors' files)

? How About You?

If applicable, do you prefer that your lover make sounds during sexual sharing or remain silent? If you enjoy sounds (moans, etc.), how about words?

Some people make a conscious effort to suppress spontaneous noises during sex play. In doing so, they deprive themselves of a potentially powerful and enjoyable form of nonverbal sexual communication. Not uncommonly, their deliberate silence also hinders their partners' sexual arousal, as the foregoing example illustrated.

In this section on nonverbal sexual communication we have acknowledged that not everything has to be spoken between lovers. However, facial expression, interpersonal distance, touching, and sounds cannot convey all our complex needs and emotions in a close relationship; words are needed, too. One writer observed, "As a supplement to verbal communication, acts and gestures are fine. As a substitute, they don't quite make it" (Zilbergeld, 1978, p. 158).

▶ Communication Patterns in Successful and Unsuccessful Relationships

What does research reveal about the patterns of communication that occur in successful, satisfying, long-lasting relationships versus communication characteristics of unhappy relationships that usually fail in the long run? The most informative research on communication patterns in relationships has been conducted by psychologist John Gottman and his colleagues (Gottman, 1994; Gottman & Silver, 2000; Gottman et al., 1976, 1998). They used a multimethod research model for building an extensive database drawn from 20 different studies of 2,000 married couples (see Chapter 14 for a description of Gottman's research methods). Gottman identified a number of communication patterns that are predictive of marital happiness or unhappiness. Happily married couples resolve conflicts by using a variety of *constructive* communicative tactics, which are described in the following section.

Gottman's Constructive Communication Tactics

Gottman identified a number of constructive communication tactics. These tactics include leveling and editing, validating, and volatile dialogue.

Leveling and Editing

Leveling involves stating our thoughts and feelings clearly, simply, and honestly while preferably using "I" language. For example, Gary is distressed because his partner, Susan, seldom initiates sex. Gary might say, "I love having sex with you, and I am concerned that most of the time it seems to be my idea that we make love. I am not sure what this means." When we begin to level with our partners, we might also need to do some editing of what we say. *Editing* means that we do not say things that would be deliberately hurtful to our partners and that we limit our comments to information relevant to the issue at hand. Even though Gary might feel some anger toward Susan, it would be counterproductive for him to say something like "Your seeming indifference to having sex with me ticks me off and makes me wonder what your problem is." It would also not be helpful to add comments irrelevant to the issues, such as "And I get real tired having to be the one who does all the shopping and makes all the decisions about what we are going to eat."

Validating

Validating involves telling our partners that, given their point of view, we can understand why they think or feel the way they do. Validating a partner's viewpoint does not mean that we invalidate our own position regarding the issue at hand. Rather, we are simply facilitating constructive dialogue by acknowledging the reasonableness of our partner's concern. For example, Susan might respond to Gary by saying, "I really enjoy our lovemaking, and I can see why you might think differently since I usually let you take the lead."

Volatile Dialogue

Even happily paired couples occasionally butt heads on certain issues, and Gottman's research suggests that some degree of conflict is actually essential to the long-term happiness of a relationship. In the process of studying couples' interaction patterns and reported levels of satisfaction over time, Gottman and his colleagues made a rather startling discovery. Couples in the early stages of a relationship who experienced some conflicts and arguments reported less satisfaction than early-stage couples who rarely or never argued. However, after 3 years the situation reversed itself and couples who occasionally argued reported significantly more relationship satisfaction than those couples who avoided arguments. What accounts for this seemingly paradoxical finding? Gottman suggests that couples who do not argue are likely ignoring important issues that should be addressed rather than left to fester and erode happiness. When problems are never discussed and resolved, both partners can harbor feelings of resentment and frustration that, when allowed to build over time, can drive a wedge between them. In contrast, conflict in a relationship fulfills the crucial role of identifying issues that need to be discussed for the relationship to thrive. Gottman found that some of his long-term happy couples actually used rather passionate or volatile dialogue to resolve conflicts.

Gottman's Destructive Communication Tactics

From his observations of hundreds of couples, Gottman also identified destructive communication tactics. These tactics include criticism, contempt, defensiveness, stonewalling, and belligerence.

Criticism

As described earlier, *criticism* is different from complaining. Criticism that involves expression of contempt and denigration can be harmful to a relationship. In contrast, complaining can be healthy because it allows expression of frustration and identifies issues that need to be discussed and resolved. Complaints are effectively registered with "I" language that focuses on the issue, whereas criticisms usually involve attacking someone's character with "you" statements. Being on the receiving end of a complaint stated as "I feel frustrated that our lovemaking has become somewhat predictable and routine" can feel very different from receiving a criticism stated as "You always want to make love in the same old way." This latter statement is likely to be taken as a personal attack, which puts the recipient in a defensive position that is clearly not beneficial to constructive dialogue.

Contempt

Contempt is similar to criticism but it degrades communication to an even more intense level of negativity by adding insults, sarcasm, and even name calling to the critical commentary. For example, someone might say, "You are so narrow and limited in your approach to lovemaking and life in general. How did I ever connect with such a stilted, boring person?" Contempt can also be expressed nonverbally by sneering, rolling one's eyes, or ignoring a partner's messages. This negative communication tactic causes emotional pain, does nothing to remedy or resolve issues, creates new problems in the form of defensiveness, anger, and resentment, and thereby erodes the quality of a relationship.

Defensiveness

A person who feels personally attacked or victimized by a partner's criticism and/or contempt is likely to respond with *defensiveness*. This involves constructing a defense rather than attempting to discuss and resolve an issue. Defensiveness can take the form of self-protective responses, such as making excuses, denying responsibility, or replying with a criticism of one's own. Thus a person on the receiving end of the contemptuous criticism described earlier might respond by saying, "You think I'm a boring lover? Take a long look at yourself. All you ever care about is your own pleasure, and you never give me a chance to say what I want!" In this situation one partner attacks and the other defends and counterattacks. Will a relationship that uses such tactics survive? Not likely.

Stonewalling

Stonewalling occurs when a partner concludes that any response to a partner's expressed criticism or complaint will not be helpful or productive and therefore decides not to respond at all. The stonewaller simply puts up a wall and refuses to communicate by responding with silence, walking out of the room, turning on the TV, picking up a book, and so on. This silent-treatment tactic communicates disapproval, distancing, and the belief that there is nothing one can do to improve the situation, so one might as well say nothing. A person who stonewalls a partner may have found that previous efforts to defuse a partner's critical attacks have been ineffective and that it is therefore no longer constructive to engage in seemingly futile dialogue.

Belligerence

The fifth destructive communication tactic involves a confrontational, "in your face" type of interaction that is likely to emerge as a relationship suffers from prolonged patterns of poor communication. *Belligerence* often entails a purposely provoking style of interaction intended to diminish or challenge a partner's right to influence patterns of interaction in the relationship. For example, a belligerent person might say to his or her partner, "So what if I always want to be on top when we have intercourse. What are you going to do about it?"

Clearly, all five of these destructive tactics erode and interfere with rather than improve a couple's communication. Such styles of communication are likely to lead to increased conflict and negativity, diminish positive exchanges between partners, and cause an escalation of hostility rather than pave the way to solving problems and resolving issues. Couples in relationships characterized by these negative, harmful exchanges may eventually decide that they would be better off ending such involvement, a conclusion supported by Gottman's research finding that long-term relationship survival rates are low for these couples.

What we can conclude from the available research on couple communication is that partners who have satisfying, long-lasting relationships clearly communicate in ways that are distinctly different from those who are involved in unhappy and often short-lived relationships. Positive communication strategies are not limited to those discussed in this section. Many of the strategies outlined in this chapter, when incorporated into a couple's communication about sex and other relationship issues, are predictive of satisfying and enduring partnerships.

▶ Impasses

Candid communication between caring, supportive partners often leads to changes that are mutually gratifying. However, even an ample supply of openness, candor, support, and understanding cannot ensure a meeting of the minds on all issues: Couples do reach impasses. Your partner simply may not want to try a new coital position. Or your suggestion to incorporate a vibrator into shared sex play may be just a bit too threatening. Perhaps the two of you cannot agree on the issue of close friendships with the other sex.

What can you do when communication results in a standoff? Continued discussion may be helpful. However, it is self-deceiving to assume that talk, even the most open and compassionate discussions, will always lead to desired changes.

Sometimes it is useful to try to put yourself in your partner's shoes. Research demonstrates that the process of trying to see things from the partner's viewpoint often results in both more positive feelings about the relationship and improved efforts to respond more constructively to dilemmas and impasses (Arriaga & Rusbult, 1998). When we consider issues from a partner's perspective, we are less likely to place blame for the dispute on her or his shoulders and thus are more inclined to respond in a positive manner. Try to see things from the other person's perspective. If you have some difficulty with this, ask your partner for help ("I am having some trouble seeing this from your point of view. Can you help me out?"). If you can understand your partner's concern, by all means say so. Acknowledging the reasonableness of the other's viewpoint is the process of **validating** described previously. Sometimes this process of trying to see the validity of another viewpoint leads to new perspectives that can help end the deadlock. However, if you continue to disagree after this effort, it may be easier to accept the idea that you can have legitimate but different opinions.

At a time of impasse a couple might also find it beneficial to take a break from each other for a while. Sometimes forced continuation of a discussion, particularly when emotions are strong, is counterproductive. Scheduling another time to talk can be a good tactic. Later, after each partner has had the opportunity to privately consider the other's feelings, it may be possible to readdress the issue more successfully.

Sometimes people cannot or will not change, often for justifiable reasons. Certainly, all of us cherish our right to refuse to do something we consider objectionable. Granting the same right to someone close to us is an important ingredient in a relationship characterized by mutual respect.

Failure to reach a solution to an impasse is not necessarily cause for despair. At least the couple has openly discussed a sensitive issue. Possibly, they have also increased their understanding of each other and the level of intimacy between them. In the event that unresolved impasses threaten to erode a relationship, professional counseling may be desirable. (Chapter 16 includes guidelines for selecting a counselor.)

Validating The process of indicating that a partner's point of view is reasonable.

InfoTrac Search Words
■ Validating

Summary

The Importance of Communication

- Sexual communication often contributes positively to the contentment and enjoyment of a sexual relationship; infrequent or ineffective sexual communication is a common reason that people feel dissatisfied with their sex lives. (p. 211)

- An excellent basis for effective sexual communication is mutual empathy—the underlying knowledge that each partner in a relationship cares for the other and knows that care is reciprocated. (p. 211)

- Childhood socialization, which often creates a sense of discomfort with sexual matters, can contribute to later difficulties in engaging in sexual communication. (pp. 211–212)

- Our language is characterized by a conspicuous absence of an effective, comfortable sexual vocabulary. (pp. 212–213)

- Differences in women's and men's styles of relating to other people can hinder communication. Men often use language to convey advice and information and to maintain a one-up status. In contrast, women typically use language to promote closeness and to achieve and share intimacy. (pp. 214–215)

- Some people object to sexual communication on the grounds that it disrupts spontaneity or that it may place one in a position of increased vulnerability to judgment, criticism, or rejection. (p. 215)

Talking: Getting Started
- It is often difficult to start talking about sex. Some suggestions for getting started include talking about talking, reading about sex and discussing the material, and sharing sexual histories. (p. 215)

Listening and Feedback
- Communication is most successful with an active listener and an effective communicator. (p. 216)
- The listener can facilitate communication by maintaining eye contact with the speaker, providing some feedback or reaction to the message, expressing appreciation for communication efforts, maintaining an attitude of unconditional positive regard, and using paraphrasing effectively. (pp. 217–218)

Discovering Your Partner's Needs
- Efforts to communicate with sexual partners are often hindered by yes/no questions, which encourage limited replies. Effective alternatives include open-ended and either/or questions. (pp. 218–219)
- Self-disclosure can make it easier for a partner to communicate her or his own needs. Sharing fantasies, beginning with mild desires, can be a particularly valuable kind of exchange. (pp. 219–220)
- Discussing sexual preferences either before or after a sexual encounter can be beneficial. (pp. 220, 222)
- Giving permission encourages partners to share feelings freely. (p. 222)

Learning to Make Requests
- Making requests is facilitated by (1) taking responsibility for one's own pleasure, (2) making sure requests are specific, and (3) using "I" language. (pp. 222–224)

Expressing and Receiving Complaints
- Be aware of your motives for complaining. Complaining that aims to hurt or blame a partner is likely to be destructive. (pp. 225–226)
- It is important to select the right time and place for expressing sexual concerns. Avoid registering complaints when anger is at its peak. (p. 226)
- Complaints are generally most effective when tempered with praise. People are usually more motivated to make changes when they are praised for their strengths as well as made aware of things that need improvement. (p. 227)
- It is beneficial to reward each small step in the process of changing undesirable behavior. (p. 228)
- "Why" questions that blame a partner do not further the process of registering constructive complaints. (p. 228)
- It is wise to direct anger toward behavior rather than toward a person's character. Anger is probably best expressed with clear, honest "I" statements rather than with accusatory "you" statements. (pp. 228–229)
- Relationships are better served when complaining is limited to one complaint per discussion. (p. 229)
- Paraphrasing a partner's complaint and acknowledging an understanding of the basis for his or her concerns can help establish a sense of empathy and lead to constructive dialogue. (pp. 229–230)

- It can be helpful to ask clarifying questions when complaints are vague. Calmly verbalizing the feelings that are aroused when one is on the receiving end of a complaint often avoids nonproductive, heated exchanges. (p. 230)
- An excellent closure to receiving a complaint is to focus on what can be done to rectify the problematic issue in a relationship. (pp. 230–231)

Saying No
- One three-step strategy for saying no to invitations for intimate involvements is expressing appreciation for the invitation, saying no in a clear, unequivocal fashion, and offering an alternative, if applicable. (p. 231)
- To avoid sending mixed messages, occasionally check for inconsistencies between verbal messages and subsequent actions. Recipients of mixed messages might find it helpful to express their confusion and to ask which of the conflicting messages they are expected to act on. (pp. 231–232)

Nonverbal Sexual Communication
- Sexual communication is not confined to words alone. Facial expressions, interpersonal distance, touching, and sounds also convey a great deal of information. (p. 232)
- The value of nonverbal communication lies primarily in its ability to supplement, not replace, verbal exchanges. (p. 234)

Communication Patterns in Successful and Unsuccessful Relationships
- Constructive communication tactics that contribute to relationship satisfaction and longevity include the strategies of leveling and editing, validating, volatile dialogue, summarizing, paraphrasing, and clarifying. (pp. 234–235)
- Destructive communication tactics include criticism, contempt, defensiveness, stonewalling, and belligerence. Such styles of communication lead to increased conflict and negativity, cause an escalation of hostility, and frequently result in relationship failure. (pp. 235–237)

Impasses
- Sexual communication does not always lead to solutions. Seeing things from a partner's perspective might help when deadlocks occur, and it might also be helpful to suspend the discussion temporarily so that each person can privately consider the other's point of view. An unresolved impasse does not necessarily threaten a relationship; if it does, counseling may be desirable. (p. 237)

▶ Suggested Readings

Goodman, Gerald, and Glenn Esterly (1988). *The Talk Book: The Intimate Science of Communication in Close Relationships.* Emmaus, PA: Rodale Press. An excellent resource for individuals seeking realistic and practical guidelines for strengthening relationships by learning to communicate more effectively.

Gottman, John (1994). *Why Marriages Succeed or Fail.* New York: Simon & Schuster. An informative book, based on 20 years of research on communication within relationships, that provides excellent suggestions for enhancing couple communication.

Gottman, John, and Nan Silver (2000). *The Seven Principles for Making Marriage Work.* New York: Crown Publishers. A practical and informative discussion of how research on patterns of marital interaction can be applied to strengthening couple relationships.

Levant, Ronald, and Gary Brooks (Eds.) (1997). *Men and Sex: New Psychological Perspectives.* New York: Wiley. A superb collection of articles that persuasively describe how men's sexuality is strongly shaped by socialization processes that discourage emotional expression and relational intimacy. The various contributors outline how this style of growing up in North America results in patterns of *nonrelational sexuality,* such as objectification of women, infidelity and womanizing, viewing sex as a commodity, and sexual victimization. A final article offers suggestions for how these potentially destructive patterns of nonrelational sexuality can be changed at both the individual and societal levels.

McKay, Matthew, Martha Davis, and Patrick Fanning (1983). *Messages: The Communication Book.* Oakland, CA: New Harbinger Publications. A practical, skills-oriented book that addresses such topics as sexual communication, conflict resolution, and family communication.

Tannen, Deborah (1990). *You Just Don't Understand: Women and Men in Conversation.* New York: Morrow. (Also available in paperback from Ballantine, 1991.) A highly readable best-selling book that uses vivid examples to outline the distinctly different conversational styles of males and females, the origins of these differing styles, and how such divergent communication modes lead to difficulties between the sexes. Throughout this book the reader will discover much to help improve his or her communication with the other sex.

▶ Web Resources

Your *Our Sexuality* Web site **http://psychology.wadsworth.com/ crooksbaur9e/** has direct links to the Web sites described below. These links are checked often for changes, dead links, and new additions.

Sexual Communication
This page from the Web site of the Counseling Center at SUNY Buffalo provides some helpful tips on building positive communication within a relationship.

Communicating About Sex
A slide show presentation on communicating about sex and intimacy is accessible on the Houghton College Web site.

The Human Awareness Institute
The Human Awareness Institute is one of many private groups that offer workshops to help couples communicate more effectively and improve relationships. Information on these workshops is available at this Web site.

Our Sexuality Web Site
For online resources directly related to this book, go to **http://psychology.wadsworth.com/ crooksbaur9e/**. You will find interactive exercises, study questions, chapter outlines, an online version of this text's glossary, and Web links and activities that complement your CD-ROM.

InfoTrac® College Edition Online Library
http://infotrac.thomsonlearning.com/
InfoTrac College Edition is an online searchable library that includes a multitude of journals, many of which are specific to human sexuality. These journals include *Archives of Sexual Behavior, Archives of Sexual Health Behavior, Canadian Journal of Human Sexuality, Hispanic Journal of the Behavioral Sciences, Journal of Cross-Cultural Psychology, Journal of Physical Education, Recreation, and Dance, Journal of Sex Research,* and *Sex Roles.* You may search topics suggested in the margins of this chapter or terms of your own.

Our Sexuality CD-ROM
Use your CD-ROM for further study of the concepts in this chapter. Your CD-ROM provides animations of difficult concepts, video clips of real people discussing sexuality, critical thinking questions, chapter quizzing, and more.

Sexual Behaviors

© Franco Vogt/CORBIS

My sexuality has had many different dimensions during my life. My childhood masturbation was a secret desire and guilt that I never did admit to the priest in the confessional. "Playing doctor" was intriguing and exciting in its "naughtiness." The hours of hot kissing and petting of my teenage and early college years developed my sexual awareness. My first intercourse experience was with a loved and trusted boyfriend. It was a profound physical and emotional experience; 30 years later the memory still brings me deep pleasure. As a young adult in the 1960s and 1970s my sexual expression alternated between periods of recreational sex and celibacy. Within marriage the comforts and challenges of commitment; combining sex with an intense desire to become pregnant; the primal experience of pregnancy, childbirth, and nursing greatly expanded the parameters of my sexuality. Now, balancing family, career, personal interests, and regular hair appointments, my sexuality is a quiet hum in the background. I'm looking forward to retirement and time and energy for more than coffee and a kiss in the morning. (Authors' files)

People express their sexuality in many ways. The emotions and meanings that they attach to sexual behavior also vary widely. In this chapter we define and explain some varieties of sexual expression and then explore meaning and context in sexual behavior. We consider individuals first and later look at couples' sexual behavior. We begin with a discussion of celibacy.

▶ Celibacy

A physically mature person who does not engage in sexual behavior is said to be *celibate*. Celibacy, or abstinence, can be a viable option until the context for a sexual relationship is appropriate and positive for a given individual. Celibacy is not commonly thought of as a form of sexual expression. However, when it represents a conscious decision not to engage in sexual behavior, this decision in itself is an expression of one's sexuality. There are two degrees of celibacy. In **complete celibacy** a person neither masturbates nor has sexual contact with another person. In **partial celibacy** the individual engages in masturbation but does not have interpersonal sexual contact.

Celibacy is most commonly thought of in connection with religious devotion: Joining a religious order or becoming a priest or nun often includes a vow of celibacy. The ideal of religious celibacy is to transform sexual energy into service to humanity (Abbott, 2000). Mother Teresa of Calcutta and Mahatma Gandhi of India exemplified this ideal and are admired for their moral leadership (Sipe, 1990).

Historically, some women embraced celibacy to free themselves from the limitations of the expected gender roles of marriage and motherhood. In the Middle Ages a nun could seek the education she desired but was unavailable to her outside the convent. In the convent nuns had access to libraries and could correspond with learned theologians, all of which was prohibited to lay women. Elizabeth I, the Virgin Queen, avoided marriage to maintain her political power, but she had several unconsummated love affairs while she led England. She entertained proposals from numerous well-connected suitors for her own political purposes, subjecting herself to repeated courtly inspections to confirm her virginity. During the Victorian Era, Florence Nightingale rebelled against her privileged family's expectations and Victorian norms of marriage to save many soldiers' lives through her determination and advanced health care practices. She established nursing as a viable profession, an accomplishment she never would have been able to pursue as a married woman of that era (Abbott, 2002).

Celibacy, especially in the form of abstinence until marriage, received more public attention in the 1990s. The media reflected this shift with characters on *Beverly Hills 90210* and *Step by Step* and with the character Cher in *Clueless,* all of whom proudly proclaimed their virginity. Julie and Matt in MTV's *Real World—New Orleans* were outspoken about their virginity. Abstinence has been promoted in school and church sex-education programs, community organizations, and groups such as Athletes for Abstinence. In 1993 the Southern Baptist convention began the "True Love Waits" campaign. Participating teens sign a pledge of chastity until marriage. Other denominations and churches across the United States have joined the campaign (Abbott, 2000; Werner, 1997).

Complete celibacy An expression of sexuality in which an individual does not engage in either masturbation or interpersonal sexual contact.

Partial celibacy An expression of sexuality in which an individual does not engage in interpersonal sexual contact but continues to engage in masturbation.

Many factors can lead a person to be celibate. Some people choose to be celibate until marriage because of religious or moral beliefs. Others maintain celibacy until their personal criteria for a good sexual relationship have been met. Some choose celibacy because they have experienced confusion or disappointment in past sexual relationships and they want to spend some time establishing new relationships without the complicating factor of sexual interaction (Elliott & Brantley, 1997). A 28-year-old man explained:

> There was a period not too long ago in my life where I had been abstinent for about four years. Part of the reason for me was that it was my preferred method of birth control. I had been on both sides of the cheating fence and began to realize that sex wasn't just something that I wanted to take, or could take, lightly. The feelings that can be created out of a physical relationship are simply too powerful to toy around with. I was terribly afraid of being hurt again, or of perhaps hurting someone else, so I chose not to get close to anyone. (Authors' files)

? How About You?

What benefits do you experience when you are not in a sexual relationship?

At times a person can be so caught up in other aspects of life that sex is simply not a priority. Health considerations, such as concerns about pregnancy or sexually transmitted diseases, also can prompt a decision not to have sexual intercourse.

Celibacy can also be an important aspect of treatment for individuals who are newly recovering from alcohol or drug dependency. Substance abusers often use drugs or alcohol in an effort to decrease their feelings of anxiety, and the anxiety created by involvement in sexual relationships can precipitate a return to drug or alcohol abuse. A period of celibacy affords individuals an opportunity to learn about their sexual feelings and desires without acting on them. Celibacy during recovery also lets people develop the skills to handle the anxiety involved in sexual relationships without turning to alcohol or drugs (Pinhas, 1989).

Some people find that a period of celibacy can be rewarding. They are often able to refocus on themselves during such a period: exploring self-pleasuring; learning to value their aloneness, autonomy, and privacy; or giving priority to work and nonsexual relationship commitments. Friendships can gain new dimensions and fulfillment.

Many people do not choose to be celibate, however, because despite its rewards for some individuals, celibacy also has a number of disadvantages. These can include lack of physical affection and loneliness for sexual intimacy. In addition, coming out of a period of celibacy can be difficult, because reestablishing sexual relationships can be awkward and frightening. It is interesting that of the many options for sexual expression, celibacy is one alternative that people sometimes have considerable trouble understanding. However, celibacy can be a personally valuable choice.

▶ Erotic Dreams and Fantasy

Some forms of sexual experience occur within a person's mind, with or without accompanying sexual behavior. These are erotic dreams and fantasies—mental experiences that arise from our imagination or life experience or that are stimulated by books, drawings, photographs, or movies.

Erotic Dreams

Erotic dreams and occasionally orgasm can occur during sleep without a person's conscious direction. As in other dreams, the content of erotic dreams can be logical or nonsensical. Explicit sexual expression in dreams varies widely, from common sexual activities to behaviors considered taboo. Both erotic dreams and waking fantasy can be ways to express and explore dimensions of experiences, feelings, and desires.

Almost all the males and two-thirds of the females in Kinsey's research populations reported experiencing erotic dreams. A person might waken during such a dream and notice signs of sexual arousal: erection, vaginal lubrication, or pelvic movements. Orgasm can also occur during sleep; this is called **nocturnal orgasm.** When orgasm occurs, males usually notice the ejaculate—hence the term *wet dream.* Women also experience orgasm during

Nocturnal orgasm Involuntary orgasm during sleep.

sleep (Renshaw, 1991), but female orgasm is more difficult to determine because of the absence of visible evidence. In one study of college women 30% reported having experienced nocturnal orgasm. Another 30% had never heard of nocturnal orgasm. Women who had a higher frequency of intercourse and of orgasm with masturbation were more likely to experience and be aware of orgasms during sleep (Wells, 1983).

Erotic Fantasy

Erotic waking fantasies commonly occur during daydreams, masturbation, or sexual encounters with a partner. A review of research studies about fantasy found that about 95% of men and women reported having had sexual fantasies (Leitenberg & Henning, 1995). The content of sexual fantasies varies greatly and can range from vague romantic images to graphic representations of imagined or actual past experiences. The fantasy content of homosexuals and heterosexuals is more similar than different, except for the sex of the imagined partner (Leitenberg & Henning, 1995).

An in-depth study of women, age 19 to 66, found six common categories of roles women played in their private fantasies. The *Pretty Maiden* is the passive woman of another's desire. She is so powerfully attractive that she is irresistible, a plot commonly found in romance novels. The *Victim* is the object of sexual humiliation or violence and can indulge her curiosity about dangerous sex without actual danger. The *Wild Woman* is the pursuer and initiator of sexual pleasure on her terms. She imagines daring situations, such as multiple partners or public places, to flout sexual convention. Singer/actress Madonna's earlier blatant sexual strutting is a good example of the wild woman role. The *Dominatrix* gets her arousal from imposing power over another, unlike the *Beloved*, who fantasizes intimacy with a cherished soul-mate partner of equal power and status. In these first five roles the women are part of the action, whereas the *Voyeur* finds arousal in imagining watching others engage in sex. Erotic tension is heightened if her fantasy includes the risk of being caught watching (Boss & Maltz, 2001).

Functions of Fantasy

Erotic fantasies serve many functions. First, they can be a source of pleasure and arousal. Erotic thoughts typically serve to enhance sexual arousal during masturbation or partner sexual activities. The following two accounts, the first by a woman and the second by a man, show how fantasy can amplify pleasurable physical and emotional feelings:

When my partner and I make love, I let my mind leave all other thoughts behind and totally experience and feel what is happening. All aromas become much more noticeable and pleasurable. The warmth increases, and I imagine my lover and me suspended in mist upon a bed of clouds. Our bodies come close together in my mind as arousal increases, and at the moment of orgasm it is as if we were mentally and physically one. I caress my lover's body, but it is as if it were part of my own. (Authors' files)

The fantasy that recurs most when I am making love is a visualization of being on an isolated tropical beach. The warm sun is baking our bodies golden brown. The rhythmic pounding of the waves eliminates all tension and worries. My partner and I are one. (Authors' files)

Sexual fantasies can also help to overcome anxiety and facilitate sexual functioning or to compensate for a somewhat negative sexual situation. Fantasies can be another way to mentally rehearse and anticipate new sexual experiences. Imagining seductive glances, that first kiss, or a novel intercourse position can help a person implement these activities more comfortably (Leitenberg & Henning, 1995).

Some sexual fantasies allow for tolerable expression of "forbidden wishes." The fact that a sexual activity in a fantasy is forbidden can make it more exciting. People in sexually exclusive relationships can fantasize about past lovers or others to whom they feel attracted, even though they are committed to a single sexual partner. In a fantasy a person can experience lustful group sex, cross-orientation sexual liaisons, brief sexual encounters with strangers, erotic relations with friends and acquaintances, incestuous experiences, sex with animals, or any other sexual activity they can imagine—all without actually engaging in them. The following anecdotes are examples of the variety of forbidden-wish fantasies. The first example is a woman's masturbation fantasy:

I fantasize about being seduced by another woman. Although I've never had an affair with another woman, it really makes me sexually excited to think of oral sex being performed on me or vice versa. (Authors' files)

A man's masturbation fantasy reflects one study's findings that one in three men have same-sex fantasies (Ellis et al., 1987):

I usually think of some woman (no one that I know), blond, beautiful, lowering herself onto me, letting me eat her out in a "69." Oftentimes, a strong and bearded man is involved and gives me oral stimulation at the same time that the woman is kissing me or letting me eat her. (Authors' files)

Another function of erotic fantasy can be to provide relief from gender-role expectations (Pinhas, 1985). In fact, in women a degree of gender-role reversal can contribute to increased fantasizing. One study found that college women with more traditional feminine attitudes report fewer sexual fantasies than women who are more independent and hold more liberal views of women's roles (Brown & Hart, 1977). Women's fantasies of being the sexual aggressor and men's fantasies of being forced to have sex can offer alternatives to stereotypical roles. In her first book about male sexual fantasy, Nancy Friday reported that one of the major themes is men's abdication of control in favor of passivity:

> It may seem lusty and dashing always to be the one who chooses the woman, who decides when, where, and how the bedroom scene will be played. But isn't her role safer? The man is like someone who has suggested a new restaurant to friends. What if it doesn't live up to expectations he has aroused? The macho stance makes the male the star performer. The hidden cost is that it puts the woman in the role of critic. (Friday, 1980, p. 274)

Although fantasies of being forced to have sex provide an alternative to gender-role expectations for men, the same type of fantasy typically means something different to women. For women, who often learn to have mixed feelings about being sexual, this type of fantasy offers sexual adventures free from the responsibility and guilt of personal choice. A research study found that women who report having fantasies of being forced to have sex had less sexual guilt and more positive feelings about sex in general than women who did not have fantasies of being forced. Also, the women who had force fantasies were no more likely to have actually experienced sexual force or coercion than the women who did not have force fantasies. This research indicates that force fantasies are not usually an indication of past abusive experiences or current negative feelings about sex (Strassberg & Lockerd, 1998).

Male–Female Similarities and Differences in Sexual Fantasy

Men's and women's fantasy lives include some common aspects. First, the frequency of fantasy is similar for both sexes during sexual activity with a partner (Leitenberg & Henning, 1995). Second, both men and women indicate a wide range of fantasy content. A research summary of male–female content of sexual fantasy (Leitenberg & Henning, 1995) found notable differences:

- Men's fantasies are more active and focus more on the woman's body and on what he wants to do to it, whereas women's fantasies are more passive and focus more on men's interest in their bodies.
- Men's sexual fantasies focus more on explicit sexual acts, nude bodies, and physical gratification, whereas women use more emotional context and romance in their sexual fantasies.
- Men are more likely to fantasize about multiple partners and group sex than are women.

- Men are more likely to have dominance fantasies, whereas women are more likely to have submission fantasies.

The frequency of fantasies of being forced or forcing someone to have sex differs significantly between males and females. Although, as we have mentioned, such fantasies can take the form of gender-role reversal, they usually reflect an exaggeration of stereotypical gender roles of the male as active and the female as receptive. Research indicates that almost twice as many women as men fantasize about being forced to have sex (Knafo & Jaffe, 1984; Maltz & Boss, 1997). It is important to note, however, that enjoyment of forced-sex fantasies does not mean women really want to be raped (Gold et al., 1991). A woman is in charge of her fantasies, but as a victim of sexual aggression she is not in control.

Fantasies: Help or Hindrance?

Erotic fantasies are generally considered a healthy and helpful aspect of sexuality (Renaud & Byers, 2001). Most people report that their sexual fantasies are pleasurable and arousing (Leitenberg & Henning, 1995). Many sex therapists encourage their clients to use sexual fantasy as a source of stimulation to help them increase interest and arousal. Sexual fantasies help many women experience arousal and orgasm during sexual activity, and a deficit of erotic fantasy is often present with problems of low sexual desire and arousal (Boss & Maltz, 2001). Research has also indicated that people who experience more guilt about sex feel less arousal to sexual fantasies than subjects who do not feel so guilty about sex (Follingstad & Kimbrell, 1986). Another study found that people who feel less guilty about sexual fantasy during intercourse reported more sexual fantasies and higher levels of sexual satisfaction and functioning than did those who felt more guilty (Cado & Leitenberg, 1990).

Although most of the available research supports erotic imagining as helpful, sexual fantasy has also been considered symptomatic of poor sexual relationships or other personal problems (Perel, 2003; Shainess & Greenwald, 1971). Private fantasies during sex with a partner can erode the trust and intimacy in a relationship. Disclosure of sexual fantasies can be problematic. One research study found that college students had a double standard with regard to the meaning of their partners' sexual fantasies compared to their own. Study participants of both sexes thought that their fantasies about someone other than their partners were normal and did not jeopardize the exclusivity of the relationship. However, the idea that their partners fantasized about someone else made the participants feel jealous and threatened, as though the fantasy was a kind of unfaithfulness. Participants commonly stated, "My partner should be satisfied with just having me." The most threatening fantasy a partner could have was about someone who actually had the potential for disrupting the relationship; that is, a fantasy about a mutual friend or classmate was much more upsetting than a fantasy about someone who was an unlikely rival, such as a movie star (Yarab & Allgeier, 1998).

MOMMA by Mell Lazarus. By permission of Mell Lazarus and Creators Syndicate, Inc.

Individuals who have experienced sexual abuse as children might use particular sexual fantasies to attempt to master their past trauma, but they can find that these fantasies actually recreate and reinforce the original abuse. Some people who have experienced sexual abuse are troubled by intrusive, unwanted sexual fantasies that emerge when they become sexually aroused. Developing new fantasies based on self-acceptance and loving relationships can be a part of the healing process for these individuals (Boss & Maltz, 2001). As with most other aspects of sexuality, what determines whether fantasizing is helpful or disturbing to a relationship is its meaning and purpose for the individuals concerned.

Some people decide to incorporate a particular fantasy into their actual sexual behavior. Acting out a fantasy can be pleasurable; however, if a fantasy is counter to one's value system or has possible negative consequences, one should consider the advantages and disadvantages of doing so. For some people fantasies are more exciting when they remain imaginary and are a disappointment in actual practice.

Most people draw a distinct boundary between their fantasy world and the real world. For example, a woman who enjoys fantasizing about having intercourse with her partner's best friend might never really consider doing so. For people who experience guilt over their fantasies, it is important to remember that thoughts and feelings are not the same as actions. So long as people feel able to refrain from acting out a fantasy that would hurt themselves or others, they probably do not need to be concerned.

In some cases fantasy can contribute to a person acting in a way that is harmful to others. This is of particular concern with people who sexually assault children or adults. A person who thinks that he or she is in danger of committing such an act should seek professional psychological assistance. We provide further information about fantasy and sexual offenders in Chapter 19.

▶ Masturbation

Masturbation Stimulation of one's own genitals to create sexual pleasure.

In this textbook the word **masturbation** is used to describe self-stimulation of one's genitals for sexual pleasure. *Autoeroticism* is another term used for masturbation. We discuss some perspectives on and purposes of masturbation and specific techniques used in masturbation.

Perspectives on Masturbation

Masturbation has been a source of social concern and censure throughout Judeo–Christian history. This state of affairs has resulted in both misinformation and considerable personal shame and fear. Many of the negative attitudes toward masturbation are rooted in early Jewish and Christian views that procreation was the only legitimate purpose of sexual behavior. Because masturbation obviously could not result in conception, it was condemned (Wiesner-Hanks, 2000). The "evils" of masturbation received a great deal of publicity in the name of science during the mid 18th century, largely as a result of the writings of a European physician named Samuel Tissot. He wrote vividly about the mind- and body-damaging effects of "self-abuse." Tissot believed that semen was made from blood and that the loss of semen was debilitating to health. This view of masturbation influenced social and medical attitudes in Europe and North America for generations, as reflected by an "encyclopedia" of health published in 1918, which describes the following "symptoms" of masturbation:

> The health soon becomes noticeably impaired; there will be general debility, a slowness of growth, weakness in the lower limbs, nervousness and unsteadiness of the hands, loss of memory, and inability to study or learn, restless disposition, weak eyes and loss of sight, headache and inability to sleep or wakefulness. Next come sore eyes, blindness, stupidity, consumption, spinal affection, emaciation, involuntary seminal emissions, loss of all energy or spirit, insanity and idiocy—the hopeless ruin of both body and mind. (Wood & Ruddock, 1918, p. 812)

In the 1800s sexual abstinence, simple foods, and fitness were lauded as crucial to health. The Reverend Sylvester Graham, who promoted the use of whole-grain flours and whose name is still attached to graham crackers, wrote that ejaculation reduced precious "vital fluids." He beseeched men to abstain from masturbation and even marital intercourse to avoid moral and physical degeneracy. John Harvey Kellogg, a physician, carried Graham's work further and developed the cornflake to help prevent masturbation and sexual desire (Kellogg believed that bland food dampened sexual interest and that spicy foods excited sexual desires). Other techniques to control masturbation included bandaging the genitals, tying one's hands at night, clitoridectomy, applying carbolic acid to the clitoris, and suturing foreskins shut, as well as employing mechanical devices (Hamilton, 2002; Planned Parenthood Federation of America, 2003a).

Freud and most other early psychoanalysts recognized that masturbation does not harm physical health, and they saw it as normal during childhood. However, they believed that masturbation in adulthood could result in "immature" sexual development and the inability to form good sexual relationships. Contemporary research indicates that masturbation is neither beneficial nor harmful to sexual adjustment in young adulthood (Leitenberg et al., 1993).

Views today reflect conflicting beliefs about masturbation, and much of the traditional condemnation still exists. In 1976 the Vatican issued a "Declaration on Certain Questions Concerning Sexual Ethics," which described masturbation as an "intrinsically and seriously disordered act." This perspective was maintained again in 1993 by Pope John Paul II's condemnation of masturbation as morally unacceptable. Indeed, some individuals abstain from masturbation because of their religious beliefs.

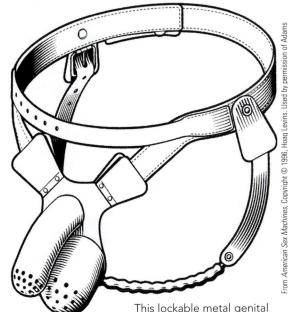

This lockable metal genital pouch with leather straps, patented in 1910, was designed to prevent masturbation by patients in mental hospitals.

I don't masturbate, because I've learned from my church and my parents that sexual love in marriage is an expression of God's love. Any other kind of sex diminishes the meaning I will find with my wife. (Authors' files)

In contrast, many view masturbation as a healthy and positive aspect of sexuality. For example, Betty Dodson, author of *Liberating Masturbation*, writes:

> Masturbation, of course, is our first natural sexual activity. It's the way we discover our eroticism, the way we learn to respond sexually, the way we learn to love ourselves and build self-esteem. Sexual skill and the ability to respond are not "natural" in our society. Doing what "comes naturally" for us is to be sexually inhibited. Sex is like any other skill—it has to be learned and practiced. (Dodson, 1974, p. 13)

Purposes of Masturbation

People masturbate for a variety of reasons, not the least of which is the pleasure of arousal and orgasm. The most commonly reported reason is to relieve sexual tension (Michael et al., 1994). At certain times the satisfaction from an autoerotic session can be more rewarding than an interpersonal sexual encounter, as the following quote illustrates:

I had always assumed that masturbation was a second-best sexual expression. One time, after reflecting back on the previous day's activities of a really enjoyable morning masturbatory experience and an unsatisfying experience that evening with a partner, I realized that first- and second-rate were very relative. (Authors' files)

Some people find that the independent sexual release available through masturbation can help them make better decisions about relating sexually with other people. Furthermore, within a relationship masturbation can help to even out the effects of dissimilar sexual interest. Masturbation can be a shared experience:

! Sexual Health

When I am feeling sexual and my partner is not, he holds me and kisses me while I masturbate. Also, sometimes after making love I like to touch myself while he embraces me. It is so much better than sneaking off to the bathroom alone. (Authors' files)

In addition, some people find masturbation valuable as a means of self-exploration. Sex educator Eleanor Hamilton recommends masturbation to adolescents as a way to release tension and to become "pleasantly at home with your own sexual organs" (1978, p. 33). Indeed, people can learn a great deal about their sexual responses from masturbation. Self-stimulation is often helpful for women learning to experience orgasms and for men experimenting with their response patterns to increase ejaculatory control. (We discuss masturbation as a tool for increasing sexual satisfaction in Chapter 16.) Finally, some people find that masturbation helps them get to sleep at night, because the same generalized feelings of relaxation that often follow a sexual encounter can also accompany self-pleasuring (Ellison, 2000). ■

A common concern about masturbation is "doing it too much." Table 9.1 shows the range in frequency of masturbation among college students. Even in writings where masturbation is said to be normal, masturbating "to excess" is often presented as unhealthy. A definition of excess rarely follows. If a person were masturbating so much that it significantly interfered with any aspect of his or her life, there might be cause for concern. However, in that case masturbation would be a symptom or manifestation of some underlying problem rather than the problem itself. For example, someone who is experiencing intense emotional anxiety might use masturbation as a way to relieve anxiety or as a form of self-comforting. The problem in this case is the intense emotional anxiety, not the masturbation.

Most men and women, both married and unmarried, masturbate on occasion. Women tend to masturbate more after they reach their 20s than they did in their teens. Kinsey hypothesized that this was due to increased erotic responsiveness, opportunities for learning about the possibility of self-stimulation through sex play with a partner, and a reduction in sexual inhibitions.

TABLE 9.1	Two Thousand College Students Answer the Question "How Often Do You Masturbate?"	
	Men (%)	**Women (%)**
Two or more times a week	50	16
Less than two times a week but more than never	38	44
Never	12	40

SOURCE: Elliott & Brantley (1997).

It is common for people to continue masturbation after they marry. In fact, individuals with a higher frequency of partnered sexual activity also masturbate more often (Laumann et al., 1994). Masturbation is often considered inappropriate when a person has a sexual partner, however. Some people believe that they should not engage in a sexual activity that excludes their partners, or that their experiencing sexual pleasure by masturbation deprives their partners of pleasure. Others mistakenly interpret their partners' desire to masturbate as a sign that there is something wrong with their relationship. But unless it interferes with mutually enjoyable sexual intimacy in the relationship, masturbation can be considered a normal part of each partner's sexual repertoire. Moreover, one study found that married women who masturbated to orgasm had greater marital and sexual satisfaction than women who did not masturbate (Hurlbert & Whittaker, 1991).

Ethnicity and Masturbation

Adults who are most likely to masturbate, and most likely to masturbate more frequently, have several characteristics in common. They have more liberal views and consider pleasure an important goal of sexuality. In addition, the higher the education level, the more likely an individual is to masturbate. White men and women masturbate more than African American men and women. Among white, African, and Hispanic Americans, Hispanic women have the lowest rate of masturbation. Contrary to expectation, people living with sexual partners are more likely to masturbate than those living alone. Given that white college-educated people who are living with a partner are most likely to masturbate, it appears that this practice is strongly influenced by a person's social group (Laumann et al., 1994).

Self-Pleasuring Techniques

In this section we offer descriptions of self-pleasuring techniques. Self-exploration exercises can help a person become more aware of genital and whole-body sensations. Readers who would like to experiment with some or all of the steps are invited to do so. Readers who have moral objections to masturbation should follow their values and not experiment with the techniques for self-pleasuring.

It is not unusual for someone who is trying self-pleasuring for the first time to feel anxious. If this happens to you, two suggestions may be helpful. First, focus for a minute on physical relaxation: Take a few slow breaths, extending your belly outward as you inhale. Another way to relax yourself is to tense a body part, such as an arm and hand, for a few seconds, then release the tension. Second, try to clear your mind of thoughts related to the "rightness" or "wrongness" of self-pleasuring, and allow yourself to concentrate instead on the positive physical sensations that can come from self-stimulation. Because the genitals are only one part of the body, we suggest involving your entire anatomy in the self-exam, to explore your sensuality as well as specific structures. Both men and women often report that their sexual feelings are enhanced by learning to be less genitally focused and more in touch with the sensual potentials that exist throughout their bodies.

Set aside a block of time (at least 1 hour for the entire exercise) when you will have privacy. Allow several minutes for your mind to quiet down from the noisy clatter of the day. A good way to begin is with a relaxing bath or shower. You can start the self-exploration while bathing, washing with soapy hands in an unhurried manner. Towel off leisurely and then explore all areas of your body with your fingertips, gently touching and stroking the skin of your face, arms, legs, stomach, and feet.

As you are touching yourself, focus on the various textures and shapes. Compare the sensations when you have your eyes open and closed. You may wish to experiment with using a body lotion, oil, or powder. After gentle stroking, try firmer, massaging pressures, paying extra attention to areas that are tense. You might like to allow yourself some pleasurable fantasies during this time. Notice whether your breathing is relaxed; let it be deep and slow. When you have completed this part, notice how you feel.

For the next step, continue the exploration with your genitals, experimenting with various kinds of pressure and stroking. Pay attention to what feels good. The following paragraphs offer descriptions of ways of touching that some people use during masturbation.

Specific techniques for masturbation vary. Males commonly grasp the penile shaft with one hand, as shown in Figure 9.1. Some men prefer to use lotion; others like the natural

▶ **Figure 9.1** Male masturbation.

friction. Up-and-down motions of differing pressures and tempos provide stimulation. A man can also stroke the glans and frenulum or caress or tug the scrotum. Or, rather than using his hands, a man can rub his penis against a mattress or pillow.

Women enjoy a variety of stimulation techniques. Typically, the hand provides circular, back-and-forth, or up-and-down movements against the mons and clitoral area (see Figure 9.2). The glans of the clitoris is rarely stimulated directly, although it can be stimulated indirectly when covered by the hood. Some women thrust the clitoral area against an object such as bedding or a pillow. Others masturbate by pressing their thighs together and tensing the pelvic floor muscles that underlie the vulva. Contrary to what is often portrayed in pornography, few women use vaginal insertion to reach orgasm during masturbation. Only 1.5% of women in Shere Hite's survey (1976) used vaginal insertion of a finger or penis-shaped object; over half of this small group had also used clitoral stimulation before insertion.

Some individuals and couples also use vibrators and other sex toys for added enjoyment or variation. Although some men enjoy using a vibrator on their genitals, women tend to be more enthusiastic about such devices. If you want to use a vibrator for sexual pleasure, experiment—both with the type of vibrator and with how it is used. By placing the vibrator on different areas of your body or genitals, you can find what is particularly arousing for you. Moving the pelvis or the vibrator can enhance your enjoyment. ■

Two types of vibrators: phallic shaped (left) and wand shaped (right).

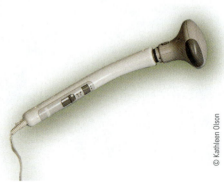

Several different types of vibrators are available, and people's preferences vary. *Good Vibrations: The New Complete Guide to Vibrators,* by Joani Blank (2000), has a detailed discussion of vibrators. The cylindrical and penis-shaped battery-operated ones usually provide less intense vibrations than do the others. These vibrators do not require an electrical outlet and are also the least expensive. Electric vibrators should never be used in or around water, because lethal electrical shock may result. Two basic kinds of handheld vibrators are the wand-shaped and the multiple-attachment types. Detachable, handheld pulsating shower heads are another alternative. Some women have long known that a stream of water coursing over their genitals can be very arousing.

The vibrator was once a time-saving medical advance. From the era of Hippocrates until the 1920s physicians treated women suffering from the common ailment "hysteria" with manual genital massage to orgasm, called "hysterical paroxysm." (The woman's postorgasmic relaxation must have verified the efficacy of the treatment to the physician.) In the 1880s the vibrator emerged as a more efficient medical instrument that could shorten the length of such office visits (Otto, 1999).

The vibrator is only one kind of sex toy for self-pleasuring and enhancing sexual interaction with one's partner. Throughout history the *dildo,* or artificial penis, has been used to enhance sexual arousal. Small dildos are also used for anal stimulation. For several thousand years women in China and Japan have used ben-wa balls for pleasure. Two spherical balls, one hollow and one filled with a heavy liquid substance, are inserted into the vagina while the woman lies on a hammock or sits in a swing in order for the motion to move the balls and create inner sensations. Until the middle of the 20th century sex toys were made by craftspeople and were used primarily by the affluent, who had the leisure and means to indulge themselves with concerns beyond the struggle for survival. Since then, factory production in Asia has resulted in the democratization of sex toys. Men can use latex or rubber simulations of female genitals for masturbation. Some more elaborately designed sex toys that stimulate several genital sites at once are also available, and more varieties are under development (Otto, 1999).

Although masturbating is valuable for many people in varied situations, not everyone wants to do it. Sometimes, in our attempts to help people who would like to eradicate their negative feelings about self-stimulation, it may sound as if the message is that people *should* masturbate. This is not the case. Masturbation is an option for sexual expression, not a mandate.

▶ Sexual Expression: The Importance of Context and Meaning

Up to this point in the chapter we have been looking at ways that people express themselves sexually as individuals. However, many of the sexual behaviors with which we are concerned take place as interactions between people. In the sections that follow we discuss some of the more common forms of shared sexual behavior. The sequence in which they are presented does not mean that such a progression is "best" in a particular sexual relationship or encounter; for example, a heterosexual couple may desire oral–genital stimulation *after* coitus rather than before. Nor is any one of these activities necessary in a given relationship or encounter: Complete sexual experience can consist of any or all of them, with or without orgasm. A sex therapist explained: "Once you've begun to think of sex as creating mutual erotic pleasure rather than as manufacturing orgasms, sex is a continuum of possibilities. You may find, for example, that low-key genital—or even nongenital—stimulation can be surprisingly erotic and relaxing" (Ellison, 2000, p. 317). The discussions of shared sexual activities, with the exception of coitus and gay and lesbian sexual expression, are directed toward all individuals, regardless of their sexual orientation. In fact, because sex between same-sex partners does not duplicate the pervasive heterosexual model's emphasis on penile–vaginal intercourse, gay men and lesbians' sexual repertoire is often more expansive and creative than heterosexuals' (Nichols, 2000; Sanders, 2000).

Some lesbians and subcultures within the lesbian community have moved beyond the typical female gender socialization of love and tenderness as essential to sexual interaction. Lesbian sex clubs have evolved where anonymous, recreational, public sex is the norm, and more lesbian couples have established nonmonogamous relationships (Iasenza, 2000).

Lesbian pornographic magazines and films have thrived for over a decade and feature scenes with dildos, bondage, and "kinky" sex. Young lesbians are more likely to practice dominant/submissive sexual activities that were considered "politically incorrect" during the 1960s and 1970s, when many lesbians viewed sexual interaction as a way to eradicate the power imbalance of sexism. The increased acceptance and practice of an extensive range of sexual behaviors among lesbians is changing notions of "female sexuality" (Nichols, 2000).

Aspects of Interactive Sexuality

Although the following sections include discussions of sexual techniques, a sexual interaction cannot stand on its own; it exists within the context of motivation and meanings of the individuals involved and the relationship as a whole. One writer explained:

> Sex can be motivated by excitement or boredom, physical need or affection, desire or duty, loneliness or complacency. It can be a bid for power or an egalitarian exchange, a purely mechanical release of tension or a highly emotional fusion, a way to wear oneself out for sleep or a way to revitalize oneself. Sex can be granted as a reward or inducement, an altruistic offering or a favor; it can also be an act of selfishness, insecurity, or narcissism. Sex can express almost anything and mean almost anything. (Fillion, 1996, p. 41)

Feelings, desires, and attitudes strongly influence choices about sexual activity. Mutual consent is an important aspect of a sexual relationship, and sexual activities that both partners are willing to engage in are more likely to provide a couple with enjoyable sexual experiences. Sensitivity to your own and your partner's sexual needs will help to develop shared pleasure and arousal more effectively than any specific technique. Because sexuality is influenced by the relationship as a whole, it may be best to think of foreplay as how partners have treated each other since their last sexual experience together (Joannides, 1996).

The Maltz Hierarchy

The context within which sexual behaviors occur is critically important for them to be self-affirming and relationship enhancing. Author and sex therapist Wendy Maltz developed a model with levels of constructive or destructive expression of sexuality (Maltz, 2001c). Maltz sees sexual energy as a neutral force; however, the intent and consequences of sexual behavior can lead in negative or positive directions. For example, marital intercourse may be intensely passionate; alternatively, it may be spousal rape.

The three positive levels of sexual interaction are built on mutual choice, caring, respect, and safety. As shown in Figure 9.3, Level +1 (Positive Role Fulfillment) reflects well-defined gender roles established by social or religious custom in which (in heterosexual relationships) the male is the initiator and the woman is receptive. Sexual interactions at this level are characterized by mutual respect and a lack of coercion and resentment; a strong sense of safety and predictability is present. Pregnancy and reduction of sexual tension are common goals for sex.

Level +2 (Making Love) emphasizes mutual pleasure through individual sexual creativity and experimentation. Traditional gender-role behavior is set aside, and sex expands to an erotic recreational experience. Partners reveal themselves more deeply through sexual self-expression and communication that create greater intimacy.

Level +3 (Authentic Sexual Intimacy) brings a shared sense of deep connection both to oneself and to one's partner, with reverence toward the body in the erotic experience. The enjoyment of sensual pleasure includes a profound expression of love for one another. A 23-year-old college man described this experience:

How About You?

Where do your sexual behaviors fall on the Maltz hierarchy?

One night we just started kissing as we were lying in bed. It was the middle of the night, and we just started making love, very nice and slow and sensuous. I felt very connected with my girlfriend because it seemed like we were just melting into each other and focusing very intensely on each other. (Authors' files)

Emotional honesty and openness are of paramount importance, and each partner gains a deeper sense of wholeness. Authentic sexual intimacy can be a momentary peak experience, or it can characterize an entire lovemaking experience.

Maltz points out that sexual interactions can also be upsetting or traumatic ordeals, often imposed on one person by another. On the negative side of her hierarchy, each level becomes increasingly destructive and abusive. Level −1 (Impersonal Interaction) is marked by a lack of respect and responsibility toward oneself and the other person. Here, individuals disregard possible negative consequences to themselves or to their partners, including consequences such as unwanted pregnancy or exposure to sexually transmitted diseases and HIV. Alcohol and drug use are often an element in sexual experiences that individuals later regret (Kaiser Family Foundation, 2003a). Enduring unpleasant sex or being dishonest about issues relevant to the partner (health status or meaning of the sexual experience) occurs at this level. These experiences result in uncomfortable, uneasy feelings.

Level −2 (Abusive Interaction) involves one person's conscious domination of another by psychological coercion. Nonviolent acquaintance rape and incest are examples. Degrading coercive communication also is included. Through distortions in thinking the exploitative person rationalizes or denies the harm he or she is inflicting on the other person. The experience usually damages the exploited person's self-esteem.

Level −3 (Violent Interaction) occurs when sexual energy is used purposefully to express hostility. Sex organs are weapons and targets. Rapists are the most extreme example.

For sexual expression to be self-affirming and relationship enhancing, it needs to be experienced at one of the positive levels and congruent with the individual's value system.

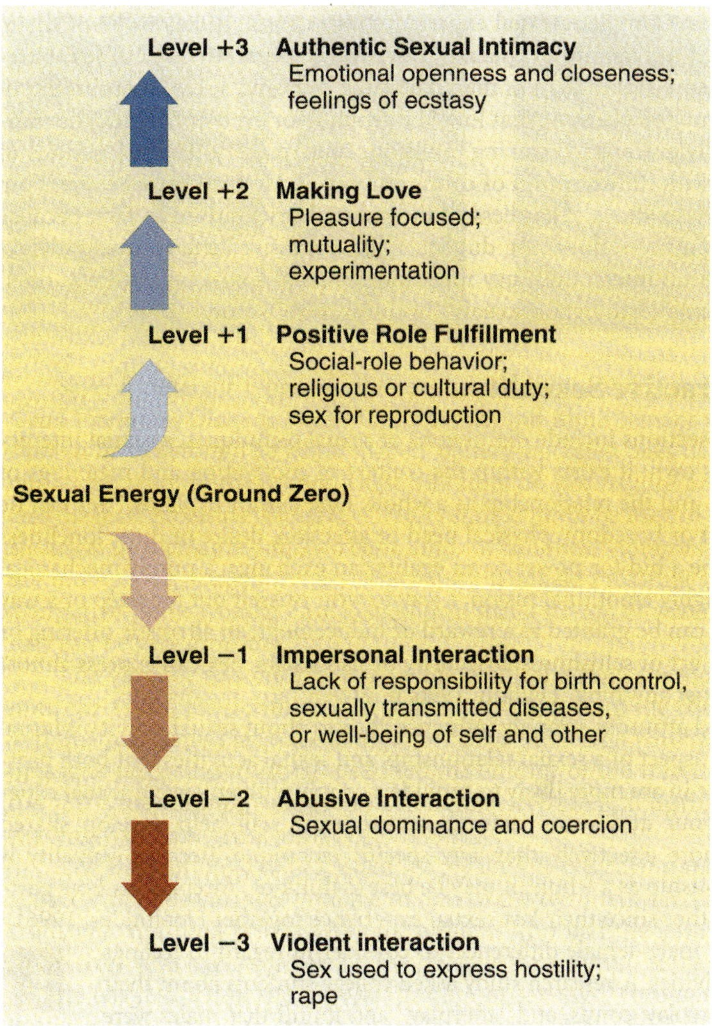

Level +3   **Authentic Sexual Intimacy**
Emotional openness and closeness; feelings of ecstasy

Level +2   **Making Love**
Pleasure focused; mutuality; experimentation

Level +1   **Positive Role Fulfillment**
Social-role behavior; religious or cultural duty; sex for reproduction

Sexual Energy (Ground Zero)

Level −1   **Impersonal Interaction**
Lack of responsibility for birth control, sexually transmitted diseases, or well-being of self and other

Level −2   **Abusive Interaction**
Sexual dominance and coercion

Level −3   **Violent interaction**
Sex used to express hostility; rape

▶ **Figure 9.3** The Maltz hierarchy of sexual interactions (Maltz, 2001c).

▶ Sexual Styles

Just as individuals differ in the sexual behaviors they prefer, they also vary in the predominant psychological state they seek during sexual experiences. A framework developed by Donald Mosher (1980) categorized three different sexual styles: sexual trance, partner engagement, and role play. These arbitrary labels identify differences in the kinds of mental focus, sexual behaviors, and interactions with the partner that an individual most enjoys and considers "good sex." One individual might prefer one sexual style almost exclusively, whereas another might enjoy all three. A couple's sexual compatibility can be influenced by their similarities or differences in these sexual styles.

The sexual-trance style is represented by the person who likes to create an altered state of consciousness by focusing inward on body sensations and arousal. Slow-paced, repetitive movements and a serene mood contribute to total focus on the sensations of sex. This person prefers taking turns giving and receiving pleasure to more fully focus on the sensations. Talking during sex is usually a distraction rather than an enhancement. Private settings with few distractions contribute to engaging fully in this style.

In the partner-engagement style individuals prefer mutual pleasuring and affection—lots of face-to-face positions and looking into one another's eyes, kissing, hugging, and full-body contact. A feeling of knowing the partner more deeply through sex and of merging and becoming one are qualities this style values. This is the style typically thought of as romantic, with sexual relating as a means of expressing tender and loving feelings.

The role-play sexual style uses sex as a stage. Settings are essential: the kitchen counter or a semipublic place is preferable to the familiar privacy, comfort, and dim lighting of a bedroom. The role-play style seeks novelty and variety. Clothing (costumes), sex toys, and fantasy scripts provide the necessary props in order for the individual's sexual expression to take on a variety of dimensions and roles (Mosher, 1980; Schnarch, 1997).

Frequency of Sexual Activity

The results of a 1998 survey of 10,000 people in the United States found that the national average of frequency of sexual activity is once a week, each episode lasting about half an hour (Robinson & Godbey, 1998). A confusing array of characteristics were correlated with a higher frequency of sex reported in this study. They included:

- Having some college education (having attended graduate school correlated with less frequency, however)
- Working 60 hours or more per week
- Watching more TV, especially PBS
- Loving jazz music
- Being married
- Defining oneself as "extremely liberal" or "extremely conservative"
- Smoking and drinking

Some of these characteristics go against the conventional wisdom for having sex more often, such as a long work week, watching more TV, smoking and drinking, and not having a college degree (Sacks, 1998). The survey did not inquire about sexual satisfaction or specific sexual behaviors that occurred during the sexual experiences. Most other research has found that people with more formal education are more likely to engage in a wider variety of sexual activities during a sexual episode than are those with less formal education. However, what is meaningful and satisfying to a given individual and couple is most important.

A major research study published in 1983 reported that lesbians had sex less often than gay male couples or married or cohabiting heterosexual couples (Blumstein & Schwartz, 1983). Despite previous research that had shown evidence to the contrary, the sexual infrequency of lesbian couples became the prevailing view and was reflected in the new expression "lesbian bed death." In the late 1990s this conclusion was challenged on several fronts. First, the results of the 1983 research were based on one question, "About how often during the last year have you and your partner had sex relations?" Frequency of sex relations is not a particularly useful measurement to use with lesbian couples because of the lack of clarity about what "sex relations" includes. Does only direct genital contact qualify? Touching breasts? Erotic kissing, touching, or holding without genital stimulation? Frequency is only one measurement of sexuality and probably not the most important in considering sexual satisfaction. The duration of sexual encounters and the subjective quality are probably better indicators of sexual fulfillment. In addition, a review of the research comparing lesbian and heterosexual women's sexual experiences found that the characteristics of sexual interactions between lesbians were those often associated with greater sexual enjoyment. For example, lesbian couples had more nongenital sexual interaction before genital contact, took more time in a sexual encounter, were more comfortable using erotic language with a partner, were more assertive sexually, and had lower rates of problems with orgasm (Iasenza, 2000).

▶ Kissing and Touching

i like my body when it is with your
body. It is so quite new a thing.
Muscles better and nerves more.
i like your body. i like what it does,
i like its hows. i like to feel the spine
of your body and its bones, and the trembling

-firm-smoothness and which i will
again and again and again
kiss, i like kissing this and that of you,
i like, slowly stroking the, shocking fuzz
of your electric fur, and what-is-it comes
over parting flesh. . . . And eyes big love-crumbs,

and possibly i like the thrill

*of under me you so quite new**

e. e. cummings

Kissing

Many of us can remember our first romantic kiss; most likely it was combined with feelings of awkwardness. Kissing can be an intense, erotic, profound experience, well suggested by the poet Tennyson: "Once he drew, with one long kiss, my whole soul through my lips."

The lips and mouth are generously endowed with sensitive, pleasure-producing nerve endings that make it feel good to kiss and to be kissed in infinite variations. Seventeen kinds of kisses are described in the *Kama Sutra,* the classical Indian text on eroticism (Ards, 2000). Kissing with closed mouths tends to be more tender and affectionate, whereas open-mouth, or deep, or French kissing is usually more sexually intense. Kissing can also run the gamut of oral activities, such as licking, sucking, and mild biting. All places on the body are possibilities for kissing. Students described some of their favorite kisses:

When my lover holds my face in her hands and tenderly kisses my eyelids, I melt.

I get so turned on when my husband thrusts his tongue into my mouth as his penis enters my vagina.

You haven't lived until you've had someone suck your toes.

In kissing my lover all over, I become intoxicated with his smell and taste. (Authors' files)

Western practices and attitudes about kissing are by no means universal. Mouth-to-mouth kissing is completely absent in the highly explicit erotic art of ancient civilizations of China and Japan. Even in the 20th century mouth kissing was viewed so negatively in Japan that Rodin's famous sculpture *The Kiss* was concealed from public view when it was displayed there in the 1920s as part of an exhibit of European art. Other cultures—the Lepcha of Eurasia, the Chewa and Thonga of Africa, and the Siriono of South America—consider kissing unhealthy and disgusting (Tiefer, 1995).

Touching

Touch is one of the first and most important senses that we experience when we emerge into this world. Infants who have been fed but deprived of this basic stimulation have died for lack of it. A classic animal study showed that when baby monkeys' and other primates' physical needs were met but they were denied their mothers' touch, they grew up to be extremely maladjusted (Harlow & Harlow, 1962). Touch forms the cornerstone of human sexuality shared with another (Kluger, 2004). In Masters and Johnson's evaluation:

Touch is an end in itself. It is a primary form of communication, a silent voice that avoids the pitfall of words while expressing the feelings of the moment. It bridges the physical separateness from which no human being is spared, literally establishing a sense

*"i like my body when it is with your." Copyright 1923, 1925, 1951, 1953, © 1991 by the Trustees for the E. E. Cummings Trust. Copyright © 1976 by George James Firmage, from COMPLETE POEMS: 1904–1962 by E. E. Cummings, edited by George J. Firmage. Used by permission of Liveright Publishing Corporation.

Touch can be pleasurable to both the giver and the receiver.

of solidarity between two individuals. Touching is sensual pleasure, exploring the textures of skin, the suppleness of muscle, the contours of the body, with no further goal than enjoyment of tactile perceptions. (Masters & Johnson, 1976, p. 253)

Touch does not need to be directed to an erogenous area to be sexual. The entire body surface is a sensory organ, and touching—almost anywhere—can enhance intimacy and sexual arousal. Because different people like different kinds of touching, it is helpful for couples to discuss their preferences openly.

The entire body responds to touching, but some specific areas are, of course, more receptive to sexual feelings than others. Preferences vary from one person to another. Many men and women report breast stimulation (especially of the nipple) to be arousing. Others find it unpleasant. A few women reach orgasm from breast stimulation alone (Masters & Johnson, 1966). The size of the breasts is not related to how erotically sensitive they are. Some women's breasts become more sensitive, even tender, during certain times of their menstrual cycles. A woman may find that a firm touch that is highly arousing one week feels uncomfortable and harsh the next. Once again, ongoing communication between partners is important.

In lesbian sexual relationships the mutual desire for and appreciation of touching can result in increased sexual arousal and orgasm compared with heterosexual relationships. Kinsey found that lesbian women had orgasms in a greater percentage of sexual encounters than did heterosexual married women. After 5 years of marriage, 55% of heterosexual women had orgasms in 60–100% of sexual contacts. In contrast, 78% of homosexual women had orgasms in 60–100% of their sexual encounters over a 5-year period. Kinsey suggested that these results might be due to a better understanding of sexual and psychological response between members of the same sex than between those of different sexes. Shere Hite stated that greater sexual satisfaction between women occurs because "lesbian sexual relations tend to be longer and involve more all-over body sensuality" (1976, p. 413). Table 9.2 compares some sexual behaviors and responses of lesbian and heterosexual women.

TABLE 9.2	Comparison of Lesbian and Heterosexual Women's Last Sexual Experience	
Experience During Last Sexual Contact	Lesbians (%)	Heterosexual Women (%)
Had more than one orgasm	32	19
Received oral sex	48	20
Lasted 15 minutes or less	4	14
Lasted more than 1 hour	39	15

SOURCES: Lesbian statistics from *Advocate* magazine survey (Lever, 1994); heterosexual statistics from the National Health and Social Life Survey (Laumann et al., 1994).

Contrary to the stereotype that sexual experiences between men are completely genitally focused, extragenital eroticism and affection are important aspects of sexual contact for many homosexual men. "Compared to other men, gay men are often able to have more diversity, self-expression, and personal enjoyment in their sexual contact" (Sanders, 2000, p. 253). Hugging, kissing, snuggling, and total-body caressing are important. A survey of gay men found that 85% liked such interactions—more than any other category of sexual behavior (Lever, 1994).

Genital stimulation is often highly pleasurable to women and men. Many people's first experience with manual genital stimulation comes from masturbation, and this self-knowledge can form the basis of further learning with a partner. People who have not previously masturbated can explore and learn what is enjoyable with each other. One partner can touch the other, or they can explore each other's sensations simultaneously, as seen in Figure 9.4. Manual stimulation can provide pleasure or orgasm by itself, or it can be a prelude to other activities.

Rubbing genitals together or against the partner's body can be included in any couple's sexual interaction and is common in lesbian lovemaking. Rubbing genitals against someone's body or genital area is called **tribadism.** Many lesbians like this form of sexual play because it involves all-over body contact and a generalized sensuality. Some women find the thrusting exciting; others straddle a partner's leg and rub gently. Some rub the clitoris on the partner's pubic bone (Loulan, 1984).

Tribadism Rubbing one's genitals against another's body or genitals.

▶ **Figure 9.4** Manual stimulation can be a highly pleasurable way for partners to explore each other's sensations.

Manual Stimulation of the Female Genitals

The kinds of genital touches that induce arousal vary from one woman to another. Even the same woman might vary in her preference from one moment to the next. Women can prefer gentle or firm movements on different areas of the vulva. Direct stimulation of the clitoris is uncomfortable for some women; touches above or along the sides are sometimes preferable. Insertion of a finger into the vagina can enhance arousal. Most, but not all, women approaching orgasm commonly need steady, consistent rhythm and pressure of touch through orgasm (Ellison, 2000).

Anal stimulation or penetration is erotic to some women but not to others. It is important not to touch the vulva or vagina with the same finger used for anal stimulation, because bacteria that are present in the rectum can cause infections if introduced into the vagina.

The vulval tissues are delicate and sensitive. If there is not enough lubrication to make the vulva slippery, it can become easily irritated. A lubricant such as K-Y Jelly, a lotion without alcohol or perfume, or saliva can be used to moisten the fingers and vulva to make the touch more pleasurable. ■

Manual Stimulation of the Male Genitals

Men also have individual preferences for manual stimulation and, as with women, might desire a firmer or softer touch—and faster or slower strokes—as their arousal increases. Gentle or firm stroking of the penile shaft and glans and light touches or tugging on the scrotum may be desired. Some men experience uncomfortable sensitivity of the penile glans when it is touched immediately following orgasm. Some men find that lubrication with a lotion or saliva increases pleasure. (With heterosexual couples, if intercourse might follow, the lotion should be nonirritating to the woman's genital tissues.) Some men also enjoy manual stimulation or penetration of the anus.

Figure 9.5 During oral sex one partner can give full attention to the experience of giving while the other can enjoy receiving.

▶ Oral–Genital Stimulation

Both the mouth and the genitals are primary biological erogenous zones, areas of the body generously endowed with sensory nerve endings. Thus couples who are psychologically comfortable with oral–genital stimulation often find both giving and receiving it to be highly pleasurable. Oral–genital contact can produce pleasure, arousal, or orgasm. As one woman stated:

I think that men put too much emphasis on a woman coming from "regular sex." A lot of women I know, including myself, have only experienced orgasm (aside from masturbation) through oral sex. I thoroughly enjoy getting and giving oral sex. I love the sounds, sights, smells, and tastes. (Authors' files)

Oral–genital stimulation can be done individually (by one partner to the other) or simultaneously. Some people prefer oral sex individually because they can focus on either giving or receiving, as in Figure 9.5. Others especially enjoy the mutuality of simultaneous oral–genital sex. Simultaneous stimulation is sometimes referred to as 69 because of the body positions suggested by that number (Figure 9.6). Besides the position illustrated in the figure, a variety of positions can be used; lying side by side and using a thigh for a pillow is another option. Because arousal becomes intense during mutual oral–genital stimulation, partners need to be careful not to suck or bite too hard.

Different terminology is used to describe oral–genital stimulation of women and oral–genital stimulation of men. **Cunnilingus** (kuh-ni-LIN-gus) is oral stimulation of the vulva—the clitoris, labia minora, vestibule, and vaginal opening. Many women find the warmth, softness, and moistness of the partner's lips and tongue to be highly pleasurable and effective in producing sexual arousal or orgasm. Variations of stimulation include rapid or slow circular or back-and-forth tongue movement on the clitoral area, sucking the clitoris or labia minora, and thrusting the tongue into the vaginal opening. Some women are especially aroused by simultaneous manual stimulation of the vagina and oral stimulation of the clitoral area.

Fellatio (fuh-LAY-shee-oh) is oral stimulation of the penis and scrotum. Both of Kinsey's studies found that, among heterosexual couples, women were less likely to stimulate their partners orally than the reverse. Among homosexual men fellatio is the most common mode of sexual expression (Lever, 1994). Options for oral stimulation of the male genitals include gently or vigorously licking and sucking the glans, the frenulum, and the penile shaft; and licking or enclosing a testicle in the mouth. Some men enjoy combined oral stimulation of the glans and manual stroking of the penile shaft, testes, or anus.

It is usually best for the partner performing fellatio to control the other's movements by grasping the penis manually below her or his lips to prevent it from going farther into the

Cunnilingus Oral stimulation of the vulva.

Fellatio Oral stimulation of the penis.

mouth than is comfortable. This helps to avoid a gag reflex. Also, too vigorous thrusting could result in lacerations of the partner's lips as he or she attempts to protect the penis from his or her teeth.

Couples differ in their preference for including ejaculation into the mouth as a part of male oral–genital stimulation. Many find it acceptable, and some find it exciting; others do not. A couple can agree beforehand that the one who is being stimulated will indicate when he is close to orgasm and withdraw from his partner's mouth. For couples who are comfortable with ejaculating into the mouth, the ejaculate can be swallowed or not, according to one's preference. The flavor of ejaculate varies from person to person and is influenced by the factors described in Table 9.3.

Some people have psychological and/or moral qualms about oral–genital stimulation. As we have seen, sexual behaviors that do not have the potential of resulting in a pregnancy within marriage have historically been labeled as unnatural acts and as immoral, and many people therefore believe that oral sex is wrong. Other qualms arise from the belief that oral–genital stimulation is unsanitary or that the genitals are unattractive. Many people also think that the genitals are dirty because they are close to the urinary opening and the anus. However, routine thorough washing of the genitals with soap and water is adequate for cleanliness. It may be difficult for someone who has a negative image of his penis or her vulva to feel comfortable receiving oral stimulation.

Another reason that some heterosexual people object to oral sex stems from the belief that it is a homosexual act—even when experienced by heterosexual couples. Although many gays and lesbians engage in oral sex, the activity is not homosexual by nature. Rather, its homosexuality or heterosexuality depends on the sexes of the partners involved.

Despite these negative attitudes, oral–genital contact is quite common and has become even more so since Kinsey's studies. A recent study found that the meaning and role of oral–genital sex have also changed greatly over time. Women born before 1950 almost never experienced oral sex in high school or before marriage. Oral sex occurred after considerable commitment and after the couple had been engaging in intercourse for some time. By contrast, in the 1990s about half of women college students had experienced oral sex, and for many oral sex occurred even before their first intercourse experience. Frequently, oral sex was used as a strategy for avoiding intercourse and technically maintaining their virginity (Ellison, 2000). A recent

TABLE	9.3	Factors Affecting Taste of Ejaculate

Taste	Source of Taste
Bitter	Coffee, alcohol, cigarettes, and marijuana (can also be due to urinary or prostate infections).
Sharp	Red meats, greasy foods, dairy products, chocolate, asparagus, broccoli, or spinach.
Moderate	Having none of the bitter factors and only one or two factors from the Sharp group.
Mild	A vegetarian diet. Fruit (especially pineapple and apples), parsley, celery, spearmint, and peppermint.
Sweet	Naturally fermented beverages or someone who is diabetic or borderline diabetic.

SOURCE: Hamilton (2002).

Sexual Health

study found that teens are more likely to have oral sex than intercourse and that they have had more oral sex partners than intercourse partners (Prinstein et al., 2003).

Because oral–genital contact often involves an exchange of bodily fluids, there is a risk of transmitting or contracting HIV (the virus that causes AIDS) (Baba et al., 1997; Torassa, 2000). This virus can enter the bloodstream through small breaks in the skin of the mouth or genitals. Although the risk of transmitting HIV through oral–genital contact is low, only monogamous partners who are both free of the virus are completely free from risk when engaging in such activities. (We discuss further precautions against transmitting HIV in Chapter 17.) ■

In American society, however, differences in oral sex experience and attitudes still exist among population segments, as shown in the following "Sexuality and Diversity" discussion.

 Sexuality and Diversity

Oral Sex Experiences Among American Men and Women

The National Health and Social Life Survey (Laumann et al., 1994) questioned men and women of different ethnic, educational, and religious backgrounds to compare their experience of oral sex. The findings, summarized in Table 9.4, show significant differences related not only to ethnic group but also to educational level and religious affiliation. In general, white Americans (both men and women) have the highest level of experience with oral sex, followed by Hispanic Americans; African Americans having the lowest rate of oral sex.

Another study, which compared African American and white American men of matched socioeconomic status, found similar rates of oral sex experience, indicating that socioeconomic status is more important than race in sexual behavior (Samuels, 1997). People with more formal education are considerably more likely to have oral sex; this difference is even more significant for women than it is for men. Findings from another study noted differences between women: Career women are more likely than homemakers to

TABLE 9.4 Oral Sex Experiences from the National Health and Social Life Survey

	Performed Oral Sex (%)[a]		Received Oral Sex (%)[a]	
	Men	Women	Men	Women
Race				
White	81	75	81	78
African American	51	34	66	49
Hispanic American	71	60	73	64
Education				
Less than high school	59	41	61	50
High school graduate	75	60	77	67
Any college	81	78	84	82
Religion				
Conservative Protestant	67	56	70	65
Other Protestant	82	74	83	77
Catholic	82	74	82	77
Other or none	79	78	83	83

[a]Rounded to nearest percentage point.

SOURCE: Laumann et al. (1994, p. 141).

consider oral sex a "normal" act (65% to 43%) (Janus & Janus, 1993). Note that, although this study found that men and women of all educational levels are today more likely to experience oral sex than were individuals in Kinsey's study, the likelihood of this behavior is still positively associated with higher educational level (Kinsey's research in the late 1940s and early 1950s revealed that 60% of college-educated couples, 20% of couples with a high-school education, and 10% of couples with a grade-school education had experienced oral–genital stimulation as part of marital sex).

▶ Anal Stimulation

Like oral–genital stimulation, anal stimulation is thought by some to be a homosexual act. In fact, anal stimulation is less common than oral sex and mutual masturbation among gay men (Lever, 1994), but penile penetration of the anus is practiced regularly by about 10% of heterosexual couples (Voeller, 1991), and an estimated 25% of adults have experienced anal intercourse at least once (Seidman & Rieder, 1994). Anal intercourse may be becoming more common among younger people. A study of 813 women enrolled in a college women's health course found that 32% had engaged in anal intercourse (Flannery et al., 2003). The anus has dense supplies of nerve endings that can respond erotically. Some women report orgasmic response from anal intercourse (Masters & Johnson, 1970), and heterosexual and homosexual men often experience orgasm from stimulation during penetration.

Individuals or couples also use anal stimulation for arousal and variety during other sexual activities. Manually stroking the outside of the anal opening or inserting one or more fingers into the anus can be pleasurable for some people during masturbation or partner sex.

Some important health risks are associated with anal intercourse. Anal intercourse is one of the riskiest of all sexual behaviors associated with transmission of HIV, particularly for the receptive partner. For women the risk of contracting this virus through unprotected anal intercourse is greater than the risk of contraction through unprotected vaginal intercourse (Silverman & Gross, 1997). Heterosexual and gay male couples who wish to reduce their risk of transmitting or contracting this deadly virus should refrain from anal intercourse or use a condom and practice withdrawal before ejaculation. In Chapter 17 we discuss more fully precautions you can take to avoid transmission of HIV.

Because the anus contains delicate tissues, special care needs to be taken in anal stimulation. A nonirritating lubricant and gentle penetration are necessary to avoid discomfort or injury. It is helpful to use lubrication on both the anus and the penis or object being inserted. The partner receiving anal insertion can bear down (as for a bowel movement) to relax the sphincter. The partner inserting needs to go slowly and gently, keeping the penis or object tilted to follow the direction of the colon (Morin, 1981). When using sex toys or other objects for anal stimulation, it is essential for the item to have a larger base to avoid a trip to the emergency room to remove an object that has slipped past the anal sphincter muscle.

Heterosexual couples should never have vaginal intercourse directly following anal intercourse, because bacteria that are present in the anus often cause vaginal infections. To prevent vaginal infections from this source, a couple should have vaginal intercourse before anal intercourse, or they should use a condom during anal intercourse and wash the man's genitals thoroughly with soap and water before moving on to penile–vaginal or penile–oral contact. Oral stimulation of the anus, known as **anilingus** (or, in slang, rimming), is extremely risky; various intestinal infections, hepatitis, and sexually transmitted diseases can be contracted or spread through oral–anal contact, even with precautions of thorough washing. Careful use of a dental dam is the best means of preventing transmission of bacteria and viruses. ■

Anilingus Oral stimulation of the anus.

▶ Coitus and Coital Positions

A heterosexual couple can choose a wide range of positions for penile–vaginal intercourse, or coitus. Table 9.5 shows college students' three favorite positions. Many people have a favored position yet enjoy others, as shown in Figures 9.7 through 9.10. A 30-year-old man stated:

Different intercourse positions usually express and evoke particular emotions for me. Being on top, I enjoy feeling aggressive; when on the bottom, I experience a special kind of receptive sensuality. In the side-by-side position, I easily feel gentle and intimate. I like sharing all these dimensions of myself with my lover. (Authors' files)

TABLE 9.5	College Students Answer the Question "What Is Your Favorite Intercourse Position?"	
	Men (%)	Women (%)
Man on top	25	48
Woman on top	45	33
Doggie style	25	15

SOURCE: Elliott & Brantley (1997).

Each position provides varying opportunities for physical and emotional expression. The desirability of a particular position can change with one's mood at the moment. Alterations in health, age, weight, pregnancy, or partners can create different preferences. In some positions one person has greater freedom to initiate and control the tempo, angle, and style of movement to create arousing stimulation. In other positions mutual control of the rhythm of thrusting works well. Some positions lend themselves to manual stimulation of the clitoris during intercourse, such as the woman above, sitting upright. Many couples like a position that allows them to have eye contact and to look at each other's bodies. For example, a common part of gay lovemaking is *interfemoral intercourse,* in which one man moves his penis between the thighs of the other. The face-to-face, side-lying position can provide a particularly relaxed connection, with each partner having one hand free to caress the other's body. Rear entry can be a good position during pregnancy when pressure against the woman's abdomen is uncomfortable.

A poem by Laura Kennedy (Maltz, 1996, p. 59) describes some of the intense feelings that can occur during intercourse:

> *I am in the most exquisite distress*
> *astride you now,*
> *sweating*
> *feeling an impetuous volcano*
> *strain at its peak*
> *inside*
> *wanting to explode*
> *my sweetest self*
> *all over you.*

▶ **Figure 9.7** Man-above, face-to-face intercourse position.

▶ **Figure 9.8** Two variations of the woman-above intercourse position.

Beyond options for position, cooperation and consideration are important, particularly at **intromission** (entry of the penis into the vagina). Often the woman can best guide her partner's penis into her vagina by moving her body or using her hand. If the penis slips out of the vagina, which can occur fairly easily in some positions, it is usually easiest for the woman to lend a helping hand to guide the penis back into the vagina. Furthermore, both nonverbal and verbal communication about preferences of position, tempo, and movement can enhance the pleasure and arousal of both partners. Intercourse can occur with or without orgasm for one or both partners.

Intromission Insertion of the penis into the vagina.

▶ **Figure 9.9** Face-to-face, side-lying intercourse position.

▶ **Figure 9.10** Rear-entry intercourse position, with pregnant woman simultaneously stimulating herself manually.

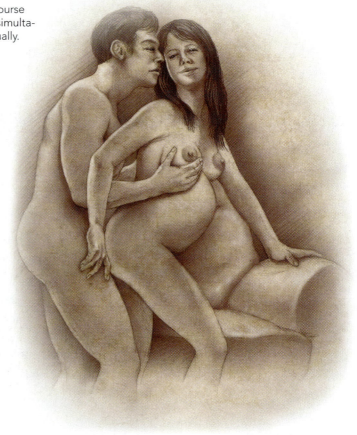

Intercourse the Tantric Way

The concept of male orgasm as the ultimate and end point of heterosexual intercourse is alien to concepts and practices of Tantric sex. Margo Anand, in her book *The Art of Sexual Ecstasy* (1991), explains that Tantra was an ancient Eastern path of spiritual enlightenment, begun in India around 5000 B.C. Tantric thought holds that an erotic act of love between a god and a goddess created the world. According to this viewpoint, sexual expression can become a spiritual meditation and a path of deep connection (Richard, 2002).

In Tantric sex the male learns to control and delay his own orgasm and to redirect the sexual energy throughout his and his partner's body. Before intercourse lovers usually slowly and erotically stimulate each other. When both partners are ready for intercourse, gentle, relaxed penetration is guided by the woman. The couple initially keeps thrusting to a minimum, generating energy by subtle inner movements, such as contractions of the muscles surrounding the opening of the vagina. The couple harmonizes their breathing, finding a common rhythm of inhaling and exhaling, while visualizing the warmth, arousal, and energy in the genitals moving upward in their bodies. Movements can become active and playful, always slowing or stopping to relax before the man experiences orgasm. The couple welcomes feelings of profound intimacy, letting go, and ecstasy, often looking in each other's eyes, creating a "deep relaxation into the heart" (Anand, 1991).

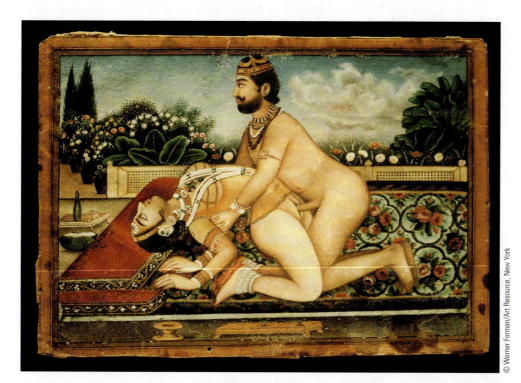

Tantric sex—the Infinite cycle.

© Werner Forman/Art Resource, New York

 ## Summary

Celibacy

- Celibacy means not engaging in sexual activities. Celibacy can be complete (no masturbation or interpersonal sexual contact) or partial (the person masturbates). There are many circumstances in which celibacy is a positive way of expressing one's sexuality. (p. 241)

Erotic Dreams and Fantasy

- Erotic dreams often accompany sexual arousal and orgasm during sleep. Erotic fantasies serve many functions: They can enhance sexual arousal, help overcome anxiety or compensate for a negative situation, allow rehearsal of new sexual experiences, permit tolerable expression of forbidden wishes, and provide relief from gender-role expectations. (pp. 242–244)

Masturbation

- Masturbation is self-stimulation of the genitals, intended to produce sexual pleasure. (p. 246)
- Past attitudes toward masturbation have been highly condemnatory. However, the meaning and purposes of masturbation are currently being more positively reevaluated. (pp. 246–247)
- Masturbation is an activity that is continuous throughout adulthood, although its frequency varies with age and sex. (p. 248)

Sexual Expression: The Importance of Context and Meaning

- The meaning of sexual expression can vary from a profound sense of love for self and other to exploitation and abuse. The Maltz hierarchy delineates six levels. (pp. 252–253)

Sexual Styles

- An individual's sexual style indicates what kind of mood, behaviors, and partner interaction are enjoyed the most. The three styles are sexual trance, partner engagement, and role play. (p. 253)
- People who have sex more often have several characteristics in common that go against conventional wisdom. (p. 254)

Kissing and Touching

- The entire body's surface is a sensory organ, and kissing and touch are basic forms of communication and shared intimacy. (pp. 255–256)
- Breast stimulation is arousing to most men and women, but some people do not find it enjoyable. (p. 256)
- Preferences as to the tempo, pressure, and location of manual genital stimulation vary from person to person. A lubricant, a nonirritating lotion, or saliva on the genitals can enhance pleasure. (pp. 257–258)

Oral–Genital Stimulation

- Oral–genital contact has become more common in recent years. Qualms about oral–genital stimulation usually stem from false ideas that it is unsanitary or solely a homosexual act or from religious beliefs that it is immoral. (pp. 258–259)
- Cunnilingus is oral stimulation of the vulva; fellatio is oral stimulation of the male genitals. (p. 258)

Anal Stimulation

• Couples engage in anal stimulation for arousal, orgasm, and variety. Careful hygiene is necessary to avoid introducing anal bacteria into the vagina. To reduce the chances of transmitting the AIDS virus, couples should avoid anal intercourse or use a condom and practice withdrawal before ejaculation. (p. 261)

Coitus and Coital Positions

• The diversity of coital positions offers potential variety during intercourse. The man-above, woman-above, side-by-side, and rear-entry positions are common. (pp. 261–263)

• Tantric sex emphasizes intense, prolonged sexual intimacy. (pp. 264–265)

▶ Suggested Readings

Abbott, Elizabeth (2000). *A History of Celibacy: From Athena to Elizabeth I, Leonardo da Vinci, Florence Nightingale, Gandhi, and Cher.* New York: Scribner. An illuminating and witty account of the potential and significance of celibacy.

Anand, Margo (1991). *The Art of Sexual Ecstasy.* Los Angeles: Tarcher. A comprehensive exploration of principles and practice of Tantric sex.

Boss, Suzie, and Wendy Maltz (2001). *Private Thoughts: Exploring the Power of Women's Sexual Fantasies.* Novato, CA: New World Library. A description of women's fantasy styles, the functions of fantasy, and steps to understand and overcome troubling fantasies.

Dodson, Betty (1996). *Sex for One.* New York: Crown Publishers. A lively, sometimes outrageous, book about masturbation.

Holstein, Lana (2001). *How to Have Magnificent Sex: The 7 Dimensions of a Vital Sexual Connection.* New York: Crown Publishers. An illuminating book about how to connect sexual energy to the various domains of physical, psychological, and spiritual experience.

Joannides, Paul (1996). *The Guide to Getting It On!* Waldport, OR: Goofy Foot Press. A humorous and instructive guide emphasizing nitty-gritty techniques and the perspective that "it doesn't matter what you've got in your pants if there's nothing in your brain to connect it to" (p. 1).

Keller, Wendy (1999). *The Cult of the Born-Again Virgin: How Single Women Can Reclaim Their Sexuality.* Deerfield Beach, FL: Health Communications. A discussion of why women choose celibacy after being sexually active and how it can be a positive step in their lives.

Laquer, Thomas (2003). *Solitary Sex: A Cultural History of Masturbation.* New York: Zone Books. A historical review of masturbation from sin and degeneracy to a pop culture mainstay that nonetheless remains the most common, harmless, and embarrassing of sexual behaviors.

Love, Patricia, and Jo Robinson (1994). *Hot Monogamy.* New York: Dutton. A step-by-step program with exercises to extend knowledge of one's sexual self to enhance a sexual relationship.

Maltz, Wendy (2001). *Intimate Kisses: The Poetry of Sexual Pleasure.* Novato, CA: New World Library. A delightful and unique collection of poems that celebrate loving sexual intimacy.

Newman, Felice (1999). *The Whole Lesbian Sex Book: A Passionate Guide for All of Us.* San Francisco: Cleis Press. A comprehensive sex manual designed for lesbians and suitable for heterosexual women who want to enhance their sexuality.

Silverstein, Charles, and Felice Picano (1993). *The New Joy of Gay Sex.* New York: Perennial. An uninhibited sex manual, including safer-sex practices.

Taylor, Emma, and Lorelei Sharkey (2003). *The Big Bang: Nerve's Guide to the New Sexual Universe.* New York: Plume Books. A sex manual, written by Nerve.com's sex and relationship advice writers, that includes often overlooked topics such as anal sex, fisting, and bondage for beginners.

▶ Web Resources

Your *Our Sexuality* Web site **http://psychology.wadsworth.com/crooksbaur9e/** has direct links to the Web sites described below. These links are checked often for changes, dead links, and new additions.

The Celibate FAQ
Frequently asked questions (FAQs) and answers about choosing a celibate lifestyle are offered at this site. Examples include how to tell people you are celibate and the advantages and disadvantages of celibacy.

Healthy Sex
This Web site, developed by the respected author and sex therapist Wendy Maltz, promotes a healthy attitude toward sex based on caring, respect, and safety. Partner communication, sexual intimacy, and sexual fantasy are among the topics explored.

Good Vibrations
This is the Web site for the Good Vibrations Store, which sells sex toys, videos, and books.

Go Ask Alice
This Web site provides lots of information about sexual behavior.

Our Sexuality Web Site
For online resources directly related to this book, go to **http://psychology.wadsworth.com/crooksbaur9e/**. You will find interactive exercises, study questions, chapter outlines, an online version of this text's glossary, and Web links and activities that complement your CD-ROM.

InfoTrac® College Edition Online Library
http://infotrac.thomsonlearning.com/
InfoTrac College Edition is an online searchable library that includes a multitude of journals, many of which are specific to human sexuality. These journals include *Archives of Sexual Behavior, Archives of Sexual Health Behavior, Canadian Journal of Human Sexuality, Hispanic Journal of the Behavioral Sciences, Journal of Cross-Cultural Psychology, Journal of Physical Education, Recreation, and Dance, Journal of Sex Research,* and *Sex Roles.* You may search topics suggested in the margins of this chapter or terms of your own.

Our Sexuality CD-ROM
Use your CD-ROM for further study of the concepts in this chapter. Your CD-ROM provides animations of difficult concepts, video clips of real people discussing sexuality, critical thinking questions, chapter quizzing, and more.

CHAPTER 10

Sexual Orientations

▶ **A Continuum of Sexual Orientations**

Approximately what percentage of men and women are exclusively homosexual? What percentage have had sex with another member of the same sex? What percentage feel attracted to others of the same sex?

What are the four different types of bisexuality?

▶ **What Determines Sexual Orientation?**

What psychosocial theories have been advanced to explain sexual orientation?

What biological factors influence sexual orientation?

▶ **Societal Attitudes**

How have Western religious views and the views of medical and psychological professionals changed concerning homosexuality?

What are some of the indications of homophobia?

What causes homophobia and hate crimes?

▶ **Lifestyles**

What is the "gay lifestyle"?

What has research shown to be the effects on children who are raised by lesbian mothers?

What steps are involved in coming out as a lesbian or gay man?

▶ **The Gay Rights Movement**

What was the Stonewall incident, and what impact did it have on the gay community?

What are some of the current decriminalization, discrimination, and positive rights successes and goals of the gay rights movement?

My life as a young lesbian was very different from the lesbian youth I see today. No one I knew talked about homosexuality, and I dated boys because my friends did. I was in my early thirties before my first sexual experience with a woman, but even that blissful experience didn't make me think of myself as a lesbian. It was several more years before I identified myself as a lesbian and had gay friends other than my partner. Today young lesbians have lots of positive information and images to help them understand and accept themselves. But they also face intense negativity from conservative reactions to gay rights. In my era the fact that homosexuality was so "hush-hush" gave us considerable privacy and protection by being overlooked. We never confronted the harassment, violence, or antigay activism that is now part of the picture. (Authors' files)

Homosexual A person whose primary erotic, psychological, emotional, and social orientation is toward members of the same sex.

Gay A homosexual, typically a homosexual male.

Lesbian A female homosexual.

Many people think of homosexuality as sexual contact between individuals of the same sex. However, this definition is incomplete. It does not take into account two important dimensions—the context within which the sexual activity is experienced and the feelings and perceptions of the people involved. Nor does it encompass all the meanings of the word **homosexual,** which can refer to erotic attraction, sexual behavior, emotional attachment, and a definition of self (Diamond, 2003b; Eliason & Morgan, 1998). The following definition incorporates a broader spectrum of elements: A homosexual person is an individual "whose primary erotic, psychological, emotional, and social interest is in a member of the same sex, even though those interests may not be overtly expressed" (Martin & Lyon, 1972, p. 1).

A common synonym for homosexual is **gay.** *Gay* was initially used as a code word between homosexuals, and it has moved into popular usage to describe homosexual men and women as well as the social and political concerns related to homosexual orientation. It has also come to be used, mainly by teens, as a negative label, as in "That is so gay!" (Caldwell, 2003b). Homosexual women are often referred to as **lesbians.** Pejorative words such as *faggot, fairy, homo, queer, lezzie,* and *dyke* have traditionally been used to demean homosexuality. However, in certain gay subcultures some gay people use these terms with each other in positive or humorous ways (Bryant & Demian, 1998).

Many nonheterosexual men and women born after 1970 call themselves queer and refer to queer culture to diffuse the negativity of the word and to blur the boundaries between subgroups of gay men, lesbians, bisexuals, and all variations of transgendered people belonging to the "queer nation." Members of "Generation Q" see themselves as different, even alienated, from lesbians and gay men over 30, partly because of their unique history of coming of age during AIDS activism (Nichols, 2000).

In this chapter we begin with a discussion of the continuum of homosexuality and heterosexuality, then move on to research and theories about what determines sexual orientation. Next, we discuss the critical issues of societal attitudes toward homosexuality, followed by information about the lives of gays and lesbians. Finally, we conclude the chapter with a clarification of the goals of the gay rights movement.

Gay and straight men laughing and getting along? Nonthreatening gay flirtation with straight men? *Queer Eye for the Straight Guy*'s funny, kind-hearted makeovers for heterosexual men may increase viewer's acceptance of homosexuality.

▶ A Continuum of Sexual Orientations

Homosexuality, bisexuality, and *heterosexuality* are words that identify one's **sexual orientation**—that is, to which of the sexes one is attracted. Attraction to same-sex partners is a homosexual orientation, and attraction to other-sex partners is a heterosexual orientation. **Bisexuality** refers to attraction to both same- and other-sex partners. Because sexual orientation is only one aspect of a person's life, we use these three terms as descriptive adjectives rather than as nouns that label one's total identity.

In our society we tend to make clear-cut distinctions between homosexuality and heterosexuality. Actually, the delineation is not so precise. A relatively small percentage of people consider themselves exclusively homosexual; over 90% of people in the United States think of themselves as exclusively heterosexual. These groups represent the opposite ends of a broad spectrum. Individuals between the ends of the spectrum exhibit varying mixtures of orientation and/or experience, which can also change over time. Sexual orientation is best evaluated by observing patterns over a life span rather than at any given time (Fox, 1990).

Figure 10.1 shows a seven-point continuum that Alfred Kinsey devised in his analysis of sexual orientations in American society (Kinsey et al., 1948). The scale ranges from 0 (exclusive contact with and erotic attraction to the other sex) to 6 (exclusive contact with and attraction to the same sex). In between are varying degrees of homosexual and heterosexual orientation; Category 3 represents equal homosexual and heterosexual attraction and experience. Research indicates variations in the pattern of where men and women fall on the Kinsey scale. Men, both homosexual and heterosexual, are typically on the far ends of the scale. Women also are at the ends of the continuum but are more likely than men to be found on the scale between Categories 2 and 5.

A limitation of the Kinsey scale is the impression it gives of a fixed, static sexual orientation when, in fact, people's placement on the scale can vary at different times in their lives. For example, because the scale is based on both feelings of attraction and behavior, someone who is bisexual would be on different sides of the center of the scale, depending on whether the current partner was male or female.

Sexual orientation Sexual attraction to one's own sex (homosexual) or the other sex (heterosexual).

Bisexuality Attraction to both same- and other-sex partners.

? How About You?

Where would you place yourself on the Kinsey scale?

Homosexuality

According to the Kinsey data, the exclusively homosexual category is composed of 2% of women and 4% of men. Kinsey's estimates were made some time ago, however, and they have been criticized. The more recent National Health and Social Life Survey (NHSLS) found somewhat lower statistics of 1.4% of women and 2.8% of men who currently identify themselves as homosexual (Table 10.1). However, two other questions elicited higher statistics. One question asked subjects whether they had had sex with another man or woman since age 18; about 5% of men and 4% of women had done so. A third question asked about feelings of sexual interest in same-sex partners. More respondents had felt sexual attraction to individuals of the same sex than had actually experienced a gay or lesbian sexual encounter; 5.5% of women and 6% of men said that they were attracted to others of the same sex. The real

▶ **Figure 10.1** Kinsey's continuum of sexual orientation.

SOURCE: Adapted from Kinsey et al. (1948, p. 638).

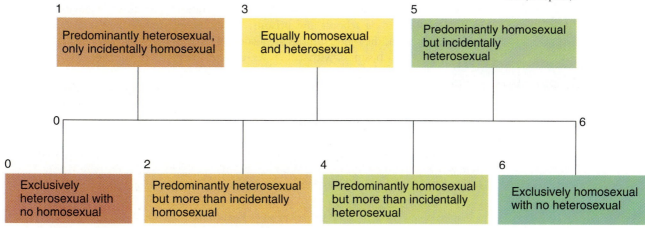

1	3	5
Predominantly heterosexual, only incidentally homosexual	Equally homosexual and heterosexual	Predominantly homosexual but incidentally heterosexual

0 ————————————————————————————— 6

0	2	4	6
Exclusively heterosexual with no homosexual	Predominantly heterosexual but more than incidentally homosexual	Predominantly homosexual but more than incidentally heterosexual	Exclusively homosexual with no heterosexual

TABLE 10.1	Who Is Straight, Gay, or Bisexual? How Do You Measure Sexual Orientation?		
Measure of Sexual Orientation		Men (%)	Women (%)
Identify self as homosexual		2.8	1.4
Sex with a same-sex partner after age 18		5.0	4.0
Feelings of attraction toward someone of the same sex		6.0	5.5

SOURCE: Laumann et al. (1994).

answer to the question of how many people are homosexual is that it depends on how you ask the question (Laumann et al., 1994).

Bisexuality

In interpreting the continuum shown in Figure 10.1, we want to caution against too broad a use of the word *bisexual*. There is a tendency to use behavior as the only criterion for sexual orientation and to use *bisexual* as a catchall term to describe the considerable number of people who fall between exclusive heterosexuality and exclusive homosexuality. This grouping fails to take into account the context within which the sexual experiences occur and the feelings and thoughts of the individuals involved. It is the context, not the contact, that is most significant. According to one definition, a bisexual person is one who can "enjoy and engage in sexual activity with members of both sexes, or recognizes a desire to do so" (MacDonald, 1981). In contrast, some people initially self-identify as lesbian or gay, then become involved in other-sex relationships and identify themselves as heterosexual. This most often occurs with women, as found in a study of 80 nonheterosexual women, age 18 to 25, who were sexually involved with other women when the research began. Within 5 years, 25% of the women were in heterosexual relationships. Although their identity and choice of sex of partners had changed, their feelings of attraction to other women remained the same (Diamond, 2003a).

On Kinsey's scale bisexual individuals are seen as a compromise between the two extremes. In another model bisexual orientation is viewed as showing high rather than moderate degrees of both homosexuality and heterosexuality (Storms, 1980). This view is supported by the type and frequency of sexual fantasies reported by subjects in the various groups. As might be expected, homosexual research participants reported more fantasy about the same sex than about the other sex, whereas heterosexual subjects reported the reverse. Contrary to what one might predict from the Kinsey scale, however, bisexual subjects reported as much same-sex fantasy as homosexual individuals and as much other-sex fantasy as heterosexual individuals. In other words, bisexual people seem to have a high degree of general erotic interest (Diamond, 2000; Lever, 1994).

Types of Bisexuality

There are several different types of bisexuality: a real orientation, a transitory orientation, a transitional orientation, and homosexual denial (Fox, 1990; Ross et al., 2003). Bisexuality as a real orientation means that some people have an attraction to both sexes that begins early in life and continues into adulthood. An individual with this orientation might or might not be sexually active with more than one partner at a time but would continue to be capable of feelings of attraction to both sexes. For example, the film *The Hours,* nominated for nine Oscars in 2003, portrayed examples of sexual fluidity in its three women characters in the woman-to-woman kisses shown in the movie (Giltz, 2003).

Bisexual behavior can also be transitory—a temporary involvement by people who are actually heterosexual or homosexual (Dykes, 2000). Transitory same-sex behavior can occur in single-sex boarding schools and prisons, yet the people involved resume heterosexual relationships when the opportunities are again available. Some prostitutes or male hustlers may do business with either sex and yet be involved in only heterosexual or homosexual relationships in their personal lives.

Bisexuality can also be a transitional state in which a person is changing from one orientation to another. This person will remain in the new orientation, as illustrated in the following account:

InfoTrac Search Words

- Bisexuality

I had led a traditional life with a husband, two kids, and community activities. My best friend and I were very active in the PTA together. Much to our surprise, we fell in love. We were initially secretive about our sexual relationship and continued our marital lives, but then we both divorced our husbands and moved away to start a life together. The best way I can describe being with her is that life is now like a color TV, instead of a black-and-white. (Authors' files)

Finally, bisexuality can sometimes be an attempt to deny exclusive homosexual interests and to avoid the full stigma of homosexual identity (MacDonald, 1981). Gay men and lesbians sometimes view the bisexual person as someone who really is homosexual but lacks the courage to identify himself or herself as such (Clausen, 1999). For example, a number of people marry to maintain a facade of heterosexuality but continue to have strong homosexual desires or secretive homosexual contacts.

Bisexuals: Their Own Category

Sexual orientation is often viewed as an either/or situation—one is either heterosexual or homosexual. Researchers have tended to categorize people who engage in sexual activity with both sexes as homosexual when they would more accurately be understood as bisexual (Leland, 1995). Self-identified bisexual individuals are sometimes met with ambivalence and suspicion and are often pressured by heterosexual or homosexual people to adhere to one orientation (Diamond, 2003a; C. Williams, 1999). One study found that few bisexual men participated in the gay community (McKirnan et al., 1995). It can be especially challenging to develop a heterosexual relationship after having had a gay or lesbian identity. For example, JoAnn Loulan, longtime lesbian activist and author of *Lesbian Sex,* received a great deal of negative reaction from other lesbians, including being branded a "hasbian," when she fell in love with and became involved with a man (White, 2003).

▶ What Determines Sexual Orientation?

A variety of theories have attempted to explain the origins of sexual orientation, particularly homosexuality. Considerable research has been done over the years, much of it contradictory, and there are still no definitive scientific answers. In the next few pages we consider some common notions about the causes of homosexuality and evaluate some of the research that has attempted to substantiate these ideas.

Psychosocial Theories

Psychosocial explanations of the development of a homosexual orientation relate to life incidents, parenting patterns, or psychological attributes of the individual. Bell and his colleagues (1981) conducted the most comprehensive study to date about the development of sexual orientation. They used a sample of 979 homosexual men and women matched to a control group of 477 heterosexual people. All research subjects were asked questions about their childhood, adolescence, and sexual practices during 4-hour face-to-face interviews. Bell then used sophisticated statistical techniques to analyze possible causal factors in the development of homosexuality or heterosexuality. This research is cited frequently throughout this section because of its excellent methodology.

"By Default" Theory

Some people believe that unhappy heterosexual experiences cause a person to become homosexual. Statements such as "All a lesbian needs is a good lay" or "He just needs to find the right woman" reflect the notion that homosexuality is a poor second choice for people who have not had satisfactory heterosexual experiences and relationships. In contrast to this myth, Bell and his colleagues found that homosexual and heterosexual groups did not differ in their frequency of dating during high school. However, the male and female homosexual subjects did tend to feel differently about dating than their heterosexual counterparts; fewer homosexual subjects reported that they enjoyed heterosexual dating. Bell's analysis of the data indicated that homosexual orientation reflects neither a lack of heterosexual experience nor a history of negative heterosexual experiences (Bell et al., 1981).

Lesbianism is sometimes assumed to be due to fear or distrust of men rather than to an attraction toward women. The illogic of this argument is clear if we turn it around and say that female heterosexuality is caused by a fear and distrust of women. Actually, research indicates that more than 70% of lesbians have had sexual experiences with men, and many report having enjoyed them. However, they prefer to be sexual and have relationships with women (Diamant et al., 1999; Klaich, 1974).

The Seduction Myth

Some people believe that young women and men become homosexual because they have been seduced by older homosexuals or because they have "caught" it from someone else, particularly a well-liked and respected teacher who is homosexual. People who believe that gay men and lesbians should not teach in schools—about 36% of Americans—probably believe in the seduction and contagion myths (Leland, 2000b). Contrary to these myths, research indicates that sexual orientation is most often established before school age and that most homosexuals have their first sexual experiences with someone close to their own age (Bell et al., 1981).

Freud's Theory

Another prevalent theory has to do with certain patterns in a person's family background. Psychoanalytic theory implicated both childhood experiences and relationships with parents. Sigmund Freud (1953 [1905]) maintained that the relationship with one's father and mother was a critical factor. Freud believed that in "normal" development we all pass through a "homoerotic" phase. He argued that boys could become fixated at this homosexual phase if they had a poor relationship with their father and an overly close relationship with their mother; the same thing might happen to a woman if she developed envy for the penis (Black, 1994). Later clinical research attempted to confirm this hypothesis (Bieber et al., 1962). Although these patterns were shown to exist in some cases (Saghir & Robins, 1973), many homosexual individuals do not fit the mold—that is, their mothers are not dominant nor are their fathers emotionally detached. At the same time, plenty of heterosexual people were reared in families where this pattern prevailed. Bell and his colleagues (1981) concluded that no particular phenomenon of family life could be singled out as "especially consequential for either homosexual or heterosexual development" (p. 190). Their findings were supported by another study of homosexual and heterosexual men who had never undergone therapy (Ross & Arrindell, 1988).

By Choice

For some individuals in same-sex relationships, choice is a significant factor (Bemporad, 1999). Although they are capable of functioning sexually with either sex, other qualities—typically gender related—lead them to find greater satisfaction in same-sex attachments. This element of choice appears to play a far greater role for women than for men (Diamond & Savin-Williams, 2000). Men usually label themselves dichotomously as gay or straight, but women are somewhat more apt to say, "It depends on who I'm with" (Bailey et al., 1993b). One study found that 58% of women in lesbian couples reported choosing the orientation of their current sexual relationship. Although they could enjoy sex with men, they preferred lesbian relationships and characterized them as less gender-role stereotyped and more intimate (Rosenbluth, 1997).

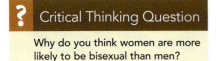
? Critical Thinking Question

Why do you think women are more likely to be bisexual than men?

Biological Theories

Researchers have explored a number of areas in an effort to establish biological causes for sexual orientation.

Adult Brain Differences

Research on differences in the brains of homosexual and heterosexual men has revealed structural differences. Some of the data are from postmortem dissections (LeVay, 1991), and other data are from live subjects obtained using magnetic resonance scanning. None of the studies have been replicated yet, and, even if they were, only a correlation would be established. It would remain unknown whether brain differences developed prenatally or during the individuals' life span. In the "Spotlight on Research" box we discuss research that indicates the influence of various factors during the prenatal period.

Prenatal Influences on the Brain

Numerous studies indicate that influences from hormones during the prenatal period affect the formation of sexual orientation. As we saw in Chapter 3, prenatal hormone levels have a masculinizing or feminizing influence on the developing fetal brain. Laboratory research with animals has demonstrated that hormones given prenatally can masculinize female fetuses and demasculinize male fetuses, which results in same-sex social and mating behavior when the animals mature. Research pertaining to some prenatal factors and human attributes associated with a homosexual orientation are described in the following sections.

Handedness

Research that shows a correlation between handedness and homosexuality indicates that it is likely that prenatal neurodevelopment contributes to sexual orientation (Lippa, 2003b; Mustanski et al., 2002). Handedness appears to be established before birth; when observed by ultrasound, a fetus indicates right- or left-handedness by thumb-sucking choice and greater movement of one arm. In a meta-analysis of studies with a combined total of almost 25,000 subjects, homosexual participants had 39% greater odds of being left-handed than heterosexuals, indicating prenatal influences in the development of some homosexuality (Lalumiere et al., 2000). However, the neurodevelopmental mechanisms that cause handedness and homosexuality have not yet been determined.

Finger Length Patterns

The influence of prenatal hormones on sexual orientation can also be revealed by the changes in sexual dimorphism sometimes related to sexual orientation. (Sexual dimorphism refers to characteristics that are typically more pronounced in one sex. For example, men typically have more body and facial hair than women, and

women have more body fat than men.) A lesser-known sex-dimorphic difference is patterns of finger length. Women's index fingers are about the same length as their ring fingers, but men's ring fingers are often considerably longer than their index fingers. Research has found that lesbians' finger lengths were more likely to follow the typical male pattern than heterosexual women's. In men, only homosexual males with at least two older brothers had finger length ratios significantly similar to heterosexual women and hence different from heterosexual men (Williams et al., 2000). Researchers attribute this reduction of the typical sex-dimorphic pattern of finger length to atypical hormone patterns during fetal development.

Age at Onset of Puberty and Cognitive Patterns

In the studies of handedness and finger length, sex-dimorphic changes occurred in both gay men and lesbians. Other studies show sex-dimorphic changes only for gay men, and the expressed characteristics tend to fall somewhere between the typical patterns for heterosexual males and heterosexual females. These studies indicate that there are some differences between men and women in the pathways to the development of homosexuality. For example, the onset of puberty is typically 12 months later for boys than for girls. However, numerous studies, including the NHSLS, have found that gay and bisexual men begin puberty earlier than heterosexual men and therefore are closer to the age that females enter puberty. In contrast, there is no evidence showing differences in age at onset of puberty with women relative to sexual orientation (Bogaert et al., 2002). Also, research on cognitive abilities in adults has demonstrated the verbal and spatial skill levels of homosexual men tend to be more similar to female patterns than is

the case with heterosexual men (McCormick et al., 1990). No differences in cognitive patterns between heterosexual and homosexual women have been found (Lalumiere et al., 2000).

Birth Order and Sex of Siblings

Birth order and the sex of siblings is another area in which research finds a correlation with male homosexuality but not with female homosexuality (Zucker et al., 2003). Research using samples of self-identified homosexuals and heterosexuals found that homosexual men had a greater number of older brothers than did heterosexual men, and each additional older brother increased the odds of homosexuality (Blanchard, 1997; Blanchard & Bogaert, 1996; Bogaert, 2003b). The first studies to use data from national probability samples—the NHSLS (Laumann et al., 1994) in the United States and an English investigation titled *Sexual Behaviour in Britain* (Wellings et al., 1994)—found that the greater the number of older brothers a man had, the more likely he was to *feel* sexual attraction toward other men. However, this group of younger brother respondents was *not* more likely to have had sexual contact with other men in response to their feelings of sexual attraction (Bogaert, 2003a). The difference between overt sexual behavior in the self-identified homosexual study and the same-sex attraction in the probability study could indicate that the effect of older brothers varies in degree in its impact on homosexual feelings or behavior. These studies found no evidence of older and younger brother sexual interaction or other learning and environmental factors that might contribute to younger brothers' feelings of attraction to other men. Furthermore, neither of these nationally representative

continued on next page

studies found a correlation between male homosexuality and older or younger sisters of any number.

Researchers hypothesize that the correlation between birth order and male homosexual orientation is due to an increasing maternal immune response to successive pregnancies of males. Some mothers develop antibodies to H-Y antigen produced by a gene on the Y chromosome. This antigen influences prenatal sexual differentiation of the brain. More maternal antibodies develop with each pregnancy, resulting in an increased effect on younger brothers. In contrast, female fetuses are the same sex as the mother; they have the same XX chromosomes as the mother and thus make an immune response unlikely (Bogaert, 2003a).

All these research findings, considered collectively, strongly suggest the important role of prenatal hormonal influences and brain development on sexual orientation. Research with human subjects indicates that higher levels of masculinizing prenatal hormones with female fetuses are associated with lesbianism and that lower levels of prenatal masculinizing hormones with male fetuses are associated with male homosexuality (Lippa, 2003a). These findings echo the previous and ongoing research with animals that demonstrates prenatal hormonal effects and subsequent adult characteristics and behavior (Vandenbergh, 2003).

Adult Hormone Levels

One line of investigation has been adult hormone levels, which some researchers have speculated contribute to homosexuality. However, no well-controlled research has found a difference in the circulating levels of sex hormones in adult heterosexual and homosexual males. And even if consistent differences could be identified, it would be difficult to tell whether they were a cause or a result of sexual orientation. The stress and anxiety that many homosexual people experience as a result of societal oppression may itself influence hormone levels. Many researchers believe that adult hormone levels will prove irrelevant because sexual orientation is established well before adulthood (Money, 1988).

Genetic Factors

A third line of research has examined the possibility that genetic factors contribute to homosexuality. Although it is not possible to completely distinguish the influences of nature from those of nurture in a given individual, analyzing family patterns has been one way to evaluate the role of heredity in homosexuality. Several studies have found that male and female homosexuality is strongly *familial,* which is to say that it appears to run in families (Bailey & Bell, 1993; Bailey & Benishay, 1993; Pattatucci & Hamer, 1995). The mere fact that homosexuality tends to be familial does not necessarily mean genetic factors are the cause; the psychosocial influences of a common family environment could just as easily be the source. Researchers often use twin studies to gain a better understanding of the relative influences of environment (nurture) and genetic (nature) influences.

Identical twins originate from a single fertilized ovum that divides into two separate entities with identical genetic codes. Because identical twins have the same genes, any differences between them must be due to environmental influences. In contrast, fraternal twins occur when a woman's ovaries release two ova and each ovum is fertilized by a different sperm cell. Because fraternal twins result from the fertilization of two separate eggs, their genetic makeup is no more alike than that of any other siblings. Physical and behavioral differences between fraternal twins may be due to genetic factors, environmental influences, or a combination of the two. Researchers attempting to understand the relative roles of genetics and environment in determining behavioral traits often compare the degree to which a particular trait is expressed by both members of a twin pair. When identical twins are more alike *(concordant)* than same-sex fraternal twins in a particular trait, we can assume that the attribute has a strong genetic basis. Conversely, when a trait shows a comparable degree of concordance in both types of twins, we can reasonably assume that environment is exerting the greater influence.

The most recent twin study recruited subjects from a twin registry in Australia (Bailey et al., 2000). A total of 1,538 twin pairs were included in this study: 312 male identical twin pairs, 182 male same-sex fraternal twin pairs, 668 female identical twin pairs, and 376 female same-sex fraternal twin pairs. All twins were recruited without respect to their co-twin's data. Each participant completed an anonymous questionnaire that addressed broad aspects of sexuality, including items pertaining to sexual orientation. Using a strict criterion for determining homosexual orientation, the researchers found a concordance rate (the percentage of pairs in which both twins are homosexual) of 20% among identical male twins and 0% among pairs of male same-sex fraternal twins. The corresponding concordance rates for female identical and same-sex fraternal pairs were 24% and 10.5%, respectively (Bailey et al., 2000). The markedly lower concordance rates for same-sex fraternal twin pairs provides strong evidence of a genetic component to sexual orientation in some individuals.

Consistent with the strong evidence from twin studies for a hereditary component in sexual orientation formation, a group of researchers reported finding evidence of a "gay gene" that might predispose men to develop a homosexual orientation (Hamer et al., 1993). In this study 33 of the 40 pairs of nontwin gay brothers studied were found to have an identical molecular structure on their X chromosomes in an area called Xq28. This concordance rate was double that of brothers in the general population. Another research team, attempting to confirm the previous findings, reported that the concordance rate for the Xq28 genetic marker among 52 male homosexual siblings was no greater than the rate in the general population (Rice et al., 1999). These discrepancies notwithstanding, researchers continue to search for a genetic marker of homosexuality (Fox, 1999).

Gender Nonconformity

Other evidence for a biological predisposition toward homosexuality comes from the strong link that exists between adult homosexuality and **gender nonconformity** as a child (Bailey et al., 2000). Gender nonconformity concerns the extent to which an individual deviates from stereotypical characteristics of masculinity or femininity during childhood; it is measured by asking respondents how traditionally masculine or feminine they were as children and how much they enjoyed conventional boys' or girls' activities.

Researchers have found that male and female homosexual adults are more likely to have experienced gender nonconformity during childhood than have heterosexual adults (Bailey & Zucker, 1995; Lippa, 2002). One-half of homosexual males but only one-quarter of heterosexual males did not conform to a typical "masculine" identity pattern, whereas about four-fifths of homosexual females but only two-thirds of heterosexual females were not highly "feminine" during childhood (Bell et al., 1981). Similar patterns have been documented cross-culturally. A comparative study of males in the United States, Guatemala, and Brazil indicated that gender nonconformity in relation to childhood toy and activity interests as well as to sexual interest in other boys was a behavioral indicator of adult homosexual orientation (Whitam, 1980). Bell and his colleagues speculated that "if there is a biological basis for homosexuality, it probably accounts for gender nonconformity as well as for sexual orientation" (1981, p. 217). A 15-year longitudinal study that compared gender-role behavior in boys and later sexual orientation found similar results (Green, 1987).

Gender nonconformity
A lack of conformity to stereotypical masculine and feminine behaviors.

Implications if Biology Is Destiny

The evidence for biological causation of homosexuality raises important issues. If homosexuality is found to be biologically based, those who assume that homosexuality is unnatural or immoral might reevaluate their beliefs. Society might thus become more accepting of homosexuality (Stein, 1999; Wood, 2000). Indeed, attitudes about gay rights are affected by whether or not people believe that homosexuality is chosen or innate. Surveys find that people who believe that homosexuals are "born that way" have more positive, accepting attitudes about issues such as homosexual teachers and equal rights in employment than do people who believe that homosexuals choose or learn to be homosexual (Wolfe, 1998). How common is the belief that homosexuality is innate? It depends on whom you ask: Approximately 33% of the general population, compared to 75% of gays, think that homosexuality is something people are born with (Leland, 2000b).

Others raise concerns about the potential negative consequences if homosexuality is proven to be the result of biological causes. If homosexuality is then labeled as biologically "defective," biological engineering to prevent or change homosexuality during pregnancy, screening techniques to prevent the birth of gay people, or medical techniques to change a person's sexual orientation might be developed and implemented (Stein, 1999; Gore, 1998). Furthermore, some maintain that the "We're born that way, so don't discriminate against us" justification for equal rights and protections under the law leads only to sympathy and tolerance for having a "defective" orientation.

This rationale for gay rights does not account for all the aspects of life that involve choice and are not biologically determined. Although feelings of attraction may be mandated by biology, whether to act on their sexual feelings, identify themselves as gay, or belong to gay organizations are choices made by homosexual individuals. The limitations inherent in basing rights on biological causation are exemplified by the beliefs of some religious conservatives. Their perspective is that homosexuals are not inherently "sinners" for having same-sex attraction feelings, which they are unable to stop. However, acting on these feelings in any way is considered a sin. Therefore the aspects of life that heterosexuals take for granted—flirting, kissing, a romantic dinner, a sexual relationship, marriage, raising children—are all considered sinful and immoral for homosexuals from this conservative religious view (Bronski, 2000; Stein, 1999; Wood, 2000). We discuss this viewpoint further in the "On the Edge" box titled "Gay Conversion Programs," later in this chapter.

In conclusion, research suggests that there is a biological predisposition to exclusive homosexuality. However, in general, the causes of sexual orientation remain speculative and most likely rely on multiple developmental pathways. It seems more appropriate to think of the continuum of sexual orientation as one influenced by an interaction of various psychosocial and biological factors, which are unique for each person, than to think in terms of a single cause for sexual orientation.

► Societal Attitudes *what's expected and what's not expected*

Around the world societal attitudes toward homosexuality vary considerably. As we can see from the following "Sexuality and Diversity" discussion, most societies consider at least some homosexual practices socially acceptable.

Sexuality and Diversity

Homosexuality in Cross-Cultural Perspective

Attitudes toward homosexuality vary considerably across cultures. A number of studies of other cultures have revealed widespread acceptance of homosexual activities. Homosexuality has been widely accepted in many earlier cultures. For example, over 50% of 225 Native American tribes accepted male homosexuality and 17% accepted female homosexuality (Pomeroy, 1965). In ancient Greece homosexual relationships between men were considered a superior intellectual and spiritual expression of love, whereas heterosexuality provided the more pragmatic benefits of children and a family unit.

Some societies *require* their members to engage in homosexual activities. For example, all male members of the Sambia society in the mountains of New Guinea engage in exclusively homosexual activities from approximately 7 years of age until their late teens or early 20s, when they marry. Sambian men believe that a prepubertal boy becomes a strong warrior and hunter by drinking as much semen as possible from postpubertal boys' penises. Once a boy reaches puberty, he must no longer fellate other boys but can experience erotic pleasure from fellatio by boys who cannot yet ejaculate. From the start of their erotic lives and during the years of peak orgasmic capacity, young men engage in frequent, obligatory, and gratifying homoeroticism. During the same period, looking at or touching females is taboo. Yet as they approach marriage, these youths create powerful erotic daydreams about women. During the first weeks of marriage, they experience only fellatio with their wives, but they then change to include intercourse as a part of their heterosexual activity. After marriage they stop homosexual activity, experience great sexual desire for women, and engage exclusively in heterosexual activity for the rest of their lives (Stoller & Herdt, 1985).

Events in Cuba demonstrate how a society can make rapid changes regarding homosexuality. During the first 35 years of the Communist revolution, lesbians and gay men were seen as deviant antirevolutionaries and were expelled from the Communist Party and state and university jobs. Some were sent to labor camps. In 1992 Castro blamed the previous homophobia on ingrained attitudes of *machismo*. He expressed support for gay rights and described homosexuality as a natural human tendency that must be respected. Gay men and lesbians now can walk down the street holding hands and join one of the several gay organizations without fear of reprisal (Otis, 1994).

However, violation of basic human rights for gays and lesbians is a common experience in many places around the globe. Amnesty International USA has increased its attention to these problems. This group has documented such abuses as the decapitation murder of a bisexual politician in Brazil, "social cleansing" death squads in Colombia, the death penalty for homosexual acts in Iran, exile to labor camps in China, and fabricated charges against gay and AIDS activists in many countries (Amnesty International, 2003; Luchsinger, 2000; Welch, 2000). The United States now grants political asylum for persecution based on sexual orientation. Before 1990 the Immigration and Naturalization Service deemed homosexuality legal grounds for exclusion from this country (Burr, 1996a).

In other places discrimination is decreasing. Fourteen countries, mostly European, have established national laws that protect gay men, lesbians, and bisexuals from discrimination (see Table 10.2). South Africa has the most comprehensive legal protection, which was included in its constitution established in 1996. (Notice that the United States is not on this list because it has yet to pass a federal law against discrimination for sexual orientation.) In 2000 Great Britain joined Australia, Canada, and New Zealand in eliminating its ban on gays in the military (Wang, 2000). Domestic partnerships have legal status in Canada, Denmark, Sweden, Norway, Spain, Iceland, Belgium, France, two cities in Italy, and Brazil, the first Latin American country to do so (Brooke, 2000; Henry, 2000; Power, 1998b). In September 2000 the Netherlands gave same-sex couples the unprecedented right to marry and adopt children (Deutsch, 2000).

TABLE 10.2	Fourteen Countries with National Laws That Protect Gays, Lesbians, and Bisexuals from Discrimination		
Canada	Ireland	Slovenia
Denmark	Israel	South Africa
Finland	The Netherlands	Spain
France	New Zealand	Sweden
Iceland	Norway	

SOURCE: Siecus (1999b).

Judeo-Christian Attitudes Toward Homosexuality

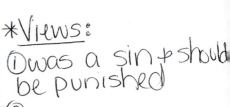

*Views:
① was a sin & should be punished
②

According to the Judeo-Christian tradition that predominates in our own North American culture, homosexuality has been viewed negatively. Many religious scholars believe that the condemnation of homosexuality increased during a reformation movement beginning in the 7th century B.C., through which Jewish religious leaders wanted to develop a distinct closed community that was different from others of the time. Homosexual activities were a part of the religious practices of many groups of people in that era, and rejecting such religious rituals was one way of enhancing the uniqueness of their religion (Fone, 2000; Kosnik et al., 1977). The Old Testament included strong prohibitive statements: "You shall not lie with a man as one lies with a female; it is an abomination" (Leviticus 18:22). We saw in Chapter 1 that the primary purpose of sexual interaction in the Judeo-Christian tradition is procreation, not pleasure. The pursuit of sexual pleasure outside that purpose, whether practiced by homosexual or heterosexual individuals, has traditionally been viewed as immoral. Currently, Jewish people are divided on their religious stance toward homosexuality. Reform Judaism sanctioned same-sex marriages in 2000 (Brinker, 2003). Conservative

Jewish leaders are reexamining their ban on same-sex weddings and the ordination of openly gay and lesbian clergy, and a decision is expected in 2004 (Friess, 2003). In Israel in 2002 the first openly gay man was appointed to the Knesset, or parliament, drawing dissent from Orthodox Jews (Landsberg, 2002).

Laws against homosexual behaviors, which stem from biblical injunctions against same-sex contact, have historically been exceedingly punitive. People with homosexual orientations have been tortured and put to death throughout Western history. In the American colonies homosexual people were condemned to death by drowning and burning. In the late 1770s Thomas Jefferson was among the political leaders who suggested reducing the punishment from death to castration for men who committed homosexual acts (Fone, 2000; Katz, 1976).

? How About You?

If you are connected to a religious denomination, what are its positions on homosexuality? Do you think that this position has influenced your own sexual orientation?

Current Christian theological positions toward homosexuality demonstrate a great range of convictions (Haffner, 2004). Different stances arise between denominations and also within the same denomination. Many mainstream denominations have groups working to open their churches to gay and lesbian parishioners and clergy, whereas others in the same denomination oppose such inclusion. The conflicts between these two positions are likely to increase in the future as denominations attempt to establish clear positions and policies about homosexuality (Johnson & Nelson, 2003).

The Unitarian Universalist Association and the United Church of Christ are the only Christian denominations that currently sanction the blessing of gay and lesbian unions (Haffner, 2000). Although many churches' official policies do not allow church bonding ceremonies for gays and lesbians, some clergy support and perform these ceremonies for homosexual couples (Dotinga, 1998). The first major American denomination to ordain an openly gay candidate was the United Church of Christ in 1972; it was followed 4 years later by an Episcopalian church. In 2003 the Reverend Gene Robinson was confirmed as an Episcopalian bishop and became the first openly gay bishop of any mainstream denomination (Freiberg, 2003). The support of churches is crucial if the civil rights movement for gay men and lesbians is to be fully successful (Sullivan, 1997).

From Sin to Sickness

In the early to mid 1900s there was a shift in societal attitudes toward homosexuality. The belief that homosexual people were sinners was replaced to some degree by the belief that they were sick. The medical and psychological professions have used drastic treatments in attempting to cure the "illness" of homosexuality. Surgical procedures such as castration were performed in the 1800s. As late as 1951 lobotomy (brain surgery that severs nerve fibers in the frontal lobe of the brain) was performed as a cure for homosexuality. Psychotherapy, drugs, hormones, hypnosis, shock treatments, and aversion therapy (pairing nausea-inducing drugs or electrical shock with homosexual stimuli) have all been used to the same end (Fone, 2000).

Actually, the research of several decades contradicts the notion that homosexual people are sick. The first major investigation to compare the adjustment of nonpatient heterosexual and homosexual individuals found no significant differences between the two groups (Hooker, 1967). Further research has supported these findings, although some research has reported that gay men have a slightly increased rate of depression and anxiety (Mills et al., 2004; Rochman, 2003; Sandfort et al., 2003). This difference is probably due to greater stigma toward homosexual men than women and the losses and stresses of coping with the AIDS epidemic. Alan Bell and Martin Weinberg summarized that "homosexual adults who have come to terms with their homosexuality, who do not regret their sexual orientation, and who can function effectively sexually and socially, are no more distressed psychologically than are heterosexual men and women" (1978, p. 216).

In 1973, after great internal conflict, the American Psychiatric Association removed homosexuality from its diagnostic categories of mental disorders. In light of contemporary research on homosexuality—and the fact that both the American Psychiatric Association and the American Psychological Association no longer categorize homosexuality as a mental illness—most therapists and counselors have changed the focus of therapy. However,

*wasn't a disease if a person was gay

Gay Conversion Programs

Can homosexual individuals alter their sexual attraction from same-sex to other-sex partners? A few mental health professionals believe so, and disagreements about conversion therapy have never been fully resolved (Green, 2003; Rosik, 2003). Difference of opinion also exists outside the professional community. About 56% of the general population believes that gay men and lesbians can change through therapy, willpower, or religious conversion. In contrast, only 11% of homosexual individuals believe a change in sexual orientation is possible (Leland, 2000b).

The goal of conversion therapy is for the homosexual individual to reduce and/or resist homosexual thoughts, feelings, and behaviors in order to live more easily in mainstream heterosexual culture (Besen, 2003). The first formal research on the effectiveness of conversion therapy was published in 2000 (Nicolosi et al., 2000b). The research participants were recruited primarily through conversion therapists, their clients, and the National Association for Research and Therapy of Homosexuality, an organization supportive of conversion therapy. The average age of the 882 participants was 38 years old, and 78% were men. Almost 90% had at least some college education. The participants were affiliated with various religions, and 96% said that religion or spirituality was very important to them. Most believed that homosexuality was sinful yet changeable.

The survey found that many of the participants reported major changes in their sexual orientation: 45% who saw themselves as exclusively homosexual before treatment considered themselves changed to either completely heterosexual or at least more heterosexual than homosexual after conversion therapy (Nicolosi et al., 2000). Conversely, up to 40% of the participants reported that they continued to struggle with unwanted homosexual thoughts and behaviors. The average length of therapy was almost three and one-half years.

Nicolosi and colleagues acknowledged several limitations of their research. First, because the sample was not random, the results cannot be generalized to all people dissatisfied with their homosexual orientation, only to those who were asked and agreed to participate in the research. In addition, results were based on retrospective self-reports, which can bias information in unknown directions. However, the primary purpose of the survey was to document whether or not conversion therapy helped any dissatisfied homosexual-oriented people. The results support Nicolosi's beliefs that conversion therapy should be available to people whose personal and religious values take priority over their homosexual desires and that mental health therapists have a professional obligation to discuss both gay affirmative and conversion therapy as viable options with homosexual clients to help them decide which approach to pursue (Nicolosi et al., 2000b).

Instead of participating in therapy, some homosexual individuals who want to convert to heterosexuality participate in ministry groups such as Exodus International, a nondenominational Christian organization with 85 agencies in 35 states (Exodus International, 1996). Religious teachings blended with group counseling focus on childhood traumas believed to have caused the participants' homosexuality—abandonment by fathers, absent mothers, sexual abuse, or violent parents. The conversion process attempts to develop heterosexual desire or, failing that, to enable the participants to abstain from same-sex sexual contact. For people who are not able to make the changes they wish for, the belief that one can only "be with God or be gay" is an often irreconcilable dilemma, which is sometimes an impetus for suicide (Clementson, 2000b; M. Miller, 2000).

Another study of 202 clients who had attempted sexual orientation conversion treatment found that only 4% of the participants reported achievement of the goal of being in a heterosexual relationship and not struggling with homosexual desires or behavior (Shidlo et al., 2001). The 96% of individuals who had failed at conversion therapy reported that the treatment had contributed to their self-hatred, and many of them had lied to their therapists about continuing homosexual activity during their treatment.

---

heterosexist bias remains a concern in mental health and family therapy treatment and research (Long & Serovich, 2003). Rather than attempting to "cure" homosexual clients by changing their sexual orientation, therapists instead provide **gay affirmative therapy** to help them live in a society that harbors considerable hostility toward them (D'Augelli, 2003; Phillips et al., 2003). This change in therapeutic practice is significant because it defines the problem as society's negativity toward homosexuality rather than as homosexuality itself (Cochran et al., 2003).

There remain, however, some mental health practitioners and religious groups who have continued to provide therapy to assist dissatisfied homosexual individuals to control, lessen, or eliminate their homosexual feelings and behavior through **conversion therapy** or **sexual reorientation therapy** (Kemena, 2000; Nicolosi et al., 2000a). This controversial issue is explored further in the "On the Edge" box, "Gay Conversion Programs."

Gay affirmative therapy
Therapy to help homosexual clients cope with negative societal attitudes.

Conversion therapy, or sexual reorientation therapy
Therapy to help homosexual men and women change their sexual orientation.

Homophobia

Homophobia Irrational fears of homosexuality, the fear of the possibility of homosexuality in oneself, or self-loathing toward one's own homosexuality.

The term **homophobia** describes antihomosexual attitudes (Wright & Cullen, 2001). Homophobia is further defined as irrational fears of homosexuals or fear and self-loathing of homosexual feelings in oneself. *Heterosexism* is a variation of homophobia; it is defined by beliefs that stigmatize and denigrate any behaviors, identities, relationships, and communities that are not heterosexual (Berkman & Zinberg, 1997; Van Voorhis & Wagner, 2002). Homophobia can be best thought of as a prejudice similar to racism, anti-Semitism, or sexism. The recognition of homophobia as a problem represents a significant shift from the view that only homosexuality itself was the problem.

Unfortunately, homophobia is still common and often plays a big role in the lives of many gay men, lesbians, and bisexuals. It is expressed in many ways, both subtle (even subconscious) and blatant (Harper & Schneider, 2003). For example, Republican Senator Rick Santorum, in a 2003 Associated Press interview, claimed that removing antisodomy laws and creating privacy protection for gay and lesbian sex is tantamount to protecting bigamy, polygamy, and incest (Mondics, 2003). A few years earlier, Senate Majority Leader Trent Lott compared homosexuality to kleptomania and alcoholism and led the opposition to antidiscrimination laws in employment because gays are "dangerous, unhealthy, or just plain wrong" (Fuller, 2000, p. E7). Some even rejoice in deaths from AIDS: The Reverend Fred Phelps and members of his church picketed funerals of people who had died from AIDS, carrying signs proclaiming "AIDS cures fags"; the group also has a Web site, www.godhatesfags.com (Boule, 1998, p. L1).

Such expressions contribute to the ongoing daily harassment and discrimination of anyone outside "acceptable" heterosexual parameters and legitimize the mind-set of people who commit *hate crimes* directed at gays. Hate crimes include assault, robbery, and murder and are committed because the victim belongs to a certain race, religion, ethnic group, or sexual orientation. Hate crimes are an extreme version of the widespread verbal and physical harassment directed at gays and lesbians (Ghent, 2003; Herek et al., 1999). The film *Soldier's Girl*, based on a murder in 1999, depicts the dynamics of hate crimes. In an army barracks an 18-year-old army private used a baseball bat to kill Private First Class Barry Winchell because of Winchell's romance with a transgendered nightclub performer (Rowe, 2003a).

© Kevin Winter/Getty Images

"If an openly gay man touches your arm in a public place and you feel uncomfortable, that doesn't make him a pervert. That makes you homophobic."—Jimmy Kimmel on *Jimmy Kimmel Live*, August 5, 2003.

*opposite of love is FEAR, not HATE

Hate Crimes

The Hate Crimes Statistics Act, passed in 1990, provides funding to document hate crimes in the United States. As a result of the data gathered, more hate crime laws have been passed, and more than 29 states now have hate crime laws that include proscriptions against antigay violence (Anti-Defamation League, 2003) (Figure 10.2). Sexual orientation was included in these laws because hate crimes are often directed at gays; 20% of adult lesbians and 25% of adult gay men have been victims of hate crimes. Survivors of hate crimes experience greater psychological distress than those of nonhate crimes. However, hate crimes are less likely to be reported than the other crimes, because survivors expect nonsupportive responses from authorities (Herek et al., 1999).

Causes of Homophobia and Hate Crimes

Murdering a gay man, voting to allow discrimination in employment for homosexuals, and calling a lesbian a dyke to insult her may seem unrelated, but they have some key elements in common. First, at the most fundamental level humankind's history reveals a poor record of accepting and valuing differences between people. The lack of acceptance toward racial, religious, or ethnic differences has fueled vicious "inhuman" events such as ethnic cleansing, the Holocaust, and the Inquisition. Homosexuality varies from the heterosexual norm and therefore requires people to expand their thinking to consider the less usual. The many religions that define homosexuality negatively also predispose groups and individuals to assume the same view. Research shows that individuals who are more religiously conservative with authoritarian beliefs have more negative attitudes toward homosexuality than people who are less conservative and authoritarian in their thinking (Kite & Whitley, 1998a; Kyes & Tumbelaka, 1994; Louderback & Whitley, 1997).

Second, homophobia and hate crimes are related to traditional gender-role stereotypes: Individuals who hold more traditional gender-role stereotypes tend to have more negative

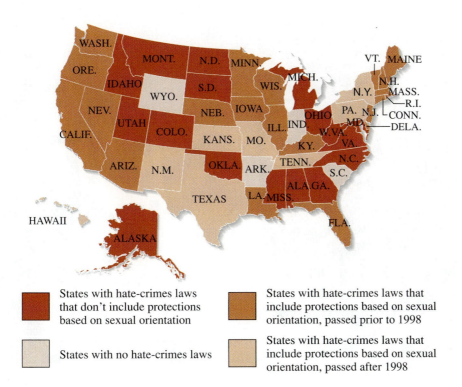

▶ **Figure 10.2** Type of hate crime laws by state.

SOURCE: Adapted from The Advocate (September 30, 2003, p. 35).

States with hate-crimes laws that don't include protections based on sexual orientation

States with hate-crimes laws that include protections based on sexual orientation, passed prior to 1998

States with no hate-crimes laws

States with hate-crimes laws that include protections based on sexual orientation, passed after 1998

feelings about homosexuality than do others (Kyes & Tumbelaka, 1994; Louderback & Whitley, 1997). Furthermore, men typically have more negative attitudes toward homosexuality than do women, reflecting, perhaps, the more rigid gender-role parameters for boys and men compared to girls and women in our culture (Kite & Whitley, 1998b; Herek & Capitanio, 1999). Bell and his colleagues discussed the idea that homosexuality confronts people with their ability to tolerate diversity in gender roles:

> In a society such as ours a special loathing is reserved for any male who appears to have forfeited the privileges and responsibilities associated with upholding the conventional imagery of males. The spectre of a group of males living outside the strict confines of "masculinity" can appear as a threat to men who are not entirely certain about their own maleness and thus heighten whatever antagonisms are expressed toward those who do not follow male "rules." (Bell et al., 1981, p. 221)

The increased collaboration for social change between transgendered individuals and groups and gay rights organizations evolved, in part, from understanding the importance of gender diversity (Coleman, 1999; Denny, 1999).

As researchers study perpetrators of hate crimes against gays, they are finding that the violence is primarily an extreme manifestation of our cultural norms, instead of hatred or fear of a specific individual. Most antigay hate-crime perpetrators—only males, to date—insist that their assaults were not motivated by hatred of homosexuals. Instead, threats to gender-role expectations, especially of masculinity, and the violation of male gender norms that homosexuality represents are the primary motivations for the violence, the same reasons transgendered individuals are frequently targets of violence (Maurer, 1999). Perpetrators, often acting in pairs or in larger groups, try to reassure themselves and their friends of their "masculinity" by assaulting a man who has stepped outside the rigid boundaries of male gender roles.

Another element involved in homophobia and hate crimes is an attempt to deny or suppress homosexual feelings in oneself. Uncomfortable with his or her own sexuality, the homophobic person focuses on what is "wrong" with the sexuality of other people (Kantor, 1998). One study found that men with strong negative attitudes toward gay men do have erotic feelings toward other men but deny both awareness and knowledge of their arousal (Adams et al., 1996). The study first evaluated men for their attitudes toward gay men. The men were

Public awareness of hate crimes against gays rose sharply after the 1998 death of Matthew Shepard. Matthew was an openly gay 21-year-old University of Wyoming student who hoped for a career in diplomacy and human rights. After two 21-year-old high school dropouts pistol-whipped Matthew, crushing his skull, and left him tied to a fence outside of town, most people were horrified. Seven hundred mourners came to his funeral. But outside the church, others carried signs with such messages as "No tears for queers" and "No fags in heaven."

© Mark Richards/PhotoEdit

then shown sexually explicit videotapes of heterosexual, lesbian, and gay male sexual interaction. While watching the videos, each man wore a penile plethysmograph to measure the increase in penile circumference during the different videos, essentially measuring his level of physical arousal to each scenario. Without knowing the results from the plethysmograph, subjects rated how sexually aroused they felt during each video. The men said that they felt aroused by the heterosexual and lesbian videos, and their reported arousal matched the findings of the plethysmograph. The most provocative results came from the discrepancy between reported arousal and physical arousal to the sexually explicit gay male video. Men who were not homophobic in their answers to the questionnaire about attitudes toward gay men said that they did not feel aroused by the video, and the plethysmograph confirmed their report. In contrast, although homophobic men also denied having any sexual arousal, the plethysmograph recorded physical arousal while they watched the gay male video (Kantor, 1998). These findings suggest that homophobic men are not aware of or are unwilling to acknowledge their homoerotic arousal. Their aggression toward gays may be a defensive reaction to their discomfort with their own unwanted feelings (Kite & Whitley, 1998a).

> ## ? Critical Thinking Question
>
> Do you think that the homophobic subjects knew they were experiencing sexual arousal during the gay male video but answered dishonestly?

Lesbians do not evoke as negative feelings in heterosexual men as gay men do. This may be, in part, because heterosexual men do not feel uncomfortable about their sexual feelings toward women in general.

Homophobia's Impact on Heterosexuals

Another expression of homophobia is the careful avoidance of any behavior that might be interpreted as homosexual. In this sense, homophobia can restrict the lives of heterosexual people. For example, during lovemaking, heterosexual men may be unable to enjoy having their nipples stimulated or may be reluctant to allow their female partners to take the lead if they believe that their enjoyment of these behaviors demonstrates homosexual tendencies (Wells, 1991). Same-sex friends or family members may refrain from spontaneous embraces, people may shun "unfeminine" or "unmasculine" clothing, or a woman may decide not to identify herself as a feminist because she fears being called a lesbian. Homophobia can have an especially significant effect on the depth of intimacy in male friendships (Plummer, 1999). Men's fear of same-sex attraction often keeps them from allowing themselves the emotional vulnerability required for deep friendship, thus limiting their relationships largely to competition and "buddyship" (Nelson, 1985).

Increasing Acceptance

Individual homophobic attitudes can change over time with deliberate effort or experience. In fact, people who personally know someone who is gay are usually more accepting of homosexuality (Leland, 2000b; Span & Vidal, 2003). However, gender-role belief systems tend to be complex and difficult to change, yet they most likely must be altered for heterosexuals, particularly men, to feel less negative toward homosexuality (Louderback & Whitley, 1997). We do see a positive trend in acceptance of homosexuality when attitudes toward homosexuality are compared by age group. Young adults (18–29 years old) are significantly more accepting of gay rights than people over 30, who are still more tolerant than those over 50 years of age. The increased acceptance may be because people younger than 50 are more likely to have a homosexual friend or acquaintance (65%) than those older than 50 (45%) (Leland, 2000b).

Education can also play a role. Most students who take courses in human sexuality become more accepting (Wright & Cullen, 2001). One of our students described how this process occurred in his life:

My own reaction to learning that one of my fraternity brothers was gay was discomfort. I increasingly avoided him. I am sorry now that I didn't confront myself as to why I felt that way. I was homophobic. And because I didn't deal with that then, it kept me from developing a closeness with my other men friends. I lost something in those relationships because I was afraid that being physically and emotionally close to another male meant that I, too, was homosexual. I finally began to explore why I felt so uncomfortable touching or being touched by another man. Today I am no longer threatened or frightened by physical closeness from another man, even if I know his sexual preference is other men. I am secure enough to deal with that honestly. (Authors' files)

Homosexuality and the Media

As noted in Chapter 1, there has been a remarkable mainstreaming of gays and lesbians over the last 10 years. Since the mid 1960s, daytime talk shows—*The Phil Donahue Show* and *Oprah* in particular—have brought previously unknown visibility to gays, lesbians, and bisexuals. Donahue's arrival in the national media coincided with lesbian and gay activism, and his focus on controversial topics gave homosexual guests unprecedented opportunities to represent their own lives and issues. Oprah Winfrey began her talk show in 1986, adding her empathic style to discussions with sexual minority guests, who were often mainstreamed into programs about common concerns, such as teens who argue with their parents (Gross, 2001).

Homosexuality became more visible—and was portrayed in a more positive light—in the 1990s cinema. The 1993 film *Philadelphia*, starring Tom Hanks, was the first major Hollywood feature to confront homophobia and AIDS and was a box-office success. Robin Williams was a partner in a longtime gay relationship in *The Birdcage*, a movie about two families with opposing social and sexual points of view. This popular film boldly proposed the acceptance of gays and was a box-office smash. These films showed the exotic and tragic sides of homosexuality. In the later 1990s movies such as *My Best Friend's Wedding* and *In and Out* began to portray homosexuals in more ordinary roles.

A watershed in the portrayal of gays as regular folks was, of course, Ellen DeGeneres's coming out on her 1997 television show, which drew a record 36.1 million viewers (DeCaro, 1997). It was the first TV program with a gay person in the starring role, and it continued to address gay issues until its end-of-season cancellation (Stockwell, 1998). The show's overall acclaim was emphasized by DeGeneres winning an Emmy for best comedy writing for the coming-out episode (Golden, 1998a). Ellen DeGeneres returned to TV in fall 2003 with her own talk-variety show.

Prime-time network television has several shows with lesbian and gay characters: *Buffy the Vampire Slayer, Dawson's Creek, ER, NYPD Blue, Will & Grace,* and *MDs* (Seomin, 2002). The character Bianca on the popular daytime show *All My Children* had the first lesbian romance and kiss on a daytime drama

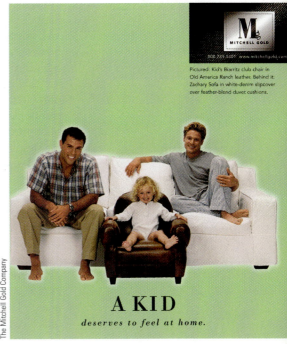

In 2003 the monthly comic *Gotham Central* brought lesbian characters out of the closet (Mangels, 2003) to join Marvel Comics' Rawhide Kid, the first gay title character in a mainstream comic book (Renna, 2002).

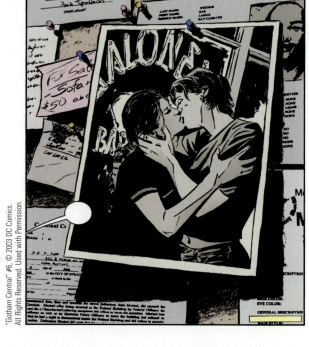

(Seomin, 2003). On cable TV *Queer As Folk* presented a no-holds-barred portrayal of gay life (Tipton, 2003) that has received criticism from gay viewers for its portrayals of recreational sex and drug use (Shelton, 2003). Two other cable reality shows, *Boy Meets Boy* and *Queer Eye for the Straight Guy*, challenge prejudices about relationships between straight and gay men, and in 2004 *Six Feet Under* and *The L Word* portrayed complex gay and lesbian characters (Goodridge, 2003; Hensley, 2004).

GLAAD (Gay and Lesbian Alliance Against Defamation) holds an annual awards show to honor each year's outstanding representations of lesbian, gay, bisexual, and transgender people in the media and entertainment and to recognize members of the media community who have promoted equal rights for sexual minorities.

By making gays more commonly known in the mainstream media, these and similar developments provide an opportunity for greater familiarity with and understanding of homosexuality.

InfoTrac Search Words

■ Homosexuality and media

▶ Lifestyles

We sometimes hear references to the "gay lifestyle" in popular vernacular. What is the gay lifestyle exactly? It probably does not imply that all gays engage in the same work, recreation, and spiritual community. The term *lifestyle* seems to be a euphemism for sexual conduct between same-sex partners (Howey & Samuels, 2000). In this discussion we will see that homosexual lifestyles are as varied as heterosexual lifestyles. All social classes, occupations, races, religions, and political persuasions are represented among homosexual people. The only characteristics that homosexual people necessarily have in common are their desire for emotional and sexual fulfillment with someone of the same sex and their shared experience of oppression from a hostile social environment.

Despite their many similarities to heterosexual people and the wide variety of their lifestyles, stereotypes about homosexual people exist (Hersch, 1991). Many of these stereotypes concern physical appearance (Terry, 1990). It is true that some homosexual individuals dress and act according to commonly held stereotypes. Characteristics often associated with an identifiable homosexual man include exaggerated "feminine" gestures and flashy clothing; in contrast, the image of a stereotypically recognizable lesbian includes such attributes as short hair and highly "masculine" clothing and gestures.

Although the incidence of people who fit such stereotypes is small, the stereotypes persist (Herek et al., 1991), in part because people who believe that homosexual individuals look a certain way notice and categorize (sometimes erroneously) those who seem to fit the image. The fact that most homosexual people do not fit the stereotype at all often goes unnoticed. One study found that neither heterosexual nor homosexual subjects could exceed chance levels of discriminating between videotaped interviews of homosexual and heterosexual men and women (Berger, 1990).

We look first at issues related to coming out and to how being secretive or open about their sexual orientation affects the lives of gays and lesbians.

Coming Out

The extent to which homosexual individuals decide to be secretive or open about their sexual orientation has a significant effect on their lifestyle. There are various degrees of being "in the closet," and several steps are involved in the process of **coming out**—acknowledging, accepting, and openly expressing one's homosexuality (Patterson, 1995). Gays, lesbians, and bisexuals base decisions about coming out on issues of safety and acceptance for themselves and others. Being openly lesbian, gay, or bisexual can be personally liberating but may not be adaptive in every situation (Anderson & Holliday, 2003; Oswald & Culton, 2003). Passing as heterosexual can help an individual avoid negative social consequences but exacts its toll in the stresses of maintaining secrecy (Berger, 1996). Individual circumstances have a significant effect on decisions about coming out, but historical context also influences coming out, as indicated in a study of three different generations of lesbians (Parks, 1999). The highlights of the study are given in Table 10.3. Parks found differences in the timing of coming out among three groups of lesbians: (1) lesbians, age 45 years and older, who were adults before the gay liberation era beginning in 1970, (2) lesbians, age 30 to 44 years old, who came of age during the gay liberation era between 1970 and 1985, and (3) lesbians younger than age 30 who achieved adulthood after 1985 during the gay rights era (Parks, 1999). The lesbians younger than 30 were unlike the older two groups in that they were typically sexual with women before having sexual experiences with men, whereas the opposite was true for the two older groups. Events such as awareness of one's sexual orientation, initial same-sexual experience, labeling oneself as lesbian, and disclosing to others happened earlier in life with each consecutively younger age group. The women's ages at first same-sex experience changed less among the generations than did other factors.

Although coming-out decisions are unique to each individual and situation, there are often some common elements: self-acknowledgment, self-acceptance, and disclosure. We look at each of these in the following sections.

Coming out The process of becoming aware of and disclosing one's homosexual identity.

Self-Acknowledgment

The initial step in coming out is usually a person's realization that she or he feels different from the heterosexual model (Meyer & Schwitzer, 1999). Some people report knowing that they were homosexual when they were small children. Many realize during adolescence that something is missing in their heterosexual involvements and that they find same-sex peers sexually attractive (Mallon, 1996). Once individuals recognize homosexual feelings, they must usually confront their own internalized homophobia as they deal

TABLE 10.3	Mean Ages of Lesbian Identity Developmental Events by Age Group			
Event	1. Mean Age for Those Born Between 1921 and 1965	2. Mean Age for Those Born Between 1958 and 1967	3. Mean Age for Those Born Between 1971 and 1977	Difference in Timing from Group 1 to Group 3
Self-awareness	18.8	17.0	14.6	4.2 years earlier
First social contact	23.9	21.7	19.3	4.6 years earlier
First sexual involvement	22.8	21.1	20.5	2.3 years earlier
First disclosure	24.9	22.6	21.0	3.9 years earlier
First self-labeling	31.9	25.5	20.3	11.6 years earlier

SOURCE: Parks (1999).

with the reality that they are members of a stigmatized minority group (Katz, 1995; Wagner et al., 1994).

Individuals become aware of their homosexual feelings at different stages of life, as shown in Table 10.4. Very closeted homosexual men and women attempt to suppress their sexual orientation, even from their own awareness, and often they succeed. These people actively seek sexual encounters with members of the other sex, and it is not uncommon for them to marry in an attempt to convince themselves of their "normalcy" (Dubé, 2000). Some homosexual individuals who have previously been married (one-third of the women and one-fifth of the men in Bell and Weinberg's 1978 study) did so to avoid openly confronting their sexual orientation. As one man, now openly homosexual, said:

TABLE 10.4	When Did You Know? When Gay or Bisexual College Students Say They Became Aware of Their Sexual Orientation	
	Female (%)	Male (%)
College	37	13
High school	46	50
Junior high	6	20
Grade school	11	17

SOURCE: Elliott & Brantley (1997).

As I look back now, I can see that my playboy lifestyle was really an attempt to convince myself that the nagging attraction I felt for John was just a good friendship. It was as if I thought I could change my feelings by having sex with enough women. (Authors' files)

Self-Acceptance

Accepting one's homosexuality is the next important step after realizing it. Self-acceptance is often difficult, because it involves overcoming the internalized negative and homophobic societal view of homosexuality:

> Initially a homosexual person often has difficulty from the pervasive condemnatory attitudes toward homosexuality. . . . His prejudice against himself is an almost exact parallel to the prejudice against homosexuals held in the larger culture. (Weinberg, 1973, p. 74)

When individuals belong to a socially stigmatized group, self-acceptance becomes a difficult but essential challenge (Ryan & Futterman, 2001).

Coming out can be problematic for teenagers (Hedgepeth, 2001). Most gay and lesbian teens experience confusion about their feelings and have few places to go for support and guidance (Rosario et al., 2002; Russell, 2001). In fact, they usually encounter considerable hostility and harassment. "That's so gay!" has become a ubiquitous insult. Middle schools and high schools are rife with homophobia, and teachers and administrators often ignore and contribute to harassment (Chesir-Teran, 2003). One survey (SIECUS, 2000) of lesbian, gay, bisexual, and transgendered students from 32 states reported that:

- 28% had experienced physical harassment (being shoved, pushed).
- 14% had experienced physical assault (being beaten, punched, kicked).
- 94% had heard other students make negative remarks ("faggot," "dyke," "queer").
- 37% had heard similar remarks from faculty and staff.
- 42% did not feel safe in their school.

At a stage of development when a sense of belonging to their peer group is so important, almost half of gay and lesbian teens lost at least one friend after they came out (Ryan & Futterman, 1997). In addition, the current generation of gay and lesbian teens came to an awareness of their own sexual identity in the midst of the controversy and stigma of the AIDS epidemic.

Judgmental families are another source of stress to gay and lesbian adolescents (Harrison, 2003; Saltzburg, 2004). Some parents throw their gay children out of the house or stop support for schooling. Young people in these kinds of families stay in the closet longer than those with accepting and supportive parents and families (Beaty, 1999). Because of these family and peer difficulties, gay young men are more likely than heterosexual males to attempt suicide, frequently because of physical and verbal abuse, rejection, and low self-esteem. Unlike young men, lesbian teens are only slightly more likely to attempt suicide than straight girls (Remafedi, 1994; Skegg et al., 2003).

Despite the discrimination that homosexual adolescents face, many of them can cope effectively and develop an integrated and positive identity (Edwards, 1996). It is helpful for gay and lesbian adolescents to find at least one supportive, nonjudgmental adult with whom to talk, and family support is especially valuable. The Internet provides these teens with connections to others to help reduce their isolation (Rodriguez, 2000). Support groups and gay teen organizations are emerging to help teens deal with the difficulties they face. About 700 high schools across the United States have gay–straight alliances—some of which were established despite great opposition from school administration, teachers, or parents—that lend support to gay students and teachers (Contemporary Sexuality, 2000h; Peyser & Lorch, 2000). The first accredited public high school for gay students, Harvey Milk School, in New York City, opened its doors in fall 2003 to provide students with a safe and supportive learning environment (Henneman, 2003).

Disclosure

Following acknowledgment and self-acceptance is the decision to be secretive or open. **Passing** is a term sometimes used for maintaining the false image of heterosexuality (Lynch, 1992). Passing as heterosexual is usually easy because most people assume that everyone is heterosexual. Being homosexual usually requires ongoing decisions about whether to be in or out of the closet, as new relationships and situations unfold (Kelly, 1998). In the "Let's Talk About It" box titled "Guidelines for Coming Out to Friends" we offer some suggestions for coming out. Heterosexuals sometimes do not understand disclosure issues, as exemplified by the following comment:

Passing Presenting a false image of being heterosexual.

I don't see any reason why they have to tell anyone. They can just lead their lives without making such a big deal out of it. (Authors' files)

In some daily interactions, sexual orientation is irrelevant, but homosexuality and heterosexuality are strong undercurrents that touch many parts of life. As one gay man noted:

My life as a gay man isn't something that takes place only in the privacy of my bedroom. It affects who my friends are, whom I choose to share my life with, the work I do, the organizations I belong to, the magazines I read, where I vacation and what I talk about. (Marcus, 1993, p. 10)

Imagine being a closeted homosexual person and hearing a friend make a derogatory reference to "fags" or "dykes," being asked, "When are you going to settle down and get married?" or being invited to bring a date to an office party. In one writer's words, "Because of its devalued status, affirmation of homosexuality (or disclaiming it) becomes a more significant act than the same would be for a heterosexual, with significant consequences for a lifestyle" (Gagnon, 1977, p. 248).

With some exceptions, the more within "the system" a person is or desires to be, the more risk there is in being open about one's sexual orientation. Jobs, social position, and friends can all be placed in jeopardy (Druzin et al., 1998; Horvath & Ryan, 2003). The conservativeness of the surrounding community or time in history can further affect one's decisions about whether or not to come out and to whom (Stein, 2001). Many more homosexuals who live in cities are out than those who live in suburbs or small rural towns. The greater ease of being open about one's homosexuality attracts people to urban life (Michael et al., 1994).

Coming out is a particularly difficult issue for homosexual adults who are parents. In fact, some stay in marriages because of their children (Green & Clunis, 1989). Approximately 60% of homosexual men and women who have been married have at least one child (Bell & Weinberg, 1978). The difficulties that a gay parent faces in attempting to attain custody or visitation rights can be severe. It is not unusual for gay parents to lose these rights strictly on the basis of their sexual orientation, regardless of their fitness as parents (Schwartz, 1990). Yet some courts hold that homosexuality itself is not proof of unfitness. The pattern of court decisions at this time is arbitrary and uncertain.

LET'S TALK ABOUT IT

 ## Guidelines for Coming Out to Friends

If you are a gay or lesbian, the unexpected is to be expected when you come out to a friend. A friend who is "liberal" may have more difficulty than another, more "conservative" person. It is essential to remember that your friend's reactions say something about his or her own strengths and weaknesses rather than anything about you. The following guidelines are meant to be a beginning to devising your own plan of disclosure. They are adapted from the book *Outing Yourself,* by Michelangelo Signorile (1995).

1. *Support network.* You should have a support network of gays in place, especially those who have come out to lots of different people in their lives. Their experiences and support will give you a solid base from which to act.
2. *First choice.* Try to make your first disclosure to a heterosexual an easy one. You might not choose your best straight friend, because the stakes are so high. Pick someone whom you would expect to be accepting. The person also needs to be trustworthy and capable of keeping your news private for a while as you come out to others.
3. *Mental practice.* Practice imagining yourself coming out in realistic detail as you plan. Picture yourself in a familiar setting where both of you will be comfortable. Envision feeling pleased with yourself for sharing something you feel good about (not something you have to apologize for). Practice saying, "There's something I want to tell you about myself, because our friendship is important to me. I trust you, and you're close to me. I am a lesbian/I am gay."

4. *Advance planning.* Plan the time—be sure to allow enough time to talk at length if things go well. Plan the place—somewhere both of you will be comfortable. Arrange to have at least one of your gay friends available for support afterward and to debrief. Be prepared to calmly answer such questions as, How do you know you're gay? How long have you known? What caused it? Can you change? Do you have AIDS?
5. *Rely on patience.* Remember that you are telling the friend something he or she has not had a chance to prepare for, whereas you have had a lot of time to prepare. Many people are surprised, shocked, and confused and need some time to think or ask questions. An initial negative reaction does not necessarily mean the friend will not accept it. If a friend reacts negatively but shows respect, stay and talk things over. Sympathize with his or her shock and confusion. "I can see this news upsets you."
6. *Control your anger.* If the person becomes hostile or insulting, politely end the meeting. "I'm sorry you aren't accepting my news well, and it's best for me to go now." Don't give your friend a real reason to be mad at you by being mean or rude or flying off the handle.

As you come out to people, you will find that some are not capable or willing to maintain their friendship with you. With others, letting them know you more fully will allow the meaning and closeness in the relationship to grow. Over time you will create a network of friends with whom you can enjoy the freedom of being your full self.

Telling the Family

Disclosing one's homosexuality to family can be more difficult than disclosing it to others. Coming out to one's family is a particularly significant step, as the following account by a 35-year-old man illustrates:

Most of my vacation at home went well, but the ending was indeed difficult. Gay people kept cropping up in conversation. My mother was very down on them (us), and I of course was disagreeing with her. Finally she asked me if I was "one of them." I said yes. It was very difficult for her to deal with. She asked a lot of questions, which I answered as calmly, honestly, and rationally as I could. We spent a rather strained day together. It was so painful for me to see her suffering so much heartache over this and not even having a clue that the issue is the oppression of gay people. I just wish my mother didn't have to suffer so much from all this. (Authors' files)

Parents often do experience difficult feelings from the revelation that a child is homosexual (A. Gottlieb, 2000; Savin-Williams & Dubé, 1998). They may react with anger or with guilt about what they "did wrong" (Woog, 1997). Conversely, a gay or lesbian closeted in a heterosexual marriage may have grave concerns about the reactions of his or her spouse and children, who indeed struggle with the disclosure (Sanders, 2000). Because telling the family is so difficult, many homosexual people do not do so. Approximately half the respondents in Bell and Weinberg's (1978) survey believed that their parents did not know about their homosexuality. Fathers were somewhat less likely to know than were mothers. Table 10.5 shows data from readers of *The Advocate,* a gay newsmagazine. The organization Parents,

Families, and Friends of Lesbians and Gays (PFLAG), which has over 400 chapters nationwide, helps parents and others develop understanding, acceptance, and support.

In the past each person usually decided if, when, and how to come out (except when his or her homosexuality was discovered by accident). Since the 1980s many homosexual men have been compelled to come out when they test positive for HIV (the AIDS virus) or if they begin to show symptoms of AIDS. Other homosexual men and women—often celebrities or prominent business or political leaders—find others abruptly opening the closet door for them. *Outing* is the term used when an individual or group publicizes the homosexual orientation of someone who would otherwise not be open about it (Rotello, 1995).

TABLE 10.5 Readers of the Newsmagazine *The Advocate* Answer the Question "Have You Come Out to Your Parents?"	
Answer	Percentage
Yes, and they took the news well.	63
Yes, and they rejected me.	11
No.	26

SOURCE: *The Advocate* (January 20, 1998, p. 22).

The Double Minority: Homosexuality and Ethnicity

Gay ethnic minority individuals have to learn to live in three different communities—ethnic, gay, and the larger society. Each of these fails to support some aspect of the person's identity (Zamora-Hernandez & Patterson, 1996). To a greater extent than white homosexuals, gays, lesbians, and bisexuals from ethnic groups with traditional values are more likely to stay in the closet with their families and community than to be open and face alienation from their families and heritage (Span & Vidal, 2003; Zea et al., 2003). They most likely will have to deal with racism in the gay communities (Paradis, 1997; Ryan & Futterman, 2001). For example, one study found that African American lesbians and gay men had a greater incidence of depressive distress than white homosexuals, most likely as a result of the doubly stigmatized status of race and sexual orientation (Cochran & Mays, 1994).

Asian cultures, in particular, place great significance on loyalty and conformity to one's family and little importance on individual needs and desires. The Asian is usually seen as a representative of his or her family rather than as an individual. Being openly homosexual is seen as shaming the family and threatening the family's future. Not marrying and creating heirs to carry on the family name is a failure for the whole extended family. However, secretly engaging in homosexual behavior while otherwise meeting family expectations may not create guilt (Matteson, 1997).

When the ethnic group places primary importance on a woman's childbearing role and subservience to men, lesbianism is a direct threat to these values (Guerrero-Pavich, 1986; Morales, 1992). This pattern commonly occurs in Hispanic and Asian cultures (Chan, 1995; Marrone, 2001). In addition, when the traditional culture expects virginity for unmarried women and views "good women" as primarily nonsexual, lesbianism is an affront to both of these traditional beliefs.

The Hispanic cultural emphasis on *machismo* often results in gay Hispanics maintaining secrecy about their sexual orientation. The emphasis in the lower socioeconomic segment of the African American community on tough masculinity as the ideal gender norm creates particular difficulty for gender-nonconforming gays. The executive director of Gay Men of African Descent in New York stated, "Holding hands walking down the street? That's not something I'd do in Harlem" (Leland, 2000b).

In general, the African American community has stronger negative views of homosexuals than does white society (Edozien, 2003; Poussaint, 1990). Although black leaders such as Coretta Scott King and Jesse Jackson support gay civil rights, the influence of strong fundamentalist Christian beliefs contributes to the higher degree of intolerance in the general black community (Gallagher, 1997a; Monroe, 1997). In addition, homosexuality is sometimes thought of as having originated from the subservient roles of slavery or imprisonment. These beliefs sometimes result in openly gay black men being viewed as traitors to their race (Franklin, 1998). This strong disapproval of homosexuality interfered with black leaders being active in the early fight against AIDS (Quimby & Friedman, 1989).

Gay ethnic self-help, social, and political organizations have been developed to manage these dilemmas and to enhance the sense of belonging (Zamora-Hernandez & Patterson, 1996).

One exception to ethnic negativity toward homosexuality is found among Native Americans. The movement to reclaim traditional Native American spiritual beliefs has led to increased tolerance for homosexuality in this group. Pre-European Native American beliefs centered around the Great Spirit, who is believed to give each person a sacred life quest. The unique tolerance of individual differences, including gender role and sexual orientation, stems from the sacredness of an individual's personal mission (Brown, 1997). This positive value for individual differences has persisted despite the assaults on the Native American culture, as indicated by the fact that the families of American Indian lesbians and gay men usually do not reject them (Epstein, 1997).

Involvement in the Gay Community

The need to belong is a deeply felt human trait. For many homosexual individuals a sense of community helps provide a sense of belonging and the affirmation and acceptance that are missing in the larger culture (Russell & Richards, 2003). Social and political involvement with other homosexual people is another step in the coming-out process. In larger cities gay and lesbian bars and cafés cater to different groups or clientele. Like heterosexual bars, these gathering places range from low-key socializing spots to establishments with reputations for casual pickups. Particularly in years past, gay bars—as well as certain designated recreational areas, restaurants, and bathhouses—served an important function: Often they were the only places where homosexual patrons could drop the facade of heterosexuality (Parks, 1999). In recent years this need has diminished to some extent. Gay people have helped to found service organizations, educational centers, and professional organizations such as the Gay and Lesbian Medical Association or the Gay and Lesbian Criminal Justice Professionals (Hayden & Peraino, 1999). About two dozen gay fraternities have formed on college campuses across the United States (DeQuine, 2003). Gay retirement communities provide alternatives to traditional retirement developments in which older gays and lesbians may have to be on their guard against negative attitudes of other residents (Rosenberg, 2001). Religious organizations for gay people have been established, including the 40,000-member Metropolitan Community Church with 400 congregations in 19 countries and denominational groups such as Dignity for Roman Catholics and Integrity for Episcopalians (Gallagher, 1994; Michael et al., 1994). In addition, the Internet has provided a gay virtual community in ways never before possible.

R Family Vacations offers a cruise package especially designed for gay and lesbian families.

My daddies are taking me on a big boat!

Courtesy of Isocurve

The AIDS crisis precipitated increased community involvement and coherence (Fineman, 1993). The gay and lesbian communities mobilized educational efforts, developed innovative programs for caring for AIDS patients, created an impressive network of volunteers to provide needed support for persons with AIDS, and lobbied—often quite visibly—for increased AIDS awareness and medical research funding.

Homosexual Relationships

Some people mistakenly think that homosexual partners always enact the stereotypically active "male" and passive "female" roles. This notion stems in part from the pervasive heterosexual model of relationships. Because this model of male–female role playing has historically been the predominant one in our culture, both heterosexual and homosexual intimate relationships have been patterned after it (O'Sullivan, 1999). However, more egalitarian relationships are being followed by both heterosexual and homosexual contemporary couples. In regard to gender roles, a homosexual relationship may well be more flexible than a heterosexual one in our society.

Aspects of Gay and Lesbian Relationships

One study that compared characteristics of homosexual and heterosexual relationships found major differences: Heterosexual couples were likely to adhere more closely to traditional gender-role expectations than were homosexual couples (Peplau, 1981). Most of the homosexual relationships studied resembled "best friendships" combined with romantic and erotic attraction. Peplau suggested that studies of homosexual couples can provide insights and models for heterosexual couples who are trying to establish more egalitarian relationships.

The Peplau study also found many similarities between homosexual and heterosexual relationships. Matched samples of homosexual females and males and heterosexual females and males indicated that being able to talk about one's most intimate feelings with a partner was most important in a love relationship. Peplau also found that partners in a love relationship, regardless of sexual orientation, must reconcile desires for togetherness and independence. For many individuals, these desires were not mutually exclusive; some people wanted both a secure love relationship and meaningful activities and friendships separate from the relationship. Responses from homosexual and heterosexual women were distinct in some ways from those of homosexual and heterosexual men. Women gave higher ratings to the importance of having an egalitarian relationship and having similar attitudes and political beliefs. Women also placed greater importance on emotional expressiveness within a relationship than did men. However, another study found that gay men who are more comfortable expressing emotions and affection experience a greater sense of well-being (Simonsen et al., 2000).

Another study used a marital satisfaction inventory to compare relationship functioning of gay and lesbian couples to cohabiting heterosexual couples (Means-Christensen et al., 2003). The results found that same- and other-sex couples that live together have more similarities than differences with each other in characteristics such as problem-solving communication, control over finances, and verbal and physical aggression. Both types of cohabiting couples were more similar to nondistressed heterosexual married couples than to heterosexual couples in therapy, which indicates that the cohabiting couples had relationships that functioned positively. However, one difference between the groups was that lesbians and heterosexual men reported higher levels of satisfaction with the quality of emotional expressiveness and shared leisure time than either gay men or heterosexual women.

Sexual Attitude and Behavior Differences of Gays and Lesbians

Homosexual men and women differ in the number of their sexual partners. Lesbians are likely to have had far fewer sexual partners, and lesbian couples are much more likely than male couples to have monogamous relationships (Dubé, 2000; Rothblum, 2000). Surveys indicate that between 45% and 80% of lesbians and between 40% and 60% of gay men are currently in a steady relationship, and many have long-term cohabiting relationships (Kurdek, 1995a, 1995b; National Gay and Lesbian Task Force, 2003).

Before the AIDS epidemic some homosexual men had frequent casual sexual encounters—sometimes hundreds or more (Bell & Weinberg, 1978; Kinsey et al., 1948). These encounters were sometimes exceedingly brief, occurring in bathhouses, public restrooms, or in film booths in pornography shops. This type of brief recreational sexual contact may be on the rise again, as AIDS has become less of an issue for some men in the gay community (Gross, 2003a; Koblin et al., 2003; Northridge, 2003).

Gender-role socialization gives more permission, even encouragement, for casual sex for males than for females. Men's and women's motivations for sexual involvement are typically different, regardless of the sex of their partners (Leigh, 1989). Homosexual women associate emotional closeness with sex more than do homosexual men, a finding consistent with the heterosexual patterns discussed in Chapter 7. In one study most of the lesbians waited to have sex with a partner until they had developed emotional intimacy. Although 46% of gay men had become friends with their partners before having sex, as a group they were more likely than lesbians to have had sexual experiences with casual acquaintances or people they had just met. Heterosexual relationships are to some extent a compromise between male and female gender-role expectations and thus might include exclusiveness for both partners. However, with gay male relationships this particular compromise is not typically as necessary, and casual sex outside an intimate and lasting relationship can occur more easily (Sanders, 2000).

The right to legal same-sex marriage is a contentious issue in the United States.

© AP/Wide World Photos

However, sexual involvement with many partners is not universal among homosexual men (Isay, 1989; Kurdek, 1995a, 1995b). Some men want to have a strong emotional relationship before becoming sexually involved. And for some men, being involved in an ongoing relationship eliminates sexual interest in other men. In some cases homosexual men's desire to modify the definition of masculinity has encouraged them to develop committed, multidimensional relationships rather than pursuing casual sexual encounters (Sullivan, 1998).

Beginning in the 1980s a lesbian "radical sex" subculture began to develop that is unparalleled in heterosexual women. Involvement in recreational sex, anonymous sex, "kinky" sex, group sex, sadomasochistic sex, and role-polarized sex went beyond the typical boundaries of female sexuality. Organizations sprang up for lesbians who pursue these sexual expressions, and this subculture continues to grow (Nichols, 2000).

Family Life

Traditionally, a family has been considered to consist of a heterosexual couple and their offspring, but many forms of family life exist in contemporary society: Homosexual individuals also form family units, either as single parents or as couples, with children included in the family through a variety of circumstances. Census data show that 33% of lesbian and female bisexual couples and 22% of gay and male bisexual couples are raising children (National Gay and Lesbian Task Force, 2003). Many have children who were born in previous heterosexual marriages (Kantrowitz, 1996). About one-third of lesbians are biological mothers from heterosexual relationships or by artificial insemination (Baker, 1990). Some homosexual individuals or couples become parents with adopted or foster children (Brooks & Goldberg, 2001; Sherman, 2002). Most laws about adoption by gay parents are ambiguous, and in many cases gays adopt as single individuals (Caldwell, 2003a; Galst & Hilty, 2003; Ryan et al., 2004). In 1998 New Jersey became the first state in the nation to allow gay and lesbian couples to jointly adopt children, and currently California, Connecticut, Illinois, Massachusetts, New York, Vermont, and the District of Columbia permit such adoptions by law or court ruling. Three states—Florida, Utah, and Mississippi—have laws banning adoption by homosexual couples (Tate, 2001).

Children are also conceived by lesbians through artificial insemination or with a partner chosen solely for this purpose. Semen can be obtained from a sperm bank or by individual arrangements with a selected donor (Galst & Hilty, 2003). One woman who became pregnant through a donor she selected reported:

A close male friend ejaculated in privacy and brought his semen to our bedroom. We put the sperm in a cervical cap and inserted it to ensure contact between the semen and the cervix. Now we have a beautiful baby boy. (Authors' files)

Another alternative for lesbian couples involves collecting ova from one partner, fertilizing them in vitro, then placing them into the other woman's uterus to carry until birth. This process might help both women to be legally recognized as parents (O'Hanlan, 1995).

A homosexual man who wants to be a father might make a personal arrangement with a woman who agrees to carry his child. Many new concepts of family are emerging, and the desire for legal and social recognition of gay and lesbian families is increasing (Campbell, 2000; Dalton & Bielby, 2000; Raab, 2001).

Some people have questioned the ability of homosexual parents to provide a positive family environment for children (McLeod et al., 1999). However, research has found that children of lesbian mothers are essentially no different from other children in terms of self-esteem, gender-related problems, gender roles, sexual orientation, and general development (Golombok et al., 2003). In addition, most children with gay or lesbian parents grow up as heterosexual (Bailey et al., 1995; Golombok & Tasker, 1996). After analyzing scientific research on the topic of gay and lesbian parenthood, the American Academy of Pediatrics decided to endorse adoption by gay and lesbian couples in order to provide the children with the security of two legally recognized parents (Contemporary Sexuality, 2002a).

Unfortunately, children with gay or lesbian parents are frequently confronted with other people's prejudices (Barovick, 2002). They often have to learn to ignore name calling, friends' parents restricting visits to their homes, and others' ignorance (Howey & Samuels, 2000). For example, when her sixth-grade teacher asked for examples of different kinds of families, a girl who lived with her mother and her female partner raised her hand and offered, "Lesbian." The teacher replied, "This is such a nice town. There wouldn't be any lesbians living here" (Kantrowitz, 1996, p. 53).

The growing gay rights movement, which began in the 1960s, has provided support for many homosexual men and women. In the following section we describe some of the movement's activities.

The Gay Rights Movement

Forty years before World War II the first organization promoting education about homosexuality and the abolition of antigay laws was founded in Germany. However, the Nazi rise to power ended the homosexual rights movement in Germany (Schoofs, 1997). It was not until the 1950s in the United States that some organizations for gay people were established, despite the conservative atmosphere of the times. The Mattachine Society had chapters in many cities and provided a national network for support and communication among homosexuals. The Daughters of Bilitis, an organization of lesbians, published a journal called *The Ladder*, which contained fiction, poetry, and political articles. The goals of both organizations were to educate homosexual and heterosexual people about homosexuality, increase understanding of homosexuality, and eliminate discriminatory laws toward homosexual individuals (Katz, 1976).

The Nazis linked homosexuality to a Jewish plot to weaken the masculinity of Aryan men. Nazi Germany decimated the base of the world's gay rights movement in Berlin. Forced to wear the pink triangle symbol on their sleeves, more than 100,000 gay men were arrested and about 50,000 were sent to death camps. The U.S. Holocaust Memorial Museum's exhibit "The Nazi Persecution of Homosexuals, 1933–1945" illustrates this persecution of homosexual men (Karlin, 2003).

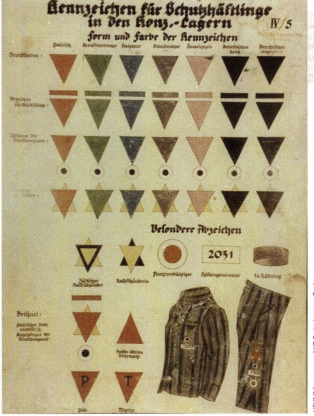

USHMM, courtesy of KZ Gedenkstaette Dachau

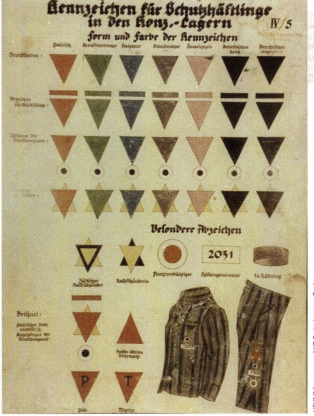

The Stonewall Incident and Beyond

During the 1960s, many people began to question traditional aspects of American life in all areas, including the sexual. In this atmosphere more gay people began to respond to social and political changes and to challenge the social problems they faced. The symbolic birth of gay activism occurred in 1969 in New York City when police raided a gay bar, the Stonewall. Police raids on gay bars were common occurrences, but this time the bar's patrons resisted and fought back. A riot ensued and did not end until the following day. The Stonewall incident served as a catalyst for the formation of gay rights groups, and activities such as Gay Pride Week and parades are held in yearly commemoration of the Stonewall riot (Herrell, 1992). In 1994 more than 1 million people gathered in New York to celebrate the 25th anniversary of the Stonewall raid.

Goals of the Gay Rights Movement

InfoTrac Search Words

■ Gay rights movement

Since the early 1970s various groups and individuals have worked to promote rights for lesbians, gays, and bisexuals. These efforts fall into three general areas: decriminalization of private sexual behavior, antidiscrimination, and positive rights (Stein, 1999).

Decriminalization of Private Sexual Behavior

The United States had a long history of laws banning "sodomy," which was defined as oral and/or anal sex between heterosexuals and homosexuals. In 2003 the U.S. Supreme Court, in *Lawrence et al.* v. *Texas*, overturned a Texas sodomy law that made private sexual contact between homosexuals illegal. The Court based its decision on the constitutional right to privacy. The ruling consequently also overturned laws in four other states that had banned sex between homosexuals and in an additional nine states that had banned "sodomy" (oral and/or anal sex) between partners of any sexual persuasion. Gay rights supporters applauded the ruling because sodomy laws had been selectively enforced against homosexuals. Before the decision a *Newsweek* magazine columnist wrote, "The sodomy laws are part of a dark tradition in this nation. . . . They are meant only to demonize and marginalize a class of human beings. . . . The sodomy laws may be the last laws standing that exist purely for the purpose of codifying and justifying bigotry" (Quindlen, 2003a, p. 72).

Antidiscrimination

The National Gay Task Force was founded in 1973 to help meet the second goal of the gay rights movement, to end various kinds of discrimination toward homosexuals. Antidiscrimination laws are not "special rights" any more so than eliminating racially segregated drinking fountains. Such laws protect the basic rights of all citizens (Stein, 1999). Gays and lesbians typically have no legal recourse when they are discriminated against in employment and housing because of their sexual orientation. Lesbian and gay community structures are also affected: Funding for lesbian and gay organizations in schools and government is often withheld. In addition, plays and artworks identified with gay culture are often banned from receiving government funds.

A major legislative goal of gay rights advocates is an amendment to the 1964 Civil Rights Act that would broaden it to include "affectional or sexual orientation" along with race, creed, color, and sex (Wildman, 2001). This would make it illegal to discriminate in housing, employment, insurance, and public accommodations on the grounds of sexual orientation (Cohn, 1992). By 2000 the Federal Civil Service Commission as well as many state and city governments, businesses, and large corporations (including Wal-Mart) had established laws and policies prohibiting antigay discrimination (Sullivan, 2003).

Most Americans, almost 85%, believe that homosexuals should have equal rights in employment and housing (Leland, 2000b; Morganthau, 1997). However, only 33% of the respondents in a survey of the general population believe that there is a lot of discrimination against gays, and even fewer, 29%, said that the government needs to do more to protect the rights of gays. These statistics contrast greatly with the survey of the gay population;

In June 2000 the U.S. Supreme Court ruled 5 to 4 that the Boy Scouts, as a private organization, have First Amendment rights to free association and therefore can exclude gays. Other youth organizations, including the Girl Scouts of America and the 4-H Club, have nondiscrimination policies and opposed the Supreme Court decision (Lindsey & Morgan, 2000). Since the decision, some individual, corporate, and civic sponsors have stopped contributing to the Boy Scouts in opposition to discrimination (Quindlen, 2000a; Zernike, 2000).

60% believe that there is a lot of discrimination, and 83% believe that the government needs to do more (Leland, 2000b).

Eliminating discrimination in the military has been far less successful than with employment and housing. Gays have always served in the U.S. military—and have always been met with hostility. After Bill Clinton's election in 1992, the status of gays and lesbians in the military became a hotly debated issue. In his first days in office Clinton moved to fulfill a campaign pledge to ban discrimination against gays and lesbians in the U.S. armed forces. In doing so, he was barraged by vocal opponents, a skeptical public, and nearly unanimous opposition by top military leaders. The "don't ask, don't tell" policy evolved. According to this policy, homosexuals were allowed to serve in the military—even though the military considered them unfit for service—provided that they kept their orientation secret by not engaging in sexual contact with or attempting to marry someone of the same sex, and by not even declaring that they are gay, lesbian, or bisexual. The need for secrecy has had adverse effects on homosexual troops serving in the 2003 Iraq war. Their partners at home did not have access to support services that the military provides to families, they were not likely to be the first to know if their loved ones were wounded, captured, or killed, and both partners had to be circumspect in communications to each other (Biederman, 2003).

Unfortunately, the "don't ask, don't tell" policy has had the reverse effect of its intent: More gays and lesbians have been forced out of the military than ever before. According to the Servicemembers Legal Defense Network, by the year 2000 discharges on the basis of sexual orientation were 73% higher than before the "don't ask, don't tell" policy (Fone, 2000; Vistica, 2000). Lesbians are more likely to be expelled from the military than gay men: almost 33% of military members discharged because of their sexual orientation were women, although women make up only 14% of the armed forces (Biederman, 2003). Typical of times of increased need for active military personnel, the rate of discharge of homosexuals decreased during the 2003 Iraq war. Closeted gay and lesbian U.S. troops served alongside openly gay troops from Great Britain and Australia, 2 of the 24 nations that allow openly homosexual soldiers (Neff, 2004). No known problems with troops working effectively together have occurred because of sexual orientation (Bull, 2003). Countless taxpayer dollars have been spent on investigating and discharging homosexual personnel (Jones &

Grammy Award winning singer-songwriter Melissa Etheridge, right, and actress Tammy Lynn Michaels exchanged vows in September 2003, one day after former California governor Gray Davis signed legislation allowing same-sex couples to register as domestic partners.

InfoTrac Search Words

■ Civil unions
■ Gay marriage

Koshes, 1995), money that could be better spent on combating sexual misbehavior and harassment—whether homosexual or heterosexual in nature.

Beyond decriminalization of gay and lesbian sexual behavior and legal protection from discrimination, positive rights provide equal recognition and protection for gays and lesbians' relationships and families. Legal adoption and marriage are positive rights issues. We discussed the benefits to a child for both parents to be legal parents in an earlier section of this chapter, and we will discuss the debate about gay marriage in Chapter 14.

The current gay rights situation is well stated by Kevin Jennings, founder of the Gay, Lesbian, and Straight Education Network: "It's the best and worst times to be gay. There's an unprecedented level of visibility and activism, but with that an unprecedented level of backlash and opposition" (Ritter, 2000, p. 3). It is our hope that progress will continue to be made and that homosexual men and women will be freer to love, work, and contribute to society.

Summary

- The word *homosexual* can be an objective or subjective appraisal of sexual behavior, emotional affiliation, and/or self-definition. (p. 268)

A Continuum of Sexual Orientations
- Kinsey's seven-point continuum ranges from exclusive heterosexuality to exclusive homosexuality. Kinsey based his ratings on a combination of overt sexual behaviors and erotic attractions. (p. 269)
- According to estimates from the National Health and Social Life Survey, approximately 2.8% of men and 1.4% of women identify themselves as homosexual. (p. 269)
- Bisexuality can be characterized by overt behaviors and/or by erotic responses to both males and females. As with heterosexuality and homosexuality, a clear-cut definition of bisexuality is difficult to establish. (p. 270)

- Four types of bisexuality are a real orientation, a transitory orientation, a transitional orientation, and homosexual denial. (pp. 271–272)

What Determines Sexual Orientation?
- A number of psychosocial and biological theories attempt to explain the development of homosexuality. Some of the psychosocial theories relate to parenting patterns, life experiences, or the psychological attributes of the person. (pp. 271–272)
- Theories of biological causation look to prenatal or adult hormone differences as well as genetic factors. A biological predisposition for some gays and lesbians is suggested by research with twins, sexual dimorphism of finger length, handedness, and gender nonconformity. (pp. 272–276)
- Sexual orientation, regardless of where it falls on the continuum of heterosexuality and homosexuality, seems to be formed from a composite of factors that are unique to each individual. (p. 276)

Societal Attitudes

- Cross-cultural attitudes toward homosexuality vary from condemnation to acceptance. Negative attitudes toward homosexuality still predominate in our society. (pp. 276–277)
- Current Judeo-Christian positions toward homosexuality vary greatly. (pp. 278–279)
- Homophobia is the irrational fear of homosexuality, the fear of homosexual feelings within oneself, or self-loathing because of one's own homosexuality. Young males often exhibit the most extreme homophobia, especially in perpetrating hate crimes. (p. 280)
- Homosexuality has been portrayed in a more positive light in the media since the early 1990s, a development that may help lead to greater familiarity with and acceptance of homosexuality. (pp. 283–284)

Lifestyles

- Contrary to popular stereotypes, homosexual individuals exhibit a wide variety of lifestyles. (p. 284)
- The choice of coming out or being "in the closet" often has a significant effect on a homosexual person's lifestyle. The steps of coming out involve recognizing one's homosexual orientation, deciding how to view oneself, and being open about one's homosexuality. (pp. 285–287)
- As gender-role stereotyping has decreased, many homosexual and heterosexual couples have developed more egalitarian relationships. Some of the differences between homosexual men and homosexual women can be attributed to general gender-role differences between men and women. Lesbian "sex radicals" are moving past typical boundaries for female sexuality. (p. 292)

The Gay Rights Movement

- Gay activism arose in the late 1960s. Its main goals are decriminalization of private sexual behavior, antidiscrimination in employment, housing, and the military and positive rights such as legal marriage and adoption. These goals are opposed by various individuals and groups. (pp. 293–296)

◆▶ Suggested Readings

Cammermeyer, Margarethe (1994). *Serving in Silence.* New York: Viking. The story of a Vietnam veteran who received the Bronze Star and the Nurse of the Year award and was discharged from the military for being homosexual after 26 years of distinguished service.

Ellis, Alan (Ed.) (2001). *Gay Men at Midlife: Age Before Beauty.* New York: Haworth Press. A collection of essays about what it means to be a gay man at midlife.

Fone, Byrne (2000). *Homophobia: A History.* New York: Metropolitan Books. A chronicle of the evolution of homophobia through the centuries and how it remains the last acceptable prejudice.

Howey, Noelle, and Ellen Samuels (2000). *Out of the Ordinary: Essays on Growing Up with Gay, Lesbian, and Transgender Parents.* A groundbreaking anthology of essays by grown children of gay, lesbian, and transgender parents.

Huegel, Kelly (2003). *GLBTQ: The Survival Guide for Queer and Questioning Teens.* Minneapolis, MN: Free Spirit Publishing. A book that covers many bases to help teens cope with outside pressures and prejudices.

Isensee, R. K. (1996). *Love Between Men: Enhancing Intimacy and Keeping Your Relationship Alive.* A collection of approaches that can be used to improve communication, solve everyday conflicts, and satisfy a partner's emotional and sexual needs.

Martin, April (1993). *The Lesbian and Gay Parenting Handbook.* New York: HarperCollins. Interviews with families and experts that discuss different options for gays becoming parents, legal considerations, and special issues related to gay family life.

Rust, Paula (Ed.) (2000). *Bisexuality in the United States.* New York: Columbia University Press. A collection of important writings on theory and research on bisexuality.

Signorile, Michelangelo (1995). *Outing Yourself: How to Come Out as Lesbian or Gay to Your Family, Friends, and Coworkers.* New York: Simon & Schuster. A 14-step program of guidance and advice about coming out.

Stein, Ed (1999). *The Mismeasure of Desire: The Science, Theory, and Ethics of Sexual Orientation.* Oxford: Oxford University Press. An in-depth analysis of research on biological causes of homosexuality. Stein critiques the limitations and liabilities of the "we're born that way" rationale for gay rights.

Sullivan, Andrew (1995). *Virtually Normal.* New York: Knopf. A gay conservative deals with his gay sexual orientation and offers unique perspectives on other conservatives.

◆▶ Resources

The National Gay and Lesbian Task Force, 1325 Massachusetts Ave. NW, Washington, DC 20005; (202) 393-5177. A group that provides information about social, political, and educational organizations in particular locales.

National Center for Lesbian Rights, 870 Market Street, Suite 570, San Francisco, CA 94102; (415) 392-6257. A legal resource center working to eradicate discrimination.

Parents, Families and Friends of Lesbians and Gays (PFLAG), 1726 M Street NW, Suite 400, Washington, DC 20036; (202) 467-8194. A group that provides support and counseling for parents and public education on gay rights.

◆▶ Web Resources

Your *Our Sexuality* Web site **http://psychology.wadsworth.com/ crooksbaur9e/** has direct links to the Web sites described below. These links are checked often for changes, dead links, and new additions.

An Encyclopedia of Gay, Lesbian, Bisexual, and Queer Culture
This Web site is a free gay and lesbian encyclopedia about gay culture.

Bisexual Resource Center
Feature articles, news updates, links, and a variety of information related to bisexuality are accessible at the Bisexual Resource Center Web site.

Sexual Orientation: Science, Education, and Policy

This Web site builds on the work of Gregory Herek at the University of California, Davis. Herek's research focuses on sexual orientation, antigay violence, homophobia, and other concerns of gay men, lesbians, and bisexuals.

Sexual Orientation and Homosexuality

This page on the Web site of the American Psychological Association provides detailed answers to commonly asked questions about what determines sexual orientation.

Human Rights Campaign

The Human Rights Campaign is an organization dedicated to securing equal rights for lesbians and gay men. The group's Web site provides news updates on legislation related to gay rights, descriptions of its public education programs, and information on such topics as coming out.

The Advocate Online

The Advocate, a weekly national news magazine covering issues of interest to lesbians and gay men, offers an up-to-date resource of news and feature articles on its Web site.

Lesbian Mothers Support Society

This Web site offers peer support and information on a range of topics related to becoming pregnant and being a lesbian parent.

Our Sexuality Web Site

For online resources directly related to this book, go to **http://psychology.wadsworth.com/crooksbaur9e/**. You will find interactive exercises, study questions, chapter outlines, an online version of this text's glossary, and Web links and activities that complement your CD-ROM.

InfoTrac® College Edition Online Library

http://infotrac.thomsonlearning.com/

InfoTrac College Edition is an online searchable library that includes a multitude of journals, many of which are specific to human sexuality. These journals include _Archives of Sexual Behavior, Archives of Sexual Health Behavior, Canadian Journal of Human Sexuality, Hispanic Journal of the Behavioral Sciences, Journal of Cross-Cultural Psychology, Journal of Physical Education, Recreation, and Dance, Journal of Sex Research,_ and _Sex Roles._ You may search topics suggested in the margins of this chapter or terms of your own.

Our Sexuality CD-ROM

Use your CD-ROM for further study of the concepts in this chapter. Your CD-ROM provides animations of difficult concepts, video clips of real people discussing sexuality, critical thinking questions, chapter quizzing, and more.

Contraception

It's a good thing that there are lots of birth control options, because I've used most of them at one time or another. I was able to be on the pill before my boyfriend and I first started having intercourse in college. That was before AIDS, so I didn't need to use anything else "embarrassing." I tried the combination pill and the minipill, then used an IUD for a while. After I was first married, we used natural family planning and the diaphragm or cervical cap successfully. After our children were born, foam and condoms filled in for us until my husband got a vasectomy. I never had any particular problems with any of the methods, and I'm very grateful to never have had an unwanted pregnancy, but it sure is nice to be free of needing to use contraceptives. (Authors' files)

▶ Historical and Social Perspectives

People's concern with controlling conception goes back at least to the beginning of recorded history. In ancient Egypt women placed dried crocodile dung next to the cervix to prevent conception. In 6th-century Greece, eating the uterus, testis, or hoof paring of a mule was recommended. In more recent historical times the 18th-century Italian adventurer Giovanni Casanova was noted for his animal-membrane condoms tied with a ribbon at the base of the penis. In 17th-century Western Europe, condoms, withdrawal of the penis from the vagina before ejaculation, and vaginal sponges soaked in a variety of solutions were used for contraception (McLaren, 1990).

Contraception in the United States

Although we may take for granted the variety of contraceptive, or birth control, methods available in the United States today, this state of affairs is quite recent. Throughout American history both the methods available for contraception and the laws concerning their use have been restrictive. In the 1870s Anthony Comstock, then secretary of the New York Society for the Suppression of Vice, succeeded in enacting national laws that prohibited the dissemination of contraceptive information through the U.S. mail on the grounds that such information was obscene; these laws were known as the Comstock Laws (Kreinen, 2002a). At that time, the only legitimate form of birth control was abstinence, and reproduction was viewed as the only acceptable reason for sexual intercourse.

Margaret Sanger was the person most instrumental in promoting the changes in birth control legislation and availability in the United States. Sanger was horrified at the misery of women who had virtually no control over their fertility and bore child after child in desperate poverty. In 1915 she opened an illegal clinic where women could obtain and learn to use the diaphragms she had shipped from Europe. She also published birth control information in her newspaper, *The Woman Rebel*. As a result, Sanger was arraigned for violating the Comstock Laws. She fled to Europe to avoid prosecution but later returned to promote research on birth control hormones, a project financed by her wealthy friend Katherine Dexter McCormack.

Sanger and McCormack wanted to develop a reliable method by which women could control their own fertility (Tone, 2002). However, it was not until 1960 that the first birth control pills came on the U.S. market, after limited testing and research in Puerto Rico. Fertility control through contraception rather than abstinence was a profound shift that implied an acceptance of female sexual expression and broadened the roles that women might choose (D'Emilio & Freedman, 1988; Harer, 2001).

In 1965 the U.S. Supreme Court ruled in *Griswold* v. *Connecticut* that states could not prohibit the use of contraceptives by married people (381 U.S. 479). The Court based its decision on the right to privacy of married couples. In 1972 the Supreme Court case *Eisenstadt* v. *Baird* extended the right to privacy to unmarried individuals by decriminalizing the use of contraception by single people (405 U.S. 438).

In the ensuing years laws governing contraceptive availability continued to change. Most states have liberalized their laws to allow the dispensing of contraceptives to adolescents without parental consent and the displaying of condoms, spermicidal foam, and contraceptive sponges on open pharmacy shelves rather than behind the counter. But many people still oppose television ads for condoms, and controversy continues on the national level about whether to require parental noti-

Margaret Sanger

Margaret Sanger was dedicated to helping women and families have every child be a wanted child.

© Bettmann/CORBIS

fication when minors receive contraceptive services from government-funded organizations. The concern, of course, is that teens who would not otherwise choose to have intercourse would do so if contraception were easily available. However, research indicates that the rate of sexual activity does not increase even when condoms are available at no cost at school (Fay & Yanoff, 2000; Guttmacher et al., 1997).

[handwritten margin note:] 1972 - the 1st time contraceptive was used by anyone

Contraception as a Contemporary Issue

In recent years the availability and use of reliable birth control have been seen as increasingly desirable for a variety of reasons. Men and women who choose *not* to be parents can avoid unwanted pregnancies more successfully with effective birth control methods. The typical heterosexual woman in the Western world is trying to become pregnant or is pregnant for only a small percentage of her reproductive life. For most of the time she is trying to prevent pregnancy. In fact, 93% of sexually active women in the United States use contraception (P. Murphy, 2003). The emphasis on having planned and wanted children has been growing. Many couples who want children wait for some years to establish their relationship and financial stability before starting a family. Birth control also enables couples and individuals to limit the size of their families. In particular, women who want to combine a career and parenthood depend on birth control. In fact, once women had access to the birth control pill in the 1970s, they entered professional programs in greater numbers, participated more in corporate America, and married later in life (Contemporary Sexuality, 2000a).

InfoTrac Search Words

■ Contraception

The use of birth control can also contribute to the physical health of the mother. Pregnancy itself has health risks, and spacing pregnancies usually results in better health for mothers and their children, particularly when nutrition and health care are inadequate (P. Murphy, 2003). In some cases, birth control is used to avoid the possibility of bearing children with hereditary diseases or birth defects.

The critical role of contraception in women's health issues has led to lawsuits and legislative bills to attempt to mandate health insurance coverage for prescription contraceptives (Espo, 2003). Some of these lawsuits cite sex discrimination as the basis of the complaint. Health insurance typically covers men's basic health care needs (including medications for erectile dysfunction), but when insurance omits contraception, women's basic health care is inadequate. Insurance coverage has increased, but is not yet universal (Sonfield et al., 2004). A writer and professor of history stated, "Apparently, enabling a man to achieve orgasm rates higher on our list of priorities than protecting a woman from the long-term consequences of his short-term delight" (Tone, 2002, p. 7).

Population growth is another concern that plays a part in some people's decision to limit their family size. The 20th century ended with a worldwide population of 6 billion people, compared to less than half that number—2.3 billion—in 1950. The United Nations projects an increase to 8.9 billion by 2050. Of that growth, 95% is expected to occur in poorer, developing countries, where the population already exceeds the availability of bare necessities—housing, food, and fuel. Furthermore, overpopulation is a dire threat to the earth's environment. For these reasons many people see birth control as necessary to combat world hunger and environmental devastation. Conversely, birth control that prevents HIV transmission—latex condoms and the microbicide contraceptive foam under development—helps to reduce the human devastation of the AIDS epidemic.

The 1994 United Nations Conference on Population and Development attempted to address these concerns. An inherent factor in controlling population levels is expanding

Nirmala Palsamy was named "Heroine of the Planet" in honor of her work in educating women about family planning and birth control.

© Baldev/Corbis Sygma

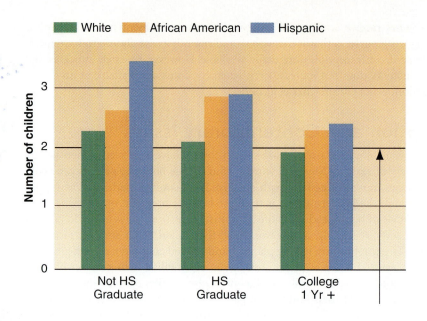

► **Figure 11.1** Average number of children by mother's education level and race or ethnicity in the United States. As the education of women increases, the number of children they have decreases. Reproductive patterns among racial groups become more similar the higher the education level (Grant, 1994).

French newspapers and the Paris Métro subway rejected an ad aimed at the vast majority of French men who were reluctant to obtain vasectomies.

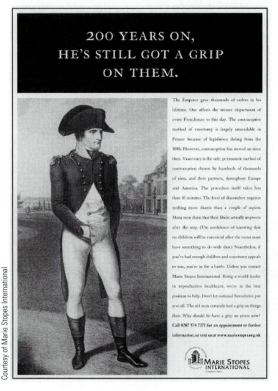

Courtesy of Marie Stopes International

women's opportunity for education and economic opportunity (Zlidar et al., 2004). Across the globe women with higher levels of education have fewer children (Morgan, 2003); and as Figure 11.1 illustrates, this pattern also holds across ethnic lines in the United States.

Cultural gender-role expectations can affect contraceptive choice and use. In male-dominated cultures it is difficult for women to use contraceptives against the objections of their partners (David & Russo, 2003; E. Murphy, 2003). For example, in Japan condoms have been the most commonly used means of contraception, but birth control pills were not available until 1999, 40 years later than in most other countries. The pill was opposed in Japan because its availability and use give women much more control over their fertility and sexuality—which is incongruent with the ideal of the traditional, docile Japanese woman. Government leaders also expressed concern that the pill would erode morals; they believed that women's lack of independence in contraceptive use would help to maintain their morals (Contemporary Sexuality, 1999b).

France provides another example of the influence of gender on contraceptive choice. Only 1% of French men obtain vasectomies, compared to 16% in Great Britain, 11% in the Netherlands, and 8% in Belgium. A family planning organization attempted to place an ad in French newspapers and in the Paris Métro subway, aimed at Frenchmen reluctant to obtain vasectomies, but the ad was rejected (Contemporary Sexuality, 2000e).

Despite these and other obstacles, an estimated 60% of couples worldwide currently use contraception, compared to 10% in 1970 (David & Russo, 2003). Although many religious groups approve of and even favor the use of birth control, objections to contraception often stem from religious mandate, and some individuals and couples do not use birth control devices because of their religious beliefs. The official doctrine of the Roman Catholic Church (and of some other religions, such as fundamentalist Islam) holds that contraceptive means other than abstinence and methods based on the menstrual cycle are immoral; this would include the use of condoms for HIV protection (Kissling, 2003; McClure, 2004). In 1995 Pope John Paul II's "Evangelium Vitae" ["Gospel of Life"] reaffirmed that contraception and sterilization were morally unacceptable. However, the discrepancy between doctrine and practice is wide: Most practicing Catholics in the

United States use some kind of artificial contraception. Seventy percent of American Catholics use contraceptive methods forbidden by the Church. Of those using prohibited methods, 40% opt for sterilization (Fehring & Schmidt, 2001).

▶ Sharing Responsibility and Choosing a Birth Control Method

Each birth control method has its advantages and disadvantages. An individual or couple might find that one method suits a certain situation best. Sharing the responsibility enhances a particular method's use.

It Takes Two

In promoting contraception, Margaret Sanger wanted to give women control over their own fertility. However, control should not mean total responsibility by the woman (Edwards, 2002). It is not wise for a man to assume that a woman has "taken care of herself." As a male student asked:

If you have sex with a girl and she tells you she's on the pill, how do you know if she's telling the truth? (Authors' files)

Many women do not regularly practice birth control, especially if they are not in a long-term relationship, and some use methods inconsistently or incorrectly (Glei, 1999; Trussell et al., 1999). Dealing with an unwanted pregnancy is difficult, and not using contraception can negatively affect both partners' sexual experience and general feelings of well-being (Brooks, 2002). It is in the best interests of both partners to be actively involved in choosing and using contraception (Wang et al., 1998). No one wants to be surprised with an unexpected pregnancy, but as the saying goes, "If you're not part of the solution, you're part of the problem."

Sharing the responsibility of contraception can enhance a relationship. Talking about birth control can be a good way to practice discussing personal and sexual topics. Failing to talk about birth control can cause women to resent men for putting the entire responsibility on them. For these reasons we recommend that women and men share the responsibility for birth control, and we are pleased to see that research shows that more couples now share contraceptive decision making (Grady et al., 2000).

The first step in sharing contraceptive responsibility may simply be for one partner to ask the other about birth control before having intercourse for the first time. Research has found that both male and female college students need to develop skills to discuss contraception. Women need to become effective in obtaining contraceptives, and men need to learn to be assertive about refusing to engage in intercourse without effective contraception (Van den Bossche & Rubinson, 1997). Openness to using condoms or to engaging in noncoital sexual activities, whether as the contraceptive method of choice or as a backup or temporary method, is another way for partners to share responsibility for birth control.

Reading about and discussing the various contraceptive methods and their side effects and choosing the one that seems best are important ways for both partners to be involved. Most birth control clinics offer classes that are open to partners. The man can also participate by accompanying his partner when a medical exam is needed. Many physicians or nurse practitioners are comfortable with the woman's partner being present during such exams. The partner can be supportive about the cramping and discomfort some women experience from insertion of an intrauterine device (IUD) and can learn to check the string. Male

Would you be more careful if it was you that got pregnant?

See your pharmacist for free information on family planning, venereal disease and other communicable diseases.

For the Clinic nearest you call your local Health Department or (800) 952-5250

! Sexual Health

Infanticide, especially neonaticide (killing an infant within 24 hours after birth), has occurred in almost every culture throughout history (Thomas, 2001). Infants were "exposed," that is, left outside to die from the cold or starvation or to be killed by predators. Moses and Oedipus are famous examples in history of infants who survived this practice (Ehrenreich, 1998). Infanticide tragically filled the gap left by the lack of safe and effective birth control. The babies who had no one willing or able to care for them were left to die. This is also a contemporary concern. For example, human rights organizations have made allegations that parents and state-run orphanages in China deliberately let children die of starvation and neglect (Birchard, 1998; Bogert & Wehrfritz, 1996).

In the modern United States contraceptives and abortion are legal and safe, and adoption is usually easy to arrange. However, each year in the United States more than 50 newborn babies are killed by their mothers shortly after birth. As the graph in this box indicates, the number of infant murders, even with population increases, decreased after oral contraceptives and abortion became legal. However, surrendering a child for adoption has always been available, but a young woman has to be able to ask for help for herself and her baby.

The murders are usually committed by young, unmarried women, many of them typical middle-class girls (Ehrenreich, 1998). Women of all races and socioeconomic classes commit this crime; most of the babies are white, but a disproportionate number, compared to the proportion in the general population, are black. Most mothers had options available to them along the way—college health clinics, high school programs for pregnant teens and mothers, and Planned Parenthood services—but failed to use them.

Some of the cases include an 18-year-old New Jersey student who delivered her son in the bathroom during her senior prom and reportedly choked him to death before tossing him in the garbage. In Los Angeles a 19-year-old was charged with dumping her baby girl in a garbage can outside her middle-class suburban home. A 20-year-old business major at the University of Southern California secretly delivered a baby girl who was later found dead in a dumpster by a USC maintenance worker.

Sometimes boyfriends are involved. An 18-year-old college freshman and her boyfriend were charged with putting their newborn son in a trash bin after killing him (Kantrowitz, 1997).

Experts in these rare homicides believe that the young women use elaborate, irrational psychological mechanisms to convince themselves that they are not pregnant. They might be stereotypical "good girls" who feel overwhelmed by shame (Ehrenreich, 1998). The thought of family and friends finding out seems worse than killing or abandoning their baby. They wear baggy clothes and isolate themselves from detection by others. The self-delusion can continue until the moment of birth in a kind of "psychotic denial." Many of these women are so disconnected from reality they do not remember feeling any pain during the delivery. They see their babies not as human but as foreign bodies that have passed through them. Most of these young women have no prior mental illness; a few may be antisocial personalities who feel no concern about their child and kill because it is more convenient for them (Kantrowitz, 1997).

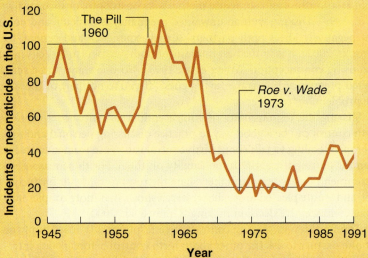

When oral contraception and abortion were legalized, the number of infant murders decreased (Kantrowitz, 1997).

partners can learn to insert the diaphragm or cervical cap and foam and to put on condoms. Expenses for both the exam and the birth control method can also be shared. We strongly believe that sharing the responsibility for birth control can help provide both better sexual relationships and improved contraceptive effectiveness.

An encouraging change in birth control use has occurred in the last several decades in the United States: More people are using contraception the first time they have intercourse. Research has shown that in the 1990s 76% of females used a contraceptive and 66% of males used a condom at first intercourse. In contrast, before 1980, 50% of females and 25% of males used contraception at their first intercourse (Alan Guttmacher Institute, 2002). ■

Choosing a Birth Control Method

Many forms of birth control are available to couples. However, an ideal method—one that is 100% effective, completely safe with no side effects, reversible, separate from sexual activity, inexpensive, easy to obtain, usable by either sex, and not dependent on the user's memory—is not available now or in the foreseeable future. Each of the methods currently available has advantages and disadvantages with regard to effectiveness, safety, cost, and convenience. It is a good idea to be familiar with the various methods available because most people will use several of them during their active sex lives.

Effectiveness   *99.9% effectiveness*

Several variables influence the effectiveness of birth control. Among the most important of these variables is human error, which is not taken into account in rating the theoretical effectiveness of a method. A health care practitioner's error could result in an improperly inserted IUD or a poorly fitted diaphragm, as discussed later in this chapter. More frequently, the user is at fault (Jones & Henshaw, 2002). Poor or improper knowledge of the correct use of the method, negative beliefs about using a method, an uninvolved partner, forgetfulness, or deciding that "this one time won't matter" all greatly increase the chances of pregnancy. In fact, about half of all unintended pregnancies occur among women using contraceptives—but not carefully enough. Unmarried women younger than 30 years old are most likely to have a contraceptive failure, and married women older than 30 are least likely to do so. In addition, low-income women experience greater failure rates than more affluent women, possibly because of limited availability of health care (Fu et al., 1999).

Research indicates that men and women who do not use contraception or who use it ineffectively or inconsistently have several characteristics in common. People who feel guilty about sex are likely to use contraception ineffectively (Strassberg & Mahoney, 1988). Negative attitudes toward sexuality often interfere with the ability to process information about sexuality and birth control; thus a person with a negative attitude is more likely to choose a less effective method and to use it inconsistently. In addition, women who are uncomfortable with their sexuality are likely to take a passive role in contraceptive decision making, leaving themselves vulnerable to their partners' contraceptive behavior. A young woman may also be concerned about whether her partner sees her as a "nice girl" or as "easy." A simple way to appear as a "nice girl" is to be unprepared with birth control (Angier, 1999). The box titled "Infanticide" describes an extreme response to guilt and denial.

Contraceptive effectiveness is best compared by looking at the **failure rate** (the number of women out of 100 who become pregnant by the end of the first year of using a particular method). Table 11.1 shows the failure rate for a large number of women or men using the most common birth control methods correctly and consistently; the table also shows the rate of accidental pregnancies resulting from improper or inconsistent use. To reduce the potential rate of failure, many couples choose to use backup methods.

Using Backup Methods to Increase Contraceptive Effectiveness

Under various circumstances, a couple may need or want to use **backup methods**—that is, more than one method of contraception used simultaneously. Backup methods can help reduce the human element in failure rates. Some examples of these circumstances include the following:

- During the first cycle of the pill.
- For the remainder of the cycle after forgetting to take two or more birth control pills, or after several days of diarrhea or vomiting while on the pill.
- The first month after changing to a new brand of pills.
- When taking medications, such as antibiotics, that reduce the effectiveness of the pill.
- During the initial 1 to 3 months after IUD insertion.
- When first learning to use a new method of birth control.
- When the couple wants to increase the effectiveness of contraception. For instance, using foam and condoms together offers effective protection.

Failure rate The number of women out of 100 who become pregnant by the end of 1 year of using a particular contraceptive.

Sexual Health

Backup methods Using a second contraceptive method simultaneously with another method.

Condoms, contraceptive foam, and the diaphragm are possible backup methods that can be combined in many ways with other birth control methods for extra contraceptive protection. ■

TABLE 11.1 Effectiveness of Various Birth Control Methods

Method	Failure Rate[a] if Used Correctly and Consistently	Typical Number[a] Who Become Pregnant Accidentally
Outercourse	0	0
Hormone-based methods		
Estrogen–progestin pills, including Seasonale	0.3	8
Progestin-only pills	0.3	8
Vaginal ring (NuvaRing)	0.3	8
Skin patch (Ortho Evra)	0.3	8
Depo-Provera injection	0.3	0.3
Lunelle	0.2	0.2
Progesterone IUDs		
Progestasert T	1.5	2
Mirena	0.1	0.1
Barrier and spermicide methods		
Male condoms	3	16
Female condoms	5	21
Vaginal spermicides	6	30
Cervical barrier methods with spermicide		
Diaphragm with spermicide	6	18
Cervical cap		
Woman has been pregnant	26	40
Woman has never been pregnant	9	18
Sponge		
Woman has been pregnant	20	40
Woman has never been pregnant	9	20
FemCap	4	15
Lea's Shield	6	18
Nonhormonal IUD		
Copper-T (Paragard)	0.6	0.8
Sterilization		
Tubal sterilization	0.5	0.5
Vasectomy	0.1	0.2
Fertility awareness		
Standard days method	5	12
Rhythm, calendar, basal temperature, and cervical mucus methods	9	20
Withdrawal	4	24
No method	85	85

[a]Number of women out of 100 who become pregnant by the end of the first year of using a particular method.

SOURCES: Akert (2003), Alan Guttmacher Institute (2002), Hutti (2003), and Long (2002).

Which Contraceptive Method Is Right for You?

Effectiveness is not the only important factor in choosing a method of birth control. Many additional factors—including cost, ease of use, and potential side effects—influence couples' decisions about whether to use a particular birth control method. Table 11.2 summarizes some of the most important factors: comparative costs and advantages and disadvantages of the most commonly used methods.

Beyond the variables listed in Table 11.2, the decision about which birth control method to use must take into account one more important factor—the individuals who will be using it (Ranjit et al., 2001). The survey presented in the boxed discussion "Which Contraceptive Method Is Best for You?" (page 310) is designed to help you take into account your own concerns, circumstances, physical condition, and personal qualities as you make this very individual decision. We discuss a number of commonly used contraceptive methods in the paragraphs that follow, and this more specific information may be helpful to you when you make your choice.

"Outercourse"

Throughout the remainder of this chapter we look at contraceptive methods designed to prevent pregnancy resulting from coitus. One important method deserves special mention because it involves a different fundamental decision at the point when a couple becomes intimate—the decision to be sexual without engaging in penile–vaginal intercourse.

Noncoital forms of sexual intimacy, which have been called **outercourse,** can be a viable form of birth control (Hatcher, 1988). Outercourse includes all avenues of sexual intimacy other than penile–vaginal intercourse, including kissing, touching, mutual masturbation, and oral and anal sex. The voluntary avoidance of coitus offers effective protection from pregnancy, provided that the male does not ejaculate near the vaginal opening, although sperm can travel from the anus to the vagina. Outercourse can be used as a primary or temporary means of preventing pregnancy, and it can also be used when it is inadvisable to have intercourse for other reasons—for example, following childbirth or abortion or during a herpes outbreak. This method has no undesirable contraceptive side effects. However, it does not eliminate the chances of spreading sexually transmitted diseases, especially if oral and anal sex are included in the sexual interaction.

Outercourse Noncoital forms of sexual intimacy.

► Hormone-Based Contraceptives

Many of the most common birth control methods used by women work by artificially altering hormone levels. Hormone-based contraceptives can have several effects, such as inhibiting ovulation, altering the mucous lining of the cervix so that it blocks the passage of sperm, or preventing the fertilized egg from implanting successfully in the uterus (see Chapter 12). In this section we look at the most popular hormone-based birth control methods: oral contraceptives, the vaginal ring, the transdermal patch, and injected contraception.

Oral Contraceptives

More than 100 million women worldwide use the pill (Blackburn et al., 2000). Oral contraceptives are the reversible method of birth control most commonly used by women in the United States today, including college-age women (Alan Guttmacher Institute, 2002). Four basic types of oral contraceptives are currently on the market: the constant-dose combination pill, the triphasic pill, Seasonale, and the progestin-only pill (currently called the mini-pill) (see Figure 11.2 on page 310).

The Pill: Four Basic Types

The **constant-dose combination pill** has been available since the early 1960s and is the most commonly used oral contraceptive in the United States today. It contains two hormones, synthetic estrogen and progestin (a progesterone-like substance). The dosage of these hormones remains constant throughout the menstrual cycle. There are more than 32 different

Constant-dose combination pills Birth control pills that contain a constant daily dose of estrogen and progestin.

TABLE 11.2 Factors to Consider When Choosing a Birth Control Method

Method	Cost per Year for 100 Occurrences of Intercourse	Advantages	Disadvantages
Outercourse	0	No medical side effects; helps develop nonintercourse sexual intimacy.	Risk of unplanned intercourse; no protection from STDs.
Hormone-based methods			
Estrogen–progestin pills, including Seasonale	$384–$516 ($32–$43 per cycle)	Very effective; no interruption of sexual experience; reduced menstrual cramps and flow. Periods 4 times per year with Seasonale. Also used for emergency contraception.	Possible side effects; increased risk of pregnancy if taken incorrectly; no protection from STDs.
Progestin-only pills	$384–$456 ($32–$38 per cycle)	Very effective; no interruption of sexual experience; no estrogen-related side effects.	Breakthrough bleeding; no protection from STDs.
Vaginal ring (NuvaRing)	$580	Do not have to remember to take daily pill; consistent, low-dose release of hormone; no interruption of sexual experience.	Increased vaginal discharge; expulsion of ring; no protection from STDs.
Skin patch (Ortho Evra)	$420	Same as vaginal ring.	Slightly higher breakthrough bleeding than oral contraceptives; skin irritation; no protection from STDs.
Depo-Provera injection	$196 ($70 per injection)	Very effective; no interruption of sexual experience; do not have to remember to take on daily basis; no estrogen-related side effects.	Breakthrough bleeding, weight gain; clinic visit and injection every 3 months; no protection from STDs.
Lunelle	$420 ($35 per injection)	Same as for Depo-Provera; may have estrogen-related side effects.	Same as for Depo-Provera, but clinic visit and injection required monthly.
Progesterone IUDs			
Progestasert T	$500 first year	Very effective; no interruption of sexual activity; don't have to remember to use.	Side effects; increased menstrual flow and cramps; may be expelled; no protection from STDs.
Mirena	$700 1st year, $140 if used for 5 years	Same as Progestasert T, except lighter periods; can be used longer than the Progestasert T.	Same as Progestasert.
Barrier and spermicide methods			
Male condoms	$100 ($1.00 each)	Some protection from STDs; available without a prescription.	Interruption of sexual experience; reduces sensation.
Female condoms	$300 ($3.00 each)	Same as male condoms.	Same as male condoms.
Vaginal spermicides	$85 (85¢ per application)	No prescription necessary.	Interruption of sexual experience; skin irritation; no protection from STDs.
Cervical barrier methods with spermicide			
Diaphragm	$50 diaphragm, $280 for fitting, $85 for spermicide	No side effects; can be put in before sexual experience; some protection from bacterial STDs.	Need practice to use correctly; can cause vaginal or cervical irritation; limited protection from STDs.
Cervical cap	Same as diaphragm.	Same as diaphragm.	Same as diaphragm.
Sponge	$200 ($2 each)	Same as diaphragm.	Same as diaphragm.

Method	Cost per Year for 100 Occurrences of Intercourse	Advantages	Disadvantages
FemCap	$65, $32.50 if used for 2 years; $85 for spermicide	Same as diaphragm; does not need to be fitted by health care practitioner; has a loop to assist removal.	Same as diaphragm.
Lea's Shield	$120 ($60 each, replaced every year); $85 for spermicide	Same as diaphragm; does not need to be fitted by health care practitioner; has a loop to assist removal.	Same as diaphragm.
Nonhormonal IUD			
Copper-T (Paragard)	$550 first year; $55 if kept for 10 years	Can be kept for 10 years; don't have to remember to use; also used for emergency contraception.	Increased menstrual flow and cramps; no protection from STDs; may be expelled.
Sterilization			
Tubal sterilization	$1,200–$2,500	Highly effective and permanent; transcervical sterilization is safest and least expensive of female sterilization procedures.	Not easy to reverse for fertility; no protection from STDs.
Vasectomy	$250–$1,000	Easier procedure than tubal sterilization.	Not easy to reverse for fertility; no protection from STDs.
Fertility awareness *(abstinence)*			
Standard days method	0	Most effective of fertility awareness methods. Acceptable to Catholic Church.	Uncertainty of safe times; periods of abstinence from intercourse or use of other methods; no protection from STDs.
Rhythm, calendar, basal temperature, and cervical mucus methods	0	Acceptable to Catholic Church; no medical side effects.	Uncertainty of safe times; periods of abstinence from intercourse or use of other methods; no protection from STDs.
Withdrawal	0	No medical side effects.	Interruption of intercourse; no protection from STDs.
No method	0	Acceptable only if pregnancy desired.	No protection from STDs.

SOURCES: Akert (2003), Alan Guttmacher Institute (2002), Hutti (2003), and Long (2002).

varieties of combination pills, and each variety contains varying amounts and ratios of the two hormones. The first pill in 1960 contained as much as 175 micrograms of estrogen. Most pills today contain about 25 micrograms (Ritter, 2003).

The **triphasic pill,** which has been on the market since 1984, is another type of oral contraceptive. Unlike the constant-dose combination pill, the triphasic pill provides fluctuations of estrogen and progesterone levels during the menstrual cycle. The triphasic pill is designed to reduce the total hormone dosage and any side effects while maintaining contraceptive effectiveness.

The newest constant-dose pill on the market, **Seasonale,** has a lower dose of estrogen and progestin than most other oral constant-dose or triphasic pills. Seasonale is designed to reduce the number of menstrual periods from 13 to 4 per year. This pill is a new take on a

Triphasic pills Birth control pills that vary the dosages of estrogen and progestin during the cycle.

Seasonale Birth control pills that reduce menstrual periods to four times a year.

◀ ▶ **Which Contraceptive Method Is Best for You?**

Answer yes or no to each statement as it applies to you and, if appropriate, your partner.

1. You have high blood pressure or cardiovascular disease.
2. You smoke cigarettes.
3. You have a new sexual partner.
4. An unwanted pregnancy would be devastating to you.
5. You have a good memory.
6. You or your partner have multiple sexual partners.
7. You prefer a method with little or no bother.
8. You have heavy, crampy periods.
9. You need protection against sexually transmitted diseases.
10. You are concerned about endometrial and ovarian cancer.
11. You are forgetful.
12. You need a method right away.
13. You are comfortable touching your and your partner's genitals.

14. You have a cooperative partner.
15. You like a little extra vaginal lubrication.
16. You have sex at unpredictable times and places.
17. You are in a monogamous relationship and have at least one child.

Scoring

Recommendations are based on *yes* answers to the following numbered statements:

- Combination pill and Lunelle: 4, 5, 6, 8, 16
- Progestin-only pill: 1, 2, 5, 7, 16
- Condoms: 1, 2, 3, 6, 9, 12, 13, 14
- Depo-Provera: 1, 2, 4, 7, 11, 16
- Cervical barrier methods: 1, 2, 13, 14
- IUD: 1, 2, 7, 11, 13, 16, 17
- Spermicides and the sponge: 1, 2, 12, 13, 14, 15

SOURCE: Hales (1994).

common off-label use of oral contraceptives. For years health care practitioners have suggested to their patients who use typical oral contraceptives that they skip the placebo pills and take the next month's worth of the hormone-containing pills. This modified use causes the women to skip a period, which can reduce menstrual problems or allow the women to avoid a period during a special event, such as a vacation or a sports competition (Yim, 2000a).

The **progestin-only pill,** which has been on the market since 1973, contains only 0.35 milligrams of progestin—about one-third the amount in an average-strength combination pill. The progestin-only pill contains no estrogen. Like the combination pill, the progestin-only pill has a constant-dose formula.

Progestin-only pills Contraceptive pills that contain a small dose of progestin and no estrogen.

▶ **Figure 11.2** Birth control pills come in many different configurations. There are currently four basic types of pills: the constant-dose pill, the triphasic pill, Seasonale, and the progestin-only pill.

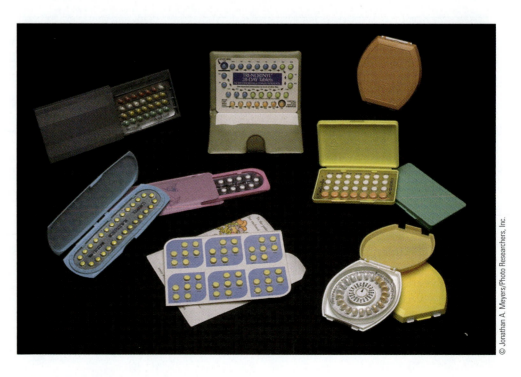

© Jonathan A. Meyers/Photo Researchers, Inc.

How Oral Contraceptives Work

The combination pill, the triphasic pill, and Seasonale prevent conception primarily by inhibiting ovulation. The estrogen in these pills affects the hypothalamus, inhibiting the release of the pituitary hormones LH and FSH (luteinizing hormone and follicle-stimulating hormone), which would otherwise begin the chain of events culminating in ovulation (see Chapter 4). The progestin in these pills provides secondary contraceptive protection by thickening and chemically altering the cervical mucus so that the passage of sperm into the uterus is hampered. Progestin also causes changes in the lining of the uterus, making it less receptive to implantation by a fertilized egg (Larimore & Stanford, 2000). In addition, progestin can inhibit ovulation by mildly disturbing hypothalamic, pituitary, and ovarian function.

The progestin-only pill works somewhat differently. Most women who take the progestin-only pill probably continue to ovulate at least occasionally. The primary effect of this pill is to alter the cervical mucus to a thick and tacky consistency that effectively blocks sperm. As with the combination pill, secondary contraceptive effects are provided by alterations in the uterine lining that make it unreceptive to implantation.

How to Use Oral Contraceptives

There are several acceptable ways to begin taking oral contraceptives; a woman who does so should carefully follow the instructions of her health care practitioner. Unlike other oral contraceptives that are taken in 28-day cycles, Seasonale is taken daily for 3 months, or 84 days, followed by 7 days of inactive tablets when menstrual flow occurs. Some women miss the reassurance that they are not pregnant that comes from their monthly flow when taking other birth control pills.

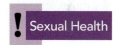

Forgetting to take one or more pills sharply reduces the effectiveness of oral contraceptives, as does taking the pill at a different time each day. Pill users should take the pill at the same time every day; taking the pill at approximately the same time each day maximizes its effectiveness. Because oral contraceptives maintain particular hormone levels in the body, missing one or more pills can lower hormone levels and allow ovulation to occur (Zlidar, 2000).

A significant number of women do forget to take the pill each day. Fifty percent of oral contraceptive users report they forget one or more pills each cycle; 22% say they miss two or more pills. However, women underestimate how often they forget their pills. A study that used electronic tracking of the time and date pills were taken from the container, rather than user self-report, found that up to 50% of users missed three or more pills per cycle, greatly reducing the contraceptive effectiveness of the method (Potter et al., 1996). To help prevent missed pills, a woman can use a pill case with a built-in clock and alarm to alert her the same time each day if she has not taken her pill.

If you are using oral contraceptives and you miss a pill, you should take the missed pill as soon as you remember and then take your next pill at the regular time. If you forget more than one pill, it is best to consult your health care practitioner. You should also use a backup method, such as contraceptive foam or condoms for the remainder of your cycle. ■

Advantages of Oral Contraceptives

Birth control pills have several advantages. They can be taken at a time separate from sexual activity, which many people believe helps maintain sexual spontaneity. In addition, the pill has the advantage of being reversible, so that a woman can easily stop using it if her needs change. If the estrogen–progestin pill is used correctly, it is a highly effective method, as Table 11.1 shows. The effectiveness is an important benefit. One student stated:

I've used the pill for 11 years. It's not a very big responsibility to take a pill every day compared to the responsibility that comes with being a parent. (Authors' files)

The combination pills also often eliminate *Mittelschmerz* (pain at ovulation) and reduce menstrual cramps (Mansour, 2004). Oral contraceptives also usually reduce the amount and duration of the menstrual flow, which is considered an advantage by most but not all users (Glasier et al., 2003). Of course, any problem associated with menstruation—headaches, anemia, heavy bleeding—will occur only four times a year if a woman is taking Seasonale.

In addition, some women notice that taking oral contraceptives diminishes premenstrual tension symptoms. Oral contraceptives can help relieve endometriosis and may decrease the incidence of benign breast disease (Hatcher & Guillebaud, 1998). Use of oral contraceptives reduces the risk of endometrial and ovarian cancer by half (Siskind et al., 2000). Other potential advantages include breast enlargement and a decrease in acne in some women (Burkman, 1995). A woman who was pleased with this method explained:

> I really like the pill I'm taking. My periods are light, and the bad cramps I used to have are gone. I hadn't been using anything before taking the pill. It's a tremendous relief to make love and not be afraid of getting pregnant. (Authors' files)

These advantages explain, in part, why the pill is more commonly used than any other reversible method of birth control (Picardo et al., 2003). In fact, the pill is the most commonly used contraception by female physicians, especially obstetrician-gynecologists (Frank, 1999).

The progestin-only pill has the advantage that it eliminates any estrogen-related side effects and reduces the likelihood of progestin-related problems because of the low progestin dosage (Hussain, 2004). Adverse reactions to the combination pill can be reduced by switching to the progestin-only pill. Progestin-only pills are sometimes used during breast feeding because they have no effect on lactation (Blackburn et al., 2000).

Disadvantages of Oral Contraceptives

One of the biggest disadvantages of the pill is that it does not protect against AIDS and other sexually transmitted diseases (STDs). Condoms should be used in conjunction with the pill when protection from these diseases is needed.

Because the hormones in birth control pills circulate in the bloodstream throughout the entire body, this form of contraception can have a variety of side effects. However, for most healthy women the benefits of oral contraceptives outweigh the risks (Blackburn et al., 2000; Gaudet et al., 2004). For women older than 35 who smoke, the risks exceed the benefits (Vessey et al., 2003; Walling, 2004). Serious problems associated with the pill can be summarized by the acronym ACHES and are described in Table 11.3. We look first at some of the problems that have been associated with the estrogen–progestin pills, then examine possible side effects of the progestin-only pill.

Use of the pill can be related to emotional changes. Some women see a correlation between their moods and use of oral contraceptives. Depression might increase or decrease from the influence of oral contraceptives. A woman who suspects that her depression is pill related can use another contraceptive method for a time and observe any changes in her moods (Sanders et al., 2001).

Many women take the pill to increase the spontaneity and enjoyment of their sexual expression, and some do experience improvement in their sexual lives. A small study of university students found that women using triphasic pills experienced greater sexual inter-

| TABLE 11.3 | Remember "ACHES" for the Pill: Symptoms of Possible Serious Problems with the Birth Control Pill |

Initial	Symptoms	Possible Problem
A	Abdominal pain (severe)	Gallbladder disease, liver tumor, or blood clot
C	Chest pain (severe) or shortness of breath	Blood clot in lungs or heart attack
H	Headaches (severe)	Stroke, high blood pressure, or migraine headache
E	Eye problems: blurred vision, flashing lights, or blindness	Stroke, high blood pressure, or temporary vascular problems at many possible sites
S	Severe leg pain (calf or thigh)	Blood clot in legs

SOURCE: Adapted from Hatcher & Guillebaud (1998).

est and response than those using constant-dose pills (McCoy & Matyas, 1996). However, a decrease in sexual motivation or vaginal lubrication during arousal can also occur (Caruso et al., 2004). A change in type of pill may help.

Oral contraceptives interact with other medications and can diminish the therapeutic effect of the medications, or the medications can diminish the contraceptive effectiveness of the pill. Some medications that can interfere with oral contraceptive effectiveness are listed in Table 11.4.

Although the reduced amount of hormones in the progestin-only pill causes fewer potential side effects, this pill also has some disadvantages. First, it must be taken consistently and regularly to be effective. Irregular and "break-through" bleeding (a light flow between menstrual periods) happens more frequently with the progestin-only pill than with the combination pill. However, the bleeding irregularities usually diminish in 2 or 3 months, as they do with the combination pill. Ectopic pregnancy, in which the zygote is implanted outside the uterus, is rare but more likely for users of progestin-only pills.

TABLE 11.4	Medications That Reduce Oral Contraceptive Effectiveness

Some medications can reduce the effectiveness of birth control pills. Tell every physician who gives you medication that you are taking oral contraceptives. Use a backup method, such as foam or condoms, when you use any of the following medications or herbal remedies:

Barbiturates	Dilantin
Ampicillin	Rifampin (for tuberculosis)
Tetracycline	Phenylbutazone (for arthritis)
Tegretol	St. John's Wort

SOURCE: Markowitz et al. (2003) and Zlidar (2000).

Additional Comments on Oral Contraceptives

Women vary in their responses to the particular hormone combinations of different oral contraceptives. Some side effects—such as nausea, fluid retention, increased appetite, acne, depression, or bleeding irregularities—can be eliminated by changing the type of pill. In general, to reduce the possibility of side effects, health practitioners prescribe a type of pill that works well for the woman and has the lowest practical hormonal potency (Akert, 2003).

Women with a history of certain conditions, however, should use a different method of contraception; these conditions include blood clots, strokes, circulation problems, heart problems, jaundice, cancer of the breast or uterus, and undiagnosed genital bleeding. In addition, a woman who currently has a liver disease or who suspects or knows that she is pregnant should not take the pill. Women who have problems with migraine headaches, depression, high blood pressure, epilepsy, diabetes or prediabetes symptoms, asthma, or varicose veins should weigh the potential risks most carefully and use the pill only under close medical supervision. ■

The Vaginal Ring and the Transdermal Patch

NuvaRing and Ortho Evra are two new hormone-based contraceptive methods that do not require taking a pill each day. Both synthetic estrogen and progestin are embedded in either a 2-inch-diameter soft and transparent vaginal ring (NuvaRing) or a beige matchbook-sized transdermal patch (Ortho Evra) (Figure 11.3).

How the Ring and Patch Work

Both NuvaRing and Ortho Evra release the hormones that are embedded in them through the vaginal lining or skin into the bloodstream. The hormones then work in the same way as the pill to prevent pregnancy.

How to Use the Ring and Patch

The ring is inserted into the vagina between Day 1 and Day 5 of a menstrual period. It is worn inside the vagina for 3 weeks, then removed for 1 week and replaced with a new ring (Novak et al., 2003). The ring can remain in place during intercourse, or it can be removed up to 3 hours at a time without reducing its contraceptive effectiveness (Long, 2002).

In using the patch, a woman chooses a specific day of the week after a menstrual period starts and identifies that day as "patch change day." She replaces the old patch with a new

▶ **Figure 11.3** The ring (top) and patch (bottom) eliminate the need to remember a birth control pill each day.

J. Darin Derstine

© Reuters/CORBIS

patch on that same day each week for 3 weeks, followed by a patch-free 7-day interval. The patch can be placed on the buttock, abdomen, upper outer arm, or upper torso (P. Murphy, 2003).

Advantages of the Ring and the Patch

The continuous low-dose release of hormone allows less hormone to be used overall. This continuous release also eliminates the daily fluctuations of hormone levels that occur with the pill. Furthermore, the ring and the patch have the same possible health benefits of oral contraceptives.

Disadvantages of the Ring and the Patch

Some women experience increased vaginal discharge with the ring. The patch can cause skin irritation for some women, which can usually be corrected by rotating the application site. The ring and the patch are not appropriate for women who weigh more than 198 pounds, because the effectiveness of the contraceptive is reduced with larger body size (Akert, 2003; Long, 2002). They have the same possible health risks of oral contraceptives, and provide no protection against STDs.

Injected Contraceptives

Depo-Provera is an injectable hormone-based contraceptive. Depo-Provera has been available worldwide for more than 20 years and was approved by the U.S. Food and Drug Administration (FDA) in 1992 (Kaunitz, 1994). Lunelle, another injected contraceptive, was approved in 2000 (Galewitz, 2000).

How Injected Contraceptives Work

The active ingredient in Depo-Provera is progestin, which inhibits the secretion of gonadotropins and prevents follicular maturation and ovulation. These actions cause the endometrial lining of the uterus to thin, preventing implantation of a fertilized egg. Progestin also alters the cervical mucus.

How to Use Injected Contraceptives

The Depo-Provera shot needs to be given once every 12 weeks, ideally within 5 days of the beginning of menstruation. It usually takes 10 months after stopping Depo-Provera for a woman to get pregnant (Galewitz, 2000).

Advantages of Injected Contraceptives

The main advantage of injected contraceptives is not needing to take a pill daily or not using a barrier method at the time of intercourse. As one student stated:

I am on Depo-Provera. I love it. It's really effective, and I can't mess it up. (Authors' files)

In some cultures or situations, injected contraceptives are advantageous for a woman who wishes to use contraception without anyone other than her health care practitioner knowing. Injections also might have a protective action against endometrial and ovarian cancer (Hatcher, 1998). Because Depo-Provera contains only progestin, estrogen-related side effects do not occur.

Disadvantages of Injected Contraceptives

Injected contraceptives provide no protection against STDs. The most common side effects are menstrual irregularities, particularly lack of menstruation. Some women report menstrual spotting, weight gain, headaches, breast tenderness, dizziness, and mood changes as other side effects (Hatcher, 1998).

▶ Barrier and Spermicide Methods

Hormone-based methods cause changes in a woman's body that inhibit conception and implantation. Another group of contraceptive devices work in a different way—by preventing healthy sperm from reaching an ovum. In this section we look at several barrier methods, including condoms, and four cervical barrier devices. In addition, we include vaginal spermicides in this section because their effect is also to prevent sperm from reaching an egg and because spermicidal creams and jellies are frequently used in conjunction with other barrier methods. Other than the condom, barrier methods do not protect against STDs, including HIV.

Condoms

Condoms, also called prophylactics and rubbers, are currently the only temporary method of birth control available for men. A condom is a sheath that fits over the erect penis. It is made of thin surgical latex or sheep membrane. A new type of condom made of polyurethane is thinner and more heat sensitive and comfortable than latex. However, it is slightly more likely to break than latex (Frezieres et al., 1999). Some condoms have special features. The world's fastest selling condom, Trojan's Extended Pleasure, has a desensitizing agent on the inside, which is intended to help delay ejaculation. Other condoms have ribs at the base to stimulate the vaginal opening. Some have ultrathin latex for more user sensation, and others use polyurethane to better conduct body heat and for use by people allergic to latex.

Condoms have a long history. A penile sheath was used in Japan during the early 1500s, and in 1564 an Italian anatomist, Fallopius, described a penile sheath made of linen. Mass production of inexpensive modern condoms began after the development of vulcanized rubber in the 1840s (Vinson & Epperly, 1991). Condoms are one of the most popular contraceptive methods used in the United States and, next to the pill, the most commonly used by college-age adults (Piccinino & Mosher, 1998). Worldwide, an estimated 6 to 9 billion condoms are used each year (Gardner et al., 1999).

Condoms are available without prescription at pharmacies and grocery stores, from family planning clinics, by mail order, in vending machines, and in some areas in school-based condom availability programs (Blake et al., 2003; Guttmacher et al., 1997). The city of Cambridge, Massachusetts, set a precedent by requiring many businesses—restaurants, theaters, hotels, and so on—to have condom machines (Ards, 2000).

Most condoms are packaged—rolled up and wrapped in foil or plastic—and come lubricated or nonlubricated in various shapes, textures, and colors (Figure 11.4). There is less chance of the condom breaking if it is lubricated, and some men report less reduction of penile sensation during intercourse with lubricated condoms. Sheep-membrane natural-skin condoms are more expensive but often interfere less with sensation than do latex condoms. However, natural-membrane condoms contain small pores that can permit passage of viruses associated with several STDs, including AIDs, genital herpes, and hepatitis.

Some condoms have a small nipple at the end, called a reservoir tip, and others have a contoured shape or textured surface. Some are made with a spermicide, nonoxynol-9, on their inner and outer surfaces. Spermicidal condoms are not as effective as the combination

Condom A sheath that fits over the penis and is used for protection against unwanted pregnancy and sexually transmitted diseases.

▶ **Figure 11.4** Condoms come in many varieties.

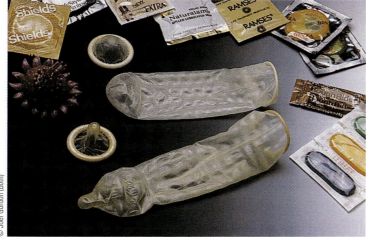

of a condom and a vaginal spermicide. Condoms have an average shelf life of about 5 years, although not all packages are dated. Condoms should not be stored in hot places, such as the glove compartment of a car or a back pocket, because heat can deteriorate the latex.

How the Condom Works

When a man uses a condom properly, both the ejaculate and the fluid from Cowper's gland secretions, sometimes called precum in slang, are contained in the tip. The condom thus serves as a mechanical barrier, effectively preventing any sperm from entering the vagina.

How to Use the Condom

Correct and consistent use of the condom is essential for its effectiveness, but studies of college students have found that user error is common. Putting a condom on after sex with penetration but before ejaculation is a common error that increases the risk of pregnancy and STD transmission (Crosby et al., 2002).

Most condoms are packaged rolled up. Correct use includes unrolling the condom over the erect penis before any contact between the penis and the vulva occurs. Sperm in the Cowper's gland secretions or in the ejaculate can travel from outside the labia to inside the vagina. For maximum comfort and sensation, an uncircumcised man can retract the foreskin before rolling the condom over the penis (Bolus, 1994). With plain-end condoms (without the reservoir tip), the end needs to be twisted before rolling the condom down over the penis, as shown in Figure 11.5. This leaves some room at the end for the ejaculate and reduces the chances of the condom breaking. If a condom breaks or slips off during intercourse, contraceptive foam, cream, or jelly should be inserted into the vagina *immediately.*

▶ **Figure 11.5** (top) The end of a plain-end condom needs to be twisted as it is rolled onto the penis in order to leave space at the tip. (bottom) A condom with a reservoir tip does not need to be twisted at the top as it is put on the penis.

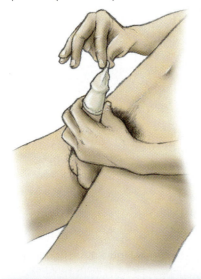

A condom breaks more easily without vaginal lubrication, so if the condom is nonlubricated, some vaginal secretion, saliva, or water-based lubricant needs to be put on the vulva and on the outside of the condom before inserting the penis into the vagina. Do *not* use oil-based lubricants (such as baby oil, Vaseline, massage oil, vegetable oil, or hand lotions) with mineral or other oils because they reduce the condom's integrity and increase the chances of breakage (Spruyt et al., 1998). Because the penis begins to lose its size and hardness soon after ejaculation, it is important to hold the condom at the base of the penis before withdrawing from the vagina. Otherwise the condom can slip off and spill semen inside the vagina:

The first time I used a rubber, I relaxed inside her after I came, holding her for a while. Then I withdrew, leaving the rubber behind. My first thought was, "Oh, no, it's dissolved." I reached inside her vagina and found the rubber. We used some foam right away but were nervous until her next period. (Authors' files)

Condoms are best disposed of in the garbage rather than the toilet, because they can clog plumbing. ■

Advantages of Condoms

Condoms have become more widely used in recent years, especially among unmarried and adolescent women (Bankole et al., 1999). Latex and polyurethane condoms provide the best protection against contracting

and spreading STDs (including HIV/AIDS) and vaginal infections (Celentano, 2004). For this reason individuals who are not in a disease-free monogamous relationship should use spermicidal condoms even if they are using other birth control methods as well (Critelli & Suire, 1998). As one student described:

I use the birth control pill and condoms. The condom just makes me feel safer against STDs and adds extra prevention against pregnancy. (Authors' files)

Strategies to encourage partner use are discussed in the "Let's Talk About It" box.

Courtesy of San Francisco AIDS Foundation

Don't Go Inside Without Your Rubbers On

The writers of a sex education book expressed their unequivocal perspectives on avoidance of effective condom use:

> If we hear any more whining about how condoms are annoying, uncomfortable deal breakers, we are going to *puke*. Could it be you've been using nonlubricated, inch-thick, five-cent prophylactics from a vending machine all your life? So condoms don't figure in your full-on, flesh-to-flesh fantasy world—we get it. We're also sure that oozing genital ulcers and child-support payments don't pop up in that utopia either. (Taylor & Sharkey, 2003, pp. 182–183)

Women's opinions of condoms have become more favorable, and women purchase 50% of condoms sold today. Eighty-eight percent of women polled said that they were likely to insist on using a condom with their next sexual partner.

These changes represent good condom sense because, along with unwanted pregnancy, women have much more to lose than men when a couple does not use a condom. A woman is much more likely to get an STD (including HIV/AIDS) from one act of intercourse than is a man, and bacterial STDs do much more damage to a woman's reproductive tract than to a man's and can ruin her subsequent ability to have a baby.

One study found that refusing to have sex unless a partner used a condom was the most common approach used by college women to encourage condom use (De Bro et al., 1994).

The book *Before You Hit the Pillow, Talk* (Foley & Nechas, 1995) offers suggestions for communicating about condoms. Basically, be clear and assertive and do not get drawn into an argument. Deciding beforehand that you will not have intercourse without using a condom will give your position the strength it needs. Some examples of specific conversations follow.

Partner's Statement	Your Response
"I'm on the pill. You don't need to use a rubber."	"I'd like to use one anyway, then we'll be doubly protected."
"It doesn't feel as good with a condom."	"It will still feel better than nothing."
"It's not very romantic."	"Neither is pregnancy or disease."
"I wouldn't do anything to hurt you."	"Great. Let me help you put it on."
"I'd rather not have sex if we have to use a condom."	"OK. What would you like to do instead?"

Nonlubricated condoms can be used for protection against infection during fellatio. However, it is important to remember that, although condoms greatly decrease the chances of contracting STDs, they do not totally eliminate this risk.

Condoms are available without prescription. No harmful side effects are associated with their use. If condoms are not used as the primary method of birth control, they are useful as a backup. Some men prefer the slightly diminished sensation they experience with condoms because it helps prolong the duration of intercourse before ejaculation. Because the semen is contained inside the condom, some women appreciate the tidiness: ■

I really like the juiciness of sex when I can bathe afterward, but when we go camping and don't have a stream or shower handy, my husband uses condoms so it's not as messy. (Authors' files)

Disadvantages of Condoms

Unless putting on a condom is incorporated as a part of sexual interaction, it can interrupt spontaneity. Some men and women see reduced penile sensitivity as a disadvantage; others believe that condom use is antithetical to good sex and will not use them for that reason. In addition, some men find that they are unable to maintain an erection while they are putting on the condom. Occasionally, people are allergic to latex condoms.

Other disadvantages of condom use have to do with effectiveness. Condoms can have pinhole-size leaks, or they can break or slip off. For this reason membrane condoms and old condoms should be avoided (if a condom is yellow or sticky, it should be discarded), and care should be taken to use condoms properly (Spruyt et al., 1998).

The Female Condom

In 1988 couples in several countries began testing a "woman's condom," which was approved for sale in the United States in 1992. However, the female condom is used more in Africa than in the United States (Tone, 2002). The female condom is made of polyurethane or latex. It resembles a regular condom (Figure 11.6) but is worn internally by the woman. A flexible plastic ring at the closed end of the sheath fits loosely against the cervix, rather like a diaphragm (discussed in the next section). Another ring encircles the labial area. Although the female condom fits the contours of the vagina, the penis moves freely inside the sheath, which is coated with a silicone-based lubricant (Macaluso et al., 2003). Used correctly, female condoms may substantially reduce the risk of transmission of some STDs (Minnis & Padian, 2001; Witte et al., 2000).

Reports vary about the user-friendliness of the female condom. Only 7% of women and 8% of men in FDA studies said that they disliked the female condom (F. Stewart, 1998c). Women in another study appreciated being able to insert the female condom before sexual activity, not needing to remove it immediately following ejaculation, and having sex be less messy. Others liked having an option they could use for protection from STDs and pregnancy instead of relying on male condom use. However, women reported frustration and difficulty with insertion, reduced pleasurable sensations, and problems with partner resistance to the method (Choi et al., 2003).

Vaginal Spermicides

Vaginal spermicides Foam, cream, jelly, suppositories, and film that contain a chemical that kills sperm.

Several types of **vaginal spermicides** are available: foam, suppositories, the sponge, creams and jellies, and contraceptive film (Figure 11.7). *Foam* is a white substance resembling shaving cream. It comes in pressurized cans and has a plastic applicator. Foam is available in pharmacies without a prescription. (Feminine-hygiene products, although often displayed along with various brands of foam, are *not* contraceptives.) *Vaginal suppositories* have an oval shape and contain the same spermicidal chemical found in foam. The *sponge* is a doughnut-shaped spermicide-containing device that absorbs and subsequently kills the sperm. Some *contraceptive creams and jellies* are made to be used without a diaphragm or

▶ **Figure 11.6** (a) The female condom. (b) A female condom consists of two flexible polyurethane rings and a soft, loose-fitting polyurethane sheath.

(a)

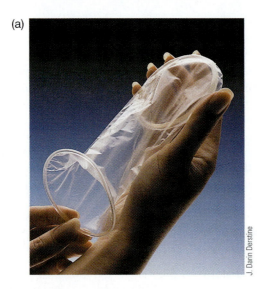

J. Darin Derstine

(b)

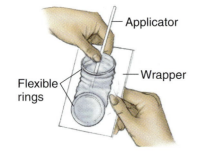

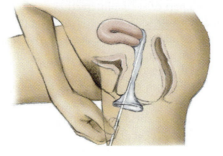

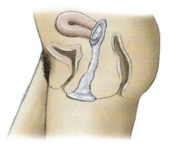

Applicator

Wrapper

Flexible rings

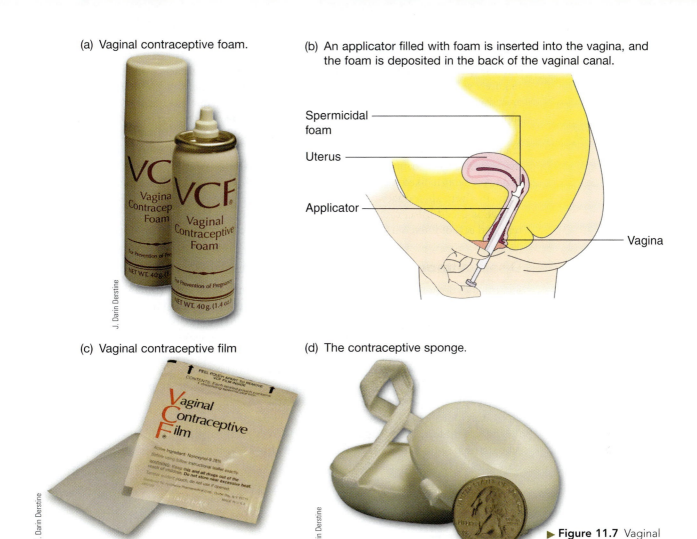

(a) Vaginal contraceptive foam.

(b) An applicator filled with foam is inserted into the vagina, and the foam is deposited in the back of the vaginal canal.

Spermicidal foam

Uterus

Applicator

Vagina

J. Darin Derstine

(c) Vaginal contraceptive film

(d) The contraceptive sponge.

J. Darin Derstine

J. Darin Derstine

▶ **Figure 11.7** Vaginal spermicides available in pharmacies without a prescription.

cervical cap. However, they are not as effective as foam, and many health care practitioners recommend that they not be used without a diaphragm or cervical cap. *VCF,* a vaginal contraceptive film, is a paper-thin, 2-inch × 2-inch sheet that is laced with spermicide. It is packaged in a matchbook-like container with 10 to 12 sheets.

How Spermicidal Methods Work

Foam, suppositories, the sponge, creams and jellies, and VCF all contain a *spermicide,* a chemical that kills sperm. When foam is inserted with the applicator, it rapidly covers the vaginal walls and the cervical os, or opening to the uterus (see Figure 11.7). Contraceptive vaginal suppositories take about 20 minutes to dissolve and cover the walls. One brand of suppository, Encare, effervesces and creates a foam inside the vagina; other brands melt. Once VCF is inserted into the vagina, next to the cervix, it dissolves into a stay-in-place gel.

How to Use Vaginal Spermicides

Complete instructions for use come with each package of vaginal spermicide. It is important to use the product as directed for maximum protection. As with spermicides used with the diaphragm, another application of spermicide is necessary before each additional act of intercourse. The sponge is an exception; it is effective for repeated acts of intercourse. It is probably better to shower rather than take a bath after sex when using a spermicide to prevent the spermicide from being rinsed out of the vagina. For highly effective contraception, vaginal spermicides and condoms should be used together.

Advantages of Vaginal Spermicides

Because spermicides and VCF are sold over the counter in pharmacies, using them does not require a visit to a physician's office. They have no known dangerous side effects for women, and some couples welcome the additional lubrication that spermicides provide. The suppository has the advantage of being small and convenient to use. VCF can be used by people who are allergic to foams and jellies; also, unlike foams and jellies, VCF dissolves gradually and almost unnoticeably. The sponge came back on the market in 1999 after having been taken off the market in 1995 because of manufacturing difficulties. The character Elaine on *Seinfeld* liked the sponge so much that she hoarded boxes of them to use only with men she deemed "spongeworthy" (Howard, 1999). Elaine apparently appreciated that the sponge is easy to use, can be inserted up to 24 hours before intercourse, is effective for repeated acts of intercourse, and can be worn for up to 24 hours afterward (Springen, 1999).

Disadvantages of Vaginal Spermicides

Spermicides do not reduce the risk of HIV. In fact, using spermicides containing nonoxynol-9 many times a day for people at risk for HIV can irritate the vaginal tissue and increase the risk of HIV and other sexually transmitted infections (Creinin, 2003; Gayle, 2000; Planned Parenthood Federation of America, 2003b). Occasionally, a woman or her partner reports irritation of genital tissues from foam or suppositories. Changing brands often alleviates this difficulty, but in some cases any brand causes discomfort. Spermicides can increase the incidence of yeast infections and urinary tract infections. Some of the suppositories do not dissolve completely and therefore feel gritty. Some women or couples dislike the additional lubrication during intercourse or the postcoital discharge following intercourse. Because of the unpleasant taste, using vaginal spermicides may limit couples who like to engage in cunnilingus after intercourse (although they can still do so before inserting the foam or suppositories). These products also have a soaplike scent that is disagreeable to some users. In addition, some people feel that insertion of spermicides interrupts spontaneity, even though the procedure takes only about 30 seconds.

Cervical Barrier Devices

The practice of covering the cervix to provide protection from pregnancy has existed for centuries. In 18th-century Europe, Casanova promoted the idea of using a squeezed-out lemon half to cover the cervix, and European women shaped beeswax to cover the cervix. In 1838 a German gynecologist took wax impressions of each patient's cervix to make custom caps out of rubber (Seaman & Seaman, 1978).

As shown in Figure 11.8, the diaphragm, cervical cap, FemCap, and Lea's Shield are four methods that combine a physical barrier that covers the cervix with vaginal spermicide to protect the cervix from contact with viable sperm. These devices are dome shaped, with a rim around the open side. The diaphragm covers the upper vaginal wall from behind the cervix to underneath the pubic bone. The cervical cap fits over the cervix only. The FemCap and the Lea's Shield have rims that rest on the vaginal wall surrounding the cervix and have removal straps. Unlike the others, the Lea's Shield allows a one-way flow of fluid from the cervix to the vagina but prevents semen from contact with the cervix.

How to Use Cervical Barrier Devices

The diaphragm and cervical cap are individually fitted by a skilled practitioner. In contrast, the FemCap and Lea's Shield do not have to be fitted, but they require a prescription in the United States. They are available over the counter in Canada, Germany, Austria, and Switzerland (Long, 2002). All barrier devices are used with spermicidal cream and jelly placed inside the dome of the cup and on the rim. Do *not* use oil-based lubricants with a diaphragm or cervical cap because these devices are made of latex and will deteriorate when used with oil-based lubricants. (The FemCap and Lea's Shield are made from silicone.)

To insert any of these barrier devices, squeeze the sides of the rim together with one hand, and use your other hand to open the lips of the vulva. Push the device into the vagina, spermicide side up. After you have inserted the barrier, you or your partner need to feel the

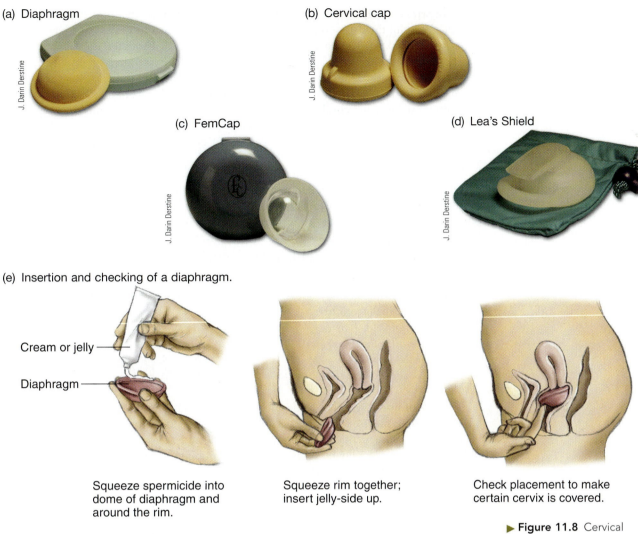

(a) Diaphragm

J. Darin Derstine

(b) Cervical cap

J. Darin Derstine

(c) FemCap

J. Darin Derstine

(d) Lea's Shield

J. Darin Derstine

(e) Insertion and checking of a diaphragm.

Cream or jelly

Diaphragm

Squeeze spermicide into dome of diaphragm and around the rim.

Squeeze rim together; insert jelly-side up.

Check placement to make certain cervix is covered.

▶ **Figure 11.8** Cervical barrier devices.

cervix to ensure that the dome is covering it. The device can be inserted just before intercourse. Some women prefer to insert the dome ahead of time, in privacy, whereas others share the insertion with their partners. As one man explained:

I have always hated "just-before" birth control devices like condoms and diaphragms. However, with my present partner, the diaphragm is part of our sexual excitement. We usually become quite stimulated before reaching for the jelly and diaphragm, and I often use manual clitoral stimulation while she inserts it. I have also learned to put it in while she continues to stimulate herself and me at the same time. Also, the leftover jelly is a good lubricant. The pause between being ready for intercourse and actually doing it seems to heighten the whole thing. (Authors' files)

All cervical barrier devices should remain in the vagina for at least 8 hours to provide time for the spermicide to kill sperm in the vaginal folds. If intercourse occurs again before 8 hours elapse, the device is left in place, and an additional application of spermicide is inserted into the vagina. Recommendations vary for the length of time before intercourse for insertion and after intercourse for removal:

	Hours Before Intercourse	**Hours After Intercourse**
Diaphragm	up to 6	at least 8, no more than 24
Cervical cap	up to 6	at least 8, no more than 24
FemCap	up to 8	at least 8, no more than 48
Lea's Shield	up to 8	at least 8, no more than 48

To remove the diaphragm or cervical cap, put a finger under the front rim to break the air seal, then pull the device out of the vagina. The FemCap and Lea's Shield have flexible loops for removal. After removal, the device should be washed with a mild soap and warm water and then dried. The diaphragm and cervical cap can last for several years, but the FemCap and Lea's Shield are usable for 1 year. All barrier devices should remain soft, flexible, and free from any tiny leaks. Check the dome periodically by holding it up to the light, stretching it slightly, and checking for leaks. Take it with you to your annual exam and Pap smear so that your health care practitioner can evaluate its fit and condition. A pregnancy (including a miscarriage or abortion) or a weight change of more than 10 pounds may require a different diaphragm.

The most important point in the effective use of cervical barrier devices is consistent use. A barrier device simply will not do any good at home in a drawer when you are at the beach for the weekend. Depending on your lifestyle, the best place for the dome may be in your purse, bedroom, or bathroom—or wherever it is most convenient.

Advantages of Cervical Barrier Methods

Through learning to use one of these methods, a woman may become more knowledgeable and comfortable with her body. She may also find these methods useful in making decisions about relating sexually to others.

Since I've been using the diaphragm, I've moved more slowly into sexual relations. I want to discuss my method with a new partner before we have intercourse. If I feel like I'm not comfortable enough to talk about birth control, then I know I'm not ready to have intercourse. (Authors' files)

The lack of hormone-related side effects is another advantage of cervical barrier methods. In addition, the use of any barrier method can help to reduce the risk of exposure to infections and subsequent cervical cell changes that can lead to cancer (Schwartz & Gabelnick, 2002b), and generally may help reduce susceptibility to bacterial STDs (Maher et al., 2004). If one of the barrier devices is difficult to fit, one of the others may perform better.

Disadvantages of Cervical Barrier Methods

The relatively high failure rates and the incomplete ability of these methods to prevent transmission of STDs are disadvantages. The device can slip during intercourse, reducing its protection against pregnancy. Some women with pelvic structure problems, such as marked loss of vaginal muscle tone and support, cannot use the diaphragm effectively, and women who have distortions of the cervix from cysts, lacerations, or pregnancy are often unsuitable candidates for the cervical cap.

▶ Intrauterine Devices

Intrauterine device (IUD)
A small, plastic device that is inserted into the uterus for contraception.

Intrauterine devices, commonly referred to as IUDs, are small plastic objects that are inserted into the uterus. The three most common IUDs are the Copper-T (ParaGard), Progestasert T, and Mirena (Figure 11.9). The Copper-T is a plastic T with a copper wire wrapped around its stem and copper sleeves on the side arms. The Progestasert T is a plastic T with slow-releasing progesterone in the plastic. Mirena, the newest IUD on the U.S. market, is a polyethylene T with a cylinder containing progesterone (Akert, 2003). All three IUDs have fine plastic threads attached; the threads are designed to hang slightly out of the cervix into the vagina.

How the IUD Works

Both the copper and the progesterone in IUDs are effective in preventing fertilization. The Copper-T seems to alter the tubal and uterine fluids, which affects the sperm and egg so fertilization does not occur. The Progestasert T has effects similar to those of hormonal contraceptive methods such as the pill and Depo-Provera. It thickens cervical mucus, alters endometrial lining, impairs tubal motility, and disrupts ovulatory patterns (G. Stewart, 1998).

How to Use the IUD

The IUD is inserted by a health care professional using sterile instruments. Most IUDs come with an inserter. The inserter and IUD are introduced through the cervical os into the uterus; the inserter is then withdrawn, leaving the IUD in place.

IUDs should be used only by women in stable, monogamous relationships who have no history of STDs or pelvic inflammatory disease, who have at least one child or have completed childbearing, who are at least 25 years old, and who have ready access to medical facilities (Greydanus et al., 2001). A woman should be screened for gonorrhea and chlamydia before IUD insertion because the procedure can cause the bacteria associated with these STDs to be pushed farther into the uterus.

While a woman is using an IUD, she or her partner needs to check each month after her menstrual period to see that the thread is the same length as when the device was inserted. To do this, one of them reaches into the vagina with a finger and finds the cervix. If the cervix is far back in the vagina and difficult to reach, the woman can squat or bear down to make it more accessible. The thread should be felt in the middle of the cervix, protruding out of the small indentation in the center. Occasionally it curls up in the os and cannot be felt, but any time a woman or her partner cannot find it, she needs to check with her health care specialist. She should also seek attention if the thread seems longer or if the plastic protrudes from the os; this probably means that her body is expelling the IUD. ■

Advantages of the IUD

The primary advantage of the IUD is that it provides a woman with highly effective contraceptive protection with little inconvenience beyond the monthly checking of the thread. The copper IUD is approved for up to 10 years of use, and the progesterone-releasing IUD is approved for 1 year. The Mirena, which was approved in 2000, can be used for 5 years. The IUD allows uninterrupted sexual interaction. Beyond the initial cost for the IUD and insertion, there are no further supplies to be purchased, making the IUD one of the least expensive contraceptives (Avecilla-Palau & Moreno, 2003). Although an IUD is usually not inserted until 2 to 3 months after childbirth, it does not interfere with breast feeding (as the pill does) once it is in place. Some women who experience initial discomfort after the insertion find that this diminishes in a month or two.

! Sexual Health

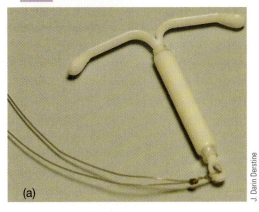
(a)

J. Darin Derstine

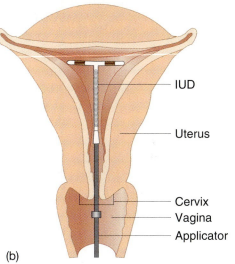
(b)

— IUD

— Uterus

— Cervix
— Vagina
— Applicator

▶ **Figure 11.9** (a) The Mirena IUD. (b) Position of the IUD after insertion by a health care practitioner.

Disadvantages of the IUD

Discomfort, cramping, bleeding, or pain can occur during insertion. The discomfort or bleeding sometimes continues for a few days and occasionally much longer. Two to 20 percent of users expel their IUDs within the first year after insertion (G. Stewart, 1998). This is most likely to occur during menstruation, so a woman needs to check her tampons or sanitary napkins before disposing of them. Also, her partner might feel the IUD protruding from the cervix during intercourse.

Serious problems associated with the IUD can be summarized by the acronym PAINS (Table 11.5). The most serious, but unlikely,

TABLE 11.5	Remember "PAINS" for the IUD: Symptoms of Possible Serious Problems with the IUD

Initial	Symptoms
P	Period late, no period
A	Abdominal pain
I	Increased temperature, fever, chills
N	Nasty discharge, foul discharge
S	Spotting, bleeding, heavy periods, clots

SOURCE: Adapted from G. Stewart (1998).

complication of IUD use is pelvic inflammatory disease (PID). Increased risk of PID has been found almost exclusively in women involved in high-risk behaviors, such as having multiple partners (Sarma, 1999). PID can occur if bacteria are introduced into the sterile environment of the uterus during insertion (P. Murphy, 2003). An IUD is likely to aggravate a gonorrhea infection and make treatment more difficult. Most physicians recommend removal of an IUD when a woman is being treated for a uterine infection. Fallopian tube problems resulting from IUD use can also be a contributing factor in infertility. If a woman becomes pregnant with an IUD in place, she has a 50% chance of a miscarriage. Removal of the IUD when a woman becomes pregnant is recommended (Backman et al., 2004).

In rare cases the IUD breaks through the uterine wall, usually at insertion (Harrison-Woolrych et al., 2003). This perforation can partially extend through the wall, or the IUD can slip completely through the uterus into the abdominal cavity. If an IUD thread seems to become shorter, this may be an indication that the IUD is perforating, and the woman should seek immediate medical attention.

Besides the IUD and hormonal and barrier methods, a number of other contraceptive options are available.

▶ Emergency Contraception

For contraception after unprotected intercourse, administration of hormone pills or insertion of a Copper-T IUD can be used for emergency contraception (EC) (Wellbery, 2000). The use of EC prevented about 51,000 abortions in 2000 in the United States (Jones et al., 2002b). Greater awareness and use of EC could prevent an estimated 2.3 million unintended pregnancies each year in the United States. Even though EC is effective, a 2002 survey found that only 49% of American voters know what EC is (Moore & Smith, 2002).

A woman may need EC because another contraceptive method failed (e.g., a condom broke or her diaphragm slipped), she neglected to use contraception, or she was sexually assaulted. One study found that the most common reason women sought EC was that a condom broke or slipped. The second most common reason was having had unplanned sex (Harvey et al., 1999).

The most common method for EC is the administration of hormone pills. The pills can be taken up to 5 days after unprotected intercourse, but they are most effective when they are taken as early as possible (Nissl, 2003). Hormonal options include two products specifically made for EC—Preven (two doses of combined estrogen and progestin) and Plan B (two doses of progestin)—and oral contraceptives used for EC. These hormone treatments work by producing impenetrable cervical mucus, inhibiting ovulation, altering tubal transport time, and affecting the uterine lining. When a woman uses EC, she should also be aware of and watch for side effects similar to those related to birth control pills (Van Look & Stewart, 1998). Nausea and vomiting are the most common side effects.

All EC methods greatly reduce the chance of pregnancy, but Plan B is the most effective and has fewer side effects. To clarify what we mean by effectiveness, we know that if 100 women have midcycle unprotected intercourse, 8 would become pregnant. Plan B would prevent 7 and Preven would prevent 6 of those 8 pregnancies (Nissl, 2003).

In 1996 the Food and Drug Administration approved the use of the emergency contraceptive pill (Sills et al., 2000). Since then EC has been available only by prescription, with the exception of an innovative program begun in Washington State in 1998 and expanded to Alaska, California, New Mexico, and Hawaii, which allows pharmacists to dispense EC without a prescription (Pollitt, 2004). Because timing is so critical to the effectiveness of EC, the FDA is considering approval of EC to join the ranks of other over-the-counter medications, such as ibuprofen, which were once available only by prescription (Lamas, 2004). It makes sense for EC to be available without prescription because women can accurately "diagnose" the problem of unprotected intercourse, and the dose is the same for all women. Making EC available over the counter would eliminate the circumstances that often interfere with immediate access to EC; need for EC often arises on weekends when doctors' offices are closed, and the costs associated with an office visit and the difficulty in taking time off from work or school can prevent a prompt appointment (Bajos et al., 2003; Lindberg, 2003).

Limited access can also be an obstacle. A survey of U.S. college health centers found that 33% did not provide EC services (Brening et al., 2003). Even a national EC hotline directory failed in 25% of its attempts to secure a prescription within 72 hours for the researchers who called requesting help (Trussell et al., 2000). In addition, only 5% of Catholic hospital emergency rooms provide EC pills to any woman who requests them, and 55% do not provide the method under any circumstances (Catholics for a Free Choice, 2002).

The Copper-T IUD is over 99% effective for EC (Golden et al., 2001). It can be inserted up to 5 days after unprotected intercourse and is appropriate for women who plan to use the IUD as an ongoing method of contraception (Long, 2002). A failure rate of less than 1% makes the Copper-T IUD the most effective form of EC. Its use is limited to women who are at low risk of PID and STDs. It is usually not desirable, however, for women who have not given birth or who have a history of ectopic pregnancy to use the IUD for EC (Van Look & Stewart, 1998).

▶ Fertility Awareness Methods

The birth control methods that we have discussed so far require the use of pills or devices. Some of these methods have side effects in some users, and there can be serious health risks associated with the use of oral contraceptives and the IUD. The barrier methods we have looked at—condoms, vaginal spermicides, and the diaphragm—have fewer side effects, but they require that the couple use them each time they have intercourse.

Many couples are interested in a birth control method that has no side effects, is inexpensive, and does not interrupt spontaneity during sexual interaction (Fehring, 2004). In the next paragraphs we look at some methods of birth control that are based on changes during the menstrual cycle. These methods, which may answer some couples' needs, are sometimes referred to as *natural family planning* or **fertility awareness methods.** They are based on the fact that a fertile woman's body reveals subtle and overt signs of cyclic fertility that can be used both to help prevent and to plan conception.

There are four different fertility awareness methods: the standard days method, the mucus method, the calendar method, and the basal body temperature method. Any of these can be used in combination to increase effectiveness. About 4% of women in the United States use natural family planning (Stanford et al., 1998). During the fertile period, couples using fertility awareness methods can abstain from intercourse and engage in other forms of sexual intimacy or can continue having intercourse and use other methods of birth control during the fertile time.

Fertility awareness methods Birth control methods that use the signs of cyclic fertility to prevent or plan conception.

Standard Days Method

The **standard days method** is the newest approach to natural family planning. It is appropriate for women who have menstrual cycles between 26 and 32 days long. Couples avoid unprotected intercourse on Days 8 through 19 of each menstrual cycle. This "fertile window" is 12 days long to take into account both the days around ovulation and the possible variations in timing of ovulation from one cycle to another. The standard days method has been clinically tested and shows the highest rate of effectiveness for natural family planning methods (Arevalo et al., 2002). A woman can keep track on a calendar or use the CycleBeads shown in Figure 11.10 to help track the days.

Standard days method A birth control method that requires couples to avoid unprotected intercourse for a 12-day period in the middle of the menstrual cycle.

▶ **Figure 11.10** Cycle-Beads, based on the standard days method, help a woman track her menstrual cycle and better know when she can and cannot get pregnant. To use the Cycle-Beads, a woman moves a black ring each day onto the next of 32 color-coded beads, which represent fertile and low-fertility days.

J. Darin Derstine

Mucus Method

The **mucus method,** also called the *ovulation method,* is based on the cyclic changes of cervical mucus that reveal periods of fertility in a woman's cycle. To use this method, a woman learns to "read" the amounts and textures of vaginal secretions and to maintain a daily chart of the changes. A woman reads her mucus by putting her fingers inside her vagina and noting the consistency of the secretions:

- After menstruation there are usually some "dry days" when there is no vaginal discharge on the vulva.
- When a yellow or white sticky discharge begins, unprotected coitus should be avoided.
- Several days later, the ovulatory mucus appears. It is clear, stringy, and stretchy in consistency, similar to egg white. A drop of this mucus will stretch between an open thumb and forefinger for at least 1 and one-half inches before breaking. A vaginal feeling of wetness and lubrication accompanies this discharge, which has a chemical balance and texture that facilitate the entry of sperm into the uterus.
- Approximately 4 days after the ovulatory mucus begins and 24 hours after a cloudy discharge resumes, it is considered safe to resume unprotected intercourse.

The fertile period usually totals 9 to 15 days out of each cycle.

In many cities classes in the mucus method are offered at a hospital or clinic. Each woman's mucus patterns vary, and a class is the best way to learn how to interpret the changes.

Calendar Method

With the **calendar method,** also called the *rhythm method,* a woman estimates the calendar time during her cycle when she is ovulating and fertile. To use the calendar method, a woman keeps a chart, preferably for 1 year, of the length of her cycles. (She cannot be using oral contraceptives during this time because they impose a cycle that may not be the same as her own.)

- The first day of menstruation is counted as Day 1. The woman counts the number of days of her cycle, the last day being the one before the onset of menstruation.
- To determine the high-risk days on which she should avoid unprotected coitus, the woman subtracts 18 from the number of days of her shortest cycle. For example, if her shortest cycle was 26 days, Day 8 would be the first high-risk day.
- To estimate when unprotected coitus can resume, the woman subtracts 10 from the number of days in her longest cycle. For example, if her longest cycle is 32 days, she would be able to resume intercourse on Day 22.

Basal Body Temperature Method

Another way of estimating high-fertility days is through temperature, using the **basal body temperature method.** Immediately before ovulation the basal body temperature (BBT, the body temperature in the resting state on waking in the morning) drops slightly. After ovulation the corpus luteum releases more progesterone, which causes the body temperature to rise slightly (0.2°F). Because these temperature changes (shown in Figure 11.11) are slight, a thermometer with easy-to-read gradations must be used. Special electronic thermometers have also been developed for measuring BBT and are effective in indicating fertile times in the cycle.

Advantages of Methods Based on the Menstrual Cycle

Major advantages of methods based on the menstrual cycle are that there are no side effects and that they are free or inexpensive. Some women and their partners report increased comfort and appreciation of their bodies' cycles and processes when they adopt these methods. Should they choose abstinence over penile–vaginal intercourse during the fertile days, this interval can provide time and motivation for noncoital sexual relating. Knowledge of cyclic changes can also help a couple plan a pregnancy. Also, fertility awareness methods are acceptable to some religious groups that oppose other contraceptive methods.

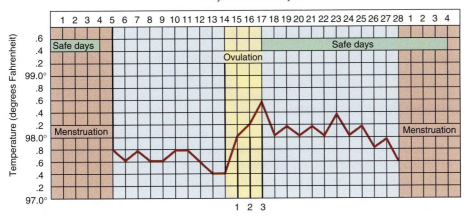

Disadvantages of Methods Based on the Menstrual Cycle

Methods based on the menstrual cycle restrict spontaneity of intercourse and ejaculation during fertile times. Furthermore, learning to accurately detect the mucus and temperature changes involves practice, and with all these methods a couple must keep accurate records for several cycles before beginning to rely on them for contraception. Considerable commitment is essential to maintain daily observation and charting. These methods are more difficult for women who have irregular cycles, and some women are unable to see mucus and temperature patterns clearly. Also, vaginal infections, semen, and contraceptive foams, jellies, and creams make it more difficult to accurately interpret mucus.

Although temperature changes are often good indicators of ovulation, this method is fallible. Slight temperature variations can result from many conditions—a low-grade infection or cold, unrestful sleep, and so forth. Also, because sperm can remain alive in the fallopian tubes for up to 72 hours, the preovulation temperature drop does not occur far enough ahead of time to safely avoid coitus. Although the temperature method is more effective in preventing an undesired pregnancy than no method, it is quite unreliable.

Even after careful arithmetic, the calendar method is also unreliable. Ovulation usually occurs about 14 days before the onset of menstruation; however, even with a woman who ordinarily has regular cycles, the timing of ovulation and menstruation may vary because of illness, fatigue, emotional extremes, or other factors. For a woman who routinely or periodically has irregular cycles, the calendar method is even less safe and requires longer abstention from coitus. Present research indicates that, other than the standard days method, fertility awareness methods are considerably less effective than most other birth control methods (Jennings et al., 1998).

▶ Sterilization

One other method of contraception has become common in recent years because of improved surgical techniques and increasing societal acceptance. *Sterilization* is the most effective method of birth control except abstinence from coitus, and its safety and permanence appeal to many who want no more children or who prefer to remain childless. Sterilization is the leading method of birth control in the United States and around the world (Landry, 2002). One million sterilizations are done each year in the United States, and half of all female sterilizations throughout the world each year are done in China (Stewart & Carignan, 1998; Tang & Chung, 1997). Although some research is being conducted on ways to reverse sterilization, at present the reversal procedures involve complicated surgery and their effectiveness is not guaranteed (Liang, 2000). Therefore sterilization is recommended only to those who desire a permanent method of birth control (Sandlow et al., 2001).

Because sterilization is best considered permanent, a person or the couple should carefully explore their situation and feelings before deciding on the procedure (Jamieson et al., 2002). Questions to consider include:

- Are there any circumstances under which I would want (more) children (e.g., if my child died or if I began a new relationship)?

Sexual Health

- Is my sense of masculinity or femininity tied to my fertility?
- What are my alternatives to sterilization?
- How does my partner feel about the decision? ■

In the following paragraphs, we look at the procedures for sterilization of females and males.

Female Sterilization

In recent years female sterilization has become a relatively safe, simple, and inexpensive procedure. Female sterilization is the most widely used contraceptive method in the United States (Tone, 2002). Worldwide, 180 million women have been sterilized (Landry, 2002). An increase in sterilization rates has occurred in Africa since the introduction of simpler procedures provided by trained nurse-midwives in family planning programs. Fifty percent of African women who have been sterilized had not previously used any other modern contraceptive method (Landry, 2002).

Sterilization can be accomplished by a variety of techniques that use small incisions and either local or general anesthesia (Robinson et al., 2001). **Tubal sterilization** can be done in several ways. A *minilaparotomy* involves a small abdominal incision. Each fallopian tube is gently pulled to this incision; then it is cut and tied, or clips or rings are applied. The tubes are then allowed to slip back into place within the abdomen. Another procedure, *laparoscopy,* is shown in Figure 11.12. One or two small incisions are made in the abdomen, usually at the navel and slightly below the pubic hairline. A narrow, lighted viewing instrument called a laparoscope is inserted into the abdomen to locate the fallopian tubes. The tubes are then tied off, cut, clipped, or cauterized to block passage of sperm and eggs. The ligated (tied) or cut tubes prevent the sperm and egg from meeting in the tube, thus preventing pregnancy. The incisions are generally so small that adhesive tape rather than stitches is used to close them after surgery. Sometimes the incision is made through the back of the vaginal wall, and the procedure is called a *culpotomy.*

A new technique not yet widely available offers women a safer and less expensive sterilization. Unlike a tubal ligation, this procedure does not require an operating room, general anesthesia, or as much recovery time (Kerin et al., 2003). During a **transcervical sterilization,** a physician inserts a tiny coil, called Essure, into the vagina, through the cervix, and

Tubal sterilization Female sterilization accomplished by severing or tying the fallopian tubes.

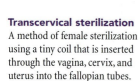

Transcervical sterilization A method of female sterilization using a tiny coil that is inserted through the vagina, cervix, and uterus into the fallopian tubes.

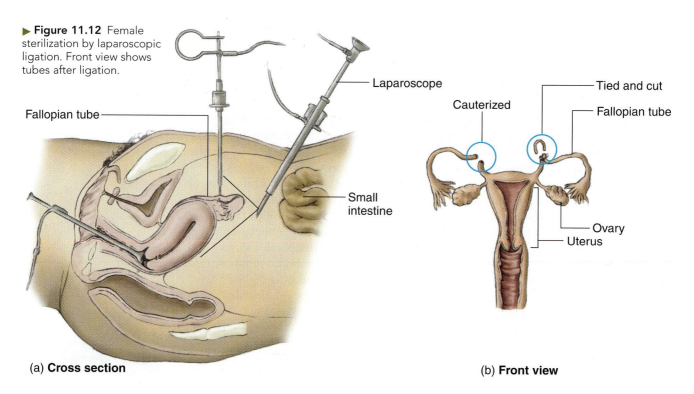

▶ **Figure 11.12** Female sterilization by laparoscopic ligation. Front view shows tubes after ligation.

Laparoscope

Fallopian tube

Small intestine

(a) **Cross section**

Cauterized

Tied and cut

Fallopian tube

Ovary

Uterus

(b) **Front view**

into the opening of each fallopian tube in the uterus. When the coil is released, it expands and anchors itself in place. The procedure takes a half-hour and is performed using local anesthesia. Essure is made of polyester fibers and nickel–titanium alloy, the same material used to make artificial heart valves. The coil promotes tissue growth that, after 3 months, blocks the fallopian tubes and prevents the ovum and sperm from meeting. Women and/or their partners should use another form of birth control during those 3 months (Ritter, 2003). The most common side effect is cramping, and in rare cases the coil is expelled or perforates the fallopian tube.

Sterilization acts only as a roadblock in the fallopian tubes. It does not further affect a woman's reproductive and sexual system. Until menopause her ovaries continue to release their eggs. The released egg simply degenerates, as do millions of other cells daily. The woman's hormone levels and the timing of menopause are not altered. Her sexuality is not physiologically changed, but she may find that her interest and arousal increase because she no longer is concerned with pregnancy or birth control methods. Research indicates that sterilization does not have a detrimental effect on a woman's sexual satisfaction (Stewart & Carignan, 1998).

Some pain or complications can result from female sterilization. The gas pains experienced during recovery in women who have undergone surgical tubal ligation can be very painful (Volm, 1997). A woman might experience some pain at the site of the incision, and if the tubes are sealed by burning, other tissue in the pelvic cavity can be accidentally burned. Postsurgical bleeding is also a possible complication (Peterson et al., 1997). To minimize the possibility of complications, it is important for a woman to choose a physician who is experienced in sterilization procedures.

Surgical reversal of female sterilization is sometimes successful. Microsurgical techniques (microscope-enhanced surgery) are usually most effective (Stewart & Carignan, 1998). To date, Conceptus is not aware of any attempts to surgically reverse the Essure method of sterilization (personal communication from Conceptus).

▶ **Figure 11.13** The Essure coil, a tiny coil that is used in female sterilization.

Courtesy of Conceptus Incorporated

Male Sterilization

In general, male sterilization is safer, has fewer complications following surgery, is considerably less expensive, and is as effective as female sterilization (Barone et al., 2004). Each year 500,000 men in the United States have vasectomies. However, three times as many married women than married men in the United States have undergone sterilization (Baill et al., 2003). **Vasectomy** is a minor surgical procedure that involves cutting and closing each vas deferens, the sperm-carrying duct (Figure 11.14). The operation is typically performed in a physician's office. Under a local anesthetic, a small incision is made in the scrotal sac, well

Vasectomy Male sterilization procedure that involves removing a section from each vas deferens.

▶ **Figure 11.14** Male sterilization by vasectomy.

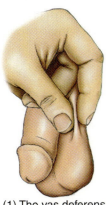

(1) The vas deferens is located.

(2) A small incision in the scrotum exposes the vas.

(3) A small section of the vas is removed, and the ends are cut and/or cauterized.

(4) The incision is closed.

(5) Steps 1–4 are repeated on the other side.

above the testis. The vas is lifted out, and a small segment is removed. The free ends are tied off, clipped, or cauterized to prevent rejoining. After the procedure is repeated on the opposite side, the incisions are closed and the operation is completed, usually in less than 20 minutes. A man can expect some short-term postoperative problems, such as swelling, inflammation, or bruising in the region of the surgery, which last from 1 day to 2 weeks. About 25% of men report some brief pain following vasectomy; a few from that group continued to experience discomfort for more than 3 months and required analgesics or medical attention (Rasheed et al., 1997).

A vasectomy procedure developed in China in 1974, known as no-scalpel vasectomy, substitutes small punctures for the conventional incision. The vas deferens is lifted out of the puncture opening and ligated. Side effects are reduced with no-scalpel vasectomy.

Sexual Health

Vasectomy prevents sperm produced in the testes from entering the semen produced by the internal reproductive organs (see Chapter 5). However, because a significant number of sperm are stored beyond the site of the incision, a man remains fertile for some time after the operation. Sperm may be present in the first 10 to 20 postoperative ejaculations, or for up to several months. Therefore effective alternative methods of birth control should be used until semen analysis reveals no sperm present in the seminal fluid. Many physicians recommend that a vasectomized man have two consecutive negative evaluations before engaging in unprotected intercourse. In general, these checks occur 6 weeks and 12 weeks after the operation (De Knijff et al., 1997). In rare cases the two free ends of the severed vas grow back together (this is called *recanalization*) (Stewart & Carignan, 1998). ■

Unlike castration, vasectomy does not alter testicular production of male sex hormones or absorption of the hormones into the bloodstream. A vasectomized man also continues to produce sperm that are absorbed and eliminated by his body. His ejaculations contain almost as much semen after the operation as before, because sperm constitute less than 1% of the total ejaculate. The characteristic odor and consistency of the semen also remain the same.

Most men report that vasectomy does not affect their sexual functioning (Stewart & Carignan, 1998). Some report improvements, often as a result of greater spontaneity of sexual expression and less fear of impregnating their partners. A few report a reduction in sexual desire, which may be related to concerns about their continued masculinity.

Vasovasostomy Surgical reconstruction of the vas deferens to reverse a vasectomy.

Between 1 and 3 men out of 1,000 who have had a vasectomy request a **vasovasostomy**, a reversal of a vasectomy (Liang, 2000). Approximately 80% of vasovasostomies are done for men in a second marriage following divorce (Fallon et al., 1981). With selected patients and experienced microsurgeons, the chances of reconnecting the vas have increased. The shorter the interval between vasectomy and vasovasostomy, the better the outcome. However, the major complication of vasovasostomy is reduced fertility following reconnection of the vas. After vasovasostomy many men have low sperm counts, reduced sperm motility, or both. Another factor in reduced postvasovasostomy fertility is that antisperm antibodies develop in some vasectomized men. The best measure of vasovasostomy success is the partner's subsequent pregnancy; various studies report an average pregnancy rate of 50% using current vasovasostomy techniques (Matthews et al., 1997).

▶ Less-Than-Effective Methods

There are other contraceptive methods that are far less effective and less commonly used than the ones we have been discussing. We mention some of them here, partly because they are used both as primary birth control methods and as backups for other methods and partly because people may have misconceptions about their effectiveness. We discuss nursing, withdrawal, and douching as methods of birth control.

Nursing

Nursing a baby delays a woman's return to fertility after childbirth when an infant is only breast-fed. However, breast feeding is not a fully reliable method of birth control because there is no way of knowing when ovulation will resume. Amenorrhea (lack of menstruation) usually occurs during nursing, but it is not a reliable indication of inability to conceive. Nearly 80% of breast-feeding women ovulate before their first menstrual period. The longer a woman breast-feeds, the more likely it is that ovulation will occur (Kennedy & Trussell, 1998).

Withdrawal

[handwritten note: NOT always safe!]

The practice of the man removing his penis from the vagina just before he ejaculates is known as *withdrawal*. Theoretically, withdrawal should be an effective method of birth control. However, this method is not very effective. It may be difficult for the man to judge exactly when he must withdraw. His likely tendency is to remain inside the vagina as long as possible, and this may be too long. Both partners may experience anxiety about whether he will withdraw in time, and this can have the effect of reducing the pleasure of sex. Furthermore, even withdrawing before ejaculation does not protect against pregnancy. The preejaculatory Cowper's gland secretions can carry sperm that remain in the urethra from a previous ejaculation, and these sperm can fertilize the egg. Also, sperm deposited on the labia after withdrawal can swim into the vagina.

Douching

[handwritten note: will mess up PHB balance]

Although some women use *douching* after intercourse as a method of birth control, it is ineffective. After ejaculation some sperm reach the inside of the uterus in a matter of 1 or 2 minutes. In addition, the movement of the water from douching may actually help sperm reach the opening of the cervix. Furthermore, frequent douching is not recommended because it can irritate vaginal tissues.

▶ New Directions in Contraception

The spectrum of choices available for contraception widened markedly with the advent of the pill and the IUD. Today, with hormonal contraceptives we have lower-dose oral contraceptives, subcutaneous capsules, and injections. As we have seen in this chapter, however, there are still potential health hazards and inconveniences associated with available methods. Unwanted pregnancies occur each year because of contraceptive and user failure. Further research is needed to improve the safety, reliability, and convenience of birth control (Nass & Strauss, 2004; Schwartz & Gabelnick, 2002).

However, research requires funding. Most clinical trials for contraception occur in foreign countries with the financial help of the United States (Benagiano & Cottingham, 1997). U.S. funds for international family planning programs to conduct clinical trials on contraception were cut for many years. The funds were made available again in July 1996, but at only 65% of previous levels. In addition, some pharmaceutical companies have dropped their contraceptive research programs because of the great expense of extensive clinical trials needed for product approval by the FDA and because of concern about product liability expenses (Tone, 2002). In fact, some companies have taken contraceptives off the market because liability insurance became unavailable or prohibitively expensive. The only new products likely to be available soon are some modified implant systems. Given these limitations, we look at some future possibilities for both men and women.

New Directions for Men

Research has shown that most men would use a male contraceptive pill (Martin et al., 2000). When discussing the possibility of a male pill, questions about whether or not women would trust their male partners to reliably use it have been raised, because contraceptive failure has greater consequences for women than for men. Research has found that most women say they would trust their partners to use such a pill; only 2% said they would not trust them to do so. In addition, women think that a male pill is a good idea because the responsibility for contraception falls too much on women (Glasier et al., 2000).

? Critical Thinking Question

Do you think women would be naive to believe men who say they are on the pill? Why or why not?

At present, male contraception is limited to condoms, vasectomy, and the withdrawal method. Some research efforts currently under way suggest that other methods may be available in the future. These efforts have concentrated on inhibiting sperm production, motility, or maturation. There is no easy solution because any drug aimed at inhibiting sperm production needs at least 10 weeks to work, the length of time of the sperm production cycle (N. Alexander, 2003). In addition, medications that impact sperm production usually impair sexual interest and function and may have other side effects.

The most promising possibility is using a combination of progestin and testosterone. A recent 5-year study in Australia of 55 men used injections of progestin every 3 months to inhibit sperm production and testosterone skin implants every 4 months to restore sex drive. The treatments prevented pregnancy, and the men's fertility was restored after treatment was stopped. However, it will be at least 10 years before a product is commercially available, especially by pill rather than injection (CNN.com, 2003).

A gonadotropin-releasing hormone inhibitor (LHRH agonist) is also under study as a male contraceptive vaccine. LHRH agonist has been shown to reduce the number and motility of sperm in men who received daily injections of the substance. Testosterone levels also dropped, and inability to achieve an erection occurred in more than half the men in the study. This side effect disappeared after treatment stopped. However, testosterone combined with LHRH agonist is effective in maintaining sexual functioning while producing temporary infertility (Gabelnick, 1998).

Medications designed for other uses can affect sperm production and might offer future possibilities for contraception. The drug N-butyldeoxynojirimycin, which is used to treat a genetic disorder, has been found to cause infertility in mice without having an effect on testosterone levels or sexual behavior. The mice regain their fertility after 4 weeks off the drug (Stephenson, 2003a). Another possible medication is a cancer drug, lonidamine, which reduces normal sperm production (Schwartz & Gabelnick, 2002).

New Directions for Women

In contrast to the limited existing and new developments for male contraception, an array of contraceptive methods for women are currently under experimentation. The search for an oral contraceptive pill without side effects and greater effectiveness continues. Implants are used outside the United States and may become available again in the United States in the future (Akert, 2003). An IUD used in Great Britain, the Gynefix, is made from six copper sleeves threaded on a length of nonbiodegradable suture material. It is flexible and has fewer side effects of bleeding, pain, and discomfort than other IUDs (Odejinmi, 2000). Variations of the original female condom are under development. Spermicides that also contain microbicides (substances that stop STD transmission) are under development (Schwartz & Gabelnik, 2002). Developing one that protects against all STDs, including HIV, is critical, especially because women are more vulnerable to contracting these diseases from intercourse than men are (D'Cruz & Uckun, 2003). Vaccines that stimulate the immune system to shut down the functions necessary for pregnancy, called *immunocontraceptives*, are also under study (Mann, 2003). Additional methods of transcervical sterilization are in clinical trials (Schwartz & Gabelnick, 2002).

Since the advent of the pill, contraceptive options have greatly increased. However, the ideal of 100% effective, reversible contraceptives for men and women that have no side effects and that protect against sexually transmitted infections will, unfortunately, not be available in the foreseeable future.

◆ Summary

Historical and Social Perspectives
- From the beginning of recorded history, humankind has been concerned with birth control. (p. 300)
- Margaret Sanger opened the first birth control clinics in the United States at a time when it was illegal to provide birth control information and devices. (p. 300)
- Objections to contraception stem from religious doctrine. However, most church members in the United States use some kind of artificial contraception. (pp. 302–303)

Sharing Responsibility and Choosing a Birth Control Method
- The male partner can share contraceptive responsibility by being informed, asking a new partner about birth control, accompanying his partner to her exam, using condoms and/or coital abstinence if the couple chooses, and sharing the expense of the exam and method. (pp. 303–304)
- Comparison of relative convenience, safety, cost, and effectiveness may influence the choice of contraception. (p. 305)

- People who feel guilty and have negative attitudes about sexuality are less likely to use contraception effectively than people who have positive attitudes about sexuality. (p. 305)

Hormone-Based Contraceptives

- Four types of oral contraceptives are currently available. The constant-dose combination pill contains steady doses of estrogen and progestin. The triphasic pill provides fluctuations of estrogen and progesterone levels throughout the cycle. Seasonale reduces menstrual cycles to four per year. The progestin-only pill consists of low-dose progestin. (pp. 307–310)
- Advantages of oral contraceptives are high effectiveness and lack of interference with sexual activity. Birth control pills are also associated with lower incidences of uterine and ovarian cancer, ovarian cysts, benign breast disease, and pelvic inflammatory disease. An additional advantage is reduction of menstrual flow and cramps. The advantage of the progestin-only pill is the reduced chance of harmful side effects. The vaginal ring, NuvaRing; the transdermal patch, Ortho Evra; and the injectable Depo-Provera are hormone-based contraceptives that do not require remembering to take a pill each day for maximum effectiveness. (pp. 311–312, 314)
- Some of the disadvantages of hormone-based contraceptives are possible side effects such as blood clots, increased probability of heart attack, high blood pressure, more rapid growth of cancer of the breast and uterus, depression, and reduced sexual interest. Disadvantages of the progestin-only pill include irregular bleeding and the possibility of additional side effects. In general, the health risks of oral contraceptives are far lower than those from pregnancy and birth. (pp. 312–313)
- Depo-Provera is an injectable contraceptive that lasts for 3 months. (p. 314)

Barrier and Spermicide Methods

- Condoms are available in a variety of styles. Advantages include protection from sexually transmitted diseases, improved ejaculatory control, and ready availability as a backup method. Disadvantages include interruption of sexual activity and reduced penile sensation. A female condom has also been developed. (pp. 315–318)
- Vaginal spermicides (including contraceptive foam, the sponge, vaginal suppositories, creams and jellies, and contraceptive film) are available without a prescription. Advantages of vaginal spermicides are lack of serious side effects and added lubrication. Disadvantages include possible irritation of genital tissues and interruption of sexual activity. (pp. 318–320)
- Advantages of cervical barrier methods include lack of side effects, high effectiveness with knowledgeable and consistent use, and possible promotion of vaginal health. Some disadvantages are interruption of sexual activity, potential irritation from the spermicidal cream or jelly, and possible misplacement during insertion or intercourse. (pp. 320–322)

Intrauterine Devices

- The Copper-T, Progestasert T, and Mirena are currently the only intrauterine devices (IUDs) on the U.S. market. Advantages of the IUD include uninterrupted sexual interaction and simplicity of use. Disadvantages include the possibility of increased cramping, spontaneous expulsion, uterine perforation, pelvic inflammatory disease, and pregnancy complications. (pp. 322–324)

Emergency Contraception

- Oral contraceptives and the Copper-T IUD can be used for emergency contraception when a woman has had unprotected intercourse. (pp. 324–325)

Fertility Awareness Methods

- Methods based on the menstrual cycle—including the standard days, mucus, calendar, and basal body temperature methods—help in planning coital activity to avoid a woman's fertile period. (pp. 325–327)

Sterilization

- At this time sterilization should be considered permanent. A decision to be sterilized should be carefully evaluated. (p. 327)
- Tubal ligation is the sterilization procedure most commonly performed for women. It does not alter a woman's hormone levels, menstrual cycle, or the timing of menopause. (pp. 328–329)
- Vasectomy, the sterilization procedure for men, is not effective for birth control immediately after surgery because sperm remain in the vas deferens above the incision. Most men report that vasectomy does not affect their sexual functioning. (pp. 329–330)

Less-Than-Effective Methods

- Breast feeding, douching, and the withdrawal method are not reliable methods of contraception. (pp. 330–331)

New Directions in Contraception

- Possible contraceptive methods for men in the future include the use of hormones or medications that would reduce the number and motility of sperm. (pp. 331–332)
- Possible future contraceptive methods for women include reintroduction of hormone-based implants, variations of the IUD, spermicides that contain microbicides effective against STDs, and immunocontraceptives (vaccines that stimulate the immune system to block pregnancy). (p. 332)

▶ Suggested Readings

Hatcher, Robert, et al. (2004). *Contraceptive Technology,* 18th edition. New York: Ardent Media. A comprehensive, up-to-date book about birth control—a must for anyone who wants the latest information about the technology and effects of contraception.

Kass-Annesse, Barbara, and Hal Danzer (1986). *The Fertility Awareness Workbook.* Atlanta: Printed Matter. A workbook containing fertility awareness charts, step-by-step instructions on how to record fertility signs, and specific advice on how to prevent pregnancy using fertility awareness.

Knowles, Jon (1998). *All About Birth Control: A Personal Guide.* New York: Three Rivers Press. A rich guide to virtually all the contraceptive choices and how to choose the right one for you.

Mclaren, Angus (1990). *A History of Contraception.* Oxford, England: Basil Blackwell. A scholarly and readable history of the uses and meaning of fertility control through the ages.

Tone, Andrea (2002). *Devices and Desires: A History of Contraceptives in America.* New York: Hill and Wang. An intricate history of birth control in the United States, from Victorian pessaries to alleged racism in government policies.

▶ Web Resources

Your *Our Sexuality* Web site **http://psychology.wadsworth.com/ crooksbaur9e/** has direct links to the Web sites described below. These links are checked often for changes, dead links, and new additions.

Margaret Sanger Papers Project

The life, writings, and work of the American birth control pioneer, Margaret Sanger, are highlighted on this site. The Web site also includes an extensive list of links to related sites.

Successful Contraception

The Association of Reproductive Health Professionals provides this Web site. Along with excellent information about various methods of contraception, this site includes an interactive feature to help you choose the method of birth control most appropriate for you.

International Planned Parenthood Federation

The well-known organization promoting family planning and contraception provides this Web site, which features breaking news, press releases, journal articles, and other resources.

Contraceptive Choices

A quick guide to the advantages and disadvantages of various types of contraception are included on this Web page sponsored by the Planned Parenthood Federation of America.

Emergency Contraception

Detailed information about emergency contraception, including how to use certain oral contraceptives for emergency contraception.

When Timing Is Everything

A full array of birth control pill cases with alarm notification to help women remember when to take their pill.

Condomania

Search through hundreds of different types of condoms.

Our Sexuality Web Site

For online resources directly related to this book, go to **http://psychology.wadsworth.com/ crooksbaur9e/**. You will find interactive exercises, study questions, chapter outlines, an online version of this text's glossary, and Web links and activities that complement your CD-ROM.

InfoTrac® College Edition Online Library

http://infotrac.thomsonlearning.com/

InfoTrac College Edition is an online searchable library that includes a multitude of journals, many of which are specific to human sexuality. These journals include *Archives of Sexual Behavior, Archives of Sexual Health Behavior, Canadian Journal of Human Sexuality, Hispanic Journal of the Behavioral Sciences, Journal of Cross-Cultural Psychology, Journal of Physical Education, Recreation, and Dance, Journal of Sex Research,* and *Sex Roles.* You may search topics suggested in the margins of this chapter or terms of your own.

Our Sexuality CD-ROM

Use your CD-ROM for further study of the concepts in this chapter. Your CD-ROM provides animations of difficult concepts, video clips of real people discussing sexuality, critical thinking questions, chapter quizzing, and more.

Conceiving Children: Process and Choice

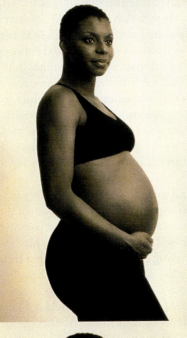
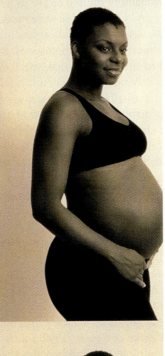

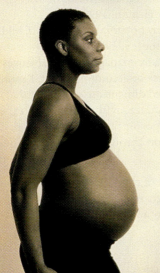

© Michael Krasowitz/Getty Images

▶ **Parenthood as an Option**

What are the pros and cons of being parents or remaining child-free?

▶ **Becoming Pregnant**

What are some of the causes of male and female infertility?

What treatments are available for infertility? How do they work?

▶ **Spontaneous and Elective Abortion**

How can a miscarriage affect a woman and couple emotionally?

What procedures are used for abortion?

▶ **The Experience of Pregnancy**

How does pregnancy affect sexuality?

▶ **A Healthy Pregnancy**

How does the fetus change in each trimester of pregnancy?

What factors can harm the fetus during pregnancy?

▶ **Childbirth**

What options are available for childbirth in the United States today?

What occurs in each of the three stages of childbirth?

▶ **After Childbirth**

What are advantages and disadvantages of breast feeding?

What criteria should a couple use to decide when to resume intercourse?

I've been an "expectant" father twice, but my role was drastically different the second time because of changes in obstetrical practices. During my first child's birth, it was the classic scene of Dad pacing the waiting room floor while my wife was in the delivery room. In my second marriage, the pregnancy was "our pregnancy" from the beginning. I went to doctor's appointments and saw our baby's ultrasound pictures. Seeing his heart beat so early in the pregnancy gave me a feeling of connection right from the start. We attended prepared childbirth classes together, and I was there from start to finish during labor and when she delivered our baby. I went with him to the nursery for all the weighing, measuring, and cleaning, then brought him back to his mother in the birthing suite. I wish I'd had those experiences with my first child's birth. (Authors' files)

One of the most important decisions you will probably make in your lifetime is whether or not to become a parent. In this chapter we address the pros and cons of parenthood. We also discuss the processes of conception, pregnancy, and birth and some of the emotions that accompany them from the viewpoints of the parents. We encourage people who desire further information to seek more extensive references or to consult a health care practitioner. As a starting point, we look at the option of parenthood and some of the alternatives that are available for people who want to become parents.

▶ Parenthood as an Option

More couples and individuals than in the past are choosing to be "kid free." In 1975 almost 9% of 40-year-old women did not have children; in 1997 almost 17% were childless (Clark, 2000). A national probability sample of 16- to 39-year-olds found that 14% of the respondents were very sure and another 14% were moderately sure that they would not have children (Schoen, 1999). Remaining childless has many potential advantages. Individuals and couples have much more time for themselves, more financial resources, and more spontaneity with regard to their recreational, social, and work patterns. Nonparents can more fully pursue careers, leaving more opportunity for fulfillment in their professional lives. At the same time, there is usually more time and energy for companionship and intimacy in an adult relationship (Carroll, 2000). As one woman who does not have children stated, "As I moved through my childbearing years, I never found a good way to reconcile . . . my longings to nurture a child and to explore the world. Over the past two decades, these desires have been irreconcilable for me—to my lingering regret at moments, but ultimately to my measured relief" (Lisle, 1996, pp. 3–4).

In general, childless marriages are less stressful; and some studies show that they are happier and more satisfying than marriages with children, especially in the years following a first child's birth (Crohan, 1996; Lavee et al., 1996). Note, however, that this discrepancy might be due in part to the fact that many unhappily married couples remain together because they have young children. Research indicates that having a baby does not help a troubled marriage. In fact, couples who had the most strain following the birth of their baby had the most marital problems before the pregnancy (Cowan & Cowan, 1992). Not having to worry about providing for the physical and psychological needs of children can make a difference, because conflict about *who* does *what* for the children is a major source of disenchantment for many couples (Cowan & Cowan, 1992; Johnson & Huston, 1998).

Having adopted or biological children also has many potential advantages. Children give as well as receive love, and their presence can enhance the love between couples as they share in the experiences of raising their offspring. Successfully managing the challenges of parenthood can also build self-esteem and provide a sense of accomplishment. Parenthood is often an opportunity for discovering new and untapped dimensions of oneself that can give one's life greater meaning and satisfaction. Many parents say that they have experienced tremendous personal growth and have become better people through parenthood. Children offer ongoing stimulation and change as they develop through childhood, as one father experienced:

> His presence . . . allowed me to experience the world of childhood, where everything is free and spontaneous. Past memories, long since forgotten, of earlier years and relationships with my own family would surface, effortlessly, to my awareness. (Greenburg, 1986, p. 7)

The potential rewards of either becoming parents or remaining childless can be romanticized or unrealistic for a given person or couple, and some people experience considerable ambivalence.

> I wish I could decide once and for all to have a baby, or even figure out whether I want one. Then I could plan the rest of my life. . . . One day I'm so absorbed by my career that I think I can't possibly have a child. Then the next day, I'm staring somewhat jealously at pregnant women. (Faux, 1984, p. 167)

There are no guarantees that the benefits of either having children or living child-free will meet your expectations. Still, it is important to consciously consider the options beforehand, because parenthood is a permanent and major life decision and responsibility. And because we all change, your feelings about parenthood may very well change during your life. As one writer put it, having children changes your life—but so does not having them (Cole, 1987). ■

▶ Becoming Pregnant

There are, of course, several options for becoming parents without actually experiencing pregnancy and childbirth. However, most people who have children are biological parents. In the remainder of this chapter we look at some of the developments, experiences, and feelings involved in the physiological process of becoming parents, starting with becoming pregnant. This first step can be difficult for some couples.

Enhancing the Possibility of Conception

Picking the right time for intercourse is important in increasing the probability of conception. Conception is most likely to occur during a 6-day period ending on the day of ovulation, but, of course, the data also suggest that conception is more likely when the interval between sexual activity and ovulation is short (Wilcox et al., 1995). It is difficult to predict the exact time of ovulation, but several methods permit a reasonable approximation. One is the mucus method discussed in Chapter 11, in which coital activity is timed according to the fertile period in the woman's menstrual cycle. Body temperature and the principles of the calendar method can also be used to estimate ovulation time. Ovulation predictor tests, which measure the rise in luteinizing hormone (LH) in urine before ovulation, can accurately identify the best time for conception and can be purchased over the counter (Perris, 2000). ■

The first stage of pregnancy—only one of the sperm surrounding this ovum will fertilize it.

Some individuals and couples are interested in enhancing the possibility of conceiving a child of a specific sex, as discussed in the "Sexuality and Diversity" section.

▶ Sexuality and Diversity

Preselecting the Baby's Sex: Technology and Cross-Cultural Issues

The desire to have a child of a certain sex has existed since ancient times, when sex selection was done after the fact. For example, in ancient Roman society infanticide was practiced against unwanted female babies (Faerman et al., 1997). Superstitions about determining the sex of the child during intercourse are part of Western folk tradition—for example, the belief that if a man wears a hat during intercourse, he will father a male child or that if a man hangs his trousers on the left bedpost, he will sire a girl.

The most recent technique for sex selection, preimplantation genetic diagnosis (PGD), creates embryos in the laboratory. The sex of the embryos is tested, and a physician subsequently inserts the embryos of the desired sex into the woman's uterus. The approximately $20,000 procedure offers almost 100% certainty of the sex of the baby (Kalb, 2004). Less certain results occur with the more commonly used laboratory techniques that can separate X-chromosome-bearing sperm from Y-chromosome-bearing sperm. Once the laboratory separation process is complete, the desired X or Y fraction is introduced into the vagina by artificial insemination. Success rates are about 90% for female babies and 70% for male babies. However, the rather "unromantic" nature of semen collection and artificial insemination will probably limit the use of such sperm-separation techniques unless parents have compelling reasons to conceive a child of a particular sex (Berkowitz, 2000). Sex preselection offers benefits to couples at risk for passing on X-chromosome-linked diseases to their children. Additional technology for sex preselection is being developed (Kahn, 1999b).

In some Asian countries—China, India, and South Korea—the preference for a son is particularly strong, and infanticide and selective abortion of female fetuses are common (Carmichael, 2004). Prenatal ultrasound and amniocentesis make sex-selection abortion possible. Laws banning the use of prenatal testing for sex-selection abortion have been passed in these countries, but it still occurs illegally (Faison, 1997; Kumar, 1994). Economic and cultural factors contribute to the importance of sons. For example, in India daughters are a financial liability to the family. They will belong to the family into which they marry and require the expense of a dowry. However, sons provide for parents through their old age, offering security in the absence of governmental social support (Hwang & Saenz, 1997). In Hindu and Confucian religious traditions in Asia, only sons can pray for and release the souls of dead parents (McCauley et al., 1994). China's one-child policy has greatly reduced the birthrate—from 4.8 children per family in 1970 to 1.8 today—but parents' desire to have that one child be male has altered the natural birth ratio from 100 girls to 105 boys to 100 girls to 118 boys (Robinson, 1999).

Infertility

Sixty percent of couples become pregnant within 3 months, but if attempts at impregnation are unsuccessful after 6 months, a couple should consult a physician (Ono, 1994). It has been estimated that as many as 1 in 6 U.S. couples attempting pregnancy experiences fertility problems, defined as not conceiving after at least 1 year (Sandlow, 2000). Because approximately 50% of infertility cases involve male factors, it is important that both partners be evaluated (Jegalian & Lahn, 2001b). We usually think of infertility as the inability to conceive any children, but secondary infertility—the inability to conceive a second child—occurs in 10% of couples (Diamond et al., 1999).

Infertility is a complex and distressing problem (Higgins, 2003). It can have a demoralizing effect on the infertile individual's sense of self and on the couple's sense of their integrity as a healthy unit (Scharf & Weinshel, 2000). Its causes are sometimes difficult to determine and remain unidentified in as many as 15% of cases (Nilsson et al., 1994). In addition, most couples seeking treatment for infertility are ultimately unsuccessful in their efforts to conceive, despite trying various avenues of treatment (Toner, 2002). In this section we look briefly at some common causes of female and male infertility and at the effects that infertility can have on individuals and their sexuality.

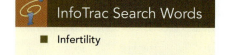

InfoTrac Search Words

■ Infertility

Female Infertility

A woman can have difficulty conceiving or be unable to conceive for a number of reasons. Failure to ovulate at regular intervals is common. This can be caused by a variety of factors, including age (Chuang et al., 2003; Gibbs, 2002), hormone imbalances, severe vitamin deficiencies, metabolic disturbances, poor nutrition, genetic factors, emotional stress, or medical conditions (Marx & Mehta, 2003). Ovulation and thus pregnancy can also be inhibited by a below-normal percentage of body fat that results from excessive dieting or exercise. Even 10–15% below normal weight is sufficient to inhibit ovulation (Frisch, 1988). Women who smoke cigarettes are less fertile and take longer to become pregnant than nonsmokers (Matikainen, 2001). Smokers are also more likely to experience ectopic pregnancy (Bouyer et al., 2003). Alcohol and drug abuse reduces fertility in women, and environmental toxins can also impair female fertility (Clarke, 2001; Thomson, 2000). Ovulation problems can sometimes be treated with a variety of medications that stimulate ovulation. Although often successful and generally safe, these drugs can produce certain complications, including a greatly increased chance of multiple births (Filicori, 2003).

If tests indicate that the woman is ovulating and that her partner's semen quality is satisfactory, the next step often is a postcoital test to see whether the sperm remain viable and motile in the cervical mucus (Chretien, 2003). A woman's cervical mucus can contain antibodies that attack her partner's sperm, or it can form a plug that blocks their passage (Ginsburg et al., 1997). Intrauterine insemination, placing semen directly into the uterus, can be helpful in some cases.

Infections and abnormalities of the cervix, vagina, uterus, fallopian tubes, or ovaries can destroy sperm or prevent them from reaching the egg (Rebar, 2004). Problems with the fallopian tubes account for as much as 36% of cases of female infertility (Healy et al., 1994). Scar tissue from old infections—in the fallopian tubes or in or around the ovaries—can block the passage of sperm and eggs. Sexually transmitted diseases (STDs) are a common cause of these problems. Tubal problems can sometimes be resolved by surgically removing the scar tissue around the fallopian tubes and ovaries. Defects in the uterine cavity can also result in infertility (Faerstein et al., 2001).

Male Infertility

Most causes of male infertility are related to abnormalities in sperm number and/or motility (i.e., sperm cells that do not

Some fertility specialists think that celebrity moms who have babies later in life, such as Susan Sarandon, give the false impression that conception at any age is easy.

propel themselves with sufficient vigor). Male infertility can result from a number of causes, including nutritional deficits (W. Wong et al., 2000). Infectious diseases of the male reproductive tract can alter sperm production, viability, and transport (Villanueva-Diaz et al., 1999). For instance, mumps, when it occurs in adulthood, can affect the testes, lowering sperm output; and infection of the vas deferens can block the passage of sperm. Infections caused by STDs are another major cause of infertility. Smoking, alcohol, and drug use and abuse reduce fertility as well (Kunzle et al., 2003; Sandlow, 2000). Cocaine use decreases spermatogenesis, and marijuana impedes sperm motility (Leibowitz & Hoffman, 2000).

Environmental toxins, such as chemicals, pollutants, and radiation, can also produce low sperm counts and abnormal sperm cells (Duty et al., 2003; Pearson, 2002; Rosa et al., 2003). Recent studies have found that traffic pollution and chemicals used during the Gulf War negatively affect sperm. Men who had a high exposure to auto exhaust because of their work as tollbooth attendants had damaged sperm compared to matched control subjects (Rosa et al., 2003). Animal studies of the insecticides and anti–nerve gas chemicals that Gulf War soldiers used have found deterioration in testicular structure and sperm production (Abou-Donia et al., 2003). Sperm absorb and metabolize environmental toxins more easily than do other body cells, which can also result in birth defects (Tanenbaun, 1997).

Congenital abnormalities of the vas deferens, epididymus, and seminal vesicles can result in infertility (Vohra & Morgentaler, 1997). A major cause of infertility in men is a damaged or enlarged vein in the testis or vas deferens, called a **varicocele** (Ehrenfeld, 2002). The varicocele causes blood to pool in the scrotum, which elevates temperature in the area, impairing sperm production (Stephenson, 2003b).

Varicocele A damaged or enlarged vein in the testis or vas deferens.

An unlikely cause of male sterility is undescended testes. If this condition is not corrected before puberty, sperm will be less likely to mature because of the higher temperatures in the abdomen. Hormone deficiencies can also result in an inadequate number of sperm cells in the semen. This situation can sometimes be remedied by hormone therapy.

When the sperm count is low, the optimal frequency of ejaculation during intercourse is usually every other day, beginning 6 days before ovulation and during the week that the woman is ovulating, to increase the concentration of sperm (Speroff et al., 1989). Under such circumstances it is especially important for a couple to chart the woman's cycle so that they can reasonably predict her most fertile time. A man with a borderline sperm count might also want to avoid taking hot baths, wearing tight clothing and undershorts, and riding bicycles long distances, because these and similar environments subject the testes to higher than normal temperatures. ■

Sexual Health

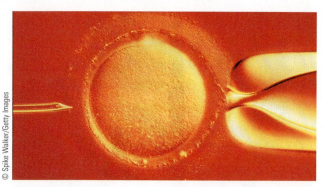

An ovum is injected with a single sperm in intracytoplasmic sperm injection (ICSI).

Intracytoplasmic sperm injection (ICSI) Procedure in which a sperm is injected into an egg.

For poor semen quality or quantity, two new reproductive technologies have made pregnancy possible in previously untreatable cases of male infertility. The first procedure is a simple surgical biopsy or needle aspiration of the testes or epididymus to retrieve sperm. The second technology is **intracytoplasmic sperm injection (ICSI).** ICSI involves injecting each harvested egg with a single sperm. Fertilization rates are comparable to in vitro (in a laboratory dish) fertilization with sperm from normal ejaculation. Before the advent of these two technologies, the only options were donor insemination or adoption (Gibbs, 2002).

Infertility and Sexuality

Most people grow up believing that they can conceive children when they decide to begin a family. Confronting infertility is an unanticipated shock and crisis (Kossman, 2002). Women usually tend to express more emotional distress about infertility than do their male partners, but both men and women experience increased anxiety, depression, and stress (Cowen, 2003). However, the man is more likely to experience emotional distress when he is the cause of the infertility (Nasseri, 2000). As their infertility becomes more evident and undeniable, a couple may feel a great sense of isolation from others during social discussions of pregnancy, childbirth, and child rearing (Schulman, 2000). As one woman who has been unable to conceive stated:

Coffee breaks at work are the worst times; everyone brings out their pictures of their kids and discusses their latest parental trials and tribulations. When one of the women complains about having problems with something like child care, I just want to shout at her and tell her how lucky she is to be able to have such a "problem." (Authors' files)

Problems with infertility can have profoundly negative effects on a couple's relationship and sexual functioning. Partners can also become isolated from each other and believe that the other does not really understand. Each partner might feel inadequate about his or her masculinity or femininity because of problems with conceiving. Each may feel anger and guilt and wonder, "Why me?" Finally, both may feel grief over life experiences they can never have, namely, pregnancy, birth, and conceiving and rearing their own biological children (Miller, 2003). Intercourse itself can evoke these uncomfortable feelings and can become an emotionally painful rather than pleasurable experience, fraught with anxiety about failing to conceive (Raphael-Leff, 2003). Studies have found that most infertile couples experience some sexual dissatisfaction or dysfunction at one point or another (Zoldbrod, 1993).

In addition, the medical procedures used in fertility diagnosis and treatment are often disruptive to the couple's sexual spontaneity and privacy. Sex can become stressful and mechanical. Taking a daily basal body temperature and timing intercourse according to ovulation can create performance anxiety that interferes with sexual arousal and emotional closeness (Pawson, 2003). Because of these psychological and sexual stresses, health care practitioners who work with infertility problems need to be sensitive to and skilled in helping affected couples (Christie & Morgan, 2003).

Alternatives to Intercourse for Conception

Artificial insemination A medical procedure in which semen is placed in a woman's vagina, cervix, or uterus.

Surrogate mother A woman who is artificially inseminated by the male partner in a childless couple, carries the pregnancy to term, delivers the child, and gives it to the couple for adoption.

Various alternatives have been developed to help couples overcome the problem of infertility. **Artificial insemination** is one option to be considered in certain instances. In this procedure semen is mechanically introduced into the woman's vagina or cervix or, in some cases, after the semen is specially prepared, directly into her uterus, a procedure called *intrauterine insemination.* Artificial insemination can also be used when it is critical for a couple to preselect the sex of their baby. If the man is not producing adequate viable sperm or if a woman does not have a male partner, artificial insemination with a donor's semen is another option. Approximately 70,000 babies are born from sperm donor pregnancies each year in the United States, mainly to single women and lesbians (Noonan & Springen, 2001).

A **surrogate mother** is a woman who is willing to be artificially inseminated by the male partner of a childless couple or who is willing to undergo in vitro fertilization using eggs and sperm from a couple. She carries the pregnancy to term, delivers the child, and gives it to the couple for adoption. Surrogacy can be done anonymously through an attorney or privately by arrangement between the woman and the couple. Surrogate mothers typically receive a fee that can range from $0 to $20,000 (Surrogate Mothers Inc., 2003).

Advances in reproductive technology have developed methods that can be used when infertility is due to blocked fallopian tubes, severe endometriosis, very low sperm count, or inability of sperm to survive in the woman's cervix and when infertility is unexplained. These technological advances are referred to as **assisted reproductive technology (ART).** The world's first test-tube baby, born in England in 1978, provided impetus to research in this area. By 1999 about 1 out of every 100 to 150 babies born in the Western world was conceived with in vitro fertilization (Fauser & te Velde, 2000). In **in vitro fertilization (IVF)** the ovaries are stimulated by fertility drugs to produce multiple mature ova. Then mature eggs are removed from the woman's ovary and are fertilized in a laboratory dish by her partner's sperm. After 2 or 3 days several fertilized eggs of two to eight cells each are then introduced into the woman's uterus. Excess embryos are often frozen so that if the first implantation does not take place, the procedure can be repeated (Fosas et al., 2003). If this procedure is successful, at least one egg will implant and develop. Because more than one fertilized ovum is placed in the uterus, there is an increased chance of triplets or higher multiple births, unless only two embryos are transferred to the uterus (Kurdas, 1999).

Variations on IVF involve transferring cells to the fallopian tube rather than to the uterus. In a procedure known as **zygote intrafallopian transfer (ZIFT),** the egg is fertilized in the laboratory and then placed in the fallopian tube. In a more recently developed procedure, known as **gamete intrafallopian transfer (GIFT),** the sperm and ova are placed directly in the fallopian tube, where fertilization normally occurs.

Donated ova can be used for IVF when the woman does not have ovaries, does not produce her own ova, or has a heritable genetic disease. Donation of ova is analogous to donor artificial insemination. Donors are usually women in their 20s, a sister or friend of the infertile woman, or another woman undergoing IVF who donates her ova to another woman wanting the IVF procedure. Advances in ova retrieval techniques have made the procedures safe and easy enough for women who are not undergoing IVF ova retrieval for themselves to donate ova (Hummel & Kettel, 1997). In cases in which both partners are infertile, IVF can be done with both donated sperm and donated ova (Kingsberg et al., 2000).

Health and Financial Problems with Assisted Reproductive Techniques

Assisted reproductive techniques are expensive and not usually successful, as shown in Table 12.1. One attempt at IVF costs between $6,000 and $12,000. Each subsequent attempt costs

Assisted reproductive technology (ART) The techniques of extrauterine conception.

In vitro fertilization (IVF) Procedure in which mature eggs are removed from a woman's ovary and fertilized by sperm in a laboratory dish.

InfoTrac Search Words

- Assisted reproductive technologies

Zygote intrafallopian transfer (ZIFT) Procedure in which the egg is fertilized in the laboratory and then placed in the fallopian tube.

Gamete intrafallopian transfer (GIFT) Procedure in which the sperm and ova are placed directly in the fallopian tube.

? Critical Thinking Question

Do you think children conceived by donor sperm and/or egg insemination should be told about this? Why or why not?

TABLE 12.1	Against the Odds: How Assisted Reproductive Techniques Compare		
Method	**Number of Procedures Done Each Year**	**Success Rate (%)[a]**	**Cost per Attempt**
Intrauterine insemination	600,000	20–25	$100 with sperm from partner, $300 with sperm from donor
IVF (in vitro fertilization)	27,000	23	$6,000–$10,000[b]
GIFT (gamete intrafallopian transfer)	4,200	27	$6,000–$10,000[b]
ZIFT (zygote intrafallopian transfer)	1,500	28	$8,000–$10,000[b]
ICSI (intracytoplasmic sperm injection)	1,000	24	$10,000–$12,000

[a]Success rates drop dramatically with women over age 40.
[b]Donor eggs add $3,000 to $7,500 to the cost.

SOURCES: Begley (1995) and Hatcher (1998).

the same. Pregnancy and live-birth rates from ART have increased after 20 years of medical development. However, live-birth rates from ART remain low. Live-birth rates from IVF are less than 30%, donor egg live-birth rates are 40%, and cryopreservation results in 20% live births (Toner, 2002). In addition, infants conceived by the various assisted reproductive technologies are more likely than infants conceived naturally to have a lower birth weight. The lower birth weight might be related to factors involved in the parents' infertility rather than the ART itself (Gaudoin et al., 2003).

Multiple births are a significant problem with ART, posing dangers to mothers and babies. They were a rare event 20 years ago, before reproductive technologies. Since then, about 30% of pregnancies achieved with fertility treatments result in multiple births (Gorman, 2002), as shown in Figure 12.1. Multiple births often exceed twins or triplets; the much publicized McCaughey septuplets, born in 1997, highlighted this phenomenon (Cowley & Springen, 1997). Multiple embryos are implanted during IVF to increase the chances of conception. Any multiple birth increases the danger to babies, with greater incidence of prematurity, low birth weight, birth defects, and postnatal death (Kalb, 2003b; Stromberg et al.,

The Normal Ovary

During normal ovulation, one follicle matures, releasing its egg for fertilization in the fallopian tube.

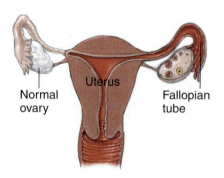

The Ovary on Drugs

Fertility drugs jump-start follicle development, increasing the likelihood that more than one follicle will release a fertile egg. Drug treatment can make the ovaries swell up to 10 times their normal volume—roughly the size of a grapefruit.

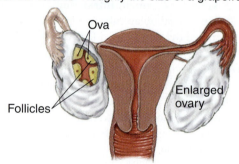

Multiple Birth

The human uterus is not designed to hold numerous fetuses. When it is forced to, the crowding causes early delivery. The consequences for babies can range from brain damage to death.

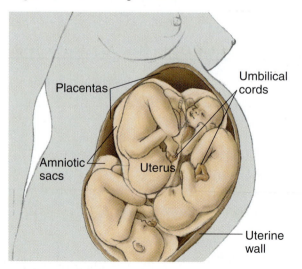

▶ **Figure 12.1** Women's hormonal rhythms normally ensure production of just one viable egg every month. By forcing the release of numerous eggs at once, fertility drugs raise the chance of multiple births (Cowley & Springen, 1997).

2002). In some cases one or more fetuses are aborted during the pregnancy to increase the likelihood that at least one other will survive. For mothers the risks of cesarean deliveries, high blood pressure, and other birth complications increase with multiple births (Dickey, 2003; Keith & Breborowicz, 2002). As a physician stated, "The human uterus is not meant to carry litters" (Heyl, 1997, p. 66). Fertility specialists have reduced the incidence of multiple births by altering their procedures (Jain et al., 2004). In the "On the Edge" box we discuss other dilemmas presented by assisted reproductive technologies.

Pregnancy Detection

The initial signs of pregnancy can provoke feelings from joy to dread, depending on the woman's desire to be pregnant, her partner's feelings, and a variety of surrounding circumstances. Although some women have either a light blood flow or spotting (irregular bleeding) after conception at the time of implantation, usually the first indications of pregnancy are fatigue and the absence of the menstrual period at the expected time. Breast tenderness, nausea, vomiting, or other nonspecific symptoms (such as extreme fatigue or change in appetite) can also accompany pregnancy in the first weeks or months.

Any or all of these clues might cause a woman to suspect that she is pregnant. Medical techniques such as blood or urine tests and pelvic exams can make the determination with greater certainty. The blood and hence urine of a pregnant woman contains the hormone **human chorionic gonadotropin** (cohr-ee-AH-nik goh-na-duh-TROH-pun) **(HCG),** which is secreted by the placenta. Sensitive blood tests for HCG have been developed that can detect pregnancy as early as 7 days after conception (G. Stewart, 1998). Commercially available at-home pregnancy urine or saliva tests can detect pregnancy shortly after a missed menstrual period (Carmichael, 2002). Because elective home pregnancy tests can yield both false-positive and false-negative results, they should always be confirmed by a health care practitioner.

Domestic partners Michael Meehan and Thomas Dysarz hold the year-old quadruplets born in 2002 to a surrogate mother and conceived through in vitro fertilization using Michael's sperm. Now active and healthy, the babies weighed about 3 pounds at birth and spent their first month of life in neonatal intensive care (DeLaMar, 2003).

Human chorionic gonadotropin (HCG) A hormone that is detectable in the urine of a pregnant woman within 1 month of conception.

▶ Spontaneous and Elective Abortion

Not every pregnancy results in a birth. Many end in spontaneous or elective abortion.

Spontaneous abortion, or miscarriage The spontaneous expulsion of the fetus from the uterus early in pregnancy, before it can survive on its own.

Miscarriage

Even when pregnancy has been confirmed, complications can prevent full-term development of the fetus. Various genetic, medical, or hormonal problems can cause a **spontaneous abortion,** or **miscarriage,** to occur, terminating the pregnancy. A miscarriage is a spontaneous abortion that occurs in the first 20 weeks of pregnancy.

About 10–15% of known pregnancies end in miscarriage (Schieve et al., 2003). Most miscarriages occur in the first trimester (the first 13 weeks) of pregnancy; many occur before the woman knows she is pregnant. Table 12.2 gives the most common causes of miscarriage, but in many cases doctors are unable to determine the specific cause (Thompson, 2003a).

Early miscarriages can appear as a heavier than usual menstrual flow; later miscarriages might involve uncomfortable cramping and heavy bleeding. Fortunately for women who desire a child, one miscarriage rarely means that a later pregnancy will be unsuccessful.

TABLE 12.2	Prime Suspects: Possible Causes of Miscarriage
More than 5 alcoholic drinks per week	
More than 375 mg of caffeine per day (2–3 cups of coffee)	
Rejection of abnormal fetus	
Cocaine use	
Damaged cervix	
Chronic kidney inflammation	
Abnormal uterus	
Infection	
Underactive thyroid gland	
Autoimmune reaction	
Diabetes	
Emotional shock	
Aspirin and nonsteroidal anti-inflammatory drugs early in pregnancy	

SOURCES: Kleiner (2000), D. Li et al. (2003), and Rasch (2003).

Ethical, Legal, and Personal Dilemmas of Assisted Reproductive Technologies

Assisted reproductive technologies have presented our society with unprecedented ethical and legal dilemmas (Haynes & Miller, 2003). The bitter battle in the 1980s between a surrogate mother and the biological father and his wife over the legal parenthood of Baby M drew attention to conflicts with assisted reproductive technologies. The husband of the couple had contributed the sperm to impregnate the surrogate mother's egg because his wife had multiple sclerosis. The surrogate mother decided she wanted to keep the baby instead of relinquishing it to the couple. The court eventually decided in favor of the couple, stipulating visitation rights to the surrogate mother.

© National Enquirer

After trying to get pregnant for 16 years, this couple had a healthy infant daughter, named Cynthia, in 1996 through assisted reproductive technology. At the time, Cynthia's birth made her mother, at age 63, the oldest woman to give birth.

Other issues have added controversy and the need to establish guidelines and laws to regulate the human complications of assisted reproductive technologies. In the late 1980s the first legal struggle over control of frozen embryos arose. A divorcing couple differed over what to do with the frozen embryos developed from their sperm and eggs before they ended their marriage. Of the 150,000 frozen embryos across the country, more than 20,000 of them are under dispute (Silvertsen, 2000). In general, courts rule against the ex-spouse who wants to implant the embryo to have a child. However, some ethicists believe that because constitutional principles give a woman the right to continue a pregnancy over her male partner's objections, a woman undergoing ART should have the same legal right to continue her pregnancy, even if the embryo has not yet been implanted (Daar, 1999). Some clinics now require an advance directive from the couple about embryo disposition before they will begin IVF, but even these directives can be legally challenged (Fuscaldo, 2000; Jones & Crocklin, 2000). In other cases, couples have put their surplus embryos up for adoption to be implanted in another woman (Stolberg, 2001).

Controversy has also arisen about spouses or family members requesting the retrieval and use of sperm for IVF from men who have just died or are in a persistent vegetative state (Strong, 1999). Some physicians will honor most requests; others will do so only if the man was married and had wanted children. The debate about the ethics of taking sperm without the explicit, written consent of the donor will intensify because the technology to retrieve, save, and fertilize an ovum taken after a woman's death will soon be available (Soules, 1999; White, 1999).

Reproductive technology has made it possible for women past the age of menopause to become pregnant, carry the pregnancy, and deliver their babies. The postmenopausal woman's own ova are not viable, so ova from a younger woman are fertilized in vitro with her husband's sperm. With hormonal assistance the woman's uterus can maintain a pregnancy. In the future the genetic material from the older mother's DNA will be transferred into the donated egg, resulting in the older mother being able to pass on her genes to her child (Budd, 2002).

Scientific and popular reactions to older men having children are quite different from attitudes about older women doing so (Eisenberg & Schenker, 1997). Only scattered criticism is directed at men who father in their 60s, 70s, and even 80s. In fact, this is often considered a confirmation of their masculinity and virility. However, attitudes toward the older woman becoming a mother are often negative, and doctors who provide reproductive assistance to postmenopausal women are accused of acting irresponsibly, tampering with nature, and playing God (Ethics Committee, American Society for Reproductive Medicine, 1997). On the other hand, others believe that it is unethical to deny women conception on the basis of age alone (Paulson, 2000). Life expectancy in the Western world enables a healthy woman who has a child in her 50s or early 60s to raise the child into adulthood.

Although no one denigrates an older woman for raising her grandchildren, this same woman's conception, pregnancy, and childbirth cause discomfort for many (Eisenberg & Schenker, 1997).

Reproductive technology in the United States is essentially market driven, with few legal restraints (Andrews & Elster, 2000). The Internet is often the way donors and recipients establish agreements (Mead, 1999). The extreme of capitalistic conception can be seen in the donor egg market (Weingarten & Hosenball, 1999). The typical payment to compensate a donor for potent hormone injections and the minor surgery to recover the eggs is $1,500 to $5,000. However, wealthy couples have offered up to $50,000 for one cycle of viable eggs from a woman who meets specific physical and intellectual criteria (Kalb, 1999).

Difficulties in defining ethical and legal parameters of ART will be exacerbated as knowledge and techniques continue to expand. Genetic alteration of embryos might be implemented in the near future (Pappert, 2000b). Genetic alterations might give parents with a known genetic defect—Alzheimer's, breast cancer, cystic fibrosis, or other illnesses with a strong genetic component—the ability to donate eggs and sperm to be fertilized in vitro, then genetically altered to remove the illness-causing material (Begley, 2001). The treated embryo is then inserted into the woman's uterus, and 9 months later the couple's baby, without the legacy of family genetic problems, is born. Many bioethicists support this development, which can shield children from disabling and life-threatening genetic problems. Others oppose this technology because it could be frivolously used to genetically engineer "designer babies" (Begley, 1998).

Fifty years ago assisted reproductive techniques were found in science fiction stories instead of at the approximately 340 assisted reproductive centers in the United States (Andrews & Elster, 2000). Scientific imagination and technological advancements will continue to expand the options for reproductive technologies as well as the quandaries that invariably accompany them (Gibbs, 2001; Krauthammer, 2001).

However, miscarriage can be a significant loss for the woman or couple. If the expectant parents strongly desired the pregnancy, have been trying to conceive for some time, or have miscarried before, the emotional effect may be particularly painful. Parents can experience grief, helplessness, guilt, and anger. As one woman explained:

> I had a miscarriage. I experienced it as the death of our child . . . and I am terrified of it happening again. . . . People minimize our loss when they say things like "You're young, you can have lots of babies," "It's God's will," or "It's for the best—there was probably something wrong with the baby." The truth is—as with any death—there is nothing one can say or do to fix it. . . . What helps me is to know that others view my child as real— for, like the Velveteen Rabbit, he was real to me. (Beck et al., 1988, p. 46)

Miscarriage can be a lonely experience. Family and friends can help by acknowledging the loss and asking what the experience has been like for the person. Listening and allowing the parents to express their emotions and unique reactions to the miscarriage, without giving advice, can also be helpful. Couples may need to grieve the loss of this hoped-for pregnancy and baby for several months before pursuing another pregnancy (Salisbury, 1991). Some parents who lose an unborn child through miscarriage find it meaningful to name the baby or have a memorial service (Beck et al., 1988). ■

! Sexual Health

Elective Abortion

In contrast to a spontaneous abortion, an **elective abortion** involves a decision to terminate a pregnancy using medical procedures. Although 50% of all pregnancies are unplanned, many of the pregnancies become wanted and welcome. However, in the United States more than one-fifth of all pregnancies end in abortion (Finer & Henshaw, 2003), and an estimated 43% of women in the United States will have had an abortion by age 45 (Kaiser Family Foundation, 2002). Most women who have abortions are young: 20% are younger than 19, and 33% are between age 20 and 25. Young, white, unmarried women obtain the most abortions, but approximately 20% of abortions are for married women. About 61% have previously given birth (Kaiser Family Foundation, 2002). Catholic women are as likely to obtain an abortion as other women, and about 18% of all abortions are obtained by born-again and evangelical Christians (Henshaw & Kost, 1996). Table 12.3 describes factors associated with higher and lower likelihood of abortion.

Elective abortion Medical procedure performed to terminate pregnancy.

TABLE 12.3	Factors Associated with Likelihood of Abortion
Characteristics of Women with Higher Likelihood of Abortion	**Characteristics of Women with Lower Likelihood of Abortion**
Age 18 to 24	Age 35 or older
Single	Married
Hispanic or black[a]	High income
Low income	Living in suburbs or rural areas
Covered by Medicaid	Born-again or evangelical Christian
Four or more children	

[a]Although white women obtain about 60% of all abortions, Hispanic and black women receive a higher proportion of abortions relative to the proportion of population size. A black woman is almost three times as likely as a white woman to have an abortion; a Hispanic woman is twice as likely as a non-Hispanic woman to experience an abortion.

SOURCES: Henshaw & Kost (1996) and Jones et al. (2002b).

Procedures for Abortion

Several different abortion procedures are used at different stages of pregnancy. Figure 12.2 shows the stages of pregnancy when abortions take place. The most common procedures are *medical abortion, suction curettage, D and E,* and *prostaglandin induction.*

In 2000 **medical abortion,** which uses medications to produce an abortion in the first 7 weeks of pregnancy, became available to women in the United States (France & Rosenberg, 2000). The procedure is known as a medical abortion because it involves medication rather than a surgical procedure. Medical abortion has been available in European countries since 1980. Currently, about half of all early abortions in France, Scotland, and Sweden are medical abortions (Jones & Henshaw, 2002). Years of antiabortion protests and political action against the U.S. manufacture and distribution of medications for abortion delayed the availability of medical abortions to U.S. women.

Medical abortion The use of medications to end a pregnancy of 7 weeks or less.

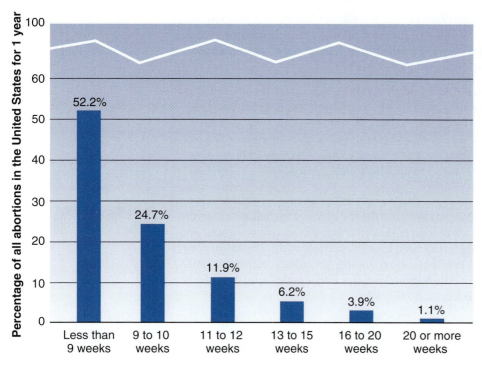

Weeks into pregnancy (full-term pregnancy usually lasts 40 weeks)

▶ **Figure 12.2** When abortions are performed (Sontag, 1997, p. A8). Eighty-eight percent of all abortions are done before 12 weeks.

Suction curettage A procedure in which the cervical os is dilated using graduated metal dilators or a laminaria; then a small plastic tube, attached to a vacuum aspirator, is inserted into the uterus, drawing the fetal tissue, placenta, and built-up uterine lining out of the uterus.

RU476- take before you are 7 weeks

Dilation and evacuation (D and E) An abortion procedure in which a curette and suction equipment are used.

Prostaglandins Hormones that are used to induce uterine contractions and fetal expulsion for second-trimester abortions.

A medical abortion must be done before 7 weeks of pregnancy. The medications block the hormone progesterone. Without progesterone the cervix softens, the lining of the uterus breaks down, and bleeding begins. A few days later the woman takes a drug that makes the uterus contract and expel the grape-size embryonic sac (Jain et al., 2002). Figure 12.3 shows how a medical abortion works. Research studies report a 92–98% effectiveness in ending pregnancies (Benson et al., 2003). Side effects can include cramping, headaches, nausea, or vomiting. However, many women experience no physical side effects (Hausknecht, 2003; Jones & Henshaw, 2002).

The personal and political impact of medical abortion is significant. A medical abortion is much safer than the surgical procedures. Women can have abortions as soon as they know they are pregnant and do not have to wait 6 to 8 weeks for a surgical abortion (Ellertson et al., 2000). Abortion may become more accessible to women because of an increase in the number of doctors willing to provide medical abortions, and a woman will be able to see her family doctor at an office instead of at an abortion clinic (Borgatta et al., 2001; Vason, 2003).

Suction curettage is usually done 7–13 weeks after the last menstrual period. A suction curettage is performed by physicians at clinics or hospitals. With suction curettage the cervical os is dilated using graduated metal dilators or a *laminaria*, a small cylinder of seaweed stem or artificial substance, which is inserted hours earlier. The laminaria slowly expands as it absorbs cervical moisture, gently opening the os. This gradual expansion reduces the chance of cervical trauma. During the abortion a small plastic tube is inserted into the uterus. The tube is attached to a vacuum aspirator, which draws the fetal tissue, placenta, and built-up uterine lining out of the uterus; the procedure takes about 10 minutes. A local anesthetic is sometimes used, but in some settings general anesthesia is available. Risks include uterine infection or perforation, hemorrhage, or incomplete removal of the uterine contents. Research data indicate that a first-trimester abortion has little effect on subsequent fertility or pregnancy; but research has also shown that having two or more abortions can lead to a higher incidence of miscarriage or ectopic pregnancy in subsequent pregnancies (Tharaux-Deneux et al., 1998).

If a pregnancy progresses past approximately 12 weeks, the suction curettage procedure is no longer as safe because the uterine walls have become thinner, making perforation and bleeding more likely. For pregnancy termination between 13 and 21 weeks, a **D and E,** or **dilation and evacuation,** is the safest and most widely used technique (Cates & Ellertson, 1998). A combination of suction equipment, special forceps, and a curette (a metal instrument used to scrape the walls of the uterus) is used. General anesthesia is usually required, and the cervix is dilated wider than with suction curettage. Second-trimester pregnancies can also be terminated using compounds such as **prostaglandins,** hormones that cause uterine contractions.

The prostaglandin can be introduced into the vagina as a suppository or into the amniotic sac by inserting a needle through the abdominal wall; the fetus and placenta are usually expelled from the vagina within 24 hours. Complications from abortion procedures that induce labor contractions include nausea, vomiting, and diarrhea; tearing of the cervix; excessive bleeding; and the possibility of shock and death. There is less than 0.3 fatality per 100,000 abortions, compared to 9.2 maternal fatalities per 100,000 live births (Adler et al., 2003).

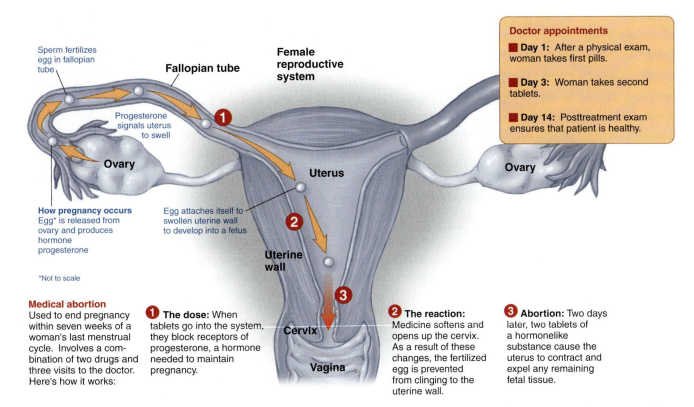

Sperm fertilizes egg in fallopian tube

Fallopian tube

Female reproductive system

Progesterone signals uterus to swell

Ovary

Ovary

1

How pregnancy occurs
Egg* is released from ovary and produces hormone progesterone

Egg attaches itself to swollen uterine wall to develop into a fetus

Uterus

2

*Not to scale

Uterine wall

3

Doctor appointments

■ **Day 1:** After a physical exam, woman takes first pills.

■ **Day 3:** Woman takes second tablets.

■ **Day 14:** Posttreatment exam ensures that patient is healthy.

Medical abortion
Used to end pregnancy within seven weeks of a woman's last menstrual cycle. Involves a combination of two drugs and three visits to the doctor. Here's how it works:

1 The dose: When tablets go into the system, they block receptors of progesterone, a hormone needed to maintain pregnancy.

Cervix

Vagina

2 The reaction: Medicine softens and opens up the cervix. As a result of these changes, the fertilized egg is prevented from clinging to the uterine wall.

3 Abortion: Two days later, two tablets of a hormonelike substance cause the uterus to contract and expel any remaining fetal tissue.

▶ **Figure 12.3** How medical abortions work.

Late-term abortion or **intact dilation and evacuation** is done after 20 weeks and before viability at 24 weeks' gestation. It is reserved for situations when serious health risks to the woman or severe fetal abnormalities exist. In this procedure the cervix is dilated, the fetus emerges feet first out of the uterus, and the fetal skull is collapsed to permit passage of the head through the cervix and vagina.

Although late-term abortions are rare and comprise less than 1% of all abortions in the United States, they are the focus of intense political controversy (Rosenberg, 2003a, 2003b). Opponents of abortion rights call this procedure partial-birth abortion and hope to make the procedure illegal. In late 2003 Congress approved a ban on late-term abortion, the first time it has prohibited a specific medical procedure (Abrams, 2003). A similar bill had been passed twice by Congress in the late 1990s, but both times it was vetoed by President Bill Clinton. President George W. Bush signed the bill on late-term abortion in 2003 (Schneider, 2003). However, several organizations, such as the Center for Reproductive Rights and the Planned Parenthood Federation of America, filed lawsuits to bring the question to the Supreme Court. In the past the Supreme Court has struck down more than 30 state laws that were passed to make late-term abortion illegal (American Civil Liberties Union, 2003; Dewar, 2003).

Late-term abortion, or intact dilation and evacuation An abortion done between 20 and 24 weeks, when serious health risks to the woman or fetal abnormalities exist.

Illegal Abortions

About 25% of the women in the world live in countries where abortion is illegal (Adler et al., 2003), and unsafe abortions kill 80,000 women each year throughout the world (E. Murphy, 2003). In countries where abortion is illegal, unsafe abortion procedures occur. Women attempt to self-induce abortions using enemas, laxatives, pills, herbs, soap, and various other substances. Illegal abortionists typically insert a catheter or sharp instrument into the uterus to induce contractions (Jewkes et al., 1997). In some countries women who are discovered to have had an abortion are charged with murder and imprisoned (S. Cohen, 2000).

Shared Responsibility

After a woman confirms that she is pregnant (assuming that she was not trying to conceive), she must then decide whether to carry the pregnancy and keep the child, give the child up for adoption, or have an abortion. A couple can share responsibility for this decision and for

! Sexual Health

the abortion itself, if that choice is made, in several ways. First, the man can help his partner clarify her feelings and can express his own regarding the unwanted pregnancy and how best to deal with it. Important topics for a couple to discuss include each person's life situation at the time; their feelings about the pregnancy, possible choices, and each other; and their future plans as individuals and as a couple. If the man and woman disagree on what to do, the final decision rests with the woman: Male partners do not have a legal right to demand or deny abortion for the woman. ■

Choosing abortion is usually a difficult decision for a woman and her partner. It means weighing and examining highly personal values and priorities. When made, the decision is usually fraught with ambivalence. Even if the pregnancy was unwanted, both partners may feel loss and sadness. They may also feel regret, depression, anxiety, guilt, or anger about the abortion or why it was necessary.

A great many factors can affect either partner's emotional response to the abortion. The timing of the abortion is important; early abortions are medically and usually emotionally much easier than are later abortions. The reactions of close friends and family, the attitude of the medical staff and physician performing the abortion, the individuals' values about abortion, the voluntariness or pressure from others about the decision, and the nature and strength of the couple's relationship all can contribute to positive or negative reactions. Women who have abortions usually experience some anxiety or depression, but relief is a common feeling once the abortion is done (Cates & Ellertson, 1998). In general, well-designed studies of psychological reactions following abortion have consistently found low risk for problems (Adler et al., 2003), and most women experience a marked improvement in their quality of life after abortion (Westhoff et al., 2003).

Pregnancy Risk Taking and Abortion

*Reasons:
*panic
parents

In many cases an unwanted pregnancy is clearly a matter of contraceptive failure. More than half of women who had an abortion were using contraception when they became pregnant (Hutti, 2003). For other women or couples seeking abortions the pregnancy can be traced to contraceptive risk taking—that is, not using contraceptives consistently or reliably, sometimes because of inconvenience, side effects of methods, or perceived low risk of pregnancy (Jones et al., 2002a).

Actively seeking and using contraception acknowledges a woman's intent to engage in intercourse, and she may not want her partner to think that she is "that kind of girl." Indeed, young women with high degrees of guilt about sex are less likely to use contraception effectively than are those who do not feel guilty (Strassberg & Mahoney, 1988). Another significant factor is being under the influence of alcohol or drugs, which reduces judgment and greatly increases contraceptive risk taking, unless the woman is using a method such as the pill or IUD.

Women of any age may avoid contraception because they fear alienating a partner by asking for his cooperation in planning and using birth control. For some women who lack strong self-esteem the loss of a relationship is a more fearful consequence than the possibility of pregnancy. Unfortunately, such women are more likely to engage in intercourse with men who refuse to take precautions and who then walk away from responsibility if a pregnancy occurs (Malloy & Patterson, 1992).

Some women take contraceptive risks because they believe that they are unlikely to become pregnant. Couples who get away with risk taking once or twice are more likely to be careless in the future. Other women take contraceptive risks because of the high social value placed on pregnancy. Pregnancy connotes adulthood in our society and is accordingly often considered a measure of a woman's worth. Pregnancy can also be a bargaining chip for marriage; it can be used to test or coerce a man's commitment to a relationship or parenthood or to try to prevent an impending breakup.

? Critical Thinking Question

Why would childhood abuse increase the likelihood of having an unintended pregnancy?

Further, women who have experienced psychological, physical, and/or sexual abuse in childhood are more than twice as likely to have an unintended pregnancy after age 20 than women whose childhoods were free from abuse. Women whose mothers suffered frequent physical abuse from their partners are also more likely to have an unwanted first pregnancy. Apparently, these childhood traumas reduce a woman's ability to effectively prevent an unintended first pregnancy (Dietz, 1999).

The Abortion Controversy

Elective abortion continues to be a highly controversial social and political issue in the United States and other countries. Beliefs regarding the beginning of life, the reproductive choices of women, and the role of law influence the stand one takes regarding elective termination of pregnancy.

Abortion: Historical Overview

Laws regulating abortion have changed over time. In ancient China and Europe abortion early in pregnancy was legal. In the 13th century St. Thomas Aquinas delineated the Catholic Church's view that the fetus developed a soul 40 days after conception for males and 90 days after conception for females. Later, in the late 1860s Pope Pius IX declared that human life begins at conception and is at any stage equally important to the mother's. The Roman Catholic Church still maintains this position. Pope John Paul II describes legal abortion as murder and a cause of grave moral decline. He also appeals to political leaders, particularly Catholics, to abolish pro-choice abortion laws (Jones & Crocklin, 2000).

Attitudes and practices regarding abortion can vary even in countries with the same predominant religion. For example, Islamic law prohibits the killing of a soul, and the fetus is generally considered to develop a soul when the mother can feel fetal movement, or *quickening,* during the fourth or fifth month. However, some Islamic countries permit abortion before quickening, whereas other prohibit it completely (Adler et al., 2003).

Early American law, based on English common law, allowed abortion until the pregnant woman felt quickening. During the 1860s abortion became illegal in the United States, except when necessary to save the woman's life. Reasons for this change included the high mortality rate resulting from crude abortion procedures, the belief that population growth was important to the country's developing economy, and, perhaps, the male-dominated political system's response to the emerging movement of middle-class white women seeking independence and equality (Sheeran, 1987). The result was that women, desperate to terminate unwanted pregnancies, were forced to choose among terrifying options: illegal "back alley" abortions using unsafe, unskilled, and unsanitary procedures, or self-induced abortions, sometimes using a wire coat hanger (Stubblefield & Grimes, 1994). Women who had enough money might leave the country or persuade an American physician to perform an illegal abortion.

Roe v. *Wade* and Beyond

By the 1960s advocacy groups of women and men were lobbying for change and began to win a few battles on the state level. In 1973, based on the right to privacy, the U.S. Supreme Court in *Roe* v. *Wade* legalized a woman's right to decide to terminate her pregnancy before the fetus has reached the age of viability. *Viability* is defined as the fetus's ability to survive independently of the woman's body. This usually occurs by the sixth or seventh month of pregnancy, and abortions are done before the third month. *Roe* v. *Wade* voided the remaining state laws, which treated abortion as a criminal act for both the doctor performing the abortion and the woman undergoing the procedure.

However, the legalization of abortion in 1973 did not end the controversy. Legislation in the late 1970s greatly curtailed the availability of medically safe abortions to low-income women. In July 1977 the Hyde Amendment was passed, prohibiting federal Medicaid funds for abortions; it was later upheld by the Supreme Court. (Medicaid is a joint state and federal program to provide payment of medical services for low-income citizens; 6 million women of reproductive age obtain their health care through Medicaid [Boonstra & Sonfield, 2000].) The Court also established that states are not required to provide Medicaid funds for the purpose of elective pregnancy termination. (States may use their own funds to provide abortions for low-income women; in 2003 only 16 states used their own funds to pay for abortions done for physical and mental health concerns [Smeal, 2003].) In 1993 the Hyde Amendment was modified to require states to fund abortions for rape and incest victims.

In 1988 the state of Missouri asked the U.S. Supreme Court to uphold state restrictions on abortion that had been declared unconstitutional under *Roe* v. *Wade.* In 1989 the Court ruled in favor of three restrictions states could impose

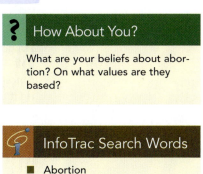

? How About You?

What are your beliefs about abortion? On what values are they based?

InfoTrac Search Words

- Abortion

on abortion: (1) Public employees can be barred from performing or assisting in abortions not necessary to save the pregnant woman's life; (2) public buildings can be restricted from use for performing abortions; and (3) doctors may be required to perform tests to determine whether the fetus is viable if they believe the woman is at least 20 weeks pregnant.

In 1991 the Supreme Court, in *Rust* v. *Sullivan,* upheld legislation barring federally funded family planning clinics from *discussing* the option of abortion with patients. This "gag rule" decision affected about 4,000 clinics serving 4.5 million mostly low-income women. Critics of the gag rule viewed the prohibition on discussing abortion as a violation of the constitutional right of free speech (McBride, 1992). Further restrictions on abortion occurred in 1992, when the Supreme Court ruled on *Planned Parenthood* v. *Casey,* which allowed states to require a 24-hour waiting period before a woman can obtain an abortion and parental notification for women younger than 18. As part of its 24-hour waiting period, Wisconsin requires women to read a booklet showing stages of fetal development and abortion providers to tell women they can listen to the fetal heartbeat before having the abortion (Gillespie, 1999).

Thirty-two states have parental consent laws that require a minor to obtain at least one parent's consent for her to have an abortion (Adler et al., 2003). Only two states and the District of Columbia have laws affirming the right of young women to have an abortion without parental consent (Meier, 2000). Most adolescents do discuss their pregnancy options with their parents. However, laws that require parental notification and consent for abortion assume that all parents are loving, responsible, and capable of having their daughters' best interests at heart. Sadly, this is not the case for abusive and neglectful parents. It is ironic that parental consent is not required for the pregnant young woman to have the baby and assume the responsibilities of parenthood, but it is required if she decides not to become a mother (Stotland, 1998). For these and other reasons many leading medical groups oppose mandatory parental consent requirements for abortion, including the American Medical Association, the American Academy of Pediatrics, and the American Academy of Family Physicians (Meier, 2000).

The Clinton administration changed a number of laws related to abortion. It lifted the gag rule that had banned funds for family planning clinics that provide abortion information and counseling. Clinton signed the Freedom of Access to Clinic Entrances Act, which prohibits interference by protesters and provides criminal penalties for obstructing entrance to clinics. Military hospitals overseas were permitted to perform abortions, provided that women pay for them. Clinton also reversed American policies cutting off aid to international family planning programs involved in abortion-related activities, but George W. Bush reinstated the policy after his election (Kreinin, 2002b). In addition, restrictions continue to be put in place; for example, in 1999, 34 states adopted 70 anti-choice measures (Cooper, 2000). For all these reasons the availability of abortion has declined since the 1980s. For example, the number of abortion providers has decreased by 37%, only 13% of all counties have an abortion provider, and 34% of women live in counties with no abortion provider (Henshaw & Finer, 2003). Access is limited most severely for young, rural, and low-income women (Borgmann & Weiss, 2003; Sotorbani et al., 2004).

Abortion continues to be a major social and political issue in the United States, characterized by highly polarized opinions (Mezin, 2001). How the present and future U.S. presidents, Congress, and the Supreme Court will support or oppose abortion remains a critical question (Clift, 2003; Rosenberg, 2003a, 2003b).

The Current Debate

Public opinion polls show that the majority of Americans—55–65%, depending on the poll—believe that women should have access to legal abortion (Cooper, 2000). The central concept in the abortion controversy is the moral debate between those arguing for the fetus's right to live and those arguing for the woman's right to choose to terminate her pregnancy. The antiabortion, or pro-life, advocates argue that life begins at conception and that the fetus is a person who should have the right to live. "The fetus is an immature, dependent form of human life which only needs time and protection to develop" (Callahan, 2002, p. 181). Consequently, abortion is seen as immoral.

Antiabortion groups want to reestablish national legislation, by constitutional amendment if necessary, to make abortion illegal and to establish the constitutional rights of the unborn fetus as an independent being. Members of this minority are waging an active battle against legal and available abortion. A primary tactic has been to target pro-choice incumbents in Congress to attempt to prevent their reelection. Antiabortion protesters also block clinic entrances and harass patients and staff. Some extreme activists have burned or bombed abortion clinics; the first reported arson and bombing was in 1978 (Palmer, 2000).

Since 1993, pro-life extremists have resorted to killing, believing that murdering physicians is justified to save unborn babies (Henshaw & Finer, 2003). The following are some of the incidents:

Abortion supporters and opponents usually believe very strongly in their positions.

- David Gunn, a physician who provided abortions in small towns in the South, was killed in March 1993 by three shots in the back by an abortion foe.
- A Florida physician, John Britton, and his security escort, retired Air Force officer James Barrett, were murdered in July 1994 by a pro-life activist who had previously picketed clinics, carrying a sign, "Abortionists are murderers. Murderers should be executed."
- A gunman in Massachusetts shot and killed abortion clinic receptionists Shannon Lowney and Leanne Nichols and wounded several others in December 1994.
- Dr. Gary Romalis was gravely wounded in November 1994 as he sat eating breakfast in his home in Vancouver, British Columbia.
- In January 1998 a homemade bomb exploded in a health care clinic in Birmingham, Alabama, killing a security guard and seriously injuring a nurse.
- In 1998 Dr. Barnett Slepian was shot in the back through the kitchen window of his home after he and his wife had returned from synagogue.

Each year, 56% of abortion clinic providers experience demonstrators picketing their clinics or homes or blocking clients' entrances, vandalism, and bomb threats (Henshaw & Finer, 2003). Doctors and clinics that provide abortion now must implement stringent security measures—metal detectors, alarms, and bulletproof glass and vests.

In contrast, pro-choice advocates see abortion as a social necessity, a result of imperfect and sometimes unavailable birth control methods and lack of education. They want abortion to be an option for women faced with the dilemma of an unwanted pregnancy who decide that terminating it is their best alternative (Willis, 2002). A columnist stated, "Mothering is so critical and so challenging that to force anyone into its service is immoral" (Quindlen, 2003b, p. 26). Pro-choice advocates support a woman's choice *not* to have an abortion, but they strongly oppose antiabortion legislation restricting others' choices. Many prestigious organizations have made public statements opposing antiabortion bills, including the National Academy of Sciences, the American Public Health Association, the American Medical Association, the American College of Obstetricians and Gynecologists, and many religious organizations.

People who support and those who oppose a woman's right to abortion tend to differ in other ways as well. One study of abortion attitudes found that people who approve of legally available abortions are more likely to support civil liberties and women's rights than are those who disapprove. People who disapprove of legal abortion are more likely than others to have strongly committed Catholic or fundamentalist Protestant affiliations (Granberg & Granberg, 1980); to have disapproving attitudes toward nonmarital sex, homosexuality, and government spending; to be politically conservative; and to have traditional attitudes about the female role (Deitch, 1983; Lynxwiler & Gay, 1994). Antiabortion activist women are more likely to be practicing Roman Catholics with large families, to have low-paying or no employment outside the home, and to base their self-esteem on their maternal roles. In contrast, women who are pro-choice activists tend to be college educated, to have well-paid careers and few children, to have few ties to formal religion, and to have a strong vested interest in their work roles. In addition, pro-choice activists believe that intimacy is the most important purpose of sexuality, whereas antiabortion activists believe that procreation is the primary purpose of sexuality (Lynxwiler & Gay, 1994).

Research examining U.S. senators' and representatives' voting records demonstrates that many who are opposed to legal abortion tend to support capital punishment, oppose handgun control, and oppose legislation that promotes the health and well-being of families and their children—such as school lunch and milk programs. Voting records of pro-choice legislative supporters have shown the opposite trends (Prescott, 1986). A recent comprehensive review of the abortion and child welfare policies in the 50 states demonstrates that states with the most restrictive abortion laws also provide the fewest resources to facilitate adoption, to provide assistance to poor children, or to educate children (Schroedel, 2000).

Research about racial differences in support for legal abortion reveals interesting findings, as described in the following "Sexuality and Diversity" discussion.

 ## Sexuality and Diversity

A Comparison of African Americans' and White Americans' Attitudes About Legal Abortion

One study of African American and white men and women over a 16-year period revealed significant differences in support for legal abortion between these groups, with the exception of women of childbearing age. The researchers hypothesized that these women realize that they may be faced with an unwanted pregnancy and must weigh their beliefs about abortion with the long-term impact of giving birth.

Although support for legal abortion has increased among both black and white men in the last 16 years, support for legal abortion was still lower among African American men than among white men during that period. However, since 1985 men of both races were similar to women of childbearing age in their attitudes. This may indicate a pattern away from more traditional gender-role beliefs commonly held by men.

Older white women reported the strongest pro-choice attitudes, whereas older African American women had the weakest support for legal abortion. The researchers conjectured that women's support for abortion shifts over their lifetime and that abortion has different meanings for women as a group. They hypothesize that white women are more likely to view abortion as a symbolic issue related to women's rights—a value that strengthens over time. Conversely, African American women may view abortion more as a practical consideration that loses its saliency after the childbearing years. It is also possible that African American women who had firsthand experience with the racial discrimination of the 1960s and 1970s and the civil rights struggle view the availability of abortion as an attempt to reduce the black population (Lynxwiler & Gay, 1994).

How Women Decide

Research indicates that the political debate over the rights of the fetus or the woman is not the important question women weigh when faced with an unwanted pregnancy. They rely on practical and emotional matters to make their decisions about their real-life dilemmas. The following are examples of the conscientious questions women asked in their process of decision making:

> Did the woman love the man with whom she had become pregnant? Would he stay with her? Could she love the baby? Could she live with herself if she had a child and turned it over to strangers to raise? If she kept her child, could she care for it properly? Did she have marketable skills, an education, income? Would she ever acquire them if she went ahead with her pregnancy? Would the birth of another baby jeopardize the welfare of

her existing children? Would the child be born with serious abnormalities? Would it suffer more than it would thrive? (Malloy & Patterson, 1992, p. 321)

It is likely that the abortion debate will remain passionate and bitter because of fundamental differences in life circumstances and values of people with strong commitments to one side or the other. However, most people experience considerable ambivalence about abortion (Connell, 1992). Many people who believe abortion is morally wrong also believe that any woman who wants an abortion should be able to obtain it legally (Stone & Waszak, 1992). As one woman stated:

> Part of my problem is that what I think and how I feel about this issue are two entirely different matters. . . . I cannot bring myself to say I am in favor of abortion. I don't want anyone to have one. I want people to use contraceptives and for those contraceptives to be foolproof. I want people to be responsible for their actions; mature in their decisions. I want children to be loved, wanted, well cared for. [At the same time,] I cannot bring myself to say I am against choice. I want women who are young, poor, single or all three to be able to direct the course of their lives. I want women who have had all the children they want or can afford or their bodies can withstand to be able to decide their future. I want women who are in bad marriages or destructive relationships to avoid being trapped by pregnancy. . . . Even as I refuse to pass judgment on other women's lives, I weep for the children who might have been. (Smith, 1985, p. 16)

▶ The Experience of Pregnancy

Pregnancy is a unique and significant experience for both the woman and her partner. In the following pages we look at the experience and the effect it has on the individuals and the couple. Many of the experiences are encountered by heterosexual and lesbian couples alike. In this section the heterosexual couple is used as a frame of reference; specific issues related to lesbians are addressed in Chapter 10.

The Woman's Experience

Each woman has different emotional and physical reactions to pregnancy, and the same woman may react differently to different pregnancies. Here are two reactions at the opposite ends of the continuum:

I loved being pregnant. My face glowed for nine months. I felt like a kindred spirit to all female mammals and discovered a new respect for my body and its ability to create life. The bigger I got, the better I liked it. (Authors' files)

If I could have babies without the pregnancy part, I'd do it. Looking fat and slowed down is a huge drag. (Authors' files)

Factors influencing a woman's emotional reactions can include how the decision for pregnancy was made, current and impending lifestyle changes, her relationship with others, her financial resources, her self-image, and hormonal changes. The woman's acquired attitudes and knowledge about childbearing and her hopes and fears about parenthood also contribute to her experience. Positive support and attention from her partner are helpful in creating a happy pregnancy.

Women sometimes feel that they should experience only positive emotions when they are pregnant. However, about 20% of women experience significant depression during pregnancy (Routh, 2000). The physical, emotional, and situational aspects of a pregnancy often elicit an array of contradictory emotions, including joy, excitement, impatience, and fear. One study of 1,000 women found this wide range of feelings about pregnancy: 35% loved being pregnant, 8% hated it, 40% had mixed feelings about the pregnancy experience, and the remainder had varying experiences with different pregnancies. The researcher concluded that the emotional and physical experiences of pregnancy were intertwined. The degree of physical discomfort influences a woman's feelings about the pregnancy and her life, and vice versa (Genevie & Margolies, 1987).

The marked changes that occur also have a significant effect on the experience of pregnancy. Several changes take place during the early stages of the first 3 months. Menstruation ceases. As the milk glands in the breasts develop, the breasts increase in size. The nipples and areola usually become darker in color. Nausea, sometimes called morning sickness, can occur (Vutyavanich et al., 2001). Many women experience a marked increase in fatigue. Vaginal secretions can change or increase. Urination can be more frequent, and bowel movements less regular. However, there is little increase in the size of the woman's abdomen during these first 3 months.

More outward signs of pregnancy appear in the middle 3 months. The waistline thickens, and the abdomen begins to protrude. Fetal movements can be felt in the fourth or fifth month, which is usually exciting and reassuring to the parents-to-be. Nausea and tiredness usually disappear in the second trimester, and a woman can experience heightened feelings of well-being. The breasts might begin to secrete a thin yellowish fluid called **colostrum** (kuh-LOSS-trum).

During the last 3 months, the uterus and abdomen increase in size. The muscles of the uterus occasionally contract painlessly. The enlarged uterus produces pressure on the woman's stomach, intestines, and bladder. This can cause discomfort, indigestion, and frequent urination. Fetal movements can be seen and felt from the outside the abdomen.

Colostrum A thin fluid secreted by the breasts during later stages of pregnancy and the first few days after delivery.

The Man's Experience

In the last several decades significant changes have occurred in the role of the woman's partner during pregnancy, childbirth, and child rearing. Once seen as predominantly the woman's domain, pregnancy is now commonly viewed as a shared experience. With the advent of the prepared childbirth movement, described later in this chapter, men frequently participate in childbirth.

An expectant father obviously does not experience the same physical sensations that a pregnant woman does (although occasionally a "pregnant father" reports psychosympathetic symptoms, such as the nausea or tiredness his partner is experiencing). However, the experiences of pregnancy and birth are often profound for the father.

What exactly does the "male pregnancy" involve? Like the woman, he often reacts with a great deal of ambivalence. He may feel ecstatic but also fearful about the woman's and the baby's well-being. Like many men, he may feel frightened about the impending birth and whether he will be able to "keep it together." He may feel especially tender toward his partner and become more solicitous. At the same time, he may feel a sense of separateness from the woman because of the physical changes that only she is experiencing. However, fetal ultrasonography allows fathers to see the fetus in utero and can create greater feelings of

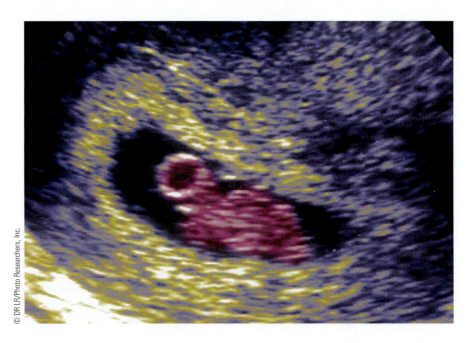

Ultrasound image of a fetus at 4 weeks.

involvement (Sandelowski, 1994). He may be proud at the prospect of becoming a father, but he may question his parenting ability. He may fear losing his wife's affection and attention to the pregnancy and baby (Brown, 1994). Most men feel concern over the impending increase in financial responsibility. In all, the expectant father has special needs, as does his partner, and it is important that the woman be aware of these needs and be willing to respond to them. One study of expectant fathers found that when men did share their feelings with their partners, the relationships deepened (Shapiro, 1987).

A man's active involvement throughout childbearing seems to initiate positive interaction between the father and the newborn. Father–newborn interaction helps develop the paternal role, and programs in the hospital to increase father–newborn contact and to teach the father caregiving skills seem to facilitate this process (Sherwen, 1987).

Sexual Interaction During Pregnancy

A woman's sexual interest and responsiveness can change throughout the course of her pregnancy. Nausea, breast tenderness, and fatigue can inhibit sexual interest during the first 3 months. A resurgence of sexual desire and arousal occurs for some women in the second trimester (Masters & Johnson, 1966), but most research shows a progressive decline in sexual interest and activity over the 9 months of pregnancy, with diminished sexual desire most common in the last 3 months (Bogren, 1991). Some of the most common reasons women give for decreasing sexual activity during pregnancy include physical discomfort, feelings of physical unattractiveness, and fear of injuring the unborn child (Colino, 1991). For some women pregnancy can result in a heightened awareness of their bodies and an increased sensuality. Others feel intensely "womanly" and are less inhibited sexually. The increased vasocongestion of the genitals during pregnancy can heighten sexual desire and response for some women. Women who have positive attitudes about sexuality to begin with tend to maintain more sexual interest, activity, and satisfaction during pregnancy than do women with negative attitudes about sexuality (Fisher & Gray, 1988). Also, a planned pregnancy results in fewer sexual problems than does an unplanned one. Many women have increased desire for nonsexual affection as pregnancy progresses (Walbroehl, 1984).

The key to sexuality and pregnancy is that feelings are highly individual: "Some feel sexier, more attractive and more easily aroused than ever before. . . . Others are completely turned off by the mere thought of sex" (Stern, 1987, p. 71).

The partner's feelings also affect the sexual relationship during pregnancy. Reactions to the woman's changing body and to the need for adjustment in the couple's sexual repertoire can vary from increased excitement to inhibition for the partner. Especially late in pregnancy, awareness of the baby can make lovemaking seem like a crowded event:

> Sex during the third trimester requires a sense of humor. It doesn't seem to matter where you touch her anymore; the baby pops up everywhere. You can't escape the little kicks and jabs, and the thought of tiny feet and fists inches away (or closer) can be disconcerting. (Stern, 1987, p. 78)

For most couples pregnancy is a time of significant emotional and physical changes. Open communication, accurate information, mutual support, and flexibility in sexual frequency and activities can help maintain and strengthen the bond between the couple.

It is now generally accepted that in pregnancies with no risk factors, sexual activity and orgasm can be continued as desired until the onset of labor (Sayle et al., 2001). Women who are at risk for bleeding or premature labor will likely be advised differently (Schrinsky, 1988). Coitus or orgasm should not occur if spotting or vaginal or abdominal pain occurs or if the amniotic sac ("water bag") breaks. As with many other areas of sexual health care, a woman, her partner, and her health care practitioner can make an informed decision.

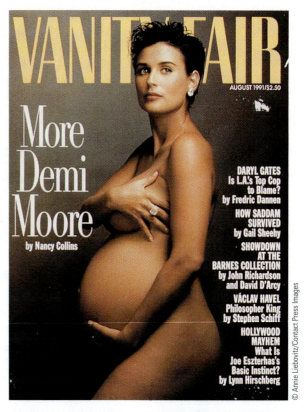

© Annie Liebovitz/Contact Press Images

Demi Moore's beautifully pregnant nude photo on the cover of *Vanity Fair* highlights the sensual richness of the pregnant woman's form.

During pregnancy it may be necessary for a couple to modify intercourse positions. The side-by-side, woman-above, and rear-entry positions are generally more comfortable than the man-above position as pregnancy progresses. Oral and manual genital stimulation as well as total body touching and holding can continue as usual. In fact, pregnancy is a time when a couple can explore and develop these dimensions of lovemaking more fully; even if intercourse is not desired, intimacy, eroticism, and sexual satisfaction can continue. ■

▶ A Healthy Pregnancy

Once a woman becomes pregnant, her own health habits and care play an important part in the development of a healthy fetus.

Fetal Development

The 9-month (40-week) span of pregnancy is customarily divided into three 13-week segments, called *trimesters.* Characteristic changes occur in each trimester.

First-Trimester Development

Zygote The single cell resulting from the union of sperm and egg cells.

Blastocyst Multicellular descendant of the united sperm and ovum that implants on the wall of the uterus.

As with all mammals, a human begins as a **zygote** (ZYE-goht), a united sperm cell and ovum. The sperm and egg unite in the fallopian tubes, where the egg's fingerlike microvilli draw the sperm to it (Begley, 1999). The zygote then develops into the multicelled **blastocyst** (BLAS-tuh-sist) that implants on the wall of the uterus about 1 week after fertilization (Fazleabas & Kim, 2003) (Figure 12.4). Growth progresses steadily. By 9–10 weeks after a woman's last menstrual period, the fetal heartbeat can be heard with a special ultrasound stethoscope known as the Doppler. By the beginning of the second month from the time of conception, the fetus is 0.5 to 1 inch long, grayish, and crescent shaped. During the second month the spinal canal and rudimentary arms and legs form, as do the beginnings of recognizable eyes, fingers, and toes. During the third month internal organs, such as the liver, kidneys, intestines, and lungs, begin limited functioning in the 3-inch fetus.

Second-Trimester Development

The second trimester begins with the fourth month of pregnancy. By now the sex of the fetus can often be distinguished. External body parts, including fingernails, eyebrows, and eyelashes, are clearly formed. The fetus's skin is covered by fine downlike hair. Future development primarily consists of growth in size and refinement of the features that already exist. Fetal movements, or quickening, can be felt by the end of the fourth month. By the end of the fifth month the fetus's weight has increased to 1 pound. Head hair can appear at this time, and subcutaneous fat develops. By the end of the second trimester, the fetus has opened its eyes.

▶ **Figure 12.4** The blastocyst implanted on the uterine wall shown (a) in diagram and (b) in photo taken by a scanning electron microscope.

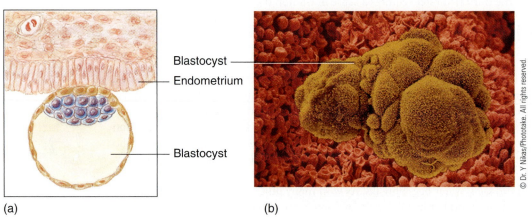

(a) (b)

Blastocyst

Endometrium

Blastocyst

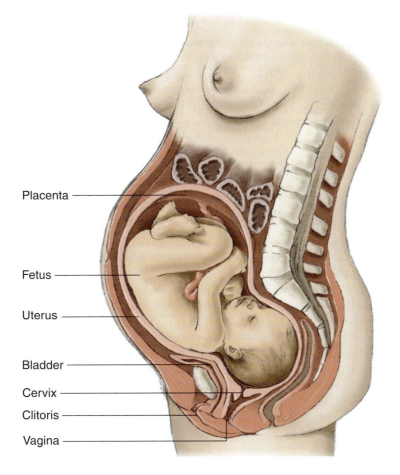

Fetal development at 9 weeks. The fetus is connected to the placenta by the umbilical cord.

© Dr. G. Moscoso/Photo Researchers, Inc.

Third-Trimester Development

In the third trimester the fetus continues to grow and to develop the size and strength it will need to live on its own (Figure 12.5). It increases in weight from 4 pounds in the seventh month to an average of over 7 pounds at birth. The downlike hair covering its body disappears, and head hair continues growing. The skin becomes smooth rather than wrinkled. The fetus is covered with a protective creamy, waxy substance called the **vernix caseosa** (VER-niks ka-see-OH-suh).

Vernix caseosa A waxy, protective substance on the fetus's skin.

▶ **Figure 12.5** Pregnancy in the ninth month. The uterus and abdomen have increased in size to accommodate the fetus.

Placenta

Fetus

Uterus

Bladder

Cervix

Clitoris

Vagina

Prenatal Care

Moderate exercise usually contributes to a healthy pregnancy and delivery. A pregnant woman should consult her health care provider for guidelines specific to her situation.

The developments just described take place in most pregnancies. Occasionally, however, something goes wrong. The fetus may not develop normally (up to 4% of infants have significant birth defects), the pregnancy may terminate early (14% of deliveries are premature), or maternal death may occur (Routh, 2000). The causes of these problems may be genetic and unpreventable, but the mother's own health and nutrition are also crucial in providing the best environment for fetal development. This is one reason it is important for a woman to have a complete physical examination and health assessment before becoming pregnant. She should also have a test to determine her immunity to rubella (German measles), a disease that can cause severe fetal defects if the mother contracts it while she is pregnant. An HIV test should also be done before or during pregnancy because HIV can be transmitted to the developing fetus during pregnancy, and therapies are available to help improve maternal and infant health (Krist, 2001).

Thorough prenatal care is essential for promoting the health of both the mother and the fetus. Components of optimal prenatal care include good nutrition, general good health, adequate rest, routine health care, exercise, and childbirth education (Thompson, 2003a). Unfortunately, many babies are born without adequate prenatal care, a situation that increases the chances of problems, including low birth weight, lung disorders, brain damage, and abnormal growth patterns. These problems can have lifelong effects (Hack, 2002). Women most likely to delay obtaining prenatal care are unmarried black or Hispanic individuals under age 20 who have not graduated from high school and are uninsured or on Medicaid. They typically live in low-income neighborhoods with a shortage of doctors' offices (Bloche, 2004; Perloff & Jaffee, 1999). Difficulties that interfere with access to care include a shortage of doctors in their low-income neighborhoods, a lack of appointments during evening and weekend times and difficulty taking time off work, long waiting times to schedule appointments, and crowded clinics. Inadequate care can affect the mother as well: Statistics indicate that four times as many black women as white women die from childbirth complications (Hoyert et al., 2000; Stolberg, 1999). Because of the wide disparity in access to health care in the United States, America ranks below 10 other countries in the world for maternal and infant mortality rates. Sweden has the lowest rates, and Switzerland, Canada, Australia, and the United Kingdom are among the other countries that have lower death rates than the United States (Cowley, 2003).

The fate of pregnant women in developing countries is severe. An African woman's risk of a pregnancy-related death is 1 in 6; an Asian woman's risk is 1 in 65, compared to a North American woman's risk of 1 in 3,700. Substandard services, women's underlying poor health, and gender-related factors resulting in women's lack of decision-making power in their families contribute to these high mortality rates (E. Murphy, 2003). ■

Risks to Fetal Development

Placenta A disk-shaped organ attached to the uterine wall and connected to the fetus by the umbilical cord. Nutrients, oxygen, and waste products pass between mother and fetus through the cell walls of the placenta.

The rapidly developing fetus is dependent on the mother for nutrients, oxygen, and waste elimination as substances pass through the **placenta** (a disk-shaped organ attached to the wall of the uterus, shown in Figure 12.6). The fetus is joined to the placenta by the umbilical cord. The fetal blood circulates independently within the closed system of the fetus and the inner part of the placenta. Maternal blood flows in the uterine walls and through the outer part of the placenta. Fetal and maternal blood do not normally intermingle. All exchanges between the fetal and maternal blood systems occur by passage of substances through the walls of the blood vessels. Nutrients and oxygen from the maternal blood pass into the fetal circulatory system; carbon dioxide and waste products from the fetus pass into the maternal blood vessels, to be removed by maternal circulation.

The placenta prevents some kinds of bacteria and viruses—but not all—from passing into the fetal blood system. Many bacteria and viruses, including HIV, do cross through the placenta. Bacterial infections of maternal tissues, the placenta, and umbilical cord can result in premature birth (Goldenberg et al., 2000). Furthermore, many substances ingested by the mother easily cross through the placenta and can damage the developing fetus (Frank et al.,

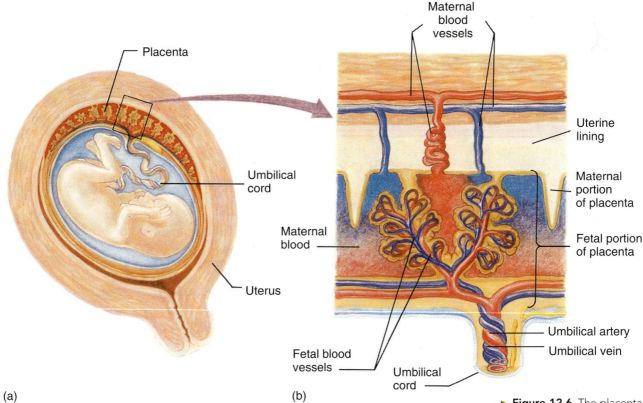

Placenta

Umbilical cord

Uterus

(a)

Maternal blood vessels

Uterine lining

Maternal portion of placenta

Fetal portion of placenta

Maternal blood

Umbilical artery

Umbilical vein

Fetal blood vessels

Umbilical cord

(b)

▶ **Figure 12.6** The placenta exchanges nutrients, oxygen, and waste products between the maternal and fetal circulatory systems. (a) The placenta attached to the uterine wall. (b) Close-up detail of the placenta.

2001; Singer, 2002). Certain medications, legal drugs such as tobacco and alcohol, and illegal drugs are all dangerous to the developing fetus, a fact that has led to controversy about whether the government can force a woman to change her behavior to protect the health of the fetus (Campbell, 2003; Harris et al., 2003). As many as one in three infants has been exposed to alcohol or other drugs in utero (Andrews & Patterson, 1995). Legal substances, such as tobacco and alcohol, affect a far greater number of pregnancies each year with more significant health consequences than illegal drugs (Pirie et al., 2000; Yuan et al., 2001).

A serious health hazard for the fetus is maternal cigarette smoking (Chavkin, 2001). Approximately 25% of U.S. women are smokers when they learn they are pregnant, and 60–75% of them continue to smoke throughout their pregnancies (Zapka et al., 2000). Smoking reduces the amount of oxygen in the bloodstream, which adversely affects the fetus, increasing the chances of miscarriage and of pregnancy complications that can result in fetal or infant death. Infants of mothers who smoked during pregnancy often weigh less, which poses even more serious health risks for twins because they are more likely to have low birth weight without maternal smoking (Haug et al., 2000; Pollack et al., 2000). Children of smoking mothers have a 50–70% greater chance of having a cleft lip or palate, significantly lower developmental scores, an increased incidence of reading disorders, and more respiratory diseases compared to matched offspring of nonsmokers (Charlton, 1994; Olds et al., 1994; Williams, 2000).

Alcohol easily crosses the placental membranes into all fetal tissues, especially brain tissue (M. Gottlieb, 2000). **Fetal alcohol syndrome (FAS)** is the leading cause of birth defects and developmental disabilities in the United States; in this country more than 8,000 infants are born with FAS each year (Stutts et al., 1997). The rate of FAS is nine times greater for Native Americans than for the general population (Goodman, 1998). Since 1981 the Food and Drug Administration has advised women to abstain *completely* from alcohol use during pregnancy to avoid the risk of damage to their babies. Any alcohol use can cause problems; even one drink per day has been associated with adverse birth effects. Binge drinking (five or more drinks per occasion) is extremely toxic to the fetus (Nanson, 1997). Women who binge drink during pregnancy often compound the insult to the fetus by also using tobacco, marijuana, cocaine, and other illicit drugs (Gladstone et al., 1997). Alcohol use can cause intrauterine death and spontaneous abortion, premature birth, congenital heart defects,

Fetal alcohol syndrome (FAS) Syndrome in infants caused by heavy maternal prenatal alcohol use; characterized by congenital heart defects, damage to the brain and nervous system, numerous physical malformations of the fetus, and below-normal IQ.

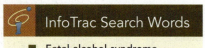
damage to the brain and nervous system, and numerous physical malformations of the fetus (Lorente et al., 2000). Babies can be born addicted to alcohol and consequently experience alcohol withdrawal for several days after birth. The effects of FAS persist through childhood; children with FAS continue to be small in size and developmentally delayed and to have behavior problems (M. Gottlieb, 2000).

Other substances known to cause harm to the mother (see Table 12.4) also pose serious hazards to a developing fetus. The babies of mothers who regularly used addictive drugs such as amphetamines, heroin, cocaine, codeine, morphine, or opium during pregnancy are often born premature, have low birth weight, and are small (Sprauve et al., 1997). In addition, after birth these babies experience withdrawal from the drug: They have tremors, disturbed feeding and sleep patterns, and abnormal muscle tension, and they often require hospitalization in neonatal intensive care units (Behnke et al., 1997). These children can experience permanent birth defects and damage to sensory, motor, and cognitive abilities that continue past infancy (Eyler et al., 1998; Zambrana & Scrimshaw, 1997).

TABLE 12.4	Things to Avoid During Pregnancy
Alcohol	
Smoking	
Secondary smoke	
Illegal drugs	
Any over-the-counter or prescription medication not approved by your health care provider	

SOURCE: Black & Hill (2003).

In a number of tragic situations children have been damaged by medications taken by their mothers during pregnancy. For example, the drug thalidomide, prescribed as a sedative to pregnant women in the early 1960s, caused severe deformities to the extremities. Some grown children of women who were given diethylstilbestrol (DES) while pregnant have developed genital tract abnormalities, including cancer (Mitka, 2003a). Antibiotics need to be prescribed selectively during pregnancy because tetracycline, a frequently used antibiotic, can damage an infant's teeth and cause stunted bone growth if it is taken after the 14th week of pregnancy (Lynch et al., 1991). Many over-the-counter medications, such as ibuprofen, aspirin, and histamines, can be detrimental to the fetus, and effects are unknown for many other nonprescription drugs and herbs (Black & Hill, 2003; Glover et al., 2003). Toxic substances found in the polluted environment can also harm fetal development (Haney, 1994).

Our knowledge about the effects of most of the drugs and other substances consumed by pregnant women is limited (Janssen & Genta, 2000). What we do know now is that we are learning of more and more potential hazards. For this reason no medications should be used during pregnancy unless they are absolutely necessary and are taken under close medical supervision. ■

Detection of Birth Defects

Amniocentesis A procedure in which amniotic fluid is removed from the uterus and tested to determine whether certain fetal birth defects exist.

Amniotic fluid The fluid inside the amniotic sac surrounding the fetus during pregnancy.

Chorionic villus sampling (CVS) A prenatal test that detects some birth defects.

If a woman and her physician have some reason to suspect that the fetus has abnormalities, a test known as **amniocentesis** (am-nee-oh-sen-TEE-sus) can help establish whether certain problems exist. The test is done during the 14th to 16th week of pregnancy. With the assistance of ultrasound guidance, the physician inserts a needle through the woman's abdominal wall into the uterine cavity to draw a sample of the **amniotic fluid** (the fluid surrounding the fetus). Fetal cells from the fluid are cultured for chromosome analysis, and the fluid is tested in procedures that take 2 to 3 weeks to produce results (Whittle, 1998). A variety of potential birth defects can be detected using amniocentesis. However, many cannot be detected (Stranc et al., 1997).

Another technique for detection of birth defects is called **chorionic villus** (kor-ee-AH-nik VIL-us) **sampling,** or **CVS.** Chorionic villi are threadlike protrusions on a membrane surrounding the placenta. To perform CVS, a physician inserts a thin catheter, with the assistance of ultrasound, through the abdomen or vagina and cervix into the uterus, where a small sample of the chorionic villi is removed for analysis. This procedure has an advantage over amniocentesis: It can be done as early as the 10th week instead of the 14th week. Amniocentesis has less than a 1% chance of inducing miscarriage, and CVS has only a slightly higher risk (Grayson, 2002).

Circumstances under which amniocentesis or CVS may be of benefit include maternal age over 35 years, a parent with a chromosomal defect, a previous child with defects such as Down syndrome (a chromosomal abnormality that results in impaired intellectual functioning and physical defects) or defects of the spine or spinal cord, or a familial background that suggests a significant risk of other disorders related to chromosomal abnormalities or metabolic defects. If the test results reveal a serious untreatable birth defect, the mother can have the pregnancy terminated. Amniocentesis and CVS involve the rare risks of damage to the fetus, induced miscarriage, and infection (Seligmann, 1992). Couples who have these procedures might also worry about harm to the fetus, the possible diagnosis of abnormality, or the possibility of having an abortion. For these reasons the procedures are not recommended unless the expected benefits outweigh the potential risks.

InfoTrac Search Words

■ Amniocentesis
■ Chorionic villus sampling

Pregnancy After Age 35

An increasing number of women are deciding to have children after 35 years of age. Births in the United States to women between age 45 and 49 nearly tripled from 1990 to 1999. In 2002 more than 5,000 women between 45 and 49 gave birth, and more than 200 women aged 50 to 54 gave birth (Budd, 2002; Tyre, 2004). Some couples are delaying childbearing for career, financial, or other reasons (Dubrzykowski & Stern, 2003).

Healthy older women have no higher risk than younger women of having a child with birth defects *not* related to abnormal chromosomes (Baird et al., 1991). However, the rate of fetal defects resulting from chromosomal abnormalities (such as Down syndrome) rises with maternal age. The estimated risk of such fetal defects is 2.6 per 1,000 before age 30; it is 5.6 at age 35, 15.8 at age 40, and 53.7 at age 45 (Hook, 1981). For women between age 35 and 44, amniocentesis and elective abortion reduce the risk of bearing an infant with a severe birth defect to a level comparable to that for younger women (Yuan et al., 2000).

There are additional increased risks to the mother and fetus with pregnancy over age 35. Slightly higher rates of maternal death, premature delivery, cesarean sections, and low-birth-weight babies occur (London, 2004). Age-related chronic illnesses such as diabetes and high blood pressure play a greater role than age itself in problems with labor, delivery, and infant health (Yuan et al., 2000). Most physicians find that pregnancy for a healthy woman over 35 is safe and not difficult to manage medically (Schrinsky, 1988). Some research even indicates that women age 35 and older felt less anxiety and depression during pregnancy than pregnant women in their mid 20s (Robinson et al., 1987).

A significant concern that women and their partners face when they consider postponing having a child until the woman is in her 30s or older is that her ability to become pregnant can be diminished. As women become older, their fertility decreases (Kalb, 2001). However, for most women who want to postpone childbearing until they have completed their education and established themselves in a career, the risks are small compared with the benefits of waiting until they are ready (Hanson, 2003).

▶ Childbirth

The full term of pregnancy usually lasts about 40 weeks from the last menstrual period, although there is some variation in length. Some women have longer pregnancies; others give birth to fully developed infants up to a few weeks before the 9-month term is over. The experience of childbirth also varies a good deal, depending on many factors: the woman's physiology, her emotional state, the baby's size and position, the kind of childbirth practices used, and the kind of support she receives.

Contemporary Childbirth

Today's parents-to-be can expect to work as part of a team with their health care provider in preparing and planning for the physical and emotional aspects of childbirth. Most hospitals and health care providers are eager to help provide a safe and positive birth experience for the entire family. Parents-to-be often participate in childbirth classes that provide thorough information about medical interventions and the process of labor and birth. The classes also

Prepared childbirth classes help prepare expectant mothers and fathers for childbirth.

provide training for the pregnant woman and her labor coach (either her partner or a friend) in breathing and relaxation exercises designed to cope with the pain of childbirth. Research has found that women assisted by a trained birth attendant during labor had fewer cesarean sections, less pain medication, shorter length of labor, and greater satisfaction with the birth experience (McNiven et al., 1992).

Approaches to contemporary childbirth began to develop when Grantly Dick-Read and Fernand Lamaze began presenting their ideas about childbirth in the late 1930s and early 1940s. They believed that certain attitudes and practices could help improve the experience of childbirth. Dick-Read believed that most of the pain during childbirth stemmed from the muscle tension caused by fear. To reduce anxiety, he advocated education about the birth process and relaxation with calm, consistent support during a woman's labor. The **Lamaze** philosophy is similar. This method consists of learning to voluntarily relax abdominal and perineal muscles and to use breathing exercises to dissociate the involuntary labor contractions from pain sensations. Although both of these methods are now incorporated into childbirth education classes throughout the United States, women in the 1950s and 1960s who wanted to use these methods frequently had difficulty finding physicians willing to support them in the hospital. Because the women questioned established obstetric practice, they were often seen as compromising the health of their infants. However, as feminists pursued women's rights in many areas, they stressed involvement in decision making about pregnancy and birth (Larimore, 1995; Wolf, 2001). Their criticisms received extensive media coverage, and the public's concept of childbirth gradually changed, creating a demand for more flexible, family-centered birth experiences—which health care practitioners also began to support (Toussie-Weingarten & Jacobwitz, 1987).

Although they are sometimes referred to as natural childbirth methods, **prepared childbirth** is a more appropriate label for the Dick-Read, Lamaze, and other childbirth approaches. A woman and her partner are indeed preparing themselves when they participate in prepared-childbirth classes and rehearse these techniques during pregnancy.

Lamaze A method of childbirth preparation using breathing and relaxation.

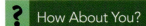 **How About You?**

What do you know about your birth? Would you be comfortable asking your parents about it to find out more?

Prepared childbirth Birth following an education process that can involve information, exercises, breathing, and working with a labor coach.

Birthplace Alternatives

Along with more options for childbirth practices have come new options for places where childbirth occurs. Not many years ago, a husband, partner, family member, or labor coach could not be with the woman during labor and childbirth. The hospital setting was cold and impersonal, and the woman had little control over the medical procedures used during the birth process. Currently, as choices about labor and birth have increased, so have options for childbirth settings. Each birthplace is unique in terms of what it offers the parents and the infant.

Hospital Births

Most hospitals now have *birthing rooms* with a homelike atmosphere. A birthing room offers families the opportunity for an emotionally supportive, homelike birth and yet provides the medical backup services of the hospital. Participation of a partner, labor coach, and others; unmedicated childbirth; and immediate postbirth parent–infant contact are common practice.

An important aspect of the hospital setting is that it provides emergency medical care should birth complications arise. The hospital is the appropriate place for childbirth in any high-risk pregnancy. Conditions that raise the risk of complication include premature labor, the infant being in a position other than head-first, blood incompatibility between mother and fetus, **toxemia** (tok-SEE-mee-uh) (water retention and high blood pressure are early symptoms—the condition can result in convulsions of the mother if untreated), **placenta previa** (pluh-SEN-tuh PREE-vee-uh) (the placenta positioned over the cervical opening), multiple births, five or more previous births, too small a pelvis, or maternal illness. Competent and thorough prenatal screening can detect most of these complications. However, even a birth that is expected to be low risk can develop complications that require medical intervention.

Toxemia A dangerous condition during pregnancy in which high blood pressure occurs.

Placenta previa A birth complication in which the placenta is between the cervical opening and the infant.

Birthing Centers

Birthing centers, available in some areas, offer the homelike atmosphere of birthing rooms in hospitals. Some are adjacent to hospitals, and others are separate, freestanding organizations. Limited emergency equipment is available at a birthing center. However, if a serious complication arises, the woman would have to be transported to a hospital—for example, if an emergency cesarean birth was required. Only women with no foreseeable birth complications should be accepted for care in a birthing center (Toussie-Weingarten & Jacobwitz, 1987).

Home Birth

Home birth became more common when families began seeking the family-centered birth experience that, in the past, hospitals did not provide. Proponents of home birth believe that with precautions—careful prenatal screening for complications, thorough preparations, a skilled attendant, and available emergency transportation—home birth can be relatively safe (Saunders, 1997).

Stages of Childbirth

Despite variations in childbirth, there are three generally recognizable stages in the process (see Figure 12.7). A woman can often tell that labor has begun when regular contractions of the uterus begin. Another indication of beginning **first-stage labor,** the gradual dilation of the cervix to 10 centimeters, is the "bloody show" (discharge of the mucus plug from the cervix). The amniotic sac can rupture in the first stage of labor, an occurrence sometimes called "breaking the bag of waters."

First-stage labor The initial stage of childbirth in which regular contractions begin and the cervix dilates.

(a) **First stage**
Dilation of cervix, followed by transition phase, when baby's head can start to pass through the cervix

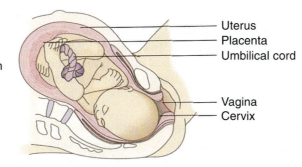
Uterus
Placenta
Umbilical cord
Vagina
Cervix

▶ **Figure 12.7** The three stages of childbirth: (a) first-stage labor, (b) second-stage labor, and (c) third-stage labor.

(b) **Second stage**
Passage of the baby through the birth canal, or vagina, and delivery into the world

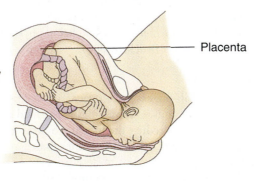
Placenta

(c) **Third stage**
Expulsion of the placenta, blood, and fluid ("afterbirth")

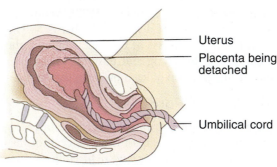
Uterus
Placenta being detached
Umbilical cord

Effacement Flattening and thinning of the cervix that occurs before and during childbirth.

© D. van Rossum/Photo Researchers, Inc.

Second-stage labor is usually the highlight of the birth process.

Second-stage labor The middle stage of labor, in which the infant descends through the vaginal canal.

Third-stage labor The last stage of childbirth, in which the placenta separates from the uterine wall and comes out of the vagina.

Afterbirth The placenta and amniotic sac following their expulsion through the vagina after childbirth.

Episiotomy An incision in the perineum that is sometimes made during childbirth.

Before the first stage begins, **effacement** (flattening and thinning) of the cervix has usually already occurred and the cervix has dilated slightly. The cervix continues to dilate throughout the first stage, and it is the extent of dilation that defines the early, late, and transition phases of first-stage labor. The cervix is dilated up to 4 centimeters during the early phase, 4 to 8 centimeters in the active phase, and 8 to 10 centimeters during the final, or transition, phase of the first stage. Each phase becomes shorter, and the contractions become stronger; transition is usually the most intense phase. The first stage is the longest of the three stages, usually lasting 10 to 16 hours for the first childbirth and 4 to 8 hours in subsequent births.

Second-stage labor begins when the cervix is fully dilated and the infant descends farther into the vaginal birth canal. Usually the descent is head first, as shown in Figure 12.7b. The second stage often lasts from a half-hour to 2 hours—although it can be shorter or longer. During this time the woman can actively push to help the baby out, and many women report their active pushing to be the best part of labor:

I knew what "labor" meant when I was finally ready to push. I have never worked so hard, so willingly. (Authors' files)

The second stage ends when the infant is born.

Third-stage labor lasts from the time of birth until the delivery of the placenta, shown in Figure 12.7c. With one or two more uterine contractions, the placenta usually separates from the uterine wall and comes out of the vagina, generally within a half-hour after the baby is born. The placenta is also called the **afterbirth.**

Medical Interventions: Pros and Cons

Women and their partners should be aware of the possible benefits and side effects of medical procedures used during childbirth. Administering or using medications, fetal heart rate monitors, and vacuum extraction and forceps, and performing an episiotomy or cesarean section are common medical interventions. The advantages and disadvantages of these procedures need to be discussed with the health care provider before labor begins.

Medications

Local and regional anesthesia (such as spinal and epidural anesthesia) have negligible effects on the fetus and can greatly help to ease labor and make the mother more comfortable (Volm, 1997). Research indicates that some medications can slow or stop labor, decrease blood pressure, and eliminate the ability to push during second-stage labor. The risks are small when medications are chosen and administered cautiously, and the woman can have a positive childbirth experience while being physically more comfortable during labor and childbirth (Faucher & Brucker, 2000).

Episiotomy

An **episiotomy** (ih-piz-ee-AH-tuh-mee), or making an incision in the perineum from the vagina toward the anus, is sometimes performed in hospital births. The rationale for episiotomies is that they reduce the pressure on the infant's head and also help prevent vaginal tearing, which is more difficult to suture than a straight incision and often heals less well. Episiotomies also are thought to help preserve pelvic muscle tone and support. However, research shows that routine episiotomy during uncomplicated labor presents greater risks than benefits (Maier & Malony, 1997). Although the procedure is common in the United States—about 39% of deliveries (Weber & Meyn, 2002)—it is used far less in most other countries (e.g., only 8% of birthing women in the Netherlands have episiotomies). Relaxation, proper breathing and pushing, physician patience, manual stretching of the perineum, and freedom of leg movement can eliminate the need for many routine incisions.

The Use of Forceps

Forceps, a medical instrument shaped like salad tongs and designed to clasp the baby's head, are sometimes used to assist the infant out of the birth canal. Forceps are often used after analgesics and anesthetics have reduced the strength of uterine contractions. Careful use of forceps is justified in appropriate circumstances but not with routine, normal births. Vacuum extraction, placing a vacuum cup on the emerging baby's head, can also be used to help pull the infant through the birth canal (Schifrin, 2003).

Delivery by Cesarean Section

A **cesarean** (sih-ZEHR-ee-un) **section,** in which the baby is removed through an incision made in the abdominal wall and uterus, can be a lifesaving surgery for the mother and child. Cesarean birth is recommended in a variety of situations, including when the fetal head is too large to pass through the mother's pelvic structure, during maternal illness, or when there are indications of fetal distress during labor or birth complications, such as a breech presentation (feet or bottom coming out of the uterus first). Mothers who experience cesarean birth often have a spinal or epidural anesthetic and are awake to greet their infants when the baby is born. In many hospitals fathers remain with the woman during cesarean births.

Cesarean section A childbirth procedure in which the infant is removed through an incision in the abdomen and uterus.

A woman can have more than one baby by cesarean section. Also, most women can have subsequent vaginal births, depending on the circumstances of the earlier cesarean birth(s) and of the subsequent birth (Dauphinee, 2004; Elkousy et al., 2003). Although many women who have cesarean births are less satisfied with their birth experiences than are women who have vaginal births, adjustment following childbirth is similar in the two groups (Padawer et al., 1988).

The percentage of cesarean sections performed in the United States increased dramatically after the mid 1960s, and it was the most common hospital surgical procedure in the United States. About 23% of live births are cesarean sections. Some maintain that high rates reflect better use of medical technology, but others believe that cesarean sections are used too readily (Springen, 2000).

▶ After Childbirth

The first several weeks following birth are referred to as the **postpartum period.** This is a time of both physical and psychological adjustment for each family member, and it is likely to be a time of intensified emotional highs and lows. The new baby affects the roles and interactions of all family members. The parents can experience an increased closeness to each other as well as some troublesome feelings. A partner might sometimes feel jealous of the close relationship between the mother and child. Both partners may want extra emotional support from the other, but each may have less than usual to give. The time and energy demands of caring for an infant can contribute to weariness and stress. Conflict about the division of household and child care labor can become problematic in the early months and years of the child's life (Cowan & Cowan, 1992). Brothers and sisters are also affected, because they often have some negative feelings about the attention given to their new sibling. Some hospitals offer classes for expectant brothers and sisters to help them anticipate and cope with changes the new baby will bring. A good support system for the new parents can be immensely helpful. Understanding that these feelings are a common response to adjustments to the new baby may help new parents cope with the stresses involved. One woman described her feelings during this time as follows:

Postpartum period The first several weeks after childbirth.

> Nothing, to be sure, had prepared me for the intensity of relationship already existing between me and a creature I had carried in my body and now held in my arms and fed from my breasts. Throughout pregnancy and nursing, women are urged to relax, to mime the serenity of madonnas. No one mentions the psychic crisis of bearing a first child, the excitation of long-buried feelings about one's own mother, the sense of confused power and powerlessness.... No one mentions the strangeness of attraction—which can be as single-minded and overwhelming as the early days of a love affair—to a being so tiny, so dependent, so folded-into itself—who is, and yet is not, part of oneself. (Rich, 1976, p. 36)

Combined with heightened excitement and happiness are often other feelings. The mother may cry easily without feeling fearful or sad (Zelkowitz & Milet, 1995). One new mother described her "postpartum euphoria":

I would cry from happiness at almost anything. I was simply overflowing with joy and amazement and love. (Authors' files)

Postpartum depression (PPD) Symptoms of depression and obsessive thoughts of hurting the baby.

Postpartum depression (PPD) affects 15% of mothers (Routh, 2000). Unlike the more common "baby blues"—short-lived tearfulness and mood swings that about 80% of new mothers feel—PPD involves classic symptoms of depression, including insomnia, anxiety, panic attacks, and hopelessness (Hanna et al., 2004; Josefsson et al., 2001). At its most extreme, women suffering from PPD lose interest in their babies or develop obsessive thoughts about harming themselves or their babies. Fortunately, PPD can be effectively treated (Formichelli, 2001; Greenberg & Westreich, 2000). Such reactions may be partly due to the sudden emotional, physical, and hormonal changes following birth. Sleep deprivation from waking many times in the night to care for the newborn also is stressful and diminishes emotional and physical reserves.

Breast Feeding

Right after birth the breasts produce a yellowish liquid, called colostrum, that contains antibodies and protein. Lactation, or milk production, begins about 1 to 3 days after birth. Pituitary hormones stimulate milk production in the breasts in response to the stimulation of the infant suckling the nipples. If a new mother does not begin or continue to nurse, milk production subsides within a matter of days.

Although exclusive breast feeding for the first 6 months is encouraged by the American Academy of Pediatrics and the World Health Organization, a nationally representative survey in the United States found that only 47% of 1-week-old children had been exclusively breast-fed and that only 10% of 6-month-old babies were breast-fed. Women most likely to have breast-fed were college graduates in the highest income level, and women least likely to have breast-fed were at the lowest education and income levels, residents of the South, teenage mothers, African American mothers, and smokers (Ruowei, 2002). Breast-feeding rates in Sweden are significantly higher than in the United States, partly due to generous maternity leave for most employees (a full year at 80% of their wages) (Gibbs, 2002).

Breast feeding has many practical and emotional advantages. Breast milk provides the infant with a digestible food filled with antibodies and other immunity-producing substances (Wold & Adlerberth, 1998). Nursing also induces uterine contractions that help speed the return of the uterus to its prepregnancy size. Breast feeding can be a positive emotional and sensual experience for the mother. For women who nurse, breast feeding is another opportunity for close physical contact with the baby.

© Erika Stone/Photo Researchers, Inc.

For women who decide to nurse, breast feeding is another opportunity for close physical contact with her baby.

Sexual Health

I love seeing the contentment spread over my baby's face as she fills her tummy with milk from my breasts. It's an awe-inspiring continuation of our physical connection during pregnancy to see her growing chubby-cheeked from nourishment my body provides her. (Authors' files)

Nursing can temporarily inhibit ovulation, particularly for women who feed their babies only breast milk (Perez et al., 1992). However, as we saw in Chapter 11, nursing is not a reliable method of birth control. Estrogen-containing birth control pills should not be used during nursing because the hormones reduce the amount of milk and affect milk quality. However, progesterone-only pills can be used because progesterone affects neither milk supply nor quality (Salisbury, 1991). However, some couples prefer foam and condoms to avoid any extra hormones during nursing. ■

Research shows that cigarette smoking reduces the amount of milk that a nursing mother produces (Horta et al., 2001). Environmental, or secondary, smoke exposure from smokers around the mother also reduces the amount of milk she makes. Women who smoke or who inhale secondary smoke tend to nurse for shorter durations than mothers who do not smoke and are in smoke-free environments (Horta et al., 1997).

Nursing also has some short-term disadvantages. For one, nursing causes reduced levels of estrogen, which conditions and maintains vulvar tissue and promotes vaginal lubrication. As a result, the nursing mother may be less interested in sexual activity, and her genitals may become sore from intercourse (Barrett et al., 2000). The woman's breasts may also be tender and sore. Milk may be ejected

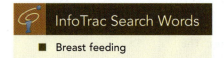

InfoTrac Search Words

■ Breast feeding

involuntarily from her nipples during sexual stimulation—a source of potential amusement or embarrassment.

Some women have negative feelings about breast feeding. Many women feel ambivalent about this activity, perhaps partly because of our society's emphasis on breasts as sex symbols. Furthermore, some mothers' lives are too demanding for the sole feeding responsibility of nursing, particularly if they return to work shortly after childbearing (Brandon, 2001; Ruben, 1992). It is often easier to share child care responsibilities by bottle feeding rather than nursing: The father can then play a greater role in holding and feeding the infant. However, a nursing mother can use a breast pump to extract her milk so that it is available to her partner or another caregiver for bottle-feeding the baby. Like other aspects of child care, breast feeding is a matter of exploration and personal preference.

Sexual Interaction After Childbirth

Couples are commonly advised that intercourse can resume after the flow of the reddish uterine discharge, called **lochia** (LOH-kee-uh), has stopped and after episiotomy incisions or vaginal tears have healed, usually about 3–4 weeks (Ono, 1994). However, most couples wait to resume intercourse until 6–8 weeks after birth (Volm, 1997). An important factor to consider is when intercourse is physically comfortable for the woman. This depends on the type of birth, the size and presentation of the baby, the extent of episiotomy or lacerations, and the individual woman's rate of healing. The postpartum decrease in hormones, especially pronounced with breast feeding, can cause discomfort during intercourse. After a cesarean birth the couple needs to wait until the incision has healed enough for intercourse to occur without discomfort. Other sexual and affectionate relations can be shared while waiting.

Lochia A reddish uterine discharge that occurs after childbirth.

Psychological readiness for sexual activity is another important factor. A new baby brings significant changes in daily life that can affect sexual intimacy. Research has found high levels of sexual difficulties after childbirth (Iovine, 1997b). Before their pregnancies, 38% of the study participants reported experiencing sexual problems. In the first 3 months after delivery, over 80% of new mothers experienced one or more sexual problems, and at 6 months 64% were still having difficulty. The most common concerns were decreased sexual interest, vaginal dryness, and painful intercourse. The researcher, who has written books about pregnancy and the first year of motherhood, warns women to be prepared for their sex lives to be "downright crummy" for up to a year: "Mother Nature is using her entire arsenal of tricks, from hormones to humility, to keep you focused on your baby and not on getting pregnant again" (Iovine, 1997a, p. 158).

Fatigue is also a major factor affecting sexuality after childbirth. The demands of caring for a new baby on both the woman and her partner may mean that there is not much time or energy left for sexual expression. Fitting lovemaking into the baby's and parents' schedules can be quite a challenge. Concern about the baby can also interfere:

It seems that every time we start to make love, the baby cries. Even though I know he's been fed and is dry, I can't focus on my sexual feelings. And when he gets quiet, I worry that he's dead! My husband has the same reactions, so lots of times we don't get much going together. (Authors' files)

Women and their partners whose sexual activity has been disrupted by pregnancy and birth may feel out of practice in their sexual relationship. It is often helpful to resume sexual activity in an unhurried, exploratory manner. Once intercourse has resumed, contraception is necessary if the woman wants to avoid another pregnancy.

Although many women experience negative effects on their sexuality after childbirth, only 15% discussed their sexual concerns with their health care provider. Apparently, health care providers overlook asking new mothers about the quality of their sexual health and instead focus on the many other concerns about the mother and baby (Barrett et al., 2000). Postpartum women and their partners may need to initiate discussions about sexual concerns. ■

Summary

Parenthood as an Option

- An increasing number of couples are choosing not to be parents. More women today choose careers over motherhood. (p. 336)
- The realities of parenthood or child-free living are difficult to predict. (p. 337)

Becoming Pregnant

- Timing intercourse to correspond to ovulation enhances the likelihood of conception. (p. 337)
- Approximately 1 in 6 couples in the United States has problems with infertility, and a cause is not found in as many as 15% of infertile couples. (p. 338)
- Failure to ovulate and blockage of the fallopian tubes are typical causes of female infertility. Low sperm count is the most common cause of male infertility. (pp. 338–340)
- Alcohol, drug use, cigarette smoking, and infections from sexually transmitted diseases reduce fertility in both women and men. (pp. 338–339)
- The emotional stress and the disruption of a couple's sexual relationship from infertility can result in sexual problems. (p. 340)
- The legal and social issues related to artificial insemination, surrogate motherhood, and assisted reproductive technologies are complex and will continue to create controversy. (pp. 340–343)
- Artificial insemination is done with donor semen when the husband is infertile. (p. 340)
- The first sign of a pregnancy is usually a missed menstrual period. Urine and blood tests and pelvic examinations are used to determine pregnancy. (p. 343)

Spontaneous and Elective Abortion

- Spontaneous abortion, or miscarriage, occurs in approximately 12–15% of pregnancies. Most miscarriages occur within the first 3 months of pregnancy. (p. 343)
- Elective abortion is a highly controversial social and political issue in the United States today. Medications, suction curettage, D and E, and prostaglandin induction are the medical techniques used to induce abortion. (p. 345)
- Contraceptive method failure is a major contributor to women having repeat abortions. (p. 348)
- Contraceptive risk taking often precedes an unplanned pregnancy and consequent abortion. (p. 348)
- In 1973 the U.S. Supreme Court legalized a woman's right to decide to terminate her pregnancy before the fetus reaches the age of viability. In 1977 the Hyde Amendment prohibited the use of federal Medicaid funds for abortion and limited low-income women's access to abortion. In the 1990s many state legislatures imposed further limitations on the availability of abortion. (pp. 349–350)
- Pro-choice and pro-life advocates have fundamental differences in their beliefs about many aspects of life. (p. 351)

The Experience of Pregnancy

- Some first-trimester physical changes include cessation of menstruation, fatigue, and breast tenderness. In the second trimester the woman's abdomen begins to protrude, and she can feel fetal movements. By the third trimester the abdomen is enlarged, and fetal movements are pronounced. Emotional reactions to pregnancy vary greatly. (pp. 356–357)
- Men have become increasingly involved in the prenatal, childbirth, and child-rearing processes. (pp. 354–355)
- Although changes of position may be necessary, sensual and sexual interaction can continue as desired during pregnancy, except in occasional cases of medical complications. (pp. 355–356)

A Healthy Pregnancy

- Pregnancy is divided into three trimesters, each of which is marked by fetal changes. (p. 356)
- Nutrient, oxygen, and waste exchange between the woman and her fetus occurs through the placenta. Substances harmful to the fetus can pass through the placenta from the mother's blood. Smoking, alcohol and drugs, and certain medications can severely damage the developing fetus. (pp. 358–360)
- Amniocentesis and chorionic villus sampling are two tests that can be done during pregnancy to screen for certain birth defects. (p. 360)
- More women are deciding to have children after age 35. These women have slightly decreased fertility and a somewhat higher risk of conceiving a fetus with chromosomal abnormalities. However, with careful monitoring of pregnancy and childbirth, their risks can be reduced to the level of those of younger women. (p. 361)

Childbirth

- Prepared childbirth, popularized by Fernand Lamaze and Grantly Dick-Read, has changed childbirth practices. Most hospitals now support participation of the woman's partner and a team approach to decision making about the birth process. (pp. 361–362)
- Birthing clinics and home birth are additional alternatives to hospital birth, but neither has the advantage of the complete emergency medical backup sometimes necessary during birth. (p. 363)
- Indications of first-stage labor are regular contractions of the uterus, discharge of the mucus plug, rupture of the amniotic sac, and cervical effacement and dilation of up to 10 cm. (p. 363)
- Second-stage labor is the descent of the infant into the birth canal, ending with birth. The placenta is delivered in the third stage. (p. 364)
- Medical interventions during birth (administering medications, using forceps, and performing episiotomies and cesarean sections) can be helpful in the birth process, but some people believe that these interventions and procedures are overused. (p. 364)

After Childbirth

- There are many physical, emotional, and family adjustments to be made following the birth of a baby. Postpartum depression affects up to 15% of new mothers. (pp. 365–366)
- Breast feeding has regained popularity in the United States. (p. 366)
- There are advantages and disadvantages to both breast and bottle feeding. (pp. 366–367)
- Intercourse after childbirth can usually resume once the flow of lochia has stopped and any vaginal tears or the episiotomy incision has healed. However, it may take longer for sexual interest and arousal to return to normal. (p. 367)

Suggested Readings

Allen, Marie, and Shelly Marks (1993). *Women Sharing from the Heart.* New York: Wiley. A book about women's experiences with miscarriage.

Carroll, Laura (2000). *Families of Two: Interviews with Happily Married Couples Without Children by Choice.* Philadelphia: Exlibris Corp. An inside look at couples who choose to live child free.

Eisenberg, Arlene, Heidi Murkoff, and Sandee Hathaway (1991). *What to Expect When You're Expecting.* New York: Workman. The current bible of pregnancy; a clear, comprehensive month-by-month guide that answers concerns of mothers- and fathers-to-be.

Gorney, Cynthia (1998). *Articles of Faith: A Frontline History of the Abortion Wars.* New York: Simon and Schuster. A thoughtful and balanced account of the battles over abortion.

Louv, Richard (1993). *Fatherlove.* New York: Pocket Books. An exploration of the fulfillment of fathering one's children and bonding with one's father, grandchildren, and community.

Miller, Juliet, and Jane Haynes (Eds.) (2003). *Inconceivable Conceptions: Psychotherapy, Fertility, and the New Reproductive Technologies.* London: Brunner-Routledge. Contributions from psychology, anthropology, literature, and medicine explore the impact of infertility diagnosis and assisted reproductive technologies.

Nilsson, Lennart (1977). *A Child Is Born.* New York: Dell. A classic book of exquisite photographs of fetal development.

Peoples, Debbie, and Harriett Ferguson (2000). *Experiencing Infertility: An Essential Resource.* New York: Norton. A comprehensive presentation of the decision-making process and emotional roller coaster of infertility. Offers sound ideas and coping methods from assessing infertility to shifting gears to adoption.

Stoppard, Miriam (2000). *Dr. Miriam Stoppard's New Pregnancy and Birth Book.* New York: Ballantine Books. A classic guide for parents-to-be.

Resources

International Childbirth Education Association, P.O. Box 20048, Minneapolis, MN 55420. Provides information and resources for childbirth education.

Resolve: The National Infertility Association, 1310 Broadway, Somerville, MA 02144; (888) 623-0744. A national nonprofit organization that provides support groups, education, and publications for couples struggling with infertility.

Web Resources

Your *Our Sexuality* Web site **http://psychology.wadsworth.com/crooksbaur9e/** has direct links to the Web sites described below. These links are checked often for changes, dead links, and new additions.

International Council on Infertility Information Dissemination (INCIID)
For those seeking more information on infertility, this Web site provides especially helpful fact sheets on various types of fertility treatments and assisted reproductive techniques.

Alan Guttmacher Institute
This well-respected nonprofit organization sponsors a great deal of research on issues related to sexuality, contraception, and abortion. Among the features of its Web site are news updates and descriptions of recent research affecting reproductive health.

NARAL Pro-Choice America
An advocacy group for abortion rights, NARAL offers a Web site promoting legal and educational efforts to guarantee reproductive rights.

Lamaze International
Lamaze International provides information promoting healthy pregnancy and childbirth on their Web site.

Our Sexuality Web Site

For online resources directly related to this book, go to **http://psychology.wadsworth.com/crooksbaur9e/**. You will find interactive exercises, study questions, chapter outlines, an online version of this text's glossary, and Web links and activities that complement your CD-ROM.

InfoTrac® College Edition Online Library

http://infotrac.thomsonlearning.com/
InfoTrac College Edition is an online searchable library that includes a multitude of journals, many of which are specific to human sexuality. These journals include *Archives of Sexual Behavior, Archives of Sexual Health Behavior, Canadian Journal of Human Sexuality, Hispanic Journal of the Behavioral Sciences, Journal of Cross-Cultural Psychology, Journal of Physical Education, Recreation, and Dance, Journal of Sex Research,* and *Sex Roles.* You may search topics suggested in the margins of this chapter or terms of your own.

Our Sexuality CD-ROM

Use your CD-ROM for further study of the concepts in this chapter. Your CD-ROM provides animations of difficult concepts, video clips of real people discussing sexuality, critical thinking questions, chapter quizzing, and more.

Sexuality During Childhood and Adolescence

▶ **Sexual Behavior During Infancy and Childhood**

What common patterns characterize emerging sexuality during childhood?

What is the nature and meaning of sex play with friends during childhood?

▶ **The Physical Changes of Adolescence**

What major physical changes accompany the onset of puberty in boys and girls?

How do the physical changes of adolescence affect sexuality?

▶ **Sexual Behavior During Adolescence**

What behavior patterns are characteristic of teenage sexuality?

What trends have been evident in adolescent coital activity over the last several decades?

▶ **Adolescent Pregnancy**

What are the major trends in and causes and implications of teenage pregnancy in the United States?

What strategies might be effective in reducing teenage pregnancy?

▶ **Sex Education**

How can parents provide valuable and effective sex education for their children?

How does sex education influence young people's sexual experimentation?

© Paul Steel/CORBIS

My earliest recollection of an experience that could be labeled as sexual in nature involved thrusting against the pillow in my crib and experiencing something that felt really good, which I now believe must have been an orgasm (actually, I remember doing this many times). I was probably around two at the time, give or take a few months. What is odd about these early experiences is that I distinctly remember sleeping in my parents' bedroom, but never being reprimanded for this "self-abuse" behavior. Either my parents were very heavy sleepers, or they were very avant-garde in their view of sex. Knowing my parents, I presume the former is true. (Authors' files)

In many Western societies, including the United States, it was once common to view the period between birth and puberty as a time when sexuality remains unexpressed. However, as many of you can no doubt attest to from your own experiences, the early years of life are by no means a period of sexual dormancy. Perhaps you can even recall sensual or sexual experiences similar to the quoted account that date from the early years of your life. In this chapter we outline many of the common sexual experiences and behaviors that take place during the formative years from infancy through adolescence.

▶ Sexual Behavior During Infancy and Childhood

Research over the last several decades has clearly demonstrated that a variety of behaviors and body functions, including sexual eroticism, develop during infancy and childhood. In some ways sexuality is especially important during this period, because many experiences during these formative years have a great effect on the future expression of adult sexuality. In this section we briefly outline some typical sexual and sensual behaviors that occur during infancy and childhood.

Infant Sexuality

For most people the capacity for sexual response is present from birth (DeLamater & Friedrich, 2002). In the first two years of life, a period generally referred to as infancy, many girls and boys discover the pleasures of genital stimulation (Lidster & Horsburgh, 1994). As reflected in the quote from our files that opened this chapter, this activity often involves thrusting or rubbing the genital area against an object, such as a doll or a pillow. Pelvic thrusting and other signs of sexual arousal in infants, such as vaginal lubrication and penile erection, are often misinterpreted or unacknowledged. However, careful observers have noted these indicators of sexuality in the very young (Lively & Lively, 1991; Montauk & Clasen, 1989; Ryan, 2000). In some cases both male and female infants have been observed experiencing what appears to be an orgasm. The infant, of course, cannot offer spoken confirmation of the sexual nature of such reactions, but the behavior is so remarkably similar to that exhibited by sexually responding adults that little doubt exists about its nature. Alfred Kinsey and his associates, in their book on female sexuality, detailed the observations of a mother who had frequently observed her 3-year old daughter engaging in unmistakably masturbatory activity:

> Lying face down on the bed, with her knees drawn up, she started rhythmic pelvic thrusts, about one second or less apart. The thrusts were primarily pelvic, with the legs tensed in a fixed position. The forward components of the thrusts were in a smooth and perfect rhythm which was unbroken except for momentary pauses during which the genitalia were readjusted against the doll on which they were pressed; the return from each thrust was convulsive, jerky. There were 44 thrusts in unbroken rhythm, a slight momentary pause, 87 thrusts followed by a slight momentary pause, concentration and intense breathing with abrupt jerks as orgasm approached. She was completely oblivious to everything during these later stages of the activity. Her eyes were glassy and fixed in a vacant stare. There was noticeable relief and relaxation after orgasm. (Kinsey et al., 1953, pp. 104–105)

Kinsey also detailed references to male infant sexuality:

> The orgasm in an infant or other young male is, except for lacking of ejaculation, a striking duplicate of orgasm in an older adult. The behavior involves a series of gradual

physiologic changes, the development of rhythmic body movements with distinct penis throbs and pelvic thrusts, an obvious change in sensory capacities, a final tension of muscles, especially of the abdomen, hips, and back, a sudden release with convulsions, including rhythmic anal contractions—followed by the disappearance of all symptoms. A fretful baby quiets down under the initial sexual stimulation, is distracted from other activities, begins rhythmic pelvic thrusts, becomes tense as climax approaches, is thrown into convulsive action, often with violent arm and leg movements, sometimes with weeping at the moment of climax. (Kinsey et al., 1948, p. 177)

It is impossible to determine what such early sexual experiences mean to infants, but it is reasonably certain that these activities are gratifying. Many infants of both sexes engage quite naturally in self-pleasuring unless such behavior produces strong negative responses from parents or other caregivers.

Clearly, an infant is unable to differentiate sexual pleasure from other forms of sensual enjoyment. Many of the natural everyday activities involved in caring for an infant, such as breast feeding and bathing, involve pleasurable tactile stimulation that, although essentially sensual in nature, stimulate a genital or sexual response (Frayser, 1994; Martinson, 1994).

Childhood Sexuality

What constitutes normal and healthy sexual behavior in children? This is a difficult question for which we have no definitive answer; the data on childhood sexuality are scarce. Research in this area is limited by a number of factors, not the least of which is political squeamishness over what "might be interpreted as exploiting children or introducing sexual ideas to them" (Contemporary Sexuality, 1998, p. 1). It is difficult to obtain financial support for basic research on childhood sexuality, and federal guidelines in the United States either prohibit such studies or make them considerably difficult to conduct. Recently, a team of researchers surmounted some of these obstacles to research in the United States by interviewing a large sample of primary caregivers (all mothers) of children, ages 2 to 12. The results of this informative study are described in the boxed discussion "Normative Sexual Behavior in Children: A Contemporary Sample."

People show considerable variation in their sexual development during childhood, and diverse influences are involved (Bancroft, 2003). Despite these differences, however, certain common features in the developmental sequence tend to emerge. As we outline our somewhat limited knowledge of some of these typical behaviors, keep in mind that each person's unique sexual history can differ in some respects from the described behaviors. It is also important to realize that, other than reports from primary caregivers, most of what we know about childhood sexual behavior is based on recollections of adults who are asked to recall their childhood experiences. As we noted in Chapter 2, accurately remembering experiences that occurred many years earlier is quite difficult.

Enjoying sexual intimacies as an adult may be related to childhood experiences of warm, pleasurable contact, particularly with parents.

A child can learn to express her or his affectionate and sensual feelings through activities such as kissing and hugging. The responses the child receives to these expressions of intimacy can have a strong influence on the manner in which he or she expresses sexuality in later years. The inclinations we have as adults toward giving and receiving affection seem to be related to our early opportunities for warm, pleasurable contact with significant others, particularly parents (DeLamater & Friedrich, 2002; Hatfield, 1994; Singer, 2002). A number of researchers believe that children who are deprived of "contact comfort" (being touched and held) during the first months and years of life can have difficulty establishing intimate relationships later in their lives (Harlow & Harlow, 1962; Montagu & Matson, 1979; Prescott, 1989). Furthermore, other research suggests that affection and physical violence are, to some extent, mutually exclusive. For example, a study of 49 separate societies found that, in cultures where children are nurtured with physical affection, instances of adult violence are few. Conversely, high levels of adult violence are manifested in those cultures in which children are deprived of physical affection (Prescott, 1975).

Normative Sexual Behavior in Children: A Contemporary Sample

Psychologist William Friedrich and his colleagues (1998) at the Mayo Clinic interviewed a large sample of mothers regarding sexual behaviors they had observed in their children. Sexual behaviors were reported for 834 children, ages 2 to 12, who were screened for the absence of sexual abuse. The mother informants were asked how often they had seen their children displaying 38 different sexual behaviors over the past 6 months. When 20 or more mothers reported observing a specific behavior, Friedrich and his associates considered it a developmentally normal form of childhood sexual expression. We outline some of the key findings of this important study in the following paragraphs.

A wide range of sexual behaviors were observed at varying levels of frequency throughout the entire age range of children. As shown in the table, the most frequently observed sexual behaviors were self-stimulation, exhibitionism (often exposure of private body parts to another child or adult), and behavior related to personal boundaries, such as touching their mother's or other women's breasts. Sexually intrusive behavior—such as a child putting his or her hand on another child's genitals—were observed less frequently.

The frequency of observed sexual behaviors was inversely related to age, with overall frequency peaking at age 5 for both sexes, and then declining over the next seven years. Two-year-old children of both sexes were observed to be more overtly sexual than children in the 10–12-year-old age range. The amount of observable sexual behaviors increased among both boys and girls up to age 5 and then began to decline. The observed decline in sexual behaviors after age 5 does not necessarily suggest that children actually engage in fewer sexual behaviors as they grow older. Rather, Friedrich and his colleagues suggested that it is likely that children

Percentage of Mothers Who Reported Observing Behavior at Least Once in the Preceding 6-Month Period

Observed Behavior	Males, Age (in Years)			Females, Age (in Years)		
	2–5	6–9	10–12	2–5	6–9	10–12
Touches sex parts in public	26.5	13.8	1.2	15.1	6.5	2.2
Touches sex parts at home	60.2	39.8	8.7	43.8	20.7	11.6
Touches other child's sex parts	4.6	8.0	1.2	8.8	1.2	1.1
Touches adult's sex parts	7.8	1.6	0.0	4.2	1.2	0.0
Touches breasts	42.4	14.3	1.2	43.7	15.9	1.1
Shows sex parts to children	9.3	4.8	0.0	6.4	2.4	1.1
Shows sex parts to adults	15.4	6.4	2.5	13.8	5.4	2.2
Masturbates with hand	16.7	12.8	3.7	15.8	5.3	7.4
Masturbates with toy/object	3.5	2.7	1.2	6.0	2.9	4.3
Talks about sex acts	2.1	8.5	8.9	3.2	7.2	8.5
Puts mouth on breasts	5.7	0.5	0.0	4.3	2.4	0.0
Knows more about sex	5.3	13.3	11.4	5.3	15.5	17.9

SOURCE: Adapted from Friedrich et al. (1998).

become more private about sexual expression as they mature. Furthermore, older children spend more time with their peers, and thus there are fewer opportunities for parental observation.

Ethnicity was not significantly related to the reported childhood sexual behaviors. There was, however, a positive association between maternal attitudes toward sexuality and frequency of observed sexual behaviors. Mothers who described themselves as having a "relaxed" approach to such things as family nudity and sleeping and/or bathing with their children reported higher levels of sexual activity in their children. The sexual behavior of children was also significantly related to maternal education level and to maternal attitude about the acceptability of sexual behavior in children. Mothers with more years of education and who reported believing that sexual feelings and behaviors in children are

normal reported observing more sexual behavior in their children.

Friedrich and his colleagues concluded that overt sexual behavior, particularly in young children, appears to be a normal part of development. This finding is especially important at a time when concern about childhood sexual abuse is understandably paramount in the minds of many parents, educators, and clinicians. In a concluding comment these researchers noted that it is important for parents (and other adults) to be aware that "simply because a 5-year-old boy touches his genitals occasionally, even after a weekend with his noncustodial parent, it does not mean he has been sexually abused. Rather, it is behavior that is seen in almost two-thirds of boys at that age" (Friedrich et al., 1998, pp. 11–12).

Childhood Masturbation

Infants fondle their genitals and masturbate by rubbing or thrusting their genital area against an object, such as a pillow or a doll, but the rhythmic manipulation of the genitals associated with adult masturbation generally does not occur until a child reaches the age of 2 and a half or 3 years old (DeLamater & Friedrich, 2002; Martinson, 1994).

Masturbation is one of the most common and natural forms of sexual expression during the childhood years. The study described in the "Spotlight on Research" box reported that approximately 16% of mothers observed their 2- to 5-year-old children masturbating with their hands (Friedrich et al., 1998). Various other studies indicate that approximately one-third of female respondents and two-thirds of males reported having masturbated before adolescence (Elias & Gebhard, 1969; Friedrich et al., 1991; Hunt, 1974). In one recently reported study of college students, a slightly larger percentage of women respondents (40%) than men respondents (38%) reported masturbating before reaching puberty (Bancroft et al., 2003a). Most boys learn about masturbating from friends, and some even receive instructions in the particulars of self-stimulation, as the following account indicates:

An older friend taught me about masturbation. One day in his basement, while we were changing from wet swimsuits, he asked me if I had ever "jerked off." Well, I hadn't, and he proceeded to soap up his penis and demonstrate his technique. When I tried it, the sensations were very good but, unlike my friend, nothing came out of my penis. He told me to keep practicing, and I did. Several months later, I had my first ejaculation. (Authors' files)

In contrast to boys, most young girls do not discuss masturbation with friends. For them, discovery of this activity is usually a solitary and often accidental event:

I discovered how to masturbate when I was about eight years old. My mother always encouraged me to thoroughly wash my "privates." One day in the tub, I decided to make them "squeaky clean." I slid my bottom under the faucet and directed a stream of warm water over my vulva. Wow! That was one kind of washing I really liked. In fact, I had my first orgasm, even though I didn't know what you called it. I soon improvised all kinds of ways to squirt water over my clitoris. (Authors' files)

? How About You?

If applicable, how did you first learn about masturbation? Were your parents or other adults aware of this activity? If so, how did they react?

! Sexual Health

Parental reactions to self-pleasuring can be an important influence on developing sexuality. Most parents and other primary caregivers in American society tend to discourage or prohibit such activities and may even describe them to other adults as unusual or problematic (Ryan, 2000). Comments about masturbation that pass from parent to child are typically either nonexistent or often negative. Think back to your youth. Did your parents ever express to you that they accepted this activity? Or did you have an intuitive sense that your parents were comfortable with self-pleasuring in their children? Probably not. Most often, a verbal message to "stop doing that," a disapproving look, or a slap on the hand is the response children receive to masturbation. These gestures may be noted even by a very young child who has not yet developed language capabilities.

How can adults convey their acceptance of this natural and normal form of self-exploration? One way to begin is by not reacting negatively to the genital fondling that is typical of infants and young children. Later, as we respond to children's questions about their bodies, it may be desirable to mention the potential for pleasure that exists in their genital anatomy ("It feels good when you touch it"). Respecting privacy—for example, knocking before entering a child's room—is another way to foster comfort with this very personal activity. Perhaps you may feel comfortable with making specific accepting responses to self-pleasuring activity in your children, as did the parent in the following account:

One day my seven-year-old son joined me on the couch to watch a football game. He was still in the process of toweling off from a shower. While he appeared to be engrossed in the activity on the screen, I noticed one hand was busy stroking his penis. Suddenly his eyes caught mine observing him. An uneasy grin crossed his face. I wasn't sure how to respond, so I simply stated, "It feels good, doesn't it?" He didn't say anything, nor did he continue touching himself, but his smile grew a little wider. I must admit I had some initial hesitancy in openly indicating my approval for such behavior. I was afraid he might begin openly masturbating in the presence of others. However, my fears were demonstrated to be groundless in that he continues to be quite private about such activity. It is gratifying to know that he can experience the pleasures of his body without the unpleasant guilt feelings that his father grew up with. (Authors' files)

Many parents are reluctant to openly express their acceptance of masturbation, afraid that their children, armed with this parental stamp of approval, will go off to some cloistered area and masturbate away the hours. Although this is an understandable concern, available evidence does not suggest that this response is likely. Children have many other activities to occupy their time.

Another concern, voiced in the previous anecdote, is that children will begin masturbating openly in front of others if they are aware that their parents accept such behavior. This also is a reasonable concern. Few of us would be enthusiastic about needing to deal with Johnny or Suzy masturbating in front of Grandma. However, children are generally aware enough of social expectations to maintain a high degree of privacy in something as emotionally laden and personal as self-pleasuring. Most of them are much more capable of making important discriminations than parents sometimes acknowledge. In the event that children do masturbate in the presence of others, it would seem reasonable for parents to voice their concerns, taking care to label the choice of location and not the activity as inappropriate. An example of how this situation can be handled with sensitivity and tact is to say to the child, "I know that feels good, but it is a private way to feel good. Let's find a place where you will have the privacy you need" (Planned Parenthood Federation of America, 2002, p. 12).

Many children masturbate. Telling them to stop this behavior rarely eliminates it, even if such requests are backed with threats of punishment or claims that masturbation causes mental or physical deterioration. Rather, these negative responses most likely succeed only in greatly magnifying the guilt and anxiety associated with this behavior (Singer, 2002). ■

Childhood Sex Play

Besides self-stimulation, prepubertal children often engage in play that can be viewed as sexual in nature (Friedrich et al., 1991; Martinson, 1994; Ryan, 2000; Sandnabba et al., 2003). Such play takes place with friends or siblings of the same or the other sex. It can occur as early as the age of 2 or 3 years but is more likely to take place between the ages of 4 and 7 (DeLamater & Friedrich, 2002). Alfred Kinsey and colleagues (1948, 1953) noted that 45% of the females and 57% of the males in their sample reported having these experiences by age 12. In another survey, parents of 6- and 7-year-old children reported that 76% of their daughters and 83% of their sons had participated in some sex play with friends or siblings (Kolodny, 1980). In other research 61% of a sample of college students reported engaging in one or more forms of sex play with another child before age 13 (Greenwald & Leitenberg, 1989), and 56% of a group of adult professionals remembered engaging in activities perceived as sexual with other children before age 12 (Ryan et al., 1988). The activities ranged from exhibition and inspection of the genitals, often under the guise of playing doctor, to simulating intercourse by rubbing genital regions together. Although most adults, particularly parents, tend to react to the apparent sexual nature of this play, for many children the play aspects of the interaction are far more significant than any sexual overtones:

> When we think of preadolescent activities that look sexual—we, as adults, looking back on it, or as parents looking at it in our children—we respond to the sexual aspect; the sex is very important; the play is unimportant. To the child, however, the balance is exactly the opposite. The play is the major part; whatever sex might be in it, is mainly interesting because it is forbidden, like mommy's jewel box or daddy's tool chest. (Gagnon, 1977, p. 85)

As this quote suggests, curiosity about what is forbidden probably plays an important role in encouraging early sexual exploration. Curiosity about the sexual equipment of others, particularly the other sex, is quite normal (Calderone & Johnson, 1989; DeLamater & Friedrich, 2002). Many day-care centers and nursery schools now have bathrooms open to both sexes so that children can learn about sexual differences in a natural, everyday way.

Besides showing interest in sexual behaviors, many children in the 5–7 age range begin to act in ways that mirror the predominant heterosexual marriage script in our society. This is apparent in the practice of playing house, which is typical of children of this age. Some of the sex play described earlier occurs within the context of this activity.

Critical Thinking Question

Assume that you are a parent of a 7-year-old and that one day you find your child playing doctor with a playmate of the same age of the other sex. Both have lowered their pants, and they seem to be involved in visually exploring each other's bodies. How would you respond? Would you react differently according to the sex of your child?

How About You?

Do you recall engaging in sex play with friends of the same or other sex? What impact, if any, did this play have on your sexual and/or social development?

Many children find the play aspects of interactions such as this one more important than any sexual overtones.

By the time children reach the age of 8 or 9, there is a pronounced tendency for boys and girls to begin to play separately, although romantic interest in the other sex may exist at the same time (DeLamater & Friedrich, 2002). Furthermore, despite an apparent decline in sex play with others, curiosity about sexual matters remains high. This is an age when many questions about reproduction and sexuality are asked (Gordon & Gordon, 1989; Parsons, 1983).

Most 10- and 11-year-olds are keenly interested in body changes, particularly those involving the genitals and secondary sex characteristics, such as underarm hair and breast development. They often wait in eager anticipation for these signs of approaching adolescence. Many prepubescent children become extremely self-conscious about their bodies and may be reticent about exposing them to the view of others. Separation from the other sex is still the general rule, and children of this age often strongly protest any suggestions of romantic interest in the other sex (Goldman & Goldman, 1982).

Sex play with friends of the same sex is common during the childhood years (DeLamater & Friedrich, 2002; Reinisch & Beasley, 1990; Sandnabba et al., 2003). In fact, during this time, when the separation of the sexes is particularly strong, same-sex activity is probably more common than heterosexual encounters (DeLamater & Friedrich, 2002; Martinson, 1994). In most instances these childhood same-sex encounters are transitory, soon replaced by the heterosexual courting of adolescence (Reinisch & Beasley, 1990; Thornburg & Aras, 1986). Nevertheless, for some of these children sex play with friends of the same sex can reflect a homosexual or bisexual orientation that will develop more fully during adolescence and adulthood. However, youthful same-sex experiences in and of themselves rarely play a determinant role in establishing a homosexual orientation (Bell et al., 1981; Van Wyk, 1984). We encourage parents who become aware of these behaviors to avoid responding in an overly negative fashion or labeling such activity as homosexual in the adult sense.

It is clear that self-discovery and peer interactions are important during childhood development of sexuality. These factors continue to be influential during the adolescent years, as we will discover later in this chapter. But first we turn our attention to the physical changes that accompany the onset of adolescence.

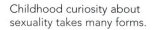

Childhood curiosity about sexuality takes many forms.

▶ The Physical Changes of Adolescence

Adolescence is a time of dramatic physiological changes and social-role development. In Western societies it is the transition between childhood and adulthood that typically spans the period between ages 12 and 20. Most of the major physical changes of adolescence take place during the first few years of this period. However, important and often profound changes in behavior and role expectations occur throughout this phase of life. By cross-cultural standards, adolescence in our society is rather extended. In many cultures (and in Western society in preindustrial times) adult roles are assumed at a much earlier age. Rather than undergoing a protracted period of child–adult status, the child is often initiated into adulthood upon reaching puberty.

Puberty (Latin *pubescere,* to be covered with hair) is a term frequently used to describe the period of rapid physical changes in early adolescence. The mechanisms that trigger the chain of developments are not fully understood. However, we do know that the hypothalamus plays a key role (Brook, 1999a; Caufriez, 1997). In general, when a child is between 8 and 14 years old, the hypothalamus increases secretions that cause the pituitary gland to release larger amounts of hormones known as **gonadotropins** into the bloodstream (Brook, 1999a). These hormones stimulate activity in the gonads, and they are chemically identical in boys and girls. However, in males they cause the testes to increase testosterone production, whereas in females they act on the ovaries to produce elevated estrogen levels. From the age of 9 or 10 years the levels of these gonadal steroid hormones begin to increase as the child approaches puberty (Bancroft, 2003).

In response to higher levels of male and female hormones, external signs of characteristic male and female sexual maturation begin to appear. The resulting developments—breasts; deepened voice; and facial, body, and pubic hair—are called **secondary sex characteristics.** Growth of pubic hair in both sexes and breast budding (slight protuberance under the nipple) in girls are usually the earliest signs of puberty. A growth spurt also follows, stimulated by an increase in sex hormones, growth hormone, and a third substance called insulin-like growth factor 1 (Caufriez, 1997). This spurt eventually terminates, again under the influence of sex hormones, which send signals to close the ends of the long bones. External genitals also undergo enlargement; the penis and testes increase in size in the male, and the labia become enlarged in the female (Figure 13.1).

The only event of puberty that is clearly different in boys and girls is growth (Brook, 1999a). Because estrogen is a much better facilitator of growth hormone secretion by the pituitary gland than is testosterone, as soon as a girl starts to show pubertal development, she starts to grow more quickly (Brook, 1999a). Even though the magnitude of the pubertal growth spurt is roughly equal in both sexes, it begins about 2 years earlier in girls. This is why the average 12-year-old girl is considerably taller than her male counterpart.

*Females are 2 yrs. ahead of males

<table>
<tr><td>InfoTrac Search Words</td></tr>
</table>

InfoTrac Search Words

■ Puberty

Puberty A period of rapid physical changes in early adolescence during which the reproductive organs mature.

Gonadotropins Pituitary hormones that stimulate activity in the gonads (testes and ovaries).

Secondary sex characteristics The physical characteristics other than genital development that indicate sexual maturity, such as body hair, breasts, and deepened voice.

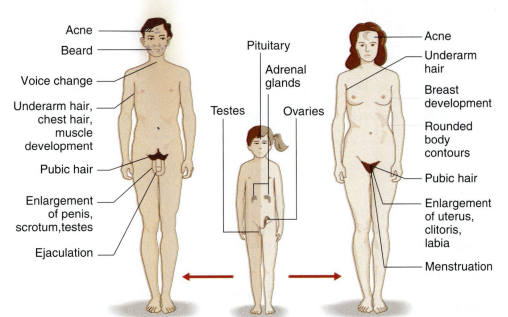

▶ **Figure 13.1** Hormonal changes during puberty, triggered by the influence of the hypothalamus over the pituitary gland, stimulate rapid growth and the development of secondary sex characteristics.

Acne
Beard
Voice change
Underarm hair, chest hair, muscle development
Pubic hair
Enlargement of penis, scrotum, testes
Ejaculation

Pituitary
Adrenal glands
Testes
Ovaries

Acne
Underarm hair
Breast development
Rounded body contours
Pubic hair
Enlargement of uterus, clitoris, labia
Menstruation

Under the influence of hormone stimulation the internal organs of both sexes undergo further development during puberty. In girls the vaginal walls become thicker, and the uterus becomes larger and more muscular. Vaginal pH changes from alkaline to acidic as vaginal and cervical secretions increase in response to the changing hormone status. Eventually, menstruation begins; the first menstrual period is called *menarche* (discussed in Chapter 4). Initial menstrual periods can be irregular and can occur without ovulation. Some adolescent girls experience irregular menstrual cycles for several years before their periods become regular and predictable. Consequently, methods of birth control based on the menstrual cycle can be particularly unreliable for females in this age group. Most girls begin menstruating around the age of 12 or 13, but there is widespread variation in the age at menarche (Chumlea et al., 2003; Herman-Giddens et al., 1997).

The median age at menarche for all girls in the United States is 12.43 years (Chumlea et al., 2003). Only 10% of U.S. girls are menstruating by age 11.1 years, but by age 13.75 years 90% are menstruating (Chumlea et al., 2003). The age at which menarche occurs has fallen steadily since the beginning of the 20th century (Anderson et al., 2003; Midyett et al., 2003). However, the rate of decline has slowed considerably over the last few decades, and there has been a downward shift of only 4 months in the last 30 years (Chumlea et al., 2003). There are significant differences in the ages at menarche for different racial and ethnic groups in the United States, as described in the "Sexuality and Diversity" discussion.

 ## Sexuality and Diversity

American Ethnic Diversity in Age at Menarche

A recent analysis of menstrual status data obtained from a nationally representative sample of 2,510 girls, age 8 to 20 years, found significant ethnic differences in age at menarche (Chumlea et al., 2003). This analysis provided estimates of the median ages at which 10%, 25%, 50%, 75%, and 90% of the population had attained menarche for each of three ethnic samples: white Americans, African Americans, and Hispanic Americans. The data, summarized in Table 13.1, reveal that African American girls start to menstruate earlier than girls in the other two ethnic groups. This difference is significant when compared with white girls at the age levels at which 10%, 25%, and 50% of the girls had started menstruating. In terms of statistical significance, Hispanic American girls began menstruating earlier than white girls only at the 25% level.

TABLE 13.1 — Age at Menarche (in Years) for Selected Percentiles of U.S. Girls

	Percentile				
	10%	25%	50%	75%	90%
Ages by race					
White	11.32	11.90	12.55	13.20	13.78
African American	10.52	11.25	12.06	12.87	13.60
Hispanic American	10.81	11.49	12.25	13.01	13.69
Overall median age	**11.11**	**11.73**	**12.43**	**13.13**	**13.75**

SOURCE: Chumlea et al. (2003).

Research has suggested that menarche is triggered when a certain minimum percentage of body fat is present (Anderson et al., 2003; Frisch & McArthur, 1974). At the onset of puberty the average ratio of lean to fatty tissue in females is 5 to 1 (i.e., approximately one-sixth of the total body weight is fat), whereas at menarche it is about 3 to 1 (about one-fourth of body weight is fat). Other evidence supporting a connection between body fat and age at menarche comes from studies of female athletes and ballet dancers who have prolonged and strenuous training schedules. These adolescents often experience delayed menarche or interrupted menstruation (Epp, 1997; Warren, 1982). Presumably, this results from having a low proportion of body fat.

In boys the prostate gland and seminal vesicles increase noticeably in size during puberty. Although boys can experience orgasms throughout childhood, ejaculation is not possible until the prostate and seminal vesicles begin functioning under the influence of increasing testosterone levels. Typically, the first ejaculation occurs a year after the growth spurt has begun, usually around age 13, but as with menstruation, the timing is highly variable (Stein & Reiser, 1994). The initial appearance of sperm in the ejaculate typically occurs at about age 14 (Kulin et al., 1989; Wheeler, 1991). Kinsey et al. (1948) reported that in two out of three boys initial ejaculation occurred during masturbation. There appears to be a period of early adolescent infertility in many girls and boys following initial menstruation or ejaculation. However, this should not be depended on for birth control. In some males sperm production occurs in the early stages of puberty, and even the first ejaculation can contain viable sperm (Abrahams, 1982).

Voice changes caused by growth of the voice box (larynx) occur in both sexes, but they are more dramatic in boys, who often experience an awkward time when their voice alternates between low and high pitch. Facial hair in boys and axillary (underarm) hair in both sexes usually appear approximately 2 years after pubic hair does. Increased activity of oil-secreting glands in the skin can cause facial blemishes, or acne.

Many of these physical developments are sources of concern or pride to the adolescent and his or her family and friends. Feeling self-conscious is a common reaction, and individuals who mature early or late often feel particularly self-conscious.

The physical changes we have been describing are dramatic and rapid. Suddenly the body a child has been living in for years undergoes mysterious changes that are often disconcerting:

I would never repeat my early teen years. My body was so unpredictable. At the most inopportune moments, my voice was cracking, my penis was erect, or a pimple was popping out on my face. Sometimes all these things would happen at the same time! (Authors' files)

Social changes also take place. Boy–girl friendships often change, and adolescents are likely to become—at least temporarily—more homosocial, relating socially primarily with members of the same sex. This phase does not last very long, however. The period of adolescence is marked not only by physical changes but also by important behavioral changes. In the following pages we look at some important areas of adolescent sexual behavior.

▶ Sexual Behavior During Adolescence

Adolescence is a period of exploration, when sexual behavior—both self-stimulation and partner-shared stimulation—generally increases. Although much of teenage sexuality is a progression from childhood behaviors, a new significance is attached to sexual expression. We will look at some areas in which important developments occur during adolescence, including the sexual double standard, masturbation, noncoital sex, development of ongoing relationships, intercourse, and homosexuality.

The Sexual Double Standard

Although children have been learning gender-role stereotypes since infancy, the emphasis on gender-role differentiation often increases during adolescence. One way that gender-role expectations for males and females are revealed is through the existence of a sexual double standard: different standards of sexual permissiveness for women and men, with more restrictive standards almost always applied to women (Crawford & Popp, 2003; Muehlenhard et al., 2003). As we will see in Chapter 15, the double standard can influence both male and female sexuality throughout our lives. Sexually emerging teenagers often receive the full brunt of this polarizing societal belief. A review of 30 studies published since 1980 found clear evidence that the sexual double standard continues to influence the sexuality of both adolescents and adults (Crawford & Popp, 2003). However, evidence gathered in recent years indicates that the sexual double standard is diminishing among adolescents and adults in

*learn through peers

North America, especially among women (Baumeister, 2000; Browning et al., 1999; Sprecher & Hatfield, 1996). Several studies have reported what appears to be a gradually emerging single standard of preference among both sexes for level of prior experiences in a desired intimate partner. For example, one investigation found that both men and women perceived individuals with high levels of sexual experience as being undesirable as either dating or marriage partners (O'Sullivan, 1995). Another study found that both sexes preferred potential marriage or dating partners to have no sexual experience rather than moderate or extensive sexual experience (Sprecher et al., 1997).

Despite these changes, research suggests that the double standard is still an influential factor in the lives of many males and females (Crawford & Popp, 2003; Milhausen & Herold, 1999; Weinberg et al., 1995). For example, in one recent study of women at a Canadian university 95% of the respondents indicated that they believed a double standard exists in which it is more acceptable for a man to have more sexual partners than a woman (Milhausen & Herold, 1999).

Because the double standard is still a factor in adolescent sexual behavior, let us briefly consider some of its potential influences. For males the focus of sexuality may be sexual conquest. Young men who are nonaggressive or sexually inexperienced are often labeled with highly negative terms such as *sissy*. On the other hand, peers often provide social reinforcement for stereotypically masculine attitudes and behaviors; for example, approval is given to aggressive and independent behaviors. For some young men, telling their peers about their sexual encounters is more important than the sexual act itself:

My own self-image was at stake. There I was—good-looking, humorous, athletic, liked to party—but still a virgin. Everybody just assumed that I was an expert at making love. I played this role and, without a doubt, always implied, "Yes, we did, and boy, was it fun." (Authors' files)

For females the message and the expectations are often very different. The following account illustrates one woman's view of both sides of the double standard:

It always seemed so strange, how society encouraged virginity in girls but it was okay for boys to lose theirs. I came from a large family, with my brother being the oldest child. I remember when word got around how much of a playboy my brother was (he was about 18). My parents were not upset, but rather seemed kind of proud. But when my sisters and I were ready to go out, our parents became suspicious. I can always remember how I felt and how if I ever became a parent I wouldn't allow such an inequality and emphasis on female virginity. (Authors' files)

Many girls face a dilemma. They may learn to appear sexy to attract males, yet they often experience ambivalence about overt sexual behavior. If a young woman refuses to have sex, she may worry that boyfriends will lose interest and stop dating her. But if she engages in sex, she may fear that she has gained a reputation for being "easy." The double standard dilemma often encompasses far more than sexual behavior. Girls may begin to define their worth by their boyfriends' accomplishments rather than by their own. Wearing her boyfriend's letter jacket may bring a girl infinitely more status than earning one herself. Her abilities may even be seen as liabilities rather than as assets. She may be concerned, for example, about getting better grades than her boyfriend.

Masturbation

Although a significant number of teenagers do not experience sexual intercourse by the age of 19, many masturbate. As we saw earlier in this chapter, masturbation is a common sexual expression during childhood. During adolescence the behavior tends to increase in frequency. A survey of teenage males revealed an average masturbation frequency of five times per week (LoPresto et al., 1985). Masturbation frequency rates among females are notably lower for all age groups, including adolescents (Leitenberg et al., 1993; Walsh, 1989). By the time they have reached the end of adolescence, almost all males and approximately three out of four females have masturbated (Coles & Stokes, 1985; Janus & Janus, 1993; Kolodny, 1980).

Masturbation can serve as an important avenue for sexual expression during adolescence. Besides providing an always available outlet for sexual tension, self-stimulation is an excellent way to learn about one's body and its sexual potential. Teenagers can experiment with different ways of pleasuring themselves, thereby increasing their self-knowledge. This information may later prove helpful during sexual interaction with a partner. ■

Noncoital Sexual Expression

Noncoital sexual expression provides an important way for many couples to relate to one another, often as an alternative to intercourse. **Noncoital sex** refers to erotic physical contact that can include kissing, holding, touching, manual stimulation, or oral–genital stimulation—but not coitus. *Petting, hooking-up, making out,* and *messing around* are other expressions for noncoital sex. Perhaps one of the most noteworthy changes in the pattern of noncoital sexual adolescent behaviors involves oral sex. A number of surveys have shown that the incidence of oral–genital stimulation among teenagers has risen dramatically, to a level two or three times higher than the rates reported in the Kinsey studies (Braverman & Strasburger, 1993a; Gagnon & Simon, 1987; Woody et al., 2000).

"How far to go" in noncoital sexual activity is often an issue. It can become a contest between the young man and woman—he trying to proceed as far as possible and she attempting to go only as far as is "respectable." Because "love" often motivates or justifies sexual behavior for girls, he may say "I love you" as a ploy to engage in further sexual behaviors.

However, making out is often not so narrowly goal oriented, and it can be a form of sexual expression that offers both members of a couple the highly valued combination of safety and enjoyment. The steps from holding hands to genital stimulation can progress with increasing emotional intimacy. Through such activity adolescents begin to learn, within an interpersonal relationship, about their own and their partners' sexual responses. They can develop a repertoire of pleasurable sexual behaviors without the risk of pregnancy, as the following account shows:

> I had a great understanding with one boy I went out with in high school. We both knew we were not ready for intercourse. Because of this mutual decision—and our mutual affection—we felt very free to experiment together and spent most of our dates making out for hours. (Authors' files)

For some young people noncoital sex is highly valued because it provides perceived opportunities to experience sexual intimacy while technically remaining virgins. However, the very notion of virginity is problematic for a number of reasons. Most important, defining virginity as the absence of a single act (coitus) perpetuates the twin beliefs that "real sex" equals penile–vaginal intercourse and that virginity involves only heterosexual coitus. What about lesbians, gay men, and heterosexuals who have not experienced coitus but who engage in other forms of sexual behavior, such as mutual masturbation, oral–genital, oral–anal, penile–anal, and genital–genital contact? Are these individuals all "technically virgins"? What about women whose only experience with penile intromission occurred during an act of rape? Are they no longer virgins despite their lack of consent?

A societal inclination to narrowly define virginity in terms of one sexual act is clearly exclusive to same-sex sexual activity. Within the confines of such a narrow conceptualization of virginity, lesbians and gay men who never have sexual contact with the other sex would be considered virgins all their lives!

The very idea that people can engage in virtually every conceivable form of sexual interaction but one and still remain virgins seems to be a questionable (antiquated?) concept. Perhaps it is time to begin de-emphasizing a term that is both value laden and exclusive.

Ongoing Sexual Relationships

Despite the lingering double standard, data indicate that early sexual experiences, both coital and noncoital, are now more likely to be shared within the context of an ongoing relationship than they were in Kinsey's time. Studies conducted in the United States have shown that from early to late adolescence the percentage of teens involved in romantic relationships approximately doubles from 30–36% in early adolescence to 67–72% in late adolescence

Noncoital sex Physical contact, including kissing, touching, and manual or oral–genital stimulation but excluding coitus.

Many adolescents form caring relationships with each other.

(Overbeek et al., 2003). Furthermore, contemporary adolescents are most likely to be sexually intimate with someone they love or to whom they feel emotionally attached (Laumann et al., 1994; Overbeek et al., 2003). In addition, noteworthy changes in the attitudes and behaviors of both sexes are narrowing the gender gap. Teenage women seem to be more comfortable with having sex with someone for whom they feel affection rather than believing they must "save themselves" for a love relationship. At the same time, adolescent males are increasingly inclined to have sex within an affectionate or loving relationship rather than engaging in sex with a casual acquaintance or stranger, which was once typical for adolescent males (Farber, 1992; Sprecher & McKinney, 1993).

Sexual Intercourse

A frequently quoted statistic in sex research is the number of people in a given category who have engaged in "premarital sex." As a statistic in sex surveys, premarital sex is defined as penile–vaginal intercourse that takes place between a couple before they are married. However, the term *premarital sex* is misleading for two reasons. First, as a measure that is frequently used to indicate the changing sexual or moral values of American youth, it excludes a broad array of noncoital heterosexual and homosexual activities. For some people, abstaining from coitus before marriage might not reflect a lack of sexual activity. Second, the term *premarital* has connotations that may seem highly inappropriate to some people:

I really hate those survey questions that ask, "Have you engaged in premarital coitus?" What about those of us who plan to remain single? Does this mean we will be engaging in "premarital sex" all of our lives? I object to the connotation that marriage is the ultimate state that all are supposed to evolve into. (Authors' files)

Because of these limitations, we avoid using the term *premarital sex* in subsequent discussions. We now turn to some of the available data on sexual intercourse during adolescence; then we look at two related areas, adolescent pregnancy and the use of contraceptives.

Incidence of Adolescent Coitus

Even though many contemporary teenagers have not experienced sexual intercourse, the results of 10 nationwide surveys reveal a strong upward trend in adolescent coitus from the 1950s through the 1970s (Table 13.2). Results of the more recent of these surveys (and other surveys) suggest that this upward trend has leveled off and even decreased somewhat over the last two decades. Data from the National Youth Risk Behavior Surveys (YRBSs) for the years 1991, 1995, 1999, and 2001, presented in Table 13.3, indicate that from 1991 to 2001 the overall percentage of high school students in the United States who had ever had sexual intercourse declined somewhat for all grade levels. The percentage of high school students currently sexually active and the number of lifetime sexual partners also declined for most grade levels. The prevalence of condom use among sexually active high school students increased somewhat during this 10-year period.

Evidence from a number of surveys indicates that the leveling-off in adolescent coital rates has not been as pronounced among young teenagers (Centers for Disease Control, 2002h; Donenberg et al., 2003; O'Donnell et al., 2003). Furthermore, data from the National Health and Social Life Survey (NHSLS) and other studies indicate that over

TABLE 13.2	Percentage of Adolescents Who Reported Experiencing Coitus by Age 19	
Study	Females (%)	Males (%)
Kinsey et al. (1948, 1953)	20	45
Sorenson (1973)	45	59
Zelnick & Kantner (1977)	55	No males in survey
Zelnick & Kantner (1980)	69	77
Mott & Haurin (1988)	68	78
Forrest & Singh (1990)	74	No males in survey
Sonenstein et al. (1991)	No females in survey	79
Centers for Disease Control (1996)	66[a]	67[a]
Centers for Disease Control (2000e)	66[a]	64[a]
Centers for Disease Control (2002h)	60[a]	61[a]

[a]Percentages reporting having had intercourse by their senior year (usually age 17 or 18).

		Ever Had Sexual Intercourse (%)	Four or More Sexual Partners During Lifetime (%)	Currently Sexually Active (%)	Condom Use During Last Sexual Intercourse (%)
Grade	Survey Year				
9	1991	39.0	12.5	22.4	53.3
	1995	36.9	12.9	23.6	62.9
	1999	38.6	11.8	26.6	66.6
	2001	34.4	9.6	22.7	67.5
10	1991	48.2	15.1	33.2	46.3
	1995	48.0	15.6	33.7	59.7
	1999	46.8	15.6	33.0	62.6
	2001	40.8	12.6	29.7	60.1
11	1991	62.4	22.1	43.3	48.7
	1995	58.6	19.0	42.4	52.3
	1999	52.5	17.3	37.5	59.2
	2001	51.9	15.2	38.1	58.9
12	1991	66.7	25.0	50.6	41.4
	1995	66.4	22.9	49.7	49.5
	1999	64.9	20.6	50.6	47.9
	2001	60.5	21.6	47.9	49.3

TABLE 13.3 Percentage of U.S. High School Students Who Reported Sexual Risk Behaviors, 1991–2001

Adapted from Centers for Disease Control (2002h).

the last several decades there has been a trend toward experiencing first coitus at an earlier age in both sexes, and this trend is consistent across a diverse range of ethnic groups (Centers for Disease Control, 2002h; Cooksey et al., 2002; Meschke et al., 2000; O'Donnell et al., 2003). However, different American ethnic groups vary in their experiences with adolescent sex; these differences are described in the following "Sexuality and Diversity" discussion.

Sexuality and Diversity

American Ethnic Diversity in Adolescent Sexual Experiences

A variety of studies have consistently reported that African American teenagers are more likely to engage in adolescent coitus than either white or Hispanic American teenagers (Centers for Disease Control, 2002h; Cooksey et al., 2002; McBride et al., 2003; O'Donnell et al., 2003). For example, a recent nationwide study reported that African American high school seniors were significantly more likely than Hispanic American seniors and white American seniors to have experienced sexual intercourse (Centers for Disease Control, 2002h). The results of this study, summarized in Table 13.4, also revealed that African American youth tend to have their initial experiences with intercourse at an earlier age than either Hispanic American or white youth.

The NHSLS also reported marked ethnic diversity in adolescent sex experiences. This nationwide survey revealed that approximately half of all African American male respondents reported having intercourse by the time they were 15, that half of all Hispanic men had experienced intercourse by about 16 and one-half years, and that half of white men had experienced coitus by the time they were 17. Figures for females revealed that half the African American women reported having intercourse by the time they were nearly 17, half the white women had experienced intercourse by about 17 and one-half, and half the Hispanic women had experienced coitus by the time they were almost 18 (Michael et al., 1994).

TABLE 13.4 Ethnicity and Percentage of Adolescents Reporting Having Had Sexual Intercourse

	Males			Females			Males and Females Combined		
	White (%)	Black (%)	Hispanic (%)	White (%)	Black (%)	Hispanic (%)	White (%)	Black (%)	Hispanic (%)
By 12th grade	45.1	68.8	53.0	41.3	53.4	44.0	43.2	60.8	48.4
Before age 13	6.2	25.7	11.4	3.3	7.6	4.1	4.7	16.3	7.6

SOURCE: Centers for Disease Control (2002h).

These ethnic differences in adolescent sexual experiences could be related more to economic status than to race or ethnicity. Poverty is a strong predictor of sexual activity among adolescents (Brewster, 1994; Kissinger et al., 1997; Singh & Darroch, 2000). Teenagers from the least affluent segments of American society are more likely to engage in sexual activity than those from more affluent classes, and African Americans and Hispanic Americans are often less affluent than white Americans. Furthermore, recent studies indicate that African American adolescents raised in more affluent homes are significantly more likely to abstain from sexual intercourse than their poorer counterparts (Henley, 1993; Leadbeater & Way, 1995; Murry, 1996).

The trend in both sexes toward having intercourse at an earlier age is a source of considerable concern for many social scientists and health practitioners. Numerous studies have linked early sexual intercourse with increased risk for adverse health outcomes, including unintended pregnancy, increased probability of exposure to HIV and other sexually transmitted diseases (STDs), and increased number of lifetime sexual partners (Donenberg et al., 2003; McBride et al., 2003; O'Donnell et al., 2003). "This link may exist because adolescents who have sex at a young age are prone to have unprotected sex, more frequent sexual encounters, and sex with multiple partners" (O'Donnell et al., 2003, p. 68).

Reasons for Engaging in Adolescent Coitus

A number of conditions motivate teenagers to engage in sexual intercourse. An accelerated output of sex hormones, especially testosterone, increases sexual desire and arousability in both sexes. Some adolescents are motivated by curiosity and a sense of readiness to experience intercourse. About half the men and one-fourth of the women in the NHSLS reported that their primary reason for engaging in their initial coital experience was curiosity and feeling ready for sex (Laumann et al., 1994). Many teenagers consider sexual intercourse a natural expression of affection or love (Sprecher & McKinney, 1993). Almost half the women and one-fourth of the men respondents in the NHSLS reported that affection for their partner was the primary reason for engaging in first intercourse (Laumann et al., 1994). A push toward "adult" behaviors, peer pressure, pressure from dating partners, and a sense of obligation to a loyal partner are other reasons that adolescents engage in coitus (Lammers et al., 2000; Rosenthal et al., 1999).

The NHSLS provides the most comprehensive available data on reasons for having first intercourse. A relatively small percentage of the subjects included in this study had their first intercourse on their wedding night (about 7% of men and 21% of women). Most of the respondents who had experienced sexual intercourse during adolescence did so by age 19. As shown in Table 13.5, about 92% of

TABLE 13.5 First Intercourse Wanted, Not Wanted, or Forced

First Intercourse	Men (%) ($n = 1,337$)	Women (%) ($n = 1,689$)
Wanted	92.1	71.3
Not wanted but not forced	7.6	24.5
Forced	0.3	4.2

n = number of subjects.

SOURCE: Laumann et al. (1994).

TABLE 13.6 Reasons for Having First Intercourse

Attributed Reason	First Coitus Wanted		First Coitus Not Wanted But Not Forced	
	Men (%) (n = 1,199)	Women (%) (n = 1,147)	Men (%) (n = 91)	Women (%) (n = 374)
Affection for partner	24.9	47.5	9.9	38.5
Peer pressure	4.2	3.3	28.6	24.6
Curiosity/readiness for sex	50.6	24.3	50.5	24.9
Wanted to get pregnant	0.5	0.6	0.0	0.0
Physical pleasure	12.2	2.8	6.6	2.1
Under influence of alcohol or drugs	0.7	0.3	3.3	7.2
Wedding night	6.9	21.1	1.1	2.7

n = number of subjects.

SOURCE: Laumann et al. (1994).

the men surveyed said that their first coitus was something they wanted to happen. However, only 71% of the women reported that they wanted their first intercourse experience to happen when it did. More than 4% of the women reported being forced into first intercourse, compared to 0.3% of men.

As indicated in Table 13.6, curiosity/readiness for sex was the most common reason reported by men for having first intercourse, followed by affection for their partner. The rankings of these two primary motivations or reasons for first coitus were reversed for women.

Factors That Predispose Teenagers to Early or Late Onset of Coitus

Just as there is a varied motivational basis for engaging in teenage coitus, researchers have also identified several factors that appear to predispose young adolescents to engage in sexual intercourse. Various psychosocial factors have been shown to be potentially powerful predisposing conditions. These include poverty, family conflict or marital disruption, teens living in single-parent or reconstituted families, parents' lack of education, lack of parental supervision, substance abuse (especially alcohol), low self-esteem, and a sense of hopelessness (Davis & Lay-Yee, 1999; Hingson et al., 2003; Lammers et al., 2000; McBride et al., 2003; Upchurch et al., 1999). Other predisposing factors that have been identified include poor academic performance and low educational expectations (Lammers et al., 2000; Steele, 1999), tolerance for antisocial behavior and association with delinquent peers (French & Dishion, 2003; Rosenthal et al., 1999; Whitbeck et al., 1999), and having been sexually victimized (molested or raped) (Boyer & Fine, 1992; Butler & Burton, 1990; Lammers et al., 2000). Adolescent females who are involved with a partner who is several years older are much more likely to experience coitus than females with same-age partners. Data from a national study of 1,975 adolescent females found that 13-year-old girls with partners who were 6 years older were 6 times more likely to have intercourse than 13-year-olds with same-age partners. Among 17-year-olds the odds of intercourse were double in age-discrepant versus age-matched relationships (Kaestle et al., 2002). Research also indicates that age differences among adolescent girls and their partners are associated with increased risks for STDs (Begley et al., 2003; Kissinger, 2003).

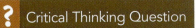

Critical Thinking Question

Assume that you are a parent of a teenager who asks, "How do I know when I should have sex?" What would you answer, and why?

Research has also provided insights into the characteristics and experiences of adolescents who choose to delay onset of sexual intercourse. A few studies suggest that strong religious beliefs, regular religious service attendance, and spiritual interconnectedness with friends lessen the likelihood of early sexual intercourse (Bancroft et al., 2003; Holder et al., 2000; Minichiello et al., 1996). Other researchers have found that adolescents' perception of maternal disapproval of teenage coitus and satisfaction with the relationship with their mothers are positively associated with adolescent sexual abstinence or less sexual activity (Althaus, 1994; Jaccard et al., 1996). Findings from a nationwide survey revealed that late onset of puberty, parental disapproval of teenage intercourse, good grades, and strong religious beliefs were all associated with delayed onset of coitus (Resnick et al., 1997). Another survey of 26,000 Minnesota students in grades 7–12 found that factors significantly associated with postponing coitus included higher socioeconomic status, good school performance, high parental expectations, and adolescents' belief that they had one or more adults in their lives who cared about them (Lammers et al., 2000). Several other studies have also found a positive link between delayed onset of teenage sexual activity and high-quality parent–child interpersonal relationships and communication (Dittus & Jaccard, 2000; Karofsky et al., 2000; Lambert et al., 2001; Rodgers, 1999). Finally, a recent analysis of data obtained from a national study of 12,000 teenagers in grades 7–12 found a strong association between higher intelligence and delayed coital experience (Halpern et al., 2000).

Homosexuality

Various studies indicate that 6–11% of girls and 11–14% of boys report having experienced same-sex contact during their adolescent years (Haffner, 1993; Hass, 1979; Sorenson, 1973). Most of these contacts took place not with older adults but between peers. These data, or the behaviors they describe, do not entirely reflect later orientation. Same-sex contact with the intent of sexual arousal can be either experimental and transitory or an expression of a lifelong sexual orientation. Many gay and lesbian adolescents do not act on their sexual feelings until adulthood, and many people with heterosexual orientations have one or more early homosexual experiences.

Some people, however, do identify themselves as gay, lesbian, or bisexual during adolescence. The process of self-identification as homosexual can begin with an awareness of having different feelings about sexual attractions than those commonly verbalized by peers. Sometimes a young person will have one or more homosexual experiences before she or he either applies a label of homosexuality to the behavior or understands its significance.

Gay, lesbian, and bisexual teenagers frequently encounter adverse societal reactions to their sexual orientation. Consequently, they may find it especially difficult to become comfortable with their developing sexuality. Unlike many other cultures in the world community, American society is not noted for embracing the fact of adolescent sexuality, even the often assumed heterosexuality of its young people. American teenagers who are at variance with the dominant heterosexual script can therefore experience a double societal rebuke of both their sexual orientation and the fact that they are sexually active.

Teenagers march in the sixth annual Gay/Straight Youth Pride March in Boston. Several thousand young people took part in the rally, demanding respect and declaring their sexuality is their own business.

For most gay, lesbian, and bisexual adolescents the process of reconciling their sexuality with the expectations of their peers and parents can be a difficult and often painful process that can create severe problems, including unusually high incidences of depression, substance abuse, and suicide attempts (Harrison, 2003; Wichstrom & Hegna, 2003). Not being "part of the crowd" can be emotionally painful for teenagers, who often find themselves scorned by their peers. Adolescents who are suspected of being homosexual are sometimes subjected to verbal and physical assault (Dover, 2000; Finz, 2000; Harrison, 2003). Many lesbian and gay adolescents are unable to talk openly with their parents about their sexual orientation. Those who do are frequently emotionally (if not physically) forsaken by their families (Dempsey, 1994; Hersch, 1991), and they may eventually leave home, voluntarily or otherwise, because their parents cannot accept their sexuality. Some gay, lesbian, and bisexual teenagers even experience antigay violence at the hands of family members (Hunter, 1990; Safren & Heimberg, 1999). In addition to being victims of violence, young people with a homosexual orientation can find it difficult to find confidants with whom they can share their concerns or find guidance (Safren & Heimberg, 1999). Parents, ministers, physicians, and teachers often are unable to offer constructive help or support. In addition, a society that generally fears and rebukes same-sex orientations has traditionally provided few positive role models for gay, lesbian, or bisexual teenagers.

It is apparent from this brief discussion that American gay, lesbian, and bisexual adolescents often must achieve self-acceptance of their sexual orientation within the context of powerful societal pressures not to accept and/or act on that orientation—not an enviable task. Fortunately, in recent years people in the United States have gradually become more accepting of behaviors that vary from the dominant scripts for sexual and gender behaviors. Information about homosexuality is becoming increasingly available, as is support for people with same-sex orientations. Many colleges and some high schools in the United States now provide a more accepting environment for the establishment of support groups for gay and lesbian students. Nationwide, there are about 700 Gay–Straight Alliances (GSAs) on high school campuses (Ness, 2000a). GSAs are clubs composed of both homosexual and heterosexual students who meet to exchange information, provide support to one another, and devise strategies for changing antigay attitudes in their schools. In this push to create a more positive school environment for gay and lesbian students, members of the GSAs "are taking on the challenge of educating not just the bullies and name callers in their classes, but the grown-ups, too—teachers, administrators and parents" (Ness, 2000a, p. 1).

Internet chat rooms and message boards can be especially helpful sources of support and constructive information for gay, lesbian, and bisexual teenagers. In addition, in recent years homosexuality has become more visible and has been portrayed in a more positive light in the media. Several prominent entertainment and sports celebrities who have openly acknowledged their homosexuality are now available as potential role models. (See Chapter 10 for more detailed information about homosexuality and the media and the gay Internet community.) Hopefully, increasing societal acceptance of homosexuality together with more positive role models and media portrayals will help make this time of life easier for adolescents with homosexual orientations.

The Effect of AIDS on Teenage Sexual Behavior

Many health professionals are concerned that American teens are particularly at risk for becoming infected with HIV, the virus that causes AIDS (Feroli & Burstein, 2003; Murphy et al., 2003; Pao et al., 2000). The largest percentage of AIDS cases in the United States occurs among people in their 20s and 30s who were infected with HIV in their teens or 20s (Murphy et al., 2003). People younger than age 25 account for one-half of new HIV infections (National Institutes of Health, 2004; Pedlow & Carey, 2003).

Various surveys have shown that most adolescents in the United States are familiar with the basic facts about AIDS and are aware that high-risk activities can lead to transmission of HIV. Unfortunately, even though most teens know the basic facts about AIDS, this knowledge has not resulted in behavior changes in many teenagers. Several recent studies of high school and college-age youths suggest that because most teenagers do not believe that they are at risk for contracting HIV, most do not significantly alter their sexual behavior to avoid

 How About You?

Did your knowledge about AIDS and other STDs have any effect on your sexual behavior during your teenage years?

infection (Clark et al., 1998; Feroli & Burstein, 2003; Lynch et al., 2000). Even some teens who believe that they are at high risk of infection with HIV or other STDs may not alter their behavior because they falsely assume that there is little they can do to prevent infection (Boyer et al., 1999). Thus knowledge of AIDS is a necessary but apparently not sufficient condition for reduction of risky teenage sexual behavior.

The notion of the "personal fable" (Elkind, 1967) is relevant to a consideration of adolescent risk taking and sexual behavior. Adolescents are particularly susceptible to a kind of cognitive egocentrism, an illusionary belief pattern in which they view themselves as somehow invulnerable and immune to the consequences of dangerous and risky behavior (Feroli & Burstein, 2003; Hillis, 1994; Murstein & Mercy, 1994). Thus large numbers of adolescents continue to engage in high-risk sexual behaviors, not because they are ignorant about AIDS and other STDs but because they falsely view themselves as being at very low (or no) risk of suffering negative consequences (Feroli & Burstein, 2003; Ku et al., 1993).

Behaviors that put young people at risk for HIV infection include engaging in intercourse without condoms; using alcohol, cocaine, and other drugs that impair judgment, reduce impulse control, and thus increase the likelihood of hazardous sexual activity; sharing needles with other intravenous drug users; exposing themselves to multiple sexual partners; and choosing sex partners in a less discriminating manner (Dittman, 2003; Dunn et al., 2003; Hingson et al., 2003). The continuing trend toward a younger age of first intercourse is disturbing because people who begin sexual activity by age 15 tend to have significantly more lifetime sexual partners than those who begin having sexual intercourse at an older age (McBride et al., 2003; O'Donnell et al., 2003; Rosenthal et al., 1999). (Exposure to multiple sex partners is a high-risk sexual behavior—see Chapter 17.) Furthermore, there is evidence that early onset of sexual intercourse is associated with risky sexual behavior later on (Davis & Lay-Yee, 1999; Greenberg et al., 1992; Halpern et al., 2000). ■

With the growing awareness that teenage women are at risk for HIV infection (and other STDs), most family clinic counselors now encourage clients, even those on birth control pills, to regularly use condoms to protect themselves against STDs. Unfortunately, this advice is often unheeded for a variety of reasons. Many young women and their partners are unwilling to deal with the minor inconvenience of condoms when they believe that they are already adequately protected from an unwanted pregnancy (Ott et al., 2002). Furthermore, some women are pressured by partners who resist using condoms. This reluctance to add STD prevention to sexual activity was reflected in one study that found that of 308 teenage women who had received a prescription for oral contraceptives at a family planning clinic, only 16% used condoms consistently over a 6-month period, even though 30% were judged to be at high risk for HIV infection because of multiple sex partners (Weisman et al., 1991). A more recent study of 436 sexually active adolescents found that condom use among teenagers who used birth control pills was much lower than condom use among adolescents who did not use oral contraceptives (Ott et al., 2002).

Finally, many heterosexual adolescents, who may use condoms when engaging in vaginal intercourse, usually do not use condoms during anal intercourse (Baldwin & Baldwin, 2000). As we describe in Chapter 17, anal intercourse is one of the riskiest of all sexual behaviors associated with HIV transmission.

▶ Adolescent Pregnancy

Recent years have brought greater availability of both contraceptive education and reproductive health care services to U.S. adolescents with a resultant moderate reduction in the incidence of adolescent pregnancy. However, the alarmingly high rate of teenage pregnancies in the United States continues to be an urgent social concern. The United States has the highest rate of teen pregnancy in the Western world (Singh & Darroch, 2000). The adolescent birthrate in the United States was quite high in 1970 (68.3 births per 1,000 adolescents), and although the rate declined to 51.0 per 1,000 in 1985, it subsequently rose to 62.1 per 1,000 in 1991. Since 1991 the teenage birthrate has declined steadily: 58.9 per 1,000 in 1994, 54.4 per 1,000 in 1996, 51.1 per 1,000 in 1998, 49.6 per 1,000 in 1999, and 45.9 per 1,000 in 2001 (Curtin & Martin, 2000; U.S. Department of Health and Human Services, 2003). The adolescent birthrate in 2000 was 26% lower than the recent high point in 1991. More effective contraception use and a decline in the number of adolescents engaging in sexual intercourse are the primary reasons for the reduction in teenage pregnancy and birthrates in recent years (Kreinin, 2002b; Oman et al., 2003).

The net decline in the adolescent birthrate in the United States (20% over the period 1970–1995) was among the smallest declines observed for this time period in a large sample of industrialized nations (Singh & Darroch, 2000). In fact, among 33 developed nations for which birth data were recently compiled, the U.S. teen birthrate was surpassed only by the Russian Federation, as indicated in the following "Sexuality and Diversity" discussion.

Sexuality and Diversity

Adolescent Pregnancy Rates and Birthrates in Developed Countries

In the 1970s studies of a wide range of developed countries revealed that both the teenage pregnancy rate and the teenage birthrate in the United States were among the highest. In contrast, these rates were low in Japan and in several Western European countries—the Netherlands, Switzerland, Sweden, Denmark, and Finland (Jones et al., 1985; Westoff et al., 1983). Since these early studies, numerous societal changes in the world's developed nations have occurred that could have an impact on teenage sexual and reproductive behaviors. Among these changes are (1) a rise in the proportion of births to unmarried women of all ages, (2) an increased acceptance or tolerance of nonmarital childbearing among adolescents and older women, (3) improved access to contraception and abortion in many developed nations, and (4) increased access to sexuality education (Donovan, 1998; Lindhal & Laack, 1996; Popova, 1996; Rahman et al., 1998; United Nations, 1998; Vilar, 1994). In addition, the radical transformation of the political structures of many Eastern European countries has had an impact on both their economies and their health care systems. This has influenced their youths' life prospects and reproductive behaviors (Burger et al., 1998; Omeragic, 1998; Prozhanova & Tantchev, 1995).

Susheela Singh and Jacqueline Darroch (2000) reported on new trends in adolescent pregnancy and birthrates in 33 developed countries in the mid-1990s. In compiling their report, Singh and Darroch used data obtained from various sources, including national vital statistics reports, official statistics, and published national and international sources. Analysis of these data revealed that the adolescent birthrate has declined in most of the surveyed industrialized nations over the last 25 years, and in some cases it has been reduced by more than 50%. This widespread trend toward lower adolescent pregnancy and birthrates "is occurring across the industrialized world, suggesting that the reasons for this general trend are broader than factors limited to any one country" (Singh & Darroch, 2000, p. 14). Singh and Darroch suggested several reasons for this widespread downward trend in teenage pregnancy and birthrates, including (1) increased importance of education as a means to achieve economic security and life satisfaction, (2) increased motivation of youth to achieve higher levels of education and career training, and (3) greater centrality of life goals other than motherhood and family formation among young women.

Examination of Table 13.7 reveals that the level of adolescent pregnancy varies greatly across the 33 developed nations, from very low rates in Japan (10 pregnancies per 1,000 adolescents per year) to an extremely high rate in the Russian Federation (more than 100 per 1,000). Most Western European countries and Israel, Japan, and Slovenia have low or very low adolescent pregnancy rates. Moderate rates occur in Australia, Canada, the Czech Republic, England and Wales, Hungary, Iceland, Latvia, New Zealand, Norway, Scotland, and the Slovak Republic. High or extremely high teenage pregnancy rates of 60 or more per 1,000 occur in Belarus, Bulgaria, Georgia, Moldova, Romania, the Russian Federation, and the United States. It is noteworthy that the United States had one of the highest teenage pregnancy rates in the mid-1990s (as it did in the late 1970s and early 1980s), second only to the Russian Federation. Similar patterns in birthrates across the 33 industrialized nations are reflected in the table. The highest teenage birthrates (50 or more births per 1,000 adolescents) occur in three nations—Georgia, Moldavia, and the United States, with the United States holding the dubious distinction of having the highest rate at the time of this investigation.

Rates of Adolescent Pregnancy and Births per Year (per 1,000 Women, Age 15–19) in 33 Developed Nations

TABLE 13.7

Country	Pregnancy Rate	Birthrate
Australia	43.7	19.8
Belarus	73.3	39.0
Belgium	14.1	9.1
Bulgaria	83.3	49.6
Canada	45.4	24.2
Czech Republic	32.4	20.1
Denmark	22.7	8.3
England and Wales	46.9	28.4
Estonia	66.2	33.4
Finland	20.5	9.8
France	20.2	10.0
Georgia	66.4	53.0
Germany	16.1	12.5
Hungary	59.1	29.5
Iceland	43.3	22.1
Ireland	19.2	15.0
Israel	27.9	18.0
Italy	12.0	6.9
Japan	10.1	3.9
Latvia	54.5	25.5
Moldova	64.8	53.2
Netherlands	12.2	8.2
New Zealand	54.0	34.0
Northern Ireland	28.4	23.7
Norway	32.3	13.5
Romania	74.0	42.0
Russian Federation	101.7	45.6
Scotland	41.6	27.1
Slovak Republic	43.3	32.3
Slovenia	19.9	9.3
Spain	12.3	7.8
Sweden	24.9	7.7
United States	83.6	54.4

Adapted from Singh & Darroch (2000).

Even though overall teen birthrates are declining in the United States, this decrease has not occurred across all ethnic subgroups in the population. Recent national data reveal significant ethnic diversity in reported birthrates per 1,000 15- to 19-year-old white Americans, African Americans, and Hispanic Americans (38.1, 89.2, and 118.2, respectively) (Goodyear et al., 2000). Data from the most recent nationwide Youth Risk Behavior Survey (see Chapter 2) revealed that African American adolescents (11.9%) were significantly more likely than Hispanic and white adolescents (6.2% and 4%, respectively) to have been pregnant (Centers for Disease Control, 2002h).

Current data indicate that approximately 900,000 unmarried American adolescents—that is, about 1 in 5 of all sexually active teenage women—become pregnant each year, accounting for about 12% of all annual births in the United States (Dittman, 2003; Hingson et al., 2003). This adolescent pregnancy rate is roughly four times higher than in several Western European nations, even though the age-specific levels of teenage sexual activity in these countries are comparable to those in the United States (Damson, 1996; Davtyan, 2000; SIECUS Fact Sheet, 2003). This finding raises the obvious question of whether contraception is either significantly underused or misused by adolescents in the United States. We address this issue in a later section of this chapter.

Of the almost 1 million teenage pregnancies annually in the United States, approximately 50% result in live births, 30% are aborted, and 20% end in spontaneous abortions or stillbirths (Alan Guttmacher Institute, 1999; Davtyan, 2000).

Negative Consequences of Teenage Pregnancy

The cited statistics on teenage pregnancy represent a great deal of human suffering. A pregnant teenager is more likely to have physical complications than a woman in her 20s. These complications include toxemia, hemorrhage, miscarriage, and even death (Hatcher et al., 1998; McGrew & Shore, 1991). Adolescent pregnancy is also associated with prenatal and infant mortality rates that are markedly higher than the rates among older pregnant women (Roye & Balk, 1997). Available data indicate that many of these negative health consequences are primarily due to inadequate prenatal care among pregnant teenagers rather than to biological immaturity.

Pregnant teenagers are also at especially high risk for STDs because of a likely reduction in the use of condoms, which are no longer needed to prevent pregnancy. Research indicates that only 8–29% of sexually active pregnant women use condoms consistently during intercourse (Byrd et al., 1998; Niccolai et al., 2003). One recent study of several hundred sexually active adolescent women, ages 14 to 19, found that the pregnant participants were four times more likely to have not used condoms during intercourse in the past 30 days compared with nonpregnant adolescents (Niccolai et al., 2003). These findings are disturbing because the resultant increase in susceptibility to STDs during pregnancy can have negative health consequences for both the youthful mother and her baby.

A teenager's unintended pregnancy and the decision to keep her child often have a serious negative effect on her education and on her financial resources (Fergusson & Woodward, 2000; Meschke et al., 2000; Shearer et al., 2002). Although it is now illegal to bar pregnant teenagers and teen mothers from public school, a large number of these young women drop out of school, and many do not return (Cassell, 2002; Stevens-Simon et al., 1996; White & DeBlassie, 1992). Faced with the burden of child care duties and the limitations of inadequate education, teenage mothers are often underemployed or unemployed and dependent on social service agencies (Davtyan, 2000; Paukku et al., 2003a; Shearer et al., 2002; Stone & Ingham, 2002). Furthermore, low education levels and limited employment skills often thwart the efforts of these young mothers to obtain economic independence as they move beyond their teenage years.

The negative effect of adolescent pregnancy is further exhibited in the lives of the resulting children. Teenage mothers often provide parenting of a lower quality than adult mothers do (Coley & Chase-Lansdale, 1998; Stier et al., 1993). In addition, the offspring of teenage mothers are at greater risk of having physical, cognitive, and emotional problems than are the children of adult mothers (Meschke et al., 2000; Shearer et al., 2002). These children of young mothers are also more likely to demonstrate deficits in intellectual ability and school performance than children of older mothers (Roye & Balk, 1997; Shearer et al., 2002).

Approximately 900,000 unmarried American teenage women become pregnant each year. Many experience considerable hardship as a result of their pregnancy.

Use of Contraceptives

Despite the physical, economic, lifestyle, and emotional stress of pregnancy and parenthood and despite the availability of birth control today, most sexually active American teenagers do not use contraceptives consistently or effectively (Davtyan, 2000; Glei, 1999; Paukku et al., 2003a). Research also reveals that a large number of adolescents do not use any contraception at all the first few times they have sexual intercourse and that only a minority consistently use a reliable method of birth control even after they have been sexually active for some time (Glei, 1999; Kahn et al., 1999).

On a more positive note, American adolescents in the late 1990s were more likely to use contraception, especially condoms, than their counterparts in the 1970s and 1980s (Davtyan, 2000; Kahn et al., 1999; Ventura et al., 1998). Data from the national Youth Risk Behavior Survey for the years 1991, 1995, 1999, and 2001 revealed that, although the percentage of U.S. high school students who had ever had sexual intercourse decreased over this 10-year period, the prevalence of condom use among currently sexually active teenagers increased (see Table 13.3). Unfortunately, teenagers experience a fairly high rate of condom failure because of either breakage or slippage. One study reported a 16.5% failure rate during 1 year of condom use by adolescents age 15 to 19 (Trussell et al., 1997). Clearly, better educational opportunities need to be provided to adolescents regarding how and when to place the condom, how and when to remove it, and how to safely store and transport it (see Chapters 11 and 17 for recommendations).

Why do so many sexually active American teenagers fail to consistently use effective contraception? A number of surveys have revealed that many adolescents, perhaps the majority, lack knowledge about effective birth control. In addition, certain myths abound, such as the belief that a woman cannot get pregnant the first time she has intercourse or the belief that infrequent coitus will not result in a pregnancy (Levinson, 1995; Trussell, 1988). The problem of knowledge deficits and false beliefs is compounded by the wide proliferation of abstinence-only sex-education programs in U.S. schools, which teach teens that abstinence is the only option for avoiding pregnancy while failing to present any positive information about effective contraceptive methods (Davtyan, 2000; Landry et al., 1999). We discuss abstinence-only school sex education in a later section of this chapter.

Many teenagers wait months after becoming sexually active to seek birth control advice, and some never seek counsel. Misconceptions about possible health risks associated with some contraceptive methods (e.g., oral contraception and IUDs), fear of the pelvic exam, embarrassment associated with seeking out and/or purchasing contraceptive devices, and concerns about confidentiality keep many teenagers from seeking birth control advice (Davtyan, 2000; Gage, 1998; Lagana, 1999). Confidentiality can be a major issue for adolescents, who are often willing to discuss their sexuality and contraception needs with their health care provider only when they know these discussions will remain confidential (Davtyan, 2000). Many teens do not use family planning clinics because they fear parental discovery (Zabin et al., 1991). Some adolescents do request contraception services from family planning clinics supported by federal Title X funding, which allows the provision of contraception to anyone regardless of age or marital status. In September 1997 the U.S. House of Representatives only narrowly rejected a bill that would have made it mandatory for clinics receiving Title X funds to notify parents if their minor children received clinic services.

Several factors or personal attributes have been found to be associated with adolescents' use or nonuse of birth control. Teenage women in less stable relationships and those who experience infrequent intercourse are likely to be ineffective contraception users (Glei, 1999; Harvey & Scrimshaw, 1988). Furthermore, teenage women age 17 or younger whose partners are more than 3 years older are significantly less likely to use birth control than are their peers who have partners closer in age (Darroch et al., 1999b; Ford et al., 2002; Glei, 1999). Adolescents who experience intercourse at an early age are less likely to use contraception than their peers who delay intercourse onset, and research has revealed an inverse relationship between pregnancy rate and age at first intercourse (Lagana, 1999). Adolescents who embrace conservative religious beliefs and oppose abortion generally use contraception less frequently and less effectively than their less conservative peers (Lagana, 1999). Sexually active adolescents are also more likely to have unprotected sex if intercourse occurs after they have consumed alcohol (Hingson et al., 2003; Stall et al., 1996). A study of almost 12,000 college students from 128 randomly selected U.S. colleges and universities found that respondents who had begun drinking by age 13 were twice as likely to experience unplanned and unprotected sex because of drinking than those who did not drink alcohol until age 19 or older (Hingson et al., 2003). Finally, many sexually active young women believe that they lack the right to communicate about and/or control aspects of their sexual interaction with men, and thus lack of sexual assertiveness is often associated with inconsistent contraceptive use (Rickert et al., 2002).

Research has shown that adolescents involved in stable, long-term relationships, in which they communicate with their partners about contraception and other issues, tend to consistently use birth control effectively (Stone & Ingham, 2002; Whitaker et al., 1999; Wilson et al., 1994). Parent–child communication about contraception has also been positively linked to adolescent contraceptive use (Jaccard et al., 2000; Stone & Ingham, 2002). One study reported that the more mothers talked to their sons about birth control, the more consistently the sons used contraception (Jaccard et al., 1996). Another study found that teenage women whose mothers discussed contraception with them were half as likely to experience coitus and three times more likely to use effective birth control than young women whose mothers did not discuss contraception with them (Newcomer & Udry, 1985b).

Other research has shown that a sense of self-competence and self-efficacy—both of which refer to the extent to which a person believes that she or he has the ability and opportunity to successfully perform an action—characterize youth who use contraceptive methods effectively (Allen et al., 1990; Kaemingk & Bootzin, 1990). These findings clearly demonstrate how important it is for parents to create a supportive and stable family environment for nurturing the acquisition of these important personal attributes. A high sense of self-esteem has also been linked with effective use of birth control among adolescents (Lagana, 1999). Research also indicates that adolescents raised in families that stress personal responsibility for behavior tend to be effective users of birth control (Whitaker et al., 1999; Wilson et al., 1994). Finally and perhaps most obviously, adolescents who are the most knowledgeable about contraceptives are the ones most likely to use them consistently and effectively (Lagana, 1999).

? Critical Thinking Question

Should parents provide birth control devices to their teenage children who are actively dating or going steady? Why or why not?

? How About You?

If applicable, what factors have influenced your decision to use contraception? Have you and your partner(s) shared responsibility for contraception? Why or why not?

Strategies for Reducing Teenage Pregnancy

Many authorities on adolescent sexuality agree that educational efforts designed to increase teenagers' awareness of contraception and other aspects of sexuality would be much more effective if they treated sexuality as a positive aspect of our humanity rather than something that is wrong or shameful. Teenagers who have a positive and accepting attitude toward their sexuality are more likely to use contraceptives in an effective manner (Baker et al., 1988; Lagana, 1999; Meschke et al., 2000). In many Western European countries, where teenage birthrates are dramatically lower than in the United States even though levels of adolescent sexual activity are equal to or greater than those in America, sex is viewed as natural and healthy and teenage sexual activity is widely accepted. This stands in sharp contrast to the United States, where sex is often romanticized and flaunted but also frequently portrayed as something sinful or dirty that should be hidden.

We offer a list of suggestions for reducing teenage pregnancy rates in the United States. These suggestions were gleaned from a large body of research on adolescent sexuality.

1. The American family planning clinic system and school-based health clinics need to be upgraded and expanded to provide free or low-cost contraceptive services to all adolescents who want them. Schools and the media should become more involved in publicizing that these services are not limited to the poor. Of equal importance is the need to publicize that clinics maintain the confidentiality of their clients.

2. The United States should follow the lead of several European nations in establishing a compulsory national sex-education curriculum that is extended to all grade levels. Safe expression of adolescent sexuality should be treated as a health issue rather than as a political or religious issue. Research clearly reveals that teenagers who are valued, respected, and expected to act responsibility often do so (Kelly & McGee, 1999). Research also indicates that teenagers who have been exposed to comprehensive sex education are considerably less likely to become pregnant than those who have had no such education, especially if exposure to sex education occurs before the young people become sexually active (Kirby, 2000; Lagana, 1999; Philliber et al., 2002).

3. Efforts to educate teenagers to prevent unwanted pregnancies must recognize that male attitudes are important for the practice and effectiveness of birth control (Goodyear et al., 2000; Marsiglio, 1993). Adolescent boys often consider birth control to be their partners' responsibility (Braverman & Strasburger, 1993b; Lagana, 1999). Sex-education programs should stress that responsibility for contraception is shared. A survey of several thousand American teenagers revealed that respondents who believed that responsibility for pregnancy prevention should be shared were more likely to have used contraception effectively than those who felt that the responsibility belonged to one partner or the other (Zabin et al., 1984). A preponderance of research on teen pregnancy has focused largely or exclusively on the young women who become pregnant rather than on the teenage men who contribute to this outcome (Goodyear et al., 2000). This has limited our understanding of the varied causes of teen pregnancy, and research efforts in the future should focus more on the sexual attitudes and behaviors of adolescent males that contribute to high teenage pregnancy rates in the United States.

4. Government agencies should continue a trend toward removing restrictions on advertising and distributing nonprescription contraceptives, especially condoms. Furthermore, condoms should be made readily available in middle schools and high schools (Crosby & Lawrence, 2000; Kirby, 2000). One study assessed the rate of condom use and sexual activity among 7,119 students in New York City public high schools, where condoms are available in school, and compared these rates to those exhibited by 5,738 high school students in Chicago, where condoms were not made available in school. The results: The availability of condoms in schools significantly increased condom use by sexually active teenage subjects but did not contribute to an increase in rates of sexual activity (Guttmacher et al., 1997). Another recent survey of a representative sample of more than 4,000 teenagers enrolled in Massachusetts high schools with and without condom availability programs found that students in schools where condoms were available were more likely to receive instruction on proper condom use and less

likely to report lifetime or recent sexual intercourse experiences than adolescents whose schools lacked condom availability programs (Blake et al., 2003). The results of these two studies suggest that school-based condom availability can reduce teenage pregnancy and lower the risk of contracting STDs, including HIV/AIDS.

▶ Sex Education

Many parents today want to provide some input into the sex education of their children. Societal values about sex are rapidly changing, and we all are exposed to contrasting opinions. How much should children see, or how much should they be told? Many parents—even some who are comfortable with their own sexuality—have difficulty judging the "best" way to react to their children's sexuality.

Perhaps the information that we offer in the following paragraphs will help modify some of this uncertainty. We do not profess to have the last word on raising sexually healthy children, so we advise you to read this material with a critical eye. Along the way, however, you may acquire some new insights that will aid you in your efforts to provide meaningful sex education for your children, either now or in the future.

Answering Children's Questions About Sex

Parents often ask us when they should start telling their children about sex. One answer is, when the child begins to ask questions. It seems typical for children to inquire about sex along with myriad other questions they ask about the world around them. Research has indicated that by about age 4, most children begin asking questions about how babies are made (Martinson, 1994). What is more natural than to ask where you came from? Yet this curiosity is often stopped short by parental response. A flushed face and a few stammering words, a cursory "Wait till your mother (or father) comes home to ask that question," or "You're not old enough to learn about such things" are a few of the common ways that communication in this vital area is blocked before it has a chance to begin. Putting off questions at this early age means that you may be confronted with the potentially awkward task of starting a dialogue on sexual matters at a later point in your children's development.

It can be helpful for parents to include information about sex (when appropriate) in everyday conversations that their children either observe or participate in. Accomplishing this with a sense of ease and naturalness can increase the comfort with which the children introduce their own questions or observations about sex.

If a child's questions either do not arise spontaneously or get sidetracked at an early age, there might be a point when you as a parent will feel it is important to begin to talk about sex. Perhaps a good starting point is to share your true feelings with your child—that possibly you are a bit uneasy about discussing sex or that maybe you are confused about some of your own feelings or beliefs. By expressing your own indecision or vulnerability, you may actually make yourself more accessible. During this initial effort, simply indicating your feelings and leaving the door open to future discussions may be all that is needed. An incubation period is often valuable, allowing a child to interpret your willingness to talk about sexuality. If no questions follow this first effort, it might be wise to select a specific area for discussion. Some suggested open-ended questions for a low-key beginning might be

- How do you feel about the changes in your body?
- What are some of the things that the kids at school say about sex?
- What are your feelings about birth control? Is it "proper"? Who should be responsible—male, female or both?

Understandably, parents sometimes tend to overload a child who expects a relatively brief, straightforward answer to his or her question. For example, 5-year-olds who inquire, "Where did I come from?" probably are not asking for a detailed treatise on the physiology of sexual intercourse and conception. It is probably more helpful to just briefly discuss the basics of sexual intercourse, perhaps including the idea of potential pleasure in such sharing. It is also a good idea to check to see whether your child has understood your answer to his or her question. In addition, you might wish to ask if you have provided the information that was desired and also to let the child know that you are open to more questions. When young children want more information, they will probably ask for it, provided that an adult has been responsive to their initial questions.

Some parents believe that it is inappropriate to tell their children that sexual interaction is pleasurable. Others conclude that there is value in discussing the joy of sex with their offspring, as revealed in the following account:

One evening, while I was sitting on my daughter's bed talking about the day's events, she expressed some concern over her next-door playmate's announcement that her father was going to purchase a stud horse. Apparently, she had been told to have me build a higher fence to protect her mare. Even though she knew all about horses mating, she asked why this was necessary. I explained the facts to her, and then she asked the real question on her mind: "Do you and Mom do that?" to which I replied, "Yes." "Do my uncle and aunt do that?" Again, "Yes," which produced the final pronouncement, "I don't think I'll get married." Clearly, she felt some strong ambivalence about what this sexual behavior meant to her. It seemed very important that I make one more statement—namely that not only did we do this but that it is a beautiful and pleasurable kind of sharing and lots of fun! (Authors' files)

Reluctance to express the message that sex can be enjoyable can stem from parents' concern that their children will rush right out to find out what kind of good times they have been missing. There is little evidence to support such apprehension. There are, however, many unhappy lovers striving to overcome early messages about the dirtiness and immorality of sex.

Initiating Conversations When Children Do Not Ask Questions

Some topics never get discussed, at least not at the proper time, unless parents are willing to take the initiative. We are referring to certain aspects of sexual maturation that the child may not consider until he or she experiences them. These include menstruation, first ejaculation, and nocturnal (nighttime) orgasms. Experience with first menstruation or ejaculation can come as quite a shock to the unprepared, as revealed in the following two anecdotes:

I hadn't even heard of menstruation when I first started bleeding. No one was home. I was so frightened I called an ambulance. (Authors' files)

I remember the first time I ejaculated during masturbation. At first I couldn't believe it when something shot out of my penis. The only thing I could figure is that I had whipped up my urine. However, considering earlier lectures from my mother about the evils of "playing with yourself," I was afraid that God was punishing me for my sinful behavior. (Authors' files)

It is important that youngsters be aware of these physiological changes before they actually happen. Children's natural curiosity about sex might cause them to discuss these topics with friends, who are usually not the most reliable sources of information. It is certainly better for parents to provide a more accurate description of these natural events.

Some parents find it relatively easy to discuss menstruation but quite difficult to talk about nocturnal orgasms or first ejaculations because of their associations with sexual activity. However, discussing these events can also provide an opportunity to talk about self-pleasuring. Females as well as males can experience nocturnal orgasms. The fact that girls have no ejaculate to deal with does not eliminate possible confusion or guilt over the meaning of these occurrences.

When I was a little girl, I began to have these incredibly erotic dreams that sometimes produced indescribably good sensations. Looking back on it now, I realize these were my first experiences with nighttime orgasms. At the time I thought it was awful to have such good feelings connected with such wicked thoughts. I wish someone had told me then that it was normal. It certainly would have eliminated a lot of unnecessary anxiety. (Authors' files)

Most young people prefer that their parents be the primary source of sex information and that their mothers and fathers share equally in this responsibility (Braverman & Strasburger, 1994a; Hutchinson & Cooney, 1998; Kreinin et al., 2001). Research indicates that fewer than 20% of parents engage in meaningful dialogue about sex with their children (Davtyan, 2000; Howard & McCabe, 1990). This is unfortunate, because children and teenagers can benefit greatly from candid discussions with their parents about sex, as exemplified by the following anecdote provided by a young woman enrolled in a sexuality class:

First my mother, and later my father, talked to me at separate times about sex. I was enlightened by these conversations, and they created a closer bond and increased confidentiality and trust among all of us. I was very thankful that both of my parents talked with me about sex. I realized that they really cared about my well-being, and I appreciated their efforts to say to me what their parents did not say to them. (Authors' files)

To the extent that parents do take an active role in the sex education of their children, mothers are far more likely than fathers to fulfill this function (Ackard & Neumark-Sztainer, 2001; Coreil & Parcel, 1983; Hutchinson & Cooney, 1998). Unfortunately, most American parents do not provide adequate sex education to their children (Kreinin et al., 2001; Meschke et al., 2000; Miller et al., 1998). Research has revealed that even where there is close and open communication between parents and children, sex often is not discussed (Fisher, 1987). Several studies have shown that friends are the principal source of information about sex for young people in the United States (Kreinin et al., 2001; Starr, 1997). Thus the gap created by lack of information in the home is likely to be filled with incorrect information from peers and other sources (Whitaker & Miller, 2000). This can have serious consequences; for example, an adolescent may hear from friends that a girl will not get pregnant if she has intercourse only now and then. Peers may also encourage traditional gender-role behavior, and they often put pressure on each other to become sexually active. Thus the challenge for parents is whether or not they want to become actively involved in their children's sex education, minimizing some of the pitfalls faced by children and adolescents who turn to their peers for sex (mis)information.

? Critical Thinking Question

Many people believe that sex education can itself cause problems, because the more children learn about sex, the more likely they are to experiment sexually. Do you think this assumption is valid? If so, do you believe that it is a good reason not to teach children about sex?

Parents might hesitate to discuss sex with their children because they are concerned that such communication will encourage early sexual experimentation. However, there is no clear evidence that sex education in the home contributes to either irresponsible sexual activity or an increased likelihood of adolescent sexual behavior. Moreover, adolescent children who openly, positively, and frequently communicate with their parents about sex are more likely to have fewer sexual partners and later and less frequent sexual activity than those teenagers who do not talk to their parents about sex (Jaccard et al., 1996, 2000; Meschke et al., 2000; K. Miller et al., 1999). Furthermore, positive parent–adolescent communication about sex has been linked to more effective and consistent use of birth control and decreased incidence of teenage pregnancies (Jaccard et al., 1996, 2000; Stone & Ingham, 2002; Whitaker et al., 1999).

School-Based Sex Education

In response to the frequent lack (or insufficiency) of information from the home and the inaccuracy of much of what children hear from peers, other social institutions in the United States, especially schools, are attempting to provide sex education. A recent nationwide study of health education policies and programs in the nation's schools found that 43% of the states, 52% of school districts, and 57% of schools required sexuality education at the elementary school level (Kann et al., 2001). These results are far from encouraging, especially because an appreciable minority of American youth begin sexual activity before their teenage years. Sometime between sixth grade and middle or junior high school many young people's intentions to become sexually involved increase and thus "the upper elementary grades provide an ideal time to positively influence children's unanswered questions about sexual issues" (Price et al., 2003, p. 9).

The quality and extent of school-based sex education programs vary considerably. Various surveys reveal that even though an overwhelming majority of parents and other adults support including sex education in schools, only a minority of U.S. schools offer comprehensive sex-education courses (Haffner & Wagoner, 1999; Landry et al., 1999; Trevor, 2002). A recent comprehensive poll of adults in the United States found that 93% of respondents supported the teaching of sex education in high school and that 84% indicated support for sex education in middle or junior high schools. Furthermore, the vast majority of polled respondents agreed that teenagers should be provided information to help them avoid STDs and unplanned pregnancies, and they collectively rejected the abstinence-only-until-marriage approach to sex education (Haffner & Wagoner, 1999). So how have U.S. schools responded to this public mandate for quality school-based sex education?

Public school sex-education programs are often hampered by pressures from well-organized and highly vocal minorities opposed to such education. In response to these pressures, many school systems completely omit sex education from their curricula, and others attempt to avert controversy by allowing only discussion of "safe" topics, such as reproduction and anatomy. As a consequence, some important areas for discussion, such as interpersonal aspects of sexuality and preventing pregnancy, are entirely overlooked.

Although opposition to sex education in the schools continues, a huge majority of parents support the idea.

A survey of a nationally representative sample of 825 public school district superintendents or their representatives found that 69% of these school districts have a districtwide policy to teach some form of sexuality education (often delayed until middle school or even high school) (Landry et al., 1999). Of the surveyed districts 35% teach "abstinence only" as their approach to preventing STDs and pregnancies in adolescents. In these programs discussions of contraception are either prohibited entirely or permitted only to emphasize the alleged shortcomings of birth control methods. An "abstinence plus" policy has been adopted in 51% of the surveyed districts, in which abstinence is presented as the preferred option for teenagers but discussions about contraceptive methods and STD prevention are allowed. Only 14% of the 825 surveyed districts have a policy of "comprehensive sex education," which treats abstinence as merely one option for teenagers in a curriculum that provides broad-based information about such topics as sexual maturation, contraception, abortion, STDs, relationships, and sexual orientation. School districts in southern states were almost five times as likely as those located in northeastern states to have abstinence-only sex-education programs.

The recent trend toward adopting abstinence-only sex education in schools is supported by numerous conservative social and political groups and has also been fueled by the power of the federal purse. In 1996 the U.S. Congress allocated $250 million to fund abstinence-only programs at a rate of $50 million per year for the period 1998–2002 (Goodson et al., 2003). The federal government has since approved additional funds for abstinence-only programs, and this approach to sex education continues to gain support. In 2003 alone, more than $100 million in federal funds was allocated to about 700 abstinence-only programs (Block, 2003). Many schools are adopting such restrictive programs as a way to avoid controversy (Kempner, 2001). What does research reveal about the efficacy of such programs, largely funded by taxpayers?

A number of comprehensive investigations of abstinence-only programs have provided no substantial evidence that such programs either delay the onset of sexual intercourse (or other sexual behaviors) or significantly change adolescents' attitudes about engaging in sexual relations (Goodson et al., 2003; Kirby, 1997, 2000; Thomas, 2000). Thus, despite the fact that abstinence-only programs enjoy substantial political and economic support, "evidence of effectiveness of this approach is scarce" (Goodson et al., 2003, p. 92). Tamara Kreinin, president of the Sexuality Information and Education Council of the United States (SIECUS), recently observed that "the dangerous and misguided attempts by countries like the United States to promote unproven abstinence-only-until-marriage education can only continue to harm and deny young people their right to information and education about sexuality" (Kreinin, 2002c, p. 6). In contrast, numerous studies provide strong evidence that comprehensive sex-education programs that stress safer sex and provide accurate information about various contraceptive methods actually increase the use of birth control, reduce teenage pregnancies, reduce high-risk sexual behavior, do not hasten the onset of intercourse (and in some cases actually delay onset), do not increase the frequency of intercourse, and do not increase the number of an adolescent's sexual partners (in some cases they reduce partner number) (Brick, 1999; Coyle, 2001; Hubbard et al., 1998; Kirby, 2000; Philliber et al., 2002).

- The traditional view of infancy and childhood as a time when sexuality remains unexpressed is not supported by research findings. (p. 371)

Sexual Behavior During Infancy and Childhood

- Infants of both sexes are born with the capacity for sexual pleasure and response, and some experience observable orgasm. (p. 371)
- Self-administered genital stimulation is common among both boys and girls during the first two years of life. (p. 371)
- The inclinations we have as adults toward giving and receiving affection seem to be related to our early opportunities for pleasurable contact with others, especially parents. (p. 372)
- Masturbation is one of the most common sexual expressions during the childhood years. Parental reactions can be an important influence on developing sexuality. (pp. 374–375)
- Sex play with other children, which can occur as early as age 2 or 3, increases in frequency during the 5–7-year-old age range. (pp. 375–376)
- Separation of the sexes tends to become pronounced by the age of 8 or 9. However, romantic interest in the other sex and curiosity about sexual matters are typically high during this stage of development. (p. 376)
- The ages of 10 and 11 are marked by keen interest in body changes, continued separation of the sexes, and a substantial incidence of homosexual encounters. (p. 376)

The Physical Changes of Adolescence

- Puberty encompasses the physical changes that occur in response to increased hormone levels. These physical developments include maturation of the reproductive organs and consequent menstruation in girls and ejaculation in boys. (pp. 377–378)

Sexual Behavior During Adolescence

- The sexual double standard often pressures males to view sex as a conquest and places females in a double bind about saying yes or no. (pp. 379–380)
- The percentage of adolescents who masturbate increases between the ages of 13 and 19. (pp. 380–381)
- Noncoital sexual expression is a common sexual behavior among adolescents. Noncoital sex refers to erotic contact that might include kissing, touching, manual stimulation, or oral–genital stimulation—but not coitus. (p. 381)
- Adolescent sexual expression is now more likely to take place within the context of an ongoing relationship than it was during Kinsey's time. (pp. 381–382)
- A significant increase in the number of both young men and young women who experience intercourse by age 19 has occurred over the last four decades. These increases have been considerably more pronounced among females. (pp. 382–383)
- During the 1990s adolescent coital rates leveled off and even decreased appreciably for all but young teenagers. (p. 382)
- Same-sex experiences during adolescence can be experiments or an expression of permanent sexual orientation. (pp. 386–387)

Adolescent Pregnancy

- The United States has the highest rate of adolescent pregnancies in the Western world and the second highest rate among a large sample of the world's developed nations. Since 1991 the teenage birthrate has declined steadily in the United States, primarily because of more effective use of contraception. (pp. 388–389)
- Approximately 900,000 unmarried U.S. adolescent females become pregnant each year. Adolescent pregnancy is often associated with social, medical, educational, and financial difficulties. (p. 390)
- Most adolescents who have intercourse do not use contraceptives consistently or effectively. (p. 390)
- The low rate of contraceptive use among U.S. adolescents is related to a number of factors, including knowledge deficits, false beliefs, inadequate home- or school-based sex education, misconceptions about health risks associated with some contraception methods, embarrassment over acquiring contraceptive devices, concerns about confidentiality, and lack of communication with partners about birth control. (p. 391)
- Strategies for reducing the teenage pregnancy rate in the United States include upgrading the family planning clinic system, establishing a compulsory national sex-education curriculum, educating males about their contraceptive responsibility, and relaxing government restrictions on the distribution and advertising of nonprescription contraceptives, especially condoms. (pp. 393–394)

Sex Education

- One answer to the question of when to start discussing sex with our children is when they start asking questions. If communication does not spontaneously occur, it may be helpful for parents to initiate dialogue, perhaps by simply sharing their feelings or asking nonstressful, open-ended questions. (p. 394)
- Some important topics—particularly menstruation, first ejaculation, and nocturnal orgasms—are rarely discussed unless parents take the initiative. (p. 395)
- Although most adolescents prefer their parents to be the primary source of sex information, evidence indicates that peers are considerably more likely than parents to provide this information, often in a biased and inaccurate manner. (p. 396)
- Even though an overwhelming majority of parents and other adults support school sex education, only a minority of American schools offer comprehensive sex-education programs. (p. 397)
- Research indicates that comprehensive school-based sex-education programs increase the use of birth control, reduce teenage pregnancies, reduce high-risk sexual behavior, do not hasten the onset or frequency of coitus, and do not increase the number of an adolescent's sexual partners. (p. 397)

Suggested Readings

Bass, Ellen, and Kate Kaufman (1996). *Free Your Mind: The Book for Gay, Lesbian, and Bisexual Youth and Their Allies.* Scranton, PA: HarperCollins. A thoughtful and informative book that provides young people with practical information about what it means to be homosexual and bisexual. The book also offers validation, reassurance, and advice.

Calderone, Mary, and Eric Johnson (1989). *The Family Book About Sexuality* (rev. ed.). New York: Harper & Row. An excellent book, helpful to both parents and children, that offers practical advice on and valuable insights into childhood sexuality.

Harris, Robie, and Michael Emberly (1996). *It's Perfectly Normal: Changing Bodies, Growing Up, Sex, and Sexual Health.* Boston: Candlewick Press. A user-friendly book written for children age 10 and older that provides accessible information about puberty and sexuality. In addition to covering sexual anatomy and physiology, the book deals with important issues for young readers, including masturbation, coitus, contraception, abortion, sexual abuse, and sexually transmitted diseases.

Kempner, Martha (2001). *Toward a Sexually Healthy America: Abstinence-Only-Until-Marriage Programs That Try to Keep Our Youth "Scared Chaste."* New York: SIECUS. A review of the educational philosophy, common curriculum characteristics, and potential harm of abstinence-only programs that attempt to control young people's sexual behavior by instilling fear, shame, and guilt. (To purchase this publication, send $10 to SIECUS, 130 West 42nd Street, Suite 350, New York, NY 10036-7802.)

Klein, Marty (1992). *Ask Me Anything.* New York: Simon & Schuster. A valuable resource book for any adult (parent, teacher, friend) who wishes to be prepared to provide factual and helpful advice to children who ask questions about sex.

Leight, Lynn (1990). *Raising Sexually Healthy Children.* New York: Avon. A well-written, insightful book that provides a wealth of information to parents who wish to provide an atmosphere conducive to the development of positive sexual attitudes and healthy sexual behavior in their children.

Moglia, Ronald, and Jan Knowles (Eds.) (1997). *All About Sex: A Family Resource on Sex and Sexuality.* Westminster, MD: Random House. A helpful book that provides valuable information about sexuality to family members, both children and adults, to enhance family communication about sexual matters.

Schwartz, Pepper (2000). *Ten Talks Parents Must Have with Their Children About Sex and Character.* Boston: Time Warner Trade Publishing. An excellent resource for parents of children in grades 4 through 12 that offers helpful advice on how to initiate conversations about sexuality with children and what to say. Topics include family values clarification, safe sex, ethics and character, peer pressure, the media, and the Internet.

▶ Web Resources

Your *Our Sexuality* Web site **http://psychology.wadsworth.com/crooksbaur9e/** has direct links to the Web sites described below. These links are checked often for changes, dead links, and new additions.

All About Sex Discussion
Information on this Web site is divided into sections for teens, preteens, and parents. For the teens and preteens, frank but sensitive explanations of such topics as sex and sexuality, masturbation, sexual orientation, and virginity are provided.

Talk to Your Kids About Sex and Relationships
Part of a larger initiative called "Talk to Your Kids About Tough Issues" (sponsored by Children Now and the Kaiser Family Foundation), this Web site offers parents practical advice and resources for talking to children about sexuality and related issues.

A Web Page by Teens for Teens
This Web site is dedicated to the discussion of sexuality and relationships for teens. Boasting an all-teen editorial board, this site also has content written by teens. It is sponsored by the Network for Family Life Education (School for Social Work, Rutgers University).

The Alan Guttmacher Institute (AGI)
A valuable source of information about a variety of topics dealing with reproductive health, including issues pertaining to adolescent pregnancy.

Hetrick-Martin Institute (HMI)
This Web site provides useful information and resources to gay, lesbian, bisexual, and transgendered youth.

Sex, etc.
This Web site provides youth with accurate and candid information about their sexuality.

Teenwire
Sponsored by the Planned Parenthood Federation of America, this Web site provides information about adolescent sexuality and relationships.

Two Web sites sponsored by the American Social Health Association
These Web sites provide answers to questions about teen sexual health and sexually transmitted diseases.

Advocates for Youth
Sections of this Web site provide information about topics important to youth, including emergency contraception, youths advocating for their right to sexual health information and services and comprehensive sex education, peer education programs, pregnancy and STD prevention, dating violence, and resources for gay, lesbian, and transgendered youth.

Our Sexuality Web Site
For online resources directly related to this book, go to **http://psychology.wadsworth.com/crooksbaur9e/**. You will find interactive exercises, study questions, chapter outlines, an online version of this text's glossary, and Web links and activities that complement your CD-ROM.

InfoTrac® College Edition Online Library
http://infotrac.thomsonlearning.com/
InfoTrac College Edition is an online searchable library that includes a multitude of journals, many of which are specific to human sexuality. These journals include *Archives of Sexual Behavior, Archives of Sexual Health Behavior, Canadian Journal of Human Sexuality, Hispanic Journal of the Behavioral Sciences, Journal of Cross-Cultural Psychology, Journal of Physical Education, Recreation, and Dance, Journal of Sex Research,* and *Sex Roles.* You may search topics suggested in the margins of this chapter or terms of your own.

Our Sexuality CD-ROM
Use your CD-ROM for further study of the concepts in this chapter. Your CD-ROM provides animations of difficult concepts, video clips of real people discussing sexuality, critical thinking questions, chapter quizzing, and more.

CHAPTER **14**

Sexuality and the Adult Years

▶ **Single Living**

How have adult single-living patterns changed in the United States?

In what ways do levels of sexual activity differ between single people and married couples?

▶ **Cohabitation**

What explains the significant increase in the number of cohabiting couples in America?

What is the relationship between premarital cohabitation and subsequent marital happiness?

▶ **Marriage**

Is it possible to successfully predict marital satisfaction?

What changes in sexual behaviors within marriage have occurred over the last few decades?

▶ **Extramarital Relationships**

What are some of the reasons people engage in extramarital relationships?

What are the possible consequences of such behavior for the marriage and for the individual?

▶ **Divorce**

How have divorce rates changed over the last 10 to 15 years?

What are some of the causes of divorce?

▶ **Sexuality and Aging**

What is the basis for the double standard in the sexuality of older men and women?

What are some psychological and lifestyle changes that occur in older individuals that can enhance their sexual lives?

Did the ratio of widows to widowers change significantly during the 20th century?

How is the postmarital adjustment of widowhood different from that of divorce?

I'm single again after my second divorce. In both marriages, sex became boring after about a year, and I love the exciting sex that comes with dating. (Authors' files)

After 44 years of marriage, with our kids in homes of their own, we can really enjoy ourselves. We often go out to dinner, come back home, dance to music from the 1940s, talk, kiss, massage each other, and then maybe even have sexual intercourse. Our lovemaking can take several hours, and we're both completely satisfied. (Authors' files)

Intimate relationships of several forms occupy a position of considerable significance in many adults' lives. An adult's relationship status—single, married, or living with someone—is an important social concern and an important element of that person's self-identity. A person's relationship status can also have considerable influence on the sexual interactions he or she experiences during the adult years. In this chapter we examine several adult lifestyles and the influences of aging on intimate relationships.

▶ Single Living

The number of single adults in the United States has increased from 10.9 million in 1970 to 28.8 million in 2002—25% of all U.S. households (U.S. Bureau of the Census, 2003). These figures represent a significant shift in adult living patterns, because in the past far fewer adults divorced or remained unmarried (Marks, 1996). What explains this change? There are many reasons, including:

Average
27 (male)
25 (female)

· A tendency to marry at a later age
· A greater emphasis on advanced education
· An increase in the number of people who choose not to marry at all
· Rising divorce rates
· More women placing career objectives ahead of marriage
· The increase in the number of women who do not depend on marriage for economic stability

The figures also reflect what may be a change in societal attitudes (Waite & Joyner, 2001). Until recently in the United States, a stigma was often attached to remaining single. This stigma applied particularly to women, as terms such as *old maid* and *spinster* indicate (Gordon, 2003; Lewis & Moon, 1997). (Single men would most likely be referred to by the less negative term *bachelor*.) Today these terms are heard less frequently. Television reflects this shift in attitude with shows about career-minded single women, such as HBO's *Sex and the City*, which shows glamorous, single New York women who pursue men for sex instead of economic security (Chang & Chambers, 1999; Yim, 2001). Although single life is still often seen as the period before, in between, or after marriage, remaining single, either as an alternative to marriage or following divorce, has become an increasingly prominent lifestyle in American culture. Therefore we see fewer people in the developed Western world who marry primarily for convention's sake or to avoid the negative perception of the single state (T. Edwards, 2000).

Single living encompasses a range of sexual lifestyles and differing levels of personal satisfaction. Levels of sexual activity among single people vary widely, just as they do among married people. Research suggests that married people experience higher levels of sexual activity and satisfaction than singles (Clements, 1994; Laumann et al., 1994). Some people who live alone remain celibate by choice or because of lack of available partners. Others are involved in a long-term, sexually exclusive

LET'S BUCK THE TREND, GET MARRIED, LIVE TOGETHER, HAVE A FAMILY...

CENSUS REPORT: UNWED COUPLES SURGE

Jeff Stahler reprinted by permission of Newspaper Enterprise Association, Inc.

Chapter Fourteen SEXUALITY AND THE ADULT YEARS **401**

relationship with one partner. Some practice *serial monogamy,* moving through a succession of sexually exclusive relationships. Still others prefer concurrent sexual and emotional involvements with a number of different partners. Some single people develop a primary relationship with one partner and have occasional sex with others.

Although being single has become more acceptable in our society and although single people can enjoy the benefits of growth and independence (Clements, 1998; Lewis & Moon, 1997), most people still choose to enter into a long-term relationship with a partner. There are several kinds of long-term sexual relationships, and we examine these various options next.

▶ Cohabitation

When I was a college student in the early 1960s, the possibility of living with someone without the sanctity of marriage simply never entered my mind. The topic of unmarried people living together was never discussed, although I occasionally heard a hushed reference to someone "living in sin." (Authors' files)

Cohabitation Living together and having a sexual relationship without being married.

Domestic partnership Unmarried couples living in the same household in committed relationships.

This account reflects a once prevalent societal attitude toward **cohabitation** (living together in a sexual relationship without being married). In the past few decades both the number of people choosing to cohabit and societal acceptance of what was once an unconventional practice have significantly increased (Kantrowitz, 2004). In fact, nearly 60% of couples who married in the early 1990s lived with each other before marriage (Teachman, 2003). The 1990 census was the first time that cohabitation was included as a category, and census figures reveal that by 2000 the number of unmarried couples living together in the United States was 5.5 million (U.S. Bureau of the Census, 2003). Cohabitation is most common among adults in their mid 20s; about 25% of this age group live together (Waite & Joyner, 2001). **Domestic partnership** is becoming a more common term applied to heterosexual and homosexual couples who live in the same household in committed relationships but who are not legally married, and businesses, cities, and states are establishing rights for access to benefits, such as health insurance, for couples in domestic partnerships.

Cohabitation has blurred the boundaries between marriage and single living and yet has distinct characteristics. Compared to their married counterparts, individuals who live together tend to have less traditional gender-role attitudes, less desire to have children, and more equity in doing household tasks. Cohabiting partners and marriage partners were similar to each other with respect to education and race. Differences were a matter of degree, with cohabiting couples reflecting less similarity than married couples. One significant difference was that cohabiting women had partners who had less than or as much education as they did, but that husbands were more likely to be better educated than their wives. The findings of this study indicate that the greater commitment between married couples may engender more restrictive requirements for a partner (Blackwell & Lichter, 2000).

Advantages of Cohabitation

At certain times in their lives many individuals prefer to be part of a couple in the relative informality of living together rather than in the more official aspects of marriage. They appreciate the sense of being together because they want to be, not because of the binding power of a legal contract. The informality of living together has other advantages. A couple may not feel as pressured to take on the new and demanding roles of wife and husband (Wineberg, 1994). As a result, the relationship is less likely to produce the sort of identity crisis that can follow when people try to live up to the social expectations attached to these roles (Elizabeth, 2000). Another perceived advantage is that the stigma of breaking up is less than with a divorce.

Many in the older generation have seen their children and grandchildren cohabit, and at this stage of their lives some allow themselves to live together without marriage even though they would not have done so in their youth (Espinoza, 2003). For example, in 1999, 75% more couples, age 65 and older, were cohabiting than in 1990. Older heterosexual couples often cohabit rather than marry to take advantage of age-specific financial benefits of cohabitation. Remarriage can mean higher income tax rates, the end of alimony payments, and the loss of spousal pension, military, and Social Security benefits. Being unmarried protects each partner from the responsibility for the other's medical expenses and debts and also prevents the partners' relatives from having any claim on the other partner's estate.

Disadvantages of Cohabitation

Although living together offers some advantages to many couples, it also poses certain unique problems. Most cohabiting couples expect sexual exclusivity of one another. However, data from a nationally representative survey found that individuals in cohabiting relationships are less likely than married people to be monogamous. The increased occurrence is attributed to the lower investment in their relationships (Treas & Giesen, 2000).

Although since the 1970s living together has not been illegal and has been less commonly referred to as "living in sin" or "shacking up," reactions from others can be nonsupportive or negative (Tolson, 2000). To peers and others the relationship often has less credibility than marriage. Disapproval of parents and other family members can place stress on one or both partners.

In Sweden 30% of couples who share a household are not married but have all the rights and obligations of married couples, unlike the legal vulnerabilities inherent in cohabitation in the United States. Some American couples, especially gay and lesbian couples, have difficulty renting or buying property together. Owning property jointly without a clear written contract results in legal rights that are less clear on dissolution of the relationship than with a divorce. Death of one or both partners can result in legal confusion in addition to the emotional trauma. Again, unless the couple has had the foresight to write a contract or to maintain up-to-date wills, there is no clearly established legal definition of partnership rights.

The Social Impact of Living Together

Living together permanently without marriage is not common in the United States, and most people see cohabitation as a precursor to marriage. Indeed, half of all cohabiting couples marry or end their relationship within 2 years. By 5 years only 10% of cohabiting couples are still together and unmarried. Living together for more than a few years apparently becomes difficult for most couples. Research has shown that the longer couples cohabit without getting married, the greater the instability, unhappiness, and lack of interaction the individuals say there is in the relationship (Brown, 2003). Ironically, gays and lesbians are criticized by some for having unstable relationships, yet if living together outside marriage does generally lead to relationship instability, then the lack of access to legal marriage between people of the same sex may, in part, foster instability in those relationships.

Many believe that cohabitation improves individuals' chances for selecting partners with whom they will experience stable and happy marriages. In this view, living together allows two people to identify their own needs and expectations as well as those of their partner before making a long-term commitment. Others argue just the opposite point—that living together has an overall negative effect on the long-term stability of a possible future marriage. Faced with conflict, couples who live together might find it easier to break up than to work together to solve their problems. Once this pattern has been established, people may be more likely to respond to marital conflict in the same way. Most research indicates that couples who lived together before getting married report more difficulty in their marriages and have an increased risk of divorce (Amato et al., 2003; Cobb et al., 2003). It is unknown whether people who cohabit have personal characteristics that make them more prone to divorce or whether the experience of cohabitation generates greater risk of divorce. Nevertheless, marriages preceded by living together are 50% more likely to end in divorce, with one exception. Couples in which the woman lived with the man she married, but never had sex with or lived with any man other than her husband, do not have an increased risk of divorce (Teachman, 2003).

Research shows that marriage has a higher degree of commitment and stability than does cohabitation (Binstock & Thornton, 2003), which may be one of the reasons that marriage continues to enjoy widespread appeal: About 90% of adults in the United States marry, many more than once (Deveny, 2003). A closer look at the institution of marriage might provide some insight into its continuing allure.

? Critical Thinking Question

Why do you think living together before marriage does not improve chances of a stable marriage?

▶ Marriage

Marriage is an institution found in virtually every society. It has traditionally served several functions, both personal and social. It typically provides societies with stable family units that serve as the primary conveyors of social norms. Most children acquire knowledge about their society's rules and mores through the teachings of their married parents or kinship groups. Marriage also structures an economic partnership that integrates child rearing, performance of household tasks, and earning into one family unit (Timmer & Orbuch, 2001). Marriage also defines inheritance rights to family property (Miya-Jervis, 2000). People have an understanding of these variables: Research finds that compatibility and a feeling of being "well matched" form a basis for a decision to marry (Surra & Hughes, 1997). However, a feeling of readiness for marriage is not just a result of finding someone compatible, but also of having factors outside the relationship in place. A person who is older and educationally and financially accomplished and who has support from friends and family for the chosen partner is more likely to feel ready to get married than someone who is not in that situation (Holman & Daoli, 1997).

Marriage tends to regulate sexual behavior to help maintain the family line. Many also hope that it will serve as a primary source of emotional and social support, the main reason most people marry. Marriage promises regular companionship, sexual gratification, a loving and enduring involvement, and parenting options, all within the security of a legitimized social institution. And on the whole, married people are generally happier and healthier, both physically and psychologically, than unmarried people (Horwitz et al., 1996; Prior & Hayes, 2003).

Although marriage is integral to most cultures, it assumes many different forms. Scientists who study culture have identified two important dimensions on which cultures differ in regard to the purpose of marriage: collectivism and individualism. *Collectivist cultures,* such as those of contemporary India, Pakistan, Thailand, and the Philippines, emphasize group or collective goals over individual aspirations. In such cultures marriage serves the purpose of uniting families rather than just two people. For this reason marriages in collectivist cultures are often arranged, with family needs taking precedence over individual feelings. This pattern also prevailed in Europe before the 19th century, when parents arranged their children's marriages to develop alliances between families and to maintain financial and social position. A benefit of arranged marriages is that the choice of a spouse made through the parents' rational deliberation instead of the individuals' passionate impulses can lend itself to greater long-term compatibility in the marriage (Razdan, 2003).

On their wedding day, a groom in Kenya lifts the veil of his bride, whose face he may have never seen before.

© Carol Beckwith/Robert Estall Photo Agency, UK

In contrast to collectivist cultures, *individualistic cultures,* such as those of contemporary Europe, Australia, European Brazil, and the United States, stress individual desires and goals over family interests. People in individualistic cultures place considerably more importance on feelings of love as a key basis for marriage than do their counterparts in collectivist cultures (Levine et al., 1995). Along with the importance of love, other elements of the contemporary Western marriage ideal are usually taken for granted. For example, sexual and emotional exclusivity between two people contrasts with other cultures that practice marriage between one man and several women (polygyny), the few cultures that recognize unions between one woman and several men (polyandry), and those cultures that permit sexual activity outside the marriage for one or both partners. The debate about legal marriage for gays and lesbians challenges the historical ideal of marriage as a legal arrangement between a man and a woman, as we discuss further in the "On the Edge" box titled "Legal Marriage for Gays and Lesbians?"

Norms for marriage also change within a culture, as we describe in the following "Sexuality and Diversity" discussion.

? Critical Thinking Question

How are arranged marriages similar to and different from professional matchmakers or reality TV shows such as *Married By America?*

Sexuality and Diversity

Interracial Marriage

As recently as 1967, interracial marriage was banned in more than a dozen states. *Miscegenation*—sex between members of different races, whether or not the couple was married—was also illegal until the U.S. Supreme Court invalidated those laws in 1967 (Moran, 2001). Since then, interracial marriage has increased dramatically, as shown in Figure 14.1: 2.2% of all marriages in the late 1990s were interracial, doubling the rate in 1980. Currently, 20% of married Asian Pacific Islanders have a non-Asian spouse, and 6% of married African Americans are wed to people outside their race (Leland & Beals, 1997).

Interracial marriage rates are higher in California than in any other state; 10% of married couples there are in mixed marriages (O'Connor, 1998).

One out of every 19 children born today—compared to 1 in 100 in 1970—is of mixed race. The standard racial and ethnic census categories of black, white, Asian, and Hispanic are simplistically out of step, and in 2000 the census provided, for the first time, the option to indicate mixed race (Clementson, 2000b).

Lack of acceptance of interracial dating and marriage in the United States is common for people of color as well as for white Americans (Cose, 2003). Ethnic and racial communities sometimes consider minority individuals who pair with white partners "race traitors" or "whitewashed" (Pan, 2000; Zia, 2003). Opinion polls show that about 30% of white Americans oppose black–white marriages (Goodheart, 2004). However, these attitudes are less common among young adults, 60% of whom have dated someone of another race (O'Connor, 1998). Well-known multi-ethnic superstars, such as singer Mariah Carey and golfer Tiger Woods, help familiarize our culture with ethnic mixing.

▶ **Figure 14.1** Increase in interracial marriages since 1960. The data for American Indians/whites was not gathered after 1990 because of small sample size.

Sources: Leland & Beals (1997, p. 60), and Fields & Caspar (2001).

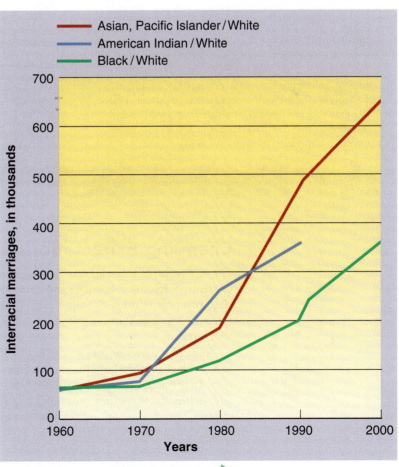

Immediately following the Supreme Court decision in 2003 that overturned the sodomy laws that remained in a few states, opponents and proponents of the right to legal civil marriage for gays and lesbians increased their efforts to ban or establish the right to marriage. Later in this chapter we will see that older heterosexual couples are increasingly deciding to live together and forgo legal marriage, yet many gays, lesbians, and gay rights advocates are striving for the United States to join Canada, Denmark, Belgium, and the Netherlands in providing the right to legal marriage (Giltz, 2004). Why is this right important? Without legal marriage gay couples do not have the same rights regarding inheritance, child custody, joint insurance policies for health, home, or auto, and status as next of kin for hospital visits or even to make funeral arrangements for a partner. Legal agreements designed by each couple can address some but not all of these practical issues. Beyond the practical issues is the symbolic meaning of marriage as recognition of the couple's relationship. When we ask whether love and commitment in gay and lesbian couples is as valid as love between straight people, the debate intensifies, as reflected in the following opposing viewpoints about gay marriage.

An opponent of gay marriage, William Bennett, editor of *The Book of Virtues* and codirector of Empower America, stated:

> The legal union of same-sex couples would shatter the conventional definition of marriage, change the rules which govern behavior, endorse practices which are completely antithetical to the tenets of all of the world's religions, send conflicting signals about marriage and sexuality, particularly to the young, and obscure marriage's enormous consequential function—procreation and child-rearing. (Bennett, 1996, p. 27)

Following the brief legalization of same-sex marriage in San Francisco in 2004, couples braved long lines for the opportunity to exchange marriage vows.

© Maggie Hallahan/CORBIS

A proponent of gay marriage, Andrew Sullivan, formerly a senior editor of *The New Republic* and author of *Virtually Normal: An Argument About Homosexuality,* stated:

> What we seek is not some special place in America but merely to be a full and equal part of America.... Some of us are lucky enough to meet the person we truly love. And we want to commit to that person in front of our family and country for the rest of our lives.... Why indeed would any conservative seek to ppose those very family values for gay people that he or she supports for everybody else? (Sullivan, 1996, p. 26)

In general, the public is less supportive of the right to marry than of civil rights for lesbians and gays. In fact, many people endorse the right

Changing Expectations and Marital Patterns

The institution of marriage has been condemned and venerated in contemporary America. Currently, a large discrepancy exists between the American marriage ideal and actual marriage practices (Corliss & Steptoe, 2004). Although cohabitation, high divorce rates, and extramarital sexual involvement are all antithetical to the traditional ideal, they are widespread.

Some of the reasons for contradictions between ideal and actual marriage practices have to do with changes in both the expectations for marriage and the social framework of marriage. In previous eras marriage fulfilled the primary function of providing an economically and socially stable environment in which to rear children. People who did not want to have children were frequently admonished not to marry (Ritter, 1919). However, contemporary couples usually marry for love and expect their marriages to provide more than a stable unit for raising children (Yalom, 2001). Most people today enter marriage with some hopes or expectations for fulfilling their financial, social, sexual, emotional, spiritual, and perhaps of gay couples to have many of the specific rights that marriage automatically brings but balk at marriage itself. Only about 25% of the general population supports legally sanctioned marriage for same-sex couples, but 40% favor legal civil unions that provide many of the legal rights of marriage. Poll results vary on whether or not most U.S. citizens support amending the Constitution to prohibit same-sex marriage (Lindlaw, 2003; Lisotta, 2004).

Most political decisions mirror the public's majority viewpoint. For example, in 1996 the U.S. Congress passed and President Clinton signed the Defense of Marriage Act, which denied federal recognition of gay marriage and gave states the right not to recognize same-sex marriages performed in other states. By 2003, 37 states had passed such laws (National Gay and Lesbian Task Force, 2003). One might question whether a defense of marriage might better be built around lowering divorce rates by preventing and treating domestic violence, providing better access to couples counseling and parenting skills training, than by excluding same-sex couples from marrying (Bouley, 2003).

In contrast to these antigay measures, in May of 2004 the Massachusetts Supreme Judicial Court affirmed a constitutional right for same-sex marriages in that state, making Massachusetts the first state to issue fully legal marriage licenses to gay and lesbian couples (Belluck & Zezima, 2004). For two months earlier in 2004, the most populous county in Oregon was the first to issue marriage licenses to same-sex couples. The 3,022 couples who obtained licenses in that county may or may not be granted recognition by the state (Cloud, 2004). These rulings were preceded by the Vermont State Supreme Court's unprecedented ruling in 2000 that it is unconstitutional to deny same-sex couples the benefits of marriage; the state legislature subsequently established a law enabling same-sex couples to form "civil unions" (Moats, 2004). The civil union entitles them to the approximately 300 rights, benefits, and responsibilities that marriage provides for heterosexual couples. In 2003 California also approved civil unions for gays and lesbians. However, these state laws do not entitle couples to recognition in other states, or to federal benefits of marriage such as spousal access to Social Security (Lisotta, 2003; Savage, 2003).

Many countries around the world have extended civil unions to gay and lesbian couples. France, Germany, most Nordic countries, and Great Britain provide legal rights for same-sex relationships (Graham, 2004). Some employers in Australia provide domestic partnership benefits, and some jurisdictions register domestic partners. Argentina allows a civil union that recognizes the couple regardless of the sex of the partners, and Buenos Aires has legalized gay and lesbian unions (Sailer, 2003).

By mid-2003 the most significant controversy focused on the possibility of Congress authorizing an amendment to the U.S. Constitution that would bar same-sex marriage. President George W. Bush supports the proposed amendment because his religious beliefs maintain that homosexual behavior is a sin. In a like-minded reaction the Vatican issued a document stating that it is the moral duty of U.S. Catholic political leaders to oppose same-sex marriage (Gambrell, 2003; Stein, 2003). Another religion-based rationale for limiting marriage to heterosexuals is the view that procreation should be the primary goal of marriage, although none of these religions forbids marriages between men and women unable to reproduce—the elderly, disabled, or sterilized, for example (Ponnuru, 2003)—or who choose not to reproduce.

Opponents of the proposed constitutional amendment emphasize the principle of separation of church and state. Religious institutions have always been and would continue to be completely free to disregard or recognize any civil marriage (Gambrell, 2003). In addition, the religious doctrine of some should not dictate a lack of rights for gay couples. Even many strongly religious individuals often have this perspective. Those against the proposed constitutional amendment also see its implementation as codifying discrimination (Lindlaw, 2003). Canadian judges who established rights to legal marriage for homosexual couples based their decision on the belief that excluding lesbian and gay couples from marriage was discriminatory and therefore unconstitutional (Hays, 2003).

The controversy over legal civil marriage for gays and lesbians will play out at the state and national level for years to come (Bergling, 2004; Sullivan, 2004). This debate asks whether people include homosexual behavior in their concept of sin and whether marriage is fundamentally a civil or religious institution (Cooperman, 2003).

parental needs (T. Edwards, 2000; Gager & Sanchez, 2003). Furthermore, many people hope that happiness is at least a likely if not guaranteed outcome of marriage. These high expectations are often difficult to fulfill (Huston et al., 2001; Jong, 2003). Succinctly stated, "The myth of marriage goes like this: Somewhere out there is the perfect soul mate, the yin that meshes easily and effortlessly with your yang. And then there is the reality of marriage, which, as any spouse knows, is not unlike what Thomas Edison once said about genius: 1% inspiration and 99% perspiration" (Kantrowitz & Wingert, 1999, p. 53).

Ironically, as people's expectations for marriage have expanded, our society's marriage support networks have seen a corresponding decline. Extended families and small communities have become less prevalent; many married couples are isolated from their families and neighbors. This loss of support places further demands on the marriage to meet a variety of human needs, because couples are often hard pressed to find outside resources for help with household tasks, child care assistance, financial aid, or emotional support. Although the challenges of sharing everyday life after marriage can enrich and fulfill some couples, the

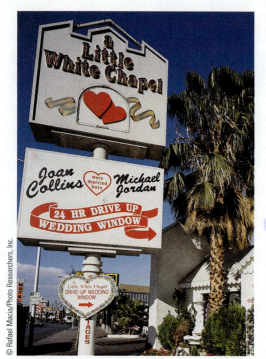

© Rafael Macia/Photo Researchers, Inc.

A Las Vegas marriage chapel offers a 24-hour drive-up window for quickie wedding ceremonies.

*5 negatives positive (5:1) for every 5 positives

? How About You?

Do you tend to be validating, volatile, or conflict avoidant in relationships?

lack of preparedness for meeting such challenges can disillusion others (Patz, 2000). Furthermore, people now live much longer than they did in the past, a condition that raises the question of how marriages can keep pace with the ever-changing needs of each partner. A "good marriage" is not necessarily a problem-free marriage but rather a relationship in which two people are committed to dealing with the problems that invariably arise.

Predicting Marital Satisfaction

Studies conducted by psychologist John Gottman and his colleagues have revealed surprisingly effective criteria for predicting marital success. Their findings, described next, are summarized and discussed in Gottman's books *Why Marriages Succeed or Fail* (1994), *What Predicts Divorce* (1993), and *The Seven Principles for Making Marriage Work* (2000). Gottman did not study long-term cohabiting heterosexuals or gay and lesbian couples, but his findings likely apply to any committed relationship.

Gottman's team used a multimethod research model to create an extensive database drawn from 20 different studies of 2,000 couples. Using videotapes of couples interacting as they discussed a problem area in their marriage, while they were monitored for physiological changes (such as heart rate and blood pressure), and using follow-up questionnaires and interviews, Gottman and his associates identified a number of patterns that predict marital discord, unhappiness, and separation. Identifying such patterns has provided the basis for predicting with better than 90% accuracy whether a couple will separate within the first few years of marriage. These patterns included:

- The ratio of positive to negative comments
- Facial expressions of disgust, fear, or misery
- High levels of heart rate
- Defensive behaviors, such as making excuses and denying responsibility for disagreement
- Verbal expressions of contempt by the wife
- "Stonewalling" by the husband (showing no response when his wife expresses her concerns)

An important variable in predicting duration and happiness in marriage was the ratio of positive to negative emotional interactions. Couples who were satisfied with their marriages demonstrated a ratio of at least five positive interactions to one negative interaction. Gottman summarized: "It is the balance between positive and negative emotional interactions in a marriage that determines its well-being—whether the good moments of mutual pleasure, passion, humor, support, kindness, and generosity outweigh the bad moments of complaining, criticism, anger, disgust, contempt, defensiveness, and coldness" (1994, p. 44). The 5:1 ratio is more important than how much a couple fights or how compatible they are socially, financially, and sexually. When couples maintain or improve this ratio, they can have long-lasting satisfying marriages regardless of their particular relationship style. The "Your Sexual Health" box contains a quiz devised by Gottman.

Gottman found three different marriage styles: *validating*, *volatile*, and *conflict avoiding*. Each style has its own unique strengths and weaknesses. Validating couples discuss problems calmly, listen to each other's viewpoints, and work out solutions, compromising when necessary, yet the partners are at risk of becoming passionless buddies. Volatile couples have intense emotional marriages characterized by frequent disagreements. They show respect for each other in their conflict and make up just as passionately as they argue. However, volatile couples can become too aggressive. Conflict-avoidant couples cannot tolerate arguments or fighting and avoid disagreements with a "peace at any price" approach that makes life run smoothly but interferes with facing problems that need to be resolved for the health of the relationship. Marriage longevity occurs equally in all three styles when the positive–negative emotional interaction ratio remains at five or more positive interactions to each negative interaction.

► Know Your Partner

Test the strength of your relationship in this quiz prepared by John Gottman.

True or False

1. I can name my partner's best friends.
2. I can tell you what stresses my partner is currently facing.
3. I know the names of some of the people who have been irritating my partner lately.
4. I can tell you some of my partner's life dreams.
5. I can tell you about my partner's basic philosophy of life.
6. I can list the relatives my partner likes the least.
7. I feel that my partner knows me pretty well.
8. When we are apart, I often think fondly of my partner.
9. I often touch or kiss my partner affectionately.
10. My partner really respects me.
11. There is fire and passion in this relationship.
12. Romance is definitely still a part of our relationship.
13. My partner appreciates the things I do in this relationship.
14. My partner generally likes my personality.
15. Our sex life is mostly satisfying.
16. At the end of the day my partner is glad to see me.
17. My partner is one of my best friends.
18. We just love talking to each other.
19. There is lots of give and take (both people have influence) in our discussions.
20. My partner listens respectfully, even when we disagree.
21. My partner is usually a great help as a problem solver.
22. We generally mesh well on basic values and goals in life.

Scoring: Give yourself 1 point for each true answer.

Above 12: You have a lot of strength in your relationship. Congratulations.

Below 12: Your relationship could stand some improvement and could probably benefit from some work on the basics, such as improving communication.

Gottman found other critical patterns of newlyweds who wind up in stable and happy marriages (Gottman et al., 1998). These successful patterns are distinct for women and men. Women typically initiate discussions about concerns and problems in the marriage. To the extent that women use a "softened start-up," a calm, kind, diplomatic beginning to the discussion, they have stable and happy marriages. Conversely, men who accept influence from their wives end up in long-term good marriages. Husbands who reject their wives' requests and concerns—in essence, husbands who refuse to share their power with their wives—find themselves in unstable, unhappy marriages that are more likely to lead to divorce. A husband's ability to accept his wife's influence is unrelated to his age, income, occupation, or educational level. Although these patterns are unique for each sex, the positive interaction between them is evident: A wife will be more inclined to use a softened start-up if she knows her husband will be responsive to her, and a husband will be more likely to accept the influence of a wife who begins a conflict discussion in a diplomatic fashion.

Another area of research involves the effectiveness of a premarital inventory called PREPARE in predicting marital satisfaction. PREPARE is a 125-item questionnaire that

Expressions of contempt can erode marital satisfaction and longevity.

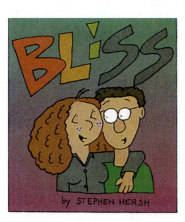

Bliss © 1998. Reprinted with permission of Stephen Hersh.

identifies strengths and weaknesses in 11 relationship areas: (1) realistic expectations, (2) personality issues, (3) communication, (4) conflict resolution, (5) financial management, (6) leisure activities, (7) sexual relationship, (8) children and marriage, (9) family and friends, (10) egalitarian roles, and (11) religious orientation (Olson et al., 1987). In studies in which couples filled out the inventory before marriage and then were revisited 3 years after they married, the PREPARE inventory had more than 80% accuracy in predicting which couples would divorce and which would have happy marriages (Murray, 1995a). Additional research has confirmed that couples who have strife-filled courtships and marriages are likely to have relatively short marriages (Huston et al., 2001).

Given that so many marriages in the United States will end in divorce, obtaining premarital counseling from professionals well versed in the use of predictive devices (such as those used by Gottman and his associates and inventories such as PREPARE) is important (Lebow, 1997). Currently, couples who choose to participate in premarital counseling have fewer risk factors for marital difficulties to begin with than couples who do not obtain premarital counseling. Therefore the couples who need the most help are obtaining the least assistance to help improve their upcoming marriages (Sullivan & Bradbury, 1997). If areas of present or potential conflict can be identified, a couple might then seek to resolve these difficulties through further counseling before taking their vows. In situations in which conflict resolution efforts do not succeed, a couple might reconsider or at least postpone marriage. See the "Let's Talk About It" box for a sample of questions used in premarital counseling.

The Good Marriage

Gottman's research found that both men and women say that the quality of the friendship with their spouse is the most important factor in marital satisfaction (Gottman & Silver, 2000). Gottman's work reinforced the findings of an earlier study of satisfying and long-lasting marriages (Wallerstein & Blakeslee, 1995), which found that happiness in marriage occurred when couples liked and respected one another. Respect was based on the integrity of the partner's honesty, compassion, decency, fairness, and loyalty to the family. Happy couples found pleasure and comfort in each other's company and treated their marriages as needing continued attention. They understood that a good marriage is a process of ongoing change, dealing with each individual's needs and wishes pertaining to work, sex, parenting, friends, and health as they evolve during the life cycle. They believed that their marriages enhanced them as individuals and that the fit between their own needs and their partner's responses was unique and irreplaceable. They felt lucky to be with their spouse and did not take each other for granted.

These couples had successfully managed the challenges of the psychological tasks that create the foundation and framework of a happy marriage. Wallerstein & Blakeslee (1995) identified each of these tasks:

- Committing to the relationship and detaching emotionally from the families of childhood while building new connections with the extended families
- Building intimacy and unity while maintaining room for autonomy
- Expanding the relationship to include children and balancing parenthood while nurturing the couple relationship
- Managing the unpredictable adversities of life—illness, death, natural disasters—in ways that enhanced the relationship
- Finding ways to resolve differences, anger, and conflict without exploiting each other or giving away one's own interests
- Establishing an imaginative and pleasurable sex life
- Sharing laughter and keeping interest alive
- Providing emotional nurturance and encouragement
- Drawing sustenance and renewal from the memories of courtship and early marriage

Individuals in happy marriages demonstrated a capacity to be sensitive to their partner's inner state of mind and a willingness to reshape the marriage in response to new circumstances. Over the course of the marriage they changed and developed personally and had a

LET'S TALK ABOUT IT

Before You Get Serious . . .

The following questions are typical of premarital counseling topics. If you and your partner decide to give them a try, the most effective approach is for each of you to write your responses in private and then to read them aloud to each other. Remember, it is not always being the same that is the most important thing. It is being able to understand and work effectively with the differences between you.

	Often	Sometimes	Rarely
Am I usually the listener in our conversations?	___	___	___
Do you interrupt me and anticipate what I wish to say?	___	___	___
Can I discuss personal problems with you?	___	___	___

Complete each of the following sentences.

The hardest subject to discuss with you is _____.

What puzzles me about you is _____.

One thing I dislike about myself is _____.

The thing I like best about myself is _____.

When we quarrel, I usually _____.

SOURCE: Adapted from Tate-O'Brien (1981).

Answer each of the following questions.

How did my father show anger or displeasure?

How did my mother show anger or displeasure?

How was physical affection shown in my family? How did I feel about it?

How did my parents handle money?

What worries do I have about our sex life?

Check items you agree with.

_____ When people are angry, it is best to keep quiet and cool down.

_____ Couples should always try to do things together.

_____ Marriage without children can be as satisfying as one with children.

_____ Household responsibilities are to be shared equally and assigned intentionally.

Place an X where your beliefs fit on the continuum.

Money is to be spent and enjoyed.	⊢——————————⊣	Money is to be spent carefully and saved for a rainy day.

sense that they had experienced many different "marriages" within the evolution of their marriage. These happy couples exemplify how "neither the legal nor the religious ceremony makes the marriage. *People* do, throughout their lives" (Wallerstein & Blakeslee, 1995, p. 331).

Sexual Behavior Within Marriage

Contemporary developments in sexual mores and behavior are often discussed in the context of nonmarital or extramarital activities. However, the greatest impact of increased sexual liberalization may be on the marital relationship itself.

Evidence of Increasing Sexual Satisfaction in Marriage

Compared with Kinsey's research groups, contemporary married women and men in the United States appear to be engaging in a wider repertoire of sexual behaviors and enjoying sexual interaction more. Several surveys have revealed significant changes in sexual activity among married couples in the years since Kinsey collected his data. The frequency and duration of sexual play before intercourse have increased, with more people focusing on these activities themselves rather than viewing them as preparation for coitus. Oral stimulation of the breasts and manual stimulation of the genitals have increased; so has oral–genital contact, both fellatio and cunnilingus (Clements, 1994; Laumann et al., 1994).

Sexual satisfaction and marital quality often are found together (Perrone & Worthington, 2001), as is also the case with relationships before marriage, in which sexual satisfaction is associated with relationship satisfaction, love commitment, and stability (Sprecher, 2002). One national survey of 7,000 American couples found that mutuality in initiating sex seems

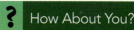

? How About You?

Of the couples you know, whose marriage most closely resembles this description by Wallerstein and Blakeslee?

© Mark Hanauer/CORBIS

Married couples are engaging in a wider variety of sexual behaviors and enjoying sexual interaction more often than in previous eras.

to contribute to the sexual satisfaction of both partners (Blumstein & Schwartz, 1983). The frequency of sexual interactions was also strongly associated with sexual satisfaction in marriage. Of the married couples who were having sex three or more times a week, 90% reported satisfaction with their sex lives. In contrast, half of those who had sex one to four times a month—and only one-third of those who had sex less than once a month—were satisfied. These researchers also found that sex is more exciting at the outset of marriage and that in long-term relationships sex tends to be more "bread and butter" rather than "champagne and caviar" (Blumstein & Schwartz, 1983). This shift may explain why, in an extensive analysis of the National Health and Social Life Survey (NHSLS) data, couples reported that the quality of sex in marriage became slightly less with greater duration of marriage (Liu, 2003).

Factors Limiting Sexual Satisfaction in Marriage

The men and women in married couples are not similarly satisfied with their sexual lives. Research indicates that married women report lower levels of sexual satisfaction than do their husbands (Liu, 2003). This difference is a complicated issue, and the causes for it are unknown. Liu (2003) speculated that the lower satisfaction wives express stems from two factors. First, wives experience orgasm in fewer sexual experiences than their husbands do. Second, because women typically invest more time and energy in the general relationship than men, women may have higher expectations for the sexual relationship.

Sexless unions are not uncommon, noted psychologist Ruthellen Josselson (1992). Josselson, who interviewed married people between the ages of 25 and 55, stated, "I was astonished at how many married couples said they hadn't had sex in years" (in Murray, 1992, p. 64). As we will see in Chapter 15, a lack of interest in sexual activity is the most frequent problem that brings people to seek sex therapy. It is important to note, however, that a lack of sexual interaction does not necessarily signify that platonic marriages are not satisfying and that they should be "fixed." For some couples sex is not and perhaps never was a high priority. And, as Josselson observed, "There are many forms of human connection. These couples are not willing to sacrifice a marriage that is working on other levels" (in Murray, 1992, p. 64).

Although some data indicate greater sexual satisfaction for married people than for single people, as shown in Table 14.1, a number of factors can interfere with marital sexual enjoyment. When people marry, their relationship often changes. They suddenly find themselves confronted with a new set of role expectations (Gager & Sanchez, 2003). They are no longer just friends and lovers but also husband and wife, and romance may be replaced by the stress of adjusting to the new identity. In addition, men and women react differently to changes in roles. One study found that an increase in the husband's share of housework improved the wives' perceptions of marital quality but decreased the husbands' perceptions (Amato et al., 2003). People often get caught up in a "rat race" lifestyle that can seriously erode the quality of marital sex. Former U.S. labor secretary Robert Reich made a point about the pressures of overworked couples in applying an acronym to many contemporary couples: DINS—dual income, no sex (Deveny, 2003). Holding down a job, doing laundry, fixing the lawn mower, socializing with two sets of relatives and friends, and countless other tasks can reduce the time and energy a couple has for intimate sharing. Couples who become parents discover that children can place unexpected

> **?** Critical Thinking Question
>
> Why do you think married women, in general, are less satisfied with their sex lives than married men are?

TABLE 14.1	Relationship Status and Orgasm Experience	
	Always or Usually Have an Orgasm with Partner	
	Men (%)	**Women (%)**
Dating	94	62
Living together	95	68
Married	95	75
(How would you explain the difference in patterns for men and women?)		

SOURCE: Laumann et al. (1994).

strains on their relationship in addition to interfering with their privacy and spontaneity (Emery & Tuer, 1993; Jouriles et al., 1991). Without the independence of living separately, the day-to-day togetherness can erode their sense of individuality and autonomy. Over time sex can become too routine and predictable. The discussion in Chapter 7 on maintaining relationship satisfaction may be helpful in enhancing sexual enjoyment in marriages and other long-term relationships.

► Extramarital Relationships

The term **extramarital relationship** is used to describe the sexual interaction of a married person with someone other than her or his spouse. The term is a general one that makes no distinction among the many ways in which extramarital sexual activity occurs. Such activity can be secret or based on an agreement between the married partners. The extramarital relationship may be casual or involve deep emotional attachment; it may last for a brief or extended time. Sometimes it occurs within the context of an alternative lifestyle, such as swinging. Most societies have restrictive norms pertaining to extramarital sex, typically more restrictive for women than men. However, some societies have formal rules allowing extramarital sex (Frayser, 1985), as discussed below in "Sexuality and Diversity."

Extramarital relationship
Sexual interaction by a married person with someone other than his or her spouse.

► Sexuality and Diversity

Attitudes Toward Extramarital Sexuality in Other Cultures

The Aborigines of western Australia's Arnhem Land openly accept extramarital sexual relationships for both wives and husbands. They welcome the variety in experience and the break in monotony offered by extramarital involvements. Many also report increased appreciation of and attachment to the spouse as a result of such experiences.

The Polynesian Marquesans, although not open advocates of extramarital affairs, nevertheless tacitly accept such activity. A Marquesan wife often takes young boys or her husband's friends or relatives as lovers. Conversely, her husband may have relations with young unmarried girls or with his sisters-in-law. Marquesan culture openly endorses the practices of partner swapping and sexual hospitality, in which unaccompanied visitors are offered sexual access to the host of the other sex. Sexual hospitality is also practiced by some Eskimo groups, in which a married female host has intercourse with a male visitor (Gebhard, 1971).

The Turu of central Tanzania regard marriage primarily as a cooperative economic and social bond. Affection between husband and wife is generally thought to be out of place; most members of this society believe that the marital relationship is endangered by the instability of love and affection. The Turu have evolved a system of romantic love, called *Mbuya,* that allows them to seek affection outside the home without threatening the stability of the primary marriage. Both husband and wife actively pursue these outside relationships (Gebhard, 1971).

Nonconsensual Extramarital Relationships

In **nonconsensual extramarital sex** the married person engages in an outside sexual relationship without the consent (or presumably the knowledge) of his or her spouse. This form of behavior has been given many labels, including cheating, adultery, infidelity, having an affair, and fooling around. These negative labels reflect the fact that more than 90% of the general U.S. public says that extramarital sex is "always" or "almost always" wrong (Treas & Giesen, 2000).

Nonconsensual extramarital sex Sexual interaction in which a married person engages in an outside sexual relationship without the consent (or presumably the knowledge) of his or her spouse.

Why Do People Have Affairs?

Varied and complex theories abound on the reasons for nonconsensual extramarital sex (Atwood & Seifer, 1997). In part, intrinsic conflicts in human nature contribute. As author Erica Jong explained, "We are pair-bonding creatures—like swans or geese. We can also be as promiscuous as baboons or bonobos. Those are the two extremes of human sexuality, and there all gradations of chastity and sensuality in between" (2003, p. 48). Another idea is that the motive is the person's desire to reestablish his or her sense of individuality and autonomy, which has been diminished within the context of marriage (Schnarch, 1991). An individual may not be developed enough emotionally to maintain being true to him- or herself in the face of a partner's discomfort or disapproval; that individual seeks a new, secret relationship to reestablish a sense of self (J. Shaw, 1997). For some, the need to confirm that they are still desirable to members of the other sex can lead them into an affair. In other cases people are highly dissatisfied with their marriages. If emotional needs are not being met within the marriage, having an "illicit lover" may seem particularly inviting (Friedman, 1994). In some situations, affairs also provide the impetus to end a marriage that is no longer satisfying (Brown, 1988). Occasionally, the reason for outside involvements is the unavailability of sex within the marriage. A lengthy separation, a debilitating illness, or a partner's inability or unwillingness to relate sexually can all influence a person to look elsewhere for sexual fulfillment. An affair may also be motivated by a desire for revenge (Sponaugle, 1989). In such instances the offending party may be quite indiscreet, to ensure that the "wronged" spouse discovers the infidelity. Sometimes nonconsensual extramarital relationships are motivated simply by a desire for excitement and variety; although they have no particular complaints about the marriage, some people want the adventure of extramarital affairs in their lives.

Indeed, the secrecy of an illicit relationship sometimes adds to its appeal. Researchers examined the allure of secrecy in relationships and found that university alumni spent more time thinking about former lovers who were kept secret than those who were known to others (Wegner et al., 1994). The researchers also set up a laboratory experiment involving male and female university students who had not met before the study. Subjects were seated in mixed-sex pairs for card games, and couples were asked to touch feet under the table while playing cards with another couple. Sometimes this game of footsie was secret; other times it was not. Couples in the "secret footsie" group reported greater attraction to each other after the game than did couples whose foot touching was not secret. The researchers concluded that secrecy often creates attraction in relationships.

Are there differences between people who are sexually exclusive and those who have sex outside their primary relationship? Most researchers who have asked this question have looked at limited variables and have based their studies on small samples that could not be generalized to the overall population. However, one study used data from the nationally representative NHSLS and examined variables that could be factors associated with a greater likelihood of extramarital sex (Treas & Giesen, 2000). The study found that most of the factors increasing the likelihood of affairs were characteristics of the person rather than of the relationship. First, age is important: Individuals between the ages of 18 and 30 were twice as likely to have an affair than people over 50. More permissive sexual attitudes and higher interest in sex were also correlated with increased extramarital sex. When men and women were matched for sexual attitudes and interest, women were as likely as men to engage in extramarital sex; this is contrary to other studies, which showed greater likelihood for men, but in those studies the sexual attitudes and interest variables were not controlled. Work and living circumstances play a role, too. People who have greater sexual opportunities through access to potential partners at work, the anonymity found in out-of-town travel, and the larger population and anonymity of living in a large city are more likely to be unfaithful. If they have weak ties to their spouses' friends, family, and activities and are not involved in a religious community, the chances are greater of betraying their commitment.

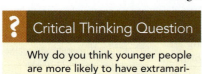

? Critical Thinking Question

Why do you think younger people are more likely to have extramarital sex?

The only variable related to the relationship rather than individual characteristics is that people who had affairs were more likely to report less subjective satisfaction with their emotional and physical relationships with their marital partners. The important issue with this variable is which came first, the dissatisfaction or the infidelity? It is just as possible for the dissatisfaction to follow the infidelity—as a consequence of guilt or in comparison to a new experience—as for dissatisfaction to have motivated the extramarital sex.

How Common Are Extramarital Affairs?

Whatever the motivation, it is difficult to estimate the incidence of extramarital sexual involvements. Kinsey's surveys reported that approximately 50% of the men and 25% of the women in his samples had experienced extramarital sexual intercourse at least once by age

40. More recent estimates vary widely. According to researchers at the Kinsey Institute in the late 1980s, roughly 40% of husbands and 30% of wives had experienced extramarital affairs (Reinisch et al., 1988). Statistics from a number of magazine surveys—including *Cosmopolitan, Playboy, Redbook,* and *New Woman*—claim higher rates, but magazine survey results are often unreliable.

The NHSLS, with its sample of 3,432 Americans, ages 18 to 59, provides more reliable rates of extramarital affairs. This survey reported extramarital involvement rates at some time during a marriage of 25% and 15% among married men and women, respectively. However, 94% of the married subjects indicated that they had been monogamous in the past year (Laumann et al., 1994).

The Internet's Role in Affairs

With access to the Internet burgeoning, the opportunity for an individual to develop intimate, secret relationships outside his or her committed relationship has taken on new dimensions. Under the guise of working online or surfing the Net, it can be easy to make contact with people for possible and actual sexual relationships (Paul, 2004). However, it can be almost as easy for the spouse (or employer) to discover these communications. Most marital therapists have seen a significant increase in couples coming to therapy following the spouse's discovery of an Internet-initiated affair (Cooper, 2004; Tangeman, 2003).

The Impact of Extramarital Sex on a Marriage

The effects of extramarital sex on a marriage vary. The dynamics of the secrecy typically have damaging effects. The secrecy and lying (even by omission) erode the connection with the spouse and amplify the illusion of closeness to the affair partner. A sex therapist elaborated, "Infidelity . . . consists of taking sexual energy of any sort—thoughts, feelings, and behaviors—outside of a committed sexual relationship in such a way that it damages the relationship, and then pretending that this drain of energy will affect neither partner nor the relationship, as long as it remains undiscovered. Hiding [these feelings] devitalizes the relationship, compromises integrity, and co-opts the other partner's choices to be responsible and responsive" (J. Shaw, 1997, p. 27).

When secret involvements are discovered, the "betrayed" spouse may feel devastated. He or she can experience a variety of emotions, including feelings of inadequacy and rejection, extreme anger, resentment, shame, and jealousy. Jealousy emerges from the belief that the spouse is giving away something that belongs exclusively to the other partner. Part of sexual jealousy stems from a misplaced sense of ownership. The fear that another person will usurp one's position of preeminence in the life of one's spouse might also be involved. However, the discovery of infidelity does not inevitably erode the quality of a marriage. In some cases it is a beneficial crisis that motivates a couple to search for and attempt to resolve sources of discord in their relationship—a process that can ultimately lead to an improved marriage (Wiviott, 2001).

Available data provide a hazy picture of the effects of extramarital sex on both the individual participant and the married couple. Blumstein and Schwartz's (1983) national survey of American couples revealed that the monogamous pairs in their sample had lower divorce rates than couples in which one or both partners had participated in extramarital relationships. This finding is consistent with the fact that extramarital relationships are often mentioned by divorced people as a cause of their marital breakup (Kelly, 1982). However, we cannot conclude that this apparent association necessarily reflects a cause-and-effect relationship. In at least some cases extramarital sex is a *symptom* of a disintegrating marriage rather than its cause. Involvement in an extramarital affair, whether or not it is discovered, can also have serious consequences for the participant, including loss of self-respect, severe guilt, stress associated with leading a secret life, damage to reputation, loss of love, and complications of sexually transmitted diseases (Humphrey, 1987; Rubenstein, 1994).

Consensual Extramarital Relationships

Consensual extramarital relationships occur in marriages where both partners know about and agree to sexual involvements outside the marriage. A variety of arrangements fall under the category of consensual extramarital involvements, including unique perspectives of other societies, previously discussed under "Attitudes Toward Extramarital Sexuality in Other Cultures." We briefly examine two arrangements: swinging and open marriage.

Consensual extramarital relationship A sexual relationship that occurs outside the marriage bond with the consent of one's spouse.

Swinging

Swinging The exchange of marital partners for sexual interaction.

Swinging, or comarital sex, refers to a form of consensual extramarital sex that a married couple shares (Atwood & Seifer, 1997). This activity was labeled wife swapping in the past, but this term came into disrepute among swingers because it implies male ownership. Husband and wife participate simultaneously and in the same location, usually in suburban living rooms, at clubs, or sometimes at "conventions" for "adventures into sensual living" with many couples. In contrast, sex clubs cater to singles or couples who pay for admission to watch others have sex or to engage in recreational sex with other club visitors themselves.

Research in the 1970s and 1980s found that about 5% of men and women in the United States had experienced swinging (Duckworth & Levitt, 1985; Tavris & Sadd, 1977). A documentary that was released in 2000, *The Lifestyle: Group Sex in the Suburbs,* provided insight into the prevalence and nature of contemporary swinging. The filmmaker found that all states except North Dakota have at least one swinging club. The clubs provide contacts for the estimated 3 million swingers in North America (Chocano, 2000). The film has one brief explicitly sexual scene. Most of its footage is devoted to interviews with typical swingers—middle-class, middle-aged suburban couples who look to the casual recreational sex of swinging for a solution to the zestless sex in their long-term marriages and for the sexual fulfillment our society emphasizes. The film shows that group sex and bisexual expression between women, but not men, are common in the swinger culture (Holden, 2000).

Open Marriage and Polyamory

Open marriage A marriage in which spouses, with each other's permission, have intimate relationships with other people as well as with the marital partner.

The 1972 book *Open Marriage,* by George and Nena O'Neill, brought widespread public attention to the concept of **open marriage,** in which couples agree to having intimate and sexual relationships outside the primary relationship. In more recent years *polyamory* has become the term many people use to describe multiple loving, consensual relationships. Polyamorists distinguish themselves from swingers by their emphasis on emotional commitment as the foundation for multiple relationships, with sex being an expression of this ability to love more than one person at the same time. Polyamorist literature emphasizes "responsible nonmonogamy," honest, ethical relationships that consist of trios, open marriages, groups of couples, and intentionally created families (Graham, 1998).

▶ Divorce

Research confirms that the proportion of marriages ending in divorce has increased dramatically since the 1950s, as shown in Table 14.2. Table 14.2a shows that the ratio of divorce to marriage was 1 to 4 in 1950; by 1977 the ratio was 1 divorce to every 2 marriages. The ratio of divorces to marriages has tended to level off and has held relatively steady since 1977. In the last few years another statistic, the *divorce rate* (number of divorces per 1,000 residents), shown in Table 14.2b, has also leveled off and has even declined slightly. There were 3.5 divorces per 1,000 U.S. residents in 1970, a rate that increased steadily until reaching a peak of 5.3 in 1980. Since then the divorce rate has slowly declined to 3.8 in 2003. It has been suggested that this leveling off of the divorce rate reflects, in part, a decrease in the marriage rate and an increase in the number of cohabiting couples in the United States whose breakups are not included in divorce statistics.

The estimated half of all marriages that end in divorce can be seen as a sign of societal rejection of the institution of marriage. This interpretation is probably not accurate, because almost 96% of adults have married during their lifetime and because most divorced people remarry. In fact, about half of all marriages involve at least one person who has been previously divorced one or more times (Amato et al., 2003).

The high divorce rate can also be seen as a vote of confidence for happy marriages. A writer explained:

> Perhaps the divorce rate doesn't mean what it seems to mean. . . . Perhaps the divorce rate measures a sentimental hopefulness, a wistful pursuit of legalized happy-ever-after in which somehow, against all odds, we continue to believe. Unrealistic, maybe, but rather sweet. Besides, despite divorce being possible for under a hundred dollars and swiftly available in many locales, half of all our married folk stay together, for richer, for poorer, till death them do part. Perhaps things have never been better. (Holland, 1998, p. 93)

TABLE 14.2   **Marriage and Divorce Rates in the United States**

(a) Number and Ratio of Divorces to Marriages

	1950	Ratio	1977	Ratio	1998	Ratio
Number of divorces	385,000		1,097,000		1,135,000	
		1:4		1:2		1:2
Number of marriages	1,667,000		2,176,000		2,256,000	

(b) Number of Marriages and Divorces per 1,000 U.S. Residents, 1970–2003

	1970	1975	1980	1985	1990	2003
Marriages	10.6	10.0	10.6	10.2	9.8	7.5
Divorces	3.5	4.8	5.2	5.0	4.7	3.8

The National Center for Health Statistics no longer publishes the yearly number of divorces.

SOURCES: (a) U.S. Bureau of the Census (1985, 1988). (b) U.S. Bureau of the Census (1985, 2000, 2003) and National Center for Health Statistics (1982, 1985, 1989, 1992, 1995, 1997, 2004).

Explaining the High Divorce Rate

A number of investigators have speculated on the factors responsible for the high divorce rate in the United States. One frequently mentioned cause is the comparative ease of obtaining no-fault divorces since the liberalization of divorce laws in the 1970s. Obtaining a divorce has become a simpler, less expensive legal process. In an attempt to help marriages last and to counter the ease of divorce under no-fault divorce laws, in 1997 Louisiana was the first state to offer the option of "covenant marriage" to couples applying for marriage licenses. Couples who choose covenant marriage agree to undergo premarital counseling and additional counseling if serious problems arise after marriage. The wait for the divorce to be final was extended from 180 days to 2 years, except in cases of a spouse committing domestic violence, child abuse, adultery, or a felony. At the least, the choice between standard marriage law and covenant marriage should promote meaningful conversations between couples contemplating marriage. A few other states have adopted covenant marriage options, and many others are considering implementing similar laws (Crary, 1999).

Further reasons for the increase in the divorce rate include a reduction in the social stigma attached to divorce (Holland, 1998). Because divorce has become legally easier to obtain and because the stigma attached to it has lessened, more children have been raised by divorced parents. Research shows that, as adults, children who were raised by divorced parents are more likely to end their own marriages in divorce than adults who were raised by parents who remained married (Amato, 2001). The causes of this correlation are unknown, but possibilities could include poor parental modeling of the skills and determination that help a marriage last.

Another factor influencing the higher divorce rate is increased expectations for marital and sexual fulfillment, which have caused people to become more disillusioned with and less willing to persist in unsatisfying marriages. The increased economic independence of women (30% of working women earn more than their husbands) may increase the importance of relationship satisfaction over financial dependence in women's decisions to divorce (Deveny, 2003). Further, a greater abundance of wealth makes it easier for some people to maintain several families, and the reduced influence of organized religion makes divorce less of a moral concern (Blackmun, 1996b).

Research has revealed two other variables that may be associated with marriages ending in divorce: age at marriage and level of education. People who marry in their teen years are more than twice as likely to divorce than those who wed in their 20s. Individuals who marry after age 30 have even lower divorce rates. The correlation between age at marriage and divorce rate is of particular interest in light of a clear upward trend in the median age at first marriage. Before 1900 most couples in the United States married while they were still in

> **? Critical Thinking Question**
>
> Why do you think adults raised by parents who divorced are more likely to end their own marriages in divorce?

"No heroic measures."

their teens. In 1950 the median marriage age was 22 for men and 20 for women; by 2000 these figures rose to 26 for men and 24 for women. Perhaps the leveling off and even slight decline in the U.S. divorce rate in recent years reflect, in part, the influence of a generalized increase in age at first marriage.

There also appears to be an inverse relationship between level of education and divorce rate; that is, the lower the educational level, the higher the divorce rate. The one exception is a disproportionately high divorce rate among women who have achieved postbaccalaureate degrees. Perhaps the increased economic and social independence of professional women with advanced degrees contributes to this exception in divorce rate patterns (Amato & Previti, 2003; Martin & Bumpass, 1989).

A recent study has provided some much needed empirical evidence of what divorced people say is the cause of their divorce (Amato & Previti, 2003). The researchers readily admit that the study cannot identify whether people's perceptions of their divorces represent actual causes or are after-the-fact reconstructions. In the randomly selected national sample of divorced individuals, the respondents gave infidelity as the most commonly reported cause of divorce. Poor general quality of the relationship—lack of communication, incompatibility, personality clashes, and growing apart—are factors people also say were reasons for ending their marriages. Serious problems such as drinking, drug use, and mental and physical abuse were further reasons.

Patterns between different groups about their reasons for divorce emerged from the research. Men and women tended to give different perspectives: Women were more likely to report that their husbands' problematic behavior led to divorce, whereas men were more likely to say that they did not know what caused the divorce. Socioeconomic status (SES) was another variable resulting in differences. High-SES divorced individuals were more likely to attribute their divorces to lack of love and communication, incompatibility, and their spouses' self-centeredness, but low-SES divorced individuals described financial problems, abuse, and drinking as major factors. In terms of positive emotional adjustment following the divorce, people who perceived that they initiated the divorce did better than those who said their partners initiated the divorces.

Helen Fisher, an anthropologist and author of *Anatomy of Love: The Natural History of Monogamy, Adultery, and Divorce* (1992), offered a controversial thesis about the course of relationships, from infatuation to divorce. Fisher contends that evolution has biologically programmed humans for serial pair bonding characterized by a natural inclination to move on after four years, a pattern she calls the four-year itch. To support this claim, Fisher cites divorce statistics from 62 cultures that reveal a peak in divorce rates around the fourth year of marriage. Fisher suggests that this "itch" is a manifestation of ancestral patterns of pair bonding in which early human couples needed to stay together just long enough for a child to be weaned from total dependence, a period of approximately four years. The birth of an additional child during this initial four-year period might then extend the union for about four more years.

? Critical Thinking Question

In the research on what reasons people give for their divorce, men are likely to say that they do not know why their marriage ended and women are likely to attribute their husbands' problematic behavior to the divorce. How do you explain this difference?

Adjusting to Divorce or Breakup of Long-Term Relationships

Although the chain of events leading to marriage is unique for each individual, most people marry with the hope that the relationship will last. Divorce often represents loss of this hope and other losses as well: one's spouse, lifestyle, the security of familiarity, part of one's identity, and sometimes custody of one's children (DeGarmo & Kitson, 1996). In the following discussion we refer to a breakup as divorce, but people who end nonmarital intimate relationships also can experience these same losses.

The loss a person feels in divorce is often comparable to the loss experienced when a loved one dies (Napolitane, 1997). In both cases the person undergoes a grieving process. There are important differences, however. When the grief is caused by death, rituals and social support may be helpful to the survivor. But no recognized grief rituals are provided by society to help the divorced person. Initially, a person may experience shock: "This cannot be happening to me." Disorganization might follow—a sense that one's entire world has turned upside down. Volatile emotions may unexpectedly surface. Feelings of guilt may become strong. Loneliness is common. Finally (usually not for several months or a year), a sense of relief and acceptance may come. After several months of separation a person who is not developing a sense of acceptance may benefit from professional help.

Although many of the feelings that accompany divorce are uncomfortable and painful, there is a potential for personal growth in the adjustment process that accompanies divorce. Many people experience a sense of autonomy for the first time in their lives. Others find that being single presents opportunities to experience more fully dimensions of themselves that had been submerged in the marriage. Learning to reach out to others for emotional support can help diminish feelings of aloneness. Divorce can offer an opportunity to reassess oneself and one's past, a process that may lead to a new life.

Making the transition from marital to postmarital sexual relationships often presents a challenge to divorced individuals. The newly divorced person may experience considerable ambivalence about intimacy. Feelings of anger, rejection, or fear remaining from the trauma of the divorce may inhibit openness to intimate relationships. To protect themselves from emotional vulnerability, some people withdraw from potential sexual relationships. Others react by seeking many superficial sexual encounters.

Despite the problems that newly single people often encounter in establishing nonmarital sexual expression, a majority of divorced individuals become sexually active within the first year following the breakup of their marriage (Stack & Gundlach, 1992). Even with the widespread concern about AIDS, people continue to be sexually active after the breakup of their marriages. In one national survey 74% of divorced and 80% of separated respondents reported being sexually active in the previous 12 months (Smith, 1991).

Approximately four out of five divorced people remarry, most within 3 years of the divorce (Lown & Dolan, 1988). Although many remarried people report that their second marriage is better than the first, evidence indicates that second marriages are more likely to end in divorce than first marriages (Ganong & Coleman, 1989; Lown et al., 1989). Remarried people are inclined to rate second marriages higher because they strive harder to achieve good communication, have fewer romantic illusions, and are more committed to effectively resolving conflicts. However, they are also inclined to monitor second marriages more closely than initial marriages and may be less willing to stick around when things turn sour. Some researchers also believe that second marriages are more prone to fail because the trauma of divorce has been lessened somewhat by having gone through it once already (Blumstein & Schwartz, 1983). Furthermore, the financial stresses associated with remarriage (alimony and child support, the high costs involved in establishing a new residence, etc.) are a major source of discord and divorce in remarried families.

▶ Sexuality and Aging

To a young adult the altered sexual expression that accompanies aging may seem remote and unimportant. However, in the later years of life most people begin to note certain changes taking place in their sexual response patterns. Some women and men who understand the nature of these variations accept them with equanimity. Others observe them with concern.

An important source of the confusion and frustration that many aging people feel is the prevailing notion that old age is a sexless time (Kellett, 2000). However, sexuality can actually improve in later life. Of a representative sample of adults over age 60, 61% said that their sex life today was either the same or more physically satisfying than in their 40s (Dunn & Cutler, 2000). As a 76-year-old woman described:

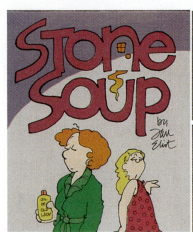

When I was married 47 years ago, my husband and I were both 29, and both virgins. I was taught that sex was for procreation only, so the adjustment to each other was not easy. The years of having babies, raising children, and, for my husband (a workaholic), getting established in his profession took much time and energy, and sex was an unimportant part of our lives. Now we are 76 years old and with the gift of time, good health, and financial security, our sex life is wonderful and very much a part of our fulfilling lives—truly, the best years of our lives. (Authors' files)

Why has aging in our society and in other societies often been associated with sexlessness? (See Figure 14.2 for a global comparison.) There are a number of reasons. Part of the answer is that American culture is still influenced by the philosophy that equates sexuality with procreation. For people beyond their reproductive years this viewpoint offers little beyond self-denial. Moreover, American society focuses on youth. The media usually link love, sex, and romance with the young. There is also an often unspoken assumption in American society that it is not quite acceptable for older people to have sexual needs (Mathias-Riegel, 1999). A human sexuality instructor and reviewer of this textbook reported that his college-age students react to discussions of sex and older adults with disbelief and disgust. With such widespread denial of the validity of sexual expression in the golden years, it is not surprising that many people are confused about aging and sexuality. As the sexual revolution generation moves into senior citizenship, these ideas will become obsolete (Kingsberg, 2002; Richard, 2002; Zilbergeld, 2001). In addition, because the percentage of seniors in the population continues to increase, the consumer market is more frequently presenting vibrant, sensual ads of older women (Jarrell, 2000).

The movie *About Schmidt* departed radically from Hollywood's usual formulas. For example, audiences were shocked by Kathy Bates's un-self-conscious disrobing and nude dip. The casting of 67-year-old June Squib as Jack Nicholson's wife departs from the standard younger woman/ older man combination.

The Double Standard and Aging

We have discussed the double standard as it relates to male and female sexual expression during adolescence and adulthood: Feelings and behaviors that are considered acceptable for males are often viewed as unacceptable or inappropriate for females. The assumptions and prejudices implicit in the sexual double standard continue into old age, imposing a particular burden on women (Scott, 2003).

One study (Stimson et al., 1981) suggested that the aspects of sexuality that contribute to a general feeling of well-being among the aged are different for men and women. For the older man both sexual performance and attractiveness to the other sex appeared to be crucial to general feelings of well-being. For older women the equation was somewhat different. Although sexual performance did not seem related to general feelings of well-being, feeling sexually attractive to the other sex was important; when the older woman no longer felt attractive, her general feelings of

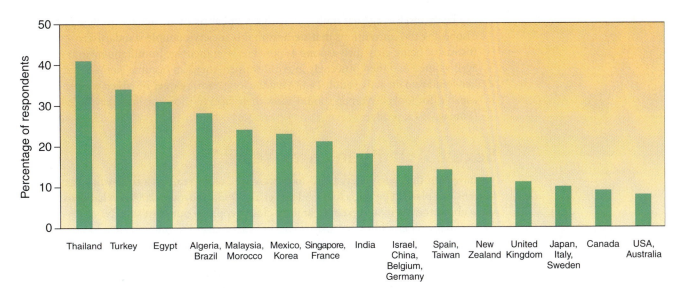

▶ **Figure 14.2** The percentage of respondents in each country who agreed with the statement "Older people no longer have sex." Adapted from *Global Study of Sexual Attitudes and Behavior* (2002).

well-being decreased. Given that attractiveness in women is often equated with youthfulness, aging may affect a woman's sense of well-being more than a man's.

Although a woman's sexual capabilities continue after menopause, it is not uncommon for a woman to be considered past her sexual prime relatively early in life. Popular media typically represent older women as either nurturing caretakers or vindictive manipulators, rarely as sexual (Daniluk, 1998). The cultural image of an erotically appealing woman is commonly one of youth. As a woman grows further away from this nubile image, she is usually considered less and less attractive (Bakos, 1999; McQuaide, 1998). In our society even young girls are sometimes advised not to frown ("You'll get wrinkles"); cosmetics, trendy clothing, and even surgery are often used to maintain a youthful appearance for as long as possible.

In contrast, the physical and sexual attractiveness of men is often considered enhanced by the aging process. Gray hair and facial wrinkles are thought to look distinguished on men—signs of accumulated life experience and wisdom. Likewise, although the professional achievements of women may be perceived as threatening to a potential male partner, it is relatively common for a man's sexual attractiveness to be closely associated with his achievements and social status, both of which may increase with age.

The pairing of powerful older men and young beautiful women reflects the double standard of aging. The marriage of a 55-year-old man and a 25-year-old woman generates a much smaller reaction than that of a 55-year-old woman and a 25-year-old man (Banks & Arnold, 2001). And as you might expect, pairings of older men and younger women occur much more commonly than the reverse. However, this pattern is changing. A recent survey found that 34% of women over age 40 were dating younger men (Mahoney, 2003).

In response to the double standard of aging, the writer Susan Sontag has presented an alternative view:

> Women have another option. They can aspire to be wise, not merely nice; to be competent, not merely helpful; to be strong, not merely graceful; to be ambitious for themselves, not merely themselves in relation to men and children. They

A great deal of media attention has been given to Demi Moore and Ashton Kutcher's romance because Demi is 15 years older than Ashton. In contrast, the 25-year age difference between Michael Douglas and Catherine Zeta-Jones has received less notice.

can let themselves age naturally and without embarrassment, actively protesting and disobeying the conventions that stem from this society's double standard about aging. Instead of being girls, girls as long as possible, who then age humiliatingly into middle-aged women and then obscenely into old women, they can become women much earlier—and remain active adults, enjoying the long, erotic career of which women are capable, for longer. Women should allow their faces to show the lives they have lived. (Sontag, 1972, p. 38)

Sexual Activity in Later Years

We have seen that our society tends to perceive the older years as a time when sexuality no longer has a place in people's lives (Adams et al., 1996; H. Brown, 2000). What does research show about the reality of sexuality among older people in our own society?

For many older adults sexuality is part of what makes life full and rich. In fact, research findings indicate that in our society sexual interest and activity continue to play a role in people's lives as a natural part of the aging process (Johnson & Scelfo, 2004; Lacy, 2001; SIECUS, 2001). A nationally representative survey of men and women, age 60 and older, found that about half are sexually active. "Sexually active" was defined as engaging in vaginal intercourse, oral sex, anal intercourse, or masturbation at least once a month (Dunn & Cutler, 2000). However, the number of people who engage in sexual activity does decline with each decade, as seen in Table 14.3. It is true that a gradual pattern of decline in frequency often accompanies advancing age and that a number of variables interfere with sexual activity, but many people remain sexually active well into their 80s and even later, adjusting successfully to the physical changes described in Chapter 6 (Budd, 1999).

Sexual activity of older adults is, unfortunately, evidenced by the rising incidence of HIV/AIDS among this group (Yared, 2004). About 10% of people older than 50 have one or more risk factors but are unlikely to request testing. Many health care professionals do not routinely screen for sexually transmitted diseases in seniors (Levy, 2001), but some public health agencies offer safe-sex seminars to seniors (McGinn & Skipp, 2002).

TABLE 14.3 Percentage of Sexually Active Adults

	Men (%)	Women (%)
Sexually active in their 60s	71	51
Sexually active in their 70s	57	30
Sexually active in their 80s	25	20

SOURCE: Dunn & Cutler (2000).

Factors in Maintaining Sexual Activity

One factor determining sexual activity levels in later years is each person's individuality. If you enjoy reading mystery novels, talking on the phone, and eating chocolate ice cream as a young adult, you probably do not expect these preferences to change when you are 60 or 70 years old. Similarly, sexuality in the older years must be viewed along the continuum of each individual's personality. Kinsey and colleagues' studies (1948, 1953) revealed a close correlation between a person's sexual activity levels in early adulthood and his or her sexual activity in later years. Other research has also reported a correlation for both sexes between level of sexual activity before middle age and in later years (Bretschneider & McCoy, 1988; Leiblum & Bachmann, 1988). These findings do not necessarily demonstrate a cause-and-effect relationship between sexual activity in young adulthood and old age; it may simply be that those people who had the strongest interest in sex in their youth maintain that interest into old age.

Another factor in maintaining sexual activity in later years is, simply put, maintaining sexual activity. Masters and Johnson (1966) reported that regularity of sexual expression throughout the adult years (whether by masturbation or activity with a partner) was a crucial factor in maintaining satisfactory sexual functioning beyond youth and middle age. People who continue to be sexually active experience less decline in the ability to function sexually than those who stop having sex. One survey found that more older people approved of masturbation (62%) than engaged in it (Brecher, 1984). This study also found that the incidence of masturbation among both male and female respondents declined with age and that a greater proportion of men than women—at all ages—reported masturbating.

A third factor influencing sexual activity in older adulthood is health. Poor health and illness have a greater effect on sexual functioning than age itself (Pope, 1999; Sander, 1999). With age, physical problems can interfere with many aspects of functioning, including sexuality; and in long-term relationships the illness of one person is likely to affect not just that individual's sexual expression but also that of the partner (Dunn & Cutler, 2000; Segraves & Segraves, 1995). Besides contributing to general and sexual health, regular physical activity (walking, jogging, swimming, etc.) and a healthy diet enhance sexual desire and erotic abilities (Bacon et al., 2003).

Far from developing a total incapacity for recreational activities, older people may simply pursue them less often and at a more leisurely pace. The same can be true of one's sex life, particularly if misconceptions and anxieties are avoided or resolved.

The need for affection and sexual intimacy extends into the older years, which can be a time of sharing and closeness.

An Emphasis on Quality over Frequency

Although older adulthood may bring some additional aches and pains and a general slowing down of physical functioning, for many people it also brings rewards. For couples who remain in a long-term relationship the opportunities for sexual expression often increase. As pressures from work, children, and fulfilling life's goals wane, there is more time for sharing with a partner (Clay, 2003). Some people find that their sex lives markedly improve because of the greater opportunities to explore relaxed and prolonged lovemaking (Golden, 2004). Genital contact may become less frequent, but interest, pleasure, and frequency of nonintercourse activities such as caressing, embracing, and kissing may remain stable or increase (Kellett, 2000). Research on sexual satisfaction of married women, age 50 and older, found that their sexual satisfaction was correlated with, in descending order of importance, overall marital satisfaction, greater frequency of orgasm for themselves and their spouses, sexual activity, and noncoital sexual activity (Young et al., 2000).

Expanding the repertoire of lovemaking can help maintain or increase enjoyment. One survey of older adults found that many respondents found new techniques for maintaining or enhancing their enjoyment of sex despite progressive physiological changes. For example, 43% of women and 56% of men provided oral stimulation to their partners. Some used fantasy or sexually explicit materials; others engaged in manual and oral stimulation of the breasts and genitals, anal stimulation, use of a vibrator, various coital positions, sex in the morning, or exclusive fondling and cuddling (Brecher, 1984).

Middle-class and upper-middle-class older adults are more likely to include options beyond intercourse than are those in lower socioeconomic groups. In one study most of the men in the lower socioeconomic group stopped all sexual activity when they were unable to have intercourse (Cogen & Steinman, 1990). These data support Kinsey's findings that the poor and working classes were strongly oriented toward intercourse, considering alternative expressions unacceptable. Openness to experimenting and developing new sexual strategies together with a supportive partner are instrumental to continuing sexual satisfaction (Bachmann, 1991). Some older individuals and couples participate in sex therapy to enhance their sexual lives (LoPiccolo, 1991).

Intimacy, a lifelong need, may find new and deeper dimensions with the personal maturity of later years (Shaw, 1994). As one man described:

> I'm closer to my wife than I ever was. We've been together seventeen years, but I don't think we were ready before to be that close. Now I guess we're secure and comfortable enough in ourselves to accept the intensity of our intimacy. We have a deep, intimate, intense closeness now—the honesty of it, I never conceived of. We could be physically touching each other, close as in sex, but if you're not emotionally there, you don't really touch each other. Now everything has come together, and both of us are really involved in our marriage. (Friedan, 1994, p. 279)

Older people also redefine their sexual and affectional relationships. Nonsexual friendships with either sex can offer affectionate physical contact, emotional closeness, intellectual stimulation, and opportunities for socializing (Harris, 1999; Jacoby, 1999). A supportive network of close friends helps to minimize loneliness and maintain enthusiasm for life, especially for the unmarried (Potts, 1997).

It is not uncommon for new sexual relationships to blossom in later adulthood. A 67-year-old woman explained:

Eight years after my husband died, I met a widower on a tour of New Orleans. The physical attraction was intense for both of us. Neither of us had had sex for many years, but two days after discovering each other we were in bed with clothes strewn all over the floor. The sex (which neither of us was sure we'd be able to achieve) was sensational. We're very much in love but have decided not to marry because we both love our homes, need "space," and are financially independent. Our children accept our lifestyle and are very happy with our respective "significant other." (Authors' files)

Homosexual Relationships in Later Years

Most of the challenges and rewards of aging are experienced by adults, regardless of sexual orientation. Some unique aspects are experienced by gay men and lesbians. The stereotypical view that homosexual people as a group face a lonely and unhappy old age is not supported by the limited research available (Woolf, 2001). In fact, some gay men and lesbians are better prepared for coping with the adjustments of aging than are many heterosexual men and women. Many homosexual individuals have planned for their own financial support and have created a network of supportive friends (Alonzo, 2003; Nystrom & Jones, 2003). Having successfully faced the adversities of belonging to a stigmatized group also helps them to deal with the losses that come with aging (Altman, 1999).

© Ferdinando Scianna/Magnum Photos

Sexual relationships can improve in later years when individuals redefine their sexual and affectional relationships.

Overall, studies find that older gays and lesbians match or exceed comparable groups in the general population on a measure of life satisfaction (Woolf, 2001). In a study of gay men there was a change over time toward fewer sexual partners, but frequency of sexual activity remained quite stable and 75% were satisfied with their current sex lives. Most of these men reported that they socialized primarily with age peers (Berger, 1996). Socializing and partnering with same-age peers is likely an important aspect of life satisfaction for older gay men, because the sexual marketplace setting of bars and bathhouses, where youth and physical appearance define desirability, is often inhospitable to older gay men (Berger, 1996).

As a group, older lesbians have some advantages over older heterosexual women (Koch, 2001). Because their partners are not statistically likely to die at a younger age, an older homosexual woman is less likely to be left alone than is a heterosexual woman—and if she is left alone, she does not face a limited pool of potentially eligible partners. Furthermore, women are less likely than men to base attraction on a physical ideal, resulting in the double standard of aging being less of an issue for lesbians (Berger, 1996). Research has revealed that most older lesbians prefer women of similar ages as partners (Daniluk, 1998; Raphael & Robinson, 1980).

Toward Androgyny in Later Life

Development toward androgyny in personal, interpersonal, and sexual styles occurs for many people in later life (A. Gottlieb, 2000; Hyde et al., 1991). On a biological level the hormonal differences between women and men tend to diminish. Estrogen levels in women decline rapidly after menopause, and androgen levels in men decline gradually starting at about age 30. The extent to which these hormonal changes contribute to increased androgyny is unknown.

On psychological and social levels the gender-role differences between heterosexual men and women also tend to diminish in later years. Expectations for gender-specific roles and responsibilities are more pronounced in younger adulthood, when the demands of supporting and rearing a family pressure men to focus on their jobs or careers and women to focus on taking care of the children. But with retirement approaching and children leaving home, such pressures tend to decline—thus freeing both women and men to develop more androgynous patterns. There is also often a shift in power in the marital relationship, with women being more likely to have increased power in later rather than earlier life stages (Chiriboga & Thurnher, 1980).

One study found that older men and women developed other-sex characteristics by age 50 without relinquishing same-sex characteristics:

> Individuals who were the psychologically healthiest at age 50 showed increased androgyny over time. Women became more assertive and analytic while remaining nurturant and open to feelings. Men became more giving and expressive while they continued to be assertive and ambitious. (Livson, 1983, p. 112)

Some older men give themselves more permission to show their feelings and personal selves more fully and to be more emotionally intimate (Friedan, 1994). One study found that men who were more emotionally expressive also experienced more sexual interest (Thomas, 1991).

These developments can help set the stage in heterosexual couples for a merging of sexual styles that can occur in later years. A more androgynous orientation allows individuals to expand their concepts of a sensuous man or woman. Older men often become more similar to women in their sexual behavior, in that fantasy and ambience become more important and orgasm less so. Older adults move away from the stereotype that women focus on the relationship and men on genital sex. Over the lives of many of the subjects in one study, women developed a greater interest in genital sex and men developed a greater interest in nongenital sexuality, thus realizing a more harmonious relationship (Bangs, 1985). In fact, a survey found that women age 75 years and older were more likely to describe their partner as "romantic" than were younger women (Jacoby, 1999).

People who continue to grow in age can develop a wholeness of self that transcends the masculine–feminine split in women and men (Shaw, 1994). Intimacy then involves a sharing of that integrated multidimensional self (Friedan, 1994; Wales & Todd, 2001). A sex and marital therapist further explained:

> The essence of sexual intimacy lies not in mastering specific sexual skills . . . but in the ability to allow oneself to deeply know and to be deeply known by one's partner. So simple to articulate, so difficult to achieve, this ability of couples to really see each other, to see inside each other during sex, requires the courage, integrity, and maturity to face oneself and, even more frightening, convey that self—all that one is capable of feeling and expressing—to the partner. . . . Adult eroticism is more a function of emotional maturation than of physiological responsiveness. (Schnarch, 1993, p. 43)

This maturity that can create powerful sexual intimacy requires life experience and self-knowledge and self-acceptance to develop. The real treasure of the "last love" of partners who have experienced enough life to deeply know themselves and each other can make the "first love" of new partners pale by comparison (Schnarch, 1993). As a Turkish proverb comments, "Young love is from the earth, and late love is from heaven" (Koch-Straube, 1982).

Widowhood

Although a spouse can die during early or middle adult years, widowhood usually occurs later in life. In most cases the man dies first, a tendency that became more pronounced during the 20th century. There are more than four widows for every widower (U.S. Bureau of the Census, 2002). Women accustomed to expressing their sexuality exclusively within marriage find themselves suddenly alone. Although older men without partners often seek younger female companions, we saw in the discussion of the double standard that older women are less likely to be

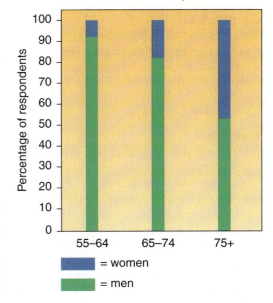

▶ **Figure 14.3** Number of men for every 100 women according to age group.

SOURCE: Mahoney (2003).

The transition period following the death of a spouse can be very traumatic, but after a period of mourning many people decide to remarry.

involved with younger men. Thus for many older heterosexual women the pool of potential new partners is limited (see Figure 14.3). In addition, for older adults who live in nursing homes the options for sexual expression may be severely curtailed by the attitudes and policies of the institution and its staff.

Many older adults remain interested in sexuality, however, even if partners are no longer available (Mulligan & Palguta, 1991). One survey of 200 healthy people, age 80 to 102, found that 88% of men and 72% of women fantasized about sex (Bretschneider & McCoy, 1988). For some older women and men, widowed or divorced, masturbation can become or continues to be a form of sexual release and expression. A study of 800 people between the age of 60 and 91 reported that women are becoming more accepting of masturbation (Starr & Weiner, 1981). As a woman of 60 stated:

I thought my life was over when my husband of 35 years died two years ago. I have learned so much in that time. I learned to masturbate. I had my first orgasm. I had an "affair." I have established intimate relationships with women for the first time in my life. (Authors' files)

The postmarital adjustment of widowhood is different in some ways from that of divorce. Widowed people typically do not have the sense of having failed at marriage. The grief may be more intense, and the quality of the emotional bond to the deceased mate is often quite high. For some people this emotional tie remains so strong that other potential relationships appear dim by comparison. However, many people who have lost a spouse through death do remarry—about half of widowed men and one-fourth of widowed women (Lown & Dolan, 1988).

► Summary

Single Living
- Although single living is often seen as a transition period before, in between, or after marriage, many people choose it as a long-term lifestyle. (p. 401)
- The proportion of individuals who have never married has increased dramatically since 1970 for men and women in their 20s. (p. 401)

Cohabitation
- Almost 5.5 million couples were cohabiting (living together without marriage) in 2000. Although cohabitors who later marry seem to have a higher risk of marital discord than couples who have not lived together before marriage, the exact nature of the relationship between cohabitation and marriage remains to be explained. (p. 402)

Marriage
- The primary element in the marriage ideal of our society is a permanent, sexually exclusive, and legal relationship between two heterosexual adults. (p. 404)
- A variety of techniques are used to predict, with a high degree of success, the probability that a couple will experience marital happiness. These assessment devices include questionnaires, videotapes of couple interaction, and physiological data that reflect arousal level. (p. 408)
- Recent changes in sexual behaviors within the marital relationship have been observed. Married couples are engaging in a wider variety of sexual behaviors than in the past. (pp. 411–412)

Extramarital Relationships
- Nonconsensual extramarital relationships occur without the partner's consent. (p. 413)
- Kinsey found that approximately 50% of married males and 25% of married females had experienced sexual intercourse outside marriage by age 40. (pp. 414–415)
- The results of magazine surveys suggest that the percentage of married American men and women who experience extramarital involvements is significantly greater than reported in Kinsey's surveys, but data from the NHSLS found lower rates of extramarital sex than Kinsey did. (p. 415)
- Consensual extramarital relationships occur with the spouse's knowledge and agreement. Examples of these involvements include sexually open marriage and swinging. (p. 415)
- Swinging, in which couples participate in sexual relations with others simultaneously and in the same location, experienced a popularity peak in the 1970s. (p. 416)
- The sexually open marriage concept and polyamory can include emotional, social, and sexual components in the extramarital relationship. (p. 416)

Divorce
- The ratio of divorces to marriages has increased from 1:4 (in 1950) to 1:2 (in 1998). (pp. 416–417)
- Since 1977 the divorce rate (divorces per 1,000 residents) has declined. (p. 417)

- Some of the causes of the high divorce rate are the liberalization of divorce laws, a reduction in the social stigma attached to divorce, unrealistic expectations for marital and sexual fulfillment, increased economic independence of women, and reduced influence of organized religion. (pp. 417–418)
- An important study found that the most common reason given by men and women for their divorces was infidelity. (p. 418)
- Divorce typically involves many emotional, sexual, interpersonal, and lifestyle changes and adjustments. (pp. 418–419)

Sexuality and Aging

- The options for sexual expression change in the older years, and many individuals find themselves without a sexual partner. Masturbation can serve as an alternative. (pp. 422–423)
- Sexual relationships can improve during later years when individuals focus on intimacy and redefine their sexual and affectional relationships. Physical health and exercise can help maintain sexual functioning and satisfaction. (pp. 423–424)
- A blurring of stereotypic gender roles, an increase in androgyny, and a consequent merging of sexual styles often occur in later life. (pp. 424–425)
- It is unlikely that the physiosexual changes of aging alone will eliminate one's capacity to maintain a satisfying sex life. (p. 423)

Suggested Readings

Berger, Raymond (1996). *Gay and Gray: The Older Homosexual Man.* New York: Haworth Press. An examination of the depth and complexity of aging among gay men, conducted with interviews and questionnaires.

Clements, Marcelle (1998). *The Improvised Woman.* New York: W. W. Norton. Engaging interviews with 100 single women describing the clarity and contradictions they experience.

Duff, Johnette, and George Truitt (1991). *The Spousal Equivalent Handbook.* Houston: Sunny Beach. A highly readable handbook that provides succinct and practical advice to unmarried people living together (other sex or same sex) regarding the legalities of partnership rights. Topics include cohabitation agreements, taxes, financial planning, durable and medical powers of attorney, and wills.

Glass, Shirley (2002). *Not Just Friends.* New York: Free Press. A discussion, by an expert on infidelity, of the increasingly common affair that starts as friendship and evolves into a passionate love affair, even when the current marriage is good.

Gottman, John, and Nan Silver (2000). *The Seven Principles for Making Marriage Work.* New York: Crown Publishers. A book that combines science and romance and that uses research findings to help couples strengthen their marriages. Includes exercises and checklists from couples workshops.

Gross, Zenith (2000). *Seasons of the Heart: Men and Women Talk About Love, Sex, and Romance After 60.* New York: New World Library. Personal stories about the sexual, romantic, and platonic joys found in relationships after 60 years of age.

Hetherington, E. Mavis (2002). *For Better or for Worse: Divorce Reconsidered.* New York: Norton. A book that presents the results of 40 years of research on 1,400 families and 2,500 children and that concludes that most children and adults do well, or thrive, years following divorce.

Real, Terrence (2002). *How Can I Get Through to You?* New York: Scribner. A book by a marital therapist that challenges the limitations that gender roles impose on marital success.

Weiner-Davis, Michelle (2003). *The Sex-Starved Marriage.* New York: Simon & Schuster. A discussion of the problems of and solutions to low sexual desire from a couple's perspective.

Web Resources

Your *Our Sexuality* Web site **http://psychology.wadsworth.com/ crooksbaur9e/** has direct links to the Web sites described below. These links are checked often for changes, dead links, and new additions.

The Couples Place

Free information on building and improving relationships is accessible to public visitors of this Web site, and additional resources are available to those who sign up as members.

DivorceSource

This Web site provides information on various aspects of divorce, including child support and custody, alimony, and counseling. In addition, there is a divorce dictionary, access to related articles and publications, and live chat rooms.

Aging and Sexuality Resource Guide

Recent literature and resources related to issues of aging and sexuality have been compiled on this Web site by the American Psychological Association. Resource directories includes books, publications, journals, and organizations.

Web MD

Search sex and aging for numerous articles on various aspects of aging.

Our Sexuality Web Site

For online resources directly related to this book, go to **http://psychology.wadsworth.com/ crooksbaur9e/**. You will find interactive exercises, study questions, chapter outlines, an online version of this text's glossary, and Web links and activities that complement your CD-ROM.

InfoTrac® College Edition Online Library

http://infotrac.thomsonlearning.com/
InfoTrac College Edition is an online searchable library that includes a multitude of journals, many of which are specific to human sexuality. These journals include *Archives of Sexual Behavior, Archives of Sexual Health Behavior, Canadian Journal of Human Sexuality, Hispanic Journal of the Behavioral Sciences, Journal of Cross-Cultural Psychology, Journal of Physical Education, Recreation, and Dance, Journal of Sex Research,* and *Sex Roles.* You may search topics suggested in the margins of this chapter or terms of your own.

Our Sexuality CD-ROM

Use your CD-ROM for further study of the concepts in this chapter. Your CD-ROM provides animations of difficult concepts, video clips of real people discussing sexuality, critical thinking questions, chapter quizzing, and more.

CHAPTER 15

Nature and Origin of Sexual Difficulties

© Eric K. K. Yu/CORBIS

I wish my first time had been better. I would have had sex with someone I at least liked, instead of just with someone who would do it with me. We were both pretty drunk, but not drunk enough to forget how fast I came. Word got around about it, and I avoided sex for a long time. My first girlfriend after that was cool about it, and after a while I could relax and last longer. (Authors' files)

In the next three chapters we are concerned with some of the difficulties that can hinder sexual functioning and discuss some ways to prevent or resolve these difficulties. In this chapter we look at a number of relatively common sexual problems and the factors that frequently contribute to them. Research indicates that sexual problems are quite common. In fact, the National Health and Social Life Survey (NHSLS) found that sexual difficulties were prevalent in its sample, as shown in Table 15.1. We first look at some common origins of problems and then discuss specific problems. The relevant materials pertain to individuals and couples regardless of sexual orientation. In Chapter 16 we build on what you will learn in this chapter by outlining sex therapy approaches and ways to enhance our sexuality, even when no specific sexual problem exists. In Chapter 17 we turn our attention to understanding and preventing sexually transmitted diseases.

As you read this chapter, it is important to remember that sexual satisfaction is a subjective perception (Ogden, 2003). A person or couple could experience some of the problems described in this chapter and yet be satisfied with their sex lives, or they could experience none of these problems and not be satisfied with their sexual experiences (Basson et al., 2003; Smith, 2003). (See Figure 15.1 for a worldwide survey of ratings of pleasure during sexual interaction.)

Inquiring about specific sexual problems or sexual satisfaction can result in different reported rates of "problems." The NHSLS asked subjects whether they experienced various sexual dysfunctions and found that 43% of women stated that they did. A subsequent random phone survey (less rigorous than the NHSLS) by the Kinsey Institute went a step further and asked women subjects whether they considered their lack of interest, arousal, or orgasm a problem. Slightly over 24% of the subjects reported distress about their sexual dysfunction (Bancroft et al., 2003b). From the results of these two studies it appears that a significant number of women can have reduced sexual functioning and not consider it a problem. The Kinsey Institute study found that a woman was most likely to report distress about sex when she reported poor personal emotional well-being and a negative emotional relationship with her partner.

| TABLE 15.1 | Prevalence of Sexual Problems by Selected Demographic Characteristics |

	Lack Interest in Sex		Cannot Achieve Orgasm		Erectile Dysfunction	Pain During Sex	Climax Too Early
	Women (%)	Men (%)	Women (%)	Men (%)	(Men) (%)	(Women) (%)	(Men) (%)
Age[a]							
18–29	32	14	26	7	7	21	30
30–39	32	13	28	7	9	15	32
40–49	30	15	22	9	11	13	28
50–59	27	17	23	9	18	8	31
Education							
Less than high school	42	19	34	11	13	18	38
High-school graduate	33	12	29	7	9	17	35
College graduate	24	14	18	7	10	10	27

[a]Sexual problems are most common among younger women and older men.

SOURCE: Laumann et al. (1999).

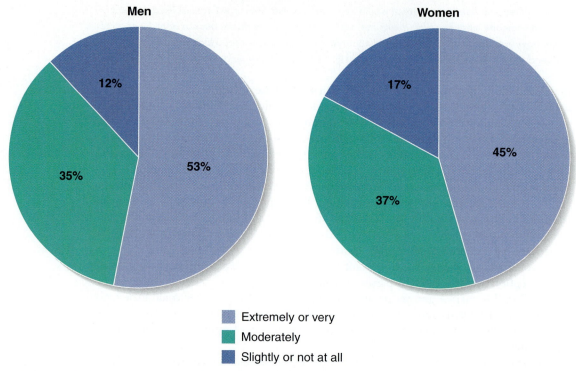

Men

Women

- ■ Extremely or very
- ■ Moderately
- ■ Slightly or not at all

▶ **Figure 15.1** Men and women worldwide were asked "How physically pleasurable is your relationship?" The Pfizer Global Study of Sexual Attitudes and Behaviors, the first worldwide study of its kind, surveyed more than 26,000 men and women in 29 countries around the globe.

For readers currently in a sexual relationship, the self-assessment inventory in the "Your Sexual Health" box will give you an indication of your level of satisfaction.

▶ Origins of Sexual Difficulties

Determining the origins of sexual problems is often difficult and complex. There are several reasons for this. First, even when a sexual difficulty has been clearly identified, it is often hard to isolate the specific causes because many varied influences and experiences contribute to sexual feelings and behavior. Second, it is usually difficult to identify a clear and consistent cause-and-effect relationship because the experiences that contribute to a specific sexual difficulty in one person may produce no such effects in another (LoPiccolo, 1989).

In the following paragraphs we examine some of the physiological, cultural, individual, and relationship factors that contribute to sexual difficulties. Significant interaction among these factors also occurs (Gregoire, 2000). For example, any degree of physiological impairment can make a person's sexual response and functioning more vulnerable to disruption by negative emotions or situations. Thus a man with moderate diabetes may have no difficulty achieving an erection when he is rested and feeling comfortable with his partner, but he may be unable to do so when he is under stress—after a hard day at work or after an argument with his partner. We hope that a clearer understanding of the events that contribute to sexual difficulties will lead to increased satisfaction, communication, and pleasure.

Physiological Factors

Physiological factors often play a role in sexual problems, so it is often desirable to have a general physical and a gynecological or urological exam to help rule out such causes (Rutherford, 2002). Any disturbances in the vascular, endocrine, or neurological systems can contribute to sexual problems (Nusbaum et al., 2003). Medications, surgeries, illnesses, disabilities, and recreational drugs can affect each of these systems, interfering with sexual interest and response, as shown in Table 15.2. Cigarette smoking can eventually make erections go up in smoke, as antismoking advertisements suggest (He, 2003). Men who smoke are five times more likely to have erectile difficulties than men who do not smoke (Manecke & Mulhall,

YOUR SEXUAL HEALTH

Self-Assessment

Index of Sexual Satisfaction

For readers who are sexually involved, this questionnaire is designed to measure the degree of satisfaction you have in the sexual relationship with your partner. It is not a test, so there are no right or wrong answers. Answer each item as carefully and accurately as you can by placing a number beside each one according to the following scale:

1 Rarely or none of the time
2 A little of the time
3 Some of the time
4 A good part of the time
5 Most or all of the time

1. I feel that my partner enjoys our sex life. _____
2. My sex life is very exciting. _____
3. Sex is fun for my partner and me. _____
4. I feel that my partner sees little in me except for the sex I can give. _____
5. I feel that sex is dirty and disgusting. _____
6. My sex life is monotonous. _____
7. When we have sex, it is too rushed and hurriedly completed. _____
8. I feel that my sex life is lacking in quality. _____
9. My partner is sexually very exciting. _____
10. I enjoy the sex techniques that my partner likes or uses. _____
11. I feel that my partner wants too much sex from me. _____
12. I think sex is wonderful. _____
13. My partner dwells on sex too much. _____
14. I try to avoid sexual contact with my partner. _____
15. My partner is too rough or brutal when we have sex. _____
16. My partner is a wonderful sex mate. _____
17. I feel that sex is a normal function of our relationship. _____
18. My partner does not want sex when I do. _____
19. I feel that our sex life really adds a lot to our relationship. _____
20. My partner seems to avoid sexual contact with me. _____
21. It is easy for me to get sexually excited by my partner. _____
22. I feel that my partner is sexually pleased with me. _____
23. My partner is very sensitive to my sexual needs and desires. _____
24. My partner does not satisfy me sexually. _____
25. I feel that my sex life is boring. _____

Scoring: Items 1, 2, 3, 9, 10, 12, 16, 17, 19, 21, 22, and 23 must be reverse-scored. (For example, if you answered 5 on one of these items, you would change that score to 1.) After these positively worded items have been reverse-scored, if there are no omitted items, the score is computed by summing the individual item scores and subtracting 25. This assessment has been shown to be valid and reliable.

Interpretation: Scores can range from 0 to 100, with a high score indicative of sexual dissatisfaction. A score of 30 or above is indicative of dissatisfaction in one's sexual relationship.

SOURCE: Adapted from Hudson et al. (1992).

1999). The effect of smoking on female sexuality has not been studied. Much more is known about the effects of illnesses, medications, and disabilities on male sexuality than on female sexuality because far more research has been conducted on male sexual function (Bancroft, 2002; Mead, 2000; Sugrue, 2000).

Chronic Illness

Many of us will confront chronic illness in our own lives. The illness may impair the nerves, hormones, or blood flow essential to sexual functioning, and any accompanying pain and fatigue can distract from erotic thoughts and sensations or limit specific sexual activities (Burt, 1995; Schover, 2000). The following paragraphs describe the sexual effects of some specific illnesses.

TABLE 15.2	Sexual Effects of Some Abused and Illicit Drugs
Drug	**Effects**
Alcohol	Chronic alcohol abuse causes hormonal alterations (reduces size of testes and suppresses hormonal function) and permanently damages the circulatory and nervous systems.
Marijuana	Reduces testosterone levels in men and decreases sexual desire in both sexes.
Tobacco	Adversely affects small blood vessels in the penis and decreases the frequency and duration of erections (Mannino et al., 1994).
Cocaine	Causes erectile disorder and inhibits orgasm in both sexes.
Amphetamines	High doses and chronic use result in inhibition of orgasm and decrease in erection and lubrication.
Barbiturates	Cause decreased desire, erectile disorders, and delayed orgasm.

SOURCE: Finger et al. (1997).

Diabetes Diabetes is a disease that occurs when the pancreas fails to secrete adequate amounts of insulin. Diabetes affects 16 million people in the United States (Tilton, 1997). This disease of the endocrine system is a leading physiological cause of erectile problems in men. Nerve damage or circulatory problems from diabetes can cause sexual problems (Johannes et al., 2000). About 50% of diabetic men experience a reduction or loss of capacity for erection (Manecke & Mulhall, 1999), and a few diabetic men experience retrograde ejaculation (ejaculating into the bladder). Heavy alcohol use and poor blood sugar control increase the chances of erectile problems in diabetic men (Romeo et al., 2000). Women with diabetes are likely to have problems with sexual desire, lubrication, and orgasm (Herter, 1998).

Arthritis Arthritis is a progressive systemic disease that causes inflammation of the joints. Chronic inflammation can cause pain, destruction of the joint, or reduced joint mobility. Nerves and muscle tissues surrounding the affected joints are also often damaged. Arthritis does not directly impair sexual response, but body image problems, depression, chronic pain and fatigue, and medicines for the arthritis can diminish a person's interest in sex (Nadler, 1997; Simon, 2001). Pain or deformities in the hands can also make masturbation difficult or impossible without assistance. Arthritic impairment of hips, knees, arms, and hands can interfere with certain intercourse positions (Schover, 2000).

Cancer Cancer and its treatment can be particularly devastating to sexuality. The disease and its therapies can impair hormonal, vascular, and neurological functions necessary for normal sexual interest and response. Pain can also greatly interfere with sexual interest and arousal (Fleming & Pace, 2001). Chemotherapy and radiation therapy can cause hair loss, skin changes, nausea, and fatigue, all of which can negatively affect sexual feelings. Some cancer surgeries result in permanent scars, loss of body parts, or an ostomy (a surgically created opening for evacuation of body wastes after removal of the colon or bladder), all of which can result in a negative body image (Burt, 1995). Although all forms of cancer can affect sexual functioning, cancers of the reproductive organs can be especially devastating and therefore are of particular concern to many people (Hamilton, 2001; Penson et al., 2003).

Multiple Sclerosis Multiple sclerosis (MS) is a neurological disease of the brain and spinal cord in which damage occurs to the myelin sheath that covers nerve fibers; vision, sensation, and voluntary movement are affected. Studies have found that most MS patients experience changes in their sexual functioning and that at least half have sexual problems (Stenager et al., 1990). A person with MS can experience either a reduction or a loss of sexual interest, genital sensation, arousal, or orgasm; he or she can also have uncomfortable hypersensitivity to genital stimulation. Sexual arousal by means of genital stimulation may not be possible because of sensory losses (Smeltzer & Kelley, 1997). Vaginal dryness can affect women. These symptoms vary and become worse over time.

Cerebrovascular Accidents Cerebrovascular accidents, commonly called strokes, occur when brain tissue is destroyed as a result of either blockage of the blood supply to the brain or hemorrhage (breakage of a vessel, causing internal bleeding). Strokes often result in residual impairments of motor, sensory, emotional, and cognitive functioning, and these impairments can have a negative effect on sexuality. Stroke survivors frequently report a decline in their frequency of interest, arousal, and sexual activity (Giaquinto et al., 2003). Some factors that commonly influence the sexual behavior of people who have experienced a stroke include limited mobility, altered or lost sensation, impairment in verbal communication, and depression (Monga & Kerrigan, 1997).

Disabilities

Major disabilities such as spinal cord injury, cerebral palsy, blindness, and deafness have widely varying effects on sexual responsiveness. Some people with these disabilities are able to maintain or restore satisfying sex lives; others find that their sexual expression is reduced or impaired by their difficulties (Welner, 1997). In the following sections we look at some of these disabilities and discuss some of the sexual adjustments that people with these problems can make.

Spinal Cord Injury People with spinal cord injuries (SCIs) have reduced motor control and sensation because the damage to the spinal cord obstructs the neural pathways between body and brain. Although the SCI does not necessarily impair sexual desire and psychological arousal, a person with a SCI may have impaired ability for arousal and orgasm; this impairment varies greatly according to the specific injury. Some women and men with SCIs are able to experience arousal or orgasm from psychological or physical stimulation; others are not (Tepper, 2000; Whipple, 2001a; Whipple & Komisaruk, 1999). One study found that about half the women who experienced orgasm before their injury were able to do so after their injury (Jackson & Wadley, 1999). Overall, research indicates that 54–87% of men with SCIs are able to experience erections. However, most such men are unable to ejaculate or experience orgasm (Alexander et al., 1994). Research has found that Viagra can increase physiological and subjective arousal for men and women with SCIs (Sipski et al., 2000). Some people with SCIs report that the sensations they experience change or increase slightly over time.

Much of the sex counseling for individuals and couples faced with SCIs consists of redefining and expanding sexual expression. Thus, although genital sensations may be slight or nonexistent, developing heightened sexual responsiveness in the inner arm, breast, neck, or some other area that has retained some feeling can become an intensely satisfying substitute (a technique known as *sensory amplification*).

Cerebral Palsy Cerebral palsy (CP) is caused by damage to the brain that can occur before or during birth or during early childhood; it is characterized by mild to severe lack of muscular control. Involuntary muscle movements can disrupt speech, facial expressions, balance, and body movement. Severe involuntary muscle contractions can cause limbs to jerk or assume awkward positions. A person's intelligence may or may not be affected. Unfortunately, it is often mistakenly assumed that people with CP have low intelligence because of their physical difficulty in communicating.

Good communication and creative exploration can help individuals and couples minimize the sexual effects of disabilities and illnesses.

Genital sensation is unaffected by CP. However, spasticity and deformity of arms and hands can make masturbation difficult or impossible without assistance, and the same problems in the hips and knees can make certain intercourse positions painful or difficult (Joseph, 1991). For women with CP, chronic contraction of the muscles surrounding the vaginal opening can create pain during intercourse (Renshaw, 1987). Options that can be helpful to individuals with CP include trying different positions, propping legs up on pillows to help ease spasms, and exploring nongenital lovemaking. Partners can help with positions, and focusing on genital pleasure can help to distract from pain.

The sexual adjustment of a person with CP depends not only on what is physically possible but also on environmental support for social contacts and privacy. People with CP and SCIs may require the help of someone who can assist in preparation and positioning for sexual relations.

Blindness and Deafness The sensory losses of blindness and deafness can affect a person's sexuality in several ways. A great deal of information and many attitudes and social interaction skills are acquired by seeing or hearing others, and visual or hearing deficits impair this learning process (Mona & Gardos, 2000). By themselves, blindness and deafness do not appear to physically impair sexual interest or response (Ballan, 2001). Other senses can play an important role, as a man who was born blind explained:

> During lovemaking, my other senses—touch, smell, hearing, and taste—serve as the primary way I become aroused. The caress of my partner, and the way she touches me, is tremendously exciting, perhaps even more so than for a sighted person. The feel of her breasts on my face, the hardness of her nipples pressing into my palms, the brush of her hair across my chest . . . these are just some of the ways I experience the incredible pleasures of sex. (Kroll & Klein, 1992, p. 136)

Coping and Enhancement Strategies

Feelings of sexual well-being are often a component of overall self-esteem for people with physical disabilities (Taleporos & McCabe, 2002). Individuals and couples can best cope with the sexual limitations of their illness or disability by accepting those limitations and developing the options that remain. For example, couples can minimize the effects of pain by planning sexual activity at optimal times of the day, using methods of pain control such as moist heat or pain medication, finding comfortable positions, and focusing on genital pleasure or arousing erotic images to distract from pain (Schover & Jensen, 1988). Expanding the definition of sexuality beyond genital arousal and intercourse to include dimensions such as erotic thoughts and sensual touch is also essential. Chronically ill and disabled people can greatly benefit from flexibility in sexual roles and innovation in sexual technique. As a woman with CP explained:

> My disability kind of makes things more interesting. We have to try harder, and I think we get more out of it because we do. We both have to be very conscious of each other—we have to take time. That makes us less selfish and more considerate of each other, which helps the relationship in other areas beside sexuality. (Shaul et al., 1978, p. 5)

Exploration, experimentation, communication, and learning together are ways of relating that can contribute to pleasure and intimacy in the relationships of nondisabled couples too, as we will discuss in the next chapter.

Medication Effects on Sexual Functioning

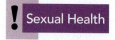

At least 200 prescription and nonprescription medications have negative effects on sexuality (Finger et al., 2000), and more is known about medication's effects on men than on women (Whipple, 2001b). Some of the more common medications that affect sexuality are psychiatric medications and antihypertensive medications, but other drugs and nonprescription remedies also can have an effect. Heath care practitioners do not always discuss potential sexual side effects of medications, so you may need to ask about the possible effects of any prescribed medicines on sexuality. Often another medication can be substituted that will have fewer or milder negative effects on sexual interest, arousal, and orgasm (Kennedy et al., 2000; Segraves & Kavoussi, 2000). Therefore individual consultation with a physician is crucial.

Psychiatric Medications Antidepressants commonly cause reduced sexual interest and arousal and delayed or absent orgasm in up to 70% of users (Nurnberg et al., 2003). The use of the antidepressant Wellbutrin (bupropion), Viagra, or ginkgo biloba (240–900 mg a day) can reverse sexual side effects from antidepressants (Bezchlibnyk-Butler & Jeffries, 2000; Holman, 2003; Nurnberg et al., 2003). Antipsychotic medications frequently result in lack of desire and erection and delay or absence of ejaculation and orgasm (Cook, 2001). Tranquilizers such as Valium and Xanax can interfere with orgasmic response (Dunsmuir & Emberton, 1997).

Antihypertensive Medications Medications prescribed for high blood pressure can result in problems with desire, arousal, and orgasm. Some hypertension medications are more likely than others to have negative sexual effects (Meston et al., 1997).

Miscellaneous Medications Prescription gastrointestinal and antihistamine medications can interfere with desire and arousal function. Methadone can cause decreased desire, arousal disorder, lack of orgasm, and delayed ejaculation. Anticancer drugs can cause gonadal damage and reduce hormone levels, resulting in loss of sexual desire both during and following treatments (Weiner & Rosen, 1997).

Nonprescription Medications Some over-the-counter antihistamines, motion sickness remedies, and gastrointestinal medications have been associated with desire and erection problems. ■

Cultural Influences

Culture strongly influences both the way we feel about our sexuality and the way we express it. In this section we examine some influences in Western society—and particularly in the United States—that affect our sexuality and can contribute to sexual problems.

Negative Childhood Learning

We learn many of our basic, important attitudes about sexuality during childhood (Barone & Wiederman, 1998). Some people's views are influenced by our cultural legacy that sex is sinful (Francoeur, 2001; Haffner, 2001). A variety of therapist researchers have reported that severe religious orthodoxy equating sex with sin is common to the backgrounds of many sexually troubled people (Slowinski, 2001).

A child may or may not be told directly that sex is shameful or sinful, but this belief can be communicated in other ways. Sex therapist Helen Singer Kaplan described some aspects of childhood sexuality and the responses they often evoke in our society:

> Infants seem to crave erotic pleasure. Babies of both genders tend to touch their genitals and express joy when their genitals are stimulated in the course of diapering and bathing, and both little boys and girls stimulate their penis or clitoris as soon as they acquire the necessary motor coordination. At the same time, sexual expression is, in our society, systematically followed by disapproval and punishment and denial. (Kaplan, 1974, p. 147)

The results are often guilt feelings about sexual pleasure from touching one's genitals (Elliott & Elliott, 2001). Kaplan summarized, "The interaction between the child's developing sexual urges and the experiences of growing up in our sexually alienating society probably produces some measure of sexual conflict in all of us" (1974, p. 145).

While growing up, we observe and integrate the models of human relationships from our families. We notice how our parents use touch and how they feel about one another (Bartlik & Goldberg, 2000). For example, one researcher found that women with low sexual desire perceived their parents' attitudes toward sex and their affectionate interaction with each other to be significantly more negative than did those with normal sexual desire (Stuart et al., 1998).

The Sexual Double Standard

Although the rigidity of the sexual double standard is diminishing somewhat, opposing sexual expectations for women and men are still prevalent in U.S. society (Greaves, 2001). Women are encouraged to be sexually cautious to avoid acquiring a reputation of being loose, but part of stereotypical masculine sexual success is "scoring" (Morehouse, 2001; Sanders et al., 2003). Masters and Johnson noted that "sociocultural influence more often than not places a woman in a position in which she must adapt, sublimate, inhibit, or even distort her natural capacity to function sexually. . . . Herein lies a major source of woman's sexual dysfunction" (1970, p. 218).

The male side of the sexual double standard is also a function of cultural expectations. Men frequently learn that sexual conquest is a measure of "manliness":

> Erotic materials portray men as always wanting and always ready to have sex, the only problem being how to get enough of it. We have accepted this rule for ourselves and most of us believe that we should always be capable of responding sexually, regardless of the time and place, our feelings about ourselves and our partners, or any other factors. (Zilbergeld, 1978, p. 41)

As a result of these expectations, men tend to see sexual interaction as a performance for which their highest priority is to "act like a man" to confirm their male gender role in every sexual experience. Acting like a man first mandates exhibiting no "feminine" characteristics, such as tenderness or receptivity. The requirements of masculine self-reliance and dominance can make asking for guidance from a sexual partner untenable (Kilmartin, 1999; Tiefer, 1999). The restrictions of these gender-role expectations can produce feelings of inadequacy, frustration, and resentment for both sexes (McCarthy, 1998). In contrast, sexual intimacy that transcends gender-role stereotypes—when both individuals are active and receptive, wild and tender, playful and serious—moves beyond caricatures of men and women and expresses the richness of humanness (Kasl, 1999; McCarthy, 2001).

Same-sex couples do not have to struggle with opposing gender-role expectations in their sexual expression. They tend to have a more varied sexual repertoire than heterosexuals, in part because of the lack of rigid gender-role scripts and of a concept of how sex "should" happen (Nichols, 2000).

© Maya Barnes/The Image Works

The way others react to childhood genital exploration can affect how children learn to feel about their sexual anatomy.

A Narrow Definition of Sexuality

Besides early socialization experiences and continuing exposure to the sexual double standard, popular opinions about the appropriateness of sexual behaviors also influence our expressions of sexuality. Although attitudes about what is normal appear to have changed in recent years, certain assumptions still strongly affect sexual expression.

As we have seen repeatedly in this textbook, the notion that sex equals penile–vaginal intercourse can contribute to inadequate stimulation for women and place burdensome and anxiety-provoking expectations on intercourse. Sex therapist Leonore Tiefer observes that the current emphasis on medical treatments that enhance erection, such as Viagra, reinforces the overemphasis on intercourse. "For every dollar devoted to perfecting the phallus, I would like to insist that a dollar be devoted to assisting women with their complaints about partner impairments in kissing, tenderness, talk, hygiene, and general eroticism. Too many men still can't dance, write love poems, erotically massage the clitoris, or diaper the baby and let Mom get some rest" (Tiefer, 1995, p. 170). Sex therapist Bernie Zilbergeld described how many men can overlook other sensual enjoyments: "Many men, when asked how it felt to touch their partners or be touched by them, have said that they didn't know because they were so busy thinking about getting to intercourse" (1978, p. 45).

Performance Anxiety

Arbitrary definitions of sexuality that impose external standards of success and failure reduce the opportunities for individuals and couples to determine what is satisfactory based on their own feelings (Leiblum, 2001). A wide variety of goals have been prescribed for sexuality throughout history. A common one has been procreation. Another is the man's physiological release, with the woman providing it as her duty. Once the woman's pleasure began to be considered a legitimate aspect of sexual contact, her orgasm and the ideal of the simultaneous orgasm became new goals to achieve. Now, as women's sexuality receives more attention, vaginal orgasms, multiple orgasms, and stimulation of the G spot are seen as essential to the sexual experience (Kohn & Kaplan, 2000). The contemporary message about sexuality often seems to be "Sex is OK for both males and females, and you better be good at it" (LoPiccolo & Heiman, 1978, p. 56). What could and should be playful and pleasurable becomes work. Performance anxiety can block natural sexual arousal and release by diminishing the pleasurable sensations that would produce them—thus creating greater anxiety because "it's not working" (Ellison, 2000; Rowland et al., 2003).

A transitory sexual problem, such as an inability to achieve an orgasm or erection because of fatigue or just not being in the mood, can produce such concern and anxiety that the problem develops into a pattern (Benson, 2003). If a partner withdraws emotionally and

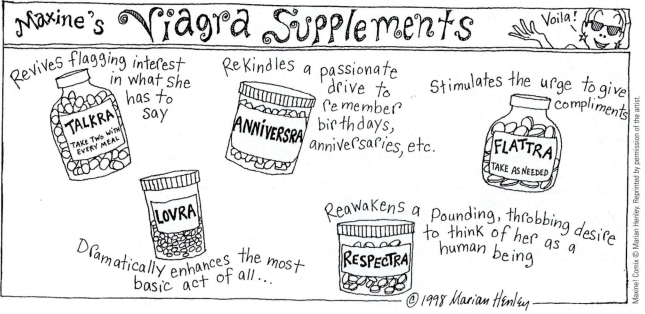

physically, blames him- or herself, or feels insecure about the relationship as a result of the other's reduced response, the problem could be worse the next time because of anxiety about it recurring. Some individuals or couples also avoid sexual activity to protect themselves from either embarrassment or a sense of failure (Slowinski, 2001).

Individual Factors

Beyond the cultural setting and the influences it has on sexual feelings and expression, sexual difficulties can also stem from psychological factors. Our sexuality begins forming in childhood and continues to develop throughout our lives. Human reactions to life experiences are highly variable; two individuals may respond in totally different ways to the same situation.

Sexual Knowledge and Attitudes

Our knowledge and attitudes about sex have a direct influence on our sexual expression. When difficulties are based on ignorance or misunderstanding, accurate information can sometimes alleviate sexual dissatisfaction. For example, if a woman knows about the function of her clitoris in sexual arousal and believes her own sexual gratification is important, she will most likely have experiences different from a woman who has neither this knowledge nor this belief. An increase in self-knowledge can contribute to women having fewer sexual problems as they get older (Leland, 2000a). Even education level and social class have an influence on sexual attitudes, behaviors, and problems. We have seen in earlier chapters that the higher the educational and occupational level of a couple, the greater their tendency to use a variety of intercourse positions and noncoital stimulation methods.

Negative attitudes about sex also contribute to poor sexual responsiveness (Birnbaum, 2003). Some people have developed a "turnoff" mechanism:

> Most of the patients I have studied tend to suppress their desire by evoking negative thoughts or by allowing spontaneously emerging negative thoughts to intrude when they have a sexual opportunity. They have learned to put themselves into negative emotional states. . . . In this manner they make themselves angry, fearful, or distracted, and so tap into the natural physiologic inhibitory mechanisms which suppress sexual desire. (Kaplan, 1979, p. 83)

Kaplan noted that people were usually not aware of the active role they played in creating their inhibitions. Their lack of desire appeared to emerge automatically and involuntarily; they did not realize that they had control over the focus of their thoughts.

Self-Concept

The term *self-concept* refers to the feelings and beliefs we have about ourselves, and our self-concept can influence our relationships and sexuality (Foley, 2003; Murray et al., 2001). Research has found that self-esteem and self-confidence are correlated with higher sexual satisfaction and lack of sexual problems (Apt et al., 1993; Hally & Pollack, 1993). For example, a woman who feels comfortable with her body, believes she is entitled to sexual pleasure, and takes an active role in attaining sexual fulfillment is likely to have a more satisfying sexual relationship than a woman who lacks those feelings about herself (Morehouse, 2001).

Body image can be an important aspect of self-concept that strongly affects sexuality. In Western cultures women's bodies are looked at, evaluated, and sexualized more than men's bodies, and thinness and beauty are often equated with sexual desirability. Women's concerns about weight begin before adulthood; research has found that even when boys and girls have the same percentage of body fat, girls express greater dissatisfaction with their body weight and body image than boys do (Rierdan et al., 1998; Wood et al., 1996).

A woman's self-consciousness about her body during physical intimacy with a male partner is quite common. One research study of college women in the Midwest found that 35%

© Joel Gordon

Various herbal treatments claiming to promote sexual functioning—harder penises, better orgasms—are available without prescription. These remedies, which are not required to have FDA approval, are sold in grocery, drug, and health food stores and are marketed extensively on the Internet. Aggressive advertising appears to be effective: Sales for sexual health supplements reached $150 million in 2001. The proclaimed sex enhancers are "heavy on testimony but light on science" (Riscol, 2003, p.4).

Courtesy of Torrid, www.torrid.com

Torrid was one of the first clothing stores to provide styles for teens who wear sizes 12 to 26 (Espinoza and Baumgartner, 2003).

? Critical Thinking Question

Why would curvaceous female bodies be the sexual ideal during one era and ultrathin bodies be considered the sexiest at another time period?

reported body-image self-consciousness during physical intimacy with a male partner, agreeing to statements such as "If a partner were to put a hand on my buttocks, I would think, 'My partner can feel my fat'" and "I would prefer having sex with my partner on top so that my partner is less likely to see my body." The research found patterns between body image and the experience of being sexual.

Women who were least self-conscious about their bodies viewed themselves as good sexual partners, were more assertive with partners, and had more heterosexual experience than women who were more self-conscious—even when their bodies were similarly sized. Of course, it is unknown whether or not there is a causal relationship with these factors; the research tells us only that there is a correlation between them (Wiederman, 2000).

The media are instrumental in shaping perceptions of female attractiveness and desirability, particularly in regard to weight. Images of women of normal weight and appearance are relatively absent in the media, and the images we usually do see have become further from the average woman over time. In the early 1980s the average model weighed 8% less than the average American woman; she now weighs 23% less (Daniluk, 1998). The curvaceous bodies of actresses in the past—Marilyn Monroe, Elizabeth Taylor, and Sophia Loren—have been replaced by ultrathin actresses—Calista Flockhart of *Ally McBeal* and Lara Flynn Boyle of *The Practice*—who widen the gap between the real and the ideal (Stein, 2000). Many women struggle to reach this thinness standard and judge themselves sharply, including in the bedroom, for the ways their bodies fail to reach it (O'Neill, 2000a).

Recent trends suggest that media images of men contribute to men's insecurity about their bodies and consequently compromise their sex lives by appearance concerns. Some men compulsively pursue ever bigger muscles through hours of weight lifting and exercise and abuse of steroids to the detriment of their relationships, work, and health. Men's dissatisfaction with their own bodies was indicated by a study of body preference; most men preferred bodies with 30 pounds more muscle than their own (O'Neill, 2000a). As the ideal female model has become thinner over time, the ideal male has become more muscular. Changes in male body dimensions were also seen over time in *Playgirl* magazine; the centerfolds lost an average of 12 pounds of fat and added 27 pounds of muscle between the 1970s and 1990s. Action figure toys, which represent the ideal male to boys, have beefed up over time. The original 1964 G.I. Joe had measurements comparable to reasonable proportions of actual men. By 1991 Joe's waist—if he had been full-sized—had shrunk from 32 to 29 inches, and his biceps bulged from 12 to 16.2 inches. G.I. Joe Extreme debuted in the mid-90s with 27-inch biceps, about the same size as his waist (Pope et al., 2000). Studies have not yet been done to assess the extent of male body-image self-consciousness and any effects on the sexual experience.

Despite the fact that most women do not put a priority on penis size, a man's concern about the size of his penis can interfere with his arousal and enjoyment. Surveys about men's satisfaction with the size of their penises show that most wish they were larger (McCarthy & McCarthy, 2003). Unlike viewing typical-sized penises in classical artwork, such as Michelangelo's nude sculpture *David*, watching pornography, where the male porn stars are selected for their oversized genitals, can contribute to a man's distorted sense of what is "normal."

Emotional Difficulties

Personal emotional difficulties, such as anxiety or depression, have a strong effect on sexuality. The NHSLS found that unhappiness with life was correlated with sexual problems. The data do not clarify if one causes the other, but women and men who were experiencing sexual problems were considerably more likely to be unhappy with their lives in general than were respondents without sexual difficulties (Laumann et al., 1999). Lack of sexual interest and response is a common symptom of depression. Moreover, life problems such as a death in the family, divorce, or extreme family or work difficulties can result in a lack of sexual interest. Severe stress and trauma, as experienced by combat veterans, also can result in sexual problems (Letourneau et al., 1997).

Discomfort with certain emotions can also affect sexuality. Particularly important are a person's feelings about intimacy and freely expressing one's feelings (Real, 2002). An individual who experiences intimacy as threatening can have considerable sexual difficulty (Schnarch, 2000). One study of individuals whose inhibited sexual desire did not improve with therapy found that the individuals had negative feelings about closeness and intimacy in general (Chapman, 1984).

Sexual Abuse and Assault

The essential conditions for positive sexual interaction—consent, equality, respect, trust, and safety—are absent in sexual abuse. Boys and girls who are sexually abused are robbed of the opportunity to explore and develop their sexuality at their own age-appropriate pace (Maltz, 2003). Both childhood sexual abuse and adult sexual assault can greatly interfere with sexuality, as this quotation exemplifies:

> In retrospect, I can see how the incest experiences of over 30 years ago still govern and pattern my sexuality. I have a very diminished sexual appetite, with little curiosity or interest. It is difficult for me to anticipate, enjoy, express, and receive love in a sexual, physical form. A wall of avoidance, fear, and dread has replaced any thrill or urge or anticipation. (Maltz & Holman, 1987, p. 75)

According to the NHSLS, 12% of men and 17% of women were sexually abused *before* adolescence. Adult men and women who experienced sexual abuse in childhood are more likely to report difficulties with sexuality (Laumann et al., 1999). Of any childhood experience, childhood sexual abuse has the greatest negative effect on adult sexual functioning (Courtois, 2000a, 2000b). The probability that one or both partners in a lesbian relationship have been abused is greater than in a heterosexual relationship, because girls are more frequently abused than boys and a lesbian relationship is composed of two women (Marvin & Miller, 2000).

Research has shown that women with a history of childhood sexual abuse are two to four times more likely than other women to have chronic pelvic pain (Reiter & Milburn, 1994) and to experience depression, anxiety, and low self-esteem (Murrey et al., 1993). In addition, sexual abuse survivors often experience specific aversion reactions to exactly what was done to them during the sexual assault. They may have flashbacks—sudden images of the smells, sounds, sights, feelings, or other reminders of the sexual abuse that dramatically interrupt any positive feelings and sexual pleasure (Courtois, 2000a, 2000b; Koehler et al., 2000). These symptoms and difficulties can also be difficult for partners of survivors to understand and to cope with effectively (Maltz, 2001c).

It is also important to note that not all sexual abuse is traumatic or all reactions severe. Each circumstance is unique and must be understood accordingly (Courtois, 2000a, 2000b).

Research has also indicated serious sexual consequences for survivors of adult sexual assault. One study of 372 female sexual assault survivors found that almost 59% experienced sexual problems after the assault—with about 70% of this group linking these problems to the assault. Fear of sex and lack of desire or arousal were the most frequently mentioned problems (Becker et al., 1986). In addition, the effects of sexual assault can be long-lasting; 60% of rape victims had sexual problems for more than 3 years after the assault (Becker & Kaplan, 1991).

Relationship Factors

Besides personal feelings and attitudes, interpersonal factors can strongly influence the satisfaction or dissatisfaction that two people experience in a sexual relationship (Real, 2002). These factors often vary according to the couple and their particular circumstances. For example, one couple may find that an argument typically ends with passionate lovemaking, whereas the partners in another couple may move to separate bedrooms for a week after a disagreement.

Unresolved Relationship Problems

The trust in yourself to express your sexual desires and the trust in your partner to be caring and responsive are essential for a good sexual relationship to evolve. In many cases a sexual difficulty is a symptom of a more general relationship problem (Alperstein, 2001). The dynamics of the whole relationship are highly significant in determining sexual satisfaction (J. Brown, 2000). As we will see in Chapter 16, this is reflected in sex therapy in the strong emphasis on working with the couple rather than with the individual. Unresolved resentments, a lack of trust or respect, dislike of a partner, lack of attraction, or poor sexual skills can easily lead to sexual dissatisfaction or disinterest. Sexual difficulties can also occur when there is insufficient independence and an overabundance of dependency within the relationship; partners need a balance of togetherness and separateness (Schnarch, 2000). In addition, a person who experiences a lack of power and control in his or her relationship can lose sexual desire or response, thereby gaining some control in the sexual aspect of the relationship (Betchen, 2001; LoPiccolo, 2000). One partner can even use his or her lack of sexual interest, consciously or unconsciously, to hurt or punish the other. A person who is frequently pressured to engage in sex or who feels guilty about saying no can become less and less interested and feel increasingly diminished desire.

Ineffective Communication

Ineffective communication can contribute to and perpetuate sexual dissatisfaction. As we discussed in Chapter 8, talking is a basic tool for learning about needs and sharing desires. Communication is also the basis for the negotiations that are often necessary to reach compromises over individual differences. The ability to communicate can often take time and effort, which can contribute to the fact that married people have fewer sexual problems than single people (Leland, 2000a). Without effective verbal communication couples must base their sexual encounters on assumptions, past experiences, and wishful thinking—all of which can be inappropriate in the immediate situation.

A frequent source of communication problems is stereotyped gender roles, in particular, the myth that "sex is exclusively the man's responsibility and that sexual assertiveness in a woman is 'unfeminine'" (Kaplan, 1974, p. 350). A woman who believes that it is not her place

"Don't be too upset. If we were meant to have good sex, we probably would have married other people."

to tell her partner that she is or is not in the mood to make love or that she would like another kind of stimulation (or any other sex-related desire) may find that the relationship becomes increasingly frustrating simply because her partner does not know what she wants. How could he? This is compounded by the popular myth that "If she/he really loved me, she/he could read my mind!" Difficulty communicating with a partner about the desire for direct clitoral stimulation is common in women who do not experience orgasm (Kelly et al., 1990).

Fears About Pregnancy or Sexually Transmitted Diseases

The fear of an unwanted pregnancy can interfere with coital enjoyment in a heterosexual relationship (Sanders et al., 2003). A 100% effective temporary method of birth control is simply not available at this time. The reality is that, unless one of the partners is surgically sterilized or infertile, there is a risk of impregnation, however small, in all instances of heterosexual intercourse.

On the other hand, emotional reactions to infertility can also create sexual difficulties. Many couples who want to conceive and have difficulties doing so often find that their sexual relationship becomes anxiety ridden, especially if they have to modify and regulate the timing and pattern of sexual interaction to enhance the possibility of conception.

Anxiety about contracting a sexually transmitted disease, particularly AIDS, can interfere with sexual arousal in both homosexual and heterosexual relationships. For people who are not in a monogamous, disease-free relationship, some risk exists. Guidelines for safer sex are outlined in Chapter 17.

Sexual Orientation

Another reason that a woman or man does not experience sexual satisfaction in a heterosexual relationship can be a desire to be involved with individuals of the same sex (Althof, 2000). Although much progress has been made for gay rights, following one's homosexual inclinations still involves facing significant societal disapproval, if not outright discrimination. To avoid these repercussions, some homosexual people attempt to relate heterosexually despite their lack of desire for such a relationship. Others have a commitment and a desire for the heterosexual relationship (often marriage) to continue and to be sexually fulfilling.

▶ Specific Sexual Difficulties

In the remainder of the chapter we consider some of the specific problems that people encounter with the desire, excitement, and orgasm phases of sexual response. In reality, there is considerable overlap: Problems with desire and arousal also affect orgasm, and orgasm difficulties can easily affect a person's interest and ability to become aroused.

The sexual problems that we will discuss can vary in duration and focus from one person to another. A specific difficulty can occur throughout life or be acquired at a specific time. A person can experience the problem in all situations with all partners (generalized type) or only in specific situations or with specific partners (situational type) (American Psychiatric Association, 2000). The categories and labels for the problems that we discuss come from the American Psychiatric Association's *Diagnostic and Statistical Manual (DSM-IV)*. A few additions of our own are also included.

Desire-Phase Difficulties

Problems with sexual desire have received increased attention in recent years. In this section we discuss inhibited sexual desire, dissatisfaction with frequency of sexual activity, and sexual aversion. Therapies for desire-phase problems are considered in Chapter 16.

Hypoactive Sexual Desire

Hypoactive sexual desire (HSD)—the lack of interest in sexual activity—is a common sexual difficulty experienced by both men and women (Sytsma & Taylor, 2001). Although it is far more common among women (see Table 15.1), by the late 1990s some sex therapy

Hypoactive sexual desire (HSD) Lack of interest in sexual activity.

? **How About You?**

When would it be normal for you to be uninterested in being sexual?

© Carol Ford/Getty Images

Hypoactive sexual desire frequently reflects relationship problems.

clinics saw equal numbers of men and women with low sexual desire (Pridal & LoPiccolo, 2000). HSD is the most frequent problem that brings people to seek sex therapy (Schnarch, 2000). Kaplan (1979) described HSD as a lack of "sexual appetite." Some people with HSD do become aroused and experience orgasm when sexually stimulated, whereas others react to physical and sexual contact with tension and anxiety instead of arousal (Lightner, 2002). Others experience HSD in a particular situation, such as with a spouse but not with a lover or when masturbating.

In general, lifelong HSD is rare: People with this condition neither masturbate nor engage in sexual fantasy, sexual activity, or the sexual aspects of a relationship. More commonly, people develop HSD at a specific point in their lives. HSD is most commonly seen as a problem when it causes distress in a relationship (Pridal & LoPiccolo, 2000).

HSD can originate from abusive personal experiences, as we illustrated on page 439. More commonly, HSD reflects unresolved relationship problems. When sex is mediocre and boring, low sexual desire actually reflects good judgment (Schnarch, 2000). One study found that women with HSD reported more dissatisfaction with relationship issues than women with other sexual problems, such as painful intercourse or difficulty reaching orgasm (discussed later in this chapter) (Stuart et al., 1998). In this study, diminished desire was associated with a few specific relationship problems:

- The woman's partner did not behave affectionately except when intercourse was expected to follow.
- Communication and conflict resolution were unsatisfactory.
- The couple did not maintain love, romance, and emotional closeness.

Stuart's study also found that women with HSD often view intercourse as an obligation. In general, they were more likely to engage in intercourse to fulfill marital obligations and to avoid hurting their spouses' feelings than were women without HSD (Stuart et al. 1998).

Lack of sexual desire can occur in homosexual men or women who have not fully accepted their sexual orientation. Internalized negative beliefs about homosexuality can interfere with joyful sexual expression, even in individuals who have accepted their homosexuality on many other levels (Nichols, 1989), as this woman explained:

It had been a 10-year struggle for me to accept myself as a lesbian. I tried dating men, but always found that a special, meaningful feeling was missing. I came out at work and to my Italian Catholic family and became involved in gay rights activities. I had several relationships with women that didn't work out. Then I met Carol. I liked her, respected her, and was very attracted to her. I was looking for a long-term relationship, and the compatibilities and feelings were right. Sex was great until she told me she loved me. A switch went off, and I stopped feeling interested. In therapy, I was able to realize that lingering feelings of my mother's disapproval had stopped me cold from allowing myself to be fully happy and complete in a "queer" relationship. I worked through those feelings and am now enjoying my sexuality in a loving, committed relationship for the first time in my life. (Authors' files)

Dissatisfaction with Frequency of Sexual Activity

Sexual partners usually have discrepancies in their preferences for amount, type, and timing of sexual activities. Sometimes the relationship can accommodate these individual differences. However, when sexual differences are a source of significant conflict or dissatisfaction, a couple can experience considerable discomfort. Instead of moving toward some compromise, the couple polarizes.

Sexual Aversion Disorder SAD

Sexual aversion disorder
Extreme and irrational fear of sexual activity.

When sexual activity includes a fear of sex and a compelling desire to avoid sexual situations, this is considered **sexual aversion disorder.** Sexual aversion can range from feelings of discomfort, repulsion, and disgust to an extreme irrational fear of sexual activity. Even the thought of sexual contact can result in intense anxiety and panic. A person who experiences sexual aversion exhibits physiological symptoms such as sweating, increased heart rate, nau-

sea, dizziness, trembling, or diarrhea as a consequence of fear. Sexual aversion is often the result of sexual abuse or trauma.

Excitement-Phase Difficulties

Both men and women can experience difficulties in sexual arousal. Of course, most of us are not responsive sexually all the time. Sometimes we are too preoccupied with another aspect of our lives, too fatigued, or feeling somewhat distant from our partners (Deveny, 2003; Leland, 2000a). However, when physiological arousal, erotic sensations, or the subjective feeling of being turned on are chronically diminished or absent, inhibited sexual excitement exists. Excitement-phase difficulties among women take the form of lack of vaginal lubrication or lack of subjective awareness of physical arousal (Basson, 2002), whereas in men an inability to achieve or maintain erection is typical.

Female Sexual Arousal Disorder

As we saw in Chapters 4 and 6, vaginal lubrication is a woman's first physiological response to sexual arousal. The persistent inability to attain or maintain the lubrication–swelling response can indicate female sexual arousal disorder. Biological factors, including low estrogen levels, can be a factor in lack of lubrication, particularly during perimenopause and menopause (Bartlik & Goldberg, 2000). Diminished lubrication is normal when a woman is breast-feeding and after menopause. Feelings of apathy, anger, or fear and ineffective sexual stimulation can also inhibit arousal and lubrication.

Male Erectile Dysfunction

The term often applied to male erection difficulty is *impotence*. The origin of this word suggests the primary reason for our opposition to its use: It comes from Latin and literally means "without power." The implication is that a man is powerless as a lover without an erection, and men who cannot experience or maintain an erection are often deeply concerned (Althof, 2000). The implication that he is without value as a lover only contributes to this distress. As the following account indicates, however, this interpretation can be far from reality:

> I met a man once whose erectile capacity was completely destroyed by a spinal-cord injury in the precise region of the lower spine where erectile function is controlled. Although he couldn't get it up, he certainly had no trouble getting it on! I've often wondered if his acquired status of highly desired lover had something to do with his discovery that erections are not essential to meaningful sexual interaction. (Authors' files)

Instead of the term *impotence*, DSM-IV uses the more neutral term **erectile dysfunction (ED),** which adequately describes this major male difficulty without the negative connotations just mentioned (T. Miller, 2000).

Erectile dysfunction is defined as the inability, for a period of 6 to 12 months, to have or maintain an erection sufficient for penetrative intercourse to the satisfaction of both partners (Nash, 1997). Erectile problems are classified broadly into two types. *Acquired erectile dysfunction* is applied to cases in which the man has previously had erections with his partner(s) but finds himself presently unable to consistently experience a functional erection. Men with *lifelong erectile dysfunction* have, throughout their lives, attempted but never experienced maintained penetration.

The advent of Viagra in 1998 dramatically increased awareness of ED (Mulcahy, 2000). Erectile disorder is a common problem among men who seek sex therapy. An estimated 30 million men in the United States have ED (Levine, 2003). The incidence of ED increases with age, as shown in Figure 15.2. A man in his 50s is over two times more likely to experience erection problems than a man in his 20s. Age itself does not cause erectile disorder; diseases such as diabetes, high blood pressure, and

Erectile dysfunction (ED)
Persistent lack of an erection sufficiently rigid for penetrative intercourse.

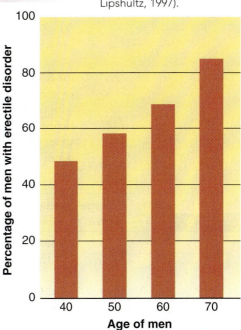

▶ **Figure 15.2** The incidence of erectile disorder related to age (Kim & Lipshultz, 1997).

cardiovascular problems that can accompany aging take their toll (Bacon et al., 2003; Mulcahy, 2000). High cholesterol that impedes blood flow to the heart can also impede blood flow to the genital area (Rim, 2000). As many as 25% of cases of ED are related to medication side effects (T. Miller, 2000). Tobacco use is another contributor to the incidence of ED.

For most men ED results from a combination of physical, psychological, and cultural interacting factors (Levine, 2003; Slowinski, 2001). Special procedures have been developed to evaluate physical factors in erection problems. Some techniques involve recording erection patterns during sleep, because erections normally occur during this time (Montague, 1998). Other instruments measure penile blood pressure and flow to determine whether erectile difficulties are caused by vascular problems. Injections of medications that produce erections can also be used to detect possible difficulties: If no erection occurs following an injection, then vascular impairment is likely (Lehmann et al., 2000; Lin et al., 2000).

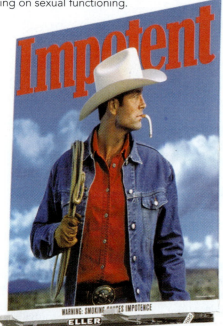

A limp cigarette makes a graphic statement about the detrimental effects of smoking on sexual functioning.

© David Young-Wolff/PhotoEdit

Anorgasmia A sexual difficulty involving the absence of orgasm in women.

Orgasm-Phase Difficulties

The problems we have been discussing are primarily ones of desire and excitement. Some other sexual difficulties specifically affect orgasmic response, and a variety of problems are reported by both women and men. Some of these difficulties are infrequency or total absence of orgasms. Others involve reaching orgasm too rapidly or too slowly. Sometimes a partner may fake orgasm to conceal its absence.

Female Orgasmic Disorder

Some women who do not achieve orgasm experience arousal, lubrication, and enjoyment from sexual contact. However, their sexual response does not increase to the point of orgasm. Some feel satisfied with their sexual experience without orgasm; others are highly disappointed and distressed. The lack of peak arousal and physical release from orgasm can result in experiences that are less and less enjoyable.

Anorgasmia (an-or-GAZ-mee-uh) means the absence of orgasm. A woman who has *generalized lifelong anorgasmia* has never experienced orgasm by masturbation or with a partner. A woman who has *situational anorgasmia* experiences orgasm rarely or in some situations but not in others; for example, she may be orgasmic when masturbating but not when stimulated by a partner.

Anorgasmia in childhood and adolescence appears to be quite common. A survey found that almost 62% of women were 18 years old or older when they first experienced orgasm (Ellison, 2000). Surveys have indicated that 5–10% of adult women in the United States have never experienced orgasm by any means of self- or partner stimulation (Spector & Carey, 1990). However, when women were asked whether they had problems with orgasm rather than whether they had ever experienced orgasm, 24% reported problems with orgasm in the last year (Laumann et al., 1994). Women who are most likely to experience difficulty with orgasm are unmarried and younger and have less education than women without problems with orgasm (Laumann et al., 1999). Table 15.3 shows the incidence of orgasm in college students. Some data have indicated that the number of lifelong anorgasmic women has decreased (LoPiccolo, 2000). This apparent decrease may be due to the accessibility of excellent self-help books and videos for women who want to learn to experience orgasm. Much of the self-help information in Chapter 16 comes from these sources.

Female Orgasm During Intercourse Most sex therapists believe that women who enjoy intercourse and experience orgasm in some way other than during coitus do not have a

TABLE 15.3	College Students Answer the Question "Have You Ever Had an Orgasm?"	
	Female (%)	Male (%)
Yes	87	94
No	13	6

SOURCE: Elliott & Brantley (1997).

sexual problem (Hamilton, 2002; LoPiccolo, 2000). The absence of routine orgasm during coitus without additional manual clitoral stimulation is a common and normal pattern for women. As sex therapist pioneer Helen Kaplan stated, "There are millions of women who are sexually responsive, and often multiply orgasmic, but who cannot have an orgasm during intercourse unless they receive simultaneous clitoral stimulation" (1974, p. 397). For many women the stimulation that occurs during coitus is simply less effective than direct manual or oral stimulation of the clitoral area (Bancroft, 2002).

Anorgasmia often reflects cultural perceptions. As we saw in Chapter 6, Freud's belief that clitoral orgasms were inferior to vaginal orgasms has lingered in popular mythology, contributing to misunderstanding among men and women (Ellison, 2000), as the following account illustrates:

I thought that there was something wrong with me because I did not have orgasm during penile–vaginal intercourse. Then I learned in my human sexuality class that I was not the only one that needs additional stimulation. But sometimes I am scared that when I get married my husband will get tired of having to do the extra work. I do not want him to think there is something wrong with me. (Authors' files)

Chapter 16 addresses ways to alleviate female orgasmic disorder.

Many advertisements imply that women can become very sexual or even orgasmic by using certain products.

© Rhydian Lewis/Getty Images

Male Orgasmic Disorder

The term **male orgasmic disorder** generally refers to the inability of a man to ejaculate during sexual activity. Eight percent of men experience this difficulty (Laumann et al., 1994). Most men who are troubled by orgasmic disorder during intercourse are able to reach orgasm through masturbation or manual or oral stimulation from their partners. *Male coital anorgasmia* or *partner anorgasmia* is a more descriptive term than the more general term male orgasmic disorder (Apfelbaum, 2000). Partner anorgasmia can develop when a man's sexual experiences with a partner do not match the idiosyncratic sexual fantasies he requires to experience orgasm during masturbation (Perleman, 2001). Extreme performance pressure and an inability to be "selfish" and pursue his own heightened arousal (instead of focusing on his partner's pleasure) interfere with his own escalation of arousal to orgasm. He might also enjoy denying his partner the satisfaction of his orgasm or feel repulsed by his partner (Apfelbaum, 2000).

Chapter 16 addresses approaches to resolving male orgasmic disorder.

Male orgasmic disorder The inability of a man to ejaculate during sexual activity.

Premature Ejaculation

A common male orgasm difficulty is **premature ejaculation (PE).** Premature ejaculation is a man's inability to consistently control, to his or his partner's satisfaction, when he has an orgasm. This condition typically leaves a man feeling intense distress about his rapid ejaculation, and his distress is reinforced by each sexual encounter (Polonsky, 2000). Needing to use intrusive and unpleasant techniques throughout intercourse to delay ejaculation is also considered a problem (Schover et al., 1982).

Almost all men ejaculate quickly in their first intercourse experience, which may be disappointing but should not be seen as a sexual problem unless it continues (Polonsky, 2000). In general, approximately 29% of men repeatedly experience PE (Laumann et al., 1994). Research indicates differences in how men with PE subjectively experience their arousal (O'Leary, 2003). Men with PE underestimate their level of physical arousal, experience rapid high arousal to penile stimulation, ejaculate before reaching full sexual arousal, and report less enjoyment of orgasm compared to men who do not have problems with rapid ejaculation. These factors indicate some degree of physiological involvement (Rowland et al., 2000).

Premature ejaculation (PE) A sexual difficulty in which a man ejaculates so rapidly as to impair his own or his partner's pleasure.

In discussing PE, it is also important to debunk myths about what intercourse "should" be:

Many men still labor under the fantasized view of intercourse in which "real" men will be able to thrust vigorously for long periods: the "engineer's view of sex," which involves a penis as hard as a rock, moving in the cylindrical vagina like a piston of a high-performance engine, generating friction and heat that would make any woman melt. Anything short of that would be mediocre and unacceptable. (Polonsky, 2000, p. 308)

Chapter 16 discusses strategies for dealing with premature ejaculation.

Faking Orgasms

Faking orgasms A sexual difficulty in which a person pretends to experience orgasm during sexual interaction.

A final orgasmic difficulty we discuss is **faking orgasms**—pretending to experience orgasm without actually doing so. This kind of sexual deception is typically discussed in reference to women, and it happens quite often, as shown in Table 15.4. Another survey found that 75% of women who had ever faked orgasm had done so up to 50 times, and about 10% had faked orgasm innumerable times (Ellison, 2000).

TABLE 15.4	College Students Answer the Question "Have You Ever Faked an Orgasm?"			
	Female Heterosexual (%)	Lesbian or Bisexual Female (%)	Male Heterosexual (%)	Gay or Bisexual Male (%)
Yes	60	71	17	27
No	40	29	83	73

SOURCE: Elliott & Brantley (1997).

Unlike some of the other difficulties that we discuss in this chapter, faking orgasm reflects a conscious decision. The most common reason given by women for pretending orgasm is to avoid disappointing or hurting their partners (Darling & Davidson, 1986; Ellison, 2000). A person is often motivated to engage in such deception by real or imagined performance pressures. Some additional factors related to faking orgasm include a desire to get sex over with, poor communication or limited knowledge of sexual techniques, a need for partner approval, and an attempt to hide a deteriorating relationship (Ellison, 2000; Lauersen & Graves, 1984). The following comments, both by women, reveal some of these motivations:

He feels badly if I don't have an orgasm during intercourse, so I fake it, even though I have real ones from oral sex. (Authors' files)

I started our sexual relationship faking, and I don't know how to stop. (Authors' files)

Although some women find faking orgasm to be an acceptable solution in their individual situations, others find that faking itself becomes troublesome, as revealed in the second of the preceding comments. At the least, faking orgasms creates emotional distance at a time of potential closeness and satisfaction (Ellison, 2000; Masters & Johnson, 1976).

A vicious cycle is often involved in faking orgasms. The person's partner is likely not to know that his or her partner has pretended to climax. Consequently, the deceived partner continues to do what he or she has been led to believe is effective, and the other partner continues to fake to prevent discovery of the deception. This makes it more difficult for the couple to talk about and discover what is gratifying to both of them. Once established, a pattern of deception can be difficult to break.

 Sexual Health

How to change this pattern of interaction is a matter of personal decision. Some people do not want to change because faking orgasm serves a purpose in a relationship. A person who does want to change might decide to discontinue faking orgasms without discussing the decision with her or his partner. Under such circumstances some of the procedures for enhancing sexual pleasure outlined in Chapter 16 might prove helpful. Another alternative is to inform one's partner of one's past deception and to discuss the reasons that pretending to climax seemed necessary. Some of the communication strategies outlined in Chapter 8 may help in this process. Perhaps some specific difficulties will surface as the motivation for deception. It may be helpful, or even necessary, to engage a counselor to help communicate with a partner. Seeing a counselor can also facilitate efforts to establish more rewarding sexual behaviors. ■

[handwritten marginal note: to expected to fake it (Negative): so when you are faking it becomes a vicious cycle when a women a vicious cycle]

Dyspareunia

The medical term for painful intercourse is **dyspareunia** (dis-puh-ROO-nee-uh). Both men and women can experience coital pain, although it is more common for women to have this problem.

Dyspareunia in Men

Painful intercourse in men is unusual but does occur. If the foreskin of an uncircumcised male is too tight, he can experience pain during an erection. Under such circumstances minor surgery may be indicated. Inadequate hygiene of an uncircumcised penis can result in the accumulation of smegma or infections beneath the foreskin, causing irritation of the glans during sexual stimulation. This problem can be prevented by routinely pulling back the foreskin and washing the glans area with soap and water. Problems and infections of the urethra, bladder, prostate gland, or seminal vesicles can induce burning, itching, or pain during or after ejaculation (Davis & Noble, 1991). Proper medical attention can generally alleviate this source of discomfort during coitus.

Another possible source of pain or discomfort for men is **Peyronie's disease** (PAY-run-eez) in which fibrous tissue and calcium deposits develop in the space above and between the cavernous bodies of the penis. This fibrosis results in pain and curvature of the penis upon erection that, in severe cases, interferes with erection and even intercourse. Peyronie's disease is usually caused by traumatic bending of the penis during intercourse or from medical procedures involving the urethra (Gholami et al., 2003; Johnson et al., 2002). There are medical treatments that can sometimes be effective in addressing this condition (Castro et al., 2003).

Dyspareunia in Women

Experiencing pain with intercourse is more common among women. At least 60% of women experience dyspareunia at some point in their lives (Jones et al., 1997). It is likely to affect a woman's sexual arousal and interest. Coital discomfort stems from a variety of causes, and for this reason it is important that the woman work with a multidisciplinary team of physicians, physical therapists, and sex therapists to evaluate and treat the pain (Binik et al., 2000; Jensen et al., 2003).

Discomfort at the vaginal entrance or inside the vaginal walls is commonly caused by inadequate arousal and lubrication. Physiological conditions such as insufficient hormones can reduce lubrication. Using a lubricating jelly can provide a temporary solution so that intercourse can take place comfortably, but this may bring only short-term relief. A permanent solution is more likely if the woman discovers the cause of her discomfort and takes steps to remedy the situation.

A variety of other factors can cause vaginal discomfort during intercourse. Yeast, bacterial, and trichomoniasis infections cause inflammations of the vaginal walls and can result in painful intercourse. Such inflammations are often related to the problem just described: Intercourse with insufficient lubrication can irritate the vaginal walls and increases the possibility of vaginal infections. Foam, contraceptive cream or jelly, condoms, and diaphragms sometimes irritate the vaginas of some women. Pain at the opening of the vagina can also be attributed to an intact or inadequately ruptured hymen, a Bartholin's gland infection, or scar tissue at the opening (Brashear & Munsick, 1991). Inflammation of the bladder wall can cause moderate to severe pain during intercourse.

Severe pain at the entrance of the vagina can be caused by a condition known as *vulvodynia* (Harlow & Stewart, 2003; Reed et al., 2003). Typically, a small reddened area is painful, even with light pressure, but the area may be so small that it is difficult even for the health care practitioner to see (Koglin, 1996). Another area where there can be discomfort is the clitoral glans. Occasionally smegma collects under the clitoral hood and causes distress when the hood is moved during sexual stimulation. Gentle washing of the clitoris and hood can help prevent this.

Pain deep in the pelvis during coital thrusting can be due to jarring of the ovaries or stretching of the uterine ligaments. A woman may experience this type of discomfort only in certain positions or at certain times in her menstrual cycle. Some women report that such pain occurs only around the time they are ovulating. Avoiding positions or movements that aggravate the pain is the first solution. If a woman has more control of pelvic movements during coitus, she may feel more secure about being able to avoid pain.

Another source of deep pelvic pain is *endometriosis*, a condition in which tissue that normally grows on the walls of the uterus implants on various parts of the abdominal cavity. This extra tissue can prevent internal organs from moving freely, resulting in pain during coitus. Birth control pills are sometimes prescribed to control the buildup of tissue during the monthly cycle (Reiter & Milburn, 1994). Gynecological surgeries for uterine and ovarian cancer can also cause dyspareunia.

Infections in the uterus, such as from gonorrhea, can also result in painful intercourse. In fact, pelvic pain is often the first physical symptom noticed by a woman who has gonorrhea. If the infection has caused considerable scar tissue to develop, surgery may be necessary. Childbirth and rape can tear the ligaments that hold the uterus in the pelvic cavity, which can result in pain during coitus. Surgery can relieve this difficulty partially or completely.

Psychological factors can also contribute to dyspareunia. Early influences that create negative and fearful feelings about intercourse or relationship problems that affect the sexual experience can result in painful intercourse. Most commonly, dyspareunia involves a combination of physical and psychological factors (Binik et al., 2000).

Vaginismus

Vaginismus A sexual difficulty in which a woman experiences involuntary spasmodic contractions of the muscles of the outer third of the vagina.

Vaginismus (vah-juh-NIZ-mus) is characterized by strong involuntary contractions of the muscles in the outer third of the vagina. The contractions can be so strong that attempts to insert a penis into the vagina are extremely painful to the woman. A woman with vaginismus usually, but not always, experiences the same contracting spasms during a pelvic exam (Weiss, 2001). Even the insertion of a finger into her vagina can cause great discomfort.

Some women who experience vaginismus are sexually responsive and orgasmic with manual and oral stimulation, but others are unable to experience desire and arousal (Leiblum, 2000). Because many heterosexual couples regard coitus as a highly important component of their sexual relationship, vaginismus typically causes great concern, even if the couple is sexually involved in other ways.

Milder forms of vaginismus can produce minor unpleasant sensations that are chronically irritating—enough to have an inhibiting effect on a woman's sexual interest and arousal. It is important for women and their partners to know that intercourse, tampon use, and pelvic exams should not be uncomfortable. If they are, it is essential to investigate the cause of the discomfort. The painful contractions of vaginismus are a conditioned, involuntary response to fearful, painful, or conflicted situations or feelings (van der Velde & Evraerd, 2001). Vaginismus often follows chronic painful intercourse, uncomfortable gynecological exams, repeated erectile difficulties of a woman's partner, strong orthodox religious taboos about sex, a homosexual orientation, past physical or sexual assault, or feelings of hostility or fear toward a partner (Koehler, 2002; Leiblum, 2000). It is important to note that, although a woman who experiences vaginismus can learn to prevent the contractions, she does not consciously will them to occur. In fact, the effort of deliberately trying to overcome the problem by having intercourse despite the pain can have just the opposite effect, contributing to a vicious cycle. When a woman experiences physical pain from vaginismus, she will probably be anxious about pain occurring the next time she attempts intercourse. Her apprehensions will increase the likelihood of involuntary muscle contractions, and when her expectations are once again met, she will be even more anxious on subsequent occasions (Renshaw, 1995). Ways of dealing with vaginismus are considered in Chapter 16.

In this chapter we have outlined some of the reasons and ways people encounter dissatisfactions, problems, or discomfort in what can be an experience of great pleasure and joy. It remains for us to explore ways of preventing or overcoming these difficulties. This is our focus in Chapter 16.

- Sexual problems in the general population appear to be common. The National Health and Social Life Survey found that many people reported problems in their sex lives. (p. 429)

Origins of Sexual Difficulties

- Physiological conditions can be the primary causes of sexual problems or can combine with psychological factors to result in sexual dysfunction. It is important to identify or rule out physiological causes of sexual problems through medical examinations. (pp. 430–431)
- Chronic illnesses and their treatments can have a great effect on sexuality. Diseases of the neurological, vascular, and endocrine systems can impair sexual functioning. Medications, pain, and fatigue can also interfere. (pp. 431–432)
- Diabetes causes damage to nerves and the circulatory system, impairing sexual arousal. (p. 432)
- Arthritis does not directly impair sexual response, but chronic pain and fatigue can lessen a person's sexual interest. (p. 432)
- Cancer and its therapies can impair the hormonal, vascular, and neurological functions necessary for normal sexual activity. Pain can also greatly interfere with sexual interest and arousal. Cancer of the reproductive organs—cervix, uterus, ovary, prostate, and testis—can greatly influence sexual response. (p. 432)
- Multiple sclerosis is a neurological disease of the brain and spinal cord that can affect sexual interest, genital sensation, arousal, or capacity for orgasm. (p. 432)
- Cerebrovascular accidents, or strokes, can reduce a person's frequency of interest, arousal, and sexual activity. (p. 432)
- Although a spinal cord injury does not necessarily impair sexual desire, a person with such an injury can have impaired ability for arousal and orgasm; this varies according to the specific injury. (pp. 432–433)
- People with cerebral palsy, which is characterized by mild to severe lack of muscular control, may need help with preparation and positioning for sexual relations. (p. 433)
- Blindness and deafness can cause depression, lowered self-esteem, and social withdrawal; however, by themselves, these conditions do not appear to physically impair sexual interest or response. (p. 433)
- Individuals and couples can best cope with the sexual limitations of their illness or disability by accepting the limitations and developing the possible options remaining to them. (pp. 433–434)
- Medications that can impair sexual functioning include drugs used to treat high blood pressure, psychiatric disorders, depression, and cancer. Recreational drugs (including barbiturates, narcotics, and marijuana), alcohol abuse, and even tobacco smoking can interfere with sexual interest, arousal, and orgasm. (p. 434)
- Negative attitudes about sexuality and shameful feelings about one's genitals learned during childhood can be detrimental to adult acceptance of one's body and sexual feelings. (pp. 434–435)
- The sexual double standard prescribes opposite expectations of sexual behavior for males and females. Both sets of expectations can have negative effects on sexuality. (p. 435)
- The cultural notion that sex equals coitus often limits the erotic potential of sexual interactions. (p. 436)

- Goal orientation in sexual expression is a culturally acquired attitude that can increase performance anxiety and reduce pleasurable options in lovemaking. (pp. 436–437)
- Sexual difficulties can be related to personal factors such as limited or inaccurate sexual knowledge, problems of self-concept and body image, or emotional difficulties. (p. 437)
- Experiencing sexual abuse as a child or sexual assault as an adult often leads to sexual problems. As a result of the abuse experiences, the person associates sexual activity with negative, traumatic feelings. (p. 439)
- Relationship problems, ineffective communication, and fear of pregnancy or sexually transmitted diseases can often inhibit sexual satisfaction. (pp. 439–441)
- A woman or man whose sexual orientation is homosexual will often have difficulty with sexual interest, arousal, and orgasm in a heterosexual sexual relationship. (p. 441)

Specific Sexual Difficulties

- Hypoactive sexual desire (HSD) is characterized by a lack of interest in sexual activity and fantasy. HSD most commonly reflects relationship problems but can also be caused by other physical or personal difficulties. (pp. 441–442)
- Dissatisfaction with frequency of sexual activity occurs when individual differences in sexual interest are significant and a couple is not able to compromise on their individual preferences. (p. 442)
- Sexual aversion disorder is an extreme irrational fear or dislike of sexual activity. Many individuals with sexual aversion experience physical symptoms of anxiety when they attempt to engage in sexual activity. (pp. 442–443)
- Female sexual arousal disorder is an inhibition of the vasocongestive response. This inhibition can be caused by physiological or psychological factors. Reduced lubrication is a normal occurrence during breast feeding and following menopause. (p. 443)
- Male erectile dysfunction is commonly caused by a combination of physical and psychological factors. Illnesses and medications account for the increase in erectile dysfunction in older men. A variety of procedures can help evaluate physical factors in erection problems. (pp. 443–444)
- Female orgasmic disorder, or anorgasmia, can be lifelong or temporary, generalized or situational. (p. 444)
- Generalized lifelong anorgasmia means that a woman has never experienced orgasm by any means of self- or partner stimulation. (p. 444)
- Situational anorgasmia describes a condition in which a woman can experience orgasm in one situation but not another—for example, during masturbation but not with a partner. (p. 444)
- Coitus provides mostly indirect clitoral stimulation and for many woman is not sufficient to result in orgasm. (p. 445)
- Male orgasmic disorder is the inability of a man to ejaculate (usually during coitus) and is also called male coital anorgasmia or partner anorgasmia. (p. 445)
- Premature ejaculation occurs when a man is consistently unable to control the timing of ejaculation and feels distress about this during each sexual encounter. Premature ejaculation is a common problem. (pp. 445–446)

- Both men and women fake orgasm, although women do so more often. Pretending usually perpetuates ineffective patterns of relating and reduces the intimacy of the sexual experience. (p. 446)
- Dyspareunia, or pain during coitus, is disruptive to sexual interest and arousal in both women and men. Numerous physical problems can cause painful intercourse. (pp. 447–448)
- Peyronie's disease, in which fibrous tissue and calcium deposits develop in the penis, can cause pain and curvature of the penis during erection. (p. 447)
- Vaginismus is an involuntary contraction of the outer vaginal muscles that makes penetration of the vagina difficult and painful. Many women who have vaginismus are interested in and enjoy sexual activity. (p. 448)

Suggested Readings

Kroll, Ken, and Erica Klein (1992). *Enabling Romance.* New York: Harmony Books. An exploration of sexual alternatives for people with a wide array of disabilities, written by a disabled husband and his wife.

Laken, Virginia, and Keith Laken (2002). *Making Love Again: Hope for Couples Facing Loss of Sexual Intimacy.* Sandwich, MA: Ant Hill Press. A book for couples dealing with the sexual effects following prostate surgery.

Leiblum, Sandra, and Raymond Rosen (Eds.) (2000). *Principles and Practice of Sex Therapy.* New York: Guilford Press. An up-to-date, comprehensive, authoritative book with contributions by leading clinical authorities in the field of sex therapy.

Maltz, Wendy (2001). *The Sexual Healing Journey.* New York: Quill. An excellent and sensitive book for adult survivors of sexual abuse and their partners. Explores the impact of sexual abuse on sexuality and explains the steps that survivors and their partners can take to reclaim their sexuality.

Ogden, Gina (1994). *Women Who Love Sex.* New York: Pocket Books. Personal portraits of women who find great meaning and pleasure in sexual expression.

Segraves, Robert, and Richard Balon (2003). *Sexual Pharmacology: Fast Facts.* New York: W. W. Norton. An easy-to-read, comprehensive, and up-to-date book on the sexual effects of prescription and recreational drugs.

Zilbergeld, Bernie (1992). *The New Male Sexuality: A Guide to Sexual Fulfillment.* New York: Bantam. An exceptionally well-written and informative treatment of male sexuality, including such topics as sexual functioning, self-awareness, and overcoming difficulties.

Suggested Videotape

Maltz, Wendy (1990). *Partners in Healing.* Available from Intervision, 261 East 12th Ave., Ste. 100, Eugene, OR 97401; (541) 345-3455; www.intervisionmedia.com. An excellent videotape of three couples discussing the effects of childhood sexual abuse on their intimate relationships and the steps they took to recover from their traumas.

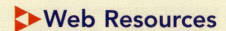

Web Resources

Your *Our Sexuality* Web site **http://psychology.wadsworth.com/ crooksbaur9e/** has direct links to the Web sites described below. These links are checked often for changes, dead links, and new additions.

Sexuality and Disability
This Web site offers information on sexuality for people with disabilities and for parents of children with disabilities. General disability information as well as disability-specific information can be found.

American Association of Sex Educators, Therapists, and Counselors
This Web site has listings of sex therapists throughout the country that the Association has certified.

American Board of Sexology
This Web site has listings of sex therapists throughout the country that the Board has certified.

Pelvic Pain
Details about pain during intercourse or menstruation are offered on this Web site.

Sex Therapy Advice
This self-help site has information and advice about sexual problems.

Our Sexuality Web Site
For online resources directly related to this book, go to **http://psychology.wadsworth.com/ crooksbaur9e/**. You will find interactive exercises, study questions, chapter outlines, an online version of this text's glossary, and Web links and activities that complement your CD-ROM.

InfoTrac® College Edition Online Library
http://infotrac.thomsonlearning.com/
InfoTrac College Edition is an online searchable library that includes a multitude of journals, many of which are specific to human sexuality. These journals include *Archives of Sexual Behavior, Archives of Sexual Health Behavior, Canadian Journal of Human Sexuality, Hispanic Journal of the Behavioral Sciences, Journal of Cross-Cultural Psychology, Journal of Physical Education, Recreation, and Dance, Journal of Sex Research,* and *Sex Roles.* You may search topics suggested in the margins of this chapter or terms of your own.

Our Sexuality CD-ROM
Use your CD-ROM for further study of the concepts in this chapter. Your CD-ROM provides animations of difficult concepts, video clips of real people discussing sexuality, critical thinking questions, chapter quizzing, and more.

CHAPTER **16**

◆

Sex Therapy and Sexual Enhancement

▶ **Basics of Sexual Enhancement and Sex Therapy**

How can individuals increase their sexual self-awareness?

What are the guidelines for sensate focus?

▶ **Specific Suggestions for Women**

What are the steps for a woman who wants to learn to experience orgasm?

What is the process for resolving vaginismus?

▶ **Specific Suggestions for Men**

How can a man learn to prolong his arousal before ejaculating?

What is the typical course of therapy for a man having difficulty with erections, and what medical options might be helpful?

▶ **Treating Hypoactive Sexual Desire**

Why does hypoactive sexual desire often require more intensive therapy than other sexual problems?

▶ **Seeking Professional Assistance**

What are the four levels of therapy in the PLISSIT model?

How might someone select a sex therapist?

© Chris Harvey/Getty Images

When I was 20, my girlfriend and I were in her room and decided to have sex. She told me to make it quick and to be quiet because her mom was in the next room. Getting an erection was no problem, but after having sex for a couple of minutes I lost it. I completely freaked out, and was in a panic for days and wouldn't let her touch me. I began placing calls to doctors specializing in penile problems, but not one would answer me over the phone, and I couldn't afford a doctor visit. It wasn't until my girlfriend showed me a book from a human sexuality class she'd taken that I mellowed out about the whole ordeal and chalked my problem up to a bad situation. (Authors' files)

In this chapter we focus on methods for increasing sexual satisfaction and on various approaches used in sex therapy. The activities we discuss can be pursued individually or by a couple; they range from expanding self-knowledge to sharing more effectively with a partner. Much of what follows embraces our belief that all of us have the potential for self-help. The suggested readings at the end of the chapter provide further self-help options.

The various suggestions offered here have proved helpful to many people. However, the same techniques do not work for everyone, and exercises often need to be individually modified. Furthermore, professional help may be called for when individual efforts, couple efforts, or both do not produce the desired results. Recognizing that therapy is sometimes necessary to promote change, we have included guidelines for seeking sex therapy in the last section of this chapter. In addition, it is important to consult a physician to rule out any physical causes for the sexual difficulty.

▶ Basics of Sexual Enhancement and Sex Therapy

Increased self-knowledge is often an important step in sexual enhancement. With this in mind, we briefly outline procedures for improving awareness and acceptance of your body and present activities that provide the most pleasurable stimulation. These basics can also be useful for individuals and couples whose sexual life is already satisfactory.

Self-Awareness

People who know themselves—their sexual feelings, their needs, and how their bodies respond—are often better able to share this valuable information with a partner than are people who are unaware of their sexual needs and potentials. Physical and emotional self-awareness and self-expression are crucial elements in satisfying sexual experiences (Morehouse, 2001; Schwartz, 2003). In the book *Women Who Love Sex,* Gina Ogden found an overall message in the stories of women she interviewed. She concluded:

> To celebrate the erotic, to feel motivated by satisfaction rather than by guilt and suffering, is a radical reframe for many women. It means women don't have to give up sex to be safe.... It means shifting from control—the ability to say "No"—to power—the ability to say "Yes."... It means sharing responsibility for initiating, for setting goals, for enjoyment.... There can be a closer meeting of minds and bodies, hearts and souls. (Ogden, 1994, p. 23)

! Sexual Health

A good way to increase self-awareness and comfort with our sexuality is to become well acquainted with our sexual anatomy. It is not unusual for women to report never having looked at their own vulvas. Men may be more familiar with their bodies, but many are still not comfortable with their genitals. You may decide to become familiar with your genitals by looking and touching, so as to be more comfortable with your own body. It can be helpful to examine all areas of your anatomy, not just the genital region. Examine yourself visually and experiment with different touches, perhaps using a massage lotion to make the movements more pleasant.

Masturbation exercises are an effective way for both men and women to learn about and experience sexual response (Everaerd et al., 2000). These exercises can be enjoyed for themselves, and the knowledge they provide can be shared with a partner. Masturbation also can help older people who do not have a current partner to maintain sexual functioning

(Leiblum & Bachmann, 1988). Further information about masturbation can be found later in this chapter, in the section "Becoming Orgasmic." ■

Communication

When you first discussed the stop–start technique [discussed later in this chapter] in class, I was excited to try it out with my partner. However, I didn't know how to talk about it. It wasn't like he had never mentioned his problem before. He would say he was sorry he was so fast, and that maybe it would get better with time. Finally, I asked him to come to class with me the day you showed the film demonstrating the technique. Man, did we do a lot of talking after it was over. He was anxious to give it a try. At first we made some mistakes. In fact, it was only when we were really talking openly that things began to work well. He showed me how he liked to be stimulated, things he had never told me before. We shared a lot of feelings. He became much more aware of my needs and what I needed to be satisfied. We really started getting into a lot of variety in our lovemaking, instead of just kissing and intercourse. By the way, the technique did work in slowing him down, but I think the biggest benefit has been breaking down the communication barriers. It sure makes sex a whole lot better! (Authors' files)

This quotation from the our files illustrates not only how difficult it can sometimes be to talk constructively about sexual problems but also how important communication can be in solving them. Research has found that couples who have better communication than other couples before sex therapy are more likely to be successful in treatment (Hawton et al., 1992). One of the primary benefits of sex therapy—whether the immediate goal is learning to have orgasms with partners, how to overcome premature ejaculation, or almost any other shared problem—is that couples participating together in the treatment process often develop more effective communication skills. The "Love Talk Exercise" box offers some suggestions, and we encourage you to review Chapter 8.

In his writings, psychologist David Schnarch notes that "intimacy during sex doesn't come 'naturally'—it's a learned ability and an acquired taste" (1993, p. 44). From this perspective adult eroticism depends more on emotional maturity than on sexual technique. A solid sense of self is needed to risk expressing oneself as fully as is necessary for intense erotic

---

LET'S TALK ABOUT IT

◆ Love Talk Exercise

Developing skills in sexual communication is one of the biggest challenges that couples face. The following sentence openers are tools to expand the all-important communication between sexual partners. If you decide to do the exercise, review Chapter 8 for using "I" language and listening skills. Do the exercise at some time other than when you are being sexual. Be sure to agree beforehand that it is okay to skip any item either of you do not feel ready to discuss. Take turns being first to read and complete the sentence openers.

Sentence openers:

Something I really like about our sexual connection is _____

What really turns me on is _____

What brings me to the most intense orgasm is _____

What I like about your orgasm is _____

Something you could do to really get me in the mood for sex is _____

Something sexual I really don't like is _____

Something I'm curious about is _____

Something sexual I've always wanted to try is _____

One thing I'd like from you sexually is _____

The thing I most want to tell you that I haven't yet is _____

Something I'd like to ask you is _____

One of my sexual fantasies is _____

One thing that worries me about our sexual relationship is _____

When we have sex I feel _____

Add your own sentence openers if there is something you would like to address that is not covered here.

SOURCE: Adapted from Linda De Villers, *Love Skills* (2004).

experiences in a long-term committed relationship or marriage. It requires the ability to risk initiating sexual behaviors and to tolerate the possibility that the partner may not respond positively. Schnarch noted, "The essence of sexual intimacy lies . . . in the ability to allow oneself to deeply know and to be deeply known by one's partner" (1993, p. 43).

Sensate Focus

One of the most useful couple-oriented activities for enhancing mutual sexual enjoyment is a series of touching exercises called **sensate focus** (Figure 16.1). "The skin is the largest sex organ, yet many of us have learned to regard as sexual only a tiny percentage of the available acreage" (Tiefer, 1999, p. 70). Masters and Johnson developed the technique of sensate focus and have used it as a basic step in treating sexual problems. Sensate focus can help to reduce anxiety caused by goal orientation and to increase communication, pleasure, and closeness.

Sensate focus A process of touching and communication used to enhance sexual pleasure and to reduce performance pressure.

This technique is by no means appropriate only for sex therapy; it can be used by all couples to enhance their sexual relationships. In the sensate focus touching exercises, partners take turns touching each other while following some essential guidelines. In the following descriptions we assume that the one doing the touching is a woman and the one being touched is a man. Of course, homosexual as well as heterosexual couples can do these exercises, and in either case the partners periodically change roles.

InfoTrac Search Words

■ Sensate focus

Sexual Health

To start, the person who will be doing the touching takes some time to "set the scene" so that the environment will be comfortable and pleasant for her; for example, she might unplug the phone and arrange a warm, cozy place with relaxing music and lighting. The two people then undress, and the toucher begins to explore her partner's body, following this important guideline: She is *not* to touch to please or arouse her partner but for her *own* interest and pleasure. The goal is for the toucher to focus on her perception of textures, shapes, and temperatures. The nondemand quality of this kind of touching helps reduce or eliminate performance anxiety, which can inhibit arousal for both partners. The person being touched remains quiet except when any touch is uncomfortable. In that case he describes the uncomfortable feeling and what the toucher could do to make it more comfortable; for example, "That feels ticklish. Please touch the other side of my arm." This guideline helps the toucher attend fully to her own sensations and perceptions without worrying about whether something she is doing is unpleasant to her partner.

In the next sensate focus exercise the two people switch roles, following the same guidelines as before. In these first sensate focus experiences, intercourse and touching the breasts and genitals are prohibited. Only after the partners have focused on touch perceptions and

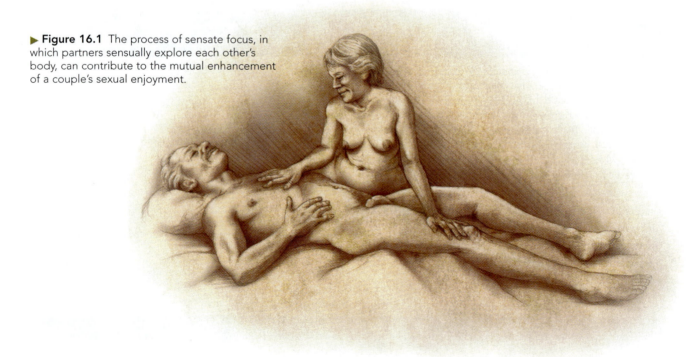

▶ **Figure 16.1** The process of sensate focus, in which partners sensually explore each other's body, can contribute to the mutual enhancement of a couple's sexual enjoyment.

on communicating uncomfortable feelings do they include breasts and genitals as part of the exercise. Again, the toucher explores for her own interest and pleasure, not her partner's. After the inclusion of breasts and genitals, the partners progress to a simultaneous sensate focus experience. Now they touch one another at the same time and experience feelings from both touching and being touched. ■

Sex therapist Leonore Tiefer explained the skepticism that some people have about sensate focus and touching:

> Couples who seek out sex therapists because of sexual disinterest or difficulty in sexual function are often thunderstruck to hear that the first homework assignment of the treatment is to pet with each other. They can't imagine how avoiding intercourse and just playing around will help. . . . But, as clients soon realize, it may be easier to have intercourse than to hug and kiss! The task is better defined. . . . It can be accomplished with a minimum of communication. With petting, the script is more vague. Over what path do the hands and mouth wander? . . . How do you know when you're through? . . . You have to like someone to enjoy petting. Because the physical sensations are less intense, much of the reward must come from the closeness. It's joyless and burdensome to cuddle and embrace with someone you neither know well nor want to know better. The petting assignment is very revealing for many couples." (Tiefer, 1999, p. 55)

Modern Western sex therapy is based on the assumption that the values of open communication, emotional intimacy, and physical pleasure for both partners guide treatment and are its goals. However, these principles are antithetical to many cultures' norms (D. Goodman, 2001), as we explain in the following "Sexuality and Diversity" discussion.

? How About You?

What kind of sexual interaction do you think is most intimate?

Sexuality and Diversity

How Modern Sex Therapy Can Clash with Cultural Values

Cultural beliefs influence sexual practices, the perception of sexual problems, and modes of treatment. In cultures in which male superiority predominates, a woman is expected to be sexual as an obligation of marriage rather than for her own pleasure. Lack of orgasm and low sexual desire would not be viewed as a problem, but vaginismus would be, because it interferes with the man's sexual activity and the possibility of conception (Lavee, 1991).

A study conducted in Saudi Arabia, where the marital relationship is based primarily on the two dimensions of male sexual potency and couple fertility, found that the most common problem leading a couple to sex therapy was erectile disorder. Females in Saudi Arabia, who are raised to inhibit their sexual desires, came to sex therapy only with problems of painful intercourse. Unlike their counterparts in Western countries, the women did not seek help for lack of desire, arousal, or orgasm. For both men and women, only when intercourse itself was impaired—not interest or pleasure—did couples seek treatment. Once again, we see that sociocultural factors affect even what kinds of sexual anxieties people experience (Osman & Al-Sawaf, 1995).

Many cultural traditions allow for little or no communication about sexual matters. Asians consider it shameful to discuss sex, especially with someone outside the family. Muslims are taught to avoid talking to the other sex (including their spouses) about sexuality. Taking a sex history can be distressing for clients with these beliefs, especially when the husband and wife are interviewed together. In cultures in which women are expected to be innocent about sex, the sex-education component of therapy conflicts with the prevailing values.

Specific sex therapy techniques often contradict cultural values (Rosenau et al., 2001; Timmerman, 2001). For example, masturbation exercises to treat anorgasmia, erectile difficulties, or premature ejaculation would conflict with religious prohibitions of Orthodox Jews. The female-above intercourse position can pose a problem in cultures in which male dominance is prevalent. The gender equality inherent in sensate focus exercises and avoidance of intercourse are also often objectionable to many ethnic groups.

Sex therapy needs to take into account the clients' cultural values and the implications they have for intimate behavior (Blass & Fagan, 2001). Therapists should attempt to adjust therapy to their clients' well-integrated ethnic and religious perspectives (Haffner, 2004; Petok, 2001). This is likely to be more helpful than attempting to impose the cultural norms inherent in Western sex therapy (Hodge, 2004).

Masturbation with a Partner Present

It can be particularly valuable for couples to let each other know what kind of touching they find arousing. Masturbating in the presence of a partner can be a way to share this kind of information. This activity can be particularly helpful for women learning to experience orgasm with a partner and for resolving premature ejaculation and erectile difficulties, as discussed further in the sections "Lasting Longer" and "Dealing with Erectile Difficulties." Also, when only one partner feels sexual, that person can masturbate with the other present, perhaps touching, perhaps kissing.

All the experiences suggested in the sensate focus section can be helpful in increasing sexual satisfaction, whether an individual or a couple has a specific difficulty or whether the goal is simply to find out more about themselves. Beyond these general exercises, though, specific exercises or techniques can sometimes aid in reducing or overcoming particular sexual difficulties. We described these difficulties in Chapter 15, and in the remainder of this chapter we look at some strategies that have been used to deal with them. For purposes of clarity and easy reference we have organized these strategies according to whether they deal with primarily female or primarily male sexual problems, except treatment of hypoactive sexual desire, which we discuss later in the chapter. We should stress, however, that these discussions are not applicable to only one sex. Men can gain some understanding of both their female partners and themselves from reading the section on specific female strategies; women can gain similarly from reading the discussions of techniques for men.

▶ Specific Suggestions for Women

In this section we suggest procedures that may help women to learn to increase sexual arousal and reach orgasm by themselves or with a partner. We also include suggestions for dealing with vaginismus. When the origins of these problems are complex, self-help may not be sufficient to resolve them.

Becoming Orgasmic

Learning effective self-stimulation is often recommended for women who have never experienced orgasm. One advantage of self-stimulation is that a woman who does not have a partner can learn to become orgasmic. For a woman with a sexual partner, becoming orgasmic first by masturbation may help develop a sense of sexual autonomy that can increase the likelihood of satisfaction with a partner.

Therapy programs for anorgasmia are based on progressive self-awareness activities that a woman does at home between therapy sessions. At the beginning of treatment, body exploration, genital self-exam, and Kegel exercises (see Chapter 4) are emphasized; then therapy and home exercises move progressively to self-stimulation exercises similar to those described in Chapter 9 (see "Self-Pleasuring Techniques").

Vibrators are sometimes used to help an anorgasmic woman experience orgasm for the first time so she knows that she can have this response. (A vibrator is often less tiring to use and supplies more intense stimulation than the fingers.) After she has experienced a few orgasms with the vibrator, it is helpful for her to return to manual stimulation. This step is important because it is easier for a partner to replicate a woman's own touch than the stimulation of a vibrator. Another method, the Eros Clitoral Therapy Device, shown in Figure 16.2, is designed to increase blood flow to and thereby arousal of the clitoris (Munarriz et al., 2003).

It can take considerable time for some women to learn to experience orgasm. However, counselors can facilitate the process by answering questions and providing personal assistance; they can also help a woman work through broader problems that contribute to anorgasmia. Information on the role of counselors in sex therapy and guidelines for seeking help appear later in this chapter.

Technology that stimulates orgasm was accidentally discovered and reported in spring 2001. A physician who specialized in pain control implanted electrodes for a spinal cord stimulator in the spine of a female patient; the goal was to use the electric impulses, controlled by a handheld remote, to reduce the pain in her back. While trying to find the correct placement of the electrodes to help with the patient's pain, the doctor stimulated an area that triggered an orgasm. The physician hopes to do research on using the device to help women with orgasmic dysfunction, including women with illnesses and disabilities that impair orgasmic response (Stenger, 2001).

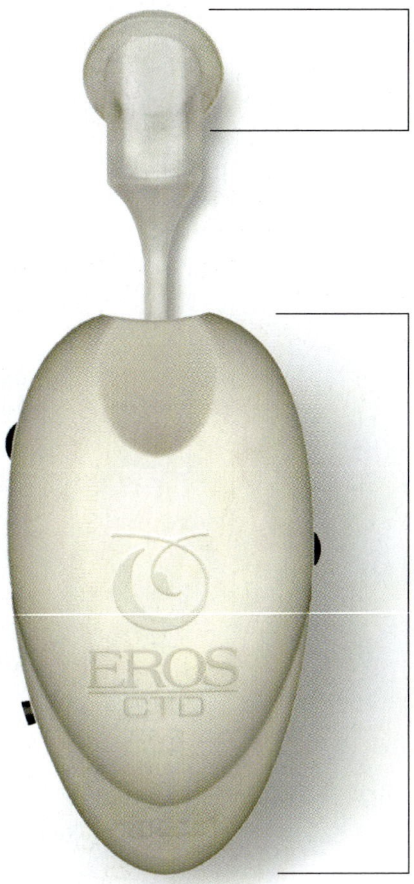

Experiencing Orgasm with a Partner

Once a woman has learned to experience orgasm through self-stimulation, sharing her discoveries with her partner can help her partner know what forms of stimulation are most pleasing to her. A woman's sexual assertiveness—initiating what is arousing to her and making her erotic wishes known—is essential to improving and maintaining her sexual experience (Apt, 1996; Ellison, 2000).

After a couple is comfortable with the sensate focus exercises described earlier, they proceed to genital exploration. Each partner takes turns visually exploring the other's genitals, locating all the parts discussed in Chapters 4 and 5. After looking thoroughly, they experiment with touch, noticing and sharing what different areas feel like.

The next step is for the woman to stimulate herself in her partner's presence. The woman can use self-stimulation methods that she has learned are effective and share her arousal with her partner, who can be holding and kissing her or lying beside her, as shown in Figure 16.3. This step is often a difficult one. One woman described how she dealt with her discomfort:

When I wanted to share with my partner what I had learned about myself through masturbation, I felt anxious about how to do it. Finally, we decided that to begin with, I would be in the bedroom, and he would be in the living room, knowing I was masturbating. Then he would sit on the bed, not looking at me. The next step was for him to hold and kiss me while I was touching myself. Then I could be comfortable showing him how I touch myself. (Authors' files)

Next the partner begins nondemanding manual genital pleasuring. The couple can do this in any position that suits them. Masters and Johnson (1970) recommended the position illustrated in Figure 16.4. (We are supposing in this discussion that the partner is a man.) The partner reclines against cushions or pillows; the woman sits between his legs with her back supported by his chest. The woman places her hand over her partner's hand on her genitals to guide the stimulation. They can use lubricants to increase sensation. The partner makes no assumptions about how to touch but rather is guided by the woman's words and hand. The purpose of the initial sessions is for the partner to discover what is arousing to the woman rather than to produce orgasm. If the woman thinks she is ready to experience orgasm, she indicates to her partner to continue the stimulation until she experiences climax. Orgasm will probably not occur until the couple has had several sessions.

Couples can use several specific techniques to increase a woman's arousal and the possibility of orgasm during intercourse. The first has to do with when to begin intercourse. Rather than beginning intercourse after a certain number of minutes of foreplay or when there is sufficient lubrication, a woman can be guided by her feeling of what might be called

Small, soft plastic cup that is placed on clitoris

Battery-operated pump that creates suction to increase blood flow to clitoris

Courtesy of Nugyn, Inc.

▶ **Figure 16.2** The Eros Clitoral Therapy Device, approved by the FDA in 2000, works by increasing vasocongestion of the clitoris.

readiness. Not all women experience this feeling of readiness, but for those who do, beginning intercourse at this time (and not before) can enhance the ensuing erotic sensations. Of course, her partner will have to cooperate by waiting for the woman to indicate when she is ready and by not attempting to begin intercourse before then.

► **Figure 16.4** The back-to-chest position for genital sensate focus.

A woman who wants increased stimulation during coitus might benefit from initiating movements herself:

> Orgasms during intercourse . . . usually seemed to result from a conscious attempt by the woman to center some kind of clitoral area contact for herself during intercourse, usually involving contact with the man's pubic area. . . . This is essentially the way men get stimulation during intercourse. They rub their penises against our vaginal walls so that the same area they stimulate during masturbation is being stimulated during intercourse. In other words, you have to get the stimulation centered where it feels good. (Hite, 1976, p. 276)

Even more direct stimulation of the clitoris can occur during intercourse. The woman can stimulate her clitoris manually during intercourse or use a vibrator, as shown in Figure 16.5. Some men report that the vibrations transmitted to their penises are pleasurable. The woman can also guide her partner in touching her clitoris. One comfortable way for him to be able to touch her clitoris is to turn his hand slightly and use his thumb. (Side-lying and rear-entry coital positions also allow either of them to touch her clitoris easily.)

The woman might find it helpful to experiment with Kegel exercises during penetration or to focus on the vaginal sensations during intercourse to increase her awareness (Brody et al., 2003).

Table 16.1 highlights how women who are routinely orgasmic facilitate experiencing orgasm (Ellison, 2000). A number of books are available for couples who want more information than we have space for here; some of these books are listed in the suggested readings at the end of this chapter.

TABLE 16.1 Facilitating Orgasm?	
2,371 women completed the sentence "In addition to getting specific physical stimulation, I often have done the following to help me reach orgasm during sex with a partner"	
Activity	**Percentage**
Positioned my body to get the stimulation I needed	90
Paid attention to my physical sensations	83
Tightened and released my pelvic muscles	75
Synchronized the rhythm of my movements to my partner's	75
Asked or encouraged my partner to do what I needed	74
Got myself in a sexy mood beforehand	71
Focused on my partner's pleasure	68
Felt/thought how much I love my partner	65

SOURCE: Ellison (2000, p. 244).

Dealing with Vaginismus

Treatment for vaginismus usually begins during a pelvic exam, with the physician demonstrating the vaginal spasm reaction to the woman or couple. Subsequent therapy starts with relaxation and self-awareness exercises, which the woman performs at home to reach a degree of comfort and control on her own. These exercises typically begin with a soothing bath, general body exploration, and manual external genital pleasuring and then proceed to dealing with vaginismus as the woman learns to insert first a fingertip, then a finger, and eventually three fingers into her vagina without experiencing muscle contractions. At each stage the woman practices relaxing and contracting the vaginal muscles, as with Kegel exercises (see Chapter 4). Dilators, which are cylindrical rods of graduated sizes, are sometimes used to accustom the vaginal walls to relaxing (Leiblum, 2000). Concurrently with these exercises, the woman meets with her therapist to discuss her reactions. Biofeedback and physical therapy treatments might also be included (Koehler, 2002).

Once the woman has completed the preceding steps, her partner can begin to participate. Together, they follow the same steps that she followed alone, starting with a visual examination of the vulva. Open communication is essential, and progress is gradual. No attempt at penile–vaginal penetration is made until the man can insert three fingers without inducing a muscle spasm. When the penis is inserted into the vagina, the purpose is for the woman to become familiar with the sensations involved in vaginal containment of the penis, so the couple remain motionless. Pelvic movements and pleasure focusing are added later, only when both partners are comfortable with penetration. Research suggests that vaginismus can sometimes be difficult to treat successfully, especially when couples have never experienced penile–vaginal intercourse (LoPiccolo, 1982). More extensive therapy may be necessary to address vaginismus (Koehler, 2002).

▶ Specific Suggestions for Men

In the following paragraphs we outline methods for dealing with the common difficulties of premature ejaculation and erectile disorder. We also discuss a way to treat the less common condition of orgasmic disorder. As in the preceding discussion of women's sexual difficulties, we caution that the origins of such problems are complex and that solutions are frequently not simple. Again, we refer readers who are interested in pursuing these topics to the suggested readings and also to the discussion in the "Seeking Professional Assistance" section.

Lasting Longer

Although premature ejaculation is a common dissatisfaction, the prospects for positive change are good. Most professional sex therapists use a multiphased program that focuses on the stop–start technique, which we discuss later in this section (McCarthy, 1994; Polonsky, 2000). The successful approaches to learning ejaculatory control are easy to implement, even, in some cases, without professional guidance. There are also simpler strategies for helping to delay ejaculation, and we discuss these first.

Some Helpful Strategies for Delaying Ejaculation

In some cases men can gain considerable control over premature ejaculation by practicing a few simple strategies. Men for whom premature ejaculation is not a problem and women readers may find the following discussion valuable simply because they would sometimes like sexual intercourse to last longer.

Sexual Health

- *Ejaculate more frequently.* Men with premature ejaculation problems sometimes find that they can delay ejaculation when they are having more frequent orgasms. If partner sex is not a viable option, frequent masturbation to orgasm can be helpful.

- *Come again!* Because of the limiting assumption that male orgasm is the end point of sexual interaction, few men or their partners consider or explore the potential for slowed responsiveness after a first climax. A couple can experiment with continuing sexual interaction after the man's ejaculation, then resume intercourse when his erection returns. This strategy is most useful for younger men who experience erections again soon after ejaculation.

ing other ways of sexual sharing. For other men unable to have erections, several types of medical treatments are available.

Viagra, a pill for erectile problems, became available in 1998. Originally developed for cardiovascular disease, it became the fastest selling prescription drug in history. Almost 40,000 prescriptions were dispensed in the first 2 weeks on the market, and since then Viagra has had $1 billion in annual worldwide sales (Holmes, 2003). By 2001, 14 million prescriptions had been written for men in the United States (Wysowski & Swann, 2003). In 2003 and 2004 the FDA approved two additional Viagra-like drugs. Levitra and Cialis are chemically similar, but the erection-enhancing effects of both last longer than Viagra's, up to 24 to 36 hours after taking the pill. Viagra and its cousins do not work for about 20% of men who take it.

Viagra ads initially represented older men with problems with erectile dysfunction. Ads now tend to appeal to a wider variety of ages, including younger men and even women who use Viagra for sexual enhancement rather than treatment.

Viagra, Levitra, and Cialis have similar side effects; the most common are flushing, headaches, and nasal congestion (Goldstein, 2001; Gotthardt, 2003). Erectile dysfunction drugs can also cause priapism, in which an erection does not subside and can result in permanent damage to penile tissue unless medical treatment is obtained (Adams, 2003). A small number of men have died after taking Viagra (49 men per 1 million prescriptions), but most of the deaths were attributed to the men's preexisting high mortality risk from cardiovascular disease. The question of Viagra's role in the deaths continues to be studied (Mitka, 2000).

For many couples erection-enhancing drugs can be wonder drugs that restore the intimacy of intercourse to the couple. In troubled relationships the availability of these medications can confront the couple with their problems, which, one hopes, would lead the couple to work toward resolving them (Steinhauer, 1998). Certainly, Viagra greatly increased general conversation and awareness about erectile problems. In fact, men who do not have erectile dysfunction are using erection-enhancing drugs for firmer and longer-lasting erections. The appeal to men to be able to extend intercourse beyond one or more ejaculations contributes to their recreational use (Naughton, 2004). The pharmaceutical companies that produce these drugs claim that they are only for treatment of erectile dysfunction, but their ads suggest otherwise. Initially, the men in the ads were older, with gray hair and wrinkles. The ads later shifted to include photos of young men and proposed that these men consider Viagra "if you're not satisfied with your sex life due to poor erections in recent months" (Tiefer, 1999, p. 64). The market segment of men who might not "be satisfied" is probably quite large and hence profitable.

Reports also indicate that Viagra has emerged as a party drug for recreational and casual sex. Mixing Viagra and recreational drugs combines enduring erections with an altered mental state during which straight and gay people often engage in high-risk sexual behaviors that they otherwise would avoid (Adams, 2003). At some teen and young adult rave parties, Viagra is available and is used to counteract erection-inhibiting effects of rave drugs such as ecstasy (Boulware, 2000b). Viagra is often present at some of the sex parties of a segment of the gay subculture. Particularly for men who have come out of the closet after age 30 or 40, Viagra helps their physical response to match the enthusiasm of their newfound sexual expression (Adams, 2003). Men use Levitra and Cialis in similar ways (Naughton, 2004).

In a double-blind placebo-controlled crossover study (each study group alternates between taking the treatment and taking the placebo), 900 milligrams of Korean red ginseng three times daily was found to significantly improve erectile function (Hong et al., 2003). Ginseng is a traditional Asian remedy for sexual dysfunction that appears to have no side effects. It is also considerably less expensive than Viagra: less than 30 cents a day for the treatment dosage.

Because vascular impairment can be a factor in erectile difficulty, one avenue of treatment is injection of the same vasoactive medications used to diagnose vascular impairment in erectile disorder (Lewis & Heaton, 2000). These medications relax smooth muscle tissue in the spongy body of the penis, causing increased blood flow, which in turn results in engorgement and erection. A physician teaches the man to inject the medication into the cavernous bodies of the penis; erection typically occurs 4–10 minutes after the almost painless injection and lasts from 1 to 4 hours. Complications include transitory numbness of the glans, infection, tissue damage at the injection site, and prolonged erection. Long-term effects of these injections are not yet known. Medication inserted into the urethra in a suppository is also available (Simon, 2003).

Yohimbine, a substance derived from the sap of the yohimbine tree that is occasionally prescribed for hypotension, can help induce erection in some cases, but it appears to be of limited value (Levy et al., 2000).

Mechanical Devices

Devices that suction blood into the penis and hold it there during intercourse have also been available since the mid-1980s (Korenman & Viosca, 1992). External vacuum constriction devices, which are available by prescription, consist of a vacuum chamber, pump, and penile constriction bands. The vacuum chamber is placed over the flaccid penis. The pump creates a negative pressure inside the chamber and draws blood into the penis. The elastic band is then placed around the base of the penis to trap the blood, and the chamber is removed (Levy et al., 2000).

A newer nonprescription product, Rejoyn, is a penile support sleeve made from soft, medical-quality rubber that fits over the penis to provide the support necessary for intercourse. A lubricated, open-ended condomlike cover fits over the sleeve. It can accommodate an erect or flaccid penis.

Surgical Treatments

A surgically implanted penile prosthesis is another option for men who are not helped by Viagra or other methods (Carson, 2003). Because the surgery is expensive and involves risks, including infection, men should evaluate this option carefully and include their partner in pre- and postsurgical counseling.

There are two basic types of penile implants. One type consists of a pair of semirigid rods made of metal wires or coils inside a silicone covering; the rods are placed inside the cavernous bodies of the penis. Although this type is easier to implant than the second type, a potential disadvantage is that the penis is always semierect. The second type of prosthesis is an inflatable device that enables the penis to change from flaccid to erect (Figure 16.6). Two inflatable cylinders are implanted into the cavernous bodies of the penile shaft. They are connected to a fluid-filled reservoir located near the bladder and to a pump in the scrotal sac. When a man wants an erection, he squeezes the pump several times, and the fluid fills the collapsed cylinders, producing an erection. When an erection is no longer desired, a release valve causes the fluid to go back into the reservoir. Neither of these devices can restore sensation or the ability to ejaculate if these have been lost as a result of medical problems. They do, however, provide an alternative for men who want to mechanically restore their ability to have erections (Garber, 1997).

Although some studies have found a high degree of satisfaction with penile implants (Mulcahy, 2000), a few cautions should be noted. In general, men with inflatable prostheses have been more satisfied than men with semirigid rods (Mohr & Beutler, 1990). In both cases altered sensations during erection can lead to dissatisfaction with the surgery (Coleman, 1998). The glans of the penis remains flaccid with the implant, and some men have

▶ **Figure 16.6** An inflatable penile prosthesis.

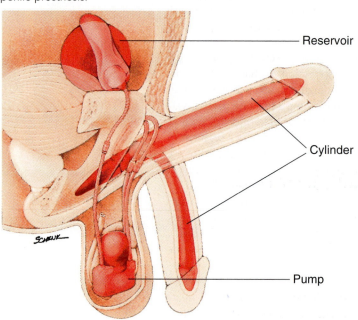

Reservoir

Cylinder

Pump

difficulty reaching orgasm. In addition, it is important for men considering penile implants to be aware that any ability to experience natural erection before surgery will be impaired by the surgery (Benet et al., 1994). Implants may need to be repaired or replaced, which requires additional surgeries.

Another surgical solution for erectile difficulties involves microsurgical vascular repairs (Kim & McVary, 1995). Revascularization surgery is done only at a few centers for carefully selected patients, but it can restore sexual functioning for a minority of people (Nash, 1997). Nerve grafts from a man's leg into his groin are an additional possibility for restoring erectile ability following prostate cancer surgery that has damaged nerves (Contemporary Sexuality, 1999c).

Reducing Male Orgasmic Disorder

A behavioral approach is generally used to treat male orgasmic disorder. In addition, psychotherapy aimed at reducing resentment in the relationship can be helpful when dislike or anger toward a partner contributes to a man's ejaculatory difficulty. The program outlined in the following paragraphs is suitable for either a heterosexual or a homosexual couple; however, for purposes of descriptive simplicity, we will assume a male–female pair.

Therapy usually begins with a few days of sensate focus, during which time the man should not attempt to have an ejaculation, either intravaginally or by some other form of stimulation. If his partner desires orgasm, this can be accomplished in whatever fashion is comfortable to both, excluding coitus. It is desirable for a man to maintain this consideration for his partner's needs throughout the program.

When the couple has become comfortable with the nondemand pleasuring of sensate focus, they may move on to the next phase of treatment. In this phase the man should experience ejaculation by whatever method is most likely to succeed. Frequently, the man begins by masturbating himself to orgasm after first being stimulated to a highly aroused state by his partner. The essential idea is for him to begin connecting his partner's presence and activity with his own pleasure.

Once both partners feel comfortable with the man's self-stimulation in the woman's presence, the couple can move on to the next phase, where she attempts to bring him to orgasm with manual or oral stimulation. Communication is especially important at this time. The man can greatly heighten his pleasure and arousal by demonstrating or verbalizing what feels best to him. It may take several days before his partner's stimulation produces an ejaculation. Most therapists agree that once he can reach orgasm by his partner's touch, an important step has been accomplished.

When the man is ejaculating consistently in response to partner stimulation, the couple can move on to the final phase of treatment, in which ejaculation takes place during vaginal penetration. The female partner sits astride the man, who is lying on his back, and stimulates him to the point where he signals that he is about to reach orgasm. She then inserts his penis and begins active pelvic thrusting. If he starts to ejaculate before insertion is completed, this should not be a cause for concern. If he does not ejaculate shortly after penetration, she should withdraw and resume manual stimulation until he is again about to ejaculate, at which point she reinserts his penis. Once the man experiences a few intravaginal ejaculations, the mental block that is usually associated with ejaculatory disorder often disappears.

▶ Treating Hypoactive Sexual Desire

Many therapists consider sexual desire problems the most complicated to treat, because multifaceted interventions are needed to help couples resolve their problems (Pridal & LoPiccolo, 2000; Sytsma & Taylor, 2001). Many aspects of the treatment for hypoactive sexual desire are similar to specific suggestions for resolving other sexual problems. These include (LoPiccolo & Friedman, 1988):

- Encouraging erotic responses through self-stimulation and arousing fantasies
- Reducing anxiety with appropriate information and sensate focus exercises

- Enhancing sexual experiences through improved communication and increased skills, both in initiating desired and in refusing undesired sexual activity
- Expanding the repertoire of affectionate and sexual activities

Therapeutic support to set aside more time for enjoyable couple activities and to prioritize a busy lifestyle (in order not to leave sex until last, when everyone is tired) can also be helpful (Weiner-Davis, 2003).

Hypoactive sexual desire is likely to require more intensive therapy than problems such as rapid ejaculation, anorgasmia, or vaginismus, and the therapy is less likely to be effective (Assalian, 1996). The goal is to modify the person's pattern of inhibiting his or her erotic impulses. To achieve this, the therapist helps the client understand the underlying motivation to suppress sexual feelings and the reasons for refusing sexual intimacy. Most therapists combine suggestions for specific activities with insight therapy, which can help the person understand and resolve unconscious conflicts about sexual pleasure and intimacy (see the next section's discussion of the PLISSIT model of sex therapy).

Hypoactive sexual desire is often a symptom of unresolved relationship problems (Leiblum, 2001). In these situations therapy focuses on the interactions between the couple that contribute to the lack of sexual desire (Alperstein, 2001). A skilled therapist helps the couple to resolve such issues as a power imbalance (where one person has most of the power and control in the relationship), fears about vulnerability and closeness, or poor sexual skills (LoPiccolo & Friedman, 1988). The therapist can also help each individual, as well as the couple together, to develop a better balance between independence and interdependence (Lobitz & Lobitz, 1996; Schnarch, 2000).

Research has found that some medications can help with low sexual desire. Testosterone supplementation increases sexual interest for many women (Apperloo et al., 2003; Lobo et al., 2003). The antidepressant buproprion (Wellbutrin) affects dopamine uptake in the brain. One study found that sexual desire and response deficits were significantly improved in 60% of women and men receiving buproprion, compared to 10% in the group receiving a placebo (Crenshaw et al., 1987). In addition, the over-the-counter steroid hormone DHEA, which is naturally produced by the adrenal glands, seems to have a positive effect. The adrenal glands produce less DHEA beginning at about age 30. In a placebo-controlled study, 50 milligrams of DHEA daily for 4 months increased sexual thoughts and sexual satisfaction (Contemporary Sexuality, 1999a). The search for a drug to increase female sexual desire, arousal, and orgasm has grown since the advent of Viagra, as we discuss in the nearby "On the Edge" box.

▶ Seeking Professional Assistance

After exploring the information and suggestions in this textbook and other readings or on the Internet, you may continue to experience considerable sexual dissatisfaction. Perhaps you find it difficult to progress beyond a particular stage in an exercise program. Although some people with sexual problems improve over time without therapy (De Amicis et al., 1984), you may decide to seek professional help. This is often a difficult step; only 10–20% of people with sexual problems seek consultation to help resolve their difficulties (Laumann et al., 1999). A skilled therapist can offer useful information, emotional support, a perspective other than your own, and specific problem-solving techniques, all of which may help you to make the desired changes in your sex life. What are the basic assumptions behind sex therapy, and how do you go about seeking professional assistance? We explore these questions in the last section of this chapter. ■

The PLISSIT Model of Sex Therapy

There are many approaches to sex therapy, and most have several elements in common (Donahey & Miller, 2001). One representative model, the PLISSIT model (Annon, 1974), specifies four levels of therapy, each of which provides treatment at an increasingly deeper level. PLISSIT is an acronym for these four levels: *permission, limited information, specific suggestions,* and *intensive therapy.*

Sex Drugs for Women?

The fact that many women report little or no sexual desire and difficulties with arousal and orgasm has been known for some time. Since the instant financial success of Viagra, commercial interests and scientists have searched for a pill to spark female sexual interest and response. Most of the research that tests whether Viagra works as well with women as it does with men has had disappointing results. Viagra does not increase blood flow to women's genital tissues as it does with men (Viagra increases blood flow by affecting an enzyme that is found throughout the penis, but that enzyme occurs in only one of the four layers of the vagina.) In addition, to the extent that vaginal blood flow did increase, most women did not notice any change in arousal or sensation. However, Viagra may be helpful to some women, but for which women and to what extent is not clear (Johnson, 2003).

The pursuit of greater sexual interest and increased blood flow to the female genitals goes beyond Viagra (Meston & Worcel, 2002). Numerous nonprescription topical products and pills are on the market. However, to date, only two of the many advertised products meet the criteria of having been researched in conformance with FDA standards and of having had their studies published in peer-reviewed professional journals. The first is Zestra, an oil with herbal extracts that is applied to the clitoris and vulva. A small study showed that it enhanced sexual response for women with and without prior problems with arousal (Ferguson et al., 2003). The second product to meet these research criteria is a nutritional supplement that contains extracts of various herbs, multivitamins, and minerals, ArginMax. This supplement is specifically designed to enhance sexual functioning. In a research study, participants using ArginMax reported increased clitoral sensation, sexual desire, vaginal lubrication, and frequency of orgasm (Ito et al., 2001). After 4 weeks almost 74% of subjects taking ArginMax were more satisfied with their sex life, compared to 37% of subjects taking a placebo.

Researchers will continue to develop and test additional products. Creams containing prostaglandins or L-argenine amino acid encourage blood flow to the genitals and are under study. Those not based on herbal preparations will require FDA approval before being made available (Gearson, 2003).

Part of the difficulty in finding a medicine for women comparable to Viagra for men is that scientific knowledge about the physiological process of female sexual functioning is rather limited (Bechara et al., 2003). To develop drugs to facilitate female sexual desire and arousal, scientists have to more fully understand the physiology of the process (Medical Ethics Advisor, 2003). Medical textbooks emphasize gynecological and pregnancy topics, and, to date, no medical textbook exists on female sexual health (Duenwald, 2003).

In addition, the negative emotional components of a sexual relationship may override the level of physiological sexual interest and enjoyment that a woman experiences. Inconsistencies in studies, especially those involving the known sex-drive hormone testosterone, may well be due to quality of relationship variables that are difficult to identify and control in research. If research on female sexual interest and arousal could identify and use only women with positive feelings about themselves and their sexual relationships, the effects of various drugs might be more easily ascertained. The importance of psychological variables may also be more significant for men than is commonly thought: half of all Viagra prescriptions are never refilled (Duenwald, 2003). Hopefully, some men do not refill them because Viagra was able to help them and their partners overcome obstacles to sexual interaction. However, many men may have found that firm erections are secondary to the less mechanical aspects of communication and intimacy.

At the first level the therapist reassures clients that thoughts, feelings, fantasies, desires, and behaviors that enhance their satisfaction and do not have potentially negative consequences are normal. Giving individuals and couples permission to appreciate their unique patterns and desires, without comparing themselves to others, is sometimes all the help they need. At the same time, people are given permission *not* to engage in certain behaviors unless they choose to do so.

At the second level, limited information, therapists provide clients with information specific to their sexual concerns. Factual information about concerns with penis size, clitoral sensitivity, or the effects of aging or medications on sexual response can alleviate anxiety and problems related to lack of knowledge (Gregoire, 2000). At the third level therapists give clients specific suggestions and recommend "homework" exercises—for instance, masturbation techniques, sensate focus, or the stop–start technique—to help the couple reach a goal. Most of these behavioral approaches are designed to reduce anxiety, enhance communication, and teach new arousal-enhancing behaviors (Heiman, 2002; McCarthy, 2001).

In some cases personal emotional difficulties or relationship problems interfere with sexual expression such that the first three therapy levels are not adequate to resolve the difficulties. In these cases the fourth level of intensive therapy may be required. In *insight-oriented*

InfoTrac Search Words

■ Psychosexual therapy

Psychosexual therapy Treatment designed to help clients gain awareness of their unconscious thoughts and feelings that contribute to their sexual problems.

Systems therapy Treatment that focuses on interactions within a couple relationship and on the functions of the sexual problems in the relationship.

EMDR (eye movement desensitization and reprocessing) A therapy technique, combining eye movements with concentrating on the problem, that may be helpful as a part of treatment for sexual difficulties.

therapy, or **psychosexual therapy,** the therapist provides interpretation and reflection to help clients gain awareness and understanding of unconscious feelings and thoughts that contribute to sexual difficulties (Kaplan, 1974). Insights gained in psychosexual therapy often pertain to patterns developed in childhood. Because intimate adult relationships can be greatly affected by the first significant relationships with parents, awareness of and insights into these early patterns are sometimes necessary to resolve sexual difficulties.

Systems therapy can be another element of intensive therapy. In contrast to psychosexual therapy, systems therapy is based on the concept that the identified problems are serving important current functions in the relationship. For instance, a person with hypoactive sexual desire can be in a relationship that is so close that a loss of sexual desire can be an unconscious response to a need to keep some distance. *Postmodern sex therapy* is the integration of the psychosexual, systems, and various behavioral approaches (LoPiccolo, 2000).

Some therapists are including **EMDR** (eye movement desensitization and reprocessing) in their treatment of sexual disorders, sexual compulsions, and sexual abuse flashbacks that occur during sexual activity. This specific technique consists of the client thinking about the problem while moving his or her eyes back and forth, following the movements of the therapist's fingers. EMDR appears to stimulate rapid and helpful informational and emotional processing in the brain, similar to what occurs during REM sleep. (During REM sleep, our eyes naturally move back and forth.) EMDR has been shown to be effective in alleviating persistent symptoms stemming from past trauma (Shapiro, 1995), and therapists have expanded its use to sexual difficulties (Koehler et al., 2000).

What Happens in Therapy?

Many people are apprehensive about going to see a sex therapist, and it can be helpful to have some idea about what to expect. Each therapist works differently, but most follow certain steps. During the first interview the therapist will help the person or couple to clarify the problem and their feelings about it and to identify their goals for the therapy. The therapist will usually ask questions about when the difficulty first began, how it has developed over time, what the person thinks has caused it, and how she or he has already tried to resolve the problem. The therapist will likely gather some information about medical history and current physical functioning and then make referrals, if necessary, for further physical screenings.

Over the next few sessions (most therapy occurs in 1-hour weekly sessions) the therapist may gather more extensive sexual, personal, and relationship histories. During these sessions the therapist will screen for psychological problems that could interfere with therapy, explore whether the clients have a lifestyle conducive to a good emotional and sexual relationship, and determine whether they have problems with substance abuse or domestic violence.

Once the therapist and the individual or couple more fully realize the nature of the difficulty and have defined the therapy goals, the therapist helps the clients understand and overcome obstacles to meeting the goals as the sessions continue. The therapist often gives assignments, such as masturbation or sensate focus exercises, for the clients to do between therapy sessions. Successes and difficulties with the assignments are discussed at subsequent meetings. Therapy is terminated when the clients reach their goals. It is often helpful for clients to leave with a plan for continuing and maintaining progress. The therapist and clients may also plan one or more follow-up sessions.

Unethical Relationships: Sex Between Therapist and Client

It is highly unethical for professional therapists to engage in sexual relationships with clients whom they have in treatment (Lamb et al., 2003; Reamer, 2003). It is the professional's responsibility to set boundaries that ensure the integrity of the therapeutic relationship (Norris et al., 2003). Psychiatry, psychology, social work, and counseling professional associations have codes of ethics against sexual relations between psychotherapists and their clients. The American Association for Marriage and Family Therapy prohibits sexual contact for 2 years after therapy has ended, and many professionals believe that sex with a former client is unethical at any time (Berkman et al., 2000). In addition, some states have criminalized sexual behavior

Critical Thinking Question

What do you think the legal and professional consequences should be for a therapist who is sexual with a client?

with patients. However, research has found that up to 3% of female therapists and 12% of male therapists admit to having sexual contact with a current client (Berkman et al., 2000).

If a sexual relationship develops in the context of therapy, attention would likely be diverted from the client's original concerns and the preexisting problems would not be resolved (Pope, 2000). In addition, the sexual involvement can have other negative effects on the client (Plaut, 1996). Research has indicated that women who experienced sexual contact with their therapists (including psychotherapists in general, not just sex therapists) felt greater mistrust of and anger toward men and therapists than did a control group of women. They also experienced more psychological and psychosomatic symptoms, including anger, shame, anxiety, and depression (Finger, 2000; Regehr & Glancy, 1995). If at any time your therapist makes verbal or physical sexual advances toward you, you have every right to leave immediately and terminate therapy. Furthermore, it would be helpful to others who might become victims of this abuse of professional power if you reported this incident to the state licensing board for the therapist's profession (Schoener, 1995). ■

Selecting a Therapist

Depending on your situation, you may wish to see a therapist alone or with your partner. Many women who want to learn to experience orgasm may not have an available partner or may decide that they prefer to attain orgasm initially by self-stimulation; the same may be true for men with ejaculation or erection problems. Others may not have a partner, or their partner may not be willing to be involved in treatment. Individual therapy can be effective, but most therapists believe that a couple's sexual functioning, including difficulties one or the other may experience, is based on their interaction. Therefore most counseling is done with both partners.

To select a therapist, you might ask your sexuality course instructor or health care practitioner for referrals or contact either the American Association of Sex Educators, Therapists, and Counselors or the American Board of Sexology (see the "Web Resources" section at the end of this chapter for links to these organizations' Web sites). You may have a preference for a male or female therapist, or one with a particular therapeutic approach.

After consulting some of these sources, you should have several potential therapists from which to choose. In making your selection, you should consider several factors. A basic criterion is training; professionals from a variety of backgrounds do sex therapy. The title "sex therapist" does not ensure competence. There are few regulations on the use of that title (McCarthy & McCarthy, 2003). At this time few advanced degree programs in sex therapy are available. Rather, a professional who has specialized in this area should have a minimum of a master's degree and credentials as a psychiatrist, psychologist, social worker, or counselor. To do sex therapy, he or she should also have participated in sex therapy training, supervision, and workshops. It is highly appropriate for you to inquire about the specific training and certification of a prospective therapist.

To help determine whether a specific therapist will meet your needs, you may wish to cover the following topics at your first meeting:

1. What do you want from therapy? You and your therapist should reach an agreement on your and the therapist's goals. This agreement is sometimes referred to as the *therapy contract.*

2. What is the therapist's approach? You can ask about the general process in the therapy sessions (what the therapist will do) and what kind of participation is expected of you.

3. How do you feel about talking with the therapist? Therapy is not intended to be a light social interaction. It can be difficult. At times it can be quite uncomfortable for a client to discuss personal sexual concerns. However, for therapy to be useful, you will want to have the sense that the therapist is open and willing to understand you.

4. What is the therapist's fee for services, and how many sessions does she or he estimate will be needed? Fees vary considerably. Psychiatrists (who are medical doctors) are usually at the upper end, psychologists (who have Ph.D.'s) are in the middle, and social workers and counselors (who have master's degrees) are usually at the lower end. A higher fee does not necessarily indicate better sex therapy skills. Some practitioners offer sliding fee schedules based on the client's income.

After the initial interview you can decide to continue with that particular therapist or ask for a referral to another therapist more appropriate to your personality or needs. If you become dissatisfied once you begin therapy, discuss your concerns with your therapist. Decide jointly, if possible, whether to continue therapy or to seek another therapist. It is usually best to continue for several sessions before making a decision to change. Occasionally, clients expect magic cures rather than the difficult but rewarding work that therapy often demands. ■

Sex therapy can be a useful tool for individuals and couples who want to resolve their sexual difficulties. The process of sex therapy can also have additional benefits. Clients often experience reduced anxiety and improved communication, marital adjustment, and satisfaction following sex therapy (Ellison, 2000; Zilbergeld & Kilmann, 1984). Couples might also be more assertive and emotionally expressive with each other (Tullman et al., 1981). Individuals and couples who have met their goals can experience increased self-confidence and emotional satisfaction (Clement & Pfäfflin, 1980). The combined efforts of the therapist and client(s) can replace doubt and anxiety with the joy of satisfying sexual intimacy.

▶ Summary

Basics of Sexual Enhancement and Sex Therapy

- Self-awareness is a good beginning for therapy. Exploring one's own body increases one's knowledge and comfort and can prepare one for exploring a partner's body. (pp. 452–453)
- Good communication between partners is an important element of therapy. It can help work out specific problems and foster stronger relationships. (pp. 453–454)
- The experience of sensate focus, nondemand pleasuring shared by sexual partners, is an excellent vehicle for mutually enhancing sexual potentials. (pp. 454–456)
- Masturbation exercises are an effective way for an individual to learn about and experience sexual response. They can be enjoyed for themselves, and the acquired knowledge can be shared with a partner. (p. 456)
- Masturbating in each other's presence can be an excellent way for a couple to indicate to each other what kind of touching they find arousing. (p. 456)

Specific Suggestions for Women

- Therapy programs for anorgasmic women are based on progressive self-awareness activities. (pp. 456–457)
- Women who wish to become orgasmic during lovemaking with a partner can benefit from programs that start with sensate focus, mutual genital exploration, masturbation, and nondemand genital pleasuring by the partner. (pp. 457–459)
- A couple can increase the probability of female orgasm during intercourse by incorporating knowledge acquired during sensate focus and nondemand pleasuring and by combining intercourse with manual stimulation of the woman's clitoris (by herself or her partner). (pp. 457–458)
- Treatment for vaginismus generally involves promoting increased self-awareness and relaxation. Insertion of a lubricated finger (first one's own and later the partner's) into the vagina is an important next step in overcoming this condition. Penile insertion is the final phase of treatment for vaginismus. (p. 460)

Specific Suggestions for Men

- A variety of approaches can help a man learn to delay his ejaculation. Potentially helpful suggestions include ejaculating more frequently, having a second orgasm, using a more relaxed inter-course position, and openly communicating a need to modulate movements and/or engage in noncoital activities to reduce stimulation. (p. 460)
- If a couple has the time and inclination to work together in resolving premature ejaculation difficulties, the stop–start or squeeze technique is often effective. Antidepressant medication can also help delay ejaculation. (p. 461)
- A behavioral approach designed to reduce anxiety has proven successful in treating psychologically based erectile dysfunction. This treatment method has several phases: sensate focus, followed by genital stimulation, then penetration. (p. 462)
- Pills to treat erectile dysfunction, such as Viagra, Levitra, and Cialis, are the newest option to stimulate blood flow to the penis. (pp. 462–464)
- Vascular surgery, vasoactive injections, external vacuum constriction devices, and surgically implanted penile prostheses are options for men who have a permanent, physiologically caused inability to experience erections. (pp. 464–465)
- A behavioral approach for the treatment of male orgasmic disorder combines sensate focus with self-stimulation and partner manual stimulation, ultimately leading to intravaginal ejaculation. (p. 465)

Treating Hypoactive Sexual Desire

- Problems with hypoactive sexual desire often require more intensive therapy to help people understand and change their suppression and avoidance of sexual feelings. (pp. 465–466)

Seeking Professional Assistance

- The PLISSIT model outlines four progressive levels of sex therapy: permission, limited information, specific suggestions, and intensive therapy. (pp. 466–468)
- Intensive therapy often combines specific behavioral techniques with insight-oriented psychosocial therapy or with a systems theory approach that focuses on the function of the problem within the relationship. The use of EMDR is also being explored. (pp. 466–468)
- Professional counseling is often helpful and sometimes necessary in overcoming sexual difficulties. (p. 466)
- A skilled therapist can offer useful information, emotional support, a more objective perspective, problem-solving strategies, and specific sex therapy techniques. (p. 466)

- A lack of regulations governing sex therapy suggests that one should be careful in selecting a therapist. Referrals can be given by sex educators, health care practitioners, or the American Association of Sex Educators, Therapists, and Counselors. (p. 469)

Suggested Readings

Berman, Jennifer, and Laura Berman (2001). *For Women Only: A Revolutionary Guide to Overcoming Sexual Dysfunction and Reclaiming Your Sex Life.* New York: Henry Holt. A comprehensive handbook about female sexual arousal and treatments for sexual problems.

Heiman, Julia, and Joseph LoPiccolo (1988). *Becoming Orgasmic: A Sexual and Personal Growth Program for Women.* Englewood Cliffs, NJ: Prentice Hall. An excellent guide for women who want to learn to experience orgasm and enhance their sexual pleasure by themselves or with a partner.

McCarthy, Barry, and Emily McCarthy (2003). *Rekindling Desire: A Step-by-Step Program to Help Low-Sex and No-Sex Marriages.* New York: Brunner-Routledge. A 10-step program to help couples revitalize the sex and intimacy in their relationships.

Renshaw, Domeena (1995). *Seven Weeks to Better Sex.* New York: Random House. A collection of questionnaires and experiences to enhance communication and sexual expression.

Schnarch, David (1997). *Passionate Marriage.* New York: W. W. Norton. A book that illustrates the connection between personal development and enhanced sexual potential.

Yaffe, Maurice, and Elizabeth Fenwick (1992). *Sexual Happiness for Men: A Practical Approach.* New York: Henry Holt. A book that offers step-by-step guidelines for men who want to enhance their sexuality or resolve specific difficulties.

Resource

Impotence Anonymous is a self-help group for men and their partners. For more information about the more than 100 chapters in the United States, call 1-800-669-1603, or send a stamped, self-addressed envelope to P.O. Box 410, Bowie, MD 20718.

Web Resources

Your *Our Sexuality* Web site **http://psychology.wadsworth.com/crooksbaur9e/** has direct links to the Web sites described below. These links are checked often for changes, dead links, and new additions.

American Association of Sex Educators, Therapists, and Counselors
This Web site has listings of sex therapists throughout the country that the Association has certified.

American Board of Sexology
This Web site has listings of sex therapists throughout the country that the Board has certified.

Pelvic Pain
Details about pain during intercourse or menstruation can be found on this Web site.

Sex Therapy Advice
Information and advice about sexual problems can be found on this self-help Web site.

Go Ask Alice!
This is a refreshingly frank and lively Web site, sponsored by Columbia University, where questions posed about common and uncommon sexual concerns are answered with sensitivity and wit. Look for Go Ask Alice's forum on sexual health as well.

Dr. Ruth
Dr. Ruth Westheimer offers a frank discussion of sexual issues in a fun and informative format. This Web page includes posted answers to visitors' questions.

Viagra Information
On this site the U.S. Food and Drug Administration provides consumers with some basic information on Viagra, including some precautions about who should not take this medication.

Our Sexuality Web Site
For online resources directly related to this book, go to **http://psychology.wadsworth.com/crooksbaur9e/**. You will find interactive exercises, study questions, chapter outlines, an online version of this text's glossary, and Web links and activities that complement your CD-ROM.

InfoTrac® College Edition Online Library
http://infotrac.thomsonlearning.com/
InfoTrac College Edition is an online searchable library that includes a multitude of journals, many of which are specific to human sexuality. These journals include *Archives of Sexual Behavior, Archives of Sexual Health Behavior, Canadian Journal of Human Sexuality, Hispanic Journal of the Behavioral Sciences, Journal of Cross-Cultural Psychology, Journal of Physical Education, Recreation, and Dance, Journal of Sex Research,* and *Sex Roles.* You may search topics suggested in the margins of this chapter or terms of your own.

Our Sexuality CD-ROM
Use your CD-ROM for further study of the concepts in this chapter. Your CD-ROM provides animations of difficult concepts, video clips of real people discussing sexuality, critical thinking questions, chapter quizzing, and more.

CHAPTER 17

Sexually Transmitted Diseases

© Bill Freeman/PhotoEdit

▶ **Bacterial Infections**

Why do health authorities now consider chlamydia infections a major health problem?

What kinds of complications can accompany gonorrhea?

Why are health authorities concerned about syphilis in the United States?

▶ **Viral Infections**

Can the herpes virus be transmitted if an open sore is not present?

Why do health practitioners consider genital warts a serious problem?

Can both hepatitis A and hepatitis B be transmitted sexually? What symptoms are associated with hepatitis?

▶ **Common Vaginal Infections**

What is a male partner's role in transmitting bacterial vaginosis?

What factors are associated with the development of candidiasis, and how is this infection treated?

How common is trichomoniasis, and what possible complications are associated with this infection?

▶ **Ectoparasitic Infections**

Can pubic lice be transmitted other than by sexual interaction?

How contagious is scabies, what are its symptoms, and how is it treated?

▶ **Acquired Immunodeficiency Syndrome (AIDS)**

How is HIV transmitted, and what behaviors put one at risk for becoming infected with HIV?

Among what portions of the population is AIDS currently increasing most rapidly? Has there been significant progress in the search for either an effective treatment or a cure for this disease?

▶ **Preventing Sexually Transmitted Diseases**

What are some effective methods of prevention that can reduce the likelihood of contracting an STD?

The possibility of getting a sexually transmitted disease has caused me to be extremely cautious and selective about whom I choose to be sexual with. It also makes every decision in a sexual relationship so critical and has made me much more careful in the choices I make. (Authors' files)

In this chapter we discuss a variety of **sexually transmitted diseases (STDs)***—that is, diseases that can be transmitted through sexual interaction. Table 17.1 summarizes the STDs described in this chapter. Some of these diseases are curable; others are not. As we will see, the consequences of STDs—such as compromised health, pain and discomfort, infertility, even death—can adversely affect the quality of our lives. It is estimated that 15 million new cases of STDs occur each year in the United States and that, globally, annual new cases of STDs probably exceed 400 million (Darroch & Frost, 1999; Tao et al., 2000).

Our purpose in including a chapter on STDs is not to discourage you from exploring the joys of sexuality. Rather, we wish to facilitate your process of making good decisions by presenting a realistic picture of what STDs are, how to recognize them, what should be done to treat them, and what measures can be taken to avoid contracting or transmitting them. We believe that this information is especially relevant to our college-age readers for the following reasons:

- A substantial majority of all STDs in the United States occur among 15- to 25-year-olds (Calvert, 2003; Whitten et al., 2003). It is estimated that two-thirds of the more than 15 million STDs diagnosed annually in the United States occur among people under the age of 25 (Guthrie & Bates, 2003; Summers et al., 2002).
- Approximately 3 million teenagers (1 in 4 sexually experienced adolescents) are infected with one or more STDs each year (Feroli & Burstein, 2003).
- About 1 in 4 people contracts an STD by age 21 (Feroli & Burstein, 2003).
- Adolescents and young adults are at considerably higher risk for acquiring STDs than older adults (Calvert, 2003; Centers for Disease Control, 2000b; Whitten et al., 2003).
- Teenage women, age 15 to 19, have the highest rates of chlamydia and gonorrhea infections (both potentially highly damaging STDs) of any age group in the United States (Calvert, 2003; Feroli & Burstein, 2003). Three-fourths of all reported cases of chlamydia occur among 15- to 24-year-olds (Ginocchio et al., 2003).
- Pelvic inflammatory disease (PID), a prevalent and serious consequence of STDs, occurs with a disproportionately high frequency in adolescent and young adult women, who account for a substantial majority of cases diagnosed each year in the United States (Feroli & Burstein, 2003; Shrier et al., 2000).
- The highest incidence of genital warts, an extremely common STD in North America, occurs among young adults, age 15 to 28 (Calvert, 2003; Sellors et al., 2003).
- The largest proportion of AIDS cases in the United States occurs among people in their 20s and 30s who were infected with the AIDS virus (HIV) in their teens or 20s (Murphy et al., 2003). Half of new HIV infections occur among people younger than 25 years (Feroli & Burstein, 2003; Whitten et al., 2003).

You may wonder why our discussion of HIV/AIDS is postponed until the later in this chapter. Certainly AIDS has received far more attention in the media in recent years than any of the other diseases discussed in this chapter. This emphasis on AIDS, although understandable in view of the continuing worldwide spread of this deadly disease, tends to obscure the fact that many other STDs are substantially more prevalent. Furthermore, many of these commonly occurring STDs, such as chlamydia and genital warts, pose major health risks that are escalating in proportion to the increasing incidence of these diseases.

Many factors contribute to the epidemic of STDs in the United States. Engaging in risky sexual behavior, such as having multiple sexual partners and unprotected (condomless) sex, is a prime reason for the high incidence of STDs. Such behavior is especially prevalent during adolescence and early adulthood, when the incidence of STDs is the highest (Feroli & Burstein, 2003). It is also believed that increased use of oral contraceptives has contributed to the epidemic of STDs both by increasing susceptibility of women to some STDs and by reducing the use of condoms, a contraceptive method known to offer some protection

---

*Some health professionals prefer to call these conditions sexually transmitted infections, or STIs. The terms STD and STI are essentially interchangeable, but STD is the preferred term in the United States and STI is the preferred term internationally.

AT A GLANCE

TABLE 17.1 Common Sexually Transmitted Diseases: Transmission, Symptoms, and Treatment

STD	Transmission	Symptoms	Treatment(s)
Chlamydia	• The *Chlamydia trachomatis* bacterium is passed through sexual contact. • Infection can spread from one body site to another via fingers.	• **Women:** Pelvic inflammatory disease, disrupted menstruation, pelvic pain, raised temperature, nausea, vomiting, headache, infertility, and ectopic pregnancy. • **Men:** Urethra infection discharge and burning during urination; with epididymitis, heaviness in and painful swelling at bottom of affected testis, inflammation of scrotum.	• Doxycycline for 7 days, or one dose of azithromycin.
Gonorrhea	• The *Neisseria gonorrhoeae* bacterium is passed through penile–vaginal, oral–genital, oral–anal, or genital–anal contact.	• **Women:** Green or yellowish discharge (usually remains undetected); pelvic inflammatory disease may develop. • **Men:** Cloudy discharge from penis and burning during urination; complications include painful swelling at bottom of affected testis and inflammation of scrotum.	• Dual therapy of one dose of ceftriaxone, cefixime, ciprofloxacin, levofloxacin, or ofloxacin plus one dose of azithromycin (or doxycycline for 7 days)
Nongonococcal urethritis (NGU)	• Primarily caused by various bacteria transmitted through coitus. • Some NGU results from allergic reactions or from *Trichomonas* infection.	• **Women:** Mild discharge of pus from vagina (often remains undetected). • **Men:** Discharge from penis and irritation during urination.	• One dose of azithromycin, or doxycycline for 7 days.
Syphilis	• The *Treponema pallidum* bacterium is passed from open lesions during penile–vaginal, oral–genital, oral–anal, or genital–anal contact.	• **Primary Stage:** Painless chancre at site where bacterium entered body. • **Secondary Stage:** Chancre disappears, and generalized skin rash appears. • **Latent Stage:** There may be no visible symptoms. • **Tertiary Stage:** Heart failure, blindness, mental disturbance, and more; death may result.	• Benzathine penicillin G, doxycycline, erythromycin, or ceftriaxone.
Chancroid	• The *Haemophilus ducreyi* bacterium is passed through penile–vaginal, oral–genital, oral–anal, or genital–anal contact.	• Small bumps in genital regions eventually rupture and form painful, soft ulcers that emit a foul-smelling discharge.	• One dose of either ceftriaxone or azithromycin, or 7 days of erythromycin, or 3 days of ciprofloxacin.
Herpes	• HSV-2 (genital herpes virus) passed primarily through penile–vaginal, oral–genital, oral–anal, or genital–anal contact. • HSV-1 (oral herpes) passed by kissing or oral–genital contact.	• Small painful red bumps appear in the genital region or mouth. • Bumps become painful blisters and eventually rupture to form wet, open sores.	• No known cure. • A variety of treatments can reduce symptoms. • Oral acyclovir, valacyclovir, or famciclovir promote healing and suppress recurrent outbreaks.
Genital warts	• Human papillomavirus (HPV) is passed primarily through penile–vaginal, oral–genital, oral–anal, or genital–anal contact.	• Hard and yellow-gray growths on dry skin areas. • Soft, pinkish-red, and cauliflower-like growths on moist areas.	• Freezing, application of topical agents, cauterization, surgical removal, or vaporization by carbon dioxide laser.

TABLE **17.1** **continued**

STD	Transmission	Symptoms	Treatment(s)
Viral hepatitis	• Hepatitis B virus can be passed through blood, semen, vaginal secretions, and saliva. • Manual, oral, or penile stimulation of anus is strongly associated with spread of hepatitis B. • Hepatitis A is spread by means of oral–anal contact, especially when the mouth encounters fecal matter. • Hepatitis C is spread through intravenous drug use and less frequently through contaminated blood products, sexual contact, or mother-to-fetus or mother-to-infant contact.	• Varies from no symptoms to mild, flulike symptoms to an incapacitating illness characterized by high fever, vomiting, and severe abdominal pain.	• No specific treatment for hepatitis A and B. • Bed rest and adequate fluid intake. • Combination therapy with interferon and ribavirin may be effective against hepatitis C.
Bacterial vaginosis	• Different types of bacterial microorganisms are passed through coitus.	• **Women:** Fishy- or musty-smelling, light-gray thin discharge (consistency of flour paste). • **Men:** Usually asymptomatic.	• Metronidazole (Flagyl) by mouth. • Intravaginal applications of topical metronidazole gel or clindamycin cream.
Candidiasis (yeast infection)	• The fungus *Candida albicans* accelerates growth when normal chemical balance of the vagina is disturbed. • Can be passed through sexual interaction.	• **Women:** White "cheesy" discharge, irritation of vaginal and vulval tissues. • **Men:** Usually asymptomatic but may have itching or reddening of the penis and burning during urination.	• Vaginal suppositories or topical cream, such as clotrimazole and miconazole. • Oral fluconazole.
Trichomoniasis	• The protozoan parasite *Trichomonas vaginalis* is usually passed through sexual contact.	• **Women:** White or yellow vaginal discharge with unpleasant odor; vulva is sore and irritated. • **Men:** Usually asymptomatic but may have urethral discharge, urge to urinate frequently, or painful urination.	• One dose of metronidazole (Flagyl) for women and men.
Pubic lice ("crabs")	• Pubic louse is spread through body contact or through shared clothing or bedding.	• Persistent itching. • Lice are visible and can be located in pubic or other body hair.	• 1% permethrin cream for body areas and 1% Lindane shampoo for hair.
Scabies	• Highly contagious. • Can be passed by close physical contact (sexual and nonsexual).	• Small bumps and a red rash that itch intensely (especially at night).	• 5% permethrin lotion or cream.
Acquired immunodeficiency syndrome (AIDS)	• Blood, semen, and vaginal fluids are the major vehicles for transmitting HIV (which attacks the immune system). • Passed primarily through penile–vaginal, oral–genital, oral–anal, or genital–anal contact or by needle sharing among injection drug users.	• Varies with the types of opportunistic infections or cancers that can afflict an infected person. • Common symptoms include fever, night sweats, weight loss, chronic fatigue, swollen lymph nodes, diarrhea and/or bloody stool, atypical bruising or bleeding, skin rashes, headache, chronic cough, and a whitish coating on the tongue or throat.	• Commence treatment with a combination of three or more antiretroviral drugs (HAART) when CD4 count is significantly low. • Specific treatments may be necessary to treat opportunistic infections and tumors.

LET'S TALK ABOUT IT

Telling a Partner

Most of us would find it difficult to discuss with our lover(s) the possibility that we have transmitted a disease to her or him during sexual activity. Because of the stigma often associated with STDs, it can be bad enough admitting to yourself that you have one of these diseases. The need to tell others that they might have "caught" something from you may seem like a formidable task. You might fear that such a revelation will jeopardize a valued relationship, or you might worry that you will be considered "dirty." In relationships presumed to be monogamous, you might fear that telling your partner about an STD will threaten mutual trust. At the same time, however, concealing a sex-related illness places a good deal more at risk in the long run.

Most important, not disclosing the existence of an STD risks the health of your partner(s). Many people may not have symptoms and thus may not become aware that they have contracted a disease until they discover it for themselves, perhaps only after they have developed serious complications. Furthermore, if a lover remains untreated, she or he may reinfect you even after you have been cured. Unlike some diseases (such as measles and chicken pox), STDs do not provide immunity against future infections. You can get one, give it to your lover, be cured, and then get it back again if he or she remains untreated.

The following suggestions provide some guidelines for telling a partner about your STD. Remember, these are only suggestions that have worked for some people; they may need to be modified to fit your particular circumstances. This sensitive issue requires thoughtful consideration and planning.

1. Be honest. There is nothing to be gained by downplaying the potential risks associated with STDs. If you tell a partner, "I have this little drip, but it probably means nothing," you may regret it. Be sure your partner understands the importance of obtaining a medical evaluation.

2. Even if you suspect that your partner may have been the source of your infection, there is little to be gained by blaming him or her. Instead, you may wish simply to acknowledge that you have the disease and are concerned that your partner gets proper medical attention.

3. Your attitude may have a considerable effect on how your partner receives the news. If you display high levels of anxiety, guilt, fear, or disgust, your partner may reflect these feelings in her or his response. Try to present the facts in as clear and calm a fashion as you can manage.

4. Be sensitive to your partner's feelings. Be prepared for reactions of anger or resentment. These are understandable initial responses. Being supportive and demonstrating a willingness to listen without becoming defensive may be the best tactics for diffusing negative responses.

5. Engaging in sexual intimacies after you become aware of your condition and before you obtain medical assurances that you are no longer contagious is clearly inappropriate. Discuss with your partner that abstinence from sexual intercourse is crucial for persons who are being treated for an STD or whose partners are undergoing treatment.

6. Medical examinations and treatments for STDs, when necessary, can be a financial burden. Offering to pay for some or all of these expenses may help to maintain (or reestablish) goodwill in your relationship.

---

against infection. Lack of adequate public health measures and limited access to effective systems for prevention and treatment of STDs also contribute to this ongoing epidemic. In addition, many health care providers in the United States "may not be diagnosing and treating STDs properly" (Kirchner & Emmert, 2000, p. 55). Furthermore, many practitioners are reluctant to ask questions about their patients' sexual behaviors, thus missing opportunities for STD-related counseling, diagnosis, and treatment. A recent nationally representative survey of 3,390 U.S. adults, ages 18 to 64, found that only 28% reported being asked about STDs during routine medical checkups (Tao et al., 2000).

The spread of STDs is facilitated by the unfortunate fact that many of these diseases do not produce obvious symptoms. In some cases, particularly among women, there may be no outward signs at all. Under these circumstances people may unknowingly infect others. In addition, feelings of guilt and embarrassment that often accompany having an STD may prevent people from seeking adequate treatment or from informing their sexual partners. In the boxed discussion "Telling a Partner" we explore why this action is important and suggest ways to more easily disclose such information.

In the following sections we focus on the most common STDs. We also provide an expanded discussion of AIDS and the progress being made in treating this dreadful disease. The Centers for Disease Control and Prevention (CDC) issue updated guidelines for treating STDs every 4 to 5 years. The most recent guidelines, issued in May 2002 (Centers for Disease Control, 2002g), are the basis for most of the treatment information provided for the diseases discussed in this chapter.

If you want more information, we recommend that you contact your county health service or STD clinic, or that you call the National STD Hotline.* These services can answer questions, send free literature, and, most important, give you the name and phone number of a local physician or public clinic that will treat STDs for free or at minimal cost.

▶ Bacterial Infections

How About You?

Have you ever told a partner or had a partner tell you about having an STD? If so, how did you or your partner respond to this disclosure?

A variety of STDs are caused by bacterial agents. We begin this section with a discussion of chlamydia, one of the most prevalent and damaging of all STDs. The other bacterial infections we describe are gonorrhea, nongonococcal urethritis, syphilis, and chancroid. We discuss bacterial vaginosis, a common vaginal infection, in a later section of this chapter.

Chlamydia Infection

Chlamydia (cluh-MID-ee-uh) is caused by *Chlamydia trachomatis,* a bacterial microorganism that grows in body cells. This organism is now recognized as the cause of a diverse group of genital infections and is a common cause of preventable blindness.

Chlamydia Urogenital infection caused by the bacterium *Chlamydia trachomatis.*

Incidence and Transmission

Chlamydia infections are among the most prevalent and most damaging of all STDs. Chlamydia is the most common bacterial STD in the United States and the most prevalent infectious disease reported to state health departments throughout the United States (Bachman et al., 2003; Paukku et al., 2003b). Furthermore, during the period 1987–1999 the annual reported rate of chlamydia infections increased 400% (Bachman et al., 2003). An estimated 3–5 million American men, women, and infants develop a chlamydia infection each year (Ginocchio et al., 2003; Schillinger et al., 2003). Sexually active teenagers have higher infection rates than any other age group (Calvert, 2003; Kirchner & Emmert, 2000). Young women who use oral contraceptives seem to be at particularly high risk for developing chlamydia infection if they are exposed to the bacterium (Ivey, 1997). Research has also identified douching as a risk factor for chlamydia infection (Peters et al., 2000; Scholes et al., 1998). Douching one or more times per month can adversely alter the balance of normal vaginal bacteria (lactobacilli) that help maintain a healthy vaginal environment, thus increasing susceptibility to infection by *Chlamydia trachomatis* and/or other bacterial agents (Ness et al., 2003).

Chlamydia disease is transmitted primarily through sexual contact (Schillinger et al., 2003; Srugo et al., 2000). It can also be spread by fingers from one body site to another, such as from the genitals to the eyes.

Symptoms and Complications

Two general types of genital chlamydia infections affect females. The first of these, infection of the mucosa of the lower reproductive tract, commonly takes the form of an inflammation of the urethral tube or an infection of the cervix. In both cases women experience few or no symptoms (Calvert, 2003; Ginocchio et al., 2003). When symptoms do occur, they include a mild irritation or itching of the genital tissues, burning during urination, and a slight vaginal discharge.

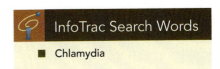
InfoTrac Search Words

■ Chlamydia

The second type of genital chlamydia infection in women is invasive infection of the upper reproductive tract, expressed as **pelvic inflammatory disease (PID).** PID typically occurs when bacteria that cause chlamydia or gonorrhea spread from the cervix upward, infecting the lining of the uterus *(endometritis),* the fallopian tubes *(salpingitis),* and possibly the ovaries and other adjacent abdominal structures (Feroli & Burstein, 2003; K. Miller et al., 2003). Approximately 10% of U.S. women will develop PID during their reproductive years (Miller & Graves, 2000). Chlamydia accounts for most of the more than 1 million

Pelvic inflammatory disease (PID) An infection in the uterus and pelvic cavity.

---

*The National Sexually Transmitted Disease Hotline can be dialed toll-free from 8:00 A.M. to 8:00 P.M. on weekdays and from 10:00 A.M. to 6:00 P.M. on weekends, Pacific time. The number is (800) 227-8922.

recognized cases of PID that occur annually in the United States (Paukku et al., 2003; Shrier et al., 2000). An estimated 20–40% of women with chlamydia will develop PID if these infections are not adequately treated (Cook et al., 2001; H. Miller et al., 1999). Adolescents and women in their early 20s have the highest PID rates in the United States (Feroli & Burstein, 2003; Messner, 2003).

InfoTrac Search Words

■ Pelvic inflammatory disease

PID resulting from chlamydia infection often produces a variety of symptoms, which can include disrupted menstrual periods, chronic pelvic pain, lower back pain, fever, nausea, vomiting, and headache. Salpingitis caused by chlamydia infection is the primary preventable cause of female infertility and ectopic pregnancy (Donovan, 2004; Magid et al., 2003; Schillinger et al., 2003). Even after PID has been effectively treated, residual scar tissue in the fallopian tubes can leave some women sterile (Hillis et al., 1997).

A woman who has had PID should be cautioned about the use of the IUD as a method of contraception. An IUD does not prevent fertilization (see Chapter 11 for an explanation of how the IUD prevents pregnancy); thus a tiny sperm cell could negotiate a partially blocked area of a scarred fallopian tube and fertilize an ovum that, because of its larger size, subsequently becomes lodged in the scarred tube. The result is an *ectopic pregnancy*, a serious hazard to the woman. The incidence of ectopic pregnancies in the United States has increased dramatically in the last two decades, largely because of an escalation in the occurrence of chlamydia infections.

In men chlamydia is estimated to be the cause of approximately half the cases of *epididymitis* (infection of the epididymis) and *nongonococcal urethritis* (NGU; infection of the urethral tube not caused by gonorrhea) (Donovan, 2004; Magid et al., 2003). The symptoms of epididymitis include a sensation of heaviness in the affected testis, inflammation of the scrotal skin, and the formation of a small area of hard, painful swelling at the bottom of the testis. Symptoms of NGU include a discharge from the penis and burning during urination (more details are provided in a later section on NGU).

One of the most disheartening aspects of chlamydia is that symptoms are either minimal or nonexistent in up to 90% of infected women and 60% of infected men (Ginocchio et al., 2003). Most women and men with rectal chlamydia infections also manifest few or no symptoms (Centers for Disease Control, 2002g). Laboratory diagnostic tests are necessary to confirm chlamydia infections. Cultures are typically not required for diagnosis, however, and the procedure is relatively simple and inexpensive. Recently introduced laboratory tests that can be performed on urine have made testing for chlamydia infection even easier (Donovan, 2004; Ginocchio et al., 2003).

Trachoma A chronic, contagious form of conjunctivitis caused by chlamydia infections.

Conjunctivitis Inflammation of the mucous membrane that lines the inner surface of the eyelid and the exposed surface of the eyeball.

Another complication associated with *Chlamydia trachomatis* is **trachoma** (truh-KOH-muh), a chronic, contagious form of **conjunctivitis** (kun-junk-ti-VIE-tus) (inflammation of the mucous membrane that lines the inner surface of the eyelid and the exposed surface of the eyeball). Trachoma is the world's leading cause of preventable blindness; it is particularly prevalent in Asia and Africa. *Chlamydia trachomatis* is also the most common cause of eye infections (conjunctivitis) in newborns, who can become infected as they pass through the birth canal (Esquivel et al., 2003; S. Wu et al., 2003). In addition, many babies of infected mothers will develop pneumonia caused by chlamydia infection during the first few months of their lives (Esquivel et al., 2003; S. Wu et al., 2003). Chlamydia infection in pregnant women can also lead to premature delivery or fetal death (Sharts-Hopco, 1997; Todd et al., 1997). The CDC recommends that pregnant women be tested for chlamydia during their first prenatal visit (Centers for Disease Control, 2002g).

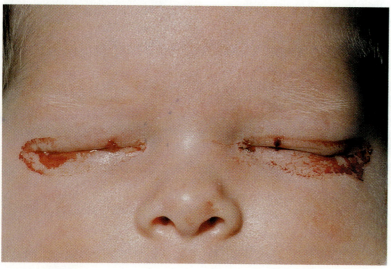

Chlamydia conjunctivitis in a newborn, acquired from an infected mother during birth.

Treatment

CDC guidelines suggest treating uncomplicated chlamydia infections with a 7-day regimen of doxycycline by mouth or a single

1-gram dose of azithromycin. All sexual partners exposed to chlamydia should be examined for STDs and treated if necessary (Ginocchio et al., 2003). Most recurrent chlamydia infections in women are the result of reexposure to infected male sex partners who were not treated (Schillinger et al., 2003).

To reduce the risk of an infant developing chlamydia conjunctivitis after passing through the birth canal of an infected mother, either erythromycin or tetracycline ointment is put into the eyes of exposed newborns as soon as possible after birth.

Gonorrhea

Gonorrhea (gah-nuh-REE-uh), known in street language as "the clap," is an STD caused by the bacterium *Neisseria gonorrhoeae* (also called gonococcus).

Gonorrhea An STD that initially causes inflammation of mucous membranes.

Incidence and Transmission

Gonorrhea is a common communicable disease. Estimates of its prevalence in the U.S. population range from 600,000 to more than 1 million new infections annually. The late 1970s witnessed the beginning of an intensified public health effort to curtail gonorrhea infections in the United States. These efforts resulted in a downward trend in the overall incidence of gonorrhea in the U.S. population, a decline that continued until 1998, when the number of reported cases rose by about 10% over the previous year (Centers for Disease Control, 2000d). Gonorrhea rates remain exceptionally high among teenagers and young adults, especially in lower socioeconomic ethnic minority communities (Calvert, 2003; Emmert & Kirchner, 2000; Mertz et al., 2000). In contrast to the general decline in U.S. gonorrhea rates that has occurred over most of the last two decades, the world's largest nation, China, has experienced a marked resurgence of gonorrhea and other STDs in recent years, as described in the following "Sexuality and Diversity" discussion.

Sexuality and Diversity

STDs in China: A Reemerging Epidemic

The overall incidence of STDs in China, a nation of more than 1.3 billion people, is considerably lower than in many other developing countries in Africa and Asia. However, this situation is changing as the prevalence of STDs in China rapidly escalates. Before the founding of the People's Republic of China in 1949, syphilis, gonorrhea, and other STDs were prevalent (X. Chen et al., 2000; M. Cohen et al., 2000). The spread of STDs in pre-revolution China was fueled by drug use, widespread commercial sex work, and poverty (M. Cohen et al., 2000). When Mao Zedong came to power, his government implemented a massive campaign to wipe out STDs. Mao's approach was heavy-handed but successful. By 1964 STDs were virtually eradicated from China (X. Chen et al., 2000; M. Cohen et al., 2000). However, this situation changed rapidly after China implemented its open-door policy in the 1980s, which encouraged contact with the Western world, promoted rapid migration of people from rural to urban areas, and led to changes in the economic and sociocultural environments of China.

In the last two decades commercial sex work has reemerged, and findings from a number of studies have demonstrated that STDs (including HIV/AIDS) and the behaviors that spread them are rapidly increasing in China (Beyrer, 2003; H. Liu et al., 2003; Parish et al., 2003). For example, one study reported incidence trends for four STDs—gonorrhea, syphilis, genital warts, and nongonococcal urethritis—for the period 1989–1998. The total combined incidence of these four STDs per 100,000 inhabitants increased from 12.32 in 1989 to 50.68 in 1998, a gain of 311%. Of the four diseases evaluated, gonorrhea was shown to have the highest prevalence in 1998 (X. Chen et al., 2000).

A more recent study of the prevalence of chlamydia infections in China provides further evidence of an epidemic of STDs in this nation and of the extent of sexual risk taking among Chinese adults. Using a nationally representative sample, investigators found relatively high incidences of chlamydia in both men (2.1%) and women (2.6%) (Parish et al., 2003). The prevalence rates of chlamydia among urban Chinese are as high as or higher than those reported in developed Western nations, and the incidence of chlamydia among rural Chinese is comparable to published prevalence rates for several African nations. Clearly, "a population prevalence of any untreated STD at the levels found in Africa is a crisis for China" (Beyrer, 2003, p. 1303).

The first case of AIDS in China was reported in 1985 (Ammann, 2000). Over the next few years HIV infection was sporadically reported in a small number of people who were either primarily foreigners granted access to China or returning "overseas Chinese" (Ammann, 2000). Rapid spread of HIV began in 1995, and an estimated 800,000 to 1,500,000 cumulative cases of HIV infection had occurred in China by the end of 2001 (Choi et al., 2003b). Major outbreaks of HIV infection among rural blood donors in several central Chinese provinces occurred in the 1990s. For-profit agencies operating in rural areas of these provinces paid poor farmers for their blood, pooled the blood and extracted profitable plasma, and then reinjected the blood back into the donors. Blood collectors cut costs by reusing equipment repeatedly without proper sterilization. In many impoverished villages a high percentage of young men and women repeatedly sold their blood, which resulted in high rates of HIV infection in some communities (Beyrer, 2003). Nearly the entire adult population of some villages was infected almost simultaneously in the 1990s, and now the victims, including many married couples, are sick and dying, often almost in unison (Rosenthal, 2002). One heartbreaking result of this horrific tragedy is the countless number of destitute orphans who lack funds for school and often go hungry.

The critical issue for HIV/AIDS in China involves China's vulnerability to a widespread heterosexual HIV epidemic. Clearly, the recent data demonstrating an overall escalation in STD rates, especially the high incidence of chlamydia infection and the increased activity of commercial sex workers in China, suggest that risky sexual behaviors are on the rise. A recent nationally representative study revealed that 9.3% of surveyed men reported inconsistent condom use in sex relations with sex workers (Parish et al., 2003). This pattern of sexual risk taking has been documented in Thailand and Cambodia, where Asia's worst HIV epidemics have occurred thus far (Rojanapithayakorn & Hannenberg, 1996; Ryan et al., 1998). In both these countries high rates of men having sex with both primary partners and sex workers, without condom protection, drove explosive heterosexual epidemics throughout the 1990s. The growing concern is that China will follow this same pattern, thus becoming the site of the next and possibly worst Asian HIV epidemic. A number of public health specialists, who are not overly optimistic about China's chance for averting an HIV epidemic, estimate that as many as 10 million Chinese will be infected with HIV by 2010 (Choi et al., 2003b; Wang et al., 2001). If current infection trends persist in China, "absolute numbers of individuals with HIV infection are projected to surpass current numbers in the United States within 2 years and those in South Africa (currently the highest) within a decade" (Parish et al., 2003, p. 1265).

National government-supported public health campaigns to encourage sex workers and their clients to use condoms have had a major effect on reducing HIV infection rates in Thailand and Cambodia in recent years (Beyrer, 2003). Unfortunately, open publicity and education about condom use by sex workers in China is difficult because prostitution remains illegal in China and police and security agencies continue to harass and arrest sex workers instead of educating them about condom use (Beyrer, 2003). We can only hope that government officials will change their tactics as the wisdom of education versus harassment becomes increasingly clear. China could mobilize an effective national campaign against HIV/AIDS similar to the successful effort in Thailand. Currently, the Chinese government controls the media, and every village has a government official who monitors menstrual cycles as part of China's one-child policy. If government officials would commit to preventing HIV infections with the same level of zealousness that they apply to preventing unauthorized births, they could curtail the spread of this disease and thus aid immeasurably in averting major expansion of the global HIV pandemic.

The gonococcus bacterium thrives in the warm mucous membrane tissues of the genitals, anus, and throat. Its mode of transmission is by sexual contact—penile–vaginal, oral–genital, oral–anal, or genital–anal.

Symptoms and Complications

Early symptoms of gonorrhea infection are more likely to be evident in men than in women (Centers for Disease Control, 2002g). Most men who experience gonococcal urethritis have some symptoms, ranging from mild to pronounced. However, it is not uncommon for men with this type of infection to have no symptoms and yet be potentially infectious. The incidence of asymptomatic gonorrhea is considerably greater in women; as many as 80% will not detect the disease until it has progressed considerably (Nicholas, 1998).

Early Symptoms in the Male In men early symptoms typically appear 1–5 days after sexual contact with an infected person. However, symptoms can show up as late as 2 weeks after contact or, in a small number of cases, may not appear at all. The two most common signs of infection are a bad-smelling cloudy discharge from the penis (see Figure 17.1) and burning sensations during urination. About 30–40% of infected men also have swollen and tender lymph glands in the groin. These early symptoms sometimes clear up on their own without treatment. However, this is no guarantee that the disease has been eradicated by the body's immune system. The bacteria may still be present, and a man may still be able to infect a partner.

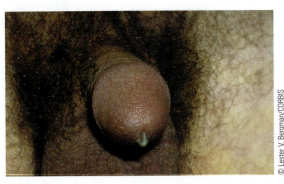

▶ **Figure 17.1** A cloudy discharge symptomatic of gonorrhea infection.

Complications in the Male If the infection continues without treatment for 2 to 3 weeks, it can spread up the genitourinary tract. Here, it can involve the prostate, bladder, kidneys, and testes. Most men who continue to harbor gonococcus have only periodic flare-ups of the minor symptoms of discharge and burning during urination. In a small number of men, however, abscesses form in the prostate. These can result in fever, painful bowel movement, difficulty urinating, and general discomfort. In approximately 1 out of 5 men who remain untreated for longer than a month, the bacteria move down the vas deferens to infect one or both of the epididymal structures that lie along the back of each testis. In general, only one side is infected initially, usually the left. (Symptoms of epididymitis were described in the discussion of chlamydia infection.) Even after successful treatment, gonococcal epididymitis leaves scar tissue, which can block the flow of sperm from the affected testis. Sterility does not usually result, because this complication typically affects only one testis. However, if treatment is still not carried out after epididymitis has occurred on one side, the infection can spread to the other testis, causing permanent sterility.

Early Symptoms in the Female An estimated 50–80% of women infected with gonorrhea are unaware of the early symptoms of this disease (H. Miller et al., 1999). The primary site of infection, the cervix, can become inflamed without producing any observable symptoms (Emmert & Kirchner, 2000). A yellow-green discharge usually results; but, because this discharge is rarely heavy, it commonly goes unnoticed. A woman who is aware of her vaginal secretions is more likely to note the infection during these early stages. Sometimes the discharge is irritating to the vulval tissues. However, when a woman seeks medical attention for an irritating discharge, her physician may fail to consider gonorrhea because many other infectious organisms produce this symptom. Also, many women who have gonorrhea also have trichomoniasis (discussed later in this chapter), and this condition can mask the presence of gonorrhea. Consequently, it is essential for any woman who thinks she may have gonorrhea to make certain that she is tested for the disease when she is examined. (A Pap smear is *not* a test for gonorrhea.)

Complications in the Female The Bartholin's glands can be invaded by the gonococcus organism. When this happens, there are usually no symptoms. Far more serious complications result from the spread of this disease to the upper reproductive tract, where it often causes PID (Mehta et al., 2001; H. Miller et al., 1999). The symptoms of PID, discussed in the section on chlamydia infection, are often more severe when the infecting organism is gonococcus rather than *Chlamydia trachomatis*. Sterility and ectopic pregnancy are serious consequences occasionally associated with gonococcal PID. Another serious complication that can result from PID is the development of tough bands of scar-tissue adhesions that may link several pelvic cavity structures (fallopian tubes, ovaries, uterus, etc.) to each other, to the abdominal walls, or to both. These adhesions can cause severe pain during coitus or when a woman is standing or walking.

Other Complications in Both Sexes In about 2% of adult men and women with gonorrhea, the gonococci enter the bloodstream and spread throughout the body to produce a variety of symptoms, including chills, fever, loss of appetite, skin lesions, and arthritic pain in the joints (Calvert, 2003; Centers for Disease Control, 2002g). If arthritic symptoms develop, quick treatment is essential to avoid permanent joint damage. In rare cases the gonococcus organism can invade the heart, liver, spinal cord, and brain.

An infant can develop a gonococcal eye infection, which may cause blindness, after passing through the birth canal of an infected woman (Sharts-Hopco, 1997). The use of silver nitrate eyedrops or erythromycin or tetracycline ophthalmic ointment immediately after birth averts this potential complication (Centers for Disease Control, 1998b). In a few rare cases adults have transmitted the bacteria to their own eyes by touching this region immediately after handling their genitals—one reason why it is important to wash with soap and water immediately after self-examination. ■

Oral contact with infected genitals can result in infection of the throat (Centers for Disease Control, 2002g; Emmert & Kirchner, 2000). Although this form of gonorrhea can cause a sore throat, most people experience no symptoms. Rectal gonorrhea can be caused by anal intercourse or, in a woman, by transmission of the bacteria from the vagina to the anal opening by means of menstrual blood or vaginal discharge. This form of gonorrhea is often asymptomatic, particularly in females, but it might be accompanied by itching, rectal discharge, and bowel disorders.

Treatment

Because gonorrhea is often confused with other ailments, it is important to make the correct diagnosis. Because coexisting chlamydia infections often accompany gonorrhea, health practitioners often use a treatment strategy that is effective against both (Centers for Disease Control, 2002g). Before 1976 gonorrhea could be effectively treated with penicillin or tetracycline. Since 1976, however, antibiotic-resistant strains of gonococcal bacteria have emerged (Burstein & Murray, 2003). Consequently, treatment guidelines suggest the use of drugs effective against both resistant and nonresistant strains. The current treatment regimen recommended by the CDC includes the dual therapy of a single dose of ceftriaxone, cefixime, ciprofloxacin, levofloxacin, or ofloxacin plus a single dose of azithromycin (or doxycycline for 7 days).

It is quite common for sexual partners of infected individuals to have also contracted gonorrhea. Consequently, all sexual partners exposed to a person with diagnosed gonorrhea should be examined, cultured, and, if necessary, treated with a drug regimen that covers both gonococcus and chlamydia infections (Centers for Disease Control, 2002g).

Nongonococcal Urethritis

Nongonococcal urethritis (NGU) An inflammation of the urethral tube caused by organisms other than gonococcus.

Any inflammation of the urethra that is not caused by gonorrhea is called **nongonococcal urethritis (NGU).** It is believed that three separate microscopic organisms, *Chlamydia trachomatis, Ureaplasma urealyticum,* and *Mycoplasma genitalium* (the last two organisms are members of a group of bacteria called mycoplasmas) are primary causes of NGU (Centers for Disease Control, 2002g; Totten et al., 2001). NGU can also result from invasion by other infectious agents, allergic reactions to vaginal secretions, or irritation from soaps, vaginal contraceptives, or deodorant sprays.

Incidence and Transmission

NGU is quite common among men: In the United States NGU occurs much more frequently than gonorrhea. Although NGU generally produces urinary tract symptoms only in men, there is evidence that women harbor the organisms that can cause NGU. The most common forms of NGU are generally transmitted through coitus. That NGU rarely occurs in men who are not involved in sexual interaction supports this contention.

Research has demonstrated that oral sex (fellatio) is strongly associated with nonchlamydia NGU in both heterosexual and homosexual men (Lafferty et al., 1997). This finding suggests that oral bacteria or other oral factors can cause NGU.

Symptoms and Complications

Men who contract NGU often manifest symptoms similar to those of gonorrhea infection, including discharge from the penis and mild burning during urination. Often the discharge is less pronounced than with gonorrhea; it may be evident only in the morning before urinating.

Women with NGU are generally unaware of the disease until they are informed that it has been diagnosed in a male partner. They frequently show no symptoms, although there may be some itching, burning during urination, and a mild discharge of pus from the vagina. A woman may unknowingly have the infection for a long time, during which she may pass it to sexual partners.

The symptoms of NGU generally disappear after 2 to 3 months without treatment. However, the disease may still be present. If left untreated in women, it can result in cervical inflammation or PID; in men it can spread to the prostate, epididymis, or both. In rare cases NGU can produce a form of arthritis.

Treatment

A single dose of azithromycin or a regimen of doxycyline for 7 days usually clears up NGU. All sexual partners of individuals diagnosed with NGU should be examined for the presence of an STD and treated if necessary.

Syphilis

Syphilis (SIH-fuh-lus) is an STD caused by a thin, corkscrewlike bacterium called *Treponema pallidum* (also commonly called a spirochete).

Syphilis A sexually transmitted disease caused by a spirochete called *Treponema pallidum.*

Incidence and Transmission

Syphilis rates declined steadily in the United States throughout the 1990s (Finelli et al., 2001). In fact, by the end of the 20th century the incidence of syphilis was so low that the CDC announced a bold plan to eliminate this disease in the United States by 2005. Unfortunately, syphilis rates rose by 2% between 2000 and 2001, the first increase since 1990 (Centers for Disease Control, 2002f). This overall increased incidence of syphilis was largely attributable to a 15% jump among men who have sex with men (MSM). Syphilis outbreaks among MSM have been recently reported in several large urban areas, such as Seattle, San Francisco, New York, and Miami. For example, health officials in New York recently reported a 50% increase in syphilis cases in 2000–2001 (Centers for Disease Control, 2002e).

The actual incidence of syphilis is undoubtedly much higher than reported. In fact, for every case of syphilis that is reported, it is estimated that three cases are not (Sharts-Hopco, 1997). Regardless of its frequency, syphilis should not be taken lightly: Unlike most STDs, syphilis can result in death.

Treponema pallidum requires a warm, moist environment for survival. It is transmitted almost exclusively from open lesions of infected individuals to the mucous membranes or skin abrasions of sexual partners through penile–vaginal, oral–genital, oral–anal, or genital–anal contacts. An infected pregnant woman can also transmit *Treponema pallidum* to her unborn child through the placental blood system. The resulting infection can cause miscarriage, stillbirth, or *congenital syphilis,* which can result in death or extreme damage to infected newborns (Donovan, 2004; Jayaraman et al., 2003). If syphilis is successfully treated before the fourth month of pregnancy, the fetus will not be affected. Therefore pregnant women should be tested for syphilis sometime during their first 3 months of pregnancy. The CDC recommends that all pregnant women be tested for syphilis at the first prenatal visit (Centers for Disease Control, 2002g).

Symptoms and Complications

If untreated, syphilis can progress through the primary, secondary, latent, and tertiary phases of development. We provide a brief description of each phase in the following paragraphs.

Primary Syphilis In its initial or primary phase syphilis is generally manifested in the form of a painless sore called a **chancre** (SHANG-kur), which usually appears about 3 weeks after

Chancre A raised, red, painless sore that is symptomatic of the primary phase of syphilis.

Figure 17.2 The first stage of syphilis. A syphilitic chancre as it appears on (a) the penis and (b) the labia.

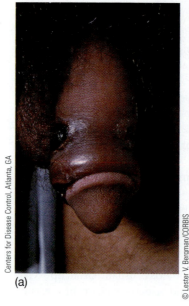

Centers for Disease Control, Atlanta, GA

(a)

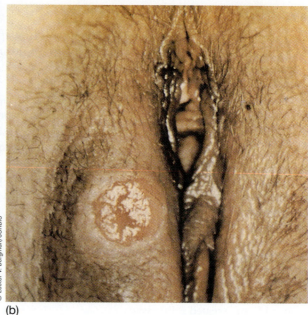

© Lester V. Bergman/CORBIS

(b)

initial infection at the site where the spirochete organism entered the body (see Figure 17.2). In women this sore most commonly appears on the inner vaginal walls or cervix. It can also appear on the external genitals, particularly the labia. In men the chancre most often occurs on the glans of the penis, but it can also show up on the penile shaft or on the scrotum. Although 95% of chancres are genital, the sores can occur in the mouth or rectum or on the anus or breast. People who have had oral sex with an infected individual might develop a sore on the lips or tongue. Anal intercourse can result in chancres appearing in the rectum or around the anus.

In view of the typically painless nature of the chancre, it often goes undiscovered when it occurs on internal structures such as the rectum, vagina, or cervix. (Occasionally, chancres may be painful, and they may occur in multiple sites.) Even when the chancre is noticed, some people do not seek treatment. Unfortunately (from the long-term perspective), the chancre generally heals without treatment 1 to 6 weeks after it first appears. For the next few weeks the person usually has no symptoms but can infect an unsuspecting partner. After about 6 weeks (although sometimes after as little as 2 weeks or as long as 6 months), the disease progresses to the secondary stage in about 50% of the people with untreated primary syphilis (Goens et al., 1994).

Secondary Syphilis In the secondary phase, which usually emerges 2 to 8 weeks after exposure, a skin rash appears on the body, often on the palms of the hands and soles of the feet (see Figure 17.3). The rash can vary from barely noticeable to severe, with raised bumps that have a rubbery, hard consistency. Although the rash may look terrible, it typically does not hurt or itch. If it is at all noticeable, it generally prompts a visit to a physician, if the earlier appearance of a chancre did not. Besides a generalized rash, a person may have flulike symptoms, such as fever, swollen lymph glands, fatigue, weight loss, and joint or bone pain. Even when not treated, these symptoms usually subside within a few weeks. Rather than being eliminated, however, the disease can enter the potentially more dangerous latent phase.

Latent Syphilis The latent stage can last for several years, during which time there may be no observable symptoms (Augenbraun, 2000; Moran, 1997b). Nevertheless, the infecting organisms continue to multiply, preparing for the final stage of syphilitic infection. After 1 year of the latent stage, the infected individual is no longer contagious to sexual partners. However, a pregnant woman with syphilis in any stage can pass the infection to her fetus.

Tertiary Syphilis Approximately 30% of those individuals who do not obtain effective treatment during the first three stages of syphilis enter the tertiary stage later in life (Augenbraun, 2000). The final manifestations of syphilis can be severe, often resulting in death.

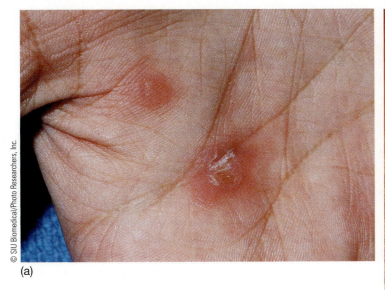
(a)

They usually occur anywhere from 5 to 25 years after initial infection and include such conditions as heart failure, blindness, ruptured blood vessels, paralysis, skin ulcers, liver damage, and severe mental disturbance (Augenbraun, 2000; Calvert, 2003). Depending on the extent of the damage, treatment even at this late stage can be beneficial (Augenbraun, 2000).

Treatment

Primary, secondary, or latent syphilis of less than 1 year's duration can be effectively treated with intramuscular injections of benzathine penicillin G (Donovan, 2004; Centers for Disease Control, 2002g). People who are allergic to penicillin can be treated with doxycycline, erythromycin, or ceftriaxone. Syphilis of more than 1 year's duration is treated with intramuscular injections of benzathine penicillin G once a week for 3 successive weeks.

All sex partners who have been exposed to a person with infectious syphilis should be treated. *All* individuals who have been treated for this disease should have several diagnostic blood tests at 3-month intervals after treatment is completed to make certain that they are completely free of the *Treponema pallidum* organism (Emmert & Kirchner, 2000; Mossad, 2003). ■

Chancroid

Chancroid (SHANG-kroyd) is an infection caused by the bacterium *Haemophilus ducreyi*.

Incidence and Transmission

Chancroid is widely prevalent in tropical and semitropical regions of the world, especially in Africa, where it is one of the most common causes of genital ulcers (Lewis, 2000). Although still relatively uncommon in the United States, the incidence of this disease has increased sharply in recent years. This has been a cause of concern among health officials, because chancroid is associated with an increased prevalence of HIV infections (Centers for Disease Control, 2002g; Lewis, 2000). The incidence of chancroid is up to 25 times higher in men than in women, and uncircumcised men seem to be especially susceptible to this infection (Lewis, 2000). This disease is usually transmitted by sexual interaction.

Symptoms and Complications

Chancroid is characterized by the formation of small bumps or papules, usually in the region of the genitals, perineum, or anus, that occur 4 to 5 days after contact with an infected person. These lesions eventually rupture and form painful, soft, craterlike ulcers that emit a

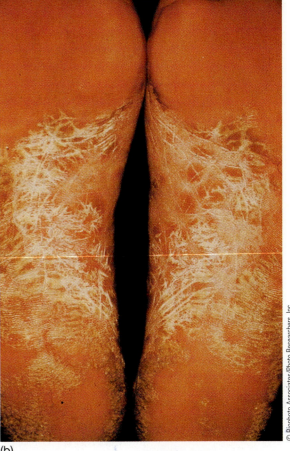
(b)

▶ **Figure 17.3** In the secondary phase of syphilis a skin rash appears on the body, often on (a) the palms and (b) the feet.

Chancroid A sexually transmitted bacterial disease characterized by small bumps in the region of the genitals, perineum, or anus that eventually rupture and form painful ulcers with a foul discharge.

foul-smelling discharge. The softness and painfulness of the chancroid ulcers distinguish them from the hard, painless chancres of syphilis. Chancroid infection frequently is accompanied by swollen lymph nodes, which can also ulcerate. The extensive ulceration associated with chancroid infections is a worrisome complication because HIV is able to gain easy access to the blood through these lesions.

Treatment

Current treatments of choice for chancroid are single doses of either ceftriaxone or azithromycin, 7 days of oral erythromycin, or 3 days of oral ciprofloxacin.

▶ Viral Infections

Viruses are the cause of several common STDs. A virus is an organism that invades, reproduces, and lives within a cell, thereby disrupting normal cellular activity. Most viruses are transmitted through direct contact with infectious blood or other body fluids. We begin our discussion with herpes, the most common viral STD. Next, we describe genital warts caused by several varieties of viruses that have reached epidemic proportions in the U.S. population. We conclude with some information about viral hepatitis. AIDS, caused by HIV infection, is described in detail later in this chapter.

Herpes

Herpes A disease characterized by blisters on the skin in the regions of the genitals or mouth. It is caused by the *Herpes simplex* virus and is easily transmitted through sexual contact.

Herpes is caused by the *Herpes simplex* virus (HSV). Eight different herpes viruses infect humans, the most common being the varicella-zoster virus (VZV) that causes chicken pox, followed in frequency by *Herpes simplex* virus type 1 (HSV-1) and *Herpes simplex* virus type 2 (HSV-2). In the following discussion we confine our attention to HSV-1 and HSV-2 because these are the two herpes viruses that are widely transmitted through sexual contact. HSV-1 typically manifests itself as lesions or sores—called cold sores or fever blisters—in the mouth or on the lips (oral herpes). HSV-2 generally causes lesions on and around the genital areas (genital herpes).

Although genital and oral herpes are usually associated with different herpes viruses, oral–genital transmission is possible. HSV-1 can affect the genital area, and, conversely, HSV-2 can produce a sore in the mouth (Emmert, 2000; Engelberg et al., 2003).

Incidence and Transmission

Current estimates indicate that more than 100 million Americans are afflicted with oral herpes, and at least 50 million have genital herpes (Calvert, 2003; Centers for Disease Control, 2002g; Turner et al., 2003). An estimated 1 million new cases of genital herpes occur each year in the United States (K. Miller et al., 2003). Genital herpes affects more people worldwide than any other STD (Gershengorn & Blower, 2000). Research indicates that 20–25% of people in the United States, age 12 years or older, are infected with HSV-2, an increase of 30% since the late 1970s (Calvert, 2003; Corey & Handsfield, 2000). This extraordinarily high incidence of genital herpes has prompted some health authorities to observe that people "who have unprotected contact with multiple partners should know that unsuspected exposure to HSV is virtually guaranteed" (Arvin & Prober, 1997, p. 1158).

InfoTrac Search Words

■ Genital herpes

Genital herpes appears to be transmitted primarily by penile–vaginal, oral–genital, genital–anal, or oral–anal contact. Oral herpes can be transmitted by kissing or through oral–genital contact. A person who receives oral sex from a partner who has a cold sore or fever blister in the mouth region can develop genital herpes of either the type 1 or type 2 variety. Recent data gathered in the United States, Europe, and Asia demonstrate a shift in the cause of genital herpes from predominantly HSV-2 infection to a significant proportion caused by HSV-1 infection (Engelberg et al., 2003). Evidence indicates that about 30% of first-episode infections of genital herpes are caused by HSV-1 (Centers for Disease Control, 2002g).

When any herpes sores are present, the infected person is highly contagious. It is extremely important to avoid bringing the lesions into contact with someone else's body through touching, sexual interaction, or kissing.

Although it was once believed that herpes could be transmitted only when lesions were present, we now know that HSV can be transmitted even when there are no symptoms (Calvert, 2003; Wald et al., 2000). In fact, research strongly indicates that asymptomatic "viral shedding" (the emission of viable HSV onto body surfaces) is likely to occur at least some of the time in many people infected with HSV. This asymptomatic viral shedding can result in transmission of the virus despite the absence of symptoms that suggest active infection. In fact, "most genital herpes infections are transmitted by persons unaware that they have the infection or who are asymptomatic when transmissions occurs" (Centers for Disease Control, 2002g).

Research has shown that HSV-2 does not pass through latex condoms. Thus condoms are effective in preventing transmission from a male whose only lesions occur on the glans or shaft of the penis (Centers for Disease Control, 2002g). Condoms are helpful but less effective in preventing transmission from a female to a male because vaginal secretions containing the virus can wash over the male's scrotal area. Nevertheless, using condoms consistently and correctly can minimize the risk of either acquiring or transmitting genital herpes (Centers for Disease Control, 2002g; Stanberry, 2000).

What can infected people do to reduce the risk that they will transmit the virus to a sexual partner? Clearly, when lesions are present, they should avoid any kind of intimate or sexual activity that will expose a partner's body to viral shedding of HSV. However, as previously described, even when no sores or other symptoms are present, infected individuals are at risk for shedding the virus. Consequently, "unprotected sex is like Russian roulette—they can never be certain regarding when they are contagious" (Stanberry, 2000, p. 268). The best strategy for people who are either infected themselves or involved with an infected partner is to consistently and correctly use condoms even when they or their partners are asymptomatic.

People can also spread the virus from one part of their bodies to another part by touching a sore and then scratching or rubbing somewhere else. However, self-infection appears to be possible only immediately after the initial appearance of infection. Soon the body produces antibodies that ward off infection at other sites. Nevertheless, it is good practice for people with herpes to wash their hands thoroughly with soap and water after touching a sore. It is better to avoid touching the sores if possible. ■

Symptoms and Complications

The symptoms associated with HSV-1 and HSV-2 infections are quite similar.

Genital Herpes (Type 2) Symptoms The incubation period of genital herpes is 2 to 14 days, and the symptoms usually last about 20 days (Kirchner & Emmert, 2000). However, some individuals with genital herpes do not experience recognizable symptoms (Donovan, 2004). When symptoms are present, they consist of one or more small, painful red bumps, called *papules,* that usually appear in the genital region. In women the areas most commonly infected are the labia. The mons veneris, clitoris, vaginal opening, inner vaginal walls, and cervix can also be affected (Donovan, 2004). In men the infected site is typically the glans or shaft of the penis. Men and women who have engaged in anal intercourse can develop eruptions in and around the anus.

Soon after their initial appearance, papules rapidly develop into tiny painful blisters filled with a clear fluid containing highly infectious virus particles. The body then attacks the virus with white blood cells, causing the blisters to fill with pus (see Figure 17.4). Soon the blisters rupture to form wet, painful, open sores surrounded by a red ring (health practitioners refer to this as the period of viral shedding). A person is highly contagious during this time. About 10 days after the first appearance of the papule, the open sore forms a crust and begins to heal, a process that can take as long as 10 more days. Sores on the cervix can continue to produce infectious material for as long as 10 days after labial sores have completely healed. Consequently, it is wise to avoid coitus for a 10-day period after all external sores have healed.

Other symptoms can accompany genital herpes, including swollen lymph nodes in the groin, fever, muscle aches, and headaches. In addition, urination may be accompanied by a burning sensation, and women may experience increased vaginal discharge.

? Critical Thinking Question

Many individuals with genital herpes, who have rare outbreaks of the disease, worry about being rejected by prospective sexual partners if they disclose their condition. Do you believe that people who carefully monitor their health and take reasonable precautions can ethically enter into sexual relationships without revealing that they have genital herpes? Why or why not?

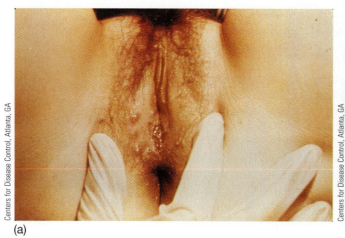
(a)

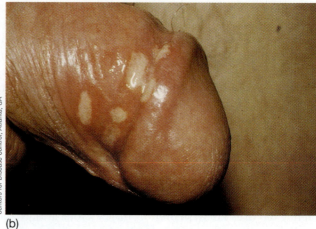
(b)

► **Figure 17.4** Genital herpes blisters as they appear on (a) the labia and (b) the penis.

Prodromal symptoms Symptoms that give advance warning of an impending herpes eruption.

Oral Herpes (Type 1) Symptoms Oral herpes is characterized by the formation of papules on the lips and sometimes on the inside of the mouth, the tongue, and the throat. (HSV-1 only infrequently occurs in the mouth and should not be confused with canker sores.) These blisters tend to crust over and heal in 10 to 16 days. Other symptoms include fever, general muscle aches, swollen lymph nodes in the neck, flulike symptoms, increased salivation, and sometimes bleeding in the mouth.

Recurrence Even after complete healing, lesions can recur. Unfortunately, the herpes virus does not typically go away; instead, it retreats up the nerve fibers leading from the infected site (Colgan et al., 2003). Ultimately, the genital herpes virus finds a resting place in nerve cells adjacent to the lower spinal column, whereas the oral herpes virus becomes lodged in nerve cells in the back of the neck. The virus can remain dormant in these cells, without causing any apparent damage, perhaps for the person's entire lifetime. However, in many cases there will be periodic flare-ups as the virus retraces its path back down the nerve fibers leading to the genitals or lips.

Although some people never experience a recurrence of herpes following the initial or primary infection, research suggests that most people who have undergone a primary episode of genital herpes infection experience at least one recurrence. Individuals who experience recurrences may do so frequently or only occasionally. Symptoms associated with recurrent attacks tend to be milder than primary episodes, and the disease tends to run its course more quickly (Eva, 2000). The recurrence rates for genital herpes caused by HSV-1 are lower than recurrence rates for genital HSV-2 infections (Engelberg et al., 2003).

Most people prone to recurrent herpes outbreaks experience some type of **prodromal symptoms** that give advance warning of an impending eruption. These indications include itching, burning, throbbing, or "pins-and-needles" tingling at the sites commonly infected by herpes blisters and sometimes pain in the legs, thighs, groin, or buttocks. Many health authorities believe that a person's degree of infectiousness increases during this stage and that it further escalates when the lesions appear. A recent study found that viral shedding is much more common on days when prodromal symptoms are present compared to days when such symptoms are absent (Krone et al., 2000). Consequently, a person should be particularly careful to avoid direct contact from the time he or she first experiences prodromal symptoms until the sores have completely healed. Even during an outbreak, it is possible to continue sexual intimacies with a partner, as long as infected skin does not come in contact with healthy skin. During this time partners may wish to experiment with other kinds of sensual pleasuring, such as sensate focus (see Chapter 16), hugging, or manual stimulation.

A variety of factors can trigger reactivation of the herpes virus, including emotional stress, anxiety, depression, acidic food, ultraviolet light, fever, menstruation, poor nutrition, being overtired or run-down, and trauma to the affected skin region (Emmert, 2000; Kirchner & Emmert, 2000). One person noted:

For several years, I have been having a herpes outbreak on my lips. It usually happens just once a year and coincides with the start of fishing season when I sit in a boat too long without protection from the sun. Now that I am aware of the pattern, I plan to take proper precautions in the future. (Authors' files)

Because triggering factors vary so widely, it is often difficult to associate a specific event with a recurrent herpes outbreak.

Some people may not experience a relapse of genital herpes until several years after the initial infection. Therefore, if you have been in what you believe is a sexually exclusive relationship and your partner shows symptoms or transmits the virus to you, it does not necessarily mean that she or he contracted the disease from someone else during the course of your relationship. Furthermore, as stated earlier, some people with genital herpes infections are asymptomatic or have such mild symptoms that they are often unrecognizable. Thus a first episode of symptomatic genital herpes may not be due to recent sexual contact with an infected person.

Other Complications Although the sores are painful and bothersome, it is unlikely that men will experience major physical complications of herpes. Women, however, face two serious, although quite uncommon, complications: cancer of the cervix and infection of a newborn. Evidence suggests that the risk of developing cervical cancer is somewhat higher among women who have had genital herpes (Centers for Disease Control, 2002g). However, genital herpes is not a direct causative agent in cervical cancer. Rather, "the role of HSV-2 in cervical cancer is at most that of a cofactor, not a primary etiologic agent" (Centers for Disease Control, 2002g, p. 15). Fortunately, the great majority of women infected with herpes will never develop cancer of the cervix. Nonetheless, it is advisable for all women, particularly those who have had genital herpes, to obtain an annual cervical Pap smear. Some authorities recommend that women with genital herpes should have this test every 6 months.

A newborn can be infected with genital herpes while passing through the birth canal (Brown et al., 2003). About 60% of newborns infected with herpes who are not treated will die or be severely damaged (Corey & Handsfield, 2000). It is believed that viral shedding from the cervix, vagina, or vulva plays the primary role in transmitting the disease perinatally from mother to infant. Most infected newborns develop typical skin sores (papules), which should be cultured to confirm a herpes diagnosis. Some health practitioners recommend treating exposed infants with acyclovir, a drug shown to be somewhat effective in suppressing herpes outbreaks. The presence of genital herpes sores when delivery is imminent poses a significant risk for transmission of HSV from an infected mother to her baby. To avert this possibility, a cesarean delivery may be performed, and the CDC recommends cesarean delivery for women in labor who have symptomatic disease, especially if it is the initial outbreak of herpes lesions (Centers for Disease Control, 2002g). Cesarean delivery has been the standard of care for more than 30 years for women who have genital herpes lesions present at the time of delivery (Brown et al., 2003). A recent large-scale study of 58,362 pregnant women clearly demonstrated that cesarean delivery reduces the risk of transmission of genital HSV-1 or HSV-2 from mother to child during delivery (Brown et al., 2003).

One additional serious complication can occur when a person transfers the virus to an eye after touching a virus-shedding sore. This can lead to a severe eye infection known as ocular herpes. The best way to prevent this complication is to avoid touching herpes sores. If you cannot avoid contact, thoroughly wash your hands with hot water and soap immediately after touching the lesions. There are effective treatments for ocular herpes, but they must be started quickly to avoid eye damage. ■

Many people who have recurrent herpes outbreaks are troubled with mild to severe psychological distress (Mills & Mindel, 2003; Romanowski et al., 2003a). In view of the physical discomfort associated with the disease, the unpredictability of recurrent outbreaks, and the lack of an effective cure (see next section), it is no small wonder that people who have herpes undergo considerable stress. We believe that becoming better informed about herpes may help to alleviate some of these emotional difficulties. In addition, talking with supportive partners might ease a person's psychological adjustment to recurrent genital herpes infections. Certainly, herpes is not the dread disease that some people believe it to be. In fact, many individuals have learned to cope effectively with it, as did the person in the following account:

When I first discovered I had herpes several years ago, my first reaction was, "Oh no, my sex life is destroyed!" I was really depressed and angry with the person who gave me the disease. However, with time I learned I could live with it, and I even began to gain some control over it. Now, on those infrequent occasions when I have an outbreak, I know what to do to hurry up the healing process. (Authors' files)

Treatment

At the time of this writing, no medical treatment has been proven effective in curing either oral or genital herpes. However, medical researchers are pursuing an effective treatment on many fronts, with mounting optimism. Current treatment strategies are designed to prevent outbreaks or to reduce discomfort and to speed healing during an outbreak.

Three separate antiviral drugs are often highly effective in the management of herpes. Acyclovir, sold under the trade name Zovirax, is the cheapest and most commonly used medication. It is available in three forms: topical (ointment), oral, and injectable. Although the ointment has not proven to be particularly helpful, a number of studies have shown that acyclovir administered orally or intravenously significantly reduces viral shedding and the duration and severity of herpes outbreaks (Colgan et al., 2003; Wald et al., 2002). Oral acyclovir taken several times daily is the most common drug treatment for genital herpes. Intravenous (injected) acyclovir is generally used only with severe infections (Centers for Disease Control, 2002g). In recent years two new antiviral agents, valacyclovir (Valtrex) and famciclovir (Famvir), taken orally, have proven effective for the treatment of genital herpes (Mills & Mindel, 2003; Romanowski et al., 2003b).

Two antiviral treatment strategies are used to manage recurrent genital herpes infections. In *suppressive therapy* medication is taken daily to prevent recurrent outbreaks. *Episodic treatment* involves treating herpes outbreaks when they occur with an antiviral agent (Romanowski et al., 2003b). Episodic treatment has been shown to reduce the duration and severity of lesion pain and time to total healing (Romanowski et al., 2003a; Wald et al., 2002). Suppressive therapy often prevents HSV reactivation and development of herpes lesions (Mills & Mindel, 2003; Romanowski et al., 2003a). A recent study compared the responses and preferences of 225 individuals with a history of recurrent genital herpes outbreaks. The participants were randomly assigned to receive 24 weeks of suppressive therapy with valacyclovir followed by 24 weeks of episodic treatment with the same drug, or vice versa. Both treatment strategies were effective. Suppressive therapy reduced the frequency of recurrences by 80%, and episodic treatment reduced the severity and duration of outbreaks. Suppressive therapy was preferred to episodic treatment by 72% of the subjects, and "overall treatment satisfaction and quality of life were significantly greater during suppressive therapy" (Romanowski et al., 2003a, p. 226).

Suppressive antiviral therapy reduces but does not eliminate asymptomatic viral shedding between outbreaks and therefore potentially decreases the risk of sexual transmission of HSV infections (Centers for Disease Control, 2002g; Romanowski et al., 2003b). Reduced transmission rates related to suppressive therapy have yet to be conclusively confirmed. However, a recent study reported that suppression with valacyclovir reduced the risk of transmission of genital herpes from an infected person to his or her disease-free partner by 48% over an 8-month period (Corey et al., 2004).

Long-term suppressive therapy with one of the three available antiviral medications is generally recommended for people who experience six or more outbreaks of genital herpes per year or for those with exceptionally severe recurrences (Colgan et al., 2003; Emmert, 2000).

A number of other measures can provide relief from the discomfort associated with herpes. The following suggestions can be helpful. Because the effectiveness of these measures varies from person to person, we encourage people to experiment to find an approach that best meets their needs.

1. Keeping herpes blisters clean and dry will lessen the possibility of secondary infections, significantly shorten the period of viral shedding, and reduce the total time of lesion healing. Washing the area with warm water and soap two to three times daily is adequate for cleaning. After bathing, dry the area thoroughly by patting it gently with a soft cotton towel or by blowing it with a hair dryer set on cool. Because the moisture that occurs naturally in the genital area can slow the healing process, sprinkling the dried area liberally with cornstarch or baby powder can help. It is desirable to wear loose cotton clothing that does not trap moisture (cotton underwear absorbs moisture, but nylon traps it).

2. Two aspirin every 3 to 4 hours might help to reduce the pain and itching. Application of a local anesthetic, such as lidocaine jelly, can also help to reduce soreness. Ice packs

applied directly to the lesions can also provide temporary relief (but avoid wetting them as the ice melts). Keeping the area liberally powdered can also alleviate itching.

3. Some people have an intense burning sensation when they urinate if the urine comes into contact with herpes lesions. This discomfort can be reduced by pouring water over the genitals while voiding or by urinating in a bathtub filled with water. It might help to dilute the acid in the urine by drinking lots of fluids (but avoid liquids that make the urine more acidic, such as cranberry juice).

4. Because stress has been implicated as a triggering event in recurrent herpes (Cohen et al., 1999), it is a good idea to try to reduce this negative influence. A variety of approaches may help reduce stress. These include relaxation techniques, yoga or meditation, and counseling about ways to cope with daily pressures.

5. If you are prone to repeated relapses of herpes, try recording events that occur immediately before an outbreak (either after the fact or as part of an ongoing journal). You may be able to recognize common precipitating events, such as fatigue, stress, or excessive sunlight, which you can then avoid in the future. ■

Researchers are currently working on vaccines to protect people from herpes infections (Cole, 2003; Stanberry et al., 2002). In one recent study the effectiveness of a vaccine against genital herpes in humans was demonstrated for the first time. However, this vaccine had a beneficial effect for only a small subgroup of women in the total study population of almost 3,000 men and women, and the vaccine was not significantly effective for any men in the study population (Stanberry et al., 2002).

It is our hope that continuing research with human subjects will eventually yield an effective vaccine, because this would offer the most cost-effective approach to curtailing the spread of this disease. However, at the time of this writing the general consensus among researchers is that a broadly effective HSV vaccine is still several years away.

Genital Warts

Genital warts are caused by a virus called the *human papillomavirus* (HPV). Application of recently developed technology has led to the identification of more than 100 types of HPV, about half of which cause genital infections (Donovan, 2004; Munoz et al., 2003).

Genital warts Viral warts that appear on the genitals and are primarily transmitted sexually.

Incidence and Transmission

The incidence of HPV infections has been increasing so rapidly in both sexes that this disease has reached epidemic proportions in recent years. HPV is presently one of the most common STDs in North America (Calvert, 2003; Sauder et al., 2003). It is estimated that at least 40 million people in the United States are infected with HPV and that over 5 million new cases occur each year (O'Neill-Morante, 2000; Sauder et al., 2003). HPV is primarily transmitted through vaginal, anal, oral, or oral–genital sexual interaction. The consensus opinion of an advisory panel of 12 world-renowned HPV researchers, scholars, and clinicians is that "most sexually active people will get HPV" (Gilbert et al., 2003, p. 194). Even condoms, which significantly reduce transmission of many bacterial and viral infections, are far from an ideal preventive measure for HPV because the virus is often present on skin not covered by a condom (Gilbert et al., 2003; Winer et al., 2003). Although condoms do provide some protection, they do not prevent transmission of viral infections on the vulva, the base of the penis, the scrotum, and any other genital area not covered by the condom (Choma, 2003).

Subclinical or asymptomatic infections with HPV are common, and viral shedding and transmission of the virus can occur during asymptomatic periods of infection (Centers for Disease Control, 2002g; Richardson et al., 2000). In fact, HPV is most commonly transmitted by asymptomatic individuals (Strand et al., 1997).

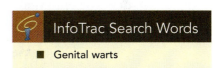

InfoTrac Search Words

■ Genital warts

Symptoms and Complications

Genital warts appear 3 weeks to 8 months after contact with an infected person, with an average incubation period of about 3 months (Vernon, 1997). In women genital warts most commonly appear on the bottom part of the vaginal opening. They can also occur on the

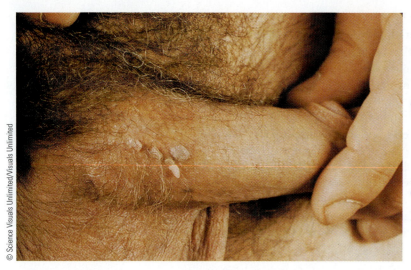

▶ **Figure 17.5** Genital warts on the penis.

perineum, the labia, the inner walls of the vagina, and the cervix. In men genital warts commonly occur on the glans, foreskin, or shaft of the penis (see Figure 17.5). Genital warts can also occur in the anus of either sex. In moist areas (such as the vaginal opening and under the foreskin), genital warts are pink or red and soft, with a cauliflower-like appearance. On dry skin areas they are generally hard and yellow-gray (O'Neill-Morante, 2000).

Many, probably most, people infected with HPV do not develop visible symptoms (Gilbert et al., 2003; Mao et al., 2003). A healthy immune system often suppresses the virus, and most infected people with an effective immune response will become HPV-negative in 6–24 months after the initial positive test for the virus. However, at present, it is unclear whether the virus is eradicated or merely suppressed to undetectable levels (Choma, 2003; Wright & Schiffman, 2003).

Genital warts are sometimes associated with serious complications. They can invade the urethra, causing urinary obstruction and bleeding. Research has also revealed an association between HPV infection and cancers of the cervix, vagina, vulva, urethra, penis, and anus (Calvert, 2003; Palefsky et al., 2001). HPV types 6 and 11 are linked to cancers of the genitals and anus, whereas HPV types 16 and 18 are most often associated with the development of cervical cancer (Gilbert et al., 2003; Munoz et al., 2003). Recent evidence indicates that HPV infections account for 85–90% of the attributable risk for the development of cervical cancer, which is the second leading cause of cancer death in women worldwide (Munoz et al., 2003; O'Neill-Morante, 2000). Women who are infected with HPV have a risk of developing cervical cancer that is somewhere on the order of 10 to 100 times greater than the risk for women who are uninfected with HPV (Stoler, 2000). It is not known whether HPV acts alone to cause these cancers of the cervix and genitalia or in conjunction with cofactors, such as other infections, smoking, immunosuppression, pregnancy, the use of oral contraceptives, and poor nutrition (Donovan, 2004; Gilbert et al., 2003; Winer et al., 2003). There is actually little risk that a woman infected with HPV will develop cervical cancer unless the virus remains undetected and untreated. This is the reason that regular Pap testing and appropriate follow-up treatment for precancerous lesions are essential to prevent most women from getting cervical cancer (Choma, 2003; Gilbert et al., 2003).

Another rare but serious complication of HPV is that pregnant women infected with the virus can transmit it to their babies during birth (Gilbert et al., 2003). Infected infants can develop a condition known as *respiratory papillomatosis,* which results from HPV infection of their upper respiratory tracts (Centers for Disease Control, 2002g). Respiratory papillomatosis can have serious health consequences that produce lifelong distress and require multiple surgeries.

Treatment

No single treatment has been shown to be uniformly effective in removing warts or in preventing them from recurring (Centers for Disease Control, 2002g; Miller & Graves, 2000). Current CDC guidelines suggest several fairly conservative approaches to HPV management that focus on the removal of visible warts. The most widely used treatments include cryotherapy (freezing) with liquid nitrogen or cryoprobe and topical applications of podofilox, imiquimod cream, or trichloroacetic acid. The response rate to these forms of therapy is only about 60–70%, and at least 20–30% of people experience recurrence after treatment (Abramowicz, 1994). Consequently, a second or extended period of treatment with freezing or topical agents may be necessary. For large or persistent warts cauterization by electric needle, vaporization by carbon dioxide laser, or surgical removal may be necessary. However, these more radical treatments can cause severe side effects. There is increasing evidence that many people treated for visible genital warts also have asymptomatic or subclinical HPV infections, which are extremely difficult or impossible to eradicate (Gilbert et al., 2003).

A vaccine effective against HPV is not currently available. However, animal studies have provided promising findings for the development of an HPV vaccine, and several human vaccine trials are currently in progress. A recent interim report on ongoing HPV vaccine research provided preliminary evidence of a vaccine with 100% effectiveness against HPV type 16, which is strongly associated with cervical cancer (Koutsky et al., 2002).

Viral Hepatitis

Viral hepatitis (heh-puh-TIE-tus) is a disease in which liver function is impaired by a viral infection. There are three major types of viral hepatitis: hepatitis A, hepatitis B, and hepatitis C. Each of these forms of viral hepatitis is caused by a different virus.

Viral hepatitis A disease in which liver function is impaired by a viral infection.

Incidence and Transmission

Hepatitis A is the most common form of viral hepatitis in the United States, followed in order of frequency by hepatitis B and hepatitis C. Estimates suggest that as many as 700,000 Americans are afflicted with acute hepatitis infections annually (Miller & Graves, 2000). Although all three types of hepatitis can be transmitted through sexual contact, types A and B are more likely to be transmitted sexually than type C. Hepatitis B is transmitted more often through sexual activity than is hepatitis A. Sexual transmission among adults accounts for most hepatitis B infections in the United States (Centers for Disease Control, 2002g). Hepatitis A is a relatively common infection of young homosexual men, especially those who have multiple sex partners and those who engage in anal intercourse (Centers for Disease Control, 2002g; Des Jarlais et al., 2003). Furthermore, both hepatitis A and hepatitis B are often transmitted by means of needle sharing among injection drug users (Centers for Disease Control, 2002g; Des Jarlais et al., 2003).

Hepatitis B can be transmitted through blood or blood products, semen, vaginal secretions, and saliva (Bertino et al., 1997). Perinatal transmission from infected mothers to untreated infants can be as high as 85% (Miller & Graves, 2000). The CDC recommends that pregnant women should be tested for hepatitis B (Centers for Disease Control, 2002g). Manual, oral, or penile stimulation of the anus are practices strongly associated with the spread of this viral agent. Hepatitis A seems to be spread primarily through the fecal–oral route. Consequently, epidemics often occur when infected handlers of food do not wash their hands properly after using the bathroom. Oral–anal sexual contact seems to be a primary mode for sexual transmission of hepatitis A (Donovan, 2004).

Recently, health officials in the United States have focused considerable attention on the most health threatening of the hepatitis viruses, hepatitis C, which is an emerging communicable disease of epidemic proportions (Des Jarlais & Schuchat, 2001; Romanowski et al., 2003a). Over the last few years hepatitis C has become a major global health problem, and it is now one of the most common chronic viral infections in North America (Romanowski et al., 2003b). It is estimated that there are more than 200 million people in the world who have chronic hepatitis C infections, 4 million of whom are in the United States (Pancholi et al., 2003). Hepatitis C is transmitted most commonly through blood-contaminated needles shared by injection drug users (Des Jarlais et al., 2003; Romanowski et al., 2003b). Other modes of transmission include transfusion of contaminated blood products, sexual contact, and perinatal transmission from an infected mother to her fetus or infant (Murray et al., 2003; Steininger et al., 2003). Whether or not transmission of hepatitis C through unprotected sexual intercourse is a significant factor in the spread of hepatitis C is controversial, but evidence indicates that some hepatitis C infections are sexually transmitted (Murray et al., 2003; Romanowski et al., 2003b). It is estimated that sexual transmission accounts for about 20% of hepatitis C infections (Centers for Disease Control, 2002g).

Symptoms and Complications

Symptoms of viral hepatitis vary from nonexistent to mild flulike symptoms (poor appetite, upset stomach, diarrhea, sore muscles, fatigue, headache) to an incapacitating illness characterized by high fever, vomiting, and severe abdominal pain. One of the most notable signs of viral hepatitis is a yellowing of the whites of the eyes; the skin of light-complexioned people can also take on a yellow, or jaundiced, look. Hospitalization is required only in severe

 no—

InfoTrac Search Words

■ Hepatitis C

cases. Chronic infections with either hepatitis B or C are a major risk factor for developing cancer of the liver, one of the most common cancers in the world (Romanowski et al., 2003b; Sun et al., 2003). About 20–30% of people infected with hepatitis C manifest rapidly progressing disease associated with severe complications, including liver cancer, cirrhosis, and end-stage liver disease culminating in liver failure (Colgan et al., 2003; Romanowski et al., 2003b). Of the estimated 16,000 deaths in the United States each year from complications of viral hepatitis, about 10,000 result from hepatitis C infections (Gunn et al., 2001).

Treatment

At present, no specific therapy is known to be effective against hepatitis A. Treatment generally consists of bed rest and adequate fluid intake to prevent dehydration. The disease generally runs its course in a few weeks, although complete recovery can take several months in cases of severe infection. Infection with hepatitis B is typically treated in the same manner as hepatitis A, and it also generally runs its course in a few weeks. However, sometimes hepatitis B infections become chronic and persist for more than 6 months. These chronic infections can be treated effectively with either the antiviral drug interferon or lamivudine, a reverse transcriptase inhibitor drug that is one of many medications used to treat HIV/AIDS (Colgan et al., 2003).

Hepatitis C presents a more serious treatment problem. About 70–80% of infected people become chronic carriers who have relatively mild disease that is stable over several decades and does not significantly erode their health. However, for the 20–30% with rapidly progressive disease, active treatment is essential to avert severe complications and/or death (Romanowski et al., 2003b). Recently, a combination therapy with the antiviral drugs interferon and ribavirin has been shown to be relatively effective in controlling hepatitis C (Colgan et al., 2003). About 40% of people treated with this approach actually remain free of the virus, with no symptoms of liver disease, 5–12 years after treatment (Lau et al., 1998; Smith & Rockey, 2004). However, the annual cost of this treatment (between $5,000 and $15,000) is a serious impediment to its widespread use, especially for people who lack adequate health insurance and residents of resource-poor countries.

An effective and safe vaccine to prevent hepatitis B infection has been available since 1982, and in 1995 the U.S. Food and Drug Administration approved an effective and safe hepatitis A vaccine. Unfortunately, at present, an effective vaccine for hepatitis C does not exist, although efforts are under way to develop this prevention tool (Liang et al., 2000; Pancholi et al., 2003). Persons at high risk for contracting hepatitis A or hepatitis B viruses should seriously consider getting immunized. These high-risk people include health care workers who are exposed to blood, injection drug users and their sex partners, homosexual and bisexual men, heterosexually active persons with multiple sexual partners, sexual partners or housemates of people infected with the hepatitis A or B virus, people with chronic liver disease, and military personnel working in field conditions (Centers for Disease Control, 2002g; Miller & Graves, 2000). In addition, the CDC recommends that all children be immunized for hepatitis B.

▶ Common Vaginal Infections

Several kinds of vaginal infections can be transmitted through sexual interaction. The infections we discuss in this section are also frequently contracted through nonsexual means. *Vaginitis* and *leukorrhea* are general terms applied to a variety of vaginal infections characterized by a whitish discharge. The secretion can also be yellow or green because of the presence of pus cells, and it often has a disagreeable odor. Additional symptoms of vaginitis include irritation and itching of the genital tissue, burning during urination, and pain around the vaginal opening during intercourse.

Vaginal infections are common. Practically every woman experiences one or more of these infections during her life. In fact, vaginitis is one of the most common reasons women consult health care providers (Calvert, 2003; Karasz & Anderson, 2003). Under typical circumstances many of the organisms that cause vaginal infections are relatively harmless. In fact, some routinely live in the vagina and cause no trouble unless something alters the normal vaginal environment and allows them to overgrow. The vagina normally houses bacteria (lactobacilli) that help maintain a healthy vaginal environment (Jeavons, 2003; Priestly et al., 1997). The pH of the vagina is usually sufficiently acidic to ward off most infections. However, certain conditions can alter the pH toward the alkaline side, which can leave a woman vulnerable to infection. Some factors that increase the likelihood of vaginal infection include antibiotic therapy, use of contraceptive pills, menstruation, pregnancy, wearing pantyhose and nylon underwear, and lowered resistance from stress or lack of sleep (Jeavons, 2003; Priestly et al., 1997). Douching also increases the risk of vaginal infections, especially bacterial vaginosis (Ness et al., 2003). Research also suggests that the alkaline nature of seminal fluid may be a factor in altering vaginal pH, thus increasing susceptibility to infections (Priestly et al., 1997).

Most women with vaginitis have an infection diagnosed as bacterial vaginosis, candidiasis, or trichomoniasis (Karasz & Anderson, 2003). Bacterial vaginosis is the most common of these infections.

Bacterial Vaginosis

Bacterial vaginosis (BV) is a vaginal infection caused by a replacement of the normal vaginal lactobacilli by an overgrowth of microorganisms, which can include anaerobic bacteria, *Mycoplasma* bacteria, and a bacterium known as *Gardnerella vaginalis.*

Bacterial vaginosis A vaginal infection caused by bacterial microorganisms that is the most common form of vaginitis among U.S. women.

Incidence and Transmission

The presence of moderate levels of bacterial microorganisms in the vaginal environment is normal. However, under conditions of decreased levels of beneficial lactobacilli, an overgrowth of other vaginal microorganisms occurs. This can result in high concentrations of one or more of the bacterial microorganisms that cause BV (Burstein & Murray, 2003; Wiesenfeld et al., 2003). BV is the most common cause of vaginitis in U.S. women (Coco & Vandenbosche, 2000). Many male partners of women with BV can also harbor the infectious microorganisms, especially *Gardnerella vaginalis,* usually without clinical symptoms (Nilsson et al., 1997). Although the role of sexual transmission in BV is not fully understood, it is believed that coitus often provides a mode of transmission for the infection. BV occurs more frequently among sexually active women compared to sexually inactive women (Feroli & Burstein, 2003). However, BV is not necessarily sexually transmitted, because this infection has been diagnosed in teenagers and women who have not experienced sexual intercourse (Coco & Vandenbosche, 2000).

Symptoms and Complications

The most prominent symptom of bacterial vaginosis in women is a foul-smelling thin discharge that resembles flour paste in consistency. The discharge is usually gray, but it can also be white, yellow, or green. The disagreeable odor, often noticed first by an infected woman's sexual partner, is typically described as fishy or musty. This smell may be particularly noticeable after coitus because the alkaline seminal fluid reacts with the bacteria, causing the release of the chemicals that produce the smell. A small number of infected women experience irritation of the genital tissues and mild burning during urination. Recent evidence suggests a link between bacterial vaginosis and both PID and adverse pregnancy outcomes, including premature rupture of the amniotic sac and preterm labor (Coco & Vandenbosche, 2000; Wiesenfeld et al., 2003). There is also evidence of a strong association between BV and gonorrhea and chlamydia infections. One recent study of several hundred women reported that subjects with BV were 4 times more likely to have gonorrhea and 3.4 times more likely to have chlamydia infection than were subjects without BV (Wiesenfeld et al., 2003). As mentioned earlier, most men are asymptomatic. However, some infected males develop inflammation of the foreskin and glans of the penis, **urethritis** (inflammation of the urethral tube), and **cystitis** (bladder infection).

Urethritis An inflammation of the urethral tube.

Cystitis An infection of the bladder.

Treatment

For many years the treatment of choice for bacterial vaginosis has been metronidazole (Flagyl) by mouth for 7 days. However, recent research indicates that intravaginal application of topical metronidazole gel or clindamycin cream are as effective as oral metronidazole (Burstein & Murray, 2003; Feroli & Burstein, 2003). Furthermore, women report more satisfaction with the topical intravaginal preparations than with the oral drug (Chambliss, 2000). Studies indicate that there is little or no proven benefit of treatment of sex partners of women diagnosed with BV (Centers for Disease Control, 2002g; Chambliss, 2000). However, some health practitioners recommend treating partners in cases of recurrent BV infection (Chambliss, 2000; Coco & Vandenbosche, 2000).

Candidiasis

Candidiasis (kan-duh-DIE-uh-sus), also commonly referred to as a yeast infection, is primarily caused by a yeastlike fungus called *Candida albicans*.

Incidence and Transmission

Candidiasis An inflammatory infection of the vaginal tissues caused by the yeastlike fungus *Candida albicans*.

Candidiasis is the second most common vaginal infection in North America (Bauters et al., 2002; Sobel et al., 1998) encountered by health practitioners. An estimated 75% of women will have at least one episode of candidiasis infection during their lifetime and 40–50% will have two or more episodes (Centers for Disease Control, 2002g). The microscopic *Candida albicans* organism is normally present in the vagina of many women; it also inhabits the mouth and large intestine of a large number of women and men. A disease state results only when certain conditions allow the yeast to overgrow in the vagina. This accelerated growth can result from pregnancy, use of oral contraceptives, or diabetes—conditions that increase the amount of sugar stored in vaginal cells (*Candida albicans* thrives in the presence of sugar) (Duerr et al., 2003; Jeavons, 2003). If a nonpregnant woman has repeated yeast infections, it may be advisable for her to be tested for diabetes or other blood sugar disorders. However, women with recurrent candidiasis are rarely found to be diabetic (Ringdahl, 2000). Another factor is the use of oral antibiotics or spermicidal jellies and creams, which reduce the number of lactobacilli (mentioned earlier as important for a healthy vaginal environment) (Jeavons, 2003). This reduction permits *Candida albicans* to multiply rapidly. ■

If the yeast organism is not already present in the woman's vagina, it can be transmitted to this area in a variety of ways. It can be conveyed from the anus by wiping back to front or on the surface of a menstrual pad, or it can be transmitted through sexual interaction because the organism can be harbored in various reservoirs in the male body, especially under the foreskin of an uncircumcised man (Ringdahl, 2000). The organism can also be passed from a partner's mouth to a woman's vagina during oral sex (Greer, 1998).

Symptoms

A woman with a yeast infection may notice that she has a white, clumpy discharge that looks something like cottage cheese. In addition, candidiasis is often associated with intense itching and soreness of the vaginal and vulval tissues, which typically become red and dry (Coco & Vandenbosche, 2000). A woman who has a yeast infection may find coitus painful, and irritation from intercourse might worsen the infection. Genital yeast infections in men are usually asymptomatic, but occasionally they cause itching and/or reddening of the penis and burning during urination.

Treatment

A variety of treatments have proved effective in combating yeast infections. Traditional treatment strategies consist of vaginal suppositories or topical creams, such as clotrimazole, miconazole, butoconazole, or terconazole. Over-the-counter intravaginal preparations of clotrimazole and miconazole are now available for treatment of candidiasis; however, these medications are recommended only for women who have previously been medically diagnosed and treated and who have a recurrence of symptoms (Coco & Vandenbosche, 2000). Research indicates that many women incorrectly diagnose themselves as having vaginal candidiasis and thus begin a course of self-treatment with over-the-counter antifungal medications (Burstein & Murray, 2003; Jeavons, 2003). Even though women who self-treat conditions mistaken for candidiasis may eventually realize their error and seek medical attention, this delay in treatment can have serious consequences, especially because other infections may be present that require different treatments (Ringdahl, 2000).

A drug taken by mouth, fluconazole, has also proven effective in treating candidiasis (Bauters et al., 2002; Burstein & Murray, 2003). Because *Candida albicans* is a hardy organism, treatment should be continued for the prescribed length of time (usually several days to 2 weeks), even though the symptoms may disappear in 2 days. Treatment of male sex partners of infected women is not recommended, because research indicates that this does not prevent recurrences of candidiasis in women (Nyirjesy, 2001; Ringdahl, 2000).

Trichomoniasis

Trichomoniasis (trih-kuh-muh-NIE-uh-sus) is caused by a one-celled protozoan parasite called *Trichomonas vaginalis.*

Trichomoniasis A form of vaginitis caused by the one-celled protozoan *Trichomonas vaginalis.*

Incidence and Transmission

In females trichomoniasis accounts for about one-fourth of all cases of vaginitis. An estimated 8 million new cases of trichomoniasis occur each year in the United States, and 20% of women experience one or more trichomoniasis infections sometime during their reproductive years (Sharts-Hopco, 1997; Wiese et al., 2000). Not all infected women have noticeable symptoms. In men trichomoniasis is more likely to be asymptomatic, but it can be associated with urethritis and other genitourinary symptoms (Burstein & Murray, 2003; Joyner et al., 2000). Nevertheless, some authorities believe that most male sex partners of infected women carry the *Trichomonas vaginalis* organism in their urethras and under the foreskin if they are uncircumcised. The primary mode of transmission of this infection is through sexual contact.

Symptoms and Complications

The most common symptom of trichomoniasis infection in women is an abundant, frothy, white or yellow-green vaginal discharge with an unpleasant odor. The discharge can irritate the tissues of the vagina and vulva, causing them to become inflamed, itchy, and sore (Burstein & Murray, 2003). The infection is usually limited to the vagina and sometimes the cervix, but occasionally the organism invades the urethra, bladder, or Bartholin's glands. Some health specialists believe that long-term trichomonal infection can damage the cells of the cervix and increase susceptibility to cervical cancer. However, prompt, effective treatment prevents permanent cervical damage. Untreated trichomoniasis infection in pregnant women is also associated with premature rupture of the amniotic sac and preterm delivery (Coco & Vandenbosche, 2000). Trichomoniasis infections in men, usually asymptomatic, may be associated with an urge to urinate frequently, painful urination, or a slight urethral discharge.

Treatment

To avoid passing the protozoan back and forth, it is important that the male partner(s) of the infected woman be treated, even if they are asymptomatic. A cure rate of 85–95% occurs when both sexual partners are treated simultaneously (Burstein & Murray, 2003). If a male partner is not treated, the couple should use condoms to prevent reinfection. The recommended drug regimen for both sexes is a single 2-gram dose of metronidazole (Flagyl), taken by mouth. ■

! Sexual Health

▶ Ectoparasitic Infections

Ectoparasites are parasitic organisms that live on the outer skin surfaces of humans and other animals (*ecto* means "outer"). Two relatively common STDs are caused by ectoparasites: pubic lice and scabies.

Ectoparasites Parasitic organisms that live on the outer skin surfaces.

Pubic Lice

Pubic lice, more commonly called crabs, belong to a group of parasitic insects called biting lice. They are known technically as *Phthirus pubis.* Although tiny, adult lice are visible to the eye. They are yellowish-gray and under magnification resemble a crab, as Figure 17.6 shows. A pubic louse generally grips a pubic hair with its claws and sticks its head into the skin, where it feeds on blood from tiny blood vessels.

Pubic lice Lice that primarily infest the pubic hair and are transmitted by sexual contact.

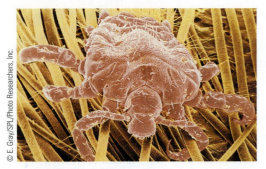

▶ **Figure 17.6** A pubic louse, or "crab."

Incidence and Transmission

Pubic lice are quite common and are seen frequently in public health clinics and by private physicians. Pubic lice are especially prevalent among young (15–25-year-old), single people and are frequently associated with the presence of other sexually transmitted infections (Varela et al., 2003). Pubic lice are often transmitted during sexual contact when two people bring their pubic areas together (Heukelbach & Feldmeier, 2004). The lice can live away from the body for as long as 1 day, particularly if their stomachs are full of blood. They may drop off onto underclothes, bedsheets, sleeping bags, and so forth. Eggs deposited by the female louse on clothing or bedsheets can survive for several days. Thus it is possible to get pubic lice by sleeping in someone else's bed or by wearing his or her clothes. Furthermore, a successfully treated person can be reinfected by being exposed to her or his own unwashed sheets or underclothes. Pubic lice do not necessarily limit themselves to the genital areas. They can be transmitted, usually by the fingers, to the armpits or scalp.

Symptoms

Most people begin to suspect something is amiss when they start itching. Suspicions become stronger when scratching brings no relief. However, a few people seem to have great tolerance for the bite of a louse, experiencing little if any discomfort. Self-diagnosis is possible simply by locating a louse on a pubic hair.

Treatment

The recommended regimen for treatment of pubic lice is 1% permethrin cream rinse applied to all affected areas and washed off after 10 minutes. It is advisable to apply the cream to all areas where there are concentrations of body hair—the genitals, armpits, scalp, and even eyebrows. Scalp hair is treated with 1% Lindane shampoo, applied for 4 minutes and then thoroughly washed off. These treatments should be repeated 7 days later (eggs take 7 days to hatch). Be sure to wash all clothes and sheets that were used before treatment.

Scabies

Scabies An ectoparasitic infestation of tiny mites.

Scabies is caused by a tortoise-shaped parasitic mite with four stubby legs called *Sarcoptes scabiei*. Unlike pubic lice, mites are too tiny to be seen by the naked eye. Scabies infestations are initiated by the female mite; after mating, she burrows beneath the skin to lay her eggs, which hatch shortly thereafter. Each hatched egg becomes a full-grown adult in 10 to 20 days. The adult mite forages for nourishment in the host's skin that is adjacent to the site of the original burrow. The average person with scabies is infested with 10 to 15 live adult female mites (Schleicher & Stewart, 1997).

Incidence and Transmission

Although scabies is not among those infectious diseases reported to health organizations in the United States and elsewhere, it affects millions of people worldwide (Heukelbach & Feldmeier, 2004). Scabies is a highly contagious condition that can be transmitted by close physical contact, both sexual and nonsexual. The mites can also be transferred on clothing or bedding, where they can remain viable for up to 48 hours (Schleicher & Stewart, 1997). In addition to sexually active people, schoolchildren, nursing home residents, and the indigent are especially at risk for scabies infestations.

Symptoms

Small vesicles or pimplelike bumps occur in the area where the female mite tunnels into the skin. A red rash around the primary lesion indicates the area where hatched adult mites are feeding. Areas of infestation itch intensely, especially at night. Favorite sites of infestation typically include the webs and sides of fingers, wrists, abdomen, genitals, buttocks, and female breasts.

Treatment

Scabies is treated with a topical scabicide that is applied from the neck down to the toes. The current scabicide of choice is 1 ounce (30 grams) of 5% permethrin lotion or cream applied at bedtime and left on for 8 to 14 hours, then washed off with soap and water. A single application is usually effective, although some physicians advocate a second treatment applied a week later. It is recommended that all household members and close contacts of an infested person, including asymptomatic ones, be treated simultaneously. In addition, all clothing and bedding used by treated people should be washed in hot water or dry cleaned.

▶ Acquired Immunodeficiency Syndrome (AIDS)

The **acquired immunodeficiency syndrome (AIDS)** epidemic, which constitutes a worldwide public health threat of rapidly increasing magnitude, is now recognized as the most serious disease pandemic of our time. An all-out research assault on this deadly disease, unprecedented in scope and extent, is being conducted throughout the world, and new findings are surfacing with startling rapidity.

AIDS results from infection with the **human immunodeficiency virus (HIV).** HIV falls into a special category of viruses called *retroviruses,* so named because they reverse the usual order of reproduction within cells they infect, a process called *reverse transcription.*

There are two forms of HIV linked with the development of AIDS—HIV-1 and HIV-2. HIV-1 was the first human immunodeficiency virus to be identified and is the one that causes the greatest number of AIDS cases in the United States and throughout the world. HIV-2 occurs in some African countries along with HIV-1. HIV-1, the more virulent of the two forms, is a formidable enemy because it is constantly mutating and is present in multiple strains or subtypes. To simplify our discussion of AIDS, we refer to the infective agent simply as HIV.

A great deal of speculation and theorizing about the origin of AIDS has occurred since the emergence of the global pandemic. It has been variously proposed that HIV came from residents of Africa or Haiti, mosquitoes, monkeys, pigs, or even from early testing of a polio vaccine in Africa in the 1950s. Recently published research appears to have solved the riddle of the origin of HIV/AIDS. Persuasive evidence that HIV was introduced to humans from chimpanzees was obtained by an international team of scientists who traced the roots of HIV to a related virus in a subspecies of chimpanzees that reside in central and southwest Africa (Gao et al., 1999). Genetic analysis revealed that this subspecies, *Pan troglodytes troglodytes,* harbors a simian immunodeficiency virus (SIV) that is the origin of HIV-1. Scientists believe that SIV genetically converted to HIV either while it was still in a chimpanzee or after a human contracted SIV, perhaps through exposure to chimpanzee blood from hunting or handling the meat during food preparation.

With evidence in hand implicating a specific subspecies of chimpanzees as the origin of HIV, another research team conducted tests that allowed them to estimate that HIV first evolved from the SIV carried by these chimpanzees sometime between 1915 and 1941, with 1931 the most likely year (Korber et al., 2000). With such an early date of origin, why was HIV not identified as the AIDS-causing virus until 1983? Scientists believe that when SIV turned into a human killer, probably in the early 1930s, it likely remained confined to a small population in an isolated area, such as a village, until migration into large cities and jet travel spread the virus worldwide. Evidence that HIV existed well before its identification in 1983 was provided by discovery of HIV in a frozen blood sample collected in 1959 from an adult African male (Zhu et al., 1998). Thus it now appears likely that HIV originated early in the 20th century, by means of cross-species transmission from a subspecies of chimpanzees to humans, and then was spread worldwide much later when Africa became less isolated.

HIV specifically targets and destroys the body's CD4 lymphocytes, also called T-helper cells or helper T-4 cells. In healthy people these cells coordinate the immune system's response to disease. The impairment of the immune system resulting from HIV infections

Acquired immunodeficiency syndrome (AIDS) A catastrophic illness in which a virus (HIV) invades and destroys the ability of the immune system to fight disease.

Human immunodeficiency virus (HIV) The immune-system-destroying virus that causes AIDS.

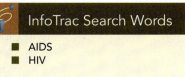

InfoTrac Search Words

- AIDS
- HIV

leaves the body vulnerable to a variety of opportunistic infections (infections that take hold because of the reduced effectiveness of the immune system) and cancers. Initially, HIV infection was diagnosed as AIDS only when the immune system became so seriously impaired that the person developed one or more severe, debilitating diseases, such as cancer or an unusual form of pneumonia caused by the protozoan *Pneumocystis carinii*. However, effective January 1, 1993, the CDC broadened this definition of AIDS to include anyone infected with HIV whose immune system is severely impaired. Now, anyone who is infected with HIV and has a CD4 count of 200 cells or less per microliter of blood is considered to have full-blown AIDS, regardless of other symptoms. (Normal CD4 counts in healthy people not infected with HIV range from 600 to 1,200 cells per microliter of blood.)

Incidence

By January 2004 over 900,000 cumulative cases of AIDS had been reported in the United States, and over 500,000 people had died of the disease since it was first diagnosed in 1981 (National Institutes of Health, 2004). The number of persons in the United States living with HIV continues to increase. An estimated 850,000 to 950,000 people in the United States are currently infected with HIV; most of them have not advanced to full-blown AIDS (Centers for Disease Control, 2003a, 2004). The CDC estimates that 25% of the infected people are unaware of their HIV-positive status (Centers for Disease Control, 2003a).

Each year about 5 million new HIV infections occur globally, and by January 2003 an estimated 42 million people worldwide were infected (UNAIDS, 2003). This disease claims more than 3 million lives in the world community each year (National Institutes of Health, 2004). Unless health professionals succeed in mounting a drastically expanded global prevention effort, experts project that an additional 45 million people worldwide will become infected with HIV by 2010 (UNAIDS, 2003).

The number of new AIDS cases reported annually in the United States grew rapidly throughout the early 1980s, increasing by about 85% each year, and reached a peak rate in the middle of the decade. The rate of new AIDS diagnoses slowed in the late 1980s. Since the early 1990s an estimated 40,000 new HIV infections have occurred annually in the United States (Centers for Disease Control, 2003a). The annual numbers of newly diagnosed cases of full-blown AIDS and deaths from AIDS have remained stable since 1998—approximately 40,000 and 16,000, respectively (Centers for Disease Control, 2003a). Although the overall incidence of new HIV infections in the U.S. population has been stable for several years, the number of new cases among teenagers, women, and racial and ethnic minorities continues to rise. Furthermore, evidence of a recent escalation in the rate at which newly diagnosed HIV infections are occurring among both heterosexuals and MSM have created concern among health officials that the incidence of new HIV infections occurring annually may no longer be stable but, in fact, might be increasing in the U.S. population (Centers for Disease Control, 2003a; Gross, 2003a, 2003b).

Many, probably most, young people with AIDS were infected during their adolescent years. The growing problem of HIV infection among adolescents has been attributed to a number of factors, including the following:

- Many teenagers have multiple sexual partners, increasing their exposure to infection.
- Many adolescents engage in sexual activity without using condoms.
- Access to condoms is generally more difficult for adolescents than for other age groups.
- Teenagers have high rates of other STDs, which are often associated with HIV infection.
- Substance abuse, which often increases risky behavior, is relatively widespread among adolescents.
- Teenagers tend to be especially likely as a group to have feelings of invulnerability (see Chapter 13).

Ethnic and racial minority groups in the United States account for a majority of the total number of AIDS cases reported since 1981 (Centers for Disease Control, 2000c, 2002c; Watkins, 2002; Williams et al., 2003). The higher AIDS rates among ethnic and racial minority groups might reflect, among other factors, (1) reduced access to health care associated with disadvantaged socioeconomic status, (2) cultural or language barriers that limit access to information about strategies for preventing STDs, and (3) differences in HIV risk behaviors, especially higher rates of injection drug use (Centers for Disease Control, 2000c; Searight & McClaren, 1997; Watkins, 2002).

Since AIDS first appeared in the United States, a majority of cases have been directly or indirectly related to two risk-exposure categories: men who have sex with men (MSM) and injection drug users. However, some significant shifting trends in exposure-risk categories have begun to emerge in recent years. Even though the prevalence of HIV infection in the United States and the rest of the Western world remains highest among MSM, in the United States the proportion of reported AIDS cases among MSM declined sharply and then leveled off in the period between the mid-1980s and the late 1990s (Centers for Disease Control, 2003a; Gross, 2003b). Unfortunately, in the early years of this century the incidence rates of HIV infection among MSM are again moving upward (Gross, 2003b; Koblin et al., 2003; Northridge, 2003). This resurgence of the HIV epidemic among MSM is especially prevalent among young MSM and among MSM of color (Gross, 2003a, 2003b; Malebranche, 2003).

A significant decline of HIV/AIDS has occurred among injection drug users in the United States over the last few years (Centers for Disease Control, 2003a). An opposite trend in HIV cases attributable to injection drug use is occurring in Russia, as described in the following "Sexuality and Diversity" discussion.

Sexuality and Diversity

Injection Drug Use and the HIV Epidemic in Russia

The Russian Federation is currently experiencing a rapidly escalating HIV epidemic associated primarily with injection drug use (Hamers & Downs, 2003; Lowndes et al., 2003). Since 1995 a series of explosive outbreaks of HIV infections have occurred among injection drug users in more than 30 major cities of the federation (Lowndes et al., 2003). This dramatic increase in rates of injection drug use is especially pronounced among young people buffeted by the enormous sociopolitical and economic changes that have occurred in Russia since the late 1990s (Dehne et al., 2000; Lowndes et al., 2003). Driven by increased poverty, social dislocation, more geographic mobility, more freedom, more drug use, and more prostitution, the HIV/AIDS epidemic has exploded exponentially in recent years in Russia. It is estimated that at least 700,000 people are HIV-positive in Russia and that most of these infections are associated with injection drug use (Lowndes et al., 2003).

In recent years there has also been an exponential increase in the number of women sex workers in Russia. In Moscow alone there may be as many as 150,000 female sex workers (Lowndes et al., 2003). Injection drug use may be a factor contributing to the increase in the number of sex workers in Russia because commercial sex appears to be a major venue for female injection drug users to obtain drugs and/or money to buy drugs (Dehne & Kobyshcha, 2000; Lowndes et al., 2003). In addition to increased vulnerability of sex workers to HIV infection through their drug use, "the potential for heterosexual transmission of HIV from sex workers to their male clients is high" (Lowndes et al., 2003, p. 47). Infected clients can also transmit HIV to their primary partners, and infected sex workers can similarly transmit infections to their nonclient sex partners. These are some of the reasons that the number of new HIV infections attributable to heterosexual contact is increasing in Russia and other areas of Eastern Europe (Lowndes et al., 2003).

In the United States, AIDS cases attributable to heterosexual transmission are accelerating (Centers for Disease Control, 2003a; Watkins, 2002). Heterosexual contact has always been the primary form of HIV transmission worldwide, especially in Africa and Asia (Ahmed et al., 2003; Betts, 2001). Of the more than 42 million people infected with HIV worldwide, approximately 70% were infected through heterosexual contact, 10% are MSM, and the rest were infected through mother-to-child transmission, injection drug use, and contaminated blood supplies (E. Murphy, 2003). In Africa, where most of the global HIV infections occur, the vast majority of infections are acquired through heterosexual transmission.

Over the last few years the number of women infected with HIV has steadily increased in the United States and worldwide, and the incidence of AIDS in the United States is now increasing more rapidly among women than among men, especially among ethnic and racial minority women (Al-Khan et al., 2003; Centers for Disease Control, 2002d; Harvey et al., 2003). In the United States 25% of all new AIDS cases and 35% of new HIV infections occur in women (Al-Khan et al., 2003). Grouped together, African American and Hispanic American women make up approximately 25% of the U.S. female population but account for about 80% of AIDS cases among U.S. women (Watkins, 2002). African American women have been especially hard hit by HIV/AIDS. Women in this category, who constitute 14% of the U.S. female population, account for 67% of all HIV-infected women and 52% of women with diagnosed AIDS (Williams et al., 2003).

What explains this upward trend in HIV/AIDS among women? Many women have sexual partners who have multiple partners, inject drugs (there are many more male than female injection drug users), or engage in bisexual activity. In addition, research indicates that HIV is not as easily transmitted from women to men as it is from men to women (Betts, 2001; Eschenbach et al., 2001; Ray & Quinn, 2000). Thus the risk of becoming infected through heterosexual intercourse appears to be much greater for a female with an HIV-infected male partner than for a male with an infected female partner.

One explanation for women's greater risk during heterosexual intercourse is that semen contains a higher concentration of HIV than vaginal fluids do, and the female mucosal surface is exposed to HIV in the ejaculate for a considerably longer time than a male's penis is exposed to HIV in vaginal secretions (Ray & Quinn, 2000). In addition, a larger area of mucosal surface is exposed on the vulva and in the vagina than on the penis, and the female mucosal surface is subjected to greater potential trauma than is typically the case with the penis (Ray & Quinn, 2000). Furthermore, some women experience unprotected anal intercourse, a high-risk behavior because HIV transmission is thought to be three to five times as likely with anal intercourse as with vaginal intercourse (Ray & Quinn, 2000; Seidman & Rieder, 1994). In fact, receiving unprotected anal intercourse has been shown to be associated with the highest risk of HIV infection through sexual activity for both men and women (Ray & Quinn, 2000; Silverman & Gross, 1997). Finally, adolescent women are especially biologically vulnerable to HIV infection because the immature cervix is highly susceptible to infection by STDs (Peters et al., 2000; Stoler, 2000; Wiesenfeld et al., 2003).

The global proportionate incidence of HIV/AIDS among women is considerably greater in Africa, Asia, and the Caribbean than in the United States. By the end of 2000 the number of HIV-infected women in sub-Saharan Africa—the epicenter of HIV/AIDS—surpassed infected men for the first time (Laurence, 2000). There has also been a dramatic rise in the number of pregnant African women infected with HIV, with rates of 20% or more found among tested populations of women in some parts of Africa (Potts, 2000; Sherfer et al., 2002). The terrible plight of Africa during these plague years is described in the following "Sexuality and Diversity" discussion.

 ## Sexuality and Diversity

AIDS in Africa: Death and Hope on a Dying Continent

To date, more than 80% of AIDS deaths have occurred in Africa, primarily in sub-Saharan nations, which collectively contain the largest concentration of people living with HIV/AIDS worldwide (Summers et al., 2002; UNAIDS, 2003). Even though countries such as India, China, and Russia have rapidly escalating HIV/AIDS epidemics, African countries are still the hardest hit by this horrific pandemic. Of the more than 14 million AIDS orphans—children who have lost their parents to the disease—over 90% live in sub-Saharan African nations (Summers et al., 2002).

In a tragedy the scope of which defies comprehension, HIV/AIDS is devastating a continent already ravaged by wars and poverty. Unless action against this disease is significantly escalated in scope and improved in focus, the damage already done will seem minor compared with what lies ahead. AIDS is poised to wipe out large portions of a generation of African people. Families are being destroyed, and skilled workers—the essence of a nation's wealth—are being cut down at an unprecedented rate.

In many sub-Saharan African nations it is estimated that more than 15% of all adults are infected with HIV (Summers et al., 2002; UNAIDS, 2003). Botswana, which has a population of 1.6 million, has one of the highest HIV infection rates in the world, with more than 1 in 3 adults being HIV-positive (Grunwald, 2002; Upton, 2003). A Botswana 15-year-old now has an estimated 80% chance of dying of AIDS, given the current infection rates in this nation and the lack of either a cure or an effective vaccine (Summers et al., 2002). South Africa now has the fastest growing AIDS epidemic in the world and the largest number of people living with HIV—over 5 million (Sherfer et al., 2002). A recent survey of pregnant women attending South African clinics revealed that more than 22% were infected with HIV, compared to less than 1% nine years earlier (Sherfer et al., 2002).

The U.S. Census Bureau estimates that AIDS will result in negative population growth in several African countries, including Botswana, Lesotho, Mozambique, South Africa, and Swaziland, before 2010 (Stanecki, 2002). Life expectancy (the average age to which a person born today can be expected to live) in many African countries devastated by HIV/AIDS has already been significantly reduced and could drop below age 30 in some countries by 2010.

Many factors account for the widespread dissemination of the AIDS plague in Africa, where HIV is transmitted primarily through heterosexual sex or mother-to-child transmission. Widespread poverty and lack of general medical care in nations that typically spend less than $10 per resident annually for health care are clearly important contributors to the African HIV/AIDS pandemic. Another important factor is that STDs that cause genital ulcers are endemic in Africa. Genital ulcers can increase the susceptibility of uninfected persons to HIV and can heighten the infectivity of people who are already HIV-positive (Ahmed et al., 2003; Feroli & Burstein, 2003). Furthermore, despite a growing awareness of HIV/AIDS throughout Africa and other developing nations in the world community, there is also widespread ignorance (especially among young people) about how to reduce one's vulnerability to HIV infection. For example, a recent study in Mozambique found that 74% of young women and 62% of young men (age 15 to 19) were unaware of any way to protect themselves against HIV infection (UNAIDS, 2001a).

Cultural factors may play an even greater role in perpetuating the African AIDS plague. African nations are male-dominated societies in which most women in ongoing or married relationships "find themselves in relations of economic dependence and sociocultural inferiority to men and are not well positioned to overcome their partner's dislike of barrier contraceptives and their refusal to discuss their other unprotected sexual relationships" (Kesby, 2000, p. 1724). Social conventions in these countries generally require that men promise material support but not sexual fidelity to their partners. Regular use of condoms is low within marriages in cultures where fertility is often central to one's identity. Condoms are also rarely used by men who engage in extramarital liaisons with sex workers or "girlfriends" (Ezzell, 2000; Kesby, 2000).

Another cultural contributor to the spread of HIV in Africa is the so-called sugar daddy syndrome, in which older men with money, many of whom are HIV-positive, look to young teenage women for sex. This cultural trend is also aided by the superstitious belief in many African societies that an HIV-infected man can be cured by having sex with a virgin (Bartholet, 2000). Finally, it is fairly common for women in southern African nations to swab their vaginal walls with cloth, paper, or cotton immediately before and during intercourse, a practice referred to as "dry sex," which is favored by many men (Ezzell, 2000). Dry sex increases the risk of HIV transmission to women by disrupting the normal balance of healthy vaginal lactobacilli, by increasing the likelihood of condom breakage, and by causing tiny tears in the vaginal walls that provide portals for HIV to access the bloodstream.

In many African nations ravaged by HIV/AIDS there is a pervasive sense of hopelessness that often erodes individual initiative to engage in safer sexual behavior. African people are often influenced by a societal narrative that poses a likely life course that includes early marriage, unprotected sex, multiple births, HIV infection, early death, and children left without means of support (Mill & Anarfi, 2002). Individuals held hostage by this life expectation are often immobilized or unmotivated to effect positive behavioral changes. Furthermore, many of the HIV prevention programs implemented thus far in African nations have resulted in limited success rates; these programs have sought to persuade individuals to make rational decisions to change their behavior based solely on the power of words, usually emanating from the mouths of "experts."

Against such a grim background, can there be any hope for Africa's future? The answer is a cautious yes. There have been a few success stories. In the last few years a limited number of programs have been designed and implemented both to combat the crippling effects of hopelessness and to move beyond more traditional information-based prevention approaches. These innovative intervention methods use trained community members, who function as *peer educators,* to reach out to their peers in a grassroots educational effort that includes providing information and resources, a format for talking openly about sexual issues, and a supportive context for positive behavior changes. A major advantage of peer education over the more traditional information-based expert-purveyor model is that peer education places health-related knowledge in the hands of ordinary people, who act not only as peer educators but also as role models for positive behavior change. A number of studies have demonstrated that such grassroots programs increase the likelihood that people will engage in health-promoting behaviors (Campbell & Mzaidume, 2001; Crooks, 2004; Galavotti et al., 2001; Ngugi et al., 1996; Wheeler, 2003). An excellent model for using peer educators to combat HIV/AIDS is provided by a successful program in Uganda that uses Muslim spiritual officials (imams) as leaders of peer education teams (Wheeler, 2003). In this innovative program community volunteers are organized into teams of peer educators and are trained to assist imams in their HIV/AIDS awareness and prevention outreach.

Another peer-educator-based HIV/AIDS intervention program was recently established in the Makindu region of southeastern Kenya by James Curtis and Bob Crooks in collaboration with a number of Kenyan citizens and with the assistance of a German NGO. This program, called Act Now, employs more than 20 Kenyan citizens and is partially funded by royalty revenues from this textbook. James Curtis, an American with extensive international experience, is program director of Act Now. Crooks's involvement includes developing a research strategy to evaluate the impact of this grassroots program (discussed in Chapter 2), designing and implementing a peer-educator-based educational strategy, and conducting 2-week training sessions for peer educator staff. There are two essential ingredients in the Act Now program: the establishment of Voluntary Counseling and Testing (VCT) Centers and the establishment of community education using peer educators drawn from the local population. VCT Centers are locations where individuals can receive voluntary and confidential counseling and testing for HIV. Clients are provided with counseling regarding the HIV test procedure and implications of test results. Simple and reliable tests are used to determine whether or not the virus is present in a sample of blood obtained by a finger stick. Results are available within 20 minutes. Clients may elect to forgo the actual test and still receive counseling on risk factors and prevention practices. For those who are tested, posttest counseling is provided and includes information on how to remain uninfected for those who test negative and information about how to avoid transmitting HIV to others for those who test positive. Act Now currently has two VCT Centers, one at the main headquarters and one satellite center. Act Now will soon add three or four mobile VCT/STD clinics, made possible by a large grant from the European Union (EU). This grant will allow Act Now to dramatically expand the scope of the program by more than doubling the staff and geographically broadening the outreach.

The second ingredient in Act Now's project involves peer educators who work in pairs, meeting with small groups of 14 to 18 people twice weekly, over a 6-week period, in various locations throughout the Makindu region. Content covered in these sessions includes assessment of risk for HIV infection and how HIV infection is transmitted, strategies for avoiding infection, communication skills (such as assertiveness training and condom negotiation skills), gender issues, and other topics pertinent to behavior change and safer sexual behavior. Group sessions use small and large group discussions, role plays, theater, games and group activities, and participatory instruction, such as practicing proper condom application using wood penis models. At the time of this writing 36 groups and almost 600 people have completed the 6-week educational outreach program. Residents of the Makindu region are reached at a rate of 150 to 200 individuals per each 6-week period. With the EU funding, the rate at which people are reached and the regions of

Kenya that can be served will greatly expand. Preliminary evidence indicates significant increases in safer sexual behavior as a direct result of the outreach program (Crooks, 2004). In addition, hundreds of people have undergone voluntary testing and counseling at Act Now's VCT Centers.

Perhaps the best hope for Africa lies in the development of the ultimate weapon against any virus—an effective preventive vaccine. However, as discussed elsewhere in this chapter, progress on this front has been slow, and the likelihood of having such a vaccine in the near future is dim at best.

Transmission

HIV has been found in the semen, blood, vaginal secretions, saliva, urine, and breast milk of infected individuals. It also can occur in any other bodily fluids that contain blood, including cerebrospinal fluid and amniotic fluid. Blood, semen, and vaginal secretions are the three bodily fluids that most consistently contain high concentrations of the virus in infected people. Most commonly, HIV enters the body when bodily fluids are exchanged during unprotected vaginal or anal intercourse or oral–genital contact with an infected person. Transmission of HIV through sexual contact is estimated to be the cause of about 80% of worldwide HIV infections. HIV is also readily transmitted by means of blood-contaminated needles shared by injection drug users.

The virus can also be passed perinatally from an infected woman to her fetus before birth, to her infant during birth, or to her baby after birth through breast feeding (Richardson et al., 2003a; Rousseau et al., 2003). Mother-to-child transmission (MTCT) is the primary way that children are infected with HIV. In 2001 approximately 800,000 children worldwide were infected with HIV, 90% of whom acquired the infection by means of MTCT (Rousseau et al., 2003a). In the United States almost all new HIV infections in children result from perinatal MTCT (Minkoff, 2003). In recent years the number of perinatally acquired cases of HIV infections in the United States has declined dramatically, in large part because of new treatment techniques used with pregnant women before and during delivery and later with their newborn infants. We discuss these prevention strategies in a later section dealing with treatment.

The likelihood of transmitting HIV during sexual contact depends on both the viral dose and the route of HIV exposure. Viral dose is a direct effect of the **viral load**—how much virus is present in an infected person's blood. The viral load measurement widely used is the number of individual viruses in a milliliter of blood. In general, the greater the viral load, the higher the chance of transmitting the infection. As common sense would suggest, when a person is in late stages of HIV/AIDS disease, with more advanced infection and thus greater viral load, he or she is highly infectious. However, many of our readers might be surprised to hear that evidence strongly indicates that in the initial period between exposure to HIV and the appearance of HIV antibodies in the blood—a period called *primary infection*, which usually lasts a few months—viral load can be extremely high, creating a state of heightened infectiousness (Koopman, 1996; Royce et al., 1997). This relatively brief peak in the transmissibility of HIV soon after a person is infected is especially troubling because most infected people are likely to remain unaware during these few months that they have been invaded by HIV. Some experts believe that transmission during primary infection accounts for a large portion of HIV infections worldwide.

The likelihood of infection during sexual activity is greater when HIV is transmitted directly into the blood (e.g., through small tears in the rectal tissues or vaginal walls) rather than onto a mucous membrane. In recent years researchers have become increasingly aware that circumcision status affects a man's risk for contracting HIV. The foreskin of the uncircumcised penis is soft and prone to tiny lacerations that may allow HIV to enter the bloodstream more easily. This could be a primary reason that circumcision provides some protection against HIV infection (J. Cohen, 2000; Quinn, 2000; Reynolds et al., 2004).

Research also suggests that HIV can be transmitted during oral sex when the virus present in semen or vaginal secretions comes into contact with mucous membrane tissues in the mouth (X. Liu et al., 2003). There has been a general tendency to view oral sex as a relatively safe practice. This viewpoint was first called into question by the results of a study with

Viral load The amount of HIV present in an infected person's blood.

monkeys in which researchers gently placed a simian version of the AIDS virus, called SIV, on the backs of the tongues of seven rhesus monkeys. Six of the monkeys became infected (Baba et al., 1997).

More recently, researchers reported that 8 out of 102 gay and bisexual men who had recently been infected contracted HIV through oral sex (Torassa, 2000). All eight of these men had engaged in no other risk behavior except oral sex, and most of them indicated that they thought oral sex had little or no risk. A recent laboratory study provided further evidence that unprotected oral sex has the potential to transmit HIV. In this investigation researchers exposed oral tissue samples obtained from more than 50 HIV-negative individuals to three strains of HIV-1. Two of the HIV strains infected and reproduced in the cells that line the surface of the mouth, and these infected cells transferred the infection to adjacent white blood cells (X. Liu et al., 2003).

Sexual Health

Current CDC recommendations for preventing HIV transmission call for using a condom during mouth-to-penis contact. However, it is extremely rare for people to use condoms during oral sex (Torassa, 2000). If you engage in unprotected oral sex with partners whose HIV status is unknown, it would be wise to take certain precautions: Make sure that your gums are in good shape (oral sores or breaks in gum tissue provide HIV with easier access to blood), avoid flossing immediately before or after sex (flossing can damage oral tissue and cause bleeding), and avoid taking ejaculated semen into your mouth. Furthermore, in light of the often substantial concentration of HIV in vaginal fluids (Money et al., 2003), you might also be cautious about engaging in cunnilingus with a female partner who has not tested negative for HIV and whose sexual history is unclear to you. ■

In the early 1980s, before the federal government required screening of donated blood for HIV, contaminated blood and blood products infected an estimated 25,000 transfusion recipients and people with blood-clotting disorders (such as hemophilia) in the United States (Graham, 1997). However, since early 1985, donated blood and blood products have been screened with extensive laboratory testing for the presence of HIV antibodies. The transition from partially paid to all-volunteer donors has further enhanced the integrity of the U.S. blood supply by eliminating persons who would donate primarily for monetary gain (Williams et al., 1997). (Health officials believe that blood donors might be less candid about their histories when offered incentives to give blood.) In addition, U.S. blood centers now use behavioral-history-based screening procedures in a format of face-to-face oral interviews by trained staff. These developments have reduced the risk of transfusion-transmitted HIV to an estimated level of approximately 2 infections per 1 million blood units. This minuscule number of infections is due almost entirely to donations made in the early stage of primary infection before antibodies are present in the blood (Williams et al., 1997).

However, precautions designed to safeguard the nation's blood supply, although admirably effective, are not foolproof. One problem is that the blood test detects antibodies to HIV rather than the virus itself. And because HIV antibodies can take months or even years in a few cases to show up in the blood, contaminated units of blood have on rare occasions slipped by. There is, however, no danger of being infected as a result of donating blood. Blood banks, the Red Cross, and other blood-collection centers use sterile equipment and a new disposable needle for each donor. Unfortunately, U.S. procedures for safeguarding the blood supply are not widely practiced globally. According to the World Health Organization (WHO), more than two-thirds of the world's countries fail to ensure safe blood supplies for their populations (Crossette, 2000). This problem is especially acute in some of the world's poorest nations, which also have high rates of blood-transmitted diseases, such as HIV and viral hepatitis.

Research indicates that a small percentage of people appear to be resistant to HIV infection (Misrahi et al., 1998; Royce et al., 1997). There are documented cases of sex workers and homosexual men who remain uninfected despite repeatedly engaging in unprotected sexual intercourse with HIV-infected partners (Cohen, 1998; Dean et al., 1996; Fowke et al., 1996). We can hope that research will someday unlock these mysteries of immunity and perhaps pave the way to development of better prevention and treatment strategies.

It is believed that the risk of transmitting HIV through saliva, tears, and urine is extremely low. Furthermore, no evidence indicates that the virus can be transmitted by casual contact such as hugging, shaking hands, cooking or eating together, or other forms of casual contact with an infected person (Courville et al., 1998). All the research to date

The late Arthur Ashe, tennis great, at a news conference announcing that he had AIDS as a result of being transfused with HIV-tainted blood.

confirms that it is sexual contact with an infected person or sharing contaminated needles that places an individual at risk for HIV infection. Furthermore, certain high-risk behaviors increase the chance of infection. These behaviors include having multiple sexual partners, engaging in unprotected sex, sexual contact with people known to be at high risk (such as injection drug users, sex workers, and people with multiple sexual partners), sharing drug injection equipment, and using noninjected drugs such as cocaine, marijuana, and alcohol.

Symptoms and Complications

As with many viruses, HIV often causes a brief flulike illness within a few weeks of initial infection. Symptoms include fevers, muscle aches, skin rashes, loss of appetite, and swollen lymph glands. These initial reactions, which represent the body's defenses at work, tend to fade fairly rapidly. However, as the virus continues to deplete the immune system, other symptoms can occur, such as persistent or periodically repeating fevers, night sweats, weight loss, chronic fatigue, persistent diarrhea or bloody stools, easy bruising, persistent headaches, a chronic dry cough, and oral candidiasis. Oral candidiasis of the mouth and throat is the most common infection in HIV-infected people. Many of these physical manifestations also indicate common, everyday ailments that are by no means life-threatening. However, observing that you have one or more of these symptoms that are persistent can alert you to seek a medical diagnosis of your ailment.

HIV Antibody Tests

Within a few months of being infected with HIV, most people develop antibodies to the virus, in a process called *seroconversion*. Seroconversion typically occurs sometime between 25 days and 6 months after initial infection. HIV infection can be detected by standard blood tests for blood serum antibodies to HIV (tests such as ELISA and Western blot). The Food and Drug Administration (2002) recently announced approval of a new HIV diagnostic test kit that uses a finger-stick sample of blood and provides results that are 99.6% accurate in as little as 20 minutes. HIV antibodies can also be detected with a high degree of accuracy in urine and saliva samples (SIECUS, 2003; Strauss et al., 2003). For more information about HIV tests and test sites, contact the CDC National Hotline at 1-800-342-2437 (English), 1-800-344-7432 (Spanish), or 1-800-243-7889 (TTY), or go online to the Web site of the American Social Health Association.

Although quite uncommon, "silent" HIV infections can be present in some individuals for 3 years or more before being detected by standard serum antibody tests. More costly and more labor intensive tests for the virus itself can be performed to detect a silent or latent infection. Once infected with HIV, a person should be considered contagious and capable of infecting others indefinitely, regardless of whether clinical signs of disease are present.

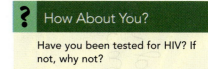

? How About You?

Have you been tested for HIV? If not, why not?

The development of better treatment strategies offers compelling reasons for people at risk to discover their HIV status as soon as possible. Presumably, once people become aware of their HIV-positive status, they will be much less likely to pass the infection on to others. This assumption was supported by a study that found that, of 615 men and women recently diagnosed with HIV infection, most adopted safer sexual behaviors after diagnosis, including regular use of condoms, less frequent or no sex, or engaging only in oral sex (Centers for Disease Control, 2000a). Another recent study found that a substantial majority of 1,363 HIV-infected men and women were using condoms during vaginal or anal intercourse with partners known to be HIV-negative and with partners of unknown HIV status (Centers for Disease Control, 2003a).

Efforts to encourage testing have been focused most directly on people at higher than normal risk for HIV infection, including MSM, injection drug users, clients at STD clinics, people who have unprotected vaginal and/or anal intercourse with multiple partners, and health care workers exposed to patients' blood. Unfortunately, despite the potential benefits of early antibody testing and the availability of treatment and counseling for infected persons, a large number of at-risk individuals, especially sexually active young people (gay, bisexual, and heterosexual), are not being tested for HIV (Maguen et al., 2000). For example, in one study that targeted a large sample of young MSM, researchers found that of the 573 study participants found to be HIV-positive, 77% were unaware that they were infected (Mackellar et al., 2002).

A recent nationally representative survey found that approximately one-third of U.S. adults have been tested for HIV. Even though people who perceive themselves to be at risk for HIV or who have engaged in high-risk behaviors are more likely than others to have been tested, a substantial number of individuals in either of these categories have never been tested for the virus (Centers for Disease Control, 2001). As described in a final section of this chapter, we believe that all couples poised on the brink of a new sexual relationship should seriously consider undergoing medical examinations and laboratory testing designed to rule out HIV and other STDs before beginning any sexual activity that might put them at risk for infection. The following account expresses one man's experience in this area:

Development of AIDS

As HIV continues to proliferate and invade healthy cells in an infected person's body, the immune system loses its capacity to defend itself against opportunistic infections. The incubation period for AIDS (i.e., the time between HIV infection and the onset of one or more severe, debilitating diseases associated with extreme impairment of the immune system) typically ranges from 8 to 11 years in adults, with a median duration of about 10 years. However, a small percentage of people infected with HIV remain symptom-free for much longer periods. Furthermore, as we will see, powerful new treatment strategies can also dramatically slow the progress of HIV/AIDS in those individuals who have access to these costly treatments.

People who experience progression to full-blown AIDS can develop a range of serious, life-threatening complications. The most common severe disease among HIV-infected people, and one that accounts for many AIDS deaths, is pneumonia caused by overgrowth of the protozoan *Pneumocystis carinii*, which normally inhabits the lungs of healthy people. Some other opportunistic infections associated with HIV include encephalitis (viral infection of the brain), severe fungal infections that cause a type of meningitis, tuberculosis, salmonella illnesses (bacterial diseases), and toxoplasmosis (caused by a protozoan). The body is also vulnerable to cancers, such as lymphomas (cancers of the lymph system), cervical cancer, and Kaposi's sarcoma, the most common cancer in male AIDS patients, which affects the skin and can also involve internal organs.

Before the advent of much-improved antiretroviral treatments, once people living with AIDS developed life-threatening illnesses, such as pneumonia or cancer, the disease tended to run a fairly rapid course. Death usually occurred within 2 years for both men and women (Suligoi, 1997). Furthermore, most people who have developed AIDS since the beginning of the epidemic in the United States have already died. However, a significant decline in the rate of AIDS deaths began in 1996 (the first year that the death rate declined since the onset of the epidemic) and has continued to the present time. In 1994 AIDS was the most common cause of death in the United States for men and women aged 25–44 years; however, by 2001 AIDS was ranked as the fifth leading cause of death for both sexes in this age group (Feinberg & Japour, 2003). This reversal in death trends was largely due to improvement in combination drug therapies, which we discuss in the next section.

The reduction in AIDS deaths seen in the United States is also occurring in other developed nations that have the resources to implement the more effective drug therapies. Unfortunately, this reversal in AIDS deaths is not occurring in developing nations, especially those

Critical Thinking Question

It has been suggested that all adolescents and adults should be required to undergo screening for the presence of HIV. Do you agree with this recommendation? How might the results of such testing be effectively used to reduce the transmission of HIV? What problems might occur as a result of compulsory screening? Do you believe that mandatory testing would be an unjustifiable violation of privacy rights?

located in Africa, Asia, and the Caribbean, where HIV/AIDS is continuing to escalate both in number of infections and number of deaths (Thaker & Snow, 2003). The high cost and difficulty of administering new and better therapies are barriers to the effective use of these treatments in poor, undeveloped nations.

Treatment

At the time of this writing, there is still no cure for HIV/AIDS. However, thousands of scientists are involved in an unprecedented worldwide effort to ultimately cure and/or prevent this horrific disease. These efforts are being waged on several fronts, including attempts to develop effective antiretroviral drugs that will kill or at least neutralize HIV and efforts to create a vaccine effective against HIV.

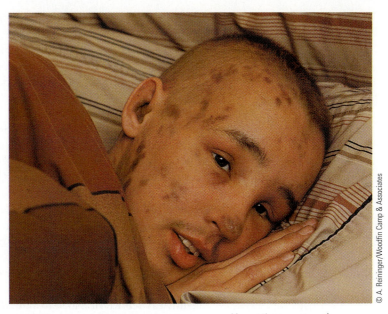

Kaposi's sarcoma, shown here with its distinctive skin lesions, is the most common cancer afflicting men with AIDS.

© A. Reininger/Woodfin Camp & Associates

As we described earlier, HIV is classified as a retrovirus because, after invading a living cell, it works backward, using an enzyme called *reverse transcriptase.* This enzyme transcribes the viral RNA into DNA, which then acts to direct further synthesis of the lethal HIV RNA. HIV also encodes another enzyme, called a *protease* (protein digesting), that is equally critical to its reproduction. Once HIV invades a host CD4 cell, it eventually takes over the host cell's genetic material and manufacturing capacity, producing additional viruses to infect other cells. During this process, HIV kills the host cell and injects copies of its own lethal RNA into the blood to invade other healthy cells.

To date, treatment strategies have focused on drug interventions designed to block the proliferation and seeding of HIV throughout the immune system and other bodily tissues and organs. Up to the mid-1990s the main class of drugs used to combat HIV were products that inhibited the action of the reverse transcriptase enzyme. These reverse transcriptase (RT) inhibitors were designed to prevent the virus from copying its own genetic material and making more viruses. A major breakthrough in drug therapy took place in 1996 with the emergence of a new class of drugs that inhibit HIV's protease enzyme, which the virus uses to assemble new copies of itself. When a protease inhibitor (PI) drug was combined with two RT inhibitor drugs in early clinical trials, the combination was shown to dramatically reduce viral load in blood to minimal or undetectable levels in most patients (Louis et al., 1997; Wong et al., 1997).

At the time of this writing 17 antiretroviral drugs—11 RT inhibitors and 6 PIs—have been approved by the FDA for the treatment of HIV/AIDS (Feinberg & Japour, 2003). The PIs are considered the most potent drugs in the treatment arsenal for HIV/AIDS (Prabu-Jeyabalan et al., 2003).

Highly Active Antiretroviral Therapy

The use of a combination of three or more drugs to combat HIV, which initially was commonly referred to as combination or triple drug therapy (or in the popular media as the "AIDS cocktail"), has more recently come to be known as **highly active antiretroviral therapy (HAART).** Most clinicians commence initial treatment of HIV/AIDS with either a combination of three RTs or a combination of two RTs and one PI according to the latest guidelines from the National Institutes of Health and the CDC (Centers for Disease Control, 2002h; Mansky et al., 2003; McNeil, 2004). A recently completed three-year study identified an ideal HAART regimen for new patients comprised of three RT drugs (Gulick et al., 2004). This drug cocktail is the same one the World Health Organization has been recommending in developing countries since 2002 and has recently been made available to people in these poorer nations in the form of low-cost generic three-in-one pills manufactured in India (McNeil, 2004).

It is generally agreed that HAART should be administered to any HIV-infected person whose CD4 count is below 200 or to anyone who manifests symptomatic disease (i.e., infections or cancers associated with HIV/AIDS). However, deciding the optimal stage of

Highly active antiretroviral therapy (HAART) A strategy for treating HIV-infected people with three or more antiretroviral drugs.

InfoTrac Search Words

■ HAART

HIV infection at which to initiate HAART among people with CD4 counts above 200 who are asymptomatic is a complex issue that is still under debate (Ahdieh-Grant et al., 2003). The potential benefits and risks of early or delayed therapy need to be carefully evaluated by both the treating clinician and the patient (Centers for Disease Control, 2002a). Table 17.2 provides a summary of these potential benefits and risks.

The cumulative evidence to date supports initiating therapy for asymptomatic HIV-infected persons with CD4 counts below 350 (Ahdieh-Grant et al., 2003; Centers for Disease Control, 2002a). However, the decision to begin HAART for asymptomatic patients with CD4 counts greater than 200 but less than 350 "is complex and must be made in the setting of careful patient counseling and education" (Centers for Disease Control, 2002a, p. 17). Some of the factors to be considered in this decision include (1) the readiness and ability of the person to begin treatment, (2) the risk for disease progression and reduced immune function without treatment, (3) the potential benefits and risks of initiating therapy for asymptomatic persons (see Table 17.2), and (4) the likelihood of adherence to the prescribed HAART regimen.

In the United States and other developed nations HAART has proven to be an effective treatment regimen for a large number of HIV/AIDS patients. Various studies have demonstrated that, when properly administered, HAART can inhibit HIV replication and frequently can reduce viral load to an undetectable level, improve immune function, and delay progression of the disease (Ahdieh-Grant et al., 2003; Centers for Disease Control, 2002a; Chesney, 2003). Current data indicate that HAART is responsible for a threefold drop in the death rate from AIDS since its introduction (Prabu-Jeyabalan et al., 2003).

The excellent clinical results produced by HAART in the early years after it was implemented led to a surge of optimism that this advance in antiretroviral therapy might not only delay HIV/AIDS progression but also ultimately eradicate the virus. Unfortunately, as we will see, these early projections were overly optimistic.

The success of HAART is directly dependent on people being able to consistently and correctly adhere to complicated medication dosing schedules for long time periods (Chesney, 2003). Unfortunately, patient adherence to the HAART regimen is often not very good. Several studies have revealed that rates of nonadherence to the regimen, range from 37% to 70% (Murphy et al., 2000).

Several factors have been shown to influence patient adherence or compliance to HAART. One important variable is the complexity of the treatment itself. The more complex the drug

TABLE 17.2	Potential Benefits and Risks of Early or Delayed HAART Initiation for Asymptomatic HIV-Infected Persons		
Potential Benefits of Early Treatment	**Potential Risks of Early Treatment**	**Potential Benefits of Delayed Treatment**	**Potential Risks of Delayed Treatment**
• Earlier suppression of viral replication. • Preservation of immune function. • Prolongation of disease-free survival. • Decrease in the risk of transmitting HIV to others.	• Adverse effects of HAART on quality of life. • Reduced adherence over time due to inconvenient and complicated drug regimens. • Development of drug resistance due to suboptimal adherence to HAART. • Limitation of future treatment options as a result of premature cycling of a patient through the available drugs. • Development of drug-resistant HIV strains. • Development of serious drug side effects.	• Minimization of adverse drug side effects and treatment-related negative effects on quality of life. • Delayed development of viral drug resistance. • Preservation of treatment options (i.e., reserving the limited number of available drugs until later in the course of HIV disease).	• Possibility of irreversible damage to the immune system, which might have been averted by earlier treatment. • Possibility that suppression of viral replication might be more difficult at a later stage of disease. • Increased risk of HIV transmission to others during a longer untreated period.

SOURCES: Ahdieh-Grant et al. (2003) and Centers for Disease Control (2002a).

regimen, the less likely it is that patients will correctly and consistently follow it, regardless of their age and educational level (Murphy et al., 2000). For people on HAART it can seem like a full-time job to strictly adhere to a rigid and difficult regimen that requires taking many pills daily at different time intervals, some on a full stomach, others before eating. This can become a daunting task. People with regular schedules, who can associate pill taking with recurring activities, generally manifest better adherence to HAART than individuals who have irregular schedules (Chesney, 2003; Murphy et al., 2000).

Another drawback of HAART that influences adherence is drug toxicity. Low compliance is often associated with adverse drug side effects, which include anemia, insomnia, mouth ulcers, diarrhea, inflammation of the pancreas, respiratory difficulties, metabolic disturbances, increased cholesterol and triglyceride levels (major risk factors for cardiovascular diseases), gastrointestinal discomfort, liver damage, excess fat accumulation in areas such as the abdomen, upper back, and breasts, fat atrophy in the face, legs, and arms, and skin rashes (Centers for Disease Control, 2002a; Chesney, 2003). Some of these side effects can be so severe that affected people are unable to tolerate HAART.

Lack of adherence to HAART because of dosing complexities and/or drug toxicity side effects can lead to less than optimal therapy, outright treatment failure, and the development of drug-resistant strains of HIV (Chesney, 2003; L. Miller et al., 2003). Successful long-term treatment of HIV/AIDS requires at least 95% adherence to a prescribed HAART regimen (Chesney, 2003). Unfortunately, many people undergoing HAART do not achieve this high level of adherence, which is so essential to optimize their prospects for long-term viral suppression (L. Miller et al., 2003). Recent improvements in medication dosing schedules (e.g., once or twice a day versus three times a day) and reductions in pill quantity (e.g., combining two or three drugs in one pill) have resulted in better adherence to HAART (Centers for Disease Control, 2002a; Chesney, 2003).

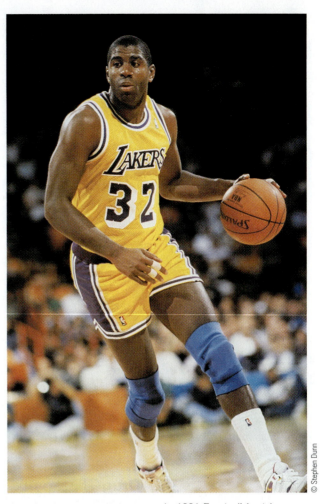

In 1991 Earvin (Magic) Johnson, Los Angeles Lakers basketball All-Star, announced that he had been infected with HIV through heterosexual contact. By April 1997, HAART had reduced HIV to undetectable levels in his body.

Treatment failure, defined as HAART drugs that no longer suppress viral loads, can occur even in people who correctly adhere to the treatment regimen (Centers for Disease Control, 2000a; Kaufmann et al., 2000). When treatment failures occur, patients are generally switched to another three-drug combination in established HAART regimens, which might reestablish effective viral load suppression.

Another problem with HAART that surfaced in recent years further dampened the optimism and excitement associated with the early years of this treatment protocol. It is now clear that HAART does not eradicate HIV from latent or silent reservoirs in the brain, lymph nodes, intestines, and other tissues, cells, and organs where the virus may reside undetected and intact, even though blood plasma viral loads drop to minimal or undetectable levels (Chesney, 2003; Kaufmann et al., 2000). Once treatment with the HAART regimen stops or is seriously compromised because a patient is too sick with toxic side effects or too confused by the complexity of dosing regimens, the virus sequestered in these lethal reservoirs typically comes roaring back, or it mutates, resulting in drug resistance in new strains of HIV that are less susceptible to the HAART drugs.

On a more positive note, the drastically reduced and sustained low viral loads that result from successful HAART treatment "substantially [reduce] the likelihood of HIV transmission" (Centers for Disease Control, 2002a). However, despite a strong association between reduced risk for HIV transmission and sustained low viral loads, a person can transmit the virus at any time after becoming infected, even while undergoing successful HAART (Centers for Disease Control, 2002a). Consequently, HAART is no substitute for safer sexual behavior or abstinence.

Has the availability of HAART influenced HIV-negative people to change their sexual behaviors? Do people undergoing this treatment regimen change their sexual behaviors after

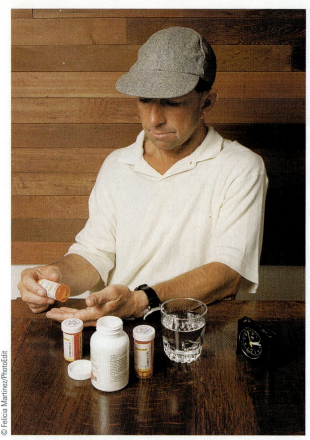

Patients undergoing HAART must strictly adhere to a rigid and difficult regimen that involves taking large daily doses of drugs spaced at different time intervals.

beginning treatment? Evidence collected in the early years of HAART indicated that at least some HIV-negative gay and bisexual men increased their involvement in risky sex as a direct result of the availability of this treatment regimen (Dilley et al., 1997; Kelly et al., 1998). More recent studies have confirmed a continuation of this trend toward increased sexual risk taking among gay and bisexual men as a result of, at least in part, improved treatment for HIV/AIDS (Kalb, 2003b; Scheer et al., 2001). A recent survey conducted by the CDC found that many people at high risk for HIV infection were less concerned about HIV/AIDS and more inclined to engage in risky behaviors since the advent of HAART. The study population of almost 2,000 HIV-negative people from several states consisted of nearly equal numbers of injection drug users, gay men, and heterosexuals who were attending STD clinics. Of these respondents, 31% said that they were less concerned about the disease and 17% indicated being less careful about drug and sexual practices because of the availability of HAART. Especially troubling was the finding that among gay men less concerned about HIV, many were engaging more frequently in unprotected receptive anal sex, the riskiest sexual behavior (Lehman, 2000).

Many persons who are aware that they are infected with HIV do refrain from engaging in risky sexual behavior. However, some HIV-positive individuals do continue to behave in a sexually reckless manner, as evidenced by research conducted in several large urban areas in the United States that indicates that "the overall rate of continued unprotected intercourse among persons living with HIV disease is 33%" (Heckman et al., 2003, p. 134).

Drug Therapy to Prevent Mother-to-Child Transmission of HIV

In 1994, research demonstrated that zidovudine, an RT inhibitor drug administered to both HIV-infected mothers and their newborns, sharply reduced perinatal mother-to-child-transmission (MTCT) by two-thirds (Connor et al., 1994). In August 1994 the U.S. Public Health Service recommended zidovudine to reduce perinatal MTCT of HIV. The standard treatment protocol involves administering zidovudine orally to pregnant women (starting between 14 and 34 weeks of gestation), intravenously during labor, and orally to the newborn for the first 6 weeks of life (Thaker & Snow, 2003). Since 1994 the number of infants infected through MTCT has declined dramatically in the United States, largely because of the widespread use of the zidovudine treatment regimen, which prevents MTCT in most instances (Minkoff, 2003).

The success of this relatively long and complex regimen of zidovudine for reducing MTCT has stimulated a search for a less costly, practical, and effective short-course antiretroviral regimen. Two recent South African studies found that infants who were provided with either (1) a single dose of the RT inhibitor drug nevirapine within 24 hours of birth or (2) a short-course regimen with this drug experienced excellent protection from HIV infection (Altman, 2002; D. Moodley et al, 2003). These findings bode well for countries with limited resources because single-dose or short-course nevirapine therapy is dramatically less costly than the longer and more complex zidovudine regimen.

Each year an estimated 800,000 infants worldwide acquire HIV infection through MTCT (Rousseau et al., 2003). Most of these infants live in resource-poor developing nations. Although the number of programs that provide zidovudine to pregnant HIV-infected women in developing nations has increased, the need for such intervention remains enormous (John et al., 2001). Moreover, preventing perinatal MTCT does not eliminate the possibility of later transmission of the virus from a mother to a child through breast feeding. Global data indicate that one-third to one-half of all HIV infections in infants occur through breast feeding (Rousseau et al., 2003). Unfortunately, at present, there is no therapeutic regimen that significantly reduces MTCT through breast feeding (Rousseau et al., 2003). Health authorities are hopeful that presenting alternatives to breast feeding, such as breast-milk substitutes or early weaning, will help reduce transmission of HIV through breast milk. Unfortunately, alternatives to breast milk are often unaffordable, or undesirable because of contaminated water, in resource-poor developing countries where breast feeding (regardless of maternal HIV status) continues to be the most prevalent form of infant feeding (Rousseau et al., 2003).

The Search for a Vaccine

We close this section on treatment with an update on efforts to develop an effective vaccine for HIV. Development of a safe, effective, and affordable vaccine is a global public health priority and remains the best long-term hope for bringing the worldwide HIV/AIDS pandemic under control. Almost a quarter-century has passed since AIDS was first reported, and the pandemic continues to spread at an astounding rate, with an estimated 14,000 new cases of HIV infection occurring daily worldwide (Hu et al., 2003).

There are two broad categories of vaccines: (1) those that prevent initial infection by HIV (prophylactic vaccines) and (2) those that delay or prevent progression of disease in those already infected (therapeutic vaccines). Despite extensive efforts, researchers so far have failed to develop vaccines from either category that are broadly effective against HIV (Hu et al., 2003; N. Russell et al., 2003).

However, recent developments in HIV vaccine research have been favorable. For example, an increasing number of vaccine candidates are entering the development pipeline, and several major efficacy trials of vaccine candidates do provide a basis for some guarded hope for future successes in this critical research area (Hu et al., 2003). A number of problems confront vaccine researchers, including the absence of an ideal animal model for research and the combined facts that HIV is extremely complicated, that the virus is present in multiple strains, and that it can change rapidly as a result of genetic mutation (Hu et al., 2003; Prabu-Jeyabalan et al., 2003).

To date, several therapeutic HIV vaccines have been tested in small-scale human studies and found to be largely ineffective. Continuing efforts in this area will hopefully yield more positive results. Testing of prophylactic vaccines is currently being conducted in the United States, Thailand, Canada, Puerto Rico, the Netherlands, and Uganda (Eaton, 2003; Hu et al., 2003; Mayor, 2003b; N. Russell et al., 2003). The first report of an apparently successful HIV vaccine was recently widely publicized by the media. This prophylactic vaccine, which has been in efficacy trials for 3 years, is a genetically engineered product derived from a protein found on the surface of HIV. Despite media reports to the contrary, the manufacturer of this vaccine recently acknowledged that efficacy trials have failed to demonstrate significant overall reduction in the development of HIV infection among more than 5,000 study subjects, all of whom were HIV-negative when they joined the study. At the end of 3 years, 5.7% of subjects in the vaccine group and 5.8% of subjects in the no-vaccine placebo group had become infected with HIV. The vaccine did, however, produce a significant reduction in HIV infection among black and Asian volunteer subjects. In these two ethnic minorities there were 67% fewer HIV infections among the vaccinated volunteers than among those receiving the placebo. The size of these two groups was small, and most of the 5,000 volunteer subjects were white (Eaton, 2003). But although this vaccine was not shown to be broadly effective, it is encouraging that it may offer hope to at least some ethnic groups.

For the sake of the world's population, especially in developing countries where minuscule per-capita health expenditures rule out costly drug therapies, we can only hope that effective, low-cost vaccines are available soon.

Prevention

The only certain way to avoid contracting HIV *sexually* is either to avoid all varieties of interpersonal sexual contact that place one at risk for infection or to be involved in a monogamous, mutually faithful relationship with one uninfected partner. If neither of these conditions is applicable, a wise person will act in a way that significantly reduces his or her risk of becoming infected with HIV.

Safer sex practices that reduce the risk of contracting HIV/AIDS and other STDs are described in some detail in the last section of this chapter. Most of these preventive methods are directly applicable to HIV/AIDS. However, it is important to note that any strategies that reduce your risk of developing any of the other STDs previously discussed will also reduce your risk of HIV infection because of the known association between HIV/AIDS and other STDs. Research throughout the world has shown that the risk of contracting HIV is elevated in people who have other STDs, such as genital herpes, gonorrhea, syphilis, chancroid, chlamydia, and trichomoniasis (Ahmed et al., 2003; Feroli & Burstein, 2003). STDs that cause genital ulcers, such as herpes, syphilis, and chancroid, have shown the highest association with HIV infection in North America and Africa (Blocker et al., 2000; C. Chen et al., 2000; P. Moodley et al., 2003), because genital ulcers allow HIV easy access to the bloodstream.

Beyond the obvious safer sex strategies of consistently and correctly using latex condoms and avoiding sex with multiple partners or with individuals at high risk for HIV, in the following list we provide some suggestions particularly relevant to avoiding HIV infection. You will note that several of these suggestions, such as avoiding oral contact with semen and vaginal fluids, are less significant for two healthy people in a monogamous relationship who apply common sense in evaluating what is most likely to be risky for them.

1. If you use injected drugs, do not share needles or syringes (boiling does not guarantee sterility). If needle sharing continues, use bleach to clean and sterilize your needles and syringes. However, be aware that research has shown that bleach has only limited effectiveness for the disinfection of injection equipment (Lurie & Drucker, 1997).

2. Injection drug users may wish to check with local health departments to see if a needle- or syringe-exchange program exists. These programs, which provide clean syringes or needles in exchange for used syringes or needles, have been shown to reduce the spread of HIV and other blood-borne infections among high-risk injection drug users (Bluthenthal et al., 2000).

3. Avoid oral, vaginal, or anal contact with semen.

4. Avoid anal intercourse, because this is one of the riskiest of all sexual behaviors associated with HIV transmission (Calzavara et al., 2003; Ray & Quinn, 2000).

5. Do not engage in insertion of fingers or fists ("fisting") into the anus as an active or receptive partner. Fingernails can easily cause tears in the rectal tissues, thereby creating a route for HIV to penetrate the blood.

6. Avoid oral contact with the anus (a practice commonly referred to as rimming).

7. Avoid oral contact with vaginal fluids.

8. Do not allow a partner's urine to enter your mouth, anus, vagina, eyes, or open cuts or sores.

9. Avoid sexual intercourse during menstruation. HIV-infected women are at increased risk for transmitting their infection, through intercourse, while menstruating (Royce et al., 1997).

10. Do not share razor blades, toothbrushes, or other implements that could become contaminated with blood.

11. In view of the remote possibility that HIV may be transmitted by means of prolonged open-mouth wet kissing, it might be wise to avoid this activity. There is no risk of HIV transmission through closed-mouth kissing.

12. Avoid sexual contact with sex workers (male or female). Research indicates that sex workers have unusually high rates of HIV infection. ■

At present, the best hope for curtailing the spread of HIV/AIDS is through education and behavior change. Because neither an effective vaccine nor a drug-based cure seems likely in the near future, the only viable available strategy for significantly curtailing this pandemic is preventing exposure through education about effective prevention and risk-reduction strategies (Hoxworth et al., 2003). A wide range of published studies of a variety of prevention strategies, directed at a broad range of target populations, have provided promising findings, indicating that intensive educational and behavioral interventions are often effective in reducing risky behaviors that increase vulnerability to HIV infection (Albarracin et al., 2003; DiClemente & Wingwood, 2003; Johnson et al., 2003; Kalichman et al., 1996).

A recent meta-analysis (a complex statistical procedure that collectively analyzes data from many studies) of 46 studies that assessed the effectiveness of persuasive communications in HIV prevention found that a number of communication strategies lead to an increase in safer sexual behavior, especially condom use (Albarracin et al., 2003). Two of the most effective strategies were (1) messages designed to teach people successful condom use strategies, such as how to negotiate with partners who refuse to use condoms, and (2) attitudinal messages that clearly described the preventive outcomes of condom use. Another recent meta-analysis of 44 studies of HIV prevention strategies applied to adolescents found that a variety of intensive behavioral interventions reduce HIV risk by accomplishing one or more of the following goals: (1) increasing condom use, (2) improving sexual communication between partners, (3) delaying sexual debut (i.e., first intercourse experience), (4) decreasing the number of sexual partners, and (5) increasing both overall knowledge of and skills in applying prevention tactics (Johnson et al., 2003).

The findings of these two meta-analyses demonstrate that HIV prevention interventions can result in safer sexual behaviors. In the absence of a cure or effective vaccine, these educational efforts provide the best weapons in the current worldwide war being waged against this devastating disease.

▶ Preventing Sexually Transmitted Diseases

Many approaches to curtailing the spread of STDs have been advocated. These range from attempting to discourage sexual activity among young people to providing easy public access to information about the symptoms of STDs, along with free medical treatment. Unfortunately, the efforts of public health agencies have not been very successful in curbing the rapid spread of STDs. For this reason, it is doubly important to stress a variety of specific preventive measures that can be taken by an individual or a couple.

Clearly, abstinence from partner sex is one virtually surefire way to avoid an STD infection. Being disease-free and monogamous yourself and having a partner who is also disease-free and monogamous is another way to prevent contracting an STD. However, it is often difficult for people to assess the disease-risk status of prospective or current partners and, for that matter, how committed their partners are to being monogamous. For example, in one study of 119 couples dating in college, investigators found that most of the participants were generally unaware of their partner's past and concurrent sexual risk behavior, despite their involvement together in a range of shared sexual activities (Seal, 1997).

Having a frank and open discussion before initial sexual interaction may seem difficult and embarrassing. However, in this era of epidemic health-damaging and/or life-threatening STDs, such discussions are essential to making sound judgments that may have profound ramifications for your physical and psychological well-being. Consequently, we address this issue early in our outline of prevention guidelines.

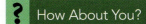

How About You?

Has the threat of contracting STDs altered your patterns of sexual interaction? If so, what changes have you made? If not, why not? Do you plan to alter your future behaviors?

Prevention Guidelines

We discuss several methods of prevention—steps that can be taken before, during, or shortly after sexual contact to reduce the likelihood of contracting an STD. Many of these methods are effective against the transmission of a variety of diseases. Several are applicable to oral–genital and anal–genital contacts in addition to genital–genital interaction. None of the methods is 100% effective, but each method acts to significantly reduce the chances of infection. Furthermore—and this cannot be overemphasized—the use of preventive measures may help to curtail the booming spread of STDs. Because many infected people have sexual contact with one or more partners before realizing that they have a disease and seeking treatment, improved prevention rather than better treatment seems to hold the key to reducing these unpleasant effects of sexual expression.

Sexual Health

Assess Your and Your Partner's Risk Status

As a result of informed concern about acquiring an STD, you may understandably focus on assessing the risk status of a prospective sexual partner. However, in doing so, you may overlook the equally important need to evaluate your own risk status. If you had previous

Health departments often provide screening and treatment for STDs.

Ryan McVay/Getty Images

sexual activity with others, is there any possibility that you may have contracted an STD from them? Have you been tested for STDs in general, not one specific infectious agent? Remember, many of the STDs discussed in this chapter produce little or no noticeable symptoms in an infected person. If you care enough to be sexually intimate with a new partner, is it not reasonable that you should also be open and willing to share information about your own physical sexual health?

Some experts maintain that one of the single most important STD prevention messages to convey to people is to spend time, ideally several months or more, getting to know prospective sexual partners before engaging in genital sex. Unfortunately, research indicates that effective communication about risk factors and safer sexual behavior seems to be "more the exception than the rule in dating couples" (Buysse & Ickes, 1999, p. 121). We strongly encourage you to take time to develop a warm, caring relationship in which mutual empathy and trust are key ingredients. Use this time to convey to the other person any relevant information from your sexual history regarding your risk status—and to inquire about your partner's present or past behavior in the areas of sex and injection drug use. As discussed in Chapter 8, self-disclosure can be an effective strategy for getting a partner to open up. Thus you might begin your dialogue about these matters by discussing why you think that such an information exchange is vitally important in the AIDS era, followed by information about your own sexual history.

Getting to know someone well enough to trust his or her answers to these important questions means taking the time to assess a person's honesty and integrity in a variety of situations. If you observe your prospective partner lying to friends, family members, or you about other matters, you may rightfully question the truthfulness of her or his responses to your risk-assessment queries.

Research suggests that we cannot always assume that potential sexual partners will accurately disclose their risk for STDs. One study found that a sizable percentage of both men and women said that they would not be fully honest when questioned about their past sexual and drug-use histories. Of more than 400 sexually experienced Southern California college students surveyed, 35% of the men and 10% of the women said that they had lied about such things as pregnancy risk and other sexual involvements in order to have sex. In addition, 47% of the men and 42% of the women said that they would report fewer previous sexual partners than they really had. Finally, 20% of the men and 4% of the women indicated that they would falsely claim that they had tested negative for HIV (Cochran & Mays, 1990). In another survey of 169 students at a large midwestern university, approximately 30% of the male respondents and 6% of the female respondents admitted to lying in order to have sex. In addition, close to half of the women and a third of the men believed that they had been lied to in order to have sex (Stebleton & Rothenberger, 1993). In still another more recent study, researchers found that 40% of 203 HIV-infected men and women (40% injection drug users, 20% homosexual or bisexual men, 39% heterosexually infected individuals) had not disclosed their HIV status to all their sexual partners in the prior 6 months. Of the 40% nondisclosers, half had not disclosed to their one and only partner. Furthermore, among those who had not disclosed, only 42% used condoms consistently (Stein et al., 1998). In general, HIV-infected individuals are more likely to disclose their status to steady sexual partners than to casual partners (Keller et al., 2000).

Obtain Prior Medical Examinations

Even when people are entirely candid about their own sexual histories, there is no way to ensure that their previous sexual partners were honest with them—or, for that matter, that they even asked previous partners about STD risk status. In view of these concerns, we strongly encourage couples who want to begin a sexual relationship to abstain from any activity that puts them at risk for STDs until both of them have had medical examinations and laboratory testing designed to rule out all STDs, including HIV (Centers for Disease Control, 2002g). It is encouraging that at least some couples currently seek testing for HIV and other STDs before starting a sexual relationship in a strategy that some health professionals have dubbed "negotiated safety" (Merson et al., 1997). Taking this step not only reduces one's chance of contracting a disease but also contributes immeasurably to a sense of mutual trust and comfort with developing intimacy. If cost is an issue, contact your campus health service or a public health clinic in your area; both of these venues can provide examinations and laboratory testing free of charge or on a sliding fee scale commensurate with your financial status.

If people in newly formed relationships do not obtain tests for STDs and are unwilling to delay the onset of sexual intercourse, health experts strongly encourage using condoms for each act of insertive intercourse (Centers for Disease Control, 2002g). This practice offers some protection against many STDs whose symptoms might emerge during the initial weeks or months of a relationship; condoms should also be used until a couple becomes more comfortable with obtaining medical examinations and laboratory tests to rule out STDs.

Use Condoms

It has been known for decades that condoms, when consistently and correctly used, help to prevent the transmission of many STDs. The condom is one of the great underrated aids to sexual interaction. Male latex condoms, when used correctly and consistently, are effective in preventing the sexual transmission of HIV, and they reduce the risk of transmission of other STDs, such as chlamydia, gonorrhea, NGU, bacterial vaginosis, and trichomoniasis, that are also transmitted by fluids from mucosal surfaces. Condoms are less effective in preventing infections that are transmitted by skin-to-skin contact, such as syphilis, chancroid, HSV, and HPV, and they have no value in combating pubic lice and scabies (Centers for Disease Control, 2002g). Condoms made from lambskin, also known as "natural skin," or "natural membrane," contain small pores that may permit passage of some STDs, including HIV, HSV, and hepatitis viruses.

Laboratory studies indicate that the female condom (see Chapter 11) is an effective barrier to viruses, including HIV. However, with the exception of one study evaluating the protective value of female condoms against trichomoniasis transmission, no properly controlled and methodologically sound clinical studies have been conducted to evaluate the effectiveness of female condoms in preventing transmission of STDs, including HIV (Centers for Disease Control, 2002g; Richardson et al., 2003b). Nevertheless, evidence gathered globally does indicate an apparent association between female condom use and reduction of STDs, including HIV, among women sex workers in the United States, France, Indonesia, Thailand, Costa Rica, Mexico, and several African nations (Witte et at., 2000). If used correctly and consistently, the female condom can substantially reduce the risk of transmission of some STDs, and when the use of male condoms is not an option, we strongly encourage our readers to consider using a female condom. The female condom can be especially valuable to sexually active women who are at substantial risk for acquiring STDs from male partners who are unwilling to use male condoms consistently or at all.

Recent evidence indicates that widely used vaginal spermicides containing non-oxynol-9 (N-9) are not effective in preventing transmission of chlamydia, gonorrhea, or HIV (Centers for Disease Control, 2002g; Roddy et al., 2002). In fact, frequent use of N-9 has been associated with genital lesions in the vagina, which can increase vulnerability to HIV infection transmitted during vaginal intercourse (van Damme, 2000). Furthermore, animal research has shown that N-9 can damage the cells lining the rectum, thus providing a portal of entry

Correctly used condoms help prevent the transmission of many STDs, including HIV.

© Michael Newman/PhotoEdit

for HIV and other STD pathogens (Phillips et al., 2000). In their recently published STD treatment guidelines, the CDC: (1) recommends against further use of condoms lubricated with N-9 spermicide, (2) indicates that condoms lubricated with spermicides are no more effective than other lubricated condoms in preventing transmission of HIV and other STDs, and (3) strongly states that N-9 should not be used as a microbicide or sexual lubricant during anal sex (Centers for Disease Control, 2002g). Information provided by the CDC also indicates that spermicide use has been associated with increased risk of bacterial urinary tract infections in women (Centers for Disease Control, 2002g).

Available barrier methods for preventing STD transmission are often disadvantageous to women because they are either male controlled (the male condom) or require male cooperation (the female condom). Consequently, researchers are actively pursuing methods for STD prevention that can be controlled solely by women. These efforts are described in the boxed discussion "New Hope for Preventing STDs: The Search for Effective Vaginal Microbicides."

We review of the proper use of condoms in the following list:

- Store condoms in a cool, dry place out of direct sunlight.
- Throw away condoms in damaged packages and any condoms that are beyond the expiration date, are brittle, sticky, discolored, or show any other signs of age.
- Handle condoms with care so that they are not punctured.
- Put on a condom before any genital contact to prevent exposure to fluids that may contain infectious agents.
- Be sure that the condom is adequately lubricated. If you need to add a lubricant, be sure to use only water-based products, such as K-Y Jelly, Astroglide, AquaLube, and glycerin. Latex is weakened by petroleum- or oil-based lubricants (such as Vaseline, baby oil, cooking oils, shortening, massage oils, and many body lotions).
- Do not blow up a condom like a balloon or fill it with water before using it to test for leaks. Such stretching weakens the latex and makes it more likely that the condom will break during use.
- If a penis is uncircumcised, pull back the foreskin before putting on the condom.
- Do not unroll the condom first and then pull it on like a sock; this also tends to weaken the latex, making it more likely that the condom will break during use. The proper way to put on a condom is to unroll it directly onto the erect penis (either while pinching the reservoir tip or while holding a twisted end to create a reservoir area).
- If a condom does break, replace it immediately.
- After ejaculation, take care that the condom does not slip off. Withdraw the condom-clad penis while the penis is still erect, holding the base of the condom firmly to prevent slippage.
- Never reuse a condom.

A final word on condoms as a preventive device: Using condoms **DOES NOT GUARANTEE** protection against STD infections. Some critics of condom campaigns assert that people too often are lulled into a sense of false complacency, thinking that as long as they use condoms they are safe. However, more than 1 out of 10 women who use condoms as their only method of birth control become pregnant in 1 year's time (Post & Botkin, 1995). We can safely assume that the actual failure rate of condoms as a result of inconsistent or improper use, breakage, slippage, and other factors must be considerably higher than indicated by pregnancy statistics. Conception can occur on only a few days each month, but an STD can be contracted any time that sexual interaction with an infected person coincides with a failure of preventive methods.

Various surveys have indicated that rates of condom slippage and breakage are considerably higher during anal intercourse than during vaginal intercourse (Silverman & Gross, 1997). We urge readers who engage in anal intercourse to be especially cautious in their use of condoms during this variety of sexual interaction (e.g., avoid rigorous thrusting, use adequate lubrication, and take special care to avoid slippage). To be effective as STD prophylactics, condoms must be used correctly *every time* a person has sex. That may be difficult to do, particularly because logic has a tendency to shut down in the heat of passion. Thus we strongly encourage you to incorporate into your sex life knowledge about the nonfoolproof

New Hope for Preventing STDs: The Search for Effective Vaginal Microbicides

The currently available barrier methods for preventing STD transmission are often disadvantageous to women. Latex condoms provide excellent protection against many STDs, but they are frequently used inconsistently and/or incorrectly and are a male-controlled method. Even use of the female condom—which is a promising device for preventing pregnancy and STD transmission—depends to some extent on cooperation and acceptance by male partners. In many resource-poor nations HIV and other STDs are epidemic, and women are often subjected to unprotected intercourse with men unwilling to use condoms (Stein et al., 2003).

Because women are often disadvantaged by gender inequity in relationships and by the limited options for disease prevention, the development of methods for preventing STDs that can be totally controlled by women is a high priority (Garg et al., 2003; Stein et al., 2003; Trager, 2003). Simply advising women to insist that their partners use condoms is often unrealistic in situations where women lack either the power or the assertive skills necessary to ensure correct and consistent use of condoms.

Research efforts are currently under way to develop safe and effective topical gel or cream products, called **microbicides,** that women can use vaginally to prevent or minimize the risk of being infected with HIV and other STDs. These products would be applied before sexual intercourse, but they would not be a substitute for condoms. Rather, they would provide extra protection at low cost. In the developing world, where financial resources are limited and women are often unable to depend on male cooperation, microbicides would offer an especially beneficial option for STD prevention. Ideally, such products will eventually be widely available at minimal cost, will be broadly effective in preventing transmission of a wide range of STDs, will not result in vaginal irritation or damage, and will have no adverse effect on vaginal lactobacilli that help to maintain a healthy vaginal environment.

Technically, the term *microbicide* means a product that kills microbes. However, there are several ways that microbicide products could function to prevent STDs. Some microbicides would kill or destroy disease-causing organisms present in semen or vaginal secretions. This class of microbicides includes many widely used spermicides with antimicrobial activity, the best known of which is nonoxynol-9 (N-9). Until recently, N-9 was widely advocated as a beneficial product for both conception control and STD prevention. However, recent evidence indicates that N-9 can actually facilitate rather than prevent the transmission of HIV by causing small lesions in the vaginal lining (van Damme, 2000). Furthermore, animal research has shown that N-9 causes changes in the cells of the rectum that increase susceptibility to HIV infection; this means that people who use lubricants containing N-9 for anal sex could be at serious risk for infection by HIV (Phillips et al., 2000).

The fact that N-9 was shown to be disadvantageous rather than beneficial as a vaginal or rectal microbicide definitely created a setback in the field of microbicide research (Trager, 2003). However, in recent years research efforts have increased to investigate microbicides that use mechanisms different from that of N-9 (Shattock & Solomon, 2004). At least 50 candidate products are being evaluated, and currently at least 5 of them are being studied in advanced clinical trials with large study populations of people in developing countries who are at high risk for infection by HIV and other STDs (Garg et al., 2003; Trager, 2003).

One of the most promising of these products is a gel made from seaweed, called Carraguard. Rather than killing cells, this gel will act as a barrier to prevent entry of viruses into cells. Efficacy trials with 6,000 women in Botswana and South Africa began in 2003 (Trager, 2003). Another gel product, PRO 2000, contains a substance that binds with the receptor sites on CD4 cells, thus preventing HIV from entering and infecting these cells (Gottemoeller, 2001). Efficacy trials with this product began in 2003 with several thousand women recruited from India and several African nations (Trager, 2003). A third product, BufferGel, is designed to work by boosting the acidity of the vagina, thus making it inhospitable to STD pathogens (Gottemoeller, 2001). This product also began efficacy trials in 2003 with several thousand women residents of third world nations (Trager, 2003). Two other potentially effective microbicides, Savvy/C31G and cellulose sulfate, also started large-scale testing in 2003 (Trager, 2003).

Some of the products currently under investigation have both spermicidal and antimicrobial activity. Health officials hope to eventually have effective products from both categories, because some users will want protection against both unwanted pregnancies and STDs, whereas others will seek only disease protection. Hopefully, one or more of these much needed products will be available soon. However, even if the substances currently undergoing large-scale efficacy trials are shown to be safe and effective, it is likely that these products will not become commercially available until 2007 at the earliest and perhaps as late as 2010 (Garg et al., 2003; Trager, 2003). Given the horrendous impact of HIV/AIDS worldwide, as well as of several other devastating STDs, we can only hope that development, testing, and approval of effective microbicides will be fast-tracked, especially because delay in any phase of this process could result in tens of thousands of avoidable deaths.

nature of condoms and how they can be used most effectively to prevent both disease transmission and conception.

Avoid Sexual Activity with Multiple Partners

You may wish to reevaluate the importance of sex with multiple partners in light of the clear and extensive evidence that having many sexual partners is one of the strongest predictors of becoming infected with HIV, HSV, chlamydia, HPV, and numerous other sexually

Microbicide A topical gel or cream product that women can use vaginally to prevent or minimize the risk of being infected with HIV or other STDs.

transmitted infections. You might also elect not to have sex with individuals who you know or suspect have had multiple partners. People with multiple partners probably know each partner less well and thus may be less successful in avoiding people who engage in high-risk behaviors.

Inspect Your Partner's Genitals

Examining your partner's genitals before coital, oral, or anal contact might reveal the symptoms of an STD. Herpes blisters, vaginal and urethral discharges, chancres and rashes associated with syphilis, genital warts, and gonorrhea may be seen. In most cases symptoms are more evident on a man. (If he is uncircumcised, be sure to retract the foreskin.) The presence of a discharge, unpleasant odor, sores, blisters, rash, warts, or anything else out of the ordinary should be viewed with some concern. "Milking" the penis is a particularly effective way to detect a suspicious discharge. This technique, sometimes called the "short-arm inspection," involves grasping the penis firmly and pulling the loose skin up and down the shaft several times, applying pressure on the base-to-head stroke. Then part the urinary opening to see if any cloudy discharge is present.

? How About You?

How do you think you would respond if, in the preliminary stages of a sexual encounter, you noticed one or more symptoms of an STD in your partner?

People frequently find it difficult to openly conduct such an inspection before sexual involvement. Sometimes the simple request "Let me undress you" can provide some opportunity to examine your partner's genitals. Sensate focus pleasuring, discussed in Chapter 16, could provide the opportunity for more detailed visual exploration. Some people suggest a shower before sex, with an eye toward examining a partner. This may be helpful for noting visible sores, blisters, and so forth, but soap and water can also remove the visual and olfactory cues associated with a discharge.

If you note signs of infection, you may justifiably and wisely elect not to have sexual relations. Your intended partner may or may not be aware of his or her symptoms. Therefore it is important that you explain your concerns. Some people may decide to continue their sexual interaction after discovering possible symptoms of an STD; they would be wise, though, to restrict their activities to kissing, hugging, touching, and manual genital stimulation.

Wash Your—and Your Partner's—Genitals Before and After Sexual Contact

There is some difference of opinion about the extent of benefits associated with soap-and-water washing of the genitals before sexual interaction. However, there can be little doubt that washing has some benefits. Washing the man's penis is generally more effective as a prophylactic measure, although washing the woman's vulva can also be helpful.

You may find it difficult to suggest that your partner wash (or allow you to wash) his or her genitals before having sex. However, you may accomplish this unobtrusively by including washing of the genitals in the sex play that occurs in the shower or bathtub. Or you may frankly announce that you are cleansing your partner's and your own genitals for your mutual protection.

After sexual contact, thorough washing of the genitals and surrounding areas with soap and water is highly recommended as a preventive procedure when the transmission of an infection is a possibility. We are not, however, suggesting that this procedure should always follow sexual activity. Many lovers with long-term monogamous relationships would find this unnecessary and possibly even offensive, implying that a person is somehow unclean after sex.

Promptness is important in postsex washing, probably as important as thoroughness. However, some people might object to jumping out of bed immediately to wash, as this may break the relaxed and intimate mood. For those who are uncomfortable letting their partners know that they are taking this precaution, perhaps simply announcing that you need to go to the bathroom (a not uncommon need after sex) will suffice. Both women and men can wash their genitals while sitting over the sink. First fill the sink with warm, soapy water, then turn your back to it and boost yourself up so that you are sitting over the sink or straddling it. In this position it is relatively easy to thoroughly wash your exposed genitals with a soapy washcloth.

Urinating after coitus may have some limited prophylactic benefits, particularly for men. Many infectious organisms do not survive in the urethra in the acidic environment created by urine. Urinating can also help to flush out disease-causing organisms.

Obtain Routine Medical Evaluations

Many authorities recommend that sexually active people with more than one partner routinely visit their health practitioner or local STD clinic for periodic checkups, even when no symptoms of disease are evident (Pace & Glass, 2001). In view of the number of people, both women and men, who are symptomless carriers of STDs, this seems like good advice. How often to have such examinations is a matter of opinion. Our advice to people who are sexually active with several partners is that they should have checkups preferably every 3 months and certainly no less often than twice a year.

Inform Your Partner(s) If You Have an STD

The high frequency of infections without symptoms makes it imperative for infected individuals to inform their sexual partner(s) once they are diagnosed with an STD (Hoxworth et al., 2003; Keller et al., 2000; Potterat, 2003). Partner notification, which is beneficial in reducing the spread of all STDs, is an especially imperative prevention tactic for curtailing the spread of HIV infections. Partner notification can be conducted by the infected person, by health care providers, or by specially trained city, state, and federal employees called disease intervention specialists (DISs) (Kissinger et al., 2003). The discussion box "Telling a Partner," which appeared earlier in this chapter, offers some suggestions that may be helpful to a person who elects to notify a partner about an STD infection. A potential benefit of partner notification conducted by a health care provider or DIS is that informed people typically receive counseling about how to reduce the risk of exposure to STDs and are often provided with options for health care services, including testing and treatment (Hoxworth et al., 2003).

A number of studies have found that partner notification often facilitates several desirable behavior changes, including increased condom use, reduction in number of sexual partners, and reduction in the incidence of STDs following notification (Hoxworth et al., 2003; Kissinger et al., 2003). Even though partner notification can be a powerful tool in the STD prevention strategy pool, we cannot assume that a previous sexual partner will be forthcoming about a diagnosed STD. For example, a recent study of 92 people diagnosed with HPV found that, although most had disclosed their infection to primary partners at the time of diagnosis, of the 60% of the participants who had new sexual partners 6 months after diagnosis, less than one-third disclosed their HPV to their new partners before engaging in sexual relations (Keller et al., 2000).

A recent survey of a national sample of 1,421 people receiving medical care for HIV infection found that 42% of gay or bisexual men, 19% of heterosexual men, and 17% of women participants reported engaging in sexual interaction without disclosing their HIV-positive status to their sex partners. This nondisclosure occurred primarily within nonexclusive partnerships (Ciccarone et al., 2003). In general, research indicates that even when people diagnosed with an STD inform a primary partner, other sexual contacts are likely to be left uninformed (Gorbach et al., 2000; Keller et al., 2000).

In recent years the U.S. legal system has witnessed the emergence of a new kind of legal action based on sexual fraud. Perhaps the most noteworthy and visible are the cases in which people who have tested positive for HIV engage in unprotected sexual contact with partners who are uninformed about their HIV status. Such actions typically result in severe legal sanctions. Several such legal proceedings have occurred in our home state of Oregon, including the first man in the United States convicted and sentenced to prison for attempted murder based on evidence that he had unprotected sexual relations with three women despite his knowledge that he was HIV-positive.

In addition to cases involving criminal prosecution, sexual-deceit civil lawsuits increasingly provide the basis for successful civil litigation in U.S. courts. In these civil proceedings it is alleged that a person has lied about an STD—either through failure to disclose the condition to a partner or by engaging in outright deception. In many states, most notably California, state appeals courts have given a green light for such legal actions, thus providing an impetus for monetary judgments and out-of-court settlements ranging well into six figures. ■

- In the United States the incidence of sexually transmitted diseases (STDs) is increasing, especially among young people age 15 to 25 years. (p. 473)

- A number of factors probably contribute to the high incidence of STDs, including more people having unprotected (condomless) sex with multiple partners, the increased use of birth control pills, limited access to effective systems for prevention and treatment of STDs, inaccurate diagnosis and treatment, and the fact that many of these diseases do not produce obvious symptoms, which results in people unknowingly infecting others. (p. 473)

Bacterial Infections

- Chlamydia infections are among the most prevalent and the most damaging of all STDs. Chlamydia is transmitted primarily through sexual contact. It can also be spread by fingers from one body site to another—for example, from the genitals to the eyes. (p. 477)

- There are two general types of genital chlamydia infections in females: infections of the lower reproductive tract, commonly manifested as urethritis or cervicitis; and invasive infections of the upper reproductive tract, expressed as PID (pelvic inflammatory disease). (p. 477)

- Most women with lower reproductive tract chlamydia infections have few or no symptoms. Symptoms of PID caused by chlamydia infection include disrupted menstrual periods, pelvic pain, elevated temperature, nausea, vomiting, and headache. (p. 478)

- Chlamydia salpingitis (infection of the fallopian tubes) is a major cause of infertility and ectopic pregnancy. (p. 478)

- In men chlamydia infections are a common cause of epididymitis and nongonococcal urethritis. Possible symptoms of chlamydia infections in men are a discharge from the penis and burning during urination. (p. 478)

- Chlamydia infection also causes trachoma, the world's leading cause of preventable blindness. (p. 478)

- Recommended drugs for treating chlamydia infections include doxycycline and azithromycin. (pp. 478–479)

- Gonorrhea, a common communicable disease in the United States, is a bacterial infection transmitted through sexual contact. The infecting organism is a gonococcus bacterium. (p. 479)

- Early symptoms of gonorrhea infection are more likely to be manifested by men, who will probably have a discharge from the penis and burning during urination. The early sign in women, often not detectable, is a mild vaginal discharge that may be irritating to vulval tissues. (p. 481)

- Complications of gonorrhea infection in men include prostate, bladder, and kidney involvement and, infrequently, gonococcal epididymitis, which can lead to sterility. In women gonorrhea can lead to PID, sterility, and abdominal adhesions. (pp. 481–482)

- Recommended treatment for gonorrhea is the dual therapy of a single dose of ceftriaxone, cefixime, cipofloxacin, levofloxacin, or ofloxacin plus a single dose of azithromycin (or doxycycline for 7 days). (p. 482)

- Nongonococcal urethritis (NGU) is a common infection of the urethral passage, typically seen in men. It is primarily caused by infectious organisms transmitted during coitus. (p. 482)

- Symptoms of NGU, most apparent in men, include penile discharge and slight burning during urination. Women may have a minor vaginal discharge and are thought to harbor the infecting organisms. (p. 483)

- Doxycycline or azithromycin therapy usually clears up NGU. (p. 483)

- Syphilis is less common but potentially more damaging than gonorrhea. It is almost always transmitted through sexual contact. (p. 483)

- If untreated, syphilis can progress through four phases: primary, characterized by the appearance of chancre sores; secondary, distinguished by the occurrence of a generalized skin rash; latent, a several-year period of no overt symptoms; and tertiary, during which the disease can produce cardiovascular disease, blindness, paralysis, skin ulcers, liver damage, and severe mental pathological conditions. (pp. 483–485)

- Syphilis can be treated with benzathine penicillin G at any stage of its development. People allergic to penicillin can be treated with doxycycline, erythromycin, or ceftriaxone. (p. 485)

- Although still relatively uncommon in the United States, the incidence of chancroid has increased sharply in recent years. Chancroid is transmitted by sexual interaction. (p. 485)

- Chancroid infection produces small papules in the genital, perineal, or anal regions that eventually rupture and form painful, soft, crater-like ulcers that emit a foul-smelling discharge. (pp. 485–486)

- Chancroid can be treated with a single dose of either ceftriaxone or azithromycin or with 7 days of oral erythromycin or 3 days of oral ciprofloxacin. (p. 486)

Viral Infections

- Some of the most common herpes viruses are type 1, which generally produces sores on or in the mouth, and type 2, which generally infects the genital area. Type 1 can be found in the genital area, and type 2 can be found in the mouth area. Type 2 is transmitted primarily through sexual contact; type 1 can be passed by sexual contact or kissing. (p. 486)

- It has been estimated that more than 100 million Americans are afflicted with oral herpes and that 50 million people in the United States have genital herpes. (p. 486)

- The presence of painful sores is the primary symptom of herpes. A person is highly contagious during a herpes eruption, but evidence indicates that herpes can also be transmitted during asymptomatic periods. (pp. 487–488)

- Genital herpes can predispose a woman to cervical cancer. It can also infect her newborn child, producing severe damage to or death of the infant. (p. 489)

- Herpes has no known cure. Treatment is aimed at reducing pain and speeding the healing process. Acyclovir, valacyclovir, or famciclovir administered orally are effective in promoting healing during first episodes and, if taken continuously, in suppressing recurrent outbreaks. (pp. 490–491)

- Genital and anal warts are an extremely common viral STD in the United States. (p. 491)

- Genital warts are primarily transmitted through vaginal, anal, or oral–genital sexual interaction. (p. 491)

- Research has revealed a strong association between genital warts and cancers of the cervix, vagina, vulva, urethra, penis, and anus. (p. 492)
- Genital warts are treated by freezing, applications of topical agents, cauterization, surgical removal, or vaporization by a carbon dioxide laser. (pp. 492–493)
- Hepatitis A, hepatitis B, and hepatitis C are three major types of viral infections of the liver. All three types can be sexually transmitted. (p. 493)
- Hepatitis B can be transmitted through blood or blood products, semen, vaginal secretions, and saliva. Manual, oral, and/or penile stimulation of the anus are practices strongly associated with the spread of this viral agent. (p. 493)
- Oral–anal contact seems to be the primary mode of sexual transmission of hepatitis A. (p. 493)
- Hepatitis C is transmitted most commonly by means of injection drug use or less frequently through contaminated blood products and sexual contact; perinatal mother-to-fetus or mother-to-infant transmission is also possible. (p. 493)
- The symptoms of viral hepatitis vary from mild to incapacitating illness. No specific therapy is available to treat the A and B types of viral hepatitis. Most infected people recover in a few weeks with adequate bed rest. (p. 493–494)
- The most health-threatening of the hepatitis viruses, hepatitis C, is an emerging communicable disease of epidemic proportions. (p. 493)
- Hepatitis C accounts for the majority of deaths from complications of viral hepatitis. Combination therapy with two antiviral drugs is relatively effective in controlling the severe complications associated with hepatitis C. (p. 494)

Common Vaginal Infections

- Bacterial vaginosis, typically caused by an overgrowth of anaerobic bacteria, *Mycoplasma* bacteria, or a bacterium known as *Gardnerella vaginalis,* is perhaps the most common cause of vaginitis (vaginal infection) in U.S. women. Male partners of infected women also harbor the infectious microorganisms, usually without clinical symptoms. Coitus often provides a mode of transmission of this infection. (p. 495)
- The most prominent symptom of bacterial vaginosis in women is a fishy- or musty-smelling, thin discharge that is like flour paste in consistency. Women can also experience irritation of the genital tissues. A small number of men develop inflammation of the foreskin and glans, urethritis, or cystitis. (p. 495)
- The treatment for bacterial vaginosis is metronidazole (Flagyl) by mouth or intravaginal applications of topical metronidazole gel or clindamycin cream. (pp. 495–496)
- Candidiasis is a yeast infection that affects many women. The *Candida albicans* organism is commonly present in the vagina but causes problems only when overgrowth occurs. Pregnancy, diabetes, and the use of birth control pills or oral antibiotics are often associated with yeast infections. The organism can be transmitted through sexual or nonsexual means. (p. 496)
- Symptoms of yeast infections include a white, clumpy discharge and intense itching of the vaginal and vulval tissues. (p. 496)
- Traditional treatment for candidiasis infection consists of vaginal suppositories or topical creams, such as clotrimazole, miconazole, or butoconazole. (pp. 496–497)
- Trichomoniasis accounts for about one-fourth of all cases of vaginitis. Male partners of infected women are thought to carry the *Trichomonas vaginalis* organism in the urethra and under the foreskin if they are uncircumcised. The primary mode of transmission of this infection is through sexual contact. (p. 497)
- Women infected with trichomoniasis and their male sexual partners can be successfully treated with metronidazole. (p. 497)

Ectoparasitic Infections

- Ectoparasites are parasitic organisms that live on the outer skin of humans and other animals. Pubic lice and scabies are two relatively common STDs caused by ectoparasites. (p. 497)
- Pubic lice ("crabs") are tiny biting insects that feed on blood from small vessels in the pubic region. They can be transmitted through sexual contact or by using bedding or clothing contaminated by an infested individual. (pp. 497–498)
- The primary symptom of a pubic lice infestation is severe itching that is not relieved by scratching. Sometimes pubic lice can be seen. (p. 498)
- Pubic lice are treated by application of 1% permethrin cream to affected body areas and 1% Lindane shampoo for hair. (p. 498)
- Scabies is caused by a tiny parasitic mite that forages for nourishment in its host's skin. Scabies is a highly contagious condition that can be transmitted by close physical contact between people, both sexual and nonsexual. (p. 498)
- The primary symptoms of scabies are small bumps and a red rash that itches intensely, especially at night. The bumps and rash indicate areas of infestation. (p. 498)
- A single application of 5% permethrin lotion or cream, applied from the neck to the toes, is usually an effective treatment. (p. 499)

Acquired Immunodeficiency Syndrome (AIDS)

- AIDS is caused by infection with a virus (HIV) that destroys the immune system, leaving the body vulnerable to a variety of opportunistic infections and cancers. (p. 499)
- It now appears likely that HIV originated early in the 20th century by means of cross-species transmission from a subspecies of African chimpanzees to humans. The virus then spread worldwide much later when Africa became less isolated. (p. 499)
- An estimated 850,000 to 950,000 people in the United States and 42 million people worldwide are infected with HIV. (p. 500)
- The number of new AIDS cases reported annually in the United States grew rapidly through the early 1980s and moderated in the late 1980s. This more moderate rate has continued to the present time. (p. 500)
- Even though the overall incidence of new HIV infections in the United States has remained relatively stable in recent years, the number of new cases among teenagers, women, and racial and ethnic minorities continues to rise. Furthermore, there is evidence of a recent escalation in the incidence of new HIV infections occurring among both heterosexuals and men who have sex with men (MSM). (pp. 500–501)
- Although most AIDS cases that have occurred in the United States since the beginning of the epidemic have involved MSM and injection drug users, cases attributable to heterosexual transmission have risen steadily. (p. 501)
- Even though the prevalence of HIV infection in the United States and the rest of the Western world remains highest among MSM, the proportion of reported AIDS cases among MSM declined sharply and then leveled off in the period extending from the mid-1980s to the late 1990s. In recent years the incidence of HIV infections among MSM has been increasing. (p. 501)

- In the United States, AIDS cases attributable to heterosexual transmission are accelerating, and heterosexual contact has always been the primary form of HIV transmission worldwide. (p. 501)
- HIV has been found in semen, blood, vaginal secretions, saliva, tears, urine, breast milk, and any other bodily fluids that can contain blood. (p. 505)
- Blood, semen, and vaginal fluids are the major vehicles for transmitting HIV, which appears to be passed primarily through sexual contact and through needle sharing among injection drug users. (p. 505)
- HIV can also be passed perinatally from an infected woman to her fetus or infant before or during birth, or after birth by breast feeding. (p. 505)
- Viral load refers to how much virus is present in an infected person's blood. In general, the greater the viral load, the higher the chance of transmitting the infection. (p. 505)
- HIV can be transmitted to the receptive partner during oral sex, when HIV comes into contact with mucous membrane tissues in the mouth. (p. 505–506)
- The present possibility of being infected with HIV by means of transfusion of contaminated blood is remote. Furthermore, there is no danger of being infected as a result of donating blood. (p. 506)
- A small percentage of people appear to be resistant to HIV infection. (p. 506)
- The risk of transmitting HIV through saliva, tears, and urine appears to be low. There is no evidence that HIV can be transmitted by casual contact. (pp. 506–507)
- High-risk behaviors that increase one's chances of becoming infected with HIV include engaging in unprotected (condomless) sex, having multiple sexual partners, having sexual contact with people known to be at high risk, and sharing injection equipment for drug use. (p. 507)
- HIV is not as easily transmitted from women to men as it is from men to women. (p. 506)
- HIV often causes a brief, flulike illness within a few weeks of initial infection. The initial illness tends to fade fairly rapidly. However, as the virus continues to deplete the immune system, other symptoms occur. (p. 507)
- Most people develop antibodies to HIV within months of being infected, but some silent infections can go undetected for 3 years or more. (p. 507)
- HIV infection can be detected by standard blood tests for blood serum antibodies to HIV. (p. 507)
- The incubation time for AIDS—defined as the time between infection with HIV and the onset of one or more severe, debilitating diseases—is estimated to range between 8 and 11 years. (p. 508)
- The symptoms of HIV/AIDS disease are many and varied, depending on the degree to which the immune system is compromised and the particular type of cancer or opportunistic infection that afflicts an infected person. (p. 508)
- A significant decline in the rate of AIDS deaths began in 1996. This reversal in death trends was due to improvement in combination drug therapies. (p. 508)
- There is still no cure for HIV/AIDS. However, when properly used, a combination of three or more antiretroviral drugs, a treatment approach known as highly active antiretroviral therapy (HAART), can dramatically reduce viral load, improve immune function, and delay progression of the disease. (pp. 509–510)
- HAART involves a complex protocol of drug dosing that is difficult to adhere to. Furthermore, drug toxicity can result in adverse side

effects that induce low compliance with the HAART protocol. (pp. 510–511)
- HAART does not eradicate HIV from latent or silent reservoirs in various bodily tissues or organs. (p. 511)
- The availability of HAART has apparently influenced some people to increase their involvement in risky sex. (pp. 511–512)
- The administration of the RT inhibitor drug zidovudine to newborns significantly reduces the incidence of mother-to-child transmission of HIV. (p. 512)
- Although progress has been made in developing HIV vaccines, many health officials believe that we may be years away from having an effective vaccine available. (p. 513)
- The best hope for curtailing the HIV/AIDS epidemic is through education and behavioral change. (pp. 513–514)
- A person can significantly reduce her or his risk of becoming infected with HIV by following safer sex strategies, which include, among other things, using condoms and avoiding sex with multiple partners or with individuals who are at high risk for HIV infection. (p. 514)

Preventing Sexually Transmitted Diseases

- Taking the time to carefully assess your and your partner's risk status for transmitting STDs is perhaps the single most important preventive strategy. (pp. 515–516)
- Because it is often difficult to accurately assess risk status from conversations alone, couples are encouraged to undergo medical examinations and laboratory testing to rule out STDs before engaging in any sexual activity that puts them at risk for STDs. (pp. 516–517)
- Condoms, when used correctly, offer good but not foolproof protection against the transmission of many STDs. (pp. 517–518)
- Avoid sex with multiple partners or with individuals who likely have had multiple partners. (pp. 519–520)
- Inspecting a partner's genitals before sexual contact may be a way to detect symptoms of an STD. (p. 520)
- Washing the genitals with soap and water both before and after sexual interaction offers additional protection against being infected with an STD. (pp. 520–521)
- Sexually active people with multiple partners should routinely visit their health practitioner or local STD clinic for periodic checkups, even when no symptoms of disease are present. (p. 521)
- It is imperative for infected individuals to tell their sexual partner(s) once they are diagnosed as having an STD. (p. 521)

▶ Suggested Readings

AIDS Education and Prevention. An interdisciplinary journal, published by the International Society for AIDS Education, that is available in many major library systems. It contains excellent information regarding the prevention of AIDS and is one of the best sources of material on AIDS education.

The MMWR (Morbidity and Mortality Weekly Report). A publication of the Centers for Disease Control and Prevention available in most major library systems (particularly medical libraries). The *MMWR* frequently contains valuable information about the nature, transmission, prevention, and treatment of STDs. It is perhaps the single best source for keeping abreast of the latest developments regarding AIDS and other STDs.

Shilts, Randy (1987). *And the Band Played On: Politics, People, and the AIDS Epidemic.* New York: St. Martin's Press. A compelling book, written by an investigative reporter, that provides shocking information about how government incompetence and infighting among research groups in the scientific and medical communities hindered efforts to mobilize an effective campaign against the AIDS epidemic. This book also humanizes the AIDS crisis by telling personal stories of people who have lived with and died from AIDS.

Resources

CDC National HIV/AIDS Hotline: (800) 342-AIDS (English), (800) 344-7432 (Spanish), (800) 243-7889 (TTY service for hearing impaired). An informative recording with current information. Those who have specific questions not answered by the recording can call (800) 447-AIDS. Many cities have a local AIDS information hotline; check your local white pages for listings.

The Herpes Resource Center, a program of the American Social Health Association, provides excellent services, including a quarterly journal complete with up-to-date information about herpes, access to local chapters (support groups), and a private telephone information, counseling, and referral service. For information about these services, call (800) 230-6039, or send $1 (postage and handling) to Herpes Resource Center, ASHA, Dept. PR46, P.O. Box 13827, Research Triangle Park, NC 27709. (No self-addressed, stamped envelope is required.)

Herpes Anonymous, P.O. Box 278, Westbury, NY 11590; (516) 334-5718. A nonprofit social organization composed of people with herpes who wish to help others overcome the difficulties associated with this disease. Herpes Anonymous assists in developing companionable associations among people who have herpes. The organization also distributes a free newsletter containing up-to-date information about this disease.

Web Resources

Your *Our Sexuality* Web site **http://psychology.wadsworth.com/ crooksbaur9e/** has direct links to the Web sites described below. These links are checked often for changes, dead links, and new additions.

American Social Health Association
This Web site contains STD resources, including a sexual health glossary, educational brochures, hotline numbers, links to support groups, a Herpes Resource Center, and an STD news bulletin.

JAMA HIV/AIDS Information Center
The *Journal of the American Medical Association* maintains this Web site with updates on the latest treatment strategies for people with HIV/AIDS. It includes a reference library and a resource center for patient and support group information.

An Introduction to Sexually Transmitted Diseases
This fact sheet from the National Institute of Allergy and Infectious Diseases (a Division of the National Institutes of Health) provides basic statistics and prevention information on sexually transmitted diseases. In addition, an index allows detailed information for specific STDs.

SaferSex.org
A comprehensive resource providing detailed information about how to have safer sex, including explicit and practical information: how to use a condom, how to talk to your kids about AIDS, how to talk to your partner about safer sex.

AIDSinfo
A comprehensive Web site that provides excellent up-to-date information about HIV/AIDS, including links to treatment guidelines and vaccine research progress.

National Herpes Resource Center
This Web site provides accurate, up-to-date information about all aspects of herpes (causes, transmission, treatment, etc.) and information about local support groups.

Centers for Disease Control and Prevention
This government Web site provides information about STDs.

Our Sexuality Web Site
For online resources directly related to this book, go to **http://psychology.wadsworth.com/ crooksbaur9e/**. You will find interactive exercises, study questions, chapter outlines, an online version of this text's glossary, and Web links and activities that complement your CD-ROM.

InfoTrac® College Edition Online Library
http://infotrac.thomsonlearning.com/
InfoTrac College Edition is an online searchable library that includes a multitude of journals, many of which are specific to human sexuality. These journals include *Archives of Sexual Behavior, Archives of Sexual Health Behavior, Canadian Journal of Human Sexuality, Hispanic Journal of the Behavioral Sciences, Journal of Cross-Cultural Psychology, Journal of Physical Education, Recreation, and Dance, Journal of Sex Research,* and *Sex Roles.* You may search topics suggested in the margins of this chapter or terms of your own.

Our Sexuality CD-ROM
Use your CD-ROM for further study of the concepts in this chapter. Your CD-ROM provides animations of difficult concepts, video clips of real people discussing sexuality, critical thinking questions, chapter quizzing, and more.

CHAPTER 18

Atypical Sexual Behavior

▶ **What Constitutes Atypical Sexual Behavior?**

What are the primary distinguishing characteristics of atypical sexual behaviors?

What impact do atypical sexual behaviors have on both the person who exhibits them and others to whom they may be directed?

▶ **Noncoercive Paraphilias**

How are noncoercive paraphilias distinct from coercive paraphilias?

How does fetishism develop?

How is transvestic fetishism distinct from female impersonation, transsexualism, and homosexuality?

What factors might motivate people to engage in sadomasochistic behavior?

▶ **Coercive Paraphilias**

What characteristics are common to individuals who engage in exhibitionism?

What are some helpful strategies for dealing with obscene phone calls?

Are there some characteristics and causative factors common to people who engage in voyeurism?

▶ **Treatment of Coercive Paraphilias**

What are some of the obstacles that can impede efforts to treat coercive paraphilias?

What kinds of therapies have been used to treat coercive paraphilias?

▶ **Sexual Addiction: Fact, Fiction, or Misnomer?**

Can people become addicted to sex?

Is there widespread support among professionals for the sexual addiction model?

My last sexual partner was very much into golden showers. Having spent a little of my time watching G. G. Allen movies, I was well acquainted with the existence of watersports, but somehow it never occurred to me that I would like to partake in them. When my partner revealed his desire to drink my urine, I was taken off guard. I have been known to try some things I would deem a little atypical, so I gave it a shot. I was very nervous about the actual art of the procedure, though. Thoughts such as "What if he was joking—he would think I'm nuts" and "What if I completely miss" entered my head. It was nerve-racking and made it especially hard to pee. Eventually, my anxiety subsided and I was able to participate. His reaction was amazing to me. He began to masturbate feverishly and lapped up my urine ecstatically. I had never seen him so turned on. More surprising, though, was how much I enjoyed it. Although I cannot imagine being on the other end, it was really an empowering and enjoyable experience. (Authors' files)

This description of a rather unusual sexual experience, provided by a student in a sexuality class, may strike our readers as reflecting an abnormal or perhaps even deviant form of sexual behavior. However, we believe it is more realistic to consider this anecdote an account of uncommon or atypical sexual behavior. One note of caution: Because HIV has been found in the urine of infected persons, it is prudent to avoid contact with a partner's urine unless he or she is known to be HIV-negative and not infected with any other STDs. Now let us consider for a moment what constitutes atypical sexual behavior.

▶ What Constitutes Atypical Sexual Behavior?

In this chapter we focus on a number of sexual behaviors that have been variously labeled as deviant, perverted, aberrant, or abnormal. More recently, the less judgmental term **paraphilia** (pair-uh-FILL-ee-uh) has been used to describe these somewhat uncommon types of sexual expression. Literally meaning "beyond usual or typical love," this term stresses that such behaviors usually are not based on an affectionate or loving relationship but rather are expressions of psychosexually disordered behavior in which sexual arousal and/or response depends on some unusual, extraordinary, or even bizarre activity (American Psychiatric Association, 2000). The term *paraphilia* is used in much of the psychological and psychiatric literature. However, in our own experience in dealing with and discussing variant sexual behaviors, the one common characteristic that stands out is that each behavior in its fully developed form is not typically expressed by most people in our society. Therefore we also categorize the behaviors discussed in this chapter as **atypical sexual behaviors.**

Several points should be noted about atypical sexual expression in general before we discuss specific behaviors. First, as with many other sexual expressions discussed in this book, the behaviors singled out in this chapter represent extreme points on a continuum. Atypical sexual behaviors exist in many gradations, ranging from mild, infrequently expressed tendencies to full-blown, regularly manifested behaviors. Although these are *atypical* behaviors, many of us may recognize some degree of such behaviors or feelings in ourselves—perhaps manifested at some point in our lives, or mostly repressed, or emerging only in private fantasies.

A second point has to do with the state of our knowledge about these behaviors. In most of the discussions that follow, the person who manifests the atypical behavior is assumed to be male, and evidence strongly indicates that in most reported cases of atypical or paraphilic behaviors, the agents of such acts are male (American Psychiatric Association, 2000; Seligman & Hardenburg, 2000). However, the tendency to assume that males are predominantly involved may be influenced by the somewhat biased nature of differential reporting and prosecution. Female exhibitionism, for example, is far less likely to be reported than is similar behavior in a male. John Money (1981) suggested that atypical sexual behavior is decidedly more prevalent among males than females because male *erotosexual differentiation* (the development of sexual arousal in response to various kinds of images or stimuli) is more complex than that of the female and subject to more errors.

Paraphilia A term used to describe uncommon types of sexual expression.

InfoTrac Search Words
■ Paraphilia

Atypical sexual behaviors Behaviors not typically expressed by most people in our society.

uncommon

A third noteworthy point is that atypical behaviors often occur in clusters. That is, the occurrence of one paraphilia appears to increase the probability that others will also be manifested, simultaneously or sequentially (Bradford et al., 1992; Durand & Barlow, 2000; Fedora et al., 1992). Research with men whose paraphilias resulted in medical or legal attention revealed that over half reported engaging in more than one paraphilia and almost one in five reported experience with four or more paraphilias (Abel & Osborn, 2000). One hypothesis offered to account for this cluster effect is that engaging in one atypical behavior, such as exhibitionism, reduces the participant's inhibitions to the point where engaging in another paraphilia, such as voyeurism, becomes more likely (Stanley, 1993).

? Critical Thinking Question

Do you think that social and cultural conditioning contributes to the much higher incidence of atypical sexual behavior among men than among women? Explain.

A final consideration is the effect of atypical behaviors both on the person who exhibits them and on the people to whom they may be directed. People who manifest atypical sexual behaviors often depend on these acts for sexual satisfaction. The behavior is frequently an end in itself. It is also possible that the unconventional behavior will alienate others. Consequently, these people often find it difficult to establish satisfying sexual and intimate relationships with partners. Instead, their sexual expression can assume a solitary, driven, even compulsive quality. Some of these behaviors do involve other people whose personal space is violated in a coercive, invasive fashion. In the following section we consider the distinction between coercive and noncoercive paraphilias.

Noncoercive versus Coercive Paraphilias

A key distinguishing characteristic of paraphilias is whether or not they involve an element of coercion. Several of the paraphilias are strictly solo activities or involve the participation of consensual adults who agree to engage in, observe, or just put up with the particular variant behavior. Because coercion is not involved and a person's basic rights are not violated, such so-called noncoercive atypical behaviors are considered relatively benign or harmless by many. Clearly, the chapter opening account falls into this category. However, as we will see, these noncoercive behaviors occasionally engender potentially adverse consequences for people drawn into their sphere of influence.

Some paraphilias are definitely coercive or invasive in that they involve unwilling recipients of behavior, such as voyeurism or exhibitionism. Furthermore, research suggests that such coercive acts can have harmful effects on the targets of such deeds, who may be psychologically traumatized by the experience. They may feel that they have been violated or that they are vulnerable to physical abuse, and they may develop fears that such unpleasant episodes will recur. This is one reason many of these coercive paraphilias are illegal. On the other hand, many people who encounter such acts are not adversely affected. Because of this and because many of these coercive behaviors do not involve physical or sexual contact with another person, many authorities view them as minor sex offenses (sometimes called nuisance offenses). However, evidence that some people progress from nuisance offenses to more serious forms of sexual abuse may lead to a reconsideration of whether these offenses are "minor" (Bradford et al., 1992; Fedora et al., 1992). We examine this issue in more detail later in this chapter and in Chapter 19.

In our discussion of both coercive and noncoercive paraphilias, we examine how each of these behaviors is expressed, some of the common characteristics of those exhibiting the paraphilia, and the various factors thought to contribute to the development of the behavior. More severe forms of sexual coercion, such as rape, incest, and child abuse, are discussed in Chapter 19.

▶ Noncoercive Paraphilias

In this section we first discuss four fairly common types of noncoercive paraphilias: fetishism, transvestic fetishism, sexual sadism, and sexual masochism. We will also describe four less common varieties of noncoercive paraphilias.

Fetishism

Fetishism A sexual behavior in which the person obtains sexual excitement primarily or exclusively from an inanimate object or a particular part of the body.

Fetishism (FET-ish-iz-um) refers to sexual behavior in which an individual becomes sexually aroused by focusing on an inanimate object or a part of the human body. As with many other atypical behaviors, it is often difficult to draw the line between normal activities that might have fetishistic overtones and those that are genuinely paraphilic. Many people are erotically aroused by the sight of undergarments and certain specific body parts, such as feet, legs, buttocks, thighs, and breasts. Many men and some women use articles of clothing and other paraphernalia as an accompaniment to masturbation or sexual activity with a partner. Only when a person becomes focused on these objects or body parts to the exclusion of everything else is the term *fetishism* truly applicable (Lowenstein, 2002). In some instances, a person is unable to experience sexual arousal and orgasm in the absence of the fetish object. In other situations where the attachment is not so strong, sexual response can occur in the absence of the object but often with diminished intensity. For some people fetish objects serve as substitutes for human contact and are dispensed with if a partner becomes available. Some common fetish objects include women's lingerie, shoes (particularly high heels), boots (often affiliated with themes of domination), hair, stockings (especially black mesh hose), and a variety of leather, silk, and rubber goods (American Psychiatric Association, 2000; Davison & Neale, 1993).

How does fetishism develop? One way is through incorporating the object or body part, often through fantasy, in a masturbation sequence where the reinforcement of orgasm strengthens the fetishistic association. This is a kind of classical conditioning in which some object or body part becomes associated with sexual arousal. This pattern of conditioning was demonstrated by Rachman (1966), who created a mild fetish among male subjects under laboratory conditions by repeatedly pairing a photograph of women's boots with erotic slides of nude females. The subjects soon began to show sexual response to the boots alone. This reaction also generalized to other types of women's shoes. Although some critics have suggested that Rachman's experiment was tainted by methodological problems (O'Donohue & Plaud, 1994), two additional studies have provided further evidence for classical conditioning of fetishism (Langevin & Martin, 1975; Rachman & Hodgson, 1968).

© Thomas Hoeffgen/Getty Images

Inanimate objects or a part of the human body, such as feet, can be sources of sexual arousal for some people.

Another possible explanation looks to childhood for the origins of some cases of fetishism. Some children learn to associate sexual arousal with objects (such as panties or shoes) that belong to an emotionally significant person, such as their mothers or older sisters (Freund & Blanchard, 1993). The process by which this occurs is sometimes called *symbolic transformation*. Here, the object of the fetish becomes endowed with the power or essence of its owner, so that the child (usually a male) responds to this object as he might react to the actual person (Gebhard et al., 1965). If these patterns become sufficiently ingrained, the person will engage in little or no sexual interaction with others during the developmental years and even as an adult may continue to substitute fetish objects for sexual contact with other humans.

Only rarely does fetishism develop into an offense that might harm someone. Occasionally, an individual may commit burglary to supply a fetish object, as in the following account:

Some years ago we had a bra stealer loose in the neighborhood. You couldn't hang your brassiere outside on the clothesline without fear of losing it. He also took panties, but bras seemed to be his major thing. I talked to other women in the neighborhood who were having the same problem. This guy must have had a roomful. I never heard that he was caught. He must have decided to move on because the thefts suddenly stopped. (Authors' files)

Burglary is the most frequent serious offense associated with fetishism (Lowenstein, 2002). Uncommonly, a person may do something bizarre, such as cut hair from an unwilling person. In extremely rare cases a man may murder and mutilate his victim, preserving certain body parts for fantasy–masturbation activities.

Common fetish items include women's lingerie and shoes. People involved in fetishism can become aroused by these common inanimate objects.

Transvestic Fetishism *mostly men

Until recently, nontranssexual cross-dressers were generally labeled *transvestites*. This term is now considered appropriately applied only to people who put on the clothes of the other sex to achieve sexual arousal. The sexual component of cross-dressing present in these individuals distinguishes them from female impersonators who cross-dress to entertain, gay men who occasionally "go in drag" to attract men or as a kind of "camp" acting out, and transsexuals who, as we discussed in Chapter 3, cross-dress to obtain a partial sense of physical and emotional completeness rather than for sexual titillation.

Transvestism comprises a range of behaviors. Some people prefer to don the entire garb of the other sex. This is often a solitary activity, occurring privately in their homes. Occasionally, a person may go out on the town while so attired, but this is unusual. In general, the cross-dressing is a momentary activity, producing sexual excitement that often culminates in gratification through masturbation or sex with a partner. In many cases of transvestism a person becomes aroused by wearing only one garment, perhaps a pair of panties or a brassiere. Because this behavior has a strong element of fetishism (Freund et al., 1996), the American Psychiatric Association (2000) formalized the link between the two conditions (transvestism and fetishism) into the diagnostic category **transvestic fetishism.** A distinguishing feature of transvestic fetishism is that the clothing article is actually worn instead of just being viewed or fondled, as is the case with fetishism.

According to the American Psychiatric Association (2000), a diagnosis of transvestic fetishism is appropriately applied to heterosexual males who experience significant psychological distress or impaired functioning as a result of recurrent sexual fantasies, urges, or behavior involving cross-dressing that persist for at least 6 months.

Today, many members of the transgendered community (see Chapter 3), who are increasingly gaining voice in both the professional literature and the popular media, contend that cross-dressing is often an appropriate and legitimate source of sexual arousal and expression rather than an indicator of disordered behavior or psychological impairment. Consequently, they reject the label of transvestic fetishism and its implication of abnormality.

The diagnostic criteria previously outlined specify that transvestic fetishism is the sole province of heterosexual males. Let us examine the evidence supporting this claim. It would appear that in most cases it is men who are attracted to transvestic fetishism. This seems true of all contemporary societies for which we have data. However, a few isolated cases of women cross-dressing for sexual pleasure also appear in the clinical literature (Bullough & Bullough, 1993; Stoller, 1982). Some writers contend that transvestic fetishism is more common among females than we are aware of because the opportunities for cross-dressing

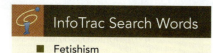

InfoTrac Search Words

■ Fetishism

Transvestic fetishism A sexual behavior in which a person derives sexual arousal from wearing clothing of the other sex.

without detection are obviously much greater for women. Although this may be true, we know that males who cross-dress are not aroused by wearing ambiguous or unisex attire. Rather, they prefer feminine apparel that only women wear, such as panties, bras, or nylons. Consequently, we might expect women engaging in transvestic fetishism to become sexually aroused while wearing something strictly identified with males, such as a pair of men's briefs or a jockstrap rather than jeans or a flannel work shirt, which are more unisex clothing. These behaviors among women are extremely rare in the clinical literature.

Several studies of both clinical and nonclinical populations suggest that transvestic fetishism occurs primarily among married men with predominantly heterosexual orientations (Brown, 1990; Doctor & Prince, 1997; Talamini, 1982). A national survey of 372 male cross-dressers reported that, although most of these men were heterosexual, a significant portion (more than 30%) classified themselves as bisexual, homosexual, or not sexually active with another person (Bullough & Bullough, 1997).

As with fetishism and some other atypical behaviors, the development of transvestic fetishism often reveals a pattern of conditioning. Reinforcement, in the form of arousal and orgasm, may accompany cross-dressing activities at an early point in the development of sexual interest, as illustrated in the following anecdote:

When I was a kid, about 11 or 12, I was fascinated and excited by magazine pictures of women modeling undergarments. Masturbating while looking at these pictures was great. Later, I began to incorporate my mother's underthings in my little masturbation rituals, at first just touching them with my free hand, and later putting them on and parading before the mirror while I did my hand-job. Now, as an adult, I have numerous sexual encounters with women that are quite satisfying without the dress-up part. But I still occasionally do the dress-up when I'm alone, and I still find it quite exciting. (Authors' files)

Many people who engage in transvestic fetishism feel that cross-dressing is an appropriate and legitimate source of arousal and expression, rather than a disorder or impairment.

© Zen Icknow/CORBIS

Sexual Sadism and Sexual Masochism

Sadism and masochism are often discussed under the common category **sadomasochistic** (SAY-doh-ma-suh-kis-tik) (SM) **behavior** because they are two variations of the same phenomenon: the association of sexual expression with pain. Furthermore, the dynamics of the two behaviors are similar and overlapping. Thus in the discussion that follows we will often refer to SM behavior or activities. However, a person who engages in one of these behaviors does not necessarily express the other, and thus sadism and masochism are actually distinct behaviors. The American Psychiatric Association (2000) underlines this distinction by listing separate categories for each of these paraphilias: **sexual sadism** and **sexual masochism.** Sexual masochism is the only paraphilia that is expressed by women with some frequency (American Psychiatric Association, 2000).

Labeling behavior as sexual sadism or sexual masochism is complicated because many people enjoy some form of aggressive interaction during sex play (such as "love bites") for which the label *sadomasochistic* seems inappropriate. Alfred Kinsey and his colleagues found that 22% of the males and 12% of the females in their sample responded erotically to stories with SM themes. Furthermore, more than 25% of both sexes reported erotic response to receiving love bites during sexual interaction. Hunt (1974) found that 10% of males and 8% of females in his sample (subjects younger than age 35) reported obtaining sexual pleasure from SM activities during interaction with a partner. A more recent survey of 975 men and women found that 25% reported occasionally engaging in a form of SM activity with a partner (Rubin, 1990). Although SM practices have the potential for being physically dangerous, most participants generally stay within mutually agreed-on limits, often confining their activities to mild or even symbolic SM acts with a trusted partner. In mild forms of sexual sadism the pain inflicted is often more symbolic than real. For example, a willing

Sadomasochistic behavior
The association of sexual expression with pain.

Sexual sadism The act of obtaining sexual arousal through giving physical or psychological pain.

Sexual masochism The act of obtaining sexual arousal through receiving physical or psychological pain.

partner may be "beaten" with a feather or a soft object designed to resemble a club. Under these conditions the receiving partner's mere feigning of suffering is sufficient to induce sexual arousal in the individual inflicting the symbolic pain.

People with masochistic inclinations are aroused by such things as being whipped, cut, pierced with needles, bound, or spanked. The degree of pain that the person must experience to achieve sexual arousal varies from symbolic or very mild to, rarely, severe beatings or mutilations. Sexual masochism is also reflected in individuals who achieve sexual arousal as a result of "being held in contempt, humiliated, and forced to do menial, filthy, or degrading service" (Money, 1981, p. 83). The common misconception that any kind of pain, physical or mental, will sexually arouse a person with masochistic inclinations is not true. The pain must be associated with a staged encounter whose express purpose is sexual gratification.

In yet another version of masochism, some individuals derive sexual pleasure from being bound, tied up, or otherwise restricted. This behavior, called **bondage,** usually takes place with a cooperative partner who binds or restrains the individual and often administers *discipline,* such as spankings or whippings. One survey of 975 heterosexual women and men revealed that bondage is a fairly common practice: One-fourth of respondents reported engaging in some form of bondage during some of their sexual encounters (Rubin, 1990).

Many individuals who engage in SM activities do not confine their participation to exclusive sadistic or masochistic behaviors. Some alternate between the two roles, often out of necessity, because it may be difficult to find a partner who prefers only to inflict or to receive pain. Most of these people seem to prefer one or the other role, but some are equally comfortable in either role (Mosher & Levitt, 1987; Weinberg et al., 1984).

Some research indicates that individuals with sexual sadistic tendencies are less common than their masochistic counterparts (Gebhard et al., 1965; Sandnabba et al., 1999). This imbalance might reflect a general social script—certainly it is more virtuous to be punished than to carry out physical or mental aggression toward another. A person who needs severe pain as a prerequisite to sexual response may have difficulty finding a cooperative partner. Consequently, such individuals may resort to causing their own pain by burning or mutilation. Likewise, a person who needs to inflict intense pain to achieve sexual arousal may find it difficult to find a willing partner, even for a price. We occasionally read of sadistic assaults against unwilling victims: The classic lust murder is often of this nature (Money, 1990). In these instances orgasmic release may be produced by the homicidal violence itself.

Many people in contemporary Western societies view sadomasochism in a highly negative light. This is certainly understandable, particularly for those who regard sexual sharing as a loving, tender interaction between partners who wish to exchange pleasure. However, much of this negativity stems from a generalized perception of SM activities as perverse forms of sexual expression that involve severe pain, suffering, and degradation. It is commonly assumed that individuals caught up in such activities are often victims rather than willing participants.

One group of researchers disputed these assumptions, suggesting that the traditional medical model of sadomasochism as a pathological condition is based on a limited sample of individuals who come to the attention of clinicians as a result of personality disorders or severe personality problems. As with some other atypical behaviors discussed in this chapter, these researchers argued that it is misleading to draw conclusions from such a sample. They conducted their own extensive fieldwork in nonclinical environments, interviewing a variety of sadomasochism participants and observing their behaviors in many different settings. Although some subjects' behaviors fit traditional perceptions, the researchers found that, for most participants, sadomasochism was simply a form of sexual enhancement involving elements of dominance and submission, role playing, and consensuality "which they voluntarily and mutually chose to explore" (Weinberg et al., 1984, p. 388). Another more recent study of 164 men who were members of sadomasochism-oriented clubs revealed that these individuals were socially well adjusted and that "sadomasochistic behavior was mainly a facilitative aspect of their sexual lives" (Sandnabba et al., 1999, p. 273).

Many people who engage in SM activities are motivated by a desire to experience dominance and/or submission rather than pain (Weinberg, 1987). This desire is reflected in the following account, recently provided by a student in a sexuality class:

Bondage A sexual behavior in which a person derives sexual pleasure from being bound, tied up, or otherwise restricted.

Some individuals derive sexual pleasure from the restrictions created by bondage attire and role-playing.

© Howard Kingsnorth/Getty Images

I fantasize about sadomasochism sometimes. I want to have wild animalistic sex under the control of my husband. I want him to "force" me to do things. Domination and mild pain would seem to fulfill the moment. I have read books and talked to people about the subject, and I am terrified at some of the things, but in the bounds of my trusting relationship I would not be afraid. It seems like a silly game, but it is so damned exciting to think about. Maybe someday it will happen. (Authors' files)

Studies of sexual behavior in other species reveal that many nonhuman animals engage in what might be labeled combative or pain-inflicting behavior before coitus. Some theorists have suggested that such activity has definite neurophysiological value, heightening accompaniments of sexual arousal such as blood pressure, muscle tension, and hyperventilation (Gebhard et al., 1965). For a variety of reasons (such as guilt, anxiety, or apathy), some people may need additional nonsexual stimuli to achieve sufficient arousal. It has also been suggested that resistance or tension between partners enhances sex and that sadomasochism is just a more extreme version of this common principle (Tripp, 1975).

Sadomasochism might also provide participants with an escape from the rigidly controlled, restrictive role they must play in their everyday public lives. This helps to explain why men who engage in SM activity are much more likely to play masochistic roles than are women (Baumeister, 1988, 1997). John Money described the scenario in which "men who may be brokers of immense political, business, or industrial power by day [become] submissive masochists begging for erotic punishment and humiliation at night" (1984, p. 169). Conversely, individuals who are normally meek may welcome the temporary opportunity to assume a powerful, dominant role within the carefully structured role playing of sadomasochism. A related theory sees sexual masochism as an attempt to escape from high levels of self-awareness. Similar to some other behaviors (such as getting drunk) in which a person may attempt to lose him- or herself, masochistic activity blocks out unwanted thoughts and feelings, particularly those that induce anxiety, guilt, or feelings of inadequacy or insecurity (Baumeister, 1988).

Clinical case studies of people who engage in sadomasochism sometimes reveal early experiences that may have established a connection between sex and pain. For example, being punished for engaging in sexual activities (such as masturbation) might result in a child or adolescent associating sex with pain. A child might even experience sexual arousal while being punished—for example, getting an erection or lubricating when one's pants are pulled down and a spanking is administered (spanking is a common SM activity).

Many people, perhaps the majority, who participate in SM behaviors do not depend on these activities to achieve sexual arousal and orgasm. Those who practice sadomasochism only occasionally find that at least some of its excitement and erotic allure stem from the fact that it represents a marked departure from more conventional sexual practices. Other people who indulge in SM acts may have acquired strong negative feelings about sex, often believing it is sinful and immoral. For such people masochistic behavior provides a guilt-relieving mechanism: Either they get their pleasure simultaneously with punishment, or they first endure the punishment to entitle them to the pleasure. Similarly, people who indulge in sadism may be punishing partners for engaging in anything so evil. Furthermore, people who have strong feelings of personal or sexual inadequacy may resort to sadistic acts of domination over their partners to temporarily alleviate these feelings.

Other Noncoercive Paraphilias

In this section we consider four additional varieties of noncoercive paraphilias that are generally uncommon or even rare. We begin our discussion by describing autoerotic asphyxia, a dangerous form of variant sexual behavior. We then offer a few brief comments about three other uncommon noncoercive paraphilias: klismaphilia, coprophilia, and urophilia.

Autoerotic Asphyxia

Autoerotic asphyxia (also called *hypoxyphilia* or *asphyxiophilia*) is a rare and life-threatening paraphilia in which an individual, almost always a male, seeks to reduce the supply of oxygen to the brain during a heightened state of sexual arousal (American Psychiatric Association,

Autoerotic asphyxia The enhancement of sexual excitement and orgasm by pressure-induced oxygen deprivation.

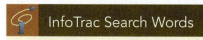

2000; Stanley, 1993). The oxygen deprivation is usually accomplished by applying pressure to the neck with a chain, leather belt, ligature, or rope noose (by means of hanging). Occasionally, a plastic bag or chest compression is used as the asphyxiating device. A person might engage in these oxygen-depriving activities while alone or with a partner.

We can only theorize from limited data what motivational dynamics underlie such behavior. People who practice autoerotic asphyxia rarely disclose this activity to relatives, friends, or therapists, let alone discuss why they engage in such behavior (Garza-Leal & Landron, 1991; Saunders, 1989). For some the goal seems to be to increase sexual arousal and to enhance the intensity of orgasm. In this situation the item used to induce oxygen deprivation (such as a rope) is typically tightened around the neck to produce heightened arousal during masturbation and is then released at the time of orgasm. Individuals often devise elaborate techniques that enable them to free themselves from the strangling device before losing consciousness.

The enhancement of sexual excitement by pressure-induced oxygen deprivation may bear some relationship to reports that orgasm is intensified by inhaling amyl nitrate ("poppers"), a drug used to treat heart pain. This substance is known to temporarily reduce brain oxygenation through peripheral dilation of the arteries that supply blood to the brain.

It has also been suggested that autoerotic asphyxia is a highly unusual variant of sexual masochism in which participants act out ritualized bondage themes (American Psychiatric Association, 2000; Cosgray et al., 1991). People who engage in this practice sometimes keep diaries of elaborate bondage fantasies and, in some cases, describe fantasies of being asphyxiated or harmed by others as they engage in this rare paraphilia.

One important fact about this seldom-seen paraphilia is quite clear: This is an extremely dangerous activity that often results in death (Cooper, 1996; Cosgray et al., 1991; Garos, 1994). Accidental deaths sometimes occur because of equipment malfunction or mistakes, such as errors in the placement of the noose or ligature. Data from the United States, England, Australia, and Canada indicate that 1 to 2 deaths per 1 million people are caused by autoerotic asphyxiation each year (American Psychiatric Association, 2000). The Federal Bureau of Investigation estimates that deaths in the United States resulting from this activity may run as high as 1,000 per year.

Klismaphilia

Klismaphilia An unusual variant in sexual expression in which an individual obtains sexual pleasure from receiving enemas.

Klismaphilia (kliz-muh-FILL-ee-uh) is an unusual variant in sexual expression in which an individual obtains sexual pleasure from receiving enemas (Agnew, 2000). Less commonly, the erotic arousal is associated with giving enemas. The case histories of many individuals who express klismaphilia reveal that as infants or young children they were frequently administered enemas by concerned and affectionate mothers. This association of loving attention with anal stimulation may eroticize the experience for some people so that as adults they may manifest a need to receive an enema as a substitute for or necessary prerequisite to genital intercourse.

Coprophilia and Urophilia

Coprophilia A sexual paraphilia in which a person obtains sexual arousal from contact with feces.

Urophilia A sexual paraphilia in which a person obtains sexual arousal from contact with urine.

Coprophilia (kah-pruh-FILL-ee-uh) and **urophilia** (yoo-roh-FILL-ee-uh) refer to activities in which people obtain sexual arousal from contact with feces and urine, respectively. Individuals who exhibit coprophilia achieve high levels of sexual excitement from watching someone defecate or by defecating on someone. In rare instances they achieve arousal when someone defecates on them. Urophilia is expressed by urinating on someone or being urinated on. This activity, reflected in the chapter opening anecdote, has been referred to as "water sports" and "golden showers." There is no consensus of opinion about the origins of these highly unusual paraphilias.

▶ Coercive Paraphilias

In this section we first discuss three common forms of coercive paraphilic behaviors: exhibitionism, obscene phone calls, and voyeurism. Three other varieties of coercive paraphilias—frotteurism, zoophilia, and necrophilia—are also discussed.

Exhibitionism

Exhibitionism, often called indecent exposure, refers to behavior in which an individual (almost always male) exposes his genitals to an involuntary observer (usually an adult woman or female child) (American Psychiatric Association, 2000; Marshall et al., 1991). Typically, a man who has exposed himself obtains sexual gratification by masturbating shortly thereafter, using mental images of the observer's reaction to increase his arousal. Some men, while having sex with a willing partner, fantasize about exposing themselves or replay mental images from previous episodes. Still others have orgasm triggered by the act of exposure, and a few masturbate while exhibiting themselves (American Psychiatric Association, 2000; Freund et al., 1988). The reinforcement of associating sexual arousal and orgasm with the actual act of exhibitionism or with mental fantasies of exposing oneself contributes significantly to the maintenance of exhibitionistic behavior (Blair & Lanyon, 1981). Exposure can occur in a variety of locations, most of which allow for easy escape. Subways, relatively deserted streets, parks, and cars with a door left open are common places for exhibitionism to occur. However, sometimes a private dwelling is the scene of an exposure, as revealed in the following account:

> One evening I was shocked to open the door of my apartment to a naked man. I looked long enough to see that he was underdressed for the occasion and then slammed the door in his face. He didn't come back. I'm sure my look of total horror was what he was after. But it is difficult to keep your composure when you open your door to a naked man. (Authors' files)

Certainly, many of us have exhibitionistic tendencies: We may go to nude beaches, parade before admiring lovers, or wear provocative clothes or scanty swimwear. However, such behavior is considered appropriate by a society that in many ways exploits and celebrates the erotically portrayed human body. The fact that legally defined exhibitionistic behavior involves generally unwilling observers sets it apart from these more acceptable variations of exhibitionism.

Our knowledge of who displays this behavior is based almost exclusively on studies of arrested offenders—a sample that may be unrepresentative. This sampling problem is common to many forms of atypical behavior that are defined as criminal. From the available data, however limited, it appears that most people who exhibit themselves are adult males in their 20s or 30s, and over half are married or have been married. They are often shy, nonassertive people who feel inadequate and insecure and suffer from problems with intimacy (Arndt, 1991; Marshall et al., 1991). They may function quite efficiently in their daily lives and be commonly characterized by others as "nice, but kind of shy." Their sexual relationships are likely to have been unsatisfactory. Many were reared in atmospheres characterized by puritanical and shame-inducing attitudes toward sexuality.

A number of factors influence the development of exhibitionistic behavior. Many individuals have such powerful feelings of personal inadequacy that they are afraid to reach out to another person out of fear of rejection (Minor & Dwyer, 1997). Their exhibitionism is thus a limited attempt to somehow involve others, however fleetingly, in their sexual expression. Limiting contact to briefly opening a raincoat before dashing off minimizes the possibility of overt rejection. Some men who expose themselves may be looking for affirmation of their masculinity. Others, feeling isolated and unappreciated, may simply be seeking attention, which they desperately crave. A few feel anger and hostility toward people, particularly women, who have failed to notice them or who they believe have caused them emotional pain. Under these circumstances exposure can be a form of reprisal, designed to shock or frighten the people they see as the source of their discomfort. In addition, exhibitionism is not uncommon in emotionally disturbed, intellectually disabled, or mentally disoriented individuals. In these cases the behavior reflects a limited awareness of what society defines as appropriate actions, a breakdown in personal ethical controls, or both.

In contrast to the public image of an exhibitionist as a person who lurks about in the shadows, ready to grab hapless victims and drag them off to ravish them, most men who engage in exhibitionism limit this activity to exposing themselves (American Psychiatric Association, 2000; Davison & Neale, 1993). Yet the word *victim* is not entirely inappropriate, in that observers of such exhibitionistic episodes

Exhibitionism The act of exposing one's genitals to an unwilling observer.

InfoTrac Search Words

- Exhibitionism

? How About You?

People typically are much less concerned about female exhibitionism than they are about male exhibitionism. For example, if a woman observed a man undressing in front of a window, the man might be accused of being an exhibitionist. However, if the roles were reversed and the woman was undressing, the man would likely be labeled a voyeur. What do you think of this sex-based inconsistency in labeling these behaviors?

Exhibitionists often want to elicit reactions of shock, disgust, fear, or terror. The best response is to calmly ignore the person and casually go about your business.

! Sexual Health

? How About You?

Have you ever encountered an exhibitionist or obscene phone caller? If so, how did you respond to this intrusive and/or threatening behavior? Would you respond the same way in the future? Why or why not?

may be emotionally traumatized by the experience (Cox, 1988; Marshall et al., 1991). Some feel that they are in danger of being raped or otherwise harmed. A few, particularly young children, can develop negative feelings about genital anatomy from such an experience.

Investigators have noted that some people who expose themselves, probably a small minority, actually physically assault their victims (R. Brown, 2000). Furthermore, it also seems probable that some men who engage in exhibitionism progress from exposing themselves to more serious offenses, such as rape and child molestation. In a one-of-a-kind study, Gene Abel (1981), a Columbia University researcher, conducted an in-depth investigation of the motives and behavior of 207 men who admitted to a variety of sexual offenses, including child molestation and rape. This research is unique because all participants were men outside the legal system who voluntarily sought treatment after being guaranteed confidentiality. Abel found that 49% of the rapists in his sample had histories of other types of variant sexual behavior, generally preceding the onset of rape behavior. The most common of these were child molestation, exhibitionism, voyeurism, incest, and sadism.

A Canadian study of 274 sex offenders, all adult males, revealed that most of them had engaged in several types of variant sexual behavior, including paraphilias and more serious forms of sexual coercion, such as child molestation and rape. Collectively, these subjects admitted to 7,677 incidents of sexual offenses, an average of 28 incidents per offender. These findings suggest that "paraphiliacs tend to have multiple types of sexual aberrations as well as a high frequency of deviant acts per individual" (Bradford et al., 1992, p. 104).

These findings do not imply that people who engage in such activities as exhibitionism and voyeurism will inevitably develop into child molesters and rapists. However, it seems clear that some people progress beyond these relatively minor acts to far more severe patterns of sexual aggression.

Although perhaps all of us would like protection against being sexually used without our consent, it seems unnecessarily harsh and punitive to imprison people for exhibitionistic behavior, particularly first-time offenders. In recent years, at least in some locales, there has been some movement toward therapy as an alternative to incarceration. Later in this chapter, we will discuss a variety of therapeutic techniques that are used to treat exhibitionism and other paraphilias.

What is an appropriate response if someone exposes himself to you? It is important to keep in mind that most people who express exhibitionist behavior want to elicit reactions of shock, fear, disgust, or terror. Although it may be difficult not to react in any of these ways, a better response is to calmly ignore the exhibitionist act and go about your business. Of course, it is also important to immediately distance yourself from the offender and to report such acts to the police or campus security as soon as possible. ■

Obscene Phone Calls

People who make obscene phone calls share similar characteristics with those who engage in exhibitionism. Thus obscene phone calling (sometimes called *telephone scatologia*) is viewed by some professionals as a subtype of exhibitionism. People who make obscene phone calls typically experience sexual arousal when their victims react in a horrified or shocked manner, and many masturbate during or immediately after a "successful" phone exchange. As one extensive study indicated, these callers are typically male, and they often suffer from pervasive feelings of inadequacy and insecurity (Matek, 1988; Nadler, 1968). Obscene phone calls are frequently the only way they can find to have sexual exchanges.

However, when relating to the other sex, they frequently show greater anxiety and hostility than do people inclined toward exhibitionism, as revealed in the following account:

One night I received a phone call from a man who sounded quite normal until he started his barrage of filth. Just as I was about to slam the phone down, he announced, "Don't hang up. I know where you live (address followed) and that you have two little girls. If you don't want to find them all mangled up, you will hear what I have to say. Furthermore, I expect you to be available for calls every night at this time." It was a nightmare. He called night after night. Sometimes he made me listen while he masturbated. Finally I couldn't take it any longer, and I contacted the police. They were unable to catch him, but they sure scared him off in short order, thank heaven. I was about to go crazy. (Authors' files)

Fortunately, a caller rarely follows up his verbal assault with a physical attack on his victim.

A survey of a nationally representative sample of several hundred U.S. women found that 16% had received at least one obscene phone call during the previous 6 months. Most of these calls appeared not to be random but rather targeted in some fashion, often at women under 65 years of age who were neither married nor widowed. The study's author suggested that her findings indicate that obscene phone calls occur in patterns similar to that of the expression of rage and perhaps can best be explained as "displaced aggression against a vulnerable population" (Katz, 1994, p. 155). Another national survey, conducted in Canada, found that 83.2% of female respondents had received obscene or threatening phone calls at some time in their lives (Smith & Morra, 1994).

What is the best way to handle obscene phone calls? Information about how to deal with obscene phone calls is available from most local phone company offices. Because they are commonly besieged by such queries, you may need to be persistent in your request. A few tips are worth knowing; they may even make it unnecessary to seek outside help.

First, quite often the caller has picked your name at random from a phone book or perhaps knows you from some other source and is just trying you out to see what kind of reaction he can get. Your initial response may be critical in determining his subsequent actions. He wants you to be horrified, shocked, or disgusted; thus the best response is usually not to react overtly. Slamming down the phone may reveal your emotional state and provide reinforcement to the caller. Simply set it down gently and go about your business. If the phone rings again immediately, ignore it. Chances are that he will seek out other, more responsive victims.

Other tactics may also be helpful. One, used successfully by a former student, is to feign deafness. "What is that you said? You must speak up. I'm hard of hearing, you know!" Setting down the phone with the explanation that you are going to another extension (which you never pick up) may be another practical solution. Finally, screening calls with an answering machine or caller ID might also prove helpful. The caller is likely to hang up in the absence of an emotionally responding person.

If you are persistently bothered by obscene phone calls, you may need to take additional steps. Your telephone company should cooperate in changing your number to an unlisted one at no charge. It is probably not a good idea to heed the common advice to blow a police whistle into the mouthpiece of the phone (which may be quite painful and even harmful to the caller's ear) because you may end up receiving the same treatment from your caller.

A service offered by many telephone companies, call tracing, may assist you in dealing with repetitive obscene or threatening phone calls. After breaking connection with the caller, you enter a designated code, such as "star 57." The telephone company then automatically traces the call. After a certain number of successful traces to the same number, a warning letter is sent to the offender indicating that he or she has been identified as engaging in unlawful behavior that must stop. The offender is warned that police intervention or civil legal action is an option if the behavior continues. Call tracing is clearly not effective when calls are placed from a public pay phone, and calls made from cellular phones cannot be traced. ■

Voyeurism

Voyeurism (voi-yur-IH-zum) refers to deriving sexual pleasure from looking at the naked bodies or sexual activities of others, usually strangers, without their consent (American Psychiatric Association, 2000). Because a degree of voyeurism is socially acceptable (witness the popularity of R- and X-rated movies and magazines such as *Playboy* and *Playgirl*), it is sometimes difficult to determine when voyeuristic behavior becomes a problem (Arndt, 1991; Forsyth, 1996). To qualify as atypical sexual behavior, voyeurism must be preferred to sexual relations with another or indulged in with some risk (or both). People who engage in this behavior are often most sexually aroused when the risk of discovery is high—which may explain why most are not attracted to such places as nudist camps and nude beaches, where looking is acceptable (Tollison & Adams, 1979).

As the common term *peeping Tom* implies, this behavior is typically, although not exclusively, expressed by males (Davison & Neale, 1993). Voyeurism includes peering in bedroom windows, stationing oneself by the entrance to women's bathrooms, and boring holes in the walls of public dressing rooms. Some men travel

! Sexual Health

© David Raymer/CORBIS

Although your initial reaction to an obscene phone call may be horror, shock, or disgust, it is usually best not to respond emotionally. A caller who doesn't receive the desired response from you is less likely to call again.

Voyeurism The act of obtaining sexual gratification by observing undressed or sexually interacting people without their consent.

G InfoTrac Search Words

■ Voyeurism

Critical Thinking Question

Are strippers and dancers who perform partially or totally nude engaging in a genuine form of exhibitionism? Why or why not? What about people who observe these performances? Are they voyeurs? What if anything differentiates diagnosed exhibitionists and voyeurs from exotic dancers and people in the audience?

Critical Thinking Question

Is it ethically acceptable to visit Web sites that offer video from hidden cameras or unauthorized videotapes of people's private lives? Why or why not?

Frotteurism A fairly common paraphilia in which a person obtains sexual pleasure by pressing or rubbing against another in a crowded public place.

Frotteurism is a fairly common paraphilia practiced in crowded public places, such as buses, subways, or outdoor concerts.

elaborate routes several nights a week for the occasional reward of a glimpse through a window of bare anatomy or, rarely, a scene of sexual interaction. In recent years we have seen the emergence of a new form of voyeurism in which small, technologically advanced video cameras are used to surreptitiously invade the personal privacy of many unaware victims. This troubling trend is described in the boxed discussion "Video Voyeurism."

Again, people inclined toward voyeurism often share some characteristics with people who expose themselves (Arndt, 1991; Langevin et al., 1979). They may have poorly developed sociosexual skills, with strong feelings of inferiority and inadequacy, particularly as directed toward potential sexual partners. They tend to be young men, usually in their early 20s (Davison & Neale, 1993; Dwyer, 1988). They rarely "peep" at someone they know, preferring strangers instead. Most individuals who engage in such activity are content merely to look, keeping their distance. However, in some instances such individuals go on to more serious offenses, such as burglary, arson, assault, and even rape (Abel, 1981; Abel & Osborn, 2000; Langevin et al., 1985).

It is difficult to isolate specific influences that trigger voyeuristic behavior, particularly because so many of us demonstrate these tendencies in a somewhat more controlled fashion. The adolescent or young adult male who displays this behavior often feels great curiosity about sexual activity (as many of us do) but at the same time feels inadequate or insecure. Voyeurism, either while physically present or by means of hidden video cameras, becomes a vicarious fulfillment because he may be unable to consummate sexual relationships with others without experiencing a great deal of anxiety. In some instances voyeuristic behavior is also reinforced by feelings of power and superiority over those who are secretly observed.

Other Coercive Paraphilias

We conclude our discussion of coercive paraphilias with a few brief comments about three additional varieties of these coercive or invasive forms of paraphilia. The first two, frotteurism and zoophilia, are actually fairly common. The third variant form, necrophilia, is rare and is an extremely aberrant form of sexual expression.

Frotteurism

Frotteurism (frah-toor-IH-zum) is a fairly common coercive paraphilia that goes largely unnoticed. It involves an individual, usually a male, who obtains sexual pleasure by pressing or rubbing against a fully clothed female in a crowded public place, such as an elevator, bus, subway, large sporting event, or outdoor concert. The most common form of contact is between the man's clothed penis and a woman's buttocks or legs. Less commonly, he may use his hands to touch a woman's thighs, pubic region, breasts, or buttocks. Often the contact seems to be inadvertent, and the woman who is touched may not notice or pay little heed to the seemingly casual contact. On the other hand, she may feel victimized and angry. In rare cases she may reciprocate (Money, 1984).

The man who engages in frotteurism may achieve arousal and orgasm during the act. More commonly, he incorporates the mental images of his actions into masturbation fantasies at a later time. Men who engage in this activity have many of the characteristics manifested by those who practice exhibitionism. They are frequently plagued with feelings of social and sexual inadequacy. Their brief, furtive contacts with strangers in crowded places allow them to include others in their sexual expression in a safe, nonthreatening manner.

As with other paraphilias, it is difficult to estimate just how common this variety of coercive paraphilia is. One study of a sample of reportedly typical or normal college men found that 21% of the respondents had engaged in one or more frotteuristic acts (Templeman & Sinnett, 1991).

Video Voyeurism

Technological advances have added a new dimension to voyeurism, perhaps best described as *video voyeurism*. Small, affordable video cameras are increasingly being used to invade and record some of our most private moments. These images might then be displayed on the Internet or on someone's VCR. High-tech video devices—hidden in such locations as smoke detectors, exit signs, ceiling fixtures, and gym bags—make it easy for unscrupulous individuals with either a penchant for peeping or an eye for a quick buck to victimize people by secretly recording them.

Video voyeurism was first brought to our attention several years ago when the media in our hometown reported that women patrons of a tanning salon had been victimized by secret video recordings while they were in the process of disrobing. A more recent instance of video voyeurism reported by the media involved the owners of a public marina located on a lake in New York who had installed hidden video cameras in the restroom and shower facilities of their establishment and subsequently played edited versions of these videotapes for the amusement of patrons of a local bar they owned and operated (Hamblett, 1999). Accounts such as these have become all too familiar in recent years as both local and national media report on a proliferation of various forms of video voyeurism, which include hidden cameras located in such places as bathrooms ("bathroomcams"), shower facilities ("showercams"), locker rooms ("lockerroomcams"), and bedrooms ("bedroomcams") and under working women's desks ("upskirtcams").

People who use "voyeurcams" do so either for their own sexual gratification or as an avenue for obtaining financial gain. Technological advances in video equipment together with the Internet have allowed the emergence of a disturbing new financial market in which unethical entrepreneurs sell secret video invasions of privacy either for home VCR viewing or for viewing at pay-per-view Web sites. In recent years there has been an explosion of both unauthorized and authorized occurrences of video displays on the Internet that appeal to voyeuristic inclinations. For example, in the late 1990s an unauthorized videotape of Pamela Anderson and her then-husband Tommy Lee, engaged in sexual activity, surfaced on the Internet. More recently, controversy erupted over the unauthorized Internet use of a sex tape involving Paris Hilton, star of Fox's *The Simple Life* series, and Rick Salomon (Rogers, 2003). There are hundreds of Web sites currently available that appeal to video voyeurs. These Web sites are set up on a pay-per-view or subscription basis, and a person can log on to watch the activities of people, often attractive women, who may or may not know that they are being taped.

Unfortunately, many embarrassed and angry victims of video voyeurism have discovered that they have little legal recourse when secret videotapes are marketed by unscrupulous entrepreneurs based in foreign countries where the legal codes allow them to function without fear of legal reprisals. Even in the United States, few states have passed new laws to cope with video voyeurs who use high-tech tools to invade personal privacy without breaking laws traditionally used to prosecute voyeurs, such as trespass laws.

Understandably, many prosecutors in criminal trials and even litigators in civil lawsuits are often reluctant to file charges against video voyeurs without laws that specifically prohibit secret videotaping. Fortunately, some states have recently enacted laws that target video voyeurism. For example, in June 2000 South Carolina amended its voyeurism laws to include prohibitions against the use of video or audio equipment in places where a person would have a reasonable expectation of privacy (State House Network–LPITR, 2000). In July 1998 Washington state also enacted a new law against video voyeurism, largely because of two widely publicized cases of video victimization (Santana, 1998). In one instance a Seattle firefighter secretly recorded female colleagues disrobing in a department locker room. In the second case an electrician who worked on the Kingdome athletic stadium in Seattle planted a secret video camera in the dressing room of the Seahawk Seagals (employees of the Seattle Seahawks, a professional football organization).

Hopefully, in the future more states will enact laws that prosecute high-tech video voyeurism, and people will generally become more aware of this serious form of personal privacy invasion. Furthermore, as we become more knowledgeable about the potential for this invasive process, we can be more aware and careful in situations where we might be victimized in this fashion. For example, when changing in a gym or health club facility, be on the lookout for clothes bags positioned in such a way that they might allow secret video recording. Clearly, some of these small, technologically advanced cameras can be hidden in ways that make detection difficult. Nevertheless, an aware person is less likely to be victimized than the uninformed individual who assumes that being alone ensures his or her personal privacy.

Zoophilia

Zoophilia (zoh-oh-FILL-ee-uh), sometimes called *bestiality*, involves sexual contact between humans and animals (American Psychiatric Association, 2000). You may wonder why we classify this as a coercive paraphilia because such behavior does not involve coercing other people into acts that they would normally avoid. In many instances of zoophilia it is reasonable to presume that the involved animals are also unwilling participants, and the performed acts are often both coercive and invasive. Consequently, assigning this paraphilia to the coercive category seems appropriate.

Zoophilia A paraphilia in which a person has sexual contact with animals.

In Kinsey's sample populations 8% of the males and almost 4% of the females reported having had sexual experience with animals at some point in their lives. The frequency of such behavior among males was highest for those raised on farms (17% of these men reported experiencing orgasm as a result of animal contact). The animals most frequently involved in sex with humans are sheep, goats, donkeys, large fowl (ducks and geese), dogs, and cats. Males are most likely to have contact with farm animals and to engage in penile–vaginal intercourse or to have their genitals orally stimulated by the animals (Hunt, 1974; Kinsey et al., 1948). Women are more likely to have contact with household pets, involving the animals licking their genitals or masturbating a male dog. Less commonly, some adult women have trained a dog to mount them and engage in coitus (Gendel & Bonner, 1988; Kinsey et al., 1953).

Sexual contact with animals is commonly only a transitory experience of young people to whom a human sexual partner is inaccessible or forbidden (Money, 1981). Most adolescent males and females who experiment with zoophilia make a transition to adult sexual relations with human partners. Occasionally, an adult may engage in such behavior as a "sexual adventure" (Tollison & Adams, 1979). True or nontransitory zoophilia exists only when sexual contact with animals is preferred, regardless of what other forms of sexual expression are available. Such behavior, which is rare, is generally expressed only by people with deep-rooted psychological problems or distorted images of the other sex. For example, a man who has a pathological hatred of women may be attempting to express his contempt for them by choosing animals in preference to women as sexual partners.

Necrophilia

Necrophilia (ne-kruh-FILL-ee-uh) is an extremely rare sexual variation in which a person obtains sexual gratification by viewing or having intercourse with a corpse. This paraphilia appears to occur exclusively among males, who may be driven to remove freshly buried bodies from cemeteries or to seek employment in morgues or funeral homes (Tollison & Adams, 1979). However, the vast majority of people who work in these settings do not have tendencies toward necrophilia.

There are a few cases on record of men with necrophilic preferences who kill someone to gain access to a corpse. The notorious Jeffrey Dahmer, the Milwaukee man who murdered and mutilated his young male victims, is believed by some experts on criminal pathology to have been motivated by uncontrollable necrophilic urges. More commonly, the difficulties associated with gaining access to dead bodies lead some men with necrophilic preferences to limit their deviant behavior to contact with simulated corpses. Some prostitutes cater to this desire by powdering themselves to produce the pallor of death, dressing in a shroud, and lying very still during intercourse. Any movement on their part may inhibit their customers' sexual arousal.

Men who engage in necrophilia almost always manifest severe emotional disorders (Goldman, 1992). They may see themselves as sexually and socially inept and may both hate and fear women. Consequently, the only "safe" woman may be one whose lifelessness epitomizes a nonthreatening, totally subjugated sexual partner (Rosman & Resnick, 1989; Stoller, 1977).

▶ Treatment of Coercive Paraphilias

In most instances noncoercive paraphilias, although clearly atypical, fall within the boundaries of acceptable modes of sexual expression. Furthermore, because they rarely cause personal anguish or harm to others, treatment is generally not called for. However, in view of the invasive nature of coercive paraphilias, which often do harm others, treatment is appropriate and often necessary. Unfortunately, getting people who engage in these paraphilias to seek or accept therapeutic intervention is another matter. People who embrace one or more of the coercive paraphilias usually do not voluntarily seek treatment, nor do they acknowledge that they are in need of and/or will benefit from treatment. These individuals are thus more likely to become involved with the mental health system only after being arrested and processed by the legal system or because of pressure from family members who have discovered their paraphilic behavior.

Treatment is difficult not only because the clients are not in therapy voluntarily, but also because paraphilic behaviors are typically a source of immense pleasure. Consequently, most people are highly motivated to continue rather than give up these acts (Money, 1988; Money & Lamacz, 1990). Therapeutic treatment, regardless of the specific techniques or strategies used, is often not very successful with clients who are resistant to change.

Finally, people who compulsively engage in one or more of the coercive paraphilias often claim that they are unable to control their urges. This perceived lack of control runs counter to a basic tenet of most mental health therapies, which, simply stated, maintains that before we can constructively change our behavior, we first must accept responsibility for our actions, no matter how driven or uncontrollable they may appear to be. Thus a first step in a successful treatment program is to break through a client's belief that he is powerless to change his behavior.

A number of different approaches have been used to treat coercive paraphilias, with varied degrees of success. We consider four of the more commonly used avenues of treatment: psychotherapy, behavior therapy, drug treatments, and social skills training.

Psychotherapy

Individual **psychotherapy**—in which a client talks with a psychologist, psychiatrist, or social worker for an hour or more each week—has generally not proven effective in treating coercive paraphilias. It is difficult to overcome years of conditioning and the resultant powerful urges to continue paraphilic behavior, however problematic, in 1 or 2 hours a week of verbal interaction.

Limited success in treating paraphilias has been reported by psychologists who use **cognitive therapies.** Cognitive therapies are based on the premise that most psychological disorders result from distortions in a person's cognitions or thoughts. Psychotherapists who operate within the cognitive framework attempt to demonstrate to their clients how their distorted or irrational thoughts have contributed to their difficulties, and they use a variety of techniques to help them change these thoughts to more appropriate ones (Johnston et al., 1997). Thus, although the goal of therapy is to change a person's maladaptive paraphilic behavior, the method in cognitive therapies is to first change what the person thinks.

Unfortunately, it is often difficult to modify the distorted ideas or thoughts that people use to justify their paraphilic behaviors. In addition to being highly invested in continuing these intensely pleasurable activities, most people who engage in coercive paraphilias believe that the problems associated with these acts result from society's intolerance of their variant behaviors and not from the fundamental inappropriateness of such acts. Changing these distorted thoughts can be a real challenge.

Behavior Therapy

Traditional models of psychotherapy have emphasized the underlying causes of psychological disorders, which are viewed as distinct from those that mold so-called normal behavior. **Behavior therapy** departs from this traditional conception. Its central thesis is that maladaptive behavior has been learned and that it can be unlearned. Furthermore, the same principles that govern the learning of normal behavior also determine the acquisition of abnormal or atypical behaviors. Behavior therapy draws heavily on the extensive body of laboratory research on strategies for helping people unlearn maladaptive behavior patterns. Behavior therapy focuses on the person's current behaviors that are creating problems. These maladaptive patterns are considered to be the problem, and behavior therapists are not interested in restructuring personalities or searching for repressed conflicts. To change these inappropriate behaviors, they enact appropriate changes in the interaction between the client and his or her environment. For example, a person who responds sexually while exposing himself might be treated through repeated exposures to an aversive stimulus paired with the situation or stimulus that elicits the inappropriate arousal pattern. This technique, called *aversive conditioning,* is one of several behavior therapy techniques.

Aversive Conditioning

The goal of **aversive conditioning** is to substitute a negative (aversive) response for a positive response to an inappropriate stimulus. For example, an undesired sexual behavior, such as masturbating while replaying mental images from previous episodes of exhibitionism, is paired repeatedly with an aversive stimulus, such as a painful but not damaging electric shock, a nausea-inducing drug, or an unpleasant odor. Similarly, an aversive stimulus can be administered to a person while he views photographs or color slides depicting the paraphilic behavior.

One study reported some success with the use of aversive conditioning to treat exhibitionism. A number of male offenders were instructed to carry smelling salts (which have an unpleasant odor) and were told to inhale deeply whenever they felt compelled to expose themselves. This approach helped some of the offenders develop some control over their paraphilic behaviors by virtue of learning to associate the aversive odor with their deviant fantasies or urges (Marshall et al., 1991).

Aversive conditioning is not a pleasant experience, and you may wonder why anyone would undergo it voluntarily. The answer is that aversive conditioning as a treatment for coercive paraphilias is most commonly used with men who are required by the legal system to undergo treatment. However, in some cases family pressures or a personal dissatisfaction with the complications associated with paraphilic behavior have led some men to voluntarily seek this therapeutic intervention.

Orgasmic Reconditioning

The goal of **orgasmic reconditioning,** another type of behavior therapy, is to increase sexual arousal and response to appropriate stimuli by pairing imagery or fantasies of socially normative or acceptable sexual behavior with the reinforcing pleasure of orgasm (Laws & Marshall, 1991; Walen & Roth, 1987). In orgasmic reconditioning the client is instructed to masturbate to his usual paraphilic images or fantasies. However, when he feels orgasm is imminent, he switches to more socially appropriate imagery, which he is told to focus on during orgasm. Ideally, after practicing this technique several times, he will become accustomed to having orgasms in conjunction with more healthy imagery or fantasies. Once this is achieved, the client is encouraged to move these more appropriate images to a progressively earlier phase of his masturbation-produced sexual arousal and response. In this fashion he can gradually become conditioned to experiencing sexual arousal and orgasm in the context of socially acceptable behaviors.

Satiation Therapy

Another, related technique for treating coercive paraphilias in which masturbation plays a central role is **satiation therapy.** In this approach to treatment the client masturbates to orgasm while fantasizing or imagining images of appropriate sexual situations. He is instructed to switch to his favorite paraphilic fantasy immediately after orgasm and to continue masturbating. The premise or theory behind this approach is that the low level of arousal and response accompanying the postorgasmic masturbation to paraphilic images will eventually result in these inappropriate stimuli becoming unarousing and perhaps even irritating (Abel et al., 1992; Laws & Marshall, 1991; Maletzky, 1998).

Drug Treatment

Antiandrogen drugs (see Chapter 6), which drastically lower testosterone levels, have been used effectively in some instances to block the inappropriate sexual arousal patterns that underlie coercive paraphilic behavior (Abel et al., 1992; Bradford, 1998; Rosler & Witztum, 1998, 2000). *Medroxyprogesterone acetate* (MPA, also known by its trade name, Depo-Provera) and *cyproterone acetate* (CPA) are two antiandrogen drugs commonly used to treat sex offenders, including those whose paraphilic behaviors have brought them into contact with legal authorities.

A different drug treatment approach to reducing paraphilic behavior is offered by the use of selective serotonin reuptake inhibitors (SSRIs), which are medications commonly used to treat depression. Several of these drugs, including fluoxetine (Prozac) and sertraline (Zoloft), have been shown to reduce the expression of various paraphilic behaviors, including fetishism, transvestic fetishism, exhibitionism, and voyeurism (Balon, 1998; Bradford, 2001; Rosler & Witztum, 2000). As we discussed in Chapter 6, SSRIs often interfere with sexual desire and sexual response (Michelson et al., 2002; Wilson, 2003). This common side effect of these antidepressant drugs may account, at least in part, for why they reduce paraphilic behaviors. However, these medications also seem to have a specific inhibitory effect on the compulsive urges characteristic of paraphilias (Gijs & Gooren, 1996).

Drug treatment of coercive paraphilias is most effective when combined with other therapeutic methods, such as psychotherapy or behavior therapy (Abel et al., 1992; Bradford & Pawlak, 1993; Rosler & Witztum, 2000). The major advantage of these drugs as adjuncts to other treatment techniques is that they markedly reduce the driven or compulsive nature of the paraphilia. This better enables the client to focus his efforts on other therapeutic procedures without being so strongly distracted by his paraphilic urges.

Social Skills Training

Finally, people who engage in paraphilias often have great difficulty forming sociosexual relationships and thus may not have access to healthy forms of sexual expression. Consequently, these individuals may benefit from **social skills training,** which is designed to teach them the skills necessary to initiate and maintain satisfying relationships with potential intimate or sexual partners. Such training, often conducted in conjunction with other therapeutic interventions, can involve practice in initiating social interaction with prospective companions, conversational skills, and techniques in how to ask someone out on a date and how to cope with perceived rejection.

Social skills training Training designed to teach socially inept clients the skills necessary to initiate and maintain satisfying relationships.

▶ Sexual Addiction: Fact, Fiction, or Misnomer?

In recent years both the professional literature and the popular media have directed considerable attention to a condition commonly referred to as sexual addiction. The idea that people can become dominated by insatiable sexual needs has been around for a long time, exemplified by the terms *nymphomania,* applied to women, and *satyriasis* or *Don Juanism,* applied to men. Many professionals have traditionally reacted negatively to these labels, suggesting that they are disparaging terms likely to induce unnecessary guilt in individuals who enjoy an active sex life. Furthermore, it has been argued that one cannot assign a label implying excessive sexual activity when no clear criteria establish what constitutes "normal" levels of sexual involvement. The criteria often used to establish alleged subconditions of *hypersexuality*—nymphomania and satyriasis—are subjective and value laden. Therefore these terms are typically defined moralistically rather than scientifically, a fact that has generated harsh criticism from a number of professionals (Klein, 1991, 2003; Levine & Troiden, 1988). Psychotherapist Marty Klein (2003) is especially critical of the sex addiction movement that, in his view, both exploits people's fear of their own sexuality and pathologizes sexual behavior and impulses that are not unhealthy. Nevertheless, the concept of compulsive sexuality achieved a heightened legitimacy with the publication of Patrick Carnes's book *Sexual Addiction* (1983), later retitled *Out of the Shadows: Understanding Sexual Addiction* (2001, 3rd ed.).

According to Carnes, many people who engage in some of the atypical or paraphilic behaviors described in this chapter (as well as extreme coercive behaviors, such as child molestation, described in Chapter 19) are manifesting the outward symptoms of a process of psychological addiction in which feelings of depression, anxiety, loneliness, and worthlessness are temporarily relieved through a sexual high not unlike the high achieved by mood-altering chemicals such as alcohol or cocaine. Carnes suggested that a typical addiction cycle progresses through four phases. Initially, the sex addict enters a trancelike state of *preoccupation,* in which obsessive thoughts about a particular sex behavior, such as exposing oneself, create a consuming need to achieve expression of the behavior. This intense preoccupation induces certain *ritualistic* behaviors, such as running a regular route through a particular neighborhood where previous incidents of exposure have occurred. These ritualistic behaviors tend to further intensify the sexual excitement that was initially aroused during the preoccupation phase. The next phase is the actual expression of the *sexual act,* in this case, exposing oneself. This is followed by the final phase, *despair,* in which sex addicts are overwhelmed by feelings of worthlessness, depression, and anxiety. One way to minimize or

ON THE EDGE

Cybersex Addiction and Compulsivity:
Harmless Sexual Outlet or Problematic Sexual Behavior?

A prominent physician in our home state recently lost his position and staff privileges at a local hospital when it was discovered that he was using a hospital computer to visit sexually explicit Internet sites that specialize in child pornography. An investigation revealed that this individual spent an inordinate amount of time, both on the job and at home, compulsively surfing sexually oriented Web sites, especially those with explicit sexual content dealing with children. This example illustrates a variety of behavior, spawned by the Internet, that has raised the concern of a number of mental health specialists.

An abundance of data obtained from studies on Internet user behavior reveals that sexually oriented Internet sites are among the most widely visited topical areas of the World Wide Web. Web sex sites constitute the third largest economic sector on the Internet (after software and computers). Research indicates that at least one-third of Internet users visit some type of sexually oriented Web site (Cooper, 2002, 2003; Cooper et al., 1999, 2000). Is this widespread incidence of "surfing for sex" indicative of problematic behavior and a cause for societal concern? Some suggest the opposite—that pursuing cybersex is a harmless, recreational pursuit that offers anonymous access to sexually oriented material that provides sexual outlets (such as chat room sex or masturbating to sexual images) that are safe from the dangers of sexually transmitted diseases and other relationship risks. In addition, the Internet can also be useful to people who wish to explore sexual fantasies online in the safety and privacy of their homes (Quittner, 2003). Certainly, for most people who log on to sexually oriented Web sites, these activities are largely recreational and relatively harmless pursuits.

A less benign view of Internet sex emerges from a growing awareness that for a small and ever increasing number of individuals who surf the Internet primarily for erotic stimulation and sexual outlets, the affordability, accessibility, and anonymity of the Internet are spawning a new breed of sexual compulsives addicted to cybersex, many of whom are using cybersex to the exclusion of other relationships. Although the exact role of the Internet in facilitating the development of sexual compulsion is unknown, several professionals who study this emerging phenomenon, including psychologist Jeff Parsons, believe that "the Internet provides a situation that is particularly good for the development of sexual compulsivity" (quoted in Quittner, 2003, p. 35).

Recently, Stanford psychologist Al Cooper and his colleagues (1999, 2000) conducted a comprehensive survey of almost 10,000 men and women who reported using the Internet to visit sexually oriented Web sites. These researchers found that about 1% of their sample was seriously hooked on or addicted to cybersex. These individuals were likely to spend endless hours each day surfing sex sites, masturbating to sexually explicit images, or engaging in mutual online sex with someone contacted through a chat room. For these individuals the Internet has become what Cooper refers to as the crack cocaine of sexual compulsivity. He

suggests that cybersex compulsives are comparable to drug addicts in that they use the Internet as their sexual outlet of choice just as drug-addicted individuals typically have a drug of choice (reported by Brody, 2000). Other professionals, for example, sexologist Mark Schwartz of the Masters and Johnson Institute, agree that cybersex is similar to addictive drugs such as heroin or cocaine because it grabs hold of people and takes over their lives (reported by Brody, 2000).

The sexual excitement, stimulation, and orgasmic outlets provided by a virtually infinite supply of Internet sexual opportunities may lead to a compulsive pursuit of cyberspace sex that can have a devastating effect on a cybersex addict's life and family (Cooper, 2002; Woodward, 2003). Partners of these individuals report feeling ignored, abandoned, devalued, or betrayed as a result of their mate's compulsive pursuit of cybersex (Brody, 2000; Cooper et al., 2000). Some people devote so much time to forays into cybersex that they end up neglecting family members and/or job responsibilities. Robin Cato, executive director of the National Council on Sexual Addiction and Compulsivity, recently stated that "when you are [a sex addict] and are on the Internet, it is all-encompassing and nothing else matters" (quoted in Quittner, 2003, p. 35). The compulsion to surf sex sites may be so strong that both men and women use computers at work to satisfy their compulsive urges. The survey of Cooper and his colleagues revealed that 20% of men respondents and 12% of women participants reported using workplace computers for sexual pursuits. As noted in the opening account of this box, this behavior can place one at serious risk of job loss, because many organizations now monitor employees' online activities.

An additional hazard faced by some cybersex addicts and compulsives who pursue online sexual relationships is that they may progress to arranging off-line meetings, which, as many news stories attest, can have seriously adverse consequences, including being exposed to STDs or sexual assault (Cooper, 2002; McFarlone et al., 2002). This potentially dangerous aspect of cybersex probably affects women more than men because women pursuers of cybersex are more inclined to visit sexually oriented chat rooms and explore online sexual relationships; men tend to prefer sexually explicit or pornographic Web sites (Cooper et al., 1999, 2000; Griffiths, 2001).

By extrapolating Cooper's survey figures to the greater population of Internet users, we estimate that cybersex compulsives and addicts now number in the hundreds of thousands, with the incidence continuing to escalate in proportion to the rapidly expanding Internet user base. Hopefully, future studies of cybersex will provide a clearer answer to the question, Is compulsive exploration of online sex a relatively harmless and safe sexual outlet or a potentially harmful variety of problematic sexual behavior? For the present, a number of professionals have raised our awareness of the potentially adverse consequences of getting hooked on cybersex.

anesthetize this despair is to start the cycle again. With each repetitive cycle the addiction behavior becomes more intense and unmanageable, "thus confirming the basic feelings of unworthiness that are the core of the addict's belief system" (Carnes, 1986, p. 5).

Carnes's conception of the sexual addict has generated considerable attention in the professional community. However, many sexologists do not believe that sexual addiction should be a distinct diagnostic category, because it is rare and lacking in distinction from other compulsive disorders, such as gambling and eating disorders, and because this label negates individual responsibility for "uncontrollable" sexual compulsions that victimize others (Barth & Kinder, 1987; Levine & Troiden, 1988; Peele & Brodsky, 1987; Satel, 1993). This position is reflected in a decision not to include a category encompassing hypersexuality in the most recent version of the *Diagnostic and Statistical Manual (DSM-IV-TR)* of the American Psychiatric Association (2000) (the most widely accepted system for classifying psychological disorders).

A number of professionals acknowledge the validity of such arguments against the addiction concept but nevertheless recognize that some people become involved in patterns of excessive sexual activity that reflect a lack of control. Noteworthy in this group is sexologist Eli Coleman (1990, 1991, 2003), who prefers to describe these behaviors as symptomatic of sexual compulsion rather than addiction. According to Coleman, a person manifesting excessive sexual behaviors often suffers from feelings of shame, unworthiness, inadequacy, and loneliness. These negative feelings cause great psychological pain, and this pain then causes the person to search for a "fix," or an agent that has pain-numbing qualities, such as alcohol, certain foods, gambling, or, in this instance, sex. Indulging oneself in this fix produces only a brief respite from the psychological pain that returns in full force, thus triggering a greater need to engage in these behaviors to obtain temporary relief. Unfortunately, these repetitive compulsive acts soon tend to be self-defeating; that is, they compound feelings of shame and lead to intimacy dysfunction by interrupting the development of normal, healthy interpersonal functioning.

Because sex has become the most sought out topic among users of the Internet, in recent years some professionals have suggested that a new variety of sexual addiction or sexual compulsivity has emerged. The boxed discussion, "Cybersex Addiction and Compulsivity: Harmless Sexual Outlet or Problematic Sexual Behavior?" examines this emerging phenomenon.

We can expect that professionals in the field of sexuality will continue to debate for some time how to diagnose, describe, and explain problems of excessive or uncontrolled sexuality. Even as this discussion continues, professional treatment programs for compulsive or addictive sexual behaviors have emerged throughout the United States (more than 2,000 programs at last count), most modeled after the 12-step program of Alcoholics Anonymous (National Council on Sexual Addiction and Compulsivity, 2002). Data pertaining to treatment outcomes for these programs are still too limited to evaluate therapeutic effectiveness. Besides formal treatment programs, a number of community-based self-help organizations have surfaced throughout the United States. Some of these groups are Sex Addicts Anonymous, Sexaholics Anonymous, Sexual Compulsives Anonymous, and Sex and Love Addicts Anonymous.

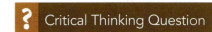

? Critical Thinking Question

Which of the atypical sexual behaviors discussed in this chapter do you find the most unacceptable? Why?

▶ Summary

What Constitutes Atypical Sexual Behavior?

- Atypical, paraphilic sexual behavior involves a variety of sexual activities that in their fully developed form are statistically uncommon in the general population. (p. 527)

- Such behaviors exist in many gradations, ranging from mild, infrequently expressed tendencies to full-blown, regularly manifested behaviors. (p. 527)

- Paraphilias are usually expressed by males, are sometimes harmful to others, may be preludes to more serious sexual offenses, and tend to occur in clusters. (p. 527)

Noncoercive Paraphilias

- Noncoercive paraphilias are often solo activities or behaviors that involve the participation of adults who agree to engage in, observe, or just put up with the particular variant behavior. (p. 528)

- Fetishism, transvestic fetishism, sexual sadism, sexual masochism, autoerotic asphyxia, klismaphilia, coprophilia, and urophilia are all varieties of noncoercive paraphilias. (pp. 528–534)

- Fetishism is a form of atypical sexual behavior in which an individual obtains arousal by focusing on an inanimate object or a part of the human body. (pp. 528–529)

- Fetishism often is a product of conditioning, in which the fetish object becomes associated with sexual arousal through the reinforcement of masturbation-produced orgasm. (p. 529)
- Transvestic fetishism involves obtaining sexual excitement by cross-dressing. It is usually a solitary activity, expressed by a heterosexual male in the privacy of his own home. (p. 530)
- Sadomasochism can be defined as obtaining sexual arousal through receiving or giving physical and/or mental pain. (p. 531)
- Most participants in sadomasochism view it as a form of sexual enhancement that they voluntarily and mutually choose to explore. (p. 531)
- People who engage in sadomasochistic behavior may be seeking additional nonsexual stimuli to achieve sufficient arousal. They may also be acting out of deeply rooted beliefs that sexual activity is sinful and immoral. (p. 533)
- For some participants, sadomasochism acts as an escape valve by which they are able to temporarily step out of the rigid, restrictive roles they play in their everyday lives. (p. 533)
- Individuals who engage in sadomasochism sometimes describe early experiences that may have established a connection between sex and pain. (p. 533)
- Autoerotic asphyxia is a rare and life-threatening paraphilia in which an individual, almost always a male, seeks to enhance sexual excitement and orgasm by pressure-induced oxygen deprivation. (pp. 533–534)
- Klismaphilia is a paraphilia that involves achieving sexual pleasure from receiving enemas. (p. 534)
- Coprophilia and urophilia are paraphilias in which the person obtains sexual arousal from contact with feces or urine, respectively. (p. 534)

Coercive Paraphilias

- Coercive paraphilias are invasive in that they involve unwilling recipients of behavior such as voyeurism or exhibitionism. Coercive acts may have harmful effects on the targets of such deeds, who may be psychologically traumatized by the experience. (p. 528)
- Exhibitionism, obscene phone calls, voyeurism, frotteurism, necrophilia, and zoophilia are all varieties of coercive paraphilias. (pp. 535–540)
- Exhibitionism is behavior in which an individual, almost always a male, exposes his genitals to an involuntary observer. (p. 535)
- People who exhibit themselves are usually young adult males who have strong feelings of inadequacy and insecurity. Sexual relationships with others, either past or present, are likely to be unsatisfactory. (p. 535)
- Gratification is usually obtained when the reaction to exhibitionism is shock, disgust, or fear. Physical assault is generally not associated with such behavior. (p. 536)
- The characteristics of individuals who make obscene phone calls are similar to those who engage in exhibitionism. (p. 536)
- Although there may be an element of vicious verbal hostility in obscene phone calls, the caller rarely follows up his verbal assault with a physical attack on his victim. (pp. 536–537)
- Voyeurism is obtaining sexual pleasure from looking at the exposed bodies or sexual activities of others, usually strangers. (p. 537)
- People inclined toward voyeurism, typically males, are often sociosexually underdeveloped, with strong feelings of inferiority and inadequacy. (p. 538)
- Frotteurism involves a person obtaining sexual pleasure by pressing or rubbing against another person in a crowded public place. (p. 538)
- Zoophilia involves sexual contact between humans and animals; it occurs most commonly as a transitory experience of young people to whom a sexual partner is inaccessible or forbidden. (pp. 539–540)
- Necrophilia involves obtaining sexual gratification by viewing or having intercourse with a corpse. (p. 540)

Treatment of Coercive Paraphilias

- People who engage in coercive paraphilias usually do not voluntarily seek treatment, nor are they likely to acknowledge that they are in need of and/or will benefit from treatment. (p. 540)
- Because paraphilic behaviors are typically a source of immense pleasure, most people are highly motivated to continue rather than give up these activities. (pp. 540–541)
- People who compulsively engage in one or more of the coercive paraphilias often claim that they are unable to control their urges. (p. 541)
- Psychotherapy has generally not proved effective in the treatment of coercive paraphilias. Limited success has been reported by cognitive therapists, who attempt to change a person's maladaptive paraphilic behaviors by changing what he thinks about these acts. (p. 541)
- Behavior therapy is based on the assumption that maladaptive paraphilic behavior has been learned and can therefore be unlearned. Varieties of behavior therapies used to treat coercive paraphilias include aversive conditioning, orgasmic reconditioning, and satiation therapy. (p. 541)
- Antiandrogen drugs and selective serotonin reuptake inhibitors have been used effectively in some instances to block the inappropriate sexual arousal patterns underlying paraphilic behavior. Drug treatment is most effective when combined with other therapeutic methods. (p. 542–543)
- People who engage in paraphilias may benefit from social skills training designed to teach them the skills necessary to initiate and maintain satisfying relationships with potential intimate or sexual partners. (p. 543)

Sexual Addiction: Fact, Fiction, or Misnomer?

- The concept of sexual addiction suggests that some people who engage in excessive sexual activity are manifesting the outward symptoms of a process of psychological addiction in which feelings of depression, anxiety, loneliness, and worthlessness are temporarily relieved through a sexual high. (p. 543)
- Many sexologists do not believe that sexual addiction should be a distinct diagnostic category because it is rare and lacking in distinction from other compulsive disorders, such as gambling and eating disorders, and because this label negates individual responsibility for "uncontrollable" sexual compulsions that victimize others. (p. 545)

▶ Suggested Readings

Arndt, William (1991). *Gender Disorders and the Paraphilias.* Madison, CT: International Universities Press. An informative book that provides an excellent overview of the scientific literature on paraphilias and a comprehensive analysis of transsexualism.

Bullough, Vern, and Bonnie Bullough (1993). *Cross-Dressing, Sex, and Gender*. Philadelphia: University of Pennsylvania Press. An informative text that provides excellent information about transvestism from a historical and cultural perspective and that describes and interprets research findings regarding cross-dressing.

Cooper, Al (Ed.) (2002). *Sex and the Internet: A Guide Book for Clinicians*. A compilation of articles by international experts on the emerging phenomenon of cybersex.

Laws, Richard, and William O'Donohue (Eds.) (1997). *Sexual Deviance: Theory, Assessment, and Treatment*. New York: Guilford Press. A collection of articles that provide insights into the causes, assessment, and treatment of a variety of atypical sexual behaviors.

Money, John, and Margaret Lamacz (1989). *Vandalized Lovemaps*. New York: Prometheus. An intriguing theory about how the erotosexual experiences we have in childhood establish patterns in the brain, called "lovemaps," and determine the kinds of sexual stimuli and activities that become sexually arousing to each of us. The primary thesis of the book is that when these lovemaps become distorted or vandalized by traumatic childhood experiences, various paraphilias result.

Weinberg, Thomas, and G. W. Levi Kamel (Eds.) (1983). *Studies in Sadomasochism*. Buffalo, NY: Prometheus Books. A collection of 18 articles that provides a considerable amount of thought-provoking information about sadomasochism.

Wilson, Glenn (Ed.) (1986). *Variant Sexuality: Research and Theory*. Baltimore: Johns Hopkins University Press. An excellent sourcebook that contains a wealth of information about the varied theoretical explanations for why people engage in atypical sexual behavior.

Web Resources

Your *Our Sexuality* Web site **http://psychology.wadsworth.com/crooksbaur9e/** has direct links to the Web sites described below. These links are checked often for changes, dead links, and new additions.

Paraphilias and Fetishes
Visitors to this Web site, part of the Human Sexuality Web site provided by the University of Missouri, Kansas City, can gain a better understanding of various paraphilias and fetishes.

Paraphilias
This Web site describes criteria, treatment, and prognosis information for different paraphilias. It is part of a larger directory of psychiatric disorders.

Tri-ESS
This Web site describes a support organization for heterosexual transvestic fetishists (cross-dressers).

National Council on Sexual Addiction and Compulsivity (NCSAC)
This Web site, maintained by the private nonprofit NCSAC, provides information designed to promote awareness and understanding of sexual addiction and sexual compulsivity. Educational material and referral sources are provided.

Our Sexuality Web Site
For online resources directly related to this book, go to **http://psychology.wadsworth.com/crooksbaur9e/**. You will find interactive exercises, study questions, chapter outlines, an online version of this text's glossary, and Web links and activities that complement your CD-ROM.

InfoTrac® College Edition Online Library
http://infotrac.thomsonlearning.com/
InfoTrac College Edition is an online searchable library that includes a multitude of journals, many of which are specific to human sexuality. These journals include *Archives of Sexual Behavior, Archives of Sexual Health Behavior, Canadian Journal of Human Sexuality, Hispanic Journal of the Behavioral Sciences, Journal of Cross-Cultural Psychology, Journal of Physical Education, Recreation, and Dance, Journal of Sex Research,* and *Sex Roles*. You may search topics suggested in the margins of this chapter or terms of your own.

Our Sexuality CD-ROM
Use your CD-ROM for further study of the concepts in this chapter. Your CD-ROM provides animations of difficult concepts, video clips of real people discussing sexuality, critical thinking questions, chapter quizzing, and more.

CHAPTER 19

Sexual Coercion

SOMEONE YOU KNOW IS A RAPE SURVIVOR

▶ **Rape**

What are some of the major false beliefs about rape?

What sociocultural factors help explain the high incidence of rape in U.S. society?

▶ **Sexual Abuse of Children**

What are some of the reasons that sexual abuse of children is so often unreported?

What can parents and other caregivers do to make children less vulnerable to sexual abuse?

▶ **Sexual Harassment**

What kinds of sexual harassment take place in the workplace and in academia?

What are some options available to someone who is being sexually harassed?

© AP/Wide World Photos

I was sexually abused by my stepbrother throughout a great part of my childhood. The abuse started the summer I was ten. He is three and a half years older than me, and he was my designated baby-sitter all summer. He usually wasn't violent. It was more coaxing and coercion, and threats of what would happen if I told. The strongest memories I have are of times when it was particularly physically painful. I put myself out of my body, and would just watch the ceiling fan go around and around. When I was 13 I saw a talk show on incest and then told a woman at my church what was happening to me, and it kind of all fell apart from there. As much as the thought of the whole experience is repulsive, what hurt the most is my parents calling it child's play and that was how it was reported to CPS [Child Protection Services]. My parents even had me believing at one point that I really had wanted it and was telling them about it for attention. Because of this reaction, I believed for a while that it was my fault and that I was dirty because of it. My stepbrother plea-bargained his case, and he was put on probation. I was taken out of the home and put in foster and group homes. I attempted suicide numerous times and was in four different psychiatric hospitals over about four years. I no longer have any contact with the "family." I am blessed to have been adopted into another loving family. My new dad is the one who saved me from hating all men forever. But I still have problems regarding sex. My boyfriend can't even hold me romantically. I have only stopped having flashbacks and nightmares fairly recently. I am in therapy for the umpteenth time, but this time it is really working. (Authors' files)

A person has been sexually victimized when she or he is deprived of free choice and is coerced or forced to comply with sexual acts under duress. Victims of coercive sexual acts often suffer grievous consequences, as revealed in the preceding account, provided by a 19-year-old college student. In this chapter we focus on three particularly abusive and exploitative forms of sexual coercion: rape, the sexual abuse of children, and sexual harassment. All these behaviors involve strong elements of coercion, sometimes even violence.

▶ Rape

Although the legal definition of **rape** varies from state to state, most state laws define rape as sexual intercourse occurring under actual or threatened forcible compulsion that overcomes the earnest resistance of the victim. This coercive act can range anywhere from the violent assault by a stranger, acquaintance, or family member to a planned romantic date that degrades into an episode of coerced sex. What these acts have in common is a disregard for the feelings of victims and a willingness to take advantage of and, often, harm them. Most writers and researchers on this topic distinguish at least three different types of rape. **Stranger rape** is rape by an unknown assailant. **Acquaintance rape,** or **date rape,** is committed by someone known to the victim. **Statutory rape** is intercourse with a person under the age of consent. (The age of consent varies by state and ranges from 14 to 18.) Statutory rape is considered to have occurred regardless of the apparent willingness of the underage partner.

Rape Sexual intercourse that occurs without consent as a result of actual or threatened force.

Stranger rape Rape of a person by an unknown assailant.

Acquaintance rape Sexual assault by a friend, acquaintance, or date—that is, someone known to the victim.

Date rape Sexual assault by an acquaintance when on a date.

Statutory rape Intercourse with a person under the age of consent.

Prevalence of Rape

Despite the fact that rape is a significant problem in our society, it has been difficult to obtain accurate statistics on its frequency. One reason is that many individuals do not report this crime. Estimates of the percentage of rapes that women victims report to police or other public agencies range from 11.9% (Hanson et al., 1999) to 28% (U.S. Department of Justice, 2001). This low percentage of reporting has led some writers to suggest that rape is the most underreported crime in the United States (Lonsway & Fitzgerald, 1994).

Victims do not report having been raped for a number of reasons. These include self-blame ("I shouldn't have had so much to drink"), fear of being blamed by others, concern for the rapist, and an attempt to block their recall of a traumatic experience (Parrot, 1991; Simonson & Subich, 1999). A person who has been raped may feel vulnerable and frightened, and reliving the experience by telling about it can be understandably difficult. Also, mistrust of the police or legal system, fear of reprisal by the offender or his family, and concern about unwanted publicity may deter individuals from reporting rapes. And, as we discuss later in this chapter, a large proportion of rapes

InfoTrac Search Words

■ Rape

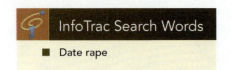
are committed by an acquaintance or partner of the victim. Under these circumstances a woman's preconceived notion of a "real" rape—a violent attack by a stranger—may not match her experience of an acquaintance rape, and therefore she may not consider it reportable criminal behavior (Cowan, 2000; Kahn et al., 1994; Rickert & Wiemann, 1998).

Previous estimates of the number of women who have experienced actual or attempted rape have varied widely and have been beset by a number of methodological problems. In an effort to overcome these problems, the National Institutes of Justice (NIJ) and the Centers for Disease Control and Prevention (CDC) commissioned a large-scale telephone survey of 8,000 women and 8,000 men (Tjaden & Thoennes, 1998). The investigators reported that more than 1 out of 6 women indicated that they had been raped or had been the victim of an attempted rape, as did 3% of men (see Table 19.1). More recently, a national survey conducted by the NIJ found that over the course of time spent in college, 20–25% of college women experience a completed or attempted rape (Fisher et al., 2000).

TABLE 19.1 Lifetime Incidence of Rape by Sex of Victim		
Rape Incident	Women (*n* = 8,000)	Men (*n* = 8,000)
Completed	14.8%	2.1%
Attempted only	2.8%	0.9%
Total	17.6%	3.0%

SOURCE: Adapted from Tjaden & Thoennes (1998).

In the following pages we look at a number of aspects of the act of rape, including the cultural context in which it occurs, the characteristics of perpetrators, and the characteristics of victims.

False Beliefs About Rape

An important factor in explaining the high incidence of rape in our society is the prevalence of misconceptions about this crime. False beliefs concerning rape, rapists, and rape victims abound (Cowan, 2000; Hall & Barongan, 1997; Lonsway & Fitzgerald, 1994, 1995; O'Donohue et al., 2003). Many people believe that roughing up a woman is acceptable, that many women are sexually aroused by such activity, and that it is impossible to rape a healthy woman against her will (Gilbert et al., 1991; Malamuth et al., 1980). The effect of such rape myths is often "to deny and justify male sexual aggression against women" (Lonsway & Fitzgerald, 1994, p. 133). Another frequent effect is to place the blame on the victim. Many victims believe that the rape was basically their fault. Even when they were simply in the wrong place at the wrong time, a pervasive sense of personal guilt often remains. The following are some of the most common false beliefs about rape.

> **Critical Thinking Question**
>
> How do false beliefs about rape perpetuate the belief that the victim is responsible?

1. *False belief: "Women can't be raped if they really don't want to be."* The belief that women can always resist a rape attempt is false, for several reasons. First, men are usually physically larger and stronger than women. Second, female gender-role conditioning often trains a woman to be compliant and submissive. These elements of gender-role conditioning can limit the options a woman believes she has in resisting rape. Third, with many rapes the rapist chooses the time and place. He has the element of surprise on his side. The fear and intimidation a woman usually experiences when attacked works to the assailant's advantage. His use of weapons, threats, or physical force further coerces her compliance.

2. *False belief: "Women say no when they mean yes."* Some rapists have distorted perceptions of their interactions with the women they rape before, during, and even after the assault. They believe that women want to be coerced into sexual activity, even to the extent of being sexually abused (Abel, 1981; Muehlenhard & Rodgers, 1998). These distorted beliefs help the rapist justify his behavior: His acts are not rape but rather "normal" sex play. Afterward, he may have little or no guilt about his behavior because, in his own mind, it was not rape. Of 114 imprisoned rapists who were interviewed in one study, over 80% did not see themselves as rapists. Those who did not deny having sexual contact with their accusers used a variety of explanations to justify their actions, including such distorted perceptions as claiming that women say no

when they mean yes, that women are seducers who "lead you on," and that most women eventually relax and enjoy it (Scully & Marolla, 1984).

3. *False belief: "Many women 'cry rape.'"* False accusations of rape are quite uncommon, and they are even less frequently carried as far as prosecution. Given the difficulties that exist in reporting and prosecuting a rape, few women (or men) could successfully proceed with an unfounded rape case. As mentioned earlier, "Women are much more likely to suffer rape victimization and not report the crime to any authorities" (Lonsway & Fitzgerald, 1994, p. 136).

4. *False belief: "All women want to be raped."* The fact that some women have rape fantasies is sometimes used to support the idea that women want to be sexually assaulted. However, it is important to understand the distinction between an erotic fantasy and a conscious desire to be harmed. In a fantasy a person retains control. A fantasy carries no threat of physical harm or death; a rape does.

5. *False belief: "Rapists are 'obviously' mentally ill."* The mistaken idea that a potential rapist somehow "looks the part" is also prevalent. "This rape myth is particularly dangerous because potential victims may feel that they can identify a rapist (the crazed stranger) or that they are safe with someone they know" (Cowan, 2000, p. 809). As we discuss later, most rapes are committed by people who are not mentally ill and who are known to the victim.

6. *False belief: "The male sex drive is so high that men often cannot control their sexual urges."* The problem with this myth is that it shifts the responsibility from the perpetrator to the victim (Cowan, 2000). Women are seen as either the precipitator of the rape ("She should not have worn that dress") or as having been careless or naive ("What did she think would happen if she went back to his apartment with him?").

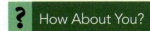

? How About You?

Which of these false beliefs about rape do you think is most dangerous and why?

Factors Associated with Rape

Women in the United States are many times more likely to be raped than women in certain other societies (Contemporary Sexuality, 1996; Sanday, 1981). In an effort to understand the underlying causes of rape, researchers have looked at a number of psychosocial and sociobiological factors.

Psychosocial Basis of Rape

Many researchers and clinicians view rape more as a product of socialization processes that occur within the fabric of "normal" society than as a product of the individual rapist's pathological condition (Hall & Barongan, 1997; Hill & Fischer, 2001; Simonson & Subich, 1999). Strong support for the view that rape is in many ways a cultural phenomenon was provided by the research of Peggy Reeves Sanday (1981), an anthropologist who compared the incidence of rape in 95 societies.

Sanday's research indicated that the frequency of rape in a given society is influenced by several factors. Foremost among these were the nature of the relations between the sexes, the status of women, and the attitudes that boys acquire during their developmental years. Sanday found that "rape-prone" societies tolerate and even glorify masculine violence, encouraging boys to be aggressive and competitive and viewing physical force as natural and exemplary. In these cultures men tend to have greater economic and political power, remaining aloof from "women's work," such as child rearing and household duties.

In contrast, relations between the sexes are quite different in societies where there is virtually no rape. Women and men in "rape-free" societies share power and authority and contribute equally to the community welfare. In addition, children of both sexes in these societies are raised to value nurturance and to avoid aggression and violence. With this cultural framework in mind, let us take a closer look at some of the aspects of male socialization in our own culture that contribute to the occurrence of rape and other forms of sexual coercion.

The United States has the highest incidence of rapes among all Western nations (Contemporary Sexuality, 1996). One important reason for this may have to do with stereotypical gender roles. Males in our society are often taught that power, aggressiveness, and getting what one wants, by force if necessary, are all part of the proper male role. Furthermore, they

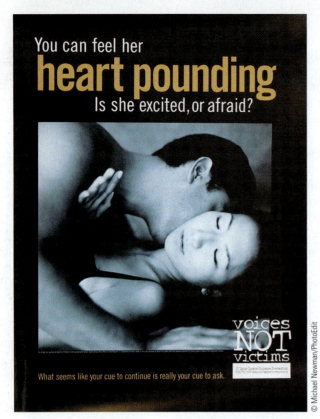

You can feel her **heart pounding**
Is she excited, or afraid?

voices NOT victims

What seems like your cue to continue is really your cue to ask.

© Michael Newman/PhotoEdit

Advertisements like this one are intended to educate men and women about rape.

frequently learn that they should seek sex and expect to be successful—often with few qualms about using unethical means to achieve their goals.

It is not surprising, therefore, that many U.S. men view aggression as a legitimate means to obtain sexual access to women. "Sexual assault is a logical extension of a system in which men are taught to fight for what they want, whereas women are taught to be passive and yielding and to put men's needs above their own" (Muehlenhard et al., 1991, p. 161).

Men whose peer groups openly legitimize and support these attitudes and behaviors are particularly likely to victimize women sexually (Sanday, 1996). In one study the best predictor of which men had engaged in sexually aggressive behavior (defined as physically forced sexual activity carried to the point that the woman was crying, fighting, or screaming) was having male friends who were sexually aggressive (Adler, 1985). In another study, which compared male college students who admitted to date rape with a control sample of nonrapists (also male college students), the rapists were much more likely to have friends who engaged in "rough sex" and who labeled certain types of females as legitimate targets for rape. The rapists in this study also reported considerably more peer pressure to acquire sexual experience than did the nonrapists (Kanin, 1985).

Despite extensive evidence supporting an interpretation of rape as a product of cultural socialization processes, this viewpoint has a few detractors. Noteworthy in this category are sociobiologists Randy Thornhill and Craig Palmer (2000), who offer a sociobiological explanation of rape:

> Learned behavior, and indeed all culture, is the result of psychological adaptations that have evolved over long periods of time. Those adaptations, like all traits of individual human beings, have both genetic and environmental components. We fervently believe that, just as the leopard's spots and the giraffe's elongated neck are the result of eons of past Darwinian selection, so also is rape. (p. 31)

Thus in Thornhill and Palmer's view there is an evolutionary advantage, which has led to a biological predisposition, to males having sex with as many women as possible. And the more partners a man has, whether or not the woman consents, the more offspring he will have and the more likely his genes will survive. Therefore, to some extent, rape is natural because it is programmed into men.

This view of our behavior as being evolutionarily determined has been vigorously disputed (Coyne & Berry, 2000; Lewontin, 1999; Stanford, 2000). In addition to attacking the science underlying the sociobiologists' assumptions regarding rape—for example, making inferences that go beyond the evidence of the studies they cite—these critics of Thornhill and Palmer raise an interesting question: If rape is "wired in" to males genetically, why do not all men rape? And why does the frequency of rape vary so much between cultures? In addition, for rape to have been "naturally selected," it must confer some evolutionary advantage; it must be an effective mating strategy. However, as Stanford (2000) pointed out, a study that Thornhill and Palmer used estimated that rapists succeed in impregnating their victims only 2% of the time and only 38% of such impregnations resulted in a birth. Thus the odds were less than 1 in 100 that a rape would confer any evolutionary advantage to the rapist. Given the cost to a rapist from imprisonment, injury, or death, Stanford believes that Thornhill and Palmer's research shows that rape is not a natural adaptation. Thus the sociobiological explanation for rape appears to rest on tenuous grounds.

Impact of the Media

The media play a powerful role in transmitting cultural values and norms. Some novels, films, videos, and computer games perpetuate the notion that women want to be raped. Often, fictionalized rape scenes begin with a woman resisting her attacker, only to melt into passionate acceptance. In the rare cases where male-to-male rape is shown, as in the films *Deliverance* and *The Shawshank Redemption,* the violation and humiliation of rape are more likely to be realistically portrayed.

A number of social scientists have suggested that sexually violent films, books, magazines, videos, and computer games contribute to some rapists' assaultive behaviors (Boeringer, 1994; Hall, 1996; Linz et al., 1988, 1992). Other evidence suggests that exposure to degrading but nonviolent pornography might also have deleterious effects on men's attitudes toward sex and women and might increase their inclinations to engage in coercive sex (Check & Guloien, 1989; Zillmann, 1989).

Boeringer (1994) found that, although exposure to nonviolent pornography was not predictive of any form of sexual coercion or rape, viewing hard-core pornography that depicted violent rape was strongly associated with judging oneself capable of sexual coercion and aggression and engaging in such coercive acts. Other research suggests that "exposure to media that combine arousing sexual images with violence may promote the development of deviant patterns of physiological sexual arousal" (Hall & Barongan, 1997, p. 5).

Is rape, then, a sexualization of violence? The evidence is equivocal. In two studies the erectile responses of matched groups of rapists and nonrapists were measured as the men listened to audiotape descriptions of rape and of mutually consenting sexual activity. In both studies rapists were more aroused by the sexual assault description than were nonrapists (Abel et al., 1977; Bernat et al., 1999). However, some other research has failed to support this conclusion, finding little difference in the erectile responses of rapists and nonrapists in similar research designs (Eccles et al., 1994; Proulx et al., 1994). Clearly, more research is needed to clarify these findings.

Characteristics of Rapists

Are rapists characterized by a singular personality or behavioral pattern? Until recently, efforts to answer this question have been hindered by both a narrow conceptualization of rape and inadequate research methods. This was because our knowledge of the characteristics and motivations of rapists was based primarily on studies of men convicted of the crime—a sample group that probably represents less than 1% of rapists. Because convicted rapists are less educated, more inclined to commit other antisocial or criminal acts, and more alienated from society than are rapists who do not pass through the criminal justice system (Smithyman, 1979), we cannot say with certainty that men who rape without being prosecuted and convicted match the profile of convicted rapists.

We can say that many of the men incarcerated for rape have a strong proclivity toward violence, one that is often reflected in their acts of rape. This fact, along with certain assumptions about male–female relationships, has led a number of writers to argue that rape is not sexually motivated but is rather an act of power and domination (Brownmiller, 1975). This viewpoint prevailed for a number of years, during which time the sexual component of rape and other assaults was de-emphasized. However, more recent research suggests that, although power and domination are often involved in sexual coercion, such acts are also frequently motivated by a desire for sexual gratification. This view has been supported by several studies of the incidence and nature of sexual coercion among nonincarcerated males (Hickman & Muehlenhard, 1999; Senn et al., 1999).

It appears that a wide range of personality characteristics and motivations underlie sexual assault and how that assault is committed. Men who embrace traditional gender roles, particularly that of male dominance, are more likely to commit rape than men who do not embrace traditional gender stereotypes (Harney & Muehlenhard, 1990; Parrot et al., 1994; Truman et al., 1996). Anger toward women is a prominent attitude among some men who sexually assault women (Anderson et al., 1997; Hall & Barongan, 1997). Alcohol can also contribute to rapists' behavior; rapists often had been drinking just before assaulting their victims (Abbey et al., 1998, 2003; Muehlenhard & Linton, 1987). Furthermore, alcohol-involved rapes are often associated with a high level of violence (Abbey et al., 2003).

Many rapists have self-centered personalities, which may render them insensitive to others' feelings (Dean & Malamuth, 1997; Marshall, 1993; Pithers, 1993). Recent research has provided strong evidence that men with a narcissistic personality trait may be especially inclined to commit rape and other acts of sexual coercion (Baumeister et al., 2002; Bushman et al., 2003). The *Diagnostic and Statistical Manual of Mental Disorders* (American

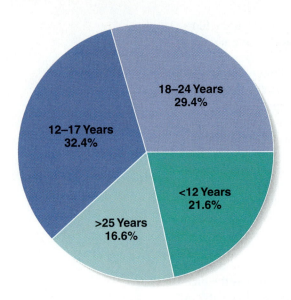

▶ **Figure 19.1** Age breakdown of women rape victims at time of first rape.

SOURCE: Tjaden & Thoennes (1998).

Pie chart labels:
18–24 Years 29.4%
12–17 Years 32.4%
<12 Years 21.6%
>25 Years 16.6%

Psychiatric Association, 2000) describes *narcissism* as being characterized by an inflated sense of self-importance, an unreasonable sense of entitlement, deficient empathy for others, and exploitative tendencies toward others. Research indicates that narcissists are also inclined to engage in aggressive retaliation against others for real or imagined slights (Baumeister et al., 2002; Bushman & Baumeister, 1998). In addition to these aggressive tendencies, narcissists' unreasonable sense of entitlement may influence them to view women as owing them sexual favors. Their lack of empathy for others would negate the impact of their victims' discomfort or suffering. Finally, their exaggerated sense of self-importance may facilitate their ability to rationalize their behavior and "convince themselves that their coercion victims had really desired sex or had expressed some form of consent" (Bushman et al., 2003, p. 1028).

Anger, power, and sexual gratification all play varying roles in rape. However, feelings of anger and a need to express power appear to occur more often in stranger rape, whereas a desire for sexual gratification seems to predominate in acquaintance or date rape.

Research also suggests that some rapists engage in a series of progressively more violent sexual offenses (Abel, 1981). While at Columbia University, psychologist Gene Abel did noteworthy work in which he developed an elaborate system of confidentiality that allowed more than 200 men who had engaged in a variety of sexual victimization behaviors to participate in his research without being identified by the criminal justice system. Approximately half the rapists in Abel's sample had histories of other types of sexual offenses, most notably sexual abuse of children, exhibitionism, voyeurism, and sadism. Abel also found that some of the rapists in his sample had extensive histories of fantasizing about rape and violence long before committing any attacks. He described a pattern in which many of these men had begun masturbating frequently to the accompaniment of rape fantasies as early as their midteens. A similar pattern was suggested by a British study in which 13 rapists reported that they had often responded to unpleasant emotional states (such as anger, loneliness, and humiliation) by masturbating to fantasies involving sexual coercion. This pattern seemed to be a precursor to rape and other aggressive sexual acts (McKibben et al., 1994).

Characteristics of Female Rape Victims

Although women of all ages are raped, more than 50% of U.S. female rape victims reported that their first rape occurred before they were 18 years old—and 22% reported that their first rape occurred before they were 12 (see Figure 19.1). Being raped before the age of 18 greatly increases the chances that a woman will be raped again (Nishith et al., 2000; Tjaden & Thoennes, 1998). The younger the age of the rape victim, the more likely it is that the perpetrator is a relative or acquaintance (U.S. Department of Justice, 2000).

As noted earlier, the frequency of reported rape varies by culture. Asian and Pacific Islander women report being raped significantly less often than do white and African American women, Hispanic women report being raped less often than non-Hispanic women, and American Indian and Alaska Native women report a much higher frequency of rape than any other group (Tjaden & Thoennes, 1998). Koss et al. (1987), however, reported similar incidences of rape across various ethnic groups when socioeconomic status (SES) was controlled, with women of lower SES more often victims of sexual assault. This finding is not surprising, because people who live in impoverished conditions are more frequent victims of all types of crimes. Given these divergent findings, however, more research is needed to ascertain whether there are cultural and ethnic variations in the frequency of rape in our society—and, if so, why.

? Critical Thinking Question

Some people perceive a woman who wears "suggestive clothing" and is then raped as somehow responsible for her own rape. In contrast, a man who dons an expensive suit, carries a lot of cash, and wears a Rolex watch is seldom, if ever, held responsible for being robbed on the street. What are your thoughts about this inconsistency in assigning the label *victim precipitation* to these two events? Is it ever appropriate to label a victim responsible for her or his own victimization?

Acquaintance Rape and Sexual Coercion

Most rapes are committed by someone who is known to the victim, by an acquaintance or a friend, not (as popularly thought) by a stranger (Fisher et al., 2000; Harney & Muehlenhard, 1990; Howard et al., 2003; Koss, 1992; Small & Kerns, 1993). A significant number of these acquaintance rapes occur in dating situations—hence the term *date rape.*

Much research has focused on the prevalence of sexual coercion in dating situations (Kalof, 1993; Small & Kerns, 1993). Thirty-five percent of 930 San Francisco women reported having been victims of either attempted or completed acquaintance rape, usually in dating situations (Russell, 1984). Twenty percent of 1,149 teenage women reported experiencing forced intercourse or some other form of unwanted sexual contact during the previous year, most commonly in dating situations (Small & Kerns, 1993). A survey of almost 200 Canadian high school students found that 30% of the female respondents reported being forced into some type of sexual activity (Rhynard et al., 1997). In a survey of eighth- to twelfth-grade students in 79 public and private schools in Vermont, 30% of almost 4,000 sexually active girls reported being forced or pressured to have sexual intercourse (Shrier et al., 1998).

Women are not the only ones to experience sexual coercion. The Canadian study mentioned previously found that 22% of the male respondents of high school age reported experiencing some form of coercive sexual activity (Rhynard et al., 1997). In the survey of Vermont middle and high school students, 10% of about 4,000 sexually active boys reported being pressured to have sexual intercourse (Shrier et al., 1998). Another survey of 433 Canadian college students found that about 25% of the men and more than 40% of the women respondents reported being pressured or forced into sexual activity during a dating experience in the past year (O'Sullivan et al., 1998). It is important to note that, although many of the women in these studies were forced to engage in unwanted sex acts, physical force is considerably less likely to be used in the sexual coercion of male respondents (Struckman-Johnson et al., 2003).

© Bob Daemmrich/The Image Works

Women in Austin, Texas, protest against sexual assault. These women, and others like them, have helped challenge societal assumptions about rape.

Acquaintance Rape: The Role of Perceptions and Communication

Earlier in this chapter we examined the relationship between sexual coercion and cultural expectations for males in our society. The socializing process that encourages men to be aggressive to get what they want is undoubtedly an important factor in rape and sexual coercion. As many have pointed out (e.g., Byers & O'Sullivan, 1996; Carpenter, 1998), in our society many males and females learn **sexual scripts** that encourage men to be aggressive and women to be passive. Yet some experts argue that in at least some cases of acquaintance rape, the picture is more complicated.

Consider the issue of men's misinterpretation of women's signals. Men often consider women's actions such as cuddling or kissing as indicating a desire to engage in intercourse (Muehlenhard, 1988; Muehlenhard & Linton, 1987). However, a woman who feels like cuddling does not necessarily want to have sex, and she may express this to her date. Even if a woman clearly expresses her desire not to have sex, her date may read her actions as "token resistance," concluding that she really wants to have sex but does not want to appear "too easy" (Krahe et al., 2000; Muehlenhard & Hollabaugh, 1989).

In some cases this "reading" is entirely motivated by exploitative self-interest. But some women do say no when they mean yes. One study of 610 female undergraduates revealed that 39.3% had engaged in token resistance to sex at least once. Reasons for saying no when they really meant yes included not wanting to appear promiscuous, uncertainty about a partner's feelings, undesirable surroundings, game playing (wanting a partner to be more physically aggressive, to persuade her to have sex, etc.), and desiring to be in control (Muehlenhard & Hollabaugh, 1989). This kind of double message may actually promote rape by providing men with a rationale for ignoring sincere refusals. The researchers in this study concluded that, if a man has had the experience of ignoring a woman's protests only to find that she actually did want to have sex, then "his belief that women's refusals are not

Sexual scripts Culturally learned ways of behaving in sexual situations.

InfoTrac Search Words

■ Sexual scripts

Critical Thinking Question

Why might people engage in unwanted sexual activity when force is not used? Do you think there are reasons that are common to both sexes? What explanations might apply to only one sex?

to be taken seriously will be strengthened" (Muehlenhard & Hollabaugh, 1989, p. 878). He may thus proceed with his sexual advances despite further protests and genuine resistance from his date. Such a man may not even define his actions as rape.

The concept of token resistance underscores the fact that many sexual interactions are beset with problems of poor communication. The ambiguity and miscommunication that often characterize sexual encounters underscore the importance of building a foundation of clear communication, the topic of Chapter 8.

Although there are times when verbal communication is misunderstood, it appears that, many times, there is little or no verbal communication at all about what people want sexually. In one study on sexual communication "both women and men reported that they most frequently signaled sexual consent by not resisting: letting their partner undress them, not stopping their partner from kissing or touching them, not saying no" (Hickman & Muehlenhard, 1999, p. 271). Although this nonverbal communication may reflect a willingness to proceed, it can also increase the chances for misunderstandings if either party finds it hard to verbally communicate what he or she does and does not want.

Even men who believe their partners when they say no may think that it is defensible to use force to obtain sex if they feel that they have been "led on." A number of studies have found that many men regard rape as justifiable, or at least hold the woman more responsible, if she leads a man on by such actions as dressing "suggestively" or going to his apartment (Muehlenhard & Linton, 1987; Muehlenhard et al., 1991; Workman & Freeburg, 1999). The implications of these findings for acquaintance rape prevention are discussed in the box "Dealing with Rape and Attempted Rape."

Date Rape Drugs

In the early 1990s reports began to circulate about the increasing use of Rohypnol (roh-HIP-nol) to facilitate sexual conquest or to incapacitate victims who are then sexually molested or raped (O'Neill, 1997; Staten, 1997). Rohypnol, commonly known on the street as "roofies," is the brand name for flunitrazepam, a powerful tranquilizer that has a sedative effect seven to ten times more potent than Valium. In addition to producing a sedative effect in 20 to 30 minutes that can last for several hours, Rohypnol also causes muscle relaxation and mild to pronounced amnesia. Rohypnol is odorless and is excreted from the victim's system in a relatively short time, making discovery and prosecution of rapists who use this drug difficult. Many cases have emerged of women being raped after their dates had given them the drug surreptitiously; hence the term *date rape drug*. When combined with alcohol, the drug's effects are greatly enhanced and can result in a dramatic "high," markedly reduced inhibitions, unconsciousness, and total amnesia concerning events that occur while a person is under its influence. Rohypnol has also led to death. In March 2000, four men were sentenced to prison for involuntary manslaughter in the death of a 15-year-old girl in Michigan (Bradsher, 2000). This is one of the many deaths reportedly caused by Rohypnol.

And Rohypnol is not alone. Other drugs, such a gamma hydroxybutyrate (GHB) and ketamine hydrochloride (Special K) have also been implicated in date rapes. GHB was developed more than 40 years ago and initially was used as an anesthetic. Its mind-altering effects soon became well known, and it has become increasingly popular as a recreational drug—often with devastating results. GHB is a central nervous system depressant that can be especially lethal when combined with alcohol (Nicholson & Balster, 2001). Since 1990, emergency rooms have reported thousands of cases of GHB overdoses, some of which have resulted in death (Dyer, 2000; Smalley, 2003). Like Rohypnol, GHB is odorless and tasteless, which makes it easy to administer to unsuspecting victims. GHB exits the body in 6 to 12 hours, which makes it an especially ideal drug for sexual predators, because a lack of toxicological evidence makes prosecution difficult.

Sexual Health

It is important to be alert for potential victimization by means of a date rape drug. Do not accept a drink (alcohol, coffee, soda, etc.), especially open-container beverages, from someone other than a trusted friend. Never leave your drink unattended. If you experience one or more of the following symptoms after ingesting a beverage, it is possible that your drink was tainted: nausea, dizziness, slurred speech, movement impairment, or euphoria. If

Dealing with Rape and Attempted Rape

Although rape is a societywide problem, it is the rape victim who experiences the direct, personal violation. The suggestions offered in the following lists present strategies for reducing the risk of acquaintance rape and for avoiding stranger rape. However, following these suggestions offers no guarantee of avoiding rape. Even a woman who leads an extremely cautious and restricted life can be assaulted. Rape prevention consists primarily of making it as difficult as possible for a rapist to victimize you. Many of the following suggestions are common-sense measures against other crimes besides rape.

Many women take self-defense training to protect themselves from assault.

© Spencer Grant/Stock Boston

Reducing the Risk of Acquaintance Rape

1. The less you know about a person before meeting, the more important it is to be cautious. For example, because the Internet has become an increasingly popular way to meet people, it is important to realize that you do not really know this person. Thus, when dating someone for the first time, seriously consider doing so in a group situation or meeting your date at a public place. This will allow you to assess your date's behavior in a relatively safe environment.

2. Watch for inclinations that your date may be a dominating person who may try to control your behavior. A man who plans all activities and makes all decisions during a date may also be inclined to dominate in a private setting.

3. If the man drives and pays for all expenses, he may think he is justified in using force to get "what he paid for." If you cover some of the expenses, he may be less inclined to use this rationale to justify acting in a sexually coercive manner (Muehlenhard & Schrag, 1991; Muehlenhard et al., 1991).

4. Avoid using alcohol or other drugs when you definitely do not wish to be sexually intimate with your date. Consumption of alcohol and/or other drugs, by both victim and perpetrator, is commonly associated with acquaintance rape (Gross & Billingham, 1998; Synovitz & Byrne, 1998). Drug intoxication can both diminish your capacity to escape from an assault and reduce your date's reluctance to engage in assaultive behavior.

5. Avoid behavior that may be interpreted as "teasing." Clearly state what you do and do not wish to do in regard to sexual contact. For example, you might say, "I hope you do not misinterpret my inviting you back to my apartment. I definitely do not want to do anything more than relax, listen to some music, and talk." If you are interested in initiating an exploration of some kind of early physical contact, you might say, "Tonight I would like to hold you and kiss, but I would not be comfortable with

anything else at this point in our relationship." Such direct communication can markedly reduce a man's inclinations to force unwanted sexual activity or to feel "led on" (Muehlenhard & Andrews, 1985; Muehlenhard et al., 1985).

6. If, despite direct communication about your intentions, your date behaves in a sexually coercive manner, you may use a "strategy of escalating forcefulness—direct refusal, vehement verbal refusal, and, if necessary, physical force" (Muehlenhard & Linton, 1987, p. 193). One study found that college students were most likely to label a scenario of date sex as rape if such activity was preceded by a clearly stated no (Sawyer et al., 1998). In another study the response rated by men as most likely to get men to stop unwanted advances was the woman vehemently saying, "This is rape, and I'm calling the cops" (Beal & Muehlenhard, 1987). If verbal protests are ineffective, reinforce your refusal with physical force such as pushing, slapping, biting, kicking, or clawing your assailant. Men are more likely to perceive their actions as at least inappropriate, if not rape, when a woman protests not only verbally but also physically (Beal & Muehlenhard, 1987; Muehlenhard & Linton, 1987).

Reducing the Risk of Stranger Rape

1. Do not advertise that you are a woman living alone. Use initials on your mailbox and in the phone book; even add a fictitious name.

2. Install and use secure locks on doors and windows, changing door locks after losing keys or moving into a new residence. A peephole in your front door can be particularly helpful.

3. Do not open your door to strangers. If a repairman or public official is at your door, ask him to identify himself and call his office to verify that he is a reputable person on legitimate business.

4. When you are in situations where strangers may be encountered, demonstrate self-confidence through your body language and speech to communicate that you will not be intimidated. Research reveals that rapists often tend to select as victims women who exhibit passivity and submissiveness (Richards et al., 1991).

5. Take a cell phone with you when you are out alone.

6. Lock your car when it is parked and while you are driving.

continued on next page

▶ **Dealing with Rape and Attempted Rape,** continued

7. Avoid dark and deserted areas and be aware of the surroundings when you are walking. This can help if you need an opportunity to escape. Should a driver ask for directions when you are a pedestrian, avoid approaching his car. Instead, call out your reply from a safe distance.

8. Have house or car keys in hand before coming to the door, and check the backseat before getting into your car.

9. Should your car break down, attach a white cloth to the antenna and lock yourself in. If someone other than a uniformed officer in an official car stops to offer help, ask this person to call the police or a garage but do not open your locked car door.

10. Never hitchhike or provide rides to hitchhikers or get into a car with a stranger.

11. Wherever you go, it can be helpful to carry a device for making a loud noise, such as a whistle, or, even better, a pint-sized compressed-air horn (available in many sporting goods and boat supply stores). Sound the noise alarm at the first sign of danger.

Many cities have crime-prevention bureaus that provide further suggestions and home-safety inspections.

What to Do in Threatening Situations Involving Strangers

If you are approached by a man or men who may intend to rape you, you will have to decide what to do. *Each situation, assailant, and woman is unique. There are no absolute rules.*

1. Run away if you can.

2. Resist if you cannot run. Make it difficult for the rapist. On locating a potential victim, many men test her to see if she is easily intimidated. Resistance by the woman is responsible for thwarting many attempts (Fischhoff, 1992; Heyden et al., 1999; Page, 1997). Active and vociferous resistance—shouting, being rude, causing a scene, running away, fighting back—may deter the attack. This was the finding of a study of 150 rapes or attempted rapes: Women who used forceful verbal or physical resistance (screaming, hitting, kicking, biting, running, and the like) were more likely to avoid being raped than women who tried pleading, crying, or offering no resistance (Zoucha-Jensen & Coyne, 1993).

3. Ordinary rules of behavior do not apply. Vomiting, screaming, or acting crazy—whatever you are willing to try—can be appropriate responses to an attempted rape.

4. Talking can be a way to stall and can give you a chance to devise an escape plan or another strategy. It can be helpful to get the attacker to start talking ("What has happened to make you so angry?"), to express some empathy ("It is really discouraging to lose a job"), or to negotiate ("Let's take time to talk about this"). Even when talking does not prevent an assault, it may reduce the degree of violence (Prentky et al., 1986).

5. Remain alert for an opportunity to escape. In some situations, initially, it may be impossible to fight or elude an attacker. However, later on you may have a chance to deter the attack and escape—for example, if the rapist becomes distracted or a passerby comes on the scene.

Self-defense classes are a resource for learning techniques of physical resistance that can injure the attacker(s) or distract him long enough for you to escape.

What to Do If You Have Been Raped

If you have been raped, you will have to decide whether to report the attack to the police.

1. It is advisable to report a rape, even an unsuccessful rape attempt. The information you provide may prevent another woman from being raped.

2. When you report a rape, any information that you can remember about the attack will be helpful—the assaulter's physical characteristics, voice, clothes, car, even an unusual smell.

3. If you have been raped, you should call the police as soon as possible; do not bathe or change your clothes. Semen, hair, and material under fingernails or on your clothing may be useful in identifying the rapist.

4. It may be helpful to contact a rape crisis center, where qualified staff members can assist you in dealing with your trauma. Most large urban communities in the United States have such programs. If you are unable to make the contact yourself, have a friend, family member, or the police make the call.

5. In addition to general counseling, there are effective treatment programs for women who have been raped. If your symptoms do not subside after a period of time, consider entering a treatment program. You do not have to continue to suffer.

6. Finally, it is important to remember that many women mistakenly blame themselves for the rape. However, being raped is not a crime—the crime has been committed by the man who raped you.

you find yourself in such a circumstance, call 911 or ask someone other than your date or companion to help you seek medical attention and, if possible, retain a sample of the beverage. ■

As a result of abuse and deaths associated with date rape drugs, the U.S. Congress has passed laws that strengthen the penalties for possessing Rohypnol, GHB, and other similar drugs and significantly increase the prison sentences for rapists who use drugs to incapacitate victims.

Wartime Rape

Although rape is most often a coercive interaction between two individuals, it has also been a strategy of war throughout history. Records abound of the mass rape of women during war, from the time of ancient Greece to the more recent atrocities in Rwanda and the former Yugoslavia. In the 20th century hundreds of thousands of women have been victimized by wartime rape (Brownmiller, 1993; Carlson, 1997; Lombardi, 2001; Shanks et al., 2001; Swiss & Giller, 1993). In the 1990s reports of mass rapes perpetrated by Serbian soldiers on thousands of Bosnian and Croatian women and girls increased the public's support for measures to label rape a war crime. Awareness was further heightened by reports that thousands of women and girls were raped during the 1994 war in Rwanda (Flanders, 1998). U.S. soldiers have also been guilty of wartime rape. Cases of gang rape of Vietnamese women appear in the records of courts-martial for American troops in Vietnam (Brownmiller, 1993). In 1996 the United Nations International Criminal Tribunal for the Former Yugoslavia ruled that wartime rape is a crime punishable by severe criminal sanctions (marking the first time that sexual assault was treated separately as a war crime). In February 2001 the United Nations tribunal for the former Yugoslavia established "sexual enslavement" as a war crime and convicted several Bosnian Serbs for the multiple rapes of Muslim women enslaved in so-called rape camps. Convicted rapists received sentences ranging from 12 to 28 years (Comiteau, 2001).

Why is rape so common during war? Wartime rape, in addition to being used as a means to dominate, humiliate, and control women, "can also be intended to disable an enemy by destroying the bonds of family and society" (Swiss & Giller, 1993, pp. 612–613). In wars instigated by ethnic conflict, as in the former Yugoslavia and Rwanda, mass rape is used as a military strategy to terrorize a whole population, to destroy its cultural integrity, and sometimes to force entire communities to flee their houses, thereby achieving the goal of "ethnic cleansing" (Carlson, 1997; Post, 1993; Rojnik et al., 1995; Shanks et al., 2001). Thus rape is an act of war that assaults not only the individual woman but also her family and her community.

The "Sexuality and Diversity" discussion on punishing women who have been raped provides insights into how societal reaction to rape, whether during wartime or otherwise, can add to the suffering of rape victims.

Sexuality and Diversity

Punishing Women Who Have Been Raped

How would it feel to be raped by your enemies, then rejected by your family and friends for being sexually violated? Shortly after the war in Kosovo ended in 1999, reports surfaced in the press of the difficulties that Kosovar women who had been raped were having as they returned to their homes and families.

Despite the fact that they had already suffered tremendously from being sexually assaulted, if these women admitted that they had been raped, they risked being disowned by their families and friends. Instead of getting the support and compassion that they deserved, which has been shown to be helpful in healing the wounds caused by trauma, they had to keep their painful memories, thoughts, and feelings locked away from others or risk being shunned by their families and communities (Lorch & Mendenhall, 2000).

Unfortunately, these attitudes are not confined to Kosovo. Research has shown that in the United States some men also tend to blame the victim of sexual abuse. In a study conducted among multiethnic groups in New York City, Cuban American men evaluated the teenage female *victim* of sexual abuse negatively (Rodriguez-Stednicki & Twaite, 1999). Another study found that Hispanic men in the United States tended to hold women more responsible for their rapes than did Caucasian men (Cowan, 2000).

Most of us would find this blaming of the victim deplorable, but others would argue that we need to accept that other cultures are different from ours and have a right to their own values. A recent investigation suggests, however, that these cultural attitudes and behaviors have a profoundly negative effect on the victims of rape and sexual assault. In a study that evaluated 157 victims of violent crime, researchers found that shame and anger play an important role in whether or not victims will develop posttraumatic stress disorder and that shame especially plays a role in the severity of the victim's subsequent symptoms (Andrews et al., 2000). Thus it would appear that cultural values that blame women who have been raped (and those who uphold and apply them) can be a major contributing factor to these victims' continued suffering.

The Aftermath of Rape

Whether a person is raped by a stranger, acquaintance, or partner, the experience can be traumatic and can have long-term repercussions. Given the characteristics of rape—the physical violation and psychological trauma that it inflicts and our societal attitudes about it—it is understandable that many rape survivors suffer long-lasting emotional effects.

Feelings of shame, anger, fear, guilt, depression, and a sense of powerlessness are common (Draucker & Stern, 2000; Golding, 1994; Koss et al., 2002; Vandeusen & Carr, 2003). One of the reasons that some women feel guilt and shame is that they are often seen, and see themselves, as being responsible—no matter what the circumstances—for not preventing unwanted sexual activity from taking place. Another reason for these uncomfortable feelings is that they may have responded physically, even to the point of orgasm, during the assault (Sarrel & Masters, 1982). Sexual response during an assault, particularly if orgasm occurs, can be a source of great distress to rape victims, and in some instances they may find their sexual response to be more upsetting than the physical and psychological trauma produced by the assault. However, as sex researcher Alfred Kinsey and his associates noted, "The physiologic mechanism of any emotional response (anger, fright, pain, etc.) may be the mechanism of sexual response" (Kinsey et al., 1948, p. 165). Thus responding sexually during an intense experience may be a normal physiological reaction for some.

In addition to the psychological impact of rape, physical symptoms such as nausea, headaches, gastrointestinal problems, genital injuries, and sleep disorders also frequently occur (Krakow et al., 2000; Leserman & Drossman, 1995; Ullman & Brecklin, 2003). Approximately 32% of women and 16% of men who were raped after age 18 reported being physically injured during the assault (Tjaden & Thoennes, 1998). For some victims these symptoms dissipate after a short period of time. For others the effects last for years (Sales et al., 1984) and include a variety of symptoms. Rape survivors may associate sexual activity with the trauma of their assault. As a result, sexual activity may induce anxiety rather than desire or arousal. In one long-term study of rape survivors, 40% refrained from sexual contact for 6 months to 1 year after the assault, and almost 75% reported decreased sexual activity for as long as 6 years (Burgess & Holmstrom, 1979).

When the emotional and physical reactions women experience following rape or attempted rape are severe, victims may be classified as suffering from **posttraumatic stress disorder (PTSD)**. PTSD, an official diagnostic category of the American Psychiatric Association (2000), refers to the long-term psychological distress that can develop after a person is subjected to a physically or psychologically traumatic event (or events). People who experience a profoundly disturbing incident, such as sexual assault, wartime combat, or a horrendous accident, often exhibit a range of distressing symptoms as an aftermath of the occurrence. These reactions include disturbing dreams, nightmares, depression, anxiety, and feelings of extreme vulnerability. In addition, just as Vietnam veterans may have flashbacks of traumatic war experiences, so too might a rape survivor have vivid flashbacks of the attack in which she reexperiences all the terror of the assault. Research indicates that rape produces one of the highest rates of PTSD among nonwartime traumatic events (Koss et al., 2002).

Victims often find that supportive counseling, either individually or in groups, can help ease the trauma caused by rape (Roth et al., 1988; Symes, 2000; Vandeusen & Carr, 2003). Research has shown that women who receive help soon after an assault experience less severe emotional repercussions than women whose treatment is delayed (Duddle, 1991; Stewart et al., 1987). Most rape survivors find that it helps to talk about their assault and the emotional upheaval they are experiencing. Often the process of reviewing the event allows them to gain control over their painful feelings and to begin the process of healing. The box "Helping a Partner or Friend Recover from Rape" provides some suggestions for ways to communicate and interact with a rape victim.

Posttraumatic stress disorder (PTSD) A psychological disorder caused by exposure to overwhelmingly painful events.

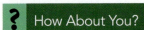

How About You?

Has anyone close to you been a victim of rape? If so, how did you react?

InfoTrac Search Words

■ Posttraumatic stress disorder

Helping a Partner or Friend Recover from Rape

The rape of a partner or friend can be a difficult experience for both partners and friends of rape survivors. To some degree, partners and close friends are also victimized by the assault. They may feel a range of emotions, including rage, disgust, and helplessness. They may also be confused and unsure about how to react to a lover or friend's victimization. This confusion can prove painful for all concerned because reactions of partners and friends can have a profound effect on a rape survivor's recovery. In the following list we offer suggestions for ways to communicate and interact with a rape victim to help her recover from this traumatic experience. Some of these suggestions are adapted from two excellent books: *Sexual Solutions* (1980), by Michael Castleman, and *"Friends" Raping Friends: Could It Happen to You?* (1987), by Jean Hughes and Bernice Sandler. Although we will frequently refer to the victim as female, our recommendations are equally applicable to male rape survivors.

1. *Listen.* Probably the most important thing a person can do to help a rape victim begin recovering is to listen to her. A person comforting a rape survivor might understandably try to divert her attention from the terrible event. However, professionals who work with survivors of sexual assault have found that many victims need to talk repeatedly about the assault to come to terms with it. A partner or friend can help by encouraging her to discuss the rape as often and in any way that she can.

2. *Let her know you believe her account of what happened.* A rape survivor needs to be believed by people she loves or feels close to. Consequently, it is essential to accept her version of the assault without questioning any of the facts. A simple statement, such as "What you describe is an intolerable violation, and I am so sorry that you had to endure such a dreadful experience," will convey both your acceptance of her account and your empathy with her pain.

3. *Let her know that it was not her fault and that she is not to blame.* Many victims of rape believe that they were somehow responsible for the attack ("I should not have invited him to my home," "I should have tried to fight him," or the like). Such impressions can lead to profound feelings of guilt. Try to head off these damaging self-recriminations by stating clearly and calmly, "I know that you are not to blame for what happened," or "You are the victim here and not responsible for what happened to you."

4. *Control your own emotions.* The last thing a rape survivor needs is the response of the partner who gets sidetracked by focusing attention on his or her own anger or imagined shortcomings ("I should have been along to protect you"). She has just been victimized by a violent man (or men), and being confronted with her own partner's or friends' outbursts will not help her regain control.

5. *Give comfort.* A rape victim is urgently in need of comfort, especially from someone she loves or cares about. She may want to be held, and the nurturing comfort of being encircled by the arms of someone she trusts may provide a powerful beginning to the process of healing. On the other hand, she also may not want to be touched at all. Respect that wish. Words can also be quite nurturing. Simply being told, "I love you very much and will be here for you in any way that is right for you," may offer a great deal of welcome comfort.

6. *Allow the victim to make decisions.* A rape survivor may recover more quickly when she is able to decide for herself how to deal with the assault. Making her own decisions about what should be done after a rape is an important step in regaining control over her life after having been stripped of control by her attacker(s). Asking some open-ended questions (see Chapter 8) may help to facilitate the process by which she regains control. Some possible queries include, "What kind of living arrangements for the next few days or weeks would you be comfortable with?" or "What can I do for you now?" Sometimes suggesting alternatives can be helpful. For example, in the process of encouraging her to take some type of positive action, you might ask, "Would you like to call the police, go to a hospital, or call a rape hotline?" Remember, the decision is hers and one that needs to be respected and not questioned even if you do not agree with it.

7. *Offer shelter.* If she does not already live with you, offer to stay with her at her home, have her stay with you, or assist in securing other living arrangements with which she is comfortable. Again, this is her choice to make.

8. *Continue to provide support.* In the days, weeks, and even months following the rape, partners and friends can continue to offer empathy, support, and reassurance to a rape survivor. They can encourage her to resume a normal life and be there for her when she feels particularly vulnerable, fearful, or angry. They can take time to listen, even if it means hearing the same things over and over again. In the event that her assailant is prosecuted, she is likely to be in need of support and understanding throughout the often arduous legal proceedings.

9. *Be patient about resuming sexual activity.* Resuming sexual activity after a rape may present problems for both the victim and her partner. Rape may precipitate sexual difficulties for the woman; she may not want to be sexually intimate for quite a while. However, some women may desire relations very soon after the attack, perhaps for assurance that their lovers still care for them and do not consider them "tainted."

   Open-ended questions may help to fuel dialogue about resuming sexual sharing. Some examples of possibly helpful queries include "What are your thoughts and feelings about being sexual with me?" or "What kinds of concerns do you have about resuming our sexual activity?"

   Some women may prefer not to have intercourse for a while but instead just want closeness and affection. Deciding when and how to engage in intimate sharing is best left up to the woman. Her partner's support in this matter is important. Even when sexual intimacy resumes, it may be some time before she is able to relax and respond the way she did before the rape. A patient, sensitive partner can help her reach the point where she is again able to experience satisfying sexual intimacy.

10. *Consider counseling.* Sometimes a rape victim needs more help than lovers, friends, and families are able to provide, no matter how supportive they are. People close to her may recognize these needs and encourage her to seek professional help. Short- or long-term therapy may help a victim recover from the emotional trauma and reconstruct her life. Similarly, partners of sexually assaulted women may also need help coping with severe conflicts and deep feelings of rage and guilt.

Sexual Assault and Rape of Males

Health professionals who work with rape survivors know that men are raped. Although the vast majority of rape victims are women, men are also targets of sexual aggression, including rape (Davies, 2002; Krahe et al., 2003). The survey conducted by Tjaden and Thoennes (1998), described earlier, found that 3% of men respondents had experienced completed or attempted rape. An exhaustive review of 120 studies of sexual victimization that collectively analyzed data from more than 100,000 respondents found an incidence rate of completed and attempted male rape by female perpetrators of 3.3% and 5.5%, respectively (Spitzberg, 1999). More recently, two German surveys of several hundred heterosexual men reported attempted and completed female-perpetrated rape percentages of 2.8% and 4.0% (study 1) and 5.2% and 2.6% (study 2), respectively (Krahe et al., 2003).

Statistics on the frequency of male sexual victimization have been difficult to obtain for a variety of reasons, not the least of which is that men are even less likely than women to report that they have been raped (Harney & Muehlenhard, 1990; Mitchell et al., 1999; Scarce, 1997). One reason for this failure to report may be that men fear that they will be judged harshly if they report abuse. At least one study supports this concern (Spencer & Tan, 1999). The investigators found that men who reported being sexually abused were viewed negatively, especially by other men. Another reason that sexual assault of males is reported less often is because it receives much less attention. The sexual assault of men is rarely reported in the media or in the psychological and medical literature (Stermac et al., 1996). The result is that little research has been conducted on the issue of sexual aggression against men (Krahe et al., 2000, 2003). In fact, it has only been in the last decade or so that many states have revised their criminal codes to include adult males as victims in the definition of rape (Isely & Gehrenbeck-Shim, 1997).

Many, probably most, rapes of males are perpetrated by heterosexual men who often commit their crime with one or more cohorts (Frazier, 1993; Isely & Gehrenbeck-Shim, 1997). As in rape of women, violence and power are often associated with the sexual assault of men. The possibility of being raped is a serious issue among male homosexuals because they are often the victims of such attacks. Although homosexual men are often raped by heterosexual men, the rapist is sometimes a homosexual man (Hickson et al., 1994).

Rape of inmates in penal institutions is a serious problem (Dumond, 1992; Hensley et al., 2003). One comprehensive survey of almost 2,000 male inmates in 7 prisons found that 21% had been sexually threatened or assaulted and 7% acknowledged being raped (Struckman-Johnson & Struckman-Johnson, 2000). Men who do the raping typically consider themselves heterosexual. When released, they usually resume sexual relations with women. The men who are raped often experience brutal gang assaults. Such a man may become the sexual partner of one particular dominant inmate for protection from others (Braen, 1980).

Only rarely do men report being sexually coerced by women who use threats of bodily harm. However, in recent years such cases have been reported with increasing frequency. The idea that mature males can be raped by women has been widely rejected because it has been assumed that a man cannot function sexually in a state of extreme anxiety or fear. However, this common impression is not accurate. Alfred Kinsey and his associates were perhaps the earliest sex researchers to note that both sexes can function sexually in a variety of severe emotional states. Sexual response during sexual assault, particularly if orgasm occurs, may be a source of great confusion and anxiety to both female and male rape survivors.

Philip Sarrel and William Masters (1982) reported on 11 men who had been raped by women. None of the victims had reported the assault, and none was able to talk about it until he became involved in therapy several years later. All of these men experienced emotional distress, sexual performance anxieties, feelings of inadequacy, and impaired sexual functioning. Other studies have also reported that, like women, men who are sexually assaulted often experience long-term emotional and sexual consequences (Frazier, 1993; Isely & Gehrenbeck-Shim, 1997; Mezy & King, 1989).

Sexual assault of males also occurs during war. However, men as victims of wartime rape and sexual assault have received only scant media coverage and limited research attention. Among the few studies in this area are investigations of male sexual assault during wars in Greece (Lindhom et al., 1980), El Salvador (Agger & Jensen, 1994), and Croatia (Medical Center for Human Rights, 1995). The widespread belief that only females can be victimized by sexual assault has led many national legal systems to bury the issue of wartime male sexual assault under the more generalized categories of torture or abuse (Carlson, 1997). However, awareness that men also can be victimized was expanded when the International Criminal Tribunal for the Former Yugoslavia reported that many men were raped or otherwise sexually assaulted during the conflict in that region (Carlson, 1997).

▶ Sexual Abuse of Children

The sexual (and physical and emotional) abuse of children in U.S. society and throughout the world is a problem of staggering proportions. Child sexual abuse can have long-lasting, painful effects. Consider the following:

When I was ten, my mother remarried, and we moved into my stepfather's house. When I was eleven he started coming upstairs to say goodnight to me. The touching began soon after and lasted for years. I used to just lie there and pray that he would go away, but he never did. For a long time I thought it was my fault. I had trouble being in a sexual relationship because I felt so guilty, so dirty. I thought that if I didn't exist this never would have happened. I think my mother may have known, but she never did anything. She didn't want to upset things, because she was afraid of being alone again, of being poor. (Authors' files)

In this section we look at the prevalence of child sexual abuse, the effects it has on many of its victims, what can be done to reduce the incidence of such abuse, and how to help those who have been abused. **Child sexual abuse** is defined as an adult engaging in sexual contact of any kind with a child (inappropriate touching, oral–genital stimulation, coitus, etc.). Even if no overt violence or threats of violence occur, such interaction is considered coercive and illegal because a child is not considered mature enough to provide informed consent to sexual involvement. Informed consent implies the possession of adequate intellectual and emotional maturity to understand fully both the meaning and possible consequences of a particular action. In recent years adults' exploitation of the naiveté of unsuspecting victims has become a serious problem for children who use the Internet, as discussed later in this chapter.

Most researchers distinguish between nonrelative child sexual abuse, referred to as **pedophilia** or **child molestation,** and **incest,** which is sexual contact between two people who are related (one of whom is often a child). Incest includes sexual contact between siblings as well as sexual contact between children and their parents, grandparents, uncles, or aunts. Incest can occur between related adults, but more commonly it involves a child and an adult relative (or older sibling) perpetrator. Although its definition varies slightly from culture to culture, incest is one of the world's most widely prohibited sexual behaviors.

Each state has its own legal codes that specify at what age sexual interaction between an adult and a younger person is considered child molestation (usually if the younger person is under age 12), statutory rape (generally age 12 to 16 or 17), or a consenting sexual act. The age of consent in the United States generally ranges from 16 to 18, but it can be as low as 14 or 15 (Findholt & Robrecht, 2002). The legal codes may appear ludicrous at times, particularly in cases involving teenage interactions where one partner is technically an adult and the other technically a minor, although only one or two years separate their ages.

Incest occurs at all socioeconomic levels and is illegal regardless of the ages of the participants. However, an incestuous relationship between consenting adult relatives is considerably less likely to precipitate legal action than one involving an adult and a child.

Although it has been commonly assumed that father–daughter incest is most prevalent, studies have shown that brother–sister and first-cousin contacts are more common (Canavan et al., 1992; Finkelhor, 1979). Sexual relations between brothers and sisters are seldom discovered, and, when they are, they do not typically elicit the extreme reactions that father–daughter sexual contacts usually do. However, coercive sibling sexual abuse and sexual abuse by a parent often have a devastating effect on the child victim.

Child sexual abuse An adult engaging in sexual contact of any kind with a child—inappropriate touching, oral–genital stimulation, coitus, and the like.

Pedophilia, or child molestation Sexual contact between an adult and a child who are not related.

Incest Sexual contact between two people who are related (one of whom is often a child), other than husband and wife.

> ### InfoTrac Search Words
> - Child sexual abuse
> - Pedophilia

The incestuous involvement of a father (or stepfather) and his daughter often begins before the child understands its significance. It may start as playful activities involving wrestling, tickling, kissing, and touching. Over time the activities may expand to include touching of the breasts and genitals, perhaps followed by oral or manual stimulation and intercourse. In most cases the father relies on his position of authority or on the pair's emotional closeness rather than on physical force to fulfill his desires. He may pressure his daughter into sexual activity by reassuring her that he is "teaching" her something important, by offering rewards, or by exploiting her need for love. Later, when she realizes that the behavior is not appropriate or when she finds her father's demands to be unpleasant and traumatizing, it may be difficult for her to escape. Occasionally, a daughter may value the relationship for the special recognition or privileges it brings her. The incestuous involvement may come to public attention when she gets angry with her father, often for nonsexual reasons, and "tells on him." Sometimes a mother may discover, to her horror, what has been transpiring between her husband and daughter. Other times, the mother may have been aware of the incest but allowed it to continue for reasons of her own. These include shame, fear of reprisals, concern about having her family disrupted, or the fact that the incestuous activity allows her to avoid her husband's demands for sex.

Father–daughter sexual abuse is more likely to be reported to authorities than other varieties of incest. However, a child often does not report being victimized because of fear that the family may be disrupted—the father being imprisoned, the mother facing economic difficulties, and perhaps the victim and other siblings being placed in foster homes. Separation or divorce may result. Sometimes, the victim herself is blamed. These potential consequences of revealing an incestuous relationship place tremendous pressures on the child to keep quiet. For these and other reasons she may be extremely reluctant to tell anyone else in her family, let alone public authorities.

Characteristics of Child Sex Offenders

No classic profile of the pedophile offender has been identified, other than that most are heterosexual males and are known to the victim (Guidry, 1995; Murray, 2000; Salter et al., 2003). Michael Seto and his colleagues (1999) did find that nonincestuous child molesters engaged in more deviant sexual behaviors, such as exhibitionism, voyeurism, and sadism, than did incestuous ones. However, child molesters cover the spectrum in terms of social class, educational achievement, intelligence, occupation, religion, and ethnic group. Some evidence suggests that many pedophile offenders, especially those who are prosecuted, tend to be shy, lonely, poorly informed about sexuality, and moralistic or religious (Bauman et al., 1984). Many are likely to have poor interpersonal and sexual relations with other adults and may feel socially inadequate and inferior (McKibben et al., 1994; Minor & Dwyer, 1997). However, it is not uncommon to encounter child sex offenders outside the legal system who are well educated, successful, socially adept, civic minded, and successful (Baur, 1995). They often pick their victims from among family friends, neighbors, or acquaintances (Murray, 2000). Relating to these children sexually may be a way of coping with powerful feelings of inadequacy that are likely to emerge in sociosexual relationships with other adults.

Other characteristics of some child molesters include alcoholism, severe marital problems, sexual difficulties, and poor emotional adjustment (Johnston, 1987; McKibben et al., 1994). These offenders have often been sexually victimized themselves during their own childhood (Gaffney et al., 1984; Murray, 2000; Seghorn et al., 1987).

Like pedophiles, incest offenders are primarily males who cannot be easily identified or categorized by a classic profile. Rather, "they are a complex, heterogeneous group of individuals who look like everyone else" (Scheela & Stern, 1994, p. 91). However, the incest offender does tend to share some of the traits of the pedophile. He is often economically disadvantaged, a heavy drinker, unemployed, devoutly religious, and emotionally immature (Rosenberg, 1988; Valliant et al., 2000). His behavior might result from general tendencies toward pedophilia, severe feelings of inadequacy in adult sexual relations, or rejection by a hostile spouse; his actions can also be an accompaniment to alcoholism or other psychological disturbances (Rosenberg, 1988). He also frequently has certain distorted ideas about adult–child sex—for example, that a child who does not resist desires sexual contact, that

In the period 1992–2000, substantiated cases of child sexual abuse reported to child protective agencies in the United States declined an astounding 41%, from 150,000 cases in 1992 to 88,000 cases in 2000 (Jones et al., 2001; Putnam, 2003). In addition, two self-report surveys of children—one using a national sample and the other using a sample in Minnesota—conducted at several points during the 1990s, reported declines in child sexual abuse during this decade (Jones & Finkelhor, 2003).

This downward trend in child sexual abuse during the 1990s is not confined solely to the United States. For example, evidence from the Canadian province of Ontario revealed a 49% decline in substantiated cases of child sexual abuse from 1993 to 1998 (Trocme et al., 2002). Recent studies conducted in Australia (Dunne et al., 2003) and Ireland (McGee et al., 2002) reported similar declines in reported cases of child sexual abuse in recent years.

What accounts for these declines in reported cases of child sexual abuse? At present, experts do not agree on the reasons for this decline in cases reported to child protective agencies or, for that matter, whether this decline represents an actual reduction in all instances of child sexual abuse in the United States, reported and not reported (Putnam, 2003). Two child abuse experts, Lisa Jones and David Finkelhor (2003), recently speculated that the apparent downward trend in the United States perhaps reflects "that the investment by the U.S. in public awareness campaigns, prevention programs, criminal justice interventions, and treatment during the 1980s and 1990s can work effectively to protect children from sexual abuse" (p. 133). Other nations, such as Canada, Australia, Great Britain, Spain, Sweden, Israel, and New Zealand, have implemented similar strategies, and this may account for the international flavor of this welcome downward trend in child sexual abuse (Jones & Finkelhor, 2003).

adult–child sex is an effective way for children to learn about sex, that a father's relationship with his daughter is enhanced by having sexual contact with her, and that a child does not report contact because she enjoys it (Abel et al., 1984).

Prevalence of Child Sexual Abuse

How high is the incidence of child sexual abuse in the United States? It is difficult to accurately estimate the incidence of either incest or pedophilia. For reasons previously mentioned, child victims of incest frequently do not reveal what is occurring at the time—and may in fact not utter a word about it until they reach adulthood, if then. Acts of child molestation are unlikely to be reported at the time they occur for several reasons. For example, a child may be unable to distinguish between expressions of affection and illicit sexual contact. Often, when a child does inform his or her parents of improper sexual advances, the parents may not believe the child or may be reluctant to expose the child, themselves, or a spouse to prosecution, with its resultant stress on the family. The fact that the offender is often a friend or acquaintance can further complicate the issue.

Because of the low reporting of child sexual abuse at the time that it occurs, researchers have relied heavily on reports provided by adults regarding their childhood experiences with sexual abuse. These estimates of child abuse in U.S. society are startling. Various surveys indicate that the proportion of girls victimized ranges from 20% to 33%, whereas comparable figures for boys range from 9% to 16% (Finkelhor, 1993, 1994; Finkelhor et al., 1990; Gorey & Leslie, 1997; Guidry, 1995). To date, the most comprehensive effort to estimate the prevalence of child sexual abuse was a 1997 meta-analysis in which data from 16 separate studies were combined and analyzed. Each of the individual investigations—14 U.S. and 2 Canadian studies—surveyed adult subjects who were asked to recall past experiences of sexual abuse that occurred before reaching age 18. Combining these diverse samples yielded an aggregate sample of about 14,000 respondents. A summarization of all the studies indicated that approximately 22% of the women and 9% of the men reported being sexually abused as children (Gorey & Leslie, 1997). Recent evidence indicates that the incidence of child sexual abuse is declining in the United States and other nations. This encouraging trend is described in the boxed discussion "Declining Trends in Child Sexual Abuse: An International Phenomenon."

We should also realize that, although the clinical literature has indicated that more girls than boys are victims of sexual abuse, the number of young boys who are sexually molested in the United States may be substantially higher than previously estimated (Denov, 2003a, 2003b; Finkelhor, 1993; Lenderking et al., 1997). In fact, two recent surveys found that almost one-fourth of male participants reported having experienced some form of sexual abuse by age 13 (Dilorio et al., 2002; Stander et al., 2002).

Awareness is increasing among mental health professionals that, although most child sexual abusers are male, some children, both male and female, are being sexually abused by women, often their mothers (Denov, 2003b; Elliott, 1992; Guidry, 1995). The belief that women sometimes sexually victimize children has been slow to emerge, both because of the prevailing notion that child sexual abuse is a male activity and because "this subject is more of a taboo because female sexual abuse is more threatening—it undermines feelings about how women should relate to children" (Elliott, 1992, p. 12).

These statistics on the prevalence of child sexual abuse have aroused significant controversy, with some claiming that they underestimate the problem and others claiming that they overestimate it. One of the most controversial types of reports has concerned the case of adults reporting so-called recovered memories of sexual abuse that happened when they were children.

Recovered Memories of Childhood Sexual Abuse

In recent years the media have reported numerous cases in which alleged perpetrators of sexual abuse have been accused and convicted based on the testimony of adult women who "recover" memories of their childhood sexual abuse. This "recovery" usually has occurred during psychotherapy. But can a person repress memories of sexual abuse that may have occurred years or decades earlier and then suddenly or gradually "recover" them after exposure to certain triggering stimuli? Or can a "memory" of an event that never happened in childhood be suggested to an adult and then remembered as true? These questions lie at the heart of an ongoing debate among clinicians, researchers, and lawyers.

Skeptics of recovered memories claim that thousands of families and individuals have been devastated by the widespread inclination to accept claims of recovered memories at face value in the absence of validating evidence. These critics offer as proof of their concern cases in which falsely accused and convicted individuals are later exonerated, either by the legal system or by victim recantation (Hoover, 1997; Johnston, 1997).

The possibility of being falsely accused of such a heinous crime is the substance of nightmares, and it has been reported that false accusations of abuse, in general, are increasing (Bowles, 2000). But just how often are the accusations false; that is, what is the probability that recovered memories are imagined? To gain some perspective on this issue, let us briefly consider some of the evidence.

Support for the legitimacy of recovered memories has been provided by several studies. In one investigation 59% of 450 clients being treated for childhood sexual abuse reported that there had been varying time periods before age 18 when they could not remember their abuse (Briere & Conte, 1993). In another study, 129 adult women who had experienced childhood sexual abuse in the 1970s were identified and interviewed in the 1990s. Of this group, 38% did not recall the abuse that had been reported and documented 17 years earlier. The author of this investigation concluded that, if having no recall of child sexual abuse is a common occurrence for adult women, as indicated by the study's results, then "later recovery of child sexual abuse by some women should not be surprising" (Williams, 1994, p. 1174). In another study, 56% of 45 adult women survivors of childhood sexual abuse indicated that they had been amnesic about their abuse for varied lengths of time, and 16% reported remembering their abuse in the context of receiving psychotherapy (Rodriguez et al., 1997). A survey of several hundred university students found that 20% of 111 victims of childhood sexual abuse reported that they had recovered previously forgotten memories of abuse (Melchert & Parker, 1997). Finally, a national survey of a sample of psychologists found that about 25% of the respondents reported being sexually abused in their childhood and that 40% of these victimized individuals stated that they had forgotten the abuse for various lengths of time (Feldman-Summers & Pope, 1994).

On the other hand, several researchers have expressed skepticism about recovered memories of childhood sexual abuse. Some have argued that "repressed memories" are inadvertently planted in suggestible clients by overzealous or poorly trained psychotherapists who believe that most psychological problems stem from childhood sexual abuse (Dawes, 1994; Lindsay & Read, 1994; Yapko, 1994). Numerous studies have demonstrated the relative ease with which "memories" of events that never occurred can be created in the research laboratory (Brainerd & Reyna, 1998; Loftus & Ketcham, 1994; Loftus et al., 1994; Porter et al., 1999). In one 11-week study, for instance, young children were asked at weekly intervals whether they had ever experienced five distinct events. Four of the events were real, and one—getting treated in the hospital for an injured finger—was fictitious. The children readily recognized the real events. However, more than one-third also became gradually convinced over the course of the 11 weeks that one of their fingers had been injured. In some cases they even "remembered" elaborate details about their injuries. Many continued to insist that these false memories were true even after being told otherwise (Ceci et al., 1994).

Clearly, the concept of client suggestibility has become central to the arguments offered by critics of recovered memories. Results of one investigation challenge the suggestibility rationale for dismissing reports of recovered memories of childhood sexual abuse. In this study suggestibility was measured in 44 women who had previously reported recovered memories of childhood sexual abuse and in a comparison group of 31 women without a history of sexual abuse. Subjects without a history of abuse were more inclined to alter memory to suggestive prompts than were the recovered memory subjects (Leavitt, 1997). In contrast, a different study reported that women who claimed to have recovered memories of childhood sexual abuse were more likely to make memory errors than those who were sexually abused as children and always remembered it (Clancy et al., 2000).

So where are we now on this controversial issue? The American Psychological Association, the American Psychiatric Association, and the American Medical Association have all issued statements supporting the belief that forgotten memories can be recovered later in life. These same professional organizations also acknowledge that a "memory" may be suggested and then remembered as true. As the controversy continues, it is important to remember that, despite the media spotlight on defendants who claim they have been falsely accused, child sexual abuse is a fact, not a question. The recovered memories debate must not turn back the clock to a time when victims of sexual abuse did not report their traumatic experiences out of fear of not being believed. In the same spirit, we must act responsibly to protect the innocent from wrongful accusations that stem from false memories.

Pedophiles in Cyberspace

Before the emergence of the Internet, pedophiles were largely isolated. Now, with several pedophile support groups online, child molesters can exchange child pornography, discuss their molestation experiences, and validate each other's abusive acts. They also have more opportunities to contact children in order to take advantage of them. These cyberspace predators can explore the bulletin boards on the Internet and cruise chat rooms designed for children. These chat rooms provide fertile hunting grounds for adults looking for unsuspecting kids in need of attention and kids with confused notions of sexuality (Durkin, 1997; Trebilcock, 1997).

Typically, pedophiles first gain a child's trust by appearing to be genuinely empathic and interested in their problems and concerns. Then they may try to get their intended victims to agree to e-mail, postal mail, or phone contacts. Next, they may send them pornographic materials that suggest that adult–child sexual interaction is normal and appropriate. The final step is to arrange a meeting. One case in which this strategy was used involved a 30-year-old Philadelphia engineer who pleaded guilty to having sexual relations in an Illinois motel room with a 13-year-old girl he had became acquainted with over the Internet. In another case, a 32-year-old Seattle engineer, who used the Internet to lure a 13-year-old girl whom he then repeatedly raped, was sentenced in February 2000 to a 23-year prison term. In New York State a 15-year-old boy's statement led police to a number of prominent local men who had been systematically abusing local boys, some as young as 13 (West, 2000).

In one of the most shocking cases of cyberspace pedophilia known to date, a 10-year-old girl was invited to a slumber party at the home of a friend in Greenfield, California, in April

1996. During the night images of her being molested by her friend's father were broadcast to other members of a sex club, who watched the live event on their computer monitors. This example of pedophiles using the Internet for real-life and real-time abuse of a child resulted in indictments of 16 members of this club. By May 1997, 14 of the 16 had elected to plead guilty, and the club leader was sentenced to life in prison (Mintz, 1997).

For many these stories bring up images of drooling, disheveled men in trench coats lurking at their computer terminals instead of around school playgrounds. However, no such easy stereotype exists. Many cyberspace offenders are upper-middle-class white males from a variety of professions who use the perceived anonymity of the Internet to explore, and, unfortunately, sometimes act out their pedophilic fantasies (Curry, 2000). What can be done to combat pedophiles in cyberspace? In September 1996 the U.S. Congress passed the Communications Decency Act (CDA), which prohibited the distribution of indecent materials to minors by computer. In July 1997 the Supreme Court overruled this legislation on constitutional grounds, concluding that the CDA would seriously erode free speech (Levy, 1997). In April 2002 the Supreme Court, in further defense of the right of free speech, struck down a section of the federal child pornography law that made it a crime to own or sell computer-created images of children engaged in sex ("virtual" child pornography). According to Justice Anthony Kennedy, making it a crime to show sexual images that only appear to be children would damage legitimate filmmakers, photographers, and advertisers (Savage, 2002). As a result of this decision, it is legal to display on the Internet both computer-generated images of children in sexual situations and depictions of minors by adult actors in sexual situations, provided that no real children are shown or "morphed" into a sex scene.

The busiest gateway to the Internet, America Online (AOL), has attempted to protect children from cyberspace predators by using "guards" to monitor kids-only chat rooms for inappropriate or suspicious dialogue. Unfortunately, these efforts are only minimally effective, because private messages cannot be screened. Knowledgeable cyberspace pedophiles are most likely to make conversations private before making inappropriate overtures.

Without effective laws or in-house procedures to curb cyberspace pedophilia, the responsibility for protecting children resides with parents. Just as most of us would not allow our children to play unsupervised in dangerous places, we should not allow them to cruise cyberspace or spend time in chat rooms without supervision. One potentially helpful strategy is to keep computers in a central location where children can be more easily monitored when they go online. It would be especially beneficial for parents to go online with a child to instruct him or her in how to identify inappropriate requests. Parents should instruct their children never to give out personal information, such as a phone number or home address, without parental approval. Parents should also be clear that a child should never meet a cyberspace acquaintance in person without a parent or other responsible adult present. Finally, parents concerned about cyberspace pornography may wish to purchase Internet filtering software designed to block children's access to Web sites with obscene pictures or vulgar words. Screening software may help to curtail children's surfing of pornographic sites, but unfortunately it offers little protection to children exposed to pedophiles in chat rooms. Parents who want to learn more about Internet safety can explore three Web sites, listed at the end of this chapter, that deal with this issue.

Effects of Child Sexual Abuse

Much research suggests that child sexual abuse can be a severely traumatizing and emotionally damaging experience, with long-term negative consequences for many of the victims (Buzi et al., 2003; Dong et al., 2003; McLean & Gallop, 2003; Noll et al., 2003; Vandeusen & Carr, 2003). Clinical contact with adult survivors of child sexual abuse often reveals memories of a childhood filled with distress and confusion. Survivors speak of their loss of childhood innocence, the contamination and interruption of normal sexual development, and a profound sense of betrayal by a family member or trusted friend.

A number of factors influence the severity of a child victim's response to sexual abuse. In general, the more intrusive or violent the assault, the closer the relationship between the victim and the perpetrator; in addition, the longer the duration of the molestation, the worse the prognosis for recovery from the trauma of the abuse (Hanson et al., 2001; McLean & Gallop, 2003; Vandeusen & Carr, 2003). Feelings of powerlessness and betrayal may be especially pronounced when physical force is used to perpetrate an act of child sexual abuse or when the victim has a close relationship to the offender. These two factors—physical force and victim–offender relationship—probably show the strongest relationship to subsequent negative consequences for child sexual abuse survivors (Banyard & Williams, 1996; Hanson et al., 2001; Rind & Tromovitch, 1997).

Many victims of child sexual abuse have difficulty forming intimate adult relationships (Collins, 1994; Rumstein-McKean & Hunsley, 2001; Vandeusen & Carr, 2003). When relationships are established, they often lack emotional and sexual fulfillment (Jackson et al., 1990; Meiselman, 1978; Rumstein-McKean & Hunsley, 2001). Sexual abuse is not uncommon in the histories of people who seek treatment for sexual difficulties (Kinzl et al., 1995; Sarwer & Durlak, 1996; Vandeusen & Carr, 2003). Other common symptoms of sexual abuse survivors include low self-esteem, guilt, shame, depression, alienation, a lack of trust in others, revulsion at being touched, drug and alcohol abuse, obesity, elevated suicide rates, a predisposition to being repeatedly victimized in a variety of ways, and long-term medical problems such as chronic pelvic pain and gastrointestinal disorders (Buzi et al., 2003; Lahoti et al., 2001; Roodman & Clum, 2001; P. Smith et al., 2003; Vandeusen & Carr, 2003).

Some research, however, suggests that the effects of sexual abuse may be less severe. In one controversial meta-analysis of 59 studies involving college students who reported having been sexually abused before the age of 18, the investigators concluded that the effects of sexual abuse appeared to have little lasting effect on men and were present in only a minority of women (Rind et al., 1998). Meston et al. (1999) also found that sexual abuse per se did not cause as much damage to later sexual functioning as others have suggested.

Critics of this research have been concerned and outraged (Ericksen, 2000; LaRue, 1999). They have expressed concern that this type of research could be used by some to justify abuse of children. They have also argued that symptoms of abuse may not show up until later in life for some victims, and thus this research with college students may underestimate the effect of abuse. Others have suggested that it gives hope to those who have been abused, because it suggests that earlier abuse does not have to lead to lifelong damage. For more on this issue, see the box "Adults Having Sexual Contact with Children."

Research indicates that there may be some sex difference in the impact of childhood sexual abuse. Two literature reviews that used meta-analysis of studies using college samples (Rind et al., 1998) and national probability samples (Rind & Tromovitch, 1997) found that males tend to be less adversely affected by child sex abuse than girls. However, not all research supports this conclusion. For example, one investigation of about 1,500 12- to 19-year-olds found that sexually abused males had more emotional and behavioral problems than their female counterparts (Garnefski & Diekstra, 1997).

A variety of treatment approaches have emerged to help survivors of child sexual abuse resolve issues regarding these experiences and their emotional aftermath (Elliott, 1999; Putnam, 2003; Vandeusen & Carr, 2003; Wolfsdorf & Zlotnick, 2001). These treatment strategies range from individual therapy to group and couple-oriented approaches. Most metropolitan areas in the United States also have self-help support organizations for sexual abuse survivors. (If you wish more information about how to seek professional therapeutic assistance, we suggest reviewing the guidelines outlined in Chapter 16.)

Preventing Child Sexual Abuse

Efforts to reduce the sexual victimization of children have focused on punishing those who have perpetrated the abuse, protecting children from them, and educating children to protect themselves. As of this writing, despite much research, treatment programs have not demonstrated much long-term effectiveness in preventing recidivism among sexual offenders (Dewhurst & Nielsen, 1999). Thus some critics of existing legal sanctions have advocated increasing the penalties for those convicted (Vachss, 1999), and several states have passed laws requiring community notification and registration of convicted pedophiles when they are released from prison. This registration and notification is often referred to as Megan's law, named for Megan Kanka, a 7-year-old New Jersey girl who was raped and murdered in 1994 by a convicted sex offender who had moved into a home across the street from her. Although concern has been expressed over the constitutionality of such laws (M. Johnson, 1998), others have argued that these laws represent a fundamental shift in the way we view

Adults Having Sexual Contact with Children

In 1998 the American Psychological Association (APA)—the country's premier organization of psychologists—published a research article by Bruce Rind, Philip Tromovitch, and Robert Bauserman titled "A Meta-Analytic Examination of Assumed Properties of Child Sexual Abuse Using College Samples." The contents of this article unleashed a firestorm against the investigators and the APA, even provoking the U.S. House of Representatives to vote unanimously to denounce the study.

There are three principal reasons that this article has been so controversial. First, Rind and his colleagues criticized much of the previous research on child sexual abuse, claiming it is beset with serious methodological and definitional problems. These problems included:

- Skewed samples, because many clinicians and researchers in the field of child sexual abuse have contact *only* with those individuals who have been damaged. Thus this research tends to exaggerate the negative impact of such abuse.

- The poor definitions of precisely what constitutes child sexual abuse.

- A frequent lack of discrimination in the research between types of adult–child sexual episodes that have occurred. For example, grouping such activities as the repeated forced violation of a 5-year-old by one adult into the same category with the willing participation of a 15-year-old with another adult obscures the true effects of child sexual abuse.

A second reason that Rind and his colleagues evoked such controversy is their claim that the available evidence does not support the views of most experts that child sexual abuse causes a host of often intense psychological problems, including anxiety, depression, eating disorders, substance abuse, low self-esteem, inappropriate sexual behavior, aggression, and suicide. Although the investigators acknowledge that child sexual abuse is indeed *correlated* with later psychological difficulties, they state that it does not appear to exert as much of a negative influence as overall family violence and emotional neglect.

Third, Rind and his associates proposed redefining the very terms used to describe sexual contact between adults and children and the criteria used for evaluating these behaviors. Especially controversial is their proposal that a *willing* encounter be labeled adult–child sex. In their view, only if children felt that they did not participate freely and if they experienced negative reactions to the sexual contact should it be labeled child sexual abuse.

Rind and his colleagues acknowledge that child sexual abuse can produce intense harm, and they are concerned that individuals or organizations might use their findings to justify sexual contact with children by underestimating the harm such contact can cause: "CSA [child sexual abuse] is potentially harmful for young persons because of their vulnerability to being misused. The current findings should thus not be interpreted by lay persons as condoning abusive behavior" (p. 245).

Nonetheless, Rind and his co-workers believe that there has been an exaggeration of the effects of

How About You?

What do you believe should happen to convicted sex offenders once they are released from prison?

these criminals. This shift is one from trying to "cure" perpetrators to protecting the community from their behaviors (Simon, 1998).

Most child sexual abuse is perpetrated by someone known to the victim. Thus some health professionals suggest that many children can avoid being victimized if they are provided with education concerning their right to say no, the difference between "okay" and "not okay" touches, and strategies for coping with an adult's attempt to coerce them into inappropriate intimate contact.

Perhaps the best prospects for reducing the high levels of child sexual abuse in our society lie in developing effective programs to be implemented in the early stages of a child's public education. School-based education programs that teach children to identify potential abuse situations and respond with effective self-protection, including telling a trusted adult, have generally been shown to be successful in increasing both children's awareness of sexual abuse and their self-protection skills (Rispens et al., 1997). One recent survey of 825 women college students found that respondents who had participated in school-based sexual abuse programs during their childhood were significantly less likely to have been sexually abused (Gibson & Leitenberg, 2000).

As indicated in Chapter 13, parents often avoid discussing sex with their children. Therefore it is probably unrealistic to expect better parent–child communication to significantly protect children. Furthermore, parents themselves are often the abusers. The following list child sexual abuse. By labeling any sexual contact between adults and children as likely to have devastating effects, they worry that we may be causing harm to those children and adolescents who have willingly participated in such activities. These participants may be made to feel that they have been irreparably damaged by such activities when they have not.

Some of Rind and his associates' conclusions have received support. One study found that parental emotional abuse and neglect played a larger role in determining distress and poor adjustment in college students than did the presence or absence of child sexual abuse (Melchert, 2000). Another inquiry determined that sexual abuse frequently occurs along with physical and emotional abuse, and the data concurred with an earlier finding that family violence had a greater effect on successful adjustment than did sexual abuse (Meston et al., 1999).

While praising Rind and his colleagues for exploring this charged issue, Julia Ericksen (2000) raised questions about the methods they

used and their suggestion to change certain definitions. Central to any understanding of whether or not sexual contact at any age is problematic is the issue of informed consent, and Ericksen argued that Rind and his associates appear to have glossed over this issue. Returning to their definition, only if a child was forced to have sex *and* experienced a negative reaction would the activities be labeled child sexual abuse. What if the child was not forced but later experienced tremendous guilt over what had happened? According to Rind's reasoning, that would not have been child sexual abuse. Moreover, what is a "willing encounter" between a child and an adult? If a 5-year-old were bribed with a chocolate bar to perform sexual activities on an adult, would that be a willing encounter? Is that 5- (or 7- or 10-) year-old capable of giving informed consent?

Rind and his colleagues suggest that the effects of adult–child sexual contact may not create lasting damage. As Carol Travis (2000) pointed out, however, the fact that children can recover from cruelties does not

mean that they should have to do so. Although the data suggest that many college students who had sexual contact with adults as children may not suffer lasting damage, we have no way of knowing how much pain these students may have gone through before college or will go through at some point in the future.

Finally, one of Rind and his coauthors' conclusions appears be based on faulty reasoning. These researchers reported that boys appear to be less harmed by adult–child sexual contact than are girls. Yet earlier in their own study they acknowledged that girls tend to be abused at a younger age than do boys and that force is more often used with girls than with boys. Thus the comparison would appear to be invalid. The only valid comparison would be to look at the effects of adult–child sexual contact on boys and girls of the same age who experienced similar levels of force or violence.

In short, better research is certainly needed in the area of child sexual abuse. So is the continued protection of children.

---

of suggestions, drawn from the writings of a number of child abuse specialists, offers some suggestions for preventing child sexual abuse that may be helpful to parents, educators, and other caregivers of children:

1. It is important to present prevention-oriented material to young children, because as many as 25% of child sexual abuse victims are younger than age 7 (Finkelhor, 1984a). Be sure to include boys, because they too can be abused.

2. Educators and parents will be more effective if they keep things simple and "translate the notions of sexual abuse into concepts that make sense within the world of the child" (Finkelhor, 1984b, p. 3).

3. Avoid making a discussion of child sexual abuse unduly frightening. It is important that children be sufficiently concerned so that they will be on the lookout for potentially abusive adult behavior. However, they should also be confident in their ability to avoid such a situation should it occur.

4. Take time to carefully explain the differences between okay touches (pats, snuggles, and hugs) and not-okay touches that make a child feel uncomfortable or confused. Not-okay touches can be explained as touching under the panties or underpants or touching areas that bathing

Elementary school students light the "Candle of Hope" in recognition of National Child Abuse Prevention Month.

© AP/Wide World Photos

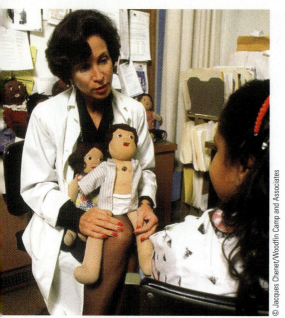

A child abuse specialist uses puppets to teach children about child abuse.

suits cover. Be sure to indicate that a child should not have to touch an adult in these areas even if the adult says it is all right. It is also a good idea to explain not-okay kisses (prolonged lip contact or tongue in mouth).

5. Encourage children to believe that they have rights—the right to control their bodies and the right to say no when they are being touched in a way that makes them uncomfortable.

6. Encourage children to tell someone right away if an adult has touched them in a way that is inappropriate or has made them do something with which they are uncomfortable. Emphasize that you will not be angry with them and that they will be okay when they tell, even if someone else has told them that they will get in trouble. Stress that no matter what happened, it was not their fault and they will not be blamed. Also, warn them that not all adults will believe them. Tell them to keep telling people until they find someone like you who will believe them.

7. Discuss with children some of the strategies that adults might use to get children to participate in sexual activities. For example, tell them to trust their own feelings when they think something is wrong, even if an adult who is a friend or relative says that it is okay and that they are "teaching" them something helpful. Given that many adults use the "this is our secret" strategy, it can be particularly helpful to explain the difference between a secret (something they are never to tell—a bad idea) and a surprise (a good idea because it is something they tell later to make someone happy).

8. Discuss strategies for getting away from uncomfortable or dangerous situations. Let them know that it is okay to scream, yell, run away, or get assistance from a friend or trusted adult.

9. Encourage children to state clearly to the adult who touches them inappropriately that they will tell a particular responsible adult about what went on. Interviews with child sexual abuse offenders have revealed that many would be deterred from their abusive actions if a child said that she or he would tell a specific adult about the assault (Budin & Johnson, 1989; Daro, 1991).

10. Perhaps one of the most important things to incorporate in this prevention discussion, particularly for parents, is the message that private touching can be a loving and pleasurable experience, as they will discover when they grow older and meet someone they care for or love. Without some discussion of the positive aspects of sexuality, there is a risk that a child will develop a negative view of any kind of sexual contact between people, regardless of the nature of their relationship.

When the Child Tells

Research demonstrates that children who have been sexually abused often either delay disclosure of the abuse to a parent or other adult or do not tell at all (Goodman-Brown et al., 2003). In fact, many children do not disclose their abuse until adulthood, if then (Berliner & Conte, 1995; Goodman-Brown et al., 2003). "Fears of retribution and abandonment, and feelings of complicity, embarrassment, guilt, and shame all conspire to silence children and inhibit their disclosures of abuse" (Goodman-Brown et al., 2003, p. 526). A recent study of 218 sexually abused children found that several factors are associated with a child's decision to delay disclosure, including (1) fear of negative consequences to self and others, (2) perceptions of responsibility for the abuse, (3) relationship to the abuser (children whose abuser was a family member took longer to disclose than children abused by someone outside the family), and (4) the child's age (older children, more fearful of negative consequences of disclosure, were slower to disclose) (Goodman-Brown et al., 2003).

As described previously, children suffer many adverse effects of sexual abuse. Their fears about potential consequences of revealing their victimization and resultant hesitancy to do so further magnify their misery. Furthermore, the emotional trauma that a child experiences as a result of a sexual encounter with an adult may be intensified by excessive parental reactions (Davies, 1995). When telling a parent what happened, children may merely be relaying a sense of discomfort over something they do not fully understand. If parents understandably react with extreme agitation, children are likely to respond with increased emotional negativity, developing a sense of being implicated in something terrible and often feeling extremely guilty about having participated in such an event. Children may feel guilty about such experiences even without parental displays of distress because they sense the guilt of the person who molested them.

It is important that parents respond appropriately to instances of child abuse involving their children. Such acts should not be ignored! While remaining calm in the face of their child's revelation, parents should take great precautions to see that the child is not alone with the offending party again. In many instances children are repeatedly molested by the same person, and they may come to feel a sense of obligation and guilt. It is essential to ensure that the child is protected from further experiences of this kind. Because it also is likely that the child will not have been the offender's only victim, it is essential to report the offender to the police to protect other children.

? Critical Thinking Question

When children have been sexually abused, what steps should be taken to reduce the potentially adverse effects of the abuse?

▶ Sexual Harassment

Whether in industry, the military, or academia, **sexual harassment** is widespread throughout U.S. society. Sexual harassment is more than just a demand for sexual favors. Sexual harassment can also occur when the actions of others create a hostile or offensive working environment. One woman offered her experience:

I was the first woman they hired at that level. I was proud of what I had accomplished and looked forward to the challenges, but it has been much harder than I expected. I have been amazed and disgusted by the jokes and the unbelievable crude remarks that some men have made. People have sent me the most disgusting e-mails, and every day I get obscene messages on my voice mail. I spoke to my boss about this and told him how upsetting it was to me, but he told me that I needed to be a "team player" and that this was just the guys' way of welcoming me to the group. Maybe it shouldn't bother me as much as it does, but it is hurting my work. I'm having trouble concentrating, and I cringe every time I listen to my messages. (Authors' files)

Sexual harassment Unwelcome sexual advances, requests for sexual favors, and other verbal or physical conduct of a sexual nature in the workplace or academic setting.

Sexual harassment gained unprecedented public attention in the early 1990s as a result of two incidents that received national media coverage: law professor Anita Hill's allegations that she had been sexually harassed by Supreme Court nominee Clarence Thomas and the U.S. Navy's Tailhook scandal, in which Pentagon investigators concluded that many women had been sexually harassed or assaulted by drunken aviators. Sexual harassment was again brought before the public by Paula Jones's sexual harassment lawsuit against President Bill Clinton. In this section we define and discuss sexual harassment with a focus on its occurrence on the job and in educational environments.

Sexual harassment in the workplace is prohibited by Title VII of the 1964 Civil Rights Act. In 1980 the Equal Employment Opportunity Commission (EEOC) issued guidelines on sexual harassment. These guidelines made it clear that both verbal and physical harassment are illegal:

Unwelcome sexual advances, requests for sexual favors, and other verbal or physical conduct of a sexual nature constitute sexual harassment when (1) submission to such conduct is made either explicitly or implicitly a term or condition of an individual's employment, (2) submission to or rejection of such conduct by an individual is used as a basis for employment decisions affecting such individual, or (3) such conduct has the purpose or effect of unreasonably interfering with an individual's work performance or creating an intimidating, hostile, or offensive working environment. (Equal Employment Opportunity Commission, 1980, pp. 74676–74677)

The EEOC guidelines describe two kinds of sexual harassment. One form, commonly labeled *quid pro quo,* is reflected in the first two situations described in the guidelines. Here, compliance with unwanted sexual advances is made a condition for securing a job or education benefits or for favorable treatment in employment or academic settings (such as receiving a promotion or high grades) (Pierce, 1994). Harassment is often evident in reprisals that follow refusals to comply (Charney & Russell, 1994).

Law professor Anita Hill, who testified during the confirmation hearings of Supreme Court Justice Clarence Thomas, triggered a national debate about the nature of sexual harassment in the workplace.

© Paul Conklin/PhotoEdit

A second form of sexual harassment, often referred to as a "hostile or offensive environment," is described in the third situation in the EEOC guidelines. This kind of sexual harassment is less clear but probably more common than the *quid pro quo* variety. Here, one or more supervisors, co-workers, teachers, or students engage in persistent, inappropriate behaviors that make the workplace or academic environment hostile, abusive, and generally unbearable. Unlike *quid pro quo* harassment, this second form does not necessarily involve power or authority differences. It may, however, involve attempts to defend status and position, because men often view the entrance of women into formerly male bastions of power and privilege as threatening (Dall'Ara & Maass, 1999).

Cases involving hostile or offensive environments have been the subject of considerable debate over what constitutes such an environment. Essentially, a hostile environment is seen as one in which a reasonable person in the same or similar circumstances would find the conduct of the harasser(s) to be intimidating, hostile, or abusive.

The reasonable person interpretation is illustrated by a decision in which the U.S. Supreme Court ruled unanimously that a Tennessee woman was subjected to sexual harassment in the form of a hostile environment "that would seriously affect a reasonable person's psychological well-being" (Justice Sandra Day O'Connor, writing for the court in *Harris* v. *Forklift Systems*, 92 U.S. 1168 [1993]). In this case the victim's male boss (the company president) (1) urged her to retrieve coins from his front pants pocket, (2) ridiculed the size of her buttocks, (3) described her as a "dumb-ass woman" in the presence of others, and (4) insinuated that she had won a large sales contract by providing sexual favors. The defendant's attorney unsuccessfully tried to pass off these behaviors as merely joking without any hostile intent. This case is noteworthy because it involved neither sexual blackmail nor unwanted touching. Nevertheless, the Supreme Court ruled that a reasonable person would find the offensive sexual speech intimidating and abusive.

Varieties and Incidence of Sexual Harassment on the Job

Sexual harassment on the job can take many forms. It can start with such things as remarks of a sexual nature; sexist comments; unwelcome attention; violations of personal space; repeated unwelcome requests for a date; inappropriate, derogatory put-downs; leering and/or whistling; offensive and crude language; and displaying sexually oriented objects, materials,

Sexual harassment creates anxiety and tension in the workplace.

or pictures that create a hostile or offensive environment. Some of these behaviors occupy a gray area because not all people would view them as genuine sexual harassment. However, they clearly become sexual harassment if they persist after the target of such acts has asked the offending person to stop.

At an intermediate level of severity, sexual harassment in the workplace can include inappropriate, graphic comments about a person's body or sexual competence, sexual propositions not directly linked to employment, verbal abuse of a sexual nature, and unwanted physical contact of a nonsexual nature. In its most severe manifestations sexual harassment on the job can involve a boss or supervisor requiring sexual services from an employee as a condition for keeping a job or getting a promotion, unwanted physical contact or conduct of a sexual nature, and, less commonly, sexual assault.

Prevalence of Sexual Harassment in the Workplace

The annual number of sexual harassment complaints filed with the EEOC more than doubled, from 5,623 in 1989 to 14,396 in 2002. The percentage of total claims filed by males has steadily increased in recent years, up from 9.1% in 1992 to 14.9% in 2002 (Equal Employment Opportunity Commission, 2003). A number of surveys have revealed that sexual harassment is all too common in the workplace (Sev'er, 1999; Welsh, 1999). Perhaps the most reliable available data come from a national survey of more than 24,000 federal employees. This survey, which adhered closely to the EEOC definition of sexual harassment, had an 85% response rate. Of the more than 20,000 respondents, 42% of women and 15% of men reported experiencing sexual harassment (U.S. Merit Systems Protection Board, 1981). In the years since this survey, these rates have increased slightly, with 44% of women and 19% of men reporting being sexually harassed (U.S. Merit Systems Protection Board, 1996). Other surveys have found sexual harassment rates among working women ranging from 50% (Gutek, 1985; Loy & Stewart, 1984) to 66% (MacKinnon, 1979). A 1995 survey of 90,000 women service members on active duty found that at least half of the respondents in each branch of the military believed that they had been sexually harassed (Firestone & Harris, 1999; Vistica, 1996).

Sexual harassment is not limited to low-paying jobs or indeed to any particular segment of the employment force. It occurs in all professions and at every level. For example, recently the army's highest-ranking woman (a general) filed a complaint of sexual harassment that was substantiated by army investigators (Myers, 2000; Ricks & Suro, 2000). Although some see sexual harassment most frequently occurring in the old economy with its more traditional values, complaints of harassment of women working in Internet companies are increasing (Ligos, 2000). Several studies have revealed high incidences of sexual harassment in medical settings as well. In one survey of 133 physicians, 73% of the female respondents and 22% of the men reported experiencing sexual harassment during their residency training (Komaromy et al., 1993). Another survey of 496 nurses revealed that 82% had experienced sexual harassment on the job (Grieco, 1987).

Same-Sex Sexual Harassment in the Workplace

In recent years sexual harassment involving members of the same sex has become an increasing issue both in the workplace and in the U.S. courts. People who are victims of same-sex sexual harassment have generally found it difficult to obtain satisfactory legal judgments regardless of their own sexual orientation. This unfortunate situation is due both to the absence of a federal law specifically prohibiting same-sex sexual harassment and to the fact that many courts have narrowly interpreted Title VII as prohibiting sex discrimination only between men and women (Landau, 1997). The courts have found this issue of same-sex harassment a difficult one, and over the years many conflicting decisions have been issued. In March 1998, however, the U.S. Supreme Court reversed an earlier decision and ruled that workplace sexual harassment involving an offender and victim of the same sex is prohibited by Title VII. Attorneys representing victims of same-sex harassment frequently find themselves in the position of needing to prove that accused same-sex harassers acted out of "sexual interest." This can be extremely difficult, because most defendants in these cases claim to be heterosexual. Furthermore, gay plaintiffs may be afraid of being "outed" or exposed, and those who are not gay may fear being thought of as gay (Gover, 1996). Nevertheless, same-sex sexual harassment claims are increasing. Over the last decade the EEOC has reported a significant increase in the proportion of sexual harassment claims that involve same-sex harassment (Hunsberger, 2003).

Effects of Workplace Sexual Harassment on the Victim

On-the-job sexual harassment can seriously erode a victim's financial status, job performance, career opportunities, psychological and physical health, and personal relationships (Charney & Russell, 1994; Rhode, 1997). The financial ramifications of refusing to endure sexual harassment may be severe, especially for people in lower-level positions. Many victims, particularly if they are supporting families, cannot afford to be unemployed. Many find it exceedingly difficult to look for other jobs while maintaining their present employment. If they are fired for resisting harassment, they may be unable to obtain unemployment compensation; and even if they do obtain compensation, it will probably provide only a fraction of their former income.

Various surveys report that the great majority of harassed workers (between 75% and 90%) report adverse psychological effects, including eating disorders, crying spells, loss of self-esteem, and feelings of anger, humiliation, shame, embarrassment, nervousness, irritability, alienation, vulnerability, helplessness, and unmotivation (Charney & Russell, 1994; Harned & Fitzgerald, 2002; Jorgenson & Wahl, 2000; Sev'er, 1999). The sense of degradation and helplessness reported by many victims of sexual harassment is similar to that experienced by many rape victims (Safran, 1976). Many victims of sexual harassment also report a variety of physical symptoms that stem directly from pressures associated with their victimization.

Dealing with Sexual Harassment on the Job

If you face sexual harassment at work, a number of options are available to you. The suggestions in the following list provide guidelines for dealing with this abuse:

1. If the harassment includes actual or attempted rape or assault, you can file criminal charges against the perpetrator.

2. If the harassment has stopped short of attempted rape or assault, consider confronting the person who is harassing you. State in clear terms that what he or she is doing is clearly sexual harassment, that you will not tolerate it, and that if it continues, you will file charges through appropriate channels. You may prefer to document what has occurred and your response to it in a letter directed to the harasser (keep a copy). In such a letter you should include specific details of previous incidents of harassment, your unequivocal rejection of such inappropriate overtures, and your intent to take more serious action if they do not stop immediately.

3. If the offender does not stop the harassment after direct verbal and/or written confrontation, it may be helpful to discuss your situation with your supervisor and/or the supervisor of the offender.

4. If neither the harasser nor the supervisors respond appropriately to your concern, you may want to gather support from your co-workers. You may discover that you are not the only victim in your company. Discussing the offense with sympathetic women and men in your workplace may produce sufficient pressure to terminate the harassment. Be very sure of your facts, though, because such actions could result in a slander lawsuit.

5. If your attempts to deal with this problem within your company are unsuccessful or if you are fired, demoted, or refused promotion because of your efforts to end harassment, you can file an official complaint with your city or state Human Rights Commission or with the Fair Employment Practices Agency (the names may vary locally). You can also ask that the local office of the federally funded EEOC investigate the situation.

6. Finally, you may wish to pursue legal action to resolve your problem with sexual harassment. Lawsuits can be filed in federal courts under the Civil Rights Act. They can also be filed under city or state laws prohibiting employment discrimination. Moreover, a single lawsuit can be filed in a number of jurisdictions. A person who has been a victim of such harassment is most likely to receive a favorable court judgment if she or he has first tried to resolve the problem within the company before going to court. ■

U.S. businesses are becoming increasingly sensitive to the issue of sexual harassment in the workplace, in part because of the damage to morale and productivity caused by such behaviors but also because of court decisions that have awarded large sums of money to victims. The estimated cost of sexual harassment for a Fortune 500 company averages at least $6 million a year (Rhode, 1997). In 1998 Mitsubishi Motor Company agreed to pay $34 million in compensation to 350 women who were allegedly sexually harassed. Because Title VII imposes liability on companies for sexual harassment perpetrated by their employees, many corporations have implemented programs designed to educate employees about sexual harassment.

Nevertheless, despite these programs in business and in the military services, many women still keep silent when they have been harassed. They do so for many reasons, including a desire to protect their career (Becker, 2000) and the fear that formal reporting will not be helpful and will lead to their being negatively evaluated by others (Marin & Guadagno, 1999). In fact, this last study indicated that, although women who reported sexual harassment were viewed more highly in qualities of assertiveness, they were also seen as less trustworthy and less feminine by both men and women.

Sexual Harassment in Academic Settings

Sexual harassment also occurs in educational settings. College students often find themselves in the unpleasant situation of experiencing unwanted sexual advances from their professors. Both sexes are vulnerable to this form of harassment. However, it is most commonly male professors or instructors who harass female students (Kelley & Parsons, 2000).

? How About You?

Have you or has anyone you know suffered from sexual harassment?

Sexual harassment also occurs in high schools and even middle schools. In 1992 the U.S. Supreme Court ruled that school districts are liable for hostile sexual environments created by school employees and can be sued for damages. However, the Supreme Court has yet to extend this liability to sexual harassment perpetrated by peers. Nevertheless, many district courts have allowed students to litigate cases of peer harassment under Title IX, a 1972 civil rights law that prohibits federally funded schools from denying students opportunities based on their sex (Scher, 1997). Furthermore, the U.S. Department of Education has published a manual outlining peer sexual harassment guidelines in which it is clearly stated that schools that do not take measures to remedy this form of harassment could lose federal funds (Scher, 1997).

Academic sexual harassment differs somewhat from harassment that occurs in the workplace. For one thing, a student who is faced with unwanted sexual advances often has the option of selecting a different instructor or adviser. In contrast, workers in an employment setting tend to have fewer alternatives for avoiding or escaping the harassment while still keeping their jobs. However, students can experience coercive pressures associated with the need to obtain a good grade, a letter of recommendation, or a desirable work or research opportunity (Riger, 1991).

Students also tend to be more naive than workers about the implications of becoming sexually involved with someone who may be important to their successful pursuit of an education or career. There is a real potential for inappropriate exploitation of youthful naiveté and awe regarding prestige and power. Furthermore, evidence has suggested that a student victim "might wonder whether her academic success has been due to her ability or her professor's sexual interest in her" (Satterfield & Muehlenhard, 1990, p. 1).

An increasing number of colleges and universities have policies prohibiting faculty from dating their students. The growing debate over professor–student romances, together with decisions to ban such relationships, is fueled largely by the belief that many relationships between faculty and students may seem consensual on the surface but actually are not. Rather, the power of professors and/or advisers to determine students' futures, through grades and recommendations, often creates pressure for students to comply to protect their classroom standing or future prospects (Begley, 1993).

Prevalence of Sexual Harassment in Academic Settings

Just how common is sexual harassment in educational settings? A survey of California high schools found that approximately 50% of the women respondents reported experiencing sexual harassment (Roscoe et al., 1994). Another survey of over 1,000 Canadian adolescent women in grades 7 through 12 found that more than 23% had experienced at least one event of sexual harassment in the previous 6 months (Bagley et al., 1997). In surveys of college and university populations, 20–40% of undergraduate women and 30–50% of graduate women report having been the target in one or more incidents of sexual harassment in their academic settings (Kalof et al., 2001; Rubin & Borgers, 1990; Sundt, 1994). Because most studies of college populations have included only female students, we have less information about harassment of male students. However, available data indicate that between 9% and 29% of male undergraduates report having been sexually harassed (Kalof et al., 2001; Mazer & Percival, 1989; Sundt, 1994). Several surveys of medical students reveal that anywhere from one-third to more than half report experiencing sexual harassment while in school, with females reporting substantially higher incidence rates (Baldwin et al., 1991; Richman et al., 1992; Wolf et al., 1991).

Dealing with Sexual Harassment on Campus

What can you do if you experience sexual harassment on campus? Some students avoid or escape the harassment by dropping a class, finding another faculty adviser, or even leaving school. However, we advise someone who feels that she or he is being harassed to report it in order to curtail these inappropriate actions and to reduce the likelihood that other students may be victimized by the same professor (it is common for people who harass students

! Sexual Health

to have several targets). You may wish to speak to the offending individual's chairperson or dean. If you are not satisfied with that person's response, contact the campus officer or department that handles matters dealing with civil rights or affirmative action. Although you may be concerned about grade discrimination or loss of position, federal affirmative action guidelines forbid discrimination against people who, in good conscience, file legitimate claims of sexual harassment. Furthermore, a professor guilty of such action will usually be closely monitored and will be less likely to continue to harass. ■

▶ Summary

Rape

- The legal definition of rape varies from state to state, but most laws define rape as sexual intercourse that occurs under actual or threatened forcible compulsion that overcomes the earnest resistance of the victim. (p. 549)

- Although evidence strongly suggests that rape is widespread, it is difficult to obtain accurate statistics on the actual number of rapes and rape victims in the United States. (p. 549)

- Many false beliefs about rape tend to hold the victim responsible for the crime and excuse the attacker. (pp. 550–551)

- Rape is often a product of socialization processes that occur in certain rape-prone societies. These processes glorify masculine violence, teach boys to be aggressive, and demean the role of women in the economic and political aspects of life. (p. 551)

- Males in U.S. society often acquire callous attitudes toward women that, when combined with a belief that "might makes right," provide a cultural foundation for rape and other acts of sexual coercion. (pp. 551–552)

- There is little support for the sociobiological viewpoint that rape is an evolutionarily determined behavior. (p. 552)

- Exposure to sexually violent media can contribute to more accepting attitudes toward rape, decrease one's sensitivity to the tragedy of rape, and perhaps even increase men's inclinations to be sexually aggressive toward women. (p. 553)

- No singular personality or behavioral pattern characterizes rapists, and a wide range of individual differences exist among rapists. (p. 553)

- Incarcerated rapists have a strong proclivity toward violence. Men who embrace traditional gender roles are more likely to commit rape than men who do not support traditional roles. Anger toward women is a prominent attitude among some rapists. Some rapists have self-centered, narcissistic personalities that may render them insensitive to the feelings of the people they victimize. (pp. 553–554)

- More than 50% of U.S. female rape victims report that their first rape occurred before they were 18 years old. (p. 554)

- Most rapes are acquaintance rapes, where the perpetrator is known to the victim. (p. 554)

- Sexual coercion in dating situations is prevalent. Both sexes experience sexual coercion, but women are more likely than men to be physically forced into unwanted sexual activity. (p. 555)

- A variety of "date rape" drugs are widely used by unscrupulous individuals to facilitate sexual conquest or to incapacitate date partners. (p. 556)

- Rape has been a strategy of war throughout history. In addition to being used as a means to humiliate and control women, wartime rape is also intended to destroy the bonds of family and society. (p. 559)

- Rape survivors often suffer severe emotional and physical difficulties that can lead to a diagnosis of posttraumatic stress disorder (PTSD). (p. 560)

- Rape victims often find that supportive counseling, either individually or in groups, can help ease the trauma caused by rape. (p. 560)

- Although the vast majority of rape victims are women, research indicates that as many as 3% of U.S. men have been raped. (p. 562)

- Men who are sexually assaulted often experience long-term adverse consequences similar to those reported by females who are sexually victimized. (p. 562)

Sexual Abuse of Children

- Child sexual abuse is sexual contact between an adult and a child. A distinction is generally made between nonrelative child sexual abuse, called pedophilia or child molestation, and incest, which involves sexual contact between an adult and a child relative. (p. 563)

- Most child sexual abusers are male relatives, friends, or neighbors of their victims. (p. 563)

- Although no classic profile of a pedophile exists other than that most are heterosexual males and known to the victim, prosecuted offenders tend to be shy, lonely, conservative, and often moralistic or religious. They frequently have poor social and sexual relations with other adults and tend to feel inadequate and inferior. (p. 564)

- Some pedophiles were sexually victimized themselves during childhood. (p. 564)

- It is difficult to obtain accurate estimates of the frequency of incest and pedophilia in U.S. society. Estimates of the number of girls sexually victimized range from 20% to 33%, whereas comparable estimates for boys range from 9% to 16%. (p. 565)

- Recent research suggests that the number of boys who are sexually molested in the United States may be substantially higher than had previously been reported. (p. 566)

- Considerable controversy exists over whether a person can repress memories of sexual abuse and then suddenly or gradually recover them after exposure to certain triggering stimuli. (pp. 566–567)

- Cyberspace pedophilia is widespread, and the responsibility for protecting children, in the absence of other effective safeguards, resides primarily with parents. (pp. 567–568)

- Child sexual abuse can be a traumatic and emotionally damaging experience, with long-term negative consequences for the child. (pp. 568–569)

- Survivors often experience a loss of childhood innocence, a disruption of their normal sexual development, and a profound sense of betrayal. Other damaging consequences include low self-esteem and difficulty establishing satisfying sexual and emotional relationships as adults. (p. 569)

- There are a number of treatment programs for survivors of child sexual abuse, ranging from individual therapy to group and couple-oriented approaches. (p. 569)
- It is important to talk to children about protecting themselves from sexual abuse. Children need to know the difference between okay and not-okay touches, the fact that they have rights, the fact that they can report abuse without fear of blame, and strategies for escaping uncomfortable situations. (p. 570)

Sexual Harassment

- Sexual harassment in the workplace or in an academic setting is any unwanted attention of a sexual nature from someone on the job or in academia that creates discomfort and/or interferes with the victim's job or education. (p. 573)
- Guidelines provided by the Equal Employment Opportunity Commission essentially describe two kinds of sexual harassment. In the *quid pro quo* variety a worker or student believes that failure to comply with sexual advances will result in job or education detriment. In the second form the actions of supervisors, co-workers, professors, or students make the workplace or academic setting a "hostile or offensive environment." (p. 573)
- Title VII of the 1964 Civil Rights Act prohibits sexual harassment. A company can be liable for such coercive actions by its employees. (p. 573)
- Estimates of the percentage of women sexually harassed on the job range from 44% to 88%. A comparable estimate for men is approximately 19%. (pp. 574–575)
- Despite increased attention to the issue of same-sex sexual harassment, victims of this form of harassment have generally found it difficult to obtain legal satisfaction in U.S. courts. (p. 575)
- Victims of sexual harassment may experience a variety of negative financial, emotional, and physical effects. (p. 575)
- Sexual harassment also occurs in educational settings. Most commonly, perpetrators are male professors or instructors who harass female students. (pp. 576–577)
- Surveys indicate that 20–40% of undergraduate women, 30–50% of graduate women, and 9–29% of male undergraduates report having been sexually harassed. (p. 577)

◢ Suggested Readings

Bass, Ellen, and Laura Davis (1988). *The Courage to Heal.* New York: Harper & Row. A powerful, moving book aimed at assisting women survivors of child sexual abuse to recover from the emotional aftermath of being sexually victimized.

Brownmiller, Susan (1975). *Against Our Will: Men, Women, and Rape.* New York: Simon & Schuster. A powerful, illuminating examination of rape from the feminist perspective that rape is an act of power and domination.

Colao, Flora, and Tamar Hosansky (1983). *Your Children Should Know.* New York: Bobbs-Merrill. A fine book, written in an engaging style, that provides a wealth of information about preventing child sexual abuse and strategies for coping with such occurrences. Children, parents, educators, and health professionals all might profit from reading this excellent text.

Francis, Leslie Pickering (2000). *Sexual Harassment as an Ethical Issue in Academic Life.* Walnut Creek, CA: Rowman & Littlefield. A discussion on a range of topics related to sexual harassment in academic settings, including philosophical, legal, and ethical issues associated with efforts to regulate and minimize campus sexual harassment.

Francke, Linda Bird (1997). *Ground Zero: The Gender Wars in the Military.* New York: Simon & Schuster. A sobering account of the extent to which women in the military are consistently subjected to demeaning and disparaging treatment, including sexual harassment and sexual assault.

Gold, Jodi, and Susan Villari (Eds.) (2000). *Just Sex: Students Rewrite the Rules on Sex, Violence, Equality, and Activism.* Walnut Creek, CA: Rowman & Littlefield. An informative collection of the writings of student activists and young scholars who are part of a student movement aimed at ending sexual violence and altering the sexual landscape of America's campuses.

Grauerholz, Elizabeth, and Mary Koralewski (Eds.) (1990). *Sexual Coercion: A Sourcebook on Its Nature, Causes, and Prevention.* Lexington, MA: Lexington Books. A valuable collection of articles that provides several illuminating perspectives on the nature of sexual coercion in its various forms, together with insights into how it can be prevented.

Groth, A. Nicholas (1979). *Men Who Rape.* New York: Plenum. A book that provides important insights into the character and motivation patterns of rapists, written by the director of a sex-offender program in Connecticut.

Maltz, Wendy (2001). *The Sexual Healing Journey.* New York: HarperCollins. An excellent book that helps sexual abuse survivors and their partners understand and recover from the effects of sexual abuse.

Parrot, Andrea, and Laurie Bechhofer (Eds.) (1991). *Acquaintance Rape: The Hidden Crime.* New York: Wiley. A fine book that provides in-depth analysis of the nature and extent of acquaintance rape, along with excellent suggestions for its treatment and prevention.

Sanday, Peggy Reeves (1996). *A Woman Scorned: Acquaintance Rape on Trial.* New York: Doubleday. A first-rate text, written by an eminent anthropologist who has conducted extensive cross-cultural research on rape, that analyzes several rape trials (such as that of boxer Mike Tyson) and describes the cultural traditions that have made the United States a "rape-prone" society.

Scarce, Michael (1997). *Male on Male Rape: The Hidden Toll of Stigma and Shame.* New York: Insight Books. A compelling book by a rape prevention educator and a survivor of such violence himself that examines the impact of same-sex rape on both the victim and society at large.

Shapiro, Francine, and Margot Forrest (1997). *EMDR: The Breakthrough Therapy for Overcoming Anxiety, Stress, and Trauma.* New York: Basic Books. An excellent introduction to eye movement desensitization and reprocessing (EMDR), one of the most effective treatments for sexual trauma.

◢ Resources

Rape crisis centers are listed in the phone books of many cities. Victims of sexual assault can also call the Rape, Abuse, and Incest National Network (RAINN) (1-800-656-HOPE), a Washington, D.C., organization that helps connect callers to local rape crisis centers.

▶ Web Resources

Your *Our Sexuality* Web site **http://psychology.wadsworth.com/crooksbaur9e/** has direct links to the Web sites described below. These links are checked often for changes, dead links, and new additions.

Rape Abuse and Incest National Network

A nonprofit organization, the Rape Abuse and Incest National Network provides news, hotlines, a list of local crisis centers, and statistics on the incidence of rape and incest on its Web site.

Sexual Assault Information Page

This Web site contains information on and links related to sexual assault, including acquaintance rape, child sexual abuse, incest, and rape. Also included is information for crisis centers and counseling and support groups, as well as university resources from across the country. Among the topics covered is Rohypnol—one of the so-called date rape drugs.

National Clearinghouse on Child Abuse and Neglect Information

This Web page is a large resource on child welfare, including issues of childhood sexual abuse. It includes statistics, state laws, fact sheets, and searchable databases.

Information on Sexual Harassment

An interactive exploration of the topic of sexual harassment is included on this Web site, which invites visitors not only to learn definitions of harassment but also to apply these definitions to everyday situations as they consider case studies and are given the opportunity to evaluate their own behavior. State and federal laws are provided, and groundbreaking legal battles are presented.

Sexual Harassment Hotline Resource List of the Feminist Majority Foundation

This Web site provides advice and resources, including links to state hotlines, for people victimized by sexual harassment.

Three Internet Sites That Deal with Web Safety:

A Parent's Guide to Internet Safety

This Web site provides valuable information to families who want to learn more about Internet safety.

American Academy of Pediatrics

Locate the "Internet and Your Family" link for important information about Web safety for children.

Get Net Wise

This Web site, a joint effort of several public-interest organizations and Internet corporations, offers Internet safety strategies for different age levels and activities.

Our Sexuality Web Site

For online resources directly related to this book, go to **http://psychology.wadsworth.com/crooksbaur9e**. You will find interactive exercises, study questions, chapter outlines, an online version of this text's glossary, and Web links and activities that complement your CD-ROM.

InfoTrac® College Edition Online Library

http://infotrac.thomsonlearning.com/
InfoTrac College Edition is an online searchable library that includes a multitude of journals, many of which are specific to human sexuality. These journals include *Archives of Sexual Behavior, Archives of Sexual Health Behavior, Canadian Journal of Human Sexuality, Hispanic Journal of the Behavioral Sciences, Journal of Cross-Cultural Psychology, Journal of Physical Education, Recreation, and Dance, Journal of Sex Research,* and *Sex Roles.*

Our Sexuality CD-ROM

Use your CD-ROM for further study of the concepts in this chapter. Your CD-ROM provides animations of difficult concepts, video clips of real people discussing sexuality, critical thinking questions, chapter quizzing, and more.

Sex for Sale

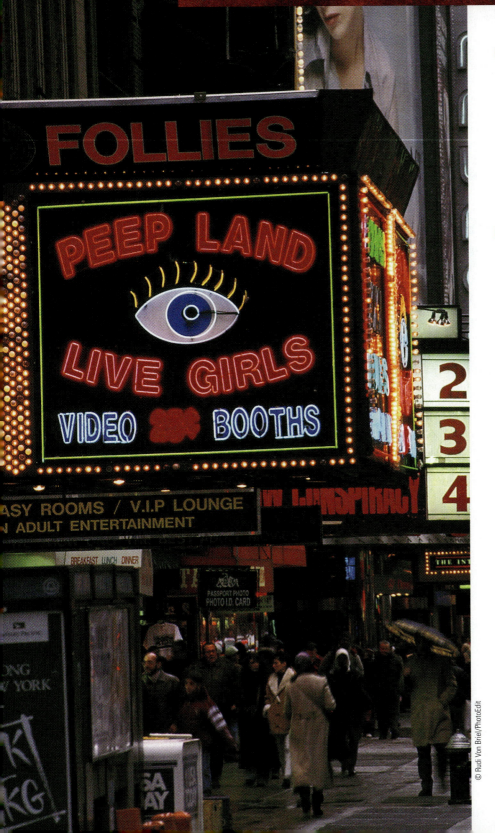

▶ **Pornography**

How is pornography defined?

Since the Middle Ages, what technological developments have made pornography more accessible to the general population?

What distinguishes erotica from pornography, and how is obscenity determined?

What different conclusions did the two federal commissions on pornography make?

What impact does the Internet have on the distribution of sexually explicit materials?

▶ **Prostitution**

How is the Internet changing prostitution?

What are the pros and cons for decriminalization or legalization of prostitution?

What are the different types of male and female prostitution?

Who profits financially from prostitution?

I view porn as dirty smut magazines and movies that old perverted men look at. I really don't appreciate pornography, it does nothing for me. I love naked women in person and in bed, but seeing magazines or movies is a pointless turn-on. Pornography is really degrading toward women, and it gives young people the wrong ideas about women. (Authors' files)

I have found that when my partner and I watch pornos I get extremely aroused and let myself go wild with my sexuality. One time I got so turned on that I took control of the evening by making him do everything I wanted, like being rough, domineering, or sensitive. We also tried different areas in the room, like the coffee table, recliner, and couch. It wore us out so bad that we fell asleep naked in the middle of the floor tangled in each other's embrace. I feel that my partner and I have really benefited from including pornos in our sex. We have become so comfortable, close, and in love knowing that sex is a good thing. (Authors' files)

Throughout this text we have explored many aspects of sexuality, from biology and behavior to sexual and social problems and their treatment. One topic we have not yet investigated is sex as business—the exchange of money for sexual stimulation. A great deal of controversy surrounds sex in the marketplace and what the consequences are of "sex for sale," as we will see in this chapter. In the following pages we examine pornography and prostitution in depth and provide an overview of other types of sex businesses. We explore some of the social and legal issues surrounding these activities. We look first at pornography, which is currently deemed worthy of scholarly analysis as a topic of undergraduate and graduate courses (Atlas, 1999).

▶ Pornography

Pornography Visual and written materials of a sexual nature that are used for purposes of sexual arousal.

In general, **pornography** is defined as any written, visual, or spoken material depicting sexual activity or genital exposure that is intended to arouse the viewer.

Historical Overview

Pictorial and written representations of sexuality are not modern inventions; even prehistoric cave drawings depict sexual activity. The ancient Indian love manual *Kama Sutra,* dating from about A.D. 400, summarized philosophies of sexuality and spirituality in its descriptions of specific sexual techniques. Graphic representations of coitus in Japanese *schunga* paintings and woodcuts from the 1600s and 1700s are regarded as art masterpieces. Ancient Greek and Roman societies extensively used sexual themes to decorate housewares and public architecture.

With the emergence of Christianity and the fall of the Roman Empire, the Catholic Church became the most significant central authority in the West. During the Middle Ages it controlled the production of the printed word and fine art to reflect its restrictive attitudes toward sex. Monks handwrote the books of that era, and the wealth of the Church enabled it to commission the majority of artworks. Johannes Gutenberg's introduction of movable metal type in Europe in 1450 ended the Church's monopoly on the written word (Lane, 2000). After the initial printings of the Bible, some presses became busy producing pornographic stories, which are credited with helping bring literacy to the masses (P. Johnson, 1998). By the middle of the 16th century, books had veered so far from the Church's influence that Pope Paul IV established the Church's first list of prohibited books (Lane, 2000).

The next technology to expand pornography was photography, developed before the Civil War. With the advent of photography, erotic photographs proliferated so extensively that Congress acted by establishing the first U.S. law prohibiting the mailing of obscenity (P. Johnson, 1998). By the mid 1800s sexually explicit "advice literature," the burgeoning production of inexpensive pornographic novels, and the U.S. publication of the notorious English novel *Fanny Hill* prompted civic leaders to establish laws against publishing and selling pornographic materials. The champion of

This Greek tomb painting of male lovers dates back to 480 B.C.

© Mimmo Jodice/CORBIS

this cause was a clerk and bookkeeper, Anthony Comstock, who was appointed to the Society for the Suppression of Vice and as a special agent for the U.S. Post Office. Although his later battle with Margaret Sanger over distribution of contraceptive information and devices in the mail was ultimately unsuccessful (see Chapter 11), Comstock claimed to have convicted more than 3,600 individuals and to have destroyed more than 160 tons of obscene literature. By the 1890s public sentiment changed from support for Comstock's moral outrage about pornography to dismissing him as old-fashioned and provincial. More important, the postal service's monopoly on the country's shipping was eliminated by the development of the railroad and automobile, private shipping companies, and the subsequent emergence of the airplane, all of which made the distribution of pornography much more difficult to control (Lane, 2000).

The transition of the pornography business from an underground enterprise to a multibillion dollar industry occurred in 1953 with the publication of the first issue of *Playboy* magazine. The World War II generation bought 50,000 copies of the first issue, and its growing readership throughout the next decade made its publisher, Hugh Hefner, a multimillionaire. Another change involved explicit sex movies. These films had been distributed only in the underground stag-film market until the 1973 film *Deep Throat*, which was the first adult film that drew mainstream audiences, including women, to X-rated movie houses. This financially successful X-rated film about a woman whose clitoris was mislocated in her throat generated $600 million in theater and video revenues. The success of *Deep Throat* launched the modern pornography industry and expanded the boundaries of sexual content in mainstream films. A 2003 documentary, *Inside Deep Throat*, examined the film's influence on the era of the early 1970s (Smith & Ordonez, 2003). Currently, the pornography industry produces about 11,000 films per year, whereas Hollywood makes 400 feature films each year (Paul, 2004).

After the 1973 U.S. Supreme Court ruling in *Miller* v. *California* established criteria for evaluating obscenity, Congress passed federal antiobscenity laws that initially dampened the production and distribution of pornography. Conservative political and religious groups focused on the damaging effects of pornography and the porn industry. The media emphasized the negative effect of pornography on individuals, the industry's mistreatment of women, and the increased crime around porn shops and adult movie theaters. However, as these censures of pornography increased, new technologies once again made pornography more difficult to control and even more lucrative to develop and sell. Furthermore, the privacy afforded by the advent of cable television and the VCR, followed closely by the Internet, extended access to pornography to people who previously would not have gone to an adult movie theater or bookstore. Rentals of X-rated videos in the United States increased from 79 million in 1985 to 759 million in 2001, an increase of more than 850% (Kloer, 2003). Nearly 1 in 5 DVD and VCR rentals are X-rated (Paul, 2004). Subsequently, consumers have turned pornography into an estimated $10 billion a year industry (Byrne & Osland, 2000; Kamalipour & Rampal, 2001).

The first home personal computers appeared along with cable TV and the VCR, and many of the Internet's technological innovations were advanced by the sex industry (Carnes, 2000). The Internet has since developed into a lucrative sex-selling business. The increase in Web pages containing the word "sex" is an indication of the growth of sex content on the Internet. In 1998 the search engine Google listed more than 70,000 Web pages containing the word sex. By 2003 over 234 million sites met the same criterion (Cooper, 2003). This market has not yet peaked, and its growth potential is immense.

Sexually explicit Web sites designed by and for women are more prevalent than in the past (Kloer, 2003). However, research has found that men

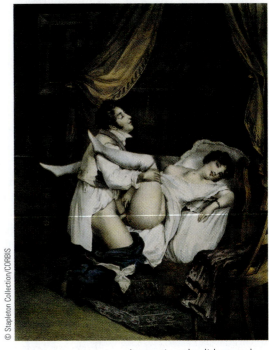

© Stapleton Collection/CORBIS

An erotic color lithograph created sometime between 1830 and 1848.

In 1973, *Deep Throat* was the first mainstream adult film to attract both men and women.

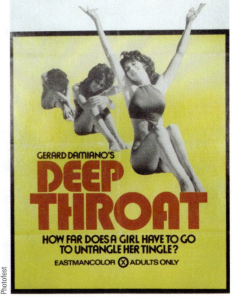

Photofest

The Internet has become a compelling source for men seeking explicit sexual content.

? Critical Thinking Question

Do you think that the Religious Alliance Against Pornography or other similar groups will be successful in deterring pornography? Why or why not?

and women tend to use the Internet differently when pursuing sexual content. Men are more likely than women to choose Web sites with visual erotica, to use online sexual materials for distraction, and to use the Internet to deal with stress. In contrast, more women than men visit chat rooms, go online to educate themselves on sexual issues, and use the Internet to get support for sexual concerns (Cooper, 2003).

DVDs are also changing the X-rated adult entertainment landscape with "interactive" movies. In these "virtual sex" movies the viewer is able to control by DVD remote some of the actors' sexual activities and emotions ("nasty" to "innocent"). The viewer can also direct the action by pressing icons of tongues, fingers, or vibrators and (as stated in an advertisement) "control this gorgeous sexual animal and enjoy her countless times" (Contemporary Sexuality, 2003a).

Because the pornography business is lucrative, major corporations and mainstream entertainment companies are closely tied to it and its annual $10 billion revenues (Dines, 2003). For example, TV viewers in the United States spent $465 million in 2001 watching adult pay-per-view movies in their homes, and most of the money goes to media companies such as AOL Time Warner and AT&T Broadband. In reaction to big business's involvement in pornography, the Religious Alliance Against Pornography has targeted three Fortune 500 companies that carry programming on the Hot Network: AT&T and AT&T/Comcast (which own cable TV systems) and General Motors (which owns Echostar satellite TV). The Alliance is seeking prosecution for violation of the "community standards" provision of federal laws on pornography (Donovan, 2002).

Types of Sexually Explicit Materials

Pornography has become an all-encompassing term to describe sexually explicit materials. Pornographic films developed for heterosexual, gay male, or lesbian consumers have some general characteristics that distinguish them. Much of straight porn is based on a formula of six or seven sex scenes of oral and anal sex and various positions of intercourse with close-up views. Male ejaculation is almost always outside the woman's mouth or vagina so that the viewer can see it. Two women having sex and threesomes or more are often part of the formula. Women are eager sexual participants, and their bodies are the primary focus. Most of the female porn stars have stereotypical underweight bodies with implant-enhanced large breasts, and the men are often, sometimes at best, ordinary looking. Eroticism of the male body is rare in straight porn (Blue, 2003).

The gay porn industry is comparable in size to the straight porn industry and shows the same range of low-cost to well-made films. Most of today's gay porn is made with well-groomed, muscle-bound, good-looking men. Gay porn emphasizes eroticism of the male body and unfettered lust that ranges from aggressive to tender. Subgenres include more variation in body style. For example, bear porn features men with extensive body hair (Blue, 2003).

Far fewer lesbian porn films are made than gay or straight films. The films tend to be low-budget and unpolished compared to straight and gay porn, but they realistically portray diverse and powerful lesbian sexual interaction instead of a performance for the viewer. Most of the lesbian porn films feature real-life lovers. A different style of beauty and sex is evident: A great variety of body types and a range of butch and femme styles pervade the films. Role playing, talking, costuming, and sex toys take precedence over plot. Safer sex practices are often included in the sexual activity (Blue, 2003).

Specialty pornography caters to the wide range of interests in bondage and discipline, sadomasochism fetishes, transgender, pregnant, old/mature, interracial, orgies, pubic shaving, and most any other imaginable topic (Blue, 2003).

The lesbian magazine *On Our Backs* broke new ground in sexual explicitness and "kinkiness" in 1984 when it first hit newsstands.

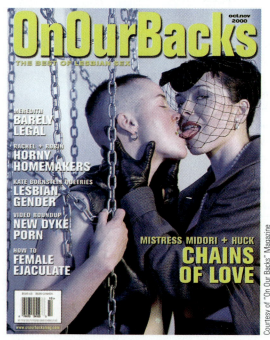

Pornography is usually considered hard-core when explicit images of genitals are shown, whereas soft-core stops short of revealing genitals. However, **erotica** is distinct from pornography irrespective of explicitness of the material. The origins of these two words clarify the differences. The root *porno* in *pornography* means "prostitution" or "female captive," and it connotes domination of women. *Erotica* is rooted in *eros*, or "passionate love" (Steinem, 1998). Erotica consists of "depictions of sexuality which display mutuality, respect, affection, and a balance of power" (Stock, 1985, p. 13). As more women become involved in the production of sexually explicit materials, erotica becomes a more dominant feature (Klinger, 2003). For example, Femme Productions' adult films emphasize sensual body lines and movements, and films such as *Nina Hartley's Guide to Better Cunnilingus* and *The Sluts and Goddesses Video Workshop* promote the development and expression of women's desire and pleasure. In addition, some sexually explicit videos are intended as adult sex education for a couple's enhancement and emphasize communication and experimentation between caring partners (Atlas, 1999). Pornography can provide a type of sex education, as seen in Table 20.1.

Erotica Respectful, affectionate depictions of sexuality.

Contrary to the notion that women find romance sexy and men find explicit sex most exciting, a study of college students 21 years old and older found a similar, rather than different, pattern to what each sex found most arousing. Researchers selected four video segments, each of which represented different combinations of high versus low expressions of love and affection in conjunction with high versus moderate sexual explicitness (hard-core versus soft-core X-rated material). The study found that men and women subjects responded similarly to displays of love and affection in highly sexually explicit videos: Both male and female subjects rated most arousing the video that was both highly romantic and highly explicit. The researchers speculated that these results indicate, at least for college-educated men, a greater integration of love and affection into sexual arousal (Quackenbush et al., 1995). Another study of interviews with 150 men in the United States, Canada, and Europe found that men most enjoyed pornography in which men and women were equal participants or in which men were recipients of female sexual assertion. For the men to enjoy watching the material, they consistently emphasized the importance of the women appearing to experience genuine pleasure (Loftus, 2002).

When we separate the erotic from pornography, we are left with an emphasis on genitals, impersonal sexual acts, an unequal balance of power, and varying degrees of aggression. The standard "plot" of heterosexual X-rated films involves women who are portrayed as sexual playthings, eager to accommodate every sexual urge of men (Zillmann & Bryant, 1982). *Degrading pornography* objectifies and denigrates its subjects. Racial stereotypes presented in interracial pornography are one form of degradation (Cowan & Campbell, 1994). *Violent pornography* involves aggression and brutality; the violence might take the form of rape, beatings, dismemberment, and even murder (Donnerstein et al., 1987). For example, *Hustler*, the hard-core pornographic magazine with the largest distribution in the world, has portrayed women hung on meat hooks with objects shoved up their genitals or a man forcing his wife to sit spread-legged while her genitals are invaded by cockroaches (Schroeder, 1995; Steinem, 1997). Violent and abusive fantasies are also common in chat rooms; titles such as "Torture Females" or "Daughter Blows Dad" can easily be found (Michaels, 1997). In fact, a study comparing

TABLE 20.1	Does Pornography Provide Sex Education? Percentage of Students Reporting That Part of Their Knowledge on Specific Topics Was Gained from Pornography[a]		
	Women (%)	Men (%)	Total (%)
Birth control	11	7	18
Foreplay	25	54	79
Homosexuality	14	21	35
Masturbation	21	31	52
Mechanics of sex	16	47	63
Oral or anal sex	31	52	83
Sexual anatomy of females	11	51	62
Sexual anatomy of males	21	21	42
Sexual attractiveness	15	35	50
Venereal disease	4	15	19

[a]University students in this study said peers were the most important source of sexual information. Pornography ranked low in its general importance but did provide knowledge about some subjects.

Source: Trostle (2003).

? Critical Thinking Question

What examples of erotica or pornography do you see in advertising?

InfoTrac Search Words

■ Erotica

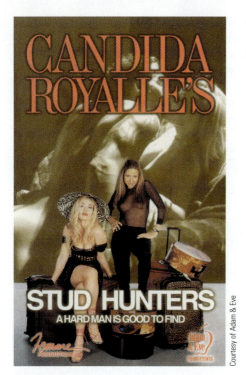

Candida Royalle began producing porn videos designed for women and couples in the 1980s. *Stud Hunters* is a lighthearted look at the adult entertainment industry.

pornographic magazines, videos, and Internet newsgroups found that newsgroups had considerably more sexual violence than the other two forms of media (Barron & Kimmel, 2000).

Several observers have expressed concern about the influence of pornography on intimate relationships between women and men. Pornography often stresses male performance and conquest rather than pleasure. It restricts male sensuality to oversized penises and overused penile performance (Castleman, 2004; Steinem, 1998). It perpetuates the myths that a real man should always be ready for sex and that he should "get it" whenever possible without regard for the other person or his own complex nature (Zilbergeld, 1978). In addition, women are usually portrayed as wildly responsive to just about any stimulation from men. When women do not react in such a manner in real life, men may feel inadequate or cheated, and men and women may doubt the normality of their own sexuality. In fact, one study found that after repeated exposure to pornography, both men and women became less satisfied with the physical appeal and sexual performance of their partners (Zillmann & Bryant, 1988).

The various categories of pornography previously described are useful as a working model to conceptualize different types of sexually explicit material, but we should stress that in real life distinctions are not always neat. "One person's pornography is another person's erotica, and one person's erotica can cause someone else to lose her lunch" (Kipnis, 1996, p. 64). And what may be harmless in one context (for instance, a couple using an erotic video to explore different ways of making love) may be potentially damaging in another (such as a child gaining access to sexually explicit material on the Internet). For reasons like these, pornography is surrounded by complex legal issues. In the next three sections we will look at three questions that have been particularly troublesome from a legal standpoint: What constitutes obscenity? Should freedom of speech protect obscene materials? How should the dissemination of pornography be regulated?

What Constitutes Obscenity?

Obscenity A term that implies a personal or societal judgment that something is offensive.

The term **obscenity** implies a judgment that something is offensive. Such a determination is difficult to establish legally. Over the years the courts have attempted to refine the definition, with incomplete success. Early U.S. courts considered material to be obscene if it depraved and corrupted the user. (The courts then faced the problem of establishing that a person had been depraved by the materials.) Since 1957, three criteria established by the U.S. Supreme Court have been used for evaluating obscenity (*Miller* v. *California*, 413 U.S. 15 [1973]; *Roth* v. *United States*, 354 U.S. 476 [1957]):

1. The dominant theme of the work as a whole must appeal to prurient interest in sex.
2. The work must be patently offensive to contemporary community standards.
3. The work must be without serious literary, artistic, political, or scientific value.

Critics point out that these criteria are still highly subjective (Penley, 1996). After all, *prurience* (an obsessive interest in sex) is in the mind of the beholder, as is the judgment of whether a work has serious artistic or other value. The subjectivity of these criteria is perhaps best reflected in Supreme Court Justice Potter Stewart's comment regarding obscenity: It is difficult to define intelligently, "but I know it when I see it" (*Jacobelis* v. *Ohio*, 379 U.S. 197 [1965]). And community standards for obscenity vary dramatically. In many large cities all manner of explicit sexual films are openly advertised and shown. However, in other areas, especially in small, rural communities, books and magazines such as *Playboy* have been banned. The books *The Color Purple* and *Our Bodies Ourselves* and *Ms.* magazine are some of the materials that have been deemed obscene in some communities and consequently banned from high school libraries (Klein, 1999). Recently, the parameters around "community" have become nebulous because of the technology of cable TV, VCRs, and the Internet, which are used in the privacy of individuals' homes, where community standards of obscenity are essentially irrelevant (Lane, 2000). However, the courts, pornographic entrepreneurs, and activists on both sides will continue to struggle with the legal definition of obscenity because of its important legal implications regarding protection by the First Amendment to the U.S. Constitution.

Should Freedom of Speech Protect Obscene Materials?

A second legal question regarding what is determined to be obscene concerns the work's standing under the U.S. Constitution's First Amendment guarantee of freedom of speech and freedom of the press. Do these constitutional protections apply to obscene materials? In a 1957 decision the Supreme Court declared that the First Amendment guarantees did not apply categorically to obscene materials.

? How About You?

What kinds of sexually explicit materials, if any, do you think should be censored?

Those who oppose limits on free speech believe that such laws can infringe on freedom of personal choice by giving the courts power to interpret and rule on a wide variety of sexual images (Hudson & Graham, 2004). Censorship is applied at the discretion of those with the most political power, and it inevitably rebounds against women, especially those who challenge their traditional roles. The use of federal antiobscenity laws of the early 20th century to prosecute Margaret Sanger for printing information about contraception is an example (McElroy, 1995). The "On the Edge" box "Pornography as Social Criticism" explores the sometimes political nature of pornography.

The Commissions on Obscenity and Pornography

Two presidential commissions have been appointed to study pornography in the past four decades, and they have come to very different conclusions. In the late 1960s President Lyndon Johnson appointed the Commission on Obscenity and Pornography to study the effects of sexually explicit materials. The commission's report was published in 1970. This commission studied the effects of legalization of pornography in Denmark (which had occurred in 1967). It also analyzed the findings of various studies in the United States and offered recommendations.

In its study of Denmark the commission found that sales of pornography to Danes decreased in the years after legalization (although sales to foreign tourists increased), and the increased availability of pornography after legalization did *not* result in an increase in sex offenses. However, a cause-and-effect relationship is difficult to establish. For example, legalization may have had the effect of increasing tolerance of lesser offenses such as exhibitionism, which could have reduced the number of cases resulting in prosecution. Studies in the United States have also not found a link between pornography laws and rape and sex offense reports (Winick & Evans, 1996).

The 1970 report also analyzed current research and found that imprisoned sex offenders had not had more exposure to pornography than had other prison inmates or nonprison populations. In its summary of research on the effects of sexually explicit materials, the commission concluded that no significant, long-lasting changes in behavior were evident in college-student volunteer research subjects after they were exposed to pornography. On the basis of this information, this commission recommended repealing all laws prohibiting access to pornography for adults. However, both President Nixon and the U.S. Senate rejected these recommendations.

The Meese Commission

In 1986 President Ronald Reagan appointed another commission to study pornography: the U.S. Attorney General's Commission on Pornography (sometimes called the Meese Commission, after then–attorney general Edwin Meese). The commission based its finding more on politics and opinion than on scientific research and reached drastically different conclusions and made radically different recommendations from the earlier commission. The Meese Commission report concluded that violent pornography caused sexually aggressive behavior toward women (U.S. Attorney General's Commission on Pornography, 1986). It also found that degrading pornography fostered

Reality TV show *Can You Be A Porn Star?* with hosts Tabitha Stevens and Mary Carey began airing on pay-per-view in early 2004, illustrating a trend toward mainstreaming of the porn industry.

Pornography as Social Criticism

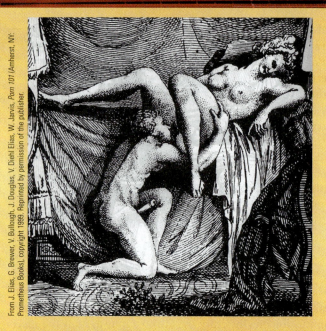

Over the course of history pornography has played the role of social critic by using sexually explicit text or images to violate social and political norms. Pornography has challenged the hypocrisy and social expectations of politics, organized religion, and the middle, professional, and upper classes (Beck, 1999; Kipnis, 1996; Penley, 1996). The degree to which people have used pornography for political, sometimes subversive, aims has varied over time. During the French Revolution, pornography helped incite the poor to rebel against the king and queen. Hundreds of pamphlets were printed and circulated that linked "degenerate" sexual activity with the material excesses and political corruption of royalty (Beck, 1999).

Pornography has also challenged the restricted sexuality of women. In the 1700s virtuous women were supposed to be repelled by sex, and female characters in novels who transgressed the established social order always met with eventual disaster. John Cleland's *Fanny Hill* was first published in Great Britain in 1748 and was far more notorious because of the happy ending in the main character's life of sexual adventure than for the sexual content itself. In keeping with this perspective, Constance Penley, a university professor who teaches a course on pornography, believes that the pervasive theme of popular pornography is men's "utopian desire for a world where women aren't socially required to say and believe that they don't like sex as much as men do" (1996, p. 18). The author of *Sex, Time, and Power,* Leonard Shlain, goes even further when he states, "Pornography would disappear tomorrow if women were as eager to have sex and behaved sexually as indiscriminately as men" (Shlain, 2003, p. 352).

The role of contemporary pornography as a social and political critic is readily evident when considered in that light. In contrast to *Playboy* and *Penthouse* magazines' consumption-oriented status-seeking fantasy of wealth and good looks, where all women are willing and all men are studs, *Hustler* magazine fuses nudity and vulgarity with attacks on "the establishment"—political power, organized religion, and class privilege. For example, stark social and political criticism are evident in a 1989 photo montage titled "Farewell to Reagan: Ronnie's Last Bash." The faces of the political elite of that era are imposed on top of naked bodies doing "obscene" things to one another. The introductory text accompanying the photo declares, "It's been eight great

Pornography can be a form of political subversion, linking "degenerate" sexual activities to political corruption. This illustration shows a man of the lower class servicing Queen Marie Antoinette's sexual appetites, implying that the King could not control his wife's sexual adventures or be certain of the paternity of his children. If he could not keep his own house in order, his ability to rule a country and its people could be challenged (Beck, 1999).

From J. Elias, G. Brewer, V. Bullough, J. Douglas, V. Diehl Elias, W. Jarvis, *Porn 101* (Amherst, NY: Prometheus Books), copyright 1999. Reprinted by permission of the publisher.

years—for the power elite, that is. . . . A radical tax plan that more than halved taxes for the rich while doubling the working man's load; . . . more than 100 appointees who resigned in disgrace over ethics or outright criminal charges . . . are all the legacies of the Reagan years . . . and we'll still get whiffs of bully-boy Ed Meese's sexual intimidation policies for years to come, particularly with conservative whores posing as Supreme Court justices" (Kipnis, 1996, pp. 152–153).

Other pornography violates conventional notions of taste, beauty, manners, and social conventions. One can find geriatric sexually explicit materials such as "Promiscuous Granny" and pornography featuring sexual interaction involving diapers, spanking, bondage and discipline, and sadomasochism. Transgender pornography wreaks havoc with any consistent concept of gender or sexual orientation because it portrays males dressed in lingerie and transsexuals with breasts and penises engaging in sexual interaction with themselves or with same- and other-sex partners.

Perhaps the most dramatic example of pornography's function of defying social norms while showcasing images banned by our contemporary culture is the subgenre of fat pornography. Fat pornography eroticizes bodies that defy social propriety. Large (between 200 and 500 pounds) naked women in sexual situations are featured in an array of magazines and videos with titles such as *Life in the Fat Lane* and *Jumbo Jezebel.* The fact that fat women have an erotic charge for some people evokes our current culture's considerable anxiety about and hostility toward obese people. Yet it is only internalized prevailing fashion that creates rigid preferences (fetishes?) for "in-shape bodies with buns of steel (on men and women), or for breasts (big ones, please), or washboard abs" (Kipnis, 1996, p. 95). Disbelief by many people that fat, fleshy bodies could be a turn-on shows how completely cultural conformity seems universally "normal." Actually, the amount of body fat considered most sexually appealing is historically and culturally relative. The 20th century's status of thinness contrasts with the previous 400 years' preference for the visual appeal of hefty, rotund body types. Thinness was not sexually attractive during those years because it connoted lower-class poverty and ill health.

accepting attitudes toward rape and had some causal relationship to sexual violence. The research on these questions is discussed in Chapter 19.

The Meese Commission went further, however. Some members also viewed nonviolent, nondegrading erotica as destructive to the moral environment of society because it promotes promiscuity and sex outside of marriage. The commission recommended:

? Critical Thinking Question

What examples have you seen of contemporary pornography that challenge social and political hypocrisy?

- That law enforcement and prosecution of pornography be vigorous.
- That citizens file complaints, pressure the legal system, and monitor and boycott businesses that sell sexually explicit materials.
- That obscene cable television programming be prohibited.
- That "dial-a-porn" telephone services be prohibited.
- That possession of child pornography be made a felony.

Many of the Meese Commission's findings were just as controversial as those of the 1970 commission. One criticism concerns the commission's conclusions about violent pornography. Leading researchers criticized the Meese Commission report because it ignored the "inescapable conclusion that it is violence, whether or not it is accompanied by sex, that has the most damaging effect.... [A]ll violent material, whether sexually explicit or not, ... promotes violence against women" (Donnerstein & Linz, 1986, p. 57).

In response to the Meese Commission's report, the American Civil Liberties Union (ACLU) argued that many of the commission's restrictions "strike not only the First Amendment directly, but intrude upon civil liberties values like due process, privacy, and choice" (American Civil Liberties Union, 1986, p. 4). As stated more graphically by the owner of *Hustler* magazine, Larry Flynt, "If the First Amendment will protect a scumbag like me, then it will protect all of you" (Alter, 1996).

The Supreme Court continues to address issues of censorship, especially in response to newer technologies. For example, it made a significant ruling regarding the Internet and sexually explicit materials in 1997 when it gave free speech protection to the Internet. The decision in *Reno* v. *American Civil Liberties Union et al.* was based on the Court's opinion that the Internet is the most participatory form of communication ever developed and therefore is entitled to the "highest protection from governmental intrusion" (Beck, 1999, p. 83). Before this ruling the nature of the technology of the Internet had already made many forms of censorship impossible because of its use in the privacy of people's homes.

How Should the Dissemination of Pornography Be Regulated?

A third difficult question regards the dissemination of pornography. How can pornography be regulated so that adults who want to use it have access to it and those who do not want to be exposed to it or may be harmed by it will be protected from it?

Possession versus Dissemination of Pornography

The distinction between possession and dissemination of pornography is a long-standing legal issue. In 1969 the U.S. Supreme Court ruled that private possession of pornography in the home was not a crime, nor was it subject to government regulation (*Stanley* v. *Georgia*, 394 U.S. 557 [1969]). However, the dissemination of pornography is regulated. Federal laws prohibit the broadcasting, mailing, importation, and transportation across state lines of obscene materials, although by the 1990s very little was held to be outrightly obscene. The Internet made these restrictions irrelevant for the vast quantity of sexually explicit materials on the Web.

The dissemination of pornography and sex-related businesses are also regulated by zoning and land-use regulations. Many cities limit the areas where adult bookstores and movie houses can be located (Bernstein, 1999; Lopez, 2000). Because of zoning ordinances, high concentrations of pornographic establishments have arisen in some cities. The Combat Zone in Boston and North Beach and the Tenderloin District in San Francisco are examples of such areas. In other states, laws prohibit zoning limitations for nude bars and adult video stores (Bates, 1995).

© Andrew Holbrooke/CORBIS

Hustler of Hollywood has a chain of four adult stores and an online e-mall specializing in sexual toys, videos, and apparel.

It can be argued that local governments should protect their citizens from unwanted exposure to sexually explicit materials in public places—such as when driving past an adult book or video store. Citizens would also be harmed by a decrease in their property values when an adult bookstore or a lingerie modeling business moves into their neighborhood. In contrast, when someone accesses the X-rated sites on the Internet in his or her own living room, the sexually explicit materials are not imposed on the community (Lane, 2000).

Child Pornography

Child pornography is not included in the First Amendment protection of free speech. The production, sale, and distribution of sexual images of children under the age of 18 is illegal under numerous state and federal laws. Federal law also prohibits the sale or distribution of images of adult women pretending to be under 18. Child pornography has been targeted for prosecution by the Attorney General's office. Internet sting operations in which federal agents pose as bookstore owners have resulted in arrests of child pornographers. In addition, records of Web site visits can help authorities identify and prosecute child pornographers.

▶ Prostitution

Prostitution The exchange of sexual services for money.

Prostitution is the exchange of sexual services for money. It is illegal in every state of the United States except Nevada, where it is legal in certain counties. Prostitution is typically thought of in terms of a woman selling sexual services to a man, although transactions between two males are also common. Payment for a man's services to a woman is less usual. Prostitutes sometimes prefer the term *sex worker*, which is a common term for people involved in related activities, such as phone sex, nude dancing, erotic massage, Internet sex, and porn movie actors.

Relationships that exchange sex for money also occur outside prostitution. Advertising frequently portrays the "trade goods for sex" theme, and one of the first "reality TV" shows in 2000, *Who Wants to Marry a Multimillionaire?*, highlighted the prostitution-like aspects sometimes present in common male–female relationships (Peyser, 2000b). Women trade sex for men's financial resources in numerous ways. A case could be made that a woman who marries a good provider instead of her heartthrob, the wife who is especially sexually pleasing before asking for extra money from her husband, or the woman who wants out of her marriage but stays for economic security all play out the dynamics of prostitution (Ridgeway, 1996).

InfoTrac Search Words

■ Prostitution

History of Prostitution

Prostitution has existed throughout history and has been called the oldest profession. However, the significance and meaning of prostitution have varied in different times and societies. In ancient Greece the practice was tolerated. During some periods of Greek history certain types of prostitutes were valued for their intellectual, social, and sexual companionship. Prostitution was part of revered religious rituals in other ancient societies. Sexual relations between prostitutes and men often took place within temples and were seen as sacred acts. In medieval Europe prostitution was tolerated, and the public baths provided opportunities for contacts between customers and prostitutes. In England during the Victorian Era, prostitution was viewed as a scandalous but necessary sexual and social outlet for men: It was a lesser evil for a middle-class man to have sexual relations with a prostitute than with another middle-class man's wife or daughter (Taylor, 1970).

As with many aspects of the sex industry, the Internet is transforming the world's oldest profession, particularly the high end of the prostitution market. Web sites offer "escorts" with a great variety of physical, intellectual, and sexual specialties (bondage, sado-masochism, fantasy enactment). The prostitute and customer negotiate through e-mail, which eliminates the role of pimps and brothels, and prostitutes keep the profits they earn. Prosecution of cyberprostitution is rare (Shuger, 2000).

Prostitutes and Their Customers

Prostitutes exist because there is a demand for their services. Customers of prostitutes are usually white, middle-aged, middle-class, and married (Adams, 1987). In one study of men who used prostitutes, 93% had contact at least once a month (Freund et al., 1991). Sex with a prostitute provides sexual contact or release without any expectation of intimacy or future commitment; it eliminates the risk of rejection and offers an opportunity to engage in sexual techniques that the customer would not do with an ongoing partner (Califia, 2002).

No single theory can explain the motivation for being a prostitute. A combination of psychological, social, environmental, and economic factors is involved, but economic necessity and incentive are usually the primary motivation for becoming a prostitute (Carter, 2003; McElroy, 1995). One study on prostitution found that "some go into prostitution as a matter of free personal choice or the right to sexual liberation, others are pressured because of dire economic conditions or the lack of remunerative alternatives, and yet others are forced through deception, violence, or debt bondage" (Lim, 1998, p. v). This last route to prostitution is of great concern, as described in the following "Sexuality and Diversity" discussion.

 ## Sexuality and Diversity

Worldwide Exploitation of Women and Children in Prostitution

Each year 1 million children worldwide are forced into prostitution (Willis & Levy, 2003). The exploitation of children and women through prostitution has become a multimillion-dollar global growth industry. A CIA–State Department report estimates that 50,000 women and children are essentially slaves in the U.S. sex industry (Leuchtag, 2003). Across the globe, poverty, political instability, wars, and the AIDS epidemic leave women and children vulnerable to exploitation (Marton, 2004). For example, after the fall of the iron curtain and communism in the mid 1990s, many women fled from the poverty of their home countries to Western Europe, only to be forced into prostitution. Furthermore, children in developing countries whose parents have died of AIDS or were killed in the ethnic and tribal wars of Eastern Europe and Africa are highly vulnerable to exploitation (Rios, 1996).

Traffickers entice women and children from Asia, Latin America, and Eastern Europe with promises of employment, only to sell them to others who force them to work as prostitutes in countries throughout the world (Brinkley, 2000; France, 2000). There has been a notable increase in young boy prostitutes to meet the demands of sex tourism (Lim, 1998). Younger and younger children are sought for prostitution because customers regard them as more likely to be free of HIV. Many then return to their homeland after they have become ill with AIDS. Adding to the tragedy of this is the fact that children are particularly vulnerable to the deadly virus; their vaginas and anuses are easily torn, creating portals of entry for HIV (Kristof, 1996).

Children are also bought from parents as indentured sexual servants. For example, an 11-year-old Cambodian girl, Sriy, was

These young prostitutes from Svay Pac in Cambodia must endure the hardships of a life they probably did not choose for themselves.

© Way Gary/Corbis Sygma

sold to a Cambodian brothel by her stepfather after her mother became ill. The brothel owner claims to prospective customers that the now 13-year-old Sriy has just lost her virginity and is "clean." The truth is that Sriy has serviced about 10 customers a night for the last 2 years. She is considered the brothel owner's property and will be locked up, beaten, and starved if she tries to escape. Other children are just kidnapped (Kristof, 1996).

The growing "sex tourism" industry, with its "clients" from industrialized countries, profits from the desperation of the urban and rural poor of developing countries. The industry is strongest in the Asian countries of Thailand, the Philippines, India, Sri Lanka, Vietnam, and Cambodia and in the South American country of Brazil. Most tours bring Japanese, German, Scandinavian, Arab, and U.S. men to these countries. Advertising builds on the stereotype of Asian women as docile and adoring. An economics professor from Thailand estimates that the sex trade earns four to five times more than the agricultural industry (Budhos, 1997).

In Egypt wealthy Arabs from oil-rich Persian Gulf countries pay "dowries" of several thousand dollars to poor families to "marry" their young daughters. The marriages last the few months that the man is in Egypt on holiday or for business. When the man returns home, he essentially abandons the woman, who is sometimes pregnant but has no recourse to any of the legal rights of marriage. This practice appears to be common; only 1 out of every 200 marriages between Egyptian women and foreigners lasts more than a few months (Gardner, 1999; Michael, 1999).

Many women's organizations and other human rights groups have consistently advocated for women's educational and economic empowerment to eradicate the connection between poverty and sexual exploitation. Unfortunately, efforts to elicit meaningful aid from governments and corporations have been met with limited success (Boulware, 2000b; Budhos, 1997). International agreements are being established to help take action against child prostitution (Leuchtag, 2003).

In contrast to the severe problem of people being forced into prostitution, most individuals in the United States who pursue prostitution come from diverse backgrounds. Some prostitutes work on a part-time basis and otherwise pursue conventional school, work, or social lifestyles. Prostitutes may be delinquent school dropouts and runaways or well-educated adults. Some sell sex to support a drug habit (Medrano et al., 2003). People who work as prostitutes on a temporary, part-time basis and have other occupational skills can leave prostitution more easily. Many of these women and men have not identified themselves as prostitutes, or "professionals." In contrast, the full-time prostitute, who is alienated from traditional values and has identified herself or himself as part of the subculture (being arrested facilitates this identification), typically has little education and few marketable skills. These people usually find it difficult to become successfully independent of prostitution (Butcher, 2003). Legal problems, health hazards, and fear of personal injury are serious concerns of prostitutes (Lane, 2000).

In contrast, sex workers on the Internet have far safer and less oppressive working conditions than other sex workers. They may be more able to have flexible part-time work schedules. The pay of high-tech sex workers is higher than entry-level service jobs; phone-sex operators earn $8 to $15 per hour, and live models on adult video-conferencing sites make $25 to $50 per hour. However, they still get only a fraction of the money they generate; the phone-sex company makes about $300 per hour from each phone-sex operator's work. Consequently, some Internet and phone-sex workers establish their own businesses instead of working for a company (Cooper, 2002; Lane, 2000).

Prostitution and the Law

The legal status of prostitution has been debated for some time in the United States. There are at least two alternatives to the criminal status of prostitution. One is legalization; the other is decriminalization. If legalized, prostitution could be regulated, licensed, and taxed by the government. Prostitutes would be registered and required to follow certain procedures, such as periodic checkups for sexually transmitted diseases to maintain their licenses, as in Nevada. (This does not, however, eliminate a customer's risk of HIV. A person can have a false-negative HIV test result because it can take up to 6 months after contracting HIV to show a positive test result.) If prostitution were decriminalized, criminal penalties for engaging in prostitution would be removed; however, prostitutes would be neither licensed nor regulated. Laws concerning solicitation and laws against the involvement of minors would remain, even if prostitution were legalized or decriminalized (McElroy, 1995).

? How About You?

What do you think the legal status of prostitution should be?

There are several arguments for maintaining the status of prostitution as a criminal offense. One view is that if prostitution were not a punishable offense, many women would take it up and it would be more difficult to enforce any restrictions on prostitution activities. Another argument is that it is the responsibility of government to regulate public morals (United Nations Commission, 1959). Some countries, such as Sweden, Vietnam, and Venezuela, have taken strong stands against prostitution by penalizing customers, pimps, and brothel owners with fines and imprisonment while providing prostitutes with medical, educational, and economic assistance to help them get out of prostitution.

Although other countries are considering similar approaches, critics claim that these laws merely drive the sex trade further underground, making it even more difficult to control sex trafficking of women from other countries (Global Agenda, 2003). For example, about 70% of prostitutes in Amsterdam lack any empowerment from legalization because they are from other countries and do not have legal papers, must operate illegally, and are not entitled to employment benefits afforded the other 30%. Instead of being protected by the regulations governing brothels, the women are vulnerable to abuse by "prostitution managers" (Leuchtag, 2003; Passariello, 2002). Furthermore, even when prostitution is not a criminal offense, customers still often refuse to wear condoms, and pimps continue to control prostitutes.

Prostitution is usually considered a "victimless crime," an act that does not harm the people engaged in it. (However, prostitution may not be victimless in all senses because the prostitute is often the victim of abuse from customers and pimps and of discriminatory laws and social stigmas [Valera et al., 2001].) Advocates for decriminalization or legalization point to the difficulty of effective and fair prosecution. Prostitution flourishes despite criminal sanctions against it, as it has throughout history in most societies where it has been prohibited. Its criminal status may encourage connections with organized crime and hamper the rehabilitation of prostitutes (who may find it difficult to find other kinds of work once they have a criminal record) (Weiner, 1996). If prostitution were legal, the victimization of prostitutes by pimps, customers, the judicial system, and others who profit at their expense would perhaps also be reduced (The Economist, 1998). Decriminalizing or legalizing prostitution could allow the criminal justice system to expend more efforts combating crimes that harm people or property.

Discrimination in applying penalties is typical: Customers and prostitutes are equally involved, but in the United States and most other countries it is the prostitute, not the customer, who is usually arrested, jailed, and prosecuted. There are some notable exceptions to this inequity. In some cities law officials seize the cars of prostitutes' customers in addition to fining them. The apprehended customer must have all other parties who are included on his vehicle registration (usually his wife or employer) sign off before the police will return his car. Many of the men forfeit their cars instead of obtaining the needed signature in order to hide their involvement with prostitutes (Chapkis, 1997). Other police departments post photos of arrested prostitutes and customers on their Web sites, hoping to deter men from involving themselves with prostitution.

Some governments are legalizing prostitution, in part to generate tax revenues. The tax revenues from legalized prostitution in the Netherlands are estimated to be $57 million per year (Global Agenda, 2003). Other countries—for example, Italy, Britain, Belgium, and Scotland—are also considering regulating or legalizing brothels to generate tax revenues and to attempt to manage the crime and health risks that accompany prostitution (Passariello, 2002). Some countries even promote prostitution as a tourist attraction: Greece is planning to increase the number of licensed brothels in Athens for the 2004 Olympics; and Cape Town, South Africa, publicizes its brothels as a tourist attraction (Global Agenda, 2003).

Some advantages occur for prostitutes under less restrictive laws. Since January 2002 in Germany, as part of new regulations for prostitution, legal brothel workers have full employment rights, including health insurance and paid vacation. Germany made these changes in part because of the health and crime concerns arising from the huge influx into Western Europe, since the fall of the Berlin Wall, of Eastern Europeans who engage in illegal prostitution.

Some prostitutes have organized for political change and mutual support. The prostitutes' union, COYOTE (Call Off Your Old Tired Ethics), was founded in 1973 and acts as a collective voice for the prostitutes' concerns; what ultimate effect this organization will have on U.S. laws pertaining to prostitution remains to be seen (Klinger, 2003).

Prostitution and HIV

AIDS is also a concern with prostitution. In parts of Africa sex with prostitutes is a primary mode of transmission of HIV. HIV infection rates among prostitutes in the United States are generally lower than in developing countries and vary greatly from one geographic area to another. Because prostitution is illegal, it is difficult to obtain reliable statistics. Prostitutes in county-licensed brothels in Nevada are required by law to be tested monthly for HIV antibodies and to use condoms to prevent HIV infection (Albert et al., 1998). Prostitutes of low socioeconomic status are much more likely to be infected with HIV than are high-priced prostitutes; HIV rates were 35% in a New York study of streetwalkers (Weiner, 1996). Prostitutes who are the most desperate for money, are in the United States illegally, or are poor, older, and drug addicted face the greatest pressures to practice unsafe sex (Chapkis, 1997). The greatest risk factor for prostitutes becoming infected with HIV is injection drug use or having sex partners who are injection drug users. Male prostitutes who service other men are also at great risk of becoming infected with and transmitting HIV (Calhoun & Weaver, 1996).

Teenage Prostitution

There are many teenage prostitutes in the United States and Canada, and teen prostitution is increasing (Franzen, 2001; Smalley, 2003). Teenagers often become prostitutes as a means of survival after they have run away from home (Carnes, 1991; Ring, 2001). As one adolescent prostitute stated:

> There's no doors opened to us. . . . How are you going to be able to hold down a job if you have no high school diploma, if you're not able to take a shower every day, if you don't have clean clothes to wear to work? And let's say you came out here because of "certain circumstances" at home. You're scared out here. (Hersch, 1988, p. 35)

Most teenage prostitutes come from unstable, problem-ridden families (McCaghy & Hou, 1994). Approximately 95% have been victims of sexual abuse, and most have been abandoned by their families (Rio, 1991). Most teenage prostitutes did not perform well in school and have poor self-images. More than 80% of girls and 60% of boys in prostitution have seriously contemplated or attempted suicide (Carnes, 1991). One study of adolescent male prostitutes found two dominant themes in their earlier lives: They were likely to have had an unstructured and unsupervised home life, and they also felt rejected by peers at school and had few friends (Price et al., 1984). However, teens from middle- and upper-class homes are increasingly involved in prostitution. Some appear to sell themselves for excitement and the quick money to spend as they wish without parental interference. After school some girls even invite customers to their homes while their parents are at work (Smalley, 2003).

The children who become prostitutes are sometimes seeking adult attention and affection, and they believe at first that prostitution is a life of glamour and adventure. However, in reality they must cope with the extreme dangers of street life, including serious risks of contracting HIV through either sexual contact or shared needles (many adolescent prostitutes are injection drug users).

Female Prostitutes

There are various types of female prostitutes who service male customers. The variations relate to such characteristics as the public visibility of the woman, the amount of money she charges, and her social class. A woman's experience as a sex worker is significantly influenced by the conditions under which she works and the control she has over her work. We look at a few different categories, defined roughly in terms of the method a woman uses to contact customers. These include *streetwalkers,* women who work in brothels or massage parlors, and *call girls.*

Streetwalkers can be seen on the streets of most large cities. They solicit customers on the street or in bars. They are often from lower socioeconomic backgrounds and charge less than do other types of prostitutes for their services (a homeless streetwalker can get as little as $5 for fellatio) (Ridgeway, 1996). They must share a large portion of their earnings with their pimps (discussed later in this chapter). Streetwalkers are at the bottom of the hierarchy of prostitution. The prostitutes in this group are most likely to have traumatic family backgrounds (Rio, 1991) and to be victims of abuse and robbery by pimps and customers (Valera et al., 2001). Street prostitutes are easy prey, and all too frequently a news story describes the discovery of a murdered prostitute or a hunt for a serial killer of sex workers (Green, 2000). Because of their visibility, streetwalkers are easily subject to arrest. Most streetwalkers repeat the cycle of arrest, short jail sentences, and release many times throughout their careers.

A **brothel** is a house in which a group of prostitutes work. Brothels were common in earlier American history and remain so in some other countries. They are legal in some areas of Nevada today. Brothels range from expensive establishments to run-down, seedy places. They are usually managed by a "madam," who acts as the hostess and business manager of the house. Prostitutes who work in brothels in areas where prostitution is illegal are somewhat more protected from arrest than are streetwalkers because they are less visible to the police. Prostitutes are also less vulnerable to physical assault from their customers within the brothel setting.

Massage parlors are often seen as a modern "quick service" version of brothels. Manual stimulation (a "local" or "hand finishing") or oral stimulation to orgasm is often arranged for a fee once the customer is in the massage room. The customer also can often dictate in what state of dress or undress he would like his masseuse to be. Intercourse may or may not occur as part of the "massage."

Call girls generally earn more than other kinds of prostitutes, up to $500,000 a year (Ridgeway, 1996). They often come from middle-class backgrounds. Call girls frequently offer social companionship as well as sexual services for their customers. Their customer contacts are usually made by personal referral or through "escort services," and they often have several regular customers (Blackmun, 1996a). Their public visibility is minimal, and their risk of arrest is much less than that of the streetwalker. Call girls provide themselves with attractive wardrobes and apartments—all part of their business expenses. They are also more likely than other types of prostitutes to be given goods, such as clothing or living accommodations by regular customers. The Hollywood madam Heidi Fleiss, arrested in 1993 in a sting operation, had an exclusive and star-studded clientele (Maxwell, 1996).

© Gilles Fonlupt/CORBIS

Streetwalkers are at high risk for abuse by customers and pimps.

Brothel A house in which a group of prostitutes work.

Male Prostitutes

Male prostitution is as old as female prostitution. Evidence exists that men sold sexual services to other men as far back as the ancient Sumerians and the ancient Greeks. In our era there is not a "typical" male prostitute in terms of cultural, socioeconomic, or personal background. Young men ranging from illiterates to middle class to wealthy work on the streets, in clubs, or through high-class escort services (Minichiello et al., 2000; Schifter, 1998).

In contrast to female prostitutes, most male prostitutes work independently, without a pimp (Calhoun & Weaver, 1996). Men who provide sexual services for women in exchange for money and gifts are called **gigolos.** The role of a gigolo is most similar to that of a call girl, because he usually acts as a social companion as well as a sexual partner. His customers are usually wealthy middle-aged women seeking the attentions of attractive young men. There is often a pretense, on the gigolo's part, of romantic interest in the woman. The exchange of money for services is less explicit than in most interactions between female prostitutes and male customers. It is unknown how common this type of male prostitution is, but it is probably far less common than female prostitution.

Gigolos Men who provide social companionship and sexual services to women for financial gain.

Male prostitutes who cater to homosexual men have not been studied as extensively as female prostitutes. Like female prostitutes, they can be classified into different groups. Street *hustlers* make contact with customers on the streets, in gay bars or bathhouses, or in public parks or restrooms (Friedman, 2003). Most hustlers come from chaotic family backgrounds and live in a social milieu of drug abuse and unstable personal relationships. One study found that male street hustlers lack knowledge about sexually transmitted diseases and do not take adequate precautions. As one young hustler said, "I always look them over, if they look clean like me, . . . then they are all right" (Calhoun & Weaver, 1996, p. 222). Male sex workers are increasingly operating through escort agencies, advertising, and the Internet (Minichiello et al., 2000). *Call boys* work similarly to call girls. They have regular customers and are often social companions as well as sexual partners. Call boys find their customers through advertisements (often in gay newspapers) or through personal referrals. *Kept boys* are partially or fully supported by an older male.

Economics and Profit from Prostitution

Many men and women who sell sexual services view their work as an economic opportunity. Recognizing the connection between prostitution and economic disadvantage, the 1959 United Nations Commission study of prostitution concluded that creating other economic opportunities for women is important for its prevention.

Although women and men usually become prostitutes to earn money for themselves, the practice also profits many other parties. In fact, it may not be as lucrative for the prostitute as it is for the other people involved, either directly or indirectly. Pimps, referral agents, hotel operators, and the criminal justice system all benefit financially from prostitution (Usry, 1995). The illegality of prostitution contributes to the prostitutes' need for a pimp. Pimps bail out the women in their "stables" from jail when they are arrested. They may offer companionship, a place to live, clothing, food, and in some cases, drugs. They often assume a highly controlling, authoritarian, sometimes abusive relationship with their prostitutes while being supported by the women's earnings. Pimps often buy ostentatious clothing and cars that represent the pimp's status and his prostitutes' earning power.

Referral agents also make money from prostitution. Cabdrivers, hotel desk clerks, and bartenders get cash tips from customers as well as from prostitutes for helping establish the contact. Prostitutes who work out of their apartments may have to give doormen, hotel proprietors, and elevator operators an ongoing supply of tips, high rental fees, or sexual services (or any combination thereof) so that they will not report them to the authorities. Where prostitution is legal, as in Nevada, taxes from brothel revenues contribute to the county budget, and brothel management maintains community support by donating generously to local projects.

Because prostitution is illegal, police officers, attorneys, judges, bail bondsmen, and jailers spend part of their work time attempting to control, litigate, or process prostitutes through the judicial bureaucracy. In this way prostitution provides some of the business for the criminal justice system. Prostitution "crackdowns" are often a sham, the main purpose of which is to create the impression of an active and efficient police department (Chapkis, 1997). Some people argue that the time and money spent in actions against prostitution impede the judicial system's effectiveness in working with more serious crimes.

▶ Summary

Pornography

- Written, visual, or spoken sexually explicit materials have been used for sexual arousal. (p. 582)

- Pornography is one of the first uses of technological developments. (p. 582)

- Soon after the printing press, photography, film, cable television, the VCR, and the Internet were developed, they were used to produce pornography. (pp. 582–583)

- Characteristics of erotica include mutual affection, respect, and pleasure. Unlike violent and degrading pornography, erotica has no known significant negative effects. (p. 585)

- A clear definition of obscenity has yet to be established by the judicial system. The criteria established by the Supreme Court in attempting to decide what is obscene are that the dominant theme of the work as a whole must appeal to prurient interest, be offensive to contemporary community standards, and be without serious literary, artistic, political, or scientific value. (p. 586)

- The U.S. Constitution's First Amendment guarantee of freedom of speech and freedom of the press does not apply categorically to obscene materials. (p. 587)
- The increased availability and legalization of pornography in Denmark were not followed by an increase in reported sex offenses. (p. 587)
- Data on the effects of pornography are conflicting. The 1970 report of the Commission on Obscenity and Pornography found that pornography did not have significant, long-lasting effects. The controversial 1986 report of the Attorney General's Commission on Pornography maintained that sexually violent and degrading pornography caused sexual aggression toward women. (pp. 587, 589)
- Research has found that nonsexual violence in media materials was associated with aggressive tendencies in men. However, the Meese Commission report ignored research in this area. (p. 589)
- Computer access to sexually explicit materials raises many issues related to censorship and the protection of children. (p. 590)

Prostitution
- Prostitution refers to the exchange of sexual services for money. Sex workers have diverse backgrounds and working conditions. Streetwalkers, women in brothels or massage parlors, and call girls are general categories of female prostitutes. (p. 590)
- Two alternatives to the criminal status of prostitution are legalization and decriminalization. (p. 592)
- Prostitutes most at risk of contracting or transmitting HIV are those who are injection drug users, have sexual partners who are injection drug users, or do not use condoms consistently during sexual encounters. (p. 594)
- Male prostitutes who service women are called gigolos. Male prostitutes who service homosexual men may be categorized as hustlers, call boys, or kept boys. (pp. 595–596)
- Women or men who turn to prostitution do so, in part, for economic opportunity. However, pimps, referral agents, hotel operators, and the criminal justice system also profit from prostitution. (p. 596)

► Suggested Readings

American Civil Liberties Union (1986). *Polluting the Censorship Debate.* Washington, DC: American Civil Liberties Union. A summary and critique of the Final Report of the Attorney General's Commission on Pornography.

Butler, Anne (1985). *Daughters of Joy, Sisters of Mercy.* Urbana: University of Illinois Press. A detailed book about the lives and the socioeconomic impact of prostitutes in the American West in the late 1800s.

Chapkis, Wendy (1997). *Live Sex Acts: Women Performing Erotic Labor.* New York: Routledge. A respectful study of and interviews with female sex workers and a comprehensive analysis of political and social issues.

Green, Richard (1992). *Sexual Science and the Law.* Cambridge, MA: Harvard University Press. An examination of sexuality in a legal context related to sexual privacy, prostitution, pornography, homosexuality, and abortion written by a lawyer and sex researcher.

Kilbourne, Jean (2000). *Can't Buy My Love: How Advertising Changes the Way We Think.* New York: Simon & Schuster. An in-depth analysis of how advertising trivializes sex with its pseudo-sexual images, romanticizes material possessions, and reinforces restrictive gender norms.

Lane, Frederick (2000). *Obscene Profits: The Entrepreneurs of Pornography in the Cyber Age.* New York: Routledge. A thorough, informative look at pornography and its rapid ascendancy through technology.

McElroy, Wendy (1995). *A Woman's Right to Pornography.* New York: St. Martin's Press. A book that emphasizes the importance to women of sexual free speech.

► Web Resources

Your *Our Sexuality* Web site **http://psychology.wadsworth.com/ crooksbaur9e/** has direct links to the Web sites described below. These links are checked often for changes, dead links, and new additions.

Prostitutes' Education Network
The Prostitutes' Education Network sponsors this Web site, which is devoted to providing information about legislative, health, and cultural issues as they affect prostitutes and other sex workers. The point of view is decidedly sympathetic to prostitution.

Prostitution Research and Education
The San Francisco Women's Centers sponsor this Web site, which provides articles and data on the exploitative nature of prostitution and the poor women victimized by it.

Online Free Speech
Sponsored by the Electronic Frontier Foundation (EFF), this Web site is devoted to the Blue Ribbon Campaign for Online Free Speech, a movement that vigorously opposes censorship on the Internet.

Our Sexuality Web Site
For online resources directly related to this book, go to **http://psychology.wadsworth.com/ crooksbaur9e**. You will find interactive exercises, study questions, chapter outlines, an online version of this text's glossary, and Web links and activities that complement your CD-ROM.

InfoTrac® College Edition Online Library
http://infotrac.thomsonlearning.com/
InfoTrac College Edition is an online searchable library that includes a multitude of journals, many of which are specific to human sexuality. These journals include *Archives of Sexual Behavior, Archives of Sexual Health Behavior, Canadian Journal of Human Sexuality, Hispanic Journal of the Behavioral Sciences, Journal of Cross-Cultural Psychology, Journal of Physical Education, Recreation, and Dance, Journal of Sex Research,* and *Sex Roles.*

Our Sexuality CD-ROM
Use your CD-ROM for further study of the concepts in this chapter. Your CD-ROM provides animations of difficult concepts, video clips of real people discussing sexuality, critical thinking questions, chapter quizzing, and more.

Epilogue

Throughout this textbook we have discussed sexual attitudes, ideals, and behaviors of the past and present. We have highlighted similarities and differences in the Western world and beyond and have emphasized the controversies inherent in sexual issues.

Finding one's way through the complex and conflicting perspectives related to human sexuality is both a personal and a societal challenge. We would like to close *Our Sexuality* with the Declaration of Sexual Rights, adopted by the World Association of Sexology,* as possible unifying guidelines:

Sexuality is an integral part of the personality of every human being. Its full development depends upon the satisfaction of basic human needs such as the desire for contact, intimacy, emotional expression, pleasure, tenderness and love.

Sexuality is constructed through the interaction between the individual and social structures. Full development of sexuality is essential for individual, interpersonal, and societal well-being.

Sexual rights are universal human rights based on the inherent freedom, dignity, and equality of all human beings. Since health is a fundamental human right, so must sexual health be a basic human right. In order to assure that human beings and societies develop healthy sexuality, the following sexual rights must be recognized, promoted, respected, and defended by all societies through all means.

Sexual health is the result of an environment that recognizes, respects and exercises these sexual rights:

1. **The right to sexual freedom.** Sexual freedom encompasses the possibility for individuals to express their full sexual potential. However, this excludes all forms of sexual coercion, exploitation and abuse at any time and situations in life.

2. **The right to sexual autonomy, sexual integrity, and safety of the sexual body.** This right involves the ability to make autonomous decisions about one's sexual life within a context of one's own personal and social ethics. It also encompasses control and enjoyment of our own bodies free from torture, mutilation and violence of any sort.

3. **The right to sexual privacy.** This involves the right for individual decisions and behaviors about intimacy as long as they do not intrude on the sexual rights of others.

4. **The right to sexual equity.** This refers to freedom from all forms of discrimination regardless of sex, gender, sexual orientation, age, race, social class, religion, or physical and emotional disability.

5. **The right to sexual pleasure.** Sexual pleasure, including autoeroticism, is a source of physical, psychological, intellectual and spiritual well-being.

6. **The right to emotional sexual expression.** Sexual expression is more than erotic pleasure or sexual acts. Individuals have a right to express their sexuality through communication, touch, emotional expression and love.

7. **The right to sexually associate freely.** This means the possibility to marry or not, to divorce, and to establish other types of responsible sexual associations.

8. **The right to make free and responsible reproductive choices.** This encompasses the right to decide whether or not to have children, the number and spacing of children, and the right to full access to the means of fertility regulation.

9. **The right to sexual information based upon scientific inquiry.** This right implies that sexual information should be generated through the process of unencumbered and yet scientifically ethical inquiry, and disseminated in appropriate ways at all societal levels.

10. **The right to comprehensive sexuality education.** This is a lifelong process from birth throughout the life cycle and should involve all social institutions.

11. **The right to sexual health care.** Sexual health care should be available for prevention and treatment of all sexual concerns, problems and disorders.

*Originally declared at the 13th World Congress of Sexology, 1997, Valencia, Spain. Revised and approved by the General Assembly of the World Association for Sexology (WAS) on August 26, 1999, during the 14th World Congress of Sexology, Hong Kong, and People's Republic of China. Reprinted with permission.

Glossary

Acquaintance rape Sexual assault by a friend, acquaintance, or date—that is, someone known to the victim.

Acquired immunodeficiency syndrome (AIDS) A catastrophic illness in which a virus (HIV) invades and destroys the ability of the immune system to fight disease.

Afterbirth The placenta and amniotic sac following their expulsion through the vagina after childbirth.

Amenorrhea The absence of menstruation.

Amniocentesis A procedure in which amniotic fluid is removed from the uterus and tested to determine whether certain fetal birth defects exist.

Amniotic fluid The fluid inside the amniotic sac surrounding the fetus during pregnancy.

Anaphrodisiac A substance that inhibits sexual desire and behavior.

Androgen insensitivity syndrome (AIS) A condition resulting from a genetic defect that causes chromosomally normal males to be insensitive to the action of testosterone and other androgens. These individuals develop female external genitals of normal appearance.

Androgens A class of hormones that promote the development of male genitals and secondary sex characteristics and influence sexual motivation in both sexes. These hormones are produced by the adrenal glands in males and females and by the testes in males.

Androgyny A blending of typical male and female behaviors in one individual.

Anilingus Oral stimulation of the anus.

Anorgasmia A sexual difficulty involving the absence of orgasm in women.

Antiandrogen drugs Drugs that block inappropriate sexual arousal patterns by lowering testosterone levels.

Aphrodisiac A substance that allegedly arouses sexual desire and increases the capacity for sexual activity.

Areola The darkened circular area surrounding the nipple of the breast.

Artificial insemination A medical procedure in which semen is placed in a woman's vagina, cervix, or uterus.

Assisted reproductive technology (ART) The techniques of extrauterine conception.

Attachment Intense emotional tie between two individuals, such as an infant and a parent or adult lovers.

Atypical sexual behaviors Behaviors not typically expressed by most people in our society.

Autoerotic asphyxia The enhancement of sexual excitement and orgasm by pressure-induced oxygen deprivation.

Autosomes The 22 pairs of human chromosomes that do not significantly influence sex differentiation.

Aversive conditioning A behavior therapy method that substitutes a negative response for positive responses to inappropriate stimuli.

Backup methods Using a second contraceptive method simultaneously with another method.

Bacterial vaginosis A vaginal infection caused by bacterial microorganisms that is the most common form of vaginitis among U.S. women.

Bartholin's glands Two small glands slightly inside the vaginal opening that secrete a few drops of fluid during sexual arousal.

Basal body temperature method A birth control method based on body temperature changes before and after ovulation.

Behavior therapy Therapy based on the assumption that maladaptive behavior has been learned and can therefore be unlearned.

Bisexuality Attraction to both same- and other-sex partners.

Blastocyst Multicellular descendant of the united sperm and ovum that implants on the wall of the uterus.

Bondage A sexual behavior in which a person derives sexual pleasure from being bound, tied up, or otherwise restricted.

Brothel A house in which a group of prostitutes work.

Calendar method A birth control method based on abstinence from intercourse during calendar-estimated fertile days.

Candidiasis An inflammatory infection of the vaginal tissues caused by the yeastlike fungus *Candida albicans*.

Case study A nonexperimental research method that examines either a single subject or a small group of subjects individually and in depth.

Castration Surgical removal of the testes.

Cavernous bodies The structures in the shaft of the clitoris and the penis that engorge with blood during sexual arousal.

Celibacy Historically defined as the state of being unmarried; currently defined as not engaging in sexual behavior.

Cerebral cortex The outer layer of the brain's cerebrum that controls higher mental processes.

Cerebral hemispheres The two sides (right and left) of the cerebrum.

Cerebrum The largest part of the brain, consisting of two cerebral hemispheres.

Cervix The small end of the uterus, located at the back of the vagina.

Cesarean section A childbirth procedure in which the infant is removed through an incision in the abdomen and uterus.

Chancre A raised, red, painless sore that is symptomatic of the primary phase of syphilis.

Chancroid A sexually transmitted bacterial disease characterized by small bumps in the region of the genitals, perineum, or anus that eventually rupture and form painful ulcers with a foul discharge.

Child sexual abuse An adult engaging in sexual contact of any kind with a child— inappropriate touching, oral–genital stimulation, coitus, and the like.

Chlamydia Urogenital infection caused by the bacterium Chlamydia trachomatis.

Chorionic villus sampling (CVS) A prenatal test that detects some birth defects.

Circumcision Surgical removal of the foreskin of the penis.

Climacteric Physiological changes that occur during the transition period from fertility to infertility in both sexes.

Clitoris A highly sensitive structure of the female external genitals, the only function of which is sexual pleasure.

Cognitive therapies Approaches to therapy that are based on the premise that most psychological disorders result from distortions in cognitions, or thoughts.

Cohabitation Living together and having a sexual relationship without being married.

Colostrum A thin fluid secreted by the breasts during later stages of pregnancy and the first few days after delivery.

Coming out The process of becoming aware of and disclosing one's homosexual identity.

Commitment The thinking component of Sternberg's triangular love theory.

Companionate love A type of love characterized by friendly affection and deep attachment based on extensive familiarity with the loved one.

Complete celibacy An expression of sexuality in which an individual does not engage in either masturbation or interpersonal sexual contact.

Condom A sheath that fits over the penis and is used for protection against unwanted pregnancy and sexually transmitted diseases.

Conjunctivitis Inflammation of the mucous membrane that lines the inner surface of the eyelid and the exposed surface of the eyeball.

Consensual extramarital relationship A sexual relationship that occurs outside the marriage bond with the consent of one's spouse.

Constant-dose combination pills Birth control pills that contain a constant daily dose of estrogen and progestin.

Conversion therapy, or sexual reorientation therapy Therapy to help homosexual men and women change their sexual orientation.

Coprophilia A sexual paraphilia in which a person obtains sexual arousal from contact with feces.

Corona The rim of the penile glans.

Corpus callosum The broad band of nerve fibers that connects the left and right cerebral hemispheres.

Corpus luteum A yellowish body that forms on the ovary at the site of the ruptured follicle and secretes progesterone.

Cowper's glands Two pea-sized glands located alongside the base of the urethra in the male that secrete an alkaline fluid during sexual arousal.

Crura The innermost tips of the cavernous bodies that connect to the pubic bones.

Cryptorchidism A condition in which the testes fail to descend from the abdominal cavity to the scrotal sac.

Cunnilingus Oral stimulation of the vulva.

Cystitis An infection of the bladder.

Date rape Sexual assault by an acquaintance when on a date.

Demographic bias A kind of sampling bias in which certain segments of society (such as white, middle-class, white-collar workers) are disproportionately represented in a study population.

Dependent variable In an experimental research design, an outcome or resulting behavior that the experimenter observes and records but does not control.

DHT-deficient male A chromosomally normal (XY) male who develops external genitalia resembling those of a female as a result of a genetic defect that prevents the prenatal conversion of testosterone into dihydrotestosterone (DHT).

Dilation and evacuation (D and E) An abortion procedure in which a curette and suction equipment are used.

Direct observation A method of research in which subjects are observed as they go about their activities.

Domestic partnership Unmarried couples living in the same household in committed relationships.

Dopamine A neurotransmitter that facilitates sexual arousal and activity.

Douching Rinsing out the vagina with plain water or a variety of solutions. It is usually unnecessary for hygiene, and too frequent douching can result in vaginal irritation.

Dysmenorrhea Pain or discomfort before or during menstruation.

Dyspareunia Pain or discomfort during intercourse.

Ectoparasites Parasitic organisms that live on the outer skin surfaces.

Ectopic pregnancy A pregnancy that occurs when a fertilized ovum implants outside the uterus, most commonly in the fallopian tube.

Effacement Flattening and thinning of the cervix that occurs before and during childbirth.

Either/or question A question that allows statement of a preference.

Ejaculation The process by which semen is expelled from the body through the penis.

Ejaculatory ducts Two short ducts located within the prostate gland.

Elective abortion Medical procedure performed to terminate pregnancy.

EMDR (eye movement desensitization and reprocessing) A therapy technique that combines eye movements with concentrating on the problem that may be helpful as a part of treatment for sexual difficulties.

Emission phase The first stage of male orgasm, in which the seminal fluid is gathered in the urethral bulb.

Endometriosis A condition in which uterine tissue grows on various parts of the abdominal cavity.

Endometrium The tissue that lines the inside of the uterine walls.

Epididymis The structure along the back of each testis in which sperm maturation occurs.

Episiotomy An incision in the perineum that is sometimes made during childbirth.

Erectile dysfunction (ED) Persistent lack of an erection sufficiently rigid for penetrative intercourse.

Erection The process by which the penis or clitoris engorges with blood and increases in size.

Erogenous zones Areas of the body that are particularly responsive to sexual stimulation.

Erotica Respectful, affectionate depictions of sexuality.

Estrogens A class of hormones that produce female secondary sex characteristics and affect the menstrual cycle.

Excitement phase Masters and Johnson's term for the first phase of the sexual response cycle, in which engorgement of the sexual organs and increases in muscle tension, heart rate, and blood pressure occur.

Exhibitionism The act of exposing one's genitals to an unwilling observer.

Experimental research Research conducted in precisely controlled laboratory conditions so that subjects' reactions can be reliably measured.

Expulsion phase The second stage of male orgasm, during which the semen is expelled from the penis by muscular contractions.

Extramarital relationship Sexual interaction by a married person with someone other than his or her spouse.

Failure rate The number of women out of 100 who become pregnant by the end of 1 year of using a particular contraceptive.

Faking orgasms A sexual difficulty in which a person pretends to experience orgasm during sexual interaction.

Fallopian tubes Two tubes, extending from the sides of the uterus, in which the egg and sperm travel.

Fellatio Oral stimulation of the penis.

Fertility awareness methods Birth control methods that use the signs of cyclic fertility to prevent or plan conception.

Fetal alcohol syndrome (FAS) Syndrome in infants caused by heavy maternal prenatal alcohol use; characterized by congenital heart defects, damage to the brain and nervous system, numerous physical malformations of the fetus, and below-normal IQ.

Fetally androgenized female A chromosomally normal (XX) female who, as a result of excessive exposure to androgens during prenatal sex differentiation, develops external genitalia resembling those of a male.

Fetishism A sexual behavior in which the person obtains sexual excitement primarily or exclusively from an inanimate object or a particular part of the body.

Fimbriae Fringelike ends of the fallopian tubes into which the released ovum enters.

First-stage labor The initial stage of childbirth in which regular contractions begin and the cervix dilates.

Follicle-stimulating hormone (FSH) A pituitary hormone secreted by a female during the secretory phase of the menstrual cycle. FSH stimulates the development of ovarian follicles. In males it stimulates sperm production.

Foreskin A covering of skin over the penile glans.

Frenulum A highly sensitive thin strip of skin that connects the glans to the shaft on the underside of the penis.

Frotteurism A fairly common paraphilia in which a person obtains sexual pleasure by pressing or rubbing against another in a crowded public place.

Gamete intrafallopian transfer (GIFT) Procedure in which the sperm and ova are placed directly in the fallopian tube.

Gay A homosexual, typically a homosexual male.

Gay affirmative therapy Therapy to help homosexual clients cope with negative societal attitudes.

Gender The psychological and sociocultural characteristics associated with our sex.

Gender assumptions Assumptions about how people are likely to behave based on their maleness or femaleness.

Gender dysphoria Unhappiness with one's biological sex or gender role.

Gender identity How one psychologically perceives oneself as either male or female.

Gender-identity disorder A disorder characterized by a cross-gender identification that produces persistent discomfort with one's sex and impaired functioning.

Gender nonconformity A lack of conformity to stereotypical masculine and feminine behaviors.

Gender role A collection of attitudes and behaviors that are considered normal and appropriate in a specific culture for people of a particular sex.

Genital warts Viral warts that appear on the genitals and are primarily transmitted sexually.

Gigolos Men who provide social companionship and sexual services to women for financial gain.

Giving permission Providing reassurance to one's partner that it is okay to talk about specific feelings or needs.

Glans The head of the clitoris or penis, which is richly endowed with nerve endings.

Gonadotropins Pituitary hormones that stimulate activity in the gonads (testes and ovaries).

Gonads The male and female sex glands—ovaries and testes.

Gonorrhea An STD that initially causes inflammation of mucous membranes.

Grafenberg spot Glands and ducts located in the anterior wall of the vagina. Some women experience sexual pleasure, arousal, orgasm, and an ejaculation of fluids from stimulation of the Grafenberg spot.

Gynecology The medical practice specializing in women's health and in diseases of the female reproductive and sexual organs.

Herpes A disease characterized by blisters on the skin in the regions of the genitals or mouth. It is caused by the Herpes simplex virus and is easily transmitted through sexual contact.

Highly active antiretroviral therapy (HAART) A strategy for treating HIV-infected people with three or more anti-retroviral drugs.

Homophobia Irrational fears of homosexuality, the fear of the possibility of homosexuality in oneself, or self-loathing toward one's own homosexuality.

Homosexual A person whose primary erotic, psychological, emotional, and social orientation is toward members of the same sex.

Hormone therapy (HT) The use of supplemental hormones during and after menopause or following surgical removal of the ovaries.

Human chorionic gonadotropin (HCG) A hormone that is detectable in the urine of a pregnant woman within 1 month of conception.

Human immunodeficiency virus (HIV) The immune-system-destroying virus that causes AIDS.

Hymen Tissue that partially covers the vaginal opening.

Hypoactive sexual desire (HSD) Lack of interest in sexual activity.

Hypogonadism Impaired hormone production in the testes that results in testosterone deficiency.

Hypothalamus A small structure located in the central core of the brain that controls the pituitary gland and regulates motivated behavior and emotional expression.

Hysterectomy Surgical removal of the uterus.

In vitro fertilization (IVF) Procedure in which mature eggs are removed from a woman's ovary and fertilized by sperm in a laboratory dish.

Incest Sexual contact between two people who are related (one of whom is often a child), other than husband and wife.

Independent variable In an experimental research design, a condition or component that is under the control of the researcher, who manipulates or determines its value.

Intersexed A term applied to people who possess biological attributes of both sexes.

Interstitial cells Cells located between the seminiferous tubules that are the major source of androgen in males.

Intimacy The emotional component of Sternberg's triangular love theory.

Intracytoplasmic sperm injection (ICSI) Procedure in which a sperm is injected into an egg.

Intrauterine device (IUD) A small, plastic device that is inserted into the uterus for contraception.

Introitus The opening to the vagina.

Intromission Insertion of the penis into the vagina.

Kegel exercises A series of exercises that strengthen the muscles underlying the external female or male genitals.

Klinefelter's syndrome A condition characterized by the presence of two X chromosomes and one Y chromosome (XXY) in which affected individuals have undersized external male genitals.

Klismaphilia An unusual variant in sexual expression in which an individual obtains sexual pleasure from receiving enemas.

Labia majora The outer lips of the vulva.

Labia minora The inner lips of the vulva, one on each side of the vaginal opening.

Lamaze A method of childbirth preparation using breathing and relaxation.

Late-term abortion, or intact dilation and evacuation An abortion done between 20 and 24 weeks, when serious health risks to the woman or fetal abnormalities exist.

Lesbian A female homosexual.

Limbic system A subcortical brain system composed of several interrelated structures that influences the sexual behavior of humans and other animals.

Lochia A reddish uterine discharge that occurs after childbirth.

Luteinizing hormone (LH) The hormone secreted by the pituitary gland that stimulates ovulation in the female. In males it is called interstitial cell hormone (ISCH) and stimulates production of androgens by the testes.

Male orgasmic disorder The inability of a man to ejaculate during sexual activity.

Mammary glands Glands in the female breast that produce milk.

Mammography A highly sensitive X-ray test for the detection of breast cancer.

Mastectomy Surgical removal of the breast(s).

Masturbation Stimulation of one's own genitals to create sexual pleasure.

Medical abortion The use of medications to end a pregnancy of 7 weeks or less.

Menarche The initial onset of menstrual periods in a young woman.

Menopause Cessation of menstruation as a result of the aging process or surgical removal of the ovaries.

Menstrual phase The phase of the menstrual cycle when menstruation occurs.

Menstrual synchrony Simultaneous menstrual cycles that sometimes occur among women who live in close proximity.

Menstruation The sloughing off of the built-up uterine lining that takes place if conception has not occurred.

Mere exposure effect The phenomenon by which repeated exposure to novel stimuli tends to increase an individual's liking for such stimuli.

Microbicide A topical gel or cream product that women can use vaginally to prevent or minimize the risk of being infected with HIV or other STDs.

Mons veneris A triangular mound over the pubic bone above the vulva.

Mucosa Collective term for the mucous membranes; moist tissue that lines certain body areas such as the penile urethra, vagina, and mouth.

Mucus method A birth control method based on determining the time of ovulation by means of the cyclical changes of the cervical mucus.

Multiple orgasms More than one orgasm experienced within a short time period.

Mutual empathy The underlying knowledge that each partner in a relationship cares for the other and knows that the care is reciprocated.

Myometrium The smooth muscle layer of the uterine wall.

Myotonia Muscle tension.

Necrophilia A rare sexual paraphilia in which a person obtains sexual gratification by viewing or having intercourse with a corpse.

Neuropeptide hormones Chemicals produced in the brain that influence sexuality and other behavioral functions.

Nipple The central pigmented area of the breast; it contains numerous nerve endings and milk ducts.

Nocturnal emission Involuntary ejaculation during sleep, also known as a wet dream.

Nocturnal orgasm Involuntary orgasm during sleep.

Noncoital sex Physical contact, including kissing, touching, and manual or oral-genital stimulation but excluding coitus.

Nonconsensual extramarital sex Sexual interaction in which a married person engages in an outside sexual relationship without the consent (or presumably the knowledge) of his or her spouse.

Nongonococcal urethritis (NGU) An inflammation of the urethral tube caused by organisms other than gonococcus.

Nonresponse The refusal to participate in a research study.

Obscenity A term that implies a personal or societal judgment that something is offensive.

Oophorectomy Surgical removal of the ovaries.

Open-ended question A question that allows a respondent to share any feelings or information she or he thinks is relevant.

Open marriage A marriage in which spouses, with each other's permission, have intimate relationships with other people as well as with the marital partner.

Orchidectomy The surgical procedure for removing the testes.

Orgasm A series of muscular contractions of the pelvic floor muscles occurring at the peak of sexual arousal.

Orgasmic reconditioning A behavior therapy technique in which a client is instructed to switch from paraphilic to healthy fantasies at the moment of masturbatory orgasm.

Os The opening in the cervix that leads to the interior of the uterus.

Outercourse Noncoital forms of sexual intimacy.

Ovaries Female gonads that produce ova and sex hormones.

Ovulation The release of a mature ovum from the ovary.

Ovum The female reproductive cell.

Oxytocin A neuropeptide produced in the hypothalamus that influences sexual response and interpersonal attraction.

Pap smear A screening test for cancer of the cervix.

Paraphilia A term used to describe uncommon types of sexual expression.

Paraphrasing A listener's summarization of the speaker's message in his or her own words.

Partial celibacy An expression of sexuality in which an individual does not engage in interpersonal sexual contact but continues to engage in masturbation.

Passing Presenting a false image of being heterosexual.

Passion The motivational component of Sternberg's triangular love theory.

Passionate love State of extreme absorption in another person. Also known as romantic love.

Pedophilia, or child molestation Sexual contact between an adult and a child who are not related.

Pelvic inflammatory disease (PID) An infection in the uterus and pelvic cavity.

Penis A male sexual organ consisting of the internal root and the external shaft and glans.

Perimenopause The time period before menopause when estrogen is decreasing.

Perimetrium The thin membrane covering the outside of the uterus.

Perineum The area between the vagina and anus of the female and the scrotum and anus of the male.

Peyronie's disease Abnormal fibrous tissue and calcium deposits in the penis.

Pheromones Certain odors produced by the body that relate to reproductive functions.

Phimosis A condition characterized by an extremely tight penile foreskin.

Physical attractiveness Physical beauty, which is a powerful factor in attracting lovers to each other.

Placenta A disk-shaped organ attached to the uterine wall and connected to the fetus by the umbilical cord. Nutrients, oxygen, and waste products pass between mother and fetus through the cell walls of the placenta.

Placenta previa A birth complication in which the placenta is between the cervical opening and the infant.

Plateau phase Masters and Johnson's term for the second phase of the sexual response cycle, in which muscle tension, heart rate, blood pressure, and vasocongestion increase.

Pornography Visual and written materials of a sexual nature that are used for purposes of sexual arousal.

Postpartum depression (PPD) Symptoms of depression and obsessive thoughts of hurting the baby.

Postpartum period The first several weeks after childbirth.

Posttraumatic stress disorder (PTSD) A psychological disorder caused by exposure to overwhelmingly painful events.

Premature ejaculation (PE) A sexual difficulty in which a man ejaculates so rapidly as to impair his own or his partner's pleasure.

Premenstrual dysphoric disorder (PMDD) Premenstrual symptoms severe enough to significantly disrupt a woman's functioning.

Premenstrual syndrome (PMS) Symptoms of physical discomfort and emotional irritability that occur 2 to 12 days before menstruation.

Prepared childbirth Birth following an education process that can involve information, exercises, breathing, and working with a labor coach.

Prepuce The foreskin or fold of skin over the clitoris.

Primary erogenous zones Areas of the body that contain dense concentrations of nerve endings.

Prodromal symptoms Symptoms that give advance warning of an impending herpes eruption.

Progestational compounds A class of hormones, including progesterone, that are produced by the ovaries.

Progestin-only pills Contraceptive pills that contain a small dose of progestin and no estrogen.

Proliferative phase The phase of the menstrual cycle in which the ovarian follicles mature.

Prostaglandins Hormones that are used to induce uterine contractions and fetal expulsion for second-trimester abortions.

Prostate gland A gland located at the base of the bladder that produces about 30% of the seminal fluid released during ejaculation.

Prostitution The exchange of sexual services for money.

Proximity The geographic nearness of one person to another, which is an important factor in interpersonal attraction.

Pseudohermaphrodites Individuals whose gonads match their chromosomal sex but whose internal and external reproductive anatomy has a mixture of male and female structures or structures that are incompletely male or female.

Psychosexual therapy Treatment designed to help clients gain awareness of their unconscious thoughts and feelings that contribute to their sexual problems.

Psychosocial Refers to a combination of psychological and social factors.

Psychotherapy A noninvasive procedure involving verbal interaction between a client and a therapist that is designed to improve a person's adjustment to life.

Puberty A period of rapid physical changes in early adolescence during which the reproductive organs mature.

Pubic lice Lice that primarily infest the pubic hair and are transmitted by sexual contact.

Random sample A randomly chosen subset of a population.

Rape Sexual intercourse that occurs without consent as a result of actual or threatened force.

Reciprocity The principle which states that when we are recipients of expressions of liking or loving, we tend to respond in kind.

Refractory period The period of time following orgasm in the male during which he cannot experience another orgasm.

Representative sample A type of limited research sample that provides an accurate representation of a larger target population of interest.

Resolution phase The fourth phase of the sexual response cycle, as outlined by Masters and Johnson, in which the sexual systems return to their nonexcited state.

Retrograde ejaculation The process by which semen is expelled into the bladder instead of out of the penis.

Root The portion of the penis that extends internally into the pelvic cavity.

Rugae The folds of tissue in the vagina.

Sadomasochistic behavior The association of sexual expression with pain.

Satiation therapy A technique for reducing arousal to inappropriate stimuli by first masturbating to orgasm while imagining appropriate stimuli and then continuing to masturbate while fantasizing about paraphilic images.

Scabies An ectoparasitic infestation of tiny mites.

Scrotum The pouch of skin of the external male genitals that encloses the testes.

Seasonale Birth control pills that reduce menstrual periods to four times a year.

Second-stage labor The middle stage of labor, in which the infant descends through the vaginal canal.

Secondary erogenous zones Areas of the body that have become erotically sensitive through learning and experience.

Secondary sex characteristics The physical characteristics other than genital development that indicate sexual maturity, such as body hair, breasts, and deepened voice.

Secretory phase The phase of the menstrual cycle in which the corpus luteum develops and secretes progesterone.

Self-selection The bias introduced into a research study results because of participants' willingness to respond.

Semen or seminal fluid A viscous fluid ejaculated through the penis that contains sperm and fluids from the prostate, seminal vesicles, and Cowper's glands.

Seminal vesicles Small glands adjacent to the terminals of the vas deferens that secrete an alkaline fluid (conducive to sperm motility) that constitutes the greatest portion of the volume of seminal fluid released during ejaculation.

Seminiferous tubules Thin, coiled structures in the testes in which sperm are produced.

Sensate focus A process of touching and communication used to enhance sexual pleasure and to reduce performance pressure.

Serotonin A neurotransmitter that inhibits sexual arousal and activity.

Sex Biological maleness and femaleness.

Sex chromosomes A single set of chromosomes that influences biological sex determination.

Sex flush A pink or red rash that can appear on the chest or breasts during sexual arousal.

Sexology The study of sexuality.

Sexual aversion disorder Extreme and irrational fear of sexual activity.

Sexual harassment Unwelcome sexual advances, requests for sexual favors, and other verbal or physical conduct of a sexual nature in the workplace or academic setting.

Sexual masochism The act of obtaining sexual arousal through receiving physical or psychological pain.

Sexual orientation Sexual attraction to one's own sex (homosexual) or the other sex (heterosexual).

Sexual sadism The act of obtaining sexual arousal through giving physical or psychological pain.

Sexual scripts Culturally learned ways of behaving in sexual situations.

Sexually transmitted diseases (STDs) Diseases that are transmitted by sexual contact.

Shaft The length of the clitoris or the penis between the glans and the body.

Similarity The similarity of beliefs, interests, and values, which is a factor in attracting people to one another.

Smegma A cheesy substance of glandular secretions and skin cells that sometimes accumulates under the foreskin of the penis or the hood of the clitoris.

Social skills training Training designed to teach socially inept clients the skills necessary to initiate and maintain satisfying relationships.

Socialization The process by which our society conveys behavioral expectations to the individual.

Speculum An instrument used to open the vaginal walls during a gynecological exam.

Sperm The male reproductive cell.

Spermatic cord A cord attached to the testis that contains the vas deferens, blood vessels, nerves, and cremasteric muscle fibers.

Spongy body A cylinder that forms a bulb at the base of the penis, extends up into the penile shaft, and forms the penile glans.

Spontaneous abortion, or miscarriage The spontaneous expulsion of the fetus from the uterus early in pregnancy, before it can survive on its own.

Standard days method A birth control method that requires couples to avoid unprotected intercourse for a 12-day period in the middle of the menstrual cycle.

Statutory rape Intercourse with a person under the age of consent.

Stereotype A generalized notion of what a person is like based only on that person's sex, race, religion, ethnic background, or similar criterion.

Steroid hormones The sex hormones and the hormones of the adrenal cortex.

Stop–start technique A treatment technique for premature ejaculation, consisting of stimulating the penis to the point of impending orgasm and then stopping until the preejaculatory sensations subside.

Stranger rape Rape of a person by an unknown assailant.

Suction curettage A procedure in which the cervical os is dilated using graduated metal dilators or a laminaria; then a small plastic tube, attached to a vacuum aspirator, is inserted into the uterus, drawing the fetal tissue, placenta, and built-up uterine lining out of the uterus.

Surrogate mother A woman who is artificially inseminated by the male partner in a childless couple, carries the pregnancy to term, delivers the child, and gives it to the couple for adoption.

Survey A research method in which a sample of people are questioned about their behaviors and/or attitudes.

Swinging The exchange of marital partners for sexual interaction.

Syphilis A sexually transmitted disease caused by a spirochete called *Treponema pallidum.*

Systems therapy Treatment that focuses on interactions within a couple relationship and on the functions of the sexual problems in the relationship.

Testes Male gonads inside the scrotum that produce sperm and sex hormones.

Third-stage labor The last stage of childbirth, in which the placenta separates from the uterine wall and comes out of the vagina.

Toxemia A dangerous condition during pregnancy in which high blood pressure occurs.

Toxic shock syndrome (TSS) A disease that occurs most commonly in menstruating women and that can cause a person to go into shock.

Trachoma A chronic, contagious form of conjunctivitis caused by chlamydia infections.

Transcervical sterilization A method of female sterilization using a tiny coil that is inserted through the vagina, cervix, and uterus into the fallopian tubes.

Transgendered A term applied to people whose appearance and/or behaviors do not conform to traditional gender roles.

Transsexual A person whose gender identity is opposite to his or her biological sex.

Transvestic fetishism A sexual behavior in which a person derives sexual arousal from wearing clothing of the other sex.

Tribadism Rubbing one's genitals against another's body or genitals.

Trichomoniasis A form of vaginitis caused by the one-celled protozoan *Trichomonas vaginalis.*

Triphasic pills Birth control pills that vary the dosages of estrogen and progestin during the cycle.

True hermaphrodites Exceedingly rare individuals who have both ovarian and testicular tissue in their bodies; their external genitals are often a mixture of male and female structures.

Tubal sterilization Female sterilization accomplished by severing or tying the fallopian tubes.

Turner's syndrome A relatively rare condition, characterized by the presence of one unmatched X chromosome (XO), in which affected individuals have normal female external genitals but their internal reproductive structures do not develop fully.

Unrequited love The experience of one person loving someone who does not return that love.

Urethra The tube through which urine passes from the bladder to outside the body.

Urethritis An inflammation of the urethral tube.

Urology The medical specialty dealing with reproductive health and genital diseases of the male and urinary tract diseases in both sexes.

Urophilia A sexual paraphilia in which a person obtains sexual arousal from contact with urine.

Uterus A pear-shaped organ inside the female pelvis, within which the fetus develops.

Vagina A stretchable canal in the female that opens at the vulva and extends about 4 inches into the pelvis.

Vaginal spermicides Foam, cream, jelly, suppositories, and film that contain a chemical that kills sperm.

Vaginismus A sexual difficulty in which a woman experiences involuntary spasmodic contractions of the muscles of the outer third of the vagina.

Vaginitis Inflammation of the vaginal walls caused by a variety of vaginal infections.

Validating The process of indicating that a partner's point of view is reasonable.

Varicocele A damaged or enlarged vein in the testis or vas deferens.

Vas deferens A sperm-carrying tube that begins at the testis and ends at the urethra.

Vasectomy Male sterilization procedure that involves removing a section from each vas deferens.

Vasocongestion The engorgement of blood vessels in particular body parts in response to sexual arousal.

Vasovasostomy Surgical reconstruction of the vas deferens to reverse a vasectomy.

Vernix caseosa A waxy, protective substance on the fetus's skin.

Vestibular bulbs Two bulbs, one on each side of the vaginal opening, that engorge with blood during sexual arousal.

Vestibule The area of the vulva inside the labia minora.

Viral hepatitis A disease in which liver function is impaired by a viral infection.

Viral load The amount of HIV present in an infected person's blood.

Voyeurism The act of obtaining sexual gratification by observing undressed or sexually interacting people without their consent.

Vulva The external genitals of the female, including the pubic hair, mons veneris, labia majora, labia minora, clitoris, and urinary and vaginal openings.

Yes/no question A question that asks for a one-word answer (yes or no) and thus provides little opportunity for discussing an issue.

Zoophilia A paraphilia in which a person has sexual contact with animals.

Zygote The single cell resulting from the union of sperm and egg cells.

Zygote intrafallopian transfer (ZIFT) Procedure in which the egg is fertilized in the laboratory and then placed in the fallopian tube.

Bibliography

AAUW (American Association of University Women) (1992). *Shortchanging Girls, Shortchanging America.* Washington, DC: American Association of University Women.

Abbey, A., Clinton-Sherrod, A., McAuslan, P., Zawacki, T., & Buck, P. (2003). The relationship between the quantity of alcohol consumed and the severity of sexual assaults committed by college men. *Journal of Interpersonal Violence, 18,* 813–833.

Abbey, A., McAuslan, P., & Ross, L. (1998). Sexual assault perpetuation by college men: The role of alcohol, misperception of sexual intent, and sexual beliefs and experiences. *Journal of Social and Clinical Psychology, 17,* 167–195.

Abbott, E. (2000). *A History of Celibacy.* New York: Scribner.

Abel, G. (1981). *The Evaluation and Treatment of Sexual Offenders and Their Victims.* Paper presented at St. Vincent Hospital and Medical Center, Portland, Oregon, October 15.

Abel, G. (2000). *How to Avoid Professional Sexual Misconduct.* Paper presented at the 32nd Annual Conference of the American Association of Sex Educators, Counselors, and Therapists, Atlanta, Georgia, May 10–14.

Abel, G., Barlow, D., Blanchard, E., & Guild, D. (1977). The components of rapists' sexual arousal. *Archives of General Psychiatry, 34,* 895–903.

Abel, G., Becker, J., & Cunningham-Ratder, J. (1984). Complications, consent, and cognitions in sex between children and adults. *International Journal of Law and Psychiatry, 7,* 89–103.

Abel, G., & Osborn, C. (2000). The paraphilias. In M. Gelder, J. Lopez-Ibor, & N. Andreasen (Eds.), *New Oxford Textbook of Psychiatry.* Oxford: Oxford University Press.

Abel, G., Osborn, C., Anthony, D., & Gardos, P. (1992). Current treatment of paraphiliacs. *Annual Review of Sex Research, 3,* 255–290.

Abou-Donia, M., Suliman, H., Khan, W., & Abdel-Rahman, S. (2003). Testicular germ-cell apoptosis in stressed rates following combined exposure to pyridostigmine bromide,N,N-diethyl m-toluamide (Deet), and permethrin. *Journal of Toxicology and Environmental Health, 66,* 57–63.

Abrahams, J. (1982). Azoospermia before puberty. *Medical Aspects of Human Sexuality, 1,* 13.

Abramowicz, M. (Ed.) (1994). Drugs for sexually transmitted diseases. *The Medical Letter, 36,* 1–6.

Abrams, J. (2003). *Bush to Sign Partial Birth Abortion Bill.* Retrieved October 23, 2003, from http://www.guardian.co.uk/uslatest/story/0,1282,3296103,00.html

Absi-Semaan, N., Crombie, G., & Freeman, C. (1993). Masculinity and femininity in middle childhood: Developmental and factor analysis. *Sex Roles, 28,* 187–202.

Ackard, D., & Neumark-Sztainer, D. (2001). Health care information sources for adolescents: Age and gender differences on use, concerns, and needs. *Journal of Adolescent Health, 29,* 170–176.

Acker, M., & Davis, M. (1992). Intimacy, passion, and commitment in adult romantic relationships: A test of the triangular theory of love. *Journal of Social and Personal Relationships, 9,* 21–50.

Ackerman, M., Montague, D., & Morganstern, S. (1994). Impotence: Help for erectile dysfunction. *Patient Care,* March, 22–56.

Acosta-Belen, E., & Bose, C. (2003). U.S. Latinas: Active at the intersections of gender, nationality, race, and class. In R. Morgan (Ed.), *Sisterhood Is Forever.* New York: Washington Square Press.

Adam, B., Sears, A., & Schellenberg, E. (2000). Accounting for unsafe sex: Interviews with men who have sex with men. *Journal of Sex Research, 37,* 24–36.

Adami, H., & Trichopoulos, D. (2002). Cervical cancer and the elusive male factor. *New England Journal of Medicine, 346,* 1160–1161.

Adams, B. (2003). Keeping it up. *The Advocate,* November 11, 38–40.

Adams, F. (1987). The role of prostitution in AIDS and other STDs. *Medical Aspects of Human Sexuality, 21,* 27–33.

Adams, N., & Bettis, P. (2003). Commanding the room in short skirts: Cheering as the embodiment of ideal girlhood. *Gender and Society, 17,* 73–91.

Adams, S., Jr., Dubbert, P., Chupurdia, K., Jones, A., Jr., Lofland, K., & Leermakers, E. (1996). Assessment of sexual beliefs and information in aging couples with sexual dysfunction. *Archives of Sexual Behavior, 25,* 249–260.

Adamson, A. (2003). *Scents to Raise Your . . . Blood Pressure.* Retrieved April 5, 2003, from http://www.philly.com/mld/philly/living/food/5161648.htm

Addiego, F., Belzer, E., Comolli, J., Moger, W., Perry, J., & Whipple, B. (1981). Female ejaculation: A case study. *Journal of Sex Research, 17,* 13–21.

Adducci, C., & Ross, L. (1991). Common urethral injuries in men. *Medical Aspects of Human Sexuality,* October, 32–44.

Adelman, W., & Joffe, A. (2000). Revisiting the adolescent male genital examination. *Patient Care,* February, 83–98.

Adler, C. (1985). An exploration of self-reported sexually aggressive behavior. *Crime and Delinquency, 31,* 306–331.

Adler, N., Hendrick, S., & Hendrick, C. (1989). Male sexual preference and attitudes toward love and sexuality. *Journal of Sex Education and Therapy, 12,* 27–30.

Adler, N., Ozer, E., & Tschann, J. (2003). Abortion among adolescents. *American Psychologist, 58,* 211–217.

Agbayani-Siewert, P. (2004). Assumptions of Asian American similarity: The case of Filipino and Chinese students. *Social Work, 49,* 39–51.

Agger, I., & Jensen, S. (1994). Sexuality as a tool of political repression. In H. Riguelme (Ed.), *Era in Twilight: Psychocultural Situation Under State Terrorism in Latin America.* Bilbao, Spain: Instituto Horizonte.

Agnew, J. (2000). Klismaphilia. *Venereology, 13,* 75–79.

Ahdieh-Grant, L., Yamashita, T., Phair, J., Detels, R., Wolinsky, S., Margolick, J., Rinaldo, C., & Jacobson, L. (2003). When to initiate highly active antiretroviral therapy: A cohort approach. *American Journal of Epidemiology, 157,* 738–746.

Ahmed, H., Mbwana, J., Gunnarsson, E., Ahlman, K., Guerino, C., Svensson, L., Mhalu, F., & Lagergard, T. (2003). Etiology of genital ulcer disease and association with human immunodeficiency virus infections in two Tanzanian cities. *Sexually Transmitted Diseases, 30,* 114–119.

Ainsworth, M. (1979). Infant–mother attachment. *American Psychologist, 34,* 932–937.

Ainsworth, M. (1989). Attachments beyond infancy. *American Psychologist, 44,* 709–716.

Ainsworth, M., Blehar, M., Waters, E., & Walls, S. (1978). *Patterns of Attachment: A Psychological Study of the Strange Situation.* Hillsdale, NJ: Erlbaum.

Akert, J. (2003). A new generation of contraceptives. *RN, 66,* 54–61.

Alan Guttmacher Institute (1999). *Teenage Pregnancy: Overall Trends and State-by-State Information.* New York: Author.

Alan Guttmacher Institute. (2002). *Facts in Brief: Contraceptive Use.* Retrieved June 20, 2003, from http://www.agi-usa.org/pubs/fb_contr/use.html

Albarracin, D., McNatt, P., Klein, C., Ho, R., Mitchell, A., & Kumkale, G. (2003). Persuasive communications to change actions: An analysis of behavioral and cognitive impact in HIV prevention. *Health Psychology, 22,* 166–177.

Albert, A., Warner, D., & Hatcher, R. (1998). Facilitating condom use with clients during commercial sex in Nevada's legal brothels. *American Journal of Public Health, 88(4),* 64.

Albertsen, P., Aaronson, N., Muller, M., Keller, S., & Ware, J. (1997). Health-related quality of life among patients with metastatic prostate cancer. *Urology, 49,* 207–217.

Alexander, C., Sipski, M., & Findley, T. (1994). Sexual activities, desire, and satisfaction in males pre- and post-spinal cord injury. *Archives of Sexual Behavior, 22,* 217–228.

Alexander, G. (2003). An evolutionary perspective of sex-typed toy preferences: Pink, blue, and the brain. *Archives of Sexual Behavior, 32,* 7–14.

Alexander, N. (2003). No pill, but other male birth control likely in not-too-distant future. *Contemporary Sexuality,* January, 8.

Al-Khan, A., Colon, J., Palta, V., & Bardequez, A. (2003). Assisted reproductive technology for men and women infected with human immunodeficiency virus type I. *Clinical Infectious Diseases, 36,* 195–200.

Al-Krenawi, A., & Wiesel-Lev, R. (1999). Attitudes toward and perceived psychosocial impact of female circumcision as practiced among the Bedouin-Arabs of the Negev. *Family Process, 38,* 431–443.

Allen, J. (2003). Return of silicone breast implants stirs debate. *Sunday Oregonian,* January 26, L5.

Allen, J., Leadbeater, B., & Aber, J. (1990). The relationship of adolescents' expectations and values to delinquency, hard drug use, and unprotected sexual intercourse. *Development and Psychopathology, 2,* 85–98.

Allen, L., & Gorski, R. (1990). Sex difference in the bed nucleus of the stria terminalis of the human brain. *Journal of Comparative Neurology, 302,* 697–706.

Allen, L., Hines, M., Shryne, J., & Gorski, R. (1989). Two sexually dimorphic cell groups. *Journal of Neurosciences, 9,* 497–506.

Allen, L., Richey, M., Chai, Y., & Gorski, R. (1991). Sex differences in the corpus callosum of the living human being. *Journal of Neuroscience, 11,* 933–942.

Allgeier, E. (1981). The influence of androgynous identification on heterosexual relations. *Sex Roles, 7,* 321–330.

Alonzo, D. (2003). *Dancing in the Autumn Light: Gay Men, Sexuality, and the Mid-Life Transition.* Paper presented at the Western Region Annual Conference Society for the Scientific Study of Sexuality, Los Angeles, April.

Alperstein, L. (2001). *For Two: Some Basic Perspectives and Skills for Couples Therapy.* Paper presented at the 33rd Annual Conference of the American Association of Sex Educators, Counselors, and Therapists, San Francisco, May 2–6.

Alter, J. (1996). The right to be wrong. *Newsweek,* December 23, 64.

Althaus, F. (1994). Age at which young men initiate intercourse is tied to sex education and mother's presence in the home. *Family Planning Perspectives, 26,* 141–143.

Althof, S. (2000). Erectile dysfunction: Psychotherapy with men and couples. In S. Leiblum & R. Rosen (Eds.), *Principles and Practice of Sex Therapy.* New York: Guilford Press.

Altman, C. (1999). Gay and lesbian seniors: Unique challenges of coming out in later life. *SIECUS Report, 27,* 14–17.

Altman, L. (2002). Inexpensive drug prevents HIV in newborns, study shows. *The Oregonian,* July 14, AJO.

Alzate, H. (1990). Vaginal erogeneity, the "G spot," and "female ejaculation." *Journal of Sex Education and Therapy, 16,* 137–140.

Amato, P. (2001). What children learn from divorce. *Population Today, 29,* 1.

Amato, P., Johnson, D., Booth, A., & Rogers, S. (2003). Continuity and change in marital quality between 1980 and 2000. *Journal of Marriage and the Family, 65,* 1–22.

Amato, P., & Previti, D. (2003). People's reasons for divorcing: Gender, social class, the life course, and adjustment. *Journal of Family Issues, 24,* 602–626.

American Academy of Pediatrics (2001a). Adolescents and human immunodeficiency virus infection: The role of the pediatrician in prevention and intervention. *Pediatrics, 107,* 188–190.

American Academy of Pediatrics. (2001b). *Sexuality, Contraception, and the Media.* Retrieved January 29, 2001, from http://www.aap.org/policy/re0038.html

American Cancer Society. (2003). *How is Breast Cancer Staged?* Retrieved June 11, 2003, from http://www.cancer.org/docroot/CRI/content/CRI_2_4_3X_How_is_breast_cancer_staged_5.asp?sitearea=CRI

American Civil Liberties Union (1986). *Polluting the Censorship Debate.* Washington, DC: American Civil Liberties Union.

American Civil Liberties Union. (2003). *Senate Passes First-Ever Federal Ban on Safe Abortion Procedures; ACLU Promises Lawsuit to Protect Women and Doctors.* Retrieved October 26, 2003, from http://www.aclu.org/neews/NewsPrint.cfm?ID=14161&c=148

American Psychiatric Association (2000). *Diagnostic and Statistical Manual of Mental Disorders* (4th ed., Text Revision). Washington, DC: American Psychiatric Association.

American Psychological Association. (2002, June 17). *Televised Sex Impairs Memory for TV Ads Just Like Violence Does.* Retrieved from http://www.newswise.com/articles/2002/6/TVADS.PSY.html

Ammann, A. (2000). HIV in China: An opportunity to halt an emerging epidemic. *AIDS Patient Care and STDs, 14,* 109–112.

Amnesty International. (2003, March 13). *Egypt: Free Those Imprisoned for Their Sexual Orientation.* Retrieved May 6, 2003, from http://web.amnesty.org/library/index/ENGMDE120092003

Anand, M. (1991). *The Art of Sexual Ecstasy.* Los Angeles: Tarcher.

Anderson, K., Cooper, H., & Okamura, L. (1997). Individual differences and attitudes toward rape: A meta-analytic review. *Personality and Social Psychology Bulletin, 23,* 295–315.

Anderson, S., Dallal, G., & Must, A. (2003). Relative weight and race influence average age at menarche: Results from two nationally representative surveys of U.S. girls studied 25 years apart. *Pediatrics, 111,* 844–850.

Anderson, S., & Holliday, M. (2003). *Normative Passing in the Lesbian Community: An Exploratory Study.* Paper presented at the Portland State University symposium "Constructing Solutions: Blueprints for Social Work Practice," Tualatin, Oregon, May.

Anderson-Hunt, M., & Dennerstein, L. (1994). Increased female sexual response after oxytocin. *British Medical Journal, 309,* 929.

Andrews, A., & Patterson, E. (1995). Searching for solutions to alcohol and other drug abuse during pregnancy: Ethics, values, and constitutional principles. *Journal of the National Association of Social Workers, 40,* 55–63.

Andrews, B., Brewin, C. Rose, S., & Kirk, M. (2000). Predicting PTSD symptoms in victims of violent crime: The role of shame, anger, and childhood abuse. *Journal of Abnormal Psychology, 109,* 69–73.

Andrews, L., & Elster, N. (2000). Regulating reproductive technologies. *Journal of Legal Medicine, 21,* 35–65.

Angier, N. (1996). Intersexual healing: An anomaly finds a group. *New York Times,* February 4, E14.

Angier, N. (1999). *Woman: An Intimate Geography.* Boston: Houghton Mifflin.

Annon, J. (1974). *The Behavioral Treatment of Sexual Problems,* v. 1. Honolulu: Enabling Systems.

Anti-Defamation League. (2003). *State Hate Crime Statutory Provisions.* Retrieved from http://www.adl.org/99hatecrime/intro.asp.com

Apfelbaum, B. (2000). Retarded ejaculation: A much misunderstood syndrome. In S. Leiblum & R. Rosen (Eds.), *Principles and Practice of Sex Therapy.* New York: Guilford Press.

Apperloo, M., Van Der Stege, J., Hoek, A., & Schultz, W. (2003). In the mood for sex: The value of androgens. *Journal of Sex and Marital Therapy, 29,* 87–102.

Apt, C. (1996). *Outcome Research on the Treatment of Female Sexual Disorders.* Paper presented at the 21st annual meeting of the Society for Sex Therapy and Research, Miami, March.

Apt, C., Hurlbert, D., & Powell, D. (1993). Men with hypoactive sexual desire disorder: The role of interpersonal dependency and assertiveness. *Journal of Sex Education and Therapy, 19(2),* 108–116.

Ards, A. (2000). Dating and mating. *Ms.,* June–July, 10.

Arevalo, M., Jenning, V., & Sinai, I. (2002). Efficacy of a new method of family planning: The standard days method. *Contraception, 65,* 333–338.

Argiolas, A. (1999). Neuropeptides and sexual behavior. *Neuroscience Biobehavioral Review, 23,* 1127–1142.

Armstrong, K., Eisen, A., & Weber, B. (2000). Assessing the risk of breast cancer. *New England Journal of Medicine, 342,* 564–571.

Armstrong, S. (2003). Not my daughter. *Ms.,* Summer, 22–23.

Arndt, W. (1991). *Gender Disorders and the Paraphilias.* Madison, CT: International Universities Press.

Aronson, A. (1998). Arabesque: A new twist on the romance novel. *Ms.,* March–April, 77–78.

Arriaga, X., & Rusbult, C. (1998). Standing in my partner's shoes: Partner perspective taking and reactions to accommodate dilemmas. *Personality and Social Psychology Bulletin, 24,* 927–948.

Arvin, A., & Prober, C. (1997). Herpes simplex virus type 2: A persistent problem. *New England Journal of Medicine, 337,* 1158–1159.

Aspelmeier, J., & Kerns, K. (2003). Love and school: Attachment/ exploration dynamics in college. *Journal of Social and Personal Relationships, 20,* 5–30.

Assalian, P. (1996). *Research Outcome in Sex Therapy.* Paper presented at the 21st annual meeting of the Society for Sex Therapy and Research, Miami, March.

Athanasiou, R., Shaver, P., & Tavris, C. (1970). Sex. *Psychology Today,* July, 39–52.

Atlas, J. (1999). The loose canon: Why higher learning has embraced pornography. *The New Yorker,* March 29, 60–65.

Atwood, J., & Seifer, M. (1997). Extramarital affairs and constructed meanings: A social constructionist therapeutic approach. *American Journal of Family Therapy, 25,* 55–75.

Aucoin, D. (2000). Feminist report says "sexist stereotypes" abound in prime time. *The Oregonian,* May 25, E9.

Augenbraun, M. (2000). Treatment of latent and tertiary syphilis. *Hospital Practice,* April 15, 89–95.

Austoni, E., & Guarneri, G. (1999). Penile elongation and thickening: A myth? Is there a cosmetic or medical indication? *Andrologia, 31(suppl. 1),* 45–51.

Avecilla-Palau, A., & Moreno, V. (2003). Uterine factors and risk of pregnancy in IUD users: A nested case–control study. *Contraception, 67,* 235–239.

Avis, N., Stellato, R., & Crawford, S. (2001). Is there a menopausal syndrome? Menopausal status and symptoms across racial/ethnic groups. *Social Science and Medicine, 52,* 345–356.

Azar, B. (1997). Environment can mitigate differences in spatial ability. *APA Monitor, 28,* 28.

Baba, T., Trichel, A., An, L., Liska, V., Martin, L., Murphey-Corb, M., & Ruprecht, R. (1997). Infection and AIDS in adult macaques after non-traumatic oral exposure to cell-free SIV. *Science, 272,* 1486–1489.

Bachman, L., Macaluso, M., & Hook, E. (2003). Demonstration of declining community prevalence of chlamydia trachomatis infection using sentinel surveillance. *Sexually Transmitted Diseases, 30,* 20–24.

Bachmann, G. (1991). Sexual dysfunction in the older woman. *Medical Aspects of Human Sexuality,* February, 42–45.

Bachmann, G., & Nevadansky, N. (2000). Diagnosis and treatment of atrophic vaginitis. *American Family Physician, 61,* 3090–3096.

Backman, T., Rauramo, I., & Huhtala, S. (2004). Pregnancy during the use of levonorgestrel intrauterine system. *American Journal of Obstetrics and Gynecology, 190,* 50–54.

Bacon, C., Mittleman, M., Kawachi, I., Giovannucci, E., Gasser, D., & Rimm, E. (2003). Sexual function in men older than 50 years of age: Results from the health professionals follow-up study. *Annals of Internal Medicine, 139,* 161–168.

Bagley, C., Bolitho, F., & Bertrand, L. (1997). Sexual assault in school, mental health and suicidal behaviors in adolescent women in Canada. *Adolescence, 32,* 361–366.

Bailey, J., & Bell, A. (1993). Familiality of female and male homosexuality. *Behavior Genetics, 23,* 313–322.

Bailey, J., & Benishay, D. (1993). Familial aggregation of female sexual orientation. *American Journal of Psychiatry, 150,* 272–277.

Bailey, J., Bobrow, D., Wolfe, M., & Mikach, S. (1995). Sexual orientation of adult sons of gay fathers. *Developmental Psychology, 31,* 124–129.

Bailey, J., Dunne, M., & Martin, N. (2000). Genetic and environmental influences on sexual orientation and its correlates in an Australian twin sample. *Journal of Personality and Social Psychology, 78,* 524–536.

Bailey, J., Gaulin, S., Agyei, Y., & Gladue, B. (1994). Effects of gender and sexual orientation on evolutionarily relevant aspects of human mating psychology. *Journal of Personality and Social Psychology, 66,* 1081–1093.

Bailey, J., Pillard, R., Neale, M., & Agyei, Y. (1993). Heritable factors influence sexual orientation in women. *Archives of General Psychiatry, 50,* 217–223.

Bailey, J., & Zucker, K. (1995). Childhood sex-typed behavior and sexual orientation: A conceptual analysis and quantitative review. *Developmental Psychology, 31,* 43–55.

Baill, I., Cullins, V., & Pati, S. (2003). Counseling issues in tubal sterilization. *American Family Physician, 67,* 1287–1294.

Bain, J. (2001). Andropause: Testosterone replacement therapy for aging men. *Canadian Family Physician, 47,* 91–97.

Baird, P., Sadovnick, A., & Yee, I. (1991). Maternal age and birth defects: A population study. *The Lancet, 337,* 527.

Bajos, N., Goulard, H., Job-Spira, N., & COCON Group. (2003). Emergency contraception: From accessibility to counseling. *Contraception, 67,* 39–40.

Baker, J. (1990). Lesbians: Portrait of a community. *Newsweek,* March 12, 24.

Baker, S., Thalberg, S., & Morrison, D. (1988). Parents' behavioral norms as predictors of adolescent sexual activity and contraceptive use. *Adolescence, 23,* 278–281.

Bakos, S. (1999). From lib to libido: How women are reinventing sex for grown-ups. *Modern Maturity,* September–October, 54.

Baldwin, D., Daugherty, S., & Eckenfels, E. (1991). Student perceptions of mistreatment and harassment during medical school: A survey of ten United States schools. *Western Journal of Medicine, 155,* 140–145.

Baldwin, J., & Baldwin, J. (2000). Heterosexual anal intercourse. *Archives of Sexual Behavior, 29,* 357–373.

Ballan, M. (2001). Parents as sexuality educators for their children with developmental disabilities. *SIECUS Report, 29,* 14–19.

Balon, R. (1998). Pharmacological treatment of paraphilias with a focus on antidepressants. *Journal of Sex Research, 24,* 241–254.

Bancroft, J. (2002a). Biological factors in human sexuality. *Journal of Sex Research, 39,* 15–21.

Bancroft, J. (2002b). The medicalization of female sexual dysfunction: The need for caution. *Archives of Sexual Behavior, 31,* 451–455.

Bancroft, J. (Ed.) (2003). *Sexual Development in Childhood.* Bloomington: Indiana University Press.

Bancroft, J., Herbenick. D., & Reynolds, M. (2003a). Masturbation as a marker of sexual development. In J. Bancroft (Ed.), *Sexual Development in Childhood.* Bloomington: Indiana University Press.

Bancroft, J., Loftus, J., & Long, J. (2003b). Distress about sex: A national survey of women in heterosexual relationships. *Archives of Sexual Behavior, 32,* 193–209.

Bangs, L. (1985). *Aging and Positive Sexuality: A Descriptive Approach.* Ph.D. dissertation, U.S. International University, San Diego.

Bankole, A., Darroch, J., & Singh, S. (1999). Determinants of trends in condom use in the United States, 1988–1995. *Family Planning Perspectives, 31,* 264–271.

Banks, C., & Arnold, P. (2001). Opinions towards sexual partners with a large age difference. *Marriage and Family Review, 33,* 5–17.

Banyard, V., & Williams, L. (1996). Characteristics of child sexual abuse as correlates of women's adjustment: A prospective study. *Journal of Marriage and the Family, 58,* 853–865.

Baran, S., & Davis, D. (2003). *Mass Communication Theory: Foundations, Ferment, and Future* (3rd ed.). Belmont, CA: Wadsworth.

Barbach, L. (1975). *For Yourself: The Fulfillment of Female Sexuality.* Garden City, NY: Doubleday.

Barbach, L. (1982). *For Each Other: Sharing Intimacy.* New York: Anchor Press/Doubleday.

Barbaree, H., Marshall, W., & Lanthier, R. (1979). Deviant sexual arousal in rapists. *Behavior Research and Therapy, 17,* 215–222.

Bardoni, B., Zanaria, E., Guioli, S., Floridia, G., Worley, K., Tonini, G., Ferrante, E., Chiumello, G., McCabe, E., Fraccaro, M., Zuffardi, O., & Camerino, G. (1994). A dosage sensitive locus at chromosome Xp21 is involved in male to female sex reversal. *Nature Genetics, 7,* 497–501.

Barfield, R., Wilson, C., & Mcdonald, P. (1975). Sexual behavior: Extreme reduction of postejaculatory refractory period by midbrain lesions in male rats. *Science, 189,* 147–149.

Barker, R. (1987). *The Green-Eyed Marriage: Surviving Jealous Relationships.* New York: Free Press.

Barkley, B., & Mosher, E. (1995). Sexuality and Hispanic culture: Counseling with children and their parents. *Journal of Sex Education and Therapy, 21,* 255–267.

Barner, M. (1999). Sex-role stereotyping in FCC-mandated children's educational television. *Journal of Broadcasting and Electronic Media, 43,* 551–564.

Barnhart, K., Furman, I., & Devoto, L. (1995). Attitudes and practice of couples regarding sexual relations during the menses and spotting. *Contraception, 51,* 93–98.

Barone, M., Johnson, C., Luick, M., Teutonico, D., & Magnani, R. (2004). Characteristics of men receiving vasectomies in the United States, 1998–1999. *Perspectives on Sexual and Reproductive Health, 36,* 27–33.

Barone, N., & Wiederman, M. (1998). Young women's sexuality as a function of perceptions of maternal sexual communication during childhood. *Journal of Sex Education and Therapy, 22(3)*, 33–38.

Barovick, H. (2002). Rainbow network. *Families*, April, F10.

Barrett, G., Pendry, E., & Peacock, J. (2000). Women's sexual health after childbirth. *British Journal of Gynecology, 107*, 186–195.

Barron, M., & Kimmel, M. (2000). Sexual violence in three pornographic media: Toward a sociological explanation. *Journal of Sex Research, 37*, 161–168.

Barstow, A. (1994). *Witchcraze*. San Francisco: Pandora.

Barth, R., & Kinder, B. (1987). The mislabeling of sexual impulsivity. *Journal of Sex and Marital Therapy, 13*, 15–23.

Bartholet, J. (2000). The plague years. *Newsweek*, January 17, 32–38.

Bartholomew, K. (1990). Avoidance of intimacy: An attachment perspective. *Journal of Social and Personal Relationships, 7*, 147–178.

Bartholomew, R. (2001). *Exotic Devices: Medicalizing Cultural Idioms from Strangeness to Illness*. Boulder: University of Colorado Press.

Bartlik, B., & Goldberg, J. (2000). Female sexual arousal disorder. In S. Leiblum & R. Rosen (Eds.), *Principles and Practice of Sex Therapy*. New York: Guilford Press.

Basoff, E., & Glass, G. (1982). The relationship between sex roles and mental health: A meta-analysis of twenty-six studies. *Counseling Psychologist, 10*, 105–112.

Basow, S. (1992). *Gender: Stereotypes and Roles* (3rd ed.). Pacific Grove, CA: Brooks/Cole.

Basson, R. (2002). A model of women's sexual arousal. *Journal of Sex and Marital Therapy, 28*, 1–10.

Basson, R., Leiblum, S., Brotto, L., Derogatis, L., Fourcroy, J., Fugl-Meyer, K., Graziottin, A., Heiman, J., Laan, E., Meston, C., Schover, L., van Lankveld, J., & Schultz W. (2003). Definitions of women's sexual dysfunction reconsidered: Advocating expansion and revision. *Journal of Psychsomatic Obstetrics and Gynecology, 24*, 221–229.

Bastian, L., Smith, C., & Nanda, K. (2003). Is this woman perimenopausal? *Journal of the American Medical Association, 289*, 895–901.

Bates, T. (1995). Oregon XXX-rated. *The Oregonian*, May 7, D1–D4.

Bauman, R., Kasper, C., & Alford, J. (1984). The child sex abusers. *Corrective and Social Psychiatry, 30*, 76–81.

Baumeister, R. (1988). Masochism as escape from self. *Journal of Sex Research, 25*, 28–59.

Baumeister, R. (1997). The enigmatic appeal of sexual masochism: Why people desire pain, bondage, and humiliation in sex. *Journal of Social and Clinical Psychology, 16*, 133–150.

Baumeister, R. (2000). Gender differences in erotic plasticity: The female sex drive as socially flexible and responsive. *Psychological Bulletin, 126*, 347–374.

Baumeister, R., Catanese, K., & Wallace, H. (2002). Conquest by force: A narcissistic reactance theory of rape and sexual coercion. *Review of General Psychology, 6*, 92–135.

Baumeister, R., & Leary, M. (1995). The need to belong: Desire for interpersonal attachments as a fundamental human motivation. *Psychological Bulletin, 11*, 497–529.

Baumeister, R., Wotman, S., & Stillwell, A. (1993). Unrequited love: On heartbreak, anger, guilt, scriptlessness, and humiliation. *Journal of Personality and Social Psychology, 64*, 377–394.

Baur, K. (1995). Socioeconomic and personality traits of nonadjudicated child sex offenders in a clinical practice. Unpublished.

Bauters, T., Dhont, M., Temmerman, M., & Nelis, H. (2002). Prevalence of vulvovaginal candidiasis and susceptibility to fluconazole in women. *American Journal of Obstetrics and Gynecology, 187*, 569–574.

Beach, F. (Ed.) (1978). *Human Sexuality in Four Perspectives*. Baltimore: Johns Hopkins University Press.

Beal, G., & Muehlenhard, C. (1987). *Getting Sexually Aggressive Men to Stop Their Advances: Information for Rape Prevention Programs*. Paper presented at the Annual Meeting of the Association for Advancement of Behavior Therapy, Boston, November.

Beard, M., Hartmann, L., & Atkinson, E. (2000). The epidemiology of ovarian cancer: A population-based study in Olmsted County, Minnesota, 1935–1991. *Annals of Epidemiology, 10*, 14–23.

Beaty, L. (1999). Identity development of homosexual youth and parental and familial influences on the coming-out process. *Adolescence, 34*, 597–601.

Bechara, A., Bertolino, M., Casabe, A., Munarriz, R., Goldstein, I., Morin, A., Secin, F., Literat, B., Pesaresi, M., & Fredatovich, N. (2003). Duplex Doppler ultrasound assessment of clitoral hemodynamics after topical administration of Alprostadil in women with arousal and orgasmic disorders. *Journal of Sex and Marital Therapy, 29(suppl.)*, 1–10.

Beck, M. (1999). The pornographic tradition: Formative influences in sixteenth- to nineteenth-century European literature. In J. Elias, V. Elias, V. Bullough, G. Brewer, J. Douglas, & W. Jarvis (Eds.), *Porn 101: Eroticism, Pornography, and the First Amendment*. Amherst, NY: Prometheus Books.

Beck, M., Wickelgren, I., Quade, V., & Wingert, P. (1988). Miscarriages. *Newsweek*, August 15, 46–49.

Becker, E. (2000). Women in military say silence on harassment protects careers. *New York Times*, May 12, AI.

Becker, J., & Kaplan, M. (1991). Rape victims: Issues, theories, and treatment. *Annual Review of Sex Research, 2*, 267–272.

Becker, J., Skinner, L., Abel, G., & Axelrod, R. (1986). Level of postassault sexual functioning in rape and incest victims. *Archives of Sexual Behavior, 15*, 37–49.

Begley, E., Crosby, R., DiClemente, R., Wingood, G., & Rose, E. (2003). Older partners and STD prevalence among pregnant African American teens. *Sexually Transmitted Diseases, 30*, 211–213.

Begley, S. (1993). Hands off Mr. Chips! *Newsweek*, May 3, 58.

Begley, S. (1995). The baby myth. *Newsweek*, September 4, 38–47.

Begley, S. (1998). Designer babies. *Newsweek*, November 9, 61–62.

Begley, S. (1999). From both sides now. *Newsweek*, June 14, 52–53.

Begley, S. (2000a). Stop blaming your genes. *Newsweek*, July 24, 53.

Begley, S. (2000b). Understanding perimenopause. *Newsweek*, Special Issue, 31–34.

Begley, S. (2001). Brave new monkey. *Newsweek*, January 22, 50–52.

Behnke, M., Eyler, F., Conlon, M., Casanova, O., & Woods, N. (1997). How fetal cocaine exposure increases neonatal hospital costs. *Pediatrics, 99*, 204–208.

Beji, N. (2003). The effect of pelvic floor training on sexual function. *Nursing Standard, 16*, 33–36.

Bell, A., & Weinberg, M. (1978). *Homosexualities: A Study of Diversity Among Men and Women*. New York: Simon & Schuster.

Bell, A., Weinberg, M., & Hammersmith, S. (1981). *Sexual Preference: Its Development in Men and Women*. Bloomington: Indiana University Press.

Beller, M., & Gafni, N. (2000). Can item format (multiple choice vs. open-ended) account for gender differences in mathematics achievement? *Sex Roles, 42*, 1–21.

Belluck, P., & Zezima, K. (2004). Gays to cross wedding threshold. *The Oregonian*, May 16, A2.

Belsey, E., & Pinol, A. (1997). Menstrual bleeding patterns in untreated women. *Contraception, 55*, 57–65.

Belzer, E., Whipple, B., & Moger, W. (1984). A female ejaculation. *Journal of Sex Research, 20*, 403–406.

Bem, S. (1974). The measurement of psychological androgyny. *Journal of Consulting and Clinical Psychology, 42*, 155–162.

Bem, S. (1975). Sex role adaptability: One consequence of psychological androgyny. *Journal of Personality and Social Psychology, 31*, 634–643.

Bem, S. (1993). *The Lenses of Gender*. New Haven, CT: Yale University Press.

Bemporad, J. (1999). Epigenesis and sexual orientation: A report of five bisexual males. *Journal of the American Academy of Psychoanalysis, 27*, 221–237.

Benagiano, G., & Cottingham, J. (1997). Contraceptive methods: Potential for abuse. *International Journal of Gynecology and Obstetrics, 56*, 39–46.

Bendich, A. (2000). The potential for dietary supplements to reduce premenstrual syndrome (PMS) symptoms. *Journal of the American College of Nutrition, 19*, 3–12.

Benet, A., Sharaby, J., & Melman, A. (1994). Male erectile dysfunction assessment and treatment options. *Comprehensive Therapy, 20(12)*, 669–673.

Bennett, W. (1996). Leave marriage alone. *Newsweek*, June 3, 27.

Benson, E. (2003). The science of sexual arousal. *Monitor on Psychology, 34*, 50–52.

Benson, J., Clark, K., Gerhardt, A., & Randall, L. (2003). Early abortion services in the United States: A provider survey. *Contraception, 67*, 287–294.

Benson, R. (1985). Vacuum cleaner injury to penis: A common urologic problem? *Urology, 25*, 41–44.

Berenbaum, S., & Snyder, E. (1995). Early hormonal influences on childhood sex-typed activity and playmate preferences: Implications for the development of sexual orientation. *Developmental Psychology, 31*, 31–42.

Berger, R. (1990). Passing: Impact on the quality of same-sex couple relationships. *Social Work, 35,* 328–332.

Berger, R. (1996). *Gay and Gray: The Older Homosexual Man.* New York: Haworth Press.

Bergling, T. (2004). Closeted in the capital. *The Advocate,* May 11, 45–46.

Berkman, C., Turner, S., & Cooper, M. (2000). Sexual contact with clients: Assessment of social workers' attitudes and educational preparation. *Social Work, 45,* 223–235.

Berkman, C., & Zinberg, G. (1997). Homophobia and heterosexism in social workers. *Journal of the National Association of Social Workers, 42(4),* 319–332.

Berkowitz, J. (2000). Personal view: Two boys and a girl please and hold the mustard. *Public Health, 114,* 5–7.

Berlin, M. (2003). *Understanding Health Research Studies as Reported in the Media.* Paper presented at the Oregon Health Sciences University Speaking of Women Series, Portland, Oregon, March.

Berliner, L., & Conte, J. (1995). The effects of disclosure and intervention on sexually abused children. *Child Abuse and Neglect, 27,* 525–540.

Berman, J., & Berman, L. (2001). *For Women Only: A Revolutionary Guide to Overcoming Sexual Dysfunction and Reclaiming Your Sex Life.* New York: Henry Holt and Company.

Berman, L., & Berman, J. (2000). Viagra and beyond: Where sex educators and therapists fit in from a multidisciplinary perspective. *Journal of Sex Education and Therapy, 25,* 17–24.

Bernat, J., Calhoun, K., & Adams, H. (1999). Sexually aggressive and nonaggressive men: Sexual arousal and judgments in response to acquaintance rape and consensual analogues. *Journal of Abnormal Psychology, 108,* 662–673.

Bernstein, J. (1999). *In Whose Back Yards Should Sex Shops Go?* Retrieved June 7, 1999, from http://www.oregonlive.com/oped/99/06/ed060704.html

Bernstein, W., Stephenson, B., Snyder, M., & Wicklund, R. (1983). Causal ambiguity and heterosexual affiliation. *Journal of Experimental Social Psychology, 19,* 78–92.

Bertino, J., Tirrell, P., Greenberg, R., Keyserling, H., Poland, G., Gump, D., Kumar, M., & Ramsey, K. (1997). A comparative trial of standard or high-dose S subunit recombinant hepatitis B vaccine versus a vaccine containing S subunit, pre-S, and pre-S2 particles for revaccination of healthy adult nonresponders. *Journal of Infectious Diseases, 175,* 678–681.

Besen, T. (2003). *Anything But Straight: Unmasking the Scandals and Lies Behind the Ex-Gay Myth.* New York: Harrington Park Press.

Best, D., & Davis, S. (1997). Testicular cancer education: Differences in approaches. *American Journal of Health Behavior, 21,* 83–87.

Betchen, S. (2001). Premature ejaculation as symptomatic of age difference in a husband and wife with underlying power and control conflicts. *Journal of Sex Education and Therapy, 26,* 34–44.

Betts, A. (2001). Role of semen in female-to-male transmission of HIV. *Annals of Epidemiology, 11,* 154–155.

Beyrer, C. (2003). Hidden epidemic of sexually transmitted diseases in China: Crises and opportunity. *Journal of the American Medical Association, 289,* 1303–1305.

Bezchlibnyk-Butler, K., & Jeffries, S. (2000). *Clinical Handbook of Psychotropic Drugs.* Seattle: Hogrefe & Huber.

Bieber, I., Dain, H., Dince, P., Drellich, M., Grand, H., Gundlach, R., Kremer, M., Rifkin, A., Wilbur, C., & Bieber, T. (1962). *Homosexuality.* New York: Vintage Books.

Biederman, P. (2003, April 17). *For Gays, Secrecy in Love, War.* Retrieved April 22, 2003, from http://www.sldn.org/templates/press/record.html?record=882

Bierce, A. (1943). *The Devil's Dictionary.* New York: World.

Bingham, S., Luben, R., Welch, A., & Wareham, N. (2003). Are imprecise methods obscuring a relation between fat and breast cancer? *The Lancet, 362,* 212–214.

Binik, Y., Bergeron, S., & Khalife, S. (2000). Dyspareunia. In S. Leiblum & R. Rosen (Eds.), *Principles and Practice of Sex Therapy.* New York: Guilford Press.

Binik, Y., Mah, K., & Kiesler, S. (1999). Ethical issues in conducting sex research on the Internet. *Journal of Sex Research, 36,* 82–90.

Binstock, G., & Thornton, A. (2003). Separations, reconciliations, and living apart in cohabiting and marital unions. *Journal of Marriage and the Family, 65,* 432–443.

Birchard, K. (1998). China plans to change policy on one-child limit to families. *The Lancet, 351,* 890.

Birnbaum, G. (2003). The meaning of heterosexual intercourse among women with female orgasmic disorder. *Archives of Sexual Behavior, 32,* 61–71.

Bjorklund, D., & Pellegrini, A. (2000). Child development and evolutionary psychology. *Child Development, 71,* 1687–1708.

Black, A. (1994). Perverting the diagnosis: The lesbian and the scientific basis of stigma. *Historical Reflections, 20,* 201–216.

Black, R., & Hill, D. (2003). Over-the-counter medications in pregnancy. *American Family Physician, 67,* 2517–2524.

Blackburn, R., Cunkelman, J., & Zlidar, V. (2000). Oral contraceptives: An update. *Population Reports, 28,* 1–39.

Blackless, M., Charuvastra, A., Derryck, A., Fausto-Sterling, A., Lauzanne, K., & Lee, E. (2000). How sexually dimorphic are we? Review and synthesis. *American Journal of Human Biology, 12,* 151–166.

Blackmun, M. (1996a). Escort services: Look all you want but don't touch. *The Oregonian,* June 16, D1, D4.

Blackmun, M. (1996b). The tie that binds knots later in life. *The Oregonian,* March 13, A9.

Blackwell, D., & Lichter, D. (2000). Mate selection among married and cohabiting couples. *Journal of Family Issues, 21,* 275–302.

Blaicher, W., Gruber, D., Bieglmayer, C., Blaicher, A., Knogler, W., & Huber, J. (1999). The role of oxytocin in relation to female sexual arousal. *Gynecology and Obstetrics Investigations, 47,* 125–126.

Blair, C., & Lanyon, R. (1981). Exhibitionism: Etiology and treatment. *Psychological Bulletin, 89,* 439–463.

Blake, A., Ledsky, R., Goodenow, C., Sawyer, R., Lohrman, D., & Windsor, R. (2003). Condom availability programs in Massachusetts high schools: Relationships with condom use and sexual behavior. *American Journal of Public Health, 93,* 955–962.

Blakeslee, S. (1993). Cryptic sensory system gains attention. *The Oregonian,* September 15, B10 & B11.

Blanchard, R. (1997). Birth order and sibling sex ratio in homosexual versus heterosexual males and females. *Annual Review of Sex Research, 8,* 27–67.

Blanchard, R., & Bogaert, A. F. (1996). Homosexuality in men and number of older brothers. *American Journal of Psychiatry, 153,* 27–31.

Blanchard, R., Steiner, B., & Clemmensen, L. (1985). Gender dysphoria, gender reorientation, and the clinical management of transsexualism. *Journal of Consulting and Clinical Psychology, 53,* 295–304.

Blank, J. (2000). *Good Vibrations: The New Complete Guide to Vibrators.* San Francisco: Down There Press.

Blass, D., & Fagan P. (2001). The treatment of orthodox Jewish patients in sex therapy. *Journal of Sex Education and Therapy, 26,* 267–271.

Blee, K., & Tickamyer, A. (1995). Racial differences in men's attitudes about women's gender roles. *Journal of Marriage and the Family, 57,* 21–30.

Bloche, M. (2004). Health care disparities: Science, politics, and race. *New England Journal of Medicine, 350,* 1568–1570.

Block, J. (1983). Differential premises arising from differential socialization of the sexes: Some conjectures. *Child Development, 54,* 1335–1354.

Block, J. (2003). Science gets sacked. *The Nation,* September 1–8, 5–6.

Blocker, M., Levine, W., & St. Louis, M. (2000). HIV prevalence in patients with syphilis, United States. *Sexually Transmitted Diseases, 27,* 53–59.

Blue, V. (2003). *The Ultimate Guide to Adult Videos: How to Watch Adult Videos and Make Your Sex Life Sizzle.* San Francisco: Cleis Press.

Blumstein, P., & Schwartz, P. (1983). *American Couples.* New York: Morrow.

Bluthenthal, R., Kral, A., Gee, L., Erringer, E., & Edlin, B. (2000). The effect of syringe exchange use on high-risk injection drug users: A cohort study. *AIDS 2000, 14,* 605–611.

Boekhout, B., Hendrick, S., & Hendrick, C. (1999). Relationship infidelity: A loss of perspective. *Journal of Personal and Interpersonal Loss, 4,* 97–124.

Boeringer, S. (1994). Pornography and sexual aggression: Association of violent and nonviolent depictions with rape and rape proclivity. *Deviant Behavior: An Interdisciplinary Journal, 15,* 289–304.

Bogaert, A. (2003a). Interaction of older brothers and sex typing in the prediction of sexual orientation in men. *Archives of Sexual Behavior, 32,* 129–134.

Bogaert, A. (2003b). Number of older brothers and sexual orientation: New tests and the attraction/behavior distinction in two national probability samples. *Journal of Personality and Social Psychology, 84,* 644–652.

Bogaert, A., Friesen, C., & Klentrou, P. (2002). Age of puberty and sexual orientation in a national probability sample. *Archives of Sexual Behavior, 31,* 73–81.

Bogert, C., & Wehrfritz, G. (1996). Rethinking family values. *Newsweek*, January 22, 44–45.

Boggess, J. (2002). How can pharmacies improve access to emergency contraception? *Perspectives on Sexual and Reproductive Health, 34*, 162–165.

Bogren, L. (1991). Changes in sexuality in women and men during pregnancy. *Archives of Sexual Behavior, 20*, 35–46.

Bolin, A. (1997). Transforming transvestism and transsexualism: Polarity, politics, and gender. In B. Bullough, V. Bullough, and J Elias (Eds.), *Gender Blending* . New York: Prometheus Books.

Bolus, J. (1994). Teaching teens about condoms. *Registered Nurse*, March, 44–47.

Bondurant, S., Ernster, V., & Herdman, R. (2000). *Safety of Silicone Breast Implants*. Washington, DC: National Academy Press.

Boonstra, H., & Sonfield, A. (2000). Rights without access: Revisiting public funding of abortion for poor women. *Guttmacher Report, 3*, 1–5.

Borgatta, L., Burnhill, M., & Tyson, J. (2001). Early medical abortion with methotrexate and misoprostol. *Obstetrics and Gynecology, 97*, 11–16.

Borgmann, C., & Weiss, C. (2003). Beyond apocalypse and apology: A moral defense of abortion. *Perspectives on Sexual and Reproductive Health, 35*, 40–43.

Bornstein, R. (1989). Exposure and effect: Overview and meta-analysis of research, 1968–1987. *Psychological Bulletin, 106*, 265–289.

Boss, S., & Maltz, W. (2001). *Private Thoughts: Exploring the Power of Women's Sexual Fantasies*. Novato, CA: New World Library.

Boston Women's Health Collective (1971). *Our Bodies, Ourselves*. New York: Simon & Schuster.

Boswell, J. (1980). *Christianity, Social Tolerance, and Homosexuality*. Chicago: University of Chicago Press.

Boule, M. (1998). Hate from around the country surrounded that fence in Wyoming. *The Sunday Oregonian*, October 18, L1.

Bouley, C. (2003, October 22). *Defending Marriage*. Retrieved November 1, 2003, from http://www.advocate.com/html/stories/901/901_bouley.asp

Boulware, J. (2000a). *Just Say Don't*. Retrieved October 5, 2000, from http://www.salon.com/sex/world/2000/10/05/cambodia/index.html

Boulware, J. (2000b). *Viagra Rave*. Retrieved May 30, 2000, from http://www.salon1999.com/sex/world/2000/05/30/viagra_rave/index.html

Bouyer, J., Coste, J., Shojaei, T., & Pouly, J. (2003). Risk factors for ectopic pregnancy: A comprehensive analysis based on a large case–control, population-based study in France. *American Journal of Epidemiology, 157*, 185–194.

Bowles, S. (2000). False accusations against teachers soar. *USA Today*, March 21, A10.

Boyer, C., Tschann, J., & Shafer, M. (1999). Predictors of risk for sexually transmitted diseases in ninth grade urban high school students. *Journal of Adolescent Research, 14*, 448–465.

Boyer, D., & Fine, D. (1992). Sexual abuse as a factor in adolescent pregnancy and child maltreatment. *Family Planning Perspectives, 24*, 4–11.

Boyers, S., & Gilbert, W. (1998). Elective repeat caesarean section versus trial of labour: The neonatologist's view. *The Lancet, 351*, 155.

Boynton, P. (2003). "I'm just a girl who can't say no"? Women, consent, and sex research. *Journal of Sex and Marital Therapy, 29(suppl.)*, 23–32.

Brackett, N., Bloch, W., & Abae, M. (1994). Neurological anatomy and physiology of sexual function. In C. Singer & W. Weiner (Eds.), *Sexual Dysfunction: A Neuromedical Approach*. New York: Futura.

Bradford, J. (1998). Treatment of men with paraphilia. *New England Journal of Medicine, 338*, 464–465.

Bradford, J., (2001). The neurobiology, neuropharmacology, and pharmacological treatment of the paraphilias and compulsive sexual behavior. *Canadian Journal of Psychiatry, 46*, 26– 34.

Bradford, J., Boulet, J., & Pawlak, A. (1992). The paraphilias: A multiplicity of deviant behaviors. *Canadian Journal of Psychiatry, 37*, 104–107.

Bradford, J., & Pawlak, A. (1993). Double-blind placebo crossover study of cyproterone acetate in the treatment of paraphilias. *Archives of Sexual Behavior, 22*, 383–402.

Bradley, S., & Zucker, K. (1997). Gender identity disorder: A review of the past 10 years. *Journal of the American Academy of Child and Adolescent Psychology, 36*, 872–880.

Bradshaw, C. (1994). Asia and Asian American women: Historical and political considerations in psychotherapy. In L. Comas-Diaz & B. Greene (Eds.), *Women of Color*. New York: Guilford Press.

Bradsher, K. (2000). Four get prison time in death of girl from date rape drug. *New York Times*, March 31, A15.

Braen, G. (1980). Examination of the accused: The heterosexual and homosexual rapist. In C. Warner (Ed.), *Rape and Sexual Assault*. Germantown, MD: Aspen Systems.

Brainerd, C., & Reyna, V. (1998). When things that were never experienced are easier to "remember" than things that were. *Psychological Science, 9*, 484–489.

Brandon, K. (2001). Nursing mothers hit office obstacles. *The Sunday Oregonian*, April 15, L11.

Brashear, D., & Munsick, R. (1991). Hymenal dyspareunia. *Journal of Sex Education and Therapy, 17*, 27–31.

Braunstein, G. (1999). *Patch Found to Restore Sex Drive After Hysterectomy*. Retrieved June 16, 1999, from http://www.cnn.com/Health/women/testosterone.patch.women.ap/

Braverman, P., & Strasburger, V. (1993a). Adolescent sexual activity. *Clinical Pediatrics, 32*, 658–668.

Braverman, P., & Strasburger, V. (1993b). Contraception. *Clinical Pediatrics, 33*, 100–109.

Braverman, P., & Strasburger, V. (1994a). The practitioner's role. *Clinical Pediatrics, 33*, 100–109.

Braverman, P., & Strasburger, V. (1994b). Sexually transmitted diseases. *Clinical Pediatrics*, January, 26–37.

Brecher, E. (1984). *Love, Sex, and Aging*. Boston: Little, Brown.

Bremer, J. (1959). *Asexualization*. New York: Macmillan.

Brening, R., Dalve-Endres, A., & Patrick, K. (2003). Emergency contraception pills (ECPs): Current trends in United States college health centers. *Contraception, 67*, 449–456.

Bretschneider, J., & McCoy, N. (1988). Sexual interest and behavior in healthy 80- to 102-year-olds. *Archives of Sexual Behavior, 17*, 109.

Brewster, K. (1994). Race differences in sexual activity among adolescent women: The role of neighborhood characteristics. *American Sociological Review, 59*, 408–424.

Brewster, W., DiSaia, P., & Grosen, E. (1999). An experience with estrogen replacement therapy in breast cancer survivors. *International Journal of Fertility, 44*, 186–192.

Brick, P. (1999). Success stories: What statistics don't tell about sexuality education. *SIECUS Report, 27*, 15–21.

Briddell, D., & Wilson, G. (1976). Effects of alcohol and expectancy set on male sexual arousal. *Journal of Abnormal Psychology, 85*, 225–234.

Briere, J., & Conte, J. (1993). Self-reported amnesia for abuse in adults molested as children. *Journal of Traumatic Stress, 6*, 21–31.

Bringle, R., & Buunk, B. (1991). Extradyadic relationships and sexual jealousy. In K. McKinney & S. Sprecher (Eds.), *Sexuality in Close Relationships*. Hillsdale, NJ: Erlbaum.

Brinker, L. (2003). Jewish-American literature. In C. Summers (Ed.), *An Encyclopedia of Gay, Lesbian, Bisexual, Transgender, and Queer Culture*. Chicago: GLBTQ Inc.

Brinkley, J. (2000). Trafficking in girls, women extensive, CIA survey finds. *The Oregonian*, April 2, A3.

Britton, G., & Lumpkin, M. (1984). Battle to imprint for the 21st century. *Reading Teacher, 37*, 724–733.

Brody, J. (2000). Cybersex gives birth to a psychological disorder. *The New York Times*, May 16, F7, F12.

Brody, S., Laan, E., & Van Lunsen, R. (2003). Concordance between women's physiological and subjective sexual arousal is associated with consistency of orgasm during intercourse but not other sexual behavior. *Journal of Sex and Marital Therapy, 29*, 15–23.

Brogan, D. (2001). Implementing the Institute of Medicine report on lesbian health. *Journal of the American Medical Women's Association, 56*, 24–26.

Brogan, P. (2004). Years haven't settled abortion debate. *News Journal*, January 25, A1.

Bronski, M. (2000). Blinded by science. *The Advocate*, February 1, 64–66.

Brook, C. (1999a). Mechanism of puberty. *Hormone Research, 51(suppl.)*, 52–54.

Brook, C. (1999b). Treatment of late puberty. *Hormone Research, 51(suppl.)*, 101–103.

Brooke, J. (2000). Gay and lesbian scouts received with open arms in tolerant Canada. *San Francisco Chronicle*, September 12, D2.

Brooks, D., & Goldberg, S. (2001). Gay and lesbian adoptive and foster care placements: Can they meet the needs of waiting children? *Social Work, 46*, 147–157.

Brooks, J., & Watkins, M. (1989). Recognition memory and the mere exposure effect. *Journal of Experimental Psychology: Learning, Memory, and Cognition, 15*, 968–976.

Brooks, T. (2002). Association of adolescent risk behaviors with mental health symptoms in high school students. *Journal of Adolescent Health, 31,* 240–246.

Brown, E. (1988). Affairs: The hidden meanings have major impact on therapeutic approach. *Behavior Today,* October 24, 3–4.

Brown, G. (1990). The transvestite husband. *Medical Aspects of Human Sexuality,* June, 35–42.

Brown, H. (2000). Don't give up on sex after 60. *Newsweek,* May 29, 55.

Brown, J. (2000). *Issues Often Seen in Couple's Sex Therapy.* Paper presented at the 32nd Annual Conference of the American Association of Sex Educators, Counselors, and Therapists, Atlanta, Georgia, May 10–14.

Brown, J. (2002, February). *Mass Media Influences on Sexuality.* Retrieved April 11, 2003, from http://www.findarticles.com/cf_0/m2372/1_39/87080439/print.jhtml

Brown, J., & Hart, D. (1977). Correlates of females' sexual fantasies. *Perceptual and Motor Skills, 45,* 819–825.

Brown, J., & Keller, S. (2000). Can the mass media be healthy sex educators? *Family Planning Perspectives, 32,* 14–19.

Brown, L. (1997). Introduction. In L. Brown (Ed.), *Two Spirit People.* New York: Harrington Park Press.

Brown, M. (1994). Marital discord during pregnancy: A family systems approach. *Family Systems Medicine, 12,* 221–234.

Brown, M., Perry, A., Cheesman, A., & Pring, T. (2000). Pitch change in male-to-female transsexuals: Has phonosurgery a role to play? *International Journal of Language and Communications Disorders, 35,* 129–136.

Brown, R. (2000). Understanding the disorders of sexual preference. *The Practitioner, 244,* 438–442.

Brown, S. (2001). Silicone gel breast implant rupture, extracapsular silicone, and health status in a population of women. *Journal of the American Medical Association, 286,* 402–421.

Brown, S. (2003). Relationship quality dynamics of cohabiting unions. *Journal of Family Issues, 24,* 583–601.

Brown, T., & Fee, E. (2003). Alfred Kinsey: A pioneer of sex research. *American Journal of Public Health, 93,* 896–897.

Brown, Z., Wald, A., Morrow, R., Selke, S., Zeh, J., & Corey, L. (2003). Effect of serologic status and cesarean delivery on transmission rates of herpes simplex virus from mother to infant. *Journal of the American Medical Association, 289,* 203–209.

Browning, J., Kessler, D., Hatfield, E., & Choo, P. (1999). Power, gender, and sexual behavior. *Journal of Sex Research, 36,* 342–347.

Brownmiller, S. (1975). *Against Our Will: Men, Women, and Rape.* New York: Simon & Schuster.

Brownmiller, S. (1993). Making female bodies the battlefield. *Newsweek,* January 4, 37.

Bruner, D., Pickett, M., Joseph, A., & Burggraf, V. (2000). Prostate cancer elder alert: Epidemiology, screening, and early detection. *Journal of Gerontological Nursing,* January, 6–15.

Bryant, S., & Demian, N. (1998). Terms of same-sex endearment. *SIECUS Report, 26(4),* 10–13.

Bryjak, G., & Soroka, M. (1994). *Sociology: Cultural Diversity in a Changing World* (2nd ed.). Boston: Allyn and Bacon.

Buchanan, T. (2000). Potential of the Internet for personality research. In M. Birnbaum (Ed.), *Psychological Experiments on the Internet.* San Diego: Academic Press.

Budd, K. (1999). The facts of life: Everything you wanted to know about sex (after 50). *Modern Maturity,* September–October, 86–87.

Budd, K. (2002). Egg beaters. *AARP,* May–June, 15.

Budhos, M. (1997). Putting the heat on sex tourism. *Ms.,* March–April, 12–16.

Budin, L., & Johnson, C. (1989). Sex abuse prevention programs: Offenders' attitudes about their efficacy. *Child Abuse and Neglect, 13,* 77–87.

Bulcroft, R., Carmady, D., & Bulcroft, K. (1996). Patterns of parental independence giving to adolescents: Variations by race, age, and gender of child. *Journal of Marriage and the Family, 58,* 866–883.

Bull, C. (2003). Marriage: Confused conservatives. *The Advocate,* October 14, 30–32.

Bullough, B., & Bullough, V. (1997). Are transvestites necessarily heterosexual? *Archives of Sexual Behavior, 26,* 1–12.

Bullough, V. (2001). Religion, sex, and science: Some historical quandaries. *Journal of Sex Education and Therapy, 26,* 254–258.

Bullough, V., & Bullough, B. (1993). *Cross Dressing, Sex and Gender.* Philadelphia: University of Pennsylvania Press.

Bureau of Labor Statistics (2003). *Labor Force Statistics from the Current Population Survey.* Retrieved February 19, 2003, from http://www.stats.bls.gov

Burger, E., Field, M., & Twigg, J. (1998). From assurance to insurance in Russia health care: The problematic transition. *American Journal of Public Health, 88,* 755–758.

Burgess, A., & Holmstrom, L. (1979). Rape: Sexual disruption and recovery. *American Journal of Orthopsychiatry, 49,* 648–657.

Burke, W., Daly, M., Garber, J., Botkin, J., Kahn, M., Lynch, P., McTiernan, A., Offit, K., Perlman, J., Petersen, G., Thomson, E., & Varricchio, C. (1997). Recommendations for follow-up care of individuals with an inherited predisposition to cancer. *Journal of the American Medical Association, 277(12),* 997–1003.

Burkman, R., Jr. (1995). Oral contraceptives: An update. *Hospital Practice, 30,* 85–97.

Burn, S., O'Neil, A., & Nederend, S. (1996). Childhood tomboyism and adult androgyny. *Sex Roles, 34,* 419–428.

Burr, C. (1996a). Gimme Shelter. *The Advocate,* July 23, 37–38.

Burr, C. (1996b). *A Separate Creation.* New York: Hyperion.

Burstein, G., & Murray, P. (2003). Diagnosis and management of sexually transmitted disease pathogens among adolescents. *Pediatrics in Review, 24,* 75–81.

Burt, K. (1995). The effects of cancer on the body image and sexuality. *Nursing Times, 91(7),* 36–37.

Bush, C., Bush, J., & Jennings, J. (1988). Effects of jealousy threats on relationship perceptions and emotions. *Journal of Social and Personal Relationships, 5,* 285–303.

Bushman, B., & Baumeister, R. (1998). Threatened egoism, narcissism, self-esteem, and direct and displaced aggression: Does self-love or self-hate lead to violence? *Journal of Personality and Social Psychology, 43,* 372–384.

Bushman, B., & Bonacci, A. (2002). Violence and sex impair memory for television ads. *Journal of Applied Psychology, 87,* 27–32.

Bushman, B., Bonacci, A., Dijk, M., & Baumeister, R. (2003). Narcissism, sexual refusal, and aggression: Testing a narcissistic reactance model of sexual aggression. *Journal of Personality and Social Psychology, 84,* 1027–1040.

Buss, D. (1989). Sex differences in human mate preferences: Evolutionary hypothesis tested in 37 cultures. *Behavioral and Brain Sciences, 12,* 1–49.

Buss, D. (1994). *The Evolution of Desire: Strategies of Human Mating.* New York: Basic Books.

Buss, D. (1999). *Evolutionary Psychology: The New Science of the Mind.* Boston: Allyn and Bacon.

Buss, D. (2000). *The Dangerous Passion: Why Jealousy Is as Necessary as Love and Sex.* New York: Free Press.

Buss, D., & Barnes, M. (1986). Preferences in human mate selection. *Journal of Personality and Social Psychology, 50,* 559–570.

Buss, D., Larsen, R., & Semmelroth, J. (1992). Sex differences in jealousy: Evolution, physiology, and psychology. *Psychological Science, 3,* 251–255.

Buss, D., Larsen, R., & Westen, D. (1996). Sex differences: Not gone, not forgotten, and not explained by alternative hypotheses. *Psychological Science, 7,* 373–375.

Buss, D., & Schmitt, D. (1993). Sexual strategies theory: An evolutionary perspective on human mating. *Psychological Review, 100,* 204–232.

Bussey, K., & Bandura, A. (1999). Social cognitive theory of gender development and differentiation. *Psychological Review, 106,* 676–713.

Butcher, K. (2003). Confusion between prostitution and sex trafficking. *The Lancet, 361,* 1983.

Butler, J., & Burton, L. (1990). Rethinking teenage childbearing: Is sexual abuse a missing link? *Family Relations, 39,* 73–80.

Butts, J. (1981). Adolescent sexuality and teenage pregnancy from a black perspective. In T. Ooms (Ed.), *Teenage Pregnancy in a Family Context.* Philadelphia: Temple University Press.

Buunk, B., Angleitner, A., Oubaid, V., & Buss, D. (1996). Sex differences in jealousy in evolutionary and cultural perspective: Tests from the Netherlands, Germany, and the United States. *Psychological Science, 6,* 359–363.

Buunk, B., & Bringle, R. (1987). Jealousy in love relationships. In D. Perlman & S. Duck (Eds.), *Intimate Relationships.* Newbury Park, CA: Sage.

Buysse, A., & Ickes, W. (1999). Communication patterns in laboratory discussions of safer sex between dating versus nondating partners. *Journal of Sex Research, 36,* 121–134.

Buzi, R., Tortolero, S., Roberts, R., Ross, M., Markham, C., & Fleschler, M. (2003). Gender differences in the consequences of a coercive sexual experience among adolescents attending alternative schools. *Journal of School Health, 73,* 191–196.

Byers, E., & Demmons, S. (1999). Sexual satisfaction and sexual self-disclosure within dating relationships. *Journal of Sex Research, 36,* 180–189.

Byers, S., & O'Sullivan, L. (1996). *Sexual Coercion in Dating Relationships.* New York: Haworth Press.

Byrd, J., Hyde, J., DeLamater, J., & Plant, E. (1998). Sexuality during pregnancy and the year postpartum. *Journal of Family Practice, 47,* 305–308.

Byrne, D. (1997). An overview (and underview) and research and theory within the attraction paradigm. *Journal of Social and Personal Relationships, 14,* 417–431.

Byrne, D., Clore, G., & Smeaton, G. (1986). The attraction hypothesis: Do similar attitudes affect anything? *Journal of Personality and Social Psychology, 51,* 1,167–1,170.

Byrne, D., & Murnen, S. (1988). Maintaining loving relationships. In R. Sternberg & M. Barnes (Eds.), *The Psychology of Loving.* New Haven, CT: Yale University Press.

Byrne, D., & Osland, J. (2000). Sexual fantasy and erotica/pornography: Internal and external imagery. In L. Szuchman & F. Muscarella (Eds.), *Psychological Perspectives on Human Sexuality.* New York: Wiley.

Cado, S., & Leitenberg, H. (1990). Guilt reactions to sexual fantasies during intercourse. *Archives of Sexual Behavior, 19,* 49–71.

Caggiula, A. (1970). Analysis of the copulation–reward properties of posterior hypothalamic stimulation in male rats. *Journal of Comparative and Physiological Psychology, 70,* 399–412.

Cain, S. (2000). Breast cancer genetics and the role of tamoxifen in prevention. *Journal of the American Academy of Nurse Practitioners, 12,* 21–28.

Calderone, M., & Johnson, E. (1989). *The Family Book About Sexuality* (rev. ed.). New York: Harper & Row.

Caldwell, J. (2003a). Little victories for gay adoption. *The Advocate,* June 10, 38–41.

Caldwell, J. (2003b, March 25). *The Trouble with "Gay."* Retrieved May 6, 2003, from http://www.advocate.com/html/stories/886/886_sogay.asp

Calhoun, T., & Weaver, G. (1996). Rational decision-making among male street prostitutes. *Deviant Behavior: An Interdisciplinary Journal, 17,* 209–227.

Califia, P. (2002). Whoring in utopia. In A. Soble (Ed.), *The Philosophy of Sex: Contemporary Readings.* Lanham, MD: Rowman & Littlefield.

Callahan, S. (2002). Abortion and the sexual agenda: A case for prolife feminism. In A. Soble (Ed.), *The Philosophy of Sex: Contemporary Readings.* Lanham, MD: Rowman & Littlefield.

Calvert, H. (2003). Sexually transmitted diseases other than human immunodeficiency virus infection in older adults. *Clinical Infectious Diseases, 36,* 609–614.

Calzavara, L., Burchell, A., Remis, R., Major, C., Corey, P., Myers, T., Millson, M., Wallace, E., and the Polaris Study Team (2003). Delayed application of condoms is a risk factor for human immunodeficiency virus infection among homosexual and bisexual men. *American Journal of Epidemiology, 157,* 210–217.

Cambell, S. (2003). Prenatal cocaine exposure and neonatal/infant outcomes. *Neonatal Network, 22,* 19–21.

Campbell, C., & Mzaidume, Z. (2001). Grassroots participation, peer education, and HIV prevention by sex workers in South Africa. *American Journal of Public Health, 91,* 1978–1986.

Campbell, J. (2000). *Lesbian Wants Visitation Rights.* Retrieved July 12, 2000, from http://abcnews.go.com/sections/us/DailyNews/gaymom.html

Campo, J., Nijman, H., Merckelbach, H., & Evers, C. (2003). Psychiatric comorbidity of gender identity disorders: A survey among Dutch psychiatrists. *American Journal of Psychiatry, 160,* 1332–1336.

Canary, D., & Dindia, K. (Eds.) (1998). *Sex Differences and Similarities in Communication.* Mahwah, NJ: Erlbaum.

Canavan, M., Meyer, W., & Higgs, D. (1992). The female experience of sibling incest. *Journal of Marital and Family Therapy, 18,* 129–142.

Canavan, T., & Doshi, N. (2000). Cervical cancer. *American Family Physician, 61,* 1369–1376.

Capewell, A., McIntyre, M., & Elton, R. (1992). Post-menopausal atrophy in elderly women: Is a vaginal smear necessary for diagnosis? *Age and Aging, 21,* 117–120.

Caplan, L., May, D., & Richardson, L. (2000). Time to diagnosis and treatment of breast cancer: Results from the National Breast and Cervical Cancer Early Detection Program, 1991–1995. *American Journal of Public Health, 90,* 130–134.

Cardenas, K., & Frisch, K. (2003). Comprehensive breast cancer screening. *Postgraduate Medicine, 113,* 34–46.

Carlson, E. (1997). Sexual assault on men in war. *The Lancet, 349,* 129.

Carmichael, M. (2002). How to make a baby. *Newsweek,* July 15, 9.

Carmichael, M. (2004). No girls, please. *Newsweek,* January 26, 50.

Carmichael, M., Warburton, V., Dixen, J., & Davidson, J. (1994). Relationships among cardiovascular, muscular, and oxytocin responses during human sexual activity. *Archives of Sexual Behavior, 23,* 59–79.

Carnes, P. (1983). *Out of the Shadows: Understanding Sexual Addiction.* Minneapolis: Compcare Publications.

Carnes, P. (1986). Progress in sexual addiction: An addictive perspective. *SIECUS Report,* July, 4, 6.

Carnes, P. (1991). *Don't Call It Love.* New York: Bantam Books.

Carnes, P. (2000). Cybersex: The scope of the problem. *The Carnes Update,* Summer, 11.

Carpenter, L. (1998). From girls into women: Scripts for sexuality and romance in *Seventeen* magazine. *Journal of Sex Research, 35,* 158–168.

Carroll, L. (2000). *Families of Two: Interviews with Happily Married Couples Without Children by Choice.* Philadelphia: Xlibris.

Carroll, R. (1999). Outcomes of treatment for gender dysphoria. *Journal of Sex Education and Therapy, 24,* 128–136.

Carson, C. (2003). Penile prostheses: Are they still relevant? *British Journal of Urology International, 91,* 176–177.

Carswell, R. (1969). Historical analysis of religion and sex. *Journal of School Health, 39,* 673–683.

Carter, C. (1998). Neuroendocrine perspectives on social attachment and love. *Psychoneuroendocrinology, 13,* 779–818.

Carter, S. (2000). Math skill, confidence multiplying for girls. *The Oregonian,* March 4, A1, A11.

Carter, V. (2003). Prostitution = slavery. In R. Morgan (Ed.), *Sisterhood Is Forever.* New York: Washington Square Press.

Caruso, S., Agnello, C., & Intelisano, G. (2004). Sexual behavior of women taking low-dose oral contraceptives. *Contraception, 69,* 237–240.

Cassell, C. (2002). Let it shine: Promoting school success, life aspirations to prevent school-age parenthood. *SIECUS Report, 30,* 7–16.

Castleman, M. (1980). *Sexual Solutions.* New York: Simon & Schuster.

Castleman, M. (1997). Recipes for lust. *Psychology Today,* July–August, 50–56.

Castleman, M. (2004). *Great Sex: A Man's Guide to the Secret Principles of Total-Body Sex.* New York: St Martin's Press.

Castro, P., Vallejo, L., Lopez, R., & Curado, A. (2003). Combined treatment with vitamin E and colchicines in the early stages of Peyronie's disease. *British Journal of Urology International, 91,* 522–524.

Catania, J. (1999a). A comment on advancing the frontiers of sexological methods. *Journal of Sex Research, 36,* 1–2.

Catania, J. (1999b). A framework for conceptualizing reporting bias and its antecedents in interviews assessing human sexuality. *Journal of Sex Research, 36,* 25–38.

Catania, J., Gibson, D., Marin, B., Coates, T., & Greenblatt, R. (1990). Response bias in assessing sexual behaviors relevant to HIV transmission. *Evaluation and Program Planning, 13,* 19–29.

Cates, W., & Ellertson, C. (1998). Abortion. In R. Hatcher, J. Trussell, F. Stewart, W. Cates, G. Stewart, F. Guest, & D. Kowal (Eds.), *Contraceptive Technology.* New York: Ardent Media.

Catholics for a Free Choice. (2002). *Second Chance Denied: Emergency Contraception in Catholic Hospital Emergency Rooms.* Washington, DC: Catholics for a Free Choice.

Caufriez, A. (1997). The pubertal spurt: Effects of sex steroid on growth hormone and insulin-like growth factor I. *European Journal of Obstetrics and Gynecology and Biology, 71,* 215–217.

Ceci, S., Loftus, E., Leichtman, M., & Bruck, M. (1994). The role of source misattributions in the creation of false beliefs among preschoolers. *International Journal of Clinical and Experimental Hypnosis, 42,* 304–320.

Celentano, D. (2004). It's all in the measurement: Consistent condom use is effective in preventing sexually transmitted infections. *Sexually Transmitted Diseases, 31,* 161–162.

Centers for Disease Control (1996). Youth risk behavior surveillance: United States, 1995. *Morbidity and Mortality Weekly Report, 45(SS-4),* 1–84.

Centers for Disease Control (1997a). *Chlamydia trachomatis* genital infections: United States, 1995. *Morbidity and Mortality Weekly Report, 46,* 193–199.

Centers for Disease Control (1997b). Total and primary cesarean rates. *Monthly Vital Statistics Report, 45(11–3)*, July 16.

Centers for Disease Control (1998a). 1998 guidelines for treatment of sexually transmitted diseases. *Morbidity and Mortality Weekly Report, 47*, 1–116.

Centers for Disease Control (1998b). Trends in sexual risk behaviors among high school students: United States, 1991–1997. *Morbidity and Mortality Weekly Report, 47*, 749–752.

Centers for Disease Control (2000a). Adoption of protective behavior among persons with recent HIV infection and diagnosis: Alabama, New Jersey, and Tennessee, 1997–1998. *Morbidity and Mortality Weekly Report, 49*, 512–515.

Centers for Disease Control (2000b). Alcohol policy and sexually transmitted disease rates: United States, 1981–1995. *Morbidity and Mortality Weekly Report, 49*, 346–349.

Centers for Disease Control (2000c). HIV/AIDS among racial/ethnic minority men who have sex with men: United States, 1989–1998. *Morbidity and Mortality Weekly Report, 49*, 4–11.

Centers for Disease Control (2000d). Summary of notifiable diseases in the United States, 1998. *Morbidity and Mortality Weekly Report, 47*, 1–86.

Centers for Disease Control (2000e). Youth risk behavior surveillance: United States, 1999. *Morbidity and Mortality Weekly Report, 49*, 1–79.

Centers for Disease Control (2001). HIV testing among racial-ethnic minorities: United States, 1999. *Morbidity and Mortality Weekly Report, 50*, 1054–1057.

Centers for Disease Control (2002a). Guidelines for using antiretroviral agents among HIV-infected adults and adolescents: Recommendations of the Panel on Clinical Practices for Treatment of HIV. *Morbidity and Mortality Weekly Report, 51(RR-7)*, 1–55.

Centers for Disease Control (2002b). *HIV/AIDS Among African Americans.* Fact Sheet of the U.S. Centers for Disease Control and Prevention, National Center for HIV, STD, and TB Prevention. Atlanta: Centers for Disease Control.

Centers for Disease Control (2002c). *HIV/AIDS Among Hispanics in the United States.* Fact Sheet of the U.S. Centers for Disease Control and Prevention, National Center for HIV, STD, and TB Prevention. Atlanta: Centers for Disease Control.

Centers for Disease Control (2002d). *HIV/AIDS Among U.S. Women: Minority and Young Women at Continuing Risk.* Fact Sheet of the U.S. Centers for Disease Control and Prevention, National Center for HIV, STD, and TB Prevention. Atlanta: Centers for Disease Control.

Centers for Disease Control (2002e). Primary and secondary syphilis among men who have sex with men: New York City, 2001. *Morbidity and Mortality Weekly Report, 51*, 853–856.

Centers for Disease Control (2002f). Primary and secondary syphilis: United States, 2000–2001. *Morbidity and Mortality Weekly Report, 51*, 971–973.

Centers for Disease Control (2002g). Sexually transmitted diseases treatment guidelines, 2002. *Morbidity and Mortality Weekly Report, 51*, 36–82.

Centers for Disease Control (2002h). Youth risk behavior surveillance: United States, 2001. *Morbidity and Mortality Weekly Report, 51*, 1–62.

Centers for Disease Control (2003a). Advancing HIV prevention: New strategies for a changing epidemic—United States, 2003. *Morbidity and Mortality Weekly Report, 52*, 329–332.

Centers for Disease Control and Prevention. (2003b). Invasive cervical cancer among Hispanic and non-Hispanic women: United States, 1992–1999. *Journal of the American Medical Association, 289*, 39–40.

Centers for Disease Control (2004). *HIV/AIDS Surveillance Report.* Retrieved February 15, 2004, from http://www.cdc.gov/hiv/stats/hasr1302/commentary.htm

Chambliss, M., (2000). Bacterial vaginosis and treatment of sexual partners. *Archives of Family Medicine, 9*, 647–648.

Chan, C. (1995). Issues of sexual identity in an ethnic minority: The case of Chinese American lesbians, gay men, and bisexual people. In A. D'Augelli & C. Patterson (Eds.), *Lesbian, Gay, and Bisexual Identities over the Lifespan.* New York: Oxford University Press.

Chang, H., & Holt, G. (1991). The concept of *yuan* and Chinese interpersonal relationships. In S. Ting-Toomey & F. Korzenny (Eds.), *Cross-Cultural Interpersonal Communication.* Newbury Park, CA: Sage.

Chang, Y., & Chambers, V. (1999). Sex and the single girl. *Newsweek*, August 2, 60–61.

Chapkis, W. (1997). *Live Sex Acts: Women Performing Erotic Labor.* New York: Routledge.

Chapman, J. (1984). Sexual anhedonia: Disorders of sexual desire. *Journal of the American Osteopathic Association, 82*, 709–714.

Chappell, K., & Davis, K. (1998). Attachment, partner choice, and perception of romantic partners: An experimental test of the attachment–security hypothesis. *Personal Relationships, 5*, 327–342.

Chara, P., & Kuennen, L. (1994). Diverging gender attitudes regarding casual sex: A cross-sectional study. *Psychological Reports, 74*, 57–58.

Charlton, A. (1994). Children and passive smoking: A review. *Journal of Family Practice, 38(3)*, 267–277.

Charney, D., & Russell, R. (1994). An overview of sexual harassment. *American Journal of Psychiatry, 151*, 10–17.

Chasan-Taber, L., & Stampfer, M. (1998). Epidemiology of oral contraceptives and cardiovascular disease. *Annals of Internal Medicine, 128*, 467–477.

Chase, C. (2003). What is the agenda of the intersex advocacy movement? *Endocrinologist, 13*, 240–242.

Chavkin, W. (2001). Cocaine and pregnancy: Time to look at the evidence. *Journal of the American Medical Association, 285*, 1626–1627.

Check, J., & Guloien, T. (1989). Reported proclivity for coercive sex following repeated exposure to sexually violent pornography, nonviolent dehumanizing pornography, and erotica. In D. Zillman & J. Bryant (Eds.), *Pornography: Research Advances and Policy Considerations.* Hillsdale, NJ: Erlbaum.

Chen, C., Ballard, R., Beck-Sague, C., Dangor, Y., Radebe, F., Schmid, S., Weiss, J., Tshabalala, V., Fehler, G., & Morse, S. (2000). Human immunodeficiency virus infection and genital ulcer disease in South Africa: The herpetic connection. *Sexually Transmitted Diseases, 27*, 21–29.

Chen, X., Gong, X., Liang, G., & Zhang, G. (2000). Epidemiologic trends of sexually transmitted diseases in China. *Sexually Transmitted Diseases, 27*, 138–142.

Chesir-Teran, D. (2003). Conceptualizing and assessing heterosexism in high schools: A setting-level approach. *American Journal of Community Psychology, 31*, 267–277.

Chesney, M. (2003). Adherence to HAART regimens. *AIDS Patient Care and STDs, 17*, 169–177.

Chigbo, M. (2003). The fight for her life. *Ms.*, Summer, 26.

Chlebowski, R., Hendrix, S., Langer, R., & Stefanick, M. (2003). Influence of estrogen plus progestin on breast cancer and mammography in healthy postmenopausal women: The Women's Health Initiative randomized trial. *Journal of the American Medical Association, 289*, 3243–3253.

Chocano, C. (2000). *Swap Meat.* Retrieved April 21, 2000, from http://www.salon.com/people/feature/2000/04/21/lifestyle/index.html

Chocano, C. (2003). Sharper image: Bravo's *Queer Eye* gives the makeover-show genre an edge. *Entertainment Weekly*, August 8, 62.

Choi, K., Gregorich, S., Anderson, K., & Grinstead, O. (2003a). Patterns and predictors of female condom use among ethnically diverse women attending family planning clinics. *Sexually Transmitted Diseases*, January, 91–97.

Choi, K., Liu, H., Guo, Y., Ran, L., Mandel, J., & Rutherford, G. (2003b). Emerging HIV-I epidemic in China in men who have sex with men. *The Lancet, 361*, 2125–2126.

Choma, K. (2003). ASC-US HPV testing. *American Journal of Nursing, 103*, 42–50.

Chretien, F. (2003). Involvement of the glycoproteic meshwork of cervical mucus in the mechanism of sperm orientation. *Acta Obstetricia et Gynecologica Scandinavica, 82*, 449–461.

Chrisler, J., Johnston, I., Champagne, N., & Preston, K. (1994). Menstrual joy. *Psychology of Women Quarterly, 18*, 375–387.

Chrisler, J., & Levy, K. (1990). The media construct a menstrual monster: A content analysis of PMS articles in the popular press. *Women and Health, 16(2)*, 89–104.

Christakis, D., Harvey, E., Zerr, D., Feudtner, C., Wright, J., & Connell, F. (2000). A trade-off analysis of routine newborn circumcision. *Pediatrics, 105*, 246–249.

Christie, G., & Morgan, A. (2003). Love, hate, and the generative couple. In J. Haynes & J. Miller (Eds.), *Inconceivable Conceptions: Psychological Aspects of Infertility and Reproductive Technology.* Hove, United Kingdom: Brunner-Routledge.

Chuang, C., Chen, C., Chao, K., & Chen, S. (2003). Age is a better predictor of pregnancy potential than basal follicle-stimulating hormone levels in women undergoing in vitro fertilization. *Fertility and Sterility, 79*, 63–68.

Chumlea, W., Schubert, M., Roche, A., Kulin, H., Lee, P., Himes, J., & Sun, S. (2003). Age at menarche and racial comparisons in U.S. girls. *Pediatrics, 111,* 110–113.

Chung, W., & Choi, H. (1990). Erotic erection versus nocturnal erection. *Journal of Urology, 143,* 294–297.

Chung, W., De Vries, G., & Schaab, D. (2002). Sexual differentiation of the bed nucleus of the stria terminalis in humans may extend into adulthood. *Journal of Neurosciences, 22,* 1,027–1,033.

Ciccarone, D., Kanouse, D., Collins, R., Miu, A., Chen, J., Morton, S., & Stall, R. (2003). Sex without disclosure of positive HIV serostatus in a U.S. probability sample of persons receiving medical care for HIV infection. *American Journal of Public Health, 93,* 949–954.

Clancy, S., Schacter, D., McNally, R., & Pitman, R. (2000). False recognition in women reporting recovered memories of sexual abuse. *Psychological Science, 11,* 26–31.

Clanton, G., & Smith, L. (1977). *Jealousy.* Englewood Cliffs, NJ: Prentice Hall.

Clark, B., & Johnson, J. (2000). Advising postmenopausal women with fibroids on HRT options. *Contemporary OB/GYN,* January, 86–99.

Clark, J., Smith, E., & Davidson, J. (1984). Enhancement of sexual motivation in male rats by yohimbine. *Science, 225,* 847–849.

Clark, K. (2000). The new midlife. *U.S. News and World Report,* March 20, 70–83.

Clark, L., Brasseux, C., Richmond, D., Getson, P., & D'Angelo, L. (1998). Effect of HIV counseling and testing on sexually transmitted diseases and condom use in an urban adolescent population. *Archives of Pediatric and Adolescent Medicine, 152,* 269–273.

Clarke, T. (2001, July 13). *Pesticide Linked to Premature Births.* Retrieved July 24, 2001, from http://www.nature.com/nsu/010719/010719-3.html

Clarnette, T., Sugita, Y., & Hutson, J. (1997). Genital anomalies in human and animal models reveal the mechanisms and hormones governing testicular descent. *British Journal of Urology, 79,* 99–112.

Clausen, J. (1999). *Apples and Oranges.* Boston: Houghton Mifflin.

Clay, R. (2003). An empty nest can promote freedom, improves relationships. *Monitor on Psychology, 34,* 40–41.

Clement, U., & Pfäfflin, F. (1980). Changes in personality scores among couples subsequent to sex therapy. *Archives of Sexual Behavior, 9,* 235–244.

Clements, M. (1994). Sex in America today. *Parade,* August 7, 4–6.

Clements, M. (1996). Sex after 65. *Parade,* March 17, 4–6.

Clements, M. (1998). *The Improvised Woman: Single Women Reinventing Single Life.* New York: W. W. Norton.

Clementson, L. (2000a). Color my world. *Newsweek,* May 8, 70–74.

Clementson, L. (2000b). A search for God's welcome. *Newsweek,* March 20, 60–61.

Clift, E. (2003). The waiting game. *Newsweek,* May 19, 9.

Cloud, J. (2004). How Oregon eloped. *Time,* May 17, 56–62.

CNN.com (2003, October 6). *Male Contraceptive Tests Positive.* Retrieved October 6, 2003, from http://www.cnn.com/2003/HEALTH/10/06/male.pill/

Cobb, N., Larson, J., & Watson, W. (2003). Development of the attitudes about romance and mate selection scale. *Family Relations, 52,* 222–231.

Cochran, S., & Mays, V. (1990). Sex, lies, and HIV. *New England Journal of Medicine, 322,* 774.

Cochran, S., & Mays, V. (1994). Depressive distress among homosexually active African American men and women. *American Journal of Psychiatry, 151,* 524–529.

Cochran, S., Mays, V., & Leung, L. (1991). Sexual practices of heterosexual Asian American young adults: Implications for risk of HIV infection. *Archives of Sexual Behavior, 20,* 381–392.

Cochran, S., Mays, V., & Sullivan, J. (2003). Prevalence of mental disorders, psychological distress, and mental health services use among lesbian, gay, and bisexual adults in the United States. *Journal of Consulting and Clinical Psychology, 71,* 53–61.

Cockey, C. (2003). Breast cancer risk from HRT confirmed. *AWHONN Lifelines, 7,* 16–23.

Coco, A. (1999). Primary dysmenorrhea. *American Family Physician, 60,* 489–496.

Coco, A., & Vandenbosche, M. (2000). Infectious vaginitis. *Postgraduate Medicine, 107,* 63–74.

Cocores, J., & Gold, M. (1989). Substance abuse and sexual dysfunction. *Medical Aspects of Human Sexuality,* February, 22–31.

Coe, C., Lulbach, G., & Schneider, M. (2002). Prenatal disturbance alters the size of the corpus callosum in young monkeys. *Developmental Psychobiology, 41,* 178–185.

Cogen, R., & Steinman, W. (1990). Sexual function and practice in elderly men of lower socioeconomic status. *Journal of Family Practice, 32,* 162–166.

Cohen, E. (2000). *Estrogen/Progestin Combination Increases Risk of Breast Cancer, AMA Reports.* Retrieved January 27, 2000, from http://www.cnn.com/2000/HEALTH/cancer/01/25/hormone.cancer.risk.02/index.html

Cohen, E. (2001). *New Treatments Hold Out Hope for Breast Cancer Patients.* Retrieved January 26, 2001, from http://www.cnn.com/2001/HEALTH/cancer/01/26/breast.cancer/index.html

Cohen, F., Kemeny, M., Kearney, K., Zegans, L., Neuhaus, J., & Conant, M. (1999). Persistent stress as a predictor of genital herpes recurrence. *Archives of Internal Medicine, 159,* 2430–2436.

Cohen, J. (1998). Uninfectable. *The New Yorker,* July 6, 34–39.

Cohen, J. (2000). AIDS researchers look to Africa for new insights. *Science, 287,* 942–943.

Cohen, J. (2001). AIDS vaccines show promise after years of frustration. *Science, 291,* 1686–1688.

Cohen, M., Ping, G., Fox, K., & Henderson, G. (2000). Sexually transmitted diseases in the Peoples Republic of China in Y2K. *Sexually Transmitted Diseases, 27,* 143–145.

Cohen-Kettenis, P., & Gooren, L. (1999). Transsexualism: A review of etiology, diagnosis, and treatment. *Journal of Psychosomatic Research, 46,* 315–333.

Cohen-Kettenis, P., Owen, A., Kaijser, V., Bradley, S., & Zucker, K. (2003). Demographic characteristics, social competence, and behavioral problems in children with gender identity disorder: A cross-national, cross-clinic comparative analysis. *Journal of Abnormal Child Psychology, 31,* 41–53.

Cohn, B. (1992). Discrimination: The limits of the law. *Newsweek,* September 14, 38–39.

Colapinto, J. (2000). *As Nature Made Him: The Boy Who Was Raised as a Girl.* New York: HarperCollins.

Coldman, A., Phillips, N., & Pickles, T. (2003). Trends in prostate cancer incidence and mortality: An analysis of mortality change by screening intensity. *Canadian Medical Association Journal, 168,* 31–35.

Cole, C. (2003). Vaccine prevents genital herpes in subgroup of women. *Journal of Family Practice, 52,* 94–95.

Cole, C., & Cole, A. (1999). Marriage enrichment and prevention really works: Interpersonal competence training to maintain and enhance relationships. *Family Relations: Interdisciplinary Journal of Applied Family Studies, 48,* 273–275.

Cole, C., O'Boyle, M., Emory, L., & Meyer, W. (1997). Comorbidity of gender dysphoria and other major psychiatric diagnoses. *Archives of Sexual Behavior, 26,* 13–26.

Cole, D. (1987). It might have been: Mourning the unborn. *Psychology Today,* July, 64–65.

Cole, J. (1992). Commonalities and differences. In M. Andersen & P. Collins (Eds.), *Race, Class, and Gender.* Belmont, CA: Wadsworth.

Cole, S., Denny, D., Eyler, A., & Samons, S. (2000). Issues of transgender. In L. Szuchman & F. Muscarella (Eds.), *Psychological Perspectives on Human Sexuality.* New York: Wiley.

Coleman, E. (1990). The obsessive-compulsive model for describing compulsive sexual behavior. *American Journal of Preventive Psychiatry and Neurology, 2,* 9–14.

Coleman, E. (1991). Compulsive sexual behavior: New concepts and treatments. *Journal of Psychology and Human Sexuality, 4,* 37–51.

Coleman, E. (1998). Erectile dysfunction: A review of current medical treatments. *Canadian Journal of Human Sexuality, 7,* 231.

Coleman, E. (1999). Revolution. *Contemporary Sexuality,* September, 1–4.

Coleman, E. (2000). A new sexual revolution in health, diversity, and rights. *SIECUS Report, 28,* 4–5.

Coleman, E. (2003). Compulsive sexual behavior: What to call it, how to treat it? *SIECUS Report, 31,* 12–16.

Coleman, M., & Ganong, L. (1985). Love and sex role stereotypes: Do macho men and feminine women make better lovers? *Journal of Personality and Social Psychology, 49,* 170–176.

Coles, R., & Stokes, G. (1985). *Sex and the American Teenager.* New York: Harper & Row.

Coley, R., & Chase-Lansdale, P. (1998). Adolescent pregnancy and parenthood. *American Psychologist, 53,* 152–166.

Colgan, R., Michocki, R., Greisman, L., & Moore, T. (2003). Antiviral drugs in the immunocompetent host. Part I. Treatment of hepatitis, cytomegalovirus, and herpes infections. *American Family Physician, 67,* 757–762.

Colino, S. (1991). Sex and the expectant mother. *Parenting,* February, 111.

Collaborative Group on Hormonal Factors in Breast Cancer. (2002). Breast cancer and breastfeeding: Collaborative reanalysis of individual data from 47 epidemiological studies in 30 countries, including 50,302 women with breast cancer and 96,973 women without the disease. *The Lancet, 360,* 94–95.

Collier, M. (1991). Conflict competence within African, Mexican, and Anglo American friendships. In S. Ting-Toomey & F. Korzenny (Eds.), *Cross-Cultural Interpersonal Communication* . Newbury Park, CA: Sage.

Collins, S. (1994). The long-term effects of contact and noncontact forms of child sexual abuse in a sample of university men. *Child Abuse and Neglect, 19,* 1–6.

Comas-Diaz, L., & Greene, B. (Eds.) (1994). *Women of Color.* New York: Guilford Press.

Comfort, A. (1972). *The Joy of Sex.* New York: Crown.

Comiteau, L. (2001). "Sexual enslavement" established as a war crime. *USA Today,* February 23, A10.

Connell, J. (1992). Seeking common ground. *The Oregonian,* April 5, B1–B4.

Connor, E., Sperling, R., & Gelber, R. (1994). Reduction of maternal-infant transmission of human immunodeficiency virus type 1 with zidovudine treatment. *New England Journal of Medicine, 331,* 1173–1180.

Contemporary Sexuality (1996). U.S. has most rapes in the Western world. *Contemporary Sexuality, 30,* 5.

Contemporary Sexuality (1998). Children and healthy sexuality. *Contemporary Sexuality, 32,* 1–2.

Contemporary Sexuality (1999a). Hormone supplements help women regain libido. *Contemporary Sexuality, 33,* 12.

Contemporary Sexuality (1999b). Japanese hardly swallow the pill. *Contemporary Sexuality, 33,* 8.

Contemporary Sexuality (1999c). Nerve operation restores erectile function. *Contemporary Sexuality, 33,* 11.

Contemporary Sexuality (1999d). Playful language. *Contemporary Sexuality, 33,* 1–2.

Contemporary Sexuality (1999e). Sexual science: A discipline for the next millennium. *Contemporary Sexuality, 33,* 1–2, 17.

Contemporary Sexuality (2000a). Birth control to board room: A new study. *Contemporary Sexuality, 34,* 6.

Contemporary Sexuality (2000b). Clinton signs agreements to protect children. *Contemporary Sexuality, 34,* 8.

Contemporary Sexuality (2000c). C.U. in Vermont, cheer betrothed gays. *Contemporary Sexuality, 34,* 8.

Contemporary Sexuality (2000d). How to repeal archaic sodomy laws? *Contemporary Sexuality, 34,* 1.

Contemporary Sexuality (2000e). Marie Stopes offer raises a huff in France. *Contemporary Sexuality, 34,* 8.

Contemporary Sexuality (2000f). Minnesota's sodomy law challenged. *Contemporary Sexuality, 34,* 7.

Contemporary Sexuality (2000g). Planned Parenthood sues: Contraceptives should be covered by insurance, it says. *Contemporary Sexuality, 34,* 9.

Contemporary Sexuality (2000h). Protests against gay school club reach fever pitch in California. *Contemporary Sexuality, 34,* 8.

Contemporary Sexuality (2000i). Third "crime of honor" in Jordan in 2000, lax sentences remain. *Contemporary Sexuality, 34,* 6.

Contemporary Sexuality (2001a). China ends notorious one-child policy in some regions. *Contemporary Sexuality, 35,* 9.

Contemporary Sexuality (2001b). Gays in China no longer "sick." *Contemporary Sexuality, 35,* 8.

Contemporary Sexuality (2001c). Study confirms public health fears about teens' views of "safe" sex. *Contemporary Sexuality, 35,* 10.

Contemporary Sexuality (2002a). Pediatricians group backs gay parents. *Contemporary Sexuality, 36,* 10.

Contemporary Sexuality (2002b). Supermarkets in Britain to give morning-after pill free to teens. *Contemporary Sexuality, 36,* 9.

Contemporary Sexuality (2003a). DVDs make porn "interactive." *Contemporary Sexuality, 37,* 9.

Contemporary Sexuality (2003b). No pill, but other male birth control likely in not-too-distant future. *Contemporary Sexuality, 37,* 8.

Contemporary Sexuality (2004). China launches sex ed in schools. *Contemporary Sexuality, 38,* 7.

The Contraception Report (2002a). Leas' shield. *The Contraception Report, 13,* 4.

The Contraception Report (2002b). St. John's wort and oral contraceptives. *The Contraception Report, 13,* 12.

Cook, J. (2001). Sexuality and people with psychiatric disabilities, *SIECUS Report, 29,* 20–25.

Cook, L., Kamb, M., & Weiss, N. (1997). Perineal powder exposure and the risk of ovarian cancer. *American Journal of Epidemiology, 145,* 459–465.

Cook, L., Koutsky, L., & Holmes, K. (1994). Circumcision and sexually transmitted diseases. *American Journal of Public Health, 84,* 197–201.

Cook, R., Wiesenfeld, H., Ashton, M., Krohn, M., Zamborsky, T., & Scholle, S. (2001). Barriers to screening sexually active adolescent women for chlamydia: A survey of primary care physicians. *Journal of Adolescent Health, 28,* 204–210.

Cooksey, E., Mott, F., & Neubauer, S. (2002). Friendships and early relationships: Links to sexual initiation among American adolescents born to young mothers. *Perspectives on Sexual and Reproductive Health, 34,* 118–126.

Cooper, A. (1996). Autoerotic asphyxiation: Three case reports. *Journal of Sex and Marital Therapy, 22,* 47–53.

Cooper, A. (Ed.) (2002). *Sex and the Internet.* Philadelphia: Brunner-Routledge.

Cooper, A. (2003). *Cybersex Addictions: How to Identify and Treat the Affects of Aberrant Online Sexual Pursuits.* Paper presented at the American Society of Professional Education, Portland, Oregon, December.

Cooper, A. (2004). Online sexual activity in the new millennium. *Contemporary Sexuality, 38,* i–vii.

Cooper, A., Boies, S., Maheu, M., & Greenfield, D. (2000). Sexuality and the Internet: The next sexual revolution. In L. Szuchman & F. Muscarella (Eds.), *Psychological Perspectives on Human Sexuality.* New York: Wiley.

Cooper, A., Scherer, C., Boies, S., & Gordon, B. (1999). Sexuality on the Internet: From sexual exploration to pathological expression. *Professional Psychology: Research and Practice, 30,* 154–164.

Cooper, C. (2000). Abortion: Take back the right. *Ms.,* June–July, 17–21.

Cooperman, A. (2003). The gay marriage debate: Groups for and against same-sex unions say fight is heating up. *The Oregonian,* July 31, A10.

Coreil, J., & Parcel, G. (1983). Sociocultural determinants of parental involvement in sex education. *Journal of Sex Education and Therapy, 9,* 22–25.

Corey, L., & Handsfield, H. (2000). Genital herpes and public health: Addressing a global problem. *Journal of the American Medical Association, 283,* 791–794.

Corey, L., Tyring, S., & Beutner, K. (2002). *Once Daily Valacyclovir Reduces Transmission of Genital Herpes.* Paper presented at the 42nd Interscience Conference on Antimicrobial Agents and Chemotherapy, San Diego, September 20–30.

Corliss, R., & Steptoe, S. (2004). *Time Special Issue,* January 19, 117–122.

Cornig, M. (2003). *The Big Book of Masturbation from Angst to Zeal.* San Francisco: Down There Press.

Cose, E. (2000). Our new look: The colors of race. *Newsweek,* January 1, 28–30.

Cose, E. (2003). The black gender gap. *Newsweek,* March 3, 46–51.

Cosgray, R., Hanna, V., Fawley, R., & Money, M. (1991). Death from autoerotic asphyxiation in long-term psychiatric setting. *Perspectives in Psychiatric Care, 27,* 21–24.

Cottrell, B. (2003). Vaginal douching. *Journal of Obstetrical, Gynecological, and Neonatal Nursing, 32,* 12–18.

Couper, M., & Stinson, L. (1999). Completion of self-administered questionnaires in a sex survey. *Journal of Sex Research, 36,* 321–330.

Courtois, C. (2000a). The aftermath of child sexual abuse: The treatment of complex posttraumatic stress reactions. In L. Szuchman & F. Muscarella (Eds.), *Psychological Perspectives on Human Sexuality.* New York: Wiley.

Courtois, C. (2000b). The sexual after-effect of incest/child sexual abuse. *SIECUS Report, 29,* 11–16.

Courville, T., Caldwell, B., & Brunell, P. (1998). Lack of evidence of transmission of HIV-1 to family contacts of HIV-1 infected children. *Clinical Pediatrics, 37,* 175–178.

Coventry, M. (2000). Making the cut. *Ms.,* October–November, 52–60.

Cowan, G. (2000). Beliefs about the causes of four types of rape. *Sex Roles, 42,* 807–823.

Cowan, G., & Campbell, R. (1994). Racism and sexism in interracial pornography. *Psychology of Women Quarterly, 18,* 323–338.

Cowan, P., & Cowan C. (1992). *When Partners Become Parents.* New York: HarperCollins.

Cowen, D. (2003). Assisted reproductive technology and the fertility clinic. In J. Haynes & J. Miller (Eds.), *Inconceivable Conceptions: Psychological Aspects of Infertility and Reproductive Technology*. Hove, United Kingdom: Brunner–Routledge.

Cowley, G. (2003). Ratings: Not Mother's Day. *Newsweek*, May 12, 8.

Cowley, G., Laris, M., & Hager, M. (1996). From freedom to fear: When AIDS hits China. *Newsweek*, April 1, 49.

Cowley, G., & Springen, K. (1997). Multiplying the risks. *Newsweek*, December 1, 66.

Cowley, G., & Springen, K. (2002). Reconsidering HRT. *Newsweek*, April 29, 71.

Cox, D. (1988). Incidence and nature of male genital exposure behavior as reported by college women. *Journal of Sex Research, 24,* 227–234.

Coyle, K. (2001). Safer choices: Reducing teen pregnancies, HIV, and STDs. *Public Health Reports, 116(suppl.)*, 83–93.

Coyne, J., & Berry, A. (2000). Rape as an adaptation. *Nature*, March 9, 121–122.

Cramer, D., Xu, H., & Harlow, B. (1995). Does "incessant" ovulation increase risk for early menopause? *American Journal Obstetrics and Gynecology, 172,* 568–573.

Crary, D. (1999). The troubled state of marriage: Despite ideals, Bible Belt sets pace in breakups. *The Oregonian*, November 12, A24.

Crawford, M., & Popp, D. (2003). Sexual double standards: A review and methodological critique of two decades of research. *Journal of Sex Research, 40,* 13–26.

Creighton, S. & Liao, L. (2004). Changing attitudes to sex assignment in intersex. *British Journal of Urology International, 93,* 659–664.

Creinin, M. (2003, January). *Frequent Daily Use of Nonoxynol-9 May Increases the Risk of HIV Infection.* Retrieved October 19, 2003, from http://www.contraceptiononline.org/contrareport/article01.cfm?art=230

Crenshaw, T. (1996). *The Alchemy of Love and Lust.* New York: Putnam.

Crenshaw, T., & Goldberg, J. (1996). *Sexual Pharmacology: Drugs That Affect Sexual Function.* New York: Norton.

Crenshaw, T., Goldberg, J., & Stern, W. (1987). Pharmacologic modification of psychosexual dysfunction. *Journal of Sex and Marital Therapy, 13,* 239–252.

Critelli, J., & Suire, D. (1998). Obstacles to condom use: The combination of other forms of birth control and short-term monogamy. *Journal of American College Health, 46,* 215–221.

Crohan, S. (1996). Marital quality and conflict across the transition to parenthood in African American and white couples. *Journal of Marriage and the Family, 58,* 933–944.

Crooks, R. (2004). A "grassroots" peer-educator and VCT based HIV/AIDS program in Makindu, Kenya. Unpublished.

Crosby, R., & Lawrence, J. (2000). Adolescents' use of school-based health clinics for reproductive health services: Data from the National Longitudinal Study of Adolescent Health. *Journal of School Health, 70,* 22–27.

Crosby, R., Sanders, S., Yarber, W., Graham, C., & Dodge, B. (2002). Condom use errors and problems in college men. *Sexually Transmitted Diseases, 29,* 552–557.

Crossette, B. (2000). Two-thirds of nations fail to make sure blood supplies are safe. *The Oregonian*, April 7, A16.

Cunningham, D., & Newton, W. (2003). Early radical prostatectomy improves disease-specific but not overall survival. *Journal of Family Practice, 52,* 22–23.

Cunningham, G., Cordero, E., & Thornby, J. (1989). Testosterone replacement with transdermal therapeutic systems. *Journal of the American Medical Association, 261,* 2525–2531.

Curry, L. (2000). Net provides new expression for sexual offenders. *APA Monitor*, April, 21.

Curtin, S., & Martin, J. (2000). Births: Preliminary data for 1999. *National Vital Statistics Reports, 48,* 1–6.

Curtis, R., & Miller, K. (1997). Believing another likes or dislikes you: Behavior making the beliefs come true. *Journal of Personality and Social Psychology, 51,* 284–290.

Cutler, W. (1999). Human sex-attractant pheromones: Discovery, research, development, and application in sex therapy. *Psychiatric Annals, 29,* 54–59.

Cutler, W., Preti, G., Krieger, A., Huggins, G., Garcia, C., & Lawley, H. (1986). Human axillary secretions influence women's menstrual cycles: The role of donor extract from men. *Hormones and Behavior, 20,* 463–473.

Cuzick, J., Powles, T., Veronesi, U., & Forbes, J. (2003). Overview of the main outcomes in breast-cancer prevention trials. *The Lancet, 361,* 296–300.

Czuczka, D. (2000). The twentieth century: An American sexual history. *SIECUS Report, 28,* 15–18.

Daar, J. (1999). Assisted reproductive technologies and the pregnancy process: Developing an equality model to protect reproductive liberties. *American Journal of Law and Medicine, 25,* 455–477.

Dabbs, J. (2000). *Heroes, Rogues, and Lovers: Testosterone and Behavior.* New York: McGraw-Hill.

Dahir, M. (2003). Marriage on his mind. *The Advocate*, June 24, 46–48.

Dall'Ara, E., & Maass, A. (1999). Studying sexual harassment in the laboratory: Are egalitarian women at higher risk? *Sex Roles, 41,* 681–704.

Dalton, S., & Bielby, D. (2000). "That's our kind of constellation": Lesbian mothers negotiate institutionalized understandings of gender within the family. *Gender and Society, 14,* 36–61.

Daly, M., Wilson, M., & Weghorst, S. (1982). Male sexual jealousy. *Ethology and Sociobiology, 3,* 11–27.

Damson, P. (Ed.) (1996). *The Progress of Nations.* New York: UNICEF.

Daniluk, J. (1998). *Women's Sexuality Across the Life Span: Challenging Myths, Creating Meanings.* New York: Guilford Press.

Darling, C., Davidson, J., & Conway-Welch, C. (1990). Female ejaculation: Perceived origins, the Grafenberg spot/area, and sexual responsiveness. *Archives of Sexual Behavior, 19,* 29–47.

Daro, D. (1991). Child sexual abuse prevention: Separating fact from fiction. *Child Abuse and Neglect, 15,* 1–4.

Darroch, J., & Frost, J. (1999). Women's interest in vaginal microbicides. *Family Planning Perspectives, 31,* 16–23.

Darroch, J., Landry, D., & Oslak, S. (1999a). Age differences between sexual partners in the United States. *Family Planning Perspectives, 31,* 160–167.

Darroch, J., Landry, D., & Oslak, S. (1999b). Pregnancy rates among U.S. women and their partners in 1994. *Family Planning Perspectives, 31,* 122–126.

D'Augelli, A. (2003). Coming out in community psychology: Personal narrative and disciplinary change. *American Journal of Community Psychology, 31,* 343–353.

Dauphinee, J. (2004). VBAC: Safety for the patient and nurse. *Journal of Gynecological and Neonatal Nursing, 33,* 105–115.

David, H., & Russo, N. (2003). Psychology, population, and reproductive behavior. *American Psychologist, 58,* 193–196.

Davies, M. (1995). Parental distress and ability to cope following disclosure of extra-familial sexual abuse. *Child Abuse and Neglect, 19,* 399–408.

Davies, M. (2002). Male sexual assault victims: A selective review of the literature and implications for support services. *Aggression and Violent Behavior, 7,* 203–214.

Davis, B., & Noble, M. (1991). Putting an end to chronic testicular pain. *Medical Aspects of Human Sexuality*, April, 26–34.

Davis, D. (2000). Most cancer is made, not born. *San Francisco Chronicle*, August 10, 1–3.

Davis, K., & Latty-Mann, H. (1987). Love styles and relationship quality: A contribution to validation. *Journal of Social and Personal Relationships, 4,* 409–428.

Davis, P., & Lay-Yee, R. (1999). Early sex and its behavioral consequences in New Zealand. *Journal of Sex Research, 36,* 135–144.

Davis, S. (1999). The therapeutic use of androgens in women. *Journal of Steroid Biochemistry and Molecular Biology, 69,* 177–184.

Davis, S. (2000). Testosterone and sexual desire in women. *Journal of Sex Education and Therapy, 25,* 25–32.

Davis, S., McCloud, P., Strauss, B., & Burger, H. (1995). Testosterone enhances estradiol's effects on postmenopausal bone density and sexuality. *Maturitas, 21,* 227–236.

Davison, G., & Neale, J. (1993). *Abnormal Psychology* (6th ed.). New York: Wiley.

Davtyan, C. (2000). Contraception for adolescents. *Western Journal of Medicine, 172,* 166–171.

Dawes, R. (1994). *House of Cards: Psychology and Psychotherapy Built of Myth.* New York: Free Press.

D'Cruz, O., & Uckun, F. (2003). Contraceptive activity of a spermicidal arylphosphate derivative of bromo-methoxyzidovudine (compound WHI-07) in rabbits. *Fertility and Sterility, 79,* 864–871.

De Amicis, L., Goldberg, D., LoPiccolo, J., Friedman, J., & Davies, L. (1984). Three-year follow-up of couples evaluated for sexual dysfunction. *Journal of Sex and Marital Therapy, 10,* 215–228.

Dean, K., & Malamuth, N. (1997). Characteristics of men who aggress sexually and men who imagine aggressing: Risk and moderating variables. *Journal of Personality and Social Psychology, 72*, 449–455.

Dean, M., Carrington, M., & Winkler, C. (1996). Genetic restriction of HIV-1 infection and progression to AIDS by a deletion allele of the CKR5 structural gene. *Science, 273*, 1856–1862.

De Bro, S., Campbell, S., & Peplau, L. (1994). Influencing a partner to use a condom. *Psychology of Women Quarterly, 18*, 165–182.

DeCaro, F. (1997). Finally out, and suddenly in. *Newsweek*, May 12, 83.

Decker, D., Pettinga, J., Vander Velde, N., & Huang, R. (2003). Estrogen replacement therapy in breast cancer survivors: A matched-controlled series. *Menopause: The Journal of the North American Menopause Society, 10*, 277–285.

Deckers, P., & Ricci, A., Jr. (1992). Pain and lumps in the female breast. *Hospital Practice*, February 28, 67–94.

DeGarmo, D., & Kitson, G. (1996). Identity relevance and disruption as predictors of psychological distress for widowed and divorced women. *Journal of Marriage and the Family, 58*, 983–997.

Degler, C. (1980). *At Odds: Women and the Family in America from the Revolution to the Present*. Oxford: Oxford University Press.

Dehne, K., & Kobyshcha, Y. (2000). *The HIV Epidemic in Central and Eastern Europe: Update 2000*. Geneva: UNAIDS.

Dehne, K., Pokrovsky, V., Kobyshcha, Y., & Schwartlander, B. (2000). Update on the epidemics of HIV and other sexually transmitted infections in the newly independent states of the former Soviet Union. *AIDS 2000, 14(suppl. 3)*, 575–584.

Deitch, C. (1983). Ideology and opposition to abortion: Trends in public opinion, 1972–1980. *Alternative Lifestyles, 6*, 6–26.

Dekker, J., Everaerd, W., & Verhelst, N. (1985). Attending to stimuli or to images of sexual feelings: Effects on sexual arousal. *Behavior Research and Therapy, 23*, 139–149.

De Knijff, D., Vrijhof, H., Arends, J., & Janknegt, R. (1997). Persistence or reappearance of nonmotile sperm after vasectomy: Does it have clinical consequences? *Fertility and Sterility, 67*, 332–335.

De Lacoste, M., Adesanya, T., & Woodward, D. (1990). Measures of gender differences in the human brain and their relationship to brain weight. *Biological Psychiatry, 28*, 931–942.

DeLaMar, R. (2003). And babies make six. *The Advocate*, June 24, 73–74.

DeLamater, J., & Friedrich, W. (2002). Human sexual development. *Journal of Sex Research, 39*, 10–14.

Delaney, J., Lupton, M., & Toth, E. (1976). *The Curse: A Cultural History of Menstruation*. New York: Dutton.

Del Carmen, R. (1990). Assessment of Asian-Americans for family therapy. In F. Serafica, A. Schwebel, R. Russell, P. Isaac, & L. Myers (Eds.), *Mental Health of Ethnic Minorities*. New York: Praeger.

Deliganis, A., Maravilla, K., Heiman, J., Carter, W., Garland, P., & Weisskoff, R. (2000). Dynamic MR imaging of the female genitalia using Angiomark: Initial experience evaluating the female sexual response [abstract]. *Radiology, 214*, 611. Originally presented as an RSNA Hot Topic presentation, Chicago, November 1999.

Delzell, J., & Lefevre, M. (2000). Urinary tract infections during pregnancy. *American Family Physician, 61*, 713–721.

Démare, D., Briere, J., & Lips, H. (1988). Violent pornography and self-reported likelihood of sexual aggression. *Journal of Research in Personality, 22*, 140–153.

DeMartino, M. (1970). How women want men to make love. *Sexology*, October, 4–7.

DeMarzo, A., Nelson, W., Isaacs, W., & Epstein, J. (2003). Pathological and molecular aspects of prostate cancer. *The Lancet, 361*, 955–964.

D'Emilio, J., & Freedman, E. (1988). *Intimate Matters*. New York: Harper & Row.

Dempsey, C. (1994). Health and social issues of gay, lesbian, and bisexual adolescents. *Families in Society*, March, 160–167.

Dennerstein, L., Burrows, G., Wood, C., & Hyman, G. (1980). Hormones and sexuality: The effects of estrogen and progestogen. *Obstetrics and Gynecology, 56*, 316–322.

Dennerstein, L., Gotts, G., Brown, J., Morse, C., Farley, T., & Pinol, A. (1994). The relationship between the menstrual cycle and female sexual interest in women with PMS complaints and volunteers. *Psychoneuroendocrinology, 19*, 293–304.

Denny, D. (1997). Transgender: Some historical, cross-cultural, and contemporary models and methods of coping and treatment. In B. Bullough, V. Bullough, & J. Elias (Eds.), *Gender Blending*. New York: Prometheus Books.

Denny, D. (1999). Transgender in the United States: A brief discussion. *SIECUS Report, 27*, 8–13.

Denov, M. (2003a). *Perspectives on Female Sexual Offending: A Culture of Denial*. Brookfield, VT: Ashgate Publishing.

Denov, M. (2003b). To a safer place: Victims of sexual abuse by females and their disclosures to professionals. *Child Abuse and Neglect, 27*, 47–61.

D'Epiro, P. (1997). Complicated UTI. *Patient Care*, April 15, 196–208.

DeQuine, J. (2003). Out of the closet and on to fraternity row. *Time*, March 17, 8.

Derlego, V., Metts, S., Petronia, S., & Margulis, S. (1993). *Self-Disclosure*. Newbury Park, CA: Sage.

Des Jarlais, D., Diaz, T., Perlis, T., Vlahov, D., Maslow, C., Latka, M., Rockwell, R., Edwards, V., Friedman, S., Monterroso, E., Williams, I., & Garfein, R. (2003). Variability in the incidence of human immunodeficiency virus, hepatitis B virus, and hepatitis C virus infection among young injecting drug users in New York City. *American Journal of Epidemiology, 157*, 467–471.

Des Jarlais, D., Marmor, M., Friedmann, P., Titus, S., Aviles, E., Deren, S., Torian, L., Glebatis, D., Murrill, C., Monterroso, E., & Friedman, S. (2000). HIV incidence among injection drug users in New York City, 1992–1997: Evidence for a declining epidemic. *American Journal of Public Health, 90*, 352–359.

Des Jarlais, D., & Schuchat, A. (2001). Hepatitis C among drug users: Deja vu all over again? *American Journal of Public Health, 91*, 21–22.

Dessens, A., Cohen-Kettenis, P., Mellenbergh, G., Poll, N., Kopper, J., & Boer, K. (1999). Prenatal exposure to anticonvulsants and psychosexual development. *Archives of Sexual Behavior, 28*, 31–44.

Deutsch, A. (2000). *The Netherlands OKs Gay Marriages*. Retrieved September 12, 2000, from http://dailynews.yahoo.com/h/ap/20000912/wl/netherlands_gay_marriage.html

Deveny, K. (2003). We're not in the mood. *Newsweek*, June 30, 40–46.

Devi, K. (1977). *The Eastern Way of Love: Tantric Sex and Erotic Mysticism*. New York: Simon & Schuster.

De Villers, L. (2001). *Love Skills: More Fun Than You've Ever Had with Sex, Intimacy, and Communication*. San Luis Obispo, CA: Impact Publishers.

Dewar, H. (2003). *Senate Passes Ban on Abortion Procedure*. Retrieved October 26, 2003, from http://www.washingtonpost.com/ac2/wp-dyn/A61725-2003Oct21

Dewhurst, A., & Nielsen, K. (1999). A resiliency-based approach to working with sexual offenders. *Sexual Addiction and Compulsivity, 6*, 271–279.

Diamant, A., Schuster, M., McGuigan, K., & Lever, J. (1999). Lesbians' sexual history with men. *Archives of Internal Medicine, 159*, 2730–2736.

Diamond, L. (2000). Sexual identity, attractions, and behavior among young sexual-minority women over a 2-year period. *Developmental Psychology, 36*, 241–250.

Diamond, L. (2003a). Was it a phase? Young women's relinquishment of lesbian/bisexual identities over a 5-year period. *Journal of Personality and Social Psychology, 84*, 352–364.

Diamond, L. (2003b). What does sexual orientation orient? A biobehavioral model distinguishing romantic love and sexual desire. *Psychological Review, 110*, 173–192.

Diamond, L., & Savin-Williams, R. (2000). *Explaining Diversity in the Development of Same-Sex Sexuality Among Young Women*. Retrieved from http://infotrac-college.thomsonlearning.com/itw/infomark/684/939/38133136w6/9!xrn_3_0 . . .

Diamond, M. (1991a). Environmental influences on the young brain. In K. Gibson & A. Petersen (Eds.), *Brain Maturation and Cognitive Development: Comparative and Cross-Cultural Perspectives*. Hawthorn, NY: Aldine deGruyter.

Diamond, M. (1991b). Hormonal effects on the development of cerebral lateralization. *Psychoneuroendocrinology, 16*, 121–129.

Diamond, M. (1997). Sexual identity and sexual orientation in children with traumatized or ambiguous genitalia. *Journal of Sex Research, 34*, 199–211.

Diamond, M. (1998). Intersexuality: Recommendations for management. *Archives of Sexual Behavior, 27*, 634–641.

Diamond, M., & Sigmundson, H. (1997). Sex reassignment at birth: Long-term review and clinical implications. *Archives of Pediatric and Adolescent Medicine, 151*, 298–304.

Diamond, R., Kezur, D., Meyers, M., Scharf, C., & Weinshel, M. (1999). *Couple Therapy for Infertility*. New York: Guilford Press.

Dickerson, L., Mazyck, P., & Hunter, M. (2003). Premenstrual syndrome. *American Family Physician, 67,* 1743–1752.

Dickey, C., & Power, C. (2003). Rethinking Islam. *Newsweek,* September 15, 50–51.

Dickey, R. (2003). It has really been 15 years of inaction on high-order multiple pregnancies due to ovulation induction. *Fertility and Sterility, 79,* 28–29.

DiClemente, R., & Wingood, G. (2003). Human immunodeficiency virus prevention for adolescents. *Archives of Adolescent and Pediatric Medicine, 157,* 319–320.

Dietz, P. (1999). Unintended pregnancy among adult women exposed to abuse or household dysfunction during their childhood. *Journal of the American Medical Association, 282,* 1359–1364.

Dilley, J., Woods, W., & McFarland, W. (1997). Are advances in treatment changing views about high-risk sex? *New England Journal of Medicine, 337,* 501–502.

Dilorio, C., Hartwell, T., & Hanson, N. (2002). Childhood sexual abuse and risk behaviors among men at high risk for HIV infection. *American Journal of Public Health, 92,* 214–219.

Dines, G. (2003). From fantasy to reality: Unmasking the pornography industry. In R. Morgan (Ed.), *Sisterhood Is Forever.* New York: Washington Square Press.

Disease-a-Month (1999). Breast cancer screening, diagnosis, and treatment. *Disease-a-Month, 45,* 337–405.

Dittman, M. (2003). Sex: Worth the risk? *Monitor on Psychology, 34,* 58–60.

Dittus, P., & Jaccard, J. (2000). Adolescents' perceptions of maternal disapproval of sex: Relationships to sexual outcomes. *Journal of Adolescent Health, 26,* 268–278.

Dobosz, A. (1997). Thicker thighs by Thanksgiving. *Ms.,* November–December, 89–91.

Dobrzykowski, T., & Stern, P. (2003). Out of sync: A generation of first-time mothers over 30. *Health Care for Women International, 24,* 242–253.

Doctor, R., & Prince, V. (1997). Transvestism: A survey of 1,032 cross-dressers. *Archives of Sexual Behavior, 26,* 589–605.

Dodson, B. (1974). *Liberating Masturbation.* New York: Betty Dodson.

Donahey, K., & Miller S. (2001). Applying a common factors perspective to sex therapy. *Journal of Sex Education and Therapy, 25,* 221–230.

Donenberg, G., Bryant, F., Emerson, E., Wilson, H., & Pasch, K. (2003). Tracing the roots of early sexual debut among adolescents in psychiatric care. *Journal of the American Academy of Child and Adolescent Psychiatry, 42,* 594–608.

Dong, M., Anda, R., Dube, S., Giles, W., & Felitti, V. (2003). The relationship of exposure to childhood sexual abuse to other forms of abuse, neglect, and household dysfunction during childhood. *Child Abuse and Neglect, 27,* 625–639.

Donnelly, P., & White, C. (2000). Testicular dysfunction in men with primary hypothyroidism: Reversal of hypogonadotrophic hypogonadism with replacement thyroxine. *Clinical Endocrinology, 52,* 197–201.

Donnerstein, E., & Linz, D. (1984). Sexual violence in the media: A warning. *Psychology Today,* January, 14–15.

Donnerstein, E., & Linz, D. (1986). The question of pornography. *Psychology Today.* December, 56–59.

Donnerstein, E., Linz, D., & Penrod, S. (1987). *The Question of Pornography.* New York: Free Press.

Donovan, B. (2004). Sexually transmissible infections other than HIV. *Lancet, 363,* 545–556.

Donovan, G. (2002). Cardinal decries corporate sponsorship of pornography. *National Catholic Reporter,* December 20, 7.

Donovan, P. (1998). School-based sexuality education: The issues and challenges. *Family Planning Perspectives, 30,* 188–193.

Dormire, S. (2003). What we know about managing menopausal hot flashes: Navigating without a compass. *Journal of Obstetrical, Gynecological, and Neonatal Nursing, 32,* 455–464.

Dotinga, R. (1998). Holy matrimony. *The Advocate,* April 14, 56–57.

Douglas, K. (1999). *Sexuality and the Black Church: A Womanist Perspective.* Maryknoll, NY: Orbis Books.

Douglass, F., & Douglass, R. (1993). The validity of the Myers-Briggs Type Indicator for predicting expressed marital problems. *Family Relations, 42,* 422–426.

Dover, J. (2000). Teaching respect for differences. *Newsweek,* April 10, 18.

Dow, M., Hart, D., & Forrest, C. (1983). Hormonal treatments of unresponsiveness in post-menopausal women: A comparative study. *British Journal of Obstetrics and Gynecology, 90,* 361–366.

Dowd, M. (1997). We must correct the eros of our ways. *The Oregonian,* June 22, D3.

Doyle, J., & Paludi, M. (1991). *Sex and Gender* (2nd ed.). Dubuque, IA: Brown and Benchmark.

Draucker, C., & Stern, P. (2000). Women's responses to sexual violence by male intimates. *Western Journal of Nursing Research, 22,* 385–406.

Dreger, A. (1998). *Hermaphrodites and the Medical Invention of Sex.* Cambridge: Harvard University Press.

Dreger, A. (2003). *Notes on the Treatment of Intersex.* Retrieved February 19, 2003, from http://www.isna.org

Druzin, P., Shrier, I., Yacowar, M., & Rossignol, M. (1998). Discrimination against gay, lesbian, and bisexual family physicians by patients. *Canadian Medical Association Journal, 158(5),* 593–597.

Dubé, E. (2000). The role of sexual behavior in the identification process of gay and bisexual males. *Journal of Sex Research, 37,* 123–132.

Duckworth, J., & Levitt, E. (1985). Personality analysis of a swingers' club. *Lifestyles: A Journal of Changing Patterns, 8,* 35–45.

Duddle, M. (1991). Emotional sequelae of sexual assault. *Journal of the Royal Society of Medicine, 84,* 26–28.

Duenwald, M. (2003). Effort to make sex drug for women challenges experts. *New York Times,* March 25, D5.

Duerr, A., Heilig, C., Meikle, S., Cu-Uvin, S., Klein, R., Rompalo, A., & Sobel, J. (2003). Incident and persistent vulvovaginal candidiasis among human immunodeficiency virus-infected women: Risk factors and severity. *Obstetrics and Gynecology, 101,* 548–556.

Dumond, R. (1992). The sexual assault of male inmates in incarcerated settings. *International Journal of the Sociology of Law, 20,* 135–157.

Dunn, J., Bretherton, I., & Munn, P. (1987). Conversations about feeling states between mothers and their children. *Developmental Psychology, 23,* 132–139.

Dunn, M., Bartee, R., & Perko, M. (2003). Self-reported alcohol use and sexual behaviors of adolescents. *Psychological Reports, 92,* 339–348.

Dunn, M., & Cutler, N. (2000). Sexual issues in older adults. *AIDS Patient Care and STDs, 14,* 67–69.

Dunn, M., & Trost, J. (1989). Male multiple orgasms: A descriptive study. *Archives of Sexual Behavior, 18,* 377–388.

Dunne, M., Purdie, D., Cook, M., Boyle, F., & Najman, J. (2003). Is child sexual abuse declining? Evidence from a population-based survey of men and women in Australia. *Child Abuse and Neglect, 27,* 141–152.

Dunsmuir, W., & Emberton, M. (1997). Surgery, drugs, and the male orgasm. *British Medical Journal, 314,* 319–320.

Durand, V., & Barlow, D. (2000). *Abnormal Psychology: An Introduction.* Belmont, CA: Wadsworth/Thomson Learning.

Durkin, K. (1997). Misuse of the Internet by pedophiles: Implications for law enforcement and probation practice. *Federal Probation, 61,* 14–18.

Duty, S., Silva, M., Barr, D., & Brock, J. (2003). Phthalate exposure and human semen parameters. *Epidemiology, 14,* 269–277.

Dwyer, M. (1988). Exhibitionism/voyeurism. *Journal of Social Work and Human Sexuality, 7,* 101–112.

Dyer, J. (2000). Evolving abuse of GHB in California: Bodybuilding drug to date-rape drug. *Journal of Toxicology, 38,* 184.

Dykes, B. (2000). Problems in defining cross-culture "kinds of homosexuality"—and a solution. *Journal of Homosexuality, 38,* 1–18.

Eastham, J., & Kattan, M. (2000). Disease recurrence in black and white men undergoing radical prostatectomy for clinical stage T1-T2 prostate cancer. *Journal of Urology, 163,* 143–145.

Eaton, L. (2003). AIDS vaccine may offer hope only for some ethnic groups. *British Medical Journal, 326,* 463.

Eccles, A., Marshall, W., & Barbaree, H. (1994). Differentiating rapists and non-rapists using the rape index. *Behaviour Research and Therapy, 32,* 539–546.

Eccles, J., Barber, E., & Jozefowicz, D. (1999). Linking gender to educational, occupational, and recreational choices: Applying the Eccles et al. model of achievement-related choices. In W. Swann & J. Langlois (Eds.), *Sexism and Stereotypes in Modern Society: The Gender Science of Janet Taylor Spence.* Washington, DC: American Psychological Association.

Ecker, N. (1993). Culture and sexual scripts out of Africa. *SIECUS Report, 22,* 16.

The Economist (1998). The sex business. *The Economist,* February 14, 17–18.

Edozien, F. (2003). Fighting AIDS face to face. *The Advocate,* July 8, 46–49.

Edwards, T. (2000). Flying solo. *Time,* August 28, 47–53.

Edwards, W. (1996). Operating within the mainstream: Coping and adjustment among a sample of homosexual youths. *Deviant Behavior: An Interdisciplinary Journal, 17,* 229–251.

Ehrenfeld, T. (2002). Infertility: A guy thing. *Newsweek*, March 25, 60–61.

Ehrenreich, B. (1998). Where have all the babies gone? *Life*, January, 69–76.

Ehrenreich, B. (1999). The real truth about the female body. *Time*, March 8, 57–71.

Eisenberg, V., & Schenker, J. (1997). Pregnancy in the older woman: Scientific and ethical aspects. *International Journal of Gynecology and Obstetrics, 56*, 163–169.

Eisner, T., Conner, J., & Carrel, J. (1990). Systemic retention of ingested cantharidin by frogs. *Chemoecology, 1*, 57–62.

Eitzen, D., & Zinn, M. (2000). *Social Problems* (8th ed.). Boston: Allyn and Bacon.

Elber, L. (2000). As "NYPD" gatekeeper, Brochtrup's glances say it all. *The Oregonian*, March 21, D5.

Elber, L. (2003, February 5). *Sex, Its Risks Showing Up More on TV*. Retrieved April 8, 2003, from http://www.bayarea.com/mld/mercurynews/entertainment/television/5105418.html

Elias, J., Bullough, V., Elias, V., & Brewer, G. (Eds.) (1998). *Prostitution: On Whores, Hustlers, and Johns*. Amherst, NY: Prometheus Books.

Eliason, M., & Morgan, K. (1998). Lesbians define themselves: Diversity in lesbian identification. *Journal of Gay, Lesbian, and Bisexual Identity, 3(1)*, 47–63.

Eliasson, R., & Lindholmer, C. (1976). Functions of male accessory genital organs. In E. Hafez (Ed.), *Human Semen and Fertility Regulations in Men*. St. Louis: Mosby.

Elizabeth, V. (2000). Cohabitation, marriage, and the unruly consequences of difference. *Gender and Society, 14*, 87–110.

Elkind, D. (1967). Egocentrism in adolescence. *Child Development, 38*, 1025–1034.

Elkousy, M., Sammel, M., Stevens, E., & Peipert, J. (2003). The effect of birth weight on vaginal birth after cesarean delivery success rates. *American Journal of Obstetrics and Gynecology, 188*, 824–830.

Ellertson, C., Elul, B., & Ambardekar, S. (2000). Accuracy of assessment of pregnancy duration by women seeking early abortions. *The Lancet, 355*, 877–881.

Elliott, K. (1999). The "inner critic" as a key element in working with adults who have experienced childhood sexual abuse. *Bulletin of the Menninger Clinic, 63*, 240–241.

Elliott, K., & Elliott, J. (2001). *Unlearning Inner Critic Messages About Sexuality*. Paper presented at the 33rd Annual Conference of the American Association of Sex Educators, Counselors, and Therapists, San Francisco, May 2–6.

Elliott, L., & Brantley, C. (1997). *Sex on Campus*. New York: Random House.

Elliott, M. (1992). Tip of the iceberg? *Social Work Today*, March, 12–13.

Ellis, H. (1920). *On Life and Sex*. Garden City, NY: Garden City Publishing.

Ellis, L., Burke, D., & Ames, M. (1987). Sexual orientation as a continuous variable: A comparison between the sexes. *Archives of Sexual Behavior, 16*, 523–534.

Ellison, C. (2000). *Women's Sexualities*. Oakland, CA.: New Harbinger Publications.

Emery, R., & Tuer, M. (1993). Parenting and the marital relationship. In T. Luster & L. Okagaki (Eds.), *Parenting: An Ecological Perspective*. Hillsdale, NJ: Erlbaum.

Emmert, D. (2000). Treatment of common cutaneous herpes simplex virus infections. *American Family Physician, 61*, 1697–1704.

Emmert, D., & Kirchner, J. (2000). Sexually transmitted diseases in women: Gonorrhea and syphilis. *Postgraduate Medicine, 107*, 181–197.

Engelberg, R., Carrell, D., Krantz, E., Corey, L., & Wald, A. (2003). Natural history of genital herpes simplex virus type 1 infection. *Sexually Transmitted Diseases, 30*, 174–177.

Epp, S. (1997). The diagnosis and treatment of athletic amenorrhea. *Physician Assistant*, March, 129–144.

Epstein, A. (1997). Justices will rule on issue of same-sex harassment. *The Oregonian*, June 10, A1.

Equal Employment Opportunity Commission (1980). Guidelines on discrimination because of sex. *Federal Register, 45*, 74,676–74,677.

Equal Employment Opportunity Commission (2003). *Sexual Harassment Charges EEOC and FEPHS Combined: FYI992–FY2002*. Retrieved September 28, 2003, from http://www.eeoc.gov/stats/harass.html

Erbelding, E., Stanton, D., Quinn, T., & Rompalo, A. (2000). Behavioral and biologic evidence of persistent high-risk behavior in an HIV primary care population. *AIDS 2000, 14*, 297–301.

Ericksen, J. (2000). Sexual liberation's last frontier. *Society, 37*, 21–25.

Erlich, K. (1997). Management of herpes simplex and varicella-zoster virus infections. *Western Journal of Medicine, 166*, 211–215.

Ernst, E., & Pittler, M. (1998). Yohimbine for erectile dysfunction: A systematic review and meta-analysis of randomized clinical trials. *Journal of Urology, 159*, 433–436.

Eschenbach, D., Patton, D., Hooton, T., Meier, A., Stapleton, A., Aura, J., & Agnew, K. (2001). Effects of vaginal intercourse with and without a condom on vaginal flora and vaginal epithelium. *Journal of Infectious Diseases, 183*, 913–918.

Eskeland, B., Thom, E., & Svendsen, K. (1997). Sexual desire in men: Effects of oral ingestion of a product derived from fertilized eggs. *Journal of International Medical Research, 25*, 62–70.

Espinoza, G. (2003). There goes the bride. *AARP*, July–August, 11.

Espinoza, G., & Baumgartner, A. (2003). Next big thing. *People*, May 26, 47.

Espo, D. (2003). Birth control, health care plan fails in Senate. *The Oregonian*, March 12, A13.

Esquivel, C., Ezcanaga, M., Limones, D., Ramos, B., Salas, E., Gutierrez, A., Medrano, J., & Castellanos, S. (2003). Prevalence of chlamydia trachomatis infection in registered female sex workers in Northern Mexico. *Sexually Transmitted Diseases, 30*, 195–197.

Ethics Committee, American Society for Reproductive Medicine (1997). Ethical considerations of assisted reproductive medicine. *International Journal of Gynecology and Obstetrics, 67(5)*, 15–95.

Eva, L. (2000). A GP guide to managing vulval pain. *The Practitioner, 244*, 225–236.

Everaerd, W., Laan, E., & Both, S. (2000). Female sexuality. In L. Szuchman & F. Muscarella (Eds.), *Psychological Perspectives on Human Sexuality*. New York: Wiley.

Exodus International (1996). Focus international doctrinal and policy statements. *Exodus International, 14*, 1–2.

Eyler, F., Behnke, M., Conlon, M., Woods, N., & Wobie, K. (1998). Birth outcome from a prospective, matched study of prenatal crack cocaine use. I. Interactive and dose effects on health and growth. *Pediatrics, 101(2)*, 229–237.

Ezzell, C. (2000). Care for a dying continent. *Scientific American*, May, 96–105.

Faerman, M., Kahila, G., & Smith, P. (1997). DNA analysis reveals the sex of infanticide victims. *Nature, 385*, 212.

Faerstein, E., Szklo, M., & Rosenshein, N. (2001). Risk factors for uterine leiomyoma: A practice-based case-control study. *American Journal of Epidemiology, 153*, 11–19.

Fagot, B. (1995). Psychosocial and cognitive determinants of early gender-role development. *Annual Review of Sex Research, 6*, 1–31.

Fair, W., Fuks, Z., & Scher, H. (1993). Cancer of the urethra and penis. In V. DeVita, S. Hellman, & S. Rosenberg (Eds.), *Cancer: Principles and Practice of Oncology*, v. 1 (4th ed.). Philadelphia: Lippincott.

Faison, S. (1997). One-child limitation eases in China. *The Oregonian*, August 17, A8.

Falk, L., Lindberg, M., Jurstrand, M., Backman, A., Olcen, P., & Fredlund, H. (2003). Genotyping of chlamydia trachomatis would improve contact tracing. *Sexually Transmitted Diseases, 30*, 205–210.

Fallon, B., Miller, R., & Gerber, W. (1981). Nonmicroscopic vasovasostomy. *Journal of Urology, 126*, 361–365.

Falwell, J. (2001). Perspectives 2001. *Newsweek*, December 24, 61.

Farber, N. (1992). Sexual standards and activity: Adolescents' perceptions. *Child and Adolescent Social Work, 9*, 53–76.

Farr, L. (2000). The danger zone. *W*, June, 100–104.

Faucher, M., & Brucker, M. (2000). Intrapartum pain: Pharmacologic management. *Journal of Obstetrical, Gynecological, and Neonatal Nursing, 29*, 169–180.

Fauser, B., & te Velde, E. (2000). The brave new world of making babies. *The Lancet, 354*, 40.

Fausto-Sterling, A. (1993). The five sexes: Why male and female are not enough. *The Sciences, 33*, 20–24.

Fausto-Sterling, A. (2000). *Sexing the Body: Gender Politics and the Construction of Sexuality*. New York: Basic Books.

Faux, M. (1984). *Childless by Choice*. New York: Anchor.

Fay, J., & Yanoff, J. (2000). What are teens telling us about sexual health? Results of the Second Annual Youth Conference of the Pennsylvania Coalition to Prevent Teen Pregnancy. *Journal of Sex Education and Therapy, 25*, 169–177.

Fazleabas, A., & Kim J. (2003). What makes an embryo stick? *Science, 299*, 355–356.

Fedora, O., Reddon, J., Morrison, J., & Fedora, S. (1992). Sadism and other paraphilias in normal controls and aggressive and nonaggressive sex offenders. *Archives of Sexual Behavior, 21*, 1–15.

Feeney, J., & Noller, P. (1996). *Adult Attachment*. Thousand Oaks, CA: Sage.

Fehring, R. (2004). The future of professional education in natural family planning. *Journal of Obstetric, Gynecologic, and Neonatal Nursing, 33*, 34–43.

Fehring, R., & Schmidt, A. (2001). Trends in contraceptive use among Catholics in the United States: 1988–1995. *Linacre Quarterly*, May, 170–185.

Feinberg, J., & Japour, A. (2003). Scientific and ethical considerations in trial design for investigational agents for the treatment of human immunodeficiency virus infection. *Clinical Infectious Diseases, 36*, 201–206.

Feingold, A. (1992). Good-looking people are not what we think. *Psychological Bulletin, 111*, 304–341.

Feldman, H., Goldstein, I., Hatzichristou, D., Krane, R., & McKinlay, J. (1994). Impotence and its medical and psychosocial correlates: Results of the Massachusetts Male Aging Study. *Journal of Urology, 151*, 54–61.

Feldman-Summers, S., & Pope, K. (1994). The experience of "forgetting" childhood abuse: A national survey of psychologists. *Journal of Consulting and Clinical Psychology, 62*, 636–639.

Felix, J. (2003). The science behind the effectiveness of in vivo screening. *American Journal of Obstetrics and Gynecology, 188*, S8–S12.

Ferguson, D., Steidle, C., Singh, G., & Alexander, S. (2003). Randomized, placebo-controlled, double blind, crossover design trial of the efficacy and safety of Zestra for women in women with and without female sexual arousal disorder. *Journal of Sex and Marital Therapy, 29*, 33–44.

Fergusson, D., & Woodward, L. (2000). Teenage pregnancy and female educational underachievement: A prospective study of a New Zealand birth cohort. *Journal of Marriage and the Family, 62*, 147–161.

Feroli, K., & Burstein, G. (2003). Adolescent sexually transmitted diseases. *American Journal of Maternal/Child Nursing, 28*, 113–118.

Ferrer, F., & McKenna, P. (2000). Current approaches to the undescended testicle. *Contemporary Pediatrics, 17*, 106–112.

Ferroni, P., & Jaffee, J. (1997). Women's emotional well-being: The importance of communicating sexual needs. *Sexual and Marital Therapy, 12*, 127–138.

Fields, C., & Scout, A.. (2001). Addressing the needs of lesbian patients. *Journal of Sex Education and Therapy, 26*, 182–188.

Fields, J., & Casper, L. (2001). *America's Families and Living Arrangements: March 2000*. Washington, DC: U.S. Census Bureau.

Filicori, M. (2003). Use of luteinizing hormone in the treatment of infertility: Time for reassessment? *Fertility and Sterility, 79*, 253–255.

Fillion, K. (1996). This is the sexual revolution? *Saturday Night*, February, 36–41.

Fincham, F. (2003). Marital conflict: Correlates, structure, and context. *Current Directions in Psychological Science, 12*, 23–27.

Findholt, N., & Robrecht, L. (2002). Legal and ethical considerations in research with sexually active adolescents: The requirement to report statutory rape. *Perspectives on Sexual and Reproductive Health, 34*, 259–264.

Findlay, J., Place, V., & Snyder, P. (1989). Treatment of primary hypogonadism in men by the transdermal administration of testosterone. *Journal of Clinical Endocrinology and Metabolism, 68*, 369–373.

Finelli, L., Levine, W., Valentine, J., & St. Louis, M. (2001). Syphilis outbreak assessment. *Sexually Transmitted Diseases, 28*, 131–134.

Fineman, H. (1993). Marching to the mainstream. *Newsweek*, May 3, 42–45.

Finer, L., & Henshaw, S. (2003). Abortion incidence and services in the United States in 2000. *Perspectives on Sexual and Reproductive Health, 35*, 6–15.

Finger, W. (2000). Avoiding sexual exploitation: Guidelines for therapists. *SIECUS Report, 28*, 12–13.

Finger, W., Lund, M., & Slagle, M. (1997). Medications that may contribute to sexual disorders. *Journal of Family Practice, 44*, 33–43.

Finger, W., Quillen, J., & Slagle, M. (2000). *They Can't All Be Viagra: Medications Causing Sexual Dysfunctions*. Paper presented at the 32nd Annual Conference of the American Association of Sex Educators, Counselors, and Therapists, Atlanta, Georgia, May 10–14.

Finkelhor, D. (1979). *Sexually Victimized Children*. New York: Free Press.

Finkelhor, D. (1984a). *Child Sexual Abuse: Theory and Research*. New York: Free Press.

Finkelhor, D. (1984b). The prevention of child sexual abuse: An overview of needs and problems. *SIECUS Report, 13*, 1–5.

Finkelhor, D. (1993). Epidemiological factors in the clinical identification of child sexual abuse. *Child Abuse and Neglect, 17*, 67–70.

Finkelhor, D. (1994). The international epidemiology of child sexual abuse. *Child Abuse and Neglect, 18*, 409–417.

Finkelhor, D., Hotaling, G., Lewis, I., & Smith, C. (1990). Sexual abuse in a national sample of adult men and women: Prevalence, characteristics, and risk factors. *Child Abuse and Neglect, 14*, 19–28.

Finz, S. (2000). Emerging from a secret. *San Francisco Chronicle*, June 12, A1.

Firestone, J., & Harris, R. (1999). Changes in patterns of sexual harassment in the U.S. military: A comparison of the 1988 and 1995 DoD surveys. *Armed Forces and Society: An Interdisciplinary Journal, 25*, 613.

Fischer, J., & Heesacker, M. (1995). Men's and women's preferences regarding sex-related and nurturing traits in dating partners. *Journal of College Student Development, 36*, 260–269.

Fischhoff, B. (1992). Giving advice: Decision theory perspectives on sexual assault. *American Psychologist, 47*, 577–588.

Fischman, J. (2001). New-style mammograms detect cancer. *U.S. News & World Report*, February 5, 58–59.

Fisher, B., Cullen, F., & Turner, G. (2000). *The Sexual Victimization of College Women*. Washington, DC: National Institutes of Justice, Bureau of Justice Statistics.

Fisher, H. (1992). *Anatomy of Love: The Natural History of Monogamy, Adultery, and Divorce*. New York: Norton.

Fisher, H. (1999). *The First Sex: The Natural Talents of Women and How They Will Change the World*. New York: Random House.

Fisher, T. (1987). Family communication and the sexual behavior and attitudes of college students. *Journal of Youth and Adolescence, 16*, 481–495.

Fisher, W. (2001). *Internet Pornography: A Social Psychological Perspective on Internet Sexuality*. Retrieved April 11, 2003, from http://www.findarticles.com/cf_0/m2372/4_38/84866949/print.jhtml

Fisher, W., Branscombe, N., & Lemery, C. (1983). The bigger the better? Arousal and attributional responses to erotic stimuli that depict different size penises. *Journal of Sex Research, 19*, 377–396.

Fisher, W., & Gray, J. (1988). Erotophobia, erotophilia, and sexual behavior during pregnancy and postpartum. *Journal of Sex Research, 25*, 379–396.

Fisher-Thompson, D. (1990). Adult sex typing of children's toys. *Sex Roles, 23*, 291–303.

Flanders, L. (1998). Rwanda's living casualties. *Ms.*, March–April, 27–30.

Flannery, D., Ellingson, L., Votaw, K., & Schaefer, E. (2003). Anal intercourse and sexual risk factors among college women, 1993–2000. *American Journal of Health Behavior, 27*, 228–234.

Fleming, M., & Kleinbart, E. (2001). Breast cancer and sexuality. *Journal of Sex Education and Therapy, 26*, 215–224.

Fleming, M., & Pace, J. (2001). Sexuality and chronic pain. *Journal of Sex Education and Therapy, 26*, 204–214.

Flobbe, K., Bosch, A., Kessels, A., & Beets, G. (2003). The additional diagnostic value of ultrasonography in the diagnosis of breast cancer. *Archives of Internal Medicine, 163*, 1,194–1,199.

Foa, U., Anderson, B., Converse, J., & Urbanski, W. (1987). Gender-related sexual attitudes: Some cross-cultural similarities and differences. *Sex Roles, 16*, 511–519.

Folb, K. (2000). "Don't touch that dial!" TV as a—what!—positive influence. *SIECUS Report, 28*, 16–18.

Foley, D., & Nechas, L. (1995). *Before You Hit the Pillow, Talk*. New York: Bantam Books.

Foley, S. (2003). Women in sex therapy: Developing a sexual identity. *Contemporary Sexuality, 37*, 7–13.

Folkes, V. (1982). Forming relationships and the matching hypothesis. *Personality and Social Psychology Bulletin, 9*, 631–636.

Follingstad, D., & Kimbrell, D. (1986). Sex fantasies revisited: An expansion and further clarification of variables affecting sex fantasy production. *Archives of Sexual Behavior, 15*, 475–486.

Fone, B. (2000). *Homophobia: A History*. New York: Metropolitan Books.

Food and Drug Administration (1997). *FDA Statement on Generic Premarin*. Retrieved May 5, 2003, from http://www.fda.gov/cder/cepressrelease.htm

Food and Drug Administration (2002). *FDA Approves New Rapid HIV Test Kit*. Retrieved December 19, 2002, from http://www.fda.gov/bbs/topics/NEWS/2002/NEW00852.html

Forbes, G. (1992). Body size and composition of perimenarchal girls. *American Journal of Diseases in Children, 146*, 63–66.

Forbes, G., Adams-Curtis, L., White, K., & Holmgren, K. (2003). The role of hostile and benevolent sexism in women's and men's perceptions of the menstruating women. *Psychology of Women Quarterly, 27,* 58–63.

Ford, C., & Beach, F. (1951). *Patterns of Sexual Behavior.* New York: Harper & Row.

Ford, K., Sohn, W., & Lepowski, J. (2002). American adolescents: Sexual mixing patterns, bridge partners, and concurrency. *Sexually Transmitted Diseases, 29,* 13–19.

Formichelli, L. (2001). Baby blues: A new mother's stress can harm fetal development, new research shows. *Psychology Today,* March–April, 24.

Forrest, J., & Singh, S. (1990). The sexual and reproductive behavior of American women, 1982–1988. *Family Planning Perspectives, 22,* 206–214.

Forsyth, C. (1996). The structuring of vicarious sex. *Deviant Behavior: An Interdisciplinary Journal, 17,* 279–295.

Fosas, N., Marina, F., Torres, P., & Jove, I. (2003). The births of five Spanish babies from cryopreserved donated oocytes. *Human Reproduction, 18,* 1417–1421.

Fowke, K., Nagelkerke, N., Kiman, J., Simonsen, J., Anzala, A., Bwayo, J., MacDonald, K., Nguigi, E., & Plummer, F. (1996). Resistance to HIV-1 infection among persistently seronegative prostitutes in Nairobi, Kenya. *The Lancet, 348,* 1347–1351.

Fox, M. (1999). *Study Casts Doubt on Idea of "Gay Gene."* Retrieved April 22, 1999, from http://www.examiner.com/990422/0422gaygene.shtml

Fox, R. (1990). *Bisexuality and Sexual Orientation Self-Disclosure.* Paper presented at the Society for the Scientific Study of Sex Annual Western Region Conference, San Diego, April 25.

Fox, T. (1995). *Sexuality and Catholicism.* New York: George Braziller.

France, D. (2000). Slavery's new face. *Newsweek,* December 18, 61–66.

France, D., & Rosenberg, D. (2000). The abortion pill. *Newsweek,* October 9, 26–30.

Francoeur, R. (2001). Challenging collective religious/social beliefs about sex, marriage, and family. *Journal of Sex Education and Therapy, 26,* 281–290.

Frank, D., Augustyn, M., & Knight, W. (2001). Growth, development, and behavior in early childhood following prenatal cocaine exposure. *Journal of the American Medical Association, 285,* 1613–1625.

Frank, E. (1999). Contraceptive use by female physicians in the United States. *Obstetrics and Gynecology, 94,* 666–671.

Frankel, S., Smith, G., Donovan, J., & Neal, D. (2003). Screening for prostate cancer. *The Lancet, 361,* 1122–1128.

Franklin, K. (1998). Unassuming motivations: Contextualizing the narratives of antigay assailants. In G. Herek (Ed.), *Stigma and Sexual Orientation: Understanding Prejudice Against Lesbians, Gay Men, and Bisexuals.* Thousand Oaks, CA: Sage.

Franzen, R. (2001). No place for a child. *The Sunday Oregonian,* March 11, A1.

Fraser, L. (1999). Why more men are going under the knife. *The Ottawa Citizen,* September 6, A10.

Fraser, L. (2002). The new breast cancer hot zone. *Organic Style,* September–October, 42–50.

Fraunfelder, F. (2000). Treating your patients with breast cancer. *British Medical Journal, 320,* 457–459.

Frayser, S. (1985). *Varieties of Sexual Experience: An Anthropological Perspective on Human Sexuality.* New Haven, CT: Human Relations Area Files Press.

Frayser, S. (1994). Defining normal childhood sexuality: An anthropological approach. *Annual Review of Sex Research, 5,* 173–217.

Frazier, P. (1993). A comparative study of male and female victims seen at hospital-based rape crises programs. *Journal of Interpersonal Violence, 8,* 65–79.

Freeman, E., Bloom, D., & McGuire, E. (2001). A brief history of testosterone. *Journal of Urology, 165,* 371–373.

Freiberg, P. (2003). Gay man of God. *The Advocate,* September 16, 28–31.

French, D., & Dishion, T. (2003). Predictors of early initiation of sexual intercourse among high-risk adolescents. *Journal of Early Adolescence, 23,* 295–315.

Freud, S. (1953 [1905]). Three essays on the theory of sexuality. In *Standard Edition,* v. 7. London: Hogarth Press.

Freund, K., & Blanchard, R. (1993). Erotic target location errors in male gender dysphorics, paedophiles, and fetishists. *British Journal of Psychiatry, 162,* 558–563.

Freund, K., Seto, M., & Kuban, M. (1996). Two types of fetishism. *Behaviour Research and Therapy, 34,* 687–694.

Freund, K., Watson, R., & Rienzo, D. (1988). The value of self-reports in the study of voyeurism and exhibitionism. *Annals of Sex Research, 1,* 243–262.

Freund, M., Lee, N., & Leonard, T. (1991). Sexual behavior of clients with street prostitutes in Camden, N.J. *Journal of Sex Research, 28,* 579–591.

Frezieres, R., Walsh, T., Nelson, A., Clark, V., & Coulson, A. (1999). Evaluation of the efficacy of a polyurethane condom: Results from a randomized, controlled clinical trial. *Family Planning Perspectives, 31,* 81–87.

Friday, N. (1980). *Men in Love.* New York: Delacorte.

Friedan, B. (1994). *The Fountain of Age.* New York: Simon & Schuster.

Friedman, M. (2003). *Strapped for Cash: A History of American Hustler Culture.* Los Angeles: Aylson Publications.

Friedman, R., Hurt, S., Arnoff, M., & Clarkin, J. (1980). Behavior and the menstrual cycle. *Signs, 5,* 719–738.

Friedman, S. (1994). *Secret Lives: Women with Two Lives.* New York: Crown.

Friedrich, W., Fisher, J., Broughton, D., Houston, M., & Shafran, C. (1998). Normative sexual behavior in children: A contemporary sample. *Pediatrics, 101,* 1–13. Retrieved May 30, 2000, from http://www.pediatircs.org/cgi/content/ full/101/4/e9

Friedrich, W., Grambsch, P., Broughton, D., Kuiper, J., & Beilke, R. (1991). Normative sexual behavior in children. *Pediatrics, 88,* 456–464.

Friess, S. (2003). Jews oy, two boys? *Newsweek,* March 24, 8.

Frisch, R. (1988). Fatness and fertility. *Scientific American,* March, 88–95.

Frisch, R., & McArthur, J. (1974). Menstrual cycles: Fatness as a determinant of minimum weight for height necessary for their maintenance or onset. *Science, 185,* 949–951.

Fromm, E. (1965). *The Ability to Love.* New York: Farrar, Straus & Giroux.

Frost, M., Schaid, D., & Sellers, T. (2000). Long-term satisfaction and psychological and social function following bilateral prophylactic mastectomy. *Journal of the American Medical Association, 284,* 319–324.

Fu, H., Darroch, J., Hass, T., & Ranjit, N. (1999). Contraceptive failure rates: New estimates from the 1995 National Survey of Family Growth. *Family Planning Perspectives, 31,* 56–63.

Fuller, C. (2000). Dr. Laura's hate talk no different from John Rocker's. *The Oregonian,* March 13, E7.

Furnham, A., & Mak, T. (1999). Sex-role stereotyping in television commercials: A review and comparison of fourteen studies done on five continents over 25 years. *Sex Roles, 41,* 413–437.

Fuscaldo, G. (2000). Gamete donation: When does consent become irrevocable? *Human Reproduction, 15,* 515–519.

Gabelnick, H. (1998). Future methods. In R. Hatcher, J. Trussell, F. Stewart, W. Cates, G. Stewart, F. Guest, & D. Kowal (Eds.), *Contraceptive Technology.* New York: Ardent Media, Inc.

Gacci, M., Bartoletti, R., Figlioli, S., Sarti, E., Eisner, B., Boddi, V., & Rizzo, M. (2003). Urinary symptoms, quality of life, and sexual function in patients with benign prostatic hypertrophy before and after prostatectomy: A prospective study. *British Journal of Urology International, 91,* 196–200.

Gaffney, G., Luries, S., & Berlin, F. (1984). Is there familiar transmission of pedophilia? *Journal of Nervous and Mental Disease, 172,* 546–548.

Gage, A. (1998). Sexual activity and contraceptive use: The component of the decision making process. *Studies of Family Planning, 29,* 154–166.

Gager, C., & Sanchez, L. (2003). Two as one? *Journal of Family Issues, 24,* 21–50.

Gagnon, J. (1977). *Human Sexualities.* Glenview, IL: Scott, Foresman.

Gagnon, J., & Simon, W. (1987). The sexual scripting of oral genital contacts. *Archives of Sexual Behavior, 16,* 1–25.

Galewitz, P. (2000). *New Birth Control Method Approved.* Retrieved October 6, 2000, from http://www.salon.com/mwt/wire/2000/10/06/birth_control/index.html

Gallagher, J. (1994). Is God gay? *The Advocate,* December 13, 40–46.

Gallagher, J. (1997a). Blacks and gays: The unexpected divide. *The Advocate,* December 9, 37–41.

Gallagher, J. (1997b). Marriage compromised. *The Advocate,* May 27, 71.

Galst, L. (2003). News on lower breast cancer risks. *Ms.,* Spring, 31–32.

Galst, L., & Hilty, J. (2003). Lesbians with strollers: The gaybie boom on wheels. *Ms.,* Spring, 17–18.

Gambrell, K. (2003, August 4). *Gay Marriage Issue Sparks Debate.* Retrieved September 1, 2003, from http://infotrac-college.thomsonlearning.com/itw/infomark/760/291/35557478w7/12!ar_fmt

Gamson, J. (1999). *Freaks Talk Back: Tabloid Talk Shows and Sexual Nonconformity.* Chicago: University of Chicago Press.

Gange, S. (1999). *When Is Adult Circumcision Necessary?* Retrieved September 20, 1999, from http://www.cnn.com/HEALTH/men/circumcision.adult/index.html

Gangestad, S., & Buss, D. (1993). Pathogen prevalence and human mate preferences. *Ethology and Sociobiology, 14,* 89–96.

Gangestad, S., & Simpson, J. (2000). The evolution of human mating: Trade-offs and strategic pluralism. *Behavioral and Brain Sciences, 23,* 573–587.

Gangestad, S., & Thornhill, R. (1997). Human sexual selection and developmental stability. In J. Simpson & D. Kenrick (Eds.), *Evolutionary Social Psychology.* Mahwah, NJ: Erlbaum.

Ganong, L., & Coleman, M. (1987). Sex, sex roles, and family love. *Journal of Genetic Psychology, 148,* 45–52.

Ganong, L., & Coleman, M. (1989). Preparing for remarriage: Anticipating the issues, seeking solutions. *Family Relations, 38,* 28–33.

Gao, F., Bailes, E., Robertson, D., Chen, Y., Rodenburg, C., Michael, S., Cummings, L., Arthur, L., Peeters, M., Shaw, G., Sharp, P., & Hahn, B. (1999). Origin of HIV-1 in chimpanzee *Pan troglodytes troglodytes. Nature, 397,* 436–441.

Garber, B. (1997). Outpatient inflatable penile prosthesis insertion. *Urology, 49(4),* 600–603.

Garcia, L. (1982). Sex-role orientation and stereotypes about male female sexuality. *Sex Roles, 8,* 863–876.

Gardner, R., Blackburn, M., & Ushma, D. (1999). Closing the condom gap. *Population Reports, 27,* 1–35.

Gardner, T. (1999). Order signals curtains for Mustang Ranch, county income source. *The Oregonian,* August 8, A16.

Garg, S., Kandarapu, R., Vermani, K., Tambwekar, K., Garg, A., Waller, D., & Saneveld, L. (2003). Development pharmaceutics of microbicide formulations. Part I. Preformulation considerations and challenges. *AIDS Patient Care and STDs, 17,* 17–32.

Garnefski, N., & Diekstra, R. (1997). Child sexual abuse and emotional and behavioral problems in adolescence: Gender differences. *Journal of the Academy of Child and Adolescent Psychiatry, 36,* 323–329.

Garos, S. (1994). Autoerotic asphyxiation: A challenge to death educators and counselors. *Omega: Journal of Death and Dying, 28,* 85–99.

Garza-Leal, J., & Landron, F. (1991). Autoerotic asphyxial death initially misinterpreted as suicide and review of the literature. *Journal of Forensic Science, 36,* 1,753–1,759.

Gauch, S. (2001). Multi-tasking: Egyptian women band together to eradicate FGM. *Ms.,* February–March, 36–37.

Gaudet, L., Kives, S., & Hahn, P. (2004). What women believe about oral contraceptives and the effect of counseling. *Contraception, 69,* 31–36.

Gaudoin, M., Dobbie, R., Finlayson, A., & Chalmers, J. (2003). Ovulation induction/intrauterine insemination in infertile couples is associated with low-birth-weight infants. *American Journal of Obstetrics and Gynecology, 188,* 611–616.

Gayle, H. (2000, August 4). *Letter to Colleagues.* Retrieved October 19, 2003, from http://www.cdc.gov/hiv/pubs/mmwr/mmwr11aug00.htm

Gaynor, M. (2003). Isoflavones and the prevention and treatment of prostate disease: Is there a role? *Cleveland Clinic Journal of Medicine, 70,* 203–214.

Gearson, C. (2003). *The Search for a Female Viagra.* Retrieved August 3, 2003, from http://health.discovery.com/centers/womens/viagra/viagra_print.html

Gebhard, P. (1971). Human sexual behavior: A summary statement. In D. Marshall & R. Suggs (Eds.), *Human Sexual Behavior: Variations in the Ethnographic Spectrum.* Englewood Cliffs, NJ: Prentice Hall.

Gebhard, P., Gagnon, J., Pomery, W., & Christenson, C. (1965). *Sex Offenders: An Analysis of Types.* New York: Harper & Row.

Geer, J., & Manguno-Mire, G. (1997). Gender differences in cognitive processes in sexuality. *Annual Review of Sex Research, 7,* 90–124.

Gelfand, M. (2000). The role of androgen replacement therapy for postmenopausal women. *Contemporary Obstetrics and Gynecology,* February, 107–116.

Gendel, E., & Bonner, E. (1988). Gender identity disorders and paraphilias. In H. Goldman (Ed.), *Review of General Psychiatry.* Norwalk, CT: Appleton & Lange.

Genevie, L., & Margolies, E. (1987). *The Motherhood Report: How Women Feel About Being Mothers.* New York: Macmillan.

Gershengorn, H., & Blower, S. (2000). Impact of antivirals and emergence of drug resistance: HSV-2 epidemic control. *AIDS Patient Care and STDs, 14,* 133–142.

Ghent, B. (2003). A new day in Washington. *The Advocate,* March 18, 18.

Ghizzani, A., & Montomoli, M. (2000). Anorexia nervosa and sexual behavior in women: A review. *Journal of Sex Education and Therapy, 25,* 80–88.

Gholami, S., Gonzalez-Cadavid, N., Lin, C., & Rajfer, J. (2003). Peyronie's disease: A review. *Journal of Urology, 169,* 1234–1241.

Giaquinto, S., Buzzelli, S., Di Francesco, L., & Nolfe, G. (2003). Evaluation of sexual changes after stroke. *Journal of Clinical Psychiatry, 64,* 302–307.

Gibbons, A. (1991). The brain as a "sexual organ." *Science, 253,* 957–959.

Gibbs, N. (2001). Renegade scientists say they are ready to start applying the technology of cloning to human beings. *Time,* February 19, 47–57.

Gibbs, N. (2002). Making time for a baby. *Time,* April 15, 48–54.

Gibson, L., & Leitenberg, H. (2000). Child sexual abuse prevention programs: Do they decrease the occurrence of child sexual abuse? *Child Abuse and Neglect, 24,* 1115–1125.

Gijs, L., & Gooren, L. (1996). Hormonal and psychopharmacological interventions in the treatment of paraphilias. *Journal of Sex Research, 33,* 273–290.

Gilbert, B., Heesacker, M., & Gannon, L. (1991). Changing the sexual aggression-supportive attitudes of men: A psychoeducational intervention. *Journal of Counseling Psychology, 38,* 197–203.

Gilbert, L., Alexander, L., Grosshans, J., & Jolley, L. (2003). Answering frequently asked questions about HPV. *Sexually Transmitted Diseases, 30,* 193–194.

Gillespie, T. (1999). Abortion: A listening law. *Newsweek,* September 6, 10.

Gilmartin, B. (1977). Swinging: Who gets involved and how? In R. Libby & R. Whitehurst (Eds.), *Marriage and Alternatives: Exploring Intimate Relationships.* Glenview, IL: Scott, Foresman.

Giltz, M. (2003). The golden hours. *The Advocate,* March 18, 41–51.

Gingrich, P., & Fogel, C. (2003). Herbal therapy use by perimenopausal women. *Journal of Obstetrical, Gynecological, and Neonatal Nursing, 32,* 181–189.

Ginocchio, R., Veenstra, D., Connell, F., & Marrazzo, J. (2003). The clinical and economic consequences of screening young men for genital chlamydia infection. *Sexually Transmitted Diseases, 30,* 99–106.

Ginsburg, K., Wolf, N., & Fidel, P. (1997). Potential effects of midcycle cervical mucus on mediators of immune reactivity. *Fertility and Sterility, 67,* 46–56.

Ginsburg, M. (1999). *Cancer Groups Push for Research Change.* Retrieved December 17, 1999, from http://www.examiner.com/991217/1217stamp.html

Girman, A., Lee, R., & Kligler, B. (2003). An integrative medicine approach to premenstrual syndrome. *American Journal of Obstetrics and Gynecology, 188,* S56–S63.

Gladstone, J., Levy, M., Nulman, I., & Koren, G. (1997). Characteristics of pregnant women who engage in binge alcohol consumption. *Canadian Medical Association Journal, 156(6),* 789–794.

Glasier, A., Anakwe, R., & Everington, D. (2000). Would women trust their partners to use a male pill? *Human Reproduction, 15,* 646–649.

Glasier, A., Smith, K., van der Spuy, Z., & Ho, P. (2003). Amenorrhea associated with contraception:– An international study on acceptability. *Contraception, 67,* 1–8.

Glei, D. (1999). Measuring contraceptive use patterns among teenage and adult women. *Family Planning Perspectives, 31,* 73–80.

Glennon, L. (1999). *The 20th Century: An Illustrated History of Our Lives and Times.* North Dighton, MA: JG Press.

Glick, P., & Fiske, S. (2001). An ambivalent alliance: Hostile and benevolent sexism as complementary justifications for gender inequality. *American Psychologist,* February, 109–118.

Glitz, M. (2004). Tuxes and tales. *The Advocate,* May 11, 34.

Global Agenda. (2003). Sex for sale, legally: Prostitution, the oldest profession, goes legit. *Global Agenda,* July 11.

Global Study of Sexual Attitudes and Behaviors (2002). *Global Study of Sexual Attitudes and Behaviors.* Retrieved December 11, 2003, from http://www.pfizerglobalstudy.com/study-results.asp

Glover, D., Amonkar, M., Rybeck, B., & Tracy, T. (2003). Prescription, over-the-counter, and herbal medicine use in a rural obstetric population. *American Journal of Obstetrics and Gynecology, 188,* 1039–1045.

Gnagy, S., Ming, E., Devesa, S., Hartge, P., & Whittemore, A. (2000). Declining ovarian cancer rates in U.S. women in relation to parity and oral contraceptive use. *Epidemiology, 11,* 102–105.

Godow, A (1999). Playful sexuality. *Contemporary Sexuality, 33,* 1–2.

Goens, J., Janniger, C., & De Wolf, K. (1994a). Dermatologic and systematic manifestations of syphilis. *American Family Physician, 50,* 1013–1020.

Gold, D., Balzano, B., & Stamey, R. (1991). Two studies of females' sexual force fantasies. *Journal of Sex Education and Therapy, 17,* 15–26.

Goldberg, C. (2000). Gay couples rush to get hitched under new Vermont law. *The Oregonian,* July 2, A4.

Goldberg, D., Whipple, B., & Fishkin, R. (1983). The Grafenberg spot and female ejaculation: A review of initial hypotheses. *Journal of Sex and Marital Therapy, 9,* 27–37.

Golden, F. (2004), Still sexy after 60. *Time,* Special Issue, January 19, 110–112.

Golden, K. (1998a). Ellen DeGeneres. *Ms.,* January–February, 54–55.

Golden, K. (1998b). Rana Husseini: A voice for justice. *Ms.,* July–August, 36–9.

Golden, N., Seigel, W., & Fisher, M. (2001). Emergency contraception: Pediatricians' knowledge, attitudes, and opinions. *Pediatrics, 107,* 287–292.

Goldenberg, R., Hauth, J., & Andrews, W. (2000). Intrauterine infection and preterm delivery. *New England Journal of Medicine, 342,* 1500–1505.

Golding, J. (1994). Sexual assault history and physical health in randomly selected Los Angeles women. *Health Psychology, 13,* 130–138.

Goldman, H. (1992). *Review of General Psychiatry.* Norwalk, CT: Appleton & Lange.

Goldman, R., & Goldman, J. (1982). *Children's Sexual Thinking: A Comparative Study of Children Aged 5 to 15 Years in Australia, North America, Britain, and Sweden.* London: Routledge & Kegan Paul.

Goldstein, J. (2001). Sexual aspects of headache. *Postgraduate Medicine, 109,* 81–88.

Golombok, S., & Fivush, R. (1995). Gender is determined biologically and socially. In D. Bender & B. Leone (Eds.), *Human Sexuality: Opposing Viewpoints.* San Diego: Greenhaven Press.

Golombok, S., Perry, B., Burston, A., & Murray, C. (2003). Children with lesbian parents: A community study. *Developmental Psychology, 39,* 20–33.

Golombok, S., & Tasker, F. (1996). Do parents influence the sexual orientation of their children? Findings from a longitudinal study of lesbian families. *Developmental Psychology, 32,* 3–11.

Gomez, J. (2000). Otherwise engaged: Marriage is an offer I can refuse. *Ms.,* June–July, 67–70.

Goodheart, A. (2004). Change of heart. *AARP Bulletin,* May, 45–47.

Goodman, D. (1998). Using the empowerment model to develop sex education for Native Americans. *Journal of Sex Education and Therapy, 23,* 135–144.

Goodman, D. (2001). *Communicating with Strangers . . . or How to Become More Culturally Competent Sex Educators and Counselors.* Paper presented at the 33rd Annual Conference of the American Association of Sex Educators, Counselors, and Therapists, San Francisco, May 2–6.

Goodman-Brown, T., Edelstein, R., Goodman, G., Jones, D., & Gordon, D. (2003). Why children tell: A model of children's disclosure of sexual abuse. *Child Abuse and Neglect, 27,* 525–540.

Goodrum, J. (2000). *A Transgender Primer.* Retrieved February 16, 2000, from http://www.ntac.org/tg101.html

Goodson, P., Suther, S., Pruitt, B., & Wilson, K. (2003). Defining abstinence: Views of directors, instructors, and participants in abstinence-only-until-marriage programs in Texas. *Journal of School Health, 73,* 91–96.

Goodyear, R., Newcomb, M., & Allison, R. (2000). Predictors of Latino men's paternity in teen pregnancy: A test of a mediational model of childhood experiences, gender role attitudes, and behaviors. *Journal of Counseling Psychology, 47,* 116–128.

Gorbach, P., Aral, S., Celum, C., Stoner, B., Whittington, W., Galen, J., Coronado, N., Connor, S., & Holmes, K. (2000). STD patients' perspectives of partner notification in Seattle. *Sexually Transmitted Diseases, 27,* 193–200.

Gordon, A., & Shaughnessy, A. (2003). Saw palmetto for prostate disorders. *American Family Physician, 67,* 1281–1283.

Gordon, P. (2003). The decision to remain single: Implications for women across cultures. *Journal of Mental Health Counseling, 25,* 33–44.

Gordon, S., Brenden, J., Wyble, J., & Ivey, C. (1997). When the Dx is penile cancer. *RN,* March, 41–44.

Gordon, S., & Gordon, J. (1989). *Raising a Child Conservatively in a Sexually Permissive World.* New York: Simon & Schuster.

Gordy, M. (2000). A call to fight forced labor. *Parade Magazine,* February 20, 4–5.

Gore, A. (1998). The genetic moral code. *The Advocate,* March 31, 9.

Gorey, K., & Leslie, D. (1997). The prevalence of child sexual abuse: Integrative review adjustment for potential response and measurement biases. *Child Abuse and Neglect, 21,* 391–398.

Gorman, C. (2002). The limits of science. *Time,* April 15, 52.

Gorski, E. (2002). New Bible: Revised gender version. *The Oregonian,* February 9, C7.

Gottemoeller, M. (2001). Microbicides: Expanding the options for STD prevention. *SIECUS Report, 30,* 10–13.

Gotthardt, M. (2003). Lust and found. *AARP,* November–December, 28–31.

Gottlieb, A. (2000). *Out of the Twilight: Fathers of Gay Men Speak.* New York: Haworth Press.

Gottlieb, M. (2000). Alcohol and pregnancy: A potential for disaster. *Emergency Medicine,* February, 103–108.

Gottman, J. (1993). *What Predicts Divorce.* Hillsdale, NJ: Lawrence Erlbaum.

Gottman, J. (1994). *Why Marriages Succeed or Fail.* New York: Simon & Schuster.

Gottman, J., Coan, J., Carrere, S., & Swanson, C. (1998). Predicting marital happiness and stability from newlywed interactions. *Journal of Marriage and the Family, 60,* 5–22.

Gottman, J., Notarius, C., Gonso, J., & Markman, H. (1976). *A Couple's Guide to Communication.* Champaign, IL: Research Press.

Gottman, J., & Silver, N. (2000). *The Seven Principles for Making Marriage Work.* New York: Crown Publishers.

Gover, T. (1996). Occupational hazards. *The Advocate,* November 26, 36–38.

Grady, D. (2000). New test for cervical cancer beats Pap smear, studies find. *San Francisco Chronicle,* January 5, C1.

Grady, D. (2003). Myocardial infarction during menses: Lessons from trials and errors. *American Journal of Medicine, 114,* 611–612.

Grady, W., Klepinger, D., & Nelson-Wally, A. (2000). Contraceptive characteristics: The perceptions and priorities of men and women. *Family Planning Perspectives, 31,* 168–175.

Grady-Weliky, T. (2003). Premenstrual dysphoric disorder. *New England Journal of Medicine, 348,* 433–438.

Grafenberg, E. (1950). The role of urethra in female orgasm. *International Journal of Sexology, 3,* 145–148.

Graham, B. (1998). *Polyamorous Pollyanna.* Retrieved September 17, 1998, from http://www.phoenixnewtimes.com

Graham, C. (2004). European unions. *The Advocate,* May 26.

Graham, C., Ramos, R., Bancroft, J., Maglaya, C., & Farley, T. (1995). The effects of steroidal contraceptives on the well-being and sexuality of women: A double-blind, placebo-controlled, two-center study of combined and progestogen-only methods. *Contraception, 52,* 363–369.

Graham, N. (1997). Epidemiology of acquired immunodeficiency syndrome: Advancing to an endemic era. *American Journal of Medicine, 102(suppl. 4A),* 2–8.

Granberg, D., & Granberg, B. (1980). Abortion attitudes, 1965–1980: Trends and determinants. *Family Planning Perspectives, 12,* 250–261.

Gravholt, C., Juul, S., Naeraa, R., & Hansen, J. (1998). Morbidity in Turner syndrome. *Journal of Clinical Epidemiology, 51,* 147–158.

Gray, P. (1993). What is love? *Time,* February 15, 47–49.

Grayson, C. (2002). *Chorionic Villus Sampling.* Retrieved October 25, 2003, from http://www.ncbi.nlm.nih.gov/entrez/query.fcgi?cmd=Retrieve&db=PubMed

Greaves, K. (2001). *The Social Construction of Sexual Activity in Heterosexual Relationships: A Qualitative Analysis.* Paper presented at the 33rd Annual Conference of the American Association of Sex Educators, Counselors, and Therapists, San Francisco, May 2–6.

Green, B., DeBacker, T., Ravindron, B., & Krows, A. (1999). Goals, values, and beliefs as predictors of achievement and effort in high-school mathematics classes. *Sex Roles, 40,* 421–458.

Green, G., & Clunis, D. (1989). Married lesbians. *Women and Therapy, 8,* 41–49.

Green, J. (2000). A killer on land and sea? *Newsweek,* April 24, 65.

Green, L., Fein, D., Modahl, C., Feinstein, C., Waterhouse, L., & Morris, M. (2001). Oxytocin and autistic disorder: Alterations in peptide forms. *Biological Psychiatry, 50,* 609–613.

Green, R. (1974). *Sexual Identity Conflict in Children and Adults.* New York: Basic Books.

Green, R. (1987). *The "Sissy Boy" Syndrome and the Development of Homosexuality.* New Haven, CT: Yale University Press.

Green, R. (2003). When therapists do not want their clients to be homosexual: A response to Rosik's article. *Journal of Marital and Family Therapy, 29*, 29–38.

Greenberg, B., & Busselle, R. (1996). Soap operas and sexual activity: A decade later. *Journal of Communication, 46(4)*, 153–161.

Greenberg, B., & Woods, M. (1999). The soaps: Their sex, gratifications, and outcomes. *Journal of Sex Research, 36*, 150–157.

Greenberg, J., Magder, L., & Aral, S. (1992). Age at first coitus: A marker for risky sexual behavior in women. *Sexually Transmitted Diseases, 19*, 331–334.

Greenberg, S., & Westreich, J. (2000). Beyond the blues. *Newsweek Special Issue*, 75.

Greenburg, D. (1986). *Dan Greenburg's Confessions of a Pregnant Father.* New York: Macmillan.

Greene, B. (1994). African-American woman. In L. Comas-Diaz & B. Greene (Eds.), *Women of Color.* New York: Guilford Press.

Greenstein, A., Plymate, S., & Katz, G. (1995). Visually stimulated erection in castrated men. *Journal of Urology, 153*, 650–652.

Greenwald, E., & Leitenberg, H. (1989). Long-term effects of sexual experiences with siblings and nonsiblings during childhood. *Archives of Sexual Behavior, 18*, 389–400.

Greer, P. (1998). Vaginal thrush: Diagnosis and treatment options. *Nursing Times, 94*, 50–52.

Gregersen, E. (1996). *The World of Human Sexuality: Behaviors, Customs, and Beliefs.* New York: Irvington.

Gregoire, A. (2000). Assessing and managing male sexual problems. *Western Journal of Medicine, 172*, 49–50.

Gregorian, R., Golden, K., Bahce, A., Goodman, C., Kwong, W., & Khan, Z. (2002). Antidepressant-induced sexual dysfunction. *Annals of Pharmacotherapy, 36*, 1577–1589.

Greydanus, D., Patel, D., & Rimsza, M. (2001). Contraception in the adolescent: An update. *Pediatrics, 107*, 562–573.

Gribble, J., Miller, H., Rogers, S., & Turner, C. (1999). Interview mode and measurement of sexual behaviors: Methodological issues. *Journal of Sex Research, 36*, 16–24.

Grieco, A. (1987). Scope and nature of sexual harassment in nursing. *Journal of Sex Research, 23*, 261–266.

Griffiths, M. (2001). Sex on the Internet: Observations and implications for Internet sex addiction. *Journal of Sex Research*, November. Retrieved April 11, 2003, from http://www.findarticles.com/cf_0/m2372/4_38/84866951/print.jhtml

Grisell, T. (1988). Brief report. *Indiana Medical Journal, 81*, 252.

Grist, T., Korosec, F., Peters, D., Witte, S., Walovich, R., Dolan, R., Bridson, W., Yucel, E., & Mistretta, E. (1997). Steady-state and dynamic MR angiography with MS-325: Initial experience in humans. *Radiology, 207*, 539–544.

Gron, G., Wunderlich, A., Spitzer, M., Tomczak, R., & Riepe, M. (2000). Brain activation during human navigation: Gender-different neural networks as substrate of performance. *Nature Neuroscience, 3*, 404–408.

Gronberg, H. (2003). Prostate cancer epidemiology. *The Lancet, 361*, 859–864.

Gross, L. (2001). *Up from Invisibility: Lesbians, Gay Men, and the Media in America.* New York: Columbia University Press.

Gross, M. (2003a). The second wave will drown us. *American Journal of Public Health, 93*, 872–881.

Gross, M. (2003b). When plagues don't end. *American Journal of Public Health, 93*, 861–862.

Gross, W., & Billingham, R. (1998). Alcohol consumption and sexual victimization among college women. *Psychological Reports, 82*, 80–82.

Grunwald, M. (2002). Botswana declares the world's most intense war on AIDS. *The Oregonian*, December 3, A13.

Gu, G., Cornea, A., & Simerly, R. (2003). Sexual differentiation of projections from the principal nucleus of the bed nuclei of the stria terminalis. *Journal of Comparative Neurology, 460*, 542–562.

Gudykunst, W., Matsumoto, Y., Ting-Toomey, S., Nishida, T., Kim, K., & Keyman, S. (1996). The influence of cultural individualism-collectivism, self construals, and individual values on communication styles across cultures. *Human Communication Research, 22*, 510–543.

Guerrero-Pavich, E. (1986). A Chicano perspective on Mexican culture and sexuality. In L. Lister (Ed.), *Human Sexuality, Ethnoculture, and Social Work.* New York: Haworth Press.

Guidry, H. (1995). Childhood sexual abuse: Role of the family physician. *American Family Physician, 51*, 407–414.

Gunn, R., Murray, P., Ackers, M., Hardison, W., & Margolis, H. (2001). Screening for chronic hepatitis B and C virus infections in an urban sexually transmitted disease clinic. *Sexually Transmitted Diseases, 28*, 166–169.

Gur, R., Mozley, L., Mozley, P., Resnick, S., Karp, J., Alavi, A., Arnold, S., & Gur, R. (1995). Sex differences in regional cerebral glucose metabolism during a resting state. *Science, 267*, 528–531.

Gutek, B. (1985). *Sex and the Workplace.* San Francisco: Jossey-Bass.

Guthrie, M., & Bates, L. (2003). Sex education sources and attitudes toward sexual precautions across a decade. *Psychological Reports, 92*, 581–592.

Guthrie, P. (2000). Body/breast cancer: Radical options. *The Sunday Oregonian*, October 1, L13.

Guttmacher, S., Lieberman, L., Ward, D., Freudenberg, N., Radosh, A., & Des Jarlais, D. (1997). Condom availability in New York City public high schools: Relationships to condom use and sexual behavior. *American Journal of Public Health, 87*, 1427–1433.

Guy-Sheftall, B. (2003). African American women: The legacy of black feminism. In R. Morgan (Ed.), *Sisterhood Is Forever.* New York: Washington Square Press.

Hack, M. (2002). Outcomes in young adulthood for very-low-birth-weight infants. *New England Journal of Medicine, 346*, 149–157.

Haffner, D. (1993). Toward a new paradigm of adolescent sexual health. *SIECUS Report, 21*, 26–30.

Haffner, D. (1997). The really good news: What the Bible says about sex. *SIECUS Report, 26(1)*, 3–8.

Haffner, D. (2000). Message from the president: Sexuality issues 2010. *SIECUS Report, 28*, 2–3.

Haffner, D. (2001). *What's Religion Got to Do with It?* Paper presented at the 33rd Annual Conference of the American Association of Sex Educators, Counselors, and Therapists, San Francisco, May 2–6.

Haffner, D. (2004). Sexuality and scripture. *Contemporary Sexuality, 38*, 7–13.

Haffner, D., & Wagoner, J. (1999). Vast majority of Americans support sexuality education. *SIECUS Report, 27*, 22–23.

Hagan, P., & Knott, P. (1998). Diagnosing and treating polycystic ovary syndrome. *The Practitioner, 242*, 98–106.

Hahn, J., & Blass, T. (1997). Dating partner preferences: A function of similarity of love styles. *Journal of Social Behavior and Personality, 12*, 595–610.

Halberstadt, A. (1985). Race, socioeconomic status, and nonverbal behavior. In A. Siegman & S. Feldstein (Eds.), *Multichannel Integration of Nonverbal Behavior.* Hillsdale, NJ: Erlbaum.

Hales, D. (1994). *An Invitation to Health* (6th ed.). Redwood City, CA: Benjamin/Cummings.

Hales, D. (1999). *Just Like a Woman: How Gender Science Is Redefining What Makes Us Female.* New York: Bantam Books.

Hall, G. (1996). *Theory-Based Assessment, Treatment, and Prevention of Sexual Aggression.* New York: Oxford University Press.

Hall, G., & Barongan, C. (1997). Prevention of sexual aggression: Sociocultural risk and protective factors. *American Psychologist, 52*, 5–14.

Hally, C., & Pollack, R. (1993). The effects of self-esteem, variety of sexual experience, and erotophilia on sexual satisfaction in sexually active heterosexuals. *Journal of Sex Education and Therapy, 19(3)*, 183–192.

Halpern, C., Joyner, K., Udry, R., & Suchindran, C. (2000). Smart teens don't have sex (or kiss much either). *Society for Adolescent Medicine, 26*, 213–225.

Halpern, D., & LaMay, M. (2000). The smarter sex: A critical review of sex differences in intelligence. *Educational Psychology Review, 12*, 229–246.

Hamblett, M. (1999). No insurance for "video voyeurism." *New York Law Journal*. Retrieved December 28, 1999, from http://www.law.com

Hamelin, B., Methot, J., Arsenault, M., & Pilote, S. (2003). Influence of the menstrual cycle on the timing of acute coronary events in premenopausal women. *American Journal of Medicine, 114*, 599–601.

Hamer, D., Hu, S., Magnuson, V., Hu, N., & Pattatucci, A. (1993). A linkage between DNA markers on the X chromosome and male sexual orientation. *Science, 261*, 321–327.

Hamers, F., & Downs, A. (2003). HIV in central and eastern Europe. *The Lancet, 361*, 1035–1044.

Hamilton, A. (2001). Regaining sexual health after cervical cancer. *Journal of Sex Education and Therapy, 26*, 196–203.

Hamilton, E. (1978). *Sex, with Love.* Boston: Beacon Press.

Hamilton, E., Wallis, M., Barlow, J., & Cullen, L. (2003). Women's views of a breast screening service. *Health Care for Women International, 24*, 40–48.

Hamilton, T. (2002). *Skin Flutes and Velvet Gloves*. New York: St. Martin's Press.

Haney, D. (1994). Study strongly ties environment to birth defects. *San Francisco Examiner*, July 7, A7.

Hanna, B., Jarman, H., & Savage, S. (2004). The early detection of post-partum depression: Midwives and nurses trial a checklist. *Journal of Gynecological and Neonatal Nursing, 33*, 191–197.

Hanrahan, S. (1994). Historical review of menstrual toxic shock syndrome. *Women and Health, 21*, 141–157.

Hansen, J. (2001). Increased breast cancer risk among women who work predominantly at night. *Epidemiology, 12*, 74–77.

Hansen, L. (2003). Clinical commentary. *Journal of Family Practice, 52*, 150.

Hanson, B. (2003). Questioning the construction of maternal age as a fertility problem. *Health Care for Women International, 24*, 166–176.

Hanson, R., Resnick, H., Saunders, B., Kilpatrick, D., & Best, C. (1999). Factors related to the reporting of childhood rape. *Child Abuse and Neglect, 23*, 559–569.

Hanson, R., Saunders, B., Kilpatrick, D., Resnick, H., Crouch, J., & Duncan, R. (2001). Impact of childhood rape and aggravated assault on mental health. *American Journal of Orthopsychiatry, 71*, 108–118.

Hardesty, C., Wenk, D., & Morgan, C. (1995). Paternal involvement and the development of gender expectations in sons and daughters. *Youth and Society, 26*, 283–297.

Harer, W. (2001). A look back at women's health and ACOG, a look forward to the challenges of the future. *Obstetrics and Gynecology, 97*, 1–4.

Hargreaves, D., & Plail, R. (1994). Fracture of the penis causing a corporourethral fistula. *British Journal of Urology, 73*, 97.

Harley, V., Jackson, D., Hextall, P., Hawkins, J., Berkovitz, G., Sockanathan, S., Lovell-Badge, R., & Goodfellow, P. (1992). DNA binding activity of recombinant *SRY* from normal males and XY females. *Science, 255*, 453–456.

Harlow, B., & Stewart, E. (2003). A population-based assessment of chronic unexplained vulvar pain: Have we underestimated the prevalence of vulvodynia? *Journal of the American Medical Women's Association, 58*, 82–88.

Harlow, B., Wise, L., Otto, M., & Soares, C. (2003). Depression and its influence on reproductive endocrine and menstrual cycle markers associated with perimenopause. *Archives of General Psychiatry, 60*, 29–36.

Harlow, H., & Harlow, M. (1962). The effects of rearing conditions on behavior. *Bulletin of the Menninger Clinic, 26*, 13–24.

Harned, M., & Fitzgerald, L. (2002). Understanding a link between sexual harassment and eating disorder symptoms: A mediational analysis. *Journal of Consulting and Clinical Psychology, 70*, 1170–1181.

Harney, P., & Muehlenhard, C. (1990). Rape. In E. Grauerholz & M. Korlewski (Eds.), *Sexual Coercion: A Sourcebook on Its Nature, Causes, and Prevention*. Lexington, MA: Lexington Books.

Harper, G., & Schneider, M. (2003). Oppression and discrimination among lesbian, gay, bisexual, and transgendered people and communities: A challenge for community psychology. *American Journal of Community Psychology, 31*, 243–251.

Harris, H. (1999). Touch and go: My silent craving for body contact. *Modern Maturity*, September–October, 58.

Harris, L., Arbor, A., & Paltrow, L. (2003). The status of pregnant women and fetuses in U.S. criminal law. *Journal of the American Medical Association, 289*, 1697–1699.

Harrison, T. (2003). Adolescent homosexuality and concerns regarding disclosure. *Journal of School Health, 73*, 107–112.

Harrison-Woolrych, M., Ashton, J., & Coulter, D. (2003). Uterine perforation on intrauterine device insertion: Is the incidence higher than previously reported? *Contraception, 67*, 53–56.

Hartman, W., & Fithian, M. (1984). *Any Man Can: Multiple Orgasmic Response in Males*. Paper presented at the Regional Conference of the American Association of Sex Educators, Counselors, and Therapists, Las Vegas, October.

Hartmann, J., Albrecht, C., Schmoll, H., Kuczyk, M., Kollmannsberger, C., & Bokemeyer, C. (1999). Long-term effects on sexual function and fertility after treatment of testicular cancer. *British Journal of Cancer, 80*, 801–807.

Harvey, S. (1987). Female sexual behavior: Fluctuations during the menstrual cycle. *Journal of Psychosomatic Research, 31*, 101–110.

Harvey, S., Beckman, L., Sherman, C., & Petitti, D. (1999). Women's experience and satisfaction with emergency contraception. *Family Planning Perspectives, 31*, 237–240.

Harvey, S., Bird, S., De Rosa, C., Montgomery, S., & Rohrbach, L. (2003). Sexual decision making and safer sex behavior among female injection drug users and female partners of IDUs. *Journal of Sex Research, 40*, 50–60.

Harvey, S., & Scrimshaw, S. (1988). Coitus-dependent contraceptives: Factors associated with effective use. *Journal of Sex Research, 25*, 364–379.

Hass, A. (1979). *Teenage Sexuality*. New York: Macmillan.

Hatcher, R. (1998a). *Contraceptive Technology* (17th ed.). New York: Ardent Media.

Hatcher, R. (1998b). Depo-Provera, Norplant, and Progestin-only pills (Minipills). In R. Hatcher, J. Trussell, F. Stewart, W. Cates, G. Stewart, F. Guest, & D. Kowal (Eds.), *Contraceptive Technology*. New York: Ardent Media.

Hatcher, R., & Guillebaud, J. (1998). The pill: Combined oral contraceptives. In R. Hatcher, J. Trussell, F. Stewart, W. Cates, G. Stewart, F. Guest, & D. Kowal (Eds.), *Contraceptive Technology*. New York: Ardent Media.

Hatfield, E. (1993). *Love, Sex, and Intimacy: Their Psychology, Biology, and History*. New York: HarperCollins College.

Hatfield, E., & Rapson, R. (1993). *Love, Sex, & Intimacy: Their Psychology, Biology, and History*. New York: HarperCollins.

Hatfield, E., & Sprecher, S. (1986a). Measuring passionate love in intimate relationships. *Journal of Adolescence, 9*, 383–410.

Hatfield, E., & Sprecher, S. (1986b). *Mirror, Mirror . . . The Importance of Looks in Everyday Life*. Albany: State University of New York Press.

Hatfield, R. (1994). Touch and sexuality. In V. Bullough & B. Bullough (Eds.), *Human Sexuality: An Encyclopedia*. New York: Garland.

Haug, K., Irgens, L., & Skjaerven, R. (2000). Maternal smoking and birthweight: Effect modification of period, maternal age and paternal smoking. *Acta Obstetricia et Gynecologica Scandinavica, 79*, 485–489.

Hausknecht, R. (2003). Mifepristone and misoprostol for early medical abortion: 18 months experience in the United States. *Contraception, 67*, 463–465.

Hawton, K., Catalan, J., & Fagg, J. (1992). Sex therapy for erectile dysfunction: Characteristics of couples, treatment outcome, and prognostic factors. *Archives of Sexual Behavior, 21*, 161–175.

Hayden, T., & Peraino, K. (1999). Uncloseted cops. *Newsweek*, September 27, 10.

Haynes, J., & Miller, J. (2003). Introduction. In J. Haynes & J. Miller (Eds.), *Inconceivable Conceptions: Psychological Aspects of Infertility and Reproductive Technology*. Hove, United Kingdom: Brunner–Routledge.

Hays, M. (2003). Blame Canada: Equal marriage rights in Canada will also allow U.S. gays to wed legally. *The Advocate*, July 22, 26–29.

Hays, M. (2004). Unveiling Islam. *The Advocate*, March 2, 27.

Hazan, C., & Shaver, P. (1987). Love conceptualized as attachment process. *Journal of Personality and Social Psychology, 52*, 511–524.

Hazan, C., & Zeifman, D. (1999). Pair bonds as attachment: Evaluating the evidence. In J. Cassidy & P. Shaver (Eds.), *Handbook of Attachment: Theory, Research, and Clinical Applications*. New York: Guilford Press.

He, J. (2003). *Heavy Smoking Habits Increase Men's Risk of Erectile Dysfunction*. Paper presented at the 43rd Annual Conference on Cardiovascular Disease Epidemiology and Prevention, Chicago, March 8.

Healy, B. (2003). Whose breasts, anyway? *U.S. News & World Report*, August 11, 50.

Healy, D., Trounson, A., & Andersen, A. (1994). Female infertility: Causes and treatment. *The Lancet, 343*, 1539–1544.

Heath, D. (1984). An investigation into the origins of a copious vaginal discharge during intercourse "enough to wet the bed" that is not urine. *Journal of Sex Research, 20*, 194–215.

Heath, R. (1972). Pleasure and brain activity in man. *Journal of Nervous and Mental Disease, 154*, 3–18.

Heaton, J., & Varrin, S. (1991). The impact of alcohol ingestion on erections in rats as measured by a novel bio-assay. *Journal of Urology, 145*, 192–194.

Hecht, M., Ribeau, S., & Collier, M. (1993). *African American Communication: Ethnic Identity and Cultural Interpretation*. Thousand Oaks, CA: Sage.

Hecht, M., Ribeau, S., & Sedano, M. (1990). A Mexican American perspective on interethnic communication. *International Journal of Intercultural Relations, 14*, 31–55.

Heck, K., & Pamuk, E. (1997). Explaining the relation between education and postmenopausal breast cancer. *American Journal of Epidemiology, 145(4)*, 366–372.

Heckman, T., Silverthorn, M., Waltje, A., Meyers, M., & Yarber, W. (2003). HIV transmission risk practices in rural persons living with HIV disease. *Sexually Transmitted Diseases, 30*, 134–136.

Hedeen, A., & White, E. (2001). Breast cancer size and stage in Hispanic American women, by birthplace: 1992–1995. *American Journal of Public Health, 91,* 122–125.

Hedgepeth, E. (2001). *Counseling GLBT Youth: Understanding Their Unique Issues.* Paper presented at the 33rd Annual Conference of the American Association of Sex Educators, Counselors, and Therapists, San Francisco, May 2–6.

Heidrich, F., Berg, A., & Bergman, J. (1984). Clothing factors and vaginitis. *Journal of Family Practice, 19,* 491–494.

Heim, N. (1981). Sexual behavior of castrated sex offenders. *Archives of Sexual Behavior, 10,* 11–19.

Heiman, J. (1998). Psychophysiological models of female sexual response. *International Journal of Impotence, 10,* 584–597.

Heiman, J. (2002). Psychologic treatments for female sexual dysfunction: Are they effective and do we need them? *Archives of Sexual Behavior, 31,* 445–450.

Heimer, L., & Larsson, K. (1964). Drastic changes in the mating behavior of male rats following lesions in the junction of diencephalon and mesencephalon. *Experientia, 20,* 460–461.

Heinlein, R. (1961). *Stranger in a Strange Land.* New York: Putnam.

Helstrom, L., Sorbom, D., & Backstrom, T. (1995). Influence of partner relationship on sexuality after subtotal hysterectomy. *Acta Obstetricia et Gynecologica Scandinavica, 74,* 142–146.

Hendrick, C., & Hendrick, S. (1986). A theory and method of love. *Journal of Personality and Social Psychology, 50,* 392–402.

Hendrick, C., Hendrick, S., & Adler, N. (1988). Romantic relationships: Love, satisfaction, and staying together. *Journal of Personality and Social Psychology, 54,* 980–988.

Hendrick, S., & Hendrick, C. (1992). *Liking, Loving, and Relating,* 2nd ed. Pacific Grove, CA: Brooks/Cole.

Hendrick, S., & Hendrick, C. (1995). Gender differences and similarities in sex and love. *Personal Relationships, 2,* 5–65.

Hendricks, M. (2002). Now they tell us! Hormone replacement therapy and the broken promise of lasting youth. *AARP,* November–December, 57–63.

Henley, J. (1993). The significance of social context: The case of adolescent childbearing in the African American community. *Journal of Black Psychology, 19,* 461–477.

Henley, N. (1977). *Body Politics: Power, Sex, and Nonverbal Communication.* Englewood Cliffs, NJ: Prentice Hall.

Henneman, T. (2003). New York public. *The Advocate,* September 2, 38.

Henry, N. (2000). Voulez-vous pacser avec moi? *Ms.,* February–March, 32.

Henshaw, S., & Finer, L. (2003). The accessibility of abortion services in the United States, 2001. *Perspectives on Sexual and Reproductive Health, 35,* 16–24.

Henshaw, S., & Kost, K. (1996). Abortion patients in 1994–1995: Characteristics and contraceptive use. *Family Planning Perspectives, 28,* 140–147, 158.

Hensleigh, P., Andrews, W., Brown, Z., Greenspoon, J., Yasukawa, L., & Prober, C. (1997). Genital herpes during pregnancy: Inability to distinguish primary and recurrent infections clinically. *Obstetrics and Gynecology, 89,* 891–895.

Hensley, C., Tewksbury, R., & Castle, T. (2003). Characteristics of prison sexual assault targets in male Oklahoma's correctional facilities. *Journal of Interpersonal Violence, 18,* 595–606.

Hensley, D. (2001). Friends indeed. *The Advocate,* March 13, 43–47.

Hensley, D. (2004). L is for lesbian. *The Advocate,* February 17, 41–53.

Henson, H. (2002). Breast cancer and sexuality. *Sexuality and Disability, 20,* 261–273.

Herek, G., & Capitanio, J. (1999). Sex differences in how heterosexuals think about lesbians and gay men: Evidence from survey context effects. *Journal of Sex Research, 36,* 348–360.

Herek, G., Cogan, J., & Gillis, J. (1999). Psychological sequelae of hate-crime victimization among lesbian, gay, and bisexual adults. *Journal of Consulting and Clinical Psychology, 67,* 945–951.

Herek, G., Kimmel, D., Amaro, H., & Melton, G. (1991). Avoiding heterosexist bias in psychological research. *American Psychologist, 46,* 957–963.

Herman-Giddens, M., Slora, E., Wasserman, R., Bourdony, C., Bhapkar, M., Koch, G., & Hesemeier, C. (1997). Secondary sexual characteristics and menses in young girls seen in office practice: A study from the pediatric research office settings network. *Pediatrics, 99,* 505–512.

Herrell, R. (1992). The symbolic strategies of Chicago's Gay and Lesbian Pride Day Parade. In G. Herdt (Ed.), *Gay Culture in America.* Boston: Beacon Press.

Herrinton, L., Zhao, W., & Husson, G. (2003). Management of cryptorchidism and risk of testicular cancer. *American Journal of Epidemiology, 157,* 602–605.

Hersch, P. (1988). Coming of age on city streets. *Psychology Today,* January, 28–37.

Hersch, P. (1991). Secret lives. *Networker,* January–February, 37–40.

Herschel, M., Khoshnood, B., Ellmam, C., Maydew, N., & Mittendorf, R. (1998). Neonatal circumcision. *Archives of Pediatric and Adolescent Medicine, 152,* 279–284.

Herter, C. (1998). Sexual dysfunction in patients with diabetes. *Journal of the American Board of Family Practice, 11,* 327–330.

Heukelbach, J., & Feldmeier, H. (2004). Ectoparasites: The underestimated realm. *Lancet, 363,* 889–891.

Heyden, M., Anger, B., Tiel, T., & Ellner, T. (1999). Fighting back works: The case for advocating and teaching self-defense against rape. *Journal of Physical Education, Recreation, and Dance, 70,* 31–34.

Heyl, P. (1997). Multiplying the risks. *Newsweek,* December 1, 66.

Hickman, S., & Muehlenhard, C. (1999). "By the semi-mystical appearance of a condom": How young women and men communicate sexual consent in heterosexual situations. *Journal of Sex Research, 36,* 258–272.

Hickson, F., Davies, P., Hunt, A., Weatherburn, P., McManus, T., & Coxon, A. (1994). Gay men as victims of nonconsensual sex. *Archives of Sexual Behavior, 23,* 281–294.

Higa, G. (2000). Altering the estrogenic milieu of breast cancer with a focus on the new aromatase inhibitors. *Pharmacotherapy, 20,* 280–291.

Higginbotham, A. (1996). Teen mags: How to get a guy, drop 20 pounds, and lose your self-esteem. *Ms.,* March–April, 82–87.

Higgins, C. (1997). Screening for cervical cancer. *Nursing Times, 84,* 34–36.

Higgins, R. (2003). One man's story. In J. Haynes & J. Miller (Eds.), *Inconceivable Conceptions: Psychological Aspects of Infertility and Reproductive Technology.* Hove, United Kingdom: Brunner–Routledge.

Hill, M., & Fischer, A. (2001). Does entitlement mediate the link between masculinity and rape-related variables? *Journal of Counseling Psychology, 48,* 39–50.

Hillis, S. (1994). PID prevention: Clinical and societal stakes. *Hospital Practice, 29,* 121–130.

Hillis, S., Owens, L., Marchbanks, P., Amsterdam, L., & Mackenzie, W. (1997). Recurrent chlamydial infections increase the risks of hospitalization for ectopic pregnancy and pelvic inflammatory disease. *American Journal of Obstetrics and Gynecology, 176,* 103–107.

Himelein, M., Vogel, R., & Wachowiak, D. (1994). Nonconsensual sexual experiences in precollege women: Prevalence and risk factors. *Journal of Counseling and Development, 72,* 411–415.

Hines, M., Ahmed, S., & Hughes, I. (2003). Psychological outcomes and gender-related development in complete androgen insensitivity syndrome. *Archives of Sexual Behavior, 32,* 93–101.

Hingson, R., Heeren, T., Winter, M., & Wechsler, H. (2003). Early age of first drunkenness as a factor in college students' unplanned and unprotected sex attributable to drinking. *Pediatrics, 111,* 34–41.

Hinrichsen, D., & Robey, B. (2000). Population and the environment: The global challenge. *Population Reports, 28,* 1–31.

Hiort, O., & Holterhus, P. (2000). The molecular basis of male sexual differentiation. *European Journal of Endocrinology, 142,* 101–110.

Hirschkowitz, M., Karacan, I., Howell, J., Arcasoy, M., & Williams, R. (1992). Nocturnal penile tumescence in cigarette smokers with erectile dysfunction. *Urology, 39,* 101–107.

Hiscock, M., Inch, R., Hawryluk, J., Lyon, P., & Perachio, N. (1999). Is there a sex difference in human laterality? III. An exhaustive survey of tactile laterality studies from six neuropsychology journals. *Journal of Clinical Experimental Neuropsychobiology, 21,* 17–28.

Hitchcock, J. (1995). The witch within me. *Newsweek,* March 27, 16.

Hite, S. (1976). *The Hite Report: A Nationwide Study of Female Sexuality.* New York: Dell Books.

Hitt, J., Hendericks, S., Ginsberg, S., & Lewis, J. (1970). Disruption of male but not female sexual behavior in rats by medial forebrain bundle lesions. *Journal of Comparative and Physiological Psychology, 73,* 377–384.

Hoban, V. (2003). Tackling the taboo. *Nursing Times,* April 15, 40–41.

Hodge, D. (2004). Working with Hindu clients in a spiritually sensitive manner. *Social Work, 49,* 27–38.

Hoffman, R. (2003). An argument against routine prostate cancer screening. *Archives of Internal Medicine, 163,* 663–664.

Holden, S. (2000). Look! It's the Smiths from Elm Street. *The New York Times,* March 16, C13.

Holder, D., Durant, R., Harris, T., Daniel, J., Obeidallah, D., & Goodman, E. (2000). The association between adolescent spirituality and voluntary sexual activity. *Society for Adolescent Medicine, 26,* 295–302.

Holland, B. (1998). The long good-bye. *Smithsonian,* March, 87–93.

Holloway, R., Anderson, P., Defendini, R., & Harper, C. (1993). Sexual dimorphism of the human corpus callosum from three independent samples: Relative size of the corpus callosum. *American Journal of Physical Anthropology, 92,* 481–498.

Holman, M. (2003). *Reclaiming Your Lost Libido.* Retrieved August 3, 2003, from http://health.discovery.com/centers/womens/sexualhealth/healthysex_print.html

Holman, T., & Daoli, B. (1997). Premarital factors influencing perceived readiness for marriage. *Journal of Family Issues, 18(2),* 124–144.

Holmberg, L., Bill-Axelson, A., Helgesen, F., Salo, J., Folmerz, P., & Haggman, M. (2002). A randomized trial comparing radical prostatectomy with watchful waiting in early prostate cancer. *New England Journal of Medicine, 347,* 781–791.

Holmes, S. (2003). Tadalafil: A new treatment for erectile dysfunction. *British Journal of Urology International, 92,* 466–468.

Holmquist, N. (2000). Revisiting the effect of the Pap test on cervical cancer. *American Journal of Public Health, 90,* 620.

Hong, B., Ji, Y., Hong, J., & Nam, K. (2003). Korean red ginseng effective for treatment of erectile dysfunction. *Journal of Family Practice, 52,* 20–21.

Hook, E. (1981). Rates of chromosome abnormalities at different maternal ages. *Obstetrics and Gynecology, 11,* 282–284.

Hooker, E. (1967). The adjustment of the male overt homosexual. *Journal of Projective Techniques, 21,* 18–31.

Hooton, T. (1996). A simplified approach to urinary tract infection. *Hospital Practice,* February 15, 23–30.

Hoover, E. (1997). Memory therapy turns woman's life into nightmare. *The Oregonian,* April 13, A1, A12.

Hopkins, S. (1999). A discussion of the legal aspects of female genital mutilation. *Journal of Advanced Nursing, 30,* 926–933.

Horta, B., Kramer, M., & Platt, R. (2001). Maternal smoking and the risk of early weaning: A meta-analysis. *American Journal of Public Health, 91,* 304–307.

Horta, B., Victora, C., Menezes, A., & Barros, F. (1997). Environmental tobacco smoke and breastfeeding duration. *American Journal of Epidemiology, 146(2),* 128–133.

Horvath, M., & Ryan, A. (2003). Antecedents and potential moderators of the relationship between attitudes and hiring discrimination on the basis of sexual orientation. *Sex Roles, 48,* 115–125.

Horwitz, A., White, H., & Howell-White, S. (1996). Becoming married and mental health: A longitudinal study of a cohort of young adults. *Journal of Marriage and the Family, 58,* 895–907.

Howard, A., Riger, S., Campbell, R., & Wasco, S. (2003). Counseling services for battered women: A comparison of outcomes for physical and sexual assault survivors. *Journal of Interpersonal Violence, 18,* 717–734.

Howard, B. (1999). The return of the sponge and other new birth control options. *New Woman,* July, 30.

Howard, C., Howard, F., Garfunkel, L., de Blieck, E., & Weitzman, M. (1998). Neonatal circumcision and pain relief: Current training practices. *Pediatrics, 101,* 423–428.

Howard, M., & McCabe, J. (1990). Helping teenagers postpone sexual involvement. *Family Planning Perspectives, 22,* 929–932.

Howey, N., & Samuels, E. (2000). *Out of the Ordinary: Essays on Growing Up with Gay, Lesbian, and Transgender Parents.* New York: St. Martin's Press.

Hoxworth, T., Spencer, N., Peterman, T., Craig, T., Johnson, S., & Maher, J. (2003). Changes in partnerships and HIV risk behavior after partner notification. *Sexually Transmitted Diseases, 30,* 83–88.

Hoyert, D., Danel, I., & Tully, P. (2000). Maternal mortality, United States and Canada, 1982–1997. *Birth, 27,* 4–11.

Hu, D., Vitek, C., Bartholow, B., & Mastro, T. (2003). Key issues for a potential human immunodeficiency virus vaccine. *Clinical Infectious Diseases, 36,* 638–644.

Hubbard, B., Giese, M., & Rainey, J. (1998). A replication of reducing the risk: A theory-based sexuality curriculum for adolescents. *Journal of School Health, 68,* 243–247.

Hudson, M., & Graham, C. (2004). Censorship: The big chill. *The Advocate,* May 11, 48–53.

Hudson, W. (1992). *The WALMYR Assessment Scales Scoring Manual.* Tallahassee, FL: WALMYR Publishing.

Hughes, C., Jr., Wall, L. L., & Creasman, W. (1991). Reproductive hormone levels in gynecologic oncology patients undergoing surgical castration after spontaneous menopause. *Gynecologic Oncology, 40,* 42–45.

Hughes, J., & Sandler, B. (1987). *"Friends" Raping Friends: Could It Happen to You?* Washington, DC: Association of American Colleges.

Hughes, M., Soh, C., Brady, M., Dankner, W., & Oleske, J. (2004). Author's reply. *Lancet, 363,* 900–901.

Hull, E., Lorrain, D., Du, J., Matuszewich, L., Lumley, L., Putnam, S., & Moses, J. (1999). Hormone–neurotransmitter interactions in the control of sexual behavior. *Behavioral Brain Research, 105,* 105–116.

Hummel, W., & Kettel, L. (1997). Assisted reproductive technology: The state of the ART. *Annals of Medicine, 29,* 207–214.

Humphrey, F. (1987). Treating extramarital sexual relationships in sex and couples therapy. In G. Weeks & L. Hof (Eds.), *Integrating Sex and Marital Therapy: A Clinical Guide.* New York: Brunner/Mazel.

Humphries, K., & Gill, S. (2003). Risks and benefits of hormone replacement therapy: The evidence speaks. *Canadian Medical Association Journal, 168,* 1001–1010.

Hunsberger, B. (2003). Same-sex harassment catches firms off guard. *The Oregonian,* April 6, Cl, C5.

Hunt, M. (1974). *Sexual Behavior in the 1970s.* Chicago: Playboy Press.

Hunter, J. (1990). Violence against lesbian and gay male youths. *Journal of Interpersonal Violence, 5,* 295–300.

Hurlbert, D., & Whittaker, K. (1991). The role of masturbation in marital and sexual satisfaction: A comparative study of female masturbators and nonmasturbators. *Journal of Sex Education and Therapy, 17,* 272–282.

Hussain, S. (2004). Progesterone-only pills and high blood pressure. *Contraception, 69,* 89–97.

Huston, A., Wartella, E., & Donnerstein, E. (1998). *Measuring the Effects of Sexual Content in the Media.* Menlo Park, CA: Kaiser Family Foundation.

Huston, T., Caughlin, J., & Houts, R. (2001). The connubial crucible: Newlywed years as predictors of marital delight, distress, and divorce. *Journal of Personality and Social Psychology, 80,* 237–252.

Hutchinson, M., & Cooney, T. (1998). Patterns of parent-teen sexual risk communication: Implications for intervention. *Family Relations, 47,* 185–194.

Hutti, M. (2003). New and emerging contraceptive methods. *Association of Women's Health, Obstetric, and Neonatal Nurses Lifelines, 7,* 32–39.

Huyghe, P. (2003). *Suo Yang (Koro): The Genital Retraction Syndrome.* Retrieved March 13, 2003, from http://www.omnimag.com/antimater/new/penis.html

Hwang, S., & Saenz, R. (1997). Fertility of Chinese immigrants in the U.S.: Testing a fertility emancipation hypothesis. *Journal of Marriage and the Family, 59,* 50–61.

Hyde, J. (1996). *Half the Human Experience: The Psychology of Women* (5th ed.). Boston: Houghton Mifflin.

Hyde, J. (2001). The next decade of sexual science: Synergy from advances in related sciences. *Journal of Sex Research, 38,* 97–101.

Hyde, J., Krajnik, M., & Skuldt-Niederberger, K. (1991). Androgyny across the life span: A replication and longitudinal follow-up. *Developmental Psychology, 27,* 516–519.

Iasenza, S. (2000). Lesbian sexuality post-Stonewall to post-modernism: Putting the "Lesbian Bed Death" concept to bed. *Journal of Sex Education and Therapy, 25,* 59–69.

Imperato-McGinley, J., Peterson, R., Gautier, T., & Sturla, E. (1979). Androgens and the evolution of male-gender identity among male pseudohermaphrodites with 5-alpha-reductase deficiency. *New England Journal of Medicine, 300,* 1233–1237.

Iovine, V. (1997a). *The Girlfriends' Guide to Pregnancy.* New York: Perigee.

Iovine, V. (1997b). *The Girlfriends' Guide to Surviving the First Year of Motherhood.* New York: Perigee.

Irvine, J. (1990). *Disorders of Desire, Sex, and Gender in Modern American Sexology.* Philadelphia: Temple University Press.

Isay, R. (1989). *Being Homosexual: Gay Men and Their Development.* New York: Farrar, Straus, & Giroux.

Isely, P., & Gehrenbeck-Shim, D. (1997). Sexual assault of men in the community. *Journal of Community Psychology, 25,* 159–166.

Ishii-Kuntz, M. (1997a). Chinese American families. In M. DeGenova (Ed.), *Families in Cultural Context: Strengths and Challenges in Diversity.* Mountain View, CA: Mayfield.

Ishii-Kuntz, M. (1997b). Japanese American families. In M. DeGenova (Ed.), *Families in Cultural Context: Strengths and Challenges in Diversity.* Mountain View, CA: Mayfield.

Ito, T., Trant, A., & Polan, M. (2001). A double-blind placebo-controlled study of ArginMax, a nutritional supplement for enhancement of female sexual function. *Journal of Sex and Marital Therapy, 27,* 541–549.

Ivey, J. (1997). The adolescent with pelvic inflammatory disease: Assessment and management. *Nurse Practitioner,* February, 78–91.

Jaccard, J., Dittus, P., & Gordon, V. (1996). Maternal correlates of adolescent sexual and contraceptive behavior. *Family Planning Perspectives, 28,* 159–165.

Jaccard, J., Dittus, P., & Gordon, V. (2000). Parent–teen communication about premarital sex. *Journal of Adolescent Research, 15,* 187–208.

Jacklin, C., Dipietro, J., & Maccoby, E. (1984). Sex-typing behavior and sex-typing pressure in child–parent interaction. *Archives of Sexual Behavior, 13,* 413–425.

Jackson, A., & Wadley, V. (1999). A multicenter study of women's self-reported reproductive health after spinal cord injury. *Archives of Physical Medicine and Rehabilitation, 80,* 1420–1428.

Jackson, J., Calhoun, K., Amick, A., Maddever, H., & Habif, V. (1990). Young adult women who report childhood intrafamilial sexual abuse: Subsequent adjustment. *Archives of Sexual Behavior, 19,* 211–221.

Jacoby, S. (1999). Great sex: What's age got to do with it? *Modern Maturity,* September–October, 43–45.

Jain, J., Dutton, C., Harwood, B., & Meckstroth, K. (2002). A prospective randomized, double-blinded, placebo-controlled trial comparing mifepristone and vaginal misoprostol to vaginal misoprostol alone for elective termination of early pregnancy. *Human Reproduction, 17,* 1477–1482.

Jain, T., Missmer, S., & Hornstein, M. (2004). Trends in embryo-transfer practice and in outcomes of the use of assisted reproductive technology in the United States. *New England Journal of Medicine, 350,* 1639–1645.

Jakobsen, J., & Pellegrini, A. (2003). *Love the Sin: Sexual Regulation and the Limits of Religious Tolerance (Sexual Cultures).* New York: New York University Press.

James, T., & Cinelli. B. (2003). Exploring gender-based communication styles. *Journal of School Health, 73,* 41–42.

Jamieson, D., Kaufman, S., Costello, C., & Hillis, S. (2002). A comparison of women's regret after vasectomy versus tubal sterilization. *Obstetrics and Gynecology, 99,* 1073–1079.

Jamison, P., & Gebhard, P. (1988). Penis size increase between flaccid and erect states: An analysis of the Kinsey data. *Journal of Sex Research, 24,* 177–183.

Jani, A., & Hellman, S. (2003). Early prostate cancer: Clinical decision-making. *The Lancet, 361,* 1045–1053.

Janowsky, D., Halbreich, U., & Rausch, J. (1996). Association among ovarian hormones, other hormones, emotional disorders, and neurotransmitters. In M. Jensvold and U. Halbreich (Eds.), *Psychopharmacology and Women: Sex, Gender, and Hormones.* Washington, DC: American Psychiatric Press.

Janssen, N., & Genta, M. (2000). The effects of immunosuppressive and anti-inflammatory medications on fertility, pregnancy, and lactation. *Archives of Internal Medicine, 160,* 610–619.

Janus, S., & Janus, C. (1993). *The Janus Report on Sexual Behavior.* New York: Wiley.

Jarrell, A. (2000). Model maturity. *The Sunday Oregonian,* April 16, L13.

Jayaraman, G., Read, R., & Singh, A. (2003). Characteristics of individuals with male-to-male and heterosexually acquired infectious syphilis during an outbreak in Calgary, Alberta, Canada. *Sexually Transmitted Diseases, 30,* 315–319.

Jeavons, H. (2003). Prevention and treatment of vulvovaginal candidiasis using exogenous lactobacillus. *Journal of Obstetrical, Gynecological, and Neonatal Nursing, 32,* 287–296.

Jegalian, K., & Lahn, B. (2001a). New answers for men: Y am I infertile? *Scientific American,* February, 61.

Jegalian, K., & Lahn, B. (2001b). Why the Y is so weird. *Scientific American,* February, 56–61.

Jehl, D. (1998). Western masterpieces locked away from Iranian view. *The Oregonian,* October 4, A7.

Jennings, V., Lamprecht, V., & Kowal, D. (1998). Fertility awareness methods. In R. Hatcher, J. Trussell, F. Stewart, W. Cates, G. Stewart, F. Guest, & D. Kowal (Eds.), *Contraceptive Technology.* New York: Ardent Media.

Jensen, J., Wilder, K., Carr, K., & Romm, J. (2003). Quality of life and sexual function after evaluation and treatment at a referral center for vulvovaginal disorders. *American Journal of Obstetrics and Gynecology, 188,* 1629–1637.

Jetter, A. (2000). Rules of engagement. *Ms.,* April–May, 20.

Jewett, M., Fleshner, N., Klotz, L., Nam, R., & Trachtenberg, J. (2003). Radical prostatectomy as treatment for prostate cancer. *Canadian Medical Association Journal, 168,* 44–45.

Jewkes, R., Wood, K., & Maforah, N. (1997). Backstreet abortion in South Africa. *Southern Africa Medical Journal, 87,* 417–418.

Joannides, P. (1996). *The Guide to Getting It On!* Walport, OR: Goofy Foot Press.

Johannes, C., Araujo, A., & Feldman, H. (2000). Incidence of erectile dysfunction in men 40 to 69 years old: Longitudinal results from the Massachusetts male aging study. *Journal of Urology, 163,* 460–463.

John, G., Nduati, R., Mbori-Ngacha, D., Richardson, B., Panteleeff, D., Mwatha, A., Overbaugh, J., Bwayo, J., Ndinya-Achola, J., & Kreiss, J. (2001). Correlates of mother-to-child human immunodeficiency virus type 1 (HIV-1) transmission: Association with maternal plasma HIV-1 RNA load, genital HIV-1 DNA shedding, and breast infections. *Journal of Infectious Diseases, 183,* 206–212.

Johnson, A., Copas, A., Erens, B., Mandalia, S., Fenton, K., Korovessis, C., Willings, K., & Field, J. (2001). Effect of computer-assisted self-interviews on reporting of sexual HIV risk behaviors in a general population sample: A methodological experiment. *AIDS 2001, 15,* 111–115.

Johnson, B., Carey, M., Marsh, K., Levin, K., & Scott-Sheldon, L. (2003). Interventions to reduce sexual risk for human immunodeficiency virus in adolescents, 1985–2000. *Archives of Pediatric and Adolescent Medicine, 157,* 381–388.

Johnson, D., & Nelson, M. (2003). Gays in church and state. *Newsweek,* August 18, 34.

Johnson, D., & Scelfo, J. (2003). Sex, love, and nursing homes. *Newsweek,* December 15, 54–55.

Johnson, E., & Huston, T. (1998). The perils of love, or why wives adapt to husbands during the transition to parenthood. *Journal of Marriage and the Family, 60,* 195–204.

Johnson, H., Weerakoon, P., & Stricker, P. (2002). The incidence, aetiology, and presentation of Peyronie's disease in Sydney, Australia. *Sexuality and Disability, 20,* 109–113.

Johnson, K. (2003). Viagra may ease women's sexual arousal disorder. *Internal Medicine News, 36,* 29.

Johnson, M. (1998). Notification dilemmas: Megan's law spawned flurry of state acts, but implementation proves problematic for all. *The Quill, 86,* 9.

Johnson, P. (1998). Pornography drives technology: Why not censor the Internet. In R. Baird & S. Rosenbaum (Eds.), *Pornography: Private Right or Public Menace?* Amherst, NY: Prometheus Books.

Johnston, L., Ward, T., & Hudson, S. (1997). Deviant sexual thoughts: Mental control and the treatment of sexual offenders. *Journal of Sex Research, 34,* 121–130.

Johnston, S. (1987). The mind of the molester. *Psychology Today,* February, 60–63.

Jones, E., Forrest, J., Goldman, N., Henshaw, S., Lincoln, R., Rosoff, J., Westoff, C., & Wulf, D. (1985). Teenage pregnancy in developed countries: Determinants and policy implications. *Family Planning Perspectives, 17,* 53–63.

Jones, F., & Koshes, R. (1995). Homosexuality and the military. *American Journal of Psychiatry, 152,* 16–21.

Jones, H., & Crocklin, S. (2000). On assisted reproduction, religion, and civil law. *Fertility and Sterility, 73,* 447–452.

Jones, J. (2003). Percutaneous vasectomy: A simple modification eliminates the steep learning curve of no-scalpel vasectomy. *Journal of Urology, 169,* 1434–1436.

Jones, K., Lehr, S., & Hewell, S. (1997). Dyspareunia: Three case reports. *Journal of Obstetrical, Gynecological, and Neonatal Nursing, 26,* 19–23.

Jones, L., & Finkelhor, D. (2003). Putting together evidence on declining trends in sexual abuse: A complex puzzle. *Child Abuse and Neglect, 27,* 133–135.

Jones, L., Finkelhor, D., & Kopiec, K. (2001). Why is sexual abuse declining? A survey of state child protection administrations. *Child Sexual Abuse and Neglect, 25,* 1139–1158.

Jones, R., Darroch, J., & Henshaw, S. (2002a). Contraceptive use among U.S. women having abortions in 2000–2001. *Perspectives on Sexual and Reproductive Health, 34,* 294–303.

Jones, R., Darroch, J., & Henshaw, S. (2002b). Patterns in the socioeconomic characteristics of women obtaining abortions in 2000–2001. *Perspectives on Sexual and Reproductive Health, 34,* 226–235.

Jones, R., & Henshaw, S. (2002). Mifepristone for early medical abortion: Experiences in France, Great Britain, and Sweden. *Perspectives on Sexual and Reproductive Health, 34,* 154–161.

Jones, W., Chernovetz, M., & Hansson, R. (1978). The enigma of androgyny: Differential implications for males and females. *Journal of Consulting and Clinical Psychology, 46*, 298–313.

Jong, E. (2003). The zipless fallacy. *Newsweek,* June 30, 48.

Jorgenson, L., & Wahl, K. (2000). Psychiatrists as expert witnesses in sexual harassment cases under Daubert and Kumho. *Psychiatric Annals, 30*, 390–396.

Josefsson, A., Berg, G., & Nordin, C. (2001). Prevalence of depressive symptoms in late pregnancy and postpartum. *Acta Obstetricia et Gynecologica Scandinavica, 80*, 251–255.

Joseph, R. (1991). A case analysis in human sexuality: Counseling to a man with severe cerebral palsy. *Sexuality and Disability, 9 (2)*, 149–159.

Josselson, R. (1992). *The Space Between Us: Exploring Dimensions of Human Relationships.* San Francisco: Jossey-Bass.

Jouriles, E., Bourg, W., & Farris, A. (1991). Marital adjustment and child conduct problems: A comparison of the correlation across subsamples. *Journal of Consulting and Clinical Psychology, 59*, 354–357.

Joyner, J., Douglas, J., Ragsdale, S., Foster, M., & Judson, F. (2000). Comparative prevalence of infection with *Trichomonas vaginalis* among men attending a sexually transmitted diseases clinic. *Sexually Transmitted Diseases, 27*, 236–240.

Julien, J., Bijker, N., & Fentiman, I. (2000). Radiotherapy in breast-conserving treatment for ductal carcinoma in situ: First results of the EORTC randomised phase III trial 10853. *The Lancet, 355*, 528–533.

Kaemingk, K., & Bootzin, R. (1990). Behavior change strategies for increasing condom use. *Evaluation and Program Planning, 13*, 47–54.

Kaestle, C., Morisky, D., & Wiley, D. (2002). Sexual intercourse and age difference between adolescent females and their romantic partners. *Perspectives on Sexual and Reproductive Health, 34*, 304–309.

Kagan-Krieger, S. (1998). Women with Turner syndrome: A maturational and developmental perspective. *Journal of Adult Development, 5*, 125–135.

Kahn, J. (1999a). *Choosing Sides in the Sperm Race.* Retrieved June 15, 1999, from http://www.cnn.com/HEALTH/bioethics/9906/sperm.separation/

Kahn, J. (1999b). *Embryonic Ethics.* Retrieved June 2, 1999, from http://www.cnn.com/HEALTH/bioethics/9906/embryonic.ethics/index.html

Kahn, J., Brindis, C., & Glei, D. (1999). Pregnancies averted among U.S. teenagers by the use of contraceptives. *Family Planning Perspectives, 31*, 29–34.

Kaiser, C. (2003). Throwing the backlash off balance. *The Advocate,* October 14, 96.

Kaiser, C. (2004). Civil marriage, civil rights. *The Advocate,* March 30, 72.

Kaiser Family Foundation (2002). *Abortion in the U.S.* Fact sheet. Menlo Park, CA: Henry J. Kaiser Family Foundation.

Kaiser Family Foundation (2003a, February). *Seventeen Magazine and Kaiser Family Foundation Release New Survey of Teens About Gender Roles.* Retrieved June 12, 2003, from http://www.kff.org/content/2003/3301

Kaiser Family Foundation (2003b). *Sex on Television. 3. Content and Context.* Retrieved from http://www.kff.org/content/2003/20030204a/

Kalb, C. (1997). How old is too old? *Newsweek,* May 5, 64.

Kalb, C. (1999). Baby boom: The $50,000 egg. *Newsweek,* March 15, 64.

Kalb, C. (2001). Should you have your baby now? *Newsweek,* August 13, 40.

Kalb, C. (2003a). Farewell to "Aunt Flo." *Newsweek,* February 3, 48.

Kalb. C. (2003b). An old enemy is back. *Newsweek,* February 10, 60.

Kalb, C. (2003c). Preemies grow up. *Newsweek,* March 10, 50–51.

Kalb, C. (2004). Brave new babies. *Newsweek,* January 26, 45–51.

Kalichman, S., Carey, M., & Johnson, B. (1996), Prevention of sexually transmitted HIV infection: A meta-analytic review of the behavioral outcome literature. *Annals of Behavioral Medicine, 18*, 6–15.

Kalick, M., Zebowitz, L., Langlois, J., & Johnson, R. (1998). Does human facial attractiveness honestly advertise health? Longitudinal data on an evolutionary question. *Psychological Science, 9*, 8–13.

Kalof, L. (1993). Rape-supportive attitudes and sexual victimization experiences of sorority and nonsorority women. *Sex Roles, 29*, 767–780.

Kalof, L., Eby, K., Matheson, J., & Kroska, R. (2001). The influence of race and gender on student self-reports of sexual harassment by college professors. *Gender and Society, 15*, 282–302.

Kamalipour, Y., & Rampal, K. (2001). *Media, Sex, Violence, and Drugs in the Global Village.* Lanham, MD: Rowman & Littlefield.

Kanin, E. (1985). Date rapists: Differential sexual socialization and relative deprivation. *Archives of Sexual Behavior, 14*, 219–231.

Kann, I., Brener, N., & Allensworth, D. (2001). Results from the School Health Policies and Programs Study 2000. *Journal of School Health, 71*, 266–278.

Kantor, M. (1998). *Homophobia: Description, Development, and Dynamic of Gay Bashing.* New York: Praeger.

Kantrowitz, B. (1992). Sexism in the schoolhouse. *Newsweek,* February 24, 62–70.

Kantrowitz, B. (1996). Parents come out. *Newsweek,* November 4, 51–57.

Kantrowitz, B. (1997). A bitter new battle over partial-birth abortions. *Newsweek,* March 17, 66.

Kantrowitz, B. (2004). State of our unions. *Newsweek,* March 1, 44–45.

Kantrowitz, B., & Wingert, P. (1999). The science of a good marriage. *Newsweek,* April 19, 52–57.

Kaplan, H. (1974). *The New Sex Therapy: Active Treatment of Sexual Dysfunction.* New York: Brunner/Mazel.

Kaplan, H. (1979). *Disorders of Sexual Desire.* New York: Brunner/ Mazel.

Karasz, A., & Anderson, M. (2003). The vaginitis monologues: Women's experiences of vaginal complaints in a primary care setting. *Social Science and Medicine, 56*, 1013–1021.

Karlen, A. (1988). *Threesomes: Studies in Sex, Power, and Intimacy.* New York: Beech Tree/Morrow.

Karlin, S. (2003). Lost world. *The Advocate,* July 8, 66.

Karney, B., & Bradbury, T. (1995). The longitudinal course of marital quality and stability: A review of theory, method, and research. *Psychological Review, 118*, 3–34.

Karofsky, P., Zeng, L., & Kosorok, M. (2000). Relationship between adolescent-parental communication and initiation of first intercourse by adolescents. *Journal of Adolescent Health, 28*, 41–45.

Kasl, C. (1999). *If the Buddha Dated: Handbook for Finding Love on a Spiritual Path.* New York: Penguin/Arkana.

Kassabian, V. (2003). Sexual function in patients treated for benign prostatic hyperplasia. *The Lancet, 361*, 60–62.

Katz, J. (1976). *Gay American History.* New York: Avon Books.

Katz, J. (1994). Empirical and theoretical dimensions of obscene phone calls to women in the United States. *Human Communication Research, 21*, 155–182.

Katz, J. (1995). *The Invention of Heterosexuality.* New York: Dutton.

Katz, P., & Ksansnak, K. (1994). Developmental aspects of gender role flexibility and traditionality in middle childhood and adolescence. *Developmental Psychology, 30*, 272–282.

Kaufman, G., Bloch, M., Zaunders, J., Smith, D., & Cooper, D. (2000). Long-term immunological response in HIV-1 infected subjects receiving potent antiretroviral therapy. *AIDS 2000, 14*, 959–969.

Kaunitz, A. (1994). Long-acting injectable contraception with depot medroxyprogesterone acetate. *American Journal of Obstetrics and Gynecology, 170*, 1543–1549.

Keith, L., & Breborowicz, G. (2002). Triplet pregnancies and their aftermaths. Part I. Basic considerations. *International Journal of Fertility, 47*, 254–264.

Keller, M., Sadovszky, V., Pankratz, B., & Hermsen, J. (2000). Self-disclosure of HPV infection to sexual partners. *Western Journal of Nursing Research, 22*, 285–302.

Keller, S., & Brown, J. (2002). Media interventions to promote responsible sexual behavior. *Journal of Sex Research, 39*, 67–73.

Kellett, J. (2000). Older adult sexuality. In L. Szuchman & F. Muscarella (Eds.), *Psychological Perspectives on Human Sexuality.* New York: Wiley.

Kelley, M., & Parsons, B. (2000). Sexual harassment in the 1990s. *Journal of Higher Education, 71*, 548.

Kelly, J. (1982). Divorce: The adult perspective. In B. Wolman & G. Stricker (Eds.), *Handbook of Developmental Psychology.* Englewood Cliffs, NJ: Prentice Hall.

Kelly, J., Hoffman, R., Rompa, D., & Gray, M. (1998). Protease inhibitor combination therapies and perceptions of gay men regarding AIDS severity and the need to maintain safer sex. *AIDS, 12*, F91–F95.

Kelly, M. (1998). View from the field out in education: Where the personal and political collide. *SIECUS Report, 26(4)*, 14–15.

Kelly, M., & McGee, M. (1999). Teen sexuality education in the Netherlands, France, and Germany. *SIECUS Reports, 27*, 11–14.

Kelly, M., Strassberg, D., & Kircher, J. (1990). Attitudinal and experiential correlates of anorgasmia. *Archives of Sexual Behavior, 19*, 165–181.

Kemena, B. (2000). Changing homosexual orientation? Considering the evolving activities of change programs in the United States. *Journal of the Gay and Lesbian Medical Association, 4*, 85–93.

Kempner, M. (2001). Fewer debates about sexuality education as abstinence-only programs take foothold *SIECUS Report, 29*, 4–16.

Kennedy, K., & Trussell, J. (1998). Postpartum contraception and lactation. In R. Hatcher, J. Trussell, F. Stewart, W. Cates, G. Stewart, F. Guest, & D. Kowal (Eds.), *Contraceptive Technology*. New York: Ardent Media.

Kennedy, S., Eisfeld, B., & Dickens, S. (2000). Antidepressant-induced sexual dysfunction during treatment with moclobemide, paroxetine, sertraline, and venlafaxine. *Journal of Clinical Psychiatry, 61*, 276–281.

Kerin, J., Copper, J., Price, T., & Van Herendael, B. (2003). Hysteroscopic sterilization using a micro-insert device: Results of a multicenter Phase II study. *Human Reproduction, 18*, 1223–1230.

Kesby, M. (2000). Participatory diagramming as a means to improve communication about sex in rural Zimbabwe: A pilot study. *Social Science and Medicine, 50*, 1723–1741.

Kessler, S. (1998). *Lessons from the Intersexed*. New Brunswick, NJ: Rutgers University Press.

Kiel, R., & Nashelsky, J. (2003). Does cranberry juice prevent or treat urinary tract infection? *Journal of Family Practice, 52*, 154–155.

Kielwasser, A. (1991). Watching television: Lesbian and gay media activism. *San Francisco Bay Times*, December 5, 13.

Kilbourn, C., & Richards, C. (2001). Abnormal uterine bleeding. *Postgraduate Medicine, 109*, 137–150.

Kilmartin, C. (1999). Pleasure and performance: Male sexuality. In K. Lebacqz & D. Sinacore-Guinn (Eds.), *Sexuality: A Reader*. Cleveland: Pilgrim Press.

Kim, E., & Lipshultz, L. (1997). Advances in the treatment of organic erectile dysfunction. *Hospital Practice*, April 15, 101–120.

Kim, E., & McVary, K. (1995). Long-term results with penile vein ligation for venogenic impotence. *Journal of Urology, 153*, 655–658.

Kim, S., & Seo, K. (1998). Efficacy and safety of fluoxetine, sertraline, and clomipramine in patients with premature ejaculation: A double-blind, placebo controlled study. *Journal of Urology, 159*, 425–427.

Kimlicka, T., Cross, H., & Tarnai, J. (1983). A comparison of androgynous, feminine, masculine, and undifferentiated women on self-esteem, body satisfaction, and sexual satisfaction. *Psychology of Women Quarterly, 1*, 291–294.

Kimura, D. (1992). Sex differences in the brain. *Scientific American, 267*, 118–125.

Kingsberg, S. (2002). The impact of aging on sexual function in women and their partners. *Archives of Sexual Behavior, 31*, 431–437.

Kingsberg, S., Applegarth, L., & Janata, J. (2000). Embryo donation programs and policies in North America: Survey results and implications for health and mental health professionals. *Fertility and Sterility, 73*, 215–220.

Kinsey, A., Pomeroy, W., & Martin, C. (1948). *Sexual Behavior in the Human Male*. Philadelphia: Saunders.

Kinsey, A., Pomeroy, W., Martin, C., & Gebhard, P. (1953). *Sexual Behavior in the Human Female*. Philadelphia: Saunders.

Kinzl, J., Traweger, C., & Biebl, W. (1995). Sexual dysfunctions: Relationship to childhood sexual abuse and early family experiences in a nonclinical sample. *Child Abuse and Neglect, 19*, 785–792.

Kipnis, L. (1996). *Bound and Gagged: Pornography and the Politics of Fantasy in America*. New York: Grove Press.

Kirby, D. (2000). Making condoms available in schools. *Western Journal of Medicine, 172*, 149–151.

Kirby, R., & Fitzpatrick, J. (2003). Radical prostatectomy or watchful waiting? *British Journal of Urology International, 91*, 5.

Kirchmeyer, C. (1996). Gender roles in decision-making in demographically diverse groups: A case for reviving androgyny. *Sex Roles, 34*, 649–663.

Kirchner, J., & Emmert, D. (2000). Sexually transmitted diseases in women: *Chlamydia trachomatis* and herpes simplex infections. *Postgraduate Medicine, 107*, 55–65.

Kirkpatrick, L., & Davis, K. (1994). Attachment style, gender, and relationship stability: A longitudinal analysis. *Journal of Personality and Social Psychology, 66*, 502–512.

Kissinger, P. (2003). Do older partners place adolescent girls at higher risk for STDs? *Sexually Transmitted Diseases, 30*, 214–215.

Kissinger, P., Niccolai, L., Magnus, M., Farley, T., Maher, J., Richardson-Alston, G., Dorst, D., Myers, L., & Peterman, T. (2003). Partner notification for HIV and syphilis. *Sexually Transmitted Diseases, 30*, 75–82.

Kissinger, P., Trim, S., Williams, E., Mielke, E., Koporc, K., & Brown, R. (1997). An evaluation of initiatives to improve family planning use by African-American adolescents. *Journal of the National Medical Association, 89*, 110–114.

Kissling, E. (2002, January). *On the Rag on Screen: Menarche in Film and Television*. Retrieved May 25, 2003, from http://www.findarticles.com/cf_0/m2294/2002_Jan/90333581/p1/article.jhtml

Kissling, F. (2003). *The Vatican: Out of Touch with Catholics*. Retrieved June 22, 2003, from http://www.cath4choice.org/spanish/lowbandwidth/youthvatican.htm

Kite, M., & Whitley, B. (1998a). Do heterosexual women and men differ in their attitudes toward homosexuality? A conceptual and methodological analysis. In G. Herek (Ed.), *Stigma and Sexual Orientation: Understanding Prejudice Against Lesbians, Gay Men, and Bisexuals*. Thousand Oaks, CA: Sage.

Kite, M., & Whitley, B. (1998b). Heterosexuals' attitudes toward homosexuality. In G. Herek (Ed.), *Stigma and Sexual Orientation: Understanding Prejudice Against Lesbians, Gay Men, and Bisexuals*. Thousand Oaks, CA: Sage.

Kjerulff, K., Langenberg, P., & Rhodes, J. (2000). Effectiveness of hysterectomy. *Obstetrics and Gynecology, 95*, 319–326.

Klagsbrun, F. (1985). *Married People: Staying Together in the Age of Divorce*. New York: Bantam Books.

Klaich, D. (1974). *Woman Plus Woman: Attitudes Towards Lesbianism*. New York: Simon & Schuster.

Klein, M. (1991). Why there's no such thing as sexual addiction and why it really matters. In R. Francoeur (Ed.), *Taking Sides: Clashing Views of Controversial Issues in Human Sexuality* (3rd ed.). Guilford, CT: Dushkin.

Klein, M. (1999). Censorship and the fear of sexuality. In J. Elias, V. Elias, V. Bullough, G. Brewer, J. Douglas, & W. Jarvis (Eds.), *Porn 101: Eroticism, Pornography, and the First Amendment*. Amherst, NY: Prometheus Books.

Klein, M. (2003). Sex addiction: A dangerous clinical concept. *SIECUS Report, 31*, 8–11.

Kleiner, K. (2000). Protect and survive. *New Scientist*, January 15, 4.

Kligler, B. (2003). Black cohosh. *American Family Physician, 68*, 114–116.

Klinger, K. (2003). Prostitution, humanism, and a woman's choice. *The Humanist*, January–February, 16–19.

Kloer, P. (2003). Upscale vendors cash in on pornography. *Knight Ridder/Tribune Business News*, August 17, E2.

Kluger, J. (2004). The power of love. *Time*, January 19, 62–65.

Knafo, D., & Jaffe, Y. (1984). Sexual fantasizing in males and females. *Journal of Research in Personality, 19*, 451–462.

Koblin, B., Chesney, M., Husnik, M., Bozeman, S., Celum, C., Buchbinder, S., Mayer, K., McKirnan, D., Judson, F., Huang, Y., Coates, T., and the EXPLORE Study Team (2003). High-risk behaviors among men who have sex with men in 6 U.S. cities: Baseline data from the EXPLORE study. *American Journal of Public Health, 93*, 926–932.

Koch-Straube, U. (1982). Attitude toward sexuality in old age. *Zeitschrift für Gerontologie, 15*, 220–227.

Koehler, J. (2002). Vaginismus: Diagnosis, etiology, and intervention. *Contemporary Sexuality, 36*, i–viii.

Koehler, J., Zangwill, W., & Lotz, L. (2000). *Integrating the Power of EMDR into Sex Therapy*. Paper presented at the 32nd Annual Conference of the American Association of Sex Educators, Counselors, and Therapists, Atlanta, Georgia, May 10–14.

Koglin, O. (1996). A woman's pain. *The Oregonian*, June 20, A20.

Koglin, O. (1998). Tamoxifen prevents breast cancer. *The Oregonian*, April 7, A1, A7.

Kohl, J. (2002). *The Scent of Eros: Mysteries of Odor in Human Sexuality*. Lincoln, NE: iUniverse Inc.

Kohl, J., Atzmueller, M., Fink, B., & Grammer, K. (2001). Human pheromones: Integrating neuroendocrinology and ethology. *Neuroendocrinology Letters, 5*, 309–321.

Kohn, I., & Kaplan, S. (2000). Female sexual dysfunction: What is known and what can be done? *Contemporary OB/GYN*, February, 25–46.

Kolata, G. (2000). Contraceptive given without doctor. *The Oregonian*, October 3, D17.

Kolodny, R. (1980). *Adolescent Sexuality*. Paper presented at the Michigan Personnel and Guidance Association Annual Convention, Detroit, November.

Kolodny, R., Masters, W., & Johnson, V. (1979). *Textbook of Sexual Medicine*. Boston: Little, Brown.

Komaromy, M., Bindman, A., Haber, R., & Sande, M. (1993). Sexual harassment in medical training. *New England Journal of Medicine, 328*, 322–326.

Koopman, J. (1996). Emerging objectives and methods in epidemiology. *American Journal of Public Health, 86*, 630–632.

Korber, B., Muldoon, M., Theiler, J., Gao, F., Gupta, R., Lapedes, A., Hahn, B., Wolinsky, S., & Bhattacharya, T. (2000). Timing the ancestor of the HIV-1 pandemic strains. *Science, 288,* 1789–1796.

Korenman, S., & Viosca, S. (1992). Use of a vacuum tumescence device in the management of impotence in men with a history of penile implant or severe pelvic disease. *Journal of the American Geriatric Society, 40,* 61–64.

Kosnik, A., Carroll, W., Cunningham, A., Modras, R., & Schulte, J. (1977). *Human Sexuality: New Directions in American Catholic Thought.* New York: Paulist Press.

Koss, L., Gidycz, C., & Wisniewski, N. (1987). The scope of rape: Incidence and prevalence of sexual aggression and victimization in a national sample of higher education students. *Journal of Consulting and Clinical Psychology, 55,* 162–170.

Koss, M. (1992). The underdetection of rape: Methodological choices influence incidence estimates. *Journal of Social Issues, 48,* 61–75.

Koss, M., Figueredo, A., & Prince, R. (2002). Cognitive mediation of rape's mental, physical, and social health impact: Tests of four models in cross-sectional data. *Journal of Consulting and Clinical Psychology, 70,* 926–941.

Kossmann, D. (2002). Barren. *Psychotherapy Networker,* July–August, 40.

Koukounas, E., & McCabe, M. (1997). Sexual and emotional variables influencing sexual response to erotica. *Behavior Research and Therapy, 35,* 221–231.

Koutsky, L., Ault, K., & Wheeler, C. (2002). A controlled trial of a human papillomavirus type 16 vaccine. *New England Journal of Medicine, 347,* 1645–1651.

Krahe, B., Scheinberger-Olwig, R., & Bieneck, S. (2003). Men's reports of nonconsensual sexual interactions with women: Prevalence and impact. *Archives of Sexual Behavior, 32,* 165–175.

Krahe, B., Scheinberger-Olwig, R., & Kolpin, S. (2000). Ambiguous communication of sexual intentions as a risk marker of sexual aggression. *Sex Roles, 42,* 313–337.

Krakow, B., Germain, A., Tandberg, D., Koss, M., Schrader, R., Hollifield, M., Cheng, D., & Edmond, T. (2000). Sleep breathing and sleep movement disorders masquerading as insomnia in sexual-assault survivors. *Comprehensive Psychiatry, 41,* 49–56.

Krauthammer, C. (2001). Why pro-lifers are missing the point. *Time,* February 12, 60.

Kreinin, T. (2002a). Critical issues about pregnancy and parenting. *SIECUS Report, 30,* 5–6.

Kreinin, T. (2002b). From the president. *SIECUS Report, 31,* 3.

Kreinin, T. (2002c). Governments need to provide sexual health services to their citizens. *SIECUS Report, 30,* 5–6.

Kreinin, T. (2002d). New approaches to contraception are needed. *SIECUS Report,* December–January, 3.

Kreinin, T., Rodriquez, M., & Edwards, M. (2001). Adolescents would prefer parents as primary sexuality educators. *SIECUS Report Supplement,* December–January, 1.

Krist, A. (2001). Obstetric care in patients with HIV disease. *American Family Physician, 63,* 107–122.

Kristof, N. (1996). The youngest prostitutes. *The Oregonian,* June 12, A12.

Kritz-Silverstein, D., Von Muhlen, D., Barrett-Conner, E., & Bressel, M. (2003). Isoflavones and cognitive function in the older women: The Soy and Postmenopausal Health in Aging (SOPHIA) study. *Menopause: The Journal of the North American Menopause Society, 10,* 196–202.

Kroll, K., & Klein E. (1992). *Enabling Romance.* New York: Harmony Books.

Kroman, N., Jensen, M., Wohlfahrt, J., Mouridsen, H., Andersen, P., & Melbye, M. (2000). Factors influencing the effect of age on prognosis in breast cancer: Population based study. *British Medical Journal, 320,* 474–478.

Krone, M., Wald, A., Tabet, S., Paradise, M., Corey, L., & Celum, C. (2000). Herpes simplex virus type 2 shedding in human immunodeficiency virus-negative men who have sex with men: Frequency, patterns, and risk factors. *Clinical Infectious Diseases, 30,* 261–267.

Krujiver, F., Zhou, J., Pool, C., Hoffman, N., Gooren, L., & Swaab, D. (2000). Male-to-female transsexuals have female neuron member in a limbic nucleus. *Journal of Clinical Endocrinology, 85,* 2034–2040.

Kruse, R., Guttenbach, M., Schartmann, B., Schubert, R., van der Ven, H., Schmid, M., & Propping, P. (1998). Genetic counseling in a patient with XXY/XXXY/XY mosaic Klinefelter's syndrome: Estimates of sex chromosome aberrations in sperm before intracytoplasmic sperm injection. *Fertility and Sterility, 69,* 482–485.

Krystal, H. (1982). Alexithymia and the effectiveness of psychoanalytic treatment. *International Journal of Psychoanalytical Psychotherapy, 9,* 353–378.

Ku, L., Sonenstein, F., & Pleck, J. (1993). Young men's risk behaviors for HIV infection and sexually transmitted diseases, 1988 through 1991. *American Journal of Public Health, 83,* 1609–1615.

Kulin, H., Frontera, M., Deuers, L., Bartholomew, M., & Lloyd, T. (1989). The onset of sperm production in pubertal boys. *American Journal of Diseases of Children, 143,* 190–193.

Kumar, S. (1994). Legislation on prenatal sex-determination in India. *The Lancet, 344,* 399.

Kunkel, D., Cope, K., & Biely, E. (1999). Sexual messages on television: Comparing findings from three studies. *Journal of Sex Research, 36,* 230–236.

Kunzle, R., Mueller, M., Hanggi, W., & Birkhauser, M. (2003). Semen quality of male smokers and nonsmokers in infertile couples. *Fertility and Sterility, 79,* 287–291.

Kurdas, C. (1999). Reproductive medicine: New findings. *Contemporary OB/GYN,* November, 128–134.

Kurdek, L. (1988). Relationship quality of gay and lesbian cohabiting couples. *Journal of Homosexuality, 15,* 93–118.

Kurdek, L. (1995a). Developmental changes in relationship quality in gay and lesbian cohabiting couples. *Developmental Psychology, 31,* 86–94.

Kurdek, L. (1995b). Lesbian and gay couples. In A. D'Augelli & C. Patterson (Eds.), *Lesbian, Gay, and Bisexual Identities over the Lifespan.* New York: Oxford University Press.

Kuriansky, J. (1996). Sexuality and television advertising: An historical perspective. *SIECUS Report, 24,* 13–15.

Kurpius, S. R., Foley Nicpon, M., & Maresh, S. (2001). Mood, marriage, and menopause. *Journal of Counseling Psychology, 48,* 77–84.

Kyes, K., & Tumbelaka, L. (1994). Comparison of Indonesian and American college students' attitudes toward homosexuality. *Psychological Reports, 74,* 227–237.

Laan, E., & Everaerd, W. (1996). Determinants of female sexual arousal: Psychophysiological theory and data. *Annual Review of Sex Research, 6,* 32–76.

Laan, E., & Everaerd, W. (1998). Physiological measures of vaginal vasocongestion. *International Journal of Impotence, 10,* S107–S110.

Lacy, K. (2001). Mature sexuality: Patient realities and provider challenges. *SIECUS Report, 30,* 22–29.

Lafferty, W., Hiltunen-Back, E., Reuwala, T., Niemen, P., & Paavonen, J. (1997). Sexually transmitted diseases in men who have sex with men. *Sexually Transmitted Diseases, 24,* 272–278.

Lagana, L. (1999). Psychological correlates of contraceptive practices during late adolescence. *Adolescence, 34,* 463–482.

Lagro-Janssen, T., Rosser, W., & van Weel, C. (2003). Breast cancer and hormone-replacement therapy: Up to general practice to pick up the pieces. *The Lancet, 362,* 414–415.

Lahoti, S., McClain, N., Girardet, R., McNeese, M., & Cheung, K. (2001). Evaluating the child for sexual abuse. *American Family Physician, 63,* 883–892.

Lalumiere, M., Blanchard, R., & Zucker, K. (2000). Sexual orientation and handedness in men and women: A meta-analysis. *Psychological Bulletin, 126,* 575–592.

Lamas, D. (2004). Morning-after pill dispute apt to stir again. *Miami Herald,* January 6, E7.

Lamb, D., Catanzaro, S., & Moorman, A. (2003). Psychologists reflect on their sexual relationships with clients, supervisees, and students: Occurrence, impact, rationales, and collegial intervention. *Professional Psychology: Research and Practice, 34,* 102–107.

Lambe, E. (1999). Dyslexia, gender, and brain imaging. *Neuropsychologia, 37,* 521–536.

Lambert, E., Dykeman, M., & Rankin, A. (2001). There is such a thing as a free lunch: A model work-site parent education program. *SIECUS Report, 7,* 7–9.

Lammers, C., Ireland, M., Resnick, M., & Blum, R. (2000). Influences on adolescents' decisions to postpone onset of sexual intercourse: A survival analysis of virginity among youths ages 13 to 18 years. *Journal of Adolescent Health, 26,* 42–48.

Landau, J. (1997). Out of order: How same-sex harassers beat the rap. *New Republic, 216,* 9–10.

Landen, M., Walinder, J., & Lundstrom, B. (1998). Clinical characteristics of a total cohort of female and male applicants for sex reassignment: A descriptive study. *Acta Psychiatrica Scandinavica, 97,* 189–194.

Landry, D., Kaeser, L., & Richards, C. (1999). Abstinence promotion and the provision of information about contraception in public school district sexuality education policies. *Family Planning Perspectives, 31,* 280–286.

Landry, E. (2002). *Contraceptive Sterilization: Global Issues and Trends.* New York: EngerderHealth.

Landsberg, M. (2002). First openly gay member will serve in Israeli parliament. *The Sunday Oregonian,* October 6, A16.

Lane, F. (2000). *Obscene Profits: The Entrepreneurs of Pornography in the Cyber Age.* New York: Routledge.

Langevin, R., & Martin, M. (1975). Can erotic response be classically conditioned? *Behavior Therapy, 6,* 350–355.

Langevin, R., Paitich, D., & Ramsay, G. (1979). Experimental studies of the etiology of genital exhibitionism. *Archives of Sexual Behavior, 8,* 307–331.

Langevin, R., Paitich, D., & Russon, A. (1985). Voyeurism: Does it predict sexual aggression or violence in general? In R. Langevin (Ed.), *Erotic Preference, Gender Identity, and Aggression in Men.* Hillsdale, NJ: Erlbaum.

Langlois, J., Roggman, L., Casey, R., Ritter, J., Rieser-Danner, L., & Jenkins, Y. (1987). Infants' preferences for attractive faces: Rudiments of a stereotype? *Developmental Psychology, 23,* 363–369.

Langlois, J., Roggman, L., & Rieser-Danner, L. (1990). Infants' differential social responses to attractive and unattractive faces. *Developmental Psychology, 26,* 153–159.

Lapham, L. (1997). In the garden of tabloid delight. *Harper's Magazine,* August, 35–39, 42, 43.

Larimore, W. (1995). Family-centered birthing: History, philosophy, and need. *Family Medicine, 27(2),* 132–137.

Larimore, W., & Stanford, J. (2000). Postfertilization effects of oral contraceptives and their relationship to informed consent. *Archives of Family Medicine, 9,* 126–133.

Larkin, M. (2000a). Oestrogen fails to halt Alzheimer's disease progression. *The Lancet, 355,* 727.

Larkin, M. (2000b). Radical prostatectomy effective in skilled hands. *The Lancet, 355,* 207.

Larmer, B. (1999). Latino America. *Newsweek,* July 12, 48–52. Larmer, B. (2000). High on Sydney. *Newsweek,* October 2, 66.

Larsen, K., & Long, E. (1988). Attitudes toward sex roles: Traditional or egalitarian? *Sex Roles, 19,* 1–12.

Larson, M. (1996). Sex roles and soap operas: What adolescents learn about single motherhood. *Sex Roles, 35,* 97–110.

LaRue, J. (1999). Legitimizing pedophilia opens door to predators. *Insight of the News,* June 14, 15, 22, 28.

Latty-Mann, H., & Davis, K. (1996). Attachment theory and partner choice: Preference and actuality. *Journal of Social and Personal Relationships, 13,* 5–23.

Lau, D., Kleiner, D., Ghany, M., Park, Y., Schmid, P., & Hoofnagle, J. (1998). 10-year follow-up after interferon-alpha therapy for chronic hepatitis C. *Hepatology, 28,* 1121–1127.

Lauer, J., & Lauer, R. (1985). Marriages made to last. *Psychology Today,* June, 22–26.

Lauersen, N., & Graves, Z. (1984). Pretended orgasm. *Medical Aspects of Human Sexuality, 18,* 74–81.

Laumann, E., Gagnon, J., Michael, R., & Michaels, S. (1994). *The Social Organization of Sexuality: Sexual Practices in the United States.* Chicago: University of Chicago Press.

Laumann, E., Masi, C., & Zuckerman, E. (1997). Circumcision in the United States: Prevalence, prophylactic effects, and sexual practice. *Journal of the American Medical Association, 277,* 1052–1057.

Laumann, E., Paik, A., & Rosen, R. (1999). Sexual dysfunction in the United States. *Journal of the American Medical Association, 281,* 537–544.

Laurence, J. (2000). AIDS and the new millennium. *AIDS Patient Care and STDs, 14,* 1–2.

Laurent, B. (1995). Intersexuality: A plea for honesty and emotional support. *AHP Perspective,* November–December, 8–9, 28.

Lavee, Y. (1991). Western and non-Western human sexuality: Implications for clinical practice. *Journal of Sex and Marital Therapy, 17,* 203–213.

Lavee, Y., Sharlin, S., & Katz, R. (1996). The effect of parenting stress on marital quality. *Journal of Family Issues, 17,* 114–135.

Laws, D., & Marshall, W. (1991). Masturbatory reconditioning with sexual deviates: An evaluative review. *Advances in Behavior Research and Therapy, 13,* 13–25.

Lawton, C., & Morrin, K. (1999). Gender differences in pointing accuracy in computer-simulated 3D images. *Sex Roles, 40,* 73–92.

Leadbeater, B., & Way, N. (1995). *Urban Adolescent Girls: Resisting Stereotypes.* New York: University Press.

Leaper, C., Anderson, K., & Sanders, P. (1998). Moderators of gender effects on parents' talk to their children: A meta-analysis. *Developmental Psychology, 34,* 3–27.

Leavitt, F. (1997). False attribution of suggestibility to explain recovered memory of childhood sexual abuse following extended amnesia. *Child Abuse and Neglect, 21,* 265–272.

Lebow, J. (1997). Is couples therapy obsolete? *Networker,* September–October, 81–88.

Lee, A., & Scheurer, V. (1983). Psychological androgyny and aspects of self-image in women and men. *Sex Roles, 9,* 289–306.

Lee, J. (1974). The styles of loving. *Psychology Today, 8,* 43–51.

Lee, J. (1988). Love-styles. In R. Sternberg & M. Barnes (Eds.), *The Psychology of Love.* New Haven, CT: Yale University Press.

Lee, J. (1998). Ideologies of lovestyle and sexstyle. In V. de Munck (Ed.), *Romantic Love and Sexual Behavior.* Westport, CT: Praeger.

Lee, M., Donahoe, P., Silverman, B., Hasegawa, T., Hasegawa, Y., Gustafson, M., Chang, Y., & MacLaughlin, D. (1997). Measurements of serum Mullerian inhibitory substance in the evaluation of children with nonpalpable gonads. *New England Journal of Medicine, 336,* 1480–1486.

Lefkowitz, G., & McCullough, A. (2000). Influence of abdominal, pelvic, and genital surgery on sexual function in women. *Journal of Sex Education and Therapy, 25,* 45–48.

Lehman, S. (2000). Paper presented at the 7th Conference on Retroviruses and Opportunistic Infections, San Francisco, January 30.

Lehmann, K., Eichlisberger, R., & Gasser, T. (2000). Lack of diagnostic tools to prove erectile dysfunction: Consequences for reimbursement? *Journal of Urology, 163,* 91–94.

Leibenluft, E. (1996). Sex is complex. *American Journal of Psychiatry, 15,* 969–971.

Leiblum, S. (2000). Vaginismus: A most perplexing problem. In S. Leiblum & R. Rosen (Eds.), *Principles and Practice of Sex Therapy.* New York: Guilford Press.

Leiblum, S. (2001). Redefining female sexual response. *Contemporary OB/GYN,* November, 120–126.

Leiblum, S., & Bachmann, G. (1988). The sexuality of the climacteric woman. In B. Eskin (Ed.), *The Menopause: Comprehensive Management.* New York: Yearbook Medical Publications.

Leibowitz, D., & Hoffman, J. (2000). Fertility drug therapies: Past, present, and future. *Journal of Obstetrical, Gynecological, and Neonatal Nursing, 29,* 201–210.

Leigh, B. (1989). Reasons for having and avoiding sex: Gender, sexual orientation, and relationship to sexual behavior. *Journal of Sex Research, 26,* 199–208.

Leinders-Zufall, T., Lane, A., Puche, A., Ma, W., Novotny, M., Shipley, M., & Zufall, F. (2000). Ultrasensitive pheromone detection by mammalian vomeronasal neurons. *Nature, 405,* 792–796.

Leiner, S. (1997). Urinary tract infections in otherwise healthy nonpregnant adult women. *Physician Assistant,* May, 36–68.

Leitenberg, H., Detzer, M., & Srebnik, D. (1993). Gender differences in masturbation and the relation of masturbation experience in preadolescence and/or early adolescence to sexual behavior and sexual adjustment in young adulthood. *Archives of Sexual Behavior, 22,* 87–98.

Leitenberg, H., & Henning, K. (1995). Sexual fantasy. *Psychological Bulletin, 117(3),* 469–496.

Leland, J. (1995). Bisexuality. *Newsweek,* July 17, 44–50.

Leland, J. (2000a). The science of women and sex. *Newsweek,* May 29, 46–53.

Leland, J. (2000b). Shades of gay. *Newsweek,* March 20, 46–49.

Leland, J., & Beals, G. (1997). In living color. *Newsweek,* May 5, 58–60.

Leland, J., & Chambers, V. (1999). Raised on rock and Ricky Martin, the Latin Gen X is cruising the American mainstream, rediscovering their roots and inventing a new, bicultural identity—without losing anything in the translation. *Newsweek,* July 12, 53–58.

Lemonick, M. (2000). Teens before their time. *Time,* October 30, 65–74.

Lenderking, W., World, C., Mayer, K., Goldstein, R., Losina, E., & Seage, G. (1997). Childhood sexual abuse among homosexual men. *Journal of General Internal Medicine, 12,* 250–253.

Lerman, S., McAleer, I., & Kaplan, G. (2000). Sex assignment in cases of ambiguous genitalia and its outcome. *Urology, 55,* 8–12.

Letourneau, E., Schewe, P., & Frueh, B. (1997). Preliminary evaluation of sexual problems in combat veterans with PTSD. *Journal of Traumatic Stress, 10*, 125–132.

Leuchtag, A. (2003). Human rights, sex trafficking, and prostitution. *The Humanist*, January–February, 10–15.

Levant, R. (1997). *Men and Emotions: A Psychoeducational Approach.* New York: Newbridge Communications.

LeVay, S. (1991). A difference in hypothalamic structure between heterosexual and homosexual men. *Science, 253*, 1034–1037.

Lever, J. (1994). Sexual revelations. *The Advocate*, August 23, 17–24.

Levin, R. (2002). The physiology of sexual arousal in the human female: A recreational and procreational synthesis. *Archives of Sexual Behavior, 31*, 405–411.

Levin, R. (2003). Do women gain anything from coitus apart from pregnancy? Changes in the human female genital tract activated by coitus. *Journal of Sex and Marital Therapy, 29(suppl.)*, 59–69.

Levine, M., & Troiden, R. (1988). The myth of sexual compulsivity. *Journal of Sex Research, 25*, 347–363.

Levine, R., Sato, S., Hashomoto, T., & Verman, J. (1995). Love and marriage in eleven cultures. *Journal of Cross-Cultural Psychology, 26*, 554–571.

Levine, S. (1999). The newly revised standards of care for gender identity disorders. *Journal of Sex Education and Therapy, 24*, 117–127.

Levine, S. (2003). Erectile dysfunction: Why drug therapy isn't always enough. *Cleveland Clinic Journal of Medicine, 70*, 241–246.

Levinson, R. (1995). Reproductive and contraceptive knowledge, contraceptive self-efficacy, and contraceptive behavior among teenage women. *Adolescence, 30*, 65–85.

Levy, A., Crowley, T., & Gingell, C. (2000). Nonsurgical management of erectile dysfunction. *Clinical Endocrinology, 52*, 253–260.

Levy, J. (2001). HIV and AIDS in people over 50. *SIECUS Report, 30*, 10–15.

Levy, S. (1997). On the Net, anything goes. *Newsweek*, July 7, 28–30.Lewis, D. (2000). Chancroid: From clinical practice to basis science. *AIDS Patient Care and STDs, 14*, 19–36.

Lewis, K., & Moon, S. (1997). Always single and single again women: A qualitative study. *Journal of Marital and Family Therapy, 23(2)*, 115–134.

Lewis, R., & Heaton, J. (2000). A novel strategy for individualizing erectile dysfunction treatment. *Patient Care*, January 30, 91–99.

Lewontin, R. (1999). The problem with an evolutionary answer. *Nature, 400*, 728–729.

Li, C., Malone, K., & Daling, J. (2003a). Differences in breast cancer stage, treatment, and survival by race and ethnicity. *Archives of Internal Medicine, 163*, 49–56.

Li, C., Malone, K., Porter, P., & Weiss, N. (2003b). Relationship between long durations and different regimens of hormone therapy and risk of breast cancer. *Journal of the American Medical Association, 289*, 3254–3263.

Li, D., Liu, L., & Odouli, R. (2003). Exposure to nonsteroidal anti-inflammatory drugs during pregnancy and risk of miscarriage: Population based cohort study. *British Medical Journal, 327*, 368–374.

Li, S., Holm, K., Gulanick, M., & Lanuza, D. (2000). Perimenopause and the quality of life. *Clinical Nursing Research, 9*, 6–26.

Liang, L. (2000). Most popular birth control? Sterilization. *The Sunday Oregonian*, September 24, L13.

Liang, T., Rehermann, B., Seeff, L., & Hoofnagle, J. (2000). Pathogenesis, natural history, treatment, and prevention of hepatitis C. *Annals of Internal Medicine, 132*, 296–305.

Lidster, C., & Horsburgh, M. (1994). Masturbation: Beyond myth and taboo. *Nursing Forum, 29(3)*, 18–26.

Liebowitz, M. (1983). *The Chemistry of Love.* Boston: Little, Brown.

Lief, H., & Hubschman, L. (1993). Orgasm in the postoperative transsexual. *Archives of Sexual Behavior, 22*, 145–155.

Lightner, D. (2002). Female sexual dysfunction. *Mayo Clinic Proceedings, 77*, 698–702.

Ligos, M. (2000). Harassment suits hit the dot-coms. *New York Times*, April 12, G1.

Lim, L. (1998). *The Sex Sector.* Geneva: International Labour Office.

Lin, J., Lin, Y., & Chow, N. (2000). Novel image analysis of corpus cavernous tissue in impotent men. *Urology, 55*, 252–256.

Lindberg, C. (2003). Emergency contraception for prevention of adolescent pregnancy. *American Journal of Maternal/Child Nursing, 28*, 199–204.

Lindhal, K., & Laack, S. (1996). Sweden looks at new ways to reach and teach its young people about sexuality. *SIECUS Reports, 24*, 7–9.

Lindholm, J., Lunde, I., Rasmussen, O., & Wagner, G. (1980). Gonadal and sexual functions in tortured Greek men. *Danish Medical Bulletin, 27*, 243–245.

Lindlaw, S. (2003). The president says he respects gay people but sees marriage as between a man and woman. *The Oregonian*, July 31, A1.

Lindsay, S., & Read, D. (1994). Psychotherapy and memories of childhood sexual abuse: A cognitive perspective. *Applied Cognitive Psychology, 8*, 281–338.

Lindsey, D., & Morgan, F. (2000). *No Out Scouts.* Retrieved June 29, 2000, from http://www.salon.com/news/feature/2000/06/29/scouts/index.html

Linz, D., Donnerstein, E., & Penrod, S. (1988). Effects of long-term exposure to violent and sexually degrading depictions of women. *Journal of Personality and Social Psychology, 55*, 758–768.

Linz, D., Wilson, B., & Donnerstein, E. (1992). Sexual violence in the mass media: Legal solutions, warnings, and mitigation through education. *Journal of Social Issues, 48*, 145–171.

Lippa, R. (2002). Gender-related traits of heterosexual and homosexual men and women. *Archives of Sexual Behavior, 31*, 83–98.

Lippa, R. (2003a). Are 2D:4D finger-length ratios related to sexual orientation? Yes for men, no for women. *Journal of Personality and Social Psychology, 85*, 179–188.

Lippa, R. (2003b). Handedness, sexual orientation, and gender-related personality traits in men and women. *Archives of Sexual Behavior, 32*, 103–114.

Lips, H. (1997). *Sex and Gender* (2nd ed.). Mountain View, CA: Mayfield.

Lipsky, B., & Schaberg, D. (2000). Managing urinary tract infections in men. *Hospital Practice*, January 15, 53–60.

Lipton, M. (2000). Turned off. *People*, March 6, 66–69.

Lisk, R. (1966). Increased sexual behavior in the male rat following lesions in the mammillary region. *Journal of Experimental Zoology, 161*, 129–136.

Lisle, L. (1996). *Without Child: Challenging the Stigma of Childlessness.* New York: Ballantine Books.

Lisotta, C. (2003). Legislation: Toward perfect unions. *The Advocate*, October 14, 17.

Lisotta, C. (2004). The domino effect. *The Advocate*, March 2, 13.

Liu, C. (2003). Does quality of marital sex decline with duration? *Archives of Sexual Behavior, 32*, 55–60.

Liu, H., Jamison, D., Li, X., Ma, E., Yin, Y., & Detels, R. (2003). Is syndromic management better than the current approach for treatment of STDs in China? *Sexually Transmitted Diseases, 30*, 327–330.

Liu, M., & Meyer, M. (2000). Out into the open. *Newsweek*, December 4, 40–42.

Liu, X., Zha, J., Chen, H., Nishitani, J., Camargo, P., Cole, S., & Zack, J. (2003). Human immunodeficiency virus type I infection and replication in normal human oral keratinocytes. *Journal of Virology, 77*, 3470–3476.

Lively, V., & Lively, E. (1991). *Sexual Development of Young Children.* Albany, NY: Delmar.

Livingston, L. (1997). Personal communication.

Livson, F. (1983). Gender identity: A life-span view of sex-role development. In R. Weg (Ed.), *Sexuality in the Later Years: Roles and Behavior.* New York: Academic Press.

Lobitz, W., & Lobitz, G. (1996). Resolving the sexual intimacy paradox: A developmental model for the treatment of sexual desire disorders. *Journal of Sex and Marital Therapy, 22*, 71–84.

Lobo, R., Rosen, R., Yang, H., & Block, B. (2003). Comparative effects of oral esterified estrogens with and without methyltestosterone on endocrine profiles and dimensions of sexual function in postmenopausal women with hypoactive sexual desire. *Fertility and Sterility, 79*, 1341–1352.

Loftus, D. (2002). *Watching Sex.* New York: Thunder's Mouth Press.

Loftus, E., & Ketcham, K. (1994). *The Myth of Repressed Memory.* New York: St. Martin's Press.

Loftus, E., Polonsky, S., & Fullilove, M. (1994). Memories of childhood sexual abuse: Remembering and repressing. *Psychology of Women Quarterly, 18*, 67–84.

Lombardi, C. (2001). A court for human rights. *Ms*, October–November, 22–23

London, S. (2004). Risk of pregnancy-related death is sharply elevated for women 35 and older. *Perspectives on Sexual and Reproductive Health, 36*, 87–88.

Long, J., & Serovich, J. (2003). Incorporating sexual orientation into MFT training programs: Infusion and inclusion. *Journal of Marital and Family Therapy, 29,* 59–67.

Long, V. (2002). Contraceptives choices: New options in the U.S. market. *SIECUS Report, 31,* 13–18.

Lonsway, K., & Fitzgerald, L. (1994). Rape myths. *Psychology of Women Quarterly, 18,* 133–164.

Lonsway, K., & Fitzgerald, L. (1995). Attitudinal antecedents of rape myth acceptance: A theoretical and empirical reexamination. *Journal of Personality and Social Psychology, 68,* 704–711.

Lopez, S. (2000). Hold the pickles, please. *Time,* October 2, 6.

LoPiccolo, J. (1982, July). Personal communication.

LoPiccolo, J. (1989). *Sexual Dysfunctions: Advances in Diagnosis and Treatment.* Workshop for the Oregon Division of the American Association for Marriage and Family Therapy, Portland, Oregon, April.

LoPiccolo, J. (1991). Counseling and therapy for sexual problems in the elderly. *Clinics in Geriatric Medicine, 7,* 161–179.

LoPiccolo, J. (2000). *Post-Modern Sex Therapy: An Integrated Approach.* Paper presented at the 32nd Annual Conference of the American Association of Sex Educators, Counselors, and Therapists, Atlanta, Georgia, May 10–14.

LoPiccolo, J., & Friedman, J. (1988). Broad-spectrum treatment of low sexual desire: Integration of cognitive, behavioral, and systemic therapy. In S. Leiblum & R. Rosen (Eds.), *Sexual Desire Disorders.* New York: Guilford Press.

LoPiccolo, J., & Heiman, J. (1978). The role of cultural values in the prevention and treatment of sexual problems. In C. Qualls, J. Wincze, & D. Barlow (Eds.), *The Prevention of Sexual Disorders.* New York: Plenum.

LoPresto, C., Sherman, M., & Sherman, N. (1985). The effects of a masturbation seminar on high school males' attitudes, false beliefs, guilt, and behavior. *Journal of Sex Research, 21,* 142–156.

Lorber, J. (1995). Gender is determined by social practices. In D. Bender & B. Leone (Eds.), *Human Sexuality: Opposing Viewpoints.* San Diego: Greenhaven Press.

Lorch, D., & Mendenhall, P. (2000). A war's hidden tragedy. *Newsweek,* August, 35–36.

Lorente, C., Cordier, S., & Goujard, J. (2000). Tobacco and alcohol use during pregnancy and risk of oral clefts. *American Journal of Public Health, 90,* 415–419.

Louderback, L., & Whitley, B., Jr. (1997). Perceived erotic value of homosexuality and sex-role attitudes as mediators of sex differences in heterosexual college students' attitudes toward lesbians and gay men. *Journal of Sex Research, 34(2),* 175–182.

Louis, M., Wasserheit, J., & Gayle, H. (1997). Janus considers the HIV pandemic: Harnessing recent advances to enhance AIDS prevention [editorial]. *American Journal of Public Health, 87,* 10–12.

Loulan, J. (1984). *Lesbian Sex.* San Francisco: Spinsters Ink.

Love, P. (2001). *The Truth About Love.* New York: Simon & Schuster.

Love, S. (1997). A surgeon's challenge. *Newsweek,* February 24, 60.

Lowenstein, L. (2002). Fetishes and their associated behavior. *Sexuality and Disability, 20,* 135–147.

Lown, J., & Dolan, E. (1988). Financial challenges in remarriage. *Lifestyles: Family and Economic Issues, 9,* 73–88.

Lown, J., McFadden, J., & Crossman, S. (1989). Family life education for remarriage focus on financial management. *Family Relations, 38,* 40–45.

Lowndes, C., Alary, M., & Platt, L. (2003). Injection drug use, commercial sex work, and the HIV/STI epidemic in Russia. *Sexually Transmitted Diseases, 30,* 46–48.

Loy, P., & Stewart, L. (1984). The extent and effects of the sexual harassment of working women. *Sociological Focus, 17,* 31–43.

Luchsinger, G. (2000). Out in Africa. *Ms.,* April–May, 23–24.

Lukwago, S., Kreuter, M., Holt, C., & Steger-May, K. (2003). Sociocultural correlates of breast cancer knowledge and screening in urban African American women. *American Journal of Public Health, 93,* 1271–1274.

Lurie, P., & Drucker, E. (1997). An opportunity lost: HIV infections associated with lack of a national needle-exchange programme in the U.S.A. *The Lancet, 349,* 604–608.

Lynch, C., Sinnott, J., Holt, D., & Herold, A. (1991). Use of antibiotics during pregnancy. *American Family Physician, 43,* 1365–1368.

Lynch, D., Krantz, S., Russell, J., Hornberger, L., & Van Ness, C. (2000). HIV infection: A retrospective analysis of adolescent high-risk behaviors. *Journal of Pediatric Health Care, 14,* 20–25.

Lynch, F. (1992). Nonghetto gays: An ethnography of suburban homosexuals. In G. Herdt (Ed.), *Gay Culture in America.* Boston: Beacon Press.

Lynxwiler, J., & Gay, D. (1994). Reconsidering race differences in abortion attitudes. *Social Science Quarterly, 75,* 67–84.

Lytton, H., & Romney, D. (1991). Parents' differential socialization of boys and girls: A meta-analysis. *Psychological Bulletin, 109,* 267–296.

Macaluso, M., Lawson, M., Hortin, G., & Duerr, A. (2003). Efficacy of the female condom as a barrier to semen during intercourse. *American Journal of Epidemiology, 157,* 289–297.

Maccoby, E. (1988). Gender as a social category. *Developmental Psychology, 26,* 755–765.

Maccoby, E. (1990). Gender and relationships: A developmental account. *American Psychologist, 45,* 513–520.

Maccoby, E. (1998). *The Two Sexes: Growing Up Apart, Coming Together.* Cambridge: Harvard University Press.

Maccoby, E., & Jacklin, C. (1987). Gender segregation in childhood. *Advances in Child Development and Behavior, 20,* 239–287.

MacDonald, A., Jr. (1981). Bisexuality: Some comments on research and theory. *Journal of Homosexuality, 6,* 21–35.

MacDonald, T., MacDonald, G., Zanna, M., & Fong, G. (2000). Alcohol, sexual arousal, and intentions to use condoms in young men: Applying alcohol myopia theory to risky sexual behavior. *Health Psychology, 19,* 290–298.

Mackellar, D., Valleroy, L., Secura, G., & Behel, S. (2002). *Unrecognized HIV Infection, Risk Behaviors, and Misperceptions of Risk Among Young Men Who Have Sex with Men: 6 United States Cities, 1994–2000.* Paper presented at the 14th International AIDS Conference, Barcelona, Spain, July 5–12.

MacKinnon, C. (1979). *Sexual Harassment of Working Women.* New Haven, CT: Yale University Press.

MacKinnon, C. (1986). Pornography: Not a moral issue. *Women's Studies International Forum, 9,* 63–78.

Macklon, N., & Fauser, B. (1999). Aspects of ovarian follicle development throughout life. *Hormone Research, 52,* 161–170.

MacLean, R. (2004). Most women are unlikely to experience premenstrual mood change with pill use. *Perspectives on Sexual and Reproductive Health, 36,* 89–90.

Magid, D., Stiffman, M., Anderson, L., Irwin, K., & Lyons, E. (2003). Adherence to CDC STD Guideline Recommendations for the treatment of chlamydia trachomatis infection in two managed care organizations. *Sexually Transmitted Diseases, 30,* 30–32.

Maguen, S., Armistead, L., & Kalichman, S. (2000). Predictors of HIV antibody testing among gay, lesbian, and bisexual youth. *Journal of Adolescent Health, 26,* 252–257.

Maher, J., Harvey, L., Bird, S., Stevens, V., & Beckman, L. (2004). Acceptability of the vaginal diaphragm among current users. *Perspectives on Sexual and Reproductive Health, 36,* 64–71.

Mahmoodian, S. (1997). Cervical and breast cancer screening rates in Sioux Indian women. *Southern Medical Journal, 90 (3),* 316–320.

Mahoney, S. (2003). Seeking love: The 50-plus dating game has never been hotter. *AARP,* November–December, 57–66.

Maier, J., & Malony, J. (1997). Nurse advocacy for selective versus routine episiotomy. *Journal of Obstetrical, Gynecological, and Neonatal Nursing, 26,* 155–161.

Majewska, M. (1996). Sex differences in brain morphology and pharmacodynamics. In M. Jensvold & U. Halbreich (Eds.), *Psychopharmacology and Women: Sex, Gender, and Hormones.* Washington, DC: American Psychiatric Press.

Malamuth, N., & Check, J. (1981). The effects of mass media exposure on acceptance of violence against women: A field experiment. *Journal of Research in Personality, 15,* 436–446.

Malamuth, N., Haber, S., & Feshback, S. (1980). Testing hypotheses regarding rape: Exposure to sexual violence, sex differences, and the normality of rapists. *Journal of Research in Personality, 14,* 121–137.

Malatesta, C., Culver, C., Tesman, J., & Shephard, B. (1989). The development of emotion expression during the first two years of life. *Monographs of the Society for Research in Child Development, 50(1–2),* Serial 219.

Malcahy, J. (2001). The merits of salvage procedures for infected penile implants. *Contemporary Urology, 13,* 45–50.

Malebranche, D. (2003). Black men who have sex with men and the HIV epidemic: Next steps for public health. *American Journal of Public Health, 93,* 862–864.

Maletzky, B. (1998). The paraphilias: Research and treatment. In P. Nathan & J. Gorman (Eds.), *A Guide to Treatments That Work.* New York: Oxford University Press.

Mallon, G. (1996). Don't ask, don't tell: Gay and lesbian adolescents in residential treatment. *Treatment Today,* Spring, 19–20.

Malloy, K., & Patterson, M. (1992). *Birth or Abortion? Private Struggles in a Political World.* New York: Plenum Press.

Maltz, W. (1996). *Passionate Hearts.* Novato, CA: New World Library.

Maltz, W. (2001a). *Healthy Sexuality After Abuse and Addiction.* Paper presented at the 33rd Annual Conference of the American Association of Sex Educators, Counselors, and Therapists, San Francisco, May 2–6.

Maltz, W. (2001b). *Intimate Kisses: The Poetry of Sexual Pleasure.* Novato, CA: New World Library.

Maltz, W. (2001c). *The Sexual Healing Journey: A Guide for Survivors of Sexual Abuse.* New York: Quill.

Maltz, W. (2003). Treating the sexual intimacy concerns of sexual abuse. *Contemporary Sexuality, 37,* I–vii.

Maltz, W., & Boss, S. (1997). *In the Garden of Desire.* New York: Broadway Books.

Maltz, W., & Holman, B. (1987). *Incest and Sexuality: A Guide to Understanding and Healing.* Lexington, MA: Lexington Books.

Mandoki, M., Sumner, G., Hoffman, R., & Riconda, D. (1991). A review of Klinefelter's syndrome in children and adolescents. *Journal of the American Academy of Child and Adolescence Psychiatry, 30,* 167–172.

Manecke, R., & Mulhall, J. (1999). Medical treatment of erectile dysfunction. *Annals of Medicine, 31,* 388–398.

Mangels, A. (2003). Outed in Batman's backyard. *The Advocate,* May 27, 62–63.

Mann, D. (2003, July 17). *The Future of Birth Control.* Retrieved from http://my.webmd.com/content/Article/71/81245.htm

Mann, K., Klingler, T., Noe, S., Roeschke, J., Mueller, S., & Benkert, O. (1996). Effects of yohimbine on sexual experiences and nocturnal tumescence and rigidity in erectile dysfunction. *Archives of Sexual Behavior, 25,* 1–16.

Mannino, D., Klevens, R., & Flanders, W. (1994). Cigarette smoking: An independent risk factor for impotence? *American Journal of Epidemiology, 140,* 1003–1008.

Mansfield, P., Voda, A., & Koch, P. (1995). Predictors of sexual response changes in heterosexual midlife women. *Health Values: The Journal of Health Behavior, Education, and Promotion, 19,* 10–20.

Mansky, L., Rouzic, E., Benichou, S., & Gajary, L. (2003). Influence of reverse transcriptase variants, drugs, and Vpr on human immunodeficiency virus type 1 mutant frequencies. *Journal of Virology, 77,* 2071–2080.

Mansour, D. (2004). Off-license prescribing in contraception. *Journal of Family Planning and Reproductive Health Care, 30,* 9–10.

Mao, C., Hughes, J., Kiviat, N., Kuypers, J., Lee, S., Adam, D., & Koutsky, L. (2003). Clinical findings among young women with genital human papillomavirus infection. *American Journal of Obstetrics and Gynecology, 188,* 677–684.

Maravilla, K., Cao, Y., Garland, P., Echelard, D., Heiman, J., Hart, L., Peterson, B., & Weisskoff, R. (2000). Reproducibility of serial MR measurement of female sexual arousal response. RSNA Hot Topic presentation, Chicago, November 2000. Abstract available in *Radiology, 218,* 610 (2000).

Maravilla, K., Heiman, J., Garland, P., Cao, Y., Carter, W., Peterson, B., & Weisskoff, R. (2003). Dynamic MR imaging of the sexual arousal response in women. *Journal of Sex and Marital Therapy, 29(suppl.),* 71–76.

Marbella, A., & Layde, P. (2001). Racial trends in age-specific breast cancer mortality rates in U.S. women. *American Journal of Public Health, 91,* 118–121.

Marchione, M. (2003). Breast cancer risk falls with aspirin, ibuprofen use. *The Oregonian,* April 10, A15.

Marcus, E. (1993). Ignorance is not bliss. *Newsweek,* April 14, 65–67.

Margolis, L. (2000). Ethical principles for analyzing dilemmas in sex research. *Health Education and Behavior, 27,* 24–27.

Marin, A., & Guadagno, R. (1999). Perceptions of sexual harassment as a function of labeling and reporting. *Sex Roles, 41,* 921–940.

Marin, R., & Miller, S. (1997). Ellen steps out. *Newsweek,* April 14, 65–67.

Markowitz, J., Donovan, J., DeVane, C., & Ruan, R. (2003). Effect of St John's wort on drug metabolism by induction of cytochrome P450 3A4 enzyme. *Journal of the American Medical Association, 290,* 1500–1504.

Marks, N. (1996). Flying solo at midlife: Gender, marital status, and psychological well-being. *Journal of Marriage and the Family, 58,* 917–932.

Marrone, N. (2001). Advice to Latino parents of LGBT children. *SIECUS Report, 29,* 32–41.

Marshall, D. (1971). Sexual behavior on Mangaia. In D. Marshall & R. Suggs (Eds.), *Human Sexual Behavior: Variations in the Ethnographic Spectrum.* Englewood Cliffs, NJ: Prentice Hall.

Marshall, W. (1988). The use of sexually explicit stimuli by rapists, child molesters, and nonoffenders. *Journal of Sex Research, 25,* 267–288.

Marshall, W. (1993). A revised approach to the treatment of men who sexually assault adult females. In G. Hall, R. Hirschman, J. Graham, & M. Zaragoza (Eds.), *Sexual Aggression: Issues in Etiology, Assessment, and Treatment.* Washington, DC: Taylor & Francis.

Marshall, W., Eccles, A., & Barbaree, H. (1991). The treatment of exhibitionists: A focus on sexual deviance versus cognitive and relationship features. *Behaviour Research and Therapy, 29,* 129–135.

Marsiglio, W. (1993). Adolescent males' orientation toward paternity and contraception. *Family Planning Perspectives, 25,* 22–31.

Martin, C., Anderson, R., & Cheng, L. (2000). Potential impact of hormonal male contraception: Cross-cultural implications for development of novel preparations. *Human Reproduction, 15,* 637–645.

Martin, D., & Lyon, P. (1972). *Lesbian-Woman.* New York: Bantam Books.

Martin, T., & Bumpass, L. (1989). Recent friends in marital disruption. *Demography, 26,* 37–51.

Martinson, F. (1994). *The Sexual Life of Children.* Westport, CT: Bergin & Garvey.

Marton, K. (2004). A worldwide gender gap. *Newsweek,* May 10, 94.

Marvin, C., & Miller, D. (2000). Lesbian couples entering the 21st century. In P. Papp (Ed.), *Couples on the Fault Line.* New York: Guilford Press.

Marx, T., & Mehta, A. (2003). Polycystic ovary syndrome: Pathogenesis and treatment over the short and long term. *Cleveland Clinic Journal of Medicine, 70,* 31–41.

Massad, L., Meyer, P., & Hobbs, J. (1997). Knowledge of cervical cancer screening among women attending urban colposcopy clinics. *Cancer Detection and Prevention, 21(1),* 103–109.

Masters, W., & Johnson, V. (1961). Orgasm, anatomy of the female. In A. Ellis & A. Abarbonel (Eds.), *Encyclopedia of Sexual Behavior,* v. 2. New York: Hawthorn.

Masters, W., & Johnson, V. (1966). *Human Sexual Response.* Boston: Little, Brown.

Masters, W., & Johnson, V. (1970). *Human Sexual Inadequacy.* Boston: Little, Brown.

Masters, W., & Johnson, V. (1976). *The Pleasure Bond.* New York: Bantam Books.

Matek, O. (1988). Obscene phone callers. *Journal of Social Work and Human Sexuality, 7,* 113–130.

Mathes, E., & Verstrate, C. (1993). Jealous aggression: Who is the target, the beloved or the rival? *Psychological Reports, 72,* 1071–1074.

Mathias-Riegel, B. (1999). Intimacy 101: A refresher course in the language of love. *Modern Maturity,* September–October, 46.

Matikainen, T. (2001). Aromatic hydrocarbon receptor-driven Bax gene expression is required for premature ovarian failure caused by biohazardous environmental chemicals. *Nature Genetics, 28,* 355–360.

Matteo, S., & Rissman, E. (1984). Increased sexual activity during the midcycle portion of the human menstrual cycle. *Hormones and Behavior, 18,* 249–255.

Matteson, D. (1997). Bisexual and homosexual behavior and HIV risk among Chinese-, Filipino-, and Korean-American men. *Journal of Sex Research, 34,* 93–104.

Matthews, G., McGee, K., & Goldstein, M. (1997). Microsurgical reconstruction following failed vasectomy reversal. *Journal of Urology, 157,* 844–846.

Matthews, T., Ventura, S., Curtin, S., & Martin, J. (1998). *Births of Hispanic Origin, 1989–95.* Monthly Vital Statistics Report, 46 (6). Washington, DC: Centers for Disease Control and Prevention and National Center for Health Statistics.

Maurer, L. (1999). Transgressing sex and gender: Deconstruction zone ahead? *SIECUS Report, 27,* 14–21.

Maxwell, K. (1996). *A Sexual Odyssey: From Forbidden Fruit to Cybersex.* New York: Plenum Press.

May, R. (1969). *Love and Will.* New York: Norton.

Mayo Clinic Health Oasis (1999). *Urinary Tract Infections.* Retrieved November 23, 1999, from http://cnn.com/HEALTH/mayo/9911/23/uti/

Mayor, S. (2003a). Adjuvant chemotherapy improves survival in early ovarian cancer. *British Medical Journal, 326,* 181.

Mayor, S. (2003b). AIDS vaccine trial begins in Uganda. *British Medical Journal, 326,* 414.

Mazer, D., & Percival, E. (1989). Students' experiences of sexual harassment at a small university. *Sex Roles, 20,* 1–22.

McAninch, C., Milich, R., Crumb, G., & Funtowicz, M. (1996). Children's perception of gender-role–congruent and –incongruent behavior in peers: Fisher-Price meets Price Waterhouse. *Sex Roles, 35,* 619–638.

McBride, C., Paikoff, R., & Holmbeck, G. (2003). Individual and familial influences on the onset of sexual intercourse among urban African American adolescents. *Journal of Consulting* and *Clinical Psychology, 71,* 159–167.

McBride, G. (1992). U.S. Supreme Court will decide women's right to abortion. *British Medical Journal, 304,* 271–272.

McCabe, M. (1999). The interrelationship between intimacy, relationship functioning, and sexuality among men and women in committed relationships. *Canadian Journal of Human Sexuality, 8,* 31–39.

McCaghy, C., & Hou, C. (1994). Family affiliation and prostitution in a cultural context: Career onsets of Taiwanese prostitutes. *Archives of Sexual Behavior, 23,* 251–265.

McCarthy, B. (1994). Etiology and treatment of early ejaculation. *Journal of Sex Education and Therapy, 20(1),* 5–6.

McCarthy, B. (2001). *Primary and Secondary Prevention of Sexual Problems and Dysfunction.* Paper presented at the 33rd Annual Conference of the American Association of Sex Educators, Counselors, and Therapists, San Francisco, May 2–6.

McCarthy, B., & McCarthy, E. (2003). *Rekindling Desire: A Step-by-Step Program to Help Low-Sex and No-Sex Marriages.* New York: Brunner-–Routledge.

McCarthy, S. (1998). The hard facts. *Ms.,* May–June, 96.

McCauley, A., Robey B., Blanc, A., & Geller, J. (1994). Family planning saves lives. *Population Reports, 22,* 4–9.

McCormack, F. (2001). SiaAmma. *Ms.,* February–March, 13.

McCormick, C., Witelson, S., & Kingstone, E. (1990). Left-handedness in homosexual men and women: Neuroendocrine implications. *Psychoneuroendocrinology, 15,* 69–76.

McCormick, N. (1996). Our feminist future: Women affirming sexuality research in the late twentieth century. *Journal of Sex Research, 33,* 99–102.

McCormick, S. (2002). Breast cancer activism: Moving beyond the mammography debate. *Ms.,* Summer, 4–5.

McCoy, N., & Matyas, J. (1996). Oral contraceptives and sexuality in university women. *Archives of Sexual Behavior, 25,* 73–89.

McCoy, N., & Pitino, L. (2001). *Pheromonal Influences on Sociosexual Behavior in Women.* Paper presented at the Scientific Study of Sexuality Western Region Meeting, San Diego, April 20.

McElroy, W. (1995). *A Woman's Right to Pornography.* New York: St. Martin's Press.

McEwen, B. (1997). Meeting report: Is there a neurobiology of love? *Molecular Psychiatry, 2,* 15–16.

McFarlane, J., Martin, C., & Williams, T. (1988). Mood fluctuations: Women versus men and menstrual versus other cycles. *Psychology of Women Quarterly, 12,* 201–224.

McFarlane, M., Bull, S., & Rietmeijer, C. (2002). Young adults on the Internet: Risk behaviors for sexually transmitted diseases and HIV. *Journal of Adolescent Health, 31,* 11–16.

McGee, R., Garavan de Barra, M., Byrne, J., & Conroy, R. (2002). *The SAV 1 Report: Sexual Abuse and Violence in Ireland—A National Study of Irish Experiences, Beliefs, and Attitudes Concerning Sexual Violence.* Dublin: Liffey Press.

McGinn, S., & Skipp, C. (2002). Does Gran get it on? *Newsweek,* June 3, 10.

McGrew, M., & Shore, W. (1991). The problem of teenage pregnancy. *Journal of Family Practice, 32,* 17–25.

McHale, S., Bartko, W., Crouter, A., & Perry-Jenkins, M. (1990). Children's housework and psychosocial functioning: The mediating effect of parents' sex-role behaviors and attitudes. *Child Development, 61,* 1413–1426.

McKenna, K., & Bargh, J. (2000). Plan 9 from cyberspace: The implications of the Internet for personality and social psychology. *Journal of Personality and Social Psychology, 4,* 57–75.

McKibben, A., Proulx, J., & Lusignan, R. (1994). Relationships between conflict, affect, and deviant sexual behaviors in rapists and pedophiles. *Behavior Research and Therapy, 32,* 571–575.

McKirnan, D., Stokes, J., Doll, L., & Burzette, R. (1995). Bisexually active men: Social characteristics and sexual behavior. *Journal of Sex Research, 32,* 65–76.

McLaren, A. (1990). *A History of Contraception: From Antiquity to the Present Day.* Cambridge, MA: Basil Blackwell.

McLean, L., & Gallop, R. (2003). Implications of childhood sexual abuse for adult borderline personality disorder and complex posttraumatic stress disorder. *American Journal of Psychiatry, 160,* 369–371.

McLeod, A., Crawford, I., & Zechmeister, J. (1999). Heterosexual undergraduates' attitudes toward gay fathers and their children. *Journal of Psychology and Human Sexuality, 11,* 43–62.

McNeil, E., & Rubin, Z. (1977). *The Psychology of Being Human.* San Francisco: Canfield Press.

McNeill, B., Prieto, L., Niemann, Y., Pizarro, M., Vera, E., & Gomez, S. (2001). Current directions in Chicana/o psychology. *Counseling Psychologist, 29,* 5–17.

McNicholas, T., Dean, J., Mulder, H., Carnegie, C., & Jones, N. (2003). Andrology. *British Journal of Urology International, 91,* 69–74.

McNiven, P., Hodnett, E., & O'Brien-Pallas, L. (1992). Supporting women in labor: A work sampling study of the activities of labor and delivery nurses. *Birth, 19,* 3–8.

McQuaide, S. (1998). Women at midlife. *Journal of the National Association of Social Workers, 43,* 21–31.

Mead, M. (1963). *Sex and Temperament in Three Primitive Societies.* New York: Morrow.

Mead, R. (1999). Eggs for sale. *The New Yorker,* August 9, 56–70.

Mead, R. (2000). Sex and sensibility. *The New Yorker,* September 18, 146–148.

Means-Christensen, A., Snyder, D., & Negy, C. (2003). Assessing nontraditional couples: Validity of the Marital Satisfaction Inventory–Revised with gay, lesbian, and cohabiting heterosexual couples. *Journal of Marital and Family Therapy, 29,* 69–83.

Media Report to Women (1993a). Depiction of women in mainstream TV shows still stereotypical, sexual. *Media Report to Women, 21,* 4.

Media Report to Women (1993b). Muppet gender gap. *Media Report to Women, 21,* 8.

Medical Center for Human Rights (1995). *Characteristics of Sexual Abuse of Men During War in the Republic of Croatia and Bosnia.* Zagreb, Croatia: Medical Center for Human Rights.

Medical Ethics Advisor (2003). Questioning the search for a Viagra for women: New quest has pros and cons. *Medical Ethics Advisor, 19,* 65.

Medrano, M., Hatch, J., Zule, W., & Desmond, D. (2003). Childhood trauma and adult prostitution behavior in a multiethnic heterosexual drug-using population. *American Journal of Drug and Alcohol Abuse, 29,* 463–475.

Meeks, B., Hendrick, S., & Hendrick, C. (1998). Communication, love, and relationship satisfaction. *Journal of Social and Personal Relationships, 15,* 755–773.

Mehta, S., Rothman, R., Kelen, G., Quinn, T., & Zenilman, J. (2001). Clinical aspects of diagnosis of gonorrhea and chlamydia infection in an acute care setting. *Clinical Infectious Diseases, 32,* 655–659.

Meier, E. (2000). RU-486 and implications for use among adolescents seeking an abortion. *Pediatric Nursing, 26,* 93–94.

Meiselman, K. (1978). *Incest.* San Francisco: Jossey-Bass.

Melby, T. (2002a). Intersex interrupted. *Contemporary Sexuality, 36,* 1–6.

Melby, T. (2002b). Pain and (possibly) a loss of pleasure. *Contemporary Sexuality, 36,* 1–6.

Melchert, T. (2000). Clarifying the effects of parental substance abuse, child sexual abuse, and parental caregiving on adult adjustment. *Professional Psychology: Research and Practice, 31,* 64–69.

Melchert, T., & Parker, R. (1997). Different forms of childhood abuse and memory. *Child Abuse and Neglect, 21,* 125–135.

Merson, M., Feldman, E., Bayer, R., & Stryker, J. (1997). Rapid self testing for HIV infection. *The Lancet, 348,* 352–353.

Mertz, K., Finelli, L., Levin, W., Mognoni, R., Berman, S., Fishbein, M., Garnett, G., & St. Louis, M. (2000). Gonorrhea in male adolescents and young adults in Newark, New Jersey. *Sexually Transmitted Diseases, 27,* 201–207.

Meschke, L., Bartholomae, S., & Zentall, S. (2000). Adolescent sexuality and parent–adolescent processes: Promoting healthy teen choices. *Family Relations, 49,* 143–154.

Messenger, J. (1971). Sex and repression in an Irish folk community. In D. Marshall & R. Suggs (Eds.), *Human Sexual Behavior: Variations in the Ethnographic Spectrum.* Englewood Cliffs, NJ: Prentice Hall.

Messner, M. (2003). When to suspect—and how to manage—pelvic inflammatory disease. *Journal of the American Academy of Physician Assistants, 16,* 18–25.

Meston, C. (2000). The psychophysiological assessment of female sexual function. *Journal of Sex Education and Therapy, 25,* 6–16.

Meston, C., Gorzalka, B., & Wright, J. (1997). Inhibition of subjective and physiological sexual arousal in women by clonidine. *Psychosomatic Medicine, 59,* 399–407.

Meston, C., Heiman, J., & Trapnell, P. (1999). The relation between early abuse and adult sexuality. *Journal of Sex Research, 36,* 385–395.

Meston, C., Trapnell, P., & Gorzalka, B. (1996). Ethnic and gender differences in sexuality: Variations in sexual behavior between Asian and non-Asian university students. *Archives of Sexual Behavior, 25,* 33–72.

Meston, C., & Worcel, M. (2002). The effects of yohimbine plus L-arginine glutamate on sexual arousal in postmenopausal women with sexual arousal disorder. *Archives of Sexual Behavior, 31,* 323–332.

Meuwissen, I., & Over, R. (1991). Multidimensionality of the content of female sexual fantasy. *Behavior Research and Therapy, 29,* 179–189.

Meyer, J., Smith, D., Lester, S., Kaelin, C., DiPiro, P., Denison, C., Christian, R., Harvey, S., Selland, D., & Durfee, S. (1999). Large-core needle biopsy of nonpalpable breast lesions. *Journal of the American Medical Association, 281,* 1638–1641.

Meyer, S., & Schwitzer, A. (1999). Stages of identity development among college students with minority sexual orientations. *Journal of College Student Psychotherapy, 13,* 41–65.

Meyer, W., Webb, A., Stuart, C., Finkelstein, J., Lawrence, B., & Walker, P. (1986). Physical and hormonal evaluation of transsexual patients: A longitudinal study. *Archives of Sexual Behavior, 15,* 121–138.

Meyer-Bahlburg, H., Gruen, R., New, M., Bell, J., Morishima, A., Shimski, M., Bueno, Y., Vargas, I., & Baker, S. (1996). Gender change from female to male in classical congenital adrenal hyperplasia. *Hormones and Behavior, 30,* 319–322.

Mezin, Z. (2001). *Pro-Choice Groups Find New Support.* Retrieved January 25, 2001, from http://www.examiner.com/news/default.jsp?story=abortion0125

Mezy, G., & King, M. (1989). The effects of sexual assault on men: A survey of 22 victims. *Psychological Medicine, 19,* 205–209.

Michael, M. (1999). Foreigners buy Egyptian girls for short-term marriages. *The Oregonian,* August 29, A11.

Michael, R., Gagnon, J., Laumann, E., & Kolata, G. (1994). *Sex in America.* Boston: Little, Brown.

Michaels, D. (1997). Cyber-rape: How virtual is it? *Ms.,* March–April, 68–72.

Michels, K. (2003). Hormone replacement therapy in epidemiologic studies and randomized clinical trials: Are we checkmate? *Epidemiology, 14,* 3–5.

Michelson, D., Kociban, K., Tamura, R., & Morrison, M. (2002). Mirtazapine, yohimbine, or olanzapine augmentation therapy for serotonin reuptake-associated female sexual dysfunction: A randomized, placebo controlled study. *Journal of Psychiatric Research, 36,* 147–152.

Midyett, L., Moore, W., & Jacobson, J. (2003). Are pubertal changes in girls before age 8 benign? *Pediatrics, 111,* 47–51.

Migeon, C., Wisniewski, A., Gearhart, J., Meyer-Bahlburg, H., Rock, J., Brown, T., Casella, S., Maret, A., Ngai, K., & Money, J. (2002). Ambiguous genitalia with perineoscrotal hypospadias in 46,XY individuals: Long-term medical, surgical, and psychosexual outcome. *Pediatrics, 110,* 616–621.

Milhausen, R., & Herold, E. (1999). Does the sexual double standard still exist? Perceptions of university women. *Journal of Sex Research, 36,* 361–368.

Mill, J., & Anarfi, J. (2002). HIV risk environment for Ghanaian women: Challenges to prevention. *Social Science and Medicine, 54,* 325–337.

Miller, B., Norton, M., Fan, X., & Christopherson, C. (1998). Pubertal development, parental communication, and sexual values in relation to adolescent sexual behaviors. *Journal of Early Adolescence, 18,* 27–52.

Miller, H., Cain, V., Rodgers, S., Gribble, J., & Turner, C. (1999). Correlates of sexually transmitted bacterial infections among U.S. women in 1995. *Family Planning Perspectives, 31,* 4–9, 23.

Miller, J. (2003). Mourning the never born and the loss of the angel. In J. Haynes & J. Miller (Eds.), *Inconceivable Conceptions: Psychological Aspects of Infertility and Reproductive Technology.* Hove, United Kingdom: Brunner-Routledge.

Miller, J., & Haynes, J. (Eds.) (2003). *Inconceivable Conceptions: Psychotherapy, Fertility, and the New Reproductive Technologies.* London: Brunner-Routledge.

Miller, K., Forehand, R., & Kotchik, B. (1999). Adolescent sexual behavior in two ethnic minority samples: The role of family variables. *Journal of Marriage and the Family, 61,* 85–98.

Miller, K., & Graves, J. (2000). Update on the prevention and treatment of sexually transmitted diseases. *American Family Physician, 61,* 379–386.

Miller, K., Ruiz, D., & Graves, J. (2003). Update on the prevention and treatment of sexually transmitted diseases. *American Family Physician, 67,* 1915–1922.

Miller, L. (2001). Continuous administration of 100 μg levonorgestrel and 20 μg ethinyl estradiol for elimination of menses: A randomized trial. *Obstetrics and Gynecology, 97,* 16S.

Miller, L., Liu, H., Hays, R., Golin, C., Ye, Z., Beck, K., Kaplan, A., & Wenger, N. (2003). Knowledge of antiretroviral regimen dosing and adherence: A longitudinal study. *Clinical Infectious Diseases, 36,* 514–518.

Miller, M., Meyer, L., Boufassa, F., Persoz, A., Sarr, A., Robain, M., & Spira, A. (2000). Sexual behavior changes and protease inhibitor therapy. *AIDS 2000, 14,* F33–F39.

Miller, T. (2000). Diagnostic evaluation of erectile dysfunction. *American Family Physician, 61,* 95–104.

Million Women Study Collaborators (2003). Breast cancer and hormone-replacement therapy in the Million Women Study. *The Lancet, 362,* 419–427.

Mills, J., & Mindel, A. (2003). Genital herpes simplex infections: Some therapeutic dilemmas. *Sexually Transmitted Diseases, 30,* 232–233.

Mills, T., Paul, J., Stall, R., & Pollack, L. (2004). Distress and depression in men who have sex with men: The Urban Men's Health Study. *American Journal of Psychiatry, 161,* 278–285.

Milow, V. (1983). Menstrual education: Past, present, and future. In S. Golub (Ed.), *Menarche.* Lexington, MA: Lexington Books.

Minichiello, V., Marino, R., & Browne, J. (2000). Commercial sex between men: A prospective diary-based study. *Journal of Sex Research, 37,* 151–160.

Minichiello, V., Paxton, S. A., & Cowling, V. (1996). Religiosity, sexual behaviour, and safe sex practices: Further evidence. *Australian and New Zealand Journal of Public Health, 20,* 321–322.

Minkoff, H. (2003). Human immunodeficiency virus infection in pregnancy. *Obstetrics and Gynecology, 101,* 797–810.

Minnis, A., & Padian, N. (2001). Choice of female-controlled barrier methods among young women and their male sexual partners. *Family Planning Perspectives, 33,* 28–34.

Minor, M., & Dwyer, S. (1997). The psychosocial development of sex offenders: Differences between exhibitionists, child molesters, and incest offenders. *International Journal of Offenders Therapy and Comparative Criminology, 41,* 36–44.

Minto, C., Liao, L., Woodhouse, C., Ransley, P., & Creighton, S. (2003). The effect of clitoral surgery on sexual outcomes in individuals who have intersex conditions with ambiguous genitalia: A cross-sectional study. *The Lancet, 361,* 1252–1257.

Mintz, H. (1997). Most alleged members of Internet child pornography ring plead guilty. *Knight-Ridder/Tribune News Service,* May 12.

Mishra, R. (2002). Vaccine fights cervical cancer. *The Oregonian,* November 21, A1.

Misrahi, M., Teglas, J., N'Go, N., Burgard, M., Mayaux, M., Rouzioux, C., Delfraissy, J., & Blanche, S. (1998). CCR5 chemokine receptor variant in HIV-1 mother-to-child transmission and disease progression in children. *Journal of the American Medical Association, 279,* 277–280.

Mitchell, D., Hirschman, R., & Hall, G. (1999). Attributions of victim responsibility, pleasure, and trauma in male rape. *Journal of Sex Research, 36,* 369–373.

Mitka, M. (2000). Some men who take Viagra die: Why? *Journal of the American Medical Association, 283,* 590–593.

Mitka, M. (2003a). CDC resource focuses on DES exposure. *Journal of the American Medical Association, 289,* 1624–1627.

Mitka, M. (2003b). Researchers seek mammography alternatives. *Journal of the American Medical Association, 290,* 450–451.

Miya-Jervis, L. (2000). Who wants to marry a feminist? *Ms.,* June–July, 63–65.

Mobley, J., McKeown, R., Jackson, K., Sy, F., Parham, J., & Brenner, E. (1998). Risk factors for congenital syphilis in infants of women with syphilis in South Carolina. *American Journal of Public Health, 88,* 597–602.

Moats, D. (2004). The tipping point. *The Advocate,* May 11, 29–35.

Modelska, K., & Cummings, S. (2003). Female sexual dysfunction in postmenopausal women: Systematic review of placebo-controlled trials. *American Journal of Obstetrics and Gynecology, 188,* 286–293.

Mohr, D., & Beutler, L. (1990). Erectile dysfunction: A review of diagnostic and treatment procedures. *Clinical Psychology Review, 10,* 123–150.

Moller, L., Hymel, S., & Rubin, K. (1992). Sex typing in play and popularity in middle childhood. *Sex Roles, 26,* 331–335.

Mona, L., & Gardos, P. (2000). Disabled sexual partners. In L. Szuchman & F. Muscarella (Eds.), *Psychological Perspectives on Human Sexuality.* New York: Wiley.

Mondics, C. (2003). Advocacy groups seek Santorum's ouster for remarks on gay sex. *Knight Ridder Newspapers,* April 21, K4893.

Money, D., Arikan, Y., Remple, V., Sherlock, C., Craib, K., Birch, P., & Burdge, D. (2003). Genital tract and plasma human immunodeficiency virus viral load throughout the menstrual cycle in women who are infected with ovulatory human immunodeficiency virus. *American Journal of Obstetrics and Gynecology, 188,* 122–128.

Money, J. (1961). Sex hormones and other variables in human eroticism. In W. Young (Ed.), *Sex and Internal Secretions* (3rd ed.). Baltimore: Williams & Wilkins.

Money, J. (1963). Cytogenetic and psychosexual incongruities with a note on space-form blindness. *American Journal of Psychiatry, 119,* 820–827.

Money, J. (1965). Psychosocial differentiation. In J. Money (Ed.), *Sex Research: New Developments.* New York: Holt, Rinehart & Winston.

Money, J. (1968). *Sex Errors of the Body: Dilemmas, Education, Counseling.* Baltimore: Johns Hopkins University Press.

Money, J. (1980). *Love and Lovesickness.* Baltimore: Johns Hopkins University Press.

Money, J. (1981). Paraphilias: Phyletic origins of erotosexual dysfunction. *International Journal of Mental Health, 10,* 75–109.

Money, J. (1984). Paraphilias: Phenomenology and classification. *American Journal of Psychotherapy, 38,* 164–179.

Money, J. (1988). *Gay, Straight, and In-Between: The Sexology of Erotic Orientation.* New York: Oxford University Press.

Money, J. (1990). Forensic sexology: Paraphilic serial rape (biastophilia) and lust murder (erotophonophilia). *American Journal of Psychotherapy, 44,* 26–37.

Money, J. (1994a). The concept of gender identity disorder in childhood and adolescence after 39 years. *Journal of Sex and Marital Therapy, 20,* 163–177.

Money, J. (1994b). *Sex Errors of the Body and Related Syndromes: A Guide to Counseling Children, Adolescents, and Their Families* (2nd ed.). Baltimore: Brookes.

Money, J., & Ehrhardt, A. (1972). Prenatal hormonal exposure: Possible effects on behavior in man. In R. Michael (Ed.), *Endocrinology and Human Behavior.* London: Oxford University Press.

Money, J., & Lamacz, M. (1990). *Vandalized Lovemaps.* Buffalo, NY: Prometheus Press.

Money, J., Lehne, G., & Pierre-Jerome, F. (1984). Micropenis: Adult follow-up and comparison of size against new norms. *Journal of Sex and Marital Therapy, 10,* 105–116.

Money, J., & Masica, D. (1968). Fetal feminization by androgen insensitivity in the testicular feminizing syndrome: Effect on marriage and maternalism. *Johns Hopkins Medical Journal, 123,* 105–114.

Monga, T., & Kerrigan, A. (1997). Cerebrovascular accidents. In M. Sipski & C. Alexander (Eds.), *Sexual Function in People with Disability and Chronic Illness.* Gaithersburg, MD: Aspen Publishers.

Monroe, I. (1997). A garden of homophobia. *The Advocate,* December 9, 9.

Monsen, R. B. (2001). Children and puberty. *Journal of Pediatric Nursing, 16,* 66–67.

Montagu, A., & Matson, F. (1979). *The Human Connection.* New York: McGraw-Hill.

Montague, D. (1998). Erectile dysfunction: The rational utilization of diagnostic testing. *Journal of Sex Education and Therapy, 23,* 194–196.

Montauk, S., & Clasen, M. (1989). Sex education in primary care: Infancy to puberty. *Medical Aspects of Human Sexuality,* January, 22–36.

Montgomery, M., & Sorell, G. (1997). Differences in love attitudes across family life stages. *Family Relations, 46,* 55–61.

Moodley, D., Moodley, J., Coovadia, H., Gray, G., McIntyre, J., Hofmyer, J., Nikodem, C., Hall, D., Gigliotti, M., Robinson, P., Boshoff, L., & Sullivan, J. (2003). A multicenter randomized controlled trial of nevirapine versus a combination of zidovudine and lamivudine to reduce intrapartum and early postpartum mother-to-child transmission of human immunodeficiency virus type 1. *Journal of Infectious Diseases, 187,* 725–735.

Moodley, P., Sturm, P., Vanmali, T., Wilkinson, D., Connolly, C., & Sturm, A. (2003). Association between HIV-1 infection, the etiology of genital ulcer disease, and response to syndromic management. *Sexually Transmitted Diseases, 30,* 241–248.

Moore, K., & Smith, K. (2002). Policies needed to increase awareness of emergency contraception. *SIECUS Report, 31,* 9–12.

Morales, A. (2003). The andropause: Bare facts for urologists. *British Journal of Urology International, 91,* 311–313.

Morales, A., Heaton, J., & Carson, C. (2000). Andropause: A misnomer for a true clinical entity. *Journal of Urology, 163,* 705–712.

Morales, E. (1992). Latino gays and Latina lesbians. In S. Dworkin & F. Gutierrez (Eds.), *Counseling Gay Men and Lesbians: Journey to the End of the Rainbow.* Alexandria, VA: American Association for Counseling and Development.

Moran, G. (1997a). Diagnosing and treating STDs. Part 2. Lesionless disorders. *Emergency Medicine,* February, 20–31.

Moran, G. (1997b). Diagnosing STDs. Part 1. Ulcerating diseases. *Emergency Medicine,* January, 63–72.

Moran, R. (2001). *Interracial Intimacy: The Regulation of Race and Romance.* Chicago: University of Chicago Press.

Morehouse, R. (2001). *Using the Crucible Approach to Enhance Women's Sexual Potential.* Paper presented at the 33rd Annual Conference of the American Association of Sex Educators, Counselors, and Therapists, San Francisco, May 2–6.

Morgan, E. (1978). The Puritans and sex. In M. Gordon (Ed.), *The American Family in Social-Historical Perspective.* New York: St. Martin's Press.

Morgan, R. (2003). Saving the world. *Ms.,* Summer, 95.

Morganthau, T. (1997). Baptists vs. Mickey. *Newsweek,* June 30, 51.

Morgentaler, A. (1999). Male impotence. *The Lancet, 354,* 1713–1718.

Morin, J. (1981). *Anal Pleasure and Health.* Burlingame, CA: Down There Press.

Morlock, R., Lafata, J., & Eisenstein, D. (2000). Cost-effectiveness of single-dose methotrexate compared with laparoscopic treatment of ectopic pregnancy. *Obstetrics and Gynecology, 95,* 407–412.

Morrell, M., Dixen, J., Carter, C., & Davidson, J. (1984). The influence of age and cycling status on sexual arousability in women. *American Journal of Obstetrics and Gynecology, 148,* 66–71.

Morris, C., Cohen, R., Schlag, R., & Wright, W. (2000). Increasing trends in the use of breast-conserving surgery in California. *American Journal of Public Health, 90,* 281.

Morris, G. (2003). Is it a boy or a girl? *Just Out,* January 17, 22–25.

Moses, S., Bailey, R., & Ronald, A. (1998). Male circumcision: Assessment of health benefits and risks. *Sexually Transmitted Infections, 74,* 368–373.

Mosher, C., & Levitt, E. (1987). An exploratory-descriptive study of a sadomasochistically oriented sample. *Journal of Sex Research, 23,* 322–337.

Mosher, C., & Tomkins, S. (1988). Scripting the macho man: Hypermasculine socialization and enculturation. *Journal of Sex Research, 25,* 60–84.

Mosher, D. (1980). Three psychological dimensions of depth of involvement in human sexual response. *Journal of Sex Research, 16,* 1–42.

Mosher, D., & MacIan, P. (1994). College men and women respond to X-rated videos intended for male or female audiences: Gender and sexual scripts. *Journal of Sex Research, 31,* 99–113.

Mossad, S. (2003). How do you manage a healthy, asymptomatic 24-year-old with positive RPR on a premarital blood test. *Cleveland Clinic Journal of Medicine, 70,* 101–102.

Mott, F., & Haurin, R. (1988). Linkages between sexual activity and alcohol and drug use among American adolescents. *Family Planning Perspectives, 20,* 128–137.

Muehlenhard, C. (1988). Misinterpreting dating behaviors and the risk of date rape. *Journal of Social and Clinical Psychology, 6,* 20–37.

Muehlenhard, C., & Andrews, S. (1985). *Open Communication About Sex: Will It Reduce Risk Factors Related to Rape?* Paper presented at the Annual Meeting of the Association for Advancement of Behavior Therapy, Houston, November.

Muehlenhard, C., Felts, A., & Andrews, S. (1985). *Men's Attitudes Toward the Justifiability of Date Rape: Intervening Variables and Possible Solutions.* Paper presented at the Midcontinent Meeting of the Society for the Scientific Study of Sex, Chicago, June.

Muehlenhard, C., Goggins, M., Jones, J., & Satterfield, A. (1991). Sexual violence and coercion in close relationships. In K. McKinney & S. Sprecher (Eds.), *Sexuality in Close Relationships.* Hillsdale, NJ: Erlbaum.

Muehlenhard, C., & Hollabaugh, L. (1989). Do women sometimes say no when they mean yes? The prevalence and correlates of women's token resistance to sex. *Journal of Personality and Social Psychology, 54,* 872–879.

Muehlenhard, C., & Linton, M. (1987). Date rape and sexual aggression in dating situations: Incidence and risk factors. *Journal of Consulting Psychology, 34,* 186–196.

Muehlenhard, C., Peterson, Z., Karwoski, L., Bryan, T., & Lee, R. (2003). Gender and sexuality: An introduction to the Special Issue. *Journal of Sex Research, 40*, 1–3.

Muehlenhard, C., & Rodgers, C. (1998). Token resistance to sex: New perspectives on an old stereotype. *Psychology of Women Quarterly, 22*, 443–463.

Muehlenhard, C., & Schrag, J. (1991). Nonviolent sexual coercion. In A. Parrot & L. Bechhofer (Eds.), *Acquaintance Rape: The Hidden Crime.* New York: Wiley.

Mulcahy, J. (2000). Erectile dysfunction: Is the incidence increasing? [editorial]. *Journal of Urology, 163*, 471.

Muller, J. (2000). *The Smart Probe: Device Could Provide Instant Breast Cancer Diagnosis.* Retrieved November 30, 2000, from http://www.abcnews.go.com/onair/CuttingEdge/wnt001128_breastcancer_feature.html

Mulligan, T., & Palguta, R., Jr. (1991). Sexual interest, activity, and satisfaction among male nursing home residents. *Archives of Sexual Behavior, 20*, 199–204.

Munarriz, R., Maitland, S., Garcia, S., Talkakoub, L., & Goldstein, I. (2003). A prospective duplex Doppler ultrasonographic study in women with sexual arousal disorder to objectively assess genital engorgement induced by EROS therapy. *Journal of Sex and Marital Therapy, 29*, 85–94.

Munoz, N., Bosch, F., Sanjose, S., Herrero, R., Castellsague, X., Shah, K., Snijders, P., & Meijer, C. (2003). Epidemiologic classification of human papillomavirus types associated with cervical cancer. *New England Journal of Medicine, 348*, 518–527.

Murnen, S., & Stockton, M. (1997). Gender and self-reported sexual arousal in response to sexual stimuli: A meta-analytic review. *Sex Roles, 37*, 135–154.

Murphy, D., Roberts, K., Martin, D., Marelich, W., & Hoffman, D. (2000). Barriers to antiretroviral adherence among HIV-infected adults. *AIDS Patient Care and STDs, 14*, 47–58.

Murphy, D., Sarr, M., Durako, S., Moscicki, A., Wilson, C., & Muenz, L. (2003). Barriers to HAART adherence among human immunodeficiency virus-infected adolescents. *Archives of Pediatric and Adolescent Medicine, 157*, 249–255.

Murphy, E. (2003). Being born female is dangerous for your health. *American Psychologist, 58*, 205–209.

Murphy, P. (2003). New methods of hormonal contraception. *Nurse Practitioner, 28*, 11–21.

Murray, J., (2000). Psychological profile of pedophiles and child molesters. *Journal of Psychology, 134*, 211–224.

Murray, K., Richardson, L., Morishima, C., Owens, J., & Gretch, D. (2003). Prevalence of hepatitis C virus infection and risk factors in an incarcerated juvenile population: A pilot study. *Pediatrics, 111*, 153–157.

Murray, L. (1992). Love and longevity. *Longevity,* August, 64.

Murray, L. (1995a). Marital "boot camps" help predict success. *The Oregonian,* October 29.

Murray, L. (1995b). The therapist can see you now: Just press "enter" to continue. *The Oregonian,* June 7, C3.

Murray, S., Holmes, J., & Griffin, D. (2001). The mismeasure of love: How self-doubt contaminates relationship beliefs. *Personality and Social Psychology Bulletin, 27*, 423–436.

Murrey, G., Bolen, J., Miller, N., Simensted, K., Robbins, M., & Truskowski, F. (1993). History of childhood sexual abuse in women with depressive and anxiety disorders: A comparative study. *Journal of Sex Education and Therapy, 19(1)*, 13–19.

Murry, V. (1996). An ecological analysis of coital timing among middle-class African American adolescent females. *Journal of Adolescent Research, 11*, 261–279.

Murstein, B., & Mercy, T. (1994). Sex, drugs, relationships, contraception, and fears of disease on a college campus over 17 years. *Adolescence, 29*, 303–22.

Murstein, B., & Tuerkheim, A. (1998). Gender differences in love, sex, and motivation for sex. *Psychological Reports, 82*, 425–450.

Mustanski, B., Bailey, J., & Kaspar, S. (2002). Dermatoglyphics, handedness, sex, and sexual orientation. *Archives of Sexual Behavior, 31*, 113–122.

Myers, S. (2000). Female general in army alleges sex harassment. *New York Times,* March 31, A1.

Nadler, R. (1968). Approach to psychodynamics of obscene telephone calls. *New York Journal of Medicine, 68*, 521–526.

Nadler, S. (1997). Arthritis and other connective tissue diseases. In M. Sipski & C. Alexander (Eds.), *Sexual Function in People with Disability and Chronic Illness.* Gaithersburg, MD: Aspen Publishers.

Nanson, J. (1997). Binge drinking during pregnancy: Who are the women at risk? *Canadian Medical Association Journal, 156(6)*, 807–808.

Napolitane, C. (1997). *Living and Loving After Divorce.* New York: Signet.

Nash, J. (1997). Personal communication.

Nass, S., & Strauss, F. (2004). *New Frontiers in Contraceptive Research: A Blueprint for Action.* Washington, DC: National Academy Press.

Nasseri, M. (2000). Cultural similarities in psychological reactions to infertility. *Psychological Reports, 86*, 375–378.

National Center for Health Statistics (1992). *Monthly Vital Statistics Report, 40,* no. 12.

National Center for Health Statistics (1995). Annual summary of births, marriages, divorces, and deaths: United States, 1994. *Monthly Vital Statistics Report, 43*, 1–7.

National Center for Health Statistics (2004). *Births, Marriages, Divorces, and Deaths.* Retrieved May 17, 2004, from http://www.cdc.gov/nchs/data/nvsr/nvsr52/nvsr52_20.pdf

National Council on Sexual Addiction and Compulsivity (2002). Information statement: Women sex addicts. *Sexual Addiction and Compulsivity, 9*, 293–295.

National Gay and Lesbian Task Force (2003, April 23). *National Gay and Lesbian Task Force Slams Santorum's "Gutter Language" Comparing Homosexuality to Pedophilia, Bestiality.* Retrieved April 26, 2003, from http://www.ngltf.org/news/printed.cfm?releaseID=534

Nattinger, A. (2000). Older women, mammography, and mortality from breast cancer. *American Journal of Medicine, 108*, 174–175.

Naughton, K. (2004). The soft sell. *Newsweek,* February 2, 46–47.

Neff, L. (2004). Gay in the navy. *The Advocate,* March 20, 32–33.

Nelson, J. (1985). Male sexuality and masculine spirituality. *SIECUS Report, 13*, 1–4.

Ness, C. (2000a). *Gay-Straight School "Alliances" Thriving.* Retrieved September 6, 2000, from http://www.examiner.com/alliances.html

Ness, C. (2000b). *Is Erotica USA Hot Enough for S.F.?* Retrieved April 3, 2000, from http://www.examiner.com/000403/0403erotica.html

Ness, R., Hillier, S., Richter, R., Soper, D., Stamm, C., Bass, D., Sweet, R., Rice, P., Downs, J., & Aral, S. (2003). Why women douche and why they may or may not stop. *Sexually Transmitted Diseases, 30*, 71–74.

Neto, F. (2001). Love styles of three generations of women. *Marriage and Family Review, 33*, 19–30.

Nevid, J. (1984). Sex differences in factors of romantic attraction. *Sex Roles, 11*, 401–411.

Newcomer, S., & Udry, J. (1985a). Oral sex in an adolescent population. *Archives of Sexual Behavior, 14*, 41–46.

Newcomer, S., & Udry, R. (1985b). Parent-child communication and adolescent sexual behavior. *Family Planning Perspectives, 17*, 169–174.

Ngugi, E., Wilson, D., Sebstad, J., Plummer, F., & Moses, S. (1996). Focused peer-mediated educational programs among female sex workers to reduce sexually transmitted disease and human immunodeficiency virus transmission in Kenya and Zimbabwe. *Journal of Infectious Diseases, 174(suppl. 2)*, S240–S247.

Niccolai, L., Ethier, K., Kershaw, T., Lewis, J., & IcKovics, J. (2003). Pregnant adolescents at risk: Sexual behaviors and sexually transmitted disease prevalence. *American Journal of Obstetrics and Gynecology, 188*, 63–70.

Nicholas, H. (1998). Gonorrhoea: Symptoms and treatment. *Nursing Times, 94*, 52–54.

Nichols, M. (1989). Sex therapy with lesbians, gay men, and bisexuals. In S. Leiblum & R. Rosen (Eds.), *Principles and Practice of Sex Therapy.* New York: Guilford Press.

Nichols, M. (2000). Therapy with sexual minorities. In S. Leiblum & R. Rosen (Eds.), *Principles and Practice of Sex Therapy.* New York: Guilford Press.

Nicholson, K., & Balster, R. (2001). A new and novel drug of abuse. *Drug and Alcohol Dependence, 63*, 1–22.

Nicolosi, J., Byrd, A., & Potts, R. (2000a). Beliefs and practices of therapists who practice sexual reorientation psychotherapy. *Psychological Reports, 86*, 689–702.

Nicolosi, J., Byrd, A., & Potts, R. (2000b). Retrospective self-reports of changes in homosexual orientation: A consumer survey of conversion therapy clients. *Psychological Reports, 86*, 1071–1088.

Nielsen Media Research (1998). *1998 Report on Television.* New York: Nielsen Media Research.

Nielson, J., & Wohlert, M. (1991). Chromosome abnormalities found among 34,910 newborn children: Results from a 13-year incidence study in Arhus, Denmark. *Human Genetics, 87*, 81–83.

Nilsson, L., Bergh, C., Bryman, I., & Thorburn, J. (1994). How do we treat unexplained infertility? *Acta Obstetricia et Gynecologica Scandinavia. 73*, 174–175.

Nilsson, U., Hellberg, D., Shoubnikova, M., Nilsson, S., & Mardh, P. (1997). Sexual behavior risk factors associated with bacterial vaginosis and chlamydial trachomatis infection. *Sexually Transmitted Diseases, 24*, 241–246.

Nishith, P., Mechanic, M., & Resnick, P. (2000). Prior interpersonal trauma: The contribution to current PTSD symptoms in female rape victims. *Journal of Abnormal Psychology, 109*, 20–25.

Nissl, J. (2003, June 1). *Emergency Contraception.* Retrieved October 23, 2003, from http://my.webmd.com/content/healthwise/16/4027.htm

Nixin, D. (2003). *Are Penises Going the Way of the Dodo?* Retrieved March 13, 2003, from http://www.mamimonline.com/grit/articles/article_3715.html

Noh, P., Cooper, C., Snyder, H., Zderic, S., Canning, D., & Huff, D. (2000). Testicular volume does not predict germ cell amount in patients with cryptorchidism. *Journal of Urology, 163*, 593–596.

Noll, J., Trickett, P., & Putnam, F. (2003). A prospective investigation of the impact of childhood sexual abuse on the development of sexuality. *Journal of Consulting and Clinical Psychology, 71*, 575–586.

Noonan, D., & Springen, K. (2001). When dad is a donor. *Newsweek,* August 13, 46.

Norris, D., Gutheil, T., & Strasburger, L. (2003). This couldn't happen to me: Boundary problems and sexual misconduct in the psychotherapy relationship. *Psychiatric Services, 54*, 517–522.

Norris, J. (1988). *Serial Killers: The Growing Menace.* New York: Doubleday.

Northridge, M. (2003). HIV returns. *American Journal of Public Health, 93*, 860.

Northrup, C. (2002, July 10). *HRT Panic? Sorting Out the Facts.* Retrieved April 14, 2003, from http://www.my.webmd.com/content/article/57/66208.htm

Nour, N. (2000). Female circumcision and genital mutilation: A practical and sensitive approach. *Contemporary OB/GYN,* March, 50–55.

Nour, N. (2003). Female genital cutting: A need for reform. *Obstetrics and Gynecology, 101*, 1051.

Novak, A., de la Loge, C., Abetz, L., & van der Meulen, E. (2003). The combined contraceptive vaginal ring, NuvaRing: An international study of user acceptability. *Contraception, 67*, 187–194.

Nurnberg, H., Hensley, P., Gelenberg, A., Lauriello, F., & Paine, T. (2003). Treatment of antidepressant-associated sexual dysfunction with Sildenafil: A randomized controlled trial. *Journal of the American Medical Association, 289*, 56–64.

Nusbaum, M., Hamilton, C., & Lenahan, P. (2003). Chronic illness and sexual functioning. *American Family Physician, 67*, 347–354.

Nussbaum, E. (2000). A question of gender. *Discover,* January, 92–99.

Nuttin, J. (1987). Affective consequences of mere ownership: The name letter effect in twelve European languages. *European Journal of Social Psychology, 17*, 381–402.

Nyirjesy, P. (2001). Chronic vulvovaginal candidiasis. *American Family Physician, 63*, 697–702.

Nystrom, N., & Jones, T. (2003). Community building with aging and old lesbians. *American Journal of Community Psychology, 31*, 293–299.

O'Brien, P., Wyatt, K., & Dimmock, P. (2000). Premenstrual syndrome is real and treatable. *The Practitioner, 244*, 185–189.

Ochs, E., & Binik, Y. (1999). The use of couple data to determine the reliability of self-reported sexual behavior. *Journal of Sex Research, 36*, 374–384.

O'Connor, A. (1998). Marriages that cross racial line increase in U.S. *The Oregonian,* May 3, A20.

Odejinmi, F. (2000). Advances in women's health. *The Practitioner, 244*, 214–222.

O'Donnell, L., Myint-U, A., O'Donnell, C., & Stueve, A. (2003). Long-term influence of sexual norms and attitudes on timing of sexual initiation among urban minority youth. *Journal of School Health, 73*, 68–75.

O'Donohue, W., & Plaud, J. (1994). The conditioning of human sexual arousal. *Archives of Sexual Behavior, 23*, 321–344.

O'Donohue, W., Yeater, E., & Fanetti, M. (2003). Rape prevention with college males: The role of rape myth acceptance, victim empathy, and outcome expectancies. *Journal of Interpersonal Violence, 18*, 513–531.

Ofman, U. (2000). Guest editor's note. *Journal of Sex Education and Therapy, 25*, 3–5.

Ogden, G. (1994). *Women Who Love Sex.* New York: Pocket Books.

Ogden, G. (2003). Spiritual dimensions of sex therapy: An integrative approach for women. *Contemporary Sexuality, 37*, i–vii.

Ogden, J. (1989). Visuospatial and other "right-hemispheric" functions after long recovery periods in left-hemispherectomized subjects. *Neuropsychologia, 27*, 765–776.

O'Hanlan, K. (1995). In the family way: Insemination 101. *The Advocate,* June 27, 49–50.

Olds, D., Henderson, C., & Tatelbaum, R. (1994). Intellectual impairment in children of women who smoke cigarettes during pregnancy. *Pediatrics, 93(2)*, 221–227.

Olds, J. (1956). Pleasure centers in the brain. *Scientific American, 193*, 105–116.

O'Leary, M. (2003). Early ejaculation. *British Journal of Urology International, 91*, 309.

Oliver, M., Sheufelt, J., Deshpande, P., Grandage, K., & St. Ann, L. (2003). Which postmenopausal women should be offered combined HRT? *Journal of Family Practice, 52*, 149–150.

Olivera, A. (1994). Sexual dysfunction due to Clomipramine and Sertraline: Nonpharmacological resolution. *Journal of Sex Education and Therapy, 20(2)*, 119–122.

Olson, B., & Douglas, W. (1997). The family on television: Evolution of gender roles in situation comedy. *Sex Roles, 36*, 409–427.

Olson, D., Fournier, D., & Druckman, J. (1987). *Counselors Manual for PREPARE/ENRICH* (rev. ed.). Minneapolis: PREPARE/ENRICH.

Oman, R., Vesely, S., Kegler, M., McLeroy, K., & Aspy, C. (2003). A youth development approach to profiling sexual abstinence. *American Journal of Health Behavior, 27(suppl. 1)*, 580–593.

Omeragic, F. (1998). Bosnia-Herzegovina: A case study in service collapse. *Entre Nous, 38*, 12.

O'Neill, P. (1997). Date-rape drug may be in Oregon. *The Oregonian,* February 26, B1, B7.

O'Neill, P. (2000a). The Adonis complex. *The Sunday Oregonian,* July 9, L11.

O'Neill, P. (2000b). Hormone replacement therapies: A treatment worse than the cure? *The Sunday Oregonian,* October 29, L11.

O'Neill-Morante, M. (2000). Human papillomavirus: A review of manifestations, diagnosis, and treatment. *Physician Assistant,* January, 19–25.

Ono, A. (1994). Personal communication.

Osman, A., & Al-Sawaf, M. (1995). Cross-cultural aspects of sexual anxieties and the associated dysfunction. *Journal of Sex Education and Therapy, 21*, 174–181.

Ostling, R. (2000). Schism threatens Southern Baptists. *The Sunday Oregonian,* October 29, A3.

Ostriker, A. (1999). Scenes from a mastectomy. In H. Raz (Ed.), *Living on the Margins.* New York: Persea Books.

O'Sullivan, L. (1995). Less is more: The effects of sexual experience on judgments of men's and women's personality characteristics and relationship desirability. *Sex Roles, 33*, 159–181.

O'Sullivan, L., Byers, E., & Finkelman, L. (1998). A comparison of male and female college students' experiences of sexual coercion. *Psychology of Women Quarterly, 22*, 177–195.

O'Sullivan, S. (1999). I don't want you anymore: Butch/femme disappointments. *Sexualities, 2*, 465–474.

Oswald, R., & Culton, L. (2003). Under the rainbow: Rural gay life and its relevance for family providers. *Family Relations, 52*, 72–81.

Otis, J. (1994). For Cuba's gays, repression is past. *San Francisco Chronicle,* October 21, A1.

Ott, M., Adler, N., Millstein, S., Tschann, J., & Ellen, J. (2002). The trade-off between hormonal contraceptives and condoms among adolescents. *Perspectives on Sexual and Reproductive Health, 34*, 6–14.

Otto, H. (1999). A short history of sex toys with an extrapolation for the new century. In J. Elias, V. Elias, V. Bullough, G. Brewer, J. Douglas, & W. Jarvis (Eds.), *Porn 101: Eroticism, Pornography, and the First Amendment.* Amherst, NY: Prometheus Books.

Overbeck, G., Vollebergh, W., Engels, R., & Meeus, W. (2003). Parental attachment and romantic relationships: Associations with emotional disturbance during late adolescence. *Journal of Counseling Psychology, 50*, 28–39.

Owen, L. (1993). *Her Blood Is Gold.* San Francisco: HarperCollins.

Pace, B. (2000). Urinary tract infections. Journal of the American Medical Association, 283, 1646.

Pace, B. (2001). Screening for breast cancer. *Journal of the American Medical Association, 285*, 246.

Pace, B., & Glass, R. (2001). Screening and prevention of sexually transmitted diseases. *Journal of the American Medical Association, 285,* 124.

Padawer, J., Fagan, C., Janoff-Bulman, R., Strickland, B., & Chorowski, M. (1988). Women's psychological adjustment following emergency cesarean versus vaginal delivery. *Psychology of Women Quarterly, 12,* 25–34.

Page, D., Mosher, R., Simpson, E., Fisher, E., Mardon, G., Pollack, J., McGillivray, B., Chapelle, A., & Brown, L. (1987). The sex-determining region of the human Y chromosome encodes a finger protein. *Cell, 51,* 1091–1104.

Page, R. (1997). Helping adolescents avoid date rape: The role of secondary education. *High School Journal, 80,* 75–80.

Palefsky, J., Holly, E., Ralston, M., DaCosta, M., & Greenblatt, R. (2001). Prevalence and risk factors for anal human papillomavirus infection in human immunodeficiency virus (HIV) positive and high-risk HIV-negative women. *Journal of Infectious Diseases, 183,* 383–391.

Palmer, J., Rao, R., Adams-Campbell, L., & Rosenberg, L. (1999). Correlates of hysterectomy among African-American women. *American Journal of Epidemiology, 150,* 1309–1315.

Palmer, J., Rosenberg, L., Wise, L., & Horton, N. (2003). Onset of natural menopause in African American women. *American Journal of Public Health, 93,* 299–306.

Palmer, L. (2000). RU-486: Changing the debate. *The Oregonian,* January 7, A16.

Pam, A., Plutchik, R., & Conte, H. (1975). Love: A psychometric approach. *Psychological Reports, 37,* 83–88.

Pan, E. (2000). Why Asian guys are on a roll. *Newsweek,* February 21, 48–51.

Pancholi, P., Perkus, M., Tricoche, N., Liu, Q., & Prince, A. (2003). DNA immunization with hepatitis C virus (HCV) polycistronic genes or immunization by HCV DNA primary-recombinant canarypox virus boosting induces immune responses and protection from recombinant HCV-Vaccinia virus infection in HLA-A2 l-transgenic mice. *Journal of Virology, 77,* 382–390.

Pao, M., Lyon, M., D'Angelo, L., Schuman, W., Tipnis, T., & Mzazek, D. (2000). Psychiatric diagnoses in adolescents seropositive for the human immunodeficiency virus. *Archives of Pediatric and Adolescent Medicine, 154,* 240–244.

Paperny, D. (1997). Computerized health assessment and education for adolescent HIV and STD prevention in health care settings and schools. *Health Education and Behavior, 24,* 54–70.

Pappas, L. (1998). China's new family values. *Newsweek,* August 24, 36.

Pappert, A. (2000a). Tamoxifen update: Has the drug been overhyped for healthy women? *Ms.,* December–January, 44–46.

Pappert, A. (2000b). What price pregnancy? A special report on the fertility industry. *Ms.,* June–July, 43–49.

Paradis, B. (1997). Multicultural identity and gay men in the era of AIDS. *American Journal of Orthopsychiatry, 67(2),* 300–307.

Pardun, C., & McKee, K. (2002). Religious and sexual images in rock videos: A second-by-second analysis. In D. Claussen (Ed.), *Sex, Religion, Media.* Lanham, MD: Rowman & Littlefield.

Paredes, R., & Baum, M. (1997). Role of the medial preoptic area/anterior hypothalamus in the control of masculine sexual behavior. *Annual Review of Sex Research, 8,* 68–101.

Parham, T., White, J., & Ajamu, A. (1999). The *Psychology of Blacks: An African-Centered Perspective* (3rd ed.). Upper Saddle, NY: Prentice Hall.

Parish, W., Laumann, E., Cohen, M., Pan, S., Zheng, H., Hoffman, I., Wang, T., & Ng, K. (2003). Population-based study of chlamydial infection in China. *Journal of the American Medical Association, 289,* 1265–1273.

Parker, C., & Dearnaley, D. (2003). Hormonal therapy as an adjuvant to radical radiotherapy for locally advanced prostate cancer. *British Journal of Urology International, 91,* 6–8.

Parker, L. (1998). Ambiguous genitalia: Etiology, treatment, and nursing implications. *Journal of Obstetrical, Gynecological, and Neonatal Nursing, 27,* 15–22.

Parks, C. (1999). Lesbian identity development: An examination of differences across generations. *American Journal of Orthopsychiatry, 69,* 347–361.

Parks, C., & Vu, A. (1994). Social dilemma behavior of individuals from highly individualist and collectivist cultures. *Journal of Conflict Resolution, 38,* 708–718.

Parrot, A. (1991). Institutionalized response: How can acquaintance rape be prevented? In A. Parrot & L. Bechhofer (Eds.), *Acquaintance Rape: The Hidden Crime.* New York: Wiley.

Parrot, A., Cummings, N., Marchell, T., & Hofher, J. (1994). A rape awareness and prevention model of male athletes. *Journal of American College Health, 42,* 179–184.

Parsons, J. (1983). Sexual socialization and gender roles in childhood. In E. Allgeier & N. McCormick (Eds.), *Changing Boundaries: Gender Roles and Sexual Behavior.* Palo Alto, CA: Mayfield.

Passariello, C. (2002). A new approach to the oldest profession: More countries are trying to regulate—and tax—brothels. *Business Week,* October 7, 34.

Patel, H., Mirsadraee, S., & Emberton, M. (2003). The patient's dilemma: Prostate cancer treatment choices. *Journal of Urology, 169,* 828–833.

Pateman, B., & Johnson, M. (2000). Men's lived experiences following transurethral prostatectomy for benign prostatic hypertrophy. *Journal of Advanced Nursing, 31,* 51–58.

Pattatucci, A., & Hamer, D. (1995). Development and familiality of sexual orientation in females. *Behavior Genetics, 25,* 407–420.

Patterson, C. (1995). Sexual orientation and human development: An overview. *Developmental Psychology, 31,* 3–11.

Patz, A. (2000). Will your marriage last? *Psychology Today,* January–February, 58–65.

Paukku, M., Kilpikari, R., Puolakkainen, M., Oksanen, H., Apter, D., & Paavonen, J. (2003a). Criteria for selective screening for chlamydia trachomatis. *Sexually Transmitted Diseases, 30,* 120–123.

Paukku, M., Quan, J., Darney, P., & Raine, T. (2003b). Adolescents' contraceptive use and pregnancy history: Is there a pattern? *Obstetrics and Gynecology, 101,* 534–538.

Paul, L., & Galloway, J. (1994). Sexual jealousy: Gender differences in response to partner and rival. *Aggressive Behavior, 20,* 203–211.

Paul, P. (2004). The porn factor. *Time,* Special Issue, January 19, 99–100.

Paulson, R. (2000). Should we help women over 50 conceive with donor eggs? *Contemporary OB/GYN,* January, 36–46.

Pauly, I. (1974). Female transsexualism, Part II. *Archives of Sexual Behavior, 3,* 509–526.

Pauly, I. (1990). Gender identity disorders: Evaluation and treatment. *Journal of Sex Education and Therapy, 16,* 2–24.

Pawson, M. (2003). The battle with mortality and the urge to procreate. In J. Haynes & J. Miller (Eds.), *Inconceivable Conceptions: Psychological Aspects of Infertility and Reproductive Technology.* Hove, United Kingdom: Brunner-Routledge.

Pealer, L., & Weiler, R. (2000). Web-based health survey research: A primer. *American Journal of Health Behavior, 24,* 69–72.

Pearce, J., Hawton, K., Blake, F., Barlow, D., Rees, M., Fagg, J., & Keenan, J. (1997). Psychological effects of continuation versus discontinuation of hormone replacement therapy by estrogen implants: A placebo-controlled study. *Journal of Psychosomatic Research, 42(2),* 177–186.

Pearlstein, T., Halbreich, U., & Batzar, E. (2000). Psychosocial functioning in women with premenstrual dysphoric disorder before and after treatment with Sertraline or placebo. *Journal of Clinical Psychiatry, 61,* 101–109.

Pearson, H. (2000). So that's why you can't fit into your jeans . . . *New Scientist,* April 8, 6.

Pearson, H. (2002, July 3). *Pollutants Mature Sperm Prematurely.* Retrieved July 28, 2003, from http://www.nature.com/nsu/nsu_pf/020701/020701-4.html

Pedersen, C. (1992). *Oxytocin in Maternal, Sexual, and Social Behavior.* New York: New York Academy of Sciences.

Pedlow, C., & Carey, M. (2003). HIV sexual risk-reduction interventions for youth. *Behavior Modification, 27,* 135–190.

Peele, S., & Brodsky, A. (1987). *Love and Addiction.* New York: NAL/Dutton.

Penley, C. (1996). From NASA to the 700 Club (with a detour through Hollywood): Cultural studies in the public sphere. In C. Nelson & D. Gaonkar (Eds.), *Disciplinarity and Dissent in Cultural Studies.* New York: Routledge.

Penson, D., Latini, D., Lubeck, D., & Wallace, K. (2003). Is quality of life different for men with erectile dysfunction and prostate cancer compared to men with erectile dysfunction due to other causes? Results from the Exceed data base. *Journal of Urology, 169,* 1558–1561.

Peplau, L. (1981). What homosexuals want in relationships. *Psychology Today, 15(3),* 28–38.

Peplau, L., & Conrad, E. (1989). Beyond nonsexist research: The perils of feminist methods in psychology. *Psychology of Women Quarterly, 13,* 381–402.

Perel, E. (2003). Erotic intelligence. *Psychotherapy Networker,* May–June, 24–31.

Perez, A., Labbok, M., & Queenan, J. (1992). Clinical study of the lactational amenorrhoea method for family planning. *The Lancet, 339,* 968–970.

Perleman, M. (2001). Integrating Sildenafil and sex therapy: Unconsummated marriage secondary to erectile dysfunction and retarded ejaculation. *Journal of Sex Education and Therapy, 26,* 13–21.

Perloff, J., & Jaffee, K. (1999). Late entry into prenatal care: The neighborhood context. *Social Work, 44,* 116–128.

Perris, A. (2000). *At the Pharmacy: OTC.* Retrieved December 1, 2000, from http://www.fertilitext.org/p3_pharmacy/OTCproducts.html

Perrone, K., & Worthington, E., Jr. (2001). Factors influencing ratings of marital quality by individuals within dual-career marriages: A conceptual model. *Journal of Counseling Psychology, 48,* 3–9.

Perry, J., & Whipple, B. (1981). Pelvic muscle strength of female ejaculators: Evidence in support of a new theory of orgasm. *Journal of Sex Research, 17,* 22–39.

Peters, S., Beck-Sague, C., Farshy, C., Gibson, I., Kubota, K., Solomon, F., Morse, S., Sievert, A., & Black, C. (2000). Behavior associated with *Neisseria gonorrhoeae* and *Chlamydia trachoimatis:* Cervical infection among young women attending adolescent clinics. *Clinical Pediatrics, 39,* 173–177.

Peterson, H., Xia, Z., Hughes, J., Wilcox, L., Tylor, L., & Trussell, J. (1997). The risk of ectopic pregnancy after tubal sterilization. *New England Journal of Medicine, 336,* 762–767.

Petitti, D., & Reingold, A. (1988). Tampon characteristics and menstrual toxic shock syndrome. *Journal of the American Medical Association, 259,* 686–687.

Petok, W. (2001). Religious observance and sex therapy with an orthodox Jewish couple. *Journal of Sex Education and Therapy, 26,* 22–27.

Peyser, M. (2000a). Gay all the way. *Newsweek,* November 27, 78–79.

Peyser, M. (2000b). Prime time "I do's." *Newsweek,* February 28, 48.

Peyser, M., & Lorch, D. (2000). Gay today: The schools. *Newsweek,* March 20, 55–56.

Pfafflin, F. (1992). Regrets after sex reassignment surgery. In W. Bockting & E. Coleman (Eds.), *Gender Dysphoria: Interdisciplinary Approaches in Clinical Management.* Binghamton, NY: Haworth Press.

Philliber, S., Kaye, J., Herrling, S., & West, E. (2002). Preventing pregnancy and improving health care access among teenagers: An evaluation of the Children's Aid Society–Carrera Program. *Perspectives on Sexual and Reproductive Health, 34,* 244–251.

Phillips, D., Taylor, C., Zacharopoulos, U., & Maguire, R. (2000). Nonoxynol-9 causes rapid exfoliation of sheets of rectal epithelium. *Contraception, 62,* 149–154.

Phillips, J., Ingram, K., Smith, N., & Mindes, E. (2003). Methodological and content review of lesbian-, gay-, and bisexual-related articles in counseling journals: 1990–1999. *Counseling Psychologist, 31,* 25–62.

Piantadosi, S. (2003). Larger lessons from the Women's Health Initiative. *Epidemiology, 14,* 6–7.

Picardo, C., Nichols, M., Edelman, A., & Jensen, J. (2003). Women's knowledge and sources of information on the risks and benefits of oral contraception. *Journal of the American Medical Women's Association, 58,* 112–116.

Piccinino, L., & Mosher, W. (1998). Trends in contraceptive use in the United States: 1982–1995. *Family Planning Perspectives, 30(1),* 4–10, 46.

Pickett, M., Bruner, D., Joseph, A., & Burggraf, V. (2000). Prostate cancer elder alert: Living with treatment choices and outcomes. *Journal of Gerontological Nursing,* February, 22–34.

Pierce, P. (1994). Sexual harassment: Frankly, what is it? *Journal of Intergroup Relations, 20,* 3–12.

Pinhas, V. (1995, June). Personal communication.

Pinhas, V. (1989). Treatment of sexual problems in chemically dependent women. *Female Patient, 20,* 27–30.

Pirie, P., Lando, H., & Curry, S. (2000). Tobacco, alcohol, and caffeine use and cessation in early pregnancy. *American Journal of Preventive Medicine, 18,* 54–61.

Pithers, W. (1993). Treatment of rapists: Reinterpretation of early outcome date and exploratory constructs to enhance therapeutic efficacy. In G. Hall, R. Hirschman, J. Graham, & M. Zaragoza (Eds.), *Sexual Aggression: Issues in Etiology, Assessment, and Treatment.* Washington, DC: Taylor & Francis.

Planned Parenthood Federation of America (2002). *Masturbation: From Stigma to Sexual Health.* White Paper. New York: Katherine Dexter McCormick Library.

Planned Parenthood Federation of America (2003a). Masturbation: From myth to sexual health. *Contemporary Sexuality, 37,* i–vii.

Planned Parenthood Federation of America (2003b, October 19). *% Effective: Spermicide.* Retrieved October 19, 2003, from http://www.plannedparenthood.org/bc/cchoices5.html

Plant, E., Hyde, J., Keltner, D., & Devine, P. (2000). The gender stereotyping of emotions. *Psychology of Women Quarterly, 24,* 81–92.

Plaud, J., Gaither, G., Hegstad, H., & Rowan, L. (1999). Volunteer bias in human psychophysiological sexual arousal research: To whom do our research results apply? *Journal of Sex Research, 36,* 171–179.

Plaut, S. (1996). *Sexual Exploitation by Health Professionals: The Victim's Perspective.* Paper presented at the 21st Annual Meeting of the Society of Sex Therapy and Research, Miami, March.

Plummer, D. (1999). *One of the Boys: Masculinity, Homophobia, and Modern Manhood.* New York: Harrington Park Press.

Poirot, C. (2000). The painless hysterectomy. *The Sunday Oregonian,* November 19, L18.

Pokorny, S. (1997). Pediatric and adolescent gynecology. *Comprehensive Therapy, 23(5),* 337–344.

Polinsky, M. (1995). Functional status of long-term breast cancer survivors: Demonstrating chronicity. *Health and Social Work, 19(3),* 165–173.

Pollack, H., Lantz, P., & Frohna, J. (2000). Maternal smoking and adverse birth outcomes among singletons and twins. *American Journal of Public Health, 90,* 395–400.

Pollis, C. (1988). An assessment of the impacts of feminism on sexual science. *Journal of Sex Research, 25,* 85–105.

Pollitt, K. (2004). Toothpaste, cough drops, aspirin, contraception. *The Nation, 278,* 9.

Polonsky, D. (2000). Premature ejaculation. In S. Leiblum & R. Rosen (Eds.), *Principles and Practice of Sex Therapy.* New York: Guilford Press.

Pomeroy, W. (1965). Why we tolerate lesbians. *Sexology,* May, 652–654.

Poniewozik, J. (1999). Sex on TV is . . . not sexy! Shows from HBO's *Sex in the City* to MTV's *Undressed* have angst in their pants. *Time,* August 2, 86.

Ponnuru, R. (2003). Coming out ahead: Why gay marriage is on the way. *National Review,* July 28, 1.

Pope, E. (1999). When illness takes sex out of a relationship. *SIECUS Report, 27,* 8–11.

Pope, H., Phillips, K., & Olivardia, R. (2000). *The Adonis Complex: The Secret Crisis of Male Body Obsession.* New York: Free Press.

Pope, K. (2000). Therapists' sexual feelings and behaviors: Research, trends, and quandaries. In L. Szuchman & F. Muscarella (Eds.), *Psychological Perspectives on Human Sexuality.* New York: Wiley.

Popova, V. (1996). Sexuality education moves forward in Russia. *SIECUS Reports, 24,* 14–17.

Porter, S., Yuille, J., & Lehman, D. (1999). The nature of real, implanted, and fabricated childhood emotion events: Implications for the recovered memory debate. *Law and Human Behavior, 23,* 517–537.

Post, S., & Botkin, J. (1995). Adolescents and HIV prevention. *Clinical Pediatrics, 34,* 41–45.

Post, T. (1993). A pattern of rape. *Newsweek,* January 4, 32–36.

Potter, J., & Ship, A. (2001). Survivors of breast cancer. *New England Journal of Medicine, 344,* 309–314.

Potter, L., Oakley, D., & de Leon-Wong, E. (1996). Measuring compliance among oral contraceptive users. *Family Planning Perspectives, 28,* 154–158.

Potterat, J. (2003). Partner notification for HIV: Running out of excuses. *Sexually Transmitted Diseases, 30,* 89–90.

Potts, M. (1997). Social support and depression among older adults living alone: The importance of friends within and outside of a retirement community. *Journal of the National Association of Social Workers, 42(3),* 348–362.

Potts, M. (2000). Thinking about vaginal microbicide testing. *American Journal of Public Health, 90,* 188–190.

Poussaint, A. (1990). An honest look at black gays and lesbians. *Ebony,* September, 124, 126, 130–131.

Power, C. (1998a). The new Islam. *Newsweek,* March 16, 35–38.

Power, C. (1998b). Now it's the gay nineties? *Newsweek,* November 23, 35.

Powlishta, K., Serbin, L., & Moller, L. (1993). The stability of individual differences in gender typing: Implication for understanding gender segregation. *Sex Roles, 29,* 723–737.

Prabu-Jeyabalan, M., Nalivaika, E., King, N., & Schiffer, C. (2003). Viability of a drug-resistant human immunodeficiency virus type 1 protease variant: Structural insights for better antiviral therapy. *Journal of Virology, 77,* 1306–1315.

Prentice, R. (2003). Breast-cancer prevention: Is the risk-benefit ratio in favour of tamoxifen? *The Lancet, 362,* 183.

Prentky, R., Burgess, A., & Carter, D. (1986). Victim responses by rapist type: An empirical and clinical analysis. *Journal of Interpersonal Violence, 1,* 73–98.

Prescott, J. (1975). Body pleasure and the origins of violence. *The Futurist,* April, 64–74.

Prescott, J. (1986). The abortion of "The Silent Scream." *The Humanist, 46,* 10–17.

Prescott, J. (1989). Affectional bonding for the prevention of violent behaviors: Neurological, psychological, and religious/spiritual determinants. In L. Hertzberg (Ed.), *Violent Behavior, v. 1, Assessment and Intervention.* New York: PMA Publishing.

Price, J., Dake, J., Kirchofer, G., & Telljohann, S. (2003). Elementary school teacher's techniques of responding to student questions regarding sexuality issues. *Journal of School Health, 73,* 9–14.

Price, V., Scanlon, B., & Janus, M. (1984). Social characteristics of adolescent male prostitution. *Victimology, 9,* 211–221.

Pridal, C., & LoPiccolo, J. (2000). Multielement treatment of desire disorders: Integration of cognitive, behavioral, and systemic therapy. In S. Leiblum & R. Rosen (Eds.), *Principles and Practice of Sex Therapy.* New York: Guilford Press.

Priestly, C., Jones, B., Dhar, J., & Goodwin, L. (1997). What is normal vaginal flora? *Genitourinary Medicine, 73,* 23–28.

Prince-Gibson, E. (2000). Success story, *Ms.,* April–May, 22–23.

Prinstein, M., Meade, C., & Cohen, G. (2003). Adolescent oral sex, peer popularity, and perceptions of best friends' sexual behavior. *Journal of Pediatric Psychology, 28,* 243–249.

Prior, P., & Hayes B. (2003). The relationship between marital status and health. *Journal of Family Issues, 24,* 124–148.

Prior, P., & Waxman, J. (2000). Localized prostate cancer: can we do better? *British Medical Journal, 320,* 69–70.

Prisant, L., Carr, A., Bottini, P., Solursh, D., & Solursh, L. (1994). Sexual dysfunction with antihypertensive drugs. *Archives of Internal Medicine, 154,* 730–736.

Pritchard, K. (1997). Breast cancer: The real challenge. *The Lancet, 349,* 124–125.

Proctor, F., Wagner, N., & Butler, J. (1974). The differentiation of male and female orgasm: An experimental study. In N. Wagner (Ed.), *Perspectives on Human Sexuality.* New York: Behavioral Publications.

Propst, A., & Laufer, M. (1999). Diagnosing and treating adolescent endometriosis. *Contemporary OB/GYN,* December, 52–59.

Proulx, J., Aubut, J., McKibben, A., & Cote, M. (1994). Penile responses of rapists and nonrapists to rape stimuli involving physical violence or humiliation. *Archives of Sexual Behavior, 23,* 295–310.

Prozhanova, V., & Tantchev, S. (1995). Bulgaria: Adolescent pregnancy on the increase. *Entre Nous, 30,* 16–17.

Puente, S., & Cohen, D. (2003). Jealousy and the meaning (or nonmeaning) of violence. *Personality and Social Psychology Bulletin, 29,* 449–460.

Purnine, D., & Carey, M. (1997). Interpersonal communication and sexual adjustment: The role of understanding and agreement. *Journal of Consulting and Clinical Psychology, 65,* 1017–1025.

Putnam, F. (2003). Ten-year research update review: Child sexual abuse. *Journal of the American Academy of Child and Adolescent Psychiatry, 42,* 269–278.

Pyke, K., & Johnson, D. (2003). Asian American women and racialized femininities: "Doing" gender across cultural worlds. *Gender and Society, 17,* 33–53.

Quackenbush, D., Strassberg, D., & Turner, C. (1995). Gender effects of romantic themes in erotica. *Archives of Sexual Behavior, 24,* 21–35.

Quadagno, D., & Sprague, J. (1991). Reasons for having sex. *Medical Aspects of Human Sexuality,* June, 52.

Quimby, E., & Friedman, S. (1989). Dynamics of black mobilization against AIDS in New York City. *Social Problems, 36,* 403–415.

Quindlen, A. (2000a). The right to be ordinary. *Newsweek,* September 11, 82.

Quindlen, A. (2000b). RU-486 and the right to choose. *Newsweek,* October 9, 86.

Quindlen, A. (2003a). Getting rid of the sex police. *Newsweek,* January 13, 72.

Quindlen, A. (2003b). Out of the time warp. *Newsweek,* January 27, 26.

Quinn, T. (2000). Paper presented at the 7th Conference on Retroviruses and Opportunistic Infections, San Francisco, January 30.

Quittner, J. (2003). Addicted to dot.com sex. *The Advocate,* February 4, 34–36.

Raab, B. (2001). A family thing. *The Advocate,* January 30, 40.

Rabkin, J., Wagner, G., & Rabkin, R. (2000). A double-blind, placebo controlled trial of testosterone therapy for HIV-positive men with hypogonadal symptoms. *Archives of General Psychiatry, 57,* 141–147.

Rabock, J., Mellon, J., & Starka, L. (1979). Klinefelter's syndrome: Sexual development and activity. *Archives of Sexual Behavior, 8,* 333–340.

Rachman, S. (1966). Sexual fetishism: An experimental analogue. *Psychological Record, 16,* 293–296.

Rachman, S., & Hodgson, R. (1968). Experimentally-induced "sexual fetishism": Replication and development. *Psychological Research, 18,* 25–27.

Radar, B. (2001). *American Ways: A Brief History of American Cultures.* Sydney, Australia: Thomson Wadsworth.

Radar, B. (2003). Personal communication.

Radlove, S. (1983). Sexual response and gender roles. In E. Allgeier & N. McCormick (Eds.), *Changing Boundaries: Gender Roles and Sexual Behavior.* Mountain View, CA: Mayfield.

Rahman, A., Katzive, L., & Henshaw, S. (1998). A global review of laws on induced abortion, 1985–1997. *International Family Planning Perspectives, 24,* 56–64.

Rakic, Z., Starcevic, V., Maric, J., & Kelin, K. (1996). The outcome of sex reassignment surgery in Belgrade: 32 patients of both sexes. *Archives of Sexual Behavior, 25,* 515–525.

Rako, S. (1996). *The Hormone of Desire.* New York: Harmony Books.

Rako, S. (1999). Testosterone deficiency and supplementation for women: Matters of sexuality and health. *Psychiatric Annals, 29,* 23–26.

Ranjit, N., Bankole, A., & Darroch, J. (2001). Contraceptive failure in the first two years of use: Differences across socioeconomic subgroups. *Family Planning Perspectives, 33,* 19–27.

Rannestad, T., Eikeland, O., & Helland, H. (2001). The quality of life in women suffering from gynecological disorders is improved by means of hysterectomy. *Acta Obstetricia et Gynecologica Scandinavica, 80,* 46–51.

Raphael-Leff, J. (2003). Eros and ART. In J. Haynes & J. Miller (Eds.), *Inconceivable Conceptions: Psychological Aspects of Infertility and Reproductive Technology.* Hove, United Kingdom: Brunner–Routledge.

Rasch, V. (2003). Cigarette, alcohol, and caffeine consumption: Risk factors for spontaneous abortion. *Acta Obstetricia et Gynecologica Scandinavica, 82,* 182–188.

Rasheed, A., White, C., & Shaikh, N. (1997). The incidence of postvasectomy chronic testicular pain and the role of nerve stripping (denervation) of the spermatic cord in its management. *British Journal of Urology, 79,* 269–270.

Ray, A., & Gold, S. (1996). Gender roles, aggression, and alcohol use in dating relationships. *Journal of Sex Research, 33,* 47–55.

Ray, S., & Quinn, T. (2000). Sex and the genetic diversity of HIV-1. *Nature Medicine, 6,* 23–25.

Raz, R., Gennesin, Y., & Wasser, J. (2000). Recurrent urinary tract infections in postmenopausal women. *Clinical Infectious Diseases, 30,* 152–156.

Razdan, A. (2003). What's love got to do with it? *Utne Reader,* May–June, 69–71.

Real, T. (2002). *How Can I Get Through to You? Reconnecting Men and Women.* New York: Screbuer.

Reamer, F. (2003). Boundary issues in social work: Managing dual relationships. *Social Work, 48,* 121–133.

Rebar, R. (2004). Assisted reproductive technology in the United States. *New England Journal of Medicine, 350,* 1603–1604.

Redmond, G. (1999). Hormones and sexual function. *International Journal of Fertility, 44,* 193–197.

Reed, B., Haefner, H., & Cantor, L. (2003). Vulvar dysesthesia (vulvodynia): A follow-up study. *Journal of Reproductive Medicine, 48,* 409–416.

Reeder, H. (1996). The subjective experience of love through adult life. *International Journal of Aging and Human Development, 43,* 325–340.

Regan, P. (1998). Of lust and love: Beliefs about the role of sexual desire in romantic relationships. *Personal Relationships, 5,* 139–157.

Regan, P., & Berscheid, E. (1995). Gender differences about the causes of male and female sexual desire. *Personal Relationships, 2,* 345–358.

Regehr, C., & Glancy, G. (1995). Sexual exploitation of patients: Issues for colleagues. *American Journal of Orthopsychiatry, 65(2),* 194–202.

Reichert, T. (2003). *The Erotic History of Advertising.* New York: Prometheus Books.

Reid, P., & Bing, V. (2000). Sexual roles of girls and women: An ethnocultural lifespan perspective. In C. Travis & J. White (Eds.), *Sexuality, Society, and Feminism.* Washington, DC: American Psychological Association.

Reid, P., & Comas-Diaz, L. (1990). Gender and ethnicity: Perspectives on dual status. *Sex Roles, 22,* 397–408.

Reiner, W. (1997a). Sex assignment in the neonate with intersex or inadequate genitalia. *Archives of Pediatric and Adolescent Medicine, 151,* 1044–1045.

Reiner, W. (1997b). To be male or female: That is the question. *Archives of Pediatric and Adolescent Medicine, 151,* 224–225.

Reiner, W. (2000). *Gender and "Sex Reassignment."* Paper presented at the Lawson Wilkins Pediatric Endocrine Society meeting, Boston, May 12. Retrieved August 19, 2000, from http://mayohealth.org/mayo/headline/htm/hw000516.htm

Reinisch, J., & Beasley, R. (1990). *The Kinsey Institute's New Report on Sex.* New York: St. Martin's Press.

Reinisch, J., Sanders, S., & Ziemba-Davis, M. (1988). The study of sexual behavior in relation to the transmission of human immunodeficiency virus: Caveats and recommendations. *American Psychologist, 43,* 921–927.

Reiter, R., & Milburn, A. (1994). Exploring effective treatment for chronic pelvic pain. *Contemporary OB/GYN,* March, 84–103.

Remafedi, G. (1994). *Death by Denial: Studies of Suicide in Gay and Lesbian Teenagers.* Boston: Alyson.

Rempel, J., & Baumgartner, B. (2003). The relationship between attitudes towards menstruation and sexual attitudes, desires, and behavior in women. *Archives of Sexual Behavior, 32,* 155–163.

Renaud, C., & Byers, S. (2001). *Positive and Negative Sexual Cognitions: Subjective Experience and Relationships to Sexual Adjustment.* Retrieved September 2, 2003, from http://infotrac-college.thomsonlearning.com/itw/infomark/684/939/38133136w6/5!xrn_1_0 . . .

Renna, C. (2002, December). *LGBT Characters in Comics.* Retrieved May 6, 2003, from http://www.glaad.org/media/resource_kit_detail.php?id=3128

Renshaw, D. (1987). Painful intercourse associated with cerebral palsy. *Journal of the American Medical Association, 257,* 2086.

Renshaw, D. (1991). Female wet dreams. *Medical Aspects of Human Sexuality,* January, 63.

Renshaw, D. (1995). *Seven Weeks to Better Sex.* New York: Random House.

Renzetti, C., & Curran, D. (1992). *Women, Men, and Society* (2nd ed.). Boston: Allyn & Bacon.

Resnick, M., Bearman, P., Blum, R., Bauman, K., Harris, K., Jones, J., Tabor, J., Beuhring, T., Sieving, R., Shew, M., Ireland, M., Bearinger, L., & Udry, J. (1997). Protecting adolescents from harm: Findings from the National Longitudinal Study on Adolescent Health. *Journal of the American Medical Association, 278,* 823–832.

Reuters (2003). *Penis Extensions Top the List in Britain.* Retrieved February 18, 2003, from http://www.reuters.com/newsArticle.jhtml

Reynolds, S., Shepherd, M., Risbud, A., Gangakhedkar, R., Brookmeyer, R., Divekar, A., Mehendale, S., & Bollinger, R. (2004). Male circumcision and risk of HIV-1 and other sexually transmitted infections in India. *Lancet, 363,* 1039–1040.

Rhode, D. (1997). Harassment is alive and well and living at the water cooler. *Ms.,* November–December, 28–29.

Rhodes, S., Bowie, D., & Hergenrather, K. (2003). Collecting behavioral data using the World Wide Web: Considerations for researchers. *Journal of Epidemiology and Community Health, 57,* 68–73.

Rhodes, S., DiClemente, R., Yee, I., & Hergenrather, K. (2001a). Correlates of hepatitis B vaccination in a high-risk population: An Internet sample. *American Journal of Medicine, 110,* 628–632.

Rhodes, S., DiClemente, R., Yee, I., & Hergenrather, K. (2001b). Factors associated with testing hepatitis C in an Internet-recruited sample of men who have sex with men. *Sexually Transmitted Diseases, 28,* 515–520.

Rhynard, J., Krebs, M., & Glover, J. (1997). Sexual assault in dating relationships. *Journal of School Health, 67,* 89–93.

Ribadeneira, D. (1998). More women step up to pulpit, but they still take a back pew. *The Oregonian,* April 19, G3.

Rice, G., Anderson, C., Risch, N., & Ebers, G. (1999). Male homosexuality: Absence of linkage to microsatellite markers at Xq28. *Science,* April 23, 665–667.

Rich, A. (1976). *Of Woman Born.* New York: Norton.

Richard, D. (2002a). Senior sexuality. *Contemporary Sexuality, 36,* 1–-6.

Richard, D. (2002b). Tantra 101. *Contemporary Sexuality, 36,* 1.

Richards, L., Rollerson, B., & Phillips, J. (1991). Perceptions of submissiveness: Implications for victimization. *Journal of Psychology, 125,* 407–411.

Richardson, B., John-Stewart, G., Hughes, J., Nduati, R., Mbori-Ngacha, D., Overbaugh, J., & Kreiss, J. (2003a). Breast-mild infectivity in human immunodeficiency virus type I–infected mothers. *Journal of Infectious Diseases, 187,* 736–740.

Richardson, B., Lavreys, L., Martin, H., Stevens, C., Ntugti, E., Mandaliya, K., Bwayo, J., Ndinya-Achola, N., & Kreiss, J. (2003b). Evaluation of a low-dose nonoxynol-9 gel for the prevention of sexually transmitted diseases. *Sexually Transmitted Diseases, 30,* 394–397.

Richardson, H., Franco, E., Pintos, J., Bergeron, J., Arella, M., & Tellier, P. (2000). Determinants of low-risk and high-risk cervical human papillomavirus infections in Montreal university students. *Sexually Transmitted Diseases, 27,* 79–86.

Richman, J., Flaherty, J., Rospenda, K., & Christensen, M. (1992). Mental health consequences and correlates of reported medical student abuse. *Journal of the American Medical Association, 267,* 692–694.

Rickert, V., Sanghvi, R., & Wiemann, C. (2002). Is lack of sexual assertiveness among adolescent and young adult women a cause for concern? *Perspectives on Sexual and Reproductive Health, 34,* 178–183.

Rickert, V., & Wiemann, C. (1998). Date rape: Office-based solutions. *Contemporary OB/GYN, 43,* 133–153.

Ricks, T., & Suro, R. (2000). Army confirms harassment charge by top woman general. *The Oregonian,* May 11, A8.

Rider, E. (2000). *Our Voices: Psychology of Women.* Belmont, CA: Wadsworth/Thomson Learning.

Ridgeway, J. (1996). *Inside the Sex Industry.* New York: Powerhouse Books.

Rierdan, J., Koff, E., & Stubbs, M. (1998). Gender, depression and body image in early adolescents. *Journal of Early Adolescence, 8,* 109–117.

Riger, S. (1991). Gender dilemmas in sexual harassment policies and procedures. *American Psychologist, 46,* 497–505.

Riley, A., & Riley, E. (2000). Controlled studies on women presenting with sexual drive disorder. I. Endocrine status. *Journal of Sex and Marital Therapy, 26,* 269–283.

Rim, E. (2000). *Lifestyles Role in Potential for Impotence.* Paper presented at the Annual Meeting of the American Urological Association, Atlanta, GA.

Rind, B., & Tromovitch, P. (1997). A meta-analytic review of findings from national samples on psychological correlates of child sexual abuse. *Journal of Sex Research, 34,* 237–255.

Rind, B., Tromovitch, P., & Bauserman, R. (1998). A meta-analytic examination of assumed properties of child sexual abuse using college samples. *Psychological Bulletin, 124,* 22–53.

Ring, W. (2001). *Vermont Teens Drawn to Prostitution.* Retrieved February 9, 2001, from http://www.salon.com/mwt/wire/2001/02/09/prostitution//index.html

Ringdahl, E. (2000). Treatment of recurrent vulvovaginal candidiasis. *American Family Physician, 61,* 3306–3312.

Rio, L. (1991). Psychological and sociological research and the decriminalization or legalization of prostitution. *Archives of Sexual Behavior, 20,* 205–217.

Rios, D. (1996). The gone girls. *The Oregonian,* November 17, E1–E3.

Riscol, L. (2003). Bigger, harder, better: Natural sex enhancers or Viagra-era snake oil? *Contemporary Sexuality, 37,* 1.

Rispens, J., Alema, A., & Goudena, P. (1997). Prevention of child sexual victimization: A meta-analysis of school programs. *Child Abuse and Neglect, 21,* 975–987.

Ritter, J. (2000). *Gay Students Stake Their Ground.* Retrieved January 18, 2000, from http://www.usatoday.com/news/acovtue.htm

Ritter, J. (2003). *More Choices Available for Birth Control.* Retrieved April 11, 2003, from http://www.suntimes.com/output/news/cst-nws-birth06.html

Ritter, T. (1919). The people's home medical book. In R. Barnum (Ed.), *The People's Home Library.* Cleveland: Barnum.

Ritts, V. (2003). *Infusing Culture into Psychopathology.* Retrieved March 13, 2003, from http://www.stlcc.cc.mo.us/mc/users/vritts/psypath.htm

Robbins, M., & Jensen, G. (1978). Multiple orgasm in males. *Journal of Sex Research, 14,* 21–26.

Robinson, D., Stewart, S., & Gist, R. (2001). Laparoscopic pomeroy: A comparison with tubal cauterization in a teaching hospital. *Obstetrics and Gynecology, 97,* 16S–17S.

Robinson, G. (1999). China: Surfeit of bachelors predicted in China. *World Press Review,* March, 18.

Robinson, G., Garner, C., Gare, D., & Crawford, B. (1987). Psychological adaptation to pregnancy in childless women more than 35 years of age. *American Journal of Obstetrics and Gynecology, 156,* 323–328.

Robinson, J., & Godbey, G. (1998). No sex, please. We're college graduates. *American Demographics, 20(2),* 18–23.

Rochman, S. (2003). Dragging us down. *The Advocate,* July 8, 43–44.

Roddy, R., Zekeng, K., Ryan, A., Tamoufe, U., & Tweedy, K. (2002). Effect of nonoxynol-9 gel on urogenital gonorrhea and chlamydial infection: A randomized controlled trial. *Journal of the American Medical Association,* March 6, 1117–1122.

Rodgers, K. (1999). Parenting processes related to sexual risk-taking behaviors of adolescent males and females. *Journal of Marriage and the Family, 61,* 99–109.

Rodriguez, M. (2000). SIECUS forum on adolescent sexuality and popular culture. *SIECUS Report, 28,* 3–5.

Rodriguez, N., Ryan, S., Vande Kemp, H., & Foy, D. (1997). Posttraumatic stress disorder in adult female survivors of childhood sexual abuse: A comparison study. *Journal of Consulting and Clinical Psychology, 65,* 53–59.

Rodriguez-Stednicki, O., & Twaite, J. (1999). Attitudes toward victims of child abuse among adults from four ethnic/cultural groups. *Journal of Child Sexual Abuse, 8,* 1–24.

Roelofs, W. (1995). Chemistry of sex attraction. *Proceedings of the National Academy of Sciences U.S.A., 92,* 44–49.

Rogers, C. (1951). *Client-Centered Therapy: Its Current Practice, Implications, and Theory.* Boston: Houghton Mifflin.

Rogers, S. (2003). *Paris Hilton Sex Video Reportedly to Be Offered via New Internet Porn Site.* Retrieved November 17, 2003, from http://www.realityworld.com/index/articles/story.php?s=1967

Rojanapithayakorn, W., & Hannenberg, R. (1996). The 100% condom program in Thailand. *AIDS, 10,* 1–7.

Rojnik, B., Andolsek-Jeras, L., & Obersnel-Kveder, D. (1995). Women in difficult circumstances: War victims and refugees. *International Journal of Gynecology and Obstetrics, 48,* 311–315.

Romanowski, B., Preiksaitis, J., Campbell, P., & Fenton, J. (2003a). Hepatitis C seroprevalence and risk behaviors in patients attending sexually transmitted disease clinics. *Sexually Transmitted Diseases, 30,* 33–38.

Romanowski, B., Valtrex HS230017 Study Group, Marina, R., & Roberts, J. (2003b). Patients' preference for valacyclovir once-daily suppressive therapy versus twice-daily episodic therapy for recurrent genital herpes: A randomized study. *Sexually Transmitted Diseases, 30,* 226–231.

Romeo, J., Seftel, A., Madhun, Z., & Aron, D. (2000). Sexual function in men with diabetes type 2: Association with glycemic control. *Journal of Urology, 163,* 788–791.

Roodman, A., & Clum, G. (2001). Revictimization rates and method variance: A meta-analysis. *Clinical Psychology Review, 21,* 183–204.

Rosa, M., Zarrilli, S., Paesano, L., & Carbone, U. (2003). Traffic pollutants affect fertility in men. *Human Reproduction, 18,* 1055–1061.

Rosario, M., Schrimshaw, E., Hunter, J., & Gwadz, M. (2002). Gay-related stress and emotional distress among gay, lesbian, and bisexual youths: A longitudinal examination. *Journal of Consulting and Clinical Psychology, 70,* 967–975.

Roscoe, B., Strouse, J., & Goodwin, M. (1994). Sexual harassment: Early adolescents' self-reports of experiences and acceptance. *Adolescence, 115,* 515–523.

Rose, A., & Montemayor, R. (1994). The relationship between gender role orientation and perceived self-competency in male and female adolescents. *Sex Roles, 31,* 579–595.

Rosen, R. (1991). Alcohol and drug effects on sexual response: Human experimental and clinical studies. *Annual Review of Sex Research, 2,* 119–179.

Rosen, R., & Ashton, A. (1993). Prosexual drugs: Empirical status of the "new aphrodisiacs." *Archives of Sexual Behavior, 22,* 521–541.

Rosen, R., & Beck, J. (1988). *Patterns of Sexual Arousal.* New York: Guilford Press.

Rosenau, D., Taylor, D., Sytsma, M., & McClusky, C. (2001). *Conducting Sex Therapy with Conservative Christian Couples.* Paper presented at the 33rd Annual Conference of the American Association of Sex Educators, Counselors, and Therapists, San Francisco, May 2–6.

Rosenberg, D. (2001). A place of their own. *Newsweek,* January 15, 54–55.

Rosenberg, D. (2003a). Chipping away at Roe. *Newsweek,* March 17, 40–41.

Rosenberg, D. (2003b). In Roe's shadow. *Newsweek,* January 27, 58–59.

Rosenberg, M. (1988). Adult behaviors that reflect childhood incest. *Medical Aspects of Human Sexuality,* May, 114–124.

Rosenbluth, S. (1997). Is sexual orientation a matter of choice? *Psychology of Women Quarterly, 21,* 595–610.

Rosenthal, D., Smith, A., & de Visser, R. (1999). Personal and social factors influencing age at first intercourse. *Archives of Sexual Behavior, 28,* 319–333.

Rosenthal, E. (2002). AIDS in rural China creating villages of destitute orphans. *The Oregonian,* August 25, A17.

Rosenzweig, J., & Daily, D. (1989). Dyadic adjustment/sexual satisfaction in women and men as a function of psychological sex role self-perception. *Journal of Sex and Marital Therapy, 15,* 42–56.

Rosik, C. (2003). Motivational, ethical, and epistemological foundations in the treatment of unwanted homoerotic attraction. *Journal of Marital and Family Therapy, 29,* 13–28.

Rosler, A., & Witztum, E. (1998). Treatment of men with paraphilia with a long-acting analogue of gonadotropin releasing hormone. *New England Journal of Medicine, 338,* 416–422.

Rosler, A., & Witztum, E. (2000). Pharmacotherapy of paraphilias in the next millennium. *Behavior Science and Law, 18,* 43–56.

Rosman, J., & Resnick, P. (1989). Sexual attraction to corpses: A psychiatric review of necrophilia. *Bulletin of the American Academy of Psychiatry and the Law, 17,* 153–163.

Ross, M., & Arrindell, W. (1988). Perceived parental rearing patterns of homosexual and heterosexual men. *Journal of Sex Research, 24,* 275–281.

Ross, M., Essien, J., Williams, M., & Fernandez-Esquer, M. (2003). Concordance between sexual behavior and sexual identity in street outreach samples of four racial/ethnic groups. *Sexually Transmitted Diseases, 30,* 110–113.

Rosser, S. (1994). *Women's Health: Missing from U.S. Medicine.* Bloomington: Indiana University Press.

Rotello, G. (1995). The inning of outing. *The Advocate,* April 18, 80.

Roth, S., Dye, E., & Lebowitz, L. (1988). Group therapy for sexual-assault victims. *Psychotherapy, 25,* 82–93.

Rothbaum, B., & Jackson, J. (1990). Religious influence on menstrual attitudes and symptoms. *Women & Health, 16(1),* 63–77.

Rothblum, E. (2000). Comments on "Lesbians' sexual activities and efforts to reduce risks for sexually transmitted diseases." *Journal of the Gay and Lesbian Medical Association, 4,* 39.

Rotheram, M., & Weiner, N. (1983). Androgyny, stress, and satisfaction. *Sex Roles, 9,* 151–158.

Rousseau, C., Nduati, R., Richardson, B., Steele, M., John-Stewart, G., Mbori-Ngacha, D., Kreiss, J., & Overbaugh, J. (2003). Longitudinal analysis of human immunodeficiency virus type I RNA in breast milk and its relationship to infant infection and maternal diseases. *Journal of Infectious Diseases, 187,* 741–747.

Routh, L. (2000). *Inside the Mind of a Woman: Neuropsychiatric Disorders and the Impact of Hormones Throughout the Female Lifecycle.* Paper presented at a workshop given by the Amen Clinic for Behavioral Medicine Inc., Fairfield, California, May 26.

Rowe, M. (2003a). Lovers in a dangerous time. *The Advocate,* May 27, 30–38.

Rowe, M. (2003b). The queer report. *The Advocate,* April 15, 41–49.

Rowland, D., Strassberg, D., de Gouveia Brazao, C., & Slob, A. (2000). Ejaculatory latency and control in men with premature ejaculation: An analysis across sexual activities using multiple sources of information. *Journal of Psychosomatic Research, 48,* 69–77.

Rowland, D., Tai, W., & Slob, A. (2003). An exploration of emotional response to erotic stimulation in men with premature ejaculation: Effects of treatment with clomipramine. *Archives of Sexual Behavior, 32,* 145–153.

Royce, R., Sena, A., Cates, W., & Cohen, M. (1997). Sexual transmission of HIV. *New England Journal of Medicine, 336,* 1072–1078.

Roye, C., & Balk, S. (1997). Evaluation of an intergenerational program for pregnant and parenting adolescents. *Maternal-Child Nursing Journal, 24,* 32–36.

Ruan, F. (1998). *Sex in China: Studies in Sexology in Chinese Culture.* New York: Plenum.

Rubble, D., & Martin, C. (1998). Gender development. In W. Damon & N. Eisenberg (Eds.), *Handbook of Child Psychology,* v. 3, *Social, Emotional, and Personality Development* (5th ed.). New York: Wiley.

Ruben, D. (1992). Saying no to nursing. *Parenting,* March, 21.

Rubenstein, C. (1994). The 1994 infidelity report. *New Woman,* March, 65–69.

Rubin, J., Provenzano, F., & Luria, Z. (1974). The eye of the beholder: Parents' views on sex of newborns. *American Journal of Orthopsychiatry, 44,* 512–519.

Rubin, L. (1990). *Erotic Wars.* New York: Farrar, Straus & Giroux.

Rubin, L., & Borgers, S. (1990). Sexual harassment in the universities during the 1980s. *Sex Roles, 23,* 397–411.

Rubin, Z. (1970). Measurement of romantic love. *Journal of Personality and Social Psychology, 16,* 265–273.

Rubin, Z. (1973). *Liking and Loving.* New York: Holt, Rinehart & Winston.

Rubinsky, H., Eckerman, D., Rubinsky, E., & Hoover, C. (1987). Early-phase physiological response patterns to psychosexual stimuli: Comparisons of male and female patterns. *Archives of Sexual Behavior, 16,* 45–55.

Rumstein-McKean, O., & Hunsley, J. (2001). Interpersonal and family functioning of female survivors of childhood sexual abuse. *Clinical Psychology Review, 21,* 471–490.

Ruowei, L. (2002). Prevalence of exclusive breastfeeding among U.S. infants. *American Journal of Public Health, 92,* 1107–1110.

Russell, D. (1984). *Sexual Exploitation: Rape, Child Sexual Abuse, and Workplace Harassment.* Beverly Hills, CA: Sage.

Russell, G., & Richards, J. (2003). Stressor and resilience factors for lesbians, gay men, and bisexuals confronting antigay politics. *American Journal of Community Psychology, 31,* 313–327.

Russell, K., Swenson, M., Skelton, A., & Shedd-Steele, R. (2003). The meaning of health in mammography screening for African American women. *Health Care for Women International, 24,* 27–39.

Russell, N., Hudgens, M., Ha, R., Havenar-Daughton, C., & McElrath, M. (2003). Moving to human immunodeficiency virus type 1 vaccine efficacy trials: Defining T cell responses as potential correlates of immunity. *Journal of Infectious Diseases, 187,* 226–242.

Russell, S. (2001). LGBTQ youth are at risk in U.S. school environment. *SIECUS Report, 29,* 19–21.

Rutherford, D. (2002). Erectile dysfunction: Assessment, treatment, and prescribing issues. *Nursing Times, 98,* 30–33.

Ryan, C., & Futterman, D. (1997). Lesbian and gay youth: Care and counseling. *Adolescent Medicine: State of the Art Reviews, 8,* 221.

Ryan, C., & Futterman, D. (2001). Social and developmental challenges for lesbian, gay, and bisexual youth. *SIECUS Report, 29,* 5–6.

Ryan, C., Vathing, O., & Gorbach, P. (1998). Explosive spread of HIV-1 and sexually transmitted diseases in Cambodia. *The Lancet, 351,* 1175–1180.

Ryan, G. (2000). Childhood sexuality: A decade of study. Part I. Research and curriculum development. *Child Abuse and Neglect, 24,* 33–48.

Ryan, G. Miyoshi, T., & Krugman, R. (1988). *Early Childhood Experience of Professionals Working in Child Abuse.* Paper presented at the 17th Annual Symposium on Child Sexual Abuse and Neglect, Keystone, Colorado.

Ryan, S., Pearlmutter, S., & Groza, V. (2004). Coming out of the closet: Opening agencies to gay and lesbian adoptive parents. *Social Work, 49,* 85–95.

Saario, T., Jacklin, C., & Tittle, C. (1973). Sex role stereotyping in public schools. *Harvard Educational Review, 43,* 386–416.

Sacks, M. (1998). Sex survey's results raise eyebrows. *The Oregonian,* February 22, L10.

Sadker, M., & Sadker, D. (1990). Confronting sexism in the college classroom. In S. Gabriel & I. Smithson (Eds.), *Gender in the Classroom: Power and Pedagogy.* Chicago: University of Chicago Press.

Sadker, M., & Sadker, D. (1994). *Failing at Fairness: How America's Schools Cheat Girls.* New York: Scribners.

Safran, C. (1976). What men do to women on the job: A shocking look at sexual harassment. *Redbook,* November, 148.

Safren, S., & Heimberg, R. (1999). Depression, hopelessness, suicidality, and related factors in sexual minority and heterosexual adolescents. *Journal of Consulting and Clinical Psychology, 67,* 859–866.

Saghir, M., & Robins, E. (1973). *Male and Female Homosexuality: A Comprehensive Investigation* Baltimore: Williams & Wilkins.

Sailer, S. (2003, July 15). *Gay Marriage Around the Globe.* Retrieved September 1, 2003, from http://infotrac-college.thomsonlearning.com/itw/infomark/760/291/35557478w7/27!ar_fmt

Sales, E., Baum, M., & Shore, B. (1984). Victim readjustment following assault. *Journal of Social Issues, 40,* 117–136.

Salisbury, N. (1991). Personal communication.

Salovey, P., & Rodin, J. (1985). The heart of jealousy. *Psychology Today,* September, 22–29.

Salter, D., McMillan, D., Richards, M., Talbot, T., Hodges, J., Bentovim, A., Hastings, R, Stevenson, J., & Skuse, D. (2003). Development of sexually abusive behavior in sexually victimized males: A longitudinal study. *The Lancet, 361,* 471–476.

Salzburg, S. (2004). Learning that an adolescent child is gay or lesbian: The parent experience. *Social Work, 49,* 109–118.

Sampson, E. (1985). The decentralization of identity: Toward a revised concept of personal and social order. *American Psychologist, 40,* 1203–1211.

Samuels, A., Croal, N., & Gates, D. (2000). Battle for the soul of hip-hop. *Newsweek,* October 9, 57–66.

Samuels, H. (1997). The relationships among selected demographics and conventional and unconventional sexual behaviors among black and white heterosexual men. *Journal of Sex Research, 34,* 85–92.

Sanchez, Y. (1997). Families of Mexican origin. In M. DeGenova (Ed.), *Families in Cultural Context: Strengths and Challenges in Diversity.* Mountain View, CA: Mayfield.

Sanday, P. (1981). The sociocultural context of rape: A cross-cultural study. *Journal of Social Issues, 37,* 5–27.

Sanday, P. (1996). *A Woman Scorned: Acquaintance Rape on Trial.* New York: Doubleday.

Sandelowski, M. (1994). Separate but less unequal: Fetal ultrasonography and the transformation of expectant mother/fatherhood. *Gender and Society, 8,* 230–245.

Sandelowski, M. (2000). "This most dangerous instrument": Propriety, power, and the vaginal speculum. *Journal of Obstetrical, Gynecological, and Neonatal Nursing, 29,* 73–82.

Sander, S. (1999). Mid-life sexuality: The need to integrate biological, psychological, and social perspectives. *SIECUS Report, 27,* 3–7.

Sanders, G. (1982). Social comparison as a basis for evaluating others. *Journal of Research in Personality, 16,* 21–31.

Sanders, G. (2000). Men together: Working with gay couples in contemporary times. In P. Papp (Ed.), *Couples on the Fault Line.* New York: Guilford Press.

Sanders, G., Sjodin, M., & de Chastelaine, M. (2002). On the elusive nature of sex differences in cognition: Hormonal influences contributing to within-sex variation. *Archives of Sexual Behavior, 31,* 145–152.

Sanders, S., Graham, C., Bass, J., & Bancroft, J. (2001). A prospective study of the effects of oral contraceptives on sexuality and well-being and their relationship to discontinuation. *Contraception, 64,* 51–58.

Sanders, S., Graham, C., & Janssen, E. (2003). *Factors Affecting Sexual Arousal in Women.* Retrieved March 8, 2003, from http://www.kinseyinstitute.org/research/focus_group.html

Sanders, S., & Reinisch, J. (1999). Would you say you "had sex" if . . . ? *Journal of the American Medical Association, 281,* 275–277.

Sandfort, T., de Graaf, R., & Bijl, R. (2003). Same-sex sexuality and quality of life: Findings from the Netherlands Mental Health Survey and Incidence Study. *Archives of Sexual Behavior, 32,* 15–22.

Sandlow, J. (2000). Shattering the myths about male infertility. *Postgraduate Medicine, 107,* 235–242.

Sandnabba, N., Santtila, P., & Nordling, N. (1999). Sexual behavior and social adaptation among sadomasochistically oriented males. *Journal of Sex Research, 36,* 273–282.

Sandnabba, N., Santtila, P., Wannas, M., & Krook, K. (2003). Age and gender specific sexual behaviors in children. *Child Abuse and Neglect, 27,* 579–605.

Santana, A. (1998). *Loopholes Help Ex-Firefighter Avoid Voyeurism Charges.* Retrieved October 29, 1998, from http://www.seattletimes.com

Sapunar, F., & Smith, I. (2000). Neoadjuvant chemotherapy for breast cancer. *Annals of Medicine, 32,* 43–50.

Sarma, S. (1999). Relationship between use of the intrauterine device and pelvic inflammatory disease. *Archives of Family Medicine, 8,* 197.

Sarrel, P. (1988). *Sex and Menopause.* Paper presented at the 21st Annual Meeting of the American Association of Sex Educators, Counselors, and Therapists, San Francisco, April.

Sarrel, P., & Masters, W. (1982). Sexual molestation of men by women. *Archives of Sexual Behavior, 11,* 117–131.

Sarwer, D., & Durlak, J. (1996). Childhood sexual abuse as a predictor of adult female sexual dysfunction: A study of couples seeking sex therapy. *Child Abuse and Neglect, 20,* 963–972.

Satel, S. (1993). The diagnostic limits of addiction. *Journal of Clinical Psychiatry, 54,* 237.

Satterfield, A., & Muehlenhard, C. (1990). *Flirtation in the Classroom: Negative Consequences on Women's Perceptions of Their Ability.* Paper presented at the annual meeting of the Society for the Scientific Study of Sex, Minneapolis, November.

Sauder, D., Skinner, R., Fox, T., & Owens, M. (2003). Topical imiquimod 5% cream as an effective treatment for external genital and perianal warts in different patient populations. *Sexually Transmitted Diseases, 30,* 124–128.

Saulnier, C. (2002). Deciding who to see: Lesbians discuss their preferences in health and mental health care providers. *Social Work, 47,* 355–365.

Saunders, E. (1989). Life-threatening autoerotic behavior: A challenge for sex educators and therapists. *Journal of Sex Education and Therapy, 15,* 77–81.

Saunders, N. (1997). Pregnancy in the 21st century: Back to nature with a little assistance. *The Lancet, 349,* s17–s19.

Savage, D. (2002). Justices void law on child sex images. *The Oregonian,* April 17, A1, A7.

Savage, T. (2003). Belgium says "I do." *The Advocate,* March 18, 15.

Savin-Williams, R., & Dubé, E. (1998). Parental reactions to their child's disclosure of a gay/lesbian identity. *Family Relations, 47,* 7–13.

Sawyer, R., Pinciaro, P., & Jessell, J. (1998). Effects of coercion and verbal consent on university students' perception of date rape. *American Journal of Health Behavior, 22,* 46–53.

Sayle, A., Savitz, D., & Thorp, J. (2001). Sexual activity during late pregnancy and risk of preterm delivery. *Obstetrics and Gynecology, 97,* 283–289.

Scarabin, P., Oger, E., & Plu-Bureau, G. (2003). Differential association of oral and transdermal oestrogen-replacement therapy with venous thromboembolism risk. *The Lancet, 362,* 428–432.

Scarce, M. (1997). Same-sex rape of male college students. *Journal of American College Health, 45,* 171–173.

Schaefer, A. (1990). Editorial comment. *Journal of Urology, 143,* 226.

Schairer, C., Lubin, J., Troisi, R., Sturgeon, S., Brinton, L., & Hoover, R. (2000). Menopausal estrogen and estrogen-progestin replacement therapy and breast cancer risk. *Journal of the American Medical Association, 283,* 485–491.

Scharf, C., & Weinshel, M. (2000). Infertility and late-life pregnancies. In P. Papp (Ed.), *Couples on the Fault Line.* New York: Guilford Press.

Scharfe, E., & Bartholomew, K. (1995). Accommodation and attachment representations in young couples. *Journal of Social and Personal Relationships, 12,* 389–401.

Scheela, R., & Stern, P. (1994). Falling apart: A process integral to the remodeling of male incest offenders. *Archives of Psychiatric Nursing, 8,* 91–100.

Scheer, S., Chu, P., Klausner, J., Katz, M., & Schwarcz, S. (2001). Effects of highly active antiretroviral therapy on diagnoses of sexually transmitted diseases in people with AIDS. *The Lancet, 357,* 432–435.

Scher, H. (1997). The drive to stop harassment in schools. *Ms.,* March–April, 22.

Schieve, L., Tathan, L., Peterson, H., Toner, J., & Jeng, G. (2003). Spontaneous abortion among pregnancies conceived using assisted reproductive technology in the United States. *Obstetrics and Gynecology, 101,* 959–967.

Schifeling, D., & Hamblin, J. (1991). Early diagnosis of breast cancer. *Postgraduate Medicine, 89(3),* 55–61.

Schifrin, B. (2003). Adverse effects of vacuum-assisted delivery devices. *Journal of Obstetrics and Gynecology, 101,* 7S.

Schifter, J. (1998). *Lila's House.* New York: Harrington Park Press.

Schillinger, J., Kissinger, P., Calvert, H., Whittington, W., Ranson, R., Sternberg, M., Berman, S., Kent, C., Martin, D., Oh, M., Handsfield, H., Bolan, G., Markowitz, L., & Fortenberry, J. (2003). Patient-delivered partner treatment with azithromycin to prevent repeated chlamydia trachomatis infection among women. *Sexually Transmitted Diseases, 30,* 49–56.

Schleicher, S., & Stewart, P. (1997). Scabies: The mite that roars. *Emergency Medicine,* June, 54–58.

Schmitt, D. (2003). Universal sex differences in the desire for sexual variety: Tests from 52 nations, 6 continents, and 13 islands. *Journal of Personality and Social Psychology, 85,* 85–104.

Schmitt, D., Shackelford, T., Duntley, J., Tooke, W., & Buss, D. (2001). The desire for sexual variety as a key to understanding basic human mating strategies. *Personal Relationships, 8,* 425–455.

Schnarch, D. (1991). *Constructing the Sexual Crucible.* New York: Norton.

Schnarch, D. (1993). Inside the sexual crucible. *Networker,* March–April, 40–48.

Schnarch, D. (1997). Sex, intimacy, and the Internet. *Journal of Sex Education and Therapy, 22(1),* 15–20.

Schnarch, D. (2000). Desire problems: A systemic perspective. In S. Leiblum & R. Rosen (Eds.), *Principles and Practice of Sex Therapy.* New York: Guilford Press.

Schneider, M. (2003). Bush signs partial-birth abortion ban: Legal challenges underway. *OB/GYN News,* December 1, 5.

Schoen, E., Anderson, G., Bohon, C., Hinman, F., Poland, R., & Wakeman, E. (1989). Report of the Task Force on Circumcision. *Pediatrics, 84,* 388–391.

Schoen, E., Wiswell, T., & Moses, S. (2000). New policy on circumcision: Cause for concern. *Pediatrics, 105,* 620–623.

Schoen, R. (1999). Do fertility intentions affect fertility behavior? *Journal of Marriage and the Family, 61,* 790–799.

Schoener, G. (1995). Assessment of professionals who have engaged in boundary violations. *Psychiatric Annals, 25(2),* 95–99.

Scholes, D., Stergachis, A., & Ichikawa, L. (1998). Vaginal douching as a risk factor for cervical *Chlamydia trachomatis* infection. *Obstetrics and Gynecology, 91,* 993–997.

Schoofs, M. (1997). Berlin. *The Advocate,* June 24, 115–116.

Schorge, J., Lea, J., Garner, E., & Duska, L. (2003). Cervical adenocarcinoma survival among Hispanic and white women: A multicenter cohort study. *American Journal of Obstetrics and Gynecology, 188,* 640–644.

Schover, L. (2000). Sexual problems in chronic illness. In S. Leiblum & R. Rosen (Eds.), *Principles and Practice of Sex Therapy.* New York: Guilford Press.

Schover, L., Friedman, J., Weiler, S., Heiman, J., & LoPiccolo, J. (1982). Multiaxial problem-oriented system for sexual dysfunctions. *Archives of General Psychiatry, 39,* 614–619.

Schover, L., & Jensen, S. (1988). *Sexuality and Chronic Illness.* New York: Guilford Press.

Schrag, D., Kuntz, K., Garber, J., & Weeks, J. (2000). Life expectancy gains from cancer prevention strategies for women with breast cancer and BRCA1 or BRCA2 mutations. *Journal of the American Medical Association, 283,* 617–624.

Schrinsky, D. (1998, January). Personal communication.

Schroder, M., & Carroll, R. (1999). New women: Sexological outcomes of male-to-female gender reassignment surgery. *Journal of Sex Education and Therapy, 24,* 137–146.

Schroedel, J. (2000). *Is the Fetus a Person: A Comparison of Policies Across the Fifty States.* Ithaca, NY: Cornell University Press.

Schroeder, J. (1995). Offensive attack. *The Advocate,* August 22, 34–38.

Schubach, G. (1996). *Urethral Expulsions During Sensual Arousal and Bladder Catherization in Seven Human Females.* Ed.D. thesis, Institute for Advanced Study of Human Sexuality, San Francisco.

Schulberg, P. (1999). Sweeping up. *The Oregonian,* December 1, B1.

Schulman, A. (2000). Inconceivable: When we couldn't get pregnant, everyone assumed the problem was mine. *Ms.,* July, 51–53.

Schwartz, J., & Gabelnick, H. (2002). Current contraceptive research. *Perspectives on Sexual and Reproductive Health, 34,* 310–315.

Schwartz, P. (1990). *The Future Is the Past: Gay Custody Decisions.* Paper presented at the Annual Western Region Conference of the Society for the Scientific Study of Sex, San Diego, April 25.

Schwartz, R.. (2003). Pathways to sexual intimacy. *Psychotherapy Networker,* May–June 36–43.

Scully, D., & Marolla, J. (1984). Convicted rapists' vocabulary of motives, excuses, and justifications. *Social Problems, 31,* 530–544.

Seal, D. (1997). Interpartner concordance of self-reported sexual behavior among college dating couples. *Journal of Sex Research, 34,* 39–55.

Seal, D., Bloom, F., & Somlai, A. (2000). Dilemmas in conducting qualitative sex research in applied field settings. *Health Education and Behavior, 27,* 10–23.

Seaman, B., & Seaman, G. (1978). *Women and the Crisis in Sex Hormones.* New York: Bantam Books.

Searight, H., & McClaren, A. (1997). Behavioral and psychiatric aspects of HIV infection. *American Family Physician,* March, 1227–1237.

Seghorn, T., Prentky, R., & Boucher, R. (1987). Childhood sexual abuse in the lives of sexually aggressive offenders. *Journal of the American Academy of Child and Adolescent Psychiatry, 26,* 262–267.

Segovia, S., Guillamon, A., del Cerro, M., Ortega, E., Perez-Laso, C., Rodriquez-Zafra, M., & Beyer, C. (1999). The development of brain sex differences: A multisignaling process. *Behavioral Brain Research, 105,* 69–80.

Segraves, R., & Balon, R. (2003). *Sexual Pharmacology: Fast Facts.* New York: W. W. Norton.

Segraves, R., & Kavoussi, R. (2000). Evaluation of sexual functioning in depressed outpatients: A double-blind comparison of sustained-release bupropion and sertraline treatment. *Journal of Clinical Psychopharmacology, 20,* 122–128.

Segraves, R., & Segraves, K. (1995). Human sexuality and aging. *Journal of Sex Education and Therapy, 21,* 88–102.

Seibert, C., Barbouche, E., Fagan, J., & Myint, E. (2003). Prescribing oral contraceptives for women older than 35 years of age. *Annals of Internal Medicine, 138,* 54–64.

Seidman, S., & Rieder, R. (1994). A review of sexual behavior in the United States. *American Journal of Psychiatry, 151,* 330–341.

Seligman, L., & Hardenburg, S. (2000). Assessment and treatment of paraphilias. *Journal of Counseling and Development, 78,* 107–113.

Seligmann, J. (1992). A condom for women moves one step closer to reality. *Newsweek,* February 10, 45.

Sellors, J., Karwalajtyus, T., Kaczorowski, J., Mahony, J., Lytwyn, A., Chang, S., Sparrow, J., & Lorincz, A. (2003). Incidence, clearance and predictors of human papillomavirus viral infection in women. *Canadian Medical Association Journal, 168,* 421–425.

Selvin, E., & Brett, K. (2003). Breast and cervical cancer screening: Sociodemographic predictors among white, black, and Hispanic women. *American Journal of Public Health, 93,* 618–623.

Sem-Jacobsen, C. (1968). *Depth-Electrographic Stimulation of the Human Brain and Behavior.* Springfield, IL: Thomas.

Semans, J. (1956). Premature ejaculation: A new approach. *Southern Medical Journal, 49,* 353–358.

Senn, C., Desmarais, S., Verberg, N., & Wood, E. (1999). Predicting coercive sexual behavior across the lifespan in a random sample of Canadian men. *Journal of Social and Personal Relationships, 17,* 95–113.

Seomin, S. (2002, September 16). *Where Have All the Gay Characters Gone?* Retrieved April 22, 2003, from http://www.glaad.org/media/release_detail.php?id=3

Seomin, S. (2003, April 12). *ABC Daytime Debuts Lesbian Romance April 23 on* All My Children. Retrieved May 6, 2003, from http://www.glaad.org/media/newspops_detail.php?id=3355

Serbin, L. (1980). *The Pinks and the Blues.* Boston: WGBH Transcripts.

Seto, M., Lalumiere, M., & Kuban, M. (1999). The sexual preferences of incest offenders. *Journal of Abnormal Psychology, 108,* 267–272.

Sev'er, A. (1999). Sexual harassment: Where we are and prospects for the new millennium. *Canadian Review of Sociology and Anthropology, 36,* 469–482.

Severn, J., Belch, G., & Belch, M. (1990). The effects of sexual and non-sexual advertising appeals and information level on cognitive processing and communication effectiveness. *Journal of Advertising, 19,* 14–22.

Shah, S. (2003). *Drug Industry Seeks Viagra-Like Remedy for Women.* Retrieved June 30, 2003, from http://www.womensnews.org.article.cfm/dyn/aid/620/context/archive

Shainess, N., & Greenwald, H. (1971). Debate: Are fantasies during sexual relations a sign of difficulty? *Sexual Behavior, 1,* 38–54.

Shanks, L., Ford, N., Schull, M., & de Jong, K. (2001). Responding to rape. *The Lancet, 357,* 304.

Shapiro, F. (1995). Remarks presented at the opening ceremony of the International EMDR Conference, Santa Monica, California, June 23–25.

Shapiro, J. (1987). The expectant father. *Psychology Today,* January, 36–42.

Sharpsteen, D. (1995). *Sex, Attachment, and Infidelity: The Context of Jealousy.* Paper presented at the annual meeting of the Southwestern Psychological Association, Austin, Texas, April.

Sharpsteen, D., & Kirkpatrick, L. (1997). Romantic jealousy and adult romantic attachment. *Journal of Personality and Social Psychology, 72,* 627–640.

Sharts-Hopco, N. (1997). STDs in women: What you need to know. *American Journal of Nursing, 97,* 46–54.

Shattock, R., & Solomon, S. (2004). Microbicides: Aids to safer sex. *Lancet, 363,* 1002–1003.

Shaul, S., Bogle, J., Hale-Harbaugh, J., & Norman, A. (1978). *Toward Intimacy: Family Planning and Sexuality Concerns of Physically Disabled Women.* New York: Human Sciences Press.

Shaver, P., Hazan, C., & Bradshaw, D. (1988). Love as attachment: The integration of three behavioral systems. In R. Sternberg & M. Barnes (Eds.), *The Psychology of Love.* New Haven, CT: Yale University Press.

Shaw, C. (1997). The perimenopausal hot flash: Epidemiology, physiology, and treatment. *Nurse Practitioner, 22(3),* 55–66.

Shaw, J. (1994). Aging and sexual potential. *Journal of Sex Education and Therapy, 20(2),* 134–139.

Shaw, J. (1997). Treatment rationale for Internet infidelity. *Journal of Sex Education and Therapy, 22(1),* 21–28.

Shearer, B., Mulvihill, B., Klerman, L., Wallander, J., Hovinga, M., & Redden, D. (2002). Association of early childbearing and low cognitive ability. *Perspectives on Sexual and Reproductive Health, 34,* 236–243.

Sheeran, P. (1987). *Women, Society, the State, and Abortion: A Structuralist Analysis.* New York: Praeger.

Sheets, V., Fredendall, L., & Claypool, H. (1997). Jealousy evocation, partner reassurance, and relationship stability: An exploration of the potential benefits of jealousy. *Evolution and Human Behavior, 18,* 387–402.

Shell-Duncan, B. (2001). The medicalization of female "circumcision": Harm reduction or promotion of a dangerous practice? *Social Science and Medicine, 52,* 1,013–1,028.

Shelton, J. (2003). Folks on folk. *The Advocate,* May 13, 4.

Sherfer, T., Strebel, A., Wilson, T., Shabalala, N., Simbayi, L., Ratele, K., Potgieter, C., & Andipatin, M. (2002). The social construction of sexually transmitted infections (STIs) in South African communities. *Qualitative Health Research, 12,* 1373–1390.

Sherfey, M. (1972). *The Nature and Evolution of Female Sexuality.* New York: Random House.

Sherman, R., & Jones, J. (1994). A response to the article on "The validity of the Myers-Briggs Type Indicator for predicting marital problems." *Family Relations, 43,* 94–95.

Sherman, S. (2002). If our son is happy, what else matters? *Newsweek,* September 16, 12.

Sherwen, L. (1987). *Psychosocial Dimensions of the Pregnant Family.* New York: Springer.

Shidlo, A., Schroeder, M., Drescher, J. (2003). *Sexual Conversion Therapy: Ethical, Clinical, and Research Perspectives.* Binghamton, NY: Haworth Medical Press.

Shifen, J., Braunstein, G., Simon, J., Casson, P., Buster, J., Redmond, G., Burki, R., Ginsburg, E., Rosen, R., Leiblum, S., Carmelli, K., & Mazer, N. (2000). Transdermal testosterone treatment in women with impaired sexual function after oophorectomy. *New England Journal of Medicine, 34,* 682–688.

Shimonaka, Y., Nakazato, K., Kawaai, C., & Sato, S. (1997). Androgyny and successful adaptation across the life span among Japanese adults. *Journal of Genetic Psychology, 158,* 389–400.

Shlain, L. (2003). *Sex, Time, and Power: How Women's Sexuality Changed the Course of Human Evolution.* New York: Penguin.

Shotorbani, S., Zimmerman, F., Bell, J., Ward, D., & Assefi, N. (2004). Attitudes and intentions of future health care providers toward abortion provision. *Perspectives on Sexual and Reproductive Health, 36,* 50–57.

Shrier, L., Moszczenski, S., Emans, S., Laufer, M., & Woods, E. (2000). Three years of a clinical practice guideline for uncomplicated pelvic inflammatory disease in adolescents. *Journal of Adolescent Health, 27,* 57–62.

Shrier, L., Pierce, J., Emans, S., & DuRant, R. (1998). Gender differences in risk behaviors associated with forced or pressured sex. *Archives of Pediatric and Adolescent Medicine, 152,* 57–63.

Shuger, S. (2000). *Hookers.Com: How E-Commerce Is Transforming the Oldest Profession.* Retrieved January 31, 2000, from http://www.slate.msn.com/Features/intpro/intpro.asp

Shuit, D. (1996). Penile enlargement patients sue, say they were disfigured. *Los Angeles Times,* March 4, B1, B3.

SIECUS (1999a). Fact sheet on sexuality education. *SIECUS Report, 27,* 29–33.

SIECUS (1999b). Worldwide antidiscrimination laws and policies based on sexual orientation. *SIECUS Report, 27,* 19–22.

SIECUS (2000). Adding sexual orientation and gender identity to discrimination and harassment policies in schools. *SIECUS Report, 28,* 17–18.

SIECUS (2001). Sexuality in middle and later life. *SIECUS Report, 30(suppl.),* 1–6.

SIECUS (2003). *SIECUS Fact Sheet: The Truth About STDs.* New York: SIECUS.

SIECUS Fact Sheet (2002). Teenage pregnancy, birth, and abortion. *SIECUS Report, 30,* 39–43.

Siegal, M. (1987). Are sons and daughters treated more differently by fathers than by mothers? *Developmental Review, 7,* 183–209.

Siegel, K., Krauss, B., & Karus, D. (1994). Reporting recent sexual practices: Gay men's disclosure of HIV risk by questionnaire and interview. *Archives of Sexual Behavior, 23,* 217–230.

Siemens, R. (2003). Radical prostatectomy or watchful waiting in early prostate cancer. *Canadian Medical Association Journal, 168,* 67.

Sieving, R., Resnick, M., Bearinger, L., Remafedi, G., Taylor, B., & Harmon, B. (1997). Cognitive and behavioral predictors of sexually transmitted disease risk behavior among sexually active adolescents. *Archives of Pediatric and Adolescent Medicine, 151,* 243–252.

Signorile, M. (1995). *Outing Yourself.* New York: Fireside.

Sills, M., Chamberlain, J., & Teach, S. (2000). The associations among pediatricians' knowledge, attitudes, and practices regarding emergency contraception. *Pediatrics, 105,* 954–956.

Silver, M. (2002). What they're seeing: Yes, popular culture is as full of sex as ever, but kids are smarter about it than you might think. *U.S. News & World Report,* June 10, 41.

Silverman, B., & Gross, T. (1997). Use and effectiveness of condoms during anal intercourse. *Sexually Transmitted Diseases, 24,* 11–17.

Silvertsen, C. (2000). *Court: Discard Embryos.* Retrieved June 2, 2000, from http://abcnews.go.com/sections/us/DailyNews/embryos000602.html

Simon, H. (2003). Alternatives to Viagra. *Newsweek,* June 16, 63.

Simon, J. (1998). Managing the monstrous: Sex offenders and the new penology. *Psychology, Public Policy, and Law, 4,* 452–467.

Simon, J. (2001). *The Effects of Chronic Pain on Sexuality and Self-Esteem.* Paper presented at the 33rd Annual Conference of the American Association of Sex Educators, Counselors, and Therapists, San Francisco, May 2–6.

Simons, M. (2000). Bosnian Serb trial opens, first on wartime sex crimes. *New York Times,* March 21, A3.

Simonsen, G., Blazina, C., & Watkins, C. (2000). Gender role conflict and psychological well-being among gay men. *Journal of Counseling Psychology, 47,* 85–89.

Simonson, K., & Subich, L. (1999). Rape perceptions as a function of gender-role traditionality and victim-perpetrator association. *Sex Roles, 40,* 617–633.

Simunic, V., Banovic, I., & Ciglar, S. (2003). Local estrogen treatment in patients with urogenital symptoms. *International Journal of Gynecology and Obstetrics, 82,* 187–197.

Singer, L. (2002). Cognitive and motor outcomes of cocaine-exposed infants. *Journal of the American Medical Association, 287,* 1952–1960.

Singh, S., & Darroch, J. (2000). Adolescent pregnancy and childbearing levels and trends in developed countries. *Family Planning Perspectives, 32,* 14–23.

Sinnott, J. (1986). *Sex Roles and Aging: Theory and Research from a Systems Perspective.* Basel, Switzerland: Karger.

Sipe, A. (1990). *A Secret World: Sexuality and the Search for Celibacy.* New York: Brunner/Mazel.

Sipski, M., Rosen, R., Alexander, C., & Hamer, R. (2000). Sildenafil effects on sexual and cardiovascular responses in women with spinal cord injury. *Urology, 55,* 812–815.

Sirovich, B., Schwartz, L., & Woloshin, S. (2003). Screening men for prostate and colorectal cancer in the United States. *Journal of the American Medical Association, 289,* 1414–1420.

Siskind, V., Green, A., Bain, C., & Purdie, D. (2000). Beyond ovulation: Oral contraceptives and epithelial ovarian cancer. *Epidemiology, 11,* 106–110.

Skegg, K., Nada-Raja, S., & Dickson, N. (2003). Sexual orientation and self-harm in men and women. *American Journal of Psychiatry, 160,* 541–546.

Skene, A. (1880). Two important glands of the urethra. *American Journal of Obstetrics, 265,* 265–270.

Skolnick, A. (1992). *The Intimate Environment: Exploring Marriage and the Family.* New York: HarperCollins.

Slijper, F., Drop, S., Molenaar, J., & Keizer-Schrama, S. (1998). Long-term psychological evaluation of intersex children. *Archives of Sexual Behavior, 27,* 125–143.

Sloane, E. (1985). *Biology of Women* (2nd ed.). New York: Wiley.

Slowinski, J. (2001a). *The Sexual Male: Problems and Solutions.* Paper presented at the 33rd Annual Conference of the American Association of Sex Educators, Counselors, and Therapists, San Francisco, May 2–6.

Slowinski, J. (2001b). Therapeutic dilemmas: Solving sexual difficulties in the context of religion. *Journal of Sex Education and Therapy, 26,* 272–280.

Sluzki, C. (1982). The Latin lover revisited. In M. McGoldrick & J. Giordano (Eds.), *Ethnicity and Family Therapy.* New York: Guilford Press.

Small, M. (1999). Nosing out a mate. *Scientific American Presents, 10,* 52–55.

Small, S., & Kerns, D. (1993). Unwanted sexual activity among peers during early and middle adolescence: Incidence and risk factors. *Journal of Marriage and the Family, 55,* 941–952.

Smalley, S. (2003a). The perfect crime. *Newsweek,* February 3, 52.

Smalley, S. (2003b). "This could be your kid." *Newsweek,* August 18, 44–47.

Smeal, E. (2003). *Roe v. Wade* at 30: A bittersweet celebration. *Ms.,* December–January, 27–30.

Smeltzer, S., & Kelley, C. (1997). Multiple sclerosis. In M. Sipski & C. Alexander (Eds.), *Sexual Function in People with Disability and Chronic Illness.* Gaithersburg, MD: Aspen Publishers.

Smith, A., & Rockey, D. (2004). Viral hepatitis C. *Lancet, 363,* 661.

Smith, D. (1995). The dynamics of culture. *Treatment Today,* Spring, 15.

Smith, D. (2003). Women and sex: What is "dysfunctional"? *Monitor on Psychology, 34,* 54–56.

Smith, D., & Over, R. (1987). Correlates of fantasy-induced and film-induced male sexual arousal. *Archives of Sexual Behavior, 16,* 395–409.

Smith, M., & Morra, N. (1994). Obscene and threatening telephone calls to women: Data from a Canadian national survey. *Gender and Society, 8,* 584–596.

Smith, P., White, J., & Holland, L. (2003). A longitudinal perspective on dating violence among adolescent and college-age women. *American Journal of Public Health, 93,* 1104–1109.

Smith, R. (1985). Abortion, right and wrong. *Newsweek,* March 25, 16.

Smith, R., Saslow, D., Sawyer, K., & Burke, W. (2003). *American Cancer Society Guidelines for Breast Cancer Screening: Update 2003.* Retrieved October 6, 2003, from http://caonline.amcancersoc.org/cgi/content/full/53/3/141

Smith, S., & Ordonez, J. (2003). Now, that's what we call oral history. *Newsweek,* September 1, 63.

Smith, T. (1991). Adult sexual behavior in 1989: Number of partners, frequency of intercourse, and risk of AIDS. *Family Planning Perspectives, 23,* 102–107.

Smith, T., & Bhatnagar, K. (2000). The human vomeronasal organ. Part II. Prenatal development. *Journal of Anatomy, 197,* 421–436.

Smith, W. (2000). Balance of power in Washington presents both challenges and opportunities. *SIECUS Report, 29,* 19–20.

Smith-Bindman, R., Kerlikowske, K., Gebretsadik, T., & Newman, J. (2000). Is screening mammography effective in elderly women? *American Journal of Medicine, 108,* 112–119.

Smithyman, S. (1979). Characteristics of undetected rapists. In W. Parsonage (Ed.), *Perspectives on Victimology.* Beverly Hills, CA: Sage.

Snyder, H. (1991). To circumcise or not. *Hospital Practice,* January 15, 201–207.

Sobel, J., Faro, S., Force, R., Foxman, B., Ledger, W., Nyirjesy, P., Reed, B., & Summers, P. (1998). Vulvovaginal candidiasis: Epidemiologic, diagnostic, and therapeutic considerations. *American Journal of Obstetrics and Gynecology, 178,* 203–211.

Solomini, C. (1991). Cures for yeast infections. *New Woman,* May, 129.

Solomon, R. (1981). The love lost in cliches. *Psychology Today,* October, 83–94.

Sonenstein, F., Pleck, J., & Ku, L. (1991). Levels of sexual activity among adolescent males in the United States. *Family Planning Perspectives, 23,* 162–167.

Sonfield, A., Gold, R., Frost, J., & Darroch, J. (2004). U.S. insurance coverage of contraceptive coverage mandates, 2002. *Perspectives on Sexual and Reproductive Health, 36,* 72–77.

Sontag, D. (1997). Partial birth abortions. *The Oregonian,* March 22, A8.

Sontag, S. (1972). The double standard of aging. *Saturday Review,* September 23, 29–38.

Sorenson, R. (1973). *Adolescent Sexuality in Contemporary America.* New York: World.

Soules, M. (1999). Commentary: Posthumous harvesting of gametes—a physician's perspective. *Journal of Law, Medicine, and Ethics, 27,* 362–365.

South-Paul, J. (2003). Cross-cultural issues concerning sexuality, fertility, and childbirth. *Journal of the American Board of Family Practice, 16,* 180–181.

Soutter, W., De Barros Lopes, A., Fletcher, A., Monaghan, J., Duncan, I., Paraskevaidis, E., & Kitchener, H. (1997). Invasive cervical cancer after conservative therapy for cervical intraepithelial neoplasia. *The Lancet, 349,* 978–980.

Spake, A. (2001). Natural hazards. *U.S. News & World Report,* February 12, 43–49.

Span, S., & Vidal, L. (2003). Cross-cultural differences in female university students' attitudes toward homosexuals: A preliminary study. *Psychological Reports, 92,* 565–572.

Spector, I., & Carey, M. (1990). Incidence and prevalence of the sexual dysfunctions: A critical review of the empirical literature. *Archives of Sexual Behavior, 19,* 389–408.

Speed, A., & Gangestad, S. (1997). Romantic popularity and mate preferences: A peer-nomination study. *Personality and Social Psychology Bulletin, 23,* 928–936.

Spence, J., & Helmreich, R. (1978). *Masculinity and Femininity.* Austin: University of Texas Press.

Spencer, T., & Tan, J. (1999). Undergraduate students' reactions to analogue male disclosure of sexual abuse. *Journal of Child Sexual Abuse, 8,* 73–90.

Speroff, L., Blas, R., & Kase, N. (1989). *Clinical Gynecologic Endocrinology and Infertility.* Baltimore: Williams & Wilkins.

Spitzberg, B. (1999). An analysis of empirical estimates of sexual aggression, victimization, and perpetration. *Violence and Victims, 14,* 241–260.

Sponaugle, G. (1989). Attitudes toward extramarital relations. In K. McKinney & S. Sprecher (Eds.), *Human Sexuality: The Societal and Interpersonal Context.* Norwood, NJ: Ablex.

Sprauve, M., Lindsay, M., Herbert, S., & Graves, W. (1997). Adverse perinatal outcome in parturients who use crack cocaine. *Obstetrics and Gynecology, 89,* 674–678.

Sprecher, S. (2002). Sexual satisfaction in premarital relationships: Associations with satisfaction, love, commitment, and stability. *Journal of Sex Research, 39,* 190–196.

Sprecher, S., & Hatfield, E. (1996). Premarital sexual standards among U.S. college students: Comparison with Russian and Japanese students. *Archives of Sexual Behavior, 25,* 261–288.

Sprecher, S., & McKinney, K. (1993). *Sexuality.* Newbury Park, CA: Sage.

Sprecher, S., Metts, S., Burleson, B., Hatfield, E., & Thompson, A. (1995). Domains of expressive interaction in intimate relationships: Associations with satisfaction and commitment. *Family Relations, 44,* 203–210.

Sprecher, S., & Regan, P. (1998). Passionate and companionate love in courting and young married couples. *Sociological Inquiry, 68,* 163–185.

Sprecher, S., Regan, P., McKinney, K., Maxwell, K., & Wazienski, R. (1997). Preferred level of sexual experience in a date or mate: The merging of two methodologies. *Journal of Sex Research, 34,* 327–337.

Sprecher, S., Sullivan, Q., & Hatfield, E. (1994). Mate selection preferences: Gender differences examined in a national sample. *Journal of Personality and Social Psychology, 66,* 1074–1080.

Spring-Mills, E., & Hafez, E. (1980). Male accessory sexual organs. In E. Hafez (Ed.), *Human Reproduction.* New York: Harper & Row.

Springen, K. (1999). Comeback of a contraceptive: The sponge returns. *Newsweek,* April 12, 69.

Springen, K. (2000). The right to choose. *Newsweek,* December 4, 73–74.

Springen, K. (2003). New year, new breasts? *Newsweek,* January 13, 65–66.

Spruyt, A., Steiner, M., Joanis, C., Glover, L., Piedrahita, C., Alvarado, G., Ramos, R., Maglaya, C., & Cordero, M. (1998). Identifying condom users at risk for breakage and slippage: Findings from three international sites. *American Journal of Public Health, 88,* 239–244.

Srivastava, A., & Krieger, N. (2000). Relation of physical activity to risk of testicular cancer. *American Journal of Epidemiology, 151,* 78–87.

Sroufe, L. (1985). Attachment classification from the perspective of infant–caregiver relationships and infant temperament. *Child Development, 56,* 1–14.

Sroufe, L., Fox, N., & Pancake, V. (1983). Attachment and dependency in a developmental perspective. *Child Development, 54,* 1615–1627.

Srugo, I., Gershtein, R., Madjar, S., Elias, I., Tal, J., & Nativ, O. (2000). Acute primary *Chlamydia trachomatis* infection in male adolescents after their first sexual contact. *Archives of Pediatric Adolescent Medicine, 154,* 169–172.

Stack, S., & Gundlach, J. (1992). Divorce and sex. *Archives of Sexual Behavior, 21,* 359–368.

Stahlberg, C., Pedersen, A., Lynge, E., Ottesen, B. (2003). Hormone replacement therapy and risk of breast cancer: The role of progestins. *Acta Obstetricia et Gynecologica Scandinavica, 82,* 335–344.

Stall, R., McResnick, L., Wiley, J., Coates, T., & Ostrow, D. (1996). Alcohol and drug use during sexual activity and compliance with safe sex guidelines for AIDS. *Health Education Quarterly, 13,* 359–371.

Stanberry, L. (2000). Asymptomatic herpes simplex virus shedding and Russian roulette. *Clinical Infectious Diseases, 30,* 268–269.

Stanberry, L., Spruance, S., & Cunningham, A. (2002). Glycoprotein-D-adjuvant vaccine to prevent genital herpes. *New England Journal of Medicine, 347,* 1652–1661.

Stander, V., Olson, C., & Merrill, L. (2002). Self-definition as a survivor of childhood sexual abuse among navy recruits. *Journal of Consulting and Clinical Psychology, 70,* 369–377.

Stanecki, K. (2002). The AIDS pandemic in the 21st century. Washington, DC: U.S. Census Bureau. Unpublished data cited by T. Summers, J. Kates, & G. Murphy in "The global impact of HIV/AIDS on young people," *SIECUS Report, 31,* 14–23 (2002).

Stanford, C. (2000). Darwinians look at rape, sex, and war. *American Scientist, 88,* 360.

Stanford, J., Lemaire, J., & Thurman, P. (1998). Women's interest in natural family planning. *Journal of Family Practice, 46,* 65–71.

Stanley, D. (1993). To what extent is the practice of autoerotic asphyxia related to other paraphilias? In K. Haas & A. Haas (Eds.), *Understanding Sexuality.* St. Louis: Mosby.

Staropoli, C., Flaws, J., Bush, T., & Moulton, A. (1997). *Cigarette Smoking and Frequency of Menopausal Hot Flashes.* Abstract for the 30th Annual Meeting of the Society for Epidemiologic Research, Edmonton, Alberta, Canada, 71.

Starr, B., & Weiner, M. (1981). *The Starr Weiner Report on Sex and Sexuality in the Mature Years.* New York: Stein & Day.

Starr, C. (1997). Beyond the birds and the bees: Talking to teens about sex. *Patient Care,* April 15, 103–129.

State House Network–LPITR (2000). *State of South Carolina, Bill 470.* Retrieved September 13, 2000, from http://www.scstatehouse.net

Staten, C. (1997). "Roofies": The new "date rape" drug of choice. *Emergency Net News,* October 21.

Stearns, S. (2001). PMS and PMDD in the domain of mental health nursing. *Journal of Psychosocial Nursing, 39,* 16–27.

Stearns, V., Beebe, K., Iyengar, M., & Dube, E. (2003). Paroxetine controlled release in the treatment of menopausal hot flashes: A randomized controlled trial. *Journal of the American Medical Association, 289,* 2827–2834.

Stebleton, M., & Rothenberger, J. (1993). Truth or consequences: Dishonesty in dating and HIV/AIDS-related issues in a college-age population. *Journal of American College Health, 42,* 51–54.

Steele, B. (2003). The gay rights makeover. *The Advocate,* September 2, 42–43.

Steele, J. (1999). Teenage sexuality and media practice: Factoring in the influences of family, friends, and school. *Journal of Sex Research, 36,* 331–341.

Stein, A. (2001). *The Stranger Next Door.* Boston: Beacon Press.

Stein, E. (1999). *The Mismeasure of Desire.* Oxford: Oxford University Press.

Stein, J. (2000). Body: Matters of weight. *The Sunday Oregonian,* July 16, L13.

Stein, J., & Reiser, L. (1994). A study of white middle-class adolescent boys' responses to "semenarche" (the first ejaculation). *Journal of Youth and Adolescence, 23,* 373–384.

Stein, L. (2003, August 11). *Gay Marriage.* Retrieved September 1, 2003, from http://infotrac-college.thomsonlearning.com/itw/infomark/760/291/35557478w7/7!ar_fmt

Stein, M., Freedberg, K., Sullivan, L., Savetsky, J., Levenson, S., Hingson, R., & Samet, J. (1998). Disclosure of HIV-positive status to partners. *Archives of Internal Medicine, 158,* 253–257.

Stein, Z., Myer, L., & Susser, M. (2003). The design of prophylactic trails for HIV: The case for microbicides. *Epidemiology, 14,* 80–83.

Steinem, G. (1997). What's wrong with this picture? *Ms.,* March–April, 76.

Steinem, G. (1998). Erotic and pornography: A clear and present difference. In R. Baird & S. Rosenbaum (Eds.), *Pornography: Private Right or Public Menace?* Amherst, NY: Prometheus Books.

Steinhauer, J. (1998). Viagra's other side effect: Upsets in many a marriage. *New York Times,* June 23, B9.

Steininger, C., Kundi, M., Jatzko, G., Kiss, H., Lischka, A., & Holzman, H. (2003). Increased risk of mother-to-infant transmission of hepatitis C virus by intrapartum infantile exposure to maternal blood. *Journal of Infectious Diseases, 187,* 345–351.

Stenager, E., Stenager, E. N., Jensen, K., & Boldsen, J. (1990). Multiple sclerosis: Sexual dysfunctions. *Journal of Sex Education and Therapy, 16,* 262–269.

Stener-Victorin, E., Waldenstrom, U., & Tagnfors, U. (2000). Effects of electroacupuncture on anovulation in women with polycystic ovary syndrome. *Acta Obstetricia et Gynecologica Scandinavica, 79,* 180–188.

Stenger, R. (2001, February 7). *Implant Could Help Women with Sexual Dysfunction.* Retrieved from http://www.cnn.com/2001/HEALTH/02/07/orgasm.device/index.html

Stephen, T., & Harrison, T. (1985). A longitudinal comparison of couples with sex-typical and non-sex-typical orientation to intimacy. *Sex Roles, 12,* 195–206.

Stephenson, J. (2003a). A hormone-free male "pill"? *Journal of the American Medical Association, 289,* 164.

Stephenson, J. (2003b). Male infertility: Little help from varicocele repair. *Journal of the American Medical Association, 289,* 2929.

Stermac, L., Sheridan, P., Davidson, A., & Dunn, S. (1996). Sexual assault of adult males. *Journal of Interpersonal Violence, 11,* 52–64.

Stern, E. (1987). Sex during pregnancy. *American Baby,* March, 71–79.

Sternberg, R. (1986). A triangular theory of love. *Psychological Review, 93,* 119–135.

Sternberg, R. (1988). Triangulating love. In R. Sternberg & M. Barnes (Eds.), *The Psychology of Love.* New Haven, CT: Yale University Press.

Stevens-Simon, C., Kelly, L., & Singer, D. (1996). Absence of negative attitudes toward childrearing among pregnant teenagers: A risk factor for repeat pregnancy. *Archives of Pediatric and Adolescent Medicine, 150,* 1037–1043.

Stevermer, J. (2001). Is there any benefit to Papanicolaou (Pap) test screening in women who have had a hysterectomy for benign disease? *Journal of Family Practice, 50,* 111–112.

Stewart, B., Hughes, C., Frank, E., Anderson, B., Kendall, K., & West, D. (1987). The aftermath of rape: Profiles of immediate and delayed treatment seekers. *Journal of Nervous and Mental Disorders, 175,* 90–94.

Stewart, F. (1998a). Menopause. In R. Hatcher, J. Trussell, F. Stewart, W. Cates, G. Stewart, F. Guest, & D. Kowal (Eds.), *Contraceptive Technology.* New York: Ardent Media.

Stewart, F. (1998b). Pregnancy testing and management of early pregnancy. In R. Hatcher, J. Trussell, F. Stewart, W. Cates, G. Stewart, F. Guest, & D. Kowal (Eds.), *Contraceptive Technology.* New York: Ardent Media.

Stewart, F. (1998c). Vaginal barriers. In R. Hatcher, J. Trussell, F. Stewart, W. Cates, G. Stewart, F. Guest, & D. Kowal (Eds.), *Contraceptive Technology.* New York: Ardent Media.

Stewart, G. (1998). Intrauterine devices (IUDs). In R. Hatcher, J. Trussell, F. Stewart, W. Cates, G. Stewart, F. Guest, & D. Kowal (Eds.), *Contraceptive Technology.* New York: Ardent Media.

Stewart, G., & Carignan, C. (1998). Female and male sterilization. In R. Hatcher, J. Trussell, F. Stewart, W. Cates, G. Stewart, F. Guest, & D. Kowal (Eds.), *Contraceptive Technology.* New York: Ardent Media.

Stier, D., Leventhal, J., Berg, A., Johnson, L., & Mezger, J. (1993). Are children born to young mothers at increased risk of maltreatment? *Pediatrics, 91,* 642–648.

Stimson, A., Wase, J., & Stimson, J. (1981). Sexuality and self-esteem among the aged. *Research in Aging, 3,* 228–239.

Stock, W. (1985). *The Effect of Pornography on Women.* Paper presented at a hearing of the Attorney General's Commission on Pornography, Houston, September 11–12.

Stockwell, A. (1998). Yep, she rules. *The Advocate,* January 20, 92.

Stolberg, S. (1999). Racial health gap widest at childbirth. *The Sunday Oregonian,* August 8, A3.

Stolberg, S. (2001). Couple offer embryos for adoption. *The Sunday Oregonian,* February 25, A9.

Stoler, M. (2000). Human papillomaviruses and cervical neoplasmia: A model for carcinogenesis. *International Journal of Gynecological Pathology, 19,* 16–28.

Stoller, R. (1977). Sexual deviations. In F. Beach (Ed.), *Human Sexuality in Four Perspectives.* Baltimore: Johns Hopkins University Press.

Stoller, R. (1982). Transvestism in women. *Archives of Sexual Behavior, 11,* 99–115.

Stoller, R., & Herdt, G. (1985). Theories of origins of male homosexuality. *Archives of General Psychiatry, 42,* 399–404.

Stomberg, B., Dahlquist, G., & Ericson, A. (2002). Neurological sequelae in children born after in vitro fertilization: A population-based study. *The Lancet, 359,* 461–465.

Stone, N., & Ingham, R. (2002). Factors affecting British teenager's contraceptive use at first intercourse: The importance of partner communication. *Perspectives on Sexual and Reproductive Health, 34,* 191–197.

Stone, R., & Waszak, C. (1992). Adolescent knowledge and attitudes about abortion. *Family Planning Perspectives, 24,* 52–58.

Storms, M. (1980). Theories of sexual orientation. *Journal of Personality and Social Psychology, 38,* 783–792.

Stotland, N. (1998). *Abortion Facts and Feelings.* Washington, DC: American Psychiatric Press.

Stott-Kendall, N. (1997). *Torn Illusions.* Fort Lauderdale, FL: Debcar.

Stranc, L., Evans, J., & Hamerton, J. (1997). Chorionic villus sampling and amniocentesis for prenatal diagnosis. *The Lancet, 349,* 711–714.

Strand, A., Wilander, E., Zehbe, I., & Rylander, E. (1997). High risk HPV persists after treatment of genital papillomavirus infection but not after treatment of cervical intraepithelial neoplasia. *Acta Obstetricia et Gynecologica Scandinavica, 76,* 140–144.

Strassberg, D., & Lockerd, L. (1998). *Force in Women's Sexual Fantasies.* Retrieved September 2, 2003, from http://infotrac-college.thomson-learning.com/itw/infomark/684/939/38133136w6/3!xrn_4_0 . . .

Strassberg, D., & Mahoney, J. (1988). Correlates of contraceptive behavior of adolescents/young adults. *Journal of Sex Research, 25,* 531–536.

Strauss, S., Des Jarlais, D., Astone, J., & Vassilev, Z. (2003). On-site HIV testing in residential drug treatment units: Results of a nationwide survey. *Public Health Reports, 118,* 37–43.

Striar, S., & Bartlik, B. (2000). Stimulation of the libido: The use of erotica in sex therapy. *Psychiatric Annals, 29,* 60–62.

Strong, C. (1999). Ethical and legal aspects of sperm retrieval after death or persistent vegetative state. *Journal of Law, Medicine, and Ethics, 27,* 347–358.

Struckman-Johnson, C., & Struckman-Johnson, D. (2000). Sexual coercion rates in seven midwestern prison facilities for men. *Prison Journal, 80,* 379–390.

Struckman-Johnson, C., Struckman-Johnson, D., & Anderson, P. (2003). Tactics of sexual coercion: When men and women won't take no for an answer. *Journal of Sex Research, 40,* 76–86.

Stuart, F., Hammond, C., & Pett, M. (1998). Inhibited sexual desire in women. *Archives of Sexual Behavior, 16,* 91–106.

Stubblefield, P., & Grimes, D. (1994). Septic abortion. *New England Journal of Medicine, 331,* 310–313.

Stubbs, K. (1992). *Sacred Orgasms.* Berkeley, CA: Secret Garden.

Stutts, M., Patterson, L., & Hunnicutt, G. (1997). Females' perception of risks associated with alcohol consumption during pregnancy. *American Journal Health Behavior, 21(2),* 137–146.

Suggs, R. (1962). *The Hidden Worlds of Polynesia.* New York: Harcourt, Brace & World.

Sugrue, D. (2000). President's column. *Contemporary Sexuality, 34,* 3.

Suligoi, B. (1997). The natural history of human immunodeficiency virus infection among women as compared with men. *Sexually Transmitted Diseases, 24,* 77–83.

Sullivan, A. (1996). Let gays marry. *Newsweek,* June 3, 26.

Sullivan, A. (1997). Winning the religious war. *The Advocate,* October 14, 91–93.

Sullivan, A. (1998). The marriage moment. *The Advocate,* January 20, 59–67.

Sullivan, A. (2003). *Beware the Straight Backlash: Queer Eye Takes a Step Forward, but the Conflict over Gay Marriage Could Get Ugly.* Retrieved from http://infotrac-college.thomsonlearning.com/itw/infomark/760/291/35557578w7/5!ar_fmt

Sullivan, A. (2004). The sacred and the pop star. *The Advocate,* February 17, 72.

Sullivan, K., & Bradbury, T. (1997). Are premarital prevention programs reaching couples at risk for marital dysfunction? *Journal of Consulting and Clinical Psychology, 65,* 24–30.

Summers, T., Kates, J., & Murphy, G. (2002). The global impact of HIV/AIDS on young people. *SIECUS Report, 31,* 14–23.

Sun, C., Wu, D., Lin, C., Lu, S., You, S., Wong, L., Wu, M., & Chen, C. (2003). Incidence and cofactors of hepatitis C virus-related hepatacellular carcinoma: A prospective study of 12,008 men in Taiwan. *American Journal of Epidemiology, 157,* 674–682.

Sundt, M. (1994). *Identifying the Attitudes and Beliefs That Accompany Sexual Harassment.* Ph.D. dissertation, University of California, Los Angeles.

Superville, D. (1996). Genital mutilation ruled persecution. *The Oregonian,* June 15, A8.

Surra, C., & Hughes, D. (1997). Commitment processes in accounts of the development of premarital relationships. *Journal of Marriage and the Family, 59,* 5–21.

Surrogate Mothers Inc. (2003). *Surrogate Mothers Inc.: Approximate Expenses.* Retrieved August 17, 2003, from http://www.surrogatemothers.com/expense.html

Sweet, M. (2001). *Inventing the Victorians.* New York: St. Martin's Press.

Swiss, S., & Giller, J. (1993). Rape as a crime of war. *Journal of the American Medical Association, 270,* 612–615.

Symes, L. (2000). Arriving at readiness to recover emotionally after sexual assault. *Archives of Psychiatric Nursing, 14,* 30–38.

Synovitz, L., & Byrne, J. (1998). Antecedents of sexual victimization: Factors discriminating victims from nonvictims. *Journal of American College Health, 46,* 151–158.

Sytsma, M., & Taylor, D. (2001). *A Model for Addressing Low Sexual Desire in Married Couples.* Paper presented at the 33rd Annual Conference of the American Association of Sex Educators, Counselors, and Therapists, San Francisco, May 2–6.

Tabár, L., Chen, H., Duffy, S., Yen, M., Chiang, C., Dean, P., & Smith, R. (2000). A novel method for prediction of long-term outcome of women with T1a, T1b, and 10–14 mm invasive breast cancers: A prospective study. *The Lancet, 355,* 429–433.

Taddio, A., Katz, J., Ilevsich, A., & Koren, G. (1997a). Effects of neonatal circumcision on pain response during subsequent routine vaccination. *The Lancet, 349,* 599–603.

Taddio, A., Stevens, B., Craig, K., Rastogi, P., Ben-David, S., Shennan, A., Mulligan, P., & Koren, G. (1997b). Efficacy and safety of lidocaine-prilocaine cream for pain during circumcision. *New England Journal of Medicine, 336,* 1197–1201.

Talamini, J. (1982). *Boys Will Be Girls: The Hidden World of the Heterosexual Male Transvestite.* Washington, DC: University Press of America.

Taleporos, G., & McCabe, M. (2002). The impact of sexual esteem, body esteem, and sexual satisfaction on psychological well-being in people with physical disability. *Sexuality and Disability, 20,* 177–183.

Tanenbaum, L. (1997). Can sperm affect fetal health? *Ms.,* March–April, 31.

Tang, C., & Chung, T. (1997). Psychosexual adjustment following sterilization: A prospective study on Chinese women. *Journal of Psychosomatic Research, 42(2),* 187–196.

Tangeman, R. (2003). Personal communication.

Tannen, D. (1990). *You Just Don't Understand: Women and Men in Conversation.* New York: Ballantine Books (paperback edition, 1991).

Tannen, D. (1994). *Gender and Discourse.* New York: Oxford University Press.

Tao, G., Irvin, K., & Kassler, W. (2000). Missed opportunities to assess sexually transmitted diseases in U.S. adults during routine medical checkups. *American Journal of Preventive Medicine, 18,* 109–114.

Task Force on Circumcision (1999). Circumcision policy statement. *Pediatrics, 103,* 686–693.

Tate, R. (2001). The battle to be a parent. *The Advocate,* January 30, 35–39.

Tate-O'Brien, J. (1981). *Love in Deed: Manual for Engaged Couples.* St. Paul, MN: International Marriage Encounter.

Tavris, C., & Sadd, S. (1977). The Redbook *Report on Female Sexuality.* New York: Delacorte.

Taylor, E., & Sharkey, L. (2003). *The Big Bang.* New York: Plume.

Taylor, J. (1971). Introduction. In R. Haber & C. Eden (Eds.), *Holy Living* (rev. ed.). New York: Adler.

Taylor, J. (1995). The long, hard days of Dr. Dick. *Esquire,* September, 120–123.

Taylor, R. (1970). *Sex in History.* New York: Harper & Row.

Teachman, J. (2003). Premarital sex, premarital cohabitation, and the risk of subsequent marital dissolution among women. *Journal of Marriage and the Family, 65,* 444–455.

Templeman, T., & Sinnett, R. (1991). Patterns of sexual arousal and history in a "normal" sample of young men. *Archives of Sexual Behavior, 20,* 137–150.

Tennov, D. (1979). *Love and Limerence.* New York: Stein & Day.

Tenore, J. (2000). Ectopic pregnancy. *American Family Physician, 61,* 1080–1088.

Tepper, M. (2000). *Pleasure and Orgasm in Men and Women with Spinal Cord Injuries: Implication for Sexology.* Paper presented at the 32nd Annual Conference of the American Association of Sex Educators, Counselors, and Therapists, Atlanta, Georgia, May 10–14.

Terry, J. (1990). Lesbians under the medical gaze: Scientists search for remarkable differences. *Journal of Sex Research, 27,* 317–339.

Thaker, H., & Snow, M. (2003). HIV viral suppression in the era of antiretroviral therapy. *Postgraduate Medicine, 79,* 36–42.

Tharaux-Deneux, C., Bouyer, J., Job-Spira, N., Coste, J., & Spira, A. (1998). Risk of ectopic pregnancy and previous induced abortion. *American Journal of Public Health, 88(3),* 401–405.

Thomas, E. (2001). Motherhood and murder. *Newsweek,* July 2, 20–25.

Thomas, L. E. (1991). Correlates of sexual interest among elderly men. *Psychological Reports, 68,* 620–622.

Thomas, M. (2000). Abstinence-based programs for prevention of adolescent pregnancies. *Journal of Adolescent Health, 26,* 5–17.

Thompson, J. (2003a). Preconceptual care, Part 2. *Community Practitioner, 76,* 143–144.

Thompson, J. (2003b). Pregnancy, Part 4. *Community Practitioner, 76,* 269–270.

Thomson, E. (2000). New conceptions on issues of fertility. *Nursing Times, 96,* 18–19.

Thornburg, H., & Aras, A. (1986). Physical characteristics of developing adolescents. *Journal of Adolescent Research, 1,* 47–78.

Thorne, S., & Murray, C. (2000). Social constructions of breast cancer. *Health Care for Women International, 21,* 141–159.

Thornhill, R., & Palmer, C. (2000). *A Natural History of Rape: Biological Bases of Sexual Coercion.* Boston: MIT Press.

Tice, J., Ettinger, B., Ensrud, K., & Wallace R. (2003). Phytoestrogen supplements for the treatment of hot flashes: The Isoflavone Clover Extract (ICE) Study—a randomized controlled trial. *Journal of the American Medical Association, 290,* 207–214.

Tiefer, L. (1995). *Sex Is Not a Natural Act and Other Essays.* Boulder, CO: Westview Press.

Tiefer, L. (1999). In pursuit of the perfect penis: The medicalization of male sexuality. In K. Lebacqz & D. Sinacore-Guinn (Eds.), *Sexuality: A Reader.* Cleveland: Pilgrim Press.

Tilton, M. (1997). Diabetes and amputation. In M. Sipski & C. Alexander (Eds.), *Sexual Function in People with Disability and Chronic Illness.* Gaithersburg, MD: Aspen Publishers.

Timmer, S., & Orbuch, T. (2001). The links between premarital parenthood, meanings of marriage, and marital outcomes. *Family Relations, 50,* 178–185.

Timmerman, J. (2001). When religion is its own worst enemy: How therapists can help people shed hurtful notions that masquerade as good theology. *Journal of Sex Education and Therapy, 26,* 259–266.

Ting-Toomey, S., & Korzenny, F. (Eds.) (1991). *Cross-Cultural Interpersonal Communication.* Newbury Park, CA: Sage.

Tingulstad, S., Skjeldestad, F., Halvorsen, T., & Hagen, B. (2003). Survival and prognostic factors in patients with ovarian cancer. *Obstetrics and Gynecology, 101,* 885–891.

Tipton, N. (2003). American television, drama. In C. Summers (Ed.), *An Encyclopedia of Gay, Lesbian, Bisexual, Transgender, and Queer Culture.* Chicago: GLBTQ Inc.

Tjaden, P., & Thoennes, N. (1998). *Prevalence, Incidence, and Consequences of Violence Against Women: Findings from the National Violence Against Women Survey.* Washington, DC: National Institutes of Justice.

Todd, C., Jones, R., Golichowski, A., & Arno, J. (1997). *Chlamydia trachomatis* and febrile complications of postpartum tubal ligation. *American Journal of Obstetrics and Gynecology, 176,* 100–102.

Tollison, C., & Adams, H. (1979). *Sexual Disorders: Treatment, Theory, Research.* New York: Gardner.

Tolman, D., & Szalacha, L. (1999). Dimension of desire: Bridging qualitative and quantitative methods in a study of female adolescent sexuality. *Psychology of Women Quarterly, 23,* 7–40.

Tolson, J. (2000). No wedding? No ring? No problem. *U.S. News & World Report,* March 13, 48.

Tone, A. (2002). The contraceptive conundrum. *SIECUS Report, 31,* 4–8.

Toner, J. (2002). Progress we can be proud of: U.S. trends in assisted reproduction over the first 20 years. *Fertility and Sterility, 78,* 943–950.

Torassa, U. (2000). *S.F. Study: HIV Spread Through Oral Sex.* Retrieved February 1, 2000, from http://www.examiner.com/oral.html

Torpy, J. (2003). Perimenopause: Beginning of menopause. *Journal of the American Medical Association, 289,* 940.

Torres, J. (1998). Masculinity and gender roles among Puerto Rican men: Machismo on the U.S. mainland. *American Journal of Orthopsychiatry, 68,* 16–26.

Totten, P., Schwartz, M., Sjostrom, K., Kenny, G., Handsfield, H., Weiss, J., & Whittington, W. (2001). Association of *Mycoplasma genitalium* with nongonococcal urethritis in heterosexual men. *Journal of Infectious Diseases, 183,* 269–276.

Toufexis, A. (1993). The right chemistry. *Time,* February 15, 49–51.Tourangeau, R., Rasinski, K., Jobe, J., Smith, T., & Pratt, W. (1997). Sources of error in a survey on sexual behavior. *Journal of Official Statistics, 13,* 341–365.

Toussie-Weingarten, C., & Jacobwitz, J. (1987). Alternatives in childbearing: Choices and challenges. In L. Sherwen (Ed.), *Psychosocial Dimensions of the Pregnant Family.* New York: Springer.

Townsend, J. (1995). Sex without emotional involvement: An evolutionary interpretation of sex differences. *Archives of Sexual Behavior, 24,* 173–182.

Townsend, J., & Wasserman, T. (1998). Sexual attractiveness: Sex differences in assessment and criteria. *Evolution and Human Behavior, 19,* 171–191.

Trafimow, D., Triandis, H., & Goto, S. (1991). Some tests of the distinction between the private self and the collective self. *Journal of Personality and Social Psychology, 60,* 649–655.

Trager, R. (2003). Raising new barriers against HIV infection. *Science, 299,* 39.

Traish, A., Kim, K., Munarriz, R., & Goldstein, I. (2002a). Role of androgens in female genital sexual arousal: Receptor expression, structure, and function. *Fertility and Sterility, 77(suppl. 4)*, 511–518.

Traish, A., Noel, K., Min, K., Munarriz, R., & Goldstein, I. (2002b). Androgens in female genital sexual arousal functions: A biochemical perspective. *Journal of Sex and Marital Therapy, 28(suppl.)*, 233–244.

Travis, C. (2000). The uproar over sexual abuse research and its findings. *Society, 37*, 15–17.

Treas, J., & Giesen, D. (2000). Sexual infidelity among married and cohabiting Americans. *Journal of Marriage and the Family, 62*, 48–60.

Trebilcock, B. (1997). Child molesters on the Internet: Are they in your home? *Redbook*, April, 100–103, 136–138.

Trevor, C. (2002). Number of controversies decline as schools adopt conservative policies. *SIECUS Report, 30*, 4–17.

Tripp, C. (1975). *The Homosexual Matrix*. New York: McGraw-Hill.

Trivedi, N., & Sabini, J. (1998). Volunteer bias, sexuality, and personality. *Archives of Sexual Behavior, 27*, 181–195.

Trocme, N., Fallon, B., MacLaurin, B., & Copp, B. (2002). *The Changing Face of Child Welfare Investigations in Ontario: Ontario Incidence Studies of Reported Child Abuse and Neglect*. Toronto: Centre of Excellence for Child Welfare, Faculty of Social Work, University of Toronto.

Troiden, R. (1988). *Gay and Lesbian Identity: A Sociological Analysis*. New York: General Hall.

Trostle, L. (2003). Overrating pornography as a source of sex information for university students: Additional consistent findings. *Psychological Reports, 92*, 143–150.

Truitt, W., & Coolen, L. (2002). Identification of a potential ejaculation generator in the spinal cord. *Science, 297*, 1566–1599.

Trull, D. (2003). *Invasion of the Penis Snatchers*. Retrieved March 13, 2003, from http://www.noveltynat.org/paranormal/www.pariscope.com/articles7196/penis.htm

Truman, D., Tokar, D., & Fischer, A. (1996). Dimensions of masculinity: Relations to date rape supportive attitudes and sexual aggression in dating situations. *Journal of Counseling and Development, 74*, 555–562.

Trussell, J. (1988). Teenage pregnancy in the United States. *Family Planning Perspectives, 20*, 262–273.

Trussell, J., Duran, V., Shochet, T., & Moore, K. (2000). Access to emergency contraception. *Obstetrics and Gynecology, 95*, 267–270.

Trussell, J., Koenig, J., Ellertson, C., & Stewart, F. (1997). Preventing unintended pregnancy: The cost-effectiveness of three methods of emergency contraception. *American Journal of Public Health, 87*, 932–933.

Trussell, J., Vaughan, B., & Stanford, J. (1999). Are all contraceptive failures unintended pregnancies? Evidence from the 1995 National Survey of Family Growth. *Family Planning Perspectives, 31*, 246–247.

Tudge, C. (1991). Can we end rhino poaching? *New Scientist, 132*, 34–35.

Tuiten, A., Van Honk, J., Koppeschaar, H., Bernaards, C., Thijssen, J., & Verbaten, R. (2000). Time course of effects of testosterone administration on sexual arousal in women. *Archives of General Psychiatry, 57*, 149–153.

Tullman, G., Gilner, F., Kolodny, R., Dornbush, R., & Tullman, G. (1981). The pre- and post-therapy measurement of communication skills of couples undergoing sex therapy at the Masters & Johnson Institute. *Archives of Sexual Behavior, 10*, 95–99.

Turner, C., Ku, L., Rogers, S., Lindberg, L., Pleck, J., & Sonenstein, F. (1998). Adolescent sexual behavior, drug use, and violence: Increased reporting with computer surveys. *Technological Science, 280*, 867–873.

Turner, H. (1999). Participation bias in AIDS-related telephone surveys: Results from the National AIDS Behavior Study (NABS) nonresponse study. *Journal of Sex Research*, 52–58.

Turner, K., McFarland, W., Kellogg, T., Wong, E., Page-Shafer, K., Louie, B., Dilley, J., Kent, C., & Klausner, J. (2003). Incidence and prevalence of herpes simplex virus type 2 infections in persons seeking repeat HIV counseling and testing. *Sexually Transmitted Diseases, 30*, 331–334.

Tyre, P. (2004). A new generation gap. *Newsweek*, January 19, 68–75.

Ubell, E. (1984). Sex in America today. *Parade*, October 28, 11–13.

Ullman, S., & Brecklin, L. (2003). Sexual assault history and health-related outcomes in a national sample of women. *Psychology of Women Quarterly, 27*, 46–57.

UNAIDS (2001a). *Children and Young People in a World of AIDS*. New York: United Nations.

UNAIDS (2001b). *Global Crisis, Global Action*. New York: United Nations.

UNAIDS (2003). *HIV/AIDS Statistics: Global Trends in the Epidemic*. Retrieved May 30, 2003, from http://www.sfaf.org/aboutaids/statistics/global.html

Unger, J., & Molina, G. (2000). Acculturation and attitudes about contraceptive use among Latina women. *Health Care for Women International, 21*, 235–249.

Unger, R., & Crawford, M. (1992). *Women and Gender: A Feminist Psychology*. New York: McGraw-Hill.

United Nations Commission (1959). *Study on Traffic in Persons and Prostitution*. ST/SOA/5D/8. New York: United Nations.

U.S. Attorney General's Commission on Pornography (1986). *Final Report of the Attorney General's Commission on Pornography*. Washington, DC: U.S. Justice Department.

U.S. Bureau of the Census (1978). *Statistical Abstract of the United States: 1978*. Washington, DC: U.S. Government Printing Office.

U.S. Bureau of the Census (1985). *Statistical Abstract of the United States: 1985*. Washington DC: U.S. Government Printing Office.

U.S. Bureau of the Census (1988). *Statistical Abstract of the United States: 1988*. Washington, DC: U.S. Government Printing Office.

U.S. Bureau of the Census (1989). *Statistical Abstract of the United States: 1989*. Washington DC: U.S. Government Printing Office.

U.S. Bureau of the Census (1993). *Statistical Abstract of the United States: 1993*. Washington, DC: U.S. Government Printing Office.

U.S. Bureau of the Census (1997). *Statistical Abstract of the United States: 1997*. Washington, DC: U.S. Government Printing Office.

U.S. Bureau of the Census (2000). *Statistical Abstract of the United States: 2000*. Washington, DC: U.S. Government Printing Office.

U.S. Bureau of the Census (2002). *Statistical Abstract of the United States: 2002*. Washington, DC: U.S. Government Printing Office.

U.S. Department of Health and Human Services (2003). U.S. teenage birthrate continues to fall. Retrieved April 14, 2003, from http://www.hhs.gov/news/press/2002press/20020606.html

U.S. Department of Justice (2000). *Bureau of Justice Statistics Sourcebook of Criminal Justice Statistic: 1999*. Washington, DC: U.S. Government Printing Office.

U.S. Department of Justice (2001). *Criminal Victimization in the United States: 1999 Statistical Tables*. NCJ 184938. Washington, DC: U.S. Government Printing Office.

U.S. Government Working Group on Electronic Commerce (2000). *Leadership in the New Millennium: Delivering on Digital Progress and Prosperity*. Washington, DC: U.S. Department of Commerce.

U.S. Merit Systems Protection Board (1981). *Sexual Harassment in the Federal Workplace: Is It a Problem?* Washington, DC: U.S. Government Printing Office.

U.S. Merit Systems Protection Board (1996). *Sexual Harassment in the Federal Workplace: Trends, Progress, Continuing Challenges*. Washington, DC: U.S. Government Printing Office.

U.S. Preventive Services Task Force (2003a). Chemoprevention of breast cancer: Recommendations and rationale. *American Family Physician, 67*, 1309–1314.

U.S. Preventive Services Task Force (2003b). Screening for prostate cancer: Recommendation and rationale. *American Family Physician, 67*, 787–792.

Upchurch, D., Aneshensel, C., Sucoff, C., & Levy-Storms, L. (1999). Neighborhood and family contexts of adolescent sexual activity. *Journal of Marriage and the Family, 61*, 920–933.

Upton, R. (2003). Women have no tribe: Connecting carework, gender, and migration in an era of HIV/AIDS in Botswana. *Gender and Society, 17*, 314–322.

Usry, B. (1995). *Sisterhood of the Night: A True Story*. Far Hills, NJ: New Horizon Press.

Utian, W. (2003). What are the key issues women face when ending hormone replacement therapy? *Cleveland Clinic Journal of Medicine, 70*, 93–94.

Utian, W., & Schiff, I. (1994). NAMS–Gallup survey on women's knowledge, information sources, and attitudes to menopause and hormone replacement therapy. *Menopause, 1*, 39–59.

Vachss, A. (1999). If we really want to keep our children safe. Parade, May 2, 6–7.

Valera, R., Sawyer, R., & Schiraldi, G. (2001). Perceived health needs of inner-city street prostitutes: A preliminary study. *American Journal of Health and Behavior, 25*, 50–59.

Valliant, P., Gauthier, T., Pottier, D., & Kosmyna, R. (2000). Moral reasoning, interpersonal skills, and cognitions of rapists, child molesters, and incest offenders. *Psychological Reports, 86*, 67–75.

van Damme, L. (2000). *Advances in Topical Microbicides*. Paper presented at the 13th International AIDS Conference, Durban, South Africa, July 9–14.

Vandenbergh, J. (2003). Prenatal hormone exposure and sexual variation. *American Scientist, 91,* 218–225.

Van den Bossche, F., & Rubinson, L. (1997). Contraceptive self-efficacy in adolescents: A comparative study of male and female contraceptive practices. *Journal of Sex Education and Therapy, 22(2),* 23–29.

Van der Velde, J., & Everaerd, W. (2001). The relationship between involuntary pelvic floor muscle activity, muscle awareness, and experienced threat in women with and without vaginismus. *Behaviour Research and Therapy, 39,* 395–408.

Vandeusen, K., & Carr, J. (2003). Recovery from sexual assault: An innovative two-stage group therapy model. *International Journal of Group Psychotherapy, 53,* 201–223.

Van Howe, R. (1998). Circumcision and infectious diseases revisited. *Pediatric Infectious Diseases Journal, 17,* 1–6.

Van Look, P., & Stewart, F. (1998). Emergency contraception. In R. Hatcher, J. Trussell, F. Stewart, W. Cates, G. Stewart, F. Guest, & D. Kowal (Eds.), *Contraceptive Technology.* New York: Ardent Media.

Van Oss Marin, B., & Gomez, C. (1994). Latinos, HIV disease, and culture: Strategies for HIV prevention. In P. Cohen, M. Sande, & P. Volberding (Eds.), *The AIDS Knowledge Base.* New York: Little Brown.

Van Voorhis, R., & Wagner, M. (2002). Among the missing: Content on lesbian and gay people in social work journals. *Social Work, 47,* 345–354.

Van Wyk, P. (1984). Psychosocial development of heterosexual, bisexual, and homosexual behavior. *Archives of Sexual Behavior, 13,* 505–544.

Varela, J., Otero, L., Espinoza, E., Sanchez, C., Junquera, M., & Vazquez, F. (2003). Phthirus pubis in a sexually transmitted diseases unit. *Sexually Transmitted Diseases, 30,* 292–296.

Vason, E. (2003). Medical abortion with mifepristone: An update. *Official Journal of the American Academy of Physician Assistants, 16,* 49–54.

Vasquez, M. (1994). Latinas. In L. Comas-Diaz & B. Greene (Eds.), *Women of Color.* New York: Guilford Press.

Vaughn, G. (2003). *Koro: A Natural History of Penis Panics.* Retrieved March 13, 2003, from http://www.koro5hin.org/story

Ventura, S., Curtin, S., & Mathews, T. (1998). *Teenage Births in the United States: National and State Trends, 1990–1996.* Hyattsville, MD: U.S. Department of Health and Human Services.

Verloop, J., Rookus, M., van der Kooy, K., & van Leeuwen, F. (2000). Physical activity and breast cancer risk in women aged 20–54 years. *Journal of the National Cancer Institute, 92,* 128–135.

Vernon, M. (1997). Issues in the management of human papillomavirus genital disease. *American Family Physician, 55,* 1813–1820.

Vessey, M., Painter, R., & Yeates, D. (2003). Mortality in relation to oral contraceptive use and cigarette smoking. *The Lancet, 362,* 185–191.

Vilar, D. (1994). School sex education still a priority in Europe. *Planned Parenthood in Europe, 23,* 8–12.

Villanueva-Diaz, C., Flores-Reyes, G., & Beltran-Zuniga, M. (1999). Bacteriospermia and male infertility: A method for increasing the sensitivity of semen culture. *International Journal of Fertility, 44,* 198–203.

Vinardi, S., Magro, P., Manenti, M., Lala, R., Costantino, S., Cortese, M., & Canarese, F. (2001). Testicular function in men treated in childhood for undescended testes. *Journal of Pediatric Surgery, 36,* 385–388.

Vinson, R., & Epperly, T. (1991). Counseling patients on proper use of condoms. *American Family Physician, 43,* 2081–2085.

Vissandjee, B., Kantiebo, M., Levine, A., & N'Dejuru, R. (2003). The cultural context of gender identity: Female genital excision and infibulation. *Health Care for Women International, 24,* 115–124.

Vistica, G. (1996). Rape in the ranks. *Newsweek,* November 25, 28–32.

Vistica, G. (2000). One, two, three, out. *Newsweek,* March 20, 57–58.

Voelker, R. (2000). Breast cancer vaccine. *Journal of the American Medical Association, 284,* 430.

Voeller, B. (1991). AIDS and heterosexual anal intercourse. *Archives of Sexual Behavior, 20,* 233–269.

Vohra, S., & Morgentaler, A. (1997). Congenital anomalies of the vas deferens, epididymis, and seminal vesicles. *Urology, 49(3),* 313–321.

Volm, L. (1997). Personal communication.

Vonk, R., & Ashmore, R. (1993). The multifaceted self: Androgyny reassessed by open-ended self-description. *Social Psychology Quarterly, 56,* 278–287.

Wade, J., Pletsch, P., Morgan, S., & Menting, S. (2000). Hysterectomy: What do women need and want to know? *Journal of Obstetrical, Gynecological, and Neonatal Nursing, 29,* 33–42.

Wagner, G., Serafini, J., Rabkin, J., Remien, R., & Williams, J. (1994). Integration of one's religion and homosexuality: A weapon against internalized homophobia? *Journal of Homosexuality, 26(4),* 91–109.

Waite, L., & Joyner, K. (2001). Emotional satisfaction and physical pleasure in sexual unions: Time horizon, sexual behavior, and sexual exclusivity. *Journal of Marriage and the Family, 63,* 247–264.

Walbroehl, G. (1984). Sexuality during pregnancy. *American Family Physician, 29,* 273–275.

Wald, A., Carrell, D., Remington, M., Kexel, E., Zeh, J., & Corey, L. (2002). Two-day regimen of acyclovir for treatment of recurrent genital herpes simplex virus type 2 infection. *Clinical Infectious Diseases, 34,* 944–948.

Wald, A., Zeh, J., Selke, S., Warren, T., Ryncarz, A., Ashley, R., Krieger, J., & Corey, L. (2000). Reactivation of genital herpes simplex virus type 2 infection in asymptomatic seropositive persons. *New England Journal of Medicine, 342,* 844–850.

Walen, S., & Roth, D. (1987). A cognitive approach. In J. Geer & W. O'Donohue (Eds.), *Theories of Human Sexuality.* New York: Plenum.

Wales, S., & Todd, K. (2001). *Sexuality and Intimacy Across the Lifespan.* Paper presented at the 33rd Annual Conference of the American Association of Sex Educators, Counselors, and Therapists, San Francisco, May 2–6.

Walfish, S., & Myerson, M. (1980). Sex role identity and attitudes toward sexuality. *Archives of Sexual Behavior, 9,* 199–203.

Wallerstein, J., & Blakeslee, S. (1995). *The Good Marriage.* New York: Houghton Mifflin.

Walling, A. (2004). Effects of oral contraceptive use in older smokers. *American Family Physician, 69,* 1248.

Walsh, A. (1991). *The Science of Love: Understanding Love and Its Effects on Mind and Body.* Buffalo, NY: Prometheus.

Walsh, R. (1989). Premarital sex among teenagers and young adults. In K. McKinney & S. Sprecher (Eds.), *Human Sexuality: The Societal and Interpersonal Context.* Norwood, NJ: Ablex.

Wang, A. (2000). Gays in the military. *The Sunday Oregonian,* January 16, A2.

Wang, C., Vittinghoff, E., Hua, L., Yun, W., & Rong, Z. (1998). Reducing pregnancy and induced abortion rates in China: Family planning with husband participation. *American Journal of Public Health, 88(4),* 646–648.

Wang, J., Jiang, B., Siegal, H., Flack, R., & Carlson, R. (2001). Level of AIDS and HIV knowledge and sexual practices among sexually transmitted disease patients in China. *Sexually Transmitted Diseases, 28,* 171–174.

Ward, L., & Rivadeneyra, R. (1999). Contributions of entertainment television to adolescents' sexual attitudes and expectations: The role of viewing amount versus viewer involvement. *Journal of Sex Research, 36,* 237–249.

Warner, J. (2003a, January 10). *Gulf War Chemicals May Harm Testes.* Retrieved August 29, 2003, from http://my.webmd.com/content/Article/58/66569.htm

Warner, J. (2003b, February 5). *TV Shows Getting Steamier: More "Racy" Sexual Content and Safe-Sex Talk Shown on TV.* Retrieved April 8, 2003, from http://my.webmd.com/content/article/60/67092.htm

Warner, L., Rochat, R., Fichtner, R., Stoll, B., Nathan, L., & Toomey, K. (2001). Missed opportunities for congenital syphilis prevention in an urban southeastern hospital. *Sexually Transmitted Diseases, 28,* 92–94.

Warner, R., & Steel, B. (1999). Child rearing as a mechanism for social change: The relationship of child gender to parents' commitment to gender equity. *Gender and Society, 13,* 503–517.

Warren, M. (1982). Onset of puberty later in athletic girls. *Medical Aspects of Human Sexuality, 4,* 77–78.

Warren, P. (1997). Down and out. *The Advocate,* August 19, 5.

Washburn, J. (1996). Reality check: Can 400,000 women be wrong? *Ms.,* March–April, 51–57.

Waters, H., & Huck, J. (1989). Networking women. *Newsweek,* March 13, 48–54.

Watkins, S. (2002). Demographic shifts change national face of HIV/AIDS. *SIECUS Report, 31,* 10–12.

Watt, P., Hughes, R., Rettew, L., & Adams, R. (2003). A holistic programmatic approach to natural hormone replacement. *Family and Community Health, 26,* 53–63.

Wattanakumtornkul, S., Pinto, A., & Williams, D. (2003). Intranasal hormone replacement therapy. *Menopause: The Journal of the North American Menopause Society, 10,* 88–98.

Waxman, J., & Mazhar, D. (2003). How are we looking after prostate cancer? *QJM: An International Journal of Medicine, 96,* 75–79.

Weber, A. (1998). Losing, leaving, and letting go: Coping with nonmarital breakups. In B. Spitzberg & W. Cupah (eds.), *The Dark Side of Close Relationships.* Mahwah, NJ: Erlbaum.

Weber, A., & Meyn, L. (2002). Episiotomy use in the United States, 1979–1997. *Obstetrics and Gynecology, 100,* 1177–1182.

Wegner, D., Lane, J., & Dimitri, S. (1994). The allure of secret relationships. *Journal of Personality and Social Psychology, 66,* 287–300.

Wehrfritz, G. (1996). Joining the party. *Newsweek,* April 1, 46, 48.

Weinberg, G. (1973). *Society and the Healthy Homosexual.* New York: Anchor.

Weinberg, M., Lottes, I., & Shaver, F. (1995). Swedish or American heterosexual youth: Who is more permissive. *Archives of Sexual Behavior, 26,* 409–437.

Weinberg, M., Williams, C., & Moser, C. (1984). The social constituents of sadomasochism. *Social Problems, 31,* 379–389.

Weinberg, T. (1987). Sadomasochism in the United States: A review of recent sociological literature. *Journal of Sex Research, 23,* 50–69.

Weiner, A. (1996). Understanding the social needs of streetwalking prostitutes. *Journal of the National Association of Social Workers, 41,* 97–105.

Weiner, D., & Rosen, R. (1997). Medications and their impact. In M. Sipski & C. Alexander (Eds.), *Sexual Function in People with Disability and Chronic Illness.* Gaithersburg, MD: Aspen Publishers.

Weiner-Davis, M. (2003). In the mood. *Psychotherapy Networker,* May–June, 32–35.

Weingarten, R., & Hosenball, M. (1999). A fertile scheme. *Newsweek,* November 8, 78–79.

Weisman, C., Plichta, S., Nathanson, C., Ensminger, M., & Robinson, J. (1991). Consistency of condom use for disease prevention among adolescent users of oral contraceptives. *Family Planning Perspectives, 23,* 71–74.

Weiss, J. (2001). Treating vaginismus: Patient without partner. *Journal of Sex Education and Therapy, 26,* 28–33.

Welch, L. (2000). Tsitsi Tiripano. *Ms.,* June–July, 12–15.

Wellbery, C. (2000). Emergency contraception. *Archives of Family Medicine, 9,* 642–646.

Weller, A. (1998). Communication through body odour. *Nature, 392,* 126–127.

Wellings, K., Field, J., Johnson, A., & Wadsworth, J. (1994). *Sexual Behaviour in Britain: The National Survey of Sexual Attitudes and Lifestyles.* London: Penguin Books.

Wells, B. (1983). Nocturnal orgasms: Females' perceptions of a "normal" sexual experience. *Journal of Sex Education and Therapy, 9,* 32–38.

Wells, J. (1991). The effects of homophobia and sexism on heterosexual sexual relationships. *Journal of Sex Education and Therapy, 17,* 185–195.

Welner, S. (1997). Gynecologic care and sexuality issues for women with disabilities. *Sexuality and Disability, 15,* 33–39.

Welsh, S. (1999). Gender and sexual harassment. *Annual Review of Sociology, 25,* 169–190.

Werner, E. (1997). The cult of virginity. *Ms.,* March–April, 40–43.

Werness, B., & Eltabbakh, G. (2001). Familial ovarian cancer and early ovarian cancer: Biologic, pathologic, and clinical features. *International Journal of Gynecological Pathology, 20,* 48–63.

Wessells, H., Lue, T., & McAninch, J. (1996). Complications of penile lengthening and augmentation seen at one referral center. *Journal of Urology, 155,* 1617–1620.

West, D. (2000). Aftermath of incest pedophilia case: Guilt and a new awareness danger. *New York Times,* July 12, B5.

Westhoff, C., Picardo, L., & Morrow, E. (2003). Quality of life following early medical or surgical abortion. *Contraception, 67,* 41–47.

Westoff, C., Calot, G., & Foster, A. (1983). Teenage fertility in developed countries. *Family Planning Perspectives, 15,* 105–110.

Wheeler, M. (1991). Physical changes of puberty. *Endocrinology and Metabolism Clinics of North America, 20,* 1–14.

Wheeler, M. (2003). *AIDS Education Through Imams (2003).* Retrieved January 2, 2003, from http://www.unaids.org/publications/documents/sectors/religion/imamscse.pdf

Whipp, G. (2003). He can handle the truth: Jack Nicholson gets the chance to act his age, warts and all, in "About Schmidt." *The Oregonian,* January 3, B1.

Whipple, B. (2000). Beyond the G spot. *Scandinavian Journal of Sexology, 3,* 35–42.

Whipple, B. (2001a). *Beyond the G Spot: Application of Recent Research Concerning Female Sexuality to Education and Practice.* Paper presented at the 33rd Annual Conference of the American Association of Sex Educators, Counselors, and Therapists, San Francisco, May 2–6.

Whipple, B. (2001b). *Women's Health Issues.* Paper presented at the 33rd Annual Conference of the American Association of Sex Educators, Counselors, and Therapists, San Francisco, May 2–6.

Whipple, B., & Komisaruk, B. (1999). Beyond the G spot: Recent research on female sexuality. *Psychiatric Annals, 29,* 34–37.

Whipple, B., Ogden, G., & Komisaruk, B. (1992). Physiological correlates of imagery-induced orgasm in women. *Archives of Sexual Behavior, 21,* 121–133.

Whitaker, D., & Miller, K. (2000). Parent-adolescent discussions about sex and condoms: Impact on peer influence of sexual risk behavior. *Journal of Adolescent Research, 15,* 251–273.

Whitaker, D., Miller, K., May, D., & Levin, M. (1999). Teenage partners' communication about sexual risk and condom use: The importance of parent-teenagers discussions. *Family Planning Perspectives, 31,* 117–121.

Whitam, F. (1980). The prehomosexual male child in three societies: The United States, Guatemala, Brazil. *Archives of Sexual Behavior, 9,* 87–99.

Whitbeck, L., Yoder, K., Hoyt, D., & Conger, R. (1999). Early adolescent sexual activity: A developmental study. *Journal of Marriage and the Family, 61,* 934–946.

White, G. (1999). Commentary: Legal and ethical aspects of sperm retrieval. *Journal of Law, Medicine, and Ethics, 27,* 359–361.

White, G., & Helbick, R. (1988). Understanding and treating jealousy. In R. Brown & J. Fields (Eds.), *Treatment of Sexual Problems in Individuals and Couples Therapy.* Boston: PMA Publishing.

White, J. (2003). Who do you love? *Utne Reader,* May–June, 24–26.

White, S., & DeBlassie, R. (1992). Adolescent sexual behavior. *Adolescence, 27,* 183–191.

Whiteford, A., & Wordley, J. (2003). Raising awareness and detection of testicular cancer in young men. *Nursing Times, 99,* 34–36.

Whittemore, A., & McGuire, V. (2003). Observational studies and randomized trials of hormone replacement therapy: What can we learn from them? *Epidemiology, 14,* 8–10.

Whitten, K., Rein, M., Land, D., Reppucci, N., & Turkheimer, E. (2003). The emotional experience of intercourse and sexually transmitted diseases. *Sexually Transmitted Diseases, 30,* 348–356.

Whittle, M. (1998). Commentary: Early amniocentesis—time for a rethink. *The Lancet, 351,* 226–227.

Wichstrom, L., & Hegna, K. (2003). Sexual orientation and suicide attempt: A longitudinal study of the general Norwegian adolescent population. *Journal of Abnormal Psychology, 112,* 144–151.

Wiederman, M. (1993). Evolved gender differences in mate preferences: Evidence from personal advertisements. *Ethology and Sociobiology, 14,* 331–352.

Wiederman, M. (1999). Volunteer bias in sexuality research using college student participants. *Journal of Sex Research, 36,* 59–66.

Wiederman, M. (2000). Women's body image self-consciousness during physical intimacy with a partner. *Journal of Sex Research, 37,* 60–68.

Wiederman, M., & Allgeier, E. (1992). Gender differences in mate selection criteria: Sociobiological or socioeconomic explanations? *Ethology and Sociobiology, 13,* 115–124.

Wiederman, M., & Allgeier, E. (1993). Gender differences in sexual jealousy: Adaptionist or social learning explanation. *Ethology and Sociobiology, 14,* 115–140.

Wiederman, M., Maynard, C., & Fretz, A. (1996). Ethnicity in 25 years of published sexuality research: 1971–1995. *Journal of Sex Research, 33,* 339–343.

Wiederman, M., Weis, D., & Allgeier, E. (1994). The effect of question preface on response rates to a telephone survey of sexual experience. *Archives of Sexual Behavior, 23,* 203–216.

Wiegratz, I., Kutschera, E., Lee, J., Moore, C., Mellinger, U., Winkler, U., & Kuhl, H. (2003). Effect of four different oral contraceptives on various sex hormones and serum-binding globulins. *Contraception, 67,* 25–32.

Wiese, W., Patel, S. R., Patel, S. C., Ohl, C., & Estrada, C. (2000). A meta-analysis of the Papanicolaou smear and wet mount for the diagnosis of vaginal trichomoniasis. *American Journal of Medicine, 108,* 301–308.

Wiesenfeld, H., Hillier, S., Krohn, M., Landers, D., & Sweet, R. (2003). Bacterial vaginosis is a strong predictor of *Neisseria gonorrhoeae* and *Chlamydia trachomatis* infections. *Clinical Infectious Diseases, 36,* 663–668.

Wiesner-Hanks, M. (2000). *Christianity and Sexuality in the Early Modern World.* London: Routledge.

Wiest, W. (1977). Semantic differential profiles of orgasm and other experiences among men and women. *Sex Roles, 3,* 399–403.

Wiest, W., Harrison, J., Johanson, C., Laubsch, B., & Whitley, A. (1995). Paper presented at the Oregon Academy of Sciences meeting, Reed College, Portland, Oregon, February 25.

Wilcox, A., Weinberg, C., & Baird, D. (1995). Timing of sexual intercourse in relation to ovulation. Effects on the probability of conception, survival of the pregnancy, and sex of the baby. *New England Journal of Medicine, 333,* 1517–1521.

Wildman, S. (2001). Continental divide. *The Advocate,* January 16, 47–48.Willet, W., Colditz, G., & Stampfer, M. (2000). Postmenopausal estrogens: Opposed, unopposed, or none of the above. *Journal of the American Medical Association, 283,* 534–535.

Williams, A., Thomson, R., Schreiber, G., Watanabe, K., Bethel, J., Lo, A., Kleinman, S., Hollingsworth, C., & Nemo, G. (1997). Estimates of infectious disease risk factors in U.S. blood donors. *Journal of the American Medical Association, 277,* 967–972.

Williams, C. (1999). *Roman Homosexualities: Ideologies of Masculinity in Classical Antiquity.* New York: Oxford University Press.

Williams, D., & D'Alessandro, J. (1994). A comparison of three measures of androgyny and their relationship to psychological adjustment. *Journal of Social Behavior and Personality, 9,* 469–480.

Williams, E., & Donnelly, J. (2002). Older Americans and AIDS: Some guidelines for prevention. *Social Work, 47,* 105–111.

Williams, E., & Ellison, F. (1996). Culturally informed social work practice with American Indian clients: Guidelines for non-Indian social workers. *Journal of the National Association of Social Workers, 41(2),* 147–151.

Williams, L. (1994). Recall of childhood trauma: A prospective study of women's memories of child sexual abuse. *Journal of Consulting and Clinical Psychology, 62,* 1,167–1,176.

Williams, L. (1999). *Hard Core.* Berkeley: University of California Press.

Williams, P., Ekundayo, O., Udezula, I., & Omishakin, A. (2003). An ethnically sensitive and gender-specific HIV/AIDS assessment of African American women. *Family Community Health, 26,* 108–123.

Williams, P., & Smith, M. (1979). Interview in *The First Question.* London: British Broadcasting System Science and Features Department.

Williams, S. (2000). A new smoking peril. *Newsweek,* April 24, 78.

Williams, T., Pepitone, M., Christensen, S., & Cooke B. (2000). Finger-length ratios and sexual orientation. *Nature,* March 30, 455–456.

Willis, B., & Levy, B. (2003). Child prostitution: Global health burden, research needs, and interventions. *The Lancet, 359,* 1417–1422.

Willis, E. (2002). Abortion: Is a woman a person? In A. Soble (Ed.), *The Philosophy of Sex: Contemporary Readings.* Lanham, MD: Rowman & Littlefield.

Wilson, B., & Lawson, D. (1976). Effects of alcohol on sexual arousal in women. *Journal of Abnormal Psychology, 85,* 489–497.

Wilson, J. (2003). *Biological Foundations of Human Behavior.* Belmont, CA: Wadsworth/Thomson Learning.

Wilson, M., Kastrinakis, M., D'Angelo, L., & Getson, P. (1994). Attitudes, knowledge, and behavior regarding condom use in urban black adolescents males. *Adolescence, 29,* 13–26.

Wineberg, H. (1994). Marital reconciliation in the United States: Which couples are successful? *Journal of Marriage and the Family, 56,* 80–88.

Winer, R., Lee, S., Hughes, J., Adam, D., Kiviat, N., & Koutsky, L. (2003). Genital human papillomavirus infection: Incidence and risk factors in a cohort of female university students. *American Journal of Epidemiology, 157,* 218–226.

Winick, C., & Evans, J. (1996). The relationship between nonenforcement of state pornography laws and rates of sex crime arrests. *Archives of Sexual Behavior, 25(5),* 439–453.

Winters, S. (1999). Current status of testosterone replacement therapy in men. *Archives of Family Medicine, 8,* 257–263.

Wistuba, I., Maitra, A., Albores-Saavedra, J., & Gazdar, A. (2000). Molecular changes in cervical endocrine tumors. *Contemporary OB/GYN,* March, 25–34.

Wiswell, T. (1997). Circumcision circumspection. *New England Journal of Medicine, 336,* 1244–1245.

Witt, S. (1997). Parental influence on children's socialization to gender roles. *Adolescence, 32,* 253–258.

Witte, S., Wada, T., El-Bassel, N., Gilbert, L., & Wallace, J. (2000). Predictors of female condom use among women exchanging street sex in New York City. *Sexually Transmitted Diseases, 27,* 93–98.

Wiviott, G. (2001). *An Existential Approach to Marital Therapy in Cases of Marital Infidelity.* Paper presented at the 33rd Annual Conference of the American Association of Sex Educators, Counselors, and Therapists, San Francisco, May 2–6.

Wohl, R., & Kane, W. (1997). Teachers' beliefs concerning teaching about testicular cancer and testicular self-examination. *Journal of School Health, 67,* 106–111.

Wold, A., & Adlerberth, I. (1998). Does breastfeeding affect the infant's immune responsiveness? *Acta Paediatrica, 87,* 19–22.

Wolf, N. (2001). What you'd never expect when you're expecting. *Ms.,* October–November, 36–47.

Wolf, T., Randall, H., Von Almen, K., Tynes, L. (1991). Perceived mistreatment and attitude change by graduating medical students: A retrospective study. *Medical Education, 25,* 182–190.

Wolfe, A. (1998). Shut up about sex. *The Advocate,* April 14, 43–45.

Wolfsdorf, B., & Zlotnick, C. (2001). Affect management in group therapy for women with posttraumatic stress disorder and histories of childhood sexual abuse. *Journal of Clinical Psychology, 57,* 169–181.

Women on Words and Images (1972). *Dick and Jane as Victims.* Princeton, NJ: Women on Words and Images.

Women's Health Initiative (2002). Risks and benefits of estrogen plus progestin in healthy postmenopausal women: Principal results from the Women's Health Initiative randomized controlled trial. *Journal of the American Medical Association, 288,* 321–333.

Wong, J., Gunthard, H., Havlir, D., Haase, A., Zhang, Z., & Kwok, S. (1997). *Reduction of HIV in Blood and Lymph Nodes After Potent Antiretroviral Therapy.* Paper presented at the 4th Conference on Retroviruses and Other Opportunistic Infections, Washington, D.C., January.

Wong, M. (1988). The Chinese American family. In C. Mindel, R. Habenstein, & R. Wright (Eds.), *Ethnic Families in America* (3rd ed.). New York: Elsevier.

Wong, W., Thomas, C., & Merkus, J. (2000). Male factor subfertility: Possible causes and the impact of nutritional factors. *Fertility and Sterility, 73,* 435–442.

Wood, G., & Ruddock, E. (1918). *Vitalogy.* Chicago: Vitalogy Association.

Wood, K., Becker, J., & Thompson, K. (1996). Body image dissatisfaction in preadolescent children. *Journal of Applied Developmental Psychology, 17,* 85–100.

Wood, M. (2000). How we got this way: The sciences of homosexuality and the Christian right. *Journal of Homosexuality, 38,* 19–40.

Woodrum, D., Brawer, M., Partin, A., Catalona, W., & Southwick, P. (1998). Interpretation of free prostate specific antigen clinical research studies for the detection of prostate cancer. *Journal of Urology, 159,* 5–12.

Woodward, S. (2003). Him, her—and the Internet. *The Oregonian,* September 7, L1, L8.

Woody, J., Russel, R., D'Souza, H., & Woody, J. (2000). Noncoital sex among adolescent virgins and nonvirgins. *Journal of Sex Education and Therapy, 25,* 261–268.

Woog, D. (1997). Our parents. *The Advocate,* October 28, 24–31.

Woog, D. (1998). Adopting a family. *The Advocate,* January 20, 69–71.

Woolard, D., & Edwards, R. (1997). Female circumcision: An emerging concern in college health care. *Journal of American College Health, 45,* 230–232.

Woolf, L. (2001). Gay and lesbian aging. *SIECUS Report, 30,* 16–21.

Worden, M., & Worden, B. (1998). *The Gender Dance in Couples Therapy.* Pacific Grove, CA: Brooks/Cole.

Workman, J., & Freeburg, E. (1999). An examination of date rape, victim dress, and perceiver variables within the context of attribution theory. *Sex Roles, 41,* 261–277.

Worthman, C. (1999). Faster, farther, higher: Biology and the discourses on human sexuality. In D. Suggs & A. Miracle (Eds.), *Culture, Biology, and Sexuality.* Athens: University of Georgia Press.

Wright, L., & Cullen J. (2001). Reducing college students' homophobia, erotophobia, and conservatism levels through a human sexuality course. *Journal of Sex Education and Therapy, 26,* 328–333.

Wright, T., Denny, L., Kuhn, L., Pollack, A., & Lorincz, A. (2000). HPV DNA testing of self-collected vaginal samples compared with cytologic screening to detect cervical cancer. *Journal of the American Medical Association, 283,* 81.

Wright, T., & Schiffman, M. (2003). Adding a test for human papillomavirus DNA to cervical cancer screening. *New England Journal of Medicine, 348,* 489–500.

Wu, S., Yang, J., & Liu, G. (2003). A clinical study in China of neonatal conjunctivitis caused by *Chlamydia trachomatis. Clinical Pediatrics, 42,* 83–84.

Wu, T., Schiffer, C., Gonzales, M., Taylor, J., Kantor, R., Chou, S., Israelski, D., Zolopa, A., Fessel, W., & Shafer, R. (2003). Mutation patterns and structural correlates in human immunodeficiency virus type 1 protease following different protease inhibitor treatments. *Journal of Virology, 77,* 4836–4847.

Wyatt, G. (1997). *Stolen Women: Reclaiming Our Sexuality, Taking Back Our Lives.* New York: Wiley.

Wysowski, D., & Swann, J. (2003). Use of medications for erectile dysfunction in the United States, 1996 through 2001. *Journal of Urology,* March, 1040–1042.

Yaffe, K., Sawaya, G., Lieberburg, I., & Grady, D. (1998). Estrogen therapy in postmenopausal women. *Journal of the American Medical Association, 279(9),* 688–695.

Yalom, M. (2001). *A History of the Wife.* New York: HarperCollins.

Yapko, M. (1994). *Suggestions of Abuse: True and False Memories of Childhood Sexual Trauma.* New York: Simon & Schuster.

Yarab, P., & Allgeier, E. (1998). Don't even think about it: The role of sexual fantasies as perceived unfaithfulness in heterosexual dating relationships. *Journal of Sex Education and Therapy, 23,* 246–254.

Yared, R. (2004). AIDS rate surges in people 50+. *AARP Bulletin,* May, 2.

Yates, A., & Wolman, W. (1991). Aphrodisiacs: Myth and reality. *Medical Aspects of Human Sexuality,* December, 58–64.

Yim, S. (2000a). Body menstruation: Life without monthly periods. *The Sunday Oregonian,* September 24, L11.

Yim, S. (2000b). Making the choice to be child-free. *The Sunday Oregonian,* November 26, L11.

Yim, S. (2000c). "Wisdom of elders" celebrates ethnic ties. *The Oregonian,* February 20, C2.

Yim, S. (2001). Relationships/marriage. *The Sunday Oregonian,* February 4, L13.

Young, M., Denny, G., & Young, T. (2000). Sexual satisfaction among married women age 50 and older. *Psychological Reports, 86,* 1107–1122.

Yuan, C., Wang, P., Lai, C., & Tsu, E. (1999). Recurrence and survival analyses of 1,115 cervical cancer patients treated with radical hysterectomy. *Gynecologic and Obstetric Investigation, 47,* 127–132.

Yuan, W., Basso, O., & Sorensen, H. (2001). Maternal prenatal lifestyle factors and infectious disease in early childhood: A follow-up study of hospitalization within a Danish birth cohort. *Pediatrics, 107,* 357–362.

Yuan, W., Steffensen, F., & Nielsen, G. (2000). A population-based cohort study of birth and neonatal outcome in older primipara. *International Journal of Gynecology and Obstetrics, 68,* 113–118.

Zabin, L., Hirsch, M., Smith, E., & Hardy, J. (1984). Adolescent sexual attitudes and behavior: Are they consistent? *Family Planning Perspectives, 16,* 181–185.

Zabin, L., Stark, H., & Emerson, M. (1991). Reasons for delay in contraceptive clinic utilization. *Journal of Adolescent Health Care, 12,* 225–232.

Zak, A., & McDonald, C. (1997). Satisfaction and trust in intimate relationships: Do lesbians and heterosexual women differ? *Psychological Reports, 80,* 904–906.

Zambrana, R., & Scrimshaw, S. (1997). Maternal psychosocial factors associated with substance use in Mexican-origin and African American low-income pregnant women. *Pediatric Nursing, 23 (3),* 253–254.

Zamora-Hernandez, C., & Patterson, D. (1996). Homosexually active Latino men: Issues for social work practice. In J. Longres (Ed.), *Men of Color.* New York: Harrington Park Press.

Zapka, J., Pbert, L., & Stoddard, A. (2000). Smoking cessation counseling with pregnant and postpartum women: A survey of community health center providers. *American Journal of Public Health, 90,* 78–84.

Zaviacic, M., & Whipple, B. (1993). Update on the female prostate and the phenomenon of female ejaculation. *Journal of Sex Research, 30,* 148–151.

Zelkowitz, P., & Milet, T. (1995). Screening for postpartum depression in a community sample. *Canadian Journal of Psychiatry, 40,* 80–85.

Zelnick, M., & Kantner, J. (1977). Sexual and contraceptive experiences of young unmarried women in the United States, 1976 and 1971. *Family Planning Perspectives, 9,* 55–71.

Zelnick, M., & Kantner, J. (1980). Sexual activity, contraceptive use, and pregnancy among metropolitan-area teenagers: 1971–1979. *Family Planning Perspectives, 12,* 230–237.

Zernike, K. (2000). Boy Scouts' ban on gays has many donors shying away. *The Oregonian,* August 30, A3.

Zhou, J., Hofman, M., Gooren, L., & Swaab, D. (1995). A sex difference in the human brain and its relation to transsexuality. *Nature, 378,* 68–70.

Zhu, T., Korber, B., Nahmias, A., Hooper, E., Sharp, P., & Ho, D. (1998). An African HIV-1 sequence from 1959 and implications for the origin of the epidemic. *Nature, 391,* 594–597.

Zia, H. (2003). Reclaiming the past, redefining the future: Asian American and Pacific Islander women. In R. Morgan (Ed.), *Sisterhood Is Forever.* New York: Washington Square Press.

Zilbergeld, B. (1978). *Male Sexuality: A Guide to Sexual Fulfillment.* Boston: Little, Brown.

Zilbergeld, B. (1992). *The New Male Sexuality.* New York: Bantam Books.

Zilbergeld, B. (2001). *Sexuality at Midlife and Beyond.* Paper presented at the 33rd Annual Conference of the American Association of Sex Educators, Counselors, and Therapists, San Francisco, May 2–6.

Zilbergeld, B., & Kilmann, P. (1984). The scope and effectiveness of sex therapy. *Psychotherapy, 21,* 319–326.

Zillmann, D. (1989). Effects of prolonged consumption of pornography. In D. Zillman & J. Bryant (Eds.), *Pornography: Research Advances and Policy Considerations.* Hillsdale, NJ: Erlbaum.

Zillmann, D., & Bryant, J. (1982). Pornography, sexual callousness, and the trivialization of rape. *Journal of Communication,* Autumn, 10–21.

Zillmann, D., & Bryant, J. (1988). Pornography's impact on sexual satisfaction. *Journal of Applied Social Psychology, 18,* 438–453.

Zlidar, V. (2000). Helping women use the pill. *Population Reports, 28,* 1–28.

Zoldbrod, A. (1993). *Men, Women, and Infertility.* New York: Norton.

Zoucha-Jensen, J., & Coyne, A. (1993). The effects of resistance strategies on rape. *American Journal of Public Health, 83,* 1633–1634.

Zucker, K., Blanchard, R., & Siegelman, M. (2003). Birth order among homosexual men. *Psychological Reports, 92,* 117–118.

Zucker, K., Bradley, S., Oliver, G., Blake, J., Fleming, S., & Head, A. (1996). Psychosexual development of women with congenital adrenal hyperplasia. *Hormones and Behavior, 30,* 300–318.

Zucker, K., Bradley, S., & Sanikhani, M. (1997). Sex differences in referral rates of children with gender identity disorder: Some hypotheses. *Journal of Abnormal Child Psychology, 25,* 217–227.

Credits

This page constitutes an extension of the copyright page. We have made every effort to trace the ownership of all copyrighted material and to secure permission from copyright holders. In the event of any question arising as to the use of any material, we will be pleased to make the necessary corrections in future printings. Thanks are due to the following authors, publishers, and agents for permission to use the material indicated.

Photo Credits

Chapter 1: p. 1, © Joel Gordon; p. 2, Courtesy of the Museum of Sex; p. 3, Universal/The Kobal Collection; p. 4, © AP/Wide World Photos; p. 7 top, © Neema Frederic/Corbis Sygma; p. 7 bottom, © Gustavo Tomsich/CORBIS; p. 9 top, © Erich Lessing/Art Resource, NY; p. 9 bottom, © Burstein Collection/CORBIS; p. 10, © SuperStock; p. 11, 12, © Bettmann/CORBIS; p. 13 top, © CORBIS; p. 13 bottom, © Hulton-Deutsch Collection/CORBIS; p. 14, © Spencer Grant/PhotoEdit; p. 15, Terry Richardson/Art+Commerce Anthology; p. 17 top, © Kevin Winter/Getty Images; p. 17 bottom, © Rachel Epstein/The Image Works; p. 18, ® 2003, Subaru of America, Inc.

Chapter 2: p. 22, © Rob Melnychuk/Getty Images; p. 26, © David Young-Wolff/PhotoEdit; p. 29, Author Photo; p. 30, © Wallace Kirkland/Time Life Pictures/Getty Images; p. 31, © Bruce Powell; p. 35, © Bettmann/CORBIS; p. 37 top left, Hess Designs; p. 37 top right and bottom, Courtesy of Farrall Instruments; p. 39, © Francis Dean/Dean Pictures/The Image Works.

Chapter 3: p. 45, © AP/Wide World Photos; p. 48, 52, © Custom Medical Stock Photo; p. 57, From Money, John and Anke A. Ehrhardt. Man and Woman, Boy and Girl: Differentiation and Dimorphism of Gender Identity from Conception to Maturity. pp. 115 (fig. 6.2). © 1973. Reprinted with permission of the The Johns Hopkins University Press; p. 59 left, © Myrleen Ferguson Cate/PhotoEdit; p. 59 right, © Donna Day/Getty Images; p. 62, © Michael Geissinger Photography; p. 67 both, Courtesy of Dr. Daniel Greenwald; p. 71 left, © Stephen Simpson/Getty Images; p. 71 right, © Ian Shaw/Getty Images; p. 72, © Tom Rosenthal/SuperStock; p. 74, © AP/Wide World Photos.

Chapter 4: p. 81, © Erich Lessing/Art Resource, NY; p. 82 left, © Judy Chicago, 1979. Photo © Donald Woodman; p. 82 right, © Charles Marden Fitch/SuperStock; p. 84 all, © Tee Corinne; p. 85, © Dion Ogust/The Image Works; p. 87, © Marie Dorigny/Sipa Press; p. 92 top, © George DeSota/Getty Images; p. 92 bottom, PhotoDisc; p. 94, © Bettman/CORBIS; p. 111 all, © Joel Gordon; p. 113, © Francoise Sauze/SPL/Photo Researchers, Inc.; p. 116, Courtesy of Breast Cancer Fund, Obsessed with Breasts Campaign, www.breastcancerfund.org; p. 117 both, © Biophoto Associates/Photo Researchers, Inc.

Chapter 5: p. 121, © Erich Lessing/Art Resource, NY; p. 128, © Joel Gordon; p. 129, © Biophoto Associates/Photo Researchers, Inc.; p. 131, © David Phillips/Photo Researchers, Inc.; p. 134, © Erich Lessing/Art Resource, NY; p. 135 all, © Justine Hill; p. 141, © Doug Pensinger/Getty Images.

Chapter 6: p. 146, © Steve Prezant/CORBIS; p. 153 left, © Thomas S. England/Photo Researchers, Inc.; p. 153 2nd from left, © Alain Evrard/Photo Researchers, Inc.; p. 153 center left, © Monique Salabar/The Image Works; p. 153 center right, © Bill Bachmann/PhotoEdit; p. 153 2nd from right, © Robert Fried/Stock Boston; p. 153 right, © Francois Gohier/Photo Researchers, Inc.; p. 156, © Deborah Egan.

Chapter 7: p. 182, © Tom & Dee Ann McCarthy/CORBIS; p. 183, © Culver Pictures; p. 184, Thinkstock/Getty Images; p. 189, © Duomo/CORBIS; p. 195, © Jeff Greenberg/PhotoEdit; p. 200, © Dwayne Newton/PhotoEdit; p. 204, © Michaelangelo Gratton/Getty Images; p. 206, © Mark Gibson/Lonely Planet Images.

Chapter 8: p. 210, © Joyce Choo/CORBIS; p. 214, © Jose Luis Pelaez, Inc./CORBIS; p. 216, Javier Pierini/Getty Images; p. 219, © Bruce Ayres/Getty Images; p. 221, © Zigy Kaluzny; p. 226, © Peter M. Fisher/CORBIS; p. 230, © Nancy Richmond/The Image Works; p. 233 top, © Adamsmith/Getty Images; p. 233 bottom, © Darren Modricker/CORBIS; p. 234, © Robert Brenner/PhotoEdit.

Chapter 9: p. 240, © Franco Vogt/CORBIS; p. 247, from *American Sex Machines*, Copyright © 1996, Hoag Levins. Used by permission of Adams Media. All rights reserved; p. 250 left, © Mark Antman/The Image Works; p. 250 right, © Kathleen Olson; p. 256, © Esbin-Anderson/The Image Works; p. 265, © Werner Forman/Art Resource, NY.

Chapter 10: p. 267, ThinkStock LLC/Index Stock Imagery; p. 268, © Carlo Allegri/Getty Images; p. 280, © Kevin Winter/Getty Images; p. 282, © Mark Richards/PhotoEdit; p. 283, Courtesy of The Mitchell Gold Company; p. 284, "Gotham Central" #6, © 2003 DC Comics. All Rights Reserved. Used with Permission; p. 290, Courtesy of Isocurve; p. 292, © AP/Wide World Photos; p. 293, USHMM, courtesy of KZ Gedenkstaette Dachau; p. 296, © AP/Wide World Photos.

Chapter 11: p. 299, © Deborah Gilbert/Getty Images; p. 300, © Bettmann/CORBIS; p. 301, © Baldev/Corbis Sygma; p. 302, Courtesy of Marie Stopes International; p. 303, Copyright Pharmacists Planning Service Inc. (PPSI); email: PPSI@aol.com; p. 310, © Jonathan A. Meyers/Photo Researchers, Inc.; p. 313 top, J. Darin Derstine; p. 313 bottom, © Reuters/CORBIS; p. 315 both, © Joel Gordon; p. 316, Courtesy of San Francisco AIDS Foundation; p. 318, p. 319 all, p. 321 all, p. 323, p. 325, J. Darin Derstine; p. 329, Courtesy of Conceptus Incorporated.

Chapter 12: p. 335, © Michael Krasowitz/Getty Images; p. 337, © David Scharf/Peter Arnold, Inc.; p. 339, © Vince Bucci/Getty Images; p. 340, © Spike Walker/Getty Images; p. 343, © Phillips Mitchell; p. 344, © National Enquirer; p. 351, © Robert Kusel; p. 354, © DR LR/Photo Researchers, Inc.; p. 355, © Annie Liebovitz/Contact Press Images; p. 356, © Dr. Y. Nikas/Phototake. All rights reserved; p. 357, © Dr. G. Moscoso/Photo Researchers, Inc.; p. 358, © Leland

Bobbe/Getty Images; p. 362, © Jiang Jin/SuperStock; p. 364, © D. van Rossum/Photo Researchers, Inc.; p. 366, © Erika Stone/Photo Researchers, Inc.

Chapter 13: p. 370, © Paul Steel/CORBIS; p. 372, © Michael Newman/PhotoEdit; p. 376 top, © Jo Browne/Mick Smee/Getty Images; p. 376 bottom, © Fredrik D. Bodin/Stock Boston; p. 382, © Vincent Besnault/Getty Images; p. 386, © AP/Wide World Photos; p. 391, © Gale Zucker/Stock Boston; p. 397, © Will & Deni McIntyre/Photo Researchers, Inc..

Chapter 14: p. 400, Thinkstock/Getty Images; p. 404, © Carol Beckwith/Robert Estall Photo Agency, UK; p. 406, © Maggie Hallahan/CORBIS; p. 408, © Rafael Macia/Photo Researchers, Inc.; p. 412, © Mark Hanauer/CORBIS; p. 420, Photofest; p. 421 left, © Evan Agostini/Getty Images; p. 421 right, © Kevin Winter/Getty Images; p. 423, © Bruce Ayres/Getty Images; p. 424, © Ferdinando Scianna/Magnum Photos; p. 426, © David Young-Wolff/PhotoEdit.

Chapter 15: p. 428, © Eric K. K. Yu/CORBIS; p. 433, © Chuck Savage/CORBIS; p. 435, © Maya Barnes/The Image Works; p. 437, © Joel Gordon; p. 438, Courtesy of Torrid, www.torrid.com; p. 442, © Carol Ford/Getty Images; p. 444, © David Young-Wolff/PhotoEdit; p. 445, © Rhydian Lewis/Getty Images.

Chapter 16: p. 451, © Chris Harvey/Getty Images; p. 457, Courtesy of NuGyn, Inc.; p. 463, © Bob Daemmrich/The Image Works.

Chapter 17: p. 472, © Bill Freeman/PhotoEdit; p. 478, © Western Opthalmic Hospital/Science Photo Library/Custom Medical Stock Photo; p. 481, 484 left, © Lester V. Bergman/CORBIS; p. 484 right, Centers for Disease Control, Atlanta, GA; p. 485 left, © SIU Biomedical/Photo Researchers, Inc.; p. 485 right, © Biophoto Associates/Photo Researchers, Inc.; p. 488 both, Centers for Disease Control, Atlanta, GA; p. 492, © Science Visuals Unlimited/Visuals Unlimited; p. 498, © E. Gray/SPL/Photo Researchers, Inc.; p. 506, © Bettmann/CORBIS; p. 509, © A. Reininger/Woodfin Camp & Associates; p. 511, © Stephen Dunn; p. 512, © Felicia Martinez/PhotoEdit; p. 516, Ryan McVay/Getty Images; p. 517, © Michael Newman/PhotoEdit.

Chapter 18: p. 526, © Mike Diver/Getty Images; p. 529, © Thomas Hoeffgen/Getty Images; p. 530 left, Royalty-Free/CORBIS; p. 530 right, © David Muscroft/SuperStock; p. 531, © Zen Icknow/CORBIS; p. 532, © Howard Kingsnorth/Getty Images; p. 536, © Jutta Klee/CORBIS; p. 537, © David Raymer/CORBIS; p. 538, © AP/Wide World Photos.

Chapter 19: p. 548, © AP/Wide World Photos; p. 552, © Michael Newman/PhotoEdit; p. 555, © Bob Daemmrich/The Image Works; p. 557, © Spencer Grant/Stock Boston; p. 571, © AP/Wide World Photos; p. 572, © Jacques Chenet/Woodfin Camp and Associates; p. 573, © Paul Conklin/PhotoEdit; p. 574, © Willie Hill, Jr./The Image Works.

Chapter 20: p. 581, © Rudi Von Briel/PhotoEdit; p. 582, © Mimmo Jodice/CORBIS; p. 583 top, © Stapleton Collection/CORBIS; p. 583 bottom, Photofest; p. 584 top, © Cat Gwynn/CORBIS; p. 584 bottom, Courtesy of "On Our Backs" Magazine; p. 586, Courtesy of Adam & Eve; p. 587, © AP/Wide World Photos; p. 588, From J. Elias, G. Brewer, V. Bullough, J. Douglas, V. Diehl Elias, W. Jarvis, Porn 101 (Amherst, NY: Prometheus Books), copyright 1999. Reprinted by permission of the publisher; p. 590, © Andrew Holbrooke/CORBIS; p. 591, © Way Gary/Corbis Sygma; p. 595, © Gilles Fonlupt/CORBIS.

Other Credits

Chapter 1: p. 6, Figure 1.1 adapted from *Global Study of Sexual Attitudes and Behaviors* funded by Pfizer Inc. Copyright 2002 Pfizer Inc.; p. 19, Reprinted with special permission of King Features Syndicate.

Chapter 4: p. 95, Poem from "'She Shall Be Called Woman' Part 5" from *Collected Poems 1930–1933* by May Sarton. Copyright © 1993, 1988, 1984, 1980, 1974 by May Sarton. Reprinted by permission of W. W. Norton & Company, Inc.; p. 112: Figure 4.9 adapted with permission from Kaiser Foundation Health Plan of Oregon.

Chapter 6: pp. 162, 163, Figures 6.3, 6.4 from *Human Sexual Response*, by W. H. Masters and V. E. Johnson. Copyright © 1966 Little, Brown & Co. Reprinted by permission of the authors.

Chapter 8: p. 225, © The New Yorker Collection 1990 Eric Teitelbaum from cartoonbank.com. All rights reserved. Reprinted by permission.

Chapter 9: p. 245, MOMMA by Mell Lazarus. By permission of Mell Lazarus and Creators Syndicate, Inc.; p. 255, "i like my body when it is with your." Copyright 1923, 1925, 1951, 1953 © 1991 by the Trustees for the E. E. Cummings Trust. Copyright © 1976 by George James Firmage, from COMPLETE POEMS: 1904–1962 by E. E. Cummings, edited by George J. Firmage. Used by permission of Liveright Publishing Corporation; p. 262, Poem from the book *Passionate Hearts*. Copyright © 1996. Reprinted with permission of New World Library, Novato, CA. www.newworldlibrary.com.

Chapter 10: p. 285, Table 10.3 adapted from "Lesbian Identity Development: An Examination of Differences Across Generations," by C. Parks, *American Journal of Orthopsychiatry*, 1999, 69(3), 347–361. Copyright © 1999 American Journal of Orthopsychiatry. Reprinted by permission; p. 289, DOONESBURY © 1997 G. B. Trudeau. Reprinted with permission of Universal Press Syndicate. All rights reserved; p. 295, Mike Luckovich. © 2000. Reprinted by permission of Creators Syndicate.

Chapter 12: p. 347, Figure 12.3 adapted from The Alan Guttmacher Institute.

Chapter 13: p. 373, Table adapted with permission from "Normative Sexual Behavior in Children: A Contemporary Sample," by W. Friedrich, J. Fisher, D. Broughton, M. Houston, and C. Shafran, *Pediatrics*, 1998, Vol. 101, Page e9, Copyright 1998; p. 378, Table 13.1 adapted with permission from "Age at Menarche and Racial Comparisons in U.S. Girls," by W. Chumlea, C. Schubert, A. Roche, H. Kulin, P. Lee, J. Himes, and S. Sun, *Pediatrics*, Vol. 111, Pages 110–113, Copyright 2003; page 390, Table 13.7 reproduced with permission of The Alan Guttmacher Institute from: Singh S and Darroch JE, Adolescent pregnancy and childbearing: trends from developed countries, *Family Planning Perspectives*, 2000, 32(1): 14–23.

Chapter 14: p. 409, Quiz reprinted by permission of John Gottman and originally appeared in *Newsweek*, April 19, 1999.

Chapter 15: p. 430, Figure 15.1 reprinted with permission from *Global Study of Sexual Attitudes and Behaviors* funded by Pfizer Inc. Copyright 2002 Pfizer Inc. All rights reserved.

Chapter 16: p. 453, Exercise from *Love Skills*, by L. DeVillers, published by Impact Publishers, San Luis Obispo, CA. Copyright © 1997 Linda DeVillers. Reprinted by permission of the author.

Author Index

Dahir, M., 407
Daily, D., 78
D'Alessandro, J., 78
Dall'Ara, E., 574
Dalton, S., 293
Daly, M., 203
Damson, P., 390
Daniluk, J., 421, 424, 438
Daoli, B., 404
Darling, C., 91, 172, 446
Daro, D., 572
Darroch, J., 384, 388, 389, 390, 392, 473
D'Augelli, A., 279
Dauphinee, J., 365
David, H., 149, 302
Davidson, J., 446
Davies, M., 562, 572
Davis, B., 447
Davis, D., 73, 115
Davis, K., 183, 187, 196
Davis, M., 187
Davis, P., 385, 388
Davis, S., 102, 127, 147, 149, 150
Davison, G., 529, 535, 537, 538
Davtyan, C., 390, 391, 392, 396
Dawes, R., 567
D'Cruz, O., 332
De Amicis, L., 466
Dean, K., 553
Dean, M., 506
Dearnaley, D., 124, 144
DeBlassie, R., 391
De Bro, S., 317
DeCaro, F., 283
Decker, D., 106
Deckers, P., 114
DeGarmo, D., 419
Degler, C., 10
Dehne, K., 501
Deitch, C., 351
Dekker, J., 131
De Knijff, D., 330
De Lacoste, M., 53
DeLaMar, R., 343
DeLamater, J., 58, 173, 175, 371, 372, 374, 375, 376
Delaney, J., 94
Del Carmen, R., 213
Deliganis, A., 165
Delzell, J., 107
Démare, D., 34
DeMartino, M., 158
DeMarzo, A., 141
Demian, N., 268

D'Emilio, J., 10, 300
Demmons, S., 198, 211, 220
Dempsey, C., 387
Dennerstein, L., 99, 148, 151
Denny, D., 65, 281
Denov, M., 566
D'Epiro, P., 107
DeQuine, J., 290
Derlego, V., 220
Des Jarlais, D., 493
Dessens, A., 66
Deutsch, A., 277
Deveny, K., 403, 412, 417, 443
Devi, K., 152, 153
De Villers, L., 453
Dewar, H., 347
Dewhurst, A., 569
Diamant, A., 271
Diamond, L., 268, 270, 271, 272
Diamond, M., 52, 53, 60, 61, 62
Diamond, R., 338
Dickerson, L., 100
Dickey, C., 7
Dickey, R., 343
DiClemente, R., 514
Diekstra, R., 569
Dietz, P., 348
Dilley, J., 512
Dilorio, C., 566
Dindia, K., 214, 215
Dines, G., 584
Disease-a-Month, 115
Dishion, T., 385
Dittman, M., 388, 390
Dittmann, M., 159
Dittus, P., 386
Dobosz, A., 18
Dobrzykowski, T., 361
Doctor, R., 531
Dodson, B., 247
Dolan, E., 419, 426
Donahey, K., 466
Donenberg, G., 382, 384
Dong, M., 568
Donnelly, J., 422
Donnelly, P., 150
Donnerstein, E., 34, 585, 589
Donovan, G., 584
Donovan, P., 389
Dormire, S., 106, 107
Doshi, N., 109
Dotinga, R., 278
Douglas, K., 11, 12

Douglas, W., 73
Douglass, F., 190
Douglass, R., 190
Dover, J., 387
Dow, M., 148
Downs, A., 501
Doyle, J., 70, 72
Draucker, C., 560
Dreger, A., 62
Drossman, D., 560
Drucker, E., 514
Druzin, P., 287
Dubé, E., 286, 288, 291
Duckworth, J., 416
Duddle, M., 560
Duenwald, M., 467
Duerr, A., 496
Dumond, R., 562
Dunn, J., 221
Dunn, M., 132, 179, 388, 419, 422, 423
Dunne, M., 565
Dunsmuir, W., 434
Durand, V., 528
Durkin, K., 567
Durlak, J., 569
Duty, S., 339
Dwyer, M., 538
Dwyer, S., 535, 564
Dyer, J., 556
Dykes, B., 270

E
Eastham, J., 141
Eaton, L., 513
Eccles, A., 553
Eccles, J., 72
Ecker, N., 152
The Economist, 593
Edozien, F., 290
Edwards, M., 303
Edwards, R., 86
Edwards, T., 401, 407
Edwards, W., 287
Ehrenfeld, T., 339
Ehrenreich, B., 54, 95, 304
Ehrhardt, A., 60, 62
Eisenberg, V., 344
Eisner, T., 160
Eitzen, D., 74
Elber, L., 15, 16
Elias, J., 374
Eliason, M., 268
Eliasson, R., 131
Elizabeth, V., 402
Elkind, D., 388
Elkousy, M., 365

Ellertson, C., 346, 348
Elliott, J., 435
Elliott, K., 435, 569
Elliott, L., 242, 248, 262, 286, 444, 446
Elliott, M., 566
Ellis, L., 244
Ellison, C., 87, 88, 248, 251, 257, 259, 436, 444, 445, 446, 457, 459, 470
Ellison, F., 4
Elster, N., 344
Eltabbakh, G., 110
Emberton, M., 434
Emery, R., 413
Emmert, D., 476, 477, 479, 481, 482, 485, 486, 487, 488, 490
Engelberg, R., 486, 488
Epp, S., 101, 379
Epperly, T., 315
Epstein, A., 290
Equal Employment Opportunity Commission, 573, 574
Ericksen, J., 569, 571
Erlich, K., 487
Ernst, E., 159
Eschenbach, D., 502
Eskeland, B., 158
Espinoza, G., 402, 438
Espo, D., 301
Esquivel, C., 478
Ethics Committee, American Society for Reproductive Medicine, 344
Eva, L., 488
Evans, J., 587
Evaraerd, W., 448
Everaerd, W., 452
Exodus International, 279
Eyler, F., 360
Ezzell, C., 503

F
Faerman, M., 337
Faerstein, E., 110, 339
Fagan, P., 456
Fagot, B., 72
Fair, W., 140
Faison, S., 338
Falk, L., 478
Fallon, B., 330
Falwell, J., 15
Farber, N., 382
Farr, L., 111, 118
Faucher, M., 364
Fauser, B., 94, 341

LoPiccolo, J., 423, 430, 436, 440, 442, 444, 445, 460, 465, 466, 468
LoPresto, C., 380
Lorber, J., 58
Lorch, D., 287, 559
Lorente, C., 360
Louderback, L., 280, 281, 283
Louis, M., 509
Loulan, J., 256
Love, P., 151, 188
Love, S., 117
Lowenstein, L., 529
Lown, J., 419, 426
Lowndes, C., 501
Loy, P., 575
Luchsinger, G., 277
Lukwago, S., 115
Lumpkin, M., 73
Lurie, P., 514
Lynch, C., 360
Lynch, D., 388
Lynch, F., 287
Lynxwiler, J., 351, 352
Lyon, P., 268
Lytton, H., 71

M
Maass, A., 574
Macaluso, M., 318
Maccoby, E., 72, 221
MacDonald, A., Jr., 270, 271
MacDonald, T., 159
Mackellar, D., 508
MacKinnon, C., 41, 575
Macklon, N., 94
Maclan, P., 156
Magid, D., 478
Maguen, S., 507
Mahmoodian, S., 109
Mahoney, J., 305, 348
Mahoney, S., 421, 425
Maier, J., 364
Majewska, M., 53
Mak, T., 73
Malamuth, N., 36, 550, 553
Malatesta, C., 221
Malebranche, D., 501
Maletzky, B., 542
Mallon, G., 285
Malloy, K., 348, 353
Malony, J., 364
Maltz, W., 243, 245, 246, 252, 253, 262, 439
Mandoki, M., 56

Manecke, R., 131, 430, 431, 432, 444
Mangels, A., 284
Manguno-Mire, G., 53
Mann, D., 332
Mann, K., 159
Mannino, D., 161
Mansfield, P., 102, 174
Mansky, L., 509
Mansour, D., 311
Mao, C., 492
Maravilla, K., 165
Marbella, A., 115
Marchione, M., 115
Marcus, D., 192
Marcus, E., 287
Margolies, E., 353
Margolis, L., 40
Marin, A., 576
Marin, R., 15
Markowitz, J., 313
Marks, N., 401
Marolla, J., 551
Marrone, N., 289
Marshall, D., 124
Marshall, W., 24, 535, 536, 542, 553
Marsiglio, W., 393
Martin, C., 70, 331
Martin, D., 268
Martin, J., 388
Martin, M., 529
Martin, T., 418
Martinson, F., 372, 374, 375, 376, 394
Marvin, C., 439
Marx, T., 338
Massad, L., 109
Masters, W., 135, 138, 162, 163, 173, 174, 177, 178, 256, 261, 355, 422, 446, 457, 560, 562
Matek, O., 536
Mathes, E., 203
Mathias-Riegel, B., 420
Matikainen, T., 338
Matson, F., 372
Matteo, S., 99
Matteson, D., 289
Matthews, G., 330
Matyas, J., 313
Maurer, L., 281
Maxwell, K., 595
May, R., 188
Mayo Clinic Health Oasis, 107
Mayor, S., 110, 513
Mays, V., 289, 516

Mazer, D., 577
Mazhar, D., 143, 144, 148
McAninch, C., 72
McArthur, J., 378
McBride, C., 383, 384, 385, 388
McBride, G., 350
McCabe, J., 396
McCabe, M., 156, 197, 198, 433
McCaghy, C., 594
McCarthy, B., 435, 438, 460, 467, 469
McCarthy, E., 438, 469
McCarthy, S., 435
McCauley, A., 338
McClaren, A., 501
McCormick, C., 273
McCormick, F., 86
McCormick, N., 40, 41
McCormick, S., 116
McCoy, N., 157, 313, 422, 426
McCullough, A., 110
McDonald, C., 198
McElroy, W., 587, 591, 593
McEwen, B., 151, 188
McFarlane, J., 100
McFarlone, M., 544
McGee, M., 393
McGee, R., 565
McGinn, S., 422
McGrew, M., 390
McGuire, V., 106
McHale, S., 71
McKee, K., 17
McKenna, K., 38
McKenna, P., 127
McKibben, A., 554, 564
McKinney, K., 191, 382, 384
McKirnan, D., 271
McLaren, A., 300
McLean, L., 568
McLeod, A., 293
McNeil, E., 193
McNeill, B., 69
McNicholas, T., 147, 148, 150, 151
McNiven, P., 362
McQuaide, S., 421
McVary, K., 465
Mead, M., 46
Mead, R., 344, 431
Means-Christensen, A., 291
Media Report to Women, 73

Medical Center for Human Rights, 562
Medical Ethics Advisor, 467
Medrano, M., 592
Meeks, B., 188
Mehta, A., 338
Mehta, S., 481
Meier, E., 350
Meiselman, K., 569
Melby, T., 63, 123, 124, 137, 138
Melchert, T., 566, 571
Mendenhall, P., 559
Mercy, T., 388
Merson, M., 517
Mertz, K., 479
Meschke, L., 383, 391, 393, 396
Messenger, J., 153
Messner, M., 478
Meston, C., 30, 91, 103, 159, 434, 467, 569, 571
Meuwissen, I., 99
Meyer, M., 8
Meyer, S., 285
Meyer, W., 66
Meyer-Bahlburg, H., 57
Meyn, L., 364
Mezin, Z., 350
Mezy, G., 562
Michael, M., 592
Michael, R., 2, 247, 287, 290, 383
Michaels, D., 585
Michels, K., 106, 107
Michelson, D., 155, 161, 542
Midgley, C., 72
Midyett, L., 378
Migeon, C., 60
Milburn, A., 448
Milet, T., 365
Milhausen, R., 380
Mill, J., 503
Miller, B., 396
Miller, D., 439
Miller, H., 478, 481
Miller, J., 340, 344
Miller, K., 191, 396, 477, 486, 492, 493, 494
Miller, L., 101, 511
Miller, M., 279
Miller, R., 192
Miller, S., 15, 466
Miller, T., 443, 444
Million Women Study Collaborators, 105, 106
Mills, J., 489, 490

Milow, V., 94
Mindel, A., 489, 490
Minichiello, V., 385, 595, 596
Minkoff, H., 505, 512
Minnis, A., 318
Minor, M., 535, 564
Minto, C., 63
Mintz, H., 568
Mishra, R., 109
Misrahi, M., 506
Mitchell, D., 562
Mitka, M., 114, 360, 463
Miya-Jervis, L., 404
Modelska, K., 103
Mohr, D., 464
Moller, L., 72
Mona, L., 433
Mondics, C., 280
Money, D., 506
Money, J., 56, 60, 61, 62, 66, 135, 198, 274, 527, 532, 538, 540, 541
Monga, T., 432
Monroe, I., 290
Monsen, R. B., 95
Montagu, A., 372
Montague, D., 444
Montauk, S., 371
Montemayor, R., 77
Montgomery, M., 188
Montomoli, M., 101
Moodley, D., 512
Moodley, P., 514
Moon, S., 401, 402
Moore, K., 324
Morales, A., 150, 151
Morales, E., 289
Moran, G., 484
Moran, R., 11, 405
Morehouse, R., 435, 437, 452
Moreno, V., 323
Morgan, A., 340
Morgan, E., 10
Morgan, F., 295
Morgan, K., 268
Morgan, R., 302
Morganthau, T., 294
Morgentaler, A., 339
Morin, J., 261
Morlock, R., 93
Morra, N., 537
Morrell, M., 174
Morrin, K., 54
Morris, C., 117
Morris, G., 63
Moses, S., 137
Mosher, C., 58, 532

Mosher, D., 156, 253, 254
Mosher, E., 4
Mosher, W., 315
Mossad, S., 485
Mott, F., 382
Muehlenhard, C., 379, 550, 552, 553, 554, 555, 556, 557, 562, 577
Mulcahy, J., 443, 444, 464
Mulhall, J., 131, 430, 431, 432, 444
Muller, J., 116
Mulligan, T., 426
Munarriz, R., 456
Munoz, N., 491, 492
Munsick, R., 447
Murnen, S., 156, 191
Murphy, D., 5, 387, 473, 510, 511
Murphy, E., 302, 347, 358, 501
Murphy, P., 301, 314, 324
Murray, C., 116
Murray, J., 564
Murray, K., 493
Murray, L., 410, 412
Murray, P., 482, 495, 496, 497
Murray, S., 437
Murry, V., 384
Murstein, B., 197, 388
Mustanski, B., 273
Myers, S., 575
Myerson, M., 78
Mzaidume, Z., 504

N
Nadler, R., 536
Nadler, S., 432
Nanson, J., 359
Napolitane, C., 419
Nash, J., 443, 465
Nashelsky, J., 108
Nass, S., 331
Nasseri, M., 340
National Center for Health Statistics, 417
National Council on Sexual Addiction and Compulsivity, 545
National Gay and Lesbian Task Force, 291, 292, 407
Nattinger, A., 114
Naughton, K., 463
Neale, J., 529, 535, 537, 538
Nechas, L., 317
Nelson, J., 282

Nelson, M., 278
Ness, C., 387
Ness, R., 92, 477, 495
Neto, F., 184
Neumark-Sztainer, D., 396
Nevadunsky, N., 105, 106, 107
Nevid, J., 192
Newcomer, S., 392
Newton, W., 143, 144
The New Yorker Collection, 440
Ngugi, E., 504
Niccolai, L., 390, 391
Nicholas, H., 481
Nichols, M., 251, 252, 268, 292, 435, 442
Nicholson, K., 556
Nicolosi, J., 279
Nielsen, K., 569
Nielson, J., 54
Nilsson, L., 338
Nilsson, U., 495
Nishith, P., 554
Nissl, J., 324
Nixin, D., 136
Noble, M., 447
Noh, P., 127
Noll, J., 568
Noller, P., 195
Noonan, D., 340
Norris, D., 468
Norris, J., 24
Northridge, M., 501
Nour, N., 86
Novak, A., 313
Nurnberg, H., 434
Nusbaum, M., 430
Nussbaum, E., 60, 63
Nuttin, J., 189
Nyirjesy, P., 497
Nystrom, N., 424

O
O'Brien, P., 100
Ochs, E., 30
O'Connor, A., 405
Odejinmi, F., 332
O'Donnell, L., 382, 383, 384, 388
O'Donohue, W., 429, 550
Offman, U., 14
Ogden, G., 429, 452
Ogden, J., 53
O'Hanlan, K., 293
Olds, D., 359
Olds, J., 153
O'Leary, M., 445

Oliver, M., 107
Olivera, A., 161
Olson, B., 73
Olson, D., 410
Oman, R., 389
Omeragic, F., 389
O'Neill, P., 102, 438, 556
O'Neill-Morante, M., 491, 492
Ono, A., 89, 338, 367
Orbuch, T., 404
Ordonez, J., 583
Osborn, C., 528, 538
Osland, J., 583
Osman, A., 455
Ostling, R., 4
Ostriker, A., 117
O'Sullivan, L., 380, 555
O'Sullivan, S., 291
Oswald, R., 285
Otis, J., 277
Ott, M., 388
Otto, H., 251
Over, R., 99, 131
Overbeck, G., 382
Owen, L., 94

P
Pace, B., 107, 114, 521
Pace, J., 432
Padawer, J., 365
Padian, N., 318
Page, D., 49
Page, R., 558
Palefsky, J., 492
Palguta, R., Jr., 426
Palmer, C., 552
Palmer, J., 102, 110
Palmer, L., 351
Paludi, M., 70, 72
Pam, A., 183
Pan, E., 405
Pancholi, P., 493, 494
Pao, M., 387
Paperny, D., 38
Pappas, L., 8
Pappert, A., 344
Paradis, B., 289
Parcel, G., 396
Pardum, C., 17
Paredes, R., 154
Parham, T., 214
Parish, W., 479, 480
Parker, C., 124, 144
Parker, L., 54
Parker, R., 566
Parks, C., 213, 285, 290
Parrot, A., 549, 553

Subject Index

sexual responsiveness and, 25, 34, 36

Alcohol/drug dependency treatment, celibacy during, 242

Alexithymia, 221

Altruistic love style, 187, 188

AMA (American Medical Association), 40

Ambiguous external genitalia, 49, 61

Amenorrhea, 102

American Academy of Pediatrics (AAP), 138

American Cancer Society, Reach to Recovery program, 117

American Civil Liberties Union, 589

American Medical Association (AMA), 40

American Psychological Association (APA), 40, 570

Amniocentesis, 338, 360–361

Amniotic fluid, 360

Amphetamines, 188–189
  aphrodisiac qualities of, 159, 160t
  sexual effects of, 431t

Ampulla, 132

Amygdala, 153

Amyl nitrite, aphrodisiac qualities of, 160t

Anal stimulation, 9, 261

Ananga Ranga, 134

Anaphrodisiacs, 160–161

Anatomy of Love: The Natural History of Monogamy, Adultery, and Divorce, 418

Androgen-blocking drugs. *See* Antiandrogen drugs

Androgen insensitivity syndrome (AIS), 55t, 56

Androgens, 50, 147, 424. *See also* Testosterone

Androgeny, 77–78

Androgyny, in later life, 424–425

Anesthesia, during childbirth, 364

Anilingus, 261

Animals
  ground-up horns of, as aphrodisiacs, 158–159
  pheromones and, 157

Anorgasmia, 444–445
  female
    experiencing with partner, 457–459, 458f
    sex therapy programs for, 456–457, 457f
  male coital or partner, 445
  situational, 444–445

Antagonism, toward women, 10

Anteflexed uterus, 93

Antiabortion groups, 350–352

Antiandrogen drugs, 148
  for coercive paraphilias, 542
  for prostate cancer, 143, 144

Anticancer drugs, sexual functioning and, 434

Antidepressants, sexual functioning and, 434

Antidiscrimination, 294–296

Antigay marriage issues, 406–407

Antihypertensive drugs
  inhibition of sexual desire/behavior, 161
  sexual functioning and, 434

Antipsychotic drugs
  inhibition of sexual desire/behavior, 161
  sexual functioning and, 434

Anus, 84f

Anxiety
  about sexual communication, 215
  sexual function and, 438–439
  in sexual relationships, 242

Anxious-ambivalent attachment
  adult intimate relationships and, 195–196, 196t
  description of, 194

APA (American Psychological Association), 40, 570

Aphrodisiacs, 158–160

Aquinas, Thomas, 9

Areola, 112

ArginMax, 467

Arousal
  breast/nipple stimulation and, 112
  vaginal lubrication and, 91

ART. *See* Assisted reproductive technology

Arthritis, sexual function and, 432

Artificial insemination, 340
  with sperm-separation techniques, 338

Asian Americans
  gender roles of, 70
  sexual communication and, 213–214
  sexual patterns of, 3

Asians. *See also* China
  homosexuality and, 289

Assisted reproductive technology (ART), 341
  ethical, legal and personal dilemmas, 344
  health/financial problems with, 341–343, 341t, 342f

Athletes, female, amenorrhea and, 102

Attachment, 184, 194
  adult intimate relationships and, 195–196, 196t
  styles of, 194–195

Attitudes
  cultural, toward extramarital relationships, 413
  maternal, toward child sex behaviors, 373
  sexual, social groups and, 4
  sexual difficulties and, 437
  societal, toward sexual orientation, 276–284
  violent, toward females, 24–25

Attractiveness, cultural diversity in, 153

Augustine, 9

Autism, oxytocin levels in, 151

Autoerotic asphyxia, 533–534

Autoimmune symptoms, from breast implants, 118

Autosomes, 48

Aversive conditioning, for coercive paraphilias, 541–542

Avoidant attachment, 194–196, 196t

B

"Baby blues," 366

Backup methods, for birth control, 305

Bacterial infections, sexually transmitted, 474t, 477–486, 478f, 481f, 484f, 485f

Bacterial vaginosis, 495–496
  symptoms, 475t
  transmission, 475t
  treatment, 475t

Bad reputation, sexuality and, 5

Barbiturates
  aphrodisiac qualities of, 160t
  sexual effects of, 431t

Barrier contraceptive methods, 308t–309t, 314–315
  condoms. *See* Condoms
  effectiveness of, 306t

Bartholin's glands, 88

Basal body temperature method, 309t, 326, 327f

Bed nucleus of the stria terminalis, 52

Behavior therapy, for coercive paraphilias, 541

Belligerence, 236

Benign prostatic hyperplasia (BPH), 141

Ben-wa balls, 251

Berman and Berman, 16

Bianchi, Kenneth, 24

Bible
  gender-accurate wording in, 74
  sexual references in, 8–9

Biological theories, of sexual orientation, 272–276

over-the-counter, sexual
functioning and,
434
sexual functioning and,
434
Dry orgasms, 132
Dry sex, 503
*DSM-IV-TR. See Diagnostic
and Statistical Manual
of Mental Disorders*
DSS gene (femaleness
gene), 50
DVDs, X-rated, 584–584
Dysmenorrhea, 100–101
Dyspareunia, 447–448

E
Ectoparasitic infections,
sexually transmitted,
497–499, 498f
Ectopic pregnancy, 93, 313,
478
ED. *See* Erectile dysfunction
Editing, 235
EDMR (eye movement
desensitization and
reprocessing), 468
Education level
of breastfeeding moth-
ers, 366
masturbation and, 2
of mother, number of
children and, 302,
302f
sexual problems and,
429, 429t
Effacement, 364
Eisenstadt v. Baird, 300
Either/or questions, 219
Ejaculate, taste of, 259, 259t
Ejaculation, 131–133, 132f
delaying, techniques for,
460
first, 379
into mouth, 259
nongenitally induced,
133
premature. *See* Prema-
ture ejaculation
retrograde, 133
serotonin and, 154
Ejaculatory duct, 130
Elective abortion, 345, 345t
complications from,
346
procedures for, 345–347,
346f

Electronic devices, for
measuring sexual
arousal, 36–37, 37f
Embryos
frozen, legal control of,
344
preselecting sex of,
337–338
Emergency contraception,
324–325
Emission phase, of male
orgasm, 132, 132f, 168
Emotional difficulties, sexual function and,
438–439
Emotional intelligence,
development of, 221
Emotions, negative,
expressing appropri-
ately, 228–229
Empty love, 186
Endometriosis, 101, 448
Endometritis, 477
Endometrium, 93, 97
Endorphins, 189
Environmental factors,
breast cancer risk and,
115, 115t
Epididymis, 127–128
Epididymitis, 478, 481
Episiotomy, 364
Equal Employment Oppor-
tunity Commission
(EEOC), sexual
harassment guide-
lines, 573–574
Erectile dysfunction (ED),
443–444, 443t
acquired, 443
incidence of, 443t
lifelong, 443
treatment, 436, 462
mechanical devices,
464
medical, 462–464
surgical, 464–465, 464f
treatment of, 443–444
Erection, 131, 436
Erection-enhancing drugs,
462–464
Erogenous zones, 155
Eros (romantic love), 187,
188
Erotica, 156, 585
Erotic dreams, 242–243
Erotic fantasy, 243–244
Erotosexual differentiation,
527

Essure coil, 329, 329f
Estrogen-progestin pills,
308t
Estrogens, 50
in adolescence, 377
aging and, 424
breast cancer risk and,
105–106
in hormone replacement
therapy, 103
menstruation and, 97
production of, 147
therapy, sexual benefits
of, 148–149
urethral/vaginal tissues
and, 174
Ethical issues
assisted reproductive
technologies, 344
human sex research
guidelines, 40
sex research in cyber-
space, 40
Ethnicity
adolescent pregnancy
and, 390
adolescent sexual experi-
ence and, 383–384,
384t
age at menarche and,
378–379
breast cancer and, 115
childhood sexual behav-
iors and, 373
gender roles and, 69–70
homosexuality and,
289–290
inner-group variations,
2–3
legal abortion and, 352
masturbation and, 248
oral-genital sex and, 2
prostate cancer and,
141–142
sexual behavior and, 32,
33t
sexual response and,
152
variations in intimate
communication,
213–214
Evagelium Vitae, 302–303
Eve, as evil temptress, 10
Evolutionary perspective,
on gender-role social-
ization, 71
Evolutionary psychology,
71

Excitement phase, of sexual
response, 162, 162f,
164, 166
difficulties with,
443–444, 443f
female, 168f
internal genital
response, 169f
in older women,
173–174
sexual anatomy dur-
ing, 168f
in Kaplan's three-stage
model, 161–162,
162f
male
aging and, 174–175
sexual anatomy dur-
ing, 167f
physiological changes in,
166t
Exhibitionism, 535–536
Exodus International, 279
Experimental research, 25t,
35–36
Expulsion phase, of sexual
response
of male orgasm,
132–133, 132f, 168
male sexual anatomy
during, 167f
External genitalia
anatomy of, 48t
prenatal development of,
50, 51f
Extramarital relationships,
413
consensual, 415–416
cultural attitudes
toward, 413
impact on marriage, 415
incidence of, 414–415
Internet and, 415
nonconsensual sex, 413
reasons for, 413–414
Extramarital sex, 8
Eye contact, in face-to-face
communication, 217
Eye infections
chlamydial conjunctivi-
tis, 478, 478f
gonococcal, 482

F
Facial expression, in sexual
communication, 233
Facial hair, during puberty,
379

Homophobia, 280–282, 281f
Homosexuality, 9, 269–270, 270t
  in adolescence, 386–387
  antigay violence, 15
  childhood same-sex experiences and, 376
  coming out, 285, 285t
  in Cuba, 277
  denial of, 281–282
  disclosure of, 287
  ethnicity and, 289–290
  family life and, 292–293
  finger length patterns and, 273
  gender nonconformity and, 275
  genetic factors, 274–275
  handedness and, 273
  hypoactive sexual desire and, 442
  increasing acceptance of, 283
  innateness of, 275–276
  Judeo-Christian attitudes toward, 277–278
  lifestyles, 284–293
  media and, 283–284
  media portrayal of, 15
  as mental disorder, 14
  as mental illness, 278–279
  self-acceptance of, 286–287
  self-acknowledgement, 285–286, 286t
  sexually explicit materials, 584
Homosexuals, 268
  faking orgasms and, 446, 446t
  love and sex relationship, 198
  male, HIV/AIDS and, 500–501
  Nazi persecution of, 293
  relationships, 291–292, 424
  sex research on, 41
  sexual victimization of, 562–563
Honor killings, 7
Hormonal sex, 48t, 50
Hormone-based contraceptives, 308t

effectiveness of, 306t
  for emergency contraception, 324–325
  injected, 314
  oral. See Oral contraceptives
  transdermal patch, 313–314
  vaginal ring, 313–314, 313f
Hormone replacement therapy (HRT)
  alternatives, 106–107
  decision-making, 107
  delivery systems for, 104
  for menopause, 103–107
  research, challenges in, 105
  risks/benefits of, 104, 104t, 105
Hormones. See also specific hormones
  adult levels, homosexuality and, 274
  for menopause, 103–107
  pubertal changes in, 377–379, 377f
  for transsexuals, 67
Hospital births, 362
Hostile environment, sexual harassment and, 574
Hot flashes, 103, 106
HPV (human papillomavirus), 109, 491–493, 492f
HRT. See Hormone replacement therapy
HSD. See Hypoactive sexual desire
HSV (herpes simplex virus), 486
Human chorionic gonadotropin (HCG), 343
Human immunodeficiency virus (HIV), 473, 499. See also Acquired immunodeficiency syndrome
  in Africa, 502–505
  AIDS development and, 508–509
  antibody testing, 507–508
  in China, 480
  effect on teenage sexual behavior, 387–388

forms of, 499
  incidence of, 422, 500–502
  injection drug users and, 501
  Kenyan education project, 29
  mother-to-child transmission, preventing, drug therapy for, 512–513
  origin of, 499
  peer-educator-based intervention programs, 504
  prevention, 513–515
  primary infection, 505
  prostitution and, 591, 594
  resistance to, 506
  risk
    anal intercourse and, 261
    oral sex and, 260
  seroconversion, 507
  symptoms/complications, 507–509, 509f
  target cells, 499–500
  testing, prenatal, 358
  transmission, 131, 501, 505–507
    during pregnancy, 358
    prevention, contraception for, 301
  treatment, 509–513, 510t
  vaccines, 513
  women and, 502
Human papillomavirus (HPV), 109, 491–493, 492f
Human Sexual Inadequacy (Masters & Johnson), 14
Human Sexual Response (Masters & Johnson), 14, 34
H-Y antigen, homosexuality and, 274
Hyde Amendment, 349
Hymen, 87–88
Hymenalplasty, 87
Hypersexuality, 543–545
Hypoactive sexual desire (HSD)
  symptoms of, 441–442
  treatment of, 465–466
Hypogonadism, 148
Hypothalamus

anatomy of, 52, 52f
  electrical stimulation of, 153–154
  lateral, 154
  menstruation and, 96f, 97
  in sexual functioning, 154
Hysterectomy, 109–110

I
ICSI (intracytoplasmic sperm injection), 339, 341t
"I" language, 223–224
Illegal abortions, 347
Illness, chronic, sexual function and, 431–432
Immunocontraceptives, 332
Impasses, 237
Imperforate hymen, 87
Incest, 563–564
Income level, of breastfeeding mothers, 366
Independent variables, in experimental research, 35–36
Individualistic cultures (individualism), 213, 405
Infant, preselecting sex of, 337–338
Infantcide, 304, 337
Infant sexuality, 371–372
Infatuation, 186
Infertility, 338–340
  female, 338–339
  male, 339–340
  sexuality and, 340
Inguinal canal, 127
Injection drug use, HIV/AIDS and, 501
Insecure attachment, 194
Insight-oriented therapy, 467–468
Intact dilation and evacuation, 347
Interaction model of gender identity, 61
Intercourse
  during adolescence, 382
  adolescence, predisposing factors, 385–386
  coital positions, 261–265, 262f–265f, 262t
  considerations during, 134

male, 331–332
mechanism of action, 311
selection of, 310
side effects, 313
usage, method for, 311
Oral-genital stimulation, 258–260, 259f
adolescent, 381
cultural variations of, 152
ethnic differences in, 2
experiences of American men and women, 260–261, 260t
as having sex, 5
heterosexuals and, 259
HIV/AIDS transmission and, 505–506
as unnatural act, 9
Oral herpes, symptoms/ complications, 488–489
Oral sex. *See* Oral-genital stimulation
Orchidectomy, 148
Orgasm
definition of, 168
faking, 446, 446t
female, 444–445, 444t
clitoral, 23, 171
external genital response, 168f
facilitation of, 459f
internal genital response, 169f
misinformation on, 170–171
in older women, 174
sex therapy programs for, 456–457, 457f
sexual anatomy during, 168f, 169f
subjective descriptions of, 170
vaginal, 23, 171
Grafenberg spot, 91, 171–173, 172f
lesbian *vs.* heterosexual married females, 256, 256t
male, 132–133, 132f, 170
multiple, 177–179
nocturnal, 171, 242–243
of older men, 175
physiological changes in, 166t

in sexual response cycle, 162, 162f
in sexual response cycle, Kaplan's model of, 161–162, 162f
subjective descriptions of, 170
Orgasmic platform, 166
Orgasmic reconditioning, for coercive paraphilias, 542
Orgasm-phase sexual difficulties, 444–446
Orthodox Jews, sexuality and, 4
Ortho Evra (transdermal patch), 313–314
Our Bodies Ourselves (Boston Women's Health Collective), 14
Outercourse, 307, 308t
Outing, 289
Ova donation, 341
Ovarian cancer, risk, breast cancer genes and, 114
Ovaries, 49, 93–94
during menstruation, 96f, 97, 98f
surgical removal of, 109–110
Over-the-counter drugs, sexual functioning and, 434
Ovulation, 94
inhibition, by breast-feeding, 366
pain at, 311
problems, 338
time estimation for, 337
timing of, 98, 99f
Ovulation method (mucus method), 326
Ovum, 48–49
Oxygen deprivation, pressure-induced, 534
Oxytocin, 147, 151, 188

P
"PAINS," for IUD symptoms, 323, 323t
PAP (prostatic acid phosphatase), 172
Pap smear, 109
ParaGard (copper-T), 309t, 322, 325
Paraphilias, 527
coercive, 534

exhibitionism, 535–536
frotteurism, 538
necrophilia, 540
obscene phone calls, 536–537
treatment of, 540–543
voyeurism, 537–538, 539
vs. noncoercive, 528
zoophilia, 539–540
noncoercive
autoerotic asphyxia, 533–534
coprophilia, 534
fetishism, 528–529
klismaphilia, 534
sexual masochism, 531–533
sexual sadism, 531–533
transvestic fetishism, 530–531
urophilia, 534
vs. coercive, 528
Paraphrasing
in active listening, 217–218
of sexual complaints, 229–230
Parenthood, as option, 336–337
Parents
gender-role socialization and, 70–71
notification, for abortion for juvenile, 350
sex information/education from, 394–396
talking about sex to, 3
Parents, Families and Friends of Lesbians and Gays (PFLAG), 288–289
Partial celibacy, 241
Partner, sexual
choice, race and, 190–191, 191t
needs of
discovering, 218–222
giving permission for, 222
making requests for, 222–224
Partner anorgasmia, 445
Partner-engagement style, 253
Passing, 287

Passion, 185–186, 186f
Passionate love, 184–185
Passive listening, 216
PEA (phenylethylamine), 188–189
Pedophiles, in cyberspace, 567–568
Pedophilia, 563
Peeping Toms, 537–538, 539
Peer-educator-based HIV/AIDS intervention programs, 504
Peer groups, gender-role socialization and, 72
Pelvic floor muscles, 88
Pelvic inflammatory disease (PID), 473, 477–478
bacterial vaginosis and, 495
gonococcal, 481–482
risk, with IUD, 323
Pelvic thrusts, infant, 371–372
Penile augmentation, 134
Penile cancer, 137, 140
Penile implants, 464–465, 464f
Penile strain gauge, 36–37, 37f
Penile-vaginal intercourse, 5
Penis
anatomy of, 122–125, 123f
construction, in sex reassignment procedures, 67–68, 67f
ejaculation. *See* Ejaculation
erection, 131
flaccid state, 134
fractured, 139–140
health care issues, 139–140
musculature around, strengthening of, 125
size, 133–135
uncircumcised, 124, 124f
washing, 139
Penis envy, 14
Penis thievery, 136
Penitentials, 9
Performance anxiety, 436–437
Perfumes, as sexual stimulants, 157

Scabies, 475t, 498
School, gender-role socialization and, 72–73
School-based education programs
on preventing child sex abuse, 570
for sex education, 396–397
Scrotum
anatomy of, 125–126, 125f, 126f
temperature changes and, 126
Seasonale, 308t, 309–311
Secondary amenorrhea, 102
Secondary dysmenorrhea, 100–101
Secondary erogenous zones, 155
Secondary sex characteristics, 93, 110, 377
Secondary syphilis, 474t, 484, 485f
Second-stage labor, 363f, 364
Secretory phase, of menstrual cycle, 98–99
Secure attachment, 194–196, 196t
Seduction myth, 272
Selective estrogen receptor modulators (SERMs), 107
Selective serotonin reuptake inhibitors (SSRIs), 155, 542–543
Self-acceptance, of homosexuality, 286–287
Self-acknowledgement, of homosexuality, 285–286, 286t
Self-administered questionnaires, 37
Self-awareness, sexual enhancement and, 452–453
Self-concept, sexual difficulties and, 437–438
Self-consciousness, sexual difficulties and, 437–438
Self-disclosure, about sexual likes/dislikes, 219–220
Self-examinations
breast, 112, 112f, 113f

genitals
female, 84–85
male, 128
vagina, 108
Self-pleasuring. See Masturbation
Self-restaint, in Victorian era, 11
Self-selection, survey research and, 28, 30
Self-stimulation, with partner present, 457–459, 458f
Self-worth, unrequited love and, 202
Semen, 130–131
Seminal fluid, 130–131
Seminal vesicles, 130, 379
Seminiferous tubules, 127
Sensate focus, 454–455, 454f, 458f
Senses, sexual arousal and, 155–158
Sensory amplification, 433
Serial monogamy, 402
SERMs (selective estrogen receptor modulators), 107
Seroconversion, 507
Serotonin, 154–155
Sex. See specific aspects of
in advertising, 17–18
in companionate love, 185
definition of, 46
genetic vs. anatomical, 46
on Internet, 18–19
love and, 197
in magazines, 18
for procreation, 5
as sinful, 9
vs. gender, 46
Sex and Temperament in Three Primitive Societies (Mead), 59
Sex change operations, for transsexuals, 64
Sex-chromosome disorders, 54–56, 55t
Sex chromosomes, 48
Sex differentiation, sex hormones in, 50
Sex education, 394–397
in Africa, 504
national curriculum for, 393
parental, 394–396

school-based, 396–397
school-based programs, 24
sexually explicit materials and, 585, 585t
Sex flush, 164
Sex-for-procreation
in China, 7–8
cultural perspective, 6–8, 6f
in Middle Ages, 10
Sex hormones
in male sexual behavior, 147–148
prenatal process disorders, 55t, 56–58
in sex differentiation, 50
Sex in America: A Definitive Study, 32
Sex in the City, 17
Sexist language, reduction of, 74
Sexology
definition of, 23
goals of, 23–24
Sex organs, homologous, 51t
Sex play, childhood, 375–376
Sex-reassignment procedures, 60–61, 67–68, 67f
Sex research
in cyberspace, 38–40
evaluation questions for, 42
feminist theory and, 40–41
surveys. See Surveys
technologies in, 36–40
Sex roles. See Gender roles
Sex therapist
selection of, 469–470
sexual relationships with clients, 468–469
Sex therapy
cultural values and, 455–456
love talk exercises, 453
masturbation with partner present, 456
PLISSIT model of, 466–468
sensate focus technique, 454–455, 454f
sessions, 468
suggestions
for men, 460–465

for women, 456–460, 457f–459f, 459t
unethical relationships in, 468–469
Sex tourism, 592
Sex toys, 251, 261
Sexual abuse, of children, 563–564
Sexual abuse/assault, sexual difficulties and, 439
Sexual abuse/exploitation, of black women, 12
Sexual activity. See Sexual behavior
Sexual addiction, 543–545
Sexual arousal
brain and, 152–155
cultural variations in, 152–153
influencing factors, 147
measuring, electronic devices for, 36–37, 37f
senses and, 155–158
in women, MRI monitoring of, 165
Sexual assault, of males, 562–563
Sexual attitudes, social groups and, 4
Sexual aversion disorder, 442–443
Sexual behavior
during adolescence, 379–388
after childbirth, 367
anal stimulation, 261
atypical, 527–528. See also Paraphilias
behavioral changes, 228
behavior changes, future focus of, 230–231
celibacy, 241–242
during childhood, 372–373
computerized assessment of, 37–38
frequency of, 254
dissatisfaction with, 442
vs. quality, 423–424
of gay men, 256, 257f
of homosexuals, in later years, 424
during infancy, 371–372
in later years, 422–425, 422t
of lesbians, 256, 257f

Vision, sexual arousal and, 156

Voice changes, pubertal, 379

Volatile couples, 408

Volatile dialogue, 235

Volunteer bias, survey research and, 28, 30

Vomeronasal system, 157

Voyeurism, 537–538, 539

Vulva, 82, 82*f*, 85*f*

Vulvodynia, 447

W

Wartime rape, 559

Wellbutrin (bupropion), 466

Wet dream, 242–243

WHI (Women's Health Initiative), 104, 104*t*, 105, 106

White Americans, sexual practices of, 33*t*

White supremacy, 12

Widowhood, 425–426

Witchcraft, 10

Withdrawal method of contraception, 306*t*, 309*t*, 331

Wolffian ducts, 50

Wollstonecraft, Mary, 10

Women. *See* Females

Women's Health Initiative (WHI), 104, 104*t*, 105, 106

Women's Health—Missing from Medicine, 41

Workplace sexual harassment in. *See* Sexual harassment, in workplace

World War I, 13

World War II, 14

X

X chromosomes, 48–49

X-rated movies, 584

Y

Y chromosomes, 48–49

Yeast infections. *See* Candidiasis

Yeast infections, vaginal, 108

Yes/no questions, 218

Yohimbine, 160*t*, 464

Youth. *See* Adolescents

Youth Risk Behavior Survey (YRBS), 33, 382

Z

Zestra, 467

Zidovudine, 512–513

ZIFT (zygote intrafallopian transfer), 341, 341*t*

Zoophilia, 539–540

Zovirax, 490

Zygote, 93, 356

Zygote intrafallopian transfer (ZIFT), 341, 341*t*

TO THE OWNER OF THIS BOOK:

I hope that you have found *Our Sexuality, 9th Edition*, useful. So that this book can be improved in a future edition, would you take the time to complete this sheet and return it? Thank you.

School and address: _____

_____

Department: _____

Instructor's name: _____

1. What I like most about this book is:_____

_____

_____

2. What I like least about this book is: _____

_____

_____

3. My general reaction to this book is: _____

_____

_____

4. What is your reaction to the accompanying CD-ROM? Did you find it useful?_____

_____

_____

5. Did you use your InfoTrac account to help you with assignments or studying for this course?_____

6. In the space below, or on a separate sheet of paper, please write specific suggestions for improving

   this book and anything else you'd care to share about your experience in using this book.

_____

_____

_____

_____

_____

_____

FOLD HERE

BUSINESS REPLY MAIL
FIRST-CLASS MAIL   PERMIT NO. 102   MONTEREY CA

POSTAGE WILL BE PAID BY ADDRESSEE

Attn: *Marianne Taflinger, Psychology*

BrooksCole/Thomson Learning
60 Garden Ct Ste 205
Monterey CA 93940-9967

FOLD HERE

OPTIONAL:

Your name: _____   Date: _____

May we quote you, either in promotion for *Our Sexuality, 9th Edition*, or in future publishing ventures?

Yes: _____   No: _____

Sincerely yours,

Bob Crooks
Karla Baur